UNIQUE EXCEL AND MINITAB POWERPOINT TUTORIALS ON THE FREE STUDENT CD-ROM

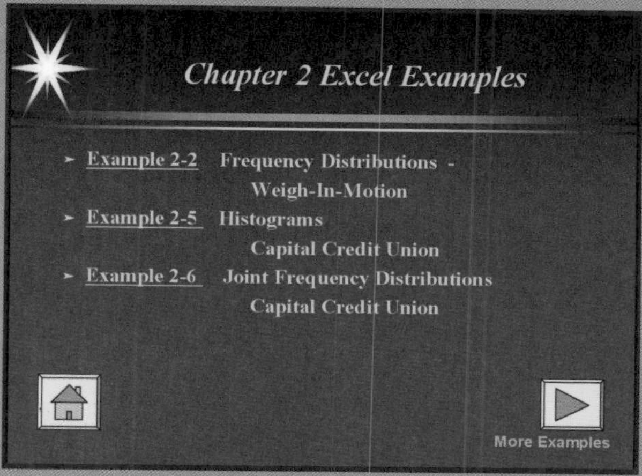

Chapter 2 Excel Examples

- Example 2-2   Frequency Distributions - Weigh-In-Motion
- Example 2-5   Histograms Capital Credit Union
- Example 2-6   Joint Frequency Distributions Capital Credit Union

More Examples

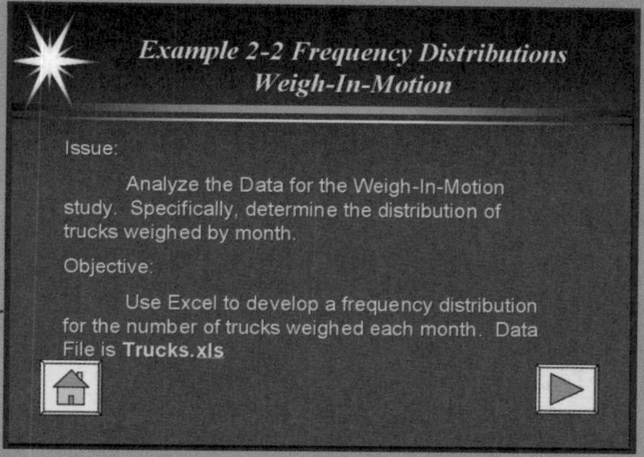

Example 2-2 Frequency Distributions Weigh-In-Motion

Issue:

Analyze the Data for the Weigh-In-Motion study. Specifically, determine the distribution of trucks weighed by month.

Objective:

Use Excel to develop a frequency distribution for the number of trucks weighed each month. Data File is **Trucks.xls**

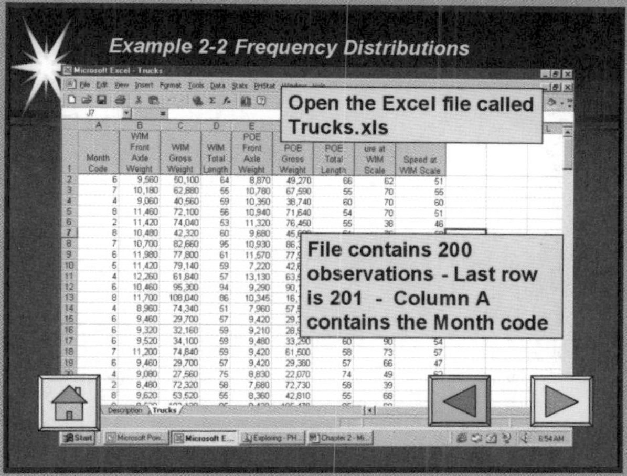

Example 2-2 Frequency Distributions

Open the Excel file called Trucks.xls

File contains 200 observations - Last row is 201 - Column A contains the Month code

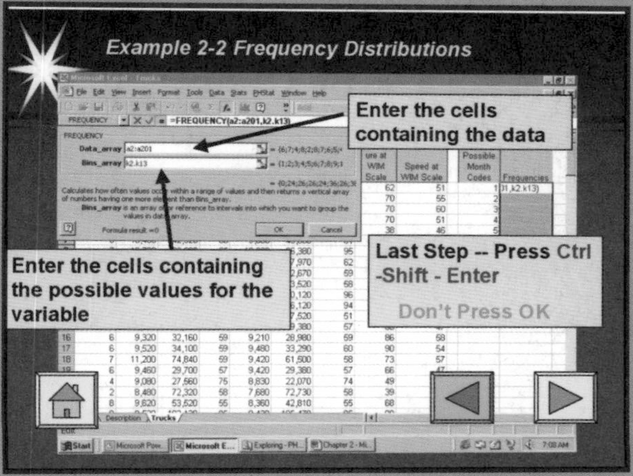

Example 2-2 Frequency Distributions

Enter the cells containing the data

Enter the cells containing the possible values for the variable

Last Step -- Press Ctrl -Shift - Enter

Don't Press OK

THESE TUTORIALS PROVIDE SPECIFIC INSTRUCTIONS FOR EACH EXAMPLE IN BOTH EXCEL AND MINITAB.

BUSINESS STATISTICS:
A DECISION-MAKING APPROACH

FIFTH EDITION

BUSINESS STATISTICS: A DECISION-MAKING APPROACH

David F. Groebner
Boise State University

Patrick W. Shannon
Boise State University

Phillip C. Fry
Boise State University

Kent D. Smith
California Polytechnic University at San Luis Obispo

Pearson
Education

Prentice Hall, UpperSaddle River, New Jersey 07458

Library of Congress Cataloging-in-Publication Data

Business statistics : a decision-making approach / David F. Groebner ... [et al.].--5th ed.
    p. cm.
    Rev. ed. of: Business statistics / David F. Groebner. 4th ed. c1993.
    Includes bibliographical references and index.
    ISBN 0–13–093491–7
      1. Commercial statistics.   2. Statistical decision.   I. Groebner, David F.   II. Grobener,
    David F. Business statistics.

    HF1017 .G73 2000
    519.5--dc21

                                                                                    00-063710

Senior Acquisitions Editor: Tom Tucker
Assistant Editor: Jennifer Surich
Media Project Manager: Cindy Harford
Senior Marketing Manager: Debbie Clare
Marketing Assistant: Jessica Pasquini
Managing Editor (Production): Cynthia Regan
Production Editor: Carol Samet
Permissions Coordinator: Suzanne Grappi
Associate Director, Manufacturing: Vincent Scelta
Production Manager: Arnold Vila
Design Manager: Patricia Smythe
Interior Design: Donna Wickes
Cover Design: Donna Wickes
Senior Print/Media Production Manager: Karen Goldsmith
Composition: Graphic World, Inc.
Full-Service Project Management: Graphic World Publishing Services
Printer/Binder: R.R. Donnelley & Sons Company

Microsoft Excel, Solver, and Windows are registered trademarks of Microsoft Corporation in the U.S.A. and other countries. Screen shots and icons reprinted with permission from the Microsoft Corporation. This book is not sponsored or endorsed by or affiliated with Microsoft Corporation.

10 9 8 7 6 5 4 3 2
ISBN 0–13–093491–7

To Jane and my family, who survived the process one more time.

David F. Groebner

*To Kathy, my wife and best friend; to our children, Jackie and Jason;
and to my parents, John and Ruth Shannon.*

Patrick W. Shannon

To my wonderful family: Susan, Alex, Allie, Candace, and Courtney.

Phillip C. Fry

To Dottie, my loving wife, who dances much better than I write.

Kent D. Smith

About the Authors

DAVID F. GROEBNER is a Professor of Production Management and Chairman of the Department of Computer Information Systems and Production Management at Boise State University. He has bachelor's and master's degrees in Engineering and a Ph.D. in Business Administration. After working as an engineer, he has taught statistics and related subjects for 27 years. In addition to writing textbooks and academic papers, he has worked extensively with both small and large organizations, including Hewlett-Packard, Boise Cascade, Albertson's, and Ore-Ida. He has worked with numerous government agencies, including Boise City and the U.S. Air Force.

PATRICK W. SHANNON, PH.D. is Professor of Production and Operations Management in the College of Business and Economics at Boise State University. He teaches graduate and undergraduate courses in business statistics, quality management, and production and operations management. In addition, Dr. Shannon has lectured and consulted in the statistical analysis and quality management areas for over 20 years. Listed among his consulting clients are Boise Cascade Corporation, Hewlett-Packard; PowerBar, Inc.; Potlatch Corporation; Woodgrain Millwork, Inc.; J.R. Simplot Company; Zilog Corporation; and numerous other public- and private-sector organizations. Professor Shannon has co-authored several university-level textbooks and has published numerous articles in such journals as *Business Horizons, Interfaces, Journal of Simulation, Journal of Production and Inventory Control, Quality Progress,* and *Journal of Marketing Research.* He obtained B.S. and M.S. degrees from the University of Montana and a Ph.D. in Statistics and Quantitative Methods from the University of Oregon.

PHILLIP C. FRY is an Associate Professor in the Department of Computer Information Systems and Production Management in the College of Business and Economics at Boise State University, where he has taught since 1988. Phil received his B.A. and M.B.A degrees from the University of Arkansas, and his M.S. and Ph.D. degrees from Louisiana State University. His teaching and research interests are in the areas of business statistics, production management, and quantitative business modeling. In addition to his academic responsibilities, Phil has consulted with and provided training to small and large organizations, including Boise Cascade Corporation; Hewlett-Packard Corporation; The J.R. Simplot Company; United Water of Idaho; Woodgrain Millwork, Inc.; Boise City; and Micron Electronics.

Phil spends most of his free time with his wife Susan, to whom he has been married for 18 years, and his four children, Phillip Alexander, age 8, Alejandra Johanna, age 7, and twins, Courtney Rene and Candace Marie, age 1.

KENT D. SMITH received a Ph.D. in Applied Statistics from the University of California, Riverside in 1981. He holds a Master of Science degree in Statistics from the University of California, Riverside and a Master of Science degree in Systems Analysis from the Air Force Institute of Technology. His Bachelor of Arts degree in Mathematics was obtained from the University of Utah. Dr. Smith has served as a University Statistical Consultant at the University of California, Riverside and at California Polytechnic State University, San Luis Obispo. While at the University of California, he served as a consultant for the Biometrical Services Unit of the Biometrical Project at the University of California, Riverside. His private consulting has ranged from serving as an expert witness in legal cases, survey sampling for corporations and private researchers, medical and orthodontic research, and assisting graduate students with analysis required for master and doctoral degrees in various disciplines.

Dr. Smith began teaching as a part-time lecturer at the California State University, San Bernardino. While completing his doctoral dissertation, he served as a lecturer at the University of California, Riverside. Currently, he is a Professor of Statistics at the California Polytechnic State University, San Luis Obispo, one of the minority of universities that offer an undergraduate degree in statistics. The subjects he teaches include upper-division courses in regression, analysis of variance, nonparametrics, linear models, and probability and mathematical statistics, as well as a full array of service courses.

BRIEF CONTENTS

Contents

PREFACE

New business school graduates face an increasingly competitive job market. While the U.S. economy continues to perform well, corporate downsizing along with competitive pressures to trim costs have affected the demand for new graduates in most business majors. In order to stand out in today's competitive job market, graduates need to bring to an organization special skills and abilities that give them the potential to hit the ground running and contribute immediately.

One area where a student can have an immediate competitive advantage over both new graduates and existing employees is in the application of statistical analysis skills to business problems. While most colleges of business require their graduates to have completed either one or two business statistics courses, too many students complete their academic programs without having mastered the statistical skills necessary to meet the needs of business. One reason for this may be that their statistics courses did not adequately prepare them in applying statistical tools and concepts to real-world decision-making problems.

Our intent in writing a fifth edition of *Business Statistics: A Decision-Making Approach* is to build on the strengths of the previous four additions (readability, decision-making focus, content coverage, pedagogical aids, etc.) and to take the text to a new level of performance. In doing so, we have made substantive changes throughout the text so that students can more fully and completely appreciate the value of business statistics to both their academic and professional careers. Dr. Phil Fry of Boise State University and Dr. Kent Smith of Cal Polytechnic State University of San Luis Obispo have joined Professors David Groebner and Patrick Shannon as co-authors. All the authors share a passion for the subject as well as a devotion to teaching, and have significant experience in applying the statistical tools in business and industry settings. Following is a description of the major improvements we have made to this edition.

◼ MOTIVATING STUDENTS USING REAL BUSINESS APPLICATIONS

The fifth edition of *Business Statistics: A Decision-Making Approach* provides real-world applications as a motivation for learning business statistics. While previous editions have focused on decision making and business applications, the new edition has more applications than ever before. Not only do the chapters focus on real companies and actual applications, increased effort has been placed on providing the student with an understanding of the role business statistics plays in decision making. This text is designed to help the instructor create a climate in which students are motivated to learn and apply statistical techniques.

We believe that students will relate well to the writing style used throughout the text. The writing style and subject presentation are intended to facilitate student interest and involvement in the material. Statistical concepts and techniques are introduced through realistic business situations and we have made every effort to communicate ideas using a nontechnical writing style. This is a business statistics text that students will actually read and use it to increase their understanding of business statistics.

■ INCREASED COMPUTER EMPHASIS

To enhance the students' appreciation for business statistics, we emphasize computer-based analysis, rather than manual computations. Toward this end, Microsoft's Excel (Office 2000 version) is featured extensively throughout the textbook. Minitab is also used as a supplement to Excel at various places throughout the text. Chapter examples, exercises, and case studies are based on real industry data or data motivated by real-world examples. In this way, students gain a greater understanding of what statistical tools to use, when and how to apply them, and how to interpret the results of their analyses to decision making.

Unlike some computer-based textbooks that provided only end-of-chapter computer instructions, this text seamlessly integrates the computer applications with the text examples, with a focus on interpreting the output. The goal is for the students to appreciate the role of spreadsheet and statistical software as business statistics tools. We do not dwell on the specifics of how the software is used within the text. However, the screen shots do show the students the key instructions needed to generate the output they are seeing. In addition, callouts highlight the important output that is being discussed in the example. The following figure from Chapter 9 is typical of this approach.

FIGURE 9-6
PHStat Test for Equality of Two Variances for Future-Vision

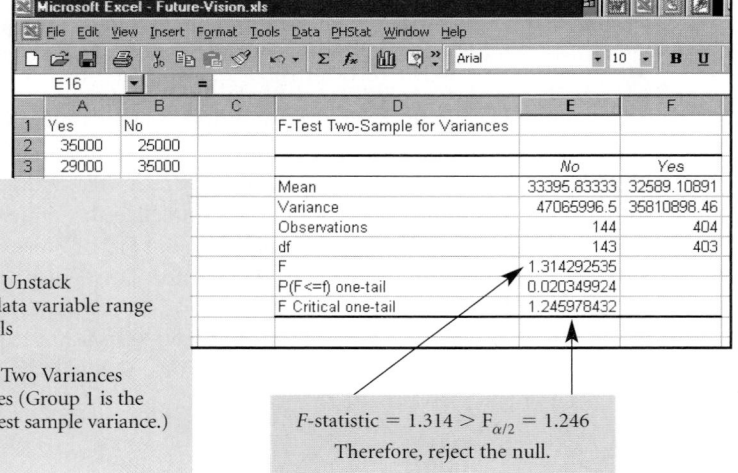

Excel Instructions:

1. Open file: Future-Vision.xls
2. Select PHStat
3. Click on Data Preparation and Unstack
4. Define grouping variable and data variable range
5. With unstacked data select Tools
6. Select Data Analysis
7. Select F-Test for Differences in Two Variances
8. Enter data range for two variables (Group 1 is the "No" Group since it has the largest sample variance.)
9. Select alpha level

F-statistic $= 1.314 > F_{\alpha/2} = 1.246$
Therefore, reject the null.

■ TOOLS OF QUALITY

Statistics have played a major role in the quality movement. The fifth edition integrates quality concepts throughout the text. For example, many chapters contain one or more "Tools of Quality" segments. These segments, which are specially marked in the text, feature applications of statistical techniques (e.g., data check sheets, Pareto charts, and process capability analysis) that are frequently employed by organizations in their quality and process improvement activities. Many other examples and applications throughout the text have a quality theme. In addition, Chapter 13 presents an overview of quality issues and introduces statistical process control charts. This SPC chapter is strategically placed to emphasize that SPC is a direct application of the important statistical concepts of estimation and hypothesis testing.

EXTENSIVE EXERCISE SETS

The Business Application Exercises at the end of each section provide realistic decision-making situations in which the statistical concepts from the section are applied. Not only do these exercises reinforce the statistical techniques presented in the book, but they also provide a useful motivation for the study of business statistics.

In addition to the end-of-section exercises, each chapter contains numerous Business Application Exercises at the end of the chapter. These end-of-chapter questions and problems require the student to identify what needs to be done and what statistical tool is required. In many instances, the problems are integrative by requiring students to draw upon material from earlier chapters. For example, problems in Chapter 3 that introduce numerical descriptive measures might also require development of appropriate charts or graphs taught in Chapter 2. In this way, students are continually reviewing and applying material learned in previous chapters, gaining a greater appreciation for how the different techniques fit together to provide an integrated set of business analysis tools.

Where appropriate, many of the Business Application Exercises include data sets to be analyzed using either Excel or Minitab. A special data set icon is used to distinguish these problems.

As a special feature, additional application problems and skill development exercises are located on the CD-ROM that accompanies the text.

CHAPTER CASES

We have included short cases at the end of each chapter. Like the Business Application Exercises, these cases are based on actual business situations. However, the cases are less directed and more open-ended than the exercises and also require the students to integrate the statistical techniques covered in the chapter into the decision-making situation. The purpose of the cases is to give the students an opportunity to apply the tools and techniques they have learned to more loosely defined business problems, requiring them to identify key issues, apply relevant statistical techniques, draw conclusions, and provide reports detailing their findings.

REVISED TABLE OF CONTENTS

For the fifth edition, we have made some changes to the order in which the chapters are presented based on feedback we have had from reviewers, students, and faculty who have used prior editions. For example, as mentioned previously, we have added a chapter on quality and statistical process control. We have moved the chapters on categorical data and nonparametric statistics to follow immediately after the quality and SPC chapter. In addition, we have added some topics, most notably an emphasis on model building in the multiple regression chapter. The ANOVA chapter now contains a section on two-factor analysis of variance. We have also expanded our discussion of descriptive statistics and data presentation, since that aspect of a business statistics course is highly relevant to graduates in the workplace.

It is always a challenge to include all the topics that professors would like to see in a business statistics textbook while keeping the text length to a manageable size. This is a special challenge to us since we have opted for a descriptive writing style with fully developed examples and applications. To help accomplish our objective in terms of topic coverage and presentation while staying within a manageable length, the fifth edition includes a number of optional topics on the CD-ROM that accompanies the text.

◼ SPECIAL FEATURES

A variety of other special features are included in this text and ancillary materials. Their brief descriptions follow.

CD-ROM

Optional CD-ROM Topic

Chapter 4

The Hypergeometric Distribution

Additional Example 9-a on CD-ROM

Estimating the Difference Between Two Population Means—Small Samples

Excel and Minitab Tutorial included on CD-ROM

Data Files

Excel Simulation

t-Distribution

Accompanying the text is a CD-ROM with many special features, including:

- **CD-ROM Topics**—Topics, listed as "Optional CD-ROM Topics" in the text. The benefit is that we are able to provide a wider array of topics and at the same time keep the length and cost of the text within acceptable limits. The CD-ROM topics tend to be of the optional variety that many faculty do not cover in their courses. However, for those who do, the topics are easily available.

- **Additional Examples**—Although among the strengths of the text are the quality and quantity of the examples and applications that are presented in each chapter, students always want more examples. At various places throughout the text we have included an icon that identifies an additional example contained on the CD-ROM. These examples are like the ones in the text and are applications involving business situations.

- **Excel and Minitab Tutorials**—Customized PowerPoint tutorials for both Minitab and Excel, which use data sets from text examples, are included on the CD-ROM. Students who need additional instruction in Excel or Minitab can access the menu-driven tutorial, which will show the exact steps needed to replicate all computer examples in the text. The benefits are that the CD-ROM tutorials free instructors from spending significant time on computer instruction during class time and the students can access specific help with the software at any time.

- **Solved Problems**—Most chapters have one or more solved problems included on the CD-ROM. In addition to providing the students with more examples and applications, these solved problems illustrate to the student a proper method for laying out their answers to the chapter exercises and problems. Another benefit is that the instructor who has computer projection in the classroom could use these solved problems in class as examples and for discussion purposes.

- **Data Files**—An extensive number of data files for examples, cases, and problems in the text are included on the CD-ROM, in both Excel and Minitab format. The text references these data files with a special icon.

- **Additional Exercises**—More exercises and application problems are included on the CD-ROM. Although the fifth edition will be among the industry leaders in the numbers of exercises and application problems provided, the CD-ROM makes it possible for instructors to select from an even greater number of problems.

- **Excel Simulations**—The CD-ROM also contains several interactive Excel simulations that are used to illustrate important statistical concepts, such as hypothesis testing and confidence interval estimation. These simulations allow the students to make changes and immediately observe the impact. The Excel simulations can also be used effectively by instructors in the classroom to illustrate statistical issues through the use of "what if" questioning.

PHStat

Included on the CD-ROM is a specially developed Excel add-in package called PHStat that can be installed on any PC running Excel 97 or higher. PHStat contains a number of statistical features that are not included with Microsoft Excel, but which are useful in the study and application of business statistics. For example, the regression section on PH-Stat contains both *All-Possible Subsets* and *Stepwise Regression* tools. Another tool is the *Box Plot* option. There are several instances in the text where the Excel output screen shows the results when a PHStat add-in has been used.

Student Solutions Manual

The Solutions Manual contains the worked-out solutions to all the odd-numbered problems in the text. More than just showing the answer, the Solutions Manual shows the detailed process that students should use to work each problem. The manual also provides interpretation of the answers and serves as a valuable learning tool for the student.

Text Web Site

This text has a Web site that can be accessed directly or as a link from the Prentice Hall Home Page. The features that are included at the Web site benefit both students and instructors.

■ ACKNOWLEDGMENTS

Publishing a textbook is a team effort and involves many people. At the risk of overlooking someone, we take this space to express our appreciation to many of the key contributors to this text. Throughout the more than two years that this revision has been in process, many faculty members from across the country have taken time from their busy schedules to provide valuable input and suggestions for improvement. We offer thanks to:

Deepinder S. Bajwa
Fayetteville State University

Fran Barbera
Louisiana State University

Ann Burns
Skyline Community College

Alan S. Chesen
Wright State University

Petro Christofi
Duquesne University

Bradford Crain
Portland State University

Christine Cring
SUNY–Morrisville

Abe Feinberg
California State University–Northridge

Wade Jackson
University of Memphis

John Lawrence
California State University–Fullerton

Catherine Lawson
Missouri Western State College

Gary Martin
DeVry Institute of Technology

Lee McClain
Western Washington University

Michael G. McMillan
Northern Virginia Community College

Glen W. Milligan
Ohio State University

Philip F. Musa
Texas Tech University

Amy V. Puelz
Southern Methodist University

Harold F. Rahmlow
St. Joseph's University

Wan Soo T. Rhee
Ohio State University

Russ Robins
Tulane Universitiy

Don R. Robinson
Illinois State University

Vartan Safarian
Winona State University

James Schmidt
University of Nebraska

Richard Twark
Penn State University

Debra K. Stiver
University of Nevada–Reno

Michael P. Wegmann
Keller Graduate School of Management

A special thanks goes to Professor Debra Stiver of the University of Nevada–Reno for her assistance all the way through the project and for agreeing to provide one last detailed review of the manuscript. Susan Reiland did a terrific job in proofing the final pages. Thanks to David Stephan for his expert work in developing the PHStat add-in for Excel.

Many people have also participated by preparing the ancillary materials that support the text and add to the students' learning experience. We wish to thank the following people: Dr. Mark Karscig, Central Missouri State University, who prepared the PowerPoint slides; Dan Cooper and staff at Active Learning Technology, who developed and continues to support the text Web page; Mohammed Z. Bsat and his team at Jackson State University, who developed the Test Bank and Interactive Study Guide, and Susan Fry, Boise State University, who prepared the Instructors and Student Solutions Manuals.

The team of professionals at Prentice Hall is the finest publishing group with whom we had the pleasure of working. Carol Samet oversaw the technical end of the publishing process and kept us on schedule; Cindy Harford coordinated the CD-ROM materials; Jennifer Surich supervised the preparation of supplements; and Debbie Clare handled the very important marketing component with great creativity and enthusiasm.

Finally, we wish to give a special thanks to Tom Tucker, Decision Sciences Editor at Prentice Hall, for his belief in our text and for his professional assistance from beginning to end. Working with him has been both a pleasure and a terrific learning experience. He has provided the resources necessary to make this fifth edition a major advance from previous editions.

David F. Groebner
Patrick W. Shannon
Phillip C. Fry
Kent D. Smith

CHAPTER 1

THE WHERE, WHY, AND HOW OF DATA COLLECTION

CHAPTER OUTCOMES

After studying the material in Chapter 1, you should:

1-1: Know the key data collection methods.

1-2: Know the difference between a population and a sample.

1-3: Understand how to categorize data by type and level of measurement.

1-4: Understand the similarities and differences between different sampling methods.

1-5: Know how to set up a computer file for data storage.

WHY YOU NEED TO KNOW

This is a good time to be entering the business world. Never before have the opportunities been so numerous. Global markets have opened up literally a world of possibilities, and job functions in businesses are changing to meet the dynamic business environment. Organizations are scrambling to find people who have the knowledge, skills, and abilities to meet the ever-increasing competitive challenges faced by businesses. While businesses have always looked to colleges and universities to help provide them with the talent they need, the trend in this direction is stronger than ever. However, these businesses are not just seeking educated people. They are seeking individuals who have the ability to understand and apply key decision-making tools to the complexities of the business environment.

Many organizations have access to massive amounts of data, but decision makers have a difficult time using these data effectively. Business statistics offers students the necessary tools for effectively converting sets of data into usable information. This is why business statistics is a required course at any accredited business school.

Business statistics offers some very important tools for data conversion. You will have the opportunity to learn about these statistical tools from your professor and from this text. This text focuses on the practical application of statistics—

we do not develop the statistical theory you would find in a standard mathematical statistics course. You will need to use math in this course, but it will be mainly basic concepts derived from college algebra.

Statistics does have its own terminology. You will need to learn various terms that have special statistical meaning. You will also learn certain do's and don'ts related to statistics. But most importantly, you will learn specific methods for effectively converting data into information. In all cases, the best way to learn is by doing. The text contains numerous problems and exercises that reinforce the concepts and methods in the chapters. Do not try to memorize the concepts; rather, go to the next level of learning, called *understanding*. Once you understand the underlying concepts, you will be able to *think statistically*.

We have taught business statistics for many years, and we are well aware that you may be approaching this course with a certain degree of apprehension. That is certainly understandable. Anything that is new is uncomfortable at first. However, we promise that once you are under way in this course, you will begin to see that business statistics is actually a logical subject area that is applicable to all areas of business. When you can think statistically, you will have truly set yourself apart from many others in the business world, and this will give you a competitive advantage for the rest of your life.

■ 1-1: WHAT IS BUSINESS STATISTICS?

When we ask people to provide examples of *statistics*, we get a variety of responses.

- A *USA Today*/CNN/Gallup poll shows that two out of three Americans still approve of the job the president is doing.
- The Conference Board reported its index of consumer confidence fell 9.1 points to 117.2 in October.
- Tiger Woods won over $4 million on the PGA tour in 1999.
- The Commerce Department announced spending on new U.S. construction increased 0.4% during the month to a $660.6 billion annual rate.
- A Dun & Bradstreet survey shows the index of employment in the construction industry rose to 16 in the fourth quarter.
- Steven Appleton, President of Micron Technology, forecasts a 49% growth rate over the next three years in the semiconductor market.

Yes, these are all examples of statistics. In fact most people are familiar with these kinds of statistics before they ever take a business statistics course. These statistics are numbers that describe certain events. Perhaps a better name for these terms is *descriptors*. Every day, your local newspaper contains stories that report descriptors such as stock prices, crime rates, and government agency budgets. Such descriptors can be found in many places. However, these descriptors are just a small part of a discipline that shares the name of statistics. Statistics as a discipline provides a wide variety of methods to assist in data analysis and decision making. Business is one important area of application for these methods. Business statistics is defined as follows:

> **BUSINESS STATISTICS**
> A collection of tools and techniques that are used to convert data into meaningful information in a business environment.

Descriptive Statistics

The tools and techniques that comprise business statistics include those specially designed to *describe data*, such as charts, graphs, and numerical measures. Also included are inferential tools that help decision makers *draw inferences* from a set of data. Inferential tools include estimation and hypothesis testing. A brief discussion of these tools and techniques follows. The following examples illustrate data that have been entered into the Microsoft Excel and Minitab software packages. Section 1-5 discusses these software packages more fully and outlines the role they will play in this text.

EXAMPLE 1-1

DESCRIBING DATA

Baker City Hospital

Healthcare companies in the United States have been faced with increased competition and the need for hospital administrators to be more efficient in managing their operations. This means they must better understand their customers.

  The financial vice president for Baker City Hospital recently collected data for 138 patients. The VP has entered these data into an Excel spreadsheet as illustrated in Figure 1-1. Each column in Figure 1-1 corresponds to a different factor for which data were collected. Each row corresponds to a different patient. Many statistical tools exist that might help the VP describe these patients' data including *charts*, *graphs*, and *numerical measures*.

CHARTS AND GRAPHS

Although we develop an extensive variety of methods to describe data using graphs and charts in Chapter 2, a few examples are offered here to give you an idea of the possibilities. Figure 1-2 shows a graph called a *histogram*. This graph gives us some insight into how long patients stay at the Baker City Hospital by visually showing how many patients are classified in each length of stay category. It describes the shape and spread of the patient length

FIGURE 1-1
Excel Spreadsheet of Baker
City Hospital Patient Data

	Length of Stay	Age (Years)	Sex (M/F/U)	Total Charges	E
1	**Length of Stay**	**Age (Years)**	**Sex (M/F/U)**	**Total Charges**	
2	3	78	F	5,419	
3	3	74	F	4,575	
4	11	89	M	12,031	
5	3	81	M	3,618	
6	9	87	F	12,807	
7	3	65	M	5,296	
8	3	90	M	3,453	
9	3	61	M	1,760	
10	3	90	F	3,290	
11	5	78	M	6,254	
12	3	78	F	3,896	
13	2	71	M	1,795	
14	3	76	M	9,265	
15	3	76	F	3,283	

Microsoft Excel - Baker.xls

File Edit View Insert Format Tools Data PHStat Window Help

Courier   10   **B** *I*

E7   =

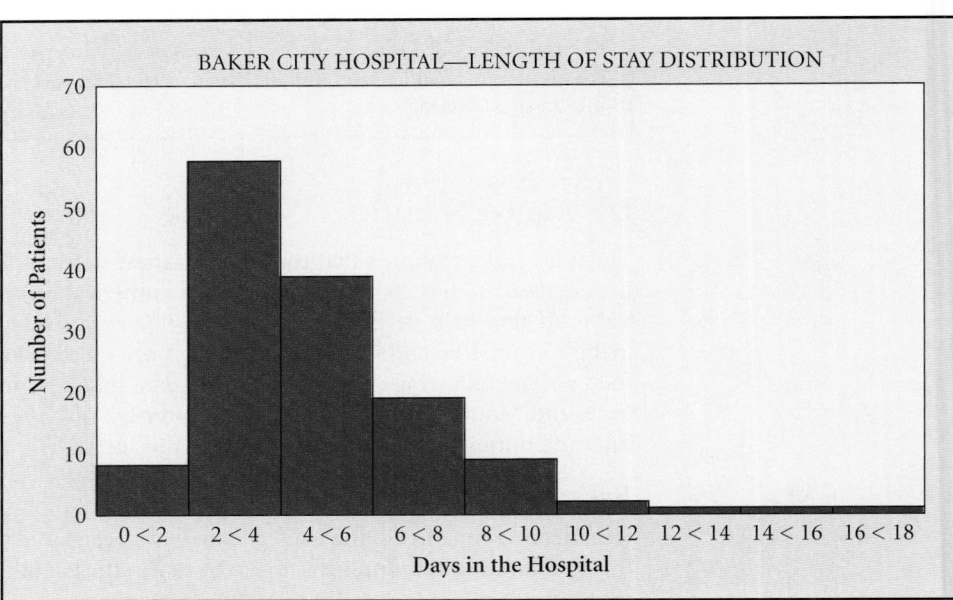

FIGURE 1-2
Histogram

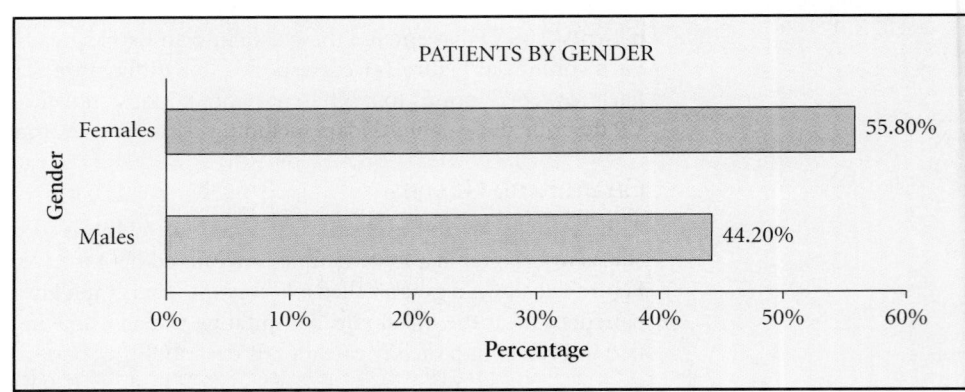

FIGURE 1-3
Bar Chart of Baker City
Hospital

of stay distribution. The *bar chart* shown in Figure 1-3 breaks down the patient data showing the percentage of male and female patients. We can tell, looking at this chart, that the mix of patients has a higher number of females.

Do you suppose the groups of men and women tend to remain in the hospital about the same length of time? Figure 1-4 presents a bar chart in which we see that, for those patients who stayed under 4 days, approximately 56% were women. Interestingly, of those patients staying over 7 days, 64% were also women. Thus, for both short and long stays there is a greater percentage of female patients than male patients. Males, however, have a higher percentage of mid-length stays than do females.

These are but a few of the graphical techniques that the Baker City Hospital VP might use to help describe her patient population. In Chapter 2 you will learn about the various graphical techniques.

NUMERICAL MEASURES

Crown Investments

During the 1990s many major changes occurred in the financial services industry. There were numerous bank mergers. Money flowed into the stock market at rates far surpassing anything the U.S. economy has previously witnessed. There were great fluctuations in the

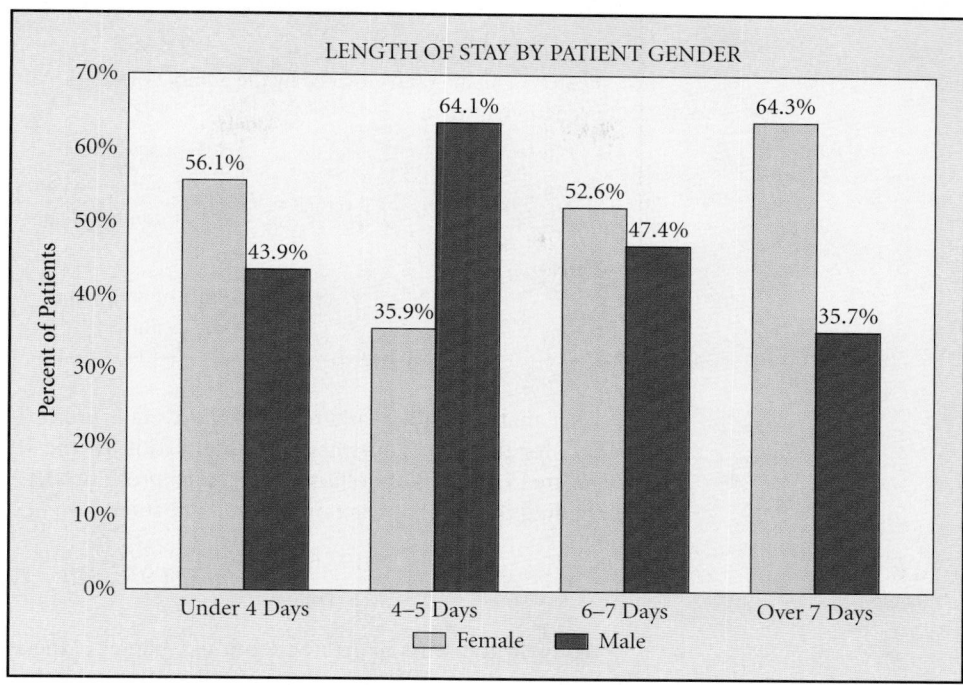

FIGURE 1-4
Baker City Hospital

international financial arena. These developments have spurred the need for more financial analysts who can critically evaluate financial data and explain these data to customers.

At Crown Investments, a senior analyst is preparing for a presentation to upper management on the 100 fastest growing companies on the Hong Kong Stock Exchange. Figure 1-5 shows a Minitab worksheet containing a subset of the data. The columns correspond to the different data items of interest (growth %, sales, etc.). The data for each company are in a single row. In addition to preparing appropriate graphs, the analyst will compute important numerical measures for the data. Chapter 3 introduces key descriptive measures and shows how they are computed, applied, and interpreted. One of the most basic and most useful measures in business statistics is one with which you are already familiar. This is the **arithmetic mean** or **average**.

FIGURE 1-5
Crown Investment Example –
Minitab Worksheet

> MINITAB - Untitled - [Fast100.MTW ***]

File Edit Manip Calc Stat Graph Editor Window Help

	C5	C6	C7	C8	C9	C10	C11	C12
↓	Growth %	Sales	EPS	Profits	Stk-Price	Last Yr Price	P/E ratio	Stk Market
1	256	185.3	-99	6.8	18.00	8.50	17	1
2	228	183.2	243	43.2	42.25	12.50	31	1
3	215	187.5	-99	26.5	21.25	11.13	17	1
4	209	229.8	129	35.4	27.38	26.25	16	1
5	209	249.9	97	8.9	23.38	15.00	53	2
6	203	399.7	18	4.2	2.31	1.13	17	1
7	200	731.4	95	77.7	11.63	10.00	24	2
8	180	93.0	116	8.6	6.63	-99.00	21	2
9	179	440.9	72	8.4	8.25	-99.00	9	1
10	167	131.8	-99	3.7	16.50	-99.00	66	1
11	156	2319.4	-99	102.1	40.25	56.88	4	3

AVERAGE

The sum of all the values divided by the number of values.
In equation form:

$$\text{Average} = \frac{\sum_{i=1}^{N} x_i}{N} = \frac{\textit{sum of all data values}}{\textit{number of data values}}$$

where:

$$N = \text{number of data values}$$
$$x_i = i\text{th data value}$$

The analyst might be interested in the average profit (i.e., mean of the column labeled Profits) for the 100 companies. The total profit for the 100 companies is $3,193.60. The profits are in millions of dollars giving a total profit of $3,193,600,000. The average is found by dividing this total by the number of companies:

$$\text{Average} = \frac{\$3,193,600,000}{100} = \$31,936,000 \text{ or } 31.936 \text{ million dollars}$$

As we will discuss in greater depth in Chapter 3, the average or mean is a measure of the center of the data. In this case, the analyst might use the average profit as an indicator—firms above the average are rated higher than firms with below average profits.

The graphical and numerical measures illustrated in this section are only some of the many descriptive tools that will be introduced in Chapters 2 and 3. The key to remember is that the purpose of the descriptive tools is to describe data. Your task will be to select the tool or tools that best accomplish this. As Figure 1-6 reminds you, the role of statistics is to convert data into meaningful information.

Inferential Tools

How do television networks determine which programs people prefer to watch? How does the network that carries the Super Bowl know how many people were watching the game? Advertisers pay for TV ads based on the audience level, so these numbers are important—millions of dollars are at stake. Clearly the networks do not check with everyone in the country. Instead, they use an area of statistics referred to as **statistical inference** to come up with the information.

STATISTICAL INFERENCE TOOLS
Tools that allow a decision maker to reach a conclusion about a population of data based on a subset of data from the population.

FIGURE 1-6
The Role of Business
Statistics

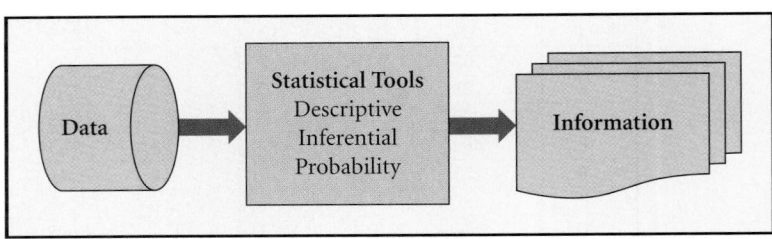

There are two primary categories of statistical inference tools: *estimation* and *hypothesis testing*. These tools are closely related but serve very different purposes.

ESTIMATION

In situations where we would like to know about all the data in a large data set but it is impractical to work with all the data, decision makers can use techniques to estimate what the larger data set looks like. The estimates are formed by looking closely at a subset of the larger data set.

ESTIMATION

TV Ratings

The television networks cannot know for sure how many people watched last year's Super Bowl. They cannot possibly ask all potential viewers if they watched. Instead, they rely on organizations like the A. C. Nielsen Company to supply program ratings. These ratings are estimates of the number of viewers who tuned in to programs during the rating period. The ratings are computed based on a rather small number of homes selected from across the country. Once the Nielsen Company knows how many people in the small group watched the program, they use that number to estimate the number for the entire population.

For example, the following article appeared in newspapers across the country on May 16, 1998:

> NEW YORK—Jerry and his three misfit friends ended "Seinfeld" arguing in a prison cell watched by an estimated 76 million people.
>
> Ratings for the comedy's final episode were below the finals for "Cheers" and "M*A*S*H" and a shade below NBC's predictions.

Advertisers enter into a contract with the television networks in which the price per ad spot is based on a certain minimum viewership. If the Nielsen ratings estimate a lower total audience, then the network must refund money to the advertiser.

In Chapter 7, we will discuss the various estimating techniques used by companies such as A. C. Nielsen.

HYPOTHESIS TESTING

Television advertising is full of product claims. For example, we might hear that "Goodyear tires will last at least 60,000 miles," or that "More doctors recommend Bayer Aspirin than any other brand." Other claims might include statements that "General Electric lightbulbs last longer than any other brand," or that "Customers prefer Burger King over McDonald's." Are these just idle boasts or are they based on actual data? Probably some of both! However, consumer research organizations such as *Consumer Reports* regularly test these types of claims. For example, in the fast food restaurant case, *Consumer Reports* might select a sample of customers who would be asked to blind taste test hamburgers from Burger King and McDonald's under the hypothesis that there is no difference in customer preferences between the two restaurants. If the sample data show a significant difference in preferences, then the hypothesis of no difference in customer preferences would be rejected. If only a slight difference in preferences is detected, then *Consumer Reports* writers could not reject the hypothesis. Chapters 8 and 9 introduce basic hypothesis testing techniques that are used to test claims about products and services using information taken from samples.

TOOLS OF QUALITY

For many years following World War II, U.S. industries dominated the world marketplace. There was little foreign competition for our growing domestic markets. Most U.S. companies could export their products abroad to customers who had few other choices. Although product quality and customer service were important, in many cases a company's priorities were focused on meeting quantity goals. If production costs increased, they could be passed on to the customers in the form of higher prices.

However, this all began to change in the late 1970s and early 1980s when overseas competition began to take large amounts of business from U.S. industries, most notably in the automobile, home electronics, and steel industries. For the first time consumers in the United States and abroad had viable alternative suppliers. U.S. managers were faced with the stark reality that their competitors, in many cases, had superior quality products, better customer service, and lower prices.

Beginning in the 1980s and extending through the 1990s, organizations across the United States have turned to quality management in an effort to meet the competitive challenges of the international marketplace. Although there is no set approach for implementing quality management, a commonality among most organizations is that employees at all levels be brought into the effort as team members to improve the production process.

Successful organizations, such as Motorola and Hewlett-Packard, realize that thrusting people together in teams and then expecting process improvement to occur will generally lead to disappointment. They know that their employees need to understand how to work together as a team. In addition to training in teamwork and team building, employees require training and education in the proper tools if they are to be successful at making lasting process improvements. Over the past several decades a number of techniques and methods for process improvement have been developed and effectively used by organizations. As a group, these are referred to as the *tools of quality*. Many of the tools of quality are merely extensions of the basic statistical tools introduced in this text. Thus, many chapters will have one or more "Tools of Quality" sections that demonstrate how the statistical techniques are applied to help improve product and service quality.

1-1: EXERCISES

ADDITIONAL EXERCISES ON YOUR CD-ROM
Try the ADDITIONAL EXERCISES and APPLICATION PROBLEMS on the CD-ROM.

1-1   In your own terms define what is meant by statistical estimation. Provide an example from your own experiences in which estimation is used.

1-2   Define what is meant by hypothesis testing. Provide an example in which you personally have tested a hypothesis (even if you did not use formal statistical techniques to do so).

1-3   It is important to know when to employ estimation and when to employ hypothesis testing. Explain under what circumstances you would use hypothesis testing as opposed to an estimation procedure.

Business Applications

1-4   Locate a business periodical such as *Fortune* or *Forbes*, or a business newspaper such as *The Wall Street Journal*. Find three examples of the use of a graph to display data. For each graph:
   a. Give the name, date, and page number of the periodical in which the graph appeared.
   b. Describe the main point made by the graph.
   c. Analyze the effectiveness of the graphs.

1-5   A group of executives at a local company is considering introducing a new product into a market area. It is important to know the age characteristics of the people in the market area.

    a. If the executives wish to calculate a number that would characterize the "center" of the age data, what statistical technique would you suggest? Explain your answer.

    b. The executives need to know the percentage of people in the market area that are senior citizens. Name the basic category of statistical inference tools they would use to provide this information.

    c. Describe a hypothesis upon which the executives might wish to conduct a test concerning the percentage of senior citizens in the market area.

1-6 An agribusiness company currently uses one brand of commercial fertilizer. However, a new fertilizer is available that the manufacturer says will produce higher than average crop yields.

    a. Name the basic category of statistical inference tools the manufacturer would use to provide this information.

    b. Describe a hypothesis upon which the manufacturer might wish to conduct a test concerning the relative effectiveness of the new fertilizer.

1-7 Locate an example from a business periodical or newspaper in which estimation has been used.

    a. What specifically was estimated?

    b. What conclusion was reached using the estimation?

    c. Describe how the data were extracted and how those data were used to produce the estimation.

    d. Keeping in mind the goal of the estimation, discuss whether you believe that the estimation was successful and why.

    e. Describe what inferences were drawn as a result of the estimation.

■ 1-2: TOOLS AND TECHNIQUES FOR COLLECTING DATA

We have defined business statistics as a set of tools that are used to transform data into information. Before you learn how to use statistical tools to transform the data, it is important that you become familiar with different types of data and data collection methods.

Primary and Secondary Data Types

There are many tools and techniques for collecting data. The appropriate tool depends on a number of factors including whether the data are considered to be **primary** or **secondary data**.

PRIMARY DATA Data that are collected by you or another person with whom you are closely associated. Primary data are collected for your specific purpose and use.	**SECONDARY DATA** Data that are collected and compiled by an outside source.

All data start out as primary data for someone. Your primary data may be someone else's secondary data. The Florida Transportation Department collects primary data at many locations on the Florida highway system. For example, data are collected on vehicle speeds, number of vehicles, vehicle weights, and vehicle types. Southwest Airlines collects primary data on pilot flying hours, fuel consumption on flights, flight on-time rates, and customer satisfaction. The Internal Revenue Service (IRS) collects primary data on taxpayer incomes, charitable deductions, and IRA deposits. A soft drink bottling company obtains primary data when it measures the number of ounces in selected cans and bottles of soft drinks.

Likewise, secondary data sources abound. Business periodicals contain many types of business data. For example, you might locate a copy of the September 28, 1998, *Fortune* magazine. Beginning on page 225, the article entitled "Surprise, It's Not Just Tech Anymore" discusses the fastest-growing companies in the United States. Included in the article is an extensive data set on the 100 fastest growing companies. Such variables as net income, earnings per share, and sales revenues are provided for each company.

Companies like Value-Line and Compustat are in the business of providing secondary financial data on every company and mutual fund that are traded on the major stock exchanges or over the counter. We can subscribe to their services and use the data for many different purposes ranging from personal investment to corporate mergers and acquisitions.

Many state and federal government agencies collect and maintain data pertaining to their general function. For example, the U.S. Department of Agriculture maintains a wide array of data on crop sizes, acres planted, water used, and so forth. These data are available for our use either in printed form or in electronic form. Another source of secondary data is the data collected by the U.S. Census Bureau. These data include employment, education, income, and many other types of data for census tracts throughout the United States.

Of course, the World Wide Web is another source of secondary data of all kinds. Be aware that not all data posted on the Web are factually correct. You should use data only if the source is known for its integrity and accuracy.

Why do we distinguish between primary and secondary data? We do so because the required data collection techniques differ. For primary data, the key issue is to determine what data is needed and how, when, and where to gather this data. For secondary data, the key issue is to determine what data are needed and where to find them.

Tools for Collecting Data

There are many methods and tools available for collecting data. The following are considered some of the most useful and frequently used data collection methods:

- experiments
- telephone surveys
- mail questionnaires
- direct observation and personal interview

EXAMPLE 1-4

EXPERIMENTS

Food Processing

Oftentimes, a specific experiment or set of experiments is needed to generate the required data to make informed decisions. For example, the J. R. Simplot Company in Idaho is a primary supplier of french fries to companies such as McDonald's. At its Caldwell factory, Simplot has a tech center that, among other things, houses a mini–french fry plant used to conduct experiments on the manufacturing process. McDonald's has strict standards on the quality of the french fries it buys. One attribute of importance is the color of the fries after cooking. They should be "golden brown"—not too light or dark, and they should be uniform in color.

French fries are made from potatoes that are peeled, sliced into strips, blanched, partially cooked, and then freeze-dried. But this is not a simple process. Potatoes differ with respect to many factors, such as sugar content and moisture. Thus, there are many decisions that must be made about blanching time, cooking temperature, and other factors in order to produce quality french fries. The Simplot Company uses its tech center miniline to conduct **experiments** that have been defined by an **experimental design**.

EXPERIMENT
Any process that generates data as its outcome.

EXPERIMENTAL DESIGN
A plan for performing an experiment in which the variable of interest is defined. One or more factors are identified to be manipulated or changed so that the impact (or influence) on the variable of interest can be measured or observed.

The tech center employees start by grouping the raw potatoes into batches with similar characteristics. They then run some of the potatoes through the line with blanch time and temperature settings set at specific levels. They measure one or more output variables for that run, then change the settings and run another batch, again measuring the output variables.

Blanch Time	Blanch Temperature	Potato Category			
		1	2	3	4
10 minutes	100°				
	110°				
	120°				
15 minutes	100°				
	110°				
	120°				
20 minutes	100°				
	110°				
	120°				
25 minutes	100°				
	110°				
	120°				

FIGURE 1-7
Experiment Data Layout

Figure 1-7 shows a typical data collection form for an experiment of this type. The output variable (for example, percent of fries without dark spots) for each combination of potato category, blanch time, and blanch temperature is recorded in the appropriate cell in the table. Chapter 10 introduces the fundamental concepts related to experimental design and analysis.

Public Issues

1-5

TELEPHONE SURVEYS

One of the common methods of obtaining data about people and their opinions is the telephone survey. Chances are that you have been on the receiving end of one or more telephone surveys. "Hello. My name is Mary Jane and I represent the XYZ organization. I am conducting a survey on...."

Telephone surveys are a relatively inexpensive and efficient data collection tool. Of course, as with any data collection tool where people are required to supply the data, some people refuse to respond to the survey. Still others are not home when the call comes. A small percentage of people will not have phones or cannot be reached by phone for one reason or another.

During election years, political groups conduct polls on issues related to the campaign and to determine how the candidates are doing. Because polling should be conducted over a short period of time, polls are usually done using a telephone survey method. Figure 1-8 shows the major steps required in conducting a telephone survey. The survey was one conducted by a Seattle television station. It was designed to determine support for using public tax dollars in the construction of a new football stadium for the NFL Seattle Seahawks. The survey is aimed at property taxpayers only.

Because most people being interviewed will not stay on the line very long, the phone survey must be relatively short—usually 1 to 3 minutes. The questions typically are known as **closed-end questions.**

CLOSED-END QUESTIONS
Questions that require the respondent to select from a short list of defined choices.

For example, a closed-end question might be, "To which political party do you belong? Republican? Democrat? Or other?" The survey instrument should have a short statement at the beginning explaining the purpose of the survey and reassuring the respondent that

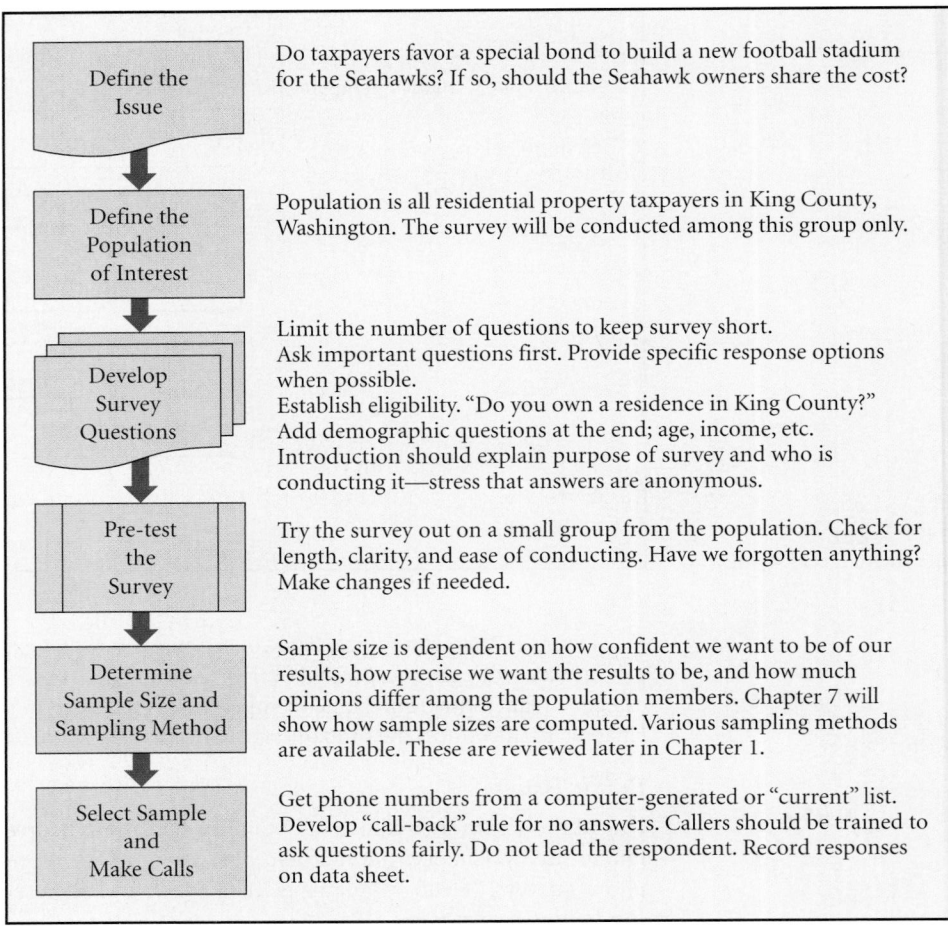

FIGURE 1-8
Major Steps for a Telephone
Survey

his or her responses will remain confidential. The initial section of the survey should contain questions relating to the central issue of the survey. The last part of the survey should contain the **demographic questions** (such as gender, income level, and education level) that will allow you to break down the responses and look deeper into the survey results.

> **DEMOGRAPHIC QUESTIONS**
> Questions relating to the respondents' own characteristics, backgrounds, and attributes.

A survey budget must be considered. For example, if you have $3,000 to spend on calls and each call costs $10 to make, you are obviously limited to making 300 calls. However, keep in mind that 300 calls may not result in 300 usable responses.

The phone survey should be conducted in a short elapsed time period. Typically, the prime calling time for a voter survey is between 7:00 P.M. and 9:00 P.M. However, some people are not home in the evening and would be excluded from the survey unless there is a plan for conducting callbacks.

MAIL QUESTIONNAIRES AND OTHER WRITTEN SURVEYS

The most frequently used method to collect opinion and factual data from people is a written survey. In some instances, the surveys are in the form of a mail questionnaire. At other times, the surveys are administered directly to the potential respondent. Written questionnaires are generally the least expensive means of collecting survey data. If the survey is mailed, the major costs include postage to and from the respondent, questionnaire development and printing costs, and data analysis.

Figure 1-9 shows the major steps in conducting a written survey. Note how written surveys are similar to telephone surveys; however, written surveys can be slightly more involved and therefore take more time to complete than those used for a telephone survey. You must be careful to construct a questionnaire that can be easily completed without requiring too much time.

A written survey can contain both closed-end and **open-end questions.**

> **OPEN-END QUESTIONS**
> Questions that allow respondents the freedom to respond with any value, words, or statements of their own choosing.

Open-end questions provide the respondent with greater flexibility in answering a question; however, the responses can be difficult to analyze. Note that telephone surveys can use open-end questions, too. However, the caller may have to transcribe a potentially long response and may misinterpret what is being said.

Written surveys also have to be formatted to make it easy for the respondent to provide accurate and reliable data. This means that proper space must be provided for the written responses. The directions must be clear as to how the survey is to be completed. A written survey needs to appear pleasing to the eye. How it looks will affect the response rate, so it

FIGURE 1-9
Written Survey Steps

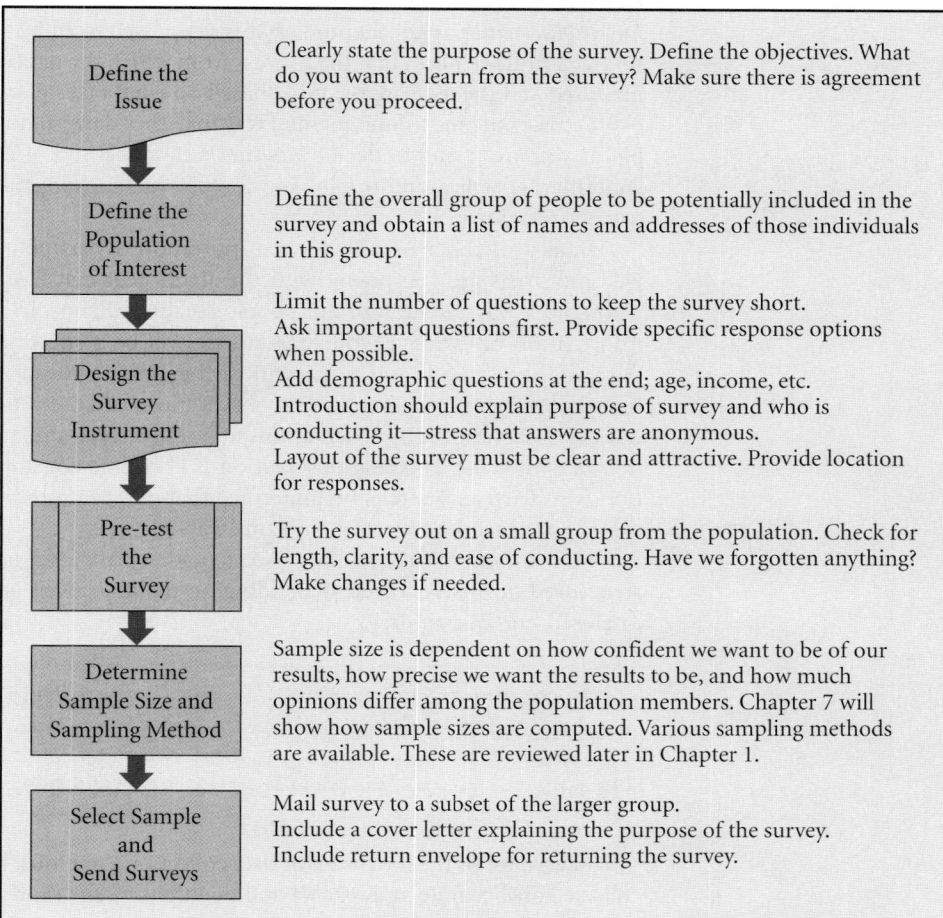

Define the Issue	Clearly state the purpose of the survey. Define the objectives. What do you want to learn from the survey? Make sure there is agreement before you proceed.
Define the Population of Interest	Define the overall group of people to be potentially included in the survey and obtain a list of names and addresses of those individuals in this group.
Design the Survey Instrument	Limit the number of questions to keep the survey short. Ask important questions first. Provide specific response options when possible. Add demographic questions at the end; age, income, etc. Introduction should explain purpose of survey and who is conducting it—stress that answers are anonymous. Layout of the survey must be clear and attractive. Provide location for responses.
Pre-test the Survey	Try the survey out on a small group from the population. Check for length, clarity, and ease of conducting. Have we forgotten anything? Make changes if needed.
Determine Sample Size and Sampling Method	Sample size is dependent on how confident we want to be of our results, how precise we want the results to be, and how much opinions differ among the population members. Chapter 7 will show how sample sizes are computed. Various sampling methods are available. These are reviewed later in Chapter 1.
Select Sample and Send Surveys	Mail survey to a subset of the larger group. Include a cover letter explaining the purpose of the survey. Include return envelope for returning the survey.

must look professional. Figure 1-10 presents the front page of the course evaluation survey administered to Boise State University students at the end of each semester. Three open-end questions are on the back of the survey asking the students to indicate the strengths and weaknesses of the course/instructor and to provide any other comments they might have. What do you think of this survey?

You also must decide whether you plan to manually enter or scan the data you gather from your written survey. The design of the survey will be affected by which approach you decide to take. If you are administering a large number of surveys, scanning is preferred—it cuts down on data-entry errors and speeds up the data-gathering process. However, you may be limited in the form of responses that are possible if you use scanning. The survey shown in Figure 1-10 is designed to be scanned after the students fill in the bubbles for their responses. The open-end questions on the back must be analyzed manually.

If the survey is administered directly to the desired respondents, you can expect a high response rate. For example, you probably have been on the receiving end of a written survey many times in your college career when you were asked to fill out a course evaluation form at the end of the term. Most students will complete the form. On the other hand, if a survey is administered through the mail you can expect a low response rate—typically 5% to 20%. So, if you want 200 responses, you should mail out 1,000 to 4,000 questionnaires.

Overall, written surveys can be a low-cost, effective means of collecting data if you can overcome the problems of low response. Be careful to pretest the survey and spend extra time on the format and look of the survey instrument.

DIRECT OBSERVATION AND PERSONAL INTERVIEWS

Direct observation is another tool that is often used to collect data. As implied by the name, this technique requires that the process from which the data are being collected is physically observed and the data are recorded based on what takes place in the process.

Possibly the most fundamental way to gather data on human behavior is to watch people. If you are trying to decide whether a new method of displaying your product at the supermarket will be more pleasing to customers, change a few displays and watch customers' reactions.

If, as a member of a state's transportation department, you want to determine how well motorists are complying with the state's seat belt laws, place observers at key spots throughout the state to monitor people's seat belt habits. If, as a movie producer, you want information on whether your new movie will be a success, hold a preview showing and observe the reactions and comments of the movie patrons as they exit the screening. The major constraints when collecting observations are the time and money it takes to carry out the observation. For observations to be effective, trained observers must be used, which increases the cost. Personal observation is also time consuming. Finally, personal perception is subjective. There is no guarantee that different observers will see a situation in the same way, much less report it the same way.

Personal interviews are often used to gather data from people. Interviews can be either **structured** or **unstructured**, depending on the objectives, and can utilize either open-end or closed-end questions.

STRUCTURED INTERVIEW Interviews in which the questions are scripted.	**UNSTRUCTURED INTERVIEW** Interviews that begin with one or more broadly stated questions with further questions being based on the responses.

Regardless of the tool used for data collection, care must be taken to ensure that the data collected are accurate and reliable and that they are the right data for the purpose at hand.

COLLEGE OF BUSINESS
FACULTY EVALUATION FORM

INSTRUCTOR _____   DATE ____ / ____ / 20 ____   COURSE NUMBER/SECTION _____

DIRECTIONS

USE NO. 2 PENCIL ONLY ⬤

| IMPROPER MARKS | PROPER MARK |

• MAKE HEAVY BLACK MARKS THAT FILL THE CIRCLE COMPLETELY.

• DO NOT MAKE ANY STRAY MARKS ON THIS ANSWER SHEET.

• ERASE CLEANLY ANY CHANGES YOU WISH TO MAKE.

	STRONGLY AGREE	AGREE	NEUTRAL	DISAGREE	STRONGLY DISAGREE	NO OPINION
1. The instructor was well prepared for class.	①	②	③	④	⑤	⑥
2. The instructor had a thorough knowledge of the subject.	①	②	③	④	⑤	⑥
3. The instructor communicated his/her subject matter well.	①	②	③	④	⑤	⑥
4. The instructor stimulated interest in the course subject(s).	①	②	③	④	⑤	⑥
5. The overall teaching ability of the instructor was high.	①	②	③	④	⑤	⑥
6. Course goals or objectives were clearly presented.	①	②	③	④	⑤	⑥
7. The course was intellectually challenging.	①	②	③	④	⑤	⑥
8. Textbook and/or other course materials aided understanding.	①	②	③	④	⑤	⑥
9. The instructor set high standards for the class.	①	②	③	④	⑤	⑥
10. Exam questions fairly reflected course content.	①	②	③	④	⑤	⑥
11. Grading was impartial.	①	②	③	④	⑤	⑥
12. I learned a great deal from the course.	①	②	③	④	⑤	⑥
13. Indicate your age: (1) under 21; (2) 21–25; (3) 26–30; (4) 31–35; (5) OVER 35.	①	②	③	④	⑤	
14. What is your class standing? (1) freshman; (2) sophomore; (3) junior; (4) senior; (5) graduate.	①	②	③	④	⑤	
15. This course is: (1) required; (2) elective.	①	②				
16. What is your overall college GPA? (1) 3.5–4.0; (2) 3.0–3.4; (3) 2.5–2.9; (4) 2.0–2.4; (5) under 2.0.	①	②	③	④	⑤	
17. What grade do you expect to receive in this class? (1) A; (2) B; (3) C; (4) D; (5) F	①	②	③	④	⑤	
18. What is your gender? (1) Male; (2) Female.	①	②				

Please Respond to Questions on the Reverse Side

FIGURE 1-10   Course Evaluation Form

Tools of Quality

DATA CHECK SHEETS

You will encounter many business situations that require measurements to be collected on the output of a process. This is especially true in quality improvement efforts. In these cases, a data collection tool known collectively as **data check sheets** can be very helpful.

> **DATA CHECK SHEETS**
> Forms designed for easy data collection. As the data are collected, they are displayed in a format that allows for immediate analysis.

Figure 1-11 illustrates three data check sheet examples. These examples are only a few of the virtually unlimited possible data check sheets. Regardless of the specific type of check sheet, the objectives are the same. Make sure the data are easy to record and that the sheets illustrate key information without the need for other specific computations and analysis.

Data Collection Issues

There are several issues involved in the collection of both primary and secondary data for which you need to be aware. When you have a need for data to aid in a decision situation, we suggest that you first look to see if appropriate secondary data exist. This is because secondary data are usually quicker and less expensive to collect than are primary data. However, before you rely on secondary data, you need to check out the source to make sure that the data were collected and recorded properly.

The Value-Lines and *Fortune* magazines of the world have built their reputations on providing quality data. And while data errors are occasionally encountered, they are few and far between. You really need to be concerned with data that come from sources with which you are not familiar. This is an issue for sources on the Web. Any organization, or any individual, can post data to the Web. Just because they are there does not mean that they are accurate. Be careful.

There are other general issues associated with data collection. One of these is the potential for *bias* in the data collection. There are many types of bias, and they can affect both primary and secondary data. For example, in a personal interview situation, the interviewer can interject bias (either accidentally or on purpose) by the way she asks the questions, by the tone of her voice, or by the way she looks at the subject being interviewed. We recently allowed ourselves to be interviewed at a trade show. The interviewer began by telling us that he would get credit for the interview only if we answered all of the questions. Next, he asked us to indicate our satisfaction with a particular display. He was not satisfied with our less than enthusiastic rating and kept asking us if we really meant what we said. He even asked us if we would consider upgrading our rating! How reliable do you think these data will be?

Another source of bias that can be interjected into a survey data collection process is called *nonresponse bias.* We stated earlier that mail surveys suffer from a high percentage of nonreturned surveys. Phone calls do not always get through or people refuse to answer. Subjects of personal interviews may refuse to be interviewed. There is a problem with nonresponse. Those who respond may provide data that would be quite different from the data that would be supplied by those who choose not to respond. If you are not careful, the responses may be heavily weighted by people who feel strongly one way or another on an issue.

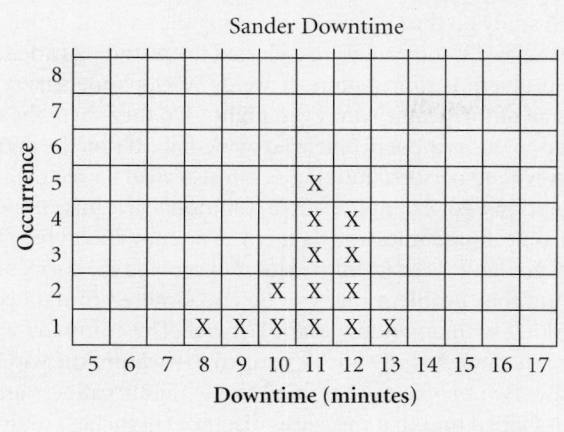

Sander Downtime

Distribution Plot

The *distribution plot* shows how data distribute over time. For example, this distribution plot shows machine down time. Each time a machine goes down, the time is measured and checked on the sheet. The pattern of downtime takes shape as the data are collected.

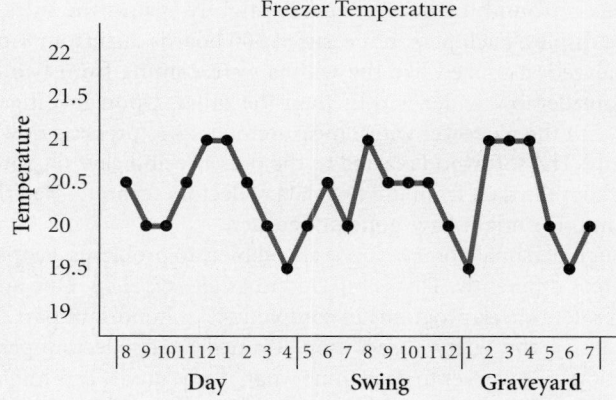

Freezer Temperature

Trend Sheet

The *trend sheet* shows data trends. For example, this trend sheet records freezer temperatures each hour of the day. As data are collected, the points are plotted and any trend analyzed. If the actual data are needed for computational purposes they can be taken from this sheet.

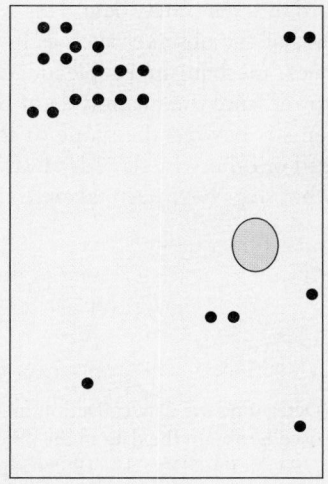

Visual Plot

The *visual plot* uses a representation of a product to depict data visually. For example, this visual plot to the left has marks showing the location of manufactured door defects. Other examples include error locations on loan applications and paint defects on automobiles.

FIGURE 1-11   Data Check Sheet Examples

Bias can be interjected by the way the subjects are selected for the data collection. This is referred to as *selection bias.* A study on the virtues of increasing the student athletic fee at your university might not be best served if the data were collected from students attending a football game. Sometimes, the problem is more subtle. If we do a telephone survey during the evening hours, we will miss all of the people who work nights. Do they share the same views, income, education levels, and so on, as those people who work days? If not, the data are biased.

Written and phone surveys and personal interviews can also yield flawed data if the interviewees *lie* in response to questions. For example, people commonly give inaccurate data about such sensitive matters as income. Sometimes, the data errors are not due to lies. The respondents may not know or may not have accurate information to provide the correct answer.

Measurement error is another problem that can be encountered in data collection. A few years ago we were working with a window manufacturer. The company was having a quality problem with one of its saws. A study was developed to measure the width of boards that had been cut by the saw. Two people were trained to use digital calipers and to record the data. This caliper is a U-shaped tool that measures distance (in inches) to three decimal places. The caliper is placed around the board, squeezed tightly against the sides, and the width is indicated on the display. Each person measured 500 boards during an 8-hour day. When the data were analyzed, it looked like the widths were coming from two different saws; one set showed considerably wider widths than the other. Upon investigation, we learned that the person with the narrower width measurements was pressing down on the calipers much more firmly. The soft wood reacted to the pressure and gave narrower reading. Fortunately, we had kept the data from the two data collectors separate. Had they been merged, the measurement error might have gone undetected.

Data collection through personal observation is also subject to problems. People tend to view the same event or item differently. This is referred to as *observer bias.* One area where this can easily occur is in safety check programs in companies. An important part of behavioral-based safety programs is the safety observation. Trained data collectors periodically conduct a safety observation on a worker to determine what, if any, unsafe acts might be taking place. We have seen situations in which two observers will conduct an observation on the same worker at the same time, yet record different safety data. This is especially true in areas where judgment is required on the part of the observer such as in judging the distance a worker is positioned from an exposed gear mechanism. People judge distance differently.

An extensive discussion of how to measure the magnitude of bias and how to reduce bias and other data collection problems is beyond the scope of this text. However, you should be aware that data may be biased or otherwise flawed. Always pose questions about the potential for bias and determine what steps have been taken to reduce its effect.

1-2: EXERCISES

1-8   RJR Nabisco reports a reduction in its work force of 16%. The U.S. Labor Department uses this information with similar data from other industries to update the unemployment rate. It announces that the unemployment rate has risen to 5.3%.
   a. Which of these two organizations would consider the 16% to be primary data? Explain your answer.
   b. Which of these two organizations would consider the 16% to be secondary data? Explain your answer.
   c. Which kind of data would the 5.3% unemployment rate be considered? By whom?

1-9   Determine the data collection method that most likely was used to obtain the data in the preceding problem.

1-10   *USA Today* (Dec. 15, 1998) reported that 8 out of 10 adults said they would give to charities during the Christmas season.
   a. Which kind of data is this?
   b. What data collection method do you think was used to collect these data? Explain your answer.

1-11   Reconsider Problem 10.
   a. Do you believe an open-end or closed-end question was used to obtain these data? Explain by writing the question you believe the researchers used.

b. If you chose "closed-end question," write an open-end question to obtain the same kind of information. If you chose "open-end question," write a closed-end question to obtain the same kind of information.

1-12 Do you believe that the data given in Problems 10 and 11 are biased data? If so, describe any bias that might exist in these data; if not, explain your reasoning.

1-13 The U.S. Department of Agriculture (USDA) estimates that the Southern fire ants spread at a rate of 4 to 5 miles a year. What data collection method do you think was used to collect these data? Explain your answer.

Business Applications

1-14 Assume that you have been given the task of conducting a survey of basketball season ticket holders at your university for the purpose of determining their satisfaction with the concessions. Describe the method of data collection you would recommend and outline the steps you would take to conduct the survey.

1-15 What are the advantages and disadvantages of using a mail questionnaire technique to survey cable TV customers regarding their preferences for a new all-sports channel?

1-16 As production manager for a personal computer maker, you want to set up a data collection process to help deal with the warranty returns problem facing your company. It has been suggested that you use a data check sheet. Develop an appropriate data check sheet and provide some sample data to show how the form will be used.

1-17 (1) Locate a written survey. (2) After reviewing the survey, prepare a critique of the survey. (3) What are its strengths and what are its weaknesses?

1-18 As manager of a department store in a local retail mall, you are interested in surveying your customers to determine whether they are pleased with the layout changes that have been made in the store. You wish to examine their attitudes concerning organization of the merchandise in the store, the ease of accessibility, locations of checkout stands, and position of walkways.
    a. Will the data you collect be considered primary or secondary data?
    b. State which of the four methods of collection (refer to page 10) you would use to collect your data.

c. Indicate the advantages and shortcomings of the method you chose in (b).

1-19 Assume you chose a telephone survey in Problem 18. Provide the following:
    a. A list of questions you will ask
    b. Your plan on how to convert data into computer readable form
    c. Your method of dealing with nonresponses

1-20 Referring to Problem 14, suppose you were to use a mail questionnaire to contact ticket holders who did not attend the basketball games in which you conducted your survey.
    a. List at least two open-end questions you would place on the survey.
    b. Describe how you would convert the answers to the open-end questions into computer readable form.

1-21 The administrator of a major city hospital in Detroit has asked you to assist in a study of the hospital's medical staff. The study is aimed at determining how satisfied these employees are and to learn what changes could be made to increase satisfaction. Suppose you choose to obtain your data using personal interviews.
    a. Adapt the six steps in Figure 1-8 to develop your personal interviews and explain how this method would be implemented at the hospital.
    b. Discuss the advantages and disadvantages of the method you have selected over other potential methods.

1-22 In your position as assistant manager for the University Food Service Company, you have been asked to collect data regarding various customer behaviors in the food line at the university cafeteria. Specifically, you are interested in the beverage and dessert selections. The cafeteria offers the same 10 dessert selections every day. Develop a check sheet to collect the data on dessert selections made by the food line customers.

1-23 The cafeteria offers a selection of the same 8 beverages every day. These beverages are served through a dispenser that regulates the proportion of syrup dispensed for each beverage.
    a. Develop a check sheet known as a trend sheet to track the proportion of syrup dispensed by one dispenser every hour for a week.
    b. Produce a sample trend sheet for some hypothetical data that you generate.

■ 1-3: POPULATIONS, SAMPLES, AND SAMPLING TECHNIQUES

Populations and Samples

Two of the most important terms in statistics are **population** and **sample**.

POPULATION	**SAMPLE**
The set of all objects or individuals of interest or the measurements obtained from all objects or individuals of interest.	A subset of the population.

The list of all objects or individuals of interest is referred to as the *frame*. The choice of the frame depends on what objects or individuals you wish to study and on the availability of the list of these objects or individuals. Once the frame is defined, it forms the list of items from which the sample will be selected. The next example illustrates what we mean.

CPA Firm

POPULATIONS AND SAMPLES

The difference between a population and a sample can be illustrated using an example involving a certified public accounting (CPA) firm. When preparing to audit the financial records of a business, the CPA firm must determine the number of accounts to examine. Traditionally, good accounting practice dictated that the auditors verify the balance of every account and trace through each financial transaction. Though this is still done in some audits, the size and complexity of most businesses have forced accountants to select only some accounts and some transactions to audit.

The accountant's first problem is to determine just what she wishes to examine. Suppose one part of the financial audit involves verifying the accounts-receivable balances. By definition a population includes all the items of interest to the data gatherer. The accountant defines the population of interest as *all accounts receivable balances* on record. The list of these accounts, possibly by account number, forms the frame. Next, she selects from this frame a subset of the accounts. The account balances for this subset of accounts is the *sample*. The accountant uses the sample results to make inferences about the population. If the sample balances look good, she might conclude that the population balances also would be acceptable. How these inferences are drawn will be discussed at greater length in later chapters.

Instead of selecting a sample of accounts receivable balances, the accountant could audit each account in the population. In this case, the accountant is taking a **census**. There are trade-offs between taking a census and a sample. Usually the trade-off is whether the information gathered in a census is worth the extra cost of taking a census. In organizations in which many census-type data are stored on computer files, the additional time and effort of gathering all information are not substantial. For the certified public accounting firm, the accounts may have to be manually checked and, if there are many accounts in the population, a census may be impractical.

> **CENSUS**
> An enumeration of the entire set of measurements taken from the whole population.

Another consideration is that the measurement error in census data may be greater than in sample data. A person obtaining data from fewer sources tends to be more complete and thorough in both gathering and tabulating the data. As a result, with a sample there are likely to be fewer human errors.

PARAMETERS AND STATISTICS

Descriptive numerical measures, such as an average or a percentage, that are computed from the entire population are called *parameters*. Corresponding measures for a sample are called *statistics*. In the previous example, if the CPA examined every accounts receivable balance, the percentage of correct balances would be a parameter since it reflects the value for the population. However, if she selected a sample of balances from the population, the percentage of accurate balances in this sample is a statistic. These concepts are more fully discussed in Chapters 3 and 6.

Sampling Techniques

Once a manager decides to gather information by sampling, he can use a sampling technique that falls into one of two categories: **statistical** or **nonstatistical**.

NONSTATISTICAL SAMPLING TECHNIQUES	STATISTICAL SAMPLING TECHNIQUES
Those methods of selecting samples using convenience, judgment, or other nonchance processes.	Those sampling methods that use selection techniques based on chance selection.

Both nonstatistical and statistical sampling techniques are commonly used by decision makers. There are some advantages to using a statistical sampling technique, as we will discuss at many places throughout this text. However, in many cases, nonstatistical sampling represents the only feasible way to sample.

J. R. Simplot Company

Recall the manufacturer of frozen french fries that we discussed earlier. The J. R. Simplot Company samples potatoes from each truck arriving at its manufacturing plant and tests these potatoes to assess their quality. The company uses the results of the sample to determine whether each truckload should be accepted. The quality control people use a nonstatistical sampling method. They select a few potatoes from the rear trap door of each truck rather than from throughout the load, as statistical sampling would require. The sheer volume of potatoes in a truck makes a statistical sample operationally impossible. Instead, Simplot relies on the idea that potatoes are evenly spread, by quality, throughout the truckload. The nonstatistical sampling method used by the Simplot Company is referred to as **convenience sampling**.

EXAMPLE 1-7

NONSTATISTICAL SAMPLING

> **CONVENIENCE SAMPLING**
> A sampling technique that selects the items from the population based on accessibility and ease of selection

There are other nonstatistical sampling methods such as *judgment sampling* and *ratio sampling* which we will not discuss here. Instead, we now turn our attention to the most frequently used statistical sampling techniques.

STATISTICAL SAMPLING

Statistical sampling methods (also called *probability sampling*) provide for every item in the population to have a known or calculable chance of being included in the sample. The fundamental statistical sample is called a *simple random sample*. Other types of statistical sampling include *stratified random sampling, systematic sampling,* and *cluster sampling.*

EXAMPLE 1-8

SIMPLE RANDOM SAMPLING

Baird Life and Casualty

A salesperson at Baird Life and Casualty in Charleston, West Virginia, wishes to estimate the percentage of people in a local subdivision who already have life insurance policies. The result would be an indication of the potential market in the subdivision. The population of interest consists of all families living in the subdivision.

For the purposes of this example, we simplify the situation by saying that there are only five families in the subdivision: James, Sanchez, Lui, White, and Fitzpatrick. We will let N be the population size and n be the sample size. From the five families ($N = 5$), we select three ($n = 3$) for the sample. There are 10 possible samples of size 3 that could be selected:

{James, Sanchez, Lui}	{James, Sanchez, White}	{James, Sanchez, Fitzpatrick}
{James, Lui, White}	{James, Lui, Fitzpatrick}	{James, White, Fitzpatrick}
{Sanchez, Lui, White}	{Sanchez, Lui, Fitzpatrick}	{Sanchez, White, Fitzpatrick}
{Lui, White, Fitzpatrick}		

This example does not allow a family to be selected more than once in a given sample. This method is called *sampling without replacement* and is the most commonly used random sampling method. If the families could be selected more than once, this would be called *sampling with replacement*.

Simple random sampling is the method most people think of when they think of random sampling.

SIMPLE RANDOM SAMPLING

A method of selecting items from a population such that *every possible sample of a specified size has an equal chance of being selected.*

Additional Example 1-a

Random Sampling Using the Lottery Method

In a correctly performed simple random sample, each of these samples would have an equal chance of being selected. A simplified way of performing this technique would be to put each sample of three names on a piece of paper in a bowl, then blindly reach in and select one piece of paper. This method would be difficult to do if the number of possible samples were large. For example, if $N = 50$ and a sample of $n = 10$ is to be selected, there are over 10 billion possible samples. Try finding a bowl big enough to hold those![1]

Simple random samples can be obtained in a variety of ways. We will present several examples to illustrate how simple random samples are selected in practice.

Nordstrom's Payroll

1-9

RANDOM NUMBERS

Suppose the personnel manager at Nordstrom's Department Store in Seattle is considering changing the pay period from once a month to every two weeks. Before doing this he plans to survey a sample of the store's 300 employees. Employees are assigned a number (001–300). Either Excel or Minitab can be used to determine which employees are to be included in the sample by taking advantage of their *random number functions*. For example, Figure 1-12 shows the results when Excel is used to create 10 random numbers assuming the Nordstrom manager wishes to survey 10 employees. The first employee to be sampled is number 115 followed by 31 and so forth. The important thing to remember is that assigning each employee a number and randomly selecting the number allows each possible sample an equal chance of being selected.

Excel and Minitab Tutorial

FIGURE 1-12
Excel Output of Random Numbers for Nordstrom's Example

	A	B	C	D
1	115			
2	31			
3	179			
4	270			
5	265			
6	288			
7	5			
8	123			
9	259			
10	42			

To convert numbers to integers, select the data in column A and click the Decrease decimal button several times.

Excel Instructions:
1. Click on the Tools tab
2. Select the Data Analysis option
3. Select Random Number Generation option
4. Select Uniform as the distribution
5. Define range as between 1 and 300
6. Indicate where the results are to go
7. Click OK

---

[1]The value is determined using a counting tool called *combinations* that is discussed in Chapter 4.

OPTIONAL CD-ROM TOPIC   Using a Random Numbers Table
Random numbers tables are one tool that decision makers use to determine which items in the population will be selected into the random sample. For more information, go to the CD-ROM.

EXAMPLE
1-10

STRATIFIED RANDOM SAMPLE

Federal Reserve Bank

Sometimes, the sample size required to obtain a certain level of information from a simple random sampling may be greater than a budget permits. At other times it may take more time than is available to collect the information. **Stratified random sampling** is an alternative method that has the potential to provide the desired information with a smaller sample size.

> **STRATIFIED RANDOM SAMPLING**
> A statistical sampling method in which the population is divided into subgroups called *strata* so that each population item belongs to only one stratum. The objective is to form strata such that the population values of interest within each stratum are as much alike as possible. Sample items are selected from each stratum using the simple random sampling method.

Each year, the Federal Reserve Board asks its staff to estimate the total cash holdings of U.S. financial institutions as of July 1. They base the estimate on a sample. The variable of interest is the total cash holdings of each of the financial institutions (banks, credit unions, etc.) in the United States as of July 1. However, not all of these financial institutions are the same size. A majority are classified as small, some are medium-sized, and only a few are large-sized. However, the few large institutions have a substantial percentage of the total cash on hand. To make sure that a simple random sample includes an appropriate number of large, medium, and small institutions, the sample size might have to be quite large.

As an alternative to the simple random sample, the Federal Reserve staff could divide the institutions into three groups called *strata*: small, medium, and large. They could then select a simple random sample of institutions from each stratum and estimate the total cash on hand for all institutions from this combined sample. Figure 1-13 shows the stratified random sampling concept. Note, the combined sample size $(n_1 + n_2 + n_3)$ is the sum of the sizes of the simple random samples taken from each stratum.

The objective of stratified sampling is to develop strata that, for the characteristic of interest (such as cash on hand), have items that are quite *homogeneous*. In this example, the size of the financial institution may be a good factor on which to stratify. If so, the combined sample size, $(n_1 + n_2 + n_3)$, will be less than the required sample size if no stratification had been done. Since sample size is directly related to cost (in both time and money), this means a stratified sample can be more cost effective than a simple random sample.

Multiple layers of stratification can be used to further reduce the overall required sample size. For example, the Federal Reserve might break the three strata in Figure 1-13 into *substrata* based on type of institution: state bank, interstate bank, credit union, and so on.

Most large-scale market research studies use stratified random sampling. The well-known political polls such as the Gallup and Harris polls also use this technique. For instance, the Gallup poll typically samples between 1,800 and 2,500 people nationwide to estimate how more than 60 million people will vote in a presidential election.

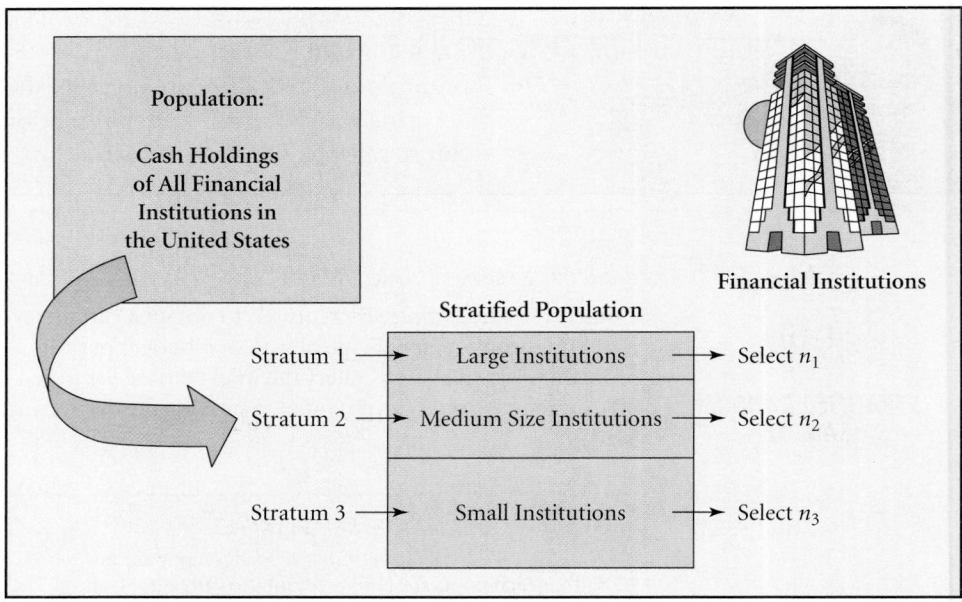

FIGURE 1-13
Stratified Sampling Example

SYSTEMATIC SAMPLING

National Association of Accountants

A few years ago, the National Association of Accountants (NAA) considered establishing a code of ethics. To determine the opinion of its 20,000 members, a questionnaire was sent to a sample of 500 members.

Although simple random sampling could have been used, an alternative method called **systematic random sampling** was chosen.

SYSTEMATIC RANDOM SAMPLING
A statistical sampling technique that involves selecting every kth item in the population after randomly selecting a starting point between 1 and k. The value of k is determined as the ratio of the population size over the desired sample size.

The NAA's systematic random sampling plan called for the group to send the questionnaire to every fortieth member ($20,000/500 = 40$) from the list of total members. The list is in alphabetical order. We could begin by using Excel or Minitab to generate a single random number in the range 1 to 40. Suppose this value is 25. Thus, the twenty-fifth person in our alphabetical list would be selected. After that, every fortieth member would be selected {25, 65, 105, 145, . . . } until we had 500 NAA members.

Systematic sampling is frequently used in business applications. Systematic sampling should be used as an alternative to simple random sampling only when the population can be assumed to be randomly ordered with respect to the measurement being addressed in the survey. In this case, peoples' views on ethics are likely unrelated to the spelling of their last name.

CLUSTER SAMPLING

Morrison-Knudsen

With a telephone survey or a mail questionnaire, the geographical location of the respondents is not a significant data collection issue. However, in some instances when physical measurement or observation is required to collect the data, location can be an important issue.

Suppose the Morrison-Knudsen Company, a large worldwide construction company, wants to develop a new corporate bidding strategy. Upper management wants input on possible new strategies from its middle-level managers. Assume that Figure 1-14 illustrates the

FIGURE 1-14   Mid-Level Managers by Location for Morrison-Knudsen Construction Company

Algeria	Illinois	Scotland	California	Alaska	New York	Florida	Idaho	Mexico	Australia
25	47	22	105	20	36	52	152	76	37

current distribution of middle-level managers throughout the world. For example, there are 25 middle-level managers in Algeria, 47 in Illinois, and so forth. Upper management decides to hold face-to-face personal interviews with a sample of these mid-level managers.

One sampling technique is to select a simple random sample of size n from the population of middle managers. Unfortunately, this technique would likely require that the interviewer(s) go to each state or country in which Morrison-Knudsen has middle-level managers. This would prove to be an expensive and time-consuming process. A systematic or stratified sampling procedure also would probably require visiting each location. The geographical spread in this case causes problems.

A sampling technique that overcomes the traveling (time and money) problem is **cluster sampling.**

> **CLUSTER SAMPLING**
> A method by which the population is divided into groups, or clusters, that are each intended to be mini-populations. A simple random sample of m clusters is selected. The items selected from a cluster can be selected using any probability sampling technique.

Ideally, the clusters would each have the same characteristics as the population as a whole. In the Morrison-Knudsen example, the states or countries where the company has managers would be the clusters.

After the clusters have been defined, a sample of m clusters is selected at random from the list of possible clusters. The number of clusters to select depends on various factors including the survey budget. Suppose Morrison-Knudsen selects $m = 3$ clusters randomly as follows:

Additional
Example 1-b

Cluster Sampling

Scotland   Florida   Illinois

These are referred to as the *primary clusters.* Next, the company can either survey all the managers in each cluster or select a simple random sample of managers from each cluster depending on time and budget considerations.

1-3: EXERCISES

ADDITIONAL EXERCISES ON YOUR CD-ROM
  Try the ADDITIONAL EXERCISES and APPLICATION PROBLEMS on the CD-ROM.

1-24 The U.S. Department of Transportation reported the average number of pieces of mishandled baggage per 1,000 passengers for October was 4.39. State whether this number is a statistic or a population parameter. Explain your answer.

1-25 In a recent trading session the NASDAQ composite fell 62 points. Since this was obtained from data for one day, would this be considered a sample? Explain.

1-26 An Ernst & Young survey of 1,363 consumers and more than 120 retailers and consumer goods manufacturers indicated that in 1997 12% of retailers sold "on line" to consumers. Is this percentage a statistic? Explain.

1-27 On October 31, Reuters news service announced that housing starts in November are estimated to be 1.68 million and were 1.695 million for October. One of these numbers is a population parameter. Indicate which number is a population parameter and give your reasons for your selection.

1-28 The Standard & Poor's 500 index on May 11, 2000, stood at 1,383.05. Give the general statistical term that is used to describe the set of measurements that was used to obtain this index.

1-29 Give the name of the kind of sampling that was most likely done in each of the following cases:
   a. A *Washington Post*/ABC News poll of 2,000 people to determine the president's approval rating
   b. A poll taken of each of the General Motors dealerships in Ohio in December 1999 to determine an estimate of the average number of 1999 model Chevrolets not yet sold by GM dealerships in the United States
   c. A quality assurance procedure within a BF Goodrich manufacturing plant that takes every thousandth tire produced to test for cord strength of the tire
   d. A sampling technique in which a random sample from each of the tax brackets is obtained by the Internal Revenue Service to audit tax returns

1-30 State the potential advantages of cluster sampling over simple random sampling.

1-31 Explain the difference between a cluster and a stratum.

1-32 A student has suggested that one could use a systematic sampling technique to sample from the primary clusters of a cluster sampling scheme. Explain why this is either a good or a bad idea.

1-33 What are the potential advantages of stratified random sampling over simple random sampling? Explain, with an example of your own indicating how this advantage might be realized.

Business Applications

1-34 The U.S. Forest Service plans to survey backcountry hikers to determine the quality of their outdoor experience. They will ask randomly selected hikers to rate the quality on a scale from 1 to 5. One indicates total dissatisfaction; 5 indicates total satisfaction. Define the population of interest. Be sure to specify the measurement of interest as part of your definition. Assume a sample of 200 is to be obtained.

1-35 Refer to Problem 34.
   a. Describe an approach you would suggest to take a random sample from the population. State which sampling technique you would use.
   b. Assuming the population size is 1,500, use either Excel or Minitab to generate the list of hikers to be selected in the sample.

1-36 The Ritz-Carlton Hotel managers wish to select a random sample of hotel guests who stayed at their Atlanta hotel on February 11. They have the list of 742 guests together with their mailing addresses. Each guest is given an identifica-

tion number (001–742). Use Excel or Minitab to generate a list of 30 guest identification numbers so that the guests with those identification numbers can be surveyed.

1-37 Referring to Problem 36, suppose the Ritz-Carlton managers wish to personally interview guests who will stay at their hotels throughout the United States on March 20.
   a. Describe an approach for using cluster sampling to select the sample.
   b. What are the potential advantages of using cluster sampling in this case instead of simple random sampling?
   c. Would it be possible to conduct a census in this situation? Why or why not?

1-38 The Fairview Title Company has over 4,000 customer files listed alphabetically in its computer system. The office manager wants to survey a sample of these customers to determine how satisfied they were with service provided by the title company. She plans to use a telephone survey of 100 customers.
   a. Describe how you would attach identification numbers to the customer files (e.g., how many digits [and which digits] would you use to indicate the first customer file?).
   b. Describe how the first random number would be obtained to begin a simple random sample method.
   c. How many random digits would you need for each random number you selected?
   d. Use Excel or Minitab to generate the list of customers to be surveyed.

1-39 Refer to Problem 38.
   a. State the advantage of conducting a systematic random sample instead of a simple random sample.
   b. Describe the method that you would use to take a systematic sample.

1-40 The Craigthorp Company is a statewide food distributor to restaurants, universities, and other establishments that prepare and sell food. The company has a very large warehouse where the food is stored until it is pulled from the shelves to be delivered to the customers. The warehouse has 64 storage racks numbered 1 to 64. Each rack is three shelves high (labeled A, B, and C). The shelves are divided into 80 sections each numbered 1 to 80. Products are located by rack number, shelf letter, and section number. For example, breakfast cereal is located at 43-A-52 (rack 43, shelf A, section 52).

Each week, employees perform an inventory for a sample of products. Certain products are selected and counted. The *actual count* is compared to the *book count* (the quantity in the records that should be in stock). To simplify things assume that the company has selected breakfast cereals to inventory. Also for sake of simplicity suppose the cereals occupy racks 1 through 5.
   a. Assume that you plan to use simple random sampling to select the sample. Use Excel or Minitab to determine the sections on each of the five racks to be sampled.
   b. Assume that you wish to use cluster random sampling to select the sample. Discuss the steps you would take to carry out the sampling.

c. In this case, why might cluster sampling be preferred over simple random sampling? Discuss.

1-41 A major retail store plans to select a sample of people entering the store on a given Saturday morning. The purpose of the sample is to determine which mode of advertising drew the customer to the store. Assume that the store manager does not care whether the survey is done using statistical or nonstatistical methods.

    a. Give reasons why you might choose a nonstatistical method for this survey.

    b. Assume 100 customers are to be sampled. Give details of how you would select the customers needed for the survey.

    c. Discuss any "bias" issues you considered in constructing your survey method.

1-42 Referring to Problem 41, suppose the manager decides that she wants a random sample of customers.

    a. Discuss the details of how this simple random sample would be obtained.

    b. How would this process impact the cost and time required to do the study? Discuss.

■ 1-4: DATA TYPES AND DATA MEASUREMENT LEVELS

Chapters 2 and 3 will introduce a variety of techniques for describing data and transforming the data into information. As you will see in those chapters, the statistical techniques deal with different forms of data. The level of measurement may vary greatly from application to application. In general, there are four types of data: *quantitative, qualitative, time series,* and *cross-sectional.*

Quantitative and Qualitative Data

In some cases, the data values are best expressed in purely numerical, or **quantitative,** terms, such as in dollars, pounds, inches, or percentages.

QUANTITATIVE DATA
Data that are numeric and which define value or quantity.

As an example, a study of college students at your campus might obtain data on the number of hours each week that students work at a paying job and the income level of the students' parents.

In other cases the observation may signify only the category to which an item belongs. Categorical data are referred to as **qualitative** data.

QUALITATIVE DATA
Data whose measurement scale is inherently categorical.

For example, a study might be interested in the class standings—*freshman, sophomore, junior, senior,* or *graduate*—of college students. The same study might also ask the students to judge the quality of their education as *very good, good, fair, poor,* or *very poor.*

Time Series Data and Cross-Sectional Data

Data may also be classified as being either **time series** or **cross-sectional.**

TIME SERIES DATA
A set of ordered data values observed at successive points in time.

CROSS-SECTIONAL DATA
A set of data values observed at a fixed point in time.

Ford Motor Company tracks the sales of its Taurus automobile on a monthly basis. Data values observed at intervals over time are referred to as time series data.

The data collected from the study of college students mentioned previously would be cross-sectional since the data from each student relate to a fixed point in time.

Data Measurement Levels

Data can also be identified as to their *level of measurement*. This is important since the higher the data level, the more sophisticated the analysis that can be performed. This will be clear when you study the material in the remaining chapters of this text.

We shall discuss and give examples of four levels of data measurements: *nominal, ordinal, interval,* and *ratio.* Figure 1-15 illustrates the hierarchy among these data levels with nominal data being the lowest level.

NOMINAL DATA

Nominal data are the lowest form of data, yet you will encounter this type of data many times. Assigning codes to categories generates nominal data. For example, a survey question that asks for marital status provides the following responses:

1. Married   2. Single   3. Divorced   4. Other

For each person, a code of 1, 2, 3, or 4 would be recorded. These codes are nominal data. Note that the values of the code numbers have no specific meaning since the order of the categories is arbitrary. We might just as well have shown it this way:

1. Single   2. Divorced   3. Married   4. Other

With nominal data we also have complete control over what codes are used. For example, we could have used:

88. Single   11. Divorced   33. Married   55. Other

All that matters is that you know which code stands for which category. Recognize also that the codes need not be numeric. We might use:

S = Single   D = Divorced   M = Married   O = Other

ORDINAL DATA

Ordinal, or **rank**, **data** are one notch above nominal data on the measurement hierarchy. At this level, the data elements can be rank-ordered on the basis of some relationship among them, with the assigned values indicating this order. For example, a typical market-research

FIGURE 1-15
Data Level Hierarchy

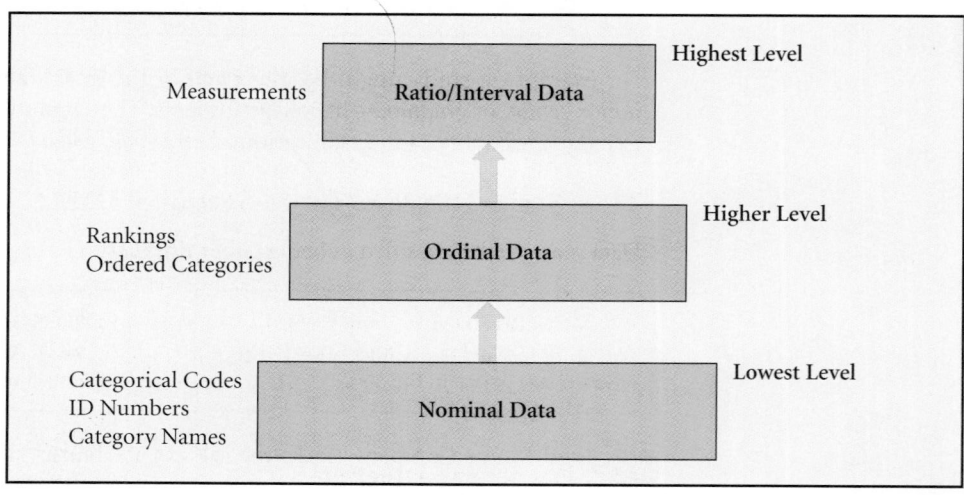

technique is to offer potential customers the chance to use two unidentified brands of a product. The customers are then asked to indicate which brand they prefer. The brand eventually offered to the general public depends on how often it was the preferred test brand. The fact that an ordering of items took place makes this an ordinal measure.

Bank loan applicants are asked to indicate the category corresponding to their household incomes:

_____ Under $20,000 _____ $20,000–$40,000 _____ over $40,000

(1)   (2)   (3)

The codes 1, 2, or 3 refer to the particular income category, with higher codes assigned to higher incomes.

Ordinal measurement allows decision makers to equate two or more observations, or to rank-order the observations. In contrast, nominal data can be compared only for equality. You cannot order nominal measurements. Thus, a primary difference between ordinal data and nominal data is that ordinal data contain both an equality ($=$) and an inequality relationship ($<, >$), whereas nominal data contain only an equality ($=$) relationship.

INTERVAL DATA

If the distance between two data items can be measured on some scale, and the data have ordinal properties ($>, <$, or $=$), the data are said to be **interval data.** The best example of interval data is the temperature scale. Both the Fahrenheit and Celsius temperature scales have ordinal properties of ">" and "=". In addition, the distances between equally spaced points are preserved. For example, 32°F $>$ 30°F and 80°F $>$ 78°F. The difference between 32°F and 30°F is the same as the difference between 80°F and 78°F, two degrees in each case. Thus, interval data allow us to precisely measure the difference between any two values. With ordinal data this is not possible since we can say only that one value is larger than another.

RATIO DATA

Data that have all the characteristics of interval data but also have a true zero point (where zero means "none") are called **ratio data.** Ratio measurement is the highest level of measurement.

Packagers of frozen foods encounter ratio measures when they pack their products by weight. Weight, whether measured in pounds or grams, is a ratio measurement because it has a unique zero point—zero meaning no weight. Many other types of data encountered in business environments involve ratio measurements, for example, distance, money, and time.

The difference between interval and ratio measurements can be confusing because it involves the definition of a true zero. If you have $5 and your brother has $10, he has twice as much money as you. If you convert your dollars to pounds, lire, yen, or marks, your brother will still have twice as much as you. If your money is lost or stolen, you have no dollars. Money has a true zero. Likewise, if you travel 100 miles today and 200 miles tomorrow, the ratio of distance traveled will be 2/1, even if you convert the distance to kilometers. If on the third day you rest, you have traveled no miles. Distance has a true zero. Conversely, if today's temperature is 35°F (1.67°C) and tomorrow's is 70°F (21.11°C), is tomorrow twice as warm as today? The answer is no. One way to see this is to convert the Fahrenheit temperature to Celsius and the ratio will no longer be 2/1 (12.64/1). Likewise, if the temperature reads 0°F (-17.78°C), this does not imply that there is no temperature—it is simply colder than 10°F (-12.22°C). Also, 0°C (32°F) is not the same temperature as 0°F. Thus, temperature, measured with either the Fahrenheit or Celsius scale (an interval level variable), does not have a true zero.

1-4: EXERCISES

1-43 For each of the following, indicate whether the data are quantitative or qualitative. Also indicate the level of data measurement.
   a. Sales regions *quant, nominal*
   b. Price to earnings ratio of a stock *quan, not ratio*
   c. Quarterly profit reported by Microsoft Corp. *quan, ratio*
   d. Response to market research survey measured on the Likert scale. The scale is in integer steps from 1 to 5; rate the level of satisfaction you have had with our service department as (1) exceptional, (2) very good, (3) good, (4) satisfactory, or (5) unsatisfactory *qualif, ord*
   e. Market share captured by Intel Corp.'s Pentium IV processor *quan, ratio*
   f. Quarterly dividend paid by Paine Webber Group Inc. *quan ratio*

1-44 Indicate whether each of the following is cross-sectional or time series data.
   a. Your income last year
   b. Weekly defect rate for one assembly line
   c. Yearly size of the population of your city since 1970
   d. Customer bank balances on December 1
   e. Students' grade point averages for the fall term of 1999
   f. Annual student enrollment from 1970 to 2000

1-45 For each of the following variables, indicate the level of data measurement.
   a. Number of years of education *ratio*
   b. Hair color *nominal*
   c. Type of business *nom*
   d. Salaries of the CEOs of the Fortune 500 companies *ratio, ord*
   e. Temperature of furnaces in steel smelteries *int ratio*
   f. Job classification *nom*

Business Applications

1-46 The company for which you work wishes to determine the percentage of Internet sales made by the companies with which it competes. You are assigned this task. You are

deciding between two survey questions to use: (1) List the percentage of your sales obtained through the Internet, or (2) The percentage of your sales obtained through the Internet is (1) 0–10, (2) 11–20 ... (10) 91–100.
   a. State the level of measurement the responses would be to each of these survey questions.
   b. State whether each survey question's responses would be qualitative or quantitative.
   c. Which of these two survey questions would allow you to calculate the average percent of sales obtained through the Internet?

1-47 In the previous problem, your supervisor tells you to assign the number in parentheses to the responses in each of the categories given above (e.g., 1 is assigned to 0–10, 2 to 11–20, ... , 10 to 91–100). He then instructs you to calculate the average of these assigned numbers and then transform the number obtained back to the appropriate category to find the average percentage of sales through the Internet.
   a. Respond to your supervisor's idea by classifying the assigned numbers as qualitative or quantitative data.
   b. Does an assigned number of 4 indicate twice as large a percentage of sales through the Internet as does a number of 2?
   c. What is the level of measurement for these assigned numbers?
   d. Would such data be classified as time series or cross-sectional data?

1-48 As part of a marketing survey, you ask customers to list the number of children they have by placing a check by the appropriate category: ___0, ___1, ___2, ___3, ___>3.
   a. Specify the level of measurement that such a response exhibits.
   b. Could you calculate the average number of children for the respondents to this survey? Indicate how you would modify the survey so that you could calculate such a statistic.

■ 1-5: USING YOUR COMPUTER

Computer hardware and software provide a major advantage to business statistics students and decision makers. There are many different software packages that can be used to aid the statistical analysis process; however, they can generally be categorized into one of two groups: *spreadsheet packages* and *statistical packages.* The best-known spreadsheet packages are Microsoft Excel, Lotus 123, and Quattro Pro. Spreadsheet packages are very versatile. They can be used for many different purposes and contain many built-in tools and functions to help you accomplish a wide range of business activities. In addition to the many financial and accounting functions available to you, spreadsheets now make available a variety of important statistics tools.

[handwritten margin notes:]
a) 1. ratio = quantitative
   2. ordinal = qualitative

b) 1. quantitative
   2. quantitative qualitative because of categories

Many high quality statistical software packages are available for PCs. The best known are Minitab, SPSS-X, and SAS. All are excellent software packages and have been developed with the pull-down menu look associated with Windows-based packages. In fact the statistical software packages also have a spreadsheet look and feel, but they contain more statistical features and fewer of the general-purpose functions found in spreadsheets.

This text emphasizes Excel but also introduces you to Minitab. Throughout the text, we illustrate the output from these two packages to help you understand how to interpret statistical output. This text focuses on the use of Excel's and Minitab's data analysis, graphical tools, and special statistical tools. Many business application exercises and cases in this text provide the opportunity to improve your skills with either or both of these software packages. While most of the output shown in this text is from Excel, the CD-ROM that accompanies your text has a Minitab and Excel tutorial that shows step-by-step how to work out each of the computer examples using each of these software packages.

Issues with Excel

The statistical features within Excel were not originally part of the software. Instead they were developed as an "add-in" package called the Analysis ToolPak, which has been included with Excel in recent versions. The Analysis ToolPak contains a number of statistical procedures that apply to the material in this course. While most of the Analysis ToolPak results are consistent with what you will find if you use true statistical software packages such as Minitab, recently statisticians have discovered certain issues with some of the statistical procedures. Some of these issues are minor aggravations such as the use of uncommon terminology and output format. Others are considered more serious. Under certain circumstances the output results are incorrect and do not match what you would get from true statistical software packages such as Minitab.

Although these problems do exist, we believe that Excel is still an excellent tool for helping students learn about statistics in their first courses. It is a software package that you will very likely have access to in your job once you graduate, and you may wish to use it for basic statistical work. However, until the Excel problems are fixed, you may wish to use a true statistical software package, such as Minitab, for more serious statistical applications. At various points throughout this text, we will point out some of the more important Excel issues that we now know about. If you are using Excel in this course, watch for these cautions.

If your college or university features a software package other than Excel or Minitab, you will still find this text useful. The statistical concepts and techniques introduced apply to any statistical software. Although the output may be formatted slightly differently with your software, the computations should be the same and the interpretation of the results will be no different.

OPTIONAL CD-ROM TOPIC   Data Format in Excel and Minitab
Both Excel and Minitab use the same row and column format for the data files. For more information, go to the CD-ROM.

■ SUMMARY AND CONCLUSIONS

Business statistics is about converting data into useful information. There are three main components in this process: *descriptive statistics*, *probability*, and *inferential statistics*. The tools for descriptive statistics include graphs, charts, tables, and various numerical measures. Chapters 2 and 3 will introduce the important descriptive tools.

Probability is the way decision makers express their uncertainty about whether some event will take place. We use probability as a means of defining the chances of any outcome occurring based on a set of business conditions. Chapters 4 and 5 introduce the key rules and concepts you will need to work effectively with probability.

Drawing inferences about a population based on sample data takes up a good portion of the remainder of the text. We will introduce you to a variety of inferential tools to help you learn to think statistically.

Businesses have access to more data than ever before. They generate much of these data internally through normal operations. In other cases the data they need are found outside the organization. We have discussed the fact that there are numerous ways to gather data. *Surveys* (phone or written)

are effective when gathering data from people. Observation and direct measurement are appropriate when collecting data from a process. The type of data that is collected varies, too. The data may be *quantitative* or *qualitative*, it may be *time series* or *cross-sectional*, and it may be *nominal, ordinal, interval* or *ratio* level. The type and level of data that we have are important factors in determining what kind of data analysis we can perform.

Many of the things you will be doing in this course can be done better using computer software. The software selected for this text is Microsoft Excel and Minitab. Although not a special-purpose statistics software package, Excel contains a great many tools and techniques for performing descriptive and inferential statistical analysis. Minitab is a fully functional statistics package with a spreadsheet look and feel. You will find that either software package used during this course will be a valuable tool, freeing you from tedious computations and allowing you to spend more time analyzing and interpreting the output for the purpose of making better business decisions.

■ KEY TERMS

Average or arithmetic mean—A measure of the center of the data, computed by summing all the data values and dividing the sum by the number of values added.

Business statistics—A collection of tools and techniques that are used to convert data into meaningful information in a business environment.

Census—An enumeration of the entire set of measurements taken from the whole population.

Closed-end questions—Questions that require the respondent to select from a short list of defined choices.

Cluster sample—A method by which the population is divided into groups, or clusters, that are each intended to be mini-populations. A simple random sample of *m* clusters is selected. The items selected from a cluster can be chosen using any probability sampling technique.

Convenience sampling—A sampling technique that selects the items from the population based on accessibility and ease of selection.

Cross-sectional data—A set of data values observed at a fixed point in time.

Data check sheets—Forms designed for easy data collection. As the data are collected, they are also displayed in a format that allows for immediate analysis.

Demographic questions—Questions relating to the respondents' own characteristics, backgrounds, and attributes.

Experiment—Any process that generates data as its outcome.

Experimental design—A plan for performing an experiment in which the variable of interest is defined. One or more factors are identified to be manipulated or changed so that the impact (or influence) on the variable of interest can be measured or observed.

Interval data—The distance between two data items can be measured, on some scale, and the data have ordinal ($\geq$) properties.

Nominal data—The lowest form of data; data assigned to categories which have no order associated with them.

Nonstatistical sampling—Those methods of selecting samples using convenience, judgment, or other nonchance processes.

Open-end questions—Questions that allow respondents the freedom to respond with any value, words, or statements of their own choosing.

Ordinal data—One notch above nominal data; the data elements can be rank-ordered on the basis of some relationship among them.

Population—The set of all objects or individuals of interest or the measurements obtained from all objects or individuals of interest.

Primary data—Data that are collected by you or another person with whom you are closely associated. Primary data are collected for your specific purpose and use.

Qualitative data—Data whose measurement scale is inherently categorical.

Quantitative data—Data that are numeric and which define value or quantity.

Ratio data—Data that have all the characteristics of interval data but also have a true zero point (where zero means "none").

Sample—A subset of the population.

Secondary data—Data that are collected and compiled by an outside source.

Simple random sampling—A method of selecting items from a population such that every possible sample of a specified size has an equal chance of being selected.

Statistical inference tools—Tools that allow a decision maker to reach a conclusion about a population of data based on a subset of data from the population.

Statistical sampling techniques—Those sampling methods that use selection techniques based on chance selection.

Stratified random sample—A statistical sampling method in which the population is divided into subgroups called *strata* so that each population item belongs to only one stratum. The objective is to form strata such that the population values of interest within each stratum are as much alike as possible. Sample items are selected from each stratum using the simple random sampling method.

Structured interview—Interview in which the questions are scripted.

Systematic random sampling—A statistical sampling technique that involves selecting every *k*th item in the population after randomly selecting a starting point between 1 and *k*. The value of *k* is determined as the ratio of the population size over the desired sample size.

Time series data—A set of ordered data values observed at successive points in time.

Unstructured interview—Interviews that begin with one or more broadly stated questions with further questions being based on the responses.

CHAPTER EXERCISES

Business Applications

1-49 Between now and when this assignment is due, make a point of listening to either television or radio commentators or newscasters. Find five examples of these individuals referring to or giving descriptive statistics. List
   (1) the commentator/newscaster's name
   (2) the time and date
   (3) network or station
   (4) descriptive statistic mentioned and
   (5) denote whether the statistic was applied to (a) the individual or object in the population or (b) to the measurement of interest

1-50 The Ford Motor Company has been advertising a series of comparisons between its cars and competitors' cars. What level of data measurement would each of the following be?
   a. The sound level measured in decibels inside the car
   b. Drivers' ratings of the handling characteristics of the car

   c. The mileage ratings in miles per gallon for the cars
   d. The indication of whether a stereo radio is standard equipment on a car

1-51 Define the difference between primary data and secondary data.

1-52 The local television station has asked its viewers to call in and respond to the question "Do you believe police officers are using too much force in routine traffic stops?"
   a. Would the results of this phone-in survey be considered a random sample?
   b. This chapter discussed problems that are often associated with surveys. Review these problems and identify any that would apply to this survey. Give your reasons.

1-53 This chapter presents four levels of data measurement. List these four levels and provide examples of each.

1-54 At the start of 1997, 41% of the 900 or so independent beer distributors affiliated with Anheuser-Busch carried only its brand. The data set that resulted in this summary parameter consists of the distributor's name and the brands of beer they carry. Describe how this information could be seen as both primary data and secondary data.

1-55 A large retail store is considering expanding into Walnut Creek, California. Before moving into a new area, the store wishes to conduct some initial survey work to determine if people in the area would shop at a store of this type.

    a. This chapter has described data collection methods. Select one of the methods that you would recommend for this survey work. Give your reasons for selecting it.

    b. Specify the population from which you would be sampling. Make sure you specify the measurement that characterizes this population.

    c. You are interested in obtaining information concerning: the type of store most often visited, the amount of money spent monthly, shopper's age, shopper's income, and shopper's rating of existing stores. Describe the level of measurement each of the above items exhibits. Write questions for the survey to provide information for each of the preceding items. Show how they can be easily entered into a spreadsheet.

1-56 A company financial manager recently made a presentation. It showed that during the previous 16 quarters (three months per quarter) the company showed a profit 12 times and a loss 4 times. It is quite likely that the presentation would contain more information than whether the company showed a profit or loss. Contemplate what this information might be.

    a. List some of the data that might have been presented. List at least one quantitative and one qualitative variable. Also provide at least one time series and one cross-sectional variable.

    b. Give the level of data for each of the preceding items.

    c. Classify each of the items above as either quantitative or qualitative.

1-57 Flowers Industries, Inc. is one of America's leading producers of fresh and frozen baked foods for retail and food service customers throughout the United States. Its 1997 annual report contains large amounts of data. For each of the following variables indicate whether it is quantitative or qualitative and the level of data measurement.

    a. Brand names of its products

    b. Years of service of board of director members

    c. Officer and staff titles

    d. Quarterly dividends for the past two years

    e. Net income for the past three years

    f. National ranking of a brand

1-58 Suppose the U.S. Post Office is interested in obtaining feedback about how satisfied the public is with its Express Mail service.

    a. Which method of data collection would you recommend and why?

    b. Outline the procedure by which the U.S. Post Office could collect the data and discuss any potential problems.

1-59 Comment on how data collected through personal interviews or observation might be inaccurate or biased. If you know of any examples of interviewer bias, discuss them.

1-60 A total of 71,123 readers participated in *USA Weekend's* February 13–15, 1998, National Forum by calling a toll-free number or voting online (*USA Weekend*, March 22, 1998). The question was "Do you support lowering the legal intoxication limit nationwide?" The results from this survey indicated that 82% were not in favor of lowering the limit while 18% were in favor of lowering the limit.

    a. Is this an example of a random sample?

    b. The chapter has discussed some of the possible data collection problems. Review Section 1-2 and indicate which of these items would apply to this type of survey.

1-61 The Basin Ski Resort is planning a telephone survey of the holders of its season lift tickets to determine their level of satisfaction with services this year. Management has a list of ticket holders in alphabetical order.

    a. Devise a sampling procedure that might be used to select the individuals to call.

    b. Consult Figure 1-8 to use as a template for the construction of the procedure. Describe each of these "major steps" in the context of this problem.

1-62 The maker of Creamy Good Ice Cream is concerned about the quality of ice cream being produced by its Illinois plant, in particular, the texture of the ice cream in each carton.

    a. Discuss a plan by which the Creamy Good managers might determine the percentage of cartons of ice cream believed to have an unacceptable texture by potential purchasers of this particular brand. (1) Define the sampling procedure to be used, (2) the randomization method to be used to select the sample, and (3) the measurement to be obtained.

    b. Explain why it would or would not be feasible (or, perhaps, possible) to take a census to address this issue.

1-63 The makers of a particular brand of skiing equipment selected a random sample of skiers at the Aspen Ski Resort. Their method for selecting the sample required that individuals waiting in one of the lift lines be asked questions about various brands of skiing equipment.

   a. Reconsider the "Data Collection Issues" in Section 1-2 of this chapter. Comment on the sampling method employed in this problem.
   b. Suggest a better sampling method and explain why it is a better method.
   c. Generate three questions of interest to this study and indicate the level of data measurement you will be obtaining.
   d. Specify whether the data are qualitative or quantitative.

1-64 A beer manufacturer is considering abandoning can containers and going exclusively to bottles because the sales manager believes beer drinkers prefer drinking beer from bottles. However, the vice president in charge of marketing is not convinced the sales manager is correct.

   a. Indicate the data collection method you would use.
   b. Indicate what procedures you would follow to apply this technique in this setting.
   c. State which level of data measurement applies to the data you would collect. Justify your answer.
   d. Are the data qualitative or quantitative? Explain.

1-65 With respect to Problem 64, how might a cluster sampling approach be used if the beer is marketed at stores in all 50 states?

1-66 If you were designing a stratified random sampling plan for a survey of city governments in your state to find out the amount of money they are spending on administrative salaries, what criteria might you use to form the strata?

1-67 A simple random sample of 10 is to be taken of the service station operators in your city. Use the random number table in Appendix A. Begin your search for your random numbers in column two, row three. (Hint: Refer to

the Optional CD-ROM Topic on Random Number Tables on your CD-ROM.)

   a. Suppose there are 29 service station operators in your city. How many digits will you need to select per random number from the random number table?
   b. Use the above starting point to obtain the 10 random numbers from the random number table. List those numbers.
   c. The last of the 10 service station operators has closed his business. Explain how you would deal with this unforeseen circumstance.

1-68 Using the random number generator in Excel or Minitab, obtain the simple random sample of service station operators in your city as indicated in Problem 67.

1-69 Student leaders often poll students to obtain opinions on topics of interest such as athletics, library hours, and so on. Using the last such poll on your campus, discuss the methods by which the sampling was performed, pointing out the strong and weak points of the process. If necessary, visit your student body officers and find out their approach to sampling student opinion.

1-70 Working women are walking away from high heels. According to a survey taken for the foot and ankle surgeons, the younger women are, the more likely they are to work in flats—or even athletic shoes. "Twenty percent of all women now wear sneakers to work," said Dr. Michael Bowman, chairman of the American Orthopedic Foot and Ankle Society's shoe wear committee (*Idaho Statesman*, March 22, 1998).

   a. State the type of sampling technique that might have been used to develop this statistic.
   b. Use Figure 1-8 as a template for describing the procedure that might have been followed to obtain the data that produced the above statistic.
   c. State the level of data measurement represented by the data in this survey.

■ GENERAL REFERENCES

1. Berenson, Mark L., and David M. Levine, *Basic Business Statistics: Concepts and Applications,* 7th ed. (Upper Saddle River, NJ: Prentice Hall, 1999).
2. Cryer, Jonathan D., and Robert B. Miller, *Statistics for Business: Data Analysis and Modeling*, 2d ed. (Belmont, CA: Duxbury Press, 1994).
3. Dodge, Mark, and Craig Stinson, *Running Microsoft Excel 2000* (Redmond, WA: Microsoft Press, 1999).
4. Groves, R. M., *Survey Errors and Survey Costs* (New York: John Wiley & Sons, 1989).
5. Hildebrand, David, and R. Lyman Ott, *Statistical Thinking for Managers*, 4th ed. (Belmont, CA: Duxbury Press, 1998).
6. Kenkel, James L., *Introductory Statistics for Management and Economics*, 4th ed. (Belmont, CA: Duxbury Press, 1996).
7. *Microsoft Excel 2000* (Redmond, WA: Microsoft Corporation, 1999).
8. *Minitab for Windows Version 13* (State College, PA: Minitab, Inc., 2000).
9. Pelosi, Marilyn K., and Theresa M. Sandifer, *Doing Statistics for Business with Excel* (New York: John Wiley & Sons, 2000).
10. Scheaffer, Richard L., William Mendenhall, and Lyman Ott, *Elementary Survey Sampling*, 5th ed. (Belmont, CA: Duxbury Press, 1996).
11. Siegel, Andrew F., *Practical Business Statistics*, 4th ed. (Burr Ridge, IL: Irwin, 2000).

CHAPTER 2

GRAPHS, CHARTS, AND TABLES—DESCRIBING YOUR DATA

CHAPTER OUTCOMES

After studying the material in Chapter 2, you should:

2-1: Be able to construct frequency distributions both manually and with your computer.

2-2: Be able to construct and interpret a frequency histogram.

2-3: Know how to construct and interpret various types of bar charts.

2-4: Understand the purpose of a Pareto chart and be able to construct one.

2-5: Be able to create a line chart and interpret the trend in the data.

2-6: Be able to construct and interpret a scatter plot.

2-7: Be able to develop and interpret joint frequency tables.

WHY YOU NEED TO KNOW

Several years ago, a vice president for General Motors spoke at the University of Montana's spring alumni and scholarship banquet. After his speech, a student asked him what factor he considered to be the most important in his rise to the position of vice president in one of the world's largest companies. He responded that a short time after joining GM he took part in a presentation to a group of upper managers. Previously he had been taught the skills to *effectively organize and present* complex data. His ability to translate the data into meaningful information caught the attention of the company's senior managers. A short time later, he was asked to coordinate another presentation. He stated that he was certain that upper management remembered his presentations for their effective display of business data. When management needed someone to lead a special project, he was selected. The success of that project led to a significant promotion and the rest was history.

Although you may not end up working at a company as large as General Motors, we are absolutely convinced that you will have numerous opportunities to organize, summarize, analyze, and present data. In fact, of all the tools and techniques introduced in this text, you will very likely use those discussed in this chapter and Chapter 3 more than any other.

Not only will you be called on to actually do the data analysis necessary to make sense out of data, you also will find yourself on the receiving end of many statistical reports. Therefore, in addition to being able to perform the appropriate data analysis, you also need to be able to question the accuracy and validity of the charts, graphs, and analyses received from others.

Business periodicals, such as *Fortune* and *Business Week*, use graphs and charts extensively in conjunction with their articles to help readers better understand key concepts. Many advertisements will even use graphs and charts to effectively convey their messages. What better proof of the potential value of descriptive statistics than to observe ads costing $50,000 or more per page using the concepts we will be discussing in this text?

This chapter introduces some of the most frequently used tools and techniques for describing data with graphs, charts, and tables. Although all this analysis can be done manually, we will provide output from Excel and Minitab showing that these software packages can be used as tools for doing the analysis easily, quickly, and with a finished quality that once required a graphic artist.

■ 2-1: FREQUENCY DISTRIBUTIONS AND HISTOGRAMS

Next time you are in your statistics class look around at your classmates. How many hours a week do they spend studying? How are the ages of the students in the class distributed? How is income distributed among the students in the class? How many credits have they completed already? A simple survey of the students would provide data to answer each of these questions. However, the data alone would not be enough. You would need to perform a descriptive analysis of the data.

One of the first steps in the analysis would be to construct a **frequency distribution** for each of the variables.

FREQUENCY DISTRIBUTION

A summary of a set of data that displays the number of observations in each of the distribution's distinct categories or classes.

Frequency Distributions

Books and Music

Consider an example involving a national book and music retailer that is considering locating into one of two cities (say, City #1 and City #2). To obtain data to aid in the decision process, the retailer has conducted a marketing study in the two cities. Among the questions asked of individuals is how many years of college they have completed. Experience in other markets indicates that cities with higher-educated populations are more profitable

EXAMPLE 2-1

FREQUENCY DISTRIBUTION

TABLE 2-1
Frequency Distribution of Years of College

CITY #1 YEARS OF COLLEGE	FREQUENCY
0	35
1	21
2	24
3	22
4	31
5	13
6	6
7	5
8	3
Total	160

TABLE 2-2
Frequency Distribution of Years of College

CITY #2 YEARS OF COLLEGE	FREQUENCY
0	187
1	62
2	34
3	19
4	14
5	7
6	3
7	4
Total	330

locations. The variable, years of college, is **discrete** since the possible responses (1, 2, 3, 4, etc.) can be counted.

DISCRETE DATA
Data whose possible values are countable.

To construct the frequency distribution for City #1, we need only count the number of times individuals in that city indicate each of these possible responses (years of education). The results are shown in Table 2-1.

This frequency distribution shows that, of the 160 people in the survey, most (125 out of 160) have spent at least one year in college.

Suppose now we wished to compare the college years variable for City #1 with the same variable for City #2. The data for City #2 can be organized into the frequency distribution shown in Table 2-2.

How do the two market areas compare? Do you see any difficulties in making this comparison? Since the surveys contained a different number of people, the frequencies of each category are difficult to compare directly. When the number of total observations differs, comparisons are aided if **relative frequencies** are computed.

Equation 2-1 is used to compute the relative frequencies. Table 2-3 shows the relative frequencies for each market area. This makes a comparison of the two market areas much easier. We see that City #2 has relatively more people without any college education (56.7%) or one year of college (18.8%) than City #1 (21.9% and 13.1%). At all other levels of education, City #1 has relatively more people than does City #2.

RELATIVE FREQUENCY
The proportion of total observations contained in a given category. Relative frequency is computed by dividing the frequency in a category by the total number of observations. The relative frequencies can be converted to percents by multiplying by 100.

$$RF = \frac{f_i}{n} \qquad \qquad RF \text{ of } 0 \text{ college} = \frac{35}{160} \qquad \qquad 2\text{-}1$$

where:

f_i = frequency of the ith value of the discrete variable

$$n = \sum_{i=1}^{k} f_i$$

k = the number of different values for the discrete variable

Years of College	CITY #1 Frequency	CITY #1 Relative Frequency	CITY #2 Frequency	CITY #2 Relative Frequency
0	35	35/160 = 0.219	187	187/330 = 0.567
1	21	21/160 = 0.131	62	62/330 = 0.188
2	24	24/160 = 0.150	34	34/330 = 0.103
3	22	22/160 = 0.138	19	19/330 = 0.058
4	31	31/160 = 0.194	14	14/330 = 0.042
5	13	13/160 = 0.081	7	7/330 = 0.021
6	6	6/160 = 0.038	3	3/330 = 0.009
7	5	5/160 = 0.031	4	4/330 = 0.012
8	3	3/160 = 0.019	0	0/330 = 0
Total	160		330	

TABLE 2-3
Relative Frequency
Distribution for the Book and
Music Example

EXAMPLE 2-2

FREQUENCY DISTRIBUTION

Excel and Minitab
Tutorial

Weigh-in-Motion

Examine the contents of the room you presently occupy. Think about all the items in your home. Chances are these things were transported by truck. Trucks play an important role in our transportation system. However, trucks adversely impact the roads and highways over which they travel. The more weight on each axle, the more damage done to the pavement. To help states compensate for this wear, truckers are charged a tax for the privilege of using the roads and highways. In many states, this tax is based on the weight of the truck and the number of miles driven—the tax is called a *ton-mile tax.*

In order to know how much tax to assess, trucks must be weighed and mileage readings must be made. Ports of Entry (POE) are placed at strategic locations throughout the state. Trucks are required to pull into the POE to be weighed and measured. This is a time-consuming, labor-intensive process when the old-style platform scales are used. The trucks must actually stop on the scale while the weight on each axle is recorded. These scales are assumed to be accurate.

In recent years, new technology has emerged for weighing trucks. This technology is called *weigh-in-motion* or WIM. The WIM scales are built to weigh trucks as they drive at highway speeds. If the WIM systems work properly, the trucks are weighed and measured without having to stop at the POE (unless there is a probable weight or length violation). Cameras capture the truck identification number so each truck can be matched to the correct weight and length.

While this sounds great, there is the issue of whether the WIM scales are accurate and should be used as a substitute for the traditional POE static weighing system. During a recent year, a test was conducted near Bliss, Idaho. A sample of trucks was weighed and measured on the WIM and then the same trucks were weighed and measured at the POE. Figure 2-1 shows the Excel worksheet with data for some of the 200 trucks in the study. The data are in a file called **Trucks** on the CD-ROM that comes with this text.

FIGURE 2-1
Excel Worksheet of the
Weigh-in-Motion Test Data

	A Month Code	B WIM Front Axle Weight	C WIM Gross Weight	D WIM Total Length	E POE Front Axle Weight	F POE Total Length	G POE Gross Weight	H WIM Gross Weight	I WIM Total Length	J Temperature at WIM Scale	K Speed at WIM Scale
2	6	9,560	50,100	64	8,870	66	49,270	50,100	64	62	51
3	7	10,180	62,880	55	10,780	55	67,500	62,880	55	70	55
4	4	9,060	40,560	59	10,35			60	59	70	60
5	8	11,460	72,100	56	10,94			00	56	70	51
6	2	11,420	74,040	53	11,32			40	53	38	46
7	8	10,480	42,320	60	9,680	61	45,600	42,320	60	76	58
8	7	10,700	82,660	95	10,930	95	86,380	82,660	95	103	46

Excel Instructions:
1. Open file: Trucks.xls

12% of all trucks were weighed in May

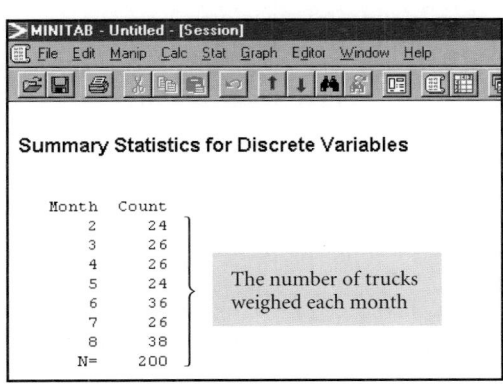

Excel Instructions:

1. Open file: Trucks.xls
2. Enter the possible values for the month variable, i.e., 1, 2, 3, . . . 12.
3. Select the cells to contain the Frequency values.
4. Click on the Function Wizard (f_x).
5. Select the Statistics—FREQUENCY function.
6. Enter the range of data A2:A201 and the bin range (the cells containing the possible values for the month variable).
7. Press **ctrl-shift-enter** to determine the frequency values.
8. Write a formula to find the relative frequencies (i.e., = N2/N\$14) in cell O2 and copy down to cell O13.

FIGURE 2-2
Excel Output of the WIM Test Frequency Distribution

Summary Statistics for Discrete Variables

Month	Count	
2	24	
3	26	
4	26	The number of trucks
5	24	weighed each month
6	36	
7	26	
8	38	
N=	200	

Minitab Instructions:

1. Open file Trucks.mtw
2. Click on the Stat tab
3. Select the Tables option
4. Select Tally
5. Identify variable to be analyzed
6. Click on the Counts box

FIGURE 2-3
Minitab Output of the WIM Test Frequency Distribution

The variable, *Month*, is a discrete, ordinal variable that designates which month of the year the data were collected: 1 = January, 2 = February, and so on. A first step in analyzing these test data might be to determine how many trucks were tested during each month. Figure 2-2 shows the frequency distribution generated using Excel. Note that we have also computed the relative frequencies. Figure 2-3 shows the corresponding Minitab frequency distribution without the relative frequencies. We see that the data collection was fairly evenly spread over the months of February through August with June and August being the months when the most trucks were sampled. The test didn't start until February and was completed by the end of August. (Note, we will revisit this example in Chapter 3 to examine whether the WIM scale is an accurate method for weighing trucks.)

Additional Example 2-a

Developing Frequency Distributions

Grouping Data by Classes

Cox Enterprises

In the previous examples, the variable of interest was a discrete variable and the number of possible values for the variable was limited to only a few possibilities. However, there are many instances where the variable of interest will be either **continuous** (weight, time,

EXAMPLE

2-3

FREQUENCY DISTRIBUTION

length) or discrete with many possible outcomes for the variable (age, income, stock prices) and yet we want to describe the variable using a frequency distribution.

CONTINUOUS DATA
Data whose possible values are uncountable and which may assume any value in an interval.

Cox Enterprises owns and operates a large cattle feedlot operation in the plains of west Texas. The company purchases young steer calves at cattle auctions and directly from cattle ranchers. The calves are moved to feedlots owned by the firm. There, the calves are kept for approximately 6 months before being sold to packing plants.

The key factor in whether Cox Enterprises makes a profit is the weight the steers gain while at the feedlots. The greater the weight gain, the greater the profit. Cox managers constantly study the growth patterns of different species of cattle to determine which species offer the best growth potential. For example, the data in Table 2-4 show the actual weight gains in pounds by a sample of 100 Polled Hereford steers. These are quantitative data. This data set is given to the nearest tenth of a pound. The range is 131.3–205.6 pounds.

The data have been sorted in order of weight from low to high forming a **data array**.

DATA ARRAY
Data that have been sorted in ascending or descending order.

Even though they are sorted, the weight gain data provide little information about these cattle. However, a good first step in understanding the data would be to construct a frequency distribution.

The variable, weight gain, is continuous and can assume many different values. If we counted the number of values at each weight, we would have many frequencies of 1 and 2. This would provide little new information. Instead, we need to group the data into *classes* and then count the number of cattle that had weight gains in each class.

The first step in this procedure is to form data groups or classes. Therefore, care needs to be taken when constructing these classes to ensure that each data point is put into one, and only one, of the possible classes. The classes must meet three criteria. First, they must be **mutually exclusive**.

MUTUALLY EXCLUSIVE CLASSES
Classes that do not overlap so that a data value can be placed in only one class.

TABLE 2-4
Cox Enterprises Cattle Weight Gain

131.3	148.3	155.9	160.2	164.5	168.7	173.2	179.3	183.0	191.7
137.2	149.4	156.2	160.5	164.6	169.5	173.7	179.6	183.1	191.7
138.2	150.8	156.3	161.5	165.1	169.6	174.8	180.1	183.5	194.9
142.3	150.8	157.3	162.1	165.2	170.0	176.7	180.4	186.4	196.0
143.4	152.0	157.4	162.3	165.3	170.4	176.8	180.7	186.7	198.3
143.9	153.3	157.7	163.2	165.5	171.1	177.0	181.4	188.0	198.8
144.6	153.7	158.4	163.6	166.4	171.7	177.3	181.4	188.6	199.6
145.8	154.2	159.0	163.9	166.5	172.0	178.1	182.4	189.1	202.9
146.6	154.6	159.6	164.3	167.2	172.0	178.4	182.4	189.6	203.1
147.2	155.3	160.2	164.4	168.7	172.1	178.9	182.9	190.1	205.6

Second, they must be **all inclusive**.

> **ALL-INCLUSIVE CLASSES**
> A set of classes that contains all the possible data values.

Third, if at all possible, they should be of **equal width**.

> **EQUAL-WIDTH CLASSES**
> The distance between the lowest possible value and the highest possible value in each class is equal for all classes.

Equal-width classes make analyzing and interpreting the frequency distribution easier. However, there are some instances where the presence of extreme high or low values makes it necessary to have an open-end class. For example, family incomes in the United States are mostly between $15,000 and $200,000 per year. However, there are some families with much higher family incomes. In order to best accommodate these higher incomes, you might consider having the highest income class be "Over $200,000" or "$200,000 and over" as a catch-all for the high income families.

STEPS FOR GROUPING DATA INTO CLASSES

There are four steps for grouping data, such as the cattle weight gain data found in Table 2-4, into classes.

STEP 1: Determine the number of groups or classes to use. Although there is no absolute right or wrong number of classes, the rule of thumb is to have *between 5 and 20 classes*. In general, use fewer classes for smaller data sets; more classes for larger data sets. However, using too few classes tends to condense the data too much and information is lost. Using too many classes spreads out the data so much that little advantage is gained over the original raw data. In this example, we will use eight classes.

 **OPTIONAL CD-ROM TOPIC   Sturges' Rule for Number of Classes**
Sturges' Rule is a mathematical formula for determining the number of classes to use in developing a frequency distribution. For more information, go to the CD-ROM.

STEP 2: Establish the class width.

> **CLASS WIDTH**
> The distance between the lowest possible value and the highest possible value for a frequency class.

The minimum **class width** is determined by Equation 2-2:

$$W = \frac{\text{Largest Value} - \text{Smallest Value}}{\text{Number of Classes}} \qquad \textbf{2-2}$$

CLASS WIDTH

For the Cox Enterprise data, we get:

$$W = \frac{205.6 - 131.3}{8} = \frac{74.3}{8} = 9.288$$

This means we could construct 8 classes that are each 9.288 pounds wide to provide mutually exclusive and all-inclusive classes. However, since our purpose is to make the data more understandable, we suggest that you *round up to a more convenient class width* such as 10 pounds or even 15 pounds. A major concern in determining class widths is to select ones that are readily understandable. Be aware that people tend to do better with multiples of 2 and 5 than they do with multiples of 3 or 4, so 10 is a better choice than 12. We will use a class width of 10.

STEP 3: Determine the class boundaries for each class.

CLASS BOUNDARIES
The upper and lower value of each class.

The **class boundaries** determine the lowest possible value and the highest possible value for each class. If we start the first class at 130 pounds, we get the class boundaries shown in the first column of Table 2-5.

Notice that the classes have been formed to be *mutually exclusive* and *all inclusive*. The weight data were recorded in pounds to one decimal place. For instance, a weight value of 149.9 pounds will fall in the second class. A value of 150 pounds will fall in the third class.

STEP 4: Count the number of values in each class. From the raw data in Table 2-4, we count the number of steers with weight gains in each class. The results are shown in the Frequency column in Table 2-5. This shows that more steers (24) gain between 160 and under 170 pounds than any other single category. The vast majority of steers (77 out of 100) in the sample gained between 150 pounds and under 190 pounds.

If the company had multiple feedlots, we might need to compute relative frequencies using Equation 2-1 as shown in the Relative Frequency column in Table 2-5. The relative frequencies can be transformed into percentages, which would mean, for example, that 19% of the steers in the sample gained between 170.1 and under 180 pounds.

Another step we can take to help analyze the steer weight gain data is to construct a **cumulative frequency distribution** and a **cumulative relative frequency distribution**.

CUMULATIVE FREQUENCY DISTRIBUTION
A summary of a set of data that displays the number of observations with values less-than-or-equal-to the upper limit of each of its classes.

CUMULATIVE RELATIVE FREQUENCY DISTRIBUTION
A summary of a set of data that displays the proportion of observations with values less-than-or-equal-to the upper limit of each of its classes.

The cumulative frequency distribution is shown in the Cumulative Frequency column in Table 2-5. We can then form the cumulative relative frequency distribution as shown in the Cumulative Relative Frequency column in Table 2-5. The cumulative relative frequency distribution indicates, as an example, that 72% of the sample steers had weight gains below 180 pounds.

CLASSES	FREQUENCY	RELATIVE FREQUENCY	CUMULATIVE FREQUENCY	CUMULATIVE RELATIVE FREQUENCY
130.0 < 140.0 lb.	3	3/100 = 0.03	3	0.03
140.0 < 150.0 lb.	9	9/100 = 0.09	12	0.12
150.0 < 160.0 lb.	17	17/100 = 0.17	29	0.29
160.0 < 170.0 lb.	24	24/100 = 0.24	53	0.53
170.0 < 180.0 lb.	19	19/100 = 0.19	72	0.72
180.0 < 190.0 lb.	17	17/100 = 0.17	89	0.89
190.0 < 200.0 lb.	8	8/100 = 0.08	97	0.97
200.0 < 210.0 lb.	3	3/100 = 0.03	100	1.00
	$\sum$ = 100	$\sum$ = 1.00		

TABLE 2-5
Cox Enterprises—Cattle Weight Gain Data

Histograms

While frequency distributions are useful for helping to analyze large sets of data, they are in a table format and may not be as visually informative as a graph. A graph called a *frequency histogram* can be used to transform a frequency distribution into a visually appealing format.

Cox Enterprises (continued)

The Cox Enterprises managers also collect sample weight gain data on steers of other breeds for comparison purposes. The frequency distributions and relative frequency distributions are helpful in understanding the sample data and in making comparisons between two or more data sets. A **frequency histogram** is another tool that is often very helpful for transforming data into useful information since it transforms data into a visually useful format.

FREQUENCY HISTOGRAM
A graph of a frequency distribution with the horizontal axis showing the classes, the vertical axis showing the frequency count, and (for equal class widths) the rectangles having a height equal to the frequency in each class.

A histogram shows three general types of information:

1. It provides a visual indication of where the approximate center of the data is—look for the center point along the horizontal axes in the histograms in Figure 2-4. Even though the shapes of the histograms are the same, there is a clear difference in where the data are centered.
2. We can gain an understanding of the degree of spread, or variation, in the data. The more the data cluster around the center, the smaller the variation in the data. If the data are spread out from the center, the data exhibit greater variation. The examples in Figure 2-5 all have the same center but are different in terms of their spread.
3. We can observe the shape of the distribution—is it reasonably flat, is it weighted to one side or the other, is it balanced around the center, or is it bell shaped?

Figure 2-6 shows the frequency histogram for the Cox Enterprises sample. We see that the weight gain data appear to be centered between 160 and 170 pounds. There is quite a bit of variation among steers in terms of weight gain, and the distribution is quite bell shaped.

Even for applications with small amounts of data like the Cox Enterprises cattle weight gain example, constructing grouped data frequency distributions and histograms is a time-consuming process. This makes decision makers hesitant to try different numbers of classes and different class limits because of the effort involved and because the "best" presentation of the data may be missed.

Additional Example 2-b

Using Histograms for Decision-making

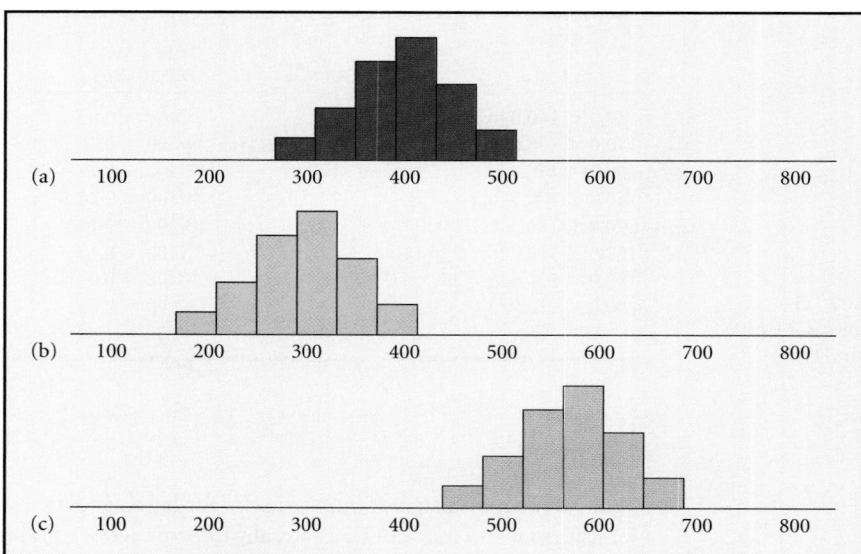

FIGURE 2-4
Histograms Showing
Different Centers

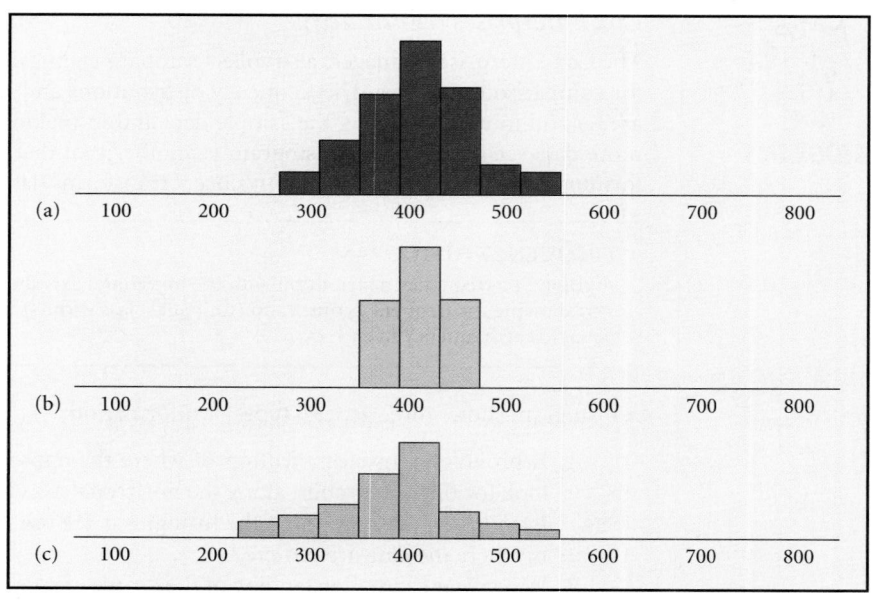

FIGURE 2-5
Histograms—Same Center,
Different Spread

We showed earlier that Excel and Minitab both provide the capability of constructing frequency distributions. Both software packages are also quite capable of generating grouped data frequency distributions and histograms.

Capital Credit Union

EXAMPLE 2-5

HISTOGRAMS

To illustrate, consider an example involving Capital Credit Union (CCU) in Mobile, Alabama, which recently began issuing a new credit card. Managers at CCU have been wondering how much customers have been charging on the card. To examine credit card use, a sample of 300 customers was selected. Data on the current credit card balance (rounded to the nearest dollar) and the gender of the cardholder were recorded in the file **Capital** that is stored on your CD-ROM. Figure 2-7 shows a portion of the data.

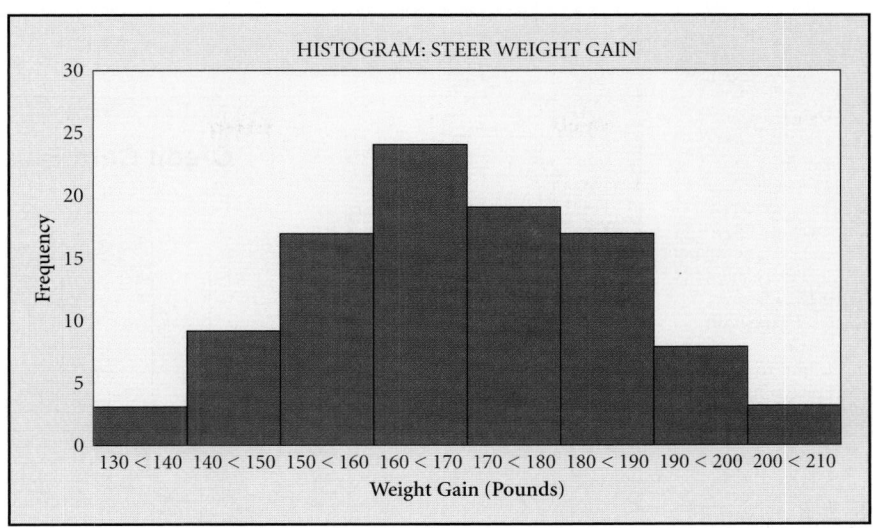

FIGURE 2-6
Cox Enterprises Example

**Excel and
Minitab Tutorial**

As with the manual process, the first step in Excel or Minitab is to determine the number of classes. Recall that the rule of thumb is to use between 5 and 20 classes depending on the amount of data. Suppose we decide to use 10 classes.

Next, we determine the class width using Equation 2-2. The highest account balance in the sample is $1,493.00. The minimum is $99.00. Thus the class width is:

$$W = \frac{1,493.00 - 99.00}{10} = 139.4$$

which we round up to $150.00.

Our classes will be:

$90 < $240
$240 < $390
$390 < $540
        etc.

**Additional
Example 2-c**

**Histograms—
Selecting the Right
Class Intervals**

The resulting histogram in Figure 2-8 shows that the data are centered in the class $690 < $840. The customers vary considerably in their credit card balances, but the distribution is quite symmetrical and bell shaped. Capital Credit Union managers will have to decide whether the usage rate for the credit card is sufficient to warrant the cost of maintaining the credit card accounts.

FIGURE 2-7
Excel Worksheet for Capital
Credit Union Data

Excel Instructions:

1. Open file: Capital.xls

Excel Instructions:

1. Open file: Capital.xls
2. Click on the Tools tab
3. Select the Data Analysis option
4. Select Histogram
5. Input Range specifies the cells containing the actual data values. Define Bin Range (upper limit of each class 239.99, 389.99, etc.).
6. Use Format Data Series, Options, to set gap width to zero.
7. Convert the bins to actual class labels by typing labels in column A.

FIGURE 2-8
Excel Output of Credit Card Balance Histogram

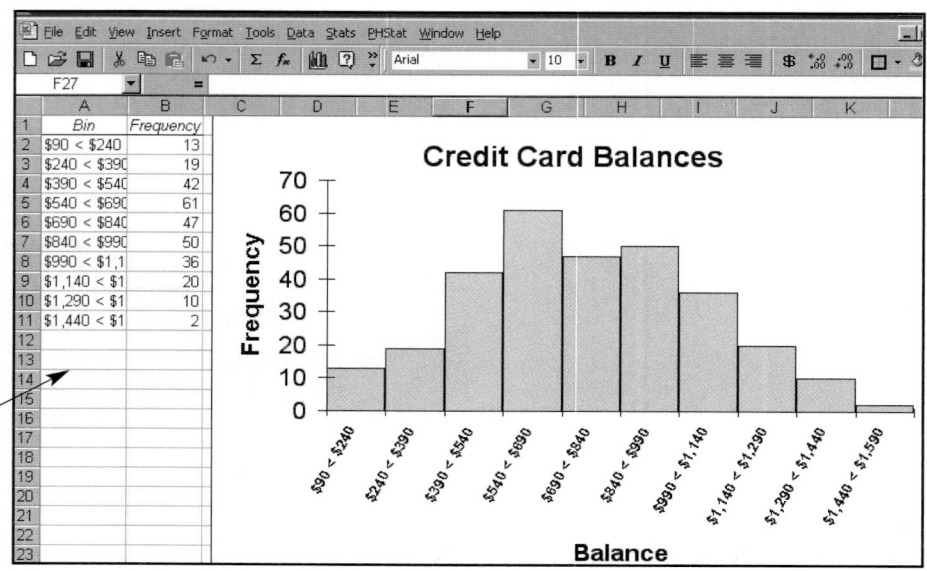

Issues with Excel

You may recall that in Chapter 1, we pointed out that Excel has some issues of which you need to be aware. One of these deals with the Histogram option under the Data Analysis menu. If you use Excel to construct a histogram as indicated in the instructions in Figure 2-8, the initial graph will come up with gaps between the bars. Since histograms illustrate the distribution of data across the range of all possible values for the variable, *histograms do not have gaps.* Therefore, to get the proper histogram format, you need to close these gaps by setting the gap width to zero as indicated in the Excel instructions shown in Figure 2-8. Minitab provides no gaps with its default output as shown in Figure 2-9.

FIGURE 2-9
Minitab Output of Credit Card Balance Histogram

Minitab Instructions:

1. Open file: Capital.mtw
2. Select Graph
3. Click on Histogram
4. Select the desired variable
5. Use Display Bar
6. Use For each Graph
7. Edit Attributes
   Fill = "Solid"
   Back Color = your choice
8. Options
   Type of Histogram = Frequency
   Type of Intervals = Cutpoint
   Definition of Intervals = Midpoint/cutpoint positions 90:1590/150
9. Annotate (Titles, etc.)

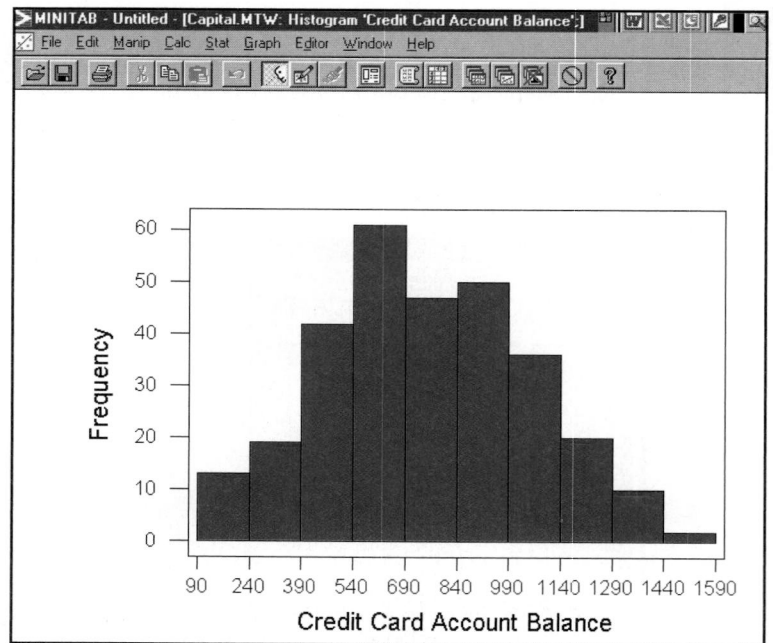

TOOLS OF QUALITY

HISTOGRAMS

Valley View Cable TV provides cable TV service to remote locations in Utah. In order to provide a clear signal, amplifiers are placed in the line at half-mile intervals. The amplifiers boost the signal to give good picture quality to customers at great distances from Valley View's signal source. However, over the past few months Valley View has received a number of complaints from customers about poor picture quality. The amplifiers are suspected to be the source of the problem.

Valley View's supplier claims that the amplifiers provide an average boost of 10 units with specifications calling for all amplifiers to deliver between 7.75 and 12.25 units. A sample of 120 amplifiers was selected. The boost ratings for each amplifier in the sample are shown as follows:

8.1	10.4	9.7	7.8	9.9	11.7	8.0	9.3	9.0	8.8
8.2	8.9	10.1	9.4	9.2	7.9	9.5	10.9	7.8	8.3
9.6	9.1	8.4	11.1	7.9	8.5	8.7	7.8	10.5	8.5
11.5	8.0	7.9	8.3	8.7	10.0	9.4	9.0	9.2	10.7
9.3	9.7	8.7	8.2	8.9	8.6	9.5	9.4	8.8	8.3
8.4	9.1	10.1	7.8	8.1	8.8	8.0	9.2	8.4	7.8
7.9	8.5	9.2	8.7	10.2	7.9	9.8	8.3	9.0	9.6
9.9	10.6	8.6	9.4	8.8	8.2	10.5	9.7	9.1	8.0
8.7	9.8	8.5	8.9	9.1	8.4	8.1	9.5	8.7	9.3
8.1	10.1	9.6	8.3	8.0	9.8	9.0	8.9	8.1	9.7
8.5	8.2	9.0	10.2	9.5	8.3	8.9	9.1	10.3	8.4
8.6	9.2	8.5	9.6	9.0	10.7	8.6	10.0	8.8	8.6

The grouped data frequency distribution for the sample data is:

CLASS	FREQUENCY	RELATIVE FREQUENCY
7.75 < 8.25	24	0.20
8.25 < 8.75	28	0.23
8.75 < 9.25	26	0.22
9.25 < 9.75	19	0.16
9.75 < 10.25	12	0.10
10.25 < 10.75	7	0.06
10.75 < 11.25	2	0.02
11.25 < 11.75	2	0.02
	120	

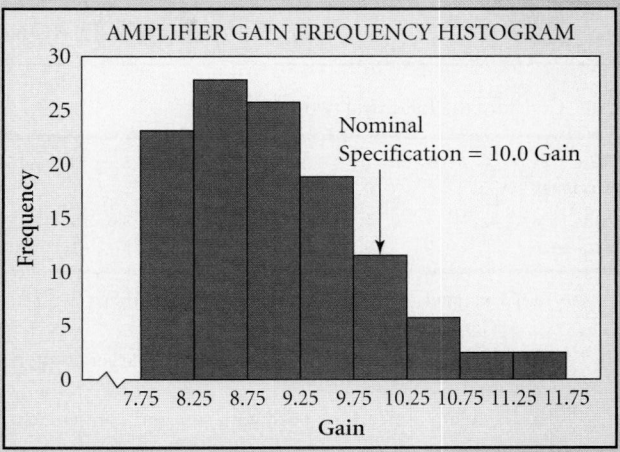

FIGURE 2-10
Valley View Cable TV Company

The first-glance analysis shows that all 120 amplifiers are within the 7.75–12.25 specification limits. Thus, the amplifiers don't appear to be the source of the picture problem. However, the frequency histogram in Figure 2-10 gives additional insight. We now see that a high percentage of the amplifiers have a gain rating well below the nominal level of 10.0 units. The amplifier gains are not evenly spread around the center. Thus, by chance, it would be possible to get a string of amplifiers with lower than average boost causing poor TV pictures. The histogram paints a clearer picture of the problem.

2-1: EXERCISES

ADDITIONAL EXERCISES ON YOUR CD-ROM
Try the ADDITIONAL EXERCISES and APPLICATION PROBLEMS on the CD-ROM.

2-1 Consider the following two sets of data.

Value	2	3	4	5	6	7	8	9	10
Frequency	5	3	10	10	10	10	5	1	6
Value	2	3	4	5	6	7	8	9	10
Frequency	1	1	10	15	13	13	5	1	1

a. Construct a frequency distribution for these two sets of data using the same classes.
b. Which distribution appears to have the larger "center" value?
c. Calculate a mean for both data sets and compare the means obtained.
d. Suppose that you had to pick one of these sets of data so that you would have the higher probability of obtaining a number larger than 6. Which set of data would you choose? Explain.
e. Explain why someone might think the answers you have given in both "c" and "d" are incongruous.

2-2 Draw a sketch of the histograms for two data sets. (Call them A and B.) Construct the sets so that A has a smaller center (say, 5) than does B (say, 6) but has a greater proportion than does B of observations larger than 8.

Business Applications

2-3 Some investors take the strategy of investing in local companies. Each day the city newspaper carries the daily closing stock prices for some of the local companies. On a recent day the closing prices for 37 companies were listed as follows:

61.00	50.06	6.50	45.56	22.13	13.88	18.13	38.75	26.94	91.44
28.38	64.56	7.13	59.94	72.94	37.88	27.75	73.19	25.88	25.38
60.06	14.63	28.88	27.31	52.75	1.69	30.25	52.38	31.81	72.98
118.00	19.88	45.31	31.00	72.63	120.00	25.88			

a. Create a data array for these data.
b. Develop a frequency distribution with five classes for these data.
c. Develop a histogram based on the frequency distribution.
d. Determine the proportion of closing stock prices that are at least 50.
e. Write a short statement that describes the stock price data.

2-4 Each month the American Automobile Association (AAA) generates a report on gasoline prices that it distributes to newspapers throughout the state. On February 17, 1999, AAA called a random sample of 51 stations to determine that day's price of unleaded gasoline. The resulting data (in dollars) are shown as follows:

1.07	1.31	1.18	1.01	1.23	1.09	1.29	1.10	1.16	1.08
0.96	1.66	1.21	1.09	1.02	1.04	1.01	1.03	1.09	1.11
1.11	1.17	1.04	1.09	1.05	0.96	1.32	1.09	1.26	1.11
1.03	1.20	1.21	1.05	1.10	1.04	0.97	1.21	1.07	1.17
0.98	1.10	1.04	1.03	1.12	1.10	1.03	1.18	1.11	1.09
1.06									

a. Create a data array with the gasoline price data.
b. Create two histograms for this data set using 5 classes for the first and 15 classes for the second. Estimate the number of prices that are at least $1.15 using each of the preceding histograms.
c. A local radio station has reported that 30% of the gas stations are charging $1.15 a gallon or more for gasoline. Use one of the histograms you have produced to respond to this report. Which histogram did you use? Why?

2-5 Refer to Problem 4. Construct the following distributions using seven classes:
a. A frequency distribution
b. A relative frequency distribution
c. A cumulative frequency distribution
d. A cumulative relative frequency distribution
e. Describe the data set by determining (1) the average, (2) approximately what percentage charges less than $1.29. (3) approximately what percentage of stations reported a price greater than $1.40.

2-6 The loan officer at Money First National Bank wants to obtain information about the loans she has made over the past 5 years. She is preparing a report for the bank's regional spring conference. As part of the report, she has decided to develop a distribution showing the loan frequency by size of loan. The data indicate that the smallest loan she made was for $1,000 and the largest loan was for $25,000.
a. If she wants to have 10 classes in her distribution, define the 10 classes in terms of lower and upper limits.

b. She knows that other loan officers will also be making similar presentations. If she wishes to compare the information in her distribution with that of the others, what kind of distribution do you recommend? Give your reasons.

2-7 Go to your university library and obtain the *Statistical Abstract of the United States.*

   a. Construct a frequency distribution for unemployment rate by state for the most current year available.

   b. Justify your choice of class limits and number of classes.

   c. Locate the unemployment rate for the state in which you are attending college. What proportion of the unemployment rates are below that of your state? Describe the distribution's shape with respect to whether it is balanced around the center. If you were planning to build a new manufacturing plant, what state would you choose in which to build? Justify your answer. Are there any unusual features of this distribution? Describe them.

2-8 The State Industrial Development Council is presently working on a financial services brochure to send to out-of-state companies. It is hoped that the brochure will be helpful in attracting companies to relocate to your state. You are given the following frequency distribution on banks in your state.

DEPOSIT SIZE (IN MILLIONS)	NUMBER OF BANKS	TOTAL DEPOSITS (IN MILLIONS)
Less than 5	2	7.2
5 to less than 10	7	52.1
10 to less than 25	6	111.5
25 to less than 50	3	95.4
50 to less than 100	2	166.6
100 to less than 500	2	529.8
Over 500	2	1663.0

   a. Does this frequency distribution violate any of the rules of construction for frequency distributions? If so, what changes would you make to the frequency distribution to remedy this violation.

   b. The Council wishes to target companies that would require financial support from banks that have at least $25 million in deposits. How would you reconstruct the frequency distribution to attract such companies to relocate to your state. Consider different classes that would accomplish such a goal.

   c. Recommend changes to the frequency distribution to attract companies that require financial support from banks that have between $5 million and $25 million in deposits.

   d. Present an eye-catching, two-paragraph summary of what the data would mean to a company considering moving to the state. Your boss has said you need to include relative frequencies in this presentation.

2-9 The data file **Wallingford** contains a sample of 60 accounts receivable balances selected from accounts at the Wallingford Department Store. Each week, the sales manager is asked to summarize the current status of the accounts receivable.

BALANCES					
39.93	33.33	27.50	68.00	70.00	11.41
72.04	107.56	29.59	15.00	96.07	37.73
69.04	146.93	98.05	11.05	150.00	44.09
87.00	107.33	27.50	24.88	9.47	80.05
55.55	80.00	141.88	105.19	25.00	99.99
19.95	47.09	12.11	110.00	11.01	19.33
53.72	72.50	19.58	8.00	76.47	49.99
125.00	16.18	20.00	9.00	19.33	52.52
75.55	33.97	126.12	30.72	62.50	27.05
97.94	56.25	16.47	14.50	90.05	66.05

   a. Decide how many classes would be appropriate for these data and justify your choice. Trial and error is a good tool in such decisions.

   b. Using the number of classes you selected, develop a frequency distribution and histogram for the accounts receivable.

   c. Suppose that the sampling procedure used for this sample was systematic sampling. The sample is one tenth of the population. If Wallingford's considers any accounts with balances under $25 to be "modest" balances, estimate the number of accounts in the population that are classified as having modest balances.

   d. Write a one-paragraph statement describing the accounts receivable balances as reflected by the sample. Specifically, (1) state the range of the account balances, (2) identify any account balances that may warrant more scrutiny by the collections department, and (3) determine the proportion of accounts larger than $100. Describe any other significant features of the data of which the manager should be made aware. (Remember that in business, report writing is an important way of conveying information.)

2-10 Comment on the pros and cons of using the following classes in connection with the data given in Problem 9.

   a. $ 9.47–$19.46
      19.47–29.46
      etc.

   b. $ 5–$15
      15–25
      25–30
      etc.

   c. $ 5 to under $35
      35 to under 45
      45 to under 55
      etc.

   d. $16<$30
      31< 45
      46< 60
      etc.

2-11 Lotteries have become very popular across the nation. Information regarding lottery sales between July 1, 1996, and June 30, 1997, are provided in the file **Lottery**. This data set was provided by the North American Association of State and Provincial Lotteries.

a. Develop a frequency distribution for the lottery sales using five classes.

b. Develop a frequency distribution for the state profits. Determine an appropriate number of classes, determine the frequency of each class, and calculate the relative frequency of each class.

c. Develop a frequency distribution for the per-capita spending on lotteries. Determine an appropriate number of classes, determine the frequency of each class, and calculate the relative frequency and the cumulative relative frequency of each class.

d. Develop histograms for parts a–c.

2-12 The Franklin Tire Company is considering whether to introduce a complete line of steel-belted radial tires. Because the company is late entering the market, the advertising campaign needs to be aggressive. As part of the advertising plan, the company wishes to demonstrate how durable the tires are. The managers have decided to put 4 new tires on each of 100 different sport utility vehicles and drive them throughout Alaska. The data collected indicate the number of miles (rounded to the nearest 1,000 miles) that each of the SUVs traveled before one of the tires on the vehicle did not meet minimum federal standards for tread thickness. The file name is **Franklin.**

61	55	57	56	69	64	56	53	57	54
74	64	58	65	58	63	58	56	64	57
63	61	58	61	65	64	57	66	56	63
58	68	66	53	65	61	63	62	58	61
59	65	61	64	59	63	57	59	58	52
65	61	53	60	59	57	63	61	66	58
58	55	55	62	54	64	63	60	52	61
54	57	67	68	61	58	69	72	65	56
58	57	58	53	57	58	67	60	66	56
54	54	55	60	52	59	68	64	63	59

a. Construct a frequency distribution and histogram using 8 classes.

b. The marketing department wishes to know the tread life of at least 50% of the tires, the 10% longest tread life, and the longest tread life of these tires. Provide this information to the marketing department. Also provide any other significant items that point out the desirability of this line of steel-belted tires.

c. Construct a frequency distribution and histogram using 12 classes. Compare your results with those in parts a and b. Which distribution gives the best information about the desirability of this line of steel-belted tires?

2-13 Refer to Problem 12. Although you do not want to be dishonest in presenting the results of your test, your job depends on showing the results in as favorable a light as possible. Organize and present the data using the methods discussed in this chapter and decide which method would be most favorable for selling the tires. Problem 12 is a beginning. You should explore several other approaches before you choose your final approach.

2-14 An example in this section discussed the weigh-in-motion project in which the state was interested in determining whether the WIM scale could be used to augment the POE scale for enforcement and data collection purposes. One of the variables collected at the Port of Entry is the length of the truck (POE length). The data are in the file called **Trucks.**

a. Develop a frequency distribution for POE length of trucks.

b. Develop a relative frequency distribution.

c. Construct both a frequency histogram and a cumulative frequency histogram.

2-15 Referring to Problem 14, the WIM scale also measures the length of the trucks. The variable is called WIM length.

a. Develop a frequency distribution for WIM length of trucks. Use the same classes as those used for the POE length of trucks' distribution so you can compare them.

b. Develop a relative frequency distribution.

c. Construct both a frequency histogram and a cumulative frequency histogram.

d. Compare these results for the WIM truck lengths to those for the POE truck lengths.

e. Comparing the two distributions, would you recommend that the WIM truck lengths be used in place of the POE truck lengths? Are there any systematic differences between the two distributions? Write a short report that discusses the similarities and differences between these two length variables.

2-2: JOINT FREQUENCY DISTRIBUTIONS

Frequency distributions are effective tools for describing data. In the previous section, we discussed how to develop grouped and ungrouped frequency distributions for one variable at a time. For instance, in the Capital Credit Union example, we were interested in customer credit card balances for all customers. We constructed a frequency distribution and histogram for that variable. However, often we need to examine the data more closely. This may involve analyzing two variables simultaneously.

Constructing Joint Frequency Distributions

Capital Credit Union (continued)

2-6

JOINT FREQUENCY DISTRIBUTIONS

Excel and
Minitab Tutorial

In the Capital Credit Union example presented in Section 2-1, the manager was interested in evaluating the success of the new credit card. Figure 2-7 showed the format for the data in the file, **Capital**, and Figures 2-8 and 2-9 showed the frequency distribution and histogram for a sample of customer credit card balances. While this information is useful, the managers would like to know more. Specifically, what does the credit card balance distribution look like for male versus female cardholders?

One way to approach this is to sort the data by the gender variable and develop frequency distributions and histograms for males and females separately. You could then make a visual comparison of the two to determine what, if any, difference exists between the credit balances of males and females. However, an alternative approach that might be preferred is to jointly analyze the two variables, gender and credit card balance.

Although the process is different for Excel and Minitab, both software packages provide methods for analyzing two variables jointly. In Figure 2-8, we constructed the frequency distribution for the 300 credit card balances using 10 classes. The class width was set at $150. Figure 2-11 shows a table that is called a **joint frequency distribution.** This type of table is also called a *cross-tabulation* table.[1]

JOINT FREQUENCY DISTRIBUTION

A summary of a bivariate set of data that displays the number of observations that exhibit the respective joint characteristics of one value taken from each of the variables that define the data set.

The Capital Credit Union managers can use a joint frequency table to analyze the credit card balances for males versus females. For instance, for the 61 customers with card balances (rounded to nearest dollar) of $540–$689, Figure 2-11 shows that 45 were males and 16 were females.

FIGURE 2-11
Excel Output—Capital Credit Union Joint Frequency Distribution

Count of Credit Card Account Balance	Gender 1 = Male 2 = Female		
Credit Card Account Balance	1	2	Grand Total
90-239	11	2	13
240-389	16	3	19
390-539	33	9	42
540-689	45	16	61
690-839	35	12	47
840-989	41	9	50
990-1139	28	8	36
1140-1289	14	6	20
1290-1439	8	2	10
1440-1589	1	1	2
Grand Total	232	68	300

Excel Instructions:

1. Open file: Capital.xls
2. Click any cell within the data
3. Click on the Data Tab
4. Select Pivot Table Report
5. Click Next—Next—Next
6. Select Layout
7. Drag Credit Card Balance to Rows
8. Drag Gender to Columns
9. Drag any variable to Data Area—(Needs to be Count)
10. Click Finish

---

[1] In Excel, the joint frequency distribution is developed using a tool called Pivot Table Report. In Minitab, the joint frequency distributions are constructed using the Cross Tabulation option.

FIGURE 2-12
Excel Output of the Joint
Relative Frequencies

Microsoft Excel - Capital.xls			
File Edit View Insert Format Tools Data PHStat Window Help			
B19	=		
	A	**B**	**C**	**D**

	A	B	C	D
1				
2				
3	Count of Credit Card Account Balance	Gender 1 = Male 2 = Female		
4	Credit Card Account Balance	1	2	Grand Total
5	90-239	3.67%	0.67%	4.33%
6	240-389	5.33%	1.00%	6.33%
7	390-539	11.00%	3.00%	14.00%
8	540-689	15.00%	5.33%	20.33%
9	690-839	11.67%	4.00%	15.67%
10	840-989	13.67%	3.00%	16.67%
11	990-1139	9.33%	2.67%	12.00%
12	1140-1289	4.67%	2.00%	6.67%
13	1290-1439	2.67%	0.67%	3.33%
14	1440-1589	0.33%	0.33%	0.67%
15	Grand Total	77.33%	22.67%	100.00%
16				

In Figure 2-12 and Figure 2-13 we have used the data field options of the PivotTable to represent the data as percentages.

In Section 2-1, we discussed the concept of relative frequency (proportions, which Excel converts to percentages) as a useful tool for making comparisons between two data sets. In this example, comparisons between males and females would be easier if the frequencies were converted to proportions (or percentages). The result is the *joint relative frequency table* shown in Figure 2-12. Notice that the percentages in each cell are percents of the total 300 people in the survey. For example, the \$540–\$689 class had 20.33% (61) of the 300 customers. The male customers with balances in the \$540–\$689 range constituted 15% (45) of the 300 customers while females with that balance level made up 5.33% (16) of all 300 customers. On the surface, this result seems to indicate a big difference between males and females at this credit balance level.

Suppose we really wanted to focus on the male versus female issue and control for the fact that there are far more males than females in the sample. We could compute the percentages differently. Rather than using a base of 300 (the entire sample size), we might instead be interested in the percentages of the males that have balances at each level, and the same for females.[2] Figure 2-13 shows the relative frequencies converted to a percentage of the column total. In general, there seems to be little difference in the male and female distributions with respect to credit card balances.

Additional
Example 2-d

Joint Frequency
Distributions—
Analyzing
Seatbelt Use

FIGURE 2-13
Excel Relative Frequency
Distributions—Males and
Females

Microsoft Excel - Capital.xls			
File Edit View Insert Format Tools Data PHStat Window Help			
C24	=		

	A	B	C	D
1				
2				
3	Count of Credit Card Account Balance	Gender 1 = Male 2 = Female		
4	Credit Card Account Balance	1	2	Grand Total
5	90-239	4.74%	2.94%	4.33%
6	240-389	6.90%	4.41%	6.33%
7	390-539	14.22%	13.24%	14.00%
8	540-689	19.40%	23.53%	20.33%
9	690-839	15.09%	17.65%	15.67%
10	840-989	17.67%	13.24%	16.67%
11	990-1139	12.07%	11.76%	12.00%
12	1140-1289	6.03%	8.82%	6.67%
13	1290-1439	3.45%	2.94%	3.33%
14	1440-1589	0.43%	1.47%	0.67%
15	Grand Total	100.00%	100.00%	100.00%
16				

Excel Instructions:

1. Place cursor anywhere in the table
2. Right click—select Wizard
3. Select layout
4. Double click on Data field item
5. For "Show Data As"—select % of Column
6. OK

[2]Such distributions are known as *marginal distributions*.

There are many options for transferring data into useful information. Thus far, we have introduced the concept of frequency distributions, joint frequency tables, and histograms. In the next section, we discuss one of the most useful graphical tools, called the bar chart.

2-2: EXERCISES

ADDITIONAL EXERCISES ON YOUR CD-ROM
Try the **ADDITIONAL EXERCISES and APPLICATION PROBLEMS** on the CD-ROM.

2-16 You have been given the following joint frequency distribution. Convert the frequencies to relative frequencies.

	YEARS OF COLLEGE				
Income	None	1–2 Years	3–4 Years	5–6 Years	>6 Years
<$20,000	16	33	30	6	4
$20,000<$40,000	22	28	40	26	5
$40,000<$60,000	9	12	21	46	9
>$60,000	3	5	15	13	6

a. Determine the proportion of those having at least 5 years of college that earn at least $40,000. Compare this proportion to a similar proportion for those having less than 5 years of college.
b. Determine the proportion of those that make over $60,000 and have at least 4 years of college.
c. Determine the proportion of the entire sample that makes less than $20,000. Compare this to the proportion of those that have not gone to college that make less than $20,000.
d. Calculate the proportion of those that have not gone to college that make over $60,000. Calculate a similar proportion for each of the years of college categories.
e. Is the proportion of those making over $60,000 dependent upon which category was selected in part d?

2-17 In a survey conducted by NFO Interactive, investors were asked to rate how knowledgeable they felt they were as investors. Both online and traditional investors were included in the survey. The survey resulted in the following data:
  • Of the online investors, 8%, 55%, and 37% responded that they were "savvy," "experienced," and "novice," respectively.
  • Of the traditional investors the percentages were 4, 29, and 67, respectively.
Six hundred investors were surveyed, of which 200 were traditional.
  a. Use the preceding information to construct a joint frequency distribution.

b. Use the preceding information to construct a joint relative frequency distribution.

2-18 Reexamine Problem 17.
  a. Calculate the proportion of investors who were online investors.
  b. Determine the proportion of investors who were both online investors and rated themselves experienced.

Business Applications

2-19 The makers of the PowerChew Energy Bar recently weighed 10 bars from each of their two production lines. The following data were observed:

Line	1	1	1	1	1	1	1	1	1	1
Weight	2.78	2.95	3.03	2.89	3.04	2.97	3.04	2.99	2.95	3.10
Line	2	2	2	2	2	2	2	2	2	2
Weight	3.02	3.11	2.98	2.90	3.02	3.05	3.01	2.97	2.98	3.00

a. Develop a joint frequency distribution showing manufacturing line and the weights broken into two categories: under 3.00 and 3.00 and over.
b. Referring to part a, convert the joint frequency distribution to a joint relative frequency distribution.
c. Write a short paragraph using the information in parts a and b to describe the output for the PowerChew company.

2-20 Recently a survey was conducted of eight companies. Three of the variables on which data were collected were: Sales increase over the previous year (Yes or No?); Public or privately held?; Manufacturer or service business? The following data were recorded.

Company	1	2	3	4
Sales Increase	Yes	Yes	No	Yes
Public or Private	Public	Public	Private	Private
Manufacturing or Service	Manufact.	Service	Service	Manufact.

Company	5	6	7	8
Sales Increase	No	No	Yes	No
Public or Private	Public	Public	Public	Private
Manufacturing or Service	Service	Manufact.	Service	Manufact.

a. Code the values for each variable with a numeric value.

b. For each variable individually, construct a frequency distribution.

c. Construct all possible joint frequency distributions for these variables. In addition, convert the frequency distributions to joint relative frequencies.

d. Using the information in parts b and c develop a short statement that describes these data for the eight companies.

2-21 Employees at the Norton Hardware Store recently completed their inventory. In the paint section, the following counts were made:

Gloss	100 gallon cans
Semi-gloss	250 gallon cans
Flat	150 gallon cans

In addition, the paint brands were distributed between four companies as follows:

Glidden	50 gallon cans
Everlast	200 gallon cans
Ponderosa	150 gallon cans
DuPont	100 gallon cans

Further, of 200 Everlast cans, 50 were gloss and 100 were semi-gloss. None of the Glidden cans were flat. Half of the flat cans were DuPont. Half of the Glidden paint cans were gloss. Of the Ponderosa cans, 100 were semi-gloss. Based on this information construct the joint frequency distribution for paint type and paint brand.

2-22 Suppose Norton Hardware attempts to have the following mix of paint types: 20% gloss, 50% semi-gloss, and 30% flat paint. Reexamining Problem 21, given the inventory they have taken, suggest to the store manager what brands and types of paint he must order so these percentages are attained for each paint brand. (Hint: Determine the number of cans needed so that the existing inventory would meet these specifications, e.g., how many cans of Glidden paint would be needed so that the 25 cans of gloss paint would be 20% of that number?)

2-23 The High Desert Banking Company is a small bank that specializes in making consumer loans, small commercial loans, and real estate loans (both home improvement and new home construction). The data file **High-Desert-Banking** contains the loans made by the bank last year. The loan types are: Consumer, Commercial, and Real Estate.

   In your position as an intern at the bank, you have been given the task of developing a presentation to the bank's loan officers. You are planning to include the following in your presentation:

a. A frequency distribution of loans by type of loan.

b. A relative frequency distribution.

c. A frequency distribution of loan amounts using class intervals of $15,000.

d. A histogram of loan amounts using the frequency distribution in part c.

e. A joint frequency distribution of loan amount and type of loan using class intervals of $15,000 for loan amount.

f. A histogram for each type of loan: consumer, commercial, and real estate.

g. Develop a written report that fully discusses the loan data. This report should be developed using a word processor. The various frequency distributions and histograms should be pasted into the document and clearly labeled. Make sure your report points out differences and similarities among the various distributions of loan data in the regions of the country. For instance, examine which regions have the largest loans, which regions have similar distributions, and how the regions' distributions are different.

2-24 The Baker Corporation is considering relocating one of its manufacturing plants. One of the criteria for relocation is the cost of living. An important factor in cost of living is the price of homes in the city. As part of an extensive relocation analysis, the Baker site selection team has data on median home prices for many U.S. cities. (Note that half the homes have a value below the median, and half the homes have values above the median.) The data are in a file called **Home-Prices.**

a. Your job is to prepare a written report that summarizes the home prices by region of the country. You will have to establish a means for allocating cities to a region. Then you will develop frequency distributions, histograms, and joint frequency distributions as appropriate. When working with home price, use a class width of $10,000. This report should be developed using a word processor. The various frequency distributions and histograms should be pasted into the document and clearly labeled.

b. Baker's management feels that there must be a substantial proportion of homes available for less than $125,000. In the summary of the report you produce in part a, address this issue and make a recommendation (based on this factor) of where the plant should relocate.

2-25 The research and development department at Hydronics, Inc. has developed two weight loss systems that they are considering introducing on the market. One month ago, the managers conducted a study in which they put a sample of people into three separate programs: #1, #2, and a placebo. They then recorded the number of pounds each person gained or lost during the month. These data are recorded in the file called **Hydronics.**

   You have been asked to analyze the weight loss data using the following statistical tools:

a. Develop a frequency distribution for each program and the placebo. Use 5.0 pound class widths.

b. Based on the results in part a, develop histograms for each program and the placebo.

c. Produce relative frequency distributions for each program and for the placebo.

d. Prepare a report that summarizes the information generated in parts a–c. You must include in your report a recommendation concerning which weight loss system they should introduce and the reasons for the recommendation.

e. Discuss whether you think it would be appropriate in this case to construct a joint frequency distribution for the weight loss by people on the two Hydronics programs.

■ 2-3: BAR CHARTS AND PIE CHARTS

Bar Charts

Sections 2-1 and 2-2 introduced some of the basic tools for describing numerical variables, both discrete and continuous, when the data were in their raw form. However, in many instances, you will be working with categorical data or data that have already been summarized to some extent. In this case, an effective presentation tool is often a **bar chart**.

> **BAR CHART**
> A graphical representation of a categorical data set in which a rectangle or bar is drawn over each category or class. The length of each bar represents the frequency or percentage of observations contained in a category. The bars may be vertical or horizontal. The bars may all be the same color or they may be different colors depicting different categories. Additionally, multiple variables can be graphed on the same bar chart.

BAR CHARTS

International Banking

In today's business climate, the U.S. economy is closely linked to the international marketplace. While the U.S. economy is extremely large and diverse, its health is tied to the economic health of foreign countries. Recently an executive for the Wall Street brokerage house Hoenig & Co. was asked to give a speech at an international economic summit in New York City. The talk was to be centered on Brazil, the world's ninth largest economy, but one that by many accounts is in great peril.[3]

A successful Brazilian economy is of vital interest to the United States and the rest of the world. Since it is an emerging market country, many American businesses generate substantial income from Brazil. In preparation for the speech, the Hoenig executive assembled the data in Table 2-6 that shows the 1997 income, in billions of dollars, derived by U.S. businesses from emerging market countries.

Although the table format contains the data and is informative, a graphical presentation is often desirable. A bar chart would work well in this instance. The bars can be vertical or horizontal. Figure 2-14 shows an example. Note, since Brazil is the focus, that bar is highlighted with a different shading than the other countries.

The bar chart shows very clearly how important Brazil is to U.S. industry as a source of income. Do you agree that the chart makes the point more effectively than the table?

People sometimes confuse histograms and bar charts. Although there are some similarities, they are two very different graphical tools. Histograms are used to represent a frequency distribution associated with a quantitative (ratio or interval level) variable. Refer to the examples in Section 2-2. In every case, the variable on the horizontal axis was numeri-

---

[3]Fox, Justin, "A Prayer for Brazil," *Fortune*, November 9, 1998, pp. 30–31.

**Additional
Example 2-e**

Bar Charts

Brazil	$4.55
Mexico	$3.97
Indonesia	$1.74
Panama	$1.30
Chile	$1.22
Malaysia	$1.21
Venezuela	$0.87
Argentina	$0.85
China	$0.81
Nigeria	$0.78

Note: Data are in billions of dollars, U.S. currency.

T A B L E   2 - 6
1997 U.S. Income from
Emerging Market Countries

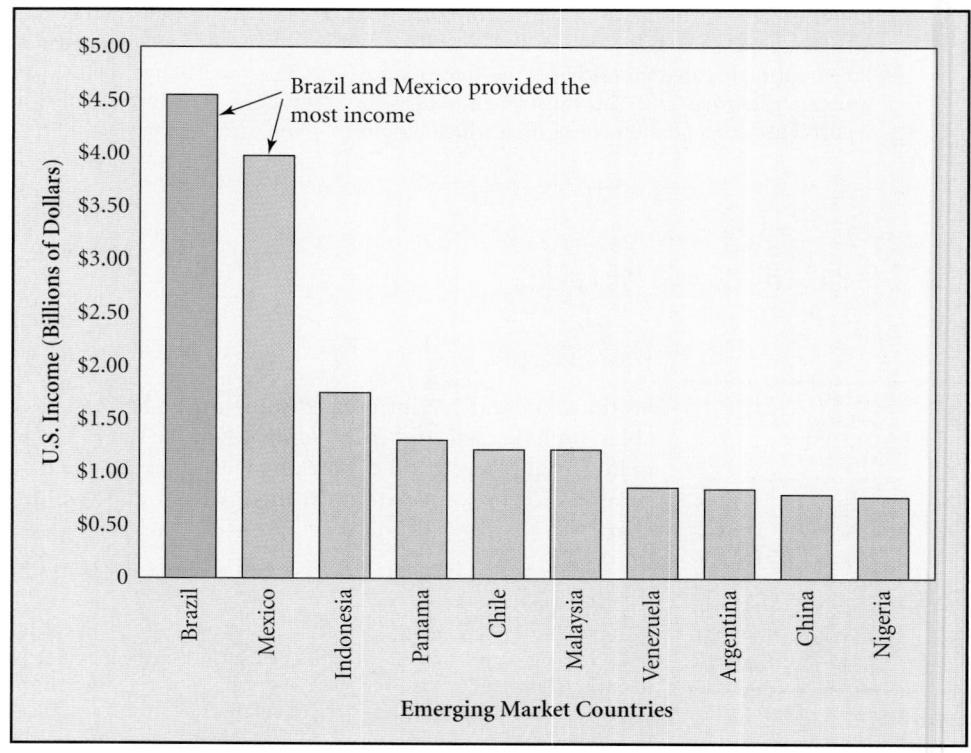

F I G U R E   2 - 1 4   Bar Chart of U.S. Income from Emerging Countries

cal with values moving from low to high. There are no gaps between the histogram bars. On the other hand, bar charts are used when the variable of interest is categorical as in this case where the category consists of the emerging countries.

Bach, Lombard & Wilson

BAR CHARTS

**Excel and
Minitab
Tutorial**

One of the most useful features of bar charts is that you can use one chart to display multiple issues. Consider an example at Bach, Lombard & Wilson, a New England law firm. In early 1999, the firm was involved in a case in which a female employee of a major electronics firm sued, claiming the company gave higher starting salaries to men than to women. Consequently, she claimed, even though the company tended to give equal percentage raises to women as men, the gap between the two groups widened.

Attorneys at Bach, Lombard & Wilson had their staff assemble massive amounts of data in preparation for the case. Table 2-7 provides an example of the type of data they collected. These data are in the file called **Bach** on your CD-ROM.

Although the table contains the data, a more effective way to convey their information is in bar chart form. Figure 2-15 illustrates a bar chart developed using Excel. From this graph we can quickly see that in all years, except 1995, the starting salaries for males did exceed that for females. The bar chart also illustrates that the general trend in starting salaries for both groups has been increasing with a slight downward turn in 1997. Thus, this one bar chart can be used to compare salaries for two groups and show the general trend in salaries for both groups. Do you think the information in Figure 2-15 alone is sufficient to rule in favor of the claimant in this lawsuit?

Suppose other data are available showing the percentage of new hires having MBA degrees by gender, as illustrated in Table 2-8. A bar chart can be used to present these data

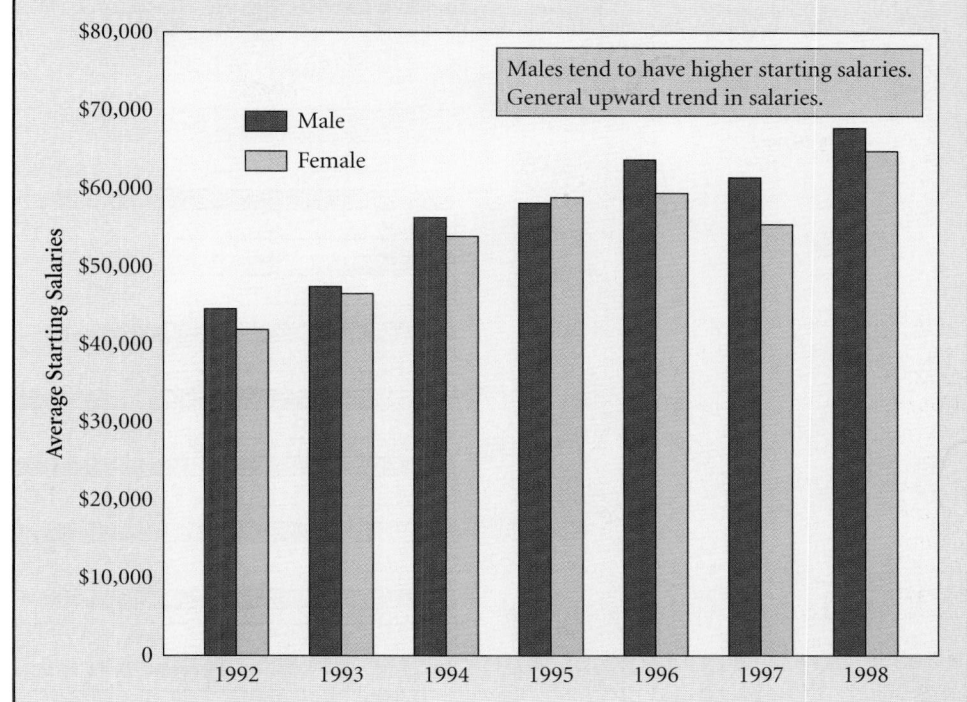

YEAR	MALES: AVERAGE STARTING SALARIES	FEMALES: AVERAGE STARTING SALARIES
1992	$44,456	$41,789
1993	$47,286	$46,478
1994	$56,234	$53,854
1995	$57,890	$58,600
1996	$63,467	$59,070
1997	$61,090	$55,321
1998	$67,543	$64,506

T A B L E   2 - 7
Salary Data for Bach,
Lombard & Wilson

F I G U R E   2 - 1 5   Bar Chart of Starting Salaries

as shown in Figure 2-16. This chart shows that every year the percentage of new hires with MBA degrees was substantially higher for male hires than for female hires. What might this imply to you about the reason for the difference in starting salaries?

After viewing the bar chart in Figure 2-16, the lead attorney had her staff look at the average starting salary for MBA and non-MBA graduates for the combined seven-year period broken down by male and female employees. Figure 2-17 contains the bar chart for those data.

Figure 2-17 shows an interesting result. Over the seven-year period, females actually had higher starting salaries than males with comparable degrees. Then how can the data in Figure 2-15 be correct? It showed that in almost every year the average male starting salaries exceeded those for females. The answer is contained in Figure 2-16 that shows that far more of the newly hired males have MBA degrees. Since MBAs tend to get substantially higher starting salaries, this brought the overall average up. Thus, the old saying, "You can't judge a book by its cover" is once again shown to be true. In this case, the initial data

T A B L E   2 - 8
Salary Data for the Bach,
Lombard & Wilson Example

YEAR	MALES: AVERAGE STARTING SALARIES	MALES: PERCENT WITH MBA	FEMALES: AVERAGE STARTING SALARIES	FEMALES: PERCENT WITH MBA
1992	$44,456	35	$41,789	18
1993	$47,286	39	$46,478	20
1994	$56,234	49	$53,854	22
1995	$57,890	40	$58,600	30
1996	$63,467	46	$59,070	25
1997	$61,090	32	$55,321	24
1998	$67,543	48	$64,506	26

Excel Instructions:

1. Open file: Bach.xls
2. Click on Chart Wizard
3. Select Bar type
4. Define Data Range
5. Label chart as desired

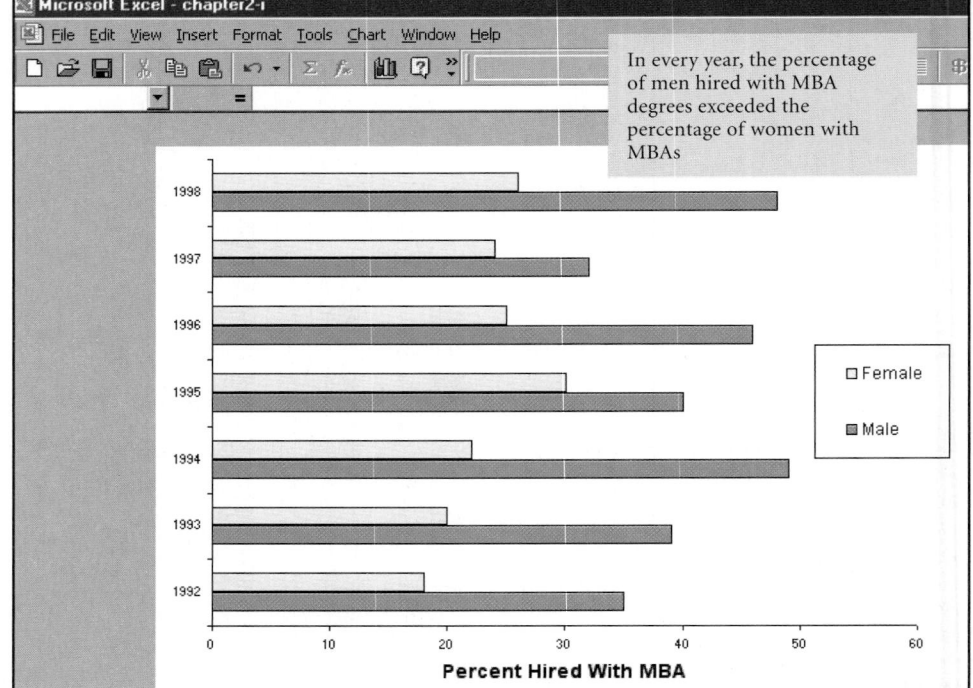

FIGURE 2-16
Excel Output—Bar Chart of
MBA Hire Data

appeared to indicate that the electronics firm had been discriminating against females by paying lower starting salaries. However, after digging deeper, we see that females actually get the higher average starting salaries with and without MBA degrees. Does this prove that the company is not discriminating in its hiring practices? Perhaps it purposefully hires fewer female MBAs or fewer females in general. More research is needed.

FIGURE 2-17
Excel Output—Bar Chart of
Average Salaries by Degree
Type

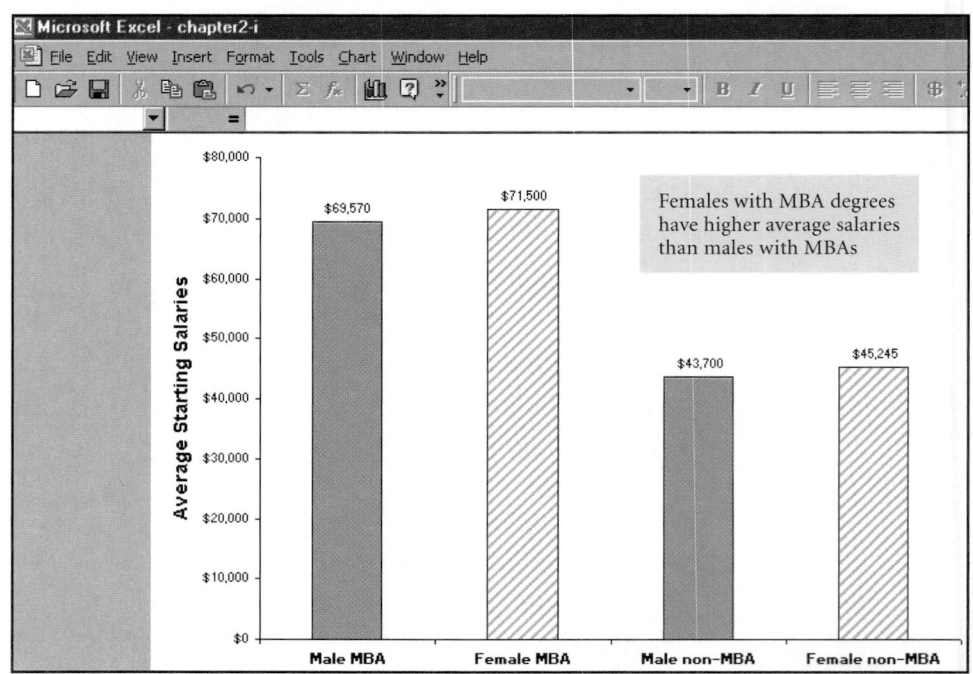

TOOLS OF QUALITY

PARETO CHARTS

Electronic Controls Company (ECCO) is one of the leading makers of backup alarms (devices that beep loudly when delivery trucks, forklifts, and other commercial vehicles are moving in reverse) and other warning products. Although the company has a sophisticated quality assurance system, sometimes alarms are returned for replacement under the company's warranty. Whenever a warranty claim is made, **ECCO** keeps detailed records on all aspects of the product. A file on your CD-ROM called **ECCO** contains data on the most recent 110 warranty cases for the XJ568 Alarm product. Figure 2-18 shows the first few cases and the variables that are tracked in the warranty file.

The variables that ECCO tracks are:

    Dollar Value of Claim
    Shift Manufactured (1 = Day, 2 = Swing,
      3 = Graveyard)
    Customer Complaint

        1 = Corrosion
        2 = Malfunction
        3 = Wiring
        4 = Sound Problem

    Manufacturing Plant

        1 = Boise
        2 = Atlanta
        3 = Reno

FIGURE 2-18
Excel Worksheet of the ECCO Warranty Data

In order to understand the warranty claims on this alarm product, ECCO will construct a **Pareto chart.**

Additional Example 2-f

Pareto Charts

80/20

PARETO CHART
A bar chart that is sorted so that the categories or classes are arranged from highest to lowest with respect to the magnitude of the displayed variable associated with each category or class.

The Pareto chart shown in Figure 2-19 shows the total dollar warranty value by complaint type. In dollar value, the biggest problem has been malfunction. Figure 2-20 shows the Pareto chart for number of claims by complaint type. Again this shows that alarm malfunction is the biggest problem. So, ECCO will focus on the malfunction issue first.

FIGURE 2-19
Excel Output—An ECCO Pareto Chart

Excel Instructions:

1. Open file: ECCO.xls
2. Click on Data
3. Select Pivot Table Report
4. Define data range
5. Use Layout—Put Complaint Type as Row and Dollar Claim as Data—then Finish
6. Use Sum of Dollar Claim option
7. Select Dollar Values in Pivot table and use Data-Sort—Descending
8. Use Chart Wizard—Bar Option

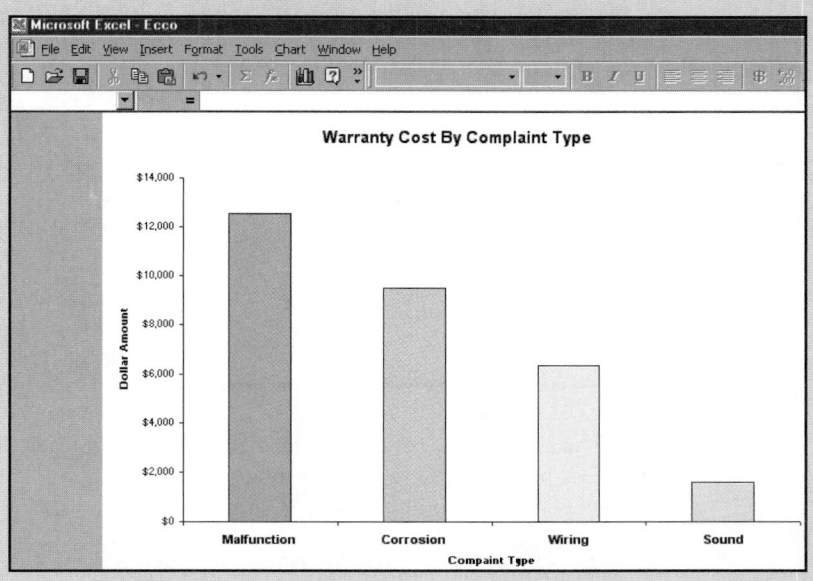

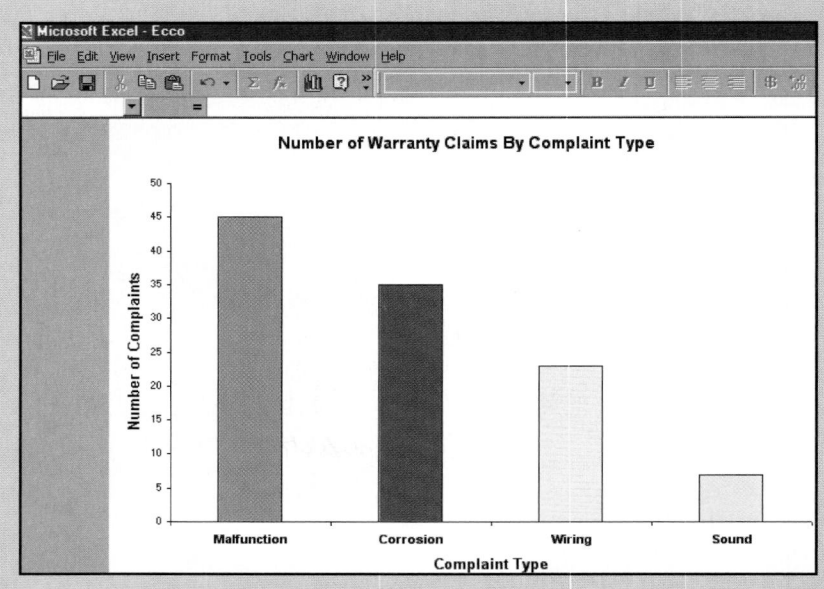

Excel Instructions:
1. Open file: ECCO.xls
2. Click on Data
3. Select Pivot Table Report
4. Define data range
5. Use Layout—Put
   Complaint Type as Row
   and Dollar Claim as
   Data—then Finish
6. Use Count of Dollar
   Claim option
7. Select Count Values in
   Pivot table and use Data-
   Sort—Descending
8. Use Chart Wizard—Bar
   Option

FIGURE 2-20
Excel Output—Another
ECCO Pareto Chart

Pie Charts

Another graphical tool that can be used to help transform data into information is the **pie chart.**

> **PIE CHART**
> A graph in the shape of a circle. The circle is divided into "slices" corresponding to the categories or classes to be displayed. The size of the slices is proportional to the magnitude of the displayed variable associated with each category or class.

2-9

PIE CHARTS

Additional
Example 2-g

Pie Charts

State Government

A pie chart is often used to display the breakdown of a budget. For example, if a state's legislature has made final approval for spending from the state's general fund, the allocations can be effectively displayed with a pie chart. Suppose the following allocations (in millions of dollars) have been made:

BUDGET CATEGORY	DOLLARS	PERCENT OF TOTAL
Health and Welfare	$ 811.7	25.37%
Education	1,477.3	46.17
Corrections	209.5	6.55
Highways	389.4	12.16
Other	312.1	9.75
Total	3,200.0	100.00%

The appropriate pie chart is formed by breaking the circle into five slices such that the slices are proportional to the percentage of the total budget that is allocated to each budget category. The output in Figure 2-21 shows that education gets the biggest share of the budget. Both Excel and Minitab have procedures for developing pie charts.

FIGURE 2-21
Pie Chart for the State
Budget Data

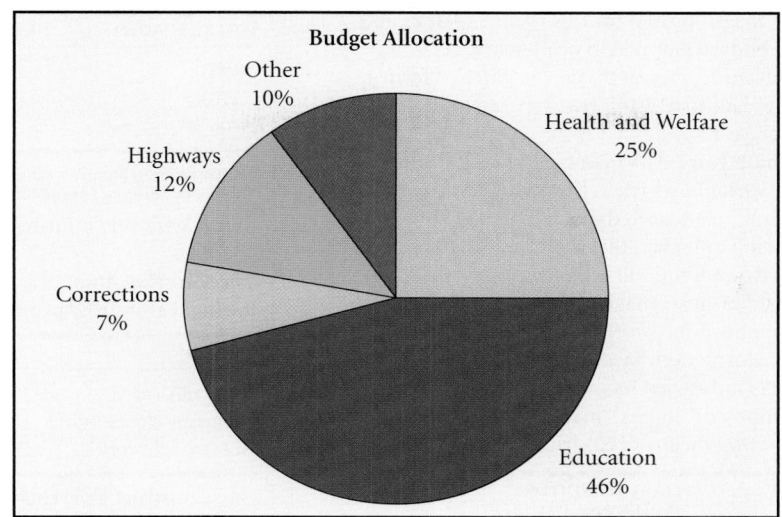

2-3: EXERCISES

 **ADDITIONAL EXERCISES ON YOUR CD-ROM**
Try the ADDITIONAL EXERCISES and APPLICATION PROBLEMS
on the CD-ROM.

2-26 You are given the following data reflecting the number of people in a study having each of the following investments.

INVESTMENTS	NO. OF PEOPLE
Mutual Fund	357
Savings Account	506
Certificate of Deposit	158
Individual Stocks	347
Bonds	86
Real Estate	169
Other	41

   a. You wish to demonstrate which investments are the most popular. Based on these data, construct a bar chart to effectively display the data.

   b. Discuss the relative merits of using a bar chart, pie chart, or Pareto chart to represent this data set.

2-27 A mutual fund recently sent a letter to its customers outlining the planned capital gain distributions for the current year. The following values reflect the per share capital gain allocation for each type of fund managed by the company:

FUND	CAPITAL GAIN DISTRIBUTIONS
Balanced	$0.13
Equity Income	0.75
Growth	0.19
Select	0.91
Utilities	0.63

   a. Construct a chart that will effectively display these data.

   b. Discuss why a pie chart would not be appropriate in this case.

   c. Discuss the relative value of using a bar chart versus a Pareto chart.

Business Applications

2-28 Ed Christianson has been asked by the director of marketing to make a presentation at next week's annual meeting of the Brown Manufacturing Company. The presentation concerns the company's advertising budget for the past year and the projected budget for the next year. In preparing for the meeting, Ed has obtained the following data:

MEDIUM	THIS YEAR'S EXPENSES	NEXT YEAR'S BUDGET
Newspaper	$35,000	$40,000
Television	60,000	80,000
Trade Publications	25,000	25,000
Miscellaneous	10,000	10,000

   a. Use these data to develop a bar chart that effectively shows both this year's expenses for advertising and next year's proposed budget.

   b. Produce a chart that highlights the media that will have the largest percentage increase in next year's budget compared to this year's expenses.

c. Determine the proportion of this year's expenses and next year's budget allocated to printed media.

2-29 Referring to Problem 28, present the data in pie chart format.

a. Present the data first using two separate pie charts, one for each year.

b. Combine both years' data in one pie chart. (Hint: create a new variable which reflects dollar change in expenses from one year to the next.)

c. Finally, develop a pie chart that shows how the increased advertising expenditure will be allocated next year.

2-30 Growing companies must make regular capital expenditures to update and improve their production facilities. The following information, taken from the 1997 Annual Report of Flowers Industries, Inc., shows the capital expenditures (in millions of dollars) made to renovate, automate, and modernize the firm's bakeries.

YEAR	CAPITAL EXPENDITURES (MILLIONS OF $)
1992	34
1993	52
1994	64
1995	73
1996	76
1997	78
1998 estimated	40

a. Prepare a bar chart using this information.

b. Suppose you wish to show how the capital expenditures for 1998 fit in the trend that had been established in the last six years. Discuss the effectiveness of the bar chart in doing this.

2-31 Real Estate Investment Trusts (REITs) were created by Congress in 1960 so that small investors could invest in real estate as shareholders rather than as landlords. Using information taken from Paine Webber and SEC filings, *The Orlando Sentinel* of April 5, 1998, reported the following proportions of REIT money invested in different categories:

CATEGORY	PERCENTAGE
Shopping Centers	20%
Multifamily	18%
Office	17%
Health Care	8%
Hotels	8%
Industrials	7%
Mixed Industry/Office	5%
Mortgage Backed	5%
Diversified	5%
Self Storage	4%
Specialty	3%

a. Present this information graphically using a pie chart and alternatively as a bar chart.

b. Which do you feel is more effective? Why?

2-32 Real Estate Investment Trusts provided investors with a convenient way to invest in real estate. Of the more than 300 U.S. REITs, 210 are publicly traded on the following exchanges:

WHERE TRADED	NUMBER
NYSE	158
AMEX	37
NASDAQ	15

Source: Paine Webber, SEC filings, *The Orlando Sentinel* (April 5, 1998).

Summarize this information using a bar chart and a pie chart.

2-33 *The Statistical Abstract of the United States* reported the following reasons why people lose their jobs.

REASON	PERCENTAGE
Job abolished	28%
Company closes/moves	42
Not enough work	30

a. Construct a pie chart displaying these results.

b. Also construct a bar chart and discuss which is the more effective tool for displaying these data.

2-34 Create both a bar chart and a pie chart of the following information taken from *The Orlando Sentinel* of April 5, 1998, concerning owners of Real Estate Investment Trusts (REITs). Which chart better illustrates REIT ownership? Explain your answer.

Individual Investors	49%
Mutual Funds	37
Banks	7
Insurance	4
Pension Funds	3

2-35 The USDA Economic Service reports that in 1970, $0.66 of the consumer food dollar was spent on food eaten at home while $0.34 was spent to eat away from home. By 1996, the amount spent for at-home dining had fallen to $0.54 while the amount spent for away-from-home dining had risen to $0.46. Produce the graphical technique which you think provides the best comparison of where consumers' food dollars were spent for these two different time periods.

2-36 Many investors prefer mutual funds to individual stocks because of the professional management and diversification that funds provide. As of December 31, 1997, the Acorn Fund, a mutual fund investing in small companies, had the portfolio diversification presented in the accompanying table. Prepare a graph that best illustrates the fund's mix of investments.

CATEGORY	PERCENT OF NET ASSETS
Information	26.6%
Health Care	7.8
Consumer Goods/Services	8.5
Finance/Real Estate/Transportation	15.9
Industrial Goods/Services	8.8
Energy/Minerals	11.1
Foreign	12.2
Cash Less Liabilities	9.1

Source: The Acorn Family of Funds 1997 Annual Report.

2-37 The Celltone Company is a provider of cellular phone service. They have two plans, a basic plan and a business plan. Recently the local Celltone store manager examined the accounts for 200 customers. The manager was interested in the total number of minutes of cell calls used by customers on each plan. He needed the information presented in an effective way for a sales meeting next week. Use the file **Celltone** located on the CD-ROM.

    a. Develop an appropriate graph and write a short statement that describes the graph.

    b. Each of the two plans was designed to evoke a certain pattern of cell call use. Plan 1 was the initial offering. However, it was felt that usage under this plan was too unpredictable. There were many heavy users (defined by at least 120 minutes usage) and many light users (defined by at most 50 minutes usage). Plan 2 was developed to encourage a more consistent usage pattern. Your presentation to the sales meeting should address this issue. Produce your presentation for this portion of the sales meeting.

2-38 The real estate loan manager for Citizens Bank uses three different appraisal companies to appraise residential property when a customer wants a home mortgage or wants to refinance an existing mortgage. Recently he conducted a test by having the same three companies appraise the same five properties. The results (in thousands of dollars) are in a file called **Citizens**.

    a. After completing the test, the manager would like your help in displaying the data in an effective way. (Hint, you might consider using total appraisal values.) Provide a graphical display to oblige the manager.

    b. Of course the manager realizes that appraisals will vary from appraiser to appraiser, however he is especially interested in determining if any of the companies show a systematic pattern of appraisals compared to the other companies. Provide this information.

PROPERTY	ALLEN & ASSOCIATES	HEIST APPRAISAL	APPRAISAL INTERNATIONAL
1	78	82	79
2	102	102	99
3	68	74	70
4	83	88	86
5	95	99	92

2-39 The Future-Vision Company is thinking of opening a TV dish franchise in a new market area. However, prior to actually securing a location and taking other necessary steps to make the move, they conducted a survey of 548 residents in the market area. The data from this survey are in the file called **Future-Vision**. As site selection manager, you have been asked to develop a presentation for next week's staff meeting.

    a. First, develop a chart that effectively displays the total number of residents in the following two categories: cable subscriber and not a cable subscriber. Be sure to do a good job labeling the graph.

    b. Then write a short statement that details the main points presented in the graph.

    c. Among the points you should address is the perception obtained from your graphs. Future-Vision classifies households with more than three occupants as a large family. (1) Does your graph give the perception that cable users have a larger proportion of large families? (2) Calculate this proportion. Explain this visual paradox.

2-40 Referring to Problem 39, suppose you are also interested in comparing total household income between cable subscribers and nonsubscribers in a graphical format.

    a. Select and produce an appropriate graph.

    b. Write a short statement that summarizes the information shown in the graph. Originally it was believed that more low-income families would be cable subscribers and that a larger proportion of high-income families would not have cable TV. As part of your summary address these issues.

2-41 Referring to Problem 39, as part of the presentation to the staff, you want to present a graph which effectively shows what the income distribution is in this market area.

    a. Select and produce an appropriate graph.

    b. Write a short statement discussing the information contained in the graph.

2-42 The file **Home-Prices** contains data on median home prices (the point below which 50% of the house prices fall) for 100 different U.S. cities. In your job with Farm-Life Insurance, you have been asked to break the cities into regions (North, South, East and West). Prepare a graphical presentation that compares the data in the study by region. Write a short summary report on your findings. Point out regions that seem to have larger proportions of low-, moderate-, and high-priced homes. Make your comments on the basis of your graphical presentation.

2-43 As an intern for the Intel Corporation suppose you have been asked to help the vice-president prepare a newsletter to the shareholders. You have been given access to the data in a file called **Intel** that contains Intel Corporation financial data for the years 1987–1996. Go to the Internet or to Intel's annual report and update the file to include the same variables for the years 1997 to the present. Then, use graphs to effectively present the data in a format that would be usable for the vice president's newsletter. Write a short article that discusses the information shown in your graphs.

	NET REVENUES (IN MILLIONS)	EMPLOYEES AT YEAR-END	RETURN ON EQUITY (%)	EARNINGS PER SHARE	RESEARCH & DEVELOPMENT (IN MILLIONS)
1987	$ 1,907	19,200	19.7%	$0.34	$ 260
1988	$ 2,875	20,800	27.0%	$0.63	$ 318
1989	$ 3,127	21,700	16.9%	$0.52	$ 365
1990	$ 3,921	23,900	21.2%	$0.80	$ 517
1991	$ 4,779	24,600	20.4%	$0.98	$ 618
1992	$ 5,844	25,800	21.6%	$1.24	$ 780
1993	$ 8,782	29,500	36.5%	$2.60	$ 970
1994	$11,521	32,600	27.3%	$2.62	$1,111
1995	$16,202	41,600	33.3%	$4.03	$1,296
1996	$20,847	48,500	35.6%	$5.81	$1,808

Source: Intel 1996 Annual Report.

2-44 In your capacity as assistant to the administrator at Freedom Hospital, you have been asked to develop a graphical presentation that focuses on the insurance carried by the geriatric patients at the hospital. The data file called **Patients** contains data for a sample of geriatric patients. In developing your presentation, please do the following:

a. Construct a pie chart that shows the percentage of patients with each health insurance payer.

b. Develop a bar chart that shows total charges for patients by insurance payer.
c. Develop a histogram for the length-of-stay variable.
d. Develop a bar chart that shows the average length of stay by insurance carrier.
e. Based on the graphs in parts a–d, develop a written report that analyzes the insurance payer issue. What conclusions can be reached? If necessary construct other graphs not requested in parts a–d.

2-4: LINE CHARTS AND SCATTER DIAGRAMS

Line Charts

Most of the examples that have been presented thus far have involved *cross-sectional data*, or data gathered from many observations, all taken at the same time. However, if you have data that are measured over time (e.g., monthly, quarterly, annually), an effective tool for presenting such data is a **line chart.**

> **LINE CHART**
> A two-dimensional chart showing time on the horizontal axis and the variable of interest on the vertical axis.

EXAMPLE 2-10

LINE CHARTS

Excel and Minitab Tutorial

McGregor Vineyards

McGregor Vineyards owns and operates a winery in the Sonoma Valley in Northern California. At a recent company meeting, the financial manager expressed concern about the company's profit trend over the past 20 weeks. He had collected weekly profit and sales data and made a presentation to McGregor management personnel. The data are on the CD-ROM that accompanies this text in a file called **McGregor**. Figure 2-22 shows the Excel worksheet containing these data.

Initially, the financial manager developed two separate line charts for this data, one for sales, the other for profits. These are displayed in Figure 2-23. These line charts provide an

FIGURE 2-22   Excel Worksheet of McGregor Financial Data

FIGURE 2-23   Excel Output Showing McGregor Line Charts

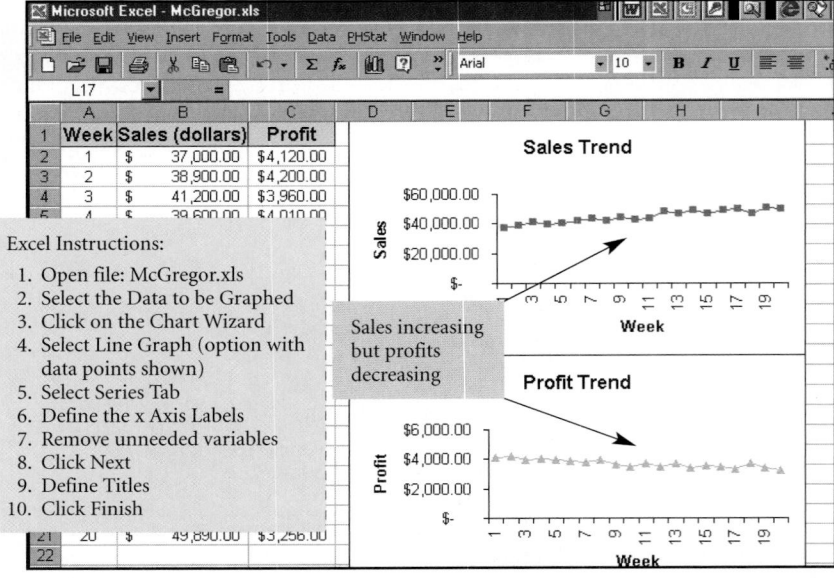

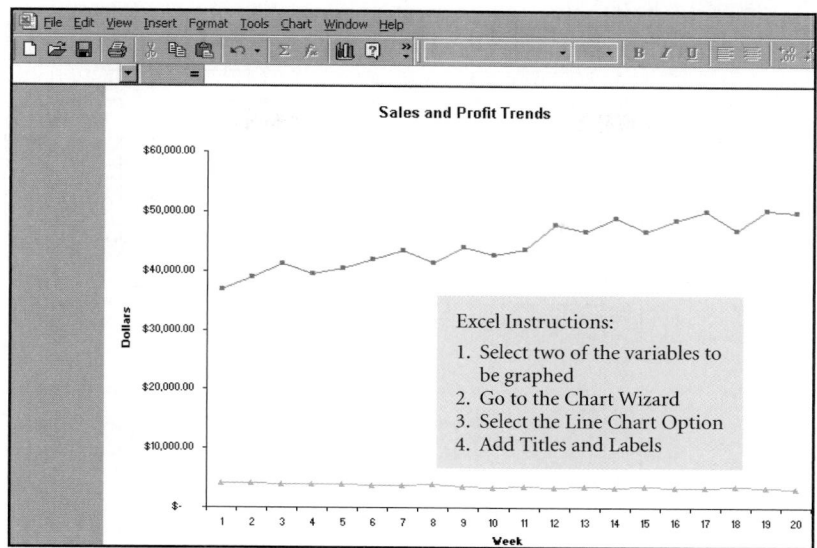

FIGURE 2-24
Excel Line Charts of
McGregor Profit and Sales

indication that, although sales have been increasing, the profit trend is downward. However, in order to fit both graphs on one page, he was forced to compress the size of the graphs. This has tended to flatten the lines somewhat, masking the magnitude of the problem.

What the financial manager needs is one graph that includes both profits and sales. Figure 2-24 shows his first attempt. This is better, but there is still a problem. The sales and profit variables are of different magnitudes. This results in the profit line being flattened out to almost a straight line. The profit trend is hidden.

To overcome this problem, the financial manager needs to construct his graph using two scales, one for each variable. Figure 2-25 shows the improved graph. We can now clearly see that while sales are moving steadily higher, profits are headed downhill. For some reason costs are rising faster than revenues, and this graph should motivate McGregor Vineyards to look into the problem.

FIGURE 2-25
Excel Sales and Profits Line
Chart

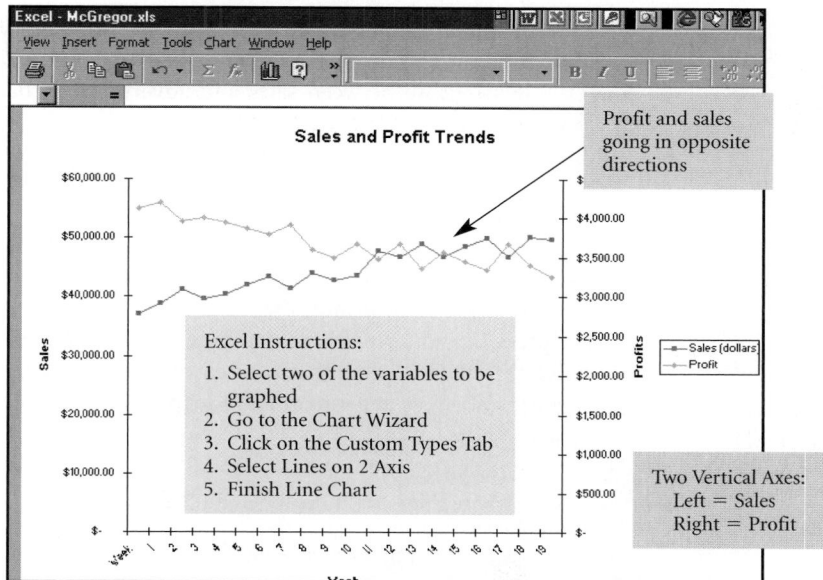

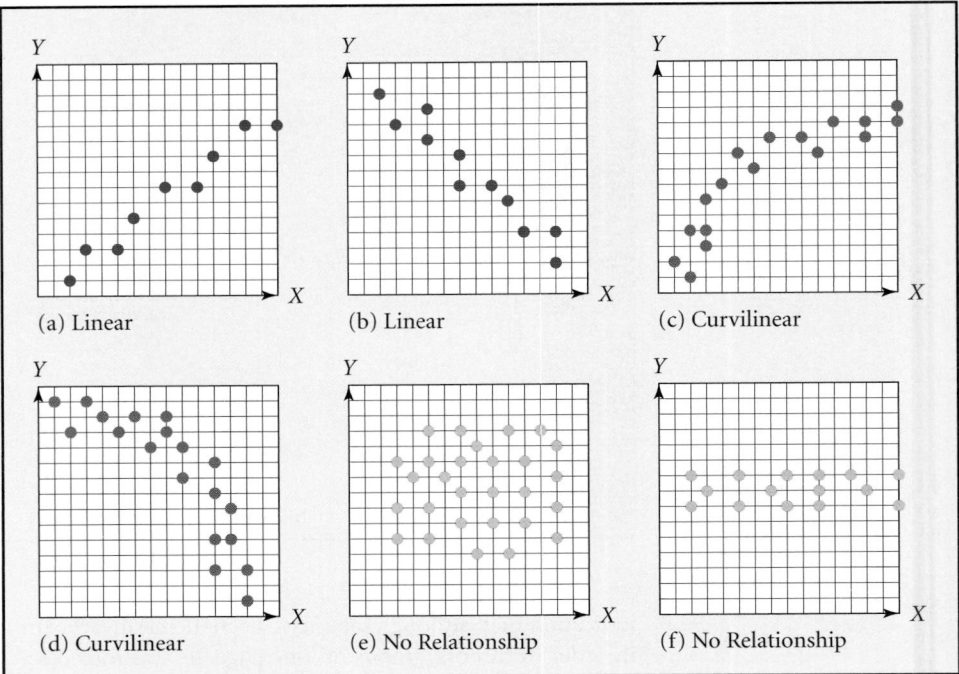

FIGURE 2-26
Scatter Diagrams Showing
Relationships Between *X* and *Y*

Scatter Diagrams

In Section 2-2 we introduced a statistical tool known as a joint frequency distribution that allow the decision maker to examine two variables at the same time. Another tool used to study two variables simultaneously is the **scatter diagram** or the **scatter plot.**

SCATTER DIAGRAM

A two-dimensional graph of plotted points in which the vertical axis represents values of one variable and the horizontal axis represents values of the other. Each plotted point has coordinates whose values are obtained from the respective variables.

There are many situations in which we are interested in understanding the *bivariate* relationship between two *quantitative* variables. For example, a company would like to know the relationship between sales and advertising. A bank might be interested in the relationship between savings account balances and credit card balances for its customers. A real estate agent might wish to know the relationship between the selling price of houses and the number of days that the houses have been on the market. The list of possibilities is almost limitless.

Regardless of the variables involved there are several key relationships for which we look when we develop a scatter diagram. Figure 2-26 shows scatter diagrams representing some key bivariate relationships that might exist between two quantitative variables.

Chapters 11 and 12 make extensive use of scatter diagrams. They introduce a statistical tool called *regression analysis* that focuses on the relationship between two variables. These variables are known as **dependent** and **independent variables.**

DEPENDENT VARIABLE

A variable whose values are thought to be a function of the values of another variable called the *independent variable.* On a scatter plot, the dependent variable is placed on the *y*-axis and is often called the response variable.

> **INDEPENDENT VARIABLE**
> A variable that is thought to have an influence on a *dependent variable*. It is often a variable that can be controlled by the decision maker. On a scatter plot, the independent variable or explanatory variable is graphed on the *x*-axis.

EXAMPLE 2-11

SCATTER DIAGRAMS

Excel and
Minitab Tutorial

Personal Computers

Can you think of any product that has increased in quality and capability as rapidly as personal computers (PCs)? Not that long ago an 8 MB RAM system with a 486 processor and a 640 K hard drive sold in the $2500 range. Now the same money would buy a much faster, higher capacity personal computer.

In January 1999 a PC industry analyst for one of the major business publications was asked to prepare an article on computer capability and price. One of the things she wished to ascertain was the relationship between PC cost and such factors as RAM and processor speed. A data file called **Computers** contains price and other information for 36 of the best-known PCs on the market.[4] The dependent variable is the price. One potential independent variable of interest is processor speed. Figure 2-27 illustrates the Excel scatter diagram for price and processor speed. The relationship is positive (i.e., as the processor speed increases, so does the price) and somewhat linear. However, the relationship is not perfectly linear.

FIGURE 2-27
Excel Output of Scatter Diagrams for Computers Data

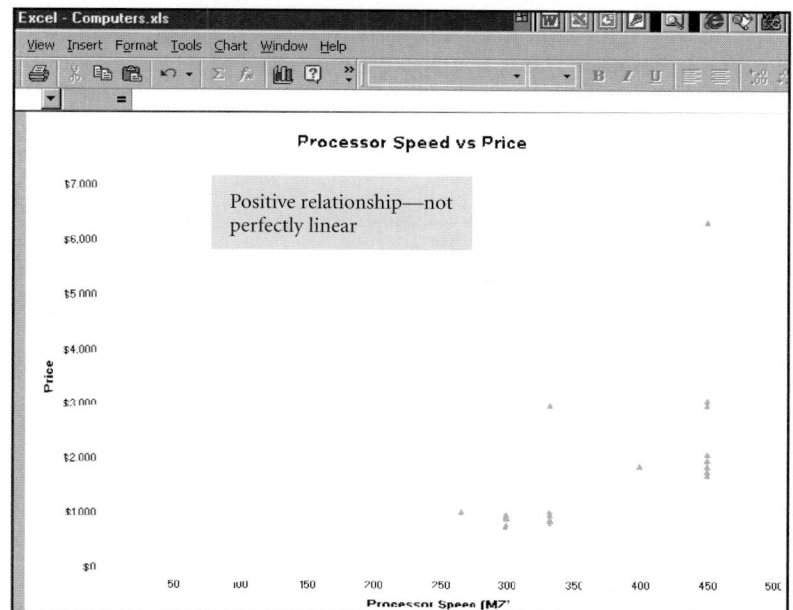

Excel Instructions:

1. Open file: Computers.xls
2. Put cursor in any data cell
3. Go to the Chart Wizard
4. Select XY Scatter Plot—default type
5. Click on the Series tab
6. Remove all but one variable from series list
7. Define X and variable data ranges
8. Go to Next
9. Add Titles, etc.

[4]*Fortune*, December 7, 1998, Special Computer Hardware Supplement

2-4: EXERCISES

ADDITIONAL EXERCISES ON YOUR CD-ROM
Try the ADDITIONAL EXERCISES and APPLICATION PROBLEMS
on the CD-ROM.

Business Applications

2-45 The following data represent expenditures on advertising over the period 1989 to 1999 by the Swanson Lumber Company.

YEAR	ADVERTISING	YEAR	ADVERTISING
1989	$12,500	1995	$18,790
1990	14,600	1996	23,500
1991	16,250	1997	24,000
1992	19,800	1998	25,600
1993	23,700	1999	27,800
1994	22,700		

a. Construct a line chart of the advertising variable.
b. Identify the range(s) of years in which a linear relationship exists between the year and the amount spent on advertising.
c. Note that there was a "downturn" in advertising expenditures from 1993 to 1995. If this pattern were to repeat itself, when would you expect the next downturn to occur?

2-46 The following data represent the number of hours individual employees spent assembling component parts and the number of parts produced.

HOURS	PARTS MADE	HOURS	PARTS MADE
5	192	3	122
3	135	2	97
2	100	4	161
4	148	6	225
6	213	2	94
4	154	8	280
3	123	6	224
2	102	3	130
2	98	3	135
1	63		

a. Assuming that the production manager wishes to estimate the number of parts that could be made in, say, 10 hours, which variable would be classified as the dependent variable and which would be the independent variable?
b. Construct and interpret a scatter plot for these two variables. What type of relationship (if any) exists for these two variables?
c. Provide the production manager an estimate of the number of parts that could be made in 10 hours.

2-47 The following data reflect the number of defective products produced each week at a local manufacturing company.

Week:	1	2	3	4	5	6	7	8	9	10	11
Defects:	80	76	79	72	68	70	64	60	64	58	52

a. From this data set, construct the appropriate graphs to display the trend in defects.
b. Note the pronounced cyclical effect in this data set. If the current pattern persists, how many defects would you expect in week 12?
c. The manufacturing company wishes to reduce the number of defects to no more than 40. In what week would you expect this to occur?

2-48 A company's human resources department recently selected a sample of 15 people. They compared the employees' performance rating (based on a 100-point scale) and the number of overtime hours the employee has worked in the past 6 months. The following data were recorded:

EMPLOYEE	RATING	OVERTIME HOURS
1	87	50
2	67	30
3	90	100
4	88	95
5	80	70
6	60	20
7	40	25
8	95	72
9	80	65
10	75	50
11	82	68
12	70	48
13	50	33
14	89	80
15	96	85

a. The human resource department wishes to estimate an employee's rating using the number of overtime hours the employee compiles. Identify the dependent and independent variables.
b. Construct the appropriate chart that can be used to determine the relationship between rating and hours worked.
c. Based on the chart developed in part b, what conclusion might be reached about how ratings are assigned in this company?

2-49 The Morrison Center for the Performing Arts has been operational since 1990. The annual ticket sales for the center for the years 1990 through 1999 are given as follows:

YEAR	TICKET SALES	YEAR	TICKET SALES
1990	$204,000	1995	$368,000
1991	275,000	1996	401,000
1992	280,000	1997	344,000
1993	299,000	1998	359,000
1994	345,000	1999	405,000

a. Prepare a time series plot for the sales data.

b. The director of the Morrison Center initially only had data from 1990 to 1996 before the downturn in 1997. He had set a goal to reach ticket sales of $500,000. If the trend in the data from 1990 to 1996 had continued, in what year could the director have expected to meet his goal?

c. Consider the magnitude of the downturn in 1997. Also note that the upturn from 1997 on seems to have approximately the same slope as that in the period 1990 to 1996. Using this information, determine the year in which the director will reach his goal.

2-50 Increasing dividends over time is an important factor for many investors when considering whether or not to purchase a company's stock. The net income and dividends paid per share of common stock for Flowers Industries, Inc. for the years 1987–1997 are shown in a table below.

YEAR	NET INCOME	DIVIDENDS
1987	$0.350	$0.163
1988	0.530	0.191
1989	0.380	0.227
1990	0.370	0.262
1991	0.310	0.291
1992	0.410	0.309
1993	0.470	0.327
1994	0.350	0.345
1995	0.500	0.362
1996	0.360	0.383
1997	0.720	0.413

Source: Flowers Industries, Inc. 1997 Annual Report.

a. Use this information to prepare a graph that best illustrates the pattern of dividends paid per share of common stock for the years 1987–1997. Based on this graph, estimate the last year in which Flowers Industries' stock paid no dividend.

b. Prepare a scatter plot that would show whether a relationship exists between net income per share of common stock and dividends per share of common stock. Does there appear to be a relationship between these two variables? If so, briefly describe the relationship. Hint: You may wish to review Figure 2-26.

c. Construct a line chart showing both net income and dividends on the same graph. Does there appear to be a relationship between these two variables? Would you

prefer a line chart or a scatter plot to determine such a relationship? Give reasons for your choice.

d. Referring to parts b and c, discuss the similarities (if any) and the differences (if any) between the scatter plot and the line graph. Under what circumstances is one preferred over the other? Hint: Pay close attention to the axes used in each of the displays.

2-51 As an intern for a local bank, you have been asked to conduct a study of the banking industry. In your research you have uncovered a data file called **Banks** that contains data for many of the major U.S. banks. As part of your study, construct the appropriate graph to determine the relationship between bank revenues and bank profits based on these data. Discuss your results. Your discussion should include two specific areas: (1) Estimate how much bank profits increase as revenue increases by one million dollars. (2) Discuss whether there are any decreasing economies of scale in the relationship between revenues and profits. That is, does the increase in profit get smaller as the bank revenues get larger?

2-52 Referring to Problem 51, construct a graph which shows the relationship between bank profits and the number of employees and discuss it. In part, you should address how much bank profits increase as the number of employees increases by one thousand, and whether the relationship between profit and number of employees is more variable than that between profit and revenues.

2-53 Suppose the manager who has reviewed your banking study (see Problems 51 and 52) would like one graph that shows the relationship between profits, revenues, and number of employees. Construct this graph and discuss how it is useful versus having two separate graphs.

2-54 The Ajax Taxi Company has collected data on the number of miles their cabs travel each week. Suppose four cabs are singled out and the miles are recorded for how much each cab was driven over a period of 40 weeks. The data are in the file called **Ajax.**

a. Combine all four taxis together by summing the miles. Construct a line chart for the total miles. Do the total miles traveled by the cabs seem to be increasing or decreasing over time?

b. Construct all possible scatter plots to show the relationship (if any) between the number of miles traveled by each pair of taxis over the 40-week period. Does the mileage traveled by any one of the cabs seem to be related to that traveled by any of the other cabs?

c. Compare the graphs in part b with the line chart generated in part a and discuss whether they show the same information.

2-55 The State Department of Commerce is in the process of generating a plan to attract new businesses to the state. You have been assigned to this team. At last week's meeting, you were given a data file called **Best-Companies.** The team leader has asked you to prepare a descriptive summary of the data in the file. Specifically, she wants you to examine the relationship between new jobs added and the companies' revenues. In addition, prepare any other graphs or tables that you think would be helpful to better understand the data.

OPTIONAL CD-ROM TOPIC 3-D Scatter Plots

3-D Scatter Plots can be an effective tool for observing the relationship between three variables at one time. For more information, go to the CD-ROM.

OPTIONAL CD-ROM TOPIC Stem and Leaf Diagrams and Area Graphs

Stem and Leaf Diagrams are used to display information about the distribution of quantitative data. For more information, go to the CD-ROM.

■ SUMMARY AND CONCLUSIONS

This chapter has introduced some of the most commonly used statistical techniques for organizing data and presenting them in a meaningful way to aid in the decision-making process. Organizing raw data into a frequency distribution is a major step in transforming data into information. We have outlined the steps for developing frequency distributions and for producing histograms.

The chapter also has introduced other graphical techniques for displaying data to make them more usable to a decision maker. The choices for effective graphical data displays are numerous. Bar charts, pie charts, scatter plots, and line graphs are among the more commonly used techniques. Software packages, such as Excel and Minitab, have made graphical representation of data much easier. You are now able to analyze large volumes of data quickly and easily. The output from these packages can be pasted directly into word processing documents to create professional-looking business reports.

EQUATIONS

Relative Frequency

$$RF = \frac{f_i}{n} \qquad\qquad 2\text{-}1$$

Class Width

$$W = \frac{\text{Largest Value} - \text{Smallest Value}}{\text{Number of Classes}} \qquad 2\text{-}2$$

■ KEY TERMS

All-Inclusive Classes—A set of classes that contains all the possible data values.

Bar Chart—A graphical representation of a categorical data set in which a rectangle or bar is drawn over each category or class. The length of each bar represents the frequency or percentage of observations contained in a category.

Class Boundaries—The upper and lower value of each class.

Class Width—The distance between the lowest possible value and the highest possible value for a frequency class.

Continuous Data—Data whose possible values are uncountable and which may assume any value in an interval.

Cumulative Frequency—The number of observations with values less-than-or-equal-to the upper limit of the class.

Cumulative Relative Frequency—The proportion of observations with values less-than-or-equal-to the upper limit of the class.

Data Array—Data that have been sorted in ascending or descending order.

Dependent Variable—A variable whose values are thought to be a function of the values of another variable called the *independent variable*. On a scatter plot, the dependent variable is placed on the *y*-axis and is often called the response variable.

Discrete Data—Data whose possible values are countable.

Equal-Width Classes—The distance between the lowest possible value and the highest possible value in each class is equal for all classes.

Frequency Distribution—A summary of a set of data that displays the number of observations in each of the distribution's distinct categories or classes.

Frequency Histogram—A graph of a frequency distribution with the horizontal axis showing the classes, the vertical axis showing the frequency count, and (for equal class widths) the rectangles having a height equal to the frequency in each class.

Independent Variable—A variable that is thought to have an influence on a *dependent variable*. It is often a variable that can be controlled by the decision maker. On a scatter plot, the independent variable or *explanatory variable* is graphed on the *x*-axis.

Joint Frequency Distribution—A summary of a bivariate set of data that displays the number of observations that exhibit the respective joint characteristics of one value taken from each of the variables that define the data set.

Line Chart—A two-dimensional chart showing time on the horizontal axis and the variable of interest on the vertical axis.

Mutually Exclusive Classes—Classes that do not overlap so that a data value can be placed in only one class.

Pareto Chart—A bar chart that is sorted so that the categories or classes are arranged from highest to lowest with respect to the magnitude of the displayed variable associated with each category or class.

Pie Chart—A graph in the shape of a circle. The circle is divided into "slices" corresponding to the categories or classes to be displayed. The size of the slices is proportional to the magnitude of the displayed variable associated with each category or class.

Relative Frequency—The proportion of total observations contained in a given category. Relative frequency is computed by dividing the frequency in a category by the total number of observations. The relative frequencies can be converted to percents by multiplying by 100.

Scatter Diagram—A two-dimensional graph of plotted points in which the vertical axis represents values of one variable and the horizontal axis represents values of the other. Each plotted point has coordinates whose values are obtained from the respective variables. Also known as a **scatter plot**.

CHAPTER EXERCISES

SOLVED PROBLEMS ON YOUR CD-ROM
Try the WORKED-OUT EXERCISES and BUSINESS APPLICATIONS on the CD-ROM.

Conceptual Questions

2-56 Several times in the chapter we stated that the number of classes to use in constructing a frequency distribution is up to the decision maker. However, some guidelines were provided and even a rule called Sturges' Rule was given on the CD-ROM to help determine the appropriate number of classes. There are potential problems with using too many or too few classes. Discuss why this is the case and use an example to illustrate your points.

2-57 In developing a scatter plot, the points on the graph are not connected. However, when developing a line chart, the data points are connected. Discuss why this difference exists between the two graphs. Would it make sense to connect the points in a scatter plot?

2-58 In developing a line chart, the choice of the scale to use on the vertical axis is very important. Locate a set of time series data for a business application and develop a line chart of the data. Adjust the scale and observe the impact on the graph. Next write a statement that explains the importance of selecting an appropriate scale.

2-59 Explain the differences and similarities between bar charts and histograms. Be sure to use examples of each to make your points.

2-60 Locate several examples of graphs, charts, or tables from business periodicals. Critique each of these for its effectiveness. What makes a graph or chart effective? Why is a graph often more useful than a table? What are some drawbacks of a graph?

Business Applications

2-61 The Green Glow Lawn Company spreads liquid fertilizer on lawns. It charges by square footage of the lawn and so has records of the lawn sizes for each of its customers. The company is now in the process of planning for next year and assumes the yard size distribution will probably be much like it was this year. Raw data on yard sizes have been converted to the following frequency distribution:

CLASS	FREQUENCY
Lawn Size (sq. ft.)	f_i
0 to less than 400	8
400 to less than 800	12
800 to less than 1,200	20
1,200 to less than 1,600	50
1,600 to less than 2,000	125
2,000 to less than 2,400	103
2,400 to less than 2,800	24

a. Develop a histogram from the frequency distribution.

b. Determine the relative frequency distribution for the lawn sizes and make a pie chart that represents the data. Be sure to label the pie chart correctly.

c. Explain why it is often useful to convert a frequency distribution to a relative frequency distribution.

d. Develop a cumulative frequency distribution and construct a histogram for the cumulative frequencies. (Note, this graph has a special name: *Ogive.*)

e. The company offers to include a crabgrass killer with the liquid fertilizer. When properly diluted with water, 8 ounces of the crabgrass killer will treat 1,000 square feet of lawn. They forecast that approximately 10% of their customers (regardless of the size of the lawn) will request this treatment. Determine the amount of crabgrass killer they should purchase for the upcoming season. (Hint: Use the midpoint of each class as a good estimate of the size of lawn for that class.)

2-62 The Minnesota State Fishing Bureau has contracted with a university biologist to study the length of walleyes (a species of fish) caught in Minnesota lakes. The biologist has collected data on a sample of 1,000 fish caught and has developed the following relative frequency distribution.

CLASS	RELATIVE FREQUENCY
Length (inches)	f_i
8 to less than 10	0.22
10 to less than 12	0.15
12 to less than 14	0.25
14 to less than 16	0.24
16 to less than 18	0.06
18 to less than 20	0.05
20 to less than 22	0.03

a. Construct a frequency distribution from this relative frequency distribution and then produce a histogram based on the frequency distribution.

b. Construct a pie chart from the relative frequency distribution. Discuss which of the two graphs, the pie chart or histogram, you think is more effective in presenting the fish length data.

c. Suppose the relative frequency distribution of these 1,000 fish is a good approximation of that for the entire population of fish that will be caught. The Fishing Bureau often publicizes that 10% of the walleyes caught in Minnesota lakes are at least 18 inches in length. Comment on this claim.

2-63 Kronos (NASDAQ: KRON) is a leader in providing employee time and attendance systems to industry. Its 1997 annual report reported the following primary net income per common share figures for 1993 to 1997.

1993	1994	1995	1996	1997
$0.50	$0.62	$1.03	$1.37	$1.34

Source: Kronos 1997 Annual Report.

a. Draw a bar chart to present these earnings per share values.

b. Develop a line chart for these data.

c. Which do you prefer in this case, a bar chart or a line chart? Discuss why.

d. Suppose you owned Kronos' stock and wish to sell your shares when the earnings per share reached

$2.60. Estimate the year in which you will sell your stock. (Hint: Draw a linear trend line through the data points and extrapolate.)

2-64 Wendy Harrington is a staff accountant at a regional accounting firm in Miami, Florida. One of her clients has had a problem with balancing the cash register at the end of the day. Because several clerks work out of the same cash register, it is not possible to determine whether only one person is at fault. Wendy has made a study of the ending shortage (indicated with parentheses) or overage for the past 30 days when the cash register did not balance and has recorded the following data (in dollars).

30-DAY STUDY OF CASH SHORTAGE OR OVERAGE ($)									
12.00	(2.55)	13.05	(55.20)	10.00	(18.00)	(11.00)	6.35	(19.02)	(33.00)
11.00	14.00	(10.00)	9.50	23.00	16.00	8.30	2.00	(24.00)	2.38
20.01	(43.50)	17.20	(41.04)	11.00	(19.33)	23.01	(0.34)	1.01	(23.04)

a. Develop a frequency distribution and histogram for these data.

b. Write a short report describing the data. Reference the frequency distribution, relative frequency distribution, cumulative frequencies, and any other pertinent factors in your report.

c. Determine the proportion of days in which the balance is missing more than the average amount.

d. If such losses were to continue, determine an estimate of the amount of money that will be missing at the end of a year—say, in 200 days.

2-65 The following data represent the commuting distances for employees of the Pay-and-Carry Department store.

COMMUTING DISTANCE (MILES)													
3.5	2.0	4.0	2.5	0.3	1.0	12.0	17.5	3.0	3.5	6.5	9.0	3.0
4.0	9.0	16.0	3.5	0.5	2.5	1.0	0.7	1.5	1.4	12.0	9.2	8.3
1.0	3.0	7.5	3.2	2.0	1.0	3.5	3.6	1.9	2.0	3.0	1.5	0.4
6.4	11.0	2.5	2.4	2.7	4.0	2.0	2.0	3.0				

a. The personnel manager for Pay-and-Carry would like you to develop a frequency distribution and histogram for these data.

b. The personnel manager has suggested that a bus be provided to those who commute more than 5 miles a day. Passes cost Pay-and-Carry $16 per person per month. Estimate the yearly cost to Pay-and-Carry for this bus pass program.

c. The personnel manager has estimated that the number of minutes a worker is late to work is approximately equal to 10% of the distance the worker commutes to work. Pay-and-Carry pays their workers about $15 an hour on average. Would the bus pass program be cost effective? Justify your answer with calculations and reasons.

2-66 A local branch of the Government Employees' Credit Union has been keeping track of the types of errors its tellers have been making. You are responsible for providing training to reduce these errors. The following data show the categories of errors and the frequency of each for the last month.

CATEGORY OF ERRORS	FREQUENCY
Errors posting debits/credits	182
Errors posting other entries	158
Entries not posted	77
Cash letter errors	31
Claims	24
Adjustment tickets	16
Multiple postings	9
Incorrect totals	7

Use these data to justify in which areas to start your training effort. (Hint: What type of graph is effective for this type of data?)

2-67 A computer software company has been looking at the amount of time customers spend on hold after their call is answered by the central switchboard. The company would like to have only 2% of the callers waiting 2 or more minutes. The company's calling service has provided the following data showing how long each of last month's callers spent on hold.

CLASS	NUMBER
Less than 15 seconds	456
15 to less than 30 seconds	718
30 to less than 45 seconds	891
45 to less than 60 seconds	823
60 to less than 75 seconds	610
75 to less than 90 seconds	449
90 to less than 105 seconds	385
105 to less than 120 seconds	221
120 to less than 150 seconds	158
150 to less than 180 seconds	124
180 to less than 240 seconds	87
240 or more seconds	153

a. Calculate the proportion of the time that callers hold for 2 or more minutes.

b. The company estimates it loses an average of $30 in business from callers that must wait 2 or more minutes before receiving assistance. The company thinks that last month's distribution of waiting times is typical. Estimate how much money the company is losing in business per day because people have to wait too long before receiving assistance.

c. The company believes that if it keeps its customers happy, business will increase. Therefore, it is willing to hire more help-desk assistants as long as it does not lose money by doing so. If the average salary of help-desk assistants is $125 a day, how many help-desk assistants can it afford to hire without losing money?

2-68 The marketing director of a company manufacturing small disk drives for notebook computers has directed her sales force to accept orders based on a projected production rate of 3,000 disk drives per day. The production manager objected strongly when hearing this and presented the following frequency distribution to support his claim that this goal was impossible given the present production process.

PRODUCTION RATE	FREQUENCY
2,000–2,499	3
2,500–2,749	7
2,750–2,999	10
3,000–3,249	15
3,250–3,499	22
3,500–3,999	11
4,000 or more	2

a. What proportion of the time does the manufacturing company produce at least 3,000 disk drives in a day? Assume the manager's data are a good approximation to the production distribution of this company.

b. Which manager do the data support? Justify your answer.

2-69 The regional sales manager for American Toys, Inc. recently collected data on weekly sales (in dollars) for the 15 stores in his region. He also collected data on the number of sales clerk work hours during the week for each of the stores. The data are as follows:

STORE	SALES	HOURS	STORE	SALES	HOURS
1	$23,300	120	9	$27,886	140
2	25,600	135	10	54,156	300
3	19,200	96	11	34,080	254
4	10,211	102	12	25,900	180
5	19,330	240	13	36,400	270
6	35,789	190	14	25,760	175
7	12,540	108	15	31,500	256
8	43,150	234			

a. Develop a scatter plot of these data.

b. Based on the scatter plot, what, if any, conclusions might the sales manager reach with respect to the relationship between sales and number of clerk hours worked? Do any stores stand out as being different? Discuss.

c. American Toys has presented its sales force with a choice with respect to their salaries. The options are either a 15% commission on their sales or an hourly wage of $25. The sales force as a group must decide. They all will get one plan or the other. What choice would you advise them to make? Back up your advice with calculations and reasoning.

d. Determine the hourly wage that would make the hourly wage equivalent, on the average, to the 15% commission.

2-70 Midlands Metal Works has recently begun supplying parts to a Japanese automaker. As part of its efforts to improve the quality of its products, the company has started keeping track of categories of defects. It has identified five general categories: incomplete (Inc), surface scars (Ss), cracks (Cks), misshapen (Mis), and others (Oth). The company has categorized the last 100 defective parts as follows:

Inc	Cks	Ss	Oth	Inc	Ss	Inc	Ss	Inc	Cks
Inc	Ss	Cks	Oth	Ss	Inc	Inc	Ss	Inc	Cks
Inc	Inc	Oth	Mis	Inc	Ss	Inc	Ss	Cks	Inc
Oth	Inc	Ss	Cks	Inc	Inc	Ss	Cks	Mis	Oth
Inc	Ss	Inc	Cks	Inc	Ss	Inc	Cks	Inc	Inc
Oth	Ss	Cks	Inc	Inc	Inc	Ss	Ss	Cks	Inc
Cks	Ss	Cks	Inc	Mis	Inc	Ss	Cks	Inc	Inc
Cks	Oth	Inc	Ss	Cks	Mis	Inc	Inc	Cks	Inc
Ss	Inc	Inc	Ss	Oth	Cks	Ss	Ss	Inc	Inc
Ss	Cks	Inc	Inc	Ss	Inc	Inc	Ss	Oth	Oth

a. Construct a frequency distribution using these data.

b. Use the values in part a to construct a Pareto chart of the types of defective parts.

c. On which area must Midlands Metal Works concentrate in order to reduce the number of defective parts?

d. Midlands has decided to focus its efforts on incomplete parts. It sets a goal that incomplete parts will account for only 25% of the defective parts. How many of the incomplete parts in the preceding sample of 100 defective parts would have to have been completed to achieve this goal?

2-71 *The Wall Street Journal* reported retail sales for February 1997 and February 1998 for many top retailers. The file **Retailers** contains sales figures for 26 different retailers divided into 4 categories. In your capacity as marketing manager for a major department store, you plan to develop a report and presentation on the retail industry using these data. To make your report complete, you plan to do the following:

a. Develop grouped frequency distributions for each year and then develop a histogram from each frequency distribution.

b. Create bar charts comparing the two years' February sales for the stores in each category. This means that you will have four different bar charts.

c. Create a pie chart for the department store category for February 1997.

d. Create a bar chart for the apparel category for February 1998.

e. Using the information generated in parts a–d, create a report on the retail industry.

2-72 The claims manager at Handover Insurance Company has been collecting data on the size of each claim paid by the company this month. A total of 500 claims were paid, with the smallest one being $44 and the largest one being $29,000.

a. If a frequency distribution were to be constructed, how many class intervals would you suggest?

b. Based on your answer to part a and assuming equal-width classes, what should the class width be for each class?

c. Discuss why the classes must not overlap. Why is it also a good idea to have equal-width classes?

2-73 The data file called **McCormick** contains selected information from the 1997 annual report for McCormick & Company, Incorporated, the leader in the manufacture, marketing, and distribution of spices, seasonings, and flavors for the food industry. Use the data to perform the following:

a. For the years 1988 to 1997, construct a line chart of net sales. Determine the relationship between the year and the net sales.

b. For the years 1988 to 1997, construct a scatter plot of net sales and capital expenditures. Briefly describe the relationship between net sales and capital expenditures for these years.

c. Choose either "capital expenditures" or the "year" as a predictor of net sales. Justify your answer.

d. Develop a line chart that displays both net sales and long-term debt. Do you prefer this display to that produced in part b? Discuss which format gives a better presentation of the relationship between the two variables.

e. Total capital consists of current debt, long-term debt, and shareholders' equity. Construct a pie chart of the various sources of total capital for each of the years 1995 to 1997. Have the component percentages changed over this period? What has happened to long-term debt as a proportion of total capital during these years?

2-74 The following information, taken from the 1997 annual report of McCormick & Company, Incorporated, reports the company's consumer sales (in millions) by region as shown:

REGION	CONSUMER SALES
Americas	$596.4
Europe	221.2
Asia/Pacific	43.2

a. Construct a bar chart of these data.

b. Construct a pie chart of these data.

c. Which graphical summary, the bar chart or the pie chart, better describes the relative proportion of total sales by geographic region? Explain the reasons that support your opinion.

2-75 The file, **Home-Prices**, contains information about single-family housing prices in 100 metropolitan areas in the United States.

a. Construct a frequency distribution of 1997 median single-family home prices.

b. Construct a relative frequency distribution for 1997 median single-family home prices.

c. Construct a histogram of 1997 median single-family home prices for the 100 metropolitan areas. What does the histogram tell you about the shape and spread of the data?

d. Increase or decrease the class intervals you used in parts a and c. How does this change the shape and spread of the data?

2-76 Stock investors often look to beat the performance of the S&P 500 Index, which generally serves as a proxy for the market as a whole. The following table shows a comparison of five-year cumulative total shareholder returns for Idaho Power Company common stock (NYSE Symbol: IDA), the S&P 500 Index, and the Edison Electric Institute (EEI) 100 Electric Utilities Index. The data assume that $100 was invested on December 31, 1992, with returns compounded monthly.

YEAR	IDAHO POWER	S&P 500	EEI 100 ELECTRIC UTILITIES
1992	$100.00	$100.00	$100.00
1993	117.38	110.08	111.15
1994	97.62	111.53	98.29
1995	134.11	153.45	128.78
1996	147.92	188.69	130.32
1997	189.73	251.63	166.00

Source: Idaho Power Company, 1997 Notice of Annual Meeting of Shareholders, p. 34.

a. Construct a graph that illustrates the performance of the three investment options for the years 1992 to 1997.

b. How well has Idaho Power Company performed during this period compared to the S&P 500?

c. How well has it performed relative to its industry?

2-77 Referring to Problem 75, the file **Home-Prices** includes information about the 1997 change in price and the 1998 forecast change in median prices of single-family homes in 100 large metropolitan areas. Develop a histogram for the 1997 change and the 1998 forecast change. Compare the two histograms. What can you say about differences in their shape, spread, and location?

2-78 A 1997 survey of human resources professionals revealed that 53% were moderately satisfied, 29% were moderately

dissatisfied, 13% were dissatisfied, and 5% were very satisfied with their company's performance evaluation system (Source: Aon Consulting and *The Detroit News*). Present this information in a graph that best summarizes and describes the findings.

2-79 The commercial banking industry is undergoing rapid changes due to advances in technology and competitive pressures in the financial services sector. The data file **Banks** contains selected information tabulated by *Fortune* magazine concerning the revenues, profitability, and number of employees for the 51 largest U.S. commercial banks in terms of revenues. Use the information in this file to do the following:

a. Construct a chart to determine whether there is a relationship between revenues and number of employees. Briefly comment on your findings.

b. Develop a frequency distribution and a relative frequency distribution of profits and number of employees. Use the distributions you developed to construct histograms and relative frequency histograms for these two variables. What do these histograms tell you about these variables?

c. Calculate a new variable: profits per employee. Develop a frequency distribution and a histogram for this new variable. Does the distribution of profits per employee differ from the distribution of profits? If so, how? How might this information be useful to a manager?

2-80 The file **Industrial Rents** contains the average annual cost per square foot for "Class A" warehouses in 51 selected cities for the fourth quarter for the years 1996 and 1997. Use this information to do the following:

a. Construct a histogram of square foot costs for each time period. Do the histograms have the same approximate shape? Are the data balanced around the center or pulled to one side or the other?

b. Referring to part a, show how the histogram changes shape if you cut the number of classes from the number you used in part a by 50%.

CASE 2-A

AJ's Fitness Center

When A. J. Reeser finished signing papers to take ownership of the fitness center previously known as The Park Center Club, he realized that he had just taken the biggest financial step in his life. Every asset he could pull together had been pledged against the mortgage. If the new AJ's Fitness Center didn't succeed, he would be in very poor shape financially.

But A. J. didn't plan on failing. After all, he had never failed at anything.

As a high school football all-American, major colleges around the country heavily recruited A. J. Although he loved football, he and his family had always put academics ahead of sports. Thus, he surprised most everyone outside those who knew him best when he chose to attend an Ivy League university not particularly noted for its football success. Although he was outstanding at football and was a member of two winning teams, he also excelled in the classroom and graduated in four years. He spent six years working for McKinsey & Company, the major consulting firm where he gained significant experience in a broad range of business situations.

He was hired away from McKinsey & Company by the Dryden Group, a management services company that specializes in running health and fitness operations and recreational resorts throughout the world. After eight years leading the Fitness Center section at Dryden, A. J. found that earning a high salary and perks associated with corporate life was not satisfying him. Besides, the travel was getting old now that he was married and had two young children. When the opportunity to purchase The Park Center Club came up, he decided that the time was right to control his own destiny.

A key aspect of the deal was that AJ's Fitness Center would keep the existing clientele consisting of 1,833 memberships. One of the things that A. J. was very concerned about was whether these members would stay with the club after the sale or move on to other fitness clubs in the area. He knew that keeping an existing customer was a lot less expensive than attracting new customers.

Within days of assuming ownership, A. J. developed a survey that was mailed to all 1,833 members. The letter that accompanied the survey discussed AJ's philosophy and asked several key questions regarding the current level of satisfaction. Respondents to the survey would be eligible to win a free lifetime membership in a drawing to be held—an inducement that was no doubt responsible for the 1,214 usable responses.

To get help with the analysis of the survey data, A. J. approached the College of Business at a local university with the idea of having a senior student serve as an intern at the AJ's Fitness Center. In addition to an hourly rate, the intern would get free use of the fitness facilities for the rest of the academic year.

The intern's first task was to key the data from the survey into a file that could be analyzed using a spreadsheet or a statistical software package. The survey contained eight questions that were keyed into eight columns as follows:

Column 1: Satisfaction with the club's weight and exercise equipment facilities
Column 2: Satisfaction with the club's staff
Column 3: Satisfaction with the club's exercise programs (aerobics, etc.)
Column 4: Satisfaction with the club's overall service

Note, Columns 1–4 were coded on an ordinal scale as follows:

1	2	3	4	5
Very Unsatisfied	Unsatisfied	Neutral	Satisfied	Very Satisfied

Column 5: Number of years that the respondent has been a member at this club
Column 6: Gender (1 = Male, 2 = Female)
Column 7: Typical number of visits to the club per week
Column 8: Age

The data, saved in a file called **AJFitness**, were clearly too much for anyone to comprehend in raw form as can be seen from the partial listing in Figure 2-28. At yesterday's meeting, A. J. requested the intern to "... make some sense of the data." When the intern asked for some direction, A. J.'s response was, "That's what I'm paying you the big bucks for. I just want you to develop a descriptive analysis of these data. For now, let's limit it to whatever charts, graphs, and tables that will help us understand our customers. After we see what that shows, maybe we will do some other analysis. For right now, give me a report that discusses the data. Why don't we set a time to get together next week to review your report?"

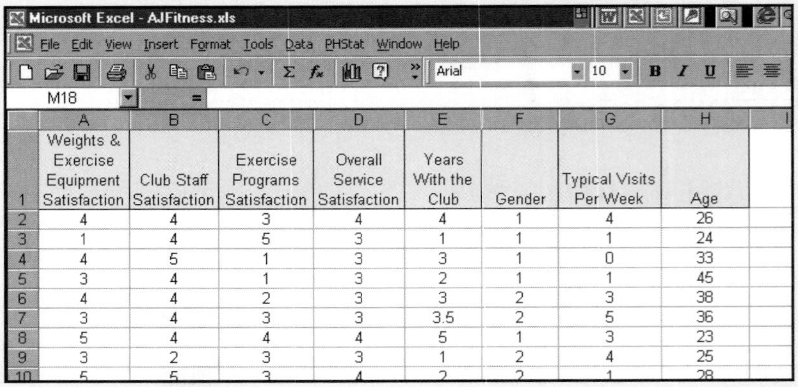

FIGURE 2-28
Excel Worksheet of AJ's Fitness Center Customer Data.

	A	B	C	D	E	F	G	H
1	Weights & Exercise Equipment Satisfaction	Club Staff Satisfaction	Exercise Programs Satisfaction	Overall Service Satisfaction	Years With the Club	Gender	Typical Visits Per Week	Age
2	4	4	3	4	4	1	4	26
3	1	4	5	3	1	1	1	24
4	4	5	1	3	3	1	0	33
5	3	4	1	3	2	1	1	45
6	4	4	2	3	3	2	3	38
7	3	4	3	3	3.5	2	5	36
8	5	4	4	4	5	1	3	23
9	3	2	3	3	1	2	4	25
10	5	5	3	4	2	2	1	28

CASE 2-B

Westbrook Graphic Arts

Lisa Westbrook founded Westbrook Graphic Arts in 1997 right after graduation. Throughout college Lisa had worked part-time for a local graphics arts company and gained significant experience in the business. She had an offer to stay with the same company and several other offers from graphics companies in the area. But her independent spirit pushed her to go out on her own. Business has been slow to develop. However, she has been able to pay her bills and sock a few dollars away for the trip to Europe she promised herself as a graduation present.

As Lisa looked at her e-mail messages in her small office on 13th Street, the phone rang. It was Charles Eddy who works for the State Department of Commerce in the International Division. Charles had called Lisa yesterday about a possible project and had promised to call back when he had more information about what his boss wanted. Charles explained that C. J. Riley, the director of the Department of Commerce, was going to give an address at a national conference. The

director was to contrast the United States with a number of other developed countries around the world. Charles further explained that he had collected quite a bit of data on various issues for each country. He, however, had not had time to create the presentation for his boss. He wanted Westbrook Graphics to prepare the presentation and speaker notes.

As Charles hung up, Lisa knew that this was a tremendous opportunity. If she could do a good job on this project, there would very likely be other work coming to her from the Department of Commerce. Charles had agreed to e-mail the data. Charles gave her total leeway in designing the presentation but did say that C. J. was big on graphs and charts. Figure 2-29 shows the data. Charles had indeed collected some interesting data on a variety of variables for each country.

Lisa sent a reply back to Charles telling him that she had received the data (that she stored in a file called **Countries**) and would have the presentation by next Tuesday. As she leaned back in her chair, she wondered where she should begin.

COUNTRY	1998 GDP GROWTH %	EXPORTS (% OF GDP)	CAR ACCIDENTS (INJURIES PER 62 MILLION MILES)	OBESITY (% OVERWEIGHT MEN)	OBESITY (% OVERWEIGHT WOMEN)	CIGARETTE SMOKERS (% OF MEN)	CIGARETTE SMOKERS (% OF WOMEN)
United States	3.50	11.30	137	19.90	24.90	25.80	24.10
Germany	2.70	23.60	87	18.20	21.30	32.00	20.00
France	3.10	23.50	36	8.60	8.40	55.70	43.10
Britain	2.70	28.50	72	16.00	17.00	26.00	28.00
Netherlands	3.80	53.30	11	8.40	8.30	53.20	46.80
Sweden	2.80	40.90	33	5.30	9.10	21.00	20.70
Italy	1.50	27.60	63	6.50	6.30	39.40	26.50
Japan	−2.60	9.40	129	1.80	2.60	57.50	14.20
South Korea	−6.50	33.10	725	NA	NA	61.00	10.80

HEALTH CARE SPENDING (% OF GDP)	PCs PER 100 PEOPLE	1994 WORLD CUP (% TV VIEWERS)	VIDEO RENTALS PER CAPITA	BOOK PURCHASES PER CAPITA	VOTERS (% VOTING LAST NATIONAL ELECTION)	HIGHEST INCOME TAX RATE	POSTAGE RATE
14.00	35	7.30	13.8	$ 95	49.10	40	$0.32
10.50	17	25.80	2.1	$122	82.20	56	$0.67
9.70	16	18.00	0.9	$ 58	68.90	54	$0.55
6.90	20	29.90	3.3	$ 63	71.50	40	$0.44
8.60	20	43.00	1.8	$ 78	78.30	60	$0.43
7.30	18	29.00	2.1	$ 56	78.60	55	$0.65
7.70	11.5	41.90	0.7	$ 39	85.00	46	$0.49
7.20	14	9.50	7.5	$ 84	58.80	50	$0.68
4.00	NA	22.30	NA	$ 62	63.90	44	$0.36

FIGURE 2-29   Worksheet for Developed Countries Data

■ GENERAL REFERENCES

1. Albright, S. Christian, Wayne L. Winston, and Christopher Zappe, *Data Analysis and Decision Making with Microsoft Excel*, (Pacific Grove, CA: Duxbury, 1999).

2. Berenson, Mark L., and David M. Levine, *Basic Business Statistics: Concepts and Applications*, 7th ed. (Upper Saddle River, NJ: Prentice Hall, 1999).

3. Cleveland, William S., and R. McGill, "Graphical Perception: Theory, Experimentation, and Application to the Development of Graphical Methods," *Journal of the American Statistical Association* 79 (September 1984), 531–554.

4. Cleveland, William S., "Graphs in Scientific Publications," *The American Statistician* 38 (November 1984), 261–269.

5. Cryer, Jonathan D., and Robert B. Miller, *Statistics for Business: Data Analysis and Modeling*, 2d ed. (Belmont, CA: Duxbury Press, 1994).

6. Dodge, Mark, and Craig Stinson, *Running Microsoft Excel 2000* (Redmond, WA: Microsoft Press, 1999).

7. *Microsoft Excel 2000* (Redmond, WA: Microsoft Corporation, 1999).

8. *Minitab for Windows Version 13* (State College, PA: Minitab, Inc., 2000).

9. Siegel, Andrew F., *Practical Business Statistics*, 4th ed. (Burr Ridge, IL: Irwin, 2000).

10. Tufte, Edward R., *The Visual Display of Quantitative Information*, reprint ed. (Cheshire, CT: Graphics Press, 1992).

11. Tufte, Edward R., *Envisioning Information* (Cheshire, CT: Graphics Press, 1990).

12. Tukey, John W., *Exploratory Data Analysis* (Reading, MA: Addison-Wesley, 1977).

DESCRIBING DATA USING NUMERICAL MEASURES

CHAPTER OUTCOMES

After studying the material in Chapter 3, you should be able to:

3-1: Compute the mean, median, and mode for a set of data and understand what these measures represent.

3-2: Compute the range, variance, and standard deviation and know what these measures mean.

3-3: Compute the coefficient of variation and z scores and understand how they are applied in decision-making situations.

3-4: Be able to use numerical measures along with graphs, charts, and tables to effectively describe data.

WHY YOU NEED TO KNOW

Graphs and charts provide effective tools for transforming data into information; however, they are only a starting point. Graphs and charts do not reveal all the information contained in a set of data. To make your descriptive toolbox complete, you need to become familiar with the key descriptive measures that quantify the center of the data and its spread.

Suppose you are an advertising manager for a major tire company and you want to develop an ad campaign touting how much longer your company's tires last than the competition's. However, you must be careful that your claims are valid. First, the Federal Trade Commission (FTC) is charged with regulating advertising and has rules requiring that advertising be truthful. Second, customers who could prove that they were misled by an incorrect claim about the tires could secure a judgment against your company. You have no choice. You must use statistical procedures to determine the validity of any claim you might want to make about tire tread life.

You might start by sampling tires from your company as well as the competition. The measurements would be the number of miles the tire lasts before a specified portion of the tread is depleted. While you might graph the data for each company in the form of a histogram, it might be difficult to make a clear comparison between the different tire brands using the graph alone. Instead, you would likely compute the tire mileage and show these values side-by-side (perhaps in a bar chart). You might also compare the wear in tire mileage for the different brands to show that your tires not only last longer on average, but that they also wear more consistently than competing products. Thus, to effectively describe data, you will need to combine the graphical tools discussed in Chapter 2 with the numerical measures introduced in this chapter.

3-1: MEASURES OF CENTRAL TENDENCY

You learned in Chapter 2 that frequency histograms are an effective way of converting quantitative data into useful information. The histogram provides a visual indication of where the data are centered and how much spread there is in the data around the center. However, to fully describe a quantitative variable, we can compute measures of its center and spread. These measures can then be coupled with the histogram to give a clear picture of the variable's distribution. This section focuses on measures of the center of the data. Section 3-2 introduces measures of the spread of the data.

Parameters and Statistics

Depending on whether we are working with a population or a sample, a numerical measure is either a **parameter** or a **statistic**.

PARAMETER
A measure computed from the entire population. As long as the population does not change, the value of the parameter will not change.

STATISTIC
A measure computed from a sample that has been selected from a population. The value of the statistic will depend on which sample is selected.

Population Mean

There are three important measures of the center of a set of data. The first of these is the **mean**, or average of the data. To find the mean, we sum the values and divide the sum by the number of data values as shown in Equation 3-1.

MEAN
A numerical measure of the center of a set of quantitative measures computed by dividing the sum of the values by the number of values in the data.

POPULATION MEAN

$$\mu = \frac{\sum_{i=1}^{N} x_i}{N}$$

3-1

where:

μ = population mean (mu)
N = population size
x_i = i^{th} individual value of variable x

The **population mean** is represented by the Greek symbol, μ, pronounced "mu." The formal notation in the numerator for the sum of the x values reads:

$$\sum_{i=1}^{N} x_i \rightarrow \text{"sum each } x_i \text{ value where } i \text{ goes from 1 to } N\text{."}$$

In other words, we are summing all N values in the population.

Since you almost always sum all the data values, to simplify notation in this text, we generally will drop the subscripts after the first time we introduce a formula. Thus the formula for the population mean will be written as

$$\mu = \frac{\sum x}{N}.$$

EXAMPLE 3-1

POPULATION MEAN

Foster City Hotel

The manager of a small hotel in Foster City, California, was asked by the corporate vice president to analyze the Sunday night registration information for the past eight weeks. Data on three variables were collected:

x_1 = The total number of rooms rented
x_2 = The total dollar revenue from the room rentals
x_3 = The number of customer complaints that came from guests each Sunday

These data are shown in Table 3-1. They are a population since they include all data of interest to the vice president.

Figure 3-1 shows the frequency histogram for the number of rooms rented. If the manager is interested in describing the data further, she could locate the center of the data by finding the balance point for the histogram. Think of the horizontal axis as a plank and the histogram bars as being weights proportional to their area. The center of the data could be defined as the point at which the plank would balance as shown in Figure 3-1. The balance point (center) seems to be at about 15 rooms.

TABLE 3-1
Foster City Hotel Data

WEEK	ROOMS RENTED	REVENUE	COMPLAINTS
1	22	$1,870.00	0
2	13	1,590.00	2
3	10	1,760.00	1
4	16	2,345.00	0
5	23	4,563.00	2
6	13	1,630.00	1
7	11	2,156.00	0
8	13	1,756.00	0

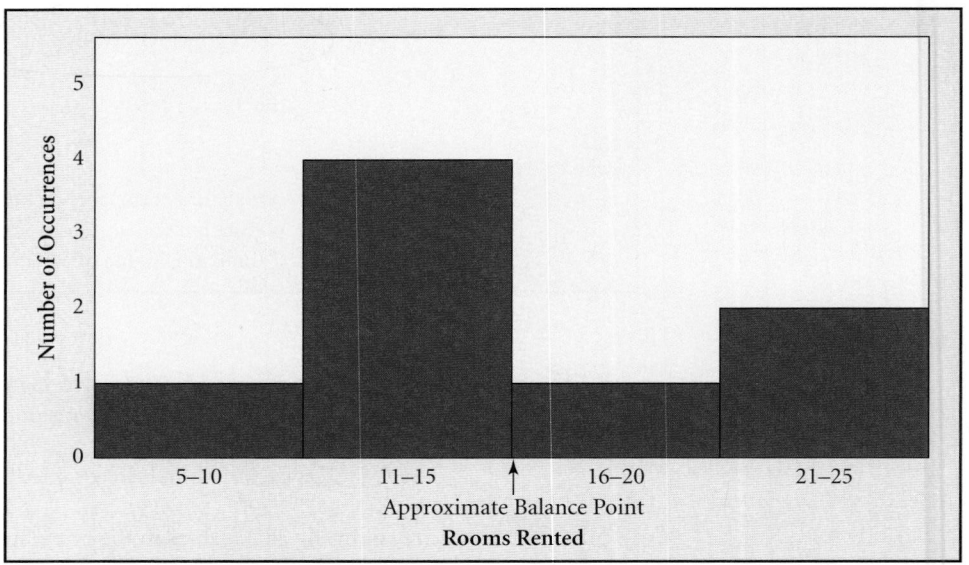

FIGURE 3-1
Balance Point, Rooms Rented
at Foster City Hotel

We might be able to get a reasonable approximation of the center by eyeing the histogram. However, computing a numerical measure of the center directly from the data is preferable. The most frequently used measure of the center is the mean.

The population mean for number of rooms rented is computed using Equation 3-1 as follows.

$$\mu = \frac{\sum x}{N} = \frac{22 + 13 + 10 + 16 + 23 + 13 + 11 + 13}{8}$$
$$= \frac{121}{8}$$
$$\mu = 15.125$$

Thus, the average number of rooms rented each Sunday for the past eight weeks is 15.125. This is the true balance point for the data. To illustrate why the mean is the true balance point, in Table 3-2 we find what is called a *deviation* $(x - \mu)$ by subtracting the mean from each value.

Note, the sum of the deviations of the data from the mean is zero. This is not a coincidence. *For any set of data, the sum of the deviations around the mean will be zero.* Because the mean has this characteristic, the mean is the true balancing point.

Foster City Hotel (continued)

In addition to collecting data on the number of rooms rented on Sunday nights, the Foster City hotel manager also collected data on the room rental revenue generated, and the number of complaints, on Sunday nights. Both Excel and Minitab have procedures for computing numerical measures such as the mean. Since these data reflect the population of all

EXAMPLE

3-2

POPULATION MEAN

Excel and
Minitab Tutorial

TABLE 3-2
Centering Concept of the
Mean Using Hotel Data

x	$x - \mu$
22	$22 - 15.125 =6.875$
13	$13 - 15.125 = -2.125$
10	$10 - 15.125 = -5.125$
16	$16 - 15.125 =0.875$
23	$23 - 15.125 =7.875$
13	$13 - 15.125 = -2.125$
11	$11 - 15.125 = -4.125$
13	$13 - 15.125 = \underline{-2.125}$
	$\sum = 0.000$

Excel Instructions:

1. Open file: Foster.xls
2. Select Tools
3. Select Data Analysis
4. Click on Descriptive Statistics
5. Define data range for the variables
6. Check Summary Statistics
7. Name output sheet

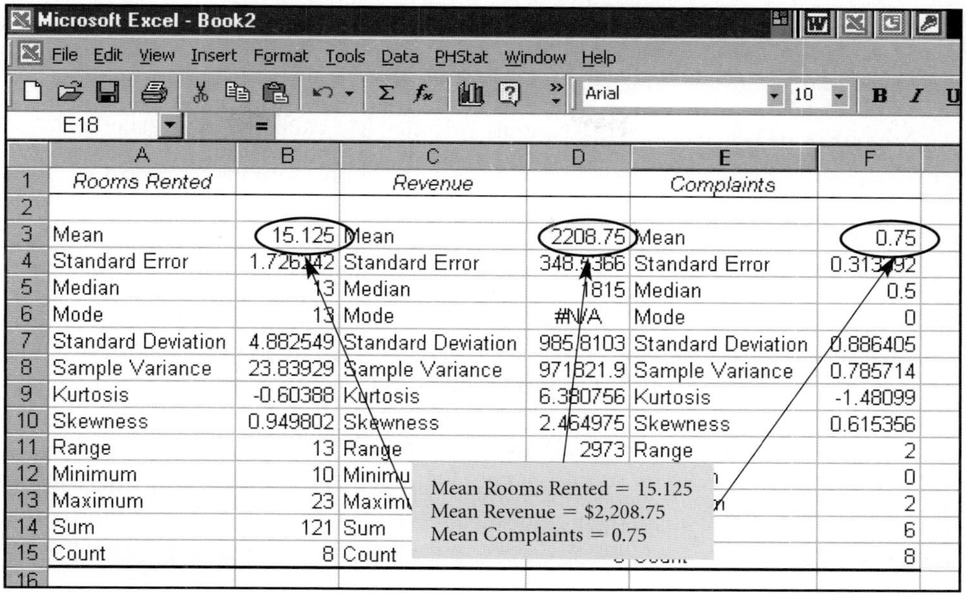

	A	B	C	D	E	F
1	*Rooms Rented*		*Revenue*		*Complaints*	
2						
3	Mean	15.125	Mean	2208.75	Mean	0.75
4	Standard Error	1.726[illegible]42	Standard Error	348.[illegible]366	Standard Error	0.313[illegible]92
5	Median	13	Median	1815	Median	0.5
6	Mode	13	Mode	#N/A	Mode	0
7	Standard Deviation	4.882549	Standard Deviation	985.8103	Standard Deviation	0.886405
8	Sample Variance	23.83929	Sample Variance	971821.9	Sample Variance	0.785714
9	Kurtosis	-0.60388	Kurtosis	6.380756	Kurtosis	-1.48099
10	Skewness	0.949802	Skewness	2.464975	Skewness	0.615356
11	Range	13	Range	2973	Range	2
12	Minimum	10	Minimu[illegible]	[illegible]	[illegible]	0
13	Maximum	23	Maxim[illegible]	[illegible]	[illegible]	2
14	Sum	121	Sum	[illegible]	[illegible]	6
15	Count	8	Count	[illegible]	[illegible]	8
16						

FIGURE 3-2
Excel Output Showing the Mean Revenue for Foster City Hotel

nights of interest to the hotel manager, she can compute the population mean μ, revenue per night. The population mean is μ = \$2,208.75 as shown in the Excel output in Figure 3-2. Likewise, the mean number of complaints is $\mu = 0.75$ per night. (Note, there are other measures shown in Figure 3-2. We will discuss several of these later in the chapter.)

Now, for these eight Sunday nights, the manager can report to the corporate vice president that the mean number of rooms rented is 15.125. This level of business generated an average nightly revenue of approximately \$2,208.75. The number of complaints averaged 0.75 (less than one) per night. These values reflect the true means for the population and are parameters.

Sample Mean

The data in the Foster City Hotel example constituted the population of interest. Thus, $\mu =$ 15.125 nights is the parameter measure. However, if we have a sample rather than a population, the mean for the sample is computed using Equation 3-2. Notice, Equation 3-2 is the same as Equation 3-1 *except* we sum the sample values, not the population values, and divide by the sample size, not the population size.

SAMPLE MEAN

$$\bar{x} = \frac{\sum_{i=1}^{n} x_i}{n} \qquad \textbf{3-2}$$

where:

$\bar{x}$ = sample mean (pronounced "*x*-bar")

n = sample size

The notation for the sample mean is $\bar{x}$. Sample descriptors (statistics) are usually assigned a Roman character. (Recall that population values are usually assigned a Greek character.)

EXAMPLE 3-3

SAMPLE MEAN

Housing Prices

Consider an example involving a sample of seven house prices in Modesto, California. The sample data are:

$$\{x_i\} = \{\text{house prices}\} = \{\$144,000; 98,000; 204,000; 177,000; 155,000; 316,000; 100,000\}$$

Using Equation 3-2, the sample mean is computed as:

$$\bar{x} = \frac{\sum x}{n} = \frac{144,000 + 98,000 + 204,000 + \cdots + 100,000}{7}$$

$$= \frac{\$1,194,000}{7} = \$170,571.43$$

So, the mean price for the sample of seven houses in Modesto is $170,571.43.

THE MEAN FOR SKEWED DATA

The fact that the mean (population or sample) is the balance point for the data is an important advantage of using the mean as a measure of the center. However, the mean does have one potential disadvantage—*the mean can be highly affected by extreme values.*

Suppose the sample of house prices in Modesto had been slightly different. If the house priced at $316,000 had actually been $1,000,000, we would get a different mean.

$$\bar{x} = \frac{\sum x}{n} = \frac{\$1,878,000}{7} = \$268,285.71$$

With only one value in the sample changed, the mean is now substantially higher than before. Thus, the mean is affected by extreme values and may be a misleading measure of the data's center. In this case, a second measure called the *median* may be more appropriate.

The Median

Another measure of the center is called the **median**. The median is found by first arranging the data in numerical order from smallest to largest. Data that are sorted in order are referred to as a **data array**.

MEDIAN The median is a center value that divides a data array into two halves.	**DATA ARRAY** Data that have been arranged in numerical order.

After the data have been sorted, we locate the value that is halfway from either end. This middle value is the median. If the number of data points in the array is odd, then the median is the middle value in the ordered list. However, if the number of data points is even, then the median is the average of the two middle values.[1]

EXAMPLE 3-4

MEDIAN

Housing Prices (continued)

Consider again the original Modesto, California, house price data:

$$\{x_i\} = \{\text{house prices}\}$$
$$= \{\$144,000; 98,000; 204,000; 177,000; 155,000; 316,000\ 100,000\}$$

---

[1]A more precise definition of the median exists. In that definition the median is defined as a data value (or possibly, a set of data values) for which at least half of the data are at least as large as that data value and at least half of the data are as small as or smaller than that data value. The definition we present in this text does, however, identify one median and will suffice as an introductory definition.

Sort the data from smallest to largest:

$$\{x_i\} = \{\text{house prices}\}$$
$$= \{\$98,000; 100,000; 144,000; 155,000; 177,000; 204,000; 316,000\}$$

Middle value

Since we have seven houses in the sample, the median sale price is $155,000. The notation for the sample median is M_d.

Data in a population or sample can be either **symmetric** or **skewed** depending on how the data are distributed around the center.

SYMMETRIC DATA Data sets whose values are evenly spread around the center. For symmetric data, the mean and the median are equal.	**SKEWED DATA** Data sets that are not symmetric. For skewed data, the mean will be larger or smaller than the median.

Recall the mean for this same sample is $170,571.43. Thus, in this example the mean and the median are not equal. This sample data set is **right skewed** since $\bar{x} = \$170,571.43 > M_d = \$155,000$. See Figure 3-3, which illustrates examples of right-skewed, left-skewed, and symmetric distributions.

RIGHT-SKEWED DATA A data distribution is right skewed if the mean for the data is larger than the median.	**LEFT-SKEWED DATA** A data distribution is left skewed if the mean for the data is smaller than the median.

Earlier, when we substituted the $1,000,000 house for the one priced at $316,000, the sample mean increased from $170,571.43 to $268,285.71. What will happen to the median? Again, here is the sample with the one change:

$$\{x_i\} = \{\text{house prices}\}$$
$$= \{\$144,000; 98,000; 204,000; 177,000; 155,000; 1,000,000; 100,000\}$$

We sort the data as follows:

$$\{x_i\} = \{\text{house prices}\}$$
$$= \{\$98,000; 100,000; 144,000; 155,000; 177,000; 204,000; 1,000,000\}$$

Since the sample size is odd ($n = 7$), the median is the center value: $M_d = \$155,000$. This is the same median we had before we substituted the extreme value. *An advantage of the*

FIGURE 3-3   Skewed and Symmetric Distributions

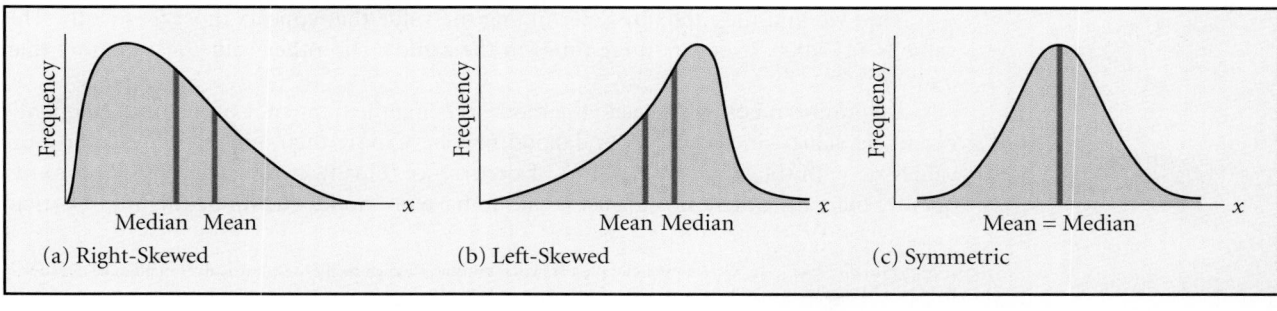

(a) Right-Skewed   Median Mean

(b) Left-Skewed   Mean Median

(c) Symmetric   Mean = Median

median over the mean is the median is not affected by extreme values. Thus, the median is particularly useful as a measure of the center when the data are highly skewed.[2]

We indicated earlier that when you have an even number of data values, the median can be approximated by the average of the two middle values. Suppose the sample of house prices in Modesto, California, is increased from 7 to 10 with the following data now available:

$$\{x_i\} = \{\text{house prices}\}$$
$$= \{\$144,000; 98,000; 204,000; 177,000; 155,000; 316,000; 100,000;$$
$$177,000; 177,000; 170,000\}$$

We first create a data array:

$$\{\$98,000; 100,000; 144,000; 155,000; 170,000; 177,000; 177,000;$$
$$177,000; 204,000; 316,000\}$$

then,

$$M_d = \frac{170,000 + 177,000}{2} = 173,500$$

These new data have resulted in a higher median indicating that the data distribution has shifted to the right.

The Mode

The mean is the most commonly used measure of central location followed closely by the median. However, the **mode** is another measure that is occasionally used as a measure of location.

MODE   *Can have more than 1 or no mode.*

The mode is the value in a data set that occurs most frequently.

EXAMPLE 3-5

MODE

Housing Prices (continued)

Consider again the sample data from Modesto with the expanded sample size of 10 sales prices:

$$\{x_i\} = \{\text{house prices}\}$$
$$= \{\$144,000; 98,000; 204,000; 177,000; 155,000; 316,000; 100,000;$$
$$177,000; 177,000; 170,000\}$$

The mean price is:

$$\bar{x} = \frac{\sum x}{n} = \frac{\$144,000 + 98,000 + \cdots + 170,000}{10} = \frac{\$1,718,000}{10} = \$171,800$$

The median was computed earlier to be $173,500.

Now, we find the mode by determining the value that appears most frequently. This value is $177,000. It occurs three times in the sample. No other value occurs more than once.

A common mistake is to state the mode as being the frequency of the most frequently occurring value—in this case 3. A data set may have more than one mode if two or more values tie with the highest frequency of occurrence. Finally, if no value occurs more frequently than any other, the data set is said to have no mode. The mode might be particu-

---

[2]Excel's Descriptive Statistics tool outputs a skewness statistic. The sign on the skewness statistic implies the direction of skewness. The higher the absolute value, the more the data are skewed.

larly useful in describing the central location value for clothing sizes. For example, shoes come in full and half sizes. Consider the following sample data that have been sorted from lowest to highest:

$$x = \{7.5, 8.0, 8.5, 9.0, 9.0, 10.0, 10.0, 10.0, 10.5, 10.5, 11.0, 11.5\}$$

The mean for these sample data is:

$$\bar{x} = \frac{\sum x}{n} = \frac{7.5 + 8.0 + \cdots + 11.5}{12} = \frac{115.5}{12} = 9.625$$

While 9.625 is the numerical average, the mode is equal to 10 since more people demanded that size shoe than any other. In making purchasing decisions, a shoe store manager would order more shoes at the modal size than at any other size. While in this case the mode is useful, in many instances it is of no practical value as a decision-making tool.

Applying the Measures of Central Tendency

Weigh-in-Motion

3-6

MEAN, MEDIAN & MODE

Excel and Minitab Tutorial

In Chapter 2, we introduced an example involving the truck weigh-in-motion test conducted by the state transportation department. Trucks were weighed on two scales: the WIM and the POE scale. The sample data are on your CD-ROM in a file called **Trucks.** Figure 3-4 shows an Excel worksheet with a portion of the 200 observations where the weights were recorded to the nearest pound.

The issue of interest in this study is whether the WIM (weigh-in-motion) scale produces weights that are close to those of the static POE (port-of-entry) scale. The POE weight is assumed to be the true weight of the truck. For the purposes of this section, we will focus on two variables:

WIM Gross Weight
POE Gross Weight

Figures 3-5 and 3-6 show the frequency histograms generated for these two variables using Excel. We have used the same class intervals for both variables. The histograms are a good place to start in our analysis of the effectiveness of the WIM scale to weigh trucks accurately. What is your initial conclusion based on the histograms in Figures 3-5 and 3-6? Do the truck weight distributions from the two scales look alike; are the distributions symmetric or skewed?

FIGURE 3-4
Excel Worksheet for Weigh-in-Motion Sample Data

Excel Instructions:

1. Open file: Trucks.xls

	A	B	C	D	E	F	G	H	I	J
1	Month Code	WIM Front Axle Weight	WIM Gross Weight	WIM Total Length	POE Front Axle Weight	POE Gross Weight	POE Total Length	Temperature at WIM Scale	Speed at WIM Scale	
2	6	9,560	50,100	64	8,870	49,270	66	62	51	
3	7	10,180	62,880	55	10,780	67,590	55	70	55	
4	4	9,060	40,560	59	10,350	38,740	60	70	60	
5	8	11,460	72,100	56	10,940	71,640	54	70	51	
6	2	11,420	74,040	53	11,320	76,450	55	38	46	
7	8	10,480	42,320	60	9,680	45,600	61	76	58	
8	7	10,700	82,660	95	10,930	86,380	95	103	46	
9	6	11,980	77,800	61	11,570	77,970	62	66	49	

Microsoft Excel - Trucks.xls

File Edit View Insert Format Tools Data PHStat Window Help

Arial   10   **B** *I* U

Excel Instructions:

1. Open file: Trucks.xls
2. Define bins (upper limit of each class)
3. Click on Tools
4. Select Data Analysis
5. Select Histogram
6. Identify data and bins range
7. Identify Output Sheet name
8. Check "Chart Output"
9. Close Gaps (Format Data Series, Options, Gap Width)
10. Modify Class Labels

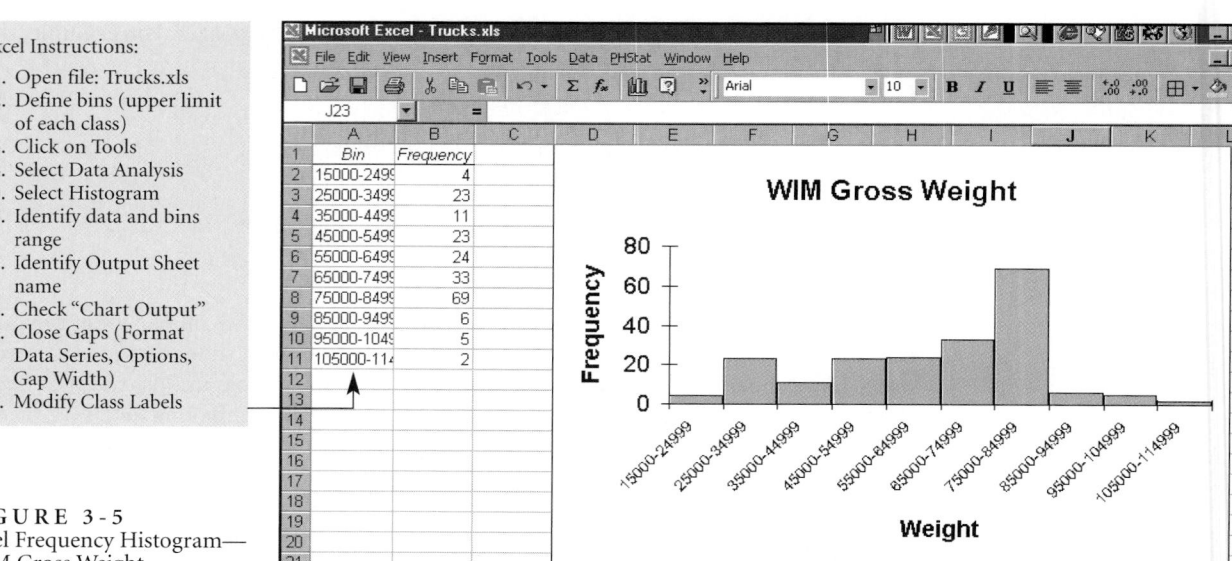

FIGURE 3-5
Excel Frequency Histogram—
WIM Gross Weight

We can extend our analysis by computing the appropriate statistical measures. Specifically, we will want to look at measures of the center. Figure 3-7 illustrates the Excel output with the descriptive measures for both WIM and POE gross weight.[3]

We first focus on the primary measures of central tendency: the mean and median.

MEASURES	WIM WEIGHT	POE WEIGHT
Mean	64,171.15 lb.	61,057.25 lb.
Median	71,380 lb.	67,655 lb.

FIGURE 3-6
Excel Frequency Histogram—
POE Gross Weight

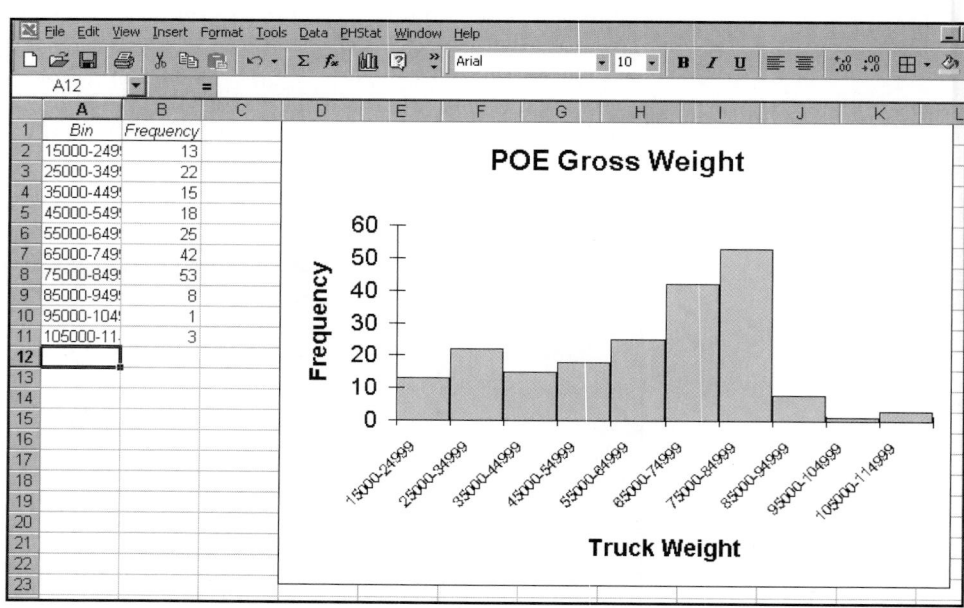

[3]Note: The Descriptive Statistics tool in Excel and Minitab provides additional statistical measures beyond the mean, median, and the mode. Several of these will be discussed later in this chapter.

Excel Instructions:

1. Open file: Trucks.xls
2. Click on the Tools button
3. Select the Data Analysis option
4. Choose Data Analysis and select the appropriate data ranges
5. Click on "Summary Statistics"

FIGURE 3-7
Excel Descriptive Statistics Output

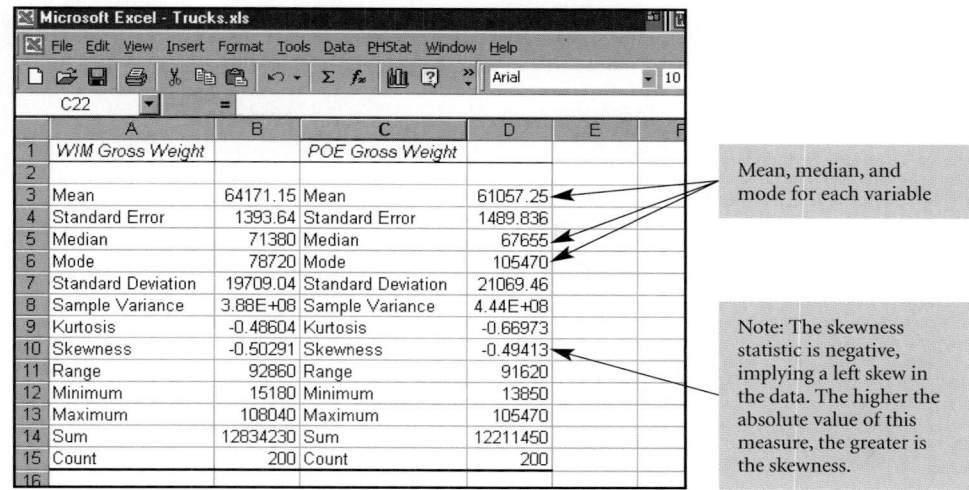

These statistics indicate that, for the sample data, the WIM scale weights are, on average, heavier than the POE scale. Likewise, the median WIM weight exceeds the median for the POE scale. In both cases, the means are less than the medians. Thus, the sample data from both scales are left skewed.

ISSUES WITH EXCEL

In many instances, data files will have "missing values." That is, the values for one or more variables may not be available for some of the observations. The data have been lost or one or more variables not measured when the other data were collected. Many times when you receive data like this, the missing values will be coded in a special way. For example, the code "N/A" might be used or a "−99" might be entered to signify that the data for that observation are missing.

Statistical software packages typically have flexible procedures for dealing with missing data. Minitab provides you with missing data options and properly adjusts the results to account for the missing data. However, *Excel does not contain a missing value option.* If you attempt to use certain data analysis options in Excel, such as Descriptive Statistics, in the presence of non-numeric ("N/A") data you will get an error message. When that happens you will need to clear the missing values, generally by deleting all rows with missing values. In some instances, you can save the good data in the row by using **Edit-Clear-All** for the cell in question. However, a bigger problem exists when the missing value has been coded as an arbitrary numeric value (−99). In this case, unless you go into the data and clear these values, Excel will use the −99 values in the computations as if they are real values. The result will be incorrect calculations.

Also, if a data set contains more than one mode, Excel will show only the first mode in the list of modes and will not warn you that multiple modes exist. (Minitab does not have a mode output option in its descriptive statistics tool.)

Other Measures of Location

PERCENTILES

Additional Example 3-a

Computing Percentiles

In some applications, we might wish to describe the location of the data in terms other than the center of the data. For example, prior to enrolling at your university you took the SAT or ACT test and received a **percentile** score in math and verbal skills. If you received word that your standardized exam score was at the 90th percentile, it means that you scored as high as or higher than 90% of the other students who took the exam. A score at the 50th percentile would indicate that you were at the median where at least 50% scored at or below your score and at least 50% scored at or above your score.[4]

PERCENTILES

The *p*th percentile in a data array is a value that divides the data set into two parts. The lower segment contains at least *p*% and the upper segment contains at least $(100 - p)$% of the data. The 50th percentile is the median.

To illustrate how to manually approximate a percentile value, consider a situation where 300 customers enter a bank during the course of a day. The time (rounded to the nearest minute) that each customer spends in the bank is recorded. If we wish to approximate the 10th percentile we would begin by first sorting the data into order from lowest to highest. Assign each data value a location indicator from 1 to 300. Next, determine the location indicator that corresponds to the 10th percentile using Equation 3-3.

PERCENTILE LOCATION VALUE

$$i = \frac{p}{100}n \qquad\qquad \textbf{3-3}$$

where:

p = desired percentile
n = number of values in the data set

If i is an integer, then the *p*th percentile is the average of the values in locations i and $i + 1$.
If i is not an integer, round i up to the next integer value; the resulting value is the location containing the *p*th percentile.

Thus, the location of the 10th percentile is

$$i = \frac{p}{100}n = \frac{10}{100}300 = 30$$

Since i is an integer, the 10th percentile is approximated by the average value in the 30th and the 30th + 1 = 31st position from the low end of the sorted data.

Additional
Example 3-b

Computing
Quartiles

QUARTILES

Quartiles are another location measure that can be used to describe data.

QUARTILES

Quartiles in a data array are those values that divide the data set into four equal-sized groups. The median corresponds to the second quartile.

The first quartile corresponds to the 25th percentile. That is, the first quartile is the value below which there is at least 25% (one quarter) of the data and above which there is at least 75% percent of the data. The third quartile is also the 75th percentile. It is the value below which there is at least 75% of the data and above which there is at least 25% of the data. The second quartile is the 50th percentile and is also the median.

---

[4]More rigorously, the percentile is that value (or set of values) such that at least *p*% of the data is as small as or smaller than that value and at least $(100 - p)$% of the data is at least as large as that value. For introductory courses, a convention has been adopted to average the largest and smallest values that qualify as a certain percentile. This is why the median was defined as it was earlier for data sets with an even number of data values.

A quartile value can be approximated manually using the same method as for percentiles with Equation 3-3. For the 300 bank customer service times, the location of the first quartile (25th percentile) value is found, after sorting the data, as:

$$i = \frac{p}{100}n = \frac{25}{100}300 = 75$$

Thus, the first quartile is approximated by the average of the values in the 75th and 76th locations from the lower end of the sorted data.

If the number of customers had been 315, the value of the third quartile is determined as follows:

$$i = \frac{p}{100}n = \frac{75}{100}315 = 236.25$$

Since this value is a noninteger, we round it up to 237. The third quartile is approximated by the value in the 237th location from the lower end of the sorted data.

APPLYING PERCENTILES AND QUARTILES

Weigh-in-Motion (continued)

3-7

PERCENTILES AND QUARTILES

Excel and Minitab Tutorial

Figure 3-7 showed that the POE scale and the WIM scale provided somewhat similar values for the mean and median weight for the 200 trucks that were studied. The officials might also be interested in comparing the two scales by examining percentiles and quartiles. Both Minitab and Excel have functions for generating percentile and quartile values. Figure 3-8 shows the Excel output and the first and third quartiles (25th and 75th percentiles) and the 10th percentile for the POE and WIM gross weight measurements. The first quartile values are nearly 5,000 pounds different for the two scales while the third quartiles are slightly more than 1,000 pounds different. The WIM scale shows heavier weights than the POE scale. Figure 3-8 also shows that at least 10% of the trucks weighed at or lower than 31,928 pounds on the WIM scale and 27,643 pounds on the POE scale. Thus at the lower weights, the WIM scale weighs heavier than the POE scale.

ISSUES WITH EXCEL

The procedure that Excel uses to compute quartiles *is not standard*. Therefore the quartile values from Excel will be slightly different than those from other statistical software packages including Minitab. For example, if Excel is used to compute the first and third quartiles for WIM gross vehicle weight in the previous example you would get:

$$Q1 = 49,885 \text{ and } Q3 = 78,125$$

Note that these values will be slightly different than those generated by Minitab which are:

$$Q1 = 49,495 \text{ and } Q3 = 78,215$$

FIGURE 3-8
Excel Output Showing First and Third Quartiles and 10th Percentile—WIM and POE Gross Weights

Excel Instructions:
1. Open file: Trucks.xls
2. Use PERCENTILE function
3. Define data range and desired percentile

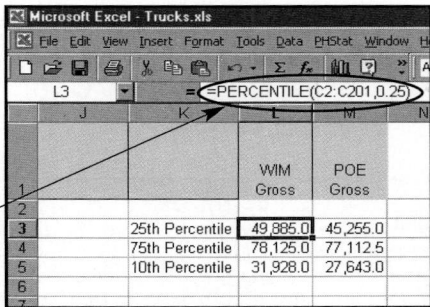

25th Percentile = First Quartile

75th Percentile = Third Quartile

Nearly a 5,000 pound difference in first quartile values

(See the Minitab Tutorial for Example 3-7 on the CD-ROM.) The methods used by Minitab are generally accepted by statisticians to be correct. Therefore, if you need precise values for the quartiles, use software such as Minitab. However, Excel will give reasonably close quartile values.

OPTIONAL CD-ROM TOPIC Box and Whiskers Plots

A Box and Whiskers Plot is an effective tool for displaying the distribution of a variable where the first and third quartiles form the left and right edges of a box and the median is shown within the box. The whiskers show the extremes in the data. For more information, go to the CD-ROM.

Common Mistakes

You need to be very aware of the level of data with which you are working prior to computing the numerical measures introduced in this chapter. A common mistake is to compute means on nominal or ordinal level data. For example, a major electronics manufacturer recently surveyed a sample of customers to determine whether they preferred black, white, or colored stereo cases. The data were coded as follows.

$$1 = \text{black}$$
$$2 = \text{white}$$
$$3 = \text{colored}$$

The sample data are:

$$\text{Color code} = \{1, 1, 3, 2, 1, 2, 2, 2, 3, 1, 1, 1, 3, 2, 2, 1, 2\}$$

Using these codes, the sample mean is:

$$\bar{x} = \frac{\sum x}{n}$$
$$= \frac{30}{17} = 1.765$$

As you can see, reporting that customers prefer a color somewhere between black and white but closer to white would be meaningless. The mean should not be used with nominal or ordinal data. This type of mistake tends to happen when people use computer software to perform their calculations. It is easy to ask Excel, Minitab, or other statistical software to compute the mean, median, and so on, for all the variables in the data set. Then a table is created and, before long, the meaningless measures creep into your report.

Figure 3-9 summarizes the three measures of the center that have been discussed in this section.

OPTIONAL CD-ROM TOPIC Computing Means for Ordinal Data

Care must be taken when computing means for ordinal data. For more information, go to the CD-ROM.

Descriptive Measure	Computation Method	Data Level	Advantages/ Disadvantages
Mean	Sum of values divided by the number of values	Ratio Interval	• Numerical center of the data • Sum of deviations from the mean is zero • Sensitive to extreme values
Median	Middle value for data that have been sorted	Ratio Interval Ordinal	• Not sensitive to extreme values • Computed only from the center values • Does not use information from all the data
Mode	Value(s) that occur most frequently in the data	Ratio Interval Ordinal Nominal	• May not reflect the center • May not exist • Might have multiple modes

FIGURE 3-9
Descriptive Measures of the Center

3-1: EXERCISES

ADDITIONAL EXERCISES ON YOUR CD-ROM
Try the ADDITIONAL EXERCISES and APPLICATION PROBLEMS on the CD-ROM.

3-1. The number of cars that went through a car wash during the noon hour over each of the past 8 days are shown as follows:

6	3	9	6	6	5	4	1

Compute the mean, median, and mode for these sample data.

3-2. The following data are the average per hour wage after deductions by the workers in an orthodontist's office:

$17.87	19.95	22.95	18.74	9.95
11.22	21.98	14.52	16.65	14.98

a. Determine the mean, median, and mode for the preceding data.
b. Give the name of the collective term given to measurements such as those in part a.

3-3. At another orthodontist's office, employees receive the following hourly wages:

$15.67	23.45	18.95	20.79	25.49	
25.49	20.79	25.49	18.95	23.45	15.67

a. Using measures of central tendency, determine the shape of these data.
b. Determine the first and third quartiles for these data.

3-4. During one weekend 11 houses were sold in Half Moon Bay, California. The prices paid for these houses are given in the following table (in thousands of dollars).

264	305	287	325	298	271
112	317	293	325	289	

a. Examine the preceding data and state which measure of central tendency you would choose to describe the "center" of these data. Give reasons for your selection.
b. Calculate the quartiles for these data.

Business Applications

3-5. The marketing director for South East Insurance has been worried about the increasing age of the company's policyholder base. She wants to determine whether the new advertising campaign has had the desired effect of attracting a larger number of younger customers. As a first step in this analysis, she has selected two samples of customers. The first sample is from the customer base prior to the new advertising campaign. The data set consists of the age of each customer at the time each policy went into effect. The second sample was taken from the new customers that were added after the advertising campaign.

PRE-ADVERTISING		POST-ADVERTISING	
33	30	23	34
44	40	31	40
52	29	40	28
34	55	28	25
25	36	26	29

a. Determine the mean, median, and mode for each sample.

b. Discuss whether either of the two data sets is skewed and show why or why not.

c. Is there any indication from these two samples that the new policyholders may tend to be younger? Write a short report that uses the findings in parts a and b to justify your answer.

3-6. The Soccer Shoppe was recently opened in Sonoma, California, to provide soccer equipment and supplies to players and teams in the area. During the first month that it was open, the managers kept track of the number of customers who entered the store each day. The following data were collected.

21	19	21	19	19	20	18	12	20	19	17	14
21	22	25	21	22	23	10	19	25	14	17	18

a. Compute the mean, median, and mode for these data.

b. Indicate whether the data are skewed or symmetrical.

c. The manager has noticed that when she has more than 20 customers a day she might be losing business because customers do not receive enough attention. Specifically, she has noted that she averages sales of $20 per person when there are more than 20 customers a day. However, when there are 20 or fewer customers a day she averages $30 per person in sales. She believes that if she were to hire one more salesperson her sales would be uniform at $30 per person. She would have to pay a salesperson approximately $12.50 an hour for an 8-hour shift. You are to advise her whether or not to hire the new salesperson. Explain your reasoning.

3-7. The Golden Calendar Company produces a variety of specialized calendars that it sells to commercial customers who then resell the calendars. The sales manager at Golden has selected a sample of 16 major customers and recorded the total number of calendars purchased by each customer last year. The following data list the number of calendars purchased. The data are also in a file called **Golden** on your CD-ROM.

Customer	1	2	3	4	5	6
Calendars	41,591	26,226	36,526	47,091	48,600	51,269

Customer	7	8	9	10	11
Calendars	51,836	31,444	48,348	21,519	40,444

Customer	12	13	14	15	16
Calendars	39,580	60,977	21,124	43,572	67,452

a. Compute the mean and median for these sales data.

b. Write a short statement that describes these sales data using the information generated in part a. Make special note of any unusually low or high number of calendar purchases since these accounts often require more attention. The company wishes to increase sales to the low accounts and keep clients who purchase large amounts.

3-8. Micron Technology, Inc., manufactures DRAM chips for the computer industry. Its stock is traded on the New York Stock Exchange under the symbol MU. Use either the Internet or financial news sources such as *The Wall Street Journal* to collect the daily close on Micron's stock price for the trading days between March 1, 2000, and April 23, 2000. Treat these data as a sample.

a. Compute the following statistics: mean, median, and mode.

b. The investment firm for which you work has asked you to advise them concerning the purchase of Micron's stock. Using the measures calculated in part a and any other methods you have learned to support your decision, provide them with some advice.

c. You have been told the company will sell the stock whenever its stock price climbs back over its 90th percentile. At what price should the stock be sold? You will have to assume that the data you have approximate the population of the stock prices here.

3-9. The Cozine Corporation operates a garbage hauling business. Up to this point the company has been charged a flat fee for each of the garbage trucks that enters the county landfill. The flat fee is based on the assumed truck weight of 45,000 pounds. In 2 weeks, the company is required to appear before the county commissioners to discuss a rate adjustment. In preparation for this meeting, Cozine has hired an independent company to weigh a sample of Cozine's garbage trucks just prior to their entering the landfill. The data file, **Cozine**, represents the data the company has collected.

a. Based on the sample data, what percentile does the 45,000 pound weight fall closest to?

b. Compute appropriate measures of central location for the data.

c. Construct a frequency histogram based on the sample data.

d. Use the information determined in parts a through c to develop a presentation to the county commissioners. Make sure the presentation attempts to answer the question of whether Cozine deserves a rate reduction.

3-10. The High Desert Bank loan manager recently selected a random sample of loan files from the bank's loan portfolio. Her objective in selecting the sample is to gain a better understanding of the relationship between commercial and real estate loans. Particularly, she wishes to analyze the loan amounts by type of loan. The data file **High-Desert Banking** contains the data on a sample of 350 loans. Determine appropriate measures of central location for the overall sample.

a. Compute the measures of central location for each category of loan.

b. Develop a frequency histogram for each loan category.

c. Develop a bar chart that displays the mean loan amount by type of loan.

d. Using the information determined in parts a through c, develop a report on loan amounts for the loan manager that emphasizes the similarities and/or differences in loan amounts for real estate and commercial loans.

3-2: MEASURES OF VARIATION

TABLE 3-3
Manufacturing Output for Bryce Lumber

DAY	PLANT A	PLANT B
1	15 units	23 units
2	25 units	26 units
3	35 units	25 units
4	20 units	24 units
5	30 units	27 units

Optional CD Topic

Relationships Between Two Variables

Consider the situation involving two manufacturing facilities for the Bryce Lumber Company. The division vice president asked the two plant managers to record their production output for the next five days. The resulting data are shown in Table 3-3.

Instead of reporting these raw data, the managers reported only the mean and median for their data. The following are the computed statistics for the two plants:

PLANT A	PLANT B
$\bar{x} = 25$ units	$\bar{x} = 25$ units
$M_d = 25$ units	$M_d = 25$ units

The division VP looked at these statistics and concluded:

1. Average production is the same at both plants.
2. At both plants, the output is at or above 25 units half the time and at or less than 25 units half the time.
3. Since the mean and median are equal, the distribution of production output at the two plants is symmetrical.
4. Based on these statistics, there is no reason to believe that the two plants are any different in terms of their production output.

However, if he had taken a close look at the raw data, he would have seen that there is a very big difference between the two plants. The difference is the production **variation** from day to day. Plant B is very stable, producing almost the same amount every day. Plant A varies considerably with some high output days and some low output days. Thus, looking at only measures of the data's central tendency can be misleading.

To fully describe a set of data, we need a measure of variation or spread.

> **VARIATION**
> A set of data exhibits variation if all the data are not the same value.

There is variation in everything that is made by humans or which occurs in nature. The variation may be small but it is there. Given a fine enough measuring instrument, we can detect the variation. Variation is either a natural part of a process (or inherent to a product), or the variation can be attributed to a special cause that is not considered random.

There are several different measures of variation that are used in business decision-making. In this section, we introduce four of these measures: range, interquartile range, variance, and standard deviation.

Range

The simplest measure of variation is the **range**. It is both easy to compute and easy to understand.

> **RANGE** = max − min
> The range is a measure of variation that is computed by finding the difference between the maximum and minimum values in a data set.

The range is computed using Equation 3-4.

> **RANGE**
> $$R = \text{Maximum Value} - \text{Minimum Value}$$ **3-4**

EXAMPLE 3-8

RANGE

Bryce Lumber

Table 3-3 showed the production volume data for the two Bryce Lumber Company plants. The range for each plant is determined as follows:

PLANT A	PLANT B
$R = \text{Maximum} - \text{Minimum}$	$R = \text{Maximum} - \text{Minimum}$
$R = 35 - 15$	$R = 27 - 23$
$R = 20$	$R = 4$

We see Plant A has a range that is 5 times as great as that of Plant B.

While the range is quick and easy to compute, it does have some limitations. First, since we use only the high and low values to compute the range, it is very sensitive to extreme values in the data. Second, regardless of how many values are in the sample or population, the range is computed from only two of these values. For these reasons, it is considered a weak measure of variation.

Interquartile Range

A measure of variation that tends to overcome the range's susceptibility to extreme values is the **interquartile range**.

> **INTERQUARTILE RANGE**
> The interquartile range is a measure of variation that is determined by computing the difference between the first and third quartiles.

Equation 3-5 is used to compute the interquartile range.

> **INTERQUARTILE RANGE**
> $$\text{Interquartile Range} = \text{Third Quartile} - \text{First Quartile}$$ **3-5**

EXAMPLE 3-9

INTERQUARTILE RANGE

Weigh-in-Motion (continued)

Refer again to the example involving the truck weigh scales. The data for a sample of 200 trucks are in the file called **Trucks**. Earlier in Figure 3-8, we used Excel to determine the first and third quartiles for gross weight on both the WIM and POE scales. These are shown again as follows:

	WIM GROSS WEIGHT	POE GROSS WEIGHT
First Quartile	49,885	45,255
Third Quartile	78,125	77,112.5

We can use Equation 3-5 to compute the interquartile range for each scale:

$$\text{WIM} = 78,125 - 49,885 = 28,240 \text{ pounds}$$
$$\text{POE} = 77,112.5 - 45,255 = 31,857.5 \text{ pounds}$$

Thus, while the weights across both scales exhibit variation, based on the interquartile range, the POE scale tends to exhibit greater variation than the WIM scale. The interquartile range is based on the middle 50% of the data and ignores the extremes at either end of the data.

Population Variance and Standard Deviation

While the range is easy to compute and understand and the interquartile range is designed to overcome the range's sensitivity to extreme values, neither measure uses all the available data in its computation. Thus, both measures ignore potentially valuable information in the data.

Two measures of variation that incorporate all the values in a data set are the **variance** and the **standard deviation**. These two measures are closely related. The standard deviation is the positive square root of the variance. The standard deviation is in the original units (dollars, pounds, etc.) while the units of measure in the variance are squared. Because dealing with the original units is easier than dealing with the square of the units, we most often use the standard deviation to measure variation in a population or sample.

VARIANCE	STANDARD DEVIATION
The population variance is the average of the squared distances of the data values from the mean.	The standard deviation is the positive square root of the variance.

EXAMPLE 3-10

VARIANCE AND STANDARD DEVIATION

Bryce Lumber (continued)

Recall the Bryce Lumber example where we compared the production output for two of the company's plants. Table 3-3 showed the data which are considered a population for our purposes here.

Previously we examined the variability in the output from these two plants by computing the ranges. While those results gave us some sense of how much more variable Plant A is than Plant B, we also pointed out some of the deficiencies of the range. The variance and standard deviation offer alternatives to the range for measuring the variation in the data.

Equation 3-6 is the formula for the population variance. Like the population mean, the population variance and standard deviation are assigned Greek symbols.

POPULATION VARIANCE

$$\sigma^2 = \frac{\sum_{i=1}^{N}(x_i - \mu)^2}{N}$$

3-6

where:

μ = population mean
N = population size
σ^2 = population variance (sigma squared)

We begin by computing the variance for the output data from Plant A. The first step in manually calculating the variance is to find the mean using Equation 3-1.

$$\mu = \frac{\sum x}{N} = \frac{15 + 25 + 35 + 20 + 30}{5} = \frac{125}{5} = 25$$

Next, subtract the mean from each value as shown in Table 3-4. Notice the sum of the deviations from the mean is 0. Recall from Section 3-1 that this will be true for any set of

TABLE 3-4
Computing the Population Variance, Squaring the Deviations for Plant A

x	$(x - \mu)$	$(x - \mu)^2$
15	$15 - 25 = -10$	100
25	$25 - 25 = \quad 0$	0
35	$35 - 25 = \quad 10$	100
20	$20 - 25 = \quad -5$	25
30	$30 - 25 = \quad 5$	25
	$\sum = 0$	$\sum = 250$

data. The positive differences are canceled out by the negative differences. To overcome this fact when computing the variance, we square each of the differences and then sum the squared differences. These calculations are also shown in Table 3-4.

The final step in computing the population variance is to divide the sum of the squared differences by the population size, $N = 5$.

$$\sigma^2 = \frac{\sum (x - \mu)^2}{N} = \frac{250}{5} = 50$$

The population variance is 50 *products-squared*. Because we squared the deviations to keep the plus values and minus values from canceling, the units of measure were also squared. The term *products-squared* doesn't have a meaning. To get back to the original units of measure, take the square root of the variance. The result is the standard deviation. Equation 3-7 shows the formula for the population standard deviation.

POPULATION STANDARD DEVIATION

$$\sigma = \sqrt{\sigma^2} = \sqrt{\frac{\sum_{i=1}^{N} (x_i - \mu)^2}{N}} \qquad 3\text{-}7$$

Therefore, the population standard deviation for Plant A's output is:

$$\sigma = \sqrt{50}$$
$$\sigma = 7.07 \text{ products}$$

The population standard deviation is a parameter and will not change unless the population values change.

We could repeat this process using the data for Plant B, which also had a mean output of 25 products. Verify that the population variance is

$$\sigma^2 = \frac{\sum (x - \mu)^2}{N} = \frac{10}{5} = 2$$

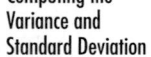

Additional Example 3-c

Computing the Variance and Standard Deviation

The standard deviation is found by taking the square root of the variance

$$\sigma = \sqrt{2}$$
$$\sigma = 1.414 \text{ products}$$

Thus, Plant A has an output standard deviation that is 5 times larger than that of Plant B. Note, the fact that Plant A's range was also 5 times the range for Plant B is merely a coincidence.

Sample Variance and Standard Deviation

Equations 3-6 and 3-7 are the equations for the population variance and standard deviation, respectively. Anytime you are working with a population, these are the equations that are used. However, in most instances, you will be describing sample data that have been selected from the population. In addition to using different notation for the sample variance and standard deviation, the equations are also slightly different. Equation 3-8 is used to find the sample variance.

The sample standard deviation is found by taking the square root of the sample variance as shown in Equation 3-9.

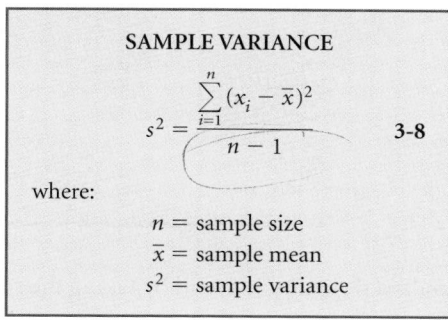

SAMPLE VARIANCE

$$s^2 = \frac{\sum_{i=1}^{n}(x_i - \bar{x})^2}{n - 1} \qquad \textbf{3-8}$$

where:

n = sample size
$\bar{x}$ = sample mean
s^2 = sample variance

SAMPLE STANDARD DEVIATION

$$s = \sqrt{\frac{\sum_{i=1}^{n}(x_i - \bar{x})^2}{n - 1}} \qquad \textbf{3-9}$$

Take note in Equations 3-8 and 3-9 that the denominator is $n - 1$ (sample size minus 1). This may seem strange given that the denominator for the population variance and standard deviation is simply N, the population size. The mathematical justification for the $n - 1$ divisor is outside the scope of this text. However, the general reason for this is that we want the average sample variance to equal the population variance. If we were to select all possible samples of size n from a given population, and for each sample we computed the sample variance using Equation 3-8, the average of all these sample variances would equal σ^2, the population variance, provided we use $n - 1$ as the divisor. Using n instead of $n - 1$ in the denominator would produce an average sample variance that would be smaller than σ^2, the population variance. Since we do not want an estimator on average to underestimate the population variance, we use $n - 1$ in the denominator of s^2.

EXAMPLE 3-11

SAMPLE VARIANCE AND STANDARD DEVIATION

Red-Line Taxi

The managers at Red-Line Taxi selected a random sample of 10 taxicabs and recorded the number of round trips made to the local international airport on November 15. The resulting data are located in Table 3-5.

The mean number of trips is three ($\frac{\sum x}{n} = \frac{30}{10} = 3$). The sample variance is found using Equation 3-8 as follows:

$$s^2 = \frac{\sum_{i=1}^{n}(x_i - \bar{x})^2}{n - 1}$$

As shown in Table 3-6, the sum of the squared deviations is $\sum(x - \bar{x})^2 = 54$. The variance formula is completed by dividing this total by $n - 1$ giving:

$$s^2 = \frac{\sum_{i=1}^{n}(x_i - \bar{x})^2}{n - 1} = \frac{54}{10 - 1} = 6 \text{ trips}^2$$

TABLE 3-5
Red-Line Taxi Trips to the Airport

CAB	ROUND TRIPS = x	CAB	ROUND TRIPS = x
1	4	6	0
2	7	7	3
3	1	8	2
4	0	9	6
5	5	10	2

CAB	TRIPS = x	$x - \bar{x}$	$(x - \bar{x})^2$
1	4	1	1
2	7	4	16
3	1	−2	4
4	0	−3	9
5	5	2	4
6	0	−3	9
7	3	0	0
8	2	−1	1
9	6	3	9
10	2	−1	1
		$\sum = 0$	$\sum = 54$

TABLE 3-6
Computing the Sample
Variance for Red-Line Taxi

The sample standard deviation is found by taking the square root of the variance (see Equation 3-9) giving:

$$s = \sqrt{\frac{\sum(x - \bar{x})^2}{n - 1}} = \frac{54}{9} = \sqrt{6}$$

$$s = 2.4495 \text{ trips}$$

This sample standard deviation measures the variation in the sample data for daily round trips to the airport for the Red-Line Taxi company.

3-12

**MEASURES OF
VARIABILITY**

Excel and
Minitab Tutorial

Weigh-in-Motion (continued)

The state transportation department has conducted a study to determine whether the weigh-in-motion (WIM) scale can be used as a substitute for the static scale located at a port-of-entry (POE). The state collected data on a sample of $n = 200$ trucks over several months. Each truck was weighed on both scales.

Previously, we computed measures of central tendency and constructed histograms in an effort to better understand the sample data. The focus was on the WIM gross vehicle weight and the POE gross vehicle weight. We saw that there were only "small" differences in the mean and median values for the two variables. This added support to the notion that the WIM scale could be used as a substitute for the POE scale.

We now turn our attention to measures of variability. The question is whether the two scales provide weight distributions that have similar amounts of variability between trucks. The range (maximum − minimum) is one measure of variability. Statistical software such as Excel and Minitab can be used to compute the range. Figure 3-10 shows the Excel descriptive statistics results for POE and WIM gross weights.

The values based on the sample data are:

WIM Scale Gross Weight: $R = 92{,}860$ pounds
POE Scale Gross Weight: $R = 91{,}620$ pounds

The ranges are reasonably close in value, which is one indication that the variability in weights for the two scales is similar.

The standard deviation is a more powerful measure of variation since it measures the deviation of all the values around the center. Again, Excel and Minitab have options for computing the standard deviation.[5] The sample standard deviations for the two scales are:

WIM Scale Gross Weight: $s = 19{,}709.04$ pounds
POE Scale Gross Weight: $s = 21{,}069.46$ pounds

On each scale, the statistics show that there is substantial variation between truck weights. (Recall the mean weights for trucks over both scales were less than 65,000

---

[5]Excel and Minitab use the formula for sample variance and sample standard deviation as the defaults.

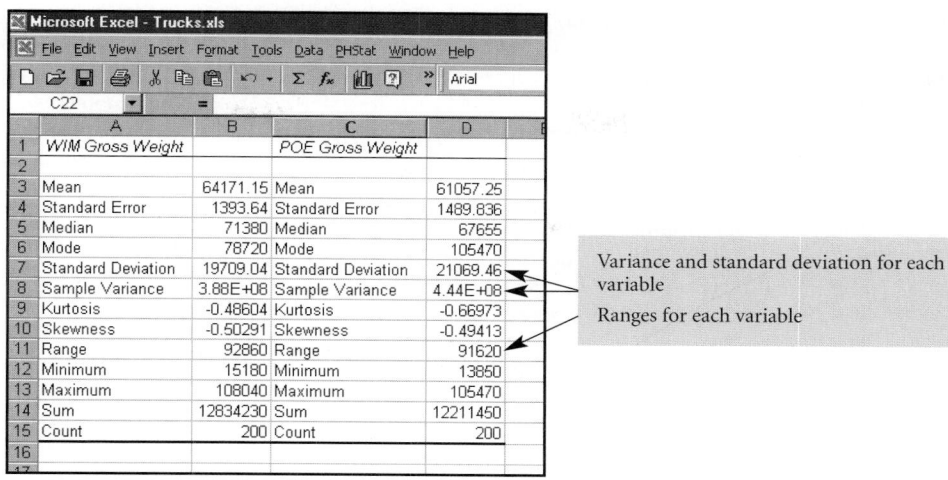

Excel Instructions:

1. Open file: Trucks.xls
2. Click on the Tools button
3. Select the Data Analysis option
4. Choose Data Analysis and select the appropriate data ranges
5. Click on "Summary Statistics"

FIGURE 3-10
Excel Descriptive Statistics Output—Truck Weight Data

pounds.) These data also indicate that the WIM scale provided less variation than the POE scale.

Up to this point, considering the graphical analyses we did in Chapter 2 and this numerical descriptive analysis, what are your conclusions about the effectiveness of the weigh-in-motion process? Are the weights produced by the two scales close enough to use? The answer probably depends on how close the weights need to be to be useful to the engineers at the transportation department. Table 3-7 summarizes the descriptive statistics.

Additional
Example 3-d

Comparing Two
Samples Using
Paired Values

TABLE 3-7
Summary Statistics—WIM versus POE Weights

STATISTICAL MEASURE	WIM SCALE	POE SCALE
Mean	64,171	61,057
Median	71,380	67,655
Mode	78,720	105,470
1st Quartile	49,885	45,255
3rd Quartile	78,125	77,113
Range	92,860	91,620
Standard Deviation	19,709	21,069

3-2: EXERCISES

ADDITIONAL EXERCISES ON YOUR CD-ROM

Try the ADDITIONAL EXERCISES and APPLICATION PROBLEMS on the CD-ROM.

3-11. You are given the following data for the number of times a population of six families dined out during the previous month:

4	6	9	4	5	7

   a. Compute the range for these data.
   b. Compute the variance and standard deviation.
   c. Assume that these data represented a sample rather than a population. Compute the variance and stan-

dard deviation. Discuss the difference between the values computed here and in part b.

3-12. For the following set of sample sales data compute the range, variance, and standard deviation.

$17.87	19.95	22.95	18.74	9.95
11.22	21.98	14.52	16.65	14.98

3-13. Refer to Problem 12.
   a. Calculate the number of standard deviations that are contained within the interquartile range.

b. Calculate the largest deviation from the mean for this data set.

3-14. Assume that the following sample represents vehicle speeds.

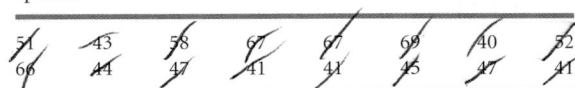

a. Determine the proportion of this data set that is within one standard deviation of the mean.
b. Determine the proportion of this data set that is within two standard deviations of the mean.
c. Determine the proportion of this data set that is within three standard deviations of the mean.

Business Applications

3-15. The Price Corporation has built six homes during the past year. The number of square feet in each home (treated as the population of interest) is listed as follows:

Square feet = {1,560; 2,340; 1,990; 1,750; 4,000; 2,200}

a. Compute the range.
b. Compute the variance.
c. Compute the standard deviation.
d. Write a short paragraph describing these data. Feel free to also compute measures of the center and include these values in your discussion.

3-16. The Stop N' Go convenience chain recently selected a random sample of 10 customers. The store monitored the number of times each customer made a purchase at the store over a two-month period. The following data were collected.

| 10 | 19 | 17 | 19 | 12 | 20 | 20 | 15 | 16 | 13 |

a. Store executives are considering a promotion in which they reward frequent purchases with a small gift. However, they do not wish to give so many gifts that it substantially reduces their profit margin. They have decided to take the advice of a consulting statistician to give gifts to only those shoppers whose number of visits in the past two-month period is above the mean plus one standard deviation. Find the minimum number of visits required to receive a prize.
b. Stop N' Go intends to give gifts that cost $5. The number of shoppers that visit one of their convenience stores per day is approximately 50. Determine the approximate cost to the company while offering this promotion for one month.

3-17. The marketing director for South East Insurance has been worried about the increasing age of the company's policy-holder base. She wants to determine whether a new advertising campaign has had the desired effect of attracting younger customers. She has taken a sample of 10 new policies and has found the following ages:

| 32 | 22 | 24 | 27 | 27 | 33 | 28 | 23 | 24 | 21 |

a. Compute the range, interquartile range, and the standard deviation for these data.
b. Before the new advertising campaign the average age of the customers was 37.8 years. Based on your calculations in part a, has the advertising campaign been effective in reducing the average age of the customers? Remember you are addressing this question for all of the company's customers, not just the customers in the sample. Discuss any problems you might have in comparing a sample value to a population value.

3-18. Grover's Pay n' Pak sells hardware supplies to "do-it-your-selfers." The company prides itself on fast service. It uses a number system and takes customers in the order that they arrive at the store. Recently, the assistant manager tracked the time customers spent in the store from the time they took a number until they left. A sample of 16 customers was selected and the following data (measured in minutes) were recorded.

| 15 | 14 | 16 | 14 | 14 | 14 | 13 | 8 |
| 12 | 9 | 7 | 17 | 10 | 15 | 16 | 16 |

a. Compute the mean, median, mode, range, interquartile range, and standard deviation.
b. Develop a frequency distribution for these data.

3-19. National Cash Register (NCR) has contacted Grover's concerning the installation of a new cash register and inventory system. Its sales force claims that the new system will reduce time spent in the store by an average of 10% per customer.

a. Determine the percentage change this reduction would have on the mean, median, and mode as well as the interquartile range and standard deviation that you calculated in Problem 18.
b. Grover's goal is to increase service so that 90% of the customers spend less than 15 minutes in their store. Would you recommend the purchase of the new cash registers? Explain and support your answer.

3-20. Welton Corporation makes dynamic random access memory chips (DRAMs) for use in personal computers. DRAMs are made on silicon wafers. The company's goal is to yield as many good chips from each wafer as possible in order to make more profit from its production operations. The following data represent the number of usable DRAM chips from a sample of 32 wafers:

488	449	510	551	548	569	413	491
544	457	472	432	426	461	469	415
477	484	505	485	487	485	554	497
493	479	579	535	595	474	566	436

Compute the following numerical measures for these yield data: (a) mean, (b) median, (c) mode, (d) range, (e) quartiles, (f) interquartile range, (g) variance, and (h) standard deviation.

3-21. The current process that Welton Corporation uses to produce DRAMs outputs an average of 485 DRAMs, a median of 490, and a standard deviation of 15 DRAMs. A new process for producing DRAMs is also available and is, in fact, the process used for the sample listed in Problem 20.

    a. If the company wished to use the process that produced the largest average number of DRAMs, which process would it use? Support your conclusion with calculations and reasons.

    b. If the company needs a process that produces at least 488 DRAMs at least half the time, determine which process the company would select. Give reasons for your answer.

3-22. Micron Technology, Inc., manufactures DRAM chips for the computer industry. Its stock is traded on the New York Stock Exchange under the symbol MU. Use either the Internet or financial news sources such as *The Wall Street Journal* to collect the daily close on Micron's stock price for 40 trading days during a recent period. Treat these data as a sample.

    a. Compute the standard deviation, range, and interquartile range for these stock prices.

    b. Combine this information with the measures of central tendency in a report for the upcoming board of directors meeting. (Note: Also research some general information about the company to include in your report.)

    c. Calculate the average of (1) the 1st to the 25th stock prices, (2) the 2d to the 26th stock prices, . . . (16) the 16th to the 40th stock prices. Examine these 16 averages and determine if there is a trend. Are the averages going up or down? Would you purchase this stock on the basis of your calculations?

3-23. Refer to the weigh-in-motion example discussed in Chapter 2 and earlier in this chapter. State officials are interested in analyzing the speeds that trucks were traveling when they crossed the WIM. The speed data for the trucks in this study are shown in the file called **Trucks**.

    a. Construct a frequency distribution and histogram with class limits that are 10 miles per hour wide.

    b. Calculate the mean and median truck speed.

    c. Compute the sample standard deviation, the range, and the interquartile range.

    d. Write a report using the information generated in parts a through c to inform the state officials about the truck speeds at the WIM scale. As part of your report, include your observations concerning the proportion of trucks that exceed 50, 60, and 70 mph.

3-24. Referring to Problem 23 involving the weigh-in-motion study, state officials are interested in determining whether the WIM scale can be used as a substitute for the static scales at port-of-entry locations. In addition to gross weight, the WIM and POE scales can measure the weight of the truck over each axle. For example, the front axle on a truck is referred to as the A axle.

    a. Create a new variable that is the paired difference in POE and WIM axle A weights. If the WIM readings can be used as a good substitute for POE readings,

what value would you expect the average of these paired differences to be? What value would you expect to see for the median of these paired differences? Calculate these two measurements and comment on the suitability of the WIM readings based solely on these measures.

    b. Calculate the standard deviation of the paired differences. If the WIM readings are a good substitute for the POE readings, would you expect a large or small standard deviation of these paired differences? Explain your answer.

    c. How would you determine if the standard deviation you calculated in part b was large or small? (Hint: Think about how this would relate to the standard deviation of the POE readings themselves.)

3-25. Refer to Problem 24. Perform a complete descriptive analysis of the paired difference variable using both appropriate graphical tools and numerical measures. When you are finished, indicate whether, based on the descriptive analysis, the WIM scale looks like a reasonable substitute for the POE scale as far as axle A weights are concerned.

3-26. Referring to Problem 25, the state officials are also interested in whether the WIM scale can be used to accurately determine the length of the truck and thus avoid having POE personnel do that manually.

    a. Compute the mean, median, and standard deviation of the POE truck length. Assume the POE lengths are accurate.

    b. Compute the mean, median, and standard deviation of the WIM truck length. Compare these with the values computed in part a.

    c. Create a new variable that is the paired difference between the WIM and POE lengths. Compute appropriate descriptive statistics and a frequency histogram for this new variable.

    d. Write a short report using the information in parts a through c to determine whether the WIM scale can be used to effectively measure truck lengths.

3-27. The managers at the Capital Credit Union have to issue a report to the state bank commission regarding credit card balances for their customers. In response to this request, the managers have selected a random sample of their customers and determined current credit card balances and gender of the cardholder. The resulting data are contained in the file called **Capital**.

    a. Compute the mean, median, range, interquartile range, variance, and standard deviation of credit card balances for all customers in the sample.

    b. Compute the mean, median, range, interquartile range, variance, and standard deviation of credit card balances for males and for females separately.

    c. Draft a report to the state bank commission that describes the credit card balances. Specifically address any notable or systematic differences in the distribution of credit card balances between males and females.

3-3: USING THE MEAN AND STANDARD DEVIATION TOGETHER

In the previous sections, we introduced several important descriptive measures that are useful for helping transform data into meaningful information. Two of the most important of these measures are the mean and standard deviation. In this section, we discuss several statistical tools that combine the mean and standard deviation.

Coefficient of Variation

The standard deviation measures the variation in a set of data. For decision makers, the standard deviation indicates how spread out, or how variable, a distribution is. For distributions having the same mean, the distribution with the largest standard deviation has the greatest relative spread. When two or more distributions have different means, the relative spread cannot be determined by merely comparing standard deviations.

The **coefficient of variation** is used to measure the relative variation for distributions with different means. The coefficient of variation for a population is computed using Equation 3-10 while Equation 3-11 is used for sample data.

> **COEFFICIENT OF VARIATION**
> The ratio of the standard deviation to the mean expressed as a percentage. The coefficient of variation is used to measure the relative variation in the data.

POPULATION COEFFICIENT OF VARIATION	SAMPLE COEFFICIENT OF VARIATION
$CV = \dfrac{\sigma}{\mu}(100\%)$ **3-10**	$CV = \dfrac{s}{\bar{x}}(100\%)$ **3-11**

When the coefficients of variation for two or more distributions are compared, the distribution with the largest CV is said to have the greatest relative spread.

EXAMPLE 3-13

COEFFICIENT OF VARIATION

Agra-Tech Industries

Agra-Tech has recently introduced feed supplements for both cattle and hogs that will increase the rate at which animals gain weight. Three years of feedlot tests indicate that steers fed the supplement will weigh an average of 125 pounds more than those not fed the supplement. However, not every steer has the same performance with the supplement. There is variation from steer to steer. The standard deviation in weight gain advantage for the steers in the three-year study has been 10 pounds.

Similar tests with hogs indicate those fed the supplement average 40 additional pounds of weight gain compared to hogs not given the supplement. The standard deviation for the hogs was also 10 pounds.

Even though the standard deviation is 10 pounds for both cattle and hogs, the fact that average added weight gain differs indicates there is a difference in the relative variation associated with the two situations. We can verify this by computing the coefficients of variation for the two groups:

$$CV(\text{cattle}) = \frac{10}{125}(100\%) = 8\%$$

$$CV(\text{hogs}) = \frac{10}{40}(100\%) = 25\%$$

These results indicate that hogs exhibit much greater relative variability in weight gain compared to cattle.

EXAMPLE 3-14

COEFFICIENT OF VARIATION

Stock Portfolios

The coefficient of variation is used in financial applications as a measure of the relative risk of a stock portfolio. If portfolio A has a collection of stocks that average 12% return with a standard deviation of 3% while portfolio B has an average return of 6% with a standard deviation of 2%, we can compute the *CV* values for each as follows:

$$CV(A) = \frac{3}{12}(100\%) = 25\%$$

and

$$CV(B) = \frac{2}{6}(100\%) = 33\%$$

Thus, even though portfolio B has a lower standard deviation, it would be considered relatively more risky than portfolio A since its *CV* is 33% compared to 25% for A.

The Empirical Rule

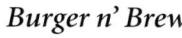

A tool that is useful for helping to describe data in certain circumstances is called the **Empirical Rule**. In order for the empirical rule to be used the frequency distribution must be bell-shaped like the one shown in Figure 3-11.

EMPIRICAL RULE

If the data distribution is bell-shaped, then the interval:

$\mu \pm 1\sigma$ contains approximately 68% of the values in the population or the sample

$\mu \pm 2\sigma$ contains approximately 95% of the values in the population or the sample

$\mu \pm 3\sigma$ contains virtually all of the data values in the population or the sample

---

EXAMPLE 3-15

EMPERICAL RULE

Burger n' Brew

The standard deviation can be thought of as a measure of distance from the mean. To illustrate, the Phoenix Burger n' Brew restaurant chain keeps records on the number of each hamburger option it sells each day at each location. The number of chili-burgers sold each day for the past 365 days are listed in the file called **BurgerNBrew**. Figure 3-12 shows the

FIGURE 3-11
Illustrating the Empirical Rule for the Bell-Shaped Distribution

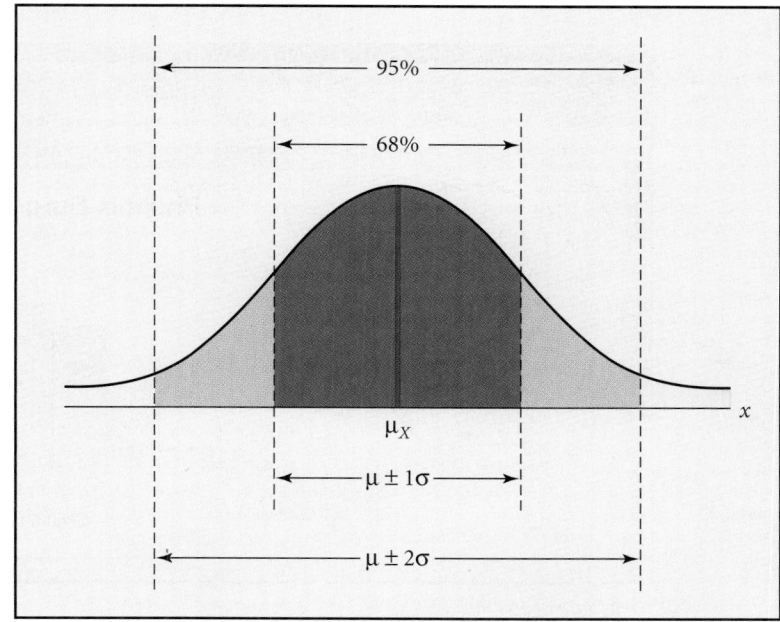

Excel and Minitab Tutorial

frequency histogram for the same data. The population distribution is nearly *symmetrical* and approximately *bell-shaped*. The mean number of chili-burgers sold was 15.1 with a standard deviation of 3.1.

The Empirical Rule is a very useful statistical concept for helping us understand the data in a bell-shaped distribution. In the Burger n' Brew example, with $\mu = 15.1$ and $\sigma = 3.1$, if we move one standard deviation in each direction from the mean, *approximately* 68% of the data should lie within the range:

$$15.1 \pm 1(3.1)$$
$$12.0 \text{- } 18.2$$

If we actually count the number of days Burger n' Brew sold between 12 and 18 chili-burgers, the number is 262. Thus, out of 365 days, 72% of the time Burger n' Brew sold between 12 and 18 chili-burgers. (Note: The reason that we didn't get exactly 68% is that the distribution in Figure 3-12 is not perfectly bell-shaped.)

If we look at the interval two standard deviations either side of the mean, we would expect approximately 95% of the data to fall within that range. The interval is:

$$15.1 \pm 2(3.1)$$
$$15.1 \pm 6.2$$
$$8.9 \text{- } 21.3$$

Counting the values between these limits, we find 353 of the 365 values or 97%. Again this is close to what the Empirical Rule predicted. Finally, according to the Empirical Rule, we would expect 99.7% (or virtually all) of the data to fall within three standard deviations. The interval is:

$$15.1 \pm 3(3.1)$$
$$15.1 \pm 9.3$$
$$5.8 \text{- } 24.4$$

Looking at the data in Figure 3-12, we find that at most one observation may fall outside this interval.

Therefore, if we know only the mean and standard deviation for a set of data, the Empirical Rule gives us a tool for describing how the data are distributed, provided the distribution is bell-shaped.

FIGURE 3-12
Excel Histogram for Burger n' Brew Data

Excel Instructions:
1. Open file: BurgerNBrew.xls
2. Set up Bins (upper limit of each class)
3. Click on Tools—Data Analysis—Histogram
4. Supply data range and bin range
5. Check Chart Output

Bin	Frequency
6-7	3
8-9	10
10-11	34
12-13	70
14-15	81
16-17	81
18-19	58
20-21	23
22-23	4
24-25	1

Phoenix Burger n' Brew

Standard Deviation S = 3.1

Mean = 15.1

Chili-Burgers Sold

Tchebysheff's Theorem

The Empirical Rule applies when the distribution is bell-shaped. But what about the many situations when the distribution is skewed and not bell-shaped? In these cases, we can use Tchebysheff's theorem.

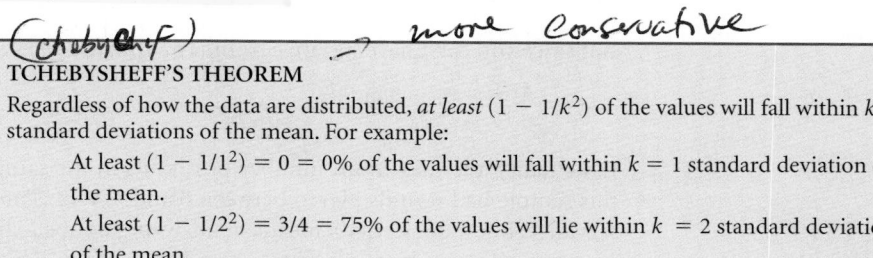

(chebycheff)   → more conservative

TCHEBYSHEFF'S THEOREM

Regardless of how the data are distributed, *at least* $(1 - 1/k^2)$ of the values will fall within k standard deviations of the mean. For example:

At least $(1 - 1/1^2) = 0 = 0\%$ of the values will fall within $k = 1$ standard deviation of the mean.

At least $(1 - 1/2^2) = 3/4 = 75\%$ of the values will lie within $k = 2$ standard deviations of the mean.

At least $(1 - 1/3^2) = 8/9 = 89\%$ of the values will lie within $k = 3$ standard deviations of the mean.

Tchebysheff's theorem is conservative. It tells us nothing about the data within one standard deviation of the mean. The theorem indicates that *at least* 75% of the data will fall within two standard deviations—it could be more. If we applied Tchebysheff's theorem to bell-shaped distributions, the percentage estimates would be very low. The thing to remember is that Tchebysheff's theorem applies to *any distribution*. This gives it great flexibility but less precision.

Warm Springs Golf Club

EXAMPLE

3-16

TCHEBYSHEFF'S EXAMPLE

Consider the Warm Springs Golf Club which has two 18-hole golf courses. On a busy spring day, 400 or more golfers may play 18 holes at the club. The data are in a file called **WarmSprings** and show the rounds played for a sample of 50 days during the spring months. Figure 3-13 shows the histogram for these golf rounds. This shows that the distribution of number of rounds played is not bell-shaped and symmetric. The sample mean for these data is 160.40 rounds and the standard deviation is 109.37 rounds.

FIGURE 3-13
Excel Output—Distribution of Rounds Played Per Day

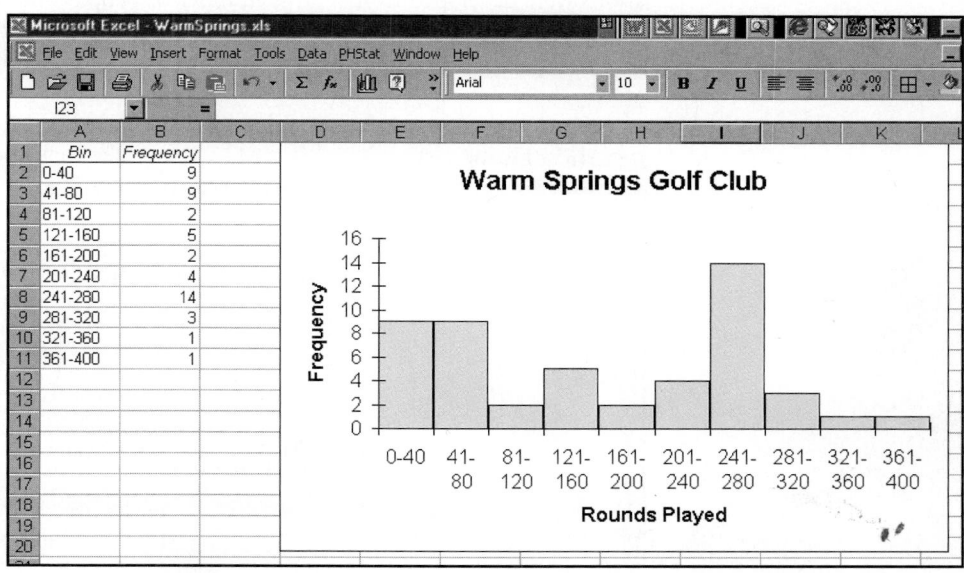

Excel Instructions:

1. Open file: Warm Springs.xls
2. Set up Bins (upper limit of each class)
3. Click on Tools—Data Analysis—Histogram
4. Supply data range and bin range
5. Check Chart Output

If we use Tchebysheff's theorem, we can expect *at least* 75% of days to have rounds played within two standard deviations of the mean:

$$160.40 \pm 2(109.37)$$

-58.34 - 379.14

But since you can't have negative rounds of golf, the 75% range is:

0 - 379.14

In actuality, the maximum number of rounds in the sample was 371 so all of the days in this sample had rounds played between 0 and 379.14. Thus Tchebysheff's theorem is conservative, but it does offer a means of analyzing nonbell-shaped distributions.

Standardized Data Values

When we are dealing with quantitative data, we will sometimes want to convert the measures to a form called **standardized data values**. This is especially useful when we wish to compare data from two or more distributions when the data scales for the two distributions are substantially different.

> **STANDARDIZED DATA VALUES**
> The number of standard deviations a value is from the mean. The standardized data values are sometimes referred to as *z*-scores.

EXAMPLE 3-17

STANDARDIZED DATA

Human Resources

Consider the situation in which the human resources department in a company uses placement exams as part of its hiring process. The company currently will accept scores from either of two tests—AIMS Hiring and BHS-Screen. The problem is that the AIMS Hiring test has an average score of 2,000 and a standard deviation of 200 while the BHS-Screen test has an average score of 80 with a standard deviation of 12. These means and standard deviations were developed from a large number of people who have taken the two tests. How can the personnel administrators compare applicants when the average scores and measures of spread are so different for the two tests? One approach is to *standardize* the test scores.

For example, suppose two applicants (John and Mary) are being considered. John took the AIMS Hiring test and scored 2,344 while Mary took the BHS-Screen and scored 95. Their scores can be standardized using Equation 3-12:

STANDARDIZED POPULATION DATA

$$z = \frac{x - \mu}{\sigma}$$ 3-12

where:

x = original data value
μ = population mean
σ = population standard deviation
z = standard score (number of standard deviations x is from μ)

If you are working with sample data rather than a population, Equation 3-13 can be used to standardize the values:

STANDARDIZED SAMPLE DATA

$$z = \frac{x - \bar{x}}{s} \qquad \qquad \textbf{3-13}$$

where:

z = standard score
$\bar{x}$ = sample mean
s = sample standard deviation
x = original data value

We can standardize the test scores for John and Mary using:

$$z = \frac{x - \mu}{\sigma}$$

For the AIMS Hiring test, the mean, μ, is 2,000 and the standard deviation, σ, equals 200. John's score of 2,344 converts to:

$$z = \frac{2,344 - 2,000}{200}$$
$$z = 1.72$$

The BHS Screen has $\mu = 80$ and $\sigma = 12$. Mary's score of 95 converts to:

$$z = \frac{95 - 80}{12}$$
$$z = 1.25$$

Compared to the average score on the AIMS Hiring test, John's score is 1.72 standard deviations higher. Mary's score is only 1.25 standard deviations higher than the average score on the BHS-Screen test. So, even though the two tests used different scales, standardizing the data allows us to conclude that John did relatively better on his test than Mary did on her test.

3-3: EXERCISES

ADDITIONAL EXERCISES ON YOUR CD-ROM

Try the **ADDITIONAL EXERCISES** and **APPLICATION PROBLEMS** on the **CD-ROM.**

3-28. Consider the following set of sample data.

| 16 | 23 | 17 | 24 | 9 | 11 | 13 | 15 | 15 | 23 | 18 | 16 | 17 |

a. Compute the mean and standard deviation for these sample data.
b. Determine the coefficient of variation for the set and interpret what it measures.
c. Without making any assumption about the shape of the distribution, supply a conservative range within which at least 75% of the data values should fall.

(Hint: Use Tchebysheff's theorem.) Count how many values actually fell in this interval and discuss whether your interval range was in fact conservative.
d. Assume that the distribution of values is bell-shaped and determine the range of values that should contain approximately 68% of the data values.

3-29. A population of unknown shape has a mean of 3,000 and a standard deviation of 200.
a. Find the minimum proportion of observations in the population that are in the range 2,600 to 3,400.

b. Determine the maximum proportion of the observations that are above 3,600.

c. What statement could you make concerning the proportion of observations that are smaller than 2,400?

3-30. A population has a mean of 400 and a standard deviation of 30.

    a. Calculate the z-score for the number 455 from this population.

    b. Determine the z-score for the mean value of 400.

    c. Find the proportion of data that have z-scores between -2 and 2. Assume that the population is bell-shaped.

    d. Referring to part c, assuming that the population is highly skewed, find the proportion of data that have z-scores between -2 and 2. Does the shape of the distribution make a difference?

Business Applications

3-31. The Miller Distributing Company is investigating two different scheduling methods for its truck drivers. The following data reflect the number of miles each driver drove to complete his or her deliveries each day for each of the scheduling methods.

Method 1:	14	11	19	6	10
Method 2:	26	5	9	6	14

    a. Compute the mean and standard deviation for each of these methods. Assume the data are sample data.

    b. Compute the coefficient of variation for each method and discuss which scheduling method seems to provide less relative variability in the distances traveled.

    c. Refer to part b. In this case would it be acceptable to compare standard deviations directly to determine relative variability? Explain why or why not.

3-32. Sportway Manufacturing has been experimenting with new materials to use for golf ball covers. Two recently developed compounds have been shown to be equally resistant to cutting, and the development lab is now looking at the distance the balls will travel during a simulated drive. However, both distance and consistency are important for a golf ball. A sample of 10 balls with each type of cover was selected and the following distances were measured (in yards) using a mechanical driver that struck each ball with the same amount of force.

Type A:	298	291	290	310	296	299	300	305	289	285
Type B:	297	315	291	292	301	286	287	290	302	323

    a. A new technician records the next ball hit as traveling only 274 yards. He says the ball was a Type B ball. Do you believe the technician? Provide calculations and reasoning to support your answer.

    b. The technician also recorded a ball hit 312 yards. However, he does not remember which type of ball it was. Help the technician decide which type of ball he used for this experiment. Give reasons and calculations to support your answer.

    c. Do you believe it is likely that one of these types of balls can be hit 325 yards? Explain your answer.

3-33. The Rippon Investment Company offers two different mutual funds. The stocks in the Growth Fund have generated an average return of 8% with a standard deviation of 2%. The stocks in the Specialized Fund have generated an average return of 18% with a standard deviation of 6%.

    a. Based on the data provided, which of these funds has exhibited greater relative variability? Use the proper statistical measure to make your determination.

    b. Suppose an investor who is very risk averse is interested in one of these two funds. Based strictly on relative variability, which fund would you recommend? Discuss.

    c. Suppose the distributions for the two stock funds had a bell-shaped distribution with the means and standard deviations previously indicated. Which fund appears to be the best one-year investment assuming future returns will mimic past returns? Explain.

3-34. The division manager for Northern Pipe and Steel Company has decided to implement a new incentive system for the managers of the three plants. The plan calls for a bonus to be paid next month to the manager whose plant has the greatest relative improvement over the average monthly production volume. The following data reflect the historical production volumes at the three plants.

PLANT 1	PLANT 2	PLANT 3
$\mu = 700$	$\mu = 2,300$	$\mu = 1,200$
$\sigma = 200$	$\sigma = 350$	$\sigma = 30$

At the close of next month, the monthly output for the three plants was:

Plant 1 = 810	Plant 2 = 2,600	Plant 3 = 1,320

Suppose the division manager has awarded the bonus to the manager of Plant 2 since her plant increased its production by 300 units over the mean. This was a higher increase than that experienced by any of the other managers. Do you agree with the selection of the Plant 2 manager to receive the bonus this month? Explain, using the appropriate statistical measures to support your position.

3-35. Each week for the past 40 weeks the Ajax Taxi Company has collected data on the miles driven by each of four taxis. These data are in a file called **Ajax**. Combine the data from the four taxis into one variable with $n = 160$ observations.

    a. Develop a frequency distribution for this new variable.

    b. Standardize the data (z-values) and develop a frequency distribution for the standardized data values. Compare this distribution to the one computed for the raw scores in part a.

3-36. The Environmental Protection Agency (EPA) tests all new cars and provides a mileage rating for both city and highway driving conditions. Thirty cars for the 1998 model year were tested and the data are contained in the file, **Automobiles**. The file contains data on several variables. In this problem, focus on the city and highway mileage data.

CAR MAKE AND MODEL	MILEAGE, CITY	MILEAGE, HIGHWAY
Dodge Stratus ES	20	29
Ford Taurus SE	19	28
Chevrolet Malibu LS	20	29
Ford Contour GL	24	32
Honda Accord LX	23	30
Mazda 626 LX	23	31
Nissan Altima GXE	22	30
Oldsmobile Cutlass GLS	20	29
Toyota Camry LE	23	30
BMW 328i	19	27
Saab 9-5	18	26
Cadillac Catera	18	24
Acura TL	19	27
Volvo S-80	18	27
Chevrolet S-10	17	22
Dodge Dakota	16	21
Ford Ranger	17	21
Nissan Frontier	20	24
Toyota Tacoma	19	23
Chevrolet Silverado LT	16	20
Dodge Ram Sport	13	18
GMC Sierra SLT	16	21
Ford F150 Lariat	14	18
Chevrolet Corvette	18	28
Dodge Viper GTS	11	21
Acura NSX	18	21
BMW 540i Sport	17	22
Chevrolet Camaro Z28 SS	19	23
Jaguar XJR	16	19
Porsche 911 Carrera	19	24

a. Calculate the sample mean miles per gallon (mpg) for both city and highway driving for the 30 cars. Also calculate the sample standard deviation for the two mileage variables. Do the data tend to support the premise that cars will get better mileage on the highway than around town? Discuss.

b. Referring to part a, what can the EPA conclude about the relative variability between car models for highway versus city driving? (Hint: Compute the appropriate measure to compare relative variability.)

c. Assume that mileage ratings are approximately bell-shaped. Approximately what proportion of cars gets at least as good a mileage in city driving conditions as the mean mileage for highway driving for all cars?

3-37. Zepolle's Bakery makes a variety of bread types that it sells to supermarket chains in the area. One of Zepolle's problems is that the number of loaves of each type of bread sold each day by the chain stores varies considerably, making it difficult to know how many loaves to bake. A sample of daily demand data is contained in the file called **Bakery**.

a. Which bread type has the highest average daily demand?

b. Develop a frequency distribution for each bread type.

c. Which bread type has the highest standard deviation in demand?

d. Which bread type has the greatest relative variability? Which type has the lowest relative variability?

e. Assuming that these sample data are representative of demand during the year, determine how many loaves of each type of bread should be made such that demand would be met on at least 75% of the days during the year.

f. Create a new variable called Total Loaves Sold. On which day of the week is the average for total loaves sold the highest?

3-38. The Woodmill Company makes windows and door trim products. The first step in the process is to rip dimension (2 × 8, 2 × 10, etc.) lumber into narrower pieces. This is an extremely important step since the value of the finished product depends on the rip width decisions that are made. Currently, the company uses a manual process in which an experienced operator quickly looks at a board and determines what rip widths to use. The decision is based on the knots and defects in the wood. The more defect-free pieces that can be cut, the higher the value generated from the board.

A company in Oregon has developed an optical scanner that can be used to determine the rip widths. The scanner is programmed to recognize defects and to determine rip widths that will "optimize" the value of the board. A test run of 100 boards was run through the scanner. The rip widths were identified. However, the boards were not actually ripped. A lumber grader determined the resulting values for each of the 100 boards assuming that the rips determined by the scanner had been made. Next, the same 100 boards were manually ripped using the normal process. The grader then determined the value for each board after the manual rip process was completed. The resulting data, in the file **Woodmill**, consist of manual rip values and scanner rip values for each of the 100 boards.

a. Develop a frequency distribution for the board values for the scanner and the manual process.

b. Compute appropriate descriptive statistics for both manual and scanner values. Use these data along with the frequency distribution developed in part a to prepare a written report that describes the results of the test. Be sure to include in your report a conclusion regarding whether the scanner outperforms the manual process.

3-39. Referring to Problem 38 involving the Woodmill Company, convert each of the two variables to z-values.

a. Which process, scanner or manual, generated the most values that were more than two standard deviations from the mean?

b. Which of the two processes has the least relative variability?

3-40. Referring to Problem 38 involving the Woodmill Company, since the same boards were used to generate the scanner and manual values, the samples are said to be dependent samples. Thus, in analyzing the effectiveness of the scanner, it would make sense to compute the paired difference (scanner − manual) between the two variables.

a. Create a new paired difference variable that is scanner value − manual value. Develop a frequency distribution for this variable.

b. Referring to the paired difference variable that you developed in part a, compute the mean and standard deviation.

c. Referring to parts a and b, convert each paired difference value to a z-score. Develop a frequency distribution for the z-score.

d. Based upon the results from parts a through c, develop a report to the Woodmill management indicating whether the company should consider purchasing the scanner. In your report, point out any other information that is needed before a final decision is made.

■ SUMMARY AND CONCLUSIONS

Transforming data into useful information is an important activity for business decision makers. Chapter 3 has introduced a variety of numerical measures that can be used either by themselves or in conjunction with the graphical techniques introduced in Chapter 2. These measures can be computed for the population as a whole or from a sample taken from the population.

Two main categories of measures were introduced. These were measures of the center and measures of spread or variation. The two most frequently used measures of central location are the mean and the median. Generally the mean is preferred except when the data are highly skewed. Other measures of location including the mode, percentiles, and quartiles were introduced.

The most frequently used measure of variation is the standard deviation. This measure uses all the data and measures the spread of the individual observations around the mean. Other measures include the range and interquartile range.

When the numerical measures introduced in this chapter are effectively combined with the graphical techniques from Chapter 2, you will have the capability of transforming data into information. These concepts and skills will be utilized throughout the remainder of this text and will be highly valuable to you in other classes and in your careers after graduation.

EQUATIONS

Population Mean

$$\mu = \frac{\sum_{i=1}^{N} x_i}{N} \qquad \text{3-1}$$

Sample Mean

$$\bar{x} = \frac{\sum_{i=1}^{n} x_i}{n} \qquad \text{3-2}$$

Percentile Location Value

$$i = \frac{p}{100} n \qquad \text{3-3}$$

Range

$$R = \text{Maximum Value} - \text{Minimum Value} \qquad \text{3-4}$$

Interquartile Range

$$\text{Interquartile Range} = \text{Third Quartile} - \text{First Quartile} \qquad \text{3-5}$$

Population Variance

$$\sigma^2 = \frac{\sum_{i=1}^{N} (x_i - \mu)^2}{N} \qquad \text{3-6}$$

Population Standard Deviation

$$\sigma = \sqrt{\frac{\sum_{i=1}^{N} (x_i - \mu)^2}{N}} \qquad \text{3-7}$$

Sample Variance

$$s^2 = \frac{\sum_{i=1}^{n} (x_i - \bar{x})^2}{n - 1} \qquad \text{3-8}$$

Sample Standard Deviation

$$s = \sqrt{\frac{\sum_{i=1}^{n} (x_i - \bar{x})^2}{n - 1}} \qquad \text{3-9}$$

Population Coefficient of Variation

$$CV = \frac{\sigma}{\mu}(100\%) \qquad \text{3-10}$$

Sample Coefficient of Variation

$$CV = \frac{s}{\bar{x}}(100\%) \qquad \text{3-11}$$

Standardized Population Data Value

$$z = \frac{x - \mu}{\sigma} \qquad \text{3-12}$$

Standardized Sample Data Value

$$z = \frac{x - \bar{x}}{s} \qquad \text{3-13}$$

■ KEY TERMS

Coefficient of Variation—The ratio of the standard deviation to the mean expressed as a percentage. The coefficient of variation is used to measure the relative variation in the data.

Data Array—Data that have been arranged in numerical order.

Empirical Rule—If the data distribution is bell-shaped, then the interval:

$\mu \pm 1\sigma$ contains approximately 68% of the values in the population or the sample

$\mu \pm 2\sigma$ contains approximately 95% of the values in the population or the sample

$\mu \pm 3\sigma$ contains virtually all of the data values in the population or the sample

Interquartile Range—The interquartile range is a measure of variation that is determined by computing the difference between the first and third quartiles.

Left-Skewed Data—A data distribution is left skewed if the mean for the data is smaller than the median.

Mean—A numerical measure of the center of a set of quantitative measures computed by dividing the sum of the values by the number of variables in the data.

Median—A center value that divides a data array into two halves.

Mode—The value in a data set that occurs most frequently.

Parameter—A measure computed from the entire population. As long as the population does not change, the value of the parameter will not change.

Percentiles—The pth percentile in a data array is a value that divides the data set into two parts. The lower segment contains at least p% and the upper segment contains at least $(100 - p)$% of the data. The 50th percentile is the median.

Quartiles—Quartiles in a data array are those values that divide the data set into four equal-sized groups. The median corresponds to the second quartile.

Range—The range is a measure of variation which is computed by finding the difference between the maximum and minimum values in a data set.

Right-Skewed Data—A data distribution is right skewed if the mean for the data is larger than the median.

Skewed Data—Data sets that are not symmetric. For skewed data, the mean will be larger or smaller than the median.

Standard Deviation—The standard deviation is the positive square root of the variance.

Standardized Data Values—The number of standard deviations a value is from the mean. The standardized data values are sometimes referred to as z-scores.

Statistic—A measure computed from a sample that has been selected from a population. The value of the statistic will depend on which sample is selected.

Symmetric Data—Data sets whose values are evenly spread around the center. For symmetric data, the mean and the median are equal.

Tchebysheff's Theorem—Regardless of how the data are distributed, *at least* $(1 - 1/k^2)$ of the values will fall within k standard deviations of the mean.

Variance—The population variance is the average of the squared distances of the data values from the mean.

Variation—A set of data exhibits variation if all the data are not the same value.

CHAPTER EXERCISES

SOLVED PROBLEMS ON YOUR CD-ROM

Try the WORKED-OUT EXERCISES and BUSINESS APPLICATIONS on the CD-ROM.

Conceptual Questions

3-41. Discuss the circumstances under which you would prefer the median to the mean as a measure of location.

3-42. Considering the relative positions of the mean, median, and mode:
   a. Draw a symmetrical distribution and label the three measures of location.
   b. Draw a left-skewed distribution and label the three measures of location.
   c. Draw a right-skewed distribution and label the three measures of location.

3-43. The marketing manager for Sweetright Cola has just received the results of two separate marketing studies performed in the Ohio Valley market region. One study was based on a random sample of 300 people and the study indicated that the mean income is $2,450.00 per month. The second study was based on a random sample of 400 people and indicated that the mean income in the region is $2,375.00 per month. The manager is confused. Should he have expected the two samples to yield exactly the same mean? Why or why not? Also, is it reasonable to believe that a sample mean should exactly equal the mean of the population? Discuss.

3-44. Discuss the advantages and disadvantages of using the range as a measure of spread in a set of data.

3-45. At almost every university in the United States, the university computes student grade point averages. The following scale is typically used by universities:

A = 4 points	B = 3 points	C = 2 points	D = 1 point	F = 0 points

Discuss what if any problems might exist when GPAs for two students are compared. What about comparing GPAs for students from two different universities?

3-46. Why is it inappropriate to compare the standard deviations of two or more distributions with different means? What measure is more appropriate? Discuss this measure and indicate what large versus small values of the measure imply.

3-47. Explain in your own terms, and through an example that you develop, why the standard deviation is considered a measure of variation.

Business Applications

3-48. Ivan Horton is a building contractor whose company builds many homes every year. In planning for each job, Ivan needs some idea about the direct labor hours required to build a home. He has collected sample information on the labor hours for 10 jobs during the past year.

645	802	791	631	653	542	418	695	552	575

a. Calculate the mean for this sample and explain what it represents.
b. Calculate the median for this sample.
c. Calculate the variance and standard deviation.
d. Ivan has asked that you determine the number of laborers he should hire. He wishes to be able to finish at least 75% of the houses he contracts to build within 2 weeks. His workers work 40 hours a week.

3-49. Refer to Problem 48. If Ivan had to select the mean or the median as the measure of location for direct labor hours, what factors about each should he consider before making the decision? Which measure would you suggest he use?

3-50. Refer to Problem 48. Assume the mean and standard deviation for the sample data are representative of the corresponding population values.
   a. Use the Empirical Rule to calculate the values between which 68, 95, and 100% of the data would be contained.
   b. Based on these sample data, does it appear that the Empirical Rule is appropriate to use? Why or why not?

3-51. The Hillside Bowling Alley manager has selected a random sample of her league customers. She asked them to record the number of lines they bowl during the month of December, including both league and open bowling. The reason for her interest in these data is that she is planning on offering a special discount to customers who bowl over a specified number of games each month. The sample of eight people produced the following data:

13	32	12	9	16	17	16	12

a. Compute the mean for these sample data.
b. Compute the median for these sample data.
c. Compute the mode for these sample data.
d. Calculate the variance and standard deviation for these sample data.
e. Note that one person in the sample bowled 32 lines. What effect, if any, does this large value have on each of the three measures of location? Discuss.
f. For these sample data, which measure of location provides the best measure of the center of the data? Discuss.
g. Given these sample data, suppose the manager wishes to give discounts to bowlers in the top quartile. What should the minimum number of games bowled be in order to receive a discount?

3-52. Referring to Problem 51, suppose the manager collected data for a second bowling alley owned by her company. These data showed an average of 10 lines bowled with a standard deviation of 2. Do the bowlers at this second alley exhibit relatively more variation in the number of games bowled in December than at the Hillside Alley? Use the appropriate measures to make your point.

3-53. The Wilnet Development Company has proposed building a new housing development in Warwick, Rhode Island. The city's planning department requires that the developer conduct a traffic study as part of the project planning. One part of that traffic study involves analyzing the trips from home made by residents in the "impact area"" located near the proposed project location. The Wilnet Company has selected 15 families at random from those in the "impact area" and has asked them to keep track of their trips from home during the next week. The data returned to the Wilnet Company are shown.

38	44	11	26	19	13	45	27	11	19	19	26	20	19	34

a. Compute the mean for these data and describe what it measures.
b. Compute the median for these data and compare it with the mean found in part a.
c. Compute the mode for these data.
d. Compute the sample standard deviation and discuss what it measures.
e. Write a short report to submit to the city's planning department describing the sample data. Use any graphical techniques you think would be helpful in transforming the data into useful information, as well as any measures of location and spread.
f. Compute the interquartile range for these data, and discuss why it is often preferred as a measure of variation over the range.

3-54. The Indiana Transportation Department recently set up a speed check station on one of the interstate highways and collected speed data on 12 vehicles selected at random during a 4-hour period. The data collected (in miles per hour) are:

62	75	81	64	81	66	70	70	69	73	72	75

a. Compute the average speed for the sample.
b. Compute the median speed for the sample data.
c. Compute the mode for these sample data.
d. Compute the variance and standard deviation of these sample data.
e. If 85% of the drivers on a specified stretch of highway are failing to obey a posted speed limit, the Highway Patrol deems this section to be a target for increased enforcement. The speed limit for this stretch of highway is 65 mph. Should the Highway Patrol target this stretch of highway?
f. Determine a speed limit that, according to the preceding data, would change your conclusion in part e.
g. As mentioned, the speed limit on the highway where the data were collected is 65 mph. Write a short report describing the sample data, and include both graphical analyses and measures of location and spread. The report should address the issue of whether the vehicles traveling on this highway tend to obey the speed limit.

3-55. The Norton Oil Company has 20 oil wells operating in the Gulf of Mexico. The output of these 20 oil wells has been recorded in terms of barrels per day pumped, as follows.

800	100	230	700	1,900	300	400	700	250	500
340	670	340	250	450	700	500	200	75	1,200

   a. Compute the mean daily production for these 20 wells. Assume the data represent the population of interest.

   b. Determine the median oil production per day for this population of oil wells.

   c. Norton Oil will cease oil production in those oil wells that are below the 33rd percentile. Determine which oil wells will be closed.

3-56. Refer to the Norton Oil Company data in Problem 55. A simple random sample of six oil wells was selected from this population. This sample was

700	700	670	700	1,200	450

   a. Describe what is meant by a simple random sample and discuss how such a sample would be selected in this situation.

   b. Compute the median for the sample.

   c. Compute the mean for the sample.

   d. Write a short report comparing the sample measures of location with the population measures.

   e. Does it trouble you that there are three "700s" contained in the sample? Before answering this question, make sure that you review the definition of a random sample. Explain why you are either troubled or not troubled.

3-57. Since deregulation has taken place, the airline industry has undergone substantial changes with respect to ticket prices. Many discount fares are available if a customer knows how to obtain the discount. Many travelers complain that they get a different price every time they call. The American Consumer Institute recently priced tickets between Spokane, Washington, and St. Louis, Missouri. The passenger was to fly coach class, round trip, staying 7 days. Calls were made directly to airlines and to travel agents with the following results. Note that the data reflect round-trip airfare.

$229.00	$345.00	$599.00	$229.00	$429.00	$605.00
$339.00	$339.00	$229.00	$279.00	$344.00	$407.00

   a. Compute the mean quoted airfare.

   b. Compute the variance and standard deviation in airfares quoted. Treat the data as a sample.

3-58. Refer to Problem 57 and suppose a second study was done where airfares were quoted between Miami, Florida, and Kansas City, Missouri. The average price quoted was $443 with a standard deviation of $58. One travel agent was involved in both studies. For the flight between Spokane and St. Louis, this agent quoted $299. For the flight between Miami and Kansas City, she quoted $502.

   a. For which route was this agent relatively closer to the mean?

   b. Which route has relatively the larger variation in air fares?

3-59. The manager of the Clark Fork Station Restaurant recently selected a random sample of 18 customers and kept track of how long the customers were required to wait from the time they arrived at the restaurant until they were actually served dinner. This study resulted from several complaints the manager had received from customers saying that their wait time was unduly long and that it appeared that the objective was to keep people waiting in the lounge for as long as possible to increase the lounge business. The following data were recorded, with time measured in minutes.

34	24	43	56	74	20	19	33	55
43	54	34	27	34	36	24	54	39

   a. Compute the mean waiting time for this sample of customers.

   b. Compute the median waiting time for this sample of customers.

   c. Compute the variance and standard deviation of waiting time for this sample of customers.

   d. Develop a frequency distribution using 6 classes each with a class width of 10. Make the lower limit of the first class 15.

   e. Develop a frequency histogram for the frequency distribution.

   f. The manager is considering giving a complimentary drink to customers whose waiting time is longer than the third quartile. Determine the minimum number of minutes a customer would have to wait in order to receive a complimentary drink.

3-60. Stock investors often look to beat the performance of the S&P 500 Index, which generally serves as a yardstick for the market as a whole. The following table shows a comparison of five-year cumulative total shareholder returns for Idaho Power Company common stock (NYSE Symbol: IDA), the S&P 500 Index, and the Edison Electric Institute (EEI) 100 Electric Utilities Index. The data assume that $100 was invested on December 31, 1992, with returns compounded monthly. Construct appropriate statistical measures that illustrate the performance of the three investment options for the years 1992 through 1997. How well has Idaho Power Company performed during this period compared to the S&P 500? How well has it performed relative to its industry?

YEAR	IDAHO POWER	S&P 500	EEI 100 ELECTRIC UTILITIES
1992	$100.00	$100.00	$100.00
1993	117.38	110.08	111.15
1994	97.62	111.53	98.29
1995	134.11	153.45	128.78
1996	147.92	188.69	130.32
1997	189.73	251.63	166.00

3-61. The C. A. Whitman Investment Company recently offered two mutual funds to its customers. A mutual fund is a group of stocks and bonds that is managed by an investment company. Individuals purchase shares of the mutual fund, and the investment company uses the money to buy stocks. Many investors feel comfortable with a mutual fund because their money is not tied up in one or two stocks but is spread over many stocks, thereby, they hope, reducing the risk.

Each of the two mutual funds offered by C. A. Whitman currently has 60 stocks. During the past 6 months the average increase in stock prices in fund A has been $3.30, with a standard deviation of $1.25. The stocks in fund B have shown an average increase of $8.00, with a standard deviation of $3.50.

   a. Based on this information, which of the two funds has stocks that have shown the greater relative variability?

   b. Explain why we cannot simply compare standard deviations in this case.

3-62. The Smithfield Agricultural Company operates in the Midwest. The company owns and leases a total of 34,000 acres of prime farmland. Most of the crops are grain. Because of its size, the company can afford to do a great amount of testing to determine what seed types produce the greatest yields. Recently, the company tested three types of corn seed on test plots. The following values were observed after the first test year.

	SEED TYPE A	SEED TYPE B	SEED TYPE C
Mean bushels/acre	88	56	100
Standard deviation	25	15	16

   a. Based on the results of this testing, which seed seems to produce the greatest average yield per acre? Comment on the type of testing controls that should have been used to make this study valid.

   b. Suppose the company is interested in consistency. Which seed type shows the least relative variability?

   c. Using the Empirical Rule, describe the production distribution for each of the three seed types.

   d. Suppose you were a farmer and had to obtain at least 135 bushels/acre to avoid bankruptcy. Which seed type would you plant? Explain your choice.

   e. Rework your answer to part d assuming the farmer needed 115 bushels/acre instead.

3-63. The B. L. Williams Company makes tennis balls. The company has two manufacturing plants. The plant in Portland, Maine, is a unionized plant with an average daily production of 34,000 tennis balls. The output varies, with a standard deviation of 4,500 tennis balls per day. The San Antonio, Texas, plant is nonunion and quite a bit smaller than the Portland plant. The San Antonio plant averages 12,000 tennis balls per day, with a standard deviation of 3,000.

Recently, the production manager was giving a speech to the Association of Sporting Goods Manufacturers. In that speech he stated that the B. L. Williams Company has been having real problems with its union plant maintaining consistency in production output and that the problem was not so great at the nonunion plant.

Based on the production data, was the manager justified in drawing the conclusions he made in the speech? Discuss and support your conclusion with any appropriate calculations.

3-64. A survey of local airline passengers shows that the mean height of male passengers is 69.5 inches with a standard deviation of 2.5 inches. The mean weight is 177 pounds with a standard deviation of 12 pounds. Which of the 2 distributions has the greater relative variability?

3-65. The Internal Revenue Service has come under a great deal of criticism in recent years for various actions it is purported to have taken against U.S. citizens related to collecting federal income taxes. The IRS is also criticized for the complexity of the tax code although the tax laws are actually written by congressional staff and passed by Congress. For the past few years, one of the country's biggest tax preparing companies has sponsored an event in which 50 certified public accountants (CPAs) from all sizes of CPA firms are asked to determine the tax owed for a fictitious citizen. The IRS is also asked to determine the "correct" tax owed. Last year, the "correct" figure stated by the IRS was $11,560. The file, **Taxes**, and the following display contain the data for the 50 accountants.

CPA FIRM	TAXES OWED	CPA FIRM	TAXES OWED
1	$16,637	26	$6,087
2	11,804	27	8,711
3	8,915	28	9,753
4	9,915	29	10,282
5	14,787	30	13,385
6	11,058	31	11,326
7	15,662	32	16,183
8	13,293	33	14,232
9	15,970	34	8,482
10	9,103	35	16,274
11	13,223	36	12,758
12	7,852	37	9,411
13	9,200	38	14,632
14	13,607	39	12,655
15	13,793	40	6,403
16	9,048	41	11,260
17	14,487	42	8,478
18	9,409	43	11,586
19	13,342	44	10,299
20	14,093	45	7,805
21	12,836	46	13,422
22	9,376	47	10,628
23	10,819	48	9,300
24	10,473	49	5,429
25	3,677	50	6,064

   a. Compute a new variable that is the difference between the IRS number and the number determined by each accountant.

   b. Develop a frequency distribution for this new variable computed in part a.

   c. Determine the mean, median, and standard deviation for the new variable computed in part a.

d. Given the data from the 50 CPA firms, at what percentile is the true value of $11,560? Describe what this implies about the agreement between returns prepared by the IRS and those prepared by tax consultants around the country.

3-66. Refer to Problem 65:

a. Using the original tax owed variable, convert the IRS "correct" amount to a z-score using the mean and standard deviation from the CPA data.

b. What, if any, relationship does this z-score have to the mean value for the new variable created in Problem 65? Discuss.

3-67. The Soft-Sole Shoe Company is considering opening a new shoe outlet in a U.S. city. As part of the company's analysis, the managers have gained access to data on a target group of cities. To avoid bias, the names of the cities have been omitted from the data file, **Cities**. The first step in the analysis is to analyze the populations of these potential franchise locations.

a. Compute the appropriate descriptive statistical measures for this variable.

b. Construct a frequency histogram.

c. The company is interested in locating outlets only in cities with populations above the 84th percentile. Determine this value for the data provided.

3-68. Referring to Problem 67, the Soft-Sole Shoe Company knows that income levels in a city will be important to the success of the new store. Locate the income variables for manufacturing workers and for white-collar workers.

a. Develop a frequency histogram for both variables.

b. Compute the means, medians, and modes for each variable.

c. Convert each income to a z-score within its own group.

d. If the Soft-Sole Shoe Company will consider only companies with white-collar and blue-collar incomes over 2.0 standard deviations above the mean for the entire group, which cities (by number) are still in the running?

3-69. Refer to Problem 68 and locate the income variables for manufacturing workers and for white-collar workers.

a. Compute a new variable that is the paired difference between manufacturing and white-collar incomes.

b. Construct a frequency distribution for the paired difference variable.

c. Compute the descriptive measures for this new variable and write a short report which summarizes your findings. Discuss primarily what your measures indicate about whether manufacturing jobs are more lucrative than white-collar incomes, any extreme values, and the proportion of cities in which manufacturing incomes are larger than white-collar incomes.

3-70. The data in the file named **Fast100** were collected by D. L. Green & Associates, a regional investment management company that specializes in working with clients who wish to invest in smaller companies with high growth potential.

To aid the investment firm in locating appropriate investments for its clients, Sandra Williams, an assistant client manager, put together the database on 100 fast-growing companies. The database consists of data on 8 variables for each of the 100 companies. Note that in some cases data are not available. A code of -99 has been used to signify missing data. These data will have to be omitted from any calculations.

a. Select the variable, sales. Develop a frequency distribution and histogram for sales.

b. Compute the mean, median, and standard deviation for the sales variable.

c. Determine the interquartile range for the sales variable.

d. Each year a goal is set for sales. Next year's goal will be to have an average sales figure that is at this year's 65th percentile. Identify next year's sales goal.

3-71. Referring to Problem 70, Sandra Williams has also been asked to prepare an analysis on the earnings per share.

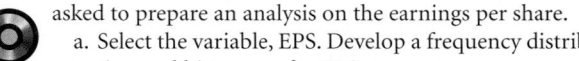

a. Select the variable, EPS. Develop a frequency distribution and histogram for EPS.

b. Compute the mean, median, and standard deviation for the EPS variable.

c. Determine the interquartile range for the EPS variable.

d. Sandra Williams is certain that the number of negative earnings per share will stand out in the data. She, therefore, wishes to determine the largest negative value and determine its percentile. Provide these measures to her for her report.

e. Because D. L. Green & Associates specialize in small, high growth potential companies, they expect their investments will produce larger variations in EPS than in more conservative portfolios. Thus, losses may be high but earnings might also be high. They like to look at the quartiles to identify the high and low portions of the EPS data. Provide these and comment on whether their strategy results in just as high a proportion of large gains as large losses.

3-72. Referring to Problems 70 and 71, the management team at D. L. Green & Associates was very impressed with Sandra's analysis of the sales and EPS data. They have now asked her to use appropriate numerical and graphical techniques to analyze all the data in the file on these 100 companies and prepare a report that can be used effectively to pull together the information contained in the data to analyze these fast growing companies.

a. One specific analysis that is needed is a descriptive breakdown on all the variables by stock market code. Are there any other breakdowns that can be performed which will allow you to dig deeper into the data?

b. As a final task, select three companies you would recommend for investments.

3-73. The following table contains selected information from the 1997 annual report for McCormick & Company, Incorporated, the leader in the manufacture, marketing, and distribution of spices, seasonings, and flavors for the food industry. Use the table data to answer the following questions. (All values are in millions.)

YEAR	NET SALES	CAPITAL EXPENDITURES	CURRENT DEBT	LONG-TERM DEBT	SHARE-HOLDERS' EQUITY
1988	$1,099.1	$50.4	$ 49.5	$229.4	$294.3
1989	1,110.2	53.4	20.3	210.5	346.2
1990	1,166.2	58.4	30.4	311.5	364.4
1991	1,276.3	73.0	78.2	207.6	389.2
1992	1,323.9	79.3	122.6	201.0	437.9
1993	1,400.9	76.1	84.7	346.4	466.8
1994	1,529.4	87.7	214.0	374.3	490.0
1995	1,691.1	82.1	297.3	349.1	519.3
1996	1,732.5	74.7	108.9	291.2	450.0
1997	1,801.0	43.9	121.3	276.5	393.1

a. For the years 1988 through 1997, compute the mean, median, and standard deviation for each variable assuming that the 10 years represent a sample.

b. Convert each value to a z-value. Then analyze the z-values for each year. Treating all variables as being on an equal footing, which year seems to stand out as most unique from the others?

3-74. The file **Home-Prices** contains information about single-family housing prices in 100 metropolitan areas in the United States. The price variable represents the median price of homes in each area. In preparation for a speech to a national real estate association, you plan to use these data to illustrate real estate patterns. Discuss why it might be appropriate to have recorded the median home price in each area rather than the mean.

a. Compute the mean of the median home prices. Is this a reasonable measure to compute? Why or why not?

b. Construct a frequency histogram for the annualized price change variable for the years 1993 through 1998.

c. Referring to part b, compute the mean, median, and standard deviation for the annualized price change of homes in the sampled areas.

d. As an investment, you have purchased a house for $109,333. This price just happens to be the median price of homes in your metropolitan area. You were hoping that you could obtain a quick profit and sell your house for $120,000. Considering the analysis you have performed in the previous steps, do you think this is realistic? Support your answer with reasons and calculations.

3-75. The commercial banking industry is undergoing rapid changes due to advances in technology and competitive pressures in the financial services sector. The data file **Banks** contains selected information tabulated by *Fortune* magazine concerning the revenues, profitability, and number of employees for the 51 largest U.S. commercial banks in terms of revenues. Use the information in this file to complete the following:

a. Compute the mean, median, and standard deviation for the three variables: revenues, profits, and number of employees.

b. Convert the data for each variable to a z-value. Consider Mellon Bank Corporation headquartered in Pittsburgh. How does it compare to the average bank in the study on the three variables? Discuss.

c. As you can see by examining the data and by looking at the statistics computed in part a, not all banks had the same revenues, same profits, or the same number of employees. Which variable had the greatest relative variation among the banks in the study?

d. Calculate a new variable: profits per employee. Develop a frequency distribution and a histogram for this new variable. Also compute the mean, median, and standard deviation for the new variable. Write a short report that describes the profits per employee for the banks.

e. Referring to part d, how many banks had a profit per employee ratio which exceeded two standard deviations from the mean?

3-76. The file **Industrial Rents** contains the average annual cost per square foot for "Class A" warehouses in 51 selected cities for the fourth quarter for the years 1996 and 1997. Use this information to do the following:

a. Construct a histogram of square foot costs for each time period.

b. Compute the mean, median, and standard deviation for cost per square foot.

c. Use the information generated in parts a and b to prepare a report on the square foot costs for Class A warehouses in the 51 cities in the sample.

CASE 3-A

Wilson Corporation

The certified letter was delivered about 4:00 PM to Andrew Wilson, CEO and principal owner of the Wilson Corporation. It was from the State Department of Environmental Services and it sent shivers down Andrew's spine. In bold-faced type at the top of the letter was the message:

"Notice of Water Quality Violation—Wilson Corporation"

The letter went on to outline the situation. The state had performed tests at the outflow location from Wilson's main processing plant and found problems with nitrates and pH levels. A hearing on the matter was scheduled in 2 weeks to outline the issues and to assess damages to be paid by the Wilson Corporation. In the meantime, all effluent from the plant was to be immediately halted.

Accompanying the letter was a computer disk file containing data from 95 water samples selected at the Wilson plant over a 3-week period. The file is labeled **Wilson Water**. Figure 3-14 illustrates the type of data that was included in the file.

Andrew reached for his phone to make two calls. The first was to Randy Glover, his production scheduler. He told Randy the problem and indicated that he was to immediately halt production and to schedule an employee meeting at 8:00 the next morning.

The second call went to Jennifer Scranton, the company's environmental liaison. Andrew explained to Jennifer the essence of the letter and the action he was taking with regard to production. He wanted Jennifer to halt all other work and

	A	B	C	D	E	F
1	Temp	pH	Nitrates	Phosphates	Oxygen	CO2
2	16.5	7.82	8.2	0.15	7.00	13
3	16.1	7.9	6.7	0.52	10.00	37
4	16.6	7.9	7.3	0.54	10.00	10
5	17	7.82	6.8	0.42	10.00	10
6	16.5	7.8	7.1	0.66	9.00	15
7	16.2	7.5	7.4	0.47	10.00	15
8	16.4	7.6	6.4	0.35	10.00	10
9	16	7.5	7.2	0.79	9.00	10
10	17	7.6	2.5	0.32	8.00	10

FIGURE 3-14   Excel Worksheet for Water Samples Data

immediately perform an analysis on the sample data supplied by the state. Andrew wanted a comprehensive descriptive analysis of the data as soon as possible so he could prepare for the hearing with the state.

CASE 3-B

Holcome Financial Planners

Marsha Holcome founded Holcome Financial Planners nearly 3 years ago after working for Merrill-Lynch for over 14 years. Although she was able to bring several clients with her, she found that getting the business started was pretty much a "chicken and the egg" problem. Potential customers would ask her how much money she had under management. When she responded with a relatively small amount, the customers would tell her to call back when she had a bigger portfolio and a better track record. However, without customers she couldn't have much money under management, so it was a circular problem.

Marsha countered this problem by attempting to provide superior service compared to major brokerage firms. One talent on which she really prided herself was her ability to analyze an industry. Recently she had been in a meeting with a potential client who was interested in the computer industry. At the close of the meeting Marsha agreed to prepare an analysis of the industry to show the client what she could do.

Marsha's assistant collected appropriate data using Standard and Poor's industry publications and generated a data file called **Computer Industry**. Figure 3-15 illustrates the type of data that were collected. Now Marsha had to get

FIGURE 3-15
Excel Worksheet for Computer Industry Financial Data

	A	B	C	D	E	F	G	H	I	J	K
1	Company	Type of Company	Risk	Rev (millions) 97	Rev (millions) 96	% change	Oper Inc. 97	Oper Inc 96	% change	Recent Price	Current Ratio
2	Compaq Computer	1	2	24584	18109	1.36	3532	2162	1.634	33.50	2.3
3	Dell Computer	1	2	12327	7759	1.59	1383	761	1.817	66.00	1.5
4	IBM	1	2	78508	75947	1.03	13116	12272	1.069	133.50	1.2
5	Micron Electronics	1	3	1956	1765	1.11	172	127	1.354	16.75	1.6
6	Apple Computer	1	2	7081	9833	0.72	-284	-1047	0.271	17.13	1.9
7	Gateway 2000, Inc.	1	3	6294	5035	1.25	377	418	0.902	54.88	1.5
8	Hewlett-Packard	1	2	42895	38420	1.12	5895	5023	1.174	54.88	1.9

121

to work. She wanted to prepare a first-rate descriptive analysis of the data using graphs, charts, and appropriate numerical measures. It would be important to break out the analysis by type of computer company, too. She decided to develop a clear written narrative to go along with the descriptive information. A key to success was the appearance of the finished product. It had to have "eye appeal" as well as be informative.

CASE 3-C

AJ's Fitness Center

A. J. Reeser was mildly surprised at the quality of the report prepared for him by the intern from the local university. (Refer to Case 2A in Chapter 2. Data file is **AJFitness**.) The report contained a wide variety of informative charts and graphs that effectively displayed the data. When A. J. had given the assignment to the intern, he had asked the intern to limit the descriptive analysis to charts and graphs. He wasn't sure what to expect. Now that he could see how good "this kid" was, A. J. wanted more analysis.

When the knock on the door came, A. J. realized how quickly time had passed as he was reading the survey report. As the intern settled into the chair to the right of A. J.'s desk,

the phone rang but A. J. ignored it. He stretched out his hand to the young intern and congratulated him on such a fine job.

"Now that I know how good you are, I need you to take this project a step further." A. J. said with a big grin. "What I need you to do now is combine the graphical analysis you have already done with a complete numerical analysis of the data. I want you to fully analyze this survey using whatever statistics will help and put your work in a full report."

After discussing the graphs and charts for a few minutes, A. J. indicated that he would like the revised report next week and suggested that they meet for dinner next Thursday to take a look at it.

■ GENERAL REFERENCES

1. Albright, S. Christian, Wayne L. Winston, and Christopher Zappe, *Data Analysis and Decision Making with Microsoft Excel* (Pacific Grove, CA: Duxbury, 1999).
2. Berenson, Mark L., and David M. Levine, *Basic Business Statistics: Concepts and Applications,* 7th ed. (Upper Saddle River, NJ: Prentice Hall, 1999).
3. Dodge, Mark, and Craig Stinson, *Running Microsoft Excel 2000* (Redmond, WA: Microsoft Press, 1999).
4. *Microsoft Excel 2000* (Redmond, WA: Microsoft Corporation, 1999).
5. *Minitab for Windows Version 13* (State College, PA: Minitab, Inc., 2000).
6. Siegel, Andrew F., *Practical Business Statistics,* 4th ed. (Burr Ridge, IL: Irwin, 2000).
7. Tukey, John W., *Exploratory Data Analysis* (Reading, MA: Addison-Wesley, 1977).

USING PROBABILITY AND DISCRETE PROBABILITY DISTRIBUTIONS

CHAPTER OUTCOMES:

After studying the material in Chapter 4, you should:

4-1: Understand the three approaches to assessing probabilities.

4-2: Be able to apply the common rules of probability.

4-3: Be able to identify the types of processes that are represented by discrete probability distributions.

4-4: Know how to determine probabilities associated with binomial and Poisson distribution applications.

WHY YOU NEED TO KNOW

Business managers must frequently choose a course of action from among several alternatives in order to move their company closer to its goals and objectives. For example, suppose the quality control manager at the American Plywood plant examines three pieces of plywood to determine whether the thickness of the boards meets specifications. The manager records her findings by labeling a good piece of plywood "G" and a defective piece of plywood "D." For the three pieces of plywood she has just sampled, she obtains the following results: G, D, G. How can this sample help her decide between the two alternatives of closing down the plant to make adjustments to the production equipment, or to keep the plant operating as it is?

Consider a second example in which an accountant randomly examines 15 accounts, and finds 14 of the 15 are accurate. What does this tell him about whether the firm has major problems in its accounting information system?

In both of these cases someone had to make a decision: about equipment operation in one case and an accounting information system in the other. Decision making means selecting among two or more alternatives. To make good decisions, managers must establish general criteria for deciding among these alternatives. Certainly the criteria must somehow be related to the objective of the decision-making situation. This objective may involve revising a plant operation, updating an accounting system, analyzing a profit or sales level, or even creating an orderly situation from near chaos. But good decisions must also be based on correctly using the available information, and initiating that discussion is the purpose of this chapter.

Chapter 1 described how managers must often operate with sample information collected from the population of interest. They are uncertain about the population, but they know a great deal about the sample. Certainly this is the case with our previous examples where we know the number of good sheets of plywood and the number of accurate accounts in the samples. Probability theory allows managers to use this knowledge about samples to make inferences about a population and to have confidence in these inferences.

In Chapter 2, we saw how a frequency distribution transforms raw data into a useful form that provides meaningful insight into the data. Frequency distributions are one way that decision makers deal with uncertainty in their decision environments. Because all managers operate in an uncertain environment, they must be able to make the connection between descriptive statistics and probability. Moving from frequency distributions to *probability distributions* makes this connection.

Constructing and analyzing a frequency distribution for every decision-making situation would be time consuming. Deciding on the correct data-gathering procedures, the appropriate class intervals, and the right methods of presenting the data are not trivial issues. Fortunately, many physical and organizational events that appear to be unrelated have the same underlying characteristics and can be described by the same probability distribution. If decision makers are dealing with an application described by a predetermined *theoretical* probability distribution, they can use a great deal of developmental statistical work already known and save considerable personal effort in analyzing their situation. Therefore, decision makers need to become comfortable with probability distributions if they are to apply them effectively in the decision-making process. Fortunately for both the quality control manager and the accountant, their situations can be described by a well-known probability distribution.

■ 4-1: THE BASICS OF PROBABILITY

Before we can apply *probability* to the decision-making process, we must first understand what it means. The mathematical study of probability originated over 300 years ago. The Chevalier de Méré, a French nobleman, who today would probably own a gaming house in Monte Carlo, began asking questions about games of chance. He was mainly interested in the probability of observing various outcomes (pairs of 1s) when a pair of dice was repeatedly rolled. The French mathematician Blaise Pascal (you may remember studying Pascal's triangle in a mathematics class) with the help of his friend, Pierre de Fermat, was able to answer de Méré's questions. Of course, Pascal began asking more and more complicated questions of himself and his colleagues, which began the formal study of probability.

Important Probability Terms

Several explanations of what probability is have come out of this mathematical study. However, the definition of probability is quite basic.[1]

---

[1]The definition given is for a countable number of events. We will see for continuous variables that an event can have a probability of zero and still occur. Similarly, an event that has a probability of one may not occur.

> **PROBABILITY**
> The chance that a particular event will occur.
>   The probability of an event will be a value in the range 0.00 to 1.00. A value of 0.00 means the event will not occur. A probability of 1.00 means the event will occur. Anything between 0.00 and 1.00 reflects the uncertainty of the event occurring.

EVENTS AND SAMPLE SPACE

As discussed in Chapter 1, data come in many forms and are gathered in many ways. In a business environment, when a sample is selected or a decision is made, there are generally many possible outcomes. In probability language, the process that produces the outcomes is an **experiment**. In business situations, the experiment can range from an investment decision to a personnel decision to a choice of warehouse location. The individual outcomes from an experiment are called **elementary events**.

> **EXPERIMENT**
> A process that produces a single outcome whose result cannot be predicted with certainty.

> **ELEMENTARY EVENTS**
> The most rudimentary outcomes resulting from a simple experiment.
> *e*

The collection of the elementary events is called the **sample space**.

> **SAMPLE SPACE**   *SS*
> The collection of all elementary outcomes that can result from a selection or decision.

The sample space for an experiment consists of all the elementary events that the experiment can produce. A collection of elementary events is called an **event**. An example will help clarify these terms.

> **EVENT**   *E*
> A collection of elementary events.

EXAMPLE 4-1

SAMPLE SPACE

Able Accounting

A regional partner for Able Accounting, a large regional accounting firm, is interested in analyzing the performance of her many audit teams. She is particularly interested in whether the audits are finished by the projected completion date. The partner can define the elementary events for one audit for one team to be:

$$e_1 = \text{Audit done early}$$
$$e_2 = \text{Audit done on time}$$
$$e_3 = \text{Audit done late}$$

The sample space (SS) for the experiment, which would be a single audit, is

$$SS = \{e_1, e_2, e_3\}$$

If the experiment is expanded to include two audits, the sample space is

$$SS = \{e_1, e_2, e_3, e_4, e_5, e_6, e_7, e_8, e_9\}$$

where the events involve what happens on both audits and are defined as:

**Additional
Example 4-a**

Sample Space

ELEMENTARY EVENT	AUDIT 1	AUDIT 2
e_1	early	early
e_2	early	on time
e_3	early	late
e_4	on time	early
e_5	on time	on time
e_6	on time	late
e_7	late	early
e_8	late	on time
e_9	late	late

Here, each elementary event consists of the combined outcomes of audit 1 and audit 2. The manager might be interested in the event "At least one audit is completed late." This event (E) is

$$E = \{e_3, e_6, e_7, e_8, e_9\}$$

MUTUALLY EXCLUSIVE EVENTS

Keeping in mind the definitions for *experiment*, *sample space*, *elementary events*, and *events*, we introduce two additional concepts in the upcoming examples. The first is **mutually exclusive events**.

MUTUALLY EXCLUSIVE EVENTS
Two events are mutually exclusive if the occurrence of one event precludes the occurrence of a second event.

**EXAMPLE
4-2**

**MUTUALLY
EXCLUSIVE EVENTS**

Able Accounting (continued)

Consider again the Able Accounting firm example. The possible elementary events for different audits done by two teams were provided in Example 4-1.

Suppose we define one event as consisting of the elementary events in which at least one of the two audits is late.

$$E_1 = \{e_3, e_6, e_7, e_8, e_9\}$$

Further, suppose we define two more events as follows:

$$E_2 = \text{neither audit is late} = \{e_1, e_2, e_4, e_5\}$$
$$E_3 = \text{both audits are completed at the same time} = \{e_1, e_5, e_9\}$$

Events E_1 and E_2 are mutually exclusive: If E_1 occurs, E_2 cannot occur, and conversely. That is, if at least one audit is late, then it is not also possible for neither audit to be late. This can be verified by observing that no elementary events in E_1 appear in E_2. This provides another way of defining mutually exclusive events: *Two events are mutually exclusive if they have no common elementary events.*

INDEPENDENT AND DEPENDENT EVENTS

The second additional probability concept is that of **independent** versus **dependent events**.

INDEPENDENT EVENTS
Two events are independent if the occurrence of one event in no way influences the probability of the occurrence of the other event.

DEPENDENT EVENTS
Two events are dependent if the occurrence of one event impacts the probability of the other event occurring.

EXAMPLE 4-3

INDEPENDENT AND DEPENDENT EVENTS

Able Accounting *(continued)*

Return to the Able Accounting example. The experiment is to check the completion times of two audits that had been assigned to different teams. Each pair of audits would be one trial of the experiment. Suppose that two audits are checked and the resulting elementary event is that both audits are late:

ELEMENTARY EVENT	AUDIT 1	AUDIT 2
e_9	late	late

If the Able Accounting manager examines a second pair of audits, one elementary event from the sample space $\{e_1, e_2, \ldots, e_9\}$ will occur. The elementary events for the two experiments would be independent if the probability of the occurrence of e_i for the pair of audits in the second experiment is in no way influenced by elementary event e_9 occurring for the first pair of audits.

This might be the case if the problems that caused the first pair of audits to be late had no impact on the second pair of audits. On the other hand, if the fact that the first pair of audits was late caused the accountants to work overtime on the second audits to make sure the same didn't happen, the trials would be considered dependent.

EXAMPLE 4-4

INDEPENDENT AND DEPENDENT EVENTS

Assembly Line Operation

Another example of dependence and independence might be an assembly line operation. Each item produced could be an experimental trial. On each trial the outcome is either a *good* or a *defective* item. Thus, the sample space is

$$SS = \{good, \ defective\}$$

As long as the machine is properly adjusted, it may produce some good outcomes and some defective outcomes with no apparent pattern, or dependency, between trials. That is, the production of one good item has no influence on the probability of the outcome of subsequent trials. However, if the machine goes out of adjustment, problems begin to occur. A defective item may cause still further adjustment problems and increase the chances that subsequent items will be defective. In this case, the trials are dependent because the probability of the outcome of one trial is in some way influenced by the outcome of a previous trial.

Methods of Assigning Probability

Part of the confusion surrounding probability may be due to the fact that probability means different things to different people. There are three common ways to assign probability to events: *classical probability assessment, relative frequency of occurrence,* and *subjective probability assessment.* The following notation is used when we refer to the probability of an event:

$$P(E_i) = \text{probability of event } E_i \text{ occurring.}$$

CLASSICAL PROBABILITY ASSESSMENT

The first method of probability measurement is **classical probability**, or *a priori* probability.

> **CLASSICAL PROBABILITY ASSESSMENT**
> The method of determining probability based on the ratio of the number of ways the event of interest can occur to the total number of ways *any* event can occur when the individual elementary events are equally likely.

You are probably already familiar with classical probability. It had its beginning with games of chance and is still most often discussed in those terms.

In those situations where all possible elementary events are *equally likely*, the classical probability measurement is defined in Equation 4-1:

CLASSICAL PROBABILITY MEASUREMENT

$$P(E_i) = \frac{\text{Number of ways } E_i \text{ can occur}}{\text{Total number of elementary events}} \qquad \textbf{4-1}$$

EXAMPLE 4-5

CLASSICAL PROBABILITY

Grover Mercantile Co.

Consider the Grover Mercantile Company in Dallas, Texas. Grover operates a large warehouse facility in support of several mail order catalog companies. The catalog companies order merchandise from suppliers who send it to the Grover warehouse. Then when the catalog company gets an order for an item, the order is transmitted electronically to Grover. Once the order is received, Grover locates the item in the warehouse and ships it to the customer directly.

One such item is a video game controller. This controller is actually manufactured by three different companies (A, B, and C) under a common label. When the controllers are received at Grover, they are put in inventory without regard to the original supplier company. Grover buys an equal number of controllers from each supplier.

When an order comes in for the controller, an item is picked from inventory in such a way that each item in inventory has an equal chance of being selected. To assess the chance that a given order is filled with a unit made by Supplier B, we use classical probability as follows:

$$P(\text{Supplier B}) = \frac{1}{3} = 0.333$$

We are interested in the chance that one supplier (B) is the manufacturer. There are three possible suppliers that are equally represented in the inventory. Thus, the classical approach is used as the ratio of the one item of interest over the three possible items that could be selected. There is, therefore, a 33.3% chance that the controller will have been made by Supplier B.

As you can see, the classical approach to probability measurement is fairly straightforward. Many games of chance are based on classical probability assessment. However, classical probability assessment is difficult to apply to most business situations. Rarely are the elementary events equally likely. For instance, you might be thinking of starting a business. The sample space listing the elementary events is:

$$SS = \{\text{Succeed, Fail}\}$$

Would it be reasonable to use classical assessment to determine the probability that your business will succeed? We would make the following assessment:

$$P(\text{Succeed}) = \frac{1}{2}$$

If this were true, then the chance of any business succeeding would be 0.50. Of course this is not true. Too many factors play a part in determining the success or failure of a business. The elementary events (Succeed, Fail) are not equally likely. Instead, we need another method of assessment in these situations.

RELATIVE FREQUENCY OF OCCURRENCE

The **relative frequency of occurrence** approach is based on actual observations.

> **RELATIVE FREQUENCY OF OCCURRENCE**
>
> The method that defines probability as the number of times an event occurs, divided by the total number of times an experiment is performed in a large number of trials.

EXAMPLE 4-6

RELATIVE FREQUENCY OF OCCURRENCE

Hathaway Heating & Air Conditioning

The sales manager at Hathaway Heating & Air Conditioning has recently developed the customer profile shown in Table 4-1. The profile is based on a total of 500 customers. As a promotion for the company, the sales manager plans to randomly select a customer once a month and offer a free service to the customer's heating and/or air-conditioning system. What is the probability that the customer selected is a residential customer? What is the probability that the customer has a heating system?

These probabilities can be assessed using relative frequency of occurrence, as shown in Equation 4-2.

> **RELATIVE FREQUENCY OF OCCURRENCE**
>
> where:
> $$RF(E_i) = \frac{\text{Number of times } E_i \text{ occurs}}{n}$$
>
> E_i = the event of interest
> $RF(E_i)$ = relative frequency of E_i occurring
> n = number of trials

4-2

To determine the probability that the customer selected is residential we determine from Table 4-1 the number of residential customers and divide by the total number of customers, both residential and commercial.

$$P(\text{Residential}) = RF(\text{Residential}) = \frac{400}{500} = 0.80$$

Additional Example 4-b

Relative Frequency of Occurrence, NFL Playing Strategies

Thus, there is an 80% chance the customer selected will be a residential customer.

The probability that the customer selected has a heating system is determined by the ratio of the number of customers with heating systems to the total number of customers.

$$P(\text{Heating}) = RF(\text{Heating}) = \frac{200}{500} = 0.40$$

There is a 40% chance the randomly selected customer will have a heating system.

TABLE 4-1
Hathaway Heating & Air Conditioning

	CUSTOMER CATEGORY		
	Commercial	*Residential*	*Total*
Heating Systems	55	145	200
Air-Conditioning Systems	45	255	300
Total	100	400	500

The sales manager hopes the customer selected is a residential customer with a heating system. Since there are 145 customers in this category, the relative frequency of occurrence method is used to assess the probability of this event occurring as follows:

$$P(\text{Residential with Heating}) = \frac{145}{500} = 0.29$$

There is a 29% chance the customer selected will be a residential customer with a heating system.

SUBJECTIVE PROBABILITY ASSESSMENT

Unfortunately, even though managers may have had some past experiences to guide their decision making, new factors always affect each decision, thus making that experience only an approximate guide to the future. In other cases, managers may have little or no past experience and, therefore, may not be able to use a relative frequency of occurrence as even a starting point in assessing the desired probability. When past experience is not available, decision makers must make a **subjective probability assessment.** A subjective probability is a measure of a personal conviction that an outcome will occur. Therefore, in this instance, probability represents a person's belief that an event will occur.

SUBJECTIVE PROBABILITY ASSESSMENT
The method that defines probability of an event as reflecting a decision maker's state of mind regarding the chances that the particular event will occur.

EXAMPLE 4-7

SUBJECTIVE PROBABILITY

Harrison Construction

The Harrison Construction Company is in the process of preparing a bid for a road construction project. The company's engineers are very good at defining all the elements of the project (labor, materials, etc.) and estimating the costs of these with a great deal of certainty. Therefore, in preparing the final bid amount, the managers take the projected costs and add a profit markup. The problem is how much markup to add. If they add too much, they won't be the low bidder and may lose the contract. If they don't mark the bid up enough, they may get the project and make less profit than they might have made had they used a higher markup. The managers are considering four possible markup values stated as a percent of base costs:

10%,   12%,   15%,   20%

In order to make their decision on the final bid amount, they need an assessment for the probability of winning the contract at each of these markup levels. Since they have never done another project exactly like this one, they can't rely on relative frequency of occurrence. Instead, they must subjectively assess the probability based on whatever information they currently have available such as who the other bidders are, the rapport Harrison has with the client, and so forth.

After considering these values, the Harrison managers make the following assessments:

$$P(\text{Win at } 10\%) = 0.30$$
$$P(\text{Win at } 12\%) = 0.25$$
$$P(\text{Win at } 15\%) = 0.15$$
$$P(\text{Win at } 20\%) = 0.05$$

These assessments reflect the managers' states of mind regarding the chances of winning the contract. If new information (e.g., a competitor drops out of the bidding) becomes available prior to submitting the bid, these assessments could change.

As indicated, each of the three methods by which probabilities are assigned to events has special advantages and specific applications. However, regardless of how decision makers arrive at a probability assessment, the rules by which these probabilities are used to assist in decision making are the same.

4-1: EXERCISES

ADDITIONAL EXERCISES ON YOUR CD-ROM
Try the ADDITIONAL EXERCISES and APPLICATION PROBLEMS on the CD-ROM.

4-1. A room contains four empty chairs. One chair is red. Assuming that the next person who enters the room will select a chair at random, what is the chance that the red chair will be the one selected?

4-2. If a paper carrier has delivered his route for 50 days and during that time he has been shorted papers by the publisher 5 times, what is the probability that he will be shorted tomorrow?

4-3. A study of weather data in a particular area reveals that measurable precipitation has occurred on 25 of the 200 days studied. Based upon this information, what is the probability that it will not rain tomorrow?

4-4. If two customers are asked their opinion on a new product and if their opinion is confined to "Like It" or "Don't Like It," list the sample space of possible responses from the two customers. How many of these events indicate a customer liking the product?

Business Applications

4-5. A shipping company can send a package through one of three cities (A, B, or C) before it gets to its final destination. Two packages are sent by the company. An elementary event will designate which city each package goes through, for example, (A, B) indicates that the first package goes through city A and the second through city B. Assume the package is equally likely to go through any of the cities. List the sample space for the possible cities through which the two packages might go.
   a. Using classical probability assessment, determine the probability that the first package did go and the second package did not go through city A.
   b. Using the classical probability assessment, determine the probability that neither of the packages went through city A.

4-6. A study of the advertisements in the classified section of a local newspaper shows that 204 are help wanted ads, 520 are real estate ads, and 306 are for other ads.
   a. If the newspaper plans to select an ad at random each week to be published free, what is the probability that the ad for a specific week will be a help wanted ad?
   b. What method of probability assessment is used to determine the probability in part a?
   c. Are the events that a help wanted ad is chosen and that an ad for other types of products or services is chosen for this promotion on a specific week mutually exclusive? Explain.

4-7. A major airline has tracked its on-time status during the past year for flights originating in San Francisco and Los Angeles. The following table reflects the data for 400 flights.

| | ON-TIME STATUS | | |
Origination	Early	On-Time	Late
San Francisco	25	50	100
Los Angeles	50	100	75

   a. Based on these data, what is the probability that a flight from one of the two cities will arrive early?
   b. What is the probability that a flight will have originated in Los Angeles?
   c. For a flight originating in Los Angeles, determine the probability that it will arrive early. What would this probability have to be if the event arriving early was independent of the event Los Angeles?
   d. If three flights are selected at random, list the sample space indicating the possible on-time status for all three.

4-8. Referring to Problem 7, suppose four flights arrive from Los Angeles each day. Define the following events: E_1 = all flights arrive early, E_2 = 1 to 3 flights arrive early, E_3 = no flights arrive early.
   a. Discuss whether the events E_1 and E_2 are mutually exclusive.
   b. List the elementary events associated with each of the three events.
   c. Discuss what, if any, differences would exist in the list of elementary events given in part b if the four flights in question originated in San Francisco instead of Los Angeles.

4-9. The manager at Filger's Furniture Store is in the process of negotiating a contract with a new supplier for dining tables. He has assessed the probability that the supplier will take the price he is willing to offer to be 0.70.

    a. Explain what type of probability assessment method the manager would use to assess this probability.

    b. Would it make sense to use the classical probability assessment approach in this case? Explain.

4-10. The Skateworld Company operates ice rinks in several major cities throughout the United States. During each session of open skating, one customer is selected at random to receive a free pass for a future open skating session. At a recent session there were 150 males and 130 females skating.

    a. What is the probability that the person selected for the free pass will be a female?

    b. Referring to part a, what method of probability assessment is used to determine the probability?

    c. Suppose the company decides to give free passes to two customers. Are the events that a female received the first pass and a male received the second pass independent? Why or why not?

4-11. A gasoline filling station recently began a promotion on its "full service" island. If the dollar value shown on the pump stops at $9.99 when the pump clicks off, the customer will get the gasoline free.

    a. If we define three events, one for each digit, can we conclude that the three events are independent? Why or why not?

    b. Are the three events referred to in part a considered to be mutually exclusive? Why or why not?

    c. What is the relationship between mutually exclusive events and independent events? (Hint: Consider two events that are mutually exclusive. If one occurs, what is the probability that the other will occur?)

4-12. Referring to Problem 11, if the station manager wants to determine the probability that a customer will hit the

$9.99, what method of probability assessment would most likely be used? Why?

4-13. A Courtyard Hotel by Marriott conducted a survey of its guests. Sixty-two surveys were completed. The data can be found in the file named **CourtyardSurvey**. Based on the data from the survey, determine the following probabilities using the relative frequency of occurrence method.

    a. What is the probability a customer either *probably will* or *definitely will* stay at a Courtyard again?

    b. What is the probability the customer is on a business trip?

    c. What is the probability the customer has stayed at a Courtyard before?

    d. What is the probability of a customer being on a business trip and rating the hotel *better* than the other hotels in the area?

4-14. The ECCO company makes backup alarms for machinery like forklifts and commercial trucks. When a customer returns one of the alarms under warranty, the quality manager logs data on the product. Using the available data found in the file named **ECCO**, use relative frequency of occurrence to find the following probabilities.

    a. What is the probability the product was made at the Salt Lake City plant?

    b. What is the probability the customer returned the product due to a wiring problem?

    c. What is the joint probability the returned item was from the Salt Lake City plant and had a wiring-related problem?

    d. What is the probability that a returned item was made on the day shift at the Salt Lake plant and had a cracked lens problem?

    e. If an item was returned, what is the most likely profile for the item including plant location, shift, and cause of problem?

4-2: THE RULES OF PROBABILITY

Measuring Probabilities

The probability attached to an event represents the likelihood the event will occur on a specified trial of an experiment. This probability also measures the perceived uncertainty about whether the event will occur.

POSSIBLE VALUES AND SUM

The probability of any event will be between 0 and 1 inclusively. If we are certain as to the outcome of an event, we will assign the event a probability of 0.0 or 1.0, where $P(E_i) = 0.0$ indicates the event E_i will not occur, and $P(E_i) = 1.0$ means that E_i will definitely occur. If we are uncertain about the result of an experiment, we measure this uncertainty by assigning a probability between 0.0 and 1.0. Probability Rule 1 shows that the probability of an event occurring is always between 0.0 and 1.0.

PROBABILITY RULE 1

For any event E_i:

$$0.0 \leq P(E_i) \leq 1.0 \text{ for all } i$$

      4-3

All possible elementary events associated with an experiment form the sample space. Therefore, the sum of the probabilities of all possible elementary events is 1.0 as shown by Probability Rule 2.

PROBABILITY RULE 2

$$\sum_{i=1}^{k} P(e_i) = 1.0$$

where:

k = Number of elementary events in the sample space
e_i = i^{th} elementary event

4-4

ADDITION RULE FOR ELEMENTARY EVENTS

If a single event is composed of two or more elementary events, then the probability of the event is found by summing the probabilities of the elementary events. This is illustrated by Probability Rule 3.

PROBABILITY RULE 3

The probability of an event E_i is equal to the *sum* of the probabilities of the elementary events forming E_i. That is, if:

$$E_i = \{e_1, e_2, e_3\}$$

then:

$$P(E_i) = P(e_1) + P(e_2) + P(e_3)$$

4-5

EXAMPLE 4-8

ADDITION RULE

Veronica's Cineplex

Veronica's Cineplex is considering opening a new 20-screen complex in Lansing, Michigan, and has recently performed a resident survey as part of its decision-making process. One question of particular interest is how often the respondent goes to a movie. Table 4-2 shows the results of the survey for this question.

The sample space for the experiment for each respondent is:

$$SS = \{e_1, e_2, e_3, e_4\}$$

where:

e_1 = ≥ 10 movies
e_2 = 3 to 9 movies
e_3 = 1 to 2 movies
e_4 = 0 movies

Using the relative frequency of occurrence approach, we assign the following probabilities.

$$
\begin{aligned}
P(e_1) &= 400/5{,}000 = 0.08 \\
P(e_2) &= 1{,}900/5{,}000 = 0.38 \\
P(e_3) &= 1{,}500/5{,}000 = 0.30 \\
P(e_4) &= 1{,}200/5{,}000 = \underline{0.24} \\
&\qquad\qquad\quad \sum = 1.00
\end{aligned}
$$

TABLE 4-2
Veronica's Cineplex Survey Results

MOVIES PER MONTH	FREQUENCY	RELATIVE FREQUENCY
≥ 10	400	0.08
3 to 9	1,900	0.38
1 to 2	1,500	0.30
0	1,200	0.24
Total	5,000	1.00

Assume we are interested in the event, "respondent attends 1 to 9 movies per month."

$$E = \text{Respondent attends 1 to 9 movies}$$

The elementary events that make up E are

$$E = \{e_2, e_3\}$$

We can find the probability $P(E)$ by using Probability Rule 3 as follows:

$$
\begin{aligned}
P(E) &= P(e_2) + P(e_3) \\
&= 0.38 + 0.30 \\
&= 0.68
\end{aligned}
$$

COMPLEMENT RULE

Closely connected with Probability Rules 1 and 2 is the **complement** of an event. The complement of an event E is the collection of all possible elementary events not contained in event E. The complement of event E is represented by $\bar{E}$. Thus, the Complement Rule is a corollary to Probability Rules 1 and 2.

COMPLEMENT RULE

$$P(\bar{E}) = 1 - P(E)$$ 4-6

That is, the probability of the complement of event E is 1.0 minus the probability of event E.

4-9

COMPLEMENT RULE

Haupert Machinery

The sales manager for Haupert Machinery in Medford, Oregon, is preparing to call on a new customer, a logging contractor. The sales manager is hoping to sell the contractor some equipment. Before making the presentation, the manager lists four possible outcomes and has subjectively assessed probabilities related to the sales prospect.

EVENTS (SALES)	P(SALES)
$ 0	0.70
2,000	0.20
15,000	0.07
50,000	0.03
	1.00

Note that each probability is between 0.0 and 1.0 and that the sum of the probabilities is 1.0 as required by Rules 1 and 2. The probability of not selling anything ($E = \$0$) to the logging contractor is:

$$P(\$0) = 0.70$$

The complement, $\bar{E}$, is all sales $> \$0$. Using the Complement Rule, the probability of sales $>\$0$ is:

$$
\begin{aligned}
P(\text{Sales} > \$0) &= 1 - P(\$0) \\
P(\text{Sales} > \$0) &= 1 - 0.70 \\
P(\text{Sales} > \$0) &= 0.30
\end{aligned}
$$

So, based on her subjective assessment, there is a 30% chance the sales manager will sell something to the logging contractor.

MOVIES PER MONTH	AGE GROUP E_5 *Less than 30*	E_6 *30 to 50*	E_7 *Over 50*	TOTAL
E_1 $\geq$10 Movies	e_1 200	e_2 100	e_3 100	400
E_2 3 to 9 Movies	e_4 600	e_5 900	e_6 400	1,900
E_3 1 to 2 Movies	e_7 400	e_8 600	e_9 500	1,500
E_4 0 Movies	e_{10} 700	e_{11} 500	e_{12} 0	1,200
Total	1,900	2,100	1,000	5,000

TABLE 4-3
Veronica's Cineplex

ADDITION RULE FOR TWO EVENTS

Veronica's Cineplex (continued)

Suppose the managers who conducted the survey for Veronica's Cineplex also asked questions about the respondent's age. Veronica's Cineplex managers consider age an important factor in the location decision since its theaters do better in areas with a younger population base. Table 4-3 shows the breakdown of the sample by age group and by the number of times the respondent goes to a movie per month.

Table 4-3 illustrates two important concepts in data analysis, namely, *joint frequencies* and *marginal frequencies*. Joint frequencies, which were discussed in Chapter 2, are represented by the values inside the table and represent information concerning age group and movie viewing jointly. Marginal frequencies are the row and column totals. These values, found in the margins, represent information concerning just the age group or just movie attendance.

For example, 2,100 people in the survey are in the 30–50 year age group. This column total is a marginal frequency for the age group between 30–50 years, which is represented by E_6. Also, 600 respondents are less than 30 years old and attend a movie from 3 to 9 times a month. Thus, 600 is a joint frequency whose elementary event is represented by e_4. The joint frequencies are the number of times their associated elementary events occur.

Table 4-4 shows the relative frequencies for the data in Table 4-3. These values represent the probabilities of the events and elementary events.

TABLE 4-4
Veronica's Cineplex—Joint Probability Table

MOVIES PER MONTH	AGE GROUP E_5 *Less than 30*	E_6 *30 to 50*	E_7 *Over 50*	TOTAL
E_1 $\geq$10 Movies	e_1 200/5,000 = 0.04	e_2 100/5,000 = 0.02	e_3 100/5,000 = 0.02	400/5,000 = 0.08
E_2 3 to 9 Movies	e_4 600/5,000 = 0.12	e_5 900/5,000 = 0.18	e_6 400/5,000 = 0.08	1,900/5,000 = 0.38
E_3 1 to 2 Movies	e_7 400/5,000 = 0.08	e_8 600/5,000 = 0.12	e_9 500/5,000 = 0.10	1,500/5,000 = 0.30
E_4 0 Movies	e_{10} 700/5,000 = 0.14	e_{11} 500/5,000 = 0.10	e_{12} 0/5,000 = 0	1,200/5,000 = 0.24
Total	1,900/5,000 = 0.38	2,100/5,000 = 0.42	1,000/5,000 = 0.20	5,000/5,000 = 1

EXAMPLE 4-10 ADDITION RULE

Suppose we wish to find the probability of E_4 (0 movies) **or** E_6 (being in the 30 to 50 age group). That is,

$$P(E_4 \text{ or } E_6) = ?$$

To find this probability, we must use Probability Rule 4.

PROBABILITY RULE 4

Addition rule for any two *events* E_1 and E_2:

$$P(E_1 \text{ or } E_2) = P(E_1) + P(E_2) - P(E_1 \text{ and } E_2) \qquad \text{4-7}$$

The key word in knowing when to use Rule 4 is *or*. The word *or* indicates addition. (You may have covered this concept as a *union* in a math class.) The word *or* is used somewhat differently in probability than it is in everyday language. For example, if you were buying a music compact disc and were told to choose one compact disc *or* another, you would understand that you could have *only one* of the compact discs. In probability, however, *or* is used as an *inclusive* term. For instance, you might be asked to calculate the probability that you would choose one *or* the other of the compact discs. From a probabilistic standpoint you would be computing the probability that you would choose one or the other of the compact discs or both of them. Probability Rule 4 is illustrated in the following example.

Referring to the Veronica Cineplex situation, suppose we wish to find the probability of E_4 (0 movies) *or* E_6 (being in the 30 to 50 age group). That is,

$$P(E_4 \text{ or } E_6) = ?$$

Table 4-5 shows the relative frequencies with the events of interest shaded. The overlap corresponds to the *joint occurrence* (intersection) of attending 0 movies *and* being in the 30 to 50 age group. The probability of the overlap is represented by $P(E_4 \text{ and } E_6)$ and must be subtracted. This is done to avoid double-counting the probabilities of the elementary events that are in both E_4 and E_6 when calculating $P(E_4 \text{ or } E_6)$. Thus,

$$
\begin{aligned}
P(E_4 \text{ or } E_6) &= 0.24 + 0.42 - 0.10 \\
&= 0.56
\end{aligned}
$$

Therefore, the probability that a respondent will be in either the 30 to 50 age group or attend no movies in a month is 0.56.

What is the probability a respondent will go to 0 movies *or* be in the over-50 age group? Again, we can use Rule 4:

$$P(E_4 \text{ or } E_7) = P(E_4) + P(E_7) - P(E_4 \text{ and } E_7)$$

TABLE 4-5
Veronica's Cineplex—
Addition Rule Example

MOVIES PER MONTH	AGE GROUP E_5 *Less than 30*	E_6 *30 to 50*	E_7 *Over 50*	TOTAL
E_1 $\geq$10 Movies	e_1 $200/5{,}000 = 0.04$	e_2 $100/5{,}000 = 0.02$	e_3 $100/5{,}000 = 0.02$	$400/5{,}000 = 0.08$
E_2 3 to 9 movies	e_4 $600/5{,}000 = 0.12$	e_5 $900/5{,}000 = 0.18$	e_6 $400/5{,}000 = 0.08$	$1{,}900/5{,}000 = 0.38$
E_3 1 to 2 movies	e_7 $400/5{,}000 = 0.08$	e_8 $600/5{,}000 = 0.12$	e_9 $500/5{,}000 = 0.10$	$1{,}500/5{,}000 = 0.30$
E_4 0 Movies	e_{10} $700/5{,}000 = 0.14$	e_{11} $500/5{,}000 = 0.10$	e_{12} $0/5{,}000 = 0$	$1{,}200/5{,}000 = 0.24$
Total	$1{,}900/5{,}000 = 0.38$	$2{,}100/5{,}000 = 0.42$	$1{,}000/5{,}000 = 0.20$	$5{,}000/5{,}000 = 1$

MOVIES PER MONTH	AGE GROUP			TOTAL
	E_5 Less than 30	E_6 30 to 50	E_7 Over 50	
E_1 ≥10 Movies	e_1 200/5,000 = 0.04	e_2 100/5,000 = 0.02	e_3 100/5,000 = 0.02	400/5,000 = 0.08
E_2 3 to 9 Movies	e_4 600/5,000 = 0.12	e_5 900/5,000 = 0.18	e_6 400/5,000 = 0.08	1,900/5,000 = 0.38
E_3 1 to 2 Movies	e_7 400/5,000 = 0.08	e_8 600/5,000 = 0.12	e_9 500/5,000 = 0.10	1,500/5,000 = 0.30
E_4 0 Movies	e_{10} 700/5,000 = 0.14	e_{11} 500/5,000 = 0.10	e_{12} 0/5,000 = 0	1,200/5,000 = 0.24
Total	1,900/5,000 = 0.38	2,100/5,000 = 0.42	1,000/5,000 = 0.20	5,000/5,000 = 1

TABLE 4-6
Veronica's Cineplex—
Addition Rule Example

Table 4-6 shows the relative frequencies for these events. We have

$$P(E_4 \text{ or } E_7) = 0.24 + 0.20 - 0.00 = 0.44$$

In this case, there were no joint occurrences so $P(E_4 \text{ and } E_7)$ was assessed as 0.0 using the relative frequency approach.

ADDITION RULE FOR MUTUALLY EXCLUSIVE EVENTS

We indicated previously that when two events are mutually exclusive, both events cannot occur at the same time. Thus for mutually exclusive events,

$$P(E_1 \text{ and } E_2) = 0.0$$

Therefore, when you are dealing with mutually exclusive events the addition rule assumes a special form shown as Rule 5.

PROBABILITY RULE 5

Addition rule for mutually exclusive events E_1, E_2:
$$P(E_1 \text{ or } E_2) = P(E_1) + P(E_2) \qquad \text{4-8}$$

Consider a situation in which a restaurant dishwasher has the chance to move into either a waiter (event W) or table busser (event B) position. Five people are being considered for the waiter position and 10 people are being considered for the busser position. Since the selection process is based on random selection, we wish to determine the probability that our dishwasher friend will receive one of the new positions. We want:

$$P(W \text{ or } B) = ?$$

This can be determined using the addition rule. However, because he can't be hired for both positions, the events W and B are mutually exclusive. Thus Rule 5 is used:

$$\begin{aligned} P(W \text{ or } B) &= P(W) + P(B) \\ &= 1/5 + 1/10 \\ &= 3/10 = 0.30 \end{aligned}$$

Thus, there is a 30% chance that he will get one of the new positions.

Conditional Probability

In dealing with probabilities, you will often need to determine the chances of two or more events occurring either at the same time or in succession. For example, a quality control manager for a manufacturing company may be interested in the probability of selecting two successive defective products from an assembly line. If the probability of this event is low, the quality control manager would be surprised when it occurs and might readjust the production process. In other instances, the decision maker may know that an event has occurred and may want to know the probability of a second event occurring. For instance, suppose that an oil company geologist believes oil will be found at a certain drilling site and makes a favorable report. Since oil is not always found at locations with a favorable report, the oil company exploration vice president might well be interested in the probability of finding oil at this drilling site given the favorable report.

Situations like this refer to a probability concept known as **conditional probability**.

CONDITIONAL PROBABILITY

The probability that an event will occur *given* that some other event has already happened.

Probability Rule 6 offers a general rule for conditional probability. The notation $P(E_1 | E_2)$ reads probability of event E_1 *given* event E_2. Thus, the probability of one event is conditional upon a second event having occurred.

PROBABILITY RULE 6

Conditional probability for any two events E_1, E_2:

$$P(E_1 | E_2) = \frac{P(E_1 \text{ and } E_2)}{P(E_2)}$$ 4-9

where:

$$P(E_2) > 0$$

Rule 6 uses *a joint probability*, $P(E_1 \text{ and } E_2)$, and *a marginal probability*, $P(E_2)$, to calculate the conditional probability, $P(E_1 | E_2)$. Note that to find a conditional probability, we find the ratio of how frequently E_1 occurs to the total number of observations, given that we restrict our observations to only those cases where E_2 has occurred.

4-11

CONDITIONAL PROBABILITY

West.net

West.net, an Internet service provider, is in an industry that is becoming increasingly competitive. The company has performed a study of its customers' Internet use habits. Among the information collected are the data shown in Table 4-7.

West.net plans on offering a series of Internet services to selected customers but not to all of its customers. The company is particularly interested in offering the services to people who presently are high-volume users. One of the factors that will influence West.net's marketing strategy is whether the time spent using the Internet is related to the customer being male or female. For example, suppose the company knows a user is female and wants

T A B L E 4 - 7
West.net Example

| HOURS PER MONTH | GENDER | | TOTAL |
	E_4 *Female*	E_5 *Male*	
E_1 <20	e_1 $f_1 = 450$	e_2 $f_2 = 500$	950
E_2 20 to 40	e_3 $f_3 = 300$	e_4 $f_4 = 800$	1,100
E_3 >40	e_5 $f_5 = 100$	e_6 $f_6 = 350$	450
Total	850	1,650	2,500

HOURS PER MONTH	GENDER		TOTAL
	E_4 Female	E_5 Male	
E_1 <20	e_1 $RF_1 = 450/2,500 = 0.18$	e_2 $RF_2 = 500/2,500 = 0.20$	950/2,500 = 0.38
E_2 20 to 40	e_3 $RF_3 = 300/2,500 = 0.12$	e_4 $RF_4 = 800/2,500 = 0.32$	1,100/2,500 = 0.44
E_3 >40	e_5 $RF_5 = 100/2,500 = 0.04$	e_6 $RF_6 = 350/2,500 = 0.14$	450/2,500 = 0.18
Total	850/2,500 = 0.34	1,650/2,500 = 0.66	2,500/2,500 = 1.00

TABLE 4-8
West.net Example

to know the probability that this user will spend between 20 and 40 hours a month on the Internet. Let:

$$E_2 = \{e_3, e_4\} = \text{Event: Person uses services 20–40 hours per month}$$
$$E_4 = \{e_1, e_3, e_5\} = \text{Event: User is female}$$

A marketing analyst needs to know the probability of E_2 *given* E_4.

Table 4-8 shows the frequencies and relative frequencies of interest. One way to find the desired probability is as follows.

1. We know E_4 has occurred (customer is female). There are 850 females in the survey.
2. Of the 850 females, 300 use Internet services 20–40 hours per month.
3. Then,

$$P(E_2 | E_4) = \frac{300}{850}$$
$$= 0.3529$$

However, we can also apply Rule 6 as follows:

$$P(E_2 | E_4) = \frac{P(E_2 \text{ and } E_4)}{P(E_4)}$$

From Table 4-8, we get $P(E_2 \text{ and } E_4) = 0.12$

and

$$P(E_4) = 0.34$$

Then,

$$P(E_2 | E_4) = \frac{0.12}{0.34} = 0.3529$$

TREE DIAGRAMS

Another way of organizing the events of an experiment that aids in the calculation of probabilities is the *tree diagram*.

West.net (continued)

EXAMPLE 4-12

TREE DIAGRAMS

Figure 4-1 illustrates the tree diagram for the West.net example. Note that the branches at each node in the tree diagram represent mutually exclusive events. Moving from left to right, the first two branches indicate the two employee types (male and female—mutually exclusive events). Three branches originate from each of these original branches, representing the three possible categories for Internet use. The probabilities for the events, male and female, are shown on the first two branches. The probabilities shown on the right of the tree are the

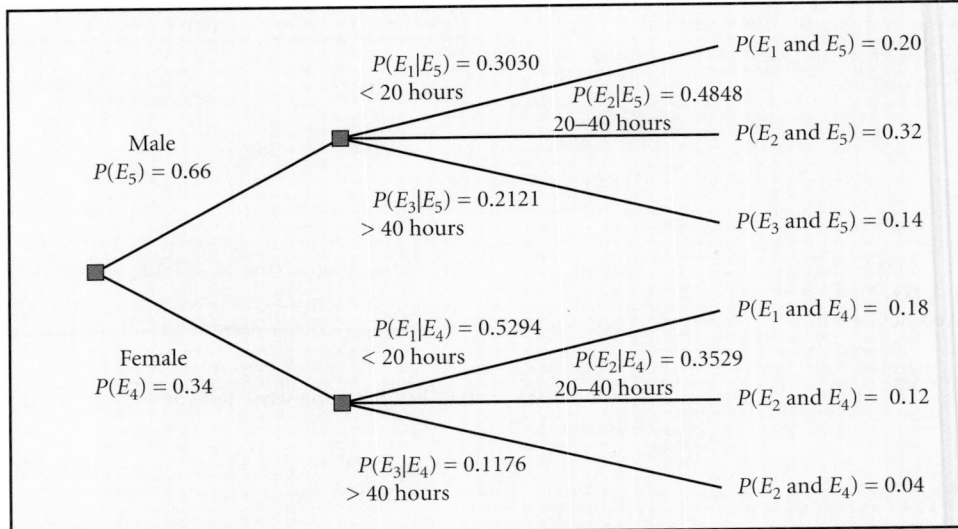

FIGURE 4-1
Tree Diagram for West.net

joint probability for each combination of gender and hours of use and are found using Table 4-8. The probabilities on the branches following the male and female branches showing hours of use are conditional probabilities. For example, the probability a customer will spend more than 40 hours on the Internet (E_3) *given* he is a male (E_5) can be found by

$$P(E_3 \mid E_5) = \frac{P(E_3 \text{ and } E_5)}{P(E_5)} = \frac{0.14}{0.66} = 0.2121$$

CONDITIONAL PROBABILITY FOR INDEPENDENT EVENTS

We earlier discussed that two events are independent if the occurrence of one event has no bearing on the probability that the second event occurs. Therefore, when two events are independent, the rule for conditional probability takes a special form, as indicated in Probability Rule 7.

PROBABILITY RULE 7

Conditional probability for independent events, E_1, E_2:

$$P(E_1 \mid E_2) = P(E_1); \quad P(E_2) > 0$$

and

$$P(E_2 \mid E_1) = P(E_2); \quad P(E_1) > 0 \qquad \textbf{4-10}$$

As Rule 7 shows, the conditional probability of one event occurring, given that a second independent event has already occurred, is simply the probability of the first event occurring.

West.net (continued)

Table 4-9 shows some additional data from the West.net survey that we can use to demonstrate Rule 7. Suppose the market analyst is also interested in knowing the probability that a male customer will use the Netscape browser.

To find this probability, let

$$E_1 = \{e_1, e_2\} = \text{Event: Uses Netscape}$$
$$E_4 = \{e_2, e_4\} = \text{Event: User is male}$$

EXAMPLE
4-13

CONDITIONAL PROBABILITY

| BROWSER USED | GENDER | | |
	E_3 Female	E_4 Male	
E_1 Netscape	e_1 $f_1 = 272$ $RF_1 = 272/2,500 = 0.1088$	e_2 $f_2 = 528$ $RF_2 = 528/2,500 = 0.2112$	$800/2,500 = 0.32$
E_2 Microsoft	e_3 $f_3 = 578$ $RF_3 = 578/2,500 = 0.2312$ $850/2,500 = 0.34$	e_4 $f_4 = 1,122$ $RF_4 = 1,122/2,500 = 0.4488$ $1,650/2,500 = 0.66$	$1,700/2,500 = 0.68$ $2,500/2,500 = 1.00$

TABLE 4-9
Relative Frequencies for West.net

Then, using Rule 6, $P(E_1 | E_4)$ is found as follows:

$$P(E_1 | E_4) = \frac{P(E_1 \text{ and } E_4)}{P(E_4)}$$

where:

$$P(E_1 \text{ and } E_4) = 0.2112$$

and

$$P(E_4) = 0.66$$

Then,

$$P(E_1 | E_4) = \frac{P(E_1 \text{ and } E_4)}{P(E_4)} = \frac{0.2112}{0.66}$$

$$= 0.32$$

However, from Table 4-9, we see that $P(E_1) = 0.32$. So,

$$P(E_1 | E_4) = P(E_1)$$
$$0.32 = 0.32$$

Therefore, since the probability of using the Netscape browser *given* that the customer is a male is equal to the probability that a customer uses Netscape without regard to gender, these two events are independent.

Multiplication Rules

We needed the joint probability of two events in the discussion on addition of two events and also in the discussion on conditional probability. In the previous example, we were able to find $P(E_1 \text{ and } E_4)$ simply by examining the joint frequency tables. However, we often need to find $P(E_1 \text{ and } E_2)$ when we do not know the joint relative frequencies. When this is the case, we can use the multiplication rule for two events.

MULTIPLICATION RULE FOR TWO EVENTS

PROBABILITY RULE 8

Multiplication rule for two events, E_1 and E_2:

$$P(E_1 \text{ and } E_2) = P(E_1)P(E_2 | E_1)$$

and

$$P(E_2 \text{ and } E_1) = P(E_2)P(E_1 | E_2)$$

4-11

To illustrate how to find a joint probability, consider an example involving classical probability.

MULTIPLICATION RULE

Real Computer Co.

Real Computer Co., a manufacturer of personal computers, uses two suppliers for CD-ROM drives. These parts are intermingled in the manufacturing floor inventory rack. When a computer is assembled, the CD-ROM unit is pulled from inventory without regard to which company made the CD-ROM. Recently a customer ordered two personal computers. At the time of assembly, the CD-ROM inventory contained 30 MATX units and 50 Quinex units. What is the probability that both computers ordered by this customer will be MATX units?

To answer this question, we must recognize that two events are required to form the desired outcome. Therefore, let

$$E_1 = \text{Event: MATX CD-ROM on first computer}$$
$$E_2 = \text{Event: MATX CD-ROM on second computer}$$

The probability that both computers contain MATX units is written as $P(E_1 \text{ and } E_2)$. The key word here is *and*, as contrasted with the addition rule, where the key word is *or*. The *and* signifies that we are interested in the joint probability of two events, as noted by $P(E_1 \text{ and } E_2)$. To find this probability, we employ Rule 8,

$$P(E_1 \text{ and } E_2) = P(E_1)P(E_2 \mid E_1)$$

We start by assuming that each CD-ROM in the inventory has the same chance of being selected for assembly. For the first computer:

$$P(E_1) = \frac{\text{Number of MATX units}}{\text{Number of CD-ROMs in inventory}}$$

$$= \frac{30}{80} = 0.375$$

Then, since we are not replacing the first CD-ROM, we find $P(E_2 \mid E_1)$ by

$$P(E_2 \mid E_1) = \frac{\text{Number of remaining MATX units}}{\text{Number of remaining CD-ROM units}}$$

$$= \frac{29}{79} = 0.3671$$

Now, by Rule 8,

$$P(E_1 \text{ and } E_2) = P(E_1)P(E_2 \mid E_1) = (0.375)(0.3671)$$
$$= 0.1377$$

Therefore, there is a 13.77% chance the two personal computers will get MATX CD-ROM drives.

Using a Tree Diagram

MULTIPLICATION RULE

Real Computer Co. (continued)

A tree diagram can be used to display the situation facing the computer manufacturer. The two branches on the left side of the tree in Figure 4-2 show the possible CD-ROM options for the first computer. The two branches coming from each of the first branches show the possible CD-ROM options for the second computer. The probabilities at the far right are the joint probabilities for the CD-ROM options for the two computers. As we determined previously, the probability that both computers will get a MATX unit is 0.1377 as shown on the top right on the tree diagram.

We can use the multiplication rule and the addition rule in one application when we determine the probability that two systems will have different CD-ROMs. Looking at Figure 4-2 we see there are two ways this can happen.

$$P[(\text{MATX } and \text{ Quinex}) \text{ or } (\text{Quinex } and \text{ MATX})] = ??$$

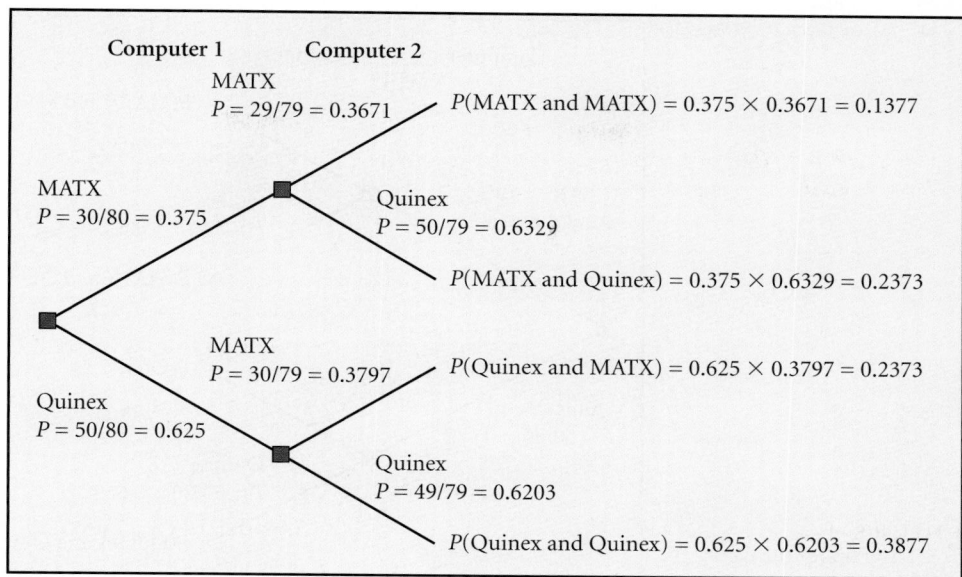

FIGURE 4-2
Tree Diagram for the CD-ROM Example

If the first CD-ROM is a MATX and the second one a Quinex, then the first cannot be a Quinex and the second a MATX. These two events are mutually exclusive and, therefore, Rule 5 can be used to calculate the required probability. The joint probabilities (generated from the multiplication rule) are shown on the right side of the tree. To find the desired probability, using Rule 5 we can add the two joint probabilities:

$$P[(\text{MATX and Quinex}) \ or \ (\text{Quinex and MATX})] =$$
$$0.2373 \quad + \quad 0.2373 \quad = 0.4746$$

The chance that a customer buying two computers will get two different CD-ROMs is 47.46%.

MULTIPLICATION RULE FOR INDEPENDENT EVENTS

When we determined the probability that two computers would have a MATX CD-ROM unit, we used the general multiplication rule (Rule 8). The general multiplication rule requires that conditional probability be used since the result for the second computer depends on the CD-ROM selected for the first computer. The chance of obtaining a MATX was lowered from 30/80 to 29/79 given the first CD-ROM was a MATX.

However, if the two events of interest are *independent*, the imposed condition does not alter the probability, and the multiplication rule takes the form shown in Probability Rule 9.

PROBABILITY RULE 9

Multiplication rule for independent events E_1, E_2:

$$P(E_1 \text{ and } E_2) = P(E_1)P(E_2) \qquad \textbf{4-12}$$

The joint probability of two independent events is simply the product of the marginal probabilities of the two events. Rule 9 is one way that you can determine whether any two events are independent. If the product of the probabilities of the two events equals the joint probability, then the events are independent. Consider the computer company example again.

**EXAMPLE
4-16

INDEPENDENT
EVENTS**

Real Computer Co. (continued)

Suppose immediately after a CD-ROM is assembled into a computer, a CD-ROM from the same supplier is replaced into the floor inventory. Now, whenever a part is selected there are

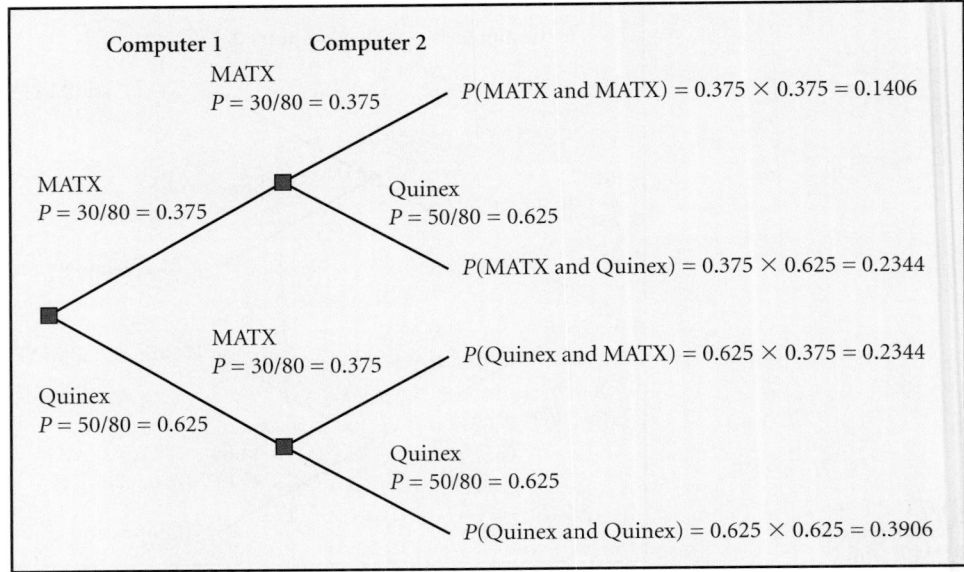

FIGURE 4-3
Tree Diagram for the CD-ROM Example

30 MATX and 50 Quinex units from which to pick. Figure 4-3 shows the tree diagram and the new probability. Now we see:

$$P(\text{MATX and MATX}) = 0.375 \times 0.375 = 0.1406$$

Bayes' Theorem

As decision makers, you will often encounter situations that require you to assess probabilities for events of interest. Your assessment may be based on relative frequency of occurrence or subjectivity. However, with new information in hand you may want to revise your probability assessment. For example, a human resources manager who has interviewed a person for a sales job might assess a low probability that the person will succeed in sales. However, after seeing the person's very high score on the company sales aptitude test, the manager might revise her assessment upward. A medical doctor might assign an 80% chance that a patient has a particular disease. However, after seeing positive results from a lab test, he might increase his assessment to 95%.

In these situations, you will need a way to formally incorporate the new information. One very useful tool for doing this is called *Bayes' theorem*, named for the Reverend Thomas Bayes who developed the special application of conditional probability in the 1700s. The general rule for determining conditional probability was shown earlier as Equation 4-9:

$$P(E_i | B) = \frac{P(E_i \text{ and } B)}{P(B)}$$

The numerator can be reformulated using the multiplication rule (Equation 4-11) as:

$$P(E_i \text{ and } B) = P(E_i)P(B|E_i)$$

The conditional probability is then:

$$P(E_i | B) = \frac{P(E_i)P(B|E_i)}{P(B)}$$

The denominator, $P(B)$, can be found by adding the probability of the k ways that event B can occur. This is:

$$P(B) = P(E_1)P(B|E_1) + P(E_2)P(B|E_2) + \cdots + P(E_k)P(B|E_k)$$

Then Bayes' theorem is formulated as Equation 4-13.

BAYES' THEOREM

$$P(E_i|B) = \frac{P(E_i)P(B|E_i)}{P(E_1)P(B|E_1) + P(E_2)P(B|E_2) + \cdots + P(E_k)P(B|E_k)}$$ **4-13**

where:

$E_i = i$th event of interest of the k possible events
$B = $ new event that might impact $P(E_i)$

EXAMPLE 4-17

BAYES' THEOREM

Varden Soap Company

The Varden Soap Company has two production facilities, one in Ohio and one in Virginia. The company makes the same type of soap at both facilities. The Ohio facility makes 60% of the company's total soap output, and the remaining 40% is made by the Virginia plant. After extensive sampling, the quality assurance manager has determined that 5% of the soap produced in Ohio and 10% of the soap produced in Virginia is unusable due to quality problems. All soap from the two facilities is sent to a central warehouse where it is intermingled rather than stored separately. When the company sells a defective product, it incurs not only the cost of replacing the item but also the loss of goodwill. The vice president for production would like to allocate these costs fairly between the two plants. To do so, he knows that he must first determine the probability that a defective item was produced by a particular production line. Specifically, he needs to answer these questions:

1. What is the probability that the soap was produced at the Ohio plant, given that the soap is defective?
2. What is the probability that the soap was produced at the Virginia plant, given that the item is defective?

In notation form, with D representing the occurrence of defective soap, what the manager wants to know is:

$P(\text{Ohio plant}|D) = ?$
$P(\text{Virginia plant}|D) = ?$

We can use Bayes' theorem to determine these probabilities as follows.

$$P(\text{Ohio}|D) = \frac{P(\text{Ohio})P(D|\text{Ohio})}{P(D)}$$

We know that D (defective soap) can happen if it is made at either the Ohio or Virginia plant. Thus,

$$P(D) = P(\text{Ohio})P(D|\text{Ohio}) + P(\text{Virginia})P(D|\text{Virginia})$$

We already know that 60% of the soap comes from Ohio and 40% from Virginia. So, $P(\text{Ohio}) = 0.60$ and $P(\text{Virginia}) = 0.40$. These are called the *prior* probabilities. Without Bayes' theorem, we would likely allocate the total cost of defects in a 60/40 split between Ohio and Virginia based on total production. However, the new information about the quality from each line is:

$$P(D|\text{Ohio}) = 0.05 \quad \text{and} \quad P(D|\text{Virginia}) = 0.10$$

which can be used to properly allocate the cost of defects. This is done using Bayes' theorem as follows.

$$P(\text{Ohio}|D) = \frac{P(\text{Ohio})P(D|\text{Ohio})}{P(\text{Ohio})P(D|\text{Ohio}) + P(\text{Virginia})P(D|\text{Virginia})}$$

EVENTS	PRIOR PROBABILITIES	CONDITIONAL PROBABILITIES	JOINT PROBABILITY	REVISED PROBABILITY
Ohio	0.60	0.05	$(0.60)(0.05) = 0.03$	$0.03/0.07 = 0.4286$
Virginia	0.40	0.10	$\underline{(0.40)(0.10) = 0.04}$	$\underline{0.04/0.07 = 0.5714}$
			0.07	1.000

TABLE 4-10
Bayes' Theorem Calculations for Varden Soap

then,

$$P(\text{Ohio}\,|D) = \frac{(0.60)(0.05)}{(0.60)(0.05) + (0.40)(0.10)} = 0.4286$$

and

$$P(\text{Virginia}\,|D) = \frac{P(\text{Virginia})P(D|\,\text{Virginia})}{P(\text{Virginia})P(D|\,\text{Virginia}) + P(\text{Ohio})P(D|\,\text{Ohio})}$$

$$P(\text{Virginia}\,|D) = \frac{(0.40)(0.10)}{(0.40)(0.10) + (0.60)(0.05)} = 0.5714$$

These probabilities are referred to as the *revised* (or posterior) probabilities. The prior probabilities have been revised given the new quality information. We now see that 42.86% of the cost of defects should be allocated to the Ohio plant and 57.14% should be allocated to the Virginia plant.

Note, the denominator, $P(D)$, is the overall probability of defective soap. This probability is:

$$P(D) = P(\text{Ohio})P(D|\,\text{Ohio}) + P(\text{Virginia})P(D|\,\text{Virginia})$$
$$= (0.60)(0.05) + (0.40)(0.10)$$
$$= 0.03 + 0.04$$
$$= 0.07$$

Thus, 7% of all the soap made by the Varden Soap Company is defective.

You might prefer to use a tabular approach like that shown in Table 4-10 when you apply Bayes' theorem. Another alternative is to use a tree diagram as illustrated in the following example.

USING A TREE DIAGRAM

IRS Audit

EXAMPLE
4-18

BAYES' THEOREM

This year projections are that 20% of all federal taxpayers will have filed an incorrect tax return. The Internal Revenue Service (IRS) audits are not perfect. They sometimes indicate there is an error when no problem exists. This is thought to happen about 10% of the time. The audits also can indicate no problem with the tax return when in fact there really is a problem. This is thought to happen about 30% of the time.

The IRS has just notified a randomly selected taxpayer that there is an error in his return. What is the probability that the return actually does have an error? We use the following notation:

$$E = \text{the return actually contains an error}$$
$$NE = \text{the return contains no error}$$
$$AE = \text{audit says an error exists}$$
$$ANE = \text{audit says no error}$$

Then, we are interested in determining the following:

$$P(E|AE) = ?$$

We know the following:

$$P(E) = 0.20 \quad P(ANE|E) = 0.30 \quad P(AE|NE) = 0.10$$
$$P(ANE|NE) = 0.90 \quad P(AE|E) = 0.70$$

FIGURE 4-4
Tree Diagram for the IRS
Audit Example

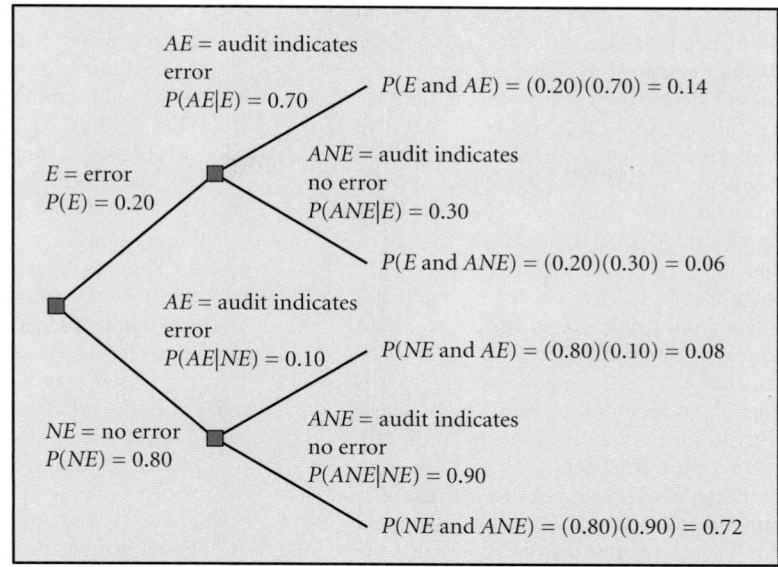

We need to use Bayes' theorem to determine the probability of interest. A tree diagram can be used to do this. Figure 4-4 shows the tree diagram and probabilities.

Now,

$$P(E|AE) = \frac{P(E \text{ and } AE)}{P(AE)} = ?$$

From Figure 4-4 we see that $P(E \text{ and } AE) = 0.14$. To find $P(AE)$, we add the probabilities of the ways in which AE occurs (audit says an error occurred) since those two ways are mutually exclusive:

$$P(AE) = P(E \text{ and } AE) + P(NE \text{ and } AE) = 0.14 + 0.08 = 0.22$$

Then,

$$P(E|AE) = \frac{P(E \text{ and } AE)}{P(AE)} = \frac{0.14}{0.22} = 0.6364$$

The chance that the return contains an error, given that the IRS audit indicates an error exists, is 63.64%.

4-2: EXERCISES

ADDITIONAL EXERCISES ON YOUR CD-ROM
Try the ADDITIONAL EXERCISES and APPLICATION PROBLEMS on the CD-ROM.

4-15. A store carries sweaters in three colors (brown, gray, and red.) Assume the store has an unlimited number of sweaters and that customers select the color at random.
    a. What is the probability that three customers will select the same color?

b. Determine the probability that the three customers do not all select the same color.

4-16. A paint store carries three brands of paint. A customer arrives and wants to buy another gallon of paint to match paint that she purchased at the store previously. She can't recall the brand name and does not wish to return home to find the old can of paint. So she selects two of the three brands of paint at random and buys them.

   a. What is the probability that she matched the paint?

   b. Her husband also goes to the paint store and fails to remember what brand to buy. So he also purchases two of the three brands of paint at random. Determine the probability that both the woman and her husband fail to get the correct brand of paint. (Hint: Are the two events independent? You may want to use a tree diagram.)

4-17. A fast-food restaurant has determined the chance that a customer will order a soft drink is 0.90. The chance that a customer will order a hamburger is 0.60. The chance that a customer will order french fries is 0.50.

   a. If a customer places an order, what is the probability that the order will include a soft drink and no fries if these two events are independent?

   b. The restaurant has also determined that if a customer orders a hamburger the chance the customer will also order fries is 0.80. Determine the probability that the order will include a hamburger and fries.

Business Applications

4-18. A local ski area offers private ski lessons by professionally qualified ski instructors. There are three ski instructors available. One is Austrian, one is German, and the third is from the United States. According to company policy, the instructors are assigned randomly. Thus, when a customer calls, a random selection is made and the selected instructor is scheduled with that customer.

   a. On a given day, five customers called for lessons. Of these, four were assigned to the German instructor and one to the American. What is the probability of this happening if the assignments are random?

   b. On a different day, three customers call for lessons and all three are assigned to the German instructor. What is the probability of this happening?

   c. Referring to parts a and b, compute the probability that both the outcome for day one and for day two happen. Based on this probability, is there any cause for concern that the ski lesson assignment may not be random? Explain.

4-19. A local photocopy shop has three black-and-white copy machines and two color copiers. Based on historical data, the chance that each black-and-white copier will be down for repairs is 10%. The color copies cause more of a problem, and those machines are down 20% of the time each.

   a. Based on this information, what is the probability that, if a customer needs a color copy, both color machines will be down for repairs?

   b. If a customer wants both a color copy and a black-and-white copy, what is the probability that the necessary machines will be available? (Assume that the color copier can also be used to make a black-and-white copy if needed.)

   c. If the manager wants to have at least a 99% chance of being able to furnish a black-and-white copy upon demand, is the present configuration sufficient? (Assume that the color copier can also be used to make a black-and-white copy if needed.) Back up your answer with appropriate probability computations.

   d. What is the probability that all five copiers will be up and running at the same time? Suppose the manager added a fourth black-and-white copier. How would the probability of all copiers being ready at any one time be affected?

4-20. Refer to Problem 19. The owners of the photocopy shop are going to open a new photocopy store. They wish to meet the increasing demand for color photocopies and have more reliable service. As a goal they would like to have at least a 99.9% chance of being able to furnish a black-and-white copy or a color copy upon demand. They also wish to purchase only four copiers. They have asked for your advice regarding the mix of black-and-white and color copiers. Supply them with your advice. Provide calculations and reasons to support your advice.

4-21. The Skiwell Manufacturing Company gets materials for its cross-country skis from two suppliers. Supplier A's materials make up 30% of what is used, with supplier B providing the rest. Past records indicate that 15% of supplier A's materials are defective and 10% of B's are defective. Since it is impossible to tell which supplier the materials came from once they are in inventory, the manager wants to know which supplier more likely supplied the defective materials the foreman has brought to his attention. Provide the manager this information.

4-22. Alpine Cannery is currently processing vegetables from the summer harvest. The manager has found a case of cans that has not been properly sealed. There are three lines that processed cans of this type, and the manager wants to know which line is most likely to be responsible for this mistake. Use the information below to provide the manager with an answer to which line is most likely responsible for the sealing mistake.

LINE	CONTRIBUTION TO TOTAL	PROPORTION DEFECTIVE
1	0.40	0.05
2	0.35	0.10
3	0.25	0.07

4-23. Cascade Paint mixes paint in three separate plants and then ships the unmarked cans to a central warehouse. Plant A supplies 50% of the paint, and past records indicate that the paint is incorrectly mixed 10% of the time. Plant B contributes 30% with a defective rate of 5%. Plant C supplies 20% with paint mixed incorrectly 20% of the time. Cascade guarantees its product and spent $10,000 replacing improperly mixed paint last year. How should the cost be distributed among the three plants?

4-24. The Chocolate House specializes in hand-dipped chocolates for special occasions. Recently, several long-time customers have complained about the quality of the chocolates. It seems there were several partially covered chocolates in each box. The defective chocolates should have been caught when the boxes were packed. The manager is wondering which of the three packers is not doing the job properly. Clerk 1 packs 40% of the boxes and usually has a 2% defective rate. Clerk 2 packs 30% with a 2.5% defective rate. Clerk 3 boxes 30% of the chocolates and her defective rate is 1.5%. Which clerk is most likely responsible for the boxes that raised the complaints?

4-25. As the owner of the Union Nursery, Kelly is concerned about the quality of some of the plants purchased from a local wholesaler, but she is not certain why the problem has suddenly cropped up. The company has been buying plants from this particular wholesaler for years, and the quality has always been excellent. A new employee of Kelly's who formerly worked for the wholesaler explains that just before he left his previous position, the wholesaler had started purchasing plants from a new grower in order to meet demand. The old grower has a good reputation and only 2% of his plants are unusable. The new grower's plants are of poor quality 30% of the time. The old grower currently supplies 80% of the wholesaler's plants. If Kelly receives another shipment of unusable plants, which grower more likely supplied the plants?

4-26. The Carlisle Medical Clinic has five doctors on staff. The doctors have agreed to keep the office open on Saturdays with just three doctors. The office manager has decided to make up Saturday schedules in such a way that no set of three doctors will be in the office together more than once.
   a. How many weeks can be covered by this schedule? (Hint: Use a tree diagram to list out the sample space.)
   b. If the office manager selects three doctors at random for four consecutive Saturdays, determine the probability that Dr. Smith and Dr. Fry will be in the office together only once.

4-27. The White Aviation Company runs a charter air service with eight planes. However, because of pilot availability, only four planes can be in the air at one time. The dispatcher has decided to set up a plane usage schedule that will include the planes to be used on a particular day in order of usage.
   a. How many different schedules are possible without repeating a schedule?
   b. If the dispatcher selects planes at random to use each day, determine the probability that a particular plane will be used on both of the first two days of the schedule.

4-28. In the late 1960s the U.S. government instituted a lottery system for determining how young men between the ages of 18 and 26 would be drafted into military service. Balls, each marked with a different day of the year (365 of them), were placed in a large drum and mixed. Balls were selected from the drum randomly.
   a. What is the probability that the first two balls selected were for birthdays in March?
   b. What is the probability that the first ball selected was a December birthday or a birthday on the first of any month?
   c. If the first ball selected was a March birthday, what is the probability that the second ball selected was a June birthday?

d. What is the probability that the first three balls selected were for birthdays in the same month?

4-29. The Ace Construction Company has submitted a bid on a state government project in Delaware. The price of the bid was predetermined in the bid specifications. The contract is to be awarded on the basis of a blind drawing from those who have bid. Five other companies have also submitted bids.
   a. What is the probability of the Ace Construction Company winning the bid?
   b. Suppose that there are two contracts to be awarded by a blind draw. What is the probability of Ace winning both contracts?
   c. Referring to part b, what is the probability of Ace not winning either contract?
   d. Referring to part b, what is the probability of Ace winning exactly one contract?
   e. Referring to part b, what is the probability of Ace winning at least one contract?

4-30. The Fortune 500 ranks the 500 largest U.S. corporations. The 1998 list revealed that 30 firms in the ranking have their headquarters in Ohio. What is the probability that a firm selected at random from the list would have its headquarters in Ohio?

4-31. If 15 of the Fortune 500 companies have their headquarters in Michigan and 6 have their headquarters in Maryland, what is the probability that 2 firms selected at random from the list of 500 would have one Michigan and one Maryland firm?

4-32. A manager of a gasoline filling station is thinking about a promotion that she hopes will bring in more business to the full-service island. She is considering the option that when a customer requests a fill-up, if the pump stops with the dollar amount at $9.99, the customer will get the gasoline free. Previous studies show that 70% of the customers require $10.00 or more when they fill up their gas tanks, so would not be eligible for the free gas. What is the probability that a customer will get free gas at this station if the promotion is implemented?

4-33. Referring to Problem 32, suppose the manager is concerned about alienating customers who buy $10.00 or more since they would not be eligible to win the free gas under the original concept. To overcome this, she is thinking about changing the contest. The customer will get free gas if any of the following happens:

$9.99, $11.11, $12.22, $13.33, $14.44, $15.55
$16.66, $17.77, $18.88, $19.99

Past data show that only 5% of all customers require $20.00 or more. If one of these big volume customers arrives, he or she will get a blind draw of a ball from a box containing 100 balls (99 red, 1 white). If the white ball is picked, the customer gets a free tank of gas. Considering this new promotion, what is the probability that a customer will get free gas?

4-34. A Courtyard Hotel by Marriott conducted a survey of its guests. Sixty-two surveys were completed. Based on the data from the survey, found in the file named **Courtyard Survey**, determine the following probabilities using the relative frequency of occurrence method.

   a. Two customers are selected. What is the probability that both will be on a business trip?

   b. What is the probability that a customer will be on a business trip or will experience a hotel problem during his or her stay at the Courtyard?

   c. What is the probability that a customer on business will have an in-state area code phone number?

   d. Based on the data in the survey, can the Courtyard manager conclude that a customer's rating regarding staff attentiveness is independent of whether he or she is traveling on business, pleasure, or both? Use the rules of probability to make this determination.

4-35. The ECCO company makes backup alarms for machinery like forklifts and commercial trucks. When a customer returns one of the alarms under warranty, the quality manager logs data on the product. Using the available data in the **ECCO** file, use relative frequency of occurrence to find the following probabilities.

   a. If a part was made in the Salt Lake plant, what is the probability the cause of the returned part was due to wiring?

   b. If the company incurs a $30 cost for each returned alarm, what percentage of the cost should be assigned to each plant if it is known that 70% of all production is done in Boise, 20% in Salt Lake, and the rest in Toronto?

■ 4-3: DISCRETE PROBABILITY DISTRIBUTIONS

As discussed earlier in this chapter, when a random experiment or trial is performed, some outcome, or event, must occur. When the trial or experiment has a quantitative characteristic, we can associate a number with each outcome. For example, an inspector who examines three sheets of plywood can judge each sheet as "acceptable" or "unacceptable." The outcome of the experiment in which three sheets of plywood are inspected defines a **random variable** where the specific number of "acceptable" sheets of plywood is:

$$x = \{0, 1, 2, 3\}$$

Although the inspector knows these are the possible values for the random variable before she samples, she would be uncertain about which value would occur in any given trial. Further, the value of the random variable will vary each time three plywood sheets are inspected.

> **RANDOM VARIABLE**
> A variable that assigns a numerical value to each outcome of a random experiment or trial.

Random Variables

In the example at the beginning of the chapter where the accountant randomly examined 15 accounts, the number of inaccurate account balances can also be represented by a random variable with the following possible values:

$$x = \{0, 1, 2, \ldots, 15\}$$

Two classes of random variables exist, namely, **discrete random variables** and **continuous random variables**.

> **DISCRETE RANDOM VARIABLE**
> A random variable that can assume only a countable number of values.

The two previous examples illustrate discrete random variables. The pieces of good plywood could assume only four values: 0, 1, 2, or 3, and the number of incorrect account balances had to be one of these 16 values: 0, 1, 2 . . ., 15.

In other situations, the random variable is said to be continuous.

> **CONTINUOUS RANDOM VARIABLES**
> Random variables that can assume any value on a continuum. Alternatively, random variables that can assume an uncountable number of values.

For example, the exact time it takes a trainee to perform a job task may be any value between two points, say 1 minute and 10 minutes. If x is the time required, then x is continuous since, if measured precisely enough, the possible values can be any point in the interval 1–10 minutes.[2] Other examples of continuous variables include measures of distance and measures of weight when measured precisely. Chapter 5 will discuss the concept of continuous random variables more fully.

In situations where the random variable can assume only a countable number of values the probability distribution is discrete. This type of distribution is illustrated in the following example.

whole #

Office Support, Inc.

Office Support, Inc. provides on-site repair for most large photocopy machines. It currently has five trained repair teams that it sends out on an on-call basis. Since the company advertises one-day service, it will not accept more than five requests for service per day. Two months ago, the vice president started considering expanding the workforce. At that time, he asked the call desk to record the actual calls for each of the next 40 days. Table 4-11 shows the resulting data. Note the discrete random variable will have possible values equal to the number of calls received per day.

The relative frequencies for each value of x have been computed in Table 4-11. For instance, over this 40-day period the company has received $x = 0$ calls on 3, or 7.5%, of the days. During 8, or 20%, of the days, $x = 3$ calls were received.

Recall that one way to assess probability is to use the relative frequency of occurrence; that is, the probability of an outcome (or value of the random variable) occurring can be assessed by the relative frequency of that outcome.

The probability distribution for a discrete random variable shows each value of the random variable (x) and its associated probability, $P(x)$. The Office Support, Inc. probability distribution is

EXAMPLE 4-19

DISCRETE DISTRIBUTIONS

x	$P(x)$
0	0.075
1	0.100
2	0.250
3	0.200
4	0.175
5	0.150
6	0.050
	$\sum = 1.000$

The probability distribution must sum to 1.0. Figure 4-5 shows this probability distribution in graphical form. The bar for each possible value of x is one unit wide. The height of

TABLE 4-11
Service Calls per Day

SERVICE CALLS = x	FREQUENCY	RELATIVE FREQUENCY
0	3	3/40 = 0.075
1	4	4/40 = 0.100
2	10	10/40 = 0.250
3	8	8/40 = 0.200
4	7	7/40 = 0.175
5	6	6/40 = 0.150
6	2	2/40 = 0.050
	40	$\sum = 40/40 = 1.000$

[2]If the time were observed to the nearest minute, then there would be only 10 possible values (a countable number) for the random variable. It would be considered, then, a discrete random variable.

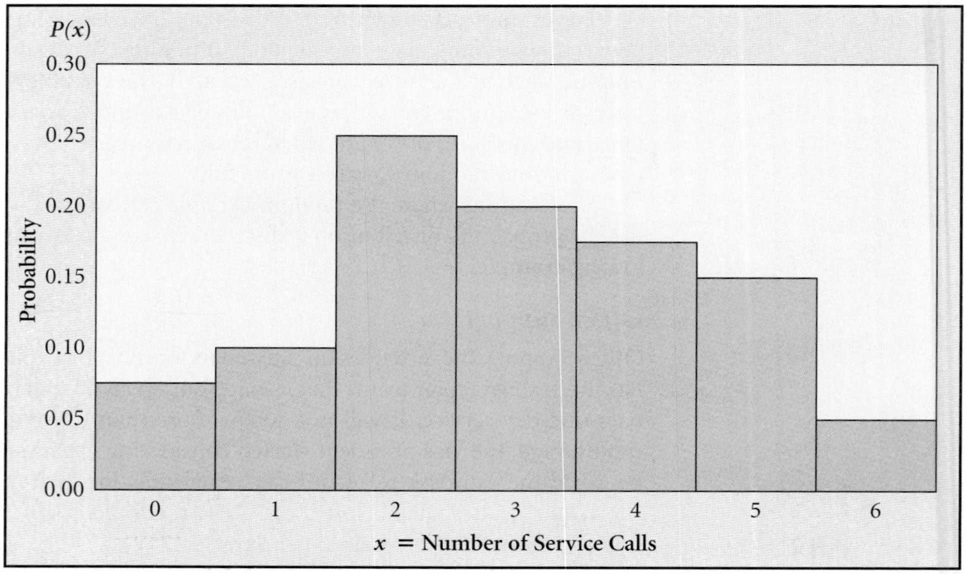

area of each bar
(w * h) = prob
of x

FIGURE 4-5
Discrete Probability
Distribution

the bars corresponds to the probability of each value of x. The area of each bar (width times height) also represents the probability of a given value of x. The sum of the areas of all the bars adds to 1.0.

As with a frequency histogram for raw data, the graph of the probability distribution provides us with a general idea where the variable is centered and how much variation there is in the possible outcomes.

Office Support, Inc. already has five service teams. According to the probability distribution, there is a 0.05 chance that a customer will be turned away given the current staffing. The manager will have to trade off his desire to serve all customers against the cost of having a sixth service team.

McMillin Manufacturing Co.

EXAMPLE

4-20

DISCRETE DISTRIBUTIONS

Consider the McMillin Manufacturing Company, which makes efficient woodburning stoves for use in homes. It manufactures all parts of the stove except for the chimney pipe, which it purchases from a supplier in Pennsylvania. The purchasing agent for McMillin has just received notification that this supplier is no longer going to make the type of chimney pipe that McMillin needs. The notification listed another company in Maryland that could supply the chimney pipe.

A call to the Maryland company confirmed that it could be used as the source of the chimney pipes. The price was comparable to that of the Pennsylvania company, but it could not guarantee a fixed time period between order and delivery. This time, referred to as *lead time*, would be anywhere between 1 and 4 weeks. Having no other information to go on, the McMillin purchasing agent developed the following discrete probability distribution for lead time.

x	$P(x)$
1 week	0.25
2 weeks	0.25
3 weeks	0.25
4 weeks	0.25
	$\sum = 1.00$

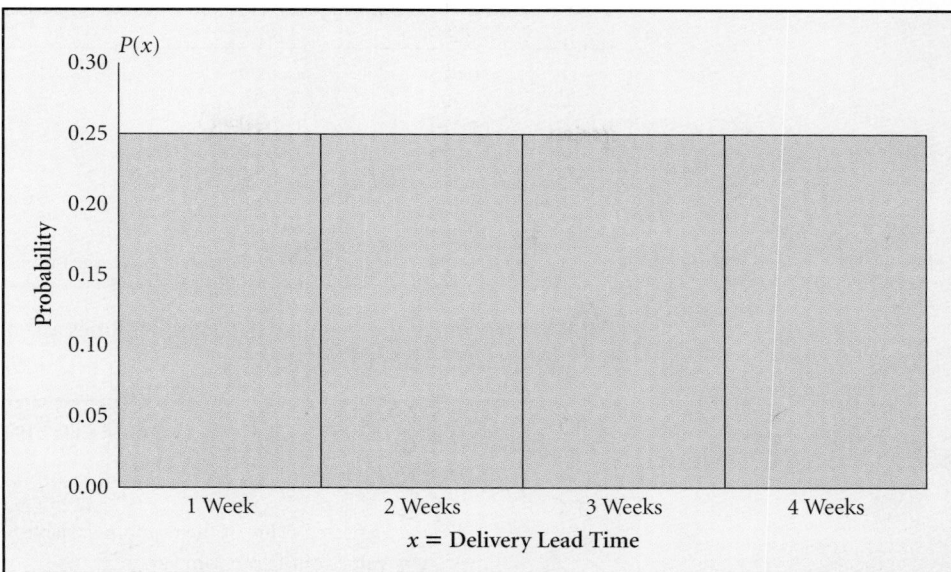

FIGURE 4-6
Uniform Probability
Distribution for the McMillin
Example

In this example, the purchasing agent subjectively assessed the probability distribution for lead time. Note that the probabilities assigned to each of the discrete outcomes of the random variable are the same. Since the purchasing agent had nothing other than the supplier's statement that lead time would be between 1 and 4 weeks, she chose to assign equal probabilities to each of the 4 outcomes. A discrete probability distribution that has equal probabilities for all possible outcomes of the random variable is called a **uniform probability distribution**. Figure 4-6 shows a graph of the uniform probability distribution for the McMillin example.

> **UNIFORM PROBABILITY DISTRIBUTION**
> A probability distribution that has equal probabilities for all possible outcomes of the random variable.

The uniform probability distribution is sometimes called the distribution of "little knowledge." In this example, the purchasing agent is unable to reflect any information in her probability assessments other than that the lead time will be either 1, 2, 3, or 4 weeks. Many instances arise in business when it is appropriate to assess a uniform probability distribution. These occur when the decision maker believes the outcomes of the random variable are equally likely.

The Mean and Standard Deviation of Discrete Distributions

A probability distribution, like a frequency distribution, can be only partially described by a graph. Often decision makers will need to calculate the distribution's *mean* and *standard deviation*. These values measure the central location and spread, respectively, of the probability distribution.

CALCULATING THE MEAN

The mean of a discrete probability distribution is also called the **expected value** of the discrete random variable. The expected value is actually a *weighted average* of the random

x	$P(x)$	$xP(x)$
0	0.075	0.00
1	0.100	0.10
2	0.250	0.50
3	0.200	0.60
4	0.175	0.70
5	0.150	0.75
6	0.050	0.30
	$\sum = 1.000$	$\sum = 2.95 = E(x)$ = average number of service calls per day

T A B L E   4 - 1 2
Expected Value Computation
for Service Calls

variable values, where the weights are the probabilities assigned to the values. The expected value is given in Equation 4-14:

EXPECTED VALUE FOR A DISCRETE DISTRIBUTION

$$E(x) = \sum xP(x)$$ 4-14

where:

$E(x)$ = Expected value of the random variable
x = Values of the random variable
$P(x)$ = Probability of the random variable taking on the value x

---

4-21

EXPECTED VALUE

Office Support (continued)

The vice president at Office Support, Inc. collected data on the actual number of calls for service. These data were used to develop a probability distribution for the number of calls (see Table 4-11). The mean (expected value) of the random variable for the Office Support, Inc. example is found using Equation 4-14 as shown in Table 4-12.

Therefore, in the long run, the average number of systems repaired per day is 2.95. Again, the expected value is just a weighted average of the random variable values. Clearly, on any one day, the actual number of calls will be higher or lower than 2.95 since the number of calls must be an integer value.

CALCULATING THE STANDARD DEVIATION

The standard deviation measures the spread, or dispersion, in a set of data. The standard deviation also measures the spread in the same units as the random variable. To calculate the standard deviation for a discrete probability distribution, use Equation 4-15.

STANDARD DEVIATION FOR A DISCRETE PROBABILITY DISTRIBUTION

$$\sigma_x = \sqrt{\sum [x - E(x)]^2 P(x)}$$ 4-15

where:

x = Values of the random variable
$E(x)$ = Expected value of the random variable
$P(x)$ = Probability of the random variable having the value x

---

4-22

**STANDARD
DEVIATION**

Office Support (continued)

As Equation 4-15 shows, the standard deviation is the positive square root of a weighted average of squared differences between each value of the random variable and the expected value of the frequency distribution. The weights are the respective probabilities.

For the Office Support, Inc. example, the standard deviation is computed as shown in Table 4-13. The standard deviation of the random variable, systems serviced, is 1.596 per day. This measures the variation around the average number of calls from day to day.

TABLE 4-13
Standard Deviation
Computation for the
Customer Service Example

Optional
CD Topic

Covariance
Analysis

x	P(x)	x − E(x)	[x − E(x)]²	[x − E(x)]²P(x)
0	0.075	0 − 2.95 = −2.95	8.7025	0.6527
1	0.100	1 − 2.95 = −1.95	3.8025	0.3803
2	0.250	2 − 2.95 = −0.95	0.9025	0.2256
3	0.200	3 − 2.95 = 0.05	0.0025	0.0005
4	0.175	4 − 2.95 = 1.05	1.1025	0.1929
5	0.150	5 − 2.95 = 2.05	4.2025	0.6304
6	0.050	6 − 2.95 = 3.05	9.3025	0.4651

$$\sum = 2.5475$$

$$\sigma = \sqrt{2.5475} = 1.596$$

OPTIONAL CD-ROM TOPIC Expected Value, and Variance Laws and Identities

There are several rules for working with expected values that you will find useful. These include the method for determining the expected value and variance for the sum of two or more random variables. For more information, go to the CD-ROM.

4-3: EXERCISES

ADDITIONAL EXERCISES ON YOUR CD-ROM

Try the ADDITIONAL EXERCISES and APPLICATION PROBLEMS on the CD-ROM.

4-36. Examine the following discrete probability distribution.

x	P(x)
10	0.05
15	0.20
25	0.40
40	0.35

a. Find the expected value, variance, and standard deviation.
b. Develop a graphical picture of the discrete probability distribution.
c. Recall that the pth percentile is a value such that at least p% of the data is at most as big as that value, and at least (100 − p)% of the data is at least as big as that value. Using this definition, produce the quartiles for this distribution.

4-37. Given the following discrete probability distribution:

x	P(x)
100	0.30
150	0.40
160	0.30

a. Find the expected value of x.
b. Find the variance of x.

c. Find the standard deviation of x.

4-38. Refer to Problems 36 and 37. Recalling the concept of coefficient of variation in Chapter 3, which distribution has the greater relative variability? Discuss why the coefficient of variation would be useful to make this determination.

Business Applications

4-39. For the past four years, Armonco Manufacturing has been offering a three-year limited warranty on all appliances it manufactures. Although all appliances are given a unique serial number when manufactured, until this year Armonco had no capability of determining how often any appliance was brought to an authorized service facility. At the beginning of the year, the long-promised computer database linking all service facilities with a central system was finally operational. A preliminary report shows the following results for one of the appliances Armonco manufactures.

TIMES BROUGHT FOR REPAIR	PROBABILITY
0	0.55
1	0.25
2	0.14
3	0.04
4	0.02

a. Find the expected number of repairs for this appliance.

b. Find the standard deviation of this repair distribution.

c. If the average cost of a service call is $40, provide an estimate for the average cost of a warranty for Armonco per year for this appliance.

4-40. The Seremonte Emergency Medical Department has recorded the number of emergency calls received each day for the past 200 days. These data are shown in frequency distribution form as follows.

CALLS	NUMBER OF DAYS	$P(x)$	$x(P_x)$
0	22	.11	0
1	20	.10	.10
2	40	.20	.4
3	55	.275	.825
4	28	.14	.56
5	20	.10	.50
6	5	.025	.15
7	10	.05	.35
	200		

$$E(x) = 2.885$$

a. Determine the probability distribution based on the given frequency distribution.

b. What is the mean of the probability distribution?

c. What is the standard deviation of the probability distribution?

d. Each emergency call requires a team of three individuals to respond. How many employees must the Seremonte Emergency Medical Department have so that they can respond to at least 75% of the emergency calls?

4-41. The Nu-Look Car Wash recently opened at a new location where customers leave cars in the morning and pick up after work. The manager at this location is concerned about staffing levels, so he has taken a sample of 100 days from the company's other location and found the following frequency distribution.

CARS	FREQUENCY
0 and under 10	10
10 and under 20	17
20 and under 30	35
30 and under 40	22
40 and under 50	16
	100

a. Determine the expected number of cars to arrive at the car wash.

b. Determine the variance and standard deviation.

c. Two employees wash each car. It takes approximately 20 minutes to wash each car. Determine the number of employees the manager must have on hand each day if the manager wishes to meet demand at least 85% of the days.

4-42. Refer to Problem 41. The manager of Nu-Look Car Wash has had complaints from his employees. He pays them each $2.00 a car. However, on some days there just aren't very many cars to wash and on others there are lots of cars. So the employees' wages vary substantially. The manager has, therefore, offered a salary of $6.00 an hour to any employee who wishes. Suppose you are advising the employees. What would you advise them to do? (Hint: You may wish to calculate the probability distribution, average dollars earned, and standard deviation under the two systems of pay.)

4-4: THE BINOMIAL PROBABILITY DISTRIBUTION

Several theoretical discrete distributions have extensive application in business decision making. A probability distribution is called *theoretical* when the mathematical properties of its random variable are used to produce its probabilities. Such distributions are different than those distributions that are obtained subjectively or from observation such as those discussed in the previous section.

The simplest theoretical probability distribution we will consider is one that describes processes whose trials have only two possible outcomes. The physical events described by this type of process are widespread. For instance, a quality control system in a manufacturing plant labels each tested item as either defective or acceptable. A firm bidding for a contract either will get the contract or it will not. A marketing research firm may receive responses to a questionnaire in the form of "Yes, I will buy" or "No, I will not buy." The personnel manager in an organization is faced with a two-stage process each time he offers a job—either the applicant accepts the offer or rejects it.

Characteristics of the Binomial Distribution

These examples are all situations that can be described by a discrete probability distribution called the **binomial distribution.**

BINOMIAL PROBABILITY DISTRIBUTION

A distribution that gives the probability of x successes in n trials of a process which meets the following conditions.

1. A trial has only two possible outcomes—a success or a failure.
2. There is a fixed number, n, of identical trials.
3. The trials of the experiment are independent of each other. This means that if one outcome is a success, this does not influence the chance of another outcome being a success.
4. The process must be consistent in generating successes and failures. That is, the probability, p, associated with a success remains constant from trial to trial.
5. The p represents the probability of a success, then $(1 - p) = q$ is the probability of a failure.

The binomial distribution requires that the trials of the experiment be independent. This can be assured in a finite population if the sampling is performed with replacement. This means that an item is sampled from a population and returned to the population, after its characteristic(s) have been recorded, before the next item is sampled. However, sampling with replacement is the exception rather than the rule in business applications. Most often the sampling is performed without replacement. Strictly speaking, when sampling is performed without replacement, the conditions for the binomial distribution cannot be satisfied. However, the conditions are approximately satisfied if the sample selected is quite small relative to the size of the population from which the sample is selected. *A commonly used rule of thumb is that the binomial distribution can be applied if the sample size is at most 5% of the population size.*

EXAMPLE 4-23

BINOMIAL DISTRIBUTION

Household Security

Household Security produces and installs home security units for both new and older houses. Business has been very good recently with Household installing 300 security units weekly. The security systems use a combination of magnetic, infrared, and sonic systems with each unit custom made for the particular house. The units are priced to include one-day installation service by two technicians. A unit with either a design or production problem must be modified on site and will require more than one day to install.

Household Security has completed an extensive study of its design and manufacturing systems. The information shows that if the company is operating at standard quality, 10% of the security systems will have problems (require more than one day to install).

The binomial distribution can be used in this situation since the following conditions exist.

1. There are only two possible outcomes when a unit is sold: it is good or it is defective (will take more than one day to install). Finding a defective system in this application will be considered a success. A success occurs when we observe the outcome of interest. If we are looking for defective systems, finding one is considered a success.
2. Each unit is designed and made in the same way.
3. The outcome of a security system (defective or good) is independent of whether the preceding system was good or defective.
4. The probability of a defective system, $p = 0.10$, remains constant from unit to unit.
5. The probability of a good system, $q = (1 - p) = 0.90$, remains constant from unit to unit.

In an effort to determine the likely cause of defects, design or production, the quality assurance group at Household Security has developed a plan for dismantling four security systems each week to help determine whether the company is maintaining its production quality standard. The sampling will be performed without replacement. Since the sample is small (4/300 = 1.33%) relative to the size of the population (300 units per week), the conditions of independence and constant probability will be approximately satisfied since the sample is less than 5% of the population. The number of defectives is limited to discrete values, $x = 0, 1, 2, 3,$ or 4.

If we let the number of defective units be the random variable of interest, we can determine the probability that the random variable will have any of the discrete values. One way of finding these probabilities is to list the sample space as shown in Table 4-14. We can find the probability of zero defectives, for instance, by employing the multiplication rule for independent events.

$$P(x = 0 \text{ defectives}) = P(G \text{ and } G \text{ and } G \text{ and } G)$$

where:

$$G = \text{Unit is good (not defective)}$$

Here:

$$P(G) = 0.90,$$

and we have assumed the units are independent. Using the multiplication rule for independent events (Rule 4-12):

$$P(G \text{ and } G \text{ and } G \text{ and } G) = P(G)P(G)P(G)P(G) = (0.90)(0.90)(0.90)(0.90)$$
$$= 0.90^4$$
$$= 0.6561$$

We can also find the probability of exactly one defective in a sample of four. This is accomplished using both the multiplication rule for independent events and the addition rule for mutually exclusive events (Rule 4-8):

$$P(1 \text{ defective}) = P(G \text{ and } G \text{ and } G \text{ and } D) + P(G \text{ and } G \text{ and } D \text{ and } G) +$$
$$P(G \text{ and } D \text{ and } G \text{ and } G) + P(D \text{ and } G \text{ and } G \text{ and } G)$$

where:

$$P(G \text{ and } G \text{ and } G \text{ and } D) = P(G)P(G)P(G)P(D) = (0.90)(0.90)(0.90)(0.10)$$
$$= (0.90^3)(0.10)$$

TABLE 4-14
Sample Space

RESULTS	NO. OF DEFECTIVES	NO. OF WAYS
G,G,G,G	0	1
G,G,G,D		
G,G,D,G		
G,D,G,G	1	4
D,G,G,G		
G,G,D,D		
G,D,G,D		
D,G,G,D		
G,D,D,G	2	6
D,G,D,G		
D,D,G,G		
D,D,D,G		
D,D,G,D		
D,G,D,D	3	4
G,D,D,D		
D,D,D,D	4	1

Likewise:
$$P(G \text{ and } G \text{ and } D \text{ and } G) = (0.90^3)(0.10)$$
$$P(G \text{ and } D \text{ and } G \text{ and } G) = (0.90^3)(0.10)$$
$$P(D \text{ and } G \text{ and } G \text{ and } G) = (0.90^3)(0.10)$$

Then:
$$P(1 \text{ defective}) = (0.90^3)(0.10) + (0.90^3)(0.10) + (0.90^3)(0.10) + (0.90^3)(0.10)$$
$$= (4)(0.90^3)(0.10)$$
$$= 0.2916$$

Factorial Notation
$$n! = n \text{ factorial}$$
$$0! = 1 \text{ by definition}$$
$$1! = 1$$
$$2! = 2 \times 1 = 2$$
$$3! = 3 \times 2 \times 1 = 6$$

Note that each of the four possible ways of finding one defective unit has the same probability $[(0.90^3)(0.10)]$. We determine the probability of one of the ways to obtain one defective unit and multiply this value by the number of ways (4) of obtaining one defective unit. This produces the overall probability of one defective unit.

COMBINATIONS

In this relatively simple example we can fairly easily list the sample space and from that count the number of ways that each possible number of defectives can occur. However, for larger examples, this approach is inefficient. A more effective method exists for counting the number of ways binomial events can occur. This method is called the *counting rule for combinations*. This rule is used to count the number of outcomes from an experiment where x objects are to be selected from a group of n objects. Equation 4-16 is used to find the number of combinations.

COUNTING RULE FOR COMBINATIONS — *order don't matter*

$$C_x^n = \frac{n!}{x!(n-x)!}$$ **4-16**

where:

i.e. - committee

$$n! = n(n-1)(n-2)\ldots(2)(1)$$
$$x! = x(x-1)(x-2)\ldots(2)(1)$$
$$0! = 1$$

Using Equation 4-16, we find the number of ways that $x = 2$ defects can occur in a sample of $n = 4$ as:

$$C_x^n = \frac{n!}{x!(n-x)!} = \frac{4!}{2!(4-2)!} = \frac{(4)(3)(2)(1)}{(2)(1)(2)(1)} = \frac{24}{4} = 6 \text{ ways}$$

Refer to Table 4-14 to see that this is the same value obtained by listing the sample space. Now we can find the probability of two defects.

$$P(2 \text{ defectives}) = (6)(0.90^2)(0.10^2)$$
$$= 0.0486$$

Use this method to verify the following:

$$P(3 \text{ defectives}) = (4)(0.90)(0.10^3)$$
$$= 0.0036$$
$$P(4 \text{ defectives}) = (0.10^4)$$
$$= 0.0001$$

The key to developing the probability distribution for a binomial process is first to determine the probability of any one way the event of interest can occur (e.g., $0.90^2 \times 0.10^2$ for two successes) and then to multiply this probability by the number of ways that event can occur (e.g., 6 in the two success example yielding $6 \times 0.90^2 \times 0.10^2$). Table 4-15 shows the binomial probability distribution for the number of defective security units in a sample of size 4 when the probability of any individual unit being defective is 0.10.

TABLE 4-15
Binomial Distribution for Household Security $n = 4$, $p = 0.10$

x = NO. OF DEFECTS	$P(x)$
0	0.6561
1	0.2916
2	0.0486
3	0.0036
4	0.0001
	$\sum P(x) = 1.0000$

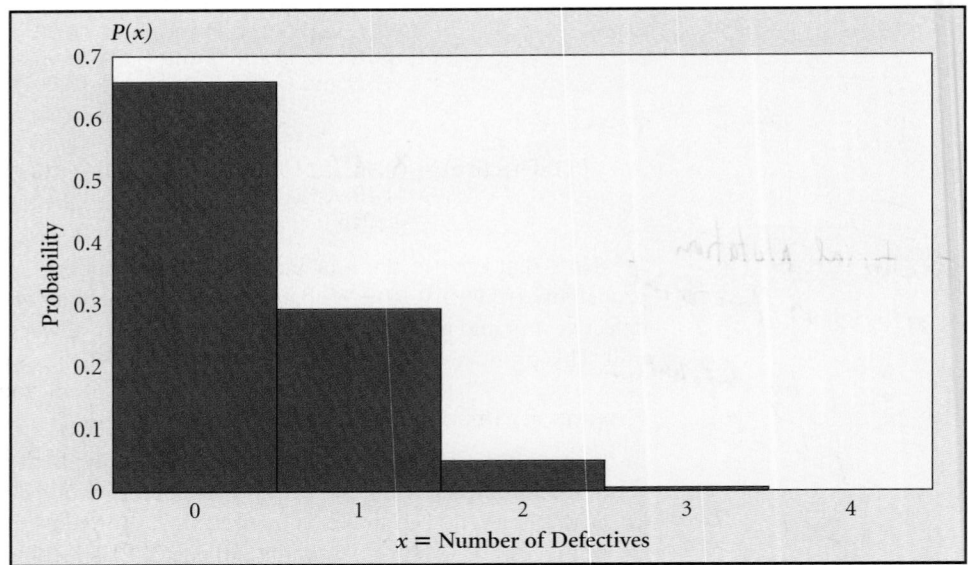

FIGURE 4-7
Binomial Distribution for
Household Security

The probability distribution is graphed in Figure 4-7. Most samples would contain zero or one defective units when the production system is functioning as designed.

BINOMIAL FORMULA

The steps that we have taken to develop this binomial probability distribution can be summarized through a formula called the **binomial formula** shown as Equation 4-17. Note that this formula is composed of two parts: the number of combinations of x items selected from n items and the probability of one of the ways that x items can occur.

BINOMIAL FORMULA

$$P(x) = \frac{n!}{x!(n-x)!}p^x q^{n-x}$$ 4-17

where:

n = Sample size
x = Number of successes (where a success is what we are looking for)
$n - x$ = Number of failures
p = Probability of a success
$q = 1 - p$ = Probability of a failure
$n! = n(n-1)(n-2)(n-3)\ldots 1$
$0! = 1$ by definition

Applying Equation 4-17 to the security system example for $n = 4$, $p = 0.10$, and $x = 2$ defects we get:

$$P(x) = \frac{n!}{x!(n-x)!}p^x q^{n-x}$$

$$P(x = 2) = \frac{4!}{2!\,2!}0.10^2 0.90^2 = 6(0.10)^2(0.90)^2 = 0.0486$$

This is the same value we obtained earlier when we listed out the sample space.

The combinations counting rule is used to help compute binomial probabilities, but there is another counting technique called *permutations* that, together with combinations, will be of value in working with certain other probability situations. A special topic on your CD-ROM is devoted to these counting techniques.

OPTIONAL CD-ROM TOPIC Counting Techniques—Permutations and Combinations

Computing probabilities is often aided by being able to count the elements in the sample space. Counting techniques exist to help with this effort. For more information go to the CD-ROM.

Using the Binomial Distribution Table

Using Equation 4-17 to develop the binomial distribution is not difficult, but it can be time consuming. To make binomial probabilities easier to find, you can use the binomial table in Appendix B. This table is constructed to give individual probabilities for different sample sizes and probabilities of success. Within the table for each specified sample size, you will find columns of probabilities. Each column is headed by a probability, p, which is the probability associated with a success. The column headings correspond to probabilities of success ranging from 0.01 to 0.50. At the bottom of each column are probabilities of successes ranging from 0.50 to 0.99. Down both sides of the table are integer values that correspond to the number of successes. The x values on the *left* side are used with values of p between 0.01 and 0.50. The x values on the *right* side are used for values of p greater than 0.50.

EXAMPLE
4-24

BINOMIAL TABLE

U. S. Bio

U.S. Bio, a pharmaceutical company, has developed a drug that has been shown to be effective in restoring hair growth in men who suffer from hair loss. Like most drugs, this product has potential side effects. One of these is increased blood pressure. The company is willing to market the drug if the increased blood pressure occurs in 2% or less of those using the drug.

The company plans to conduct a clinical test with 10 men. The number of men who exhibit increased blood pressure will be $x = 0, 1, 2, \ldots, 10$. We can use the binomial table in Appendix B to develop the probability distribution. Table 4-16 shows the portion of the binomial table we need for $n = 10$. Go to the column for $p = 0.02$. The values of x are listed down the left side of the table. For example, the probability of 3 occurrences is 0.0008. This means that it is extremely unlikely that 3 men, in a sample of 10, would exhibit increased blood pressure if the overall percentage having this side effect is 0.02.

If the test showed that 3 men did actually have elevated blood pressure after taking the new drug, the company would have serious doubts about the drug since the chance of this

TABLE 4-16
Binomial Table ($n = 10$)

x	$p = .01$	$p = .02$	$p = .03$	$p = .04$	$p = .05$	$p = .06$	$p = .07$	$p = .08$	$p = .09$	$p = .10$	$n - x$
0	.9044	.8171	.7374	.6648	.5987	.5386	.4840	.4344	.3894	.3487	10
1	.0914	.1667	.2281	.2770	.3151	.3438	.3643	.3777	.3851	.3874	9
2	.0042	.0153	.0317	.0519	.0746	.0988	.1234	.1478	.1714	.1937	8
3	.0001	.0008	.0026	.0058	.0105	.0168	.0248	.0343	.0452	.0574	7
4	.0000	.0000	.0001	.0004	.0010	.0019	.0033	.0052	.0078	.0112	6
5	.0000	.0000	.0000	.0000	.0001	.0001	.0003	.0005	.0009	.0015	5
6	.0000	.0000	.0000	.0000	.0000	.0000	.0000	.0000	.0001	.0001	4
7	.0000	.0000	.0000	.0000	.0000	.0000	.0000	.0000	.0000	.0000	3
8	.0000	.0000	.0000	.0000	.0000	.0000	.0000	.0000	.0000	.0000	2
9	.0000	.0000	.0000	.0000	.0000	.0000	.0000	.0000	.0000	.0000	1
10	.0000	.0000	.0000	.0000	.0000	.0000	.0000	.0000	.0000	.0000	0
	$q = .99$	$q = .98$	$q = .97$	$q = .96$	$q = .95$	$q = .94$	$q = .93$	$q = .92$	$q = .91$	$q = .90$	

Header for table: $n = 10$

happening is extremely low (0.0008) if the true rate is 2%. Instead, the true rate of high blood pressure likely exceeds 2%.

4-25

BINOMIAL TABLE

Excel and
Minitab Tutorial

EPA Standards

A fact of life in making decisions using probability distributions is that the decision is often not clear-cut. As an example, suppose the Environmental Protection Agency (EPA) has been given a mandate by Congress to determine whether automobiles manufactured in the United States meet pollution standards. The EPA wishes to allow no more than 5% of the cars produced by any manufacturer to receive a substandard rating. A southern U.S. state with strict pollution control standards has decided to base its enforcement policy on the EPA's 5% standard. Since the state enforcement agency cannot test every car sold in the state, it randomly samples 25 cars of each make and model. If it finds more than 1 car in the sample with a substandard pollution rating, the manufacturer receives a stiff fine. The state's rule says that if more than 1 substandard car is found, the conclusion is that the automobile company is exceeding the 5% limit.

Of course the automobile manufacturers are concerned about the chances of being unjustly accused. That is, a company may in fact be producing 5% or fewer cars with substandard pollution control devices, but the state could find, by chance, more than 1 such car in its sample of 25. The binomial probability table can be used to find the probability of this happening. We let the random variable equal the number of cars with a substandard pollution rating. We are interested in finding $P(x > 1)$. We can easily compute this probability by finding:

$$P(x > 1) = 1 - P(x \le 1)$$

Going to the binomial table with $n = 25$ and $p = 0.05$, we find that:

$$\begin{aligned} P(x > 1) &= 1 - [P(0) + P(1)] \\ &= 1 - (0.2774 + 0.3650) = 1 - 0.6424 \\ &= 0.3576 \end{aligned}$$

This means that, under the proposed sampling plan, there is over a 35% chance that automakers, in compliance with EPA standards, will be unjustly accused of making too large a proportion of substandard cars (by pollution standards).

Because of the high potential costs of being unjustly accused, the manufacturers would be likely to challenge the sampling plan. They would probably argue that more cars should be sampled and that the cutoff point for recall should be altered to reduce the probability of being unjustly accused.

To look at the situation from the state's perspective, let us consider the situation where 10% of a manufacturer's cars exceed the pollution standards. This is twice the EPA allowable rate. What is the probability that a sample of 25 cars will have only 1 or fewer cars exceed the standards and thus allow the manufacturer to pass the test? This time we want:

$$P(x \le 1)$$

Going to the binomial table with $n = 25$ and $p = 0.10$, we find:

$$\begin{aligned} P(x \le 1) &= P(0) + P(1) \\ &= 0.0718 + 0.1994 \\ &= 0.2712 \end{aligned}$$

This relatively large chance of incorrectly passing the test may lead EPA officials to argue for stricter standards.

In the dispute between the state and the automobile makers over pollution testing, both sides would benefit from a larger sample size. The only argument against testing more than 25 cars is the cost of conducting the tests. Suppose that the state obtained funding to sample 100 cars of each make and model. Based on this higher sample size, the state is considering fining the automaker if more than 4 cars fail to meet the standards. How does this new sampling plan affect the chances of the state incorrectly fining a company that is meeting the 5% EPA level?

The binomial table in Appendix B does not contain sample sizes of 100. Instead we can use Excel's **BINOMDIST** function or the binomial tool in Minitab's **Calc—Probability Distribution** menu to find the probability. Both software packages offer the user the option of computing individual or cumulative probabilities. Figure 4-8 shows the Minitab output with the cumulative binomial probabilities for $n = 100$ and $p = 0.05$.

The probability of interest is:

$$P(x > 4) = 1 - P(x \leq 4)$$

The probability distribution shown in Figure 4-8 shows the cumulative probabilities. Thus, $P(x \leq 4) = 0.4360$. The chance that the state will find more than 4 cars that don't meet the pollution standards in a sample of $n = 100$ is $1 - 0.4360 = 0.5640$. There is more than a 56% chance that a car company will be unjustly accused of having too many cars in violation of the EPA pollution standards. This is higher than when a sample of 25 cars was used and would be met with heavy resistance from the car companies.

State officials would likely agree and alter their sampling plan. Suppose they change the cutoff for fining the car company to more than 6 noncomplying cars. Now we look to the cumulative binomial probability distribution (Figure 4-8) to find the following.

$$P(x > 6) = 1 - P(x \leq 6)$$
$$P(x > 6) = 1 - 0.7660$$
$$P(x > 6) = 0.2340$$

This is clearly an improvement from the car company's standpoint. Now the chance of being unjustly fined is 0.2340.

However, the state would still be interested in the chance of properly catching a poorly performing company. If the automaker has a true rate of noncompliance equal to 10%, the state wants to find:

$$P(x > 6) = 1 - P(x \leq 6)$$

FIGURE 4-8
Minitab Binomial
Distribution Output for
Pollution Test $n = 100$,
$p = 0.05$

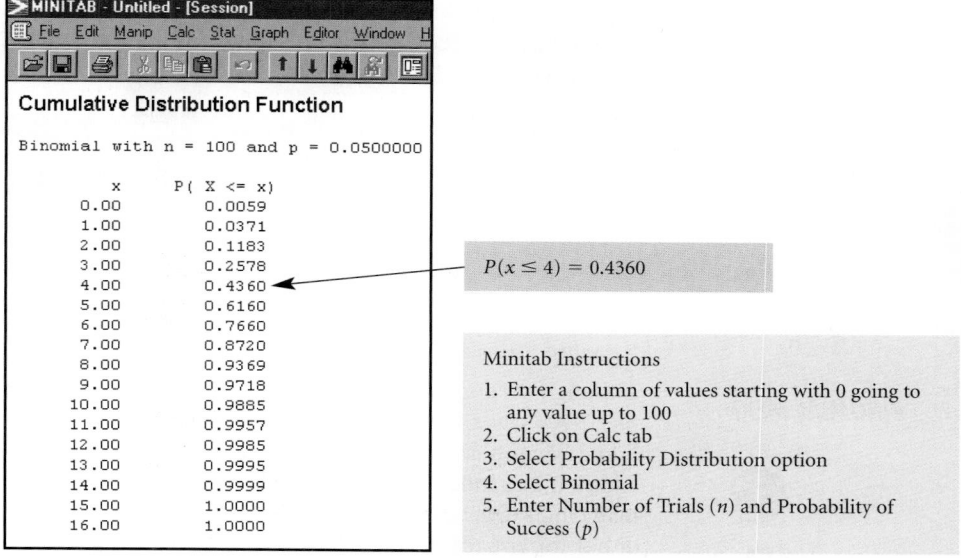

Cumulative Distribution Function

Binomial with n = 100 and p = 0.0500000

x	P(X <= x)
0.00	0.0059
1.00	0.0371
2.00	0.1183
3.00	0.2578
4.00	0.4360
5.00	0.6160
6.00	0.7660
7.00	0.8720
8.00	0.9369
9.00	0.9718
10.00	0.9885
11.00	0.9957
12.00	0.9985
13.00	0.9995
14.00	0.9999
15.00	1.0000
16.00	1.0000

$P(x \leq 4) = 0.4360$

Minitab Instructions

1. Enter a column of values starting with 0 going to any value up to 100
2. Click on Calc tab
3. Select Probability Distribution option
4. Select Binomial
5. Enter Number of Trials (n) and Probability of Success (p)

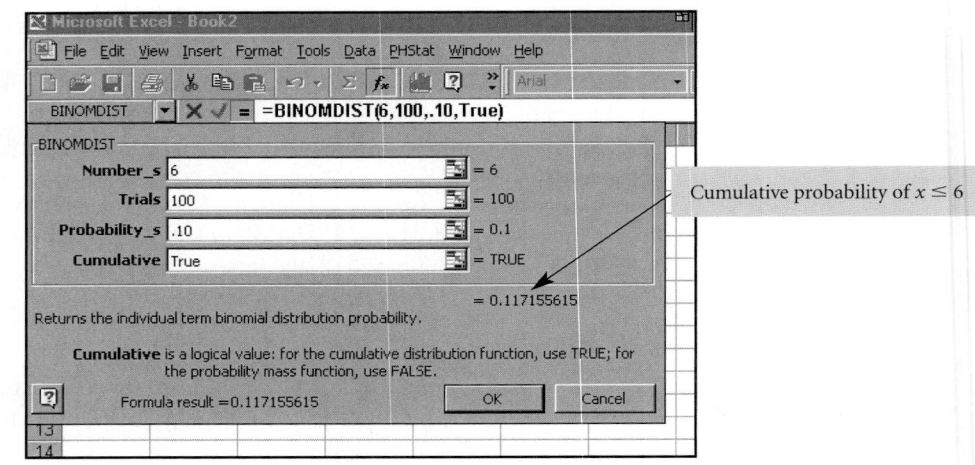

FIGURE 4-9
Excel Cumulative Binomial Probability Output $n = 100$, $p = 0.10$

Figure 4-9 shows the cumulative probability computed with Excel's **BINOMDIST** function. The chance that the state will find more than 6 noncomplying cars in a sample of 100 if the true rate of noncompliance is 10% is:

$$P(x > 6) = 1 - 0.1172 = 0.8828$$

There is only a $1 - 0.8828 = 0.1172$ chance that a poor performer will escape detection. This is a substantial improvement over the sampling plan with 25 cars. By increasing the sample size, both the automakers and the state benefit.

Mean and Standard Deviation of the Binomial Distribution

You learned earlier the mean of a discrete probability distribution is referred to as the *expected value*. Recall the expected value of a discrete random variable is found using Equation 4-14.

$$E(x) = \sum xP(x)$$

MEAN OF A BINOMIAL DISTRIBUTION

Equation 4-14 can be used with any discrete probability distribution including the binomial. However, if we are working with a binomial distribution, the mean can be found more easily using Equation 4-18.

MEAN OF THE BINOMIAL DISTRIBUTION

$$\mu_x = E(x) = np \qquad \text{4-18}$$

where:

n = Sample size
p = Probability of a success

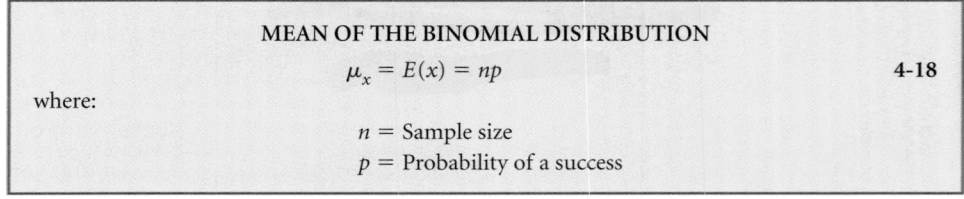

EXAMPLE 4-26

BINOMIAL MEAN

Excel and Minitab Tutorial

Catalog Sales

Although catalog sales have been a part of the U.S. economy for many years, the decade of the 1990s saw a large increase in these sales. Companies like Lands' End, L. L. Bean, and Eddie Bauer placed their merchandise into a vast number of homes across the country. In addition, the Internet has made cyber shopping an "in thing." One of the features that has made mail-order buying so popular is the ease with which customers can return merchandise if for any reason they don't want to keep it. One mail-order catalog has a goal of no more than 11% of all purchased items being returned.

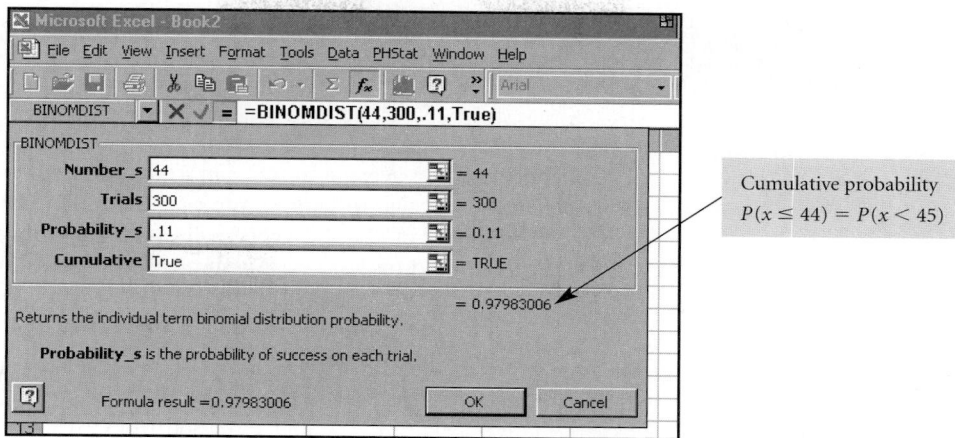

Cumulative probability
$P(x \leq 44) = P(x < 45)$

FIGURE 4-10
Output for Mail-Order Sales
Returns

The distribution that can describe the number of items returned is the binomial distribution. For instance, if in a given hour the company shipped 300 items with the probability of an item being returned at $p = 0.11$, then the expected number of items (mean) to be returned is:

$$\mu_x = E(x) = np$$
$$\mu_x = E(x) = (300)(0.11) = 33.0$$

Thus, the average number of returned items for each 300 items shipped is 33.

Suppose the company sales manager is interested in determining whether the return rate remains at 11%. To test this, she monitors 300 items and finds that 45 have been returned. This return rate exceeds the mean of 33 units, which is a cause for concern. However, before reaching a conclusion, she would be interested in the probability of observing 45 or more returns in a sample of 300.

$$P(x \geq 45) = 1 - P(x \leq 44)$$

The Excel output in Figure 4-10 shows that the cumulative probability of 44 or fewer [$P(x \leq 44)$] is equal to 0.9798. Then the probability of 45 or more returns is:

$$P(x \geq 45) = 1 - 0.9798 = 0.0202$$

There is only a 2% chance of 45 or more items being returned if the 11% return rate is still in effect. This low probability suggests that the return rate may have increased above the 11% rate.

STANDARD DEVIATION OF A BINOMIAL DISTRIBUTION

Earlier we showed that the standard deviation for a discrete probability distribution can be determined using Equation 4-15.

$$\sigma = \sqrt{\sum [x - E(x)]^2 P(x)}$$

If a discrete probability distribution meets the binomial distribution conditions, the standard deviation can be found using Equation 4-19.

STANDARD DEVIATION FOR THE BINOMIAL DISTRIBUTION

$$\sigma = \sqrt{npq}$$ 4-19

where:

n = Sample size
p = Probability of a success
$q = (1 - p)$ = Probability of a failure

BINOMIAL STANDARD DEVIATION

Catalog Sales (continued)

The catalog company sales manager had an 11% return rate goal. She tracked a sample of 300 items and observed that 45 were returned. The expected number to be returned was:

$$\mu_x = E(x) = (300)(0.11) = 33.0$$

This is considered an average number in a sample of 300 assuming the 11% rate holds. However, she knows that different samples of size 300 would yield a different number of returns. The number of items returned will vary from sample to sample. The binomial distribution can be used to describe the number of items returned. Figure 4-11 displays the binomial distribution for $n = 300$ and $p = 0.11$.

To measure the potential variation in the number of items returned, the manager needs to compute the standard deviation for the binomial distribution. We can use Equation 4-19 to find this standard deviation.

$$\sigma = \sqrt{npq} = \sqrt{(300)(0.11)(0.89)} = 5.419$$

Note that the binomial distribution shown in Figure 4-11 is bell-shaped. This means we can use the Empirical Rule (see Chapter 3) to help describe the distribution of returned items in a sample of 300. We recall that for bell-shaped distributions:

$$\mu \pm 1\sigma \text{ will include approximately 68\% of the outcomes}$$
$$\mu \pm 2\sigma \text{ will include approximately 95\% of the outcomes}$$
$$\mu \pm 3\sigma \text{ will include approximately 99.7\% of the outcomes}$$

Additional
Example 4-c

Acceptance
Sampling Using the
Binomial
Distribution

In this case,

$$\mu = 33 \text{ and } \sigma = 5.419$$

So, virtually all the possible number of returned items in a sample of 300 items should be between:

$$33 \pm 3(5.419)$$
$$16.74 - - - - - - - - - - - - - - - 49.26$$

FIGURE 4-11
Excel Binomial Distribution Output for Catalog Sales Returns Binomial, $n = 300$, $p = 0.11$

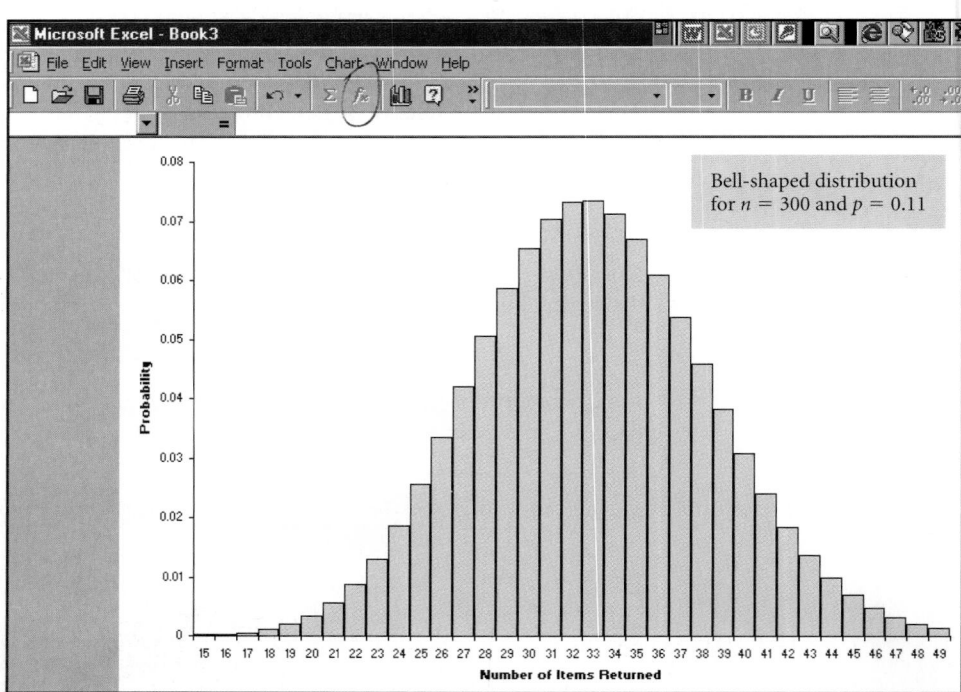

Excel Instructions:

1. Enter values in a column from 0 to 60
2. Use BINOMDIST function
3. Use Chart Wizard for column chart

The sample of 300 items the manager tracked showed 45 returns. This is within the range of possible outcomes. But as you can see in Figure 4-11, it is located in the upper tail of the distribution. While possible, it is unlikely that she would find 45 or more returns if the true return rate is 11%. Thus, the manager would have cause for concern that the 11% return rate has increased.

Additional Information About the Binomial Distribution

At this point, several comments about the binomial distribution are worth making. If p, the probability of a success, is 0.50, the binomial distribution is *symmetrical* and bell-shaped regardless of the sample size. This is illustrated in Figure 4-12, which shows probability distributions for samples of $n = 5$, $n = 10$, and $n = 50$. Notice that all three distributions are centered at the expected value, $E(x) = \mu$.

When the value of p differs from 0.50 in either direction, the binomial distribution is skewed. This was the case for the Household Security example. The skewness will be most pronounced when n is small and p approaches 0 or 1.0. However, the binomial distribution becomes more bell-shaped as n increases. The probability distributions shown in Figure 4-13 bear this out.

FIGURE 4-12 The Binomial Distribution with Varying Sample Sizes ($p = 0.50$)

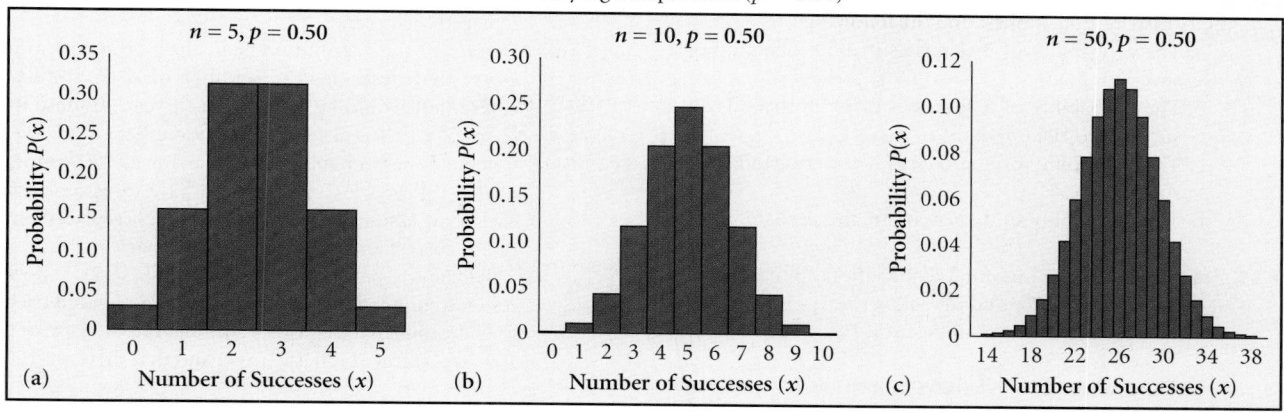

FIGURE 4-13 The Binomial Distribution with Varying Sample Sizes ($p = 0.05$)

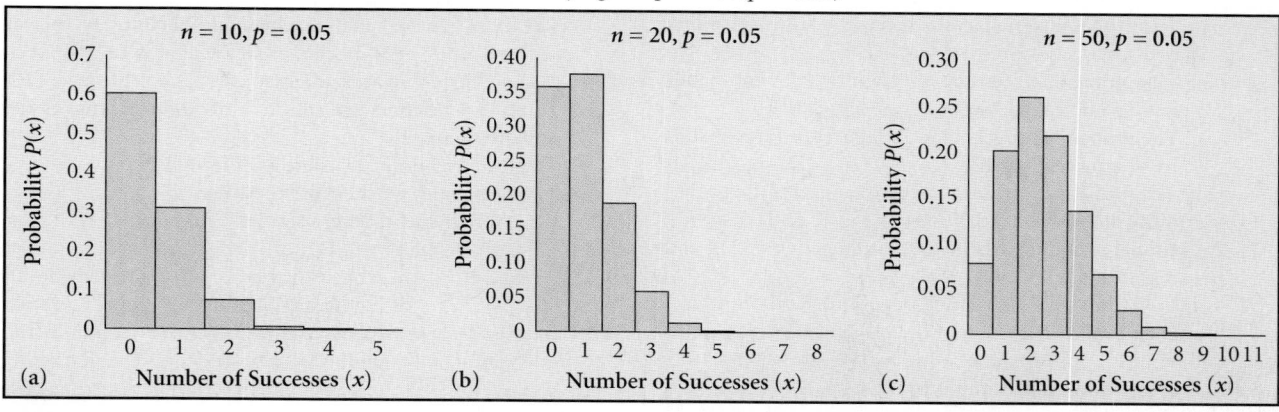

4-4: EXERCISES

 **ADDITIONAL EXERCISES ON YOUR CD-ROM**
Try the ADDITIONAL EXERCISES and APPLICATION PROBLEMS on the CD-ROM.

4-43. Use the counting rule for combinations to determine:
   a. The number of ways 4 items can be selected from 8 items
   b. The number of ways 6 items can be selected from 10 items
   c. The number of ways 3 items can be selected from 10 items
   d. The number of ways 7 items can be selected from 10 items
   e. Compare your answers to parts c and d and write a short paragraph explaining why the answers are the same.

4-44. For a sample of $n = 10$, assuming that the binomial probability distribution applies, find the following.
   a. The probability of 3 successes if the probability of a success is 0.20
   b. The probability of 3 successes if the probability of a success is 0.80
   c. The probability of 4 successes if the probability of a success is 0.33
   d. The probability of 4 successes if the probability of a success is 0.15

4-45. Assuming that the binomial distribution applies, given a sample size of $n = 25$, find the following.
   a. The probability of 5 successes if the probability of a success is 0.75
   b. The probability of 4 failures if the probability of a success is 0.20
   c. The probability of 11 successes if the probability of a failure is 0.33
   d. The probability of 5 successes if the probability of a success is 0.40
   e. The probability of at least 7 successes if the probability of a success is 0.25
   f. The probability of at most 18 failures if the probability of a failure is 0.75
   g. The probability of less than 10 failures if the probability of a success is 0.40
   h. The probability of more than 10 failures if the probability of a success is 0.60

4-46. A binomial random variable has parameters $n = 250$ and $p = 0.7$.
   a. Find the mean, variance, standard deviation, and coefficient of variation of the random variable.
   b. Find an approximate value for the 16th percentile. (Hint: Look at the graphs in Figure 4-13.)

   c. Find an approximate value for the 97.5th percentile.
   d. Determine approximately $P(175 \leq x \leq 182)$.

Business Applications

4-47. The Lexington School Board has agreed to help the A. P. Stevens School Furniture Company test a new type of elementary school chair. Using the present school furniture, school administrators have found that 15% of the chairs must be replaced each year. A. P. Stevens claims its chair will have a 10% replacement rate.
   a. In a sample of 100 chairs, determine the distribution (state the type and parameters) that describes the number of chairs presently being used that would be replaced each year.
   b. Determine the distribution (state the type and parameters) that describes the number of A. P. Stevens' chairs that would be replaced each year. Assume its claim of a 10% replacement rate is correct.
   c. Calculate the probability that as many as 12 or more of the A. P. Stevens' chairs would have to be replaced each year. Assume that its claim of a 10% replacement rate is correct and that there are 100 chairs.
   d. Calculate the probability that as many as 12 or more presently used chairs would have to be replaced each year. Assume that the school administrators' claim of a 15% replacement rate is correct and that there are 100 chairs.
   e. Assume 100 Stevens chairs are tested for 1 year and 12 need to be replaced. Comment on Stevens' claim that this proves its chair is superior to the present brand. Support your comments with probabilities and reasons.

4-48. The 1997 Tenth Planet Teachers and Technology Survey reported that 21% of elementary teachers use the Web (*Source:* http://www.usatoday.com/snapshot/life/lsnap064.htm). If 5 teachers are selected at random, what is the probability that:
   a. Exactly 3 of the teachers use the Web
   b. Less than 4 teachers use the Web
   c. More than 1 teacher uses the Web

4-49. Refer to Problem 48. Education Unlimited, an educational software organization, has targeted its newly developed software at elementary school teachers. The software is designed to make the Web more accessible and interesting to elementary school students. The marketing department has proposed a marketing program that would help sell this software to elementary schools. They believe that the marketing program will persuade half of the elementary school teachers reached by the program who presently use the Web to buy the software. The marketing program is to reach approximately 10,000 elementary teachers. The marketing program will cost $10,000. Each software copy will produce a profit of $10. Education Unlimited managers feel that they must have at least a 50% chance of making more on the software sales than the marketing program would cost. You have been asked to analyze this marketing program and give a recommendation. Respond.

4-50. A survey by KRC Research for *U.S. News* reported that 37% of people plan on spending more on eating out after they retire (*Source:* http://www.usatoday.com/snapshot/life/lsnap062.htm). If 8 people are randomly selected, determine the following probabilities.

    a. Exactly 5 people plan on spending more on eating out after they retire.

    b. Less than 4 people plan on spending more on eating out after they retire.

    c. More than 2 plan on spending more on eating out after they retire.

4-51. Gateway 2000 Inc. receives large shipments of microprocessors from Intel Corp. It must try to ensure that the proportion of microprocessors that are defective is small. Later in this text you will develop faster ways of solving this problem. For now let us illustrate the process in a scaled-down scenario. The concept will be the same as for the actual procedure used. Suppose Gateway decides to test 5 (they actually check many more than this) microprocessors out of a shipment of thousands of these microprocessors. Suppose that if at least 1 of the microprocessors is defective, the shipment is returned.

    a. Suppose that Intel Corp.'s shipment contains 10% defective microprocessors. Calculate the probability that the entire shipment will be returned.

    b. Suppose that Intel and Gateway agree that Intel will not provide more than 5% defective chips. Calculate the probability that the entire shipment will be returned even though only 5% are defective.

    c. Calculate the probability that the entire shipment will be kept by Gateway even though the shipment has 10% defective microprocessors.

4-52. A CBS News survey reported that 67% of adults said the U.S. Treasury should continue making pennies (*Source:* http://www.usatoday.com/snapshot/news/nsnap062.htm). What is the probability that for 6 adults selected at random:

    a. Exactly 5 adults would want the Treasury to continue making pennies?

    b. Three or fewer adults would want the Treasury to continue making pennies?

    c. More than 2 adults would want the Treasury to continue making pennies?

4-53. Probability is used to a great extent in quality control programs throughout industry. Quality control is a procedure used to determine when a process (usually a production process) is out of control and needs adjustment to meet quality standards. The observations obtained from the (production) process are assumed to have come from a bell-shaped population. Recall the Empirical Rule and what it states about the proportion of observations beyond one standard deviation from the mean. There are several rules used to determine when a process is going "out of control."

    a. One such rule says that a process is out of control if four out of five observations on the same side of the mean are at least one standard deviation from the mean. Calculate the probability that the process will be labeled as being out of control even if the distribution has not gone out of control—i.e., calculate the probability that four out of five observations (on the same side of the mean) from a bell-shaped curve are at least one standard deviation from the mean.

    b. Another rule is the system is out of control if two out of three observations (on the same side of the mean) are at least two standard deviations from the mean. Calculate the probability that the process will be labeled out of control even if it is not.

4-54. The 1997 Tenth Planet Teachers and Technology Survey reported that 21% of elementary teachers use the Web (*Source:* http://www.usatoday.com/snapshot/life/lsnap064.htm). If 5 teachers are selected at random, determine the:

    a. Expected number of these teachers who use the Web

    b. Standard deviation of these teachers who use the Web

4-55. Let us re-examine the quality control example from Problem 53. One additional rule that is used to determine if the process is out of control is if nine observations in a row fall on the same side of the mean. Calculate the probability that a process that was in control would be viewed as being out of control because of this rule.

4-56. A survey by KRC Research for *U.S. News* reported that 37% of people plan on spending more on eating out after they retire (*Source:* http://www.usatoday.com/snapshot/life/lsnap062.htm). If 8 people are randomly selected, then determine the:

    a. Expected number of people who plan on spending more eating out after they retire

    b. Standard deviation of the individuals who plan on spending more eating out after they retire

4-57. We have examined the contractual relationship between Gateway and Intel before. Intel also supplies memory modules (RAM). Again, an important issue for Gateway is the proportion of defective modules they receive from Intel. When Gateway enters a contract with Intel it must be very careful to negotiate a contract that will ensure the quality of its own product. Suppose that Gateway can tolerate 2.5% of its computers being returned because of failures in the memory modules. Suppose each computer has 3 memory modules installed. If any 1 of the modules malfunctions the computer will be returned for repair. Define a random variable whose value equals the number of defective memory modules in a randomly chosen Gateway computer.

a. Does the random variable have a binomial distribution? If so, list the parameters that define this specific binomial distribution.
b. If Gateway negotiates a contract that allows Intel to ship modules of which 5% are defective, calculate the probability that a randomly chosen Gateway computer with these memory modules installed will be returned for repair. Is this probability larger than the 0.025 (2.5%) required by Gateway?
c. Since the contract negotiated in part b doesn't meet with Gateway's approval, suggest a contract that would be acceptable to Gateway (i.e., specify the percent of defectives Intel can deliver so that no more than 2.5% of Gateway's computers are returned for repairs).

4-58. A CBS News survey reported that 67% of adults said the U.S. Treasury should continue making pennies (*Source:* http://www.usatoday.com/snapshot/news/nsnap062.htm). If 6 adults are selected at random, determine the expected number of adults who say the U.S. Treasury should continue making pennies.

4-5: THE POISSON PROBABILITY DISTRIBUTION

To use the binomial distribution, we must be able to count the number of successes and the number of failures. Whereas in many applications you may be able to count the number of successes, you often cannot count the number of failures. For example, suppose a company builds freeways in Vermont. The company could count the number of chuckholes that develop per mile (here a chuckhole is a success since it is what we are looking for), but how could the company count the number of non-chuckholes? Or consider the emergency medical service in Los Angeles. It could easily count the number of emergencies its units respond to in one hour, but how could it determine how many calls it did not receive? Obviously, in these cases the number of possible outcomes (successes + failures) is difficult, if not impossible, to determine. If the total number of possible outcomes cannot be determined, the binomial distribution cannot be applied.

Characteristics of the Poisson Distribution

Fortunately, the **Poisson probability distribution** can be applied in these situations without knowing the total possible outcomes. *lambda*

> **POISSON PROBABILITY DISTRIBUTION**
> A probability distribution for the possible outcomes of interest of a process where the average number of outcomes of interest per segment is λ, and the following characteristics are present:
> 1. The outcomes of interest are *rare* relative to the possible outcomes.
> 2. The number of outcomes of interest is *random,* and the occurrence of one outcome does not influence the chance of another outcome of interest.
> 3. The probability that an outcome of interest occurs in a given segment is the same for all segments.

The Poisson distribution[3] is described by a single parameter, λ (lambda), which is the average occurrence per segment. The value of λ depends on the situation being described. For instance, λ could be the average number of machine breakdowns per month or the average number of customers arriving at a checkout stand in a 10-minute period. It could also be the average number of emergency responses for the emergency medical service per hour or the average number of chuckholes in a section of freeway.

Once λ has been determined, we can calculate the average occurrence rate for any multiple segments, t. This is λt. Note that λ and t must be in compatible units. If we have $\lambda = 20$ arrivals per hour, we cannot multiply this by a time period measured in minutes.

That is, if we have:

$$\lambda = 20 \text{ arrivals per hour and } t = 30 \text{ minutes}$$

---

[3]The Poisson distribution can be derived as the limiting distribution of the binomial distribution as the number of trials, *n*, tends to infinity. It serves as a good approximation to the binomial when *n* is large.

we must convert the time units to hours:

$$t = (1/2) \text{ h}$$

Then:

$$\lambda t = 20(1/2) = 10$$

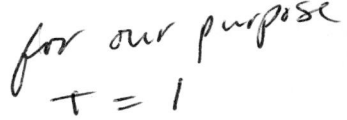

for our purpose
T = 1

The average number of occurrences is not necessarily the number we will see if we observe the process for one segment. We might expect an average of 20 people to arrive at a checkout stand in any given hour, but we do not expect to find exactly that number arriving every hour. The actual arrivals will form a distribution with an expected value, or mean, equal to λt. So, for the Poisson distribution,

$$\mu_x = \lambda t$$

The Poisson distribution is a discrete distribution. This means, for example, that if we are counting the airplane arrivals at the San Francisco International Airport in any given hour, the count must be integer valued (0, 1, 2, . . ., airplanes can arrive). In theory, there is no upper limit on the number of occurrences.

Once λt has been specified, the probability for any discrete value in the Poisson distribution can be found using Equation 4-20:

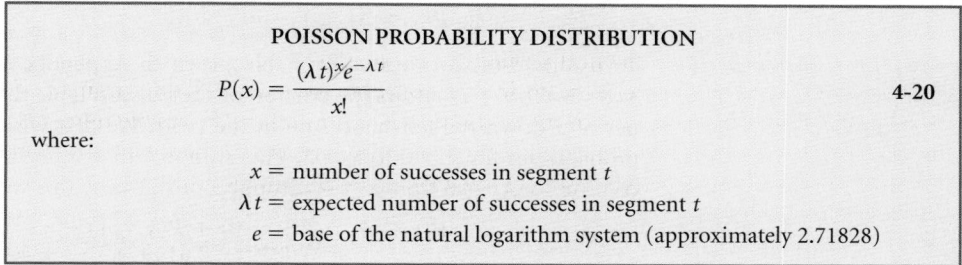

POISSON PROBABILITY DISTRIBUTION

$$P(x) = \frac{(\lambda t)^x e^{-\lambda t}}{x!}$$

4-20

where:

x = number of successes in segment t
λt = expected number of successes in segment t
e = base of the natural logarithm system (approximately 2.71828)

First City Bank

A study conducted at First City Bank has determined that the average number of arrivals to the teller section of the bank per hour is 15. Further, the distribution for the number of arrivals is considered to be Poisson distributed. Figure 4-14 shows the shape of the Poisson distribution for $\lambda = 15$. The probability of each possible number of customers arriving

EXAMPLE 4-28

POISSON DISTRIBUTION

FIGURE 4-14
Poisson Distribution for Bank Customer Arrivals with $\lambda = 15$

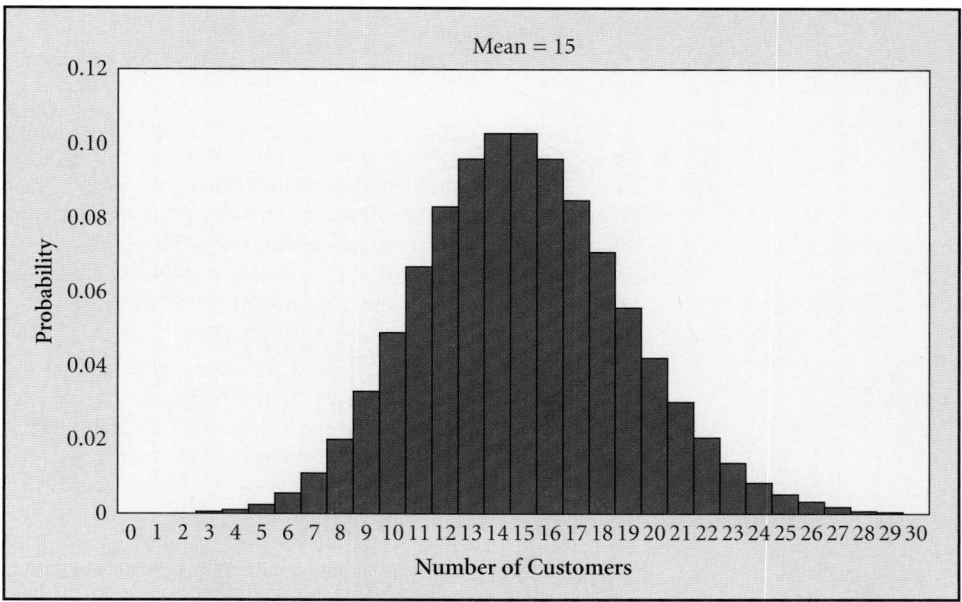

can be computed using Equation 4-20. For example, we can find the probability of $x = 12$ customers as follows.

$$P(x = 12) = \frac{(\lambda t)^x e^{-\lambda t}}{x!} = \frac{15^{12} e^{-15}}{12!} = 0.0829$$

Poisson Probability Distribution Tables

As was the case with the binomial distribution, a table of probabilities exists for the Poisson distribution. (The full Poisson table appears in Appendix C at the end of the text.) The Poisson table shows the probabilities for different λt values. The following examples illustrate how to use the Poisson table.

Acme Taxi Service

EXAMPLE 4-29

POISSON TABLE

The Acme Taxi Service has studied the demand for taxis at the local airport and found that, on average, 6 taxis are demanded per hour. Thus, $\lambda = 6$/hour. If the company is considering locating 6 taxis at the airport during each hour, what is the probability that demand will exceed 6 and people will have to wait for taxi service?

To answer this question, we recognize that the segment of interest, t, equals 1 hour, so $\lambda t = 6$. We are interested in:

$$P(x > 6) = 1 - P(x \le 6)$$

To use the Poisson probability tables, turn to Appendix C and locate the column with $\lambda t = 6$. Table 4-17 shows the portion of the Poisson table that we will need. Locate the values of x down the left-hand side of the table. We first wish to determine the sum of the probabilities for $x = 0$ to $x = 6$. This sum is found by adding the probabilities under the column for $\lambda t = 6$ from $x = 0$ through $x = 6$. Doing this we get:

$$P(x \le 6) = P(x = 0) + P(x = 1) + \cdots + P(x = 6)$$
$$= 0.0025 + 0.0149 + \cdots + 0.01606$$
$$= 0.6063$$

Therefore, the desired probability is:

$$P(x > 6) = 1 - P(x \le 6)$$
$$= 1 - 0.6063$$
$$= 0.3937$$

TABLE 4-17
Poisson Distribution Table
$\lambda t = 6$

	5.10	5.20	5.30	5.40	5.50	5.60	5.70	5.80	5.90	6.00
						λt				
0	.0061	.0055	.0050	.0045	.0041	.0037	.0033	.0030	.0027	.0025
1	.0311	.0287	.0265	.0244	.0225	.0207	.0191	.0176	.0162	.0149
2	.0793	.0746	.0701	.0659	.0618	.0580	.0544	.0509	.0477	.0446
3	.1348	.1293	.1239	.1185	.1133	.1082	.1033	.0985	.0938	.0892
4	.1719	.1681	.1641	.1600	.1558	.1515	.1472	.1428	.1383	.1339
5	.1753	.1748	.1740	.1728	.1714	.1697	.1678	.1656	.1632	.1606
6	.1490	.1515	.1537	.1555	.1571	.1584	.1594	.1601	.1605	.1606
7	.1086	.1125	.1163	.1200	.1234	.1267	.1298	.1326	.1353	.1377
8	.0692	.0731	.0771	.0810	.0849	.0887	.0925	.0962	.0998	.1033
9	.0392	.0423	.0454	.0486	.0519	.0552	.0586	.0620	.0654	.0688
10	.0200	.0220	.0241	.0262	.0285	.0309	.0334	.0359	.0386	.0413
11	.0093	.0104	.0116	.0129	.0143	0.157	0.173	0.190	0.207	0.225
12	.0039	.0045	.0051	.0058	.0065	.0073	.0082	.0092	.0102	.0113
13	.0015	.0018	.0021	.0024	.0028	.0032	.0036	.0041	.0046	.0052
14	.0006	.0007	.0008	.0009	.0011	.0013	.0015	.0017	.0019	.0022
15	.0002	.0002	.0003	.0003	.0004	.0005	.0006	.0007	.0008	.0009
16	.0001	.0001	.0001	.0001	.0001	.0002	.0002	.0002	.0003	.0003
17	.0000	.0000	.0000	.0000	.0000	.0001	.0001	.0001	.0001	.0001

Additional
Example 4-d

Poisson Distribution
at the Boise
Cascade
Corporation

Thus, there is a 0.3937 probability that demand for taxis at the airport will exceed supply if the company puts only 6 taxis at the airport. This means that in almost 4 out of every 10 hours, at least one more cab will be demanded than Acme will have available.

The Mean and Standard Deviation for the Poisson Distribution

The mean of the Poisson distribution is λt. This is the value we use to specify which Poisson distribution we are using. We must know the mean before we can find probabilities for a Poisson distribution.

Figure 4-14 illustrated that the outcome of a Poisson distribution variable is subject to variation. Like any other discrete probability distribution, the standard deviation for the Poisson can be computed using Equation 4-15:

$$\sigma_x = \sqrt{\sum [x - E(x)]^2 P(x)}$$

However, for a Poisson distribution, the standard deviation can be found using Equation 4-21.

STANDARD DEVIATION FOR THE POISSON DISTRIBUTION

$$\sigma = \sqrt{\lambda t}$$

4-21

The standard deviation of the Poisson distribution is simply the square root of the mean. Therefore, if you are working with a Poisson process, generating the mean can produce the variability measure, also.

POISSON STANDARD DEVIATION

Excel and
Minitab Tutorial

Heritage Tile

To illustrate the importance of the relationship between the mean and standard deviation of the Poisson distribution, consider Heritage Tile in New York City. The company makes ceramic tile for use in kitchens and bathrooms. The quality standards call for the number of imperfections to average 3 or fewer per tile. The distribution of imperfections is thought to be Poisson distributed. Both Minitab and Excel can be used to generate Poisson probabilities in much the same way as for the binomial distribution discussed earlier in Section 4-4. Assuming that the company is meeting the standard, Figure 4-15 shows the Poisson probability distribution generated using Excel when $\lambda t = 3.0$. Even though the average number of defects is 3, the manager is concerned about the large number of instances in which the number of imperfections will be 4, 5, 6 or more on a tile. The variability is too great. Using Equation 4-21, the standard deviation for this distribution is:

$$\sigma = \sqrt{3.0} = 1.732$$

This large standard deviation means that while some tiles will have few if any imperfections, others will have several, causing problems for installers and creating unhappy customers.

A quality improvement effort directed at reducing the average number of imperfections to 2.0 will also reduce the standard deviation to:

$$\sigma = \sqrt{2.0} = 1.414$$

Further reductions in the average will also result in reduced variation in the number of imperfections between tiles. This means more consistency for installers and higher customer satisfaction.

Excel Instructions:

1. Enter values for *x* ranging from 0 to 10.
2. Click on f_n on the tool bar
3. Select the Statistical and POISSON options
4. Supply mean and type "FALSE" for cumulative option
5. Graph using the Column chart option in the Chart Wizard

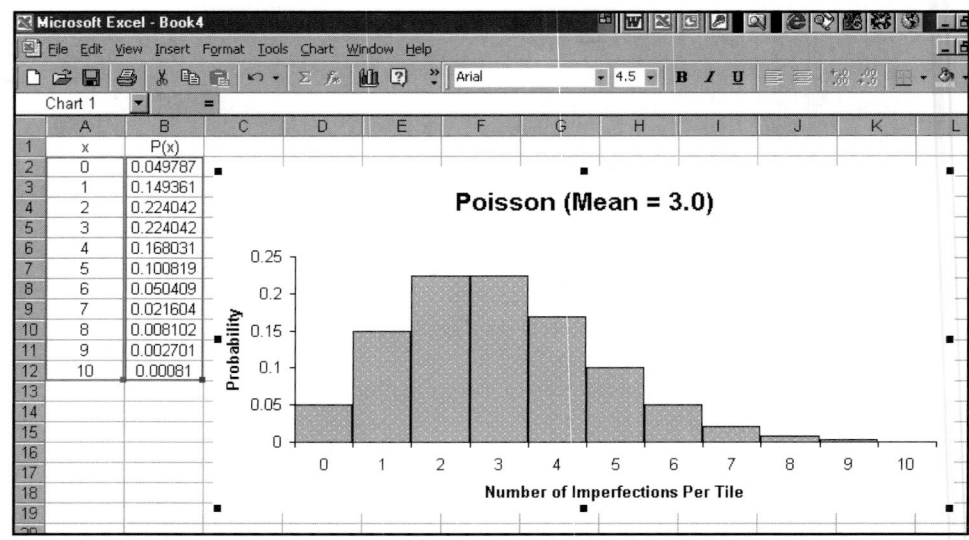

FIGURE 4-15
Excel Output for Heritage Tile Example

4-5: EXERCISES

ADDITIONAL EXERCISES ON YOUR CD-ROM
Try the ADDITIONAL EXERCISES and APPLICATION PROBLEMS on the CD-ROM.

4-59. If the mean value of a Poisson distributed variable is 5.0, find the following:
   a. $P(x = 5) =$
   b. $P(x \leq 5) =$
   c. $P(x > 3) =$

4-60. If $\lambda t = 3.5$ for a Poisson distributed variable, find the following:
   a. $P(2 \leq x \leq 5) =$
   b. $P(x = 3) =$
   c. $P(x \geq 1) =$

4-61. If $\lambda = 5$ and $t = 2$ for a Poisson distribution:
   a. Determine the mean and standard deviation of this Poisson distribution.
   b. Calculate $P(\mu_x - k\sigma_x \leq x \leq \mu_x + k\sigma_x)$ where $k = 1$, 2, and 3. Compare these values with the corresponding probabilities of the Empirical Rule.

4-62. If $\lambda = 18$ and $t = 1/3$ for a Poisson distribution:
   a. Find the expected value, variance, and standard deviation of this Poisson distribution.
   b. Calculate $P(\mu_x - k\sigma_x \leq x \leq \mu_x + k\sigma_x)$ where $k = 1$, 2, and 3. Compare these values with the corresponding values of Tchebysheff's theorem.

Business Applications

4-63. East-West Translations publishes textbooks of ancient Oriental teachings for English-speaking universities. The company is presently testing a computer-based translation service. Since Asian symbols are difficult to translate, East-West assumes the computer program will make some errors, but then so do human translators. The computer service claims its error rate will average 3 per 400 words of translation. East-West randomly selects a 1,200-word passage. If the computer company's claim is accurate:
   a. Determine the probability that no errors will be found.
   b. Calculate the probability that more than 14 errors will be found.
   c. Find the probability that fewer than 9 errors will be found.
   d. If 15 errors are found in the 1,200-word passage, what would you conclude about the computer company's claim? Why?

4-64. Your company president has told you that the company experiences product returns at the rate of two per month. Determine the probability that next month there will be:

a. No returns

b. One return

c. Two returns

d. More than two returns

e. In the last three months your company has had only one month in which the number of returns was at most two. Calculate the probability of this event occurring. What will you tell the president of your company concerning the return rate for your com-

pany? Make sure you support your statement with something other than opinion.

4-65. The O'Rilley Office Worker Company has agreed to supply 100 part-time office employees to Mid-East Insurance each day. The O'Rilley Company knows that, typically, 7% of the workers it schedules for any day will not come to work for one of many reasons. Mid-East Insurance is O'Rilley's biggest customer and so O'Rilley wants to schedule enough workers so that fewer than 100 show up less than 1 in 20 workdays per month. Assuming the Poisson distribution can be used to describe the number of workers not coming to work on any day, how many workers should O'Rilley schedule?

 **OPTIONAL CD-ROM TOPIC The Hypergeometric Distribution**

You will encounter situations in which you are sampling from a finite population and the sampling is performed without replacement. In cases where the sample size is relatively large compared to the population, a discrete distribution called the hypergeometric may be useful. For more information, go to the CD-ROM.

■ SUMMARY AND CONCLUSIONS

Probability provides decision makers with a quantitative measure of the chance a particular outcome will occur. Probability allows decision makers to quantify uncertainty. The objectives of this chapter have been to discuss the various types of probability and to provide the basic rules that govern probability operations. In addition, we have introduced the elementary concepts associated with discrete probability distributions. From a business point of view, the two most useful discrete distributions are the binomial and Poisson distribution.

The examples throughout this chapter and the exercises at the end of each section and at the end of the chapter should give you a good idea of how probability is used in business situations.

EQUATIONS

Classical Probability Measurement

$$P(E_i) = \frac{\text{Number of ways } E_i \text{ can occur}}{\text{Total number of elementary events}} \qquad \textbf{4-1}$$

Relative Frequency of Occurrence

$$RF(E_i) = \frac{\text{Number of times } E_i \text{ occurs}}{n} \qquad \textbf{4-2}$$

Probability Rule 1

For any event E_i:

$$0.0 \leq P(E_i) \leq 1.0 \text{ for all } i \qquad \textbf{4-3}$$

Probability Rule 2

$$\sum_{i=1}^{k} P(e_i) = 1.0 \qquad \textbf{4-4}$$

Probability Rule 3

Addition Rule for Elementary Events

The probability of an event E_i is equal to the *sum* of the probabilities of the elementary events forming E_i. That is, if:

$$E_i = \{e_1, e_2, e_3\}$$

then:

$$P(E_i) = P(e_1) + P(e_2) + P(e_3) \qquad \textbf{4-5}$$

Complement Rule

$$P(\bar{E}) = 1 - P(E) \qquad \textbf{4-6}$$

Probability Rule 4

Addition rule for any two *events* E_1 and E_2:

$$P(E_1 \text{ or } E_2) = P(E_1) + P(E_2) - P(E_1 \text{ and } E_2) \qquad \textbf{4-7}$$

Probability Rule 5

Addition rule for mutually exclusive events E_1, E_2:

$$P(E_1 \text{ or } E_2) = P(E_1) + P(E_2) \qquad \textbf{4-8}$$

Probability Rule 6

Conditional probability for any two events E_1, E_2:

$$P(E_1 \,|\, E_2) = \frac{P(E_1 \text{ and } E_2)}{P(E_2)} \qquad \textbf{4-9}$$

Probability Rule 7

Conditional probability for independent events, E_1, E_2:

$$P(E_1 \,|\, E_2) = P(E_1); \quad P(E_2) > 0$$

and

$$P(E_2 \,|\, E_1) = P(E_2); \quad P(E_1) > 0 \qquad \textbf{4-10}$$

Probability Rule 8

Multiplication rule for two events, E_1 and E_2:

$$P(E_1 \text{ and } E_2) = P(E_1)P(E_2 \,|\, E_1)$$

and

$$P(E_2 \text{ and } E_1) = P(E_2)\, P(E_1 | E_2) \qquad \textbf{4-11}$$

Probability Rule 9

Multiplication rule for independent events E_1, E_2:

$$P(E_1 \text{ and } E_2) = P(E_1)P(E_2) \qquad \textbf{4-12}$$

Bayes' Theorem

$$P(E_i | B) = \qquad \textbf{4-13}$$

$$\frac{P(E_i)P(B|E_i)}{P(E_1)P(B|E_1) + P(E_2)P(B|E_2) + \cdots + P(E_k)P(B|E_k)}$$

Expected Value for a Discrete Distribution

$$E(x) = \sum xP(x) \qquad \textbf{4-14}$$

Standard Deviation for a Discrete Probability Distribution

$$\sigma_x = \sqrt{\sum [x - E(x)]^2 P(x)} \qquad \textbf{4-15}$$

Counting Rule for Combinations

$$C_x^n = \frac{n!}{x!(n-x)!} \qquad \textbf{4-16}$$

Binomial Formula

$$P(x) = \frac{n!}{x!(n-x)!}p^x q^{n-x} \qquad \textbf{4-17}$$

Mean of the Binomial Distribution

$$\mu_x = E(x) = np \qquad \textbf{4-18}$$

Standard Deviation for the Binomial Distribution

$$\sigma = \sqrt{npq} \qquad \textbf{4-19}$$

Poisson Probability Distribution

$$P(x) = \frac{(\lambda t)^x e^{-\lambda t}}{x!} \qquad \textbf{4-20}$$

Standard Deviation for the Poisson Distribution

$$\sigma = \sqrt{\lambda t} \qquad \textbf{4-21}$$

■ KEY TERMS

Binomial Probability Distribution—A distribution that gives the probability of x successes in a fixed number of independent trials. Each trial must only have two possible outcomes. The probability of a success must be constant from trial to trial.

Classical Probability Assessment—The method of determining probability based on the ratio of the number of ways the event of interest can occur to the total number of ways *any* event can occur when the individual elementary events are equally likely.

Conditional Probability—The probability that an event will occur *given* that some other event has already happened.

Continuous Random Variable—Random variables that can assume any value on a continuum. Alternatively, random variables that can assume an uncountable number of values.

Dependent Events—Two events are dependent if the occurrence of one event impacts the probability of the other event occurring.

Discrete Random Variable—A random variable that can only assume only a countable number of values.

Elementary Events—The most rudimentary outcomes resulting from a simple experiment.

Event—A collection of elementary events.

Experiment—A process that produces a single outcome whose result cannot be predicted with certainty.

Independent Events—Two events are independent if the occurrence of one event in no way influences the probability of the occurrence of the other event.

Mutually Exclusive Events—The occurrence of one event precludes the occurrence of a second event.

Poisson Probability Distribution—A probability distribution for the possible outcomes of interest of a process where the average number of outcomes of interest per segment is λ, and the outcomes of interest are rare and random.

Probability—The chance that a particular event will occur. The probability of an event will be a value in the range 0.00 to 1.00. A value of 0.00 means the event will not occur. A probability of 1.00 means the event will occur. Anything between 0.00 and 1.00 reflects the uncertainty of the event occurring.

Random Variable—A variable that assigns a numerical value to each outcome of a random experiment or trial.

Relative Frequency of Occurrence—The method that defines probability as the number of times an event occurs, divided by the total number of times an experiment is performed in a large number of trials.

Sample Space—The collection of all elementary outcomes that can result from a selection or decision.

Subjective Probability Assessment—The method that defines probability of an event as reflecting a decision maker's state of mind regarding the chances that a particular event will occur.

Uniform Probability Distribution—A probability distribution that has equal probabilities for all possible outcomes of the random variables.

CHAPTER EXERCISES

SOLVED PROBLEMS ON YOUR CD-ROM
Try the WORKED-OUT EXERCISES and BUSINESS APPLICATIONS on the CD-ROM.

Conceptual Questions

4-66. Discuss what is meant by the relative frequency of occurrence approach to probability assessment. Provide a business-related example, other than those given in the text, where this method of probability assessment might be used.

4-67. Discuss the characteristics that must be present for the binomial probability distribution to apply. Relate these to a particular business application and show how the application meets the binomial requirements.

4-68. Discuss what is meant by *subjective probability*. Provide a business-related example in which subjective probability assessment would likely be used. Also provide an example of when you have personally used subjective probability assessment.

4-69. Discuss why, in the strictest sense, if the sampling is performed without replacement, the binomial distribution does not apply. Also, indicate under what conditions it is considered acceptable to use the binomial distribution even when the sampling is without replacement. Identify a business application that supports your answer.

4-70. Discuss what is meant by *classical probability assessment* and indicate why classical assessment is not often used in business applications.

4-71. How is the shape of a binomial distribution changed for a given sample size as p approaches 0.50 from either side? Discuss.

4-72. Based on your experience thus far in this class, what is the probability that you will receive an "A" grade? Discuss the factors you have used in arriving at this probability assessment. Do you believe that all students in your class will arrive at the same probability assessment that you have? Why or why not?

4-73. How is the shape of the binomial distribution changed for a given value of p as the sample size is increased? Discuss.

4-74. Define and list five business examples of each of the following:
   a. Mutually exclusive events
   b. Independent events

4-75. Discuss the basic differences and similarities between the binomial distribution and the Poisson distribution.

4-76. Use an example to discuss why the following is true: If the mean of the Poisson distribution can be reduced, the spread of the distribution can also be reduced.

Business Applications

4-77. The Goldberg Construction Company recently bid on three contracts, each of which the company could be either awarded or not awarded.
   a. Define the elementary events for a given bid.
   b. List the sample space for a bid on one contract.
   c. List the sample space for all three contracts.

4-78. The Harrison Corporation manufactures electronic components for the U.S. government. One particular component can be made without defect, with a minor defect, or with a major defect.
   a. If the company makes only one of these components, list the sample space.
   b. If the company makes three of the components, list the sample space.
   c. Grouping the minor defect and major defect elementary events together, list the sample space if the company makes six components.

4-79. Assuming customer arrivals at the Fidelity Credit Union drive-through window are Poisson-distributed with a mean of 5 per hour, find:
   a. The probability that in a given hour more than 8 customers will arrive at the drive-through window
   b. The probability that between 3 and 6 customers, inclusive, will arrive at the drive-through window in a given hour
   c. The probability that fewer than 3 customers will arrive at the window in a given 30-minute period

4-80. The Sullivan Stables Company owns and races expensive racehorses. One of its horses placed second in the Kentucky Derby two years ago. Suppose Sullivan Stables recently purchased a new racehorse from a European breeder. Sullivan plans to race the horse four times this year.
   a. If the company is interested only in winning versus losing a particular race, list the sample space for the four races. Let W indicate win and L indicate lose.
   b. Suppose the stable is interested in the chances of the horse placing first, second, third, or lower in each race. List the sample space for the first two races.

4-81. Assume that the outcomes of a lottery are equally likely.
   a. What is the probability that an individual will win if he or she holds 1 ticket out of the 500 sold?
   b. What is the probability of winning if he or she holds 3 tickets out of the 500 sold?

c. What method of probability assessment did you use to answer parts a and b?

4-82. The manager of a local convenience food and gasoline store has observed that the number of customers failing to pay for their gasoline is Poisson-distributed, with a mean of five per week.

a. What is the probability that during a given week, no customers fail to pay?

b. Suppose that during the initial week of a new employee's hire, more than nine people failed to pay for their gasoline. Based on the probability of this happening, what might the store manager conclude about the distribution of the people who fail to pay?

4-83. The Hilgren Map Company produces topographical maps covering all parts of Utah, Arizona, and New Mexico. Past studies have indicated that the number of errors per map is Poisson-distributed, with an average of 0.5 errors per map.

a. What is the probability that a map will contain no errors?

b. What is the probability that a map will contain fewer than three errors?

c. What is the probability that a series of three maps will contain no errors?

d. What is the probability that a map will have five or more errors? What would you conclude if this did occur? Discuss.

4-84. Gossage's Beverages recently sent a special advertisement to a large number of people in its marketing area. It offered a special price on root beer for purchases of between one and four packages each containing six bottles or cans. In planning for the special promotion, Jane Gossage assessed the probability distribution of the number of packages of six that each customer would buy during the promotion as follows:

NO. OF PACKAGES OF SIX	
x	P(x)
0	0.30
1	0.10
2	0.10
3	0.05
4	0.45

Based on the probability assessments, what is the expected number of packages to be sold per customer? Comment on whether any particular customer is likely to purchase exactly this amount.

4-85. The State of Maine has an inspector who checks all painting work performed by the state's painting crew. Past experience indicates that the average number of mistakes per 500 square feet of painting is 3.5 and the distribution of mistakes follows a Poisson distribution.

a. What is the probability that if the inspector checks 1,000 square feet, she will not find a mistake?

b. What is the probability in an inspection of 500 square feet that over 7 mistakes are observed? What could be concluded if this did occur?

c. Suppose the 3.5 average number of mistakes is considered to be a standard for good work. If the inspector wants at most a 10% probability of unjustly criticizing the painters, how many errors should she allow before she makes a criticism for 500 square feet of painting?

4-86. Suppose a study performed at St. Jude's Hospital shows that 30% of all patients arriving at the emergency room are subsequently admitted to the hospital for at least one night. Assuming that in a sample of seven who arrived at the emergency room, the number of people needing to be admitted to the hospital meets the requirements for the binomial distribution:

a. Determine the probabilities for each of the possible values of the random variable. Use the binomial formula.

b. What is the probability that five or more in the sample of seven will require admittance to the hospital?

c. What is the expected number of patients in the sample who will require admittance to the hospital?

4-87. The manager for the Inland Food Market chain has determined that the occurrence of spoiled fruit is Poisson-distributed, with a mean of 4 pieces per case.

a. What is the probability that in 2 cases over 10 pieces of spoiled fruit will be discovered?

b. Suppose a new employee has been assigned the task of unpacking 2 cases of fruit, and he reports that none of the pieces were spoiled. What are some conclusions you might reach and why?

4-88. It has been determined that vehicles arriving at a drive-through pharmacy window arrive according to a Poisson distribution at the rate of 12 per hour.

a. In a half-hour time period, what is the probability that 3 or fewer cars will arrive at the window?

b. In a 15-minute period, what is the probability that 3 or fewer cars will arrive at the window?

c. If the pharmacist can serve 4 cars per half-hour, what is the probability that during the first half-hour of business a customer will not be served and will still be waiting in line when the half-hour period ends?

4-89. The Telephone Company of America recently made the claim that only 10% of the people who have telephones in their residences make enough local calls during the month to justify paying the monthly bill if the calls were charged at the rate of $0.25 per call. A consumer agency decided to follow up this claim by selecting a random sample of 15 people who have telephones.

a. Assuming the binomial distribution applies, what is the probability that the survey will show fewer than 7 people actually making the necessary number of calls to justify their phone bill if in fact the true percentage in the population is 10%, as claimed by the Telephone Company of America?

b. If the binomial distribution applies, what is the probability that no customer in the sample will be found to be making enough calls to justify their bill at the rate of $0.25 per call?

4-90. A typist at Austin Company's typing pool makes errors periodically. In fact, a study has shown that errors made are random and independent of each other at an average rate of three per page ($\lambda = 3$).

    a. Develop the appropriate probability distribution for the number of errors made by the typist on a particular page.

    b. Based on the distribution developed in part a, determine the average number of errors the typist will make per page.

    c. Compute the variance and standard deviation for the probability distribution in part a.

4-91. The Town-Pump service station has performed an analysis of its customers and found that 80% pay on credit and the rest pay cash. If five customers are sampled, what is the probability that three or fewer of them will pay on credit?

4-92. The makers of Time-Tell digital watches claim that their watches are of very high quality. Specifically, they have claimed that no more than 10% of their watches will fail within the first 6 months of use. Suppose the distribution of watch failures in a sample of 10 watches has a binomial distribution.

    a. Use the binomial tables to develop the probability distribution for the number of watch failures in a sample of 10 within the first 6 months of ownership.

    b. Based on the distribution in part a, what is the mean of the probability distribution? Interpret this value.

    c. Based on the distribution developed in part a, what is the standard deviation of the random variable? Interpret this value.

4-93. Amstar Airlines has just supplied data to the U.S. federal government indicating that out of 10,000 flights, 4,900 arrived on time (within 5 minutes of schedule), 4,000 arrived late, and the remaining flights arrived early.

    a. Using the relative frequency of occurrence method, provide an assessment of the chances that an Amstar Airlines flight will arrive on time.

    b. Assess the probability that a flight will be late.

    c. Assess the chances that a flight will be early.

    d. Comment on some of the potential problems associated with using relative frequency of occurrence probability assessment in cases like this one.

4-94. After a recent freeze in Florida, the Sweetbrand Citrus Company was concerned about the quality of its grapefruit. Estimates by the Department of Agriculture (USDA) indicated that 25% of the grapefruit was damaged by the freeze. The problem is that there seems to be no pattern to indicate which grapefruit suffered freeze damage. For instance, given 2 grapefruit growing side by side on a tree, one could be perfect and the other damaged. Suppose the Sweetbrand Company selected a random sample of 50 grapefruit.

    a. What conditions must be satisfied in order that the number of damaged grapefruit has a probability distribution described by the binomial distribution?

    b. Assuming that the binomial distribution does apply, what is the probability of finding less than 5 damaged grapefruit, given that the 25% estimate is correct?

    c. Assuming that the binomial distribution applies, what is the probability of finding more than 20 damaged grapefruit if the 25% estimate is correct?

    d. Referring to your answer to part c, suppose that the company actually did observe more than 20 damaged grapefruit in a sample of 50. What might be concluded about the USDA's 25% estimate? Discuss.

4-95. The Bayhill City Council claims that 40% of the parking spaces downtown are used by employees of the downtown businesses. A sample of 5 parking spaces was selected from the 4,000 parking spaces.

    a. Assuming that the number of spaces filled by employees can be described by the binomial distribution, develop the binomial probability distribution for the sample size of 5 using the binomial formula.

    b. Suppose the sample results showed 4 or more of the spaces were actually filled by employees. What would you conclude about the council's claim? Discuss.

    c. What is the expected number of employees' cars in a sample of 5 parking spaces?

4-96. The Harris Newspaper Company sometimes makes printing errors in its advertising and is forced to provide corrected advertising in the next issue of the paper. The managing editor has done a study of this problem and found the following data:

NO. OF ERRORS x	RELATIVE FREQUENCY
0	0.56
1	0.21
2	0.13
3	0.07
4	0.03

    a. Using the relative frequencies as probabilities, what is the expected number of errors? Interpret what this value means to the managing editor.

    b. Compute the variance and standard deviation for the number of errors and explain what these values measure.

4-97. How old is your statistics instructor? Rather than trying to pick an exact age, assess a probability to each of the following categories. Make sure that the sum of the probabilities you assess equals 1.0.

Under 30
30–40
41–50
51–60
Over 60

4-98. Referring to Problem 97, compare your assessments with those of some other students in the class. Why might the assessments be different? Discuss.

4-99. The High Mountain Spring Water Company buys gallon bottles in lots of 5,000. According to the supplier, 80% of the bottles will be acceptable for use without any additional cleaning by the company's "scrubber." Assuming that the binomial distribution applies:

    a. In a sample of 200 bottles, what is the expected number of bottles that will need to be cleaned by the "scrubber"?

b. In a sample of 100 bottles, what is the expected number of bottles that will not require additional cleaning by the High Mountain Spring Water Company?

c. Suppose it costs $0.03 per bottle to use the "scrubber." What is the expected cost of scrubbing for a sample of 300 bottles?

d. Compute the standard deviation of the probability distribution for a sample of 100 bottles, where x is defined as the number of bottles that require scrubbing. Assume that the estimate of 80% acceptable clean bottles applies.

4-100. The Askot Publishing Company publishes paperback romantic novels. At the page-proof stage, it has been determined that spelling errors appear randomly and are independent of each other at an average rate of 1.3 errors per page ($\lambda = 1.3$). Suppose a proofreader has been hired to read a new book.

a. Develop the appropriate discrete probability distribution describing the number of errors in 2 pages of a book to be published.

b. If the proofreader does a perfect job, what is the average number of errors he will find for each 2 pages read?

c. What is the variance of the number of errors per 2 pages? What is the standard deviation?

d. Suppose a proofreader has just finished 4 pages and has found no errors. What are some of the possible conclusions you might reach and why?

4-101. Suppose you were given a 10-question multiple-choice examination in which each question had 4 possible answers.

a. What is the probability of getting a perfect score if you were forced to guess at each question?

b. Suppose it takes at least 7 correct answers out of 10 to pass the test. What is the probability of passing if you are forced to guess at each question? What does this indicate about studying for such an exam?

c. Suppose through some late-night studying you are able to correctly eliminate 2 answers on each question. Now answer parts a and b.

4-102. The Aims Photo Company sends photographers around to various department stores in the South to take pictures of children. The company charges only $0.99 for a sitting, which consists of 6 poses. The company then makes up 3 packages that are offered to the parents, who have a choice of buying 0, 1, 2, or all 3 of the packages. Based on his experience in the business, Samuel Aims has assessed the following probabilities of the number of packages that might be purchased by a parent.

NO. OF PACKAGES x	$P(x)$
0	0.30
1	0.40
2	0.20
3	0.10

a. What is the expected number of packages to be purchased by each parent?

b. What is the standard deviation for the random variable?

c. Suppose all of the picture packages are to be priced at the same level. Assume that the production costs are $3.00 per package. How much should they be priced if the Aims Company wants to break even? Remember that the sitting charge is $0.99.

4-103. The Dade County Emergency Services dispatcher is trained to determine whether an emergency exists or whether the problem can be handled on a non-emergency basis based on the call received. Past evidence indicates that 50% of calls are true emergencies.

a. If the binomial distribution applies, develop the probability distribution for a sample of 10, and graph the distribution in histogram form. Does the distribution appear to be symmetric? Discuss.

b. Referring to part a, suppose that the probability of a call being a true emergency is actually 70%. Develop the probability distribution, and graph the distribution in histogram form. Compare the distribution in part a with this one in terms of symmetry. Discuss.

4-104. The Iverson Investment Company recently gave a public seminar in which its representatives discussed a number of issues, including investment risk analysis. In that seminar the company reminded people that the coefficient of variation often can be used as a measure of an investment's risk. To demonstrate its point, it used two hypothetical stocks as examples. It let x equal the change in assets for a $1,000 investment in stock 1 and y reflect the change in assets for a $1,000 investment in stock 2. It showed the seminar participants the following probability distributions:

x	$P(x)$	y	$P(y)$
−$1,000	0.10	−$1,000	0.20
0	0.10	0	0.40
500	0.30	500	0.30
1,000	0.30	1,000	0.05
2,000	0.20	2,000	0.05

a. Compute the expected values for random variables.

b. Compute the standard deviations for random variables.

c. Recalling that the coefficient of variation is determined by the ratio of the standard deviation over the mean, compute the coefficient of variation for each random variable.

d. Referring to part c, suppose the seminar director said that the first stock was more risky since its standard deviation was greater than the standard deviation of the second stock. How would you respond?

4-105. A Fox News/Opinion Dynamics poll reported that 44% of all registered voters believe there is intelligent life on other planets (Source: http://www.usatoday.com/snapshot/news/nsnap006.htm). If 10 registered voters are randomly selected, what is the probability that:

a. Exactly 5 of them will believe there is intelligent life on other planets?

b. Seven or fewer will believe there is intelligent life on other planets?

c. More than 2 will believe there is intelligent life on other planets?

4-106. Referring to Problem 105, what are the expected number and standard deviation of registered voters who believe there is intelligent life on other planets?

4-107. The Bentfield Electronics Company purchases parts from a variety of vendors. In each case the company is particularly concerned with the quality of the products it purchases. Part number 34-78D is used in the company's new laser printer. The parts are sensitive to dust and can easily be damaged in shipment even if they are acceptable when they leave the vendor's plant. In a shipment of four parts, the purchasing agent has assessed the following probability distribution for the number of defective products.

x	$P(x)$
0	0.20
1	0.20
2	0.20
3	0.20
4	0.20

a. What is the expected number of defectives in a shipment of four parts? Discuss what this value really means to Bentfield.

b. Compute and interpret the standard deviation of the number of defective parts in a shipment of four.

c. Examine the probabilities as assessed and indicate what this probability distribution is called. Provide some reasons why the probabilities might all be equal, as they are in this case.

4-108. If the probability of a particular stock increasing in value is assessed at 0.60 and the probability of a second stock increasing is 0.70, are the 2 stocks independent if the probability of both stocks increasing is 0.15? Discuss.

4-109. The Question Research Company performs research work in which opinion surveys are administered. In a recent survey regarding the acceptability of a particular product, the respondents were asked to indicate (yes or no) whether they would consider using the product regularly after having tried it. The product's manufacturer thought that the chance of an individual saying yes was 0.70.

a. Assuming that the 0.70 is correct, develop a probability distribution for the number of yes responses in a sample of 5, assuming that the binomial distribution applies. Use the binomial formula.

b. Use Equation 4-14 to compute the expected value of this probability distribution. Interpret this value.

c. Suppose the Question Research Company did survey 5 people and found no one who answered yes. What is the probability of this happening, assuming the

manufacturer's 0.70 probability value is correct? What might be concluded about the manufacturer's probability value? Why?

4-110. Approximately 90% of executives indicate that Microsoft Windows is standard software at their companies (Sources: 1997 Olsten Forum and http://www.usatoday.com/snapshot/money/msnap039.htm). What is the probability that a sample of 12 executives would reveal:

a. At least 7 using Microsoft Windows?

b. No more than 10 using Microsoft Windows?

c. Exactly 6 using Microsoft Windows?

4-111. What are the expected number and standard deviation of executives from the preceding Problem 110, who say Microsoft Windows is standard software at their companies?

4-112. Of employees who work for companies that offer 401(k) retirement accounts, 57% do not participate (Source: http://www.usatoday.com/snapshot/money/msnap018.htm). If 15 workers are selected at random from companies with 401(k) plans, what is the probability that

a. Exactly 11 do not participate?

b. Exactly 5 do participate?

c. More than 4 do not participate?

d. Less than 5 participate?

4-113. The National Golf Foundation reports that a large bucket of golf balls is requested 52% of the time at golf ranges. Suppose that 12 golfers are randomly selected. What is the probability that:

a. More than 3 would request a large bucket of golf balls?

b. Less than 7 would request a large bucket of golf balls?

c. Exactly 5 would request a large bucket of golf balls?

4-114. Referring to Problem 113, what are the expected number and standard deviation of the number of golfers who request large buckets of golf balls?

4-115. In the sales business, repeat calls to finalize a sale are common. Suppose a particular salesperson has a 0.70 probability of selling on the first call and that the probability of selling drops by 0.10 on each successive call. If the salesperson is willing to make up to 4 calls on any client, what is the probability of a sale?

4-116. Recreational developers are considering opening a skiing area near a western U.S. town. They are trying to decide whether to open an area catering to family skiers or to some other group. To help make their decision, they gather the following information.

If:

A_1 = Family will ski

A_2 = Family will not ski

B_1 = Family has children but none in the 8–16 age group

B_2 = Family has children in the 8–16 age group

B_3 = Family has no children

then, for this location,

$$P(A_1) = 0.40$$
$$P(B_2) = 0.35$$
$$P(B_1) = 0.25$$
$$P(A_1 | B_2) = 0.70$$
$$P(A_1 | B_1) = 0.30$$

a. Use the probabilities given to construct a joint probability distribution table.

b. What is the probability a family will ski *and* have children who are not in the 8–16 age group? How do you write this probability?

c. What is the probability a family with children in the 8–16 age group will not ski?

d. Are the categories "skiing" and "family composition" independent?

4-117. A company is considering changing its starting hour from 8:00 A.M. to 7:30 A.M. A census of the company's 1,200 office and production workers shows 370 of its 750 production workers favor the change and a total of 715 workers favor the change. To further assess worker opinion, the region manager decides to talk with randomly selected workers.

a. What is the probability a randomly selected worker will be in favor of the change?

b. What is the probability a randomly selected worker will be against the change *and* be an office worker?

c. Is the relationship between job type and opinion independent? Explain.

4-118. The Cranston Corporation makes replacement parts for videocassette recorders (VCRs) sold under a variety of brand names. The company has a contract with one of the leading VCR manufacturers to supply a certain part. The contract calls for 95% of all parts to be "good." Before shipping a lot of 5,000 parts, Cranston selected a random sample of 50 parts and found that 4 were defective.

a. What is the probability that a sample will contain 4 or more defectives if the population of all parts meets the contract specifications? What conditions must be satisfied to employ the binomial distribution?

b. Based on the probability computed in part a, would you conclude that the shipment is likely to meet the specifications in the contract? Discuss.

4-119. Refer to Problem 118. Suppose the company sets up the following sampling plan before shipping out the parts. If a sample of 50 contains 3 or fewer defectives, the shipment will be considered acceptable. If it contains 6 or more defectives, it will be considered unacceptable. Either 4 or 5 defectives in the sample will result in a second sample of 50 items.

a. If the shipment really does meet the 95% "good" requirement, what is the probability that the first sample of 50 parts will lead the company to conclude incorrectly that the shipment is unacceptable?

b. Suppose the shipment contains only 90% good parts. What is the probability that the first sample will lead the company to thinking the shipment actually does meet the 95% requirement?

c. Based on your answers to parts a and b, what do you think of the sampling plan and why?

d. What is the probability that the sample results on the first sample will lead to the necessity of a second sample? (Assume 95% good.)

4-120. Bill Jones and Herman Smith are long-time business associates. They know that regular exercise improves their productivity and have made a practice of playing either tennis or golf every Saturday for the past 10 years. Jones enjoys tennis, but Smith prefers golf. Each Saturday they flip a coin to decide which sport to play. Jones beats Smith at tennis 80% of the time, whereas he beats Smith at golf only 30% of the time.

a. Suppose Jones walks into the Monday morning staff meeting and announces he beat Smith on Saturday. What sport do you think they played and why?

b. Assume open tennis courts are hard to find on Saturday, so instead of flipping a coin, Smith and Jones always first look for a tennis court. If they find one open, they play tennis; if not, they play golf. Further, suppose the chance of finding an open court is 30%. Given this, what sport do you think they played on Saturday, given that Jones won?

4-121. A marketing research team is considering using a mailing list for an advertising campaign. They know that 40% of the people on the list have only a MasterCard and that 10% have only an American Express card. Another 20% hold both MasterCard and American Express. Finally, 30% of those on the list have neither card. Suppose a person on the list is known to have a MasterCard. What is the probability that person also has an American Express card?

4-122. The Stevens Company in Seattle, Washington, recently did a study regarding customer satisfaction with its winter boots, which are marketed throughout the United States. A basic premise that the company has been operating under for the past several years is that 90% of its customers were satisfied with the boots they purchased. However, H. B. Stevens, the company president, felt that a survey should be taken to see if this was, in fact, the case.

a. Assuming that the characteristics of the binomial distribution are satisfied, what is the probability of finding fewer than 90 satisfied customers in a sample of 100 if the company's assumption about consumer satisfaction is correct?

b. Assuming that the binomial distribution is applicable, what is the probability of finding more than 10 dissatisfied customers in a sample of 100 if the probability of any 1 customer being satisfied is 90%?

c. Suppose the sample reveals 78 satisfied customers. What is the probability of exactly 78 satisfied customers if the probability of a customer being satisfied is 90%?

CASE 4-A

Great Air Commuter Service[4]

The Great Air Commuter Service Company originated in 1984 to provide efficient and inexpensive commuter travel between Boston and New York City. People in the airline industry know Peter Wilson, the principal owner and operating manager of the company, as "a real promoter." Before founding Great Air, Peter operated a small regional airline in the Rocky Mountain area with varying success. When Cascade Airlines offered to buy his company, Peter decided to sell and return to the East.

Peter arrived at his office near Fenway Park in Boston a little later than usual this morning. He had stopped to have a business breakfast with Aaron Little, his longtime friend and sometime partner in various business deals. Peter needed some advice and through the years had learned to rely on Aaron as a ready source of advice no matter what the subject.

Peter had explained to Aaron that his commuter service needed a promotional gimmick to improve its visibility among the business communities in both Boston and New York. Peter was thinking of running a contest on each flight and awarding the winner a prize. The idea would be that travelers who commute between Boston and New York might just as well have fun on the way and have a chance to win a nice prize.

As Aaron sat back listening to Peter outline his contest plans, his mind raced through ideas for contests. Aaron thought that a large variety of contests would be needed, since many of the passengers would likely be repeat customers and might tire of the same old thing. In addition, some of the contests should be chance-type contests, while others should be skill-based.

"Well, what do you think?" asked Peter. Aaron finished his scrambled eggs before responding. When he did, it was completely in character. "I think it will fly," Aaron said and proceeded to offer a variety of suggestions.

Peter felt good about the enthusiastic response Aaron had given to the idea and thought that the ideas discussed at breakfast presented a good basis for the promotional effort. Now back at the office, Peter did have some concerns with one part of the plan. Aaron thought that in addition to the regular in-flight contests for prizes (such as free flights, dictation equipment, business periodical subscriptions), each month on a randomly selected day, a major prize should be offered on all Great Air flights. This would encourage the reg-

ular business fliers to fly Great Air all the time. Aaron proposed that the prize could be a trip to the Virgin Islands or somewhere similar or the cash equivalent.

Great Air has three flights daily to New York and three flights returning to Boston for a total of six flights. Peter was concerned that the cost of funding six prizes of this size each month plus six daily smaller prizes might be excessive. He also believed that it might be better to increase the size of the prize to something like a new car, but use a contest that would not guarantee a winner.

But what kind of a contest could be used? Just as he was about to dial Aaron's number, Margaret Runyon, Great Air's marketing manager, entered Peter's office. He had been waiting for her to return from a meeting so he could run the contest idea past her and get her input.

Margaret's response was not as upbeat as Aaron's had been, but she did think the idea was worth looking into. She offered an idea for the large prize contest that she thought might be workable. She outlined the contest as follows.

On the first of each month she and Peter would randomly select a day for that month on which the major contest would be run. That date would not be disclosed to the public. Then on each flight on the contest day, the flight attendant would have passengers write down their birthdays (month and day). If any two people on the plane had the same birthday, they would place their names in a hat and one name would be selected to receive the grand prize.

Margaret explained that since the capacity of each flight was 40 passengers plus the crew, there was a very low chance of a birthday match and, therefore, the chance of giving away a grand prize on any one flight was small. Peter liked the idea but when he asked Margaret what the probability was that a match would occur, her response did not sound quite right. She believed the probability for a match would be 40/365 for a full plane and less than that when there are fewer than 40 passengers aboard.

After Margaret left, Peter thought that it would be useful to know the probability of one or more birthday matches on flights with 20, 30, and 40 passengers. Further, he wanted to know what the chances were that he would end up awarding two or more major prizes during a given month, assuming that the six flights carried the same number of passengers (20, 30, or 40). He realized that he would need some help from someone with a background in statistics.

---

[4]This case requires the use of counting techniques which are included as an optional CD-ROM topic. The case could be assigned if students have been introduced to combinations and permutations.

CASE 4-B

Rutledge Collections

Bob and Lisa Rutledge have operated a small collection company in New Hampshire for 14 years. Throughout this time, they have worked as agents for various companies in the area doing debt collection work. For example, they are currently under contract with Dalton Chevrolet to collect past due accounts for Dalton's service department. As with most of their contracts, Rutledge gets a percentage of all money collected. This has worked well over the years and the Rutledges have earned a decent income.

However, Bob and Lisa are now facing a major decision that involves significant risk and significant reward as well. The Bell Home Furnishings Company in Vermont recently declared bankruptcy. At the time, Bell had over 8,000 receivable accounts that had balances that were over 90 days late. This delay in collecting payments from so many customers put a cash flow strain on the company causing their lenders to call due Bell's short-term loans.

The bankruptcy judge handling the case has ordered the delinquent accounts to be sold. Bob and Lisa have the opportunity to purchase these accounts at a fraction of their face value. If they do, then any money they collect will be theirs. Bob has figured that if they can collect on 30% or more of the accounts, they will make a sizable profit. However, if the collection rate is 20% or less, they will be in big trouble themselves. The judge has agreed to allow the Rutledges the opportunity to test their collection process on a sample of 50 of Bell's accounts. Bob and Lisa agree that if they are able to collect 15 or more, they will take the deal. If they are successful on 14 or fewer, they will walk away from the opportunity.

However, they are both uneasy about this plan. If they would actually be successful in collecting on 30% or more of accounts, they don't want to miss out. On the other hand, if the collection rate is really as low as 20%, they don't want the deal. Bob wonders how effective this sampling plan might be. He decides to make a call to the local university to see if he can get some advice.

CASE 4-C

Let's Make a Deal

Quite a few years ago, a popular show called *Let's Make a Deal* appeared on network television. Contestants were selected from the audience. Each contestant would bring some silly item that he or she would trade for a cash prize or a prize behind one of three doors.

Suppose that you go back in time and have been selected as a contestant on the show. You are given a choice of three doors. Behind one door is a new sports car. Behind the other doors are a pig and chicken—booby prizes to be sure! Let's suppose that you pick door number 1. Before opening that door, the host, who knows what is behind each door, opens door 2 to show you the chicken. He then asks you: Would you be willing to trade door 1 for door 3? What should you do?

CASE 4-D

Belko Equipment Company

When Andrew Wilson was hired at the Belko Equipment Company, the company's managers considered him a top prospect. After a short introduction period in each of the company's departments, Andrew was assigned to the production control division in the Des Moines, Iowa, plant. He reported directly to Sarah Billings, who had been in charge of production control for about 3 years. Sarah was excited about having Andrew in her department because the workload had been increasing very fast during the past few months. It was becoming difficult to maintain the type of control on incoming parts that Sarah wanted with the increasing volume of orders.

Sarah assigned Andrew immediately to the task of reviewing the acceptance sampling plan for a critical part (A-67890-BCD). This part was singled out because of its high failure rate. Andrew discovered that the acceptance sampling plan involved a random sample of 250 parts from each shipment. The decision rule that had been used in the past was to accept the entire shipment if the sample contained fewer than 20 defectives. If the sample contained 20 or more defectives, the shipment was rejected and returned to the supplier.

In reviewing the contract with the supplier and Belko's work notes in the contract file, Andrew learned that the negotiated price for part A-67890-BCD assumed a maximum defective rate of 4%. Further, the notes indicated that Belko would start losing money in significant amounts if the defective rate on a shipment reached 10% defective.

Andrew leaned back in his chair and looked out his window. His concern with the acceptance sampling plan was that it be fair to the supplier by not rejecting too many good shipments, but that the plan also be fair to Belko by not letting too many shipments be accepted that contain 10% or more defectives. Andrew thought that he could apply the binomial probability distribution to help evaluate the sampling plan. He would submit his report on the plan to Sarah Billings the next morning.

■ GENERAL REFERENCES

1. Albright, S. Christian, Wayne L. Winston, and Christopher Zappe, *Data Analysis and Decision Making with Microsoft Excel*, (Pacific Grove, CA: Duxbury, 1999).
2. Blyth, C. R., "Subjective vs. Objective Methods in Statistics." *American Statistician* 26 (June 1972): 20–22.
3. Brightman, Harvey, and Howard Schneider, *Statistics for Business Problem Solving*, 2d ed. (Cincinnati, Ohio: South-Western, 1992).
4. Dodge, Mark, and Craig Stinson, *Running Microsoft Excel 2000* (Redmond, WA: Microsoft Press, 1999).
5. Hogg, R. V., and Elliot A. Tanis, *Probability and Statistical Inference*, 5th ed. (Upper Saddle River, NJ: Prentice Hall, 1997).
6. Marx, Morris L., and Richard J. Larsen, *Mathematical Statistics and Its Applications*, 3d ed. (Upper Saddle River, NJ: Prentice Hall, 2000).
7. *Microsoft Excel 2000* (Redmond, WA: Microsoft Corporation, 1999).
8. *Minitab for Windows Version 13* (State College, PA: Minitab, Inc., 2000).
9. Raiffa, H., *Decision Analysis: Introductory Lectures on Choices Under Uncertainty* (Reading, MA: Addison-Wesley, 1968).
10. Siegel, Andrew F., *Practical Business Statistics*, 4th ed. (Burr Ridge, IL: Irwin, 2000).

Continuous Probability Distributions

CHAPTER OUTCOMES:

After studying the material in Chapter 5, you should:

5-1: Be able to discuss the important properties of the normal probability distribution.

5-2: Recognize when the normal distribution might apply in a decision-making process.

5-3: Be able to calculate probabilities using the normal distribution table and be able to apply the normal distribution in appropriate business situations.

5-4: Recognize situations in which the uniform and exponential distributions apply.

WHY YOU NEED TO KNOW

Consider the case of a major wood products company that has perfected a new strain of disease-resistant Douglas Fir tree. Even though the tree seeds are clones of each other, when planted in the company tree farm, the biologists who developed the new strain find the trees exhibit different growth rates. Also consider the case of a tire manufacturer who has developed a new tread design for sport utility vehicles, and measures the tread life of the tires in terms of the number of miles driven. The testing team has found that the tires don't all wear at the same rate, even when they are tested on the same vehicle.

Unlike the discrete random variable examples introduced in Chapter 4, there are many situations in which the variable of interest is not restricted to discrete integer values. For example, the growth rates of trees can take on any value between zero and some large number, and tire tread life, measured in miles driven, could also take on values between zero and some large number. Variables that are measured in units of length, time, weight, volume, or distance are often assumed to be *continuous* variables.

Technically, a continuous variable is one that can take on an uncountably infinite number of values (measured to as many decimal places as necessary). Because of measuring limitations, some argue that there is no such thing as a truly continuous variable. They consider all variables discrete even though they can take on values containing several decimal values. However, if the variable of interest is measured such that it takes on a very large number of possible values in a specified interval, we might argue that the variable is continuous. It depends on the situation. For instance, if the time required to complete a small project that will last less than a day is tracked in hours, the time variable is not assumed to be continuous. However, if the time is measured in seconds, we would be justified in treating the variable as continuous.

Because many business applications involve continuous or quasi-continuous variables, decision makers need to become acquainted with continuous probability distributions and learn how to use them in decision making.

5-1: THE NORMAL PROBABILITY DISTRIBUTION

Variables can be classified as being either **discrete** or **continuous** depending on the number of values that the variable can assume.

DISCRETE RANDOM VARIABLE A random variable that can assume only a countable number of values.	**CONTINUOUS RANDOM VARIABLE** Random variables that can assume any value on a continuum. Alternatively, random variables that can assume an uncountable number of values.

Chapter 4 discussed a number of the decision situations that could be analyzed using discrete random variables and their associated probability distributions. In most instances, the value of a discrete random variable is determined by counting. For instance, the number of customers who arrive at a store is a discrete variable. Its value is determined by counting the customers.

In many other instances decision makers will be faced with variables that can take on a seemingly unlimited number of values. The values for these continuous random variables are typically determined by measurement instead of counting. Examples include:

Time required to perform a job Interest rates
Financial ratios Income levels
Product weights Distance between two points
Volume of soft drink in a 12-ounce can

In general, *measurement* is required to determine the value for a continuous random variable, whereas the value for a discrete random variable comes from *counting*.

Comparing Discrete and Continuous Probability Distributions Graphically

The probability distribution for an integer valued discrete random variable is composed of the values the variable can assume and the probabilities that the variable assumes those values. The probability distribution is represented by the areas of rectangles where the base is one unit wide and the height corresponds to the probability. The areas of the rectangles sum to 1.00.

The probability distribution of a continuous random variable is represented by a *probability density function* that defines a curve. The area under the curve corresponds to the probabilities for the random variable. Figure 5-1 illustrates the relationship of discrete probability distributions and a typical probability density function. Figure 5-1 (a) shows a discrete random variable with only 3 possible outcomes. Figure 5-1 (b) shows the probability distribution for a discrete variable that has 21 possible outcomes. Note, as the number of possible outcomes increases, the distribution becomes smoother. In Figure 5-1 (c), the graph of the continuous variable is a smooth curve. This smooth curve represents the probability density function for a continuous variable.

The total area (probability) under the density function curve is equal to 1.0. In addition, the probability that the variable will have a value between any two points, $P(a < x < b)$ on the continuous scale equals the area under the curve between these two points. However, for any chosen x value, $P(x) = 0$; this indicates the probability that a continuous random variable will assume a specific value is zero. Thus, when dealing with continuous random variables, we will determine probabilities for ranges of values and not for specific values.[1] For instance, we might ask, "What is the probability of a student in this class weighing 160 pounds?" If we mean exactly 160.0000 . . . pounds, the probability is zero. If we mean any weight that would round to 160 pounds, the question makes sense and we could find the probability.

The Normal Distribution

You will encounter many business situations in which the random variable of interest will be treated as a continuous variable. There are several continuous distributions that are frequently used to describe physical situations. The most useful continuous probability distribution is the **normal distribution**.[2] The reason is that the output from a great many processes (both those designed by humans and natural) is normally distributed.

FIGURE 5-1   Probability Density Functions versus Discrete Probability Distributions

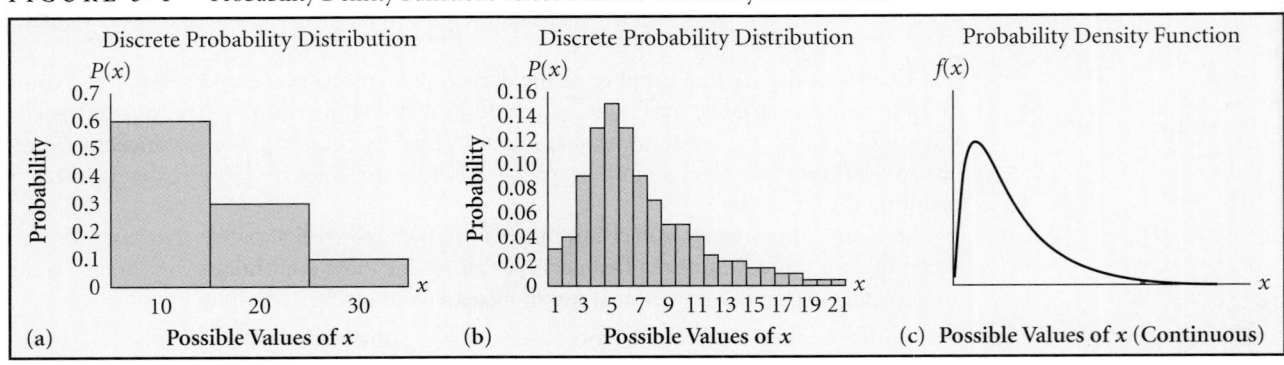

[1] The method used to determine areas under a curve is a calculus procedure called integration. We define the function for the curve and then integrate the function between two points giving the area. If we want the area above a specific point, the integration would be from a point to the same point. This integration equals zero. For more information see the optional CD-ROM topic on integration.

[2] It is common to refer to the very large family of normal distributions as "*the* normal distribution." Keep in mind, however, that "the normal distribution" really is a very large family of distributions.

NORMAL DISTRIBUTION

A bell-shaped, continuous distribution with the following properties:

1. It is *unimodal*; that is, the normal distribution peaks at a single value.
2. It is *symmetrical*; this means that 50% of the area under the curve lies left of the center and 50% lies right of the center. One side of the distribution is the mirror image of the other side.
3. The mean, median, and mode are equal.
4. The normal distribution approaches the horizontal axis on each side of the mean toward plus and minus infinity ($\pm\infty$). In more formal terms, the normal distribution is *asymptotic* to the *x*-axis.
5. The amount of variation in the random variable determines the width of the normal distribution.

Figure 5-2 illustrates a typical normal distribution and highlights the normal distribution's characteristics. All normal distributions have the same general shape as the one shown in Figure 5-2. However, they can differ in their mean value and their variation depending on the situation being considered. The process being represented determines the scale of the horizontal axis. It may be pounds, inches, dollars, or any other physical attribute with a continuous measurement. Figure 5-3 shows several normal distributions with different centers and different spreads. Note that the total area (probability) under each normal curve equals 1.0. The normal distribution is described by the rather complicated looking **probability density function** shown in Equation 5-1.

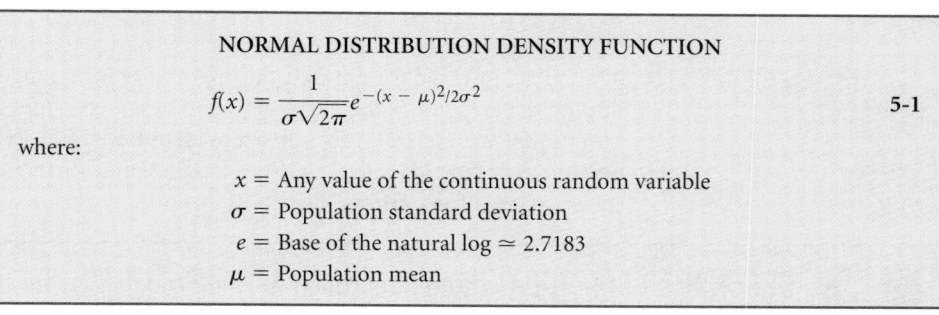

NORMAL DISTRIBUTION DENSITY FUNCTION

$$f(x) = \frac{1}{\sigma\sqrt{2\pi}}e^{-(x-\mu)^2/2\sigma^2}$$

5-1

where:

x = Any value of the continuous random variable
σ = Population standard deviation
e = Base of the natural log ≈ 2.7183
μ = Population mean

FIGURE 5-2
Characteristics of the Normal Distribution

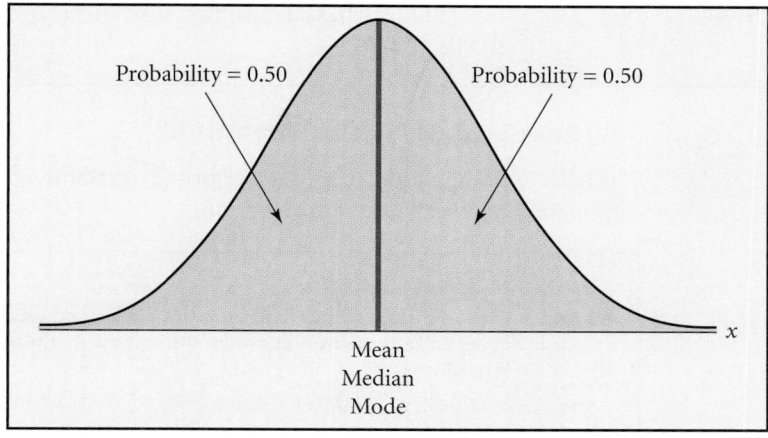

Probability = 0.50   Probability = 0.50

Mean
Median
Mode

x

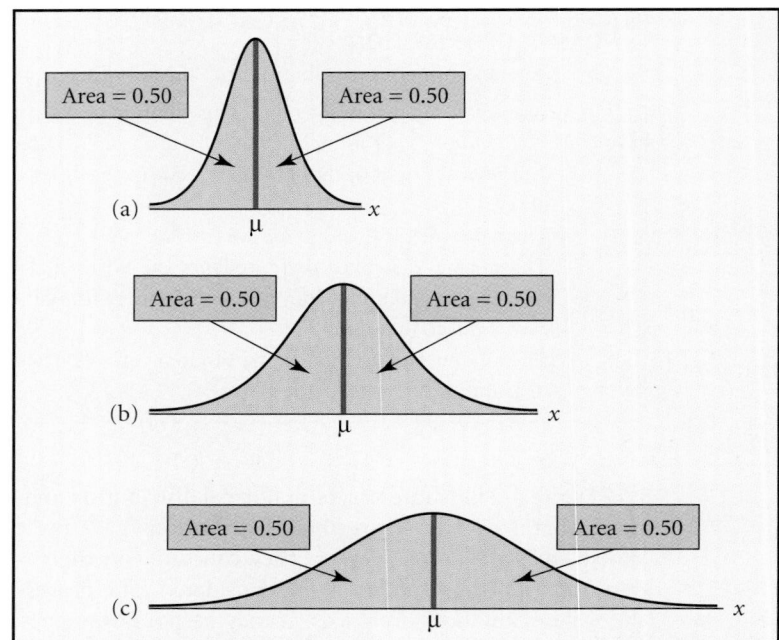

FIGURE 5-3
Different Normal
Distributions

To graph the normal distribution, we need to know the mean, μ, and the standard deviation, σ. Placing μ, σ, and a value of the variable, x, into the probability density function, we can calculate a height, $f(x)$, of the density function. If we try enough x values, we will get a curve like those shown in Figures 5-2 and 5-3.

The area under the normal curve corresponds to probability. The probability, $P(x) = 0$ for all x. However, we can find the probability for a range of values between x_1 and x_2 by finding the area under the curve between these two values. Integral calculus is used to find areas under a curve and is the subject of an optional CD-ROM topic. Alternatively, a special normal distribution called the standard normal distribution is also used to find areas (probabilities) for a normal distribution.

 **OPTIONAL CD-ROM TOPIC** Using Integration to Find Probabilities for a Continuous Distribution
To find areas between any two points for a continuous function, the technique of integral calculus is used. Although this text is not calculus based, you can find out more information by going to the CD-ROM.

The Standard Normal Distribution

The trick to finding probabilities for a normal distribution is to convert the normal distribution to a **standard normal distribution**.

STANDARD NORMAL DISTRIBUTION
A normal distribution which has a mean = 0.0 and a standard deviation = 1.0.
The horizontal axis is scaled in z-values that measure the number of standard deviations a point is from the mean.
Values above the mean have positive z-values. Values below the mean have negative z-values.

To convert a normal distribution to a standard normal distribution, the values, *x*, of the random variable are standardized as outlined in Chapter 3. The conversion formula is shown as Equation 5-2.

Excel Simulation

Normal Distribution

STANDARDIZED NORMAL Z-VALUE

$$z = \frac{x - \mu}{\sigma}$$

5-2

where:

z = Scaled value (the number of standard deviations a point x is from the mean)
x = Any point on the horizontal axis
μ = Mean of the normal distribution
σ = Standard deviation of the normal distribution

Equation 5-2 *rescales* the normal distribution axis from its true units (time, weight, dollars, barrels, and so forth) to the standard measure referred to as a *z-value*. Thus, any value of the normally distributed continuous random variable can be represented by a unique *z*-value.

Westex Oil Company

To illustrate how the standard normal distribution works, consider Westex Oil, which has home offices in Midland, Texas. Westex, an independent oil exploration and production company, was created after the oil embargo in the early 1970s. The company had some initial success in finding small deposits of new oil, but most of the company's cash flow comes from wells it owns on established, and maturing, oil fields.

Even though most oil fields in the lower 48 states are maturing and facing declining production rates, substantial oil remains that is not recoverable by conventional methods. Therefore, most oil producers experiment with ways to increase production from mature wells. One method is to inject water into a well to force out additional oil. Westex management is considering adding a newly developed enzyme to the injected water but will do so only if the increased production is sufficient to cover the additional costs. Suppose the new enzyme will increase oil output by an average of 50 barrels a day, but because of differences in rock structures this output varies and has a standard deviation of 10 barrels a day.

Assume data suggest that the number of barrels of oil is described by the normal distribution with $\mu = 50$, and a standard deviation $\sigma = 10$. Equation 5-1 will determine the height of the normal distribution curve for each possible value of the random variable. Figure 5-4 shows the resulting distribution. Suppose in the Westex example we select a level

EXAMPLE 5-1

STANDARD NORMAL EXAMPLE

FIGURE 5-4
Distribution of Oil Barrels Produced per Day for Westex Oil

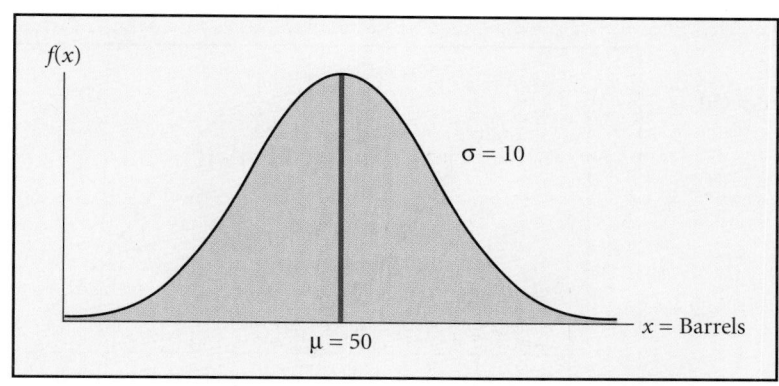

of $x = 50$ barrels per day. (Note that 50 is also μ, the mean increase.) We can find the z-value for this point using Equation 5-2:

$$z = \frac{x - \mu}{\sigma} = \frac{50 - 50}{10}$$

$$= 0.00$$

Thus, the z-value corresponding to the population mean, μ, is zero. This indicates that the mean is 0.00 standard deviations from itself.

Next, select $x = 60$ barrels per day. The z-value for this point is

$$z = \frac{x - \mu}{\sigma} = \frac{60 - 50}{10} = \frac{10}{10} = 1.00$$

Thus, for this distribution, the value 60 barrels is 1.00 standard deviation above the mean of 50. A value $x = 35$ has a standardized z-value $= -1.50$ as follows:

$$z = \frac{x - \mu}{\sigma} = \frac{35 - 50}{10} = \frac{-15}{10} = -1.50$$

This indicates that the value 35 barrels is 1.50 standard deviations below the mean of 50 barrels. Verify for yourself that $x = 40$ barrels per day corresponds to a z-value of -1.00. Note that a negative z-value indicates that the specified value of x is less than the mean.

The z-value represents the number of standard deviations a point, x, is away from the population mean. In this Westex Oil example, the standard deviation is 10 barrels per day. Therefore, an output increase of 60 barrels per day is 1 standard deviation above 50 barrels per day. Likewise, an output increase of 70 barrels per day is 2 standard deviations above the mean. Figure 5-5 shows the standard normal distribution for the Westex Oil Company example.

USING THE STANDARD NORMAL TABLE

The *standard normal table* in Appendix D provides probabilities (or areas under the normal curve) for many different z-values. The standard normal table is constructed such that the probabilities provided represent the chance of a value falling between the z-value and the population mean.

The standard normal table is also reproduced in Table 5-1. This table provides probabilities for z-values in the range $z = 0.00$ to $z = 3.09$. For example, to find the probability associated with $z = 1.45$ (i.e., $P[0 \leq z \leq 1.45]$), do the following:

1. Go down the left-hand column of the table to $z = 1.4$.
2. Go across the top row of the table to 0.05 for the second decimal place in $z = 1.45$.
3. Find the value where the row and column found in steps 1 and 2 intersect.

FIGURE 5-5
Standard Normal
Distribution for Westex Oil

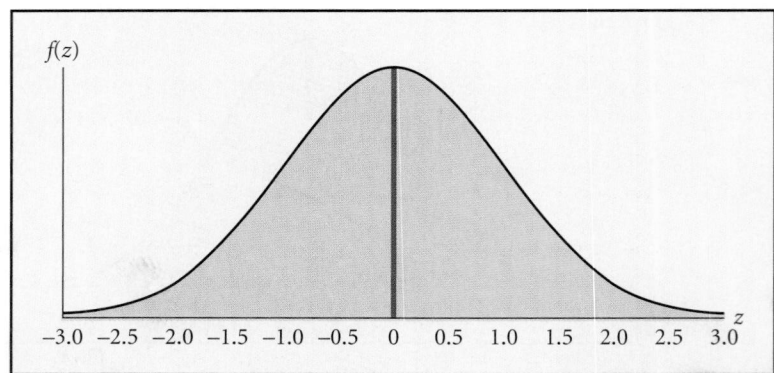

The value, 0.4265, is the probability that a value in a normal distribution will lie between the mean and 1.45 standard deviations above the mean.

For a $z = -2.07$, the probability (i.e., $P(-2.07 \le z \le 0.0)$) is found using Table 5-1 with the following steps:

1. Go down the left-hand column of the table to $z = 2.0$. (Remember, negative z-values have the same probabilities as the corresponding positive z-values.)

TABLE 5-1
Standard Normal
Distribution Table

To illustrate: 19.85% of the area under a normal curve lies between the mean, μ, and a point 0.52 standard deviation units away.

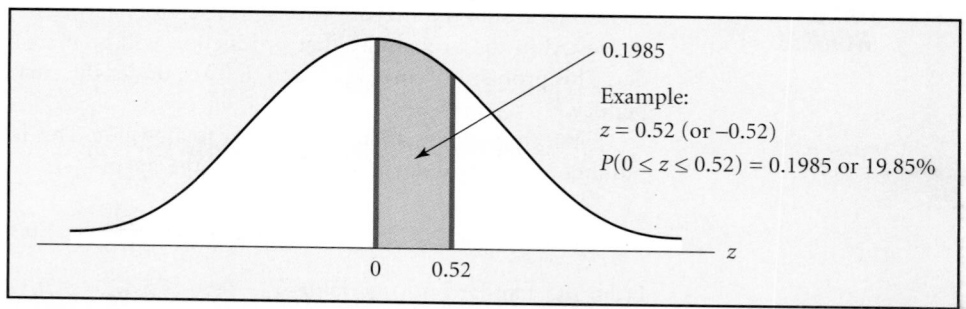

Z	.00	.01	.02	.03	.04	.05	.06	.07	.08	.09
0.0	.0000	.0040	.0080	.0120	.0160	.0199	.0239	.0279	.0319	.0359
0.1	.0398	.0438	.0478	.0517	.0557	.0596	.0636	.0675	.0714	.0753
0.2	.0793	.0832	.0871	.0910	.0948	.0987	.1026	.1064	.1103	.1141
0.3	.1179	.1217	.1255	.1293	.1331	.1368	.1406	.1443	.1480	.1517
0.4	.1554	.1591	.1628	.1664	.1700	.1736	.1772	.1808	.1844	.1879
0.5	.1915	.1950	.1985	.2019	.2054	.2088	.2123	.2157	.2190	.2224
0.6	.2257	.2291	.2324	.2357	.2389	.2422	.2454	.2486	.2517	.2549
0.7	.2580	.2611	.2642	.2673	.2704	.2734	.2764	.2794	.2823	.2852
0.8	.2881	.2910	.2939	.2967	.2995	.3023	.3051	.3078	.3106	.3133
0.9	.3159	.3186	.3212	.3238	.3264	.3289	.3315	.3340	.3365	.3389
1.0	.3413	.3438	.3461	.3485	.3508	.3531	.3554	.3577	.3599	.3621
1.1	.3643	.3665	.3686	.3708	.3729	.3749	.3770	.3790	.3810	.3830
1.2	.3849	.3869	.3888	.3907	.3925	.3944	.3962	.3980	.3997	.4015
1.3	.4032	.4049	.4066	.4082	.4099	.4115	.4131	.4147	.4162	.4177
1.4	.4192	.4207	.4222	.4236	.4251	.4265	.4279	.4292	.4306	.4319
1.5	.4332	.4345	.4357	.4370	.4382	.4394	.4406	.4418	.4429	.4441
1.6	.4452	.4463	.4474	.4484	.4495	.4505	.4515	.4525	.4535	.4545
1.7	.4554	.4564	.4573	.4582	.4591	.4599	.4608	.4616	.4625	.4633
1.8	.4641	.4649	.4656	.4664	.4671	.4678	.4686	.4693	.4699	.4706
1.9	.4713	.4719	.4726	.4732	.4738	.4744	.4750	.4756	.4761	.4767
2.0	.4772	.4778	.4783	.4788	.4793	.4798	.4803	.4808	.4812	.4817
2.1	.4821	.4826	.4830	.4834	.4838	.4842	.4846	.4850	.4854	.4857
2.2	.4861	.4864	.4868	.4871	.4875	.4878	.4881	.4884	.4887	.4890
2.3	.4893	.4896	.4898	.4901	.4904	.4906	.4909	.4911	.4913	.4916
2.4	.4918	.4920	.4922	.4925	.4927	.4929	.4931	.4932	.4934	.4936
2.5	.4938	.4940	.4941	.4943	.4945	.4946	.4948	.4949	.4951	.4952
2.6	.4953	.4955	.4956	.4957	.4959	.4960	.4961	.4962	.4963	.4964
2.7	.4965	.4966	.4967	.4968	.4969	.4970	.4971	.4972	.4973	.4974
2.8	.4974	.4975	.4976	.4977	.4977	.4978	.4979	.4979	.4980	.4981
2.9	.4981	.4982	.4982	.4983	.4984	.4984	.4985	.4985	.4986	.4986
3.0	.4987	.4987	.4987	.4988	.4988	.4989	.4989	.4989	.4990	.4990

2. Go across the top row of the table to 0.07 for the second decimal place in $z = 2.07$.
3. Find the value where the row and column found in steps 1 and 2 intersect.

The value, 0.4808, is the probability of a value falling between the mean and 2.07 standard deviations below the mean.

To find $P(-2.07 \leq z \leq 1.45)$, the probability of a value falling between $z = -2.07$ and $z = 1.45$, find the individual probabilities (0.4808 and 0.4265) and add them for a total of 0.9073.

**STANDARD
NORMAL**

Westex Oil Company (continued)

In the Westex Oil example, recall that the mean increase in oil output was 50 barrels per day and the standard deviation was 10 barrels per day. Company cost accountants have estimated that the output level must be increased by at least 45 barrels per day to pay for the additional cost of the enzyme injection. Therefore, if the enzyme is tried on one well, we are interested in the probability that production will be increased by 45 or more barrels per day. This probability corresponds to the area under the curve to the right of $x = 45$ barrels per day.

First, convert $x = 45$ barrels per day to a z-value. This is equivalent to determining the number of standard deviations 45 is from the mean.

$$z = \frac{x - \mu}{\sigma} = \frac{45 - 50}{10} = -0.50$$

From the standard normal table, $P(-0.50 \leq z \leq 0) = 0.1915$. This is shown as the area between $x = 45$ and $\mu = 50$ in Figure 5-6. Since the normal curve is symmetrical and half the total area lies on each side of the mean, we can find the probability of an increase of 45 or more barrels per day by adding 0.1915 to 0.5000:

$$0.1915 + 0.5000 = 0.6915$$

FIGURE 5-6
Probabilities from the
Normal Curve for Westex

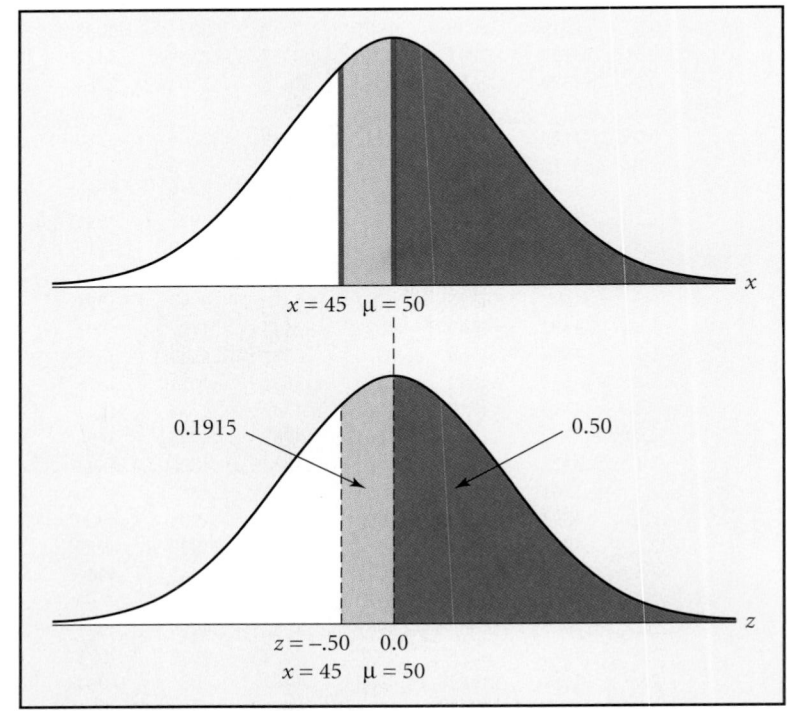

Therefore, based on the mean and standard deviation values, the probability that the well will increase production by 45 or more gallons per day is 0.6915. On the other hand, $1 - 0.6915 = 0.3085$ is the probability that increased production will be less than 45 gallons and thus unprofitable for Westex Oil.

EXAMPLE
5-3

**STANDARD
NORMAL**

Longlife Battery Company

Several states, most predominately California, have passed legislation requiring automakers to sell a certain percentage of zero emissions cars in those states. The current choice is to manufacture battery-powered cars. The major problem with battery-operated cars is the limited time they can be driven before the batteries must be recharged. Longlife Battery, a start-up company, has developed a battery pack it claims will power a car at a sustained speed of 45 miles per hour for an average of 8 hours. However, like all other manufactured products, there is variation in how long individual batteries will function without the need to be recharged. Thus, not all packs of batteries will last for 8 hours. Some will last longer and some for shorter amounts of time. Current data indicate that the standard deviation of battery operation times before a charge is needed is 0.4 hours. Data show that the distribution of uptime on these battery packs is normally distributed. Because drivers need to rely on their car to move when they want it to, automakers are concerned with the potential that batteries will run short. For example, an "8-hour" battery that lasts 7.5 hours or less might be unacceptable. What are the chances of this happening with the Longlife Battery pack?

To calculate the probability the batteries will last 7.5 hours or less, find the appropriate area under the normal curve shown in Figure 5-7. There is approximately 1 chance in 10 (10%) that a battery will last 7.5 hours or less when the vehicle is driven at 45 miles per hour.

Suppose this level of reliability is unacceptable to the automakers. Instead of a 10% chance of an "8-hour" battery lasting 7.5 hours or less, the automakers will accept no more than a 2% chance of this happening. The Longlife Battery Company recognizes that one option it might use to meet the automaker's standards is to determine a way to increase the mean life of the battery. The question is, what would the mean uptime have to be to meet the 2% requirement?

FIGURE 5-7
Longlife Battery Company

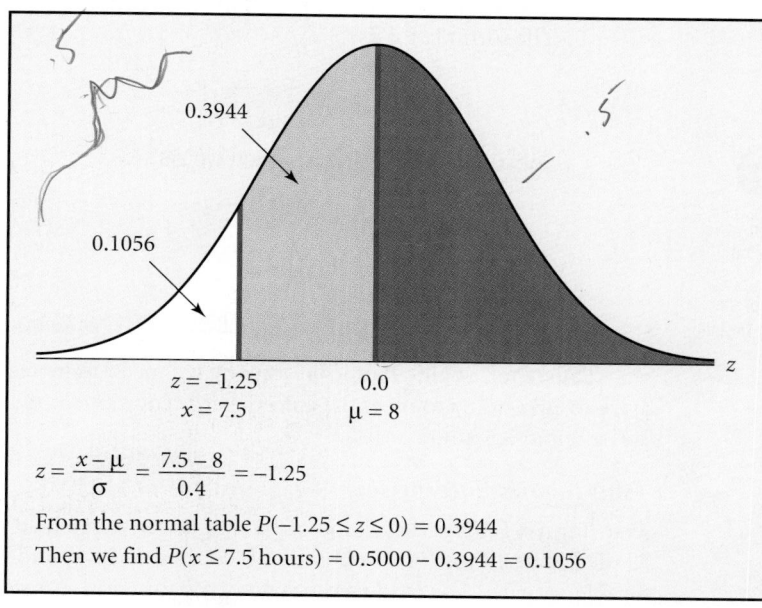

$$z = \frac{x - \mu}{\sigma} = \frac{7.5 - 8}{0.4} = -1.25$$

From the normal table $P(-1.25 \leq z \leq 0) = 0.3944$

Then we find $P(x \leq 7.5 \text{ hours}) = 0.5000 - 0.3944 = 0.1056$

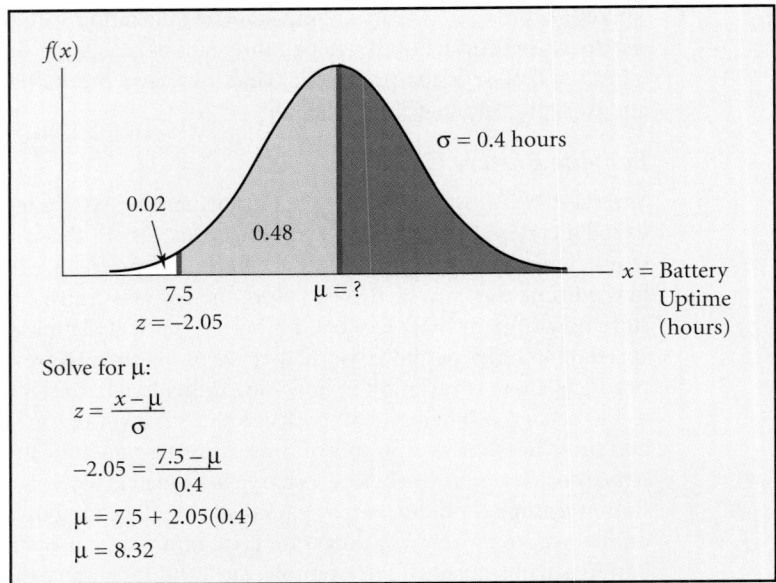

FIGURE 5-8
Longlife Battery Company,
Solving for the Mean

Assuming that the uptime distribution is normally distributed, we can answer this question by using the standard normal distribution. However, instead of using the standard normal table to find a probability, we use it in reverse to find the z-value that corresponds to a known probability. Figure 5-8 shows the uptime distribution for the battery packs. Note, the 0.02 probability is shown in the left tail of the distribution. This is the allowable probability of a battery lasting 7.5 hours or less. We must solve for μ, the mean uptime that will meet this requirement. This is done as follows:

1. Go to the standard normal table on the inside where the probabilities are located and find the probability as close to 0.48 as possible. This is 0.4798.
2. Determine the z-value associated with 0.4798. This is $z = 2.05$. Since we are below the mean, the z is negative. Thus, $z = -2.05$.
3. The formula for z is:

$$z = \frac{x - \mu}{\sigma}$$

Additional
Example 5-a

Solving for the
Standard Deviation

Substituting the known values, we get:

$$-2.05 = \frac{7.5 - \mu}{0.4}$$

4. Solve for μ:

$$\mu = 7.5 + 2.05(0.4) = 8.32 \text{ hours}$$

Thus, the Longlife Battery Company will need to increase the mean life of the battery pack to 8.32 hours to meet the automaker's requirement that no more than 2% of the batteries fail in 7.5 hours or less.

Pete Tagaris Enterprises

EXAMPLE 5-4

STANDARD NORMAL

Pete Tagaris Enterprises is one of the largest privately held agricultural operations in the United States. Most of its operation is located in Iowa and Kansas. However, it does have sizable irrigated hay land in the state of Washington. A recent study of the weight of hay bales at their Washington operation shows that bale weight is normally distributed with a

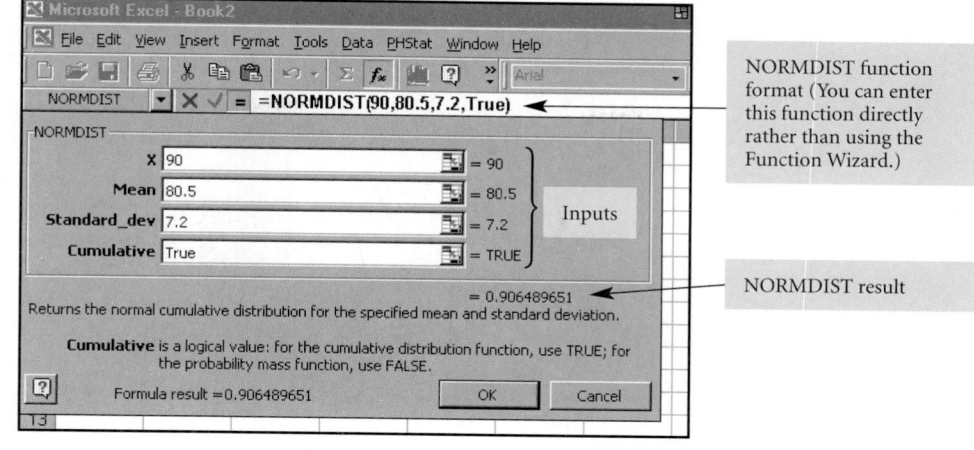

NORMDIST function format (You can enter this function directly rather than using the Function Wizard.)

Inputs

NORMDIST result

FIGURE 5-9
Excel Output for Pete Tagaris Enterprises

Excel and Minitab Tutorial

mean of 80.5 pounds and a standard deviation of 7.2 pounds. Bales that are too heavy likely have too much moisture and will spoil. Bales that are too light may be overly dry and would not have the desired feed content.

A hay bale is considered too heavy if it weighs more than 90 pounds. The hay operations manager wishes to know the probability that a bale will weigh more than 90 pounds. Excel and Minitab both have functions that can be used to determine probabilities associated with a normal distribution. Figure 5-9 shows the Excel output when the NORMDIST function is employed.

Figure 5-10 shows the area under the normal curve which Excel's NORMDIST function provides. The value 0.9064 is actually the probability of a bale weighing less than 90 pounds. The managers are interested in bales that are too heavy (90 or more pounds). We find this by subtracting 0.9064 from 1.0 giving 0.0936. Thus just over 9% of the bales will be too heavy.

If the Tagaris managers had their way, the bales would ideally weigh between 82.5 and 87.5 pounds. Given the current setting for the baler, what is the percent of bales that would fall in this range?

To calculate this we obtain the z-value for both weights. The z-value associated with 87.5 is:

$$z = \frac{x - \mu}{\sigma} = \frac{87.5 - 80.5}{7.2} = 0.97$$

From the standard normal table (Appendix D), $P(0 \leq z \leq 0.97) = 0.3340$. This area consists of both shaded areas in Figure 5-11 between $z = 0.97$ and $z = 0.00$. The next step is to

FIGURE 5-10
Excel Result for "Too Heavy" Bales Example

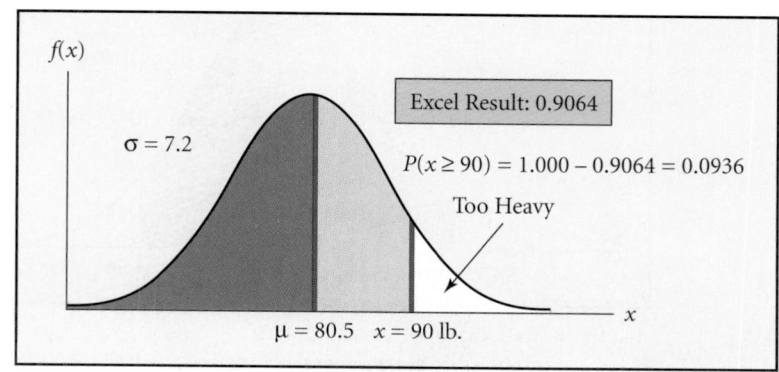

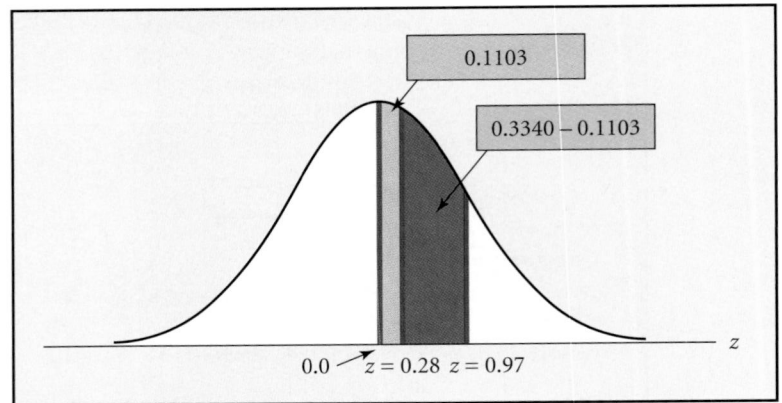

FIGURE 5-11
"Ideal" Bales Example

find the area between 82.5 pounds and the mean, 80.5 pounds. The z-value for 82.5 pounds is:

$$z = \frac{x - \mu}{\sigma} = \frac{82.5 - 80.5}{7.2} = 0.28$$

From the standard normal table, the area between a z-value of 0.00 and 0.28 is 0.1103. This area is shown as the light shaded area in Figure 5-11 between $z = 0.28$ and $z = 0.00$. The proportion of bales weighing between 87.5 pounds and 82.5 pounds is equal to $P(0.28 \le z \le 0.97)$. This probability is obtained as:

$$0.3340 - 0.1103 = 0.2237$$

Thus, approximately 22% of the bales would weigh in the ideal range.

The managers are, understandably, more concerned about the bales spoiling than not having the desired feed content. After some consideration, they conclude that they will use bales weighing between 66.5 and 91 pounds. To calculate what percentage of the bales will be used, we obtain the z-value for both values. The z-value associated with 66.5 is:

$$z = \frac{x - \mu}{\sigma} = \frac{66.5 - 80.5}{7.2} = -1.94$$

From the standard normal table,[3] $P(-1.94 \le z \le 0) = 0.4738$. This is the shaded area to the left of 0 in Figure 5-12. The next step is to find the area between 91 pounds and the mean, 80.5 pounds. The z-value for 91 pounds is:

$$z = \frac{x - \mu}{\sigma} = \frac{91 - 80.5}{7.2} = 1.46$$

FIGURE 5-12
Tagaris Hay Example

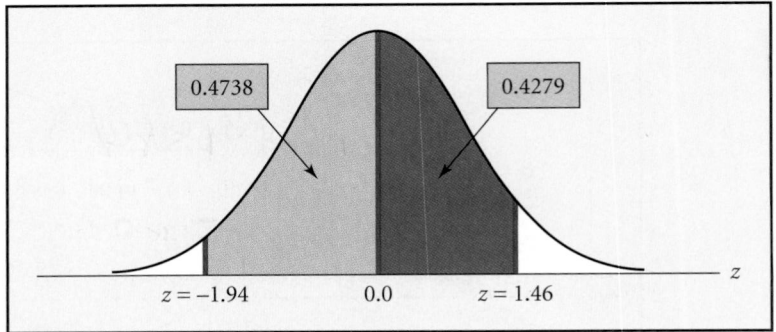

[3]Instead of using the Standard Normal Table, you could use Excel's NORMDIST or NORMSDIST functions.

From the standard normal table, $P(0 \leq z \leq 1.46) = 0.4279$. This is the proportion of bales between 91 pounds and the mean, 80.5 pounds in Figure 5-12. To obtain the proportion of bales between 66.5 and 91 pounds we add the two probabilities (areas) to obtain:

$$0.4738 + 0.4279 = 0.9017$$

EXAMPLE 5-5

STANDARD NORMAL

Excel and
Minitab Tutorial

State Bank and Trust

The director of operations for the State Bank and Trust recently performed a study of the amount of time bank customers spent in the bank from the time they arrived in the parking lot until they exited the parking lot after completing their banking business. The data file called **State Bank** contains the data for a sample of 1,045 customers randomly observed over a 4-week period. The customers in the survey were limited to those who were there for "basic bank business" such as making a deposit, a withdrawal, or cashing a check. The histogram in Figure 5-13 illustrates that the times appear to be distributed quite closely to a normal distribution.[4] The mean service time for the 1,045 customers was 22.14 minutes with a standard deviation equal to 6.09 minutes.

Based on these data, the manager is willing to assume that the service times are normally distributed with $\mu = 22.14$ and $\sigma = 6.09$. Given these assumptions, the manager is considering providing a gift certificate to a local restaurant to any customer who spends over 30 minutes in the service process for basic bank business. Before doing this, she is interested in the probability of having to pay off on this offer. Figure 5-14 shows the theoretical distribution with the area of interest identified.

FIGURE 5-13
Excel Output for State Bank
and Trust Service Times

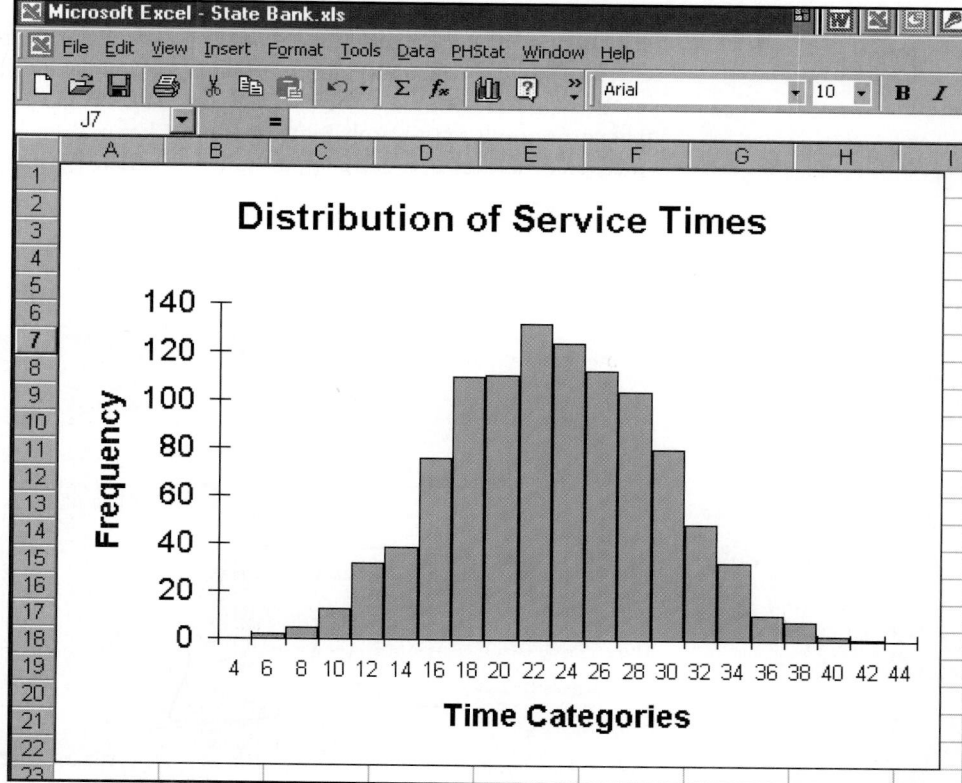

Excel Instructions:

1. Open file: State Bank.xls
2. Define Bins upper limit of each class
3. Select Tools
4. Click on Histogram
5. Identify Data range and bin range
6. Check Chart Output
7. Define output location

---

[4]A statistical technique known as the chi-square goodness-of-fit test is introduced in Chapter 14 that can be used to determine statistically whether the data follow a normal distribution.

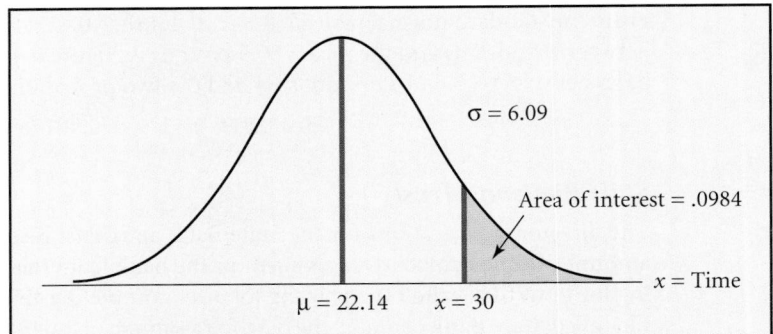

FIGURE 5-14
Normal Distribution for the
State Bank Example

The manager is interested in finding $P(x > 30 \text{ minutes})$. This can be done manually or with Excel or Minitab. Figure 5-15 shows the Excel output. Excel gives the cumulative probability, $P(x \leq 30) = 0.9016$. To find the probability of interest, we subtract this value from 1.0:

$$1.0 - 0.9016 = 0.0984$$

Thus, there are just under 10 chances in 100 that the bank would have to give out a gift certificate assuming the mean and standard deviation remain at their current levels and the times continue to be normally distributed.

Suppose the manager believes this policy is too liberal. She wants to set the time limit such that the chance of giving out the gift is only 5%. To determine the time limit, you can either use the standard normal table or the NORMSINV function in Excel.[5] To use the table, we first consider that the manager wants a 5% area in the upper tail of the normal distribution. This will leave $0.50 - 0.05 = 0.45$ between the new time limit and the mean. Given this, go to the standard normal table on the inside where the probabilities are and locate the value as close to 0.45 as possible (0.4495 or 0.4505). Next, determine the z-value that corresponds to this probability. Since 0.45 lies midway between 0.4495 and 0.4505, we interpolate halfway between $z = 1.64$ and $z = 1.65$ to get $z = 1.645$.

Using the standardization formula:

$$z = \frac{x - \mu}{\sigma}$$

FIGURE 5-15
Excel Output for State Bank
and Trust

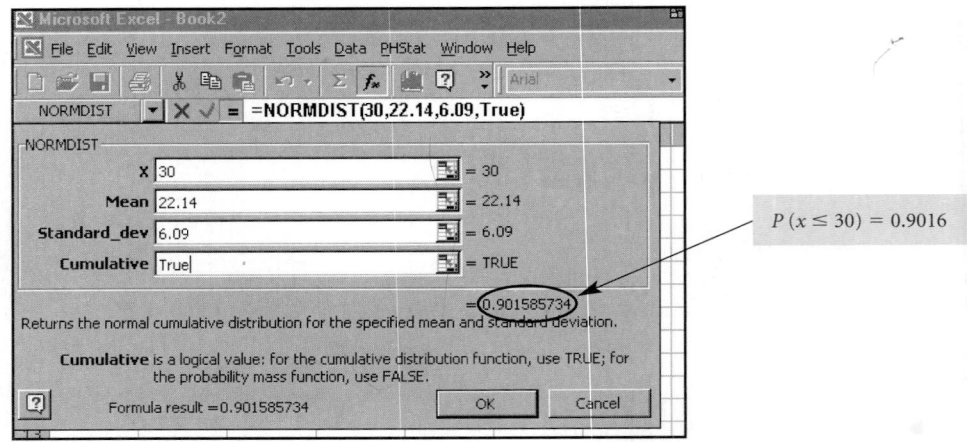

Excel Instructions:

1. Select the Function Wizard
2. Click on Statistical
3. Select NORMDIST
4. Enter the mean and standard deviation and X value
5. Set cumulative equal to TRUE
6. Click OK

[5]The function is = NORMSINV (0.95) in Excel. This will return the z-value corresponding to the area to the left of the upper tail equaling 0.05.

Additional
Example 5-b

Tools of Quality:
Quality Control
and the Normal
Distribution

We now substitute the known values and solve for x:

$$1.645 = \frac{x - 22.14}{6.09}$$

$$x = 22.14 + 1.645(6.09)$$

$$x = 32.158 \text{ minutes}$$

Therefore, any customer waiting more than 32.158 (or 32) minutes will receive the gift. This should result in about 5% of the customers receiving the gift.

OPTIONAL CD-ROM TOPIC Normal Approximation to the Binomial

Under certain circumstances, even though the binomial distribution is a discrete distribution, the normal distribution can be used to determine approximate probability values for the binomial. For more information, go to the CD-ROM.

5-1: EXERCISES

ADDITIONAL EXERCISES ON YOUR CD-ROM

Try the **ADDITIONAL EXERCISES** and **APPLICATION PROBLEMS** on the CD-ROM.

5-1. Assuming that we have a normal distribution, find the following probabilities if the mean is 60 and the standard deviation is 10.
   a. $P(x > 60)$
   b. $P(x \geq 70)$
   c. $P(50 \leq x \leq 70)$
   d. $P(x \leq 40)$

5-2. Assume a normal distribution with a mean of 15 and a standard deviation of 2.5.
   a. Determine the probability of a value exceeding 18.7.
   b. Calculate the distribution's 90th percentile.
   c. Determine the probability of a value being within 2 standard deviations of the mean.

5-3. A variable is distributed as a normal distribution with a standard deviation equal to 2.5.
   a. If the probability of a value being larger than 16.3 is to be set at 0.10, what must the mean value be? (Assume the standard deviation remains at 2.5.)
   b. Suppose the mean of the distribution is 13. Determine the value of the standard deviation so the probability that a value is larger than 16.3 is 0.10.

Business Applications

5-4. The average number of acres burned by forest and range fires in a large New Mexico county is 4,300 acres per year, with a standard deviation of 750 acres. The distribution of the number of acres burned is normal.

   a. Compute the probability in any year that more than 5,000 acres will be burned.
   b. Determine the probability in any year that fewer than 4,000 acres will be burned.
   c. What is the probability that between 2,500 and 4,200 acres will be burned?
   d. In those years when more than 5,500 acres are burned, help is needed from adjoining counties' fire teams. Determine the probability that help will be needed in any year.

5-5. Refer to Problem 4. The Bureau of Land Management and the U.S. Forest Service are responsible for estimating the amount of damage (in millions of dollars) which occurs as a result of such fires. Suppose the damage is estimated to be:

ACRES (A)	COST ($M)	# FIREFIGHTERS (F)
$0 \leq A < 2,050$	0.05	25
$2,050 \leq A < 2,800$	0.15	50
$2,800 \leq A < 3,550$	0.25	100
$3,550 \leq A < 4,300$	0.35	130
$4,300 \leq A < 5,050$	0.40	150
$5,050 \leq A < 5,600$	0.75	160
$5,600 \leq A < 6,550$	1	175
$A \geq 6,550$	1.5	200

a. Calculate the average monetary damage occurring as a result of a fire.

b. Calculate the average number of firefighters needed to combat a fire.

c. If it is desired to have enough firefighters on hand for 75% of the fires, how many firefighters are required?

d. If only 160 firefighters are available, calculate the percentage of fires that can be fought successfully.

5-6. Micron Electronics makes both desktop and laptop personal computers that it sells directly to customers by phone or over the Internet. In addition to making the computers, Micron provides customer support via a 1-800 number. Recently the manager of the service department conducted a study of the amount of time customers spent on hold waiting for a Micron representative to become available. The data showed that the distribution of time spent on hold is approximately normally distributed with a mean of 8 minutes and a standard deviation of 4 minutes.

a. Based on this information, what is the probability that a customer will have to wait more than 11.3 minutes?

b. Considering the data collected in this study, what is the probability that a customer will wait less than 2 minutes?

c. Suppose a customer has complained to the customer service manager that she was on hold for 22 minutes. Based on the data collected in the study, how would you respond to this customer? Do you think that the customer is accurate with her claim?

d. The service manager wants to make sure (for all practical purposes) that no one waits longer than 18 minutes. Determine the standard deviation that would be required to meet this goal.

5-7. A commuter airline has studied the passenger counts on a flight between Boston and Atlanta and found that the number of passengers who purchase tickets for this flight is approximately normally distributed with a mean of 72 and a standard deviation of 4. The data were determined for all days regardless of the number of tickets sold on the flight.

a. If the capacity on the plane is 85, what percentage of the time would the flight be sold out?

b. The catering manager who is responsible for snack and beverage provisions on the flight plans to stock 90 snack packs. What is the probability that there will be 8 or fewer snacks left over assuming that each passenger gets one snack pack and all passengers who buy a ticket show for their flight?

c. Comment on the potential problems in assuming that the number of passengers on a flight is normally distributed. What type of variable is the number of passengers? Discuss.

5-8. J & G Painting has been gathering data on its painting speed in an effort to be more accurate in submitting bids. Based on data gathered after considering washing, taping, painting, and clean-up, one person can paint an average of 100 square feet of indoor wall space per hour (because of extra taping time, doors and windows are counted as plain wall space), with a standard deviation of 12 square feet.

The distribution of square feet painted is considered to be normally distributed.

A painter has just started an 8-foot wide by 10-foot long room at 2:00 P.M. (assume an 8-foot high ceiling). The painter will be paid overtime if she is still working after 5:00 P.M. The ceiling is not to be painted.

a. Determine the probability overtime will not be paid.

b. Calculate the earliest the painter can expect to be finished with the room.

c. The painter is paid a "shop rate." This means that J & G Painting will charge a flat fee for the painting of the room. This charge is based on how long the particular job is expected to take. If the painter can finish the job earlier, she will receive half of the difference of the labor charged for how long the job was expected to take and how much time it actually took. The owner of the house was charged $50 an hour and was told the job should take 3 hours. What is the largest amount of money the painter can make on this job over and above her salary?

5-9. The Nelson Company makes the machines that automatically dispense soft drinks into cups. Many national fast-food chains such as McDonald's and Burger King use these machines. A study by the company shows that the actual volume of soft drink that goes into a 16-ounce cup per fill is normally distributed with a mean of 16 ounces and a standard deviation of 0.35 ounces. A new 16-ounce cup that is being considered for use actually holds 16.7 ounces of drink.

a. Calculate the proportion of cups that will be "overfilled" by the automatic dispenser.

b. The company wishes to adjust the dispenser so that the overfill percentage is no greater than 0.5%. Determine the mean required to fulfill this wish.

c. If the mean is set at 16 ounces, calculate the standard deviation that would be required to meet the stipulation in part b.

d. Which of the two procedures described in parts b and c do you prefer? Explain your answer.

5-10. Referring to the Nelson Company example in Problem 9, suppose the managers wish to have no more than 1 cup in 1,000 overfill. What should the mean fill setting on the dispenser be to assure that this takes place? (Assume the standard deviation stays at 0.35 ounces.)

5-11. Once a dispenser has been set at the value determined in Problem 10, it is put into use. After a period of time the mean amount of soft drink dispensed changes. It is important to know when this occurs so that the dispenser can be serviced and the mean level of soft drink dispensed can be adjusted. One of the decision rules developed for quality control would have the machine shut down if 2 out of 3 observations are outside 2 standard deviations from the mean (and on the same side of the mean).

a. Calculate the value that is 2 standard deviations above the mean.

b. Calculate the probability that the amount of liquid dispensed in 1 cup is above the value found in part a.

c. Now calculate the probability that at least 2 out of 3 observations are above the value found in part a. (Hint: You are counting something that assumes one of two things per trial. Refer to the optional CD-ROM topic for the normal approximation to the binomial.) For this calculation assume that the mean has not changed (i.e., the mean is still 16 ounces).

5-12. A new filter system for swimming pools is designed to filter out certain harmful particles that can get into the water. A study shows that the number of particles per gallon of water is normally distributed with a mean of 20,000 and a standard deviation of 3,000. The filter is designed to catch 25,000 particles per gallon.

a. What is the probability that a gallon of water filtered will contain one or more particles?

b. What would the filter particle limit need to be to reduce the probability computed in part a to 0.01 or less?

5-13. The Edward's Theater chain has studied its movie customers to determine how much they spend on concessions. The study based on a large number of customers shows that the spending distribution is approximately normally distributed with a mean of $4.11 and a standard deviation of $1.37.

a. Between what two values do 80% of all customers spend? (Assume that the two values are equally spaced on each side of the mean.)

b. Determine the percentiles attributed to the two numbers you produced in part a.

5-14. Refer to Problem 13. The manager of one of Edward's theaters wishes to estimate the income from the concession stand. He has engaged a very popular movie and expects to fill the theater every night for the next 2 weeks. The theater has 1,000 seats.

a. Provide the manager with an estimate of the expected income from the concession stand for the next 2 weeks.

b. Determine an estimate of the maximum income the manager might expect from the concession stand for the next 2 weeks.

5-15. Refer to Problem 14. After reviewing your calculations, the manager was somewhat disturbed. He had set a goal of taking in at least $125,000 from the concession stand in that 2-week period. He is considering offering a promotion for the concession stand to reach his goal.

a. If the promotion is successful, determine the amount the customers' spending distribution average will have to increase to reach that goal.

b. Suppose the average of the customers' spending distribution remained at $4.11. Determine the minimum value for the standard deviation so that the manager can reach his goal. Is the standard deviation you obtained realistic? (Hint: Consider the smallest amount for the spending distribution with this standard deviation.)

5-16. The length of french fries made by the J. R. Simplot Company for one of its biggest customers is normally distributed with a mean of 4.2 inches and a standard devia-

tion of 0.5 inches. The customer purchases the fries by the pound but sells to its customers by volume. Thus, the company prefers the longer fries and wants no more than a 5% chance that a fry will be shorter than 3.5 inches. Based on the current data, does the Simplot Company meet the customer's requirements? Show why or why not.

5-17. Referring to Problem 16, suppose the Simplot Company does not want to lose this customer's business. One option it is considering is changing its purchasing standards for raw potatoes in an effort to change the average length of fries. What would the average fry length have to be to meet the customer's requirement that no more than 5% of the fries will be shorter than 3.5 inches? (Assume the standard deviation does not change.)

5-18. Referring to Problems 16 and 17, suppose the Simplot Company determines that by changing the standards for raw potato purchases, the mean fry length will not be changed from the original 4.2 inches. However, the change in purchasing standards could impact the standard deviation. How much lower would the standard deviation in fry length have to be to meet the customer's requirements for no more than a 5% chance of a fry being less than 3.5 inches?

5-19. Refer to Problem 16. One of the retailers that buys from Simplot has proposed a "lot acceptance" program. You have been asked to review the program and report back to the vice president for operations. The retailer proposes selecting one box of 1,000 french fries. It will then determine the percent of the french fries in the selected box that are shorter than 3.5 inches. If the percent is greater than 10, the retailer will return the shipment of french fries to Simplot. You need to determine the proportion of shipments that will be returned. Then either make a recommendation to accept this sampling program or indicate how you would modify it. (Hint: Use Excel's Binomdist function.)

5-20. Refer to Problem 16. Another customer of Simplot has said that it will no longer accept shipments of french fries with more than 5% of the french fries longer than 5.5 inches or shorter than 3.86 inches. Simplot is considering changing its purchasing standards for raw potatoes.

a. Determine the mean for the new standards so that this customer would be satisfied.

b. Determine the distance between the 25th and the 75th percentiles (this is known as the interquartile range—IQR) for the length of french fries.

5-21. The Hydronics Company is in the business of developing health supplements. Recently, the company's R&D department came up with two weight loss plans that included products produced by Hydronics. To determine whether these products are effective, the company has conducted a test. A total of 300 people who were 30 pounds or more overweight were recruited to participate in the study. Of these, 100 people were given a placebo supplement, 100 people were given plan 1, and 100 people were given plan 2. As might be expected, some people dropped out of the study before the 4-week study period was completed. The weight loss (or gain) for each individual is listed in the data file called **Hydronics**. Note, positive values indicate that the individual actually gained weight during the study period.

a. Develop a frequency histogram for the weight loss (or gain) for those people on plan 1. Does it appear from this graph that weight loss is approximately normally distributed?

b. Referring to part a, assume that a normal distribution does apply and compute the mean and standard deviation of weight loss for the plan 1 subjects.

c. Referring to parts a and b, assume that the weight change distribution for plan 1 users is normally distributed and that the sample mean and standard deviation are used to directly represent the population mean and standard deviation. Then, what is the probability that a plan 1 user will lose over 12 pounds in a 4-week period?

d. Referring to your answer in part c, would it be appropriate for the company to claim that plan 1 users can expect to lose as much as 12 pounds in 4 weeks? Discuss.

5-22. Refer to Problem 21.

a. Develop a frequency histogram for the weight loss (or gain) for those people on plan 2. Does it appear from this graph that weight loss is approximately normally distributed?

b. Referring to part a, assume that a normal distribution does apply and compute the mean and standard deviation of weight loss for the plan 2 subjects.

c. Referring to parts a and b, assume that the weight change distribution for plan 2 users is normally distributed and that the sample mean and standard deviation are used to directly represent the population mean and standard deviation. Then, what is the probability that a plan 2 user will lose over 12 pounds in a 4-week period?

d. Referring to your answer in part c, would it be appropriate for the company to claim that plan 2 users can expect to lose as much as 12 pounds in 4 weeks? Discuss.

5-23. Refer to Problem 22.

a. Twin sisters were part of this study. One sister was put on plan 1 and the other on plan 2. Determine the probability that at least one of the sisters will lose 12 pounds.

b. The company wishes to advertise the amount of weight people can lose on plan 2. Determine the weight loss amount that corresponds to the weight lost by the upper 3% of people on plan 2.

5-24. The Future-Vision Cable TV Company recently surveyed its customers. A total of 548 responses were received. Among other things, the respondents were asked to indicate their household income. The data from the survey are found in a file named **Future-Vision**.

a. Develop a frequency histogram for the income variable. Does the graph of income appear to be approximately normally distributed? Discuss.

b. Compute the mean and standard deviation for the income variable.

c. Referring to parts a and b and assuming that income is normally distributed and the sample mean and standard deviation are good substitutes for the population values, what is the probability that a Future-Vision customer will have an income exceeding $40,000?

d. Suppose that Future-Vision managers are thinking about offering a monthly discount to customers who have a household income below a certain level. If the management wants to grant discounts to no more than 7% of the customers, what income level should be used for the cutoff?

5-25. Refer to Problem 24. Future Vision targets the $40,000 through $60,000 household income group with special advertising appealing to that income bracket. As part of the program, it offers a discount coupon of $10 off of next month's cable bill. Of those in the $40,000 through $60,000 category, 75% of the subscribers return the coupons. Determine the percent of Future-Vision's customers who both receive the promotion and send in the coupon.

■ 5-2: OTHER CONTINUOUS PROBABILITY DISTRIBUTIONS

The normal distribution is the most frequently used continuous probability distribution in statistics. However, there are other continuous distributions that have application in business decision making. This section introduces two of these: the uniform distribution and the exponential distribution.

Uniform Probability Distribution

The **uniform distribution** is sometimes referred to as the *distribution of little information* since the probability over any interval of the continuous random variable is the same as for any other interval of the same width.

> **UNIFORM DISTRIBUTION**
> A probability distribution in which the probability of a value occurring between two points, *a* and *b*, is the same as the probability between any other two points, *c* and *d*, given that the distance between *a* and *b* is equal to the distance between *c* and *d*.

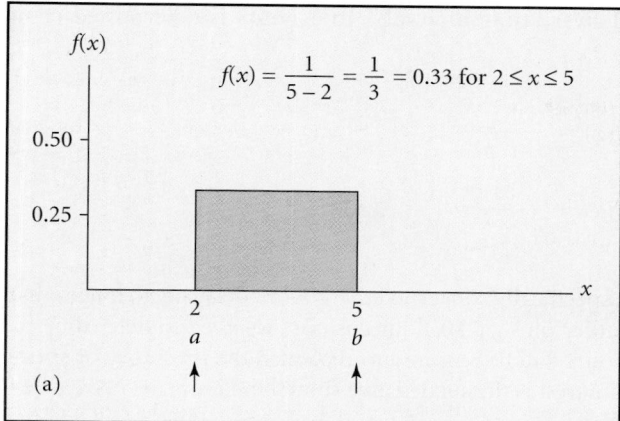

FIGURE 5-16   Uniform Distributions

Equation 5-3 defines the *continuous uniform distribution*.

CONTINUOUS UNIFORM DISTRIBUTION

$$f(x) = \begin{cases} \dfrac{1}{b-a} & \text{if } a \leq x \leq b \\ 0 & \text{otherwise} \end{cases}$$

5-3

where:

$f(x)$ = Value of the density function at any x value
a = Lower limit of the interval from a to b
b = Upper limit of the interval from a to b

Figure 5-16 illustrates two examples of uniform probability distributions with different a to b intervals. Note the height of the probability distribution is the same for all values of x between a and b for a given distribution. The graph of the uniform distribution is a rectangle.

Stern Manufacturing Company

5-6

UNIFORM DISTRIBUTION

The Stern Manufacturing Company makes seat belt buckles for all types of vehicles. The production scheduler has observed that the inventory level for a component part used in producing the buckles, the spring mechanism, has run dangerously low. In fact, she estimates that there are only enough parts to continue production for 2 more hours. The parts distributor is located nearby, but its trucks are all out on delivery and the dispatcher estimates that the springs will be delivered between 1 and 4 hours from the time they are ordered. Since the dispatcher offers no other information about the pending delivery schedule, the time needed to replenish the inventory is said to be *uniformly distributed* over the interval of 1 hour to 4 hours.

The production scheduler would prefer to continue production without any work stoppage, but she may run out of parts. If she knew that the parts were going to be more than 30 minutes late, she would call now to alert the standby crew to be ready to begin their general preventive maintenance procedures.

A first step in deciding whether to continue production and hope that the inventory arrives in time or to call the maintenance staff is to determine the probability of the inventory arriving late. For the Stern Manufacturing Company example, the height of the probability rectangle, $f(x)$, for the delivery time interval 1 to 4 hours is determined using Equation 5-3 as follows:

$$f(x) = \frac{1}{b - a}$$

$$f(x) = \frac{1}{4 - 1} = \frac{1}{3} = 0.33$$

The production scheduler is specifically concerned that a work delay be no longer than 0.50 hours. Given a 2-hour inventory plus a 0.50-hour cushion, we need to determine the probability that more than 2.5 hours will be required to replenish the inventory of spring mechanisms. The probability of interest is the shaded area shown in Figure 5-17. We determine the area (probability) as follows:

$$P(x > 2.5) = P(2.5 \le x \le 4.0)$$
$$= 0.33(4 - 2.5)$$
$$= 0.33(1.5)$$
$$= 0.50$$

Thus, there is a 0.50 probability that production will be delayed for more than 0.50 hours because of a shortage of spring mechanisms. The production scheduler will have to weigh this probability along with the costs of a work stoppage and the costs of needlessly calling in the maintenance staff before making a decision.

The Exponential Probability Distribution

Another continuous probability distribution frequently used in business situations is the **exponential distribution**. The exponential distribution is used to measure the time that elapses between two occurrences of an event such as the time between "hits" on an Internet home page. The exponential distribution might also be used to describe the time between arrivals of customers at a bank drive-in teller window or the time between failures of an electronic component.

FIGURE 5-17
Uniform Distribution for Stern Manufacturing Company

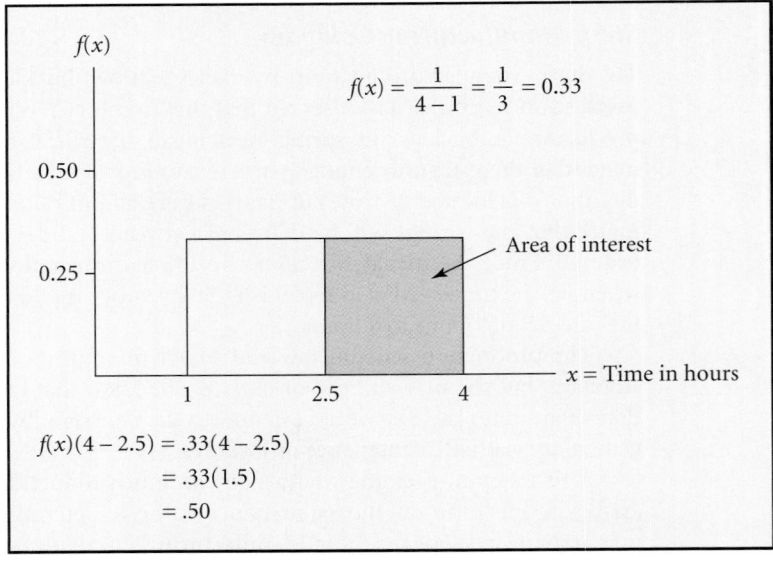

$f(x)$

$$f(x) = \frac{1}{4 - 1} = \frac{1}{3} = 0.33$$

0.50 —

0.25 —

Area of interest

1   2.5   4 x = Time in hours

$f(x)(4 - 2.5) = .33(4 - 2.5)$
$= .33(1.5)$
$= .50$

Equation 5-4 shows the probability density function for the exponential distribution.

EXPONENTIAL DISTRIBUTION

A continuous random variable that is exponentially distributed has the probability density function given by

$$f(x) = \lambda e^{-\lambda x}, \quad x \geq 0 \qquad \textbf{5-4}$$

where:

$$e = 2.71828\ldots$$
$$1/\lambda = \text{The mean time between events } (\lambda > 0)$$

Note, the parameter that defines the exponential distribution is λ (lambda). You might recall from Chapter 4 that λ is the mean value for the Poisson distribution. Thus, if the number of occurrences per time period is known to be Poisson distributed with a mean of λ, then the time between occurrences will be exponentially distributed with a mean time of $1/\lambda$.

If we select a value for λ, we can graph the exponential distribution by substituting λ and different values for x into Equation 5-4. For instance, Figure 5-18 shows exponential distributions for $\lambda = 0.5$, $\lambda = 1.0$, $\lambda = 2.0$, and $\lambda = 3.0$. Note in Figure 5-18 that for any exponential distribution, the density function, $f(0) = \lambda$ and as x increases, $f(x)$ approaches zero. It can also be shown that *the standard deviation of any exponential distribution is equal to the mean, $1/\lambda$.*

As with any continuous probability distribution, the probability that a value will fall within an interval is equal to the area under the graph between the two points defining the

FIGURE 5-18   Exponential Distributions

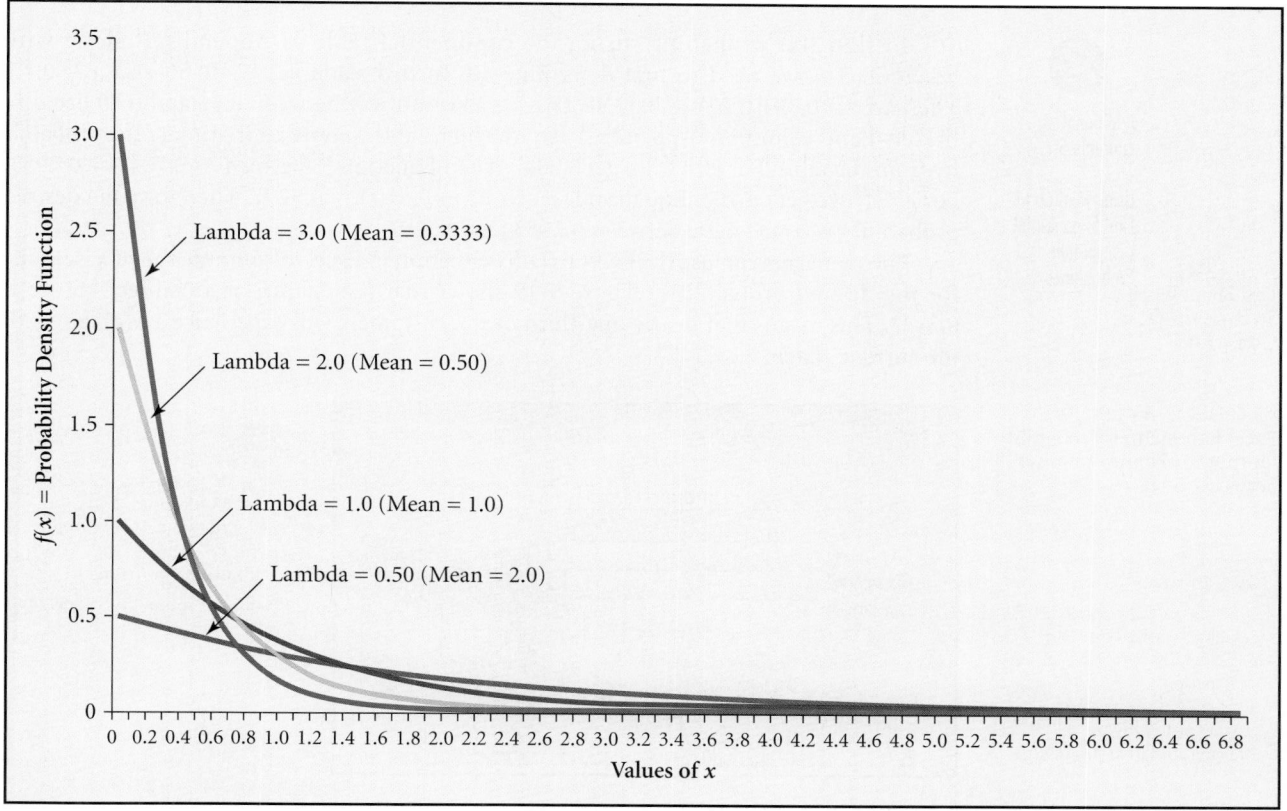

interval.[6] Equation 5-5 is used to find the probability that a value will be equal to or less than a particular value for an exponential distribution.

EXPONENTIAL PROBABILITY

$$P(x \leq a) = 1 - e^{-\lambda a}$$

5-5

Appendix E contains a table of $e^{-\lambda a}$ values for different values of λa. You can use this table and Equation 5-5 to find the probabilities when the λa of interest is contained in the table. You can also use Minitab or Excel to find exponential probabilities as the following example illustrates.

Haines Internet Services

The Haines Internet Services Company has determined that the number of customers who attempt to connect to the Internet per hour is Poisson distributed with $\lambda = 30$ per hour. The time between connect requests is exponentially distributed with a mean time between calls of 2.0 minutes computed as follows:

$$\lambda = 30 \text{ connects per 60 minutes} = 0.50 \text{ per minute}$$

Then the mean time between calls is $1/\lambda = 1/0.50 = 2.0$ minutes.

Because of the system that Haines uses, if customer requests are too close together, some customers will experience connect failures. Specifically, if the time between calls is 45 seconds or less (0.75 minutes or less), there will be a problem. The managers at Haines are analyzing whether they should purchase new equipment that will eliminate this problem. One factor of interest is the probability that a customer will experience a connect failure. Thus they want:

$$P(x \leq 0.75 \text{ minutes}) = ?$$

To find this probability using the exponential table in Appendix E along with Equation 5-5, we need to first determine λa. In this example, $\lambda = 0.50$ and $a = 0.75$. Then $\lambda \alpha = (0.50)(0.75) = 0.3750$. This value is midway between 0.35 and 0.40 listed in the left-hand column of Appendix E, so we will be able to only approximate the probability from the table. For $e^{-0.35}$ we get 0.7047. Then Equation 5-5 gives $1 - 0.7047 = 0.2953$. For $e^{-0.40}$ we get 0.6703. Equation 5-5 gives $1 - 0.6703 = 0.3297$. Therefore, the desired probability is somewhere between 0.2953 and 0.3297.

The managers can use the EXPONDIST function in Excel to compute the precise value for the desired probability.[7] Figure 5-19 shows that the chance of a connect failure is 0.3127. This means that nearly one-third of the customers will experience a problem with the current system.

Excel Instructions:

1. Click on Function Wizard
2. Select Statistics
3. Select EXPONDIST function
4. Supply x and lambda
5. Set Cumulative = TRUE for cumulative probability

Sidebar icons and labels:

EXAMPLE 5-7

EXPONENTIAL DISTRIBUTION

Excel Tutorial included on CD-ROM

Additional Example 5-c

Using Minitab to Find Exponential Distribution Probabilities

FIGURE 5-19
Excel Exponential Probability Output for Haines Internet Services

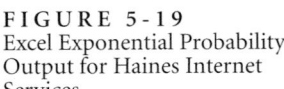

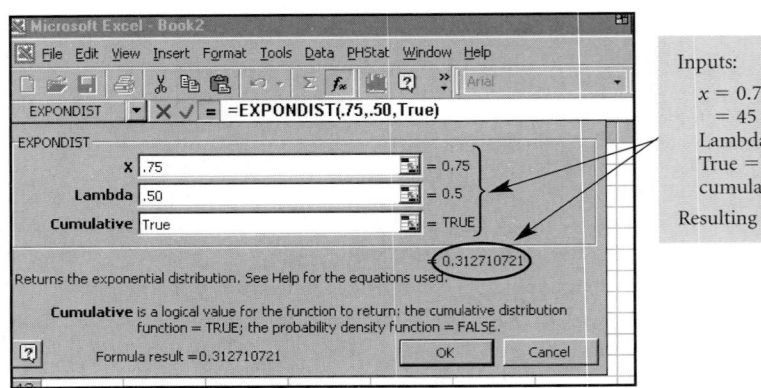

Inputs:
$x = 0.75$ minutes
    = 45 seconds
Lambda = 0.50 per minute
True = output is the cumulative probability
Resulting Probability = 0.3127

---

[6]Integral calculus is used to find the area.
[7]The Excel EXPONDIST function requires that λ be inputted rather than $1/\lambda$.

5-2: EXERCISES

ADDITIONAL EXERCISES ON YOUR CD-ROM
Try the ADDITIONAL EXERCISES and APPLICATION PROBLEMS on the CD-ROM.

5-26. A continuous random variable is uniformly distributed between 20 and 60.
   a. What is the probability a randomly selected value will be above 50?
   b. Calculate the probability a randomly selected value will be exactly 45.
   c. Determine the probability that a randomly selected value will be between 25 and 35.
   d. Find the probability that a randomly selected value will be less than 34.

5-27. A random variable is known to be exponentially distributed with a mean time between occurrences equal to 2.0 minutes.
   a. What is the probability that the time between the next two occurrences is over 2.0 minutes?
   b. Determine the probability that the time between the next two occurrences is between 1.0 and 2.0 minutes.
   c. Calculate the probability that the time between the next two occurrences is greater than 2.5 minutes.

Business Applications

5-28. When only the value-added time is considered, the time it takes to build a laser printer is thought to be uniformly distributed between 8 and 15 hours.
   a. What are the chances that it will take more than 10 value-added hours to build a printer?
   b. How likely is it that a printer will require less than 9 value-added hours to build?
   c. Suppose a single customer orders 2 printers. Determine the probability that the first and second printer each will require less than 9 value-added hours to complete.

5-29. In Western Oregon, the growth distribution for a pine tree is thought to be uniformly distributed between 5 and 8.5 inches per year. A forest products company is building a computer simulation model that they will use to help determine how many trees should be harvested each year.
   a. The modelers are thinking of using a constant growth rate of 7.0 inches per year. Based on the growth distribution, what is the probability that a tree will grow less than 7.0 inches in a year? Comment on the potential impact of using this growth level in the model. Would the model tend to understate or overstate the actual pine tree growth? Discuss.
   b. Suppose the modelers are also considering using a growth rate of 6.0 inches per year. What is the probability that a tree will grow more than 6.0 inches per

year? If they use this as their model input, what might be the general impact on tree growth projections by the model? Discuss.

5-30. The Sea Pines Golf Course is preparing for a major LPGA golf tournament. Since parking near the course is extremely limited (room for only 500 cars), the course officials have contracted with the local community to provide parking and a bus shuttle service. Sunday, the final day of the tournament, will have the largest crowd, and the officials estimate they will have between 8,000 and 12,000 cars needing parking spaces, but think no value is more likely than another. The tournament committee is discussing how many parking spots to contract from the city. If they want to limit the chance to 10% of not having enough available parking, how many spaces do they need from the city on Sunday?

5-31. The manager for Select-a-Seat, a company that sells tickets to athletic games, concerts, and other events, has determined that the number of people arriving at the Broadway location on a typical day is Poisson distributed with a mean of 12 per hour. It takes approximately 4 minutes to process a ticket request. Thus, if customers arrive in intervals that are less than 4 minutes, they will have to wait. Assuming that a customer has just arrived and the ticket agent is starting to serve that customer, what is the probability that the next customer who arrives will have to wait in line?

5-32. The Barineer Hospital in Sarasota, Florida, has determined that the time between patient arrivals to the emergency room is exponentially distributed with a mean time between arrivals of 11 minutes. Processing a patient into the hospital requires 5 minutes. A person has just begun the processing procedure, and there are no other patients waiting.
   a. What is the probability that the next arriving patient will have to wait to be processed? What does this imply about the hospital's need to add another check-in station in the emergency room? Discuss.
   b. The emergency room often has several patients arriving at once as a result of a traffic accident, fire, etc. Suppose the emergency room has 5 patients from a traffic accident arrive at the same time. How many other patients will arrive at the emergency room while the original 5 are being processed? (Hint: Recall the relationship between the Poisson distribution and the exponential distribution.) Can you visualize why at times it takes a long time to see a doctor in a hospital's emergency room?

5-33. The time to failure for a power supply unit used in a particular brand of personal computer is thought to be exponentially distributed with a mean of 4,000 hours as per the contract between the power supply vendor and the PC maker. The PC manufacturer has just had a warranty return from a customer who had the power supply fail after 2,100 hours of use.

a. What is the probability that the power supply would fail at 2,100 or less? Based on this probability, do you feel the PC maker has a right to require that the power supply vendor refund the money on this unit?

b. Assuming that the PC maker has sold 100,000 computers with this power supply, approximately how many should be returned due to failure at 2,100 hours or less?

■ SUMMARY AND CONCLUSIONS

This chapter introduced continuous probability distributions, including the normal, uniform, and exponential distributions. We showed that the normal distribution, with its special properties, is used extensively in statistical decision making. The chapter discussed in some detail the standard normal distribution. It showed how the standard normal can be used to produce probability characteristics of any normal distribution. We also illustrated the use of Excel to find probabilities for the normal and exponential distributions.

Subsequent chapters will introduce other continuous probability distributions. Among these will be the t-*distribution*, the *chi-square distribution*, and the F-*distribution*. These additional distributions play important roles in statistical decision making. The basic concept that the area under a continuous curve is equivalent to probability is true for all continuous distributions.

EQUATIONS

Normal Distribution Density Function

$$f(x) = \frac{1}{\sigma\sqrt{2\pi}} e^{-(x-\mu)^2/2\sigma^2} \qquad \text{5-1}$$

Standardized Normal z-Value

$$z = \frac{x - \mu}{\sigma} \qquad \text{5-2}$$

Continuous Uniform Distribution

$$f(x) = \begin{cases} \dfrac{1}{b-a} & \text{if } a \le x \le b \\ 0 & \text{otherwise} \end{cases} \qquad \text{5-3}$$

Exponential Distribution

$$f(x) = \lambda e^{-\lambda x}, \quad x \ge 0 \qquad \text{5-4}$$

Exponential Probability

$$P(x \le a) = 1 - e^{-\lambda a} \qquad \text{5-5}$$

■ KEY TERMS

Continuous Random Variable—Random variables that can assume any of the possible values between two points.

Discrete Random Variable—A variable that can take on a countable number of possible values along a specified interval. The values can be listed.

Exponential Distribution—A continuous probability distribution has the probability density function given by $f(x) = \lambda e^{-\lambda x}$, $x \ge 0$. It describes the distribution of times between occurrences for a Poisson distributed variable with mean = λ. The mean of the exponential is $1/\lambda$.

Normal Distribution—A bell-shaped, continuous distribution with the following properties:

1. It is *unimodal*; that is, the normal distribution peaks at a single value.
2. It is *symmetrical*; this means that 50% of the area under the curve lies left of the center and 50% lies right of the center. One side of the distribution is the mirror image of the other side.
3. The mean, median, and mode are equal.
4. The normal distribution approaches the horizontal axis on each side of the mean toward plus and minus infinity

$(\pm\infty)$. In more formal terms, the normal distribution is *asymptotic* to the *x*-axis.

5. The amount of variation in the random variable determines the width of the normal distribution.

Standard Normal Distribution—A normal distribution which has a mean = 0.0 and a standard deviation = 1.0. The horizontal axis is scaled in *z*-values that measure the number of standard deviations a point is from the mean. Values above the mean have positive *z*-values. Values below the mean have negative *z*-values.

Standard Normal Table—A table of standard normal distribution probabilities.

Uniform Distribution—A probability distribution in which the probability of a value occurring between two points, *a* and *b*, is the same as the probability between any other two points, *c* and *d*, given that the distance between *a* and *b* is equal to the distance between *c* and *d*.

z-Value—The standardized value representing the number of standard deviations a value is from the mean. A positive *z*-value indicates the value is larger than the mean and a negative *z*-value means that the value is smaller than the mean.

CHAPTER EXERCISES

SOLVED PROBLEMS ON YOUR CD-ROM
Try the WORKED-OUT EXERCISES and BUSINESS APPLICATIONS on the CD-ROM.

Conceptual Questions

5-34. The probability that a value for a normally distributed random variable will exceed the mean is 0.50. The same is true for the uniform distribution. Why is this not necessarily true for the exponential distribution? Discuss and show examples to illustrate your point.

5-35. One of your fellow students tells you that when working with a continuous distribution, it does not make sense to try to compute the probability of any specific value since it will be zero. She then says that this can't be true since when the experiment is performed some value must occur so the probability can't be zero. Your task is to respond to her statement, and in doing so, explain why it is appropriate to find the probability for specific ranges of values for a continuous distribution.

5-36. Discuss the difference between discrete and continuous probability distributions. Discuss two situations where a variable of interest may be considered either continuous or discrete.

5-37. Collect data on the daily change (up or down) in the Dow Jones Industrial Index for the New York Stock Exchange for a period of 100 days. Plot the data in a frequency histogram. Does the distribution look somewhat normally distributed? Would you expect the distribution in daily changes in this index to be normally distributed if more data were available?

Business Application Exercises

5-38. The American Testing Service has determined that examination scores on the Indiana real estate exam are uniformly distributed between scores of 40% and 80% correct.
   a. Develop a graph of the probability distribution.
   b. Determine the probability of a score under 65% correct on the exam.
   c. What is the probability of scoring 70% correct or better on the exam?
   d. What is the probability of scoring between 60% and 75% correct on the exam?
   e. Determine the score you would need to achieve the 90th percentile on this test.

5-39. A new battery designed especially for children's toys has been found to have a lifetime between 2.5 hours and 7 hours, with probabilities uniformly distributed between these two points.
   a. Develop a graph showing the probability distribution.
   b. Determine the probability that a battery will last over 6 hours.

   c. What is the probability that a battery will last between 3.5 and 5.5 hours?
   d. You have been given the task of deciding whether or not to purchase these batteries for the toy manufacturer. Your firm will purchase the batteries if you can verify the lifetime distribution claimed at the beginning of the problem. A sample of 10 batteries is tested. Only 1 battery lasted longer than 6 hours. Discuss what you will report to your superiors concerning your decision whether or not to purchase these batteries. Include probability calculations in your discussion.

5-40. Many computer simulation experiments use the uniform distribution in determining random numbers. For instance, an inventory simulation model requires that uniformly distributed random numbers with values between 30 and 90 be selected. These numbers will be used in the model to indicate the delivery time for merchandise once an order is placed.
   a. What is the probability that a random number will exceed 80?
   b. Suppose you were to use an exponential distribution, rather than a uniform distribution, that has the same mean as the uniform distribution you are using. Calculate the probability indicated in part a. Compare the two values.

5-41. Problem 40 considers a computer program used to generate random numbers that follow a uniform distribution.
   a. You are using the program to generate numbers ranging from 30 to 90, but the first 10 values you get are all less than 40. What is the probability of this occurring?
   b. Given that you have seen the 10 numbers, what conclusion might you draw with respect to the program?

5-42. The manager of consumer loans at Farwest National Bank has indicated that the distribution of account balances is a normal distribution.
   a. He has determined that the average credit card account balance is $700.00, with a median balance of $600.00. Comment on this conclusion.
   b. Having seen your comments to part a, he recounts and says, "I was mistaken. It is the standard deviation that is $600.00." Comment on this conclusion.

5-43. The time spent by patients at a particular hospital has averaged 4.2 days, which is also the median number of days.
   a. In order for the distribution of patient length of stay to be normally distributed, what must the mode for length of stay be?

b. If the mean, mode, and median are all equal does this assure us that the distribution is normally distributed? Explain.

c. Give an example in which the mean, mode, and median are all the same but the distribution is not normal.

5-44. Suppose personal daily water usage in California is normally distributed, with a mean of 18 gallons and a standard deviation of 6 gallons.

a. What percentage of the population uses more than 18 gallons?

b. What percentage of the population uses between 10 and 20 gallons?

c. What is the probability of finding a person who uses less than 10 gallons?

d. La Niña (the little sister weather pattern of her more famous brother, el Niño) has been cited as the cause of drought conditions in the southern portion of the United States. The city manager of Morro Bay, California, (population, 14,500) has been trying to gain support for Morro Bay's participation in the state of California's water project to bring water from Northern California to Southern California. He contends that the population of the city has grown to the point that the city's water needs cannot be met. Recently, he noted that the city's current water sources would provide only 350,000 gallons of water a day. Do you see a need for additional water for Morro Bay? Provide statistical evidence to support your views.

5-45. Referring to Problem 44, the daily water usage in California was thought to be normally distributed, with a mean of 18 gallons and a standard deviation of 6 gallons. Because of a perpetual water shortage in California, the governor wants to give a tax rebate to the 20% of the population that use the least amount of water.

a. What should the governor use as the maximum water limit for a person to qualify for a tax rebate?

b. Referring to your answer in part a, suppose the governor's proposed tax rebate causes a shift in the average water use from 18 gallons to 14 gallons per person per day, but causes no change in the standard deviation. What percent of the water users will now get a rebate? Assume the tax rebates will be given to those using less water than you specified in part a.

5-46. Cattle are often fattened in a feedlot before being shipped to a slaughterhouse. Suppose the weight gain per steer at a feedlot averaged 1.5 pounds per day, with a standard deviation of 0.25 pounds. Assume a normal distribution.

a. What is the probability a steer will gain over 2 pounds on a given day?

b. Determine the probability a steer will gain between 1 and 2 pounds in any given day.

c. Provide the probability of selecting 2 steers that both gain less than 1.5 pounds on a given day, assuming the 2 weight gains are independent.

d. Compute the probabilities found in parts a, b, and c assuming a standard deviation of 0.2 pounds. Why are these probabilities different?

5-47. Refer to Problem 46. A cattleman is trying to determine whether he will make a profit by taking his cattle to a feedlot before he sells his cattle. He has 4,000 head of cattle. The manager of the feedlot has agreed to feed his cattle for 5 days for $12,500. Currently slaughterhouses are buying beef for $0.40 a pound. Provide advice to this cattleman supported by statistical evidence.

5-48. The dollar amount of dairy products consumed per week by adults is thought to be normally distributed, with a mean of $4.50 and a standard deviation of $1.10.

a. What is the probability that an individual adult from the population will consume over $4.90 in dairy products in a week?

b. Determine the probability that an individual selected at random from the population will consume less than $6.25 in dairy products in a week.

c. Compute the probability that a person will consume between $3.25 and $5.75 in dairy products in a week.

5-49. Jamieson Airlines has a central office that takes reservations for all flights flown by the airline. The number of calls received during any week is approximately normally distributed, with a mean of 12,000 and a standard deviation of 2,500.

a. During what percentage of weeks does the airline receive more than 11,000 calls?

b. During what percentage of weeks does it receive fewer than 12,300 calls?

c. During what percentage of weeks does it receive between 10,800 and 13,400 calls?

d. During the last year the manager of the central office has kept track of the number of calls received each week. She has determined that the smallest number of calls was 10,800 and the largest number of calls was 13,400. If the number of calls received is normally distributed, determine the mean and standard deviation these data suggest.

5-50. The Ziegler Lumber Company sets the cut length on its 2 × 12 lumber a little longer than the specified length because its trim saw is fairly old. The mill foreman had discovered that the saw would cut any set length short by an average of 3 inches, with a standard deviation of 1.5 inches. Fortunately, the errors seem to be normally distributed.

a. If the foreman is setting up the trim saw to cut 2 × 12 boards each 10 feet long, what should the trim saw length setting be if he wants no more than a 5% chance of a board being shorter than 10 feet?

b. Suppose the machine can be fixed so that the standard deviation in cut error can be controlled to a specified level. What would the standard deviation have to be in order that the trim length could be set 1 inch shorter than the answer to part a?

5-51. Problem 50 refers to the Ziegler Lumber Company, which discovered its old trim saw would cut any set length short by an average of 3 inches, with a standard deviation of 1.5 inches. The errors seen are normally distributed. Suppose an adjustment is made to the machine that reduces the average error to 2 inches, but increases the standard deviation to 2 inches.

    a. Determine the trim saw length setting if the foreman wants no more than a 5% chance of a board being cut shorter than 10 feet.

    b. The foreman has kept track of the complaints concerning the length of the 10-foot boards. He is convinced that about 10% of the boards are more than 4.56 inches shorter than they were intended to be. Does this figure convince you that the adjustment really has been made? Provide statistical evidence to support your opinion.

5-52. The personnel manager for a large company is interested in the distribution of sick-leave hours for employees of her company. A recent study revealed the distribution to be approximately normal, with a mean of 58 hours per year and a standard deviation of 14 hours.

    An office manager in one division has reason to believe that during the past year, two of his employees have taken excessive sick leave relative to everyone else. The first employee used 74 hours of sick leave, and the second used 90 hours. What would you conclude about the office manager's claim and why?

5-53. Refer to Problem 52. Suppose the company grants 40 hours of paid sick leave per year. Given the distribution of time lost due to illness, what would you conclude about the adequacy of the company's sick-leave policy? Why?

5-54. Refer to Problems 52 and 53. Suppose the company is considering a change in its sick-leave policy for next year. The objective is to have the number of paid sick-leave hours at a level that will require 10% or fewer people to incur unpaid sick time. Assuming the historical sick-leave pattern holds true next year, how many sick-leave hours should be paid by the company?

5-55. Refer to Problems 52–54. Suppose a consultant has suggested the company hold its paid sick-leave hours to 40 hours per year and hire a physician who will serve employees at the plant in an attempt to reduce the average number of sick-leave hours used to a more acceptable level.

    a. Determine the required mean sick-leave hours if the probability of an individual needing more than 40 hours of sick leave is to be, at most, 10%. Assume the standard deviation remains 14 hours and the distribution is normal.

    b. The average salary of the 200 workers that this study addresses is approximately $25 an hour. If the doctor were able to reduce the average number of sick-leave hours to that calculated in part a, determine the annual salary the company could pay the doctor as the direct result of the money she would save the company in terms of the lost productivity due to illness. (Note: Do not try to include the money paid to the workers for sick leave.)

5-56. The Bryce Brothers Lumber Company is considering buying a machine that planes lumber to the correct thickness. The machine is advertised to produce "6-inch lumber" having a width that is normally distributed, with a mean of 6 inches and a standard deviation of 0.1 inches.

    a. If building standards in the industry require a 99% chance of a board being between 5.85 and 6.15 inches, should Bryce Brothers purchase this machine? Why or why not?

    b. To what level would the company that manufactures the machine have to reduce the standard deviation for the machine to conform to industry standards?

5-57. The manager at the Town Square Movie Theater has determined that 45 customers go to the concession stand to make purchases in the 15 minutes prior to the start of a movie, and the distribution for the number of arrivals is Poisson distributed. Based upon this information determine each of the following:

    a. Find the probability that the time between arrivals for any two customers is less than 20 seconds.

    b. Determine the probability that the time between two customers arriving is over 30 seconds.

    c. What is the probability that the time between arrivals for two customers is between 30 seconds and 1 minute?

5-58. One of the production steps for a company that makes equipment for the semiconductor industry involves polishing. The polishing machine requires a polishing disk. The amount of time this disk lasts will vary from disk to disk. Once a disk wears to a certain point, it must be replaced with a new one. Experience indicates that the time to failure is exponentially distributed with a mean of 4.5 hours. The operators are required to log the amount of time each disk lasts. One operator reported the following times for her machine on her 12-hour shift: 2.4 hours, 1.5 hours, 2.8 hours, and 3.1 hours. (Note, the fifth disk was still okay when she went off shift after 12 hours.)

    a. For each of the four disks that were replaced, determine the probability that the disk will wear out in that number of hours or less.

    b. What is the probability that an operator would find four successive disks with these hours of performance?

    c. Based on your answers to parts a and b, comment on whether you think there is evidence to suggest that the disks currently being used are not meeting the 4.5 hour mean life.

5-59. Referring to Problem 58, suppose the shift supervisor is concerned that this operator is changing polishing disks too quickly. Explain how the probabilities computed in Problem 58 could be used to help analyze the situation and reach a conclusion about the operator. How might the supervisor determine whether the problem was with the disks or with the operator? Discuss.

5-60. A small private ambulance service in Oklahoma has determined that the time between emergency calls is exponentially distributed with a mean of 41 minutes. When a unit goes on call, it is out of service for 60 minutes. If a unit is busy when an emergency call is received, the call is immediately routed to another service. The company is considering buying a second ambulance. However, before doing so, the owners are interested in determining the probability that a call will come in before the current ambulance is back in service. Without knowing the costs involved in this situation, does this probability tend to support the need for a second ambulance? Discuss.

5-61. The Cozine Corporation runs the landfill operation outside Little Rock, Arkansas. Every day, each of the company's trucks makes several trips from the city to the landfill. On each entry the truck is weighed. The data diskette contains a data file called **Cozine**, which contains a sample of 200 truck weights. Develop a grouped data frequency distribution using 20 classes. Does this distribution seem to best fit a uniform distribution, an exponential, or a normal distribution? Provide reasons for your reply.

5-62. Referring to Problem 61, determine the mean and standard deviation for the garbage truck weights. Assume that these sample values are representative of the population of all Cozine garbage trucks, and assume that the distribution is normally distributed.
   a. Determine the probability that a truck will arrive at the landfill weighing in excess of 46,000 pounds.
   b. Compare the probability in part a to the proportion of trucks in the sample that weighed over 46,000 pounds. What does this imply to you?

5-63. Referring to Problems 61 and 62, suppose the managers are concerned that trucks are returning to the landfill before they are fully loaded. If they have set a minimum weight of 38,000 pounds before the truck returns to the landfill, what is the probability that a truck will fail to meet the minimum standard?

5-64. Refer to Problem 63. The managers at Cozine want only a 2% chance of a truck coming below the 38,000 pound

minimum. What must the mean weight be if the distribution of weights is assumed to be normally distributed and the standard deviation is the same as that for the sample data in the file?

5-65. The St. Maries plywood plant is part of the Potlatch Corporation's Northwest Division. The plywood superintendent organized a study of the tree diameters that are being shipped to the mill. After collecting a large amount of data on diameters, he concluded that the distribution is approximately normally distributed with a mean of 14.25 inches and a standard deviation of 2.92 inches. Because of the way plywood is made, there is a certain amount of waste on each log because the peeling process leaves a core that is approximately 3 inches thick. For this reason, he feels that any log less than 10 inches in diameter is not profitable for making plywood.
   a. Based on the data he has collected, what is the probability that a log will be unprofitable?
   b. An alternative is to peel the log and then sell the core as "peeler logs." These peeler logs are sold as fence posts and for various landscape projects. There is not as much profit in these peeler logs, however. The superintendent has determined that he can make a profit if the peeler log's diameter is not more than 32% of the diameter of the log. Using this additional information, calculate the proportion of logs that will be unprofitable.

5-66. Referring to Problem 65, suppose the manager of the plywood mill wants no more than a 3% chance that any log will be unprofitable (less than 10 inches in diameter). One way to get to this value is to have the tree cutters do a better job of sorting the logs to reduce the standard deviation. Assume that the mean diameter does not change.
   a. What standard deviation would have to be achieved to meet the manager's requirements?
   b. Answer part a if the peeler logs defined in Problem 65 are included.

CASE 5-A

East Mercy Medical Center

Dorothy Jacobs was recently hired as assistant administrator of the East Mercy Medical Center. She is a new graduate of a well-regarded master's degree program in hospital administration and is expected to incorporate some advanced thinking into the apparently lax practices at East Mercy.

Hospitals have recently been under increasing pressure from both government and local sources because of escalating costs. Although members of the board of directors of East

Mercy feel that cost considerations are secondary to quality care, its members also are sensitive to the increasing public pressure.

East Mercy is located in a rapidly growing area and is experiencing capacity limitations. In particular, according to staff personnel, the obstetrics, adult medical/surgical, and pediatric wards are "bursting at the seams." East Mercy is considering an extensive expansion program, including expansion of the obstetric, adult medical/surgical, and pediatric wards. The board has allocated a total of $400,000 for new beds in these three wards. Dorothy is presently trying to determine how many beds current demand levels justify for each ward and how many beds to actually add, given the $400,000 cost constraint.

Dorothy and her staff have computed statistics based on the current year's patient census data in each of the three wards. These figures are as follows:

WARD	AVERAGE NO. BEDS USED PER DAY	STANDARD DEVIATION
Obstetrics	24	6.1
Surgery	13	4.3
Pediatrics	19	4.7

Histogram plots of bed usage show a close approximation to a normal distribution for each department.

The present capacity of each ward is

Obstetrics:	30
Surgery:	20
Pediatrics:	24

The hospital's architects have given the following estimates for the cost of adding one bed and all necessary supporting equipment to each of the wards:

Obstetrics:	$20,000
Surgery:	$26,000
Pediatrics:	$15,500

It is possible for a ward to exceed its capacity, but according to state guidelines, this should not occur more than 5% of the time.

Dorothy is in the process of preparing a report to the administrator showing how many beds are to be added to each of the three wards.

CASE 5-B

American Oil Company

Chad Williams, field geologist for the American Oil Company, settled into his first-class seat on the Sun-Air flight between Los Angeles and Oakland, California. Earlier that afternoon, he had attended a meeting with the design engineering group at the Los Angeles New Product Division. He was now on his way to his home office in Oakland. He was looking forward to the one-hour flight as it would give him a chance to reflect on a problem that had surfaced during the meeting. It would also give him a chance to think about the exciting opportunities that lay ahead in Australia.

Chad works with a small group of highly trained people at American Oil who literally walk the earth looking for new sources of oil. They make use of the latest in electronic equipment to take a wide range of measurements from many thousands of feet below the earth's surface. It was one of these electronic machines that was the source of Chad's current problem. Engineers in Los Angeles had designed a sophisticated enhancement that would greatly improve the equipment's ability to detect oil. The enhancement required 800 capacitors which have to operate within ±0.50 microns from the specified standard of 12 microns.

The problem is that the supplier could provide capacitors that operate according to a normal distribution with a mean of 12 microns and a standard deviation of 1 micron. Thus, Chad knew that not all capacitors would meet the specifications required by the new piece of exploration equipment. This would mean that in order to have at least 800 usable capacitors, American Oil would have to order more than 800 from the supplier. But these items are very expensive, so he wants to order as few as possible to meet their needs. At the meeting, the group agreed that they wanted a 98% chance that any order of capacitors would contain the sufficient number of usable items. If the project was going to remain on schedule, Chad had to place the order by tomorrow. He wanted the new equipment ready to go by the time he left for an exploration trip in Australia. As he reclined in his seat, sipping a cool lemonade, he wondered whether a basic statistical technique could be used to help determine how many capacitors to order.

■ GENERAL REFERENCES

1. Albright, S. Christian, Wayne L. Winston, and Christopher Zappe, *Data Analysis and Decision Making with Microsoft Excel* (Pacific Grove, CA: Duxbury, 1999).
2. Cryer, Jonathan D., and Robert B. Miller, *Statistics for Business: Data Analysis and Modeling,* 2d ed. (Belmont, CA: Duxbury Press, 1994).
3. Dodge, Mark, and Craig Stinson, *Running Microsoft Excel 2000* (Redmond, WA: Microsoft Press, 1999).
4. Hogg, R. V., and Elliot A. Tanis, *Probability and Statistical Inference,* 5th ed. (Upper Saddle River, NJ: Prentice Hall, 1997).
5. Marx, Morris L., and Richard J. Larsen, *Mathematical Statistics and Its Applications,* 3d ed. (Upper Saddle River, NJ: Prentice Hall, 2000).
6. *Microsoft Excel 2000* (Redmond, WA: Microsoft Corporation, 1999).
7. Siegel, Andrew F., *Practical Business Statistics,* 4th ed. (Burr Ridge, IL: Irwin, 2000).

CHAPTER 6

INTRODUCTION TO SAMPLING DISTRIBUTIONS

CHAPTER OUTCOMES

After studying the material in Chapter 6, you should:

6-1: Understand the concept of sampling error.

6-2: Be able to determine the mean and standard deviation for the sampling distribution of $\bar{x}$.

6-3: Be able to determine the mean and standard deviation for the sampling distribution for the sample proportion, p.

6-4: Understand the importance of the Central Limit Theorem.

6-5: Be able to apply sampling distributions for both $\bar{x}$ and p.

WHY YOU NEED TO KNOW

A marketing research executive receives a summary report from her analyst indicating that the mean dollars spent by adults on winter sports recreation activities per year is $302.45. As she reads further in the report, it indicates the mean value is based on a statistical sample of 540 adults in the state of Vermont. Thus, the $302.45 is a *statistic*, not a *parameter*, because it is based on the sample rather than on the entire population. If you were this marketing executive, you might have several questions:

- Is the actual population mean equal to $302.45?
- If the population mean is not $302.45, how close is $302.45 to the true population mean?
- Is a sample of 540 taken from a population of several million sufficient to provide a "good" estimate of the population mean?

A major manufacturer of personal computers selects a random sample of computers that are already boxed and ready for shipment to customers. These computers are unboxed and inspected to see if the contents of the box match exactly what the customer order specifies. This past week, 233 systems were sampled and 18 were found to have one or more discrepancies. This is a 7.7% defect rate. Should the quality engineer conclude that exactly 7.7% of the 13,300 computers made this week reached the customer with one or more order discrepancies? Is the actual percentage higher or lower than 7.7%, and by how much? Should the quality engineer request that more computers be sampled?

The questions facing the marketing executive and the quality engineer are common to those faced by people in business everywhere. If you haven't already, you will almost assuredly find yourself in a similar situation many times in the future. To help answer these questions, you need to have an understanding of *sampling distributions*. Whenever decisions are based on samples rather than the entire population, questions about the sample results exist. Anytime we sample from a population, there are many, many possible samples that could have been selected. Each sample will contain different items. Because of this, the sample means for each possible sample can be different or the sample percentages can be different. The sampling distribution describes the distribution of possible sample outcomes. If you know the characteristics of this distribution, it will help you understand the specific result you have obtained from the one sample you have selected.

This chapter introduces you to sampling error and sampling distributions and discusses how you can use this knowledge to help answer the questions facing the marketing executive and the quality engineer. The information presented here provides an essential building block to understanding the topics of statistical estimation and hypothesis testing to be covered in upcoming chapters.

■ 6-1: SAMPLING ERROR — WHAT IT IS AND WHY IT HAPPENS

As discussed in previous chapters, you will encounter many situations in business where a sample will be taken from a population, and you will be required to analyze the sample data. Chapter 1 introduced several different statistical sampling techniques. Chapters 2 and 3 introduced a variety of descriptive tools that are useful in analyzing the sample data. The objective of sampling is to gather data that accurately represent the population. However, we very rarely know if our objective has been achieved. In order to determine that the sample accurately represents the population, we must have access to data from the entire population. If that is the case, we do not need to sample. Because in many instances we will not be able to work with the entire population, the next best thing is to require that our sample be random so that bias is not introduced into an already difficult task.

Calculating Sampling Error

Regardless of how careful we are in using proper sampling methods, the sample likely will not be a perfect reflection of the population. For example a *statistic* such as $\bar{x}$ might be computed for the sample data. Unless the sample is a mirror image of the population, the statistic will likely not equal the *parameter*, μ. In this case, the difference between the sample mean and the population mean is called **sampling error**. In the case where we are interested in the mean value, the sampling error is computed using Equation 6-1.

> **SAMPLING ERROR—SINGLE MEAN**
>
> The difference between a value (a statistic) computed from a sample and the corresponding value (a parameter) computed from the population.
>
> $$\text{Sampling Error} = \bar{x} - \mu \qquad\qquad\qquad \textbf{6-1}$$
>
> where:
>
> $\bar{x}$ = Sample mean
> μ = Population mean

EXAMPLE 6-1

SAMPLING ERROR

Kornfield, Harrington & Sandmeyer

The architectural firm of Kornfield, Harrington & Sandmeyer has been involved in a total of 12 shopping center projects. Table 6-1 shows a list of the 12 projects and the total square footage of each project.

Since these 12 projects are all the shopping centers on which the company has performed work, the square feet for the 12 projects are considered to be the population. The data in Table 6-1 have been double-checked and are known to be the correct number of square feet in each project. Equation 6-2 is used to compute the mean square feet in the population of projects.

> **POPULATION MEAN**
>
> $$\mu = \frac{\sum_{i=1}^{N} x_i}{N} \qquad\qquad\qquad \textbf{6-2}$$
>
> where:
>
> μ = Population mean
> x_i = Values in the population
> N = Population size

The mean square feet for the 12 shopping centers is:

$$\mu = \frac{114{,}560 + 202{,}300 + \cdots + 125{,}200 + 156{,}900}{12}$$

$$\mu = 158{,}972 \text{ square feet}$$

The average size shopping center project designed by the firm is 158,972 square feet. This value is a **parameter.** No matter how many times we compute the value, assuming no arithmetic mistakes, we will get the same value for the population mean.

TABLE 6-1
Square Feet for Shopping Center Projects

PROJECT	SQUARE FEET
1	114,560
2	202,300
3	78,600
4	156,700
5	134,600
6	88,200
7	177,300
8	155,300
9	214,200
10	303,800
11	125,200
12	156,900

> **PARAMETER**
>
> A measure computed from the entire population.

The Kornfield, Harrington & Sandmeyer (KH&S) firm is a finalist to be the architect for a new shopping center project in Orlando, Florida. The developers who will be hiring the architects for the project plan to select a **simple random sample** of $n = 5$ projects from those that have been completed by each of the finalists. The developers will travel to these shopping centers and examine the designs and interview the owners and shoppers in the

> **SIMPLE RANDOM SAMPLE**
>
> A sample selected in such a manner that each possible sample of a specified size has an equal chance of being selected.

selected shopping centers. (You may want to refer to Chapter 1 to review the material on simple random samples.) Referring to the shopping center project data in Table 6-1, suppose the developer randomly selects the following 5 projects from the population:

SQUARE FEET	PROJECT
134,600	5
156,700	4
114,560	1
155,300	8
214,200	9

One of the key factors in being selected for the new project is the architect's past performance on large projects, so the developers might be interested in the mean size of the shopping centers that the architects have designed. Equation 6-3 is used to compute the sample mean.

SAMPLE MEAN

$$\bar{x} = \frac{\sum\limits_{i=1}^{n} x_i}{n}$$ 6-3

where:

$\bar{x}$ = Sample mean
x_i = Sample value selected from the population
n = Sample size

The sample mean is:

$$\bar{x} = \frac{134,600 + 156,700 + 114,560 + 155,300 + 214,200}{5} = \frac{775,360}{5} = 155,072$$

The average number of square feet in the sample of 5 shopping centers selected by the developers is 155,072. This value is a **statistic** based on the sample.

STATISTIC
A measure computed from a sample that has been selected from a population.

Recall the mean for the population, μ, is 158,972 square feet. The sample mean, $\bar{x}$, is 155,072. As you can see, the sample mean does not equal the population mean. This difference is called sampling error. Using Equation 6-1, we compute the sampling error as follows.

$$\text{Sampling error} = \bar{x} - \mu$$
$$= 155,072 - 158,972 = -3,900 \text{ square feet}$$

The sample mean for the sample of $n = 5$ shopping centers is 3,900 square feet less than the population mean. Regardless of how carefully you construct your sampling plan, you can almost always expect to see sampling error. A sample will almost never be a perfect mirror image of the population. The sample value and the population value will most likely be different.

Suppose the developer who selected the random sample throws these 5 projects back into the stack and selects a second sample of 5 as follows:

SQUARE FEET	PROJECT
214,200	9
88,200	6
134,600	5
156,900	12
303,800	10

The mean for this sample is:

$$\bar{x} = \frac{214,200 + 88,200 + 134,600 + 156,900 + 303,800}{5} = \frac{897,700}{5} = 179,540$$

This time, the sample mean is higher than the population mean. This time the sampling error is:

$$\bar{x} - \mu = 179,540 - 158,972 = 20,568 \text{ square feet}$$

This illustrates some useful fundamental statistical concepts.
- The size of the sampling error depends on which sample is selected.
- The sampling error may be positive or negative.
- There is potentially a different $\bar{x}$ for each possible sample.

If the developers wanted to use the sample mean to estimate the population mean, they might be 3,900 square feet too low in one case and 20,568 square feet too high in another.

The Role of Sample Size on Sampling Error

Kornfield, Harrington & Sandmeyer (continued)

EXAMPLE 6-2

SAMPLING ERROR

In the previous example, the developers selected a random sample of 5 shopping centers. We looked at two potential samples and the resulting sampling error. There are actually 792 possible samples of size 5 taken from 12 projects. This value is found using a counting rule called combinations discussed in Chapter 4.[1]

In actual situations, only one sample is selected and the decision maker uses the sample value to estimate the population value. A "small" amount of sampling error may be acceptable. However, if the sampling error is "too large," conclusions about the population value could be misleading.

We can look at the extremes on either end to evaluate the potential for extreme sampling error. Suppose, by chance, the developers ended up with the 5 smallest shopping centers in their sample. These would be:

PROJECT	SQUARE FEET
3	78,600
6	88,200
1	114,560
11	125,200
5	134,600

---

[1]The number of combinations of r items from a sample of n is $\dfrac{n!}{r!(n-r)!}$.

SMALLEST SHOPPING CENTERS		LARGEST SHOPPING CENTERS	
Square Feet	*Project*	*Square Feet*	*Project*
78,600	3	303,800	10
88,200	6	214,200	9
114,560	1	202,300	2
$\bar{x}$ = 93,786.67 square feet		$\bar{x}$ = 240,100 square feet	
Sampling Error:		Sampling Error:	
93,786.67 − 158,972 = −65,185.33 square feet		240,100 − 158,972 = 81,128 square feet	

TABLE 6-2
Shopping Center Example for $n = 3$ (extreme samples)

The mean of this sample is $\bar{x}$ = 108,232. Of all the possible samples, this one provides the smallest sample mean. The sampling error is:

$$108,232 − 158,972 = −50,740 \text{ square feet}$$

Thus, if this sample had been selected, the sampling error would be −50,740 square feet and the statistic would underestimate the true population mean by this amount.

On the other extreme, suppose the sample contained the 5 largest shopping centers, as follows.

PROJECT	SQUARE FEET
10	303,800
9	214,200
2	202,300
7	177,300
12	156,900

The mean for this sample is $\bar{x}$ = 210,900. This is the largest possible sample mean from all the possible samples. The sampling error in this case would be:

$$210,900 − 158,972 = 51,928 \text{ square feet}$$

The potential for extreme sampling error ranges from −50,740 to +51,928 square feet. The remaining possible samples will provide sampling error between these limits.

What happens if the sample size were larger or smaller? Suppose the developers scale back their sample size to $n = 3$ shopping centers. Table 6-2 shows the extremes for this sample size. By reducing the sample size from 5 to 3, the range of potential sampling error has increased from (−50,740 . . . +51,928 square feet) to (−65,185.33 . . . +81,128 square feet). This illustrates that the potential for extreme sampling error is greater when smaller sized samples are used.

While larger sample sizes reduce the potential for extreme sampling error, there is no guarantee that the larger sample size will always give the smallest sampling error. For example, Table 6-3 shows two further applications of the shopping center data. As illustrated, the

TABLE 6-3
Shopping Center Example with Different Sample Sizes

$n = 5$		$n = 3$	
Square Feet	*Project*	*Square Feet*	*Project*
156,700	4	156,900	12
114,560	1	156,700	4
177,300	7	155,300	8
125,200	11		
303,800	10		
$\bar{x}$ = 175,512 square feet		$\bar{x}$ = 156,300 square feet	
Sampling Error:		Sampling Error:	
175,512 − 158,972 = 16,540 square feet		156,300 − 158,972 = −2,672 square feet	

sample with a size of 3 had a sampling error of $-2{,}672$ square feet, while the sample of 5 had a sampling error of 16,540 square feet. In this case, the smaller sample was "better" than the larger sample. However, in Section 6-2 you will learn that, on average, the sampling error produced by large samples will be less than the sampling error from small samples.

EXAMPLE 6-3

SAMPLING ERROR

Lincoln Research

The previous discussion has been based around an example in which the sample mean was compared to the population mean to measure sampling error. However, the concept of sampling error extends beyond situations involving means. For example, consider the situation in which Lincoln Research, a market research firm, surveyed *every customer* in a certain region who purchased tires at a tire store during the first week of March last year. The key question in the survey was: "Are you satisfied with the tires and service received at this tire store?"

The population size was 80 customers. The number of customers who answered "Yes" to the question was 72. The value of interest in this example is the **population proportion**. Equation 6-4 is used to compute a population proportion.

POPULATION PROPORTION

The fraction of values in a population which have a specific attribute.

$$\pi = \frac{x}{N}$$

6-4

where:

π = Population proportion
x = Number of items having the attribute
N = Population size

The proportion of customers in the population who are satisfied with the tires and service is:

$$\pi = \frac{72}{80} = 0.90$$

So, 90% of the population responded "Yes" to the survey question. This is the *parameter*. It is a measurement taken from the population. It is the "true value."

Now, suppose that the market research firm wishes to do a follow-up survey for a simple random sample of $n = 20$ of the customers. What fraction of this sample will be people who had previously indicated "Yes" to the satisfaction question?

The answer depends on which sample is selected. There are a huge number of possible samples of 20 that could be selected from 80 people. However, the marketing research firm will select only one sample of 20, but it will come from the possible samples. At one extreme, suppose the 20 people selected for the sample included all 8 who answered "No" to the satisfaction question and 12 others who answered "Yes." The **sample proportion** is computed using Equation 6-5.

SAMPLE PROPORTION

The fraction of items in a sample that have the attribute of interest.

$$p = \frac{x}{n}$$

6-5

where:

p = Sample proportion
x = Number of items in the sample with the attribute
n = Sample size

For the tire store example the sample proportion of "Yes" responses is:

$$p = \frac{12}{20} = 0.60$$

The sample contains 60% who responded "Yes" while the population percentage is 90%. The difference between the sampling value and the population value, as you may recall, is called sampling error. Equation 6-6 is used to compute the sampling error involving a single proportion.

SINGLE PROPORTION SAMPLING ERROR

Sampling Error $= p - \pi$

6-6

where:

π = Population proportion
p = Sample proportion

Then for this extreme situation we get:

$$\text{Sampling Error} = 0.60 - 0.90 = -0.30$$

If a sample on the other extreme had been selected and all 20 people had been included from the original list of 72 who had responded "Yes" in the original survey, the sample proportion would be:

$$p = \frac{20}{20} = 1.00$$

For this sample, the sampling error is:

$$\text{Sampling Error} = 1.00 - 0.90 = 0.10$$

Thus, the range of sampling error in this example is from -0.30 to 0.10. As with any sampling situation, you can expect some sampling error. The sample proportion will probably not equal the population proportion because the sample selected will not be a perfect mirror image of the population.

6-1: EXERCISES

ADDITIONAL EXERCISES ON YOUR CD-ROM

Try the ADDITIONAL EXERCISES and APPLICATION PROBLEMS on the CD-ROM.

6-1. Consider the following data to be a population of $N = 20$ values.

5	3	2	6	6	7	3	3	6	7
7	9	7	5	3	12	6	10	7	2

a. Compute the population mean.
b. A random sample of $n = 6$ produced the following numbers: 6 12 10 3 2 2. Find the sample mean and determine the sampling error for this sample.
c. Find the range of extreme sampling error for a sample of 6.

6-2. Assume the following data represent a population of 50 values. Values equal to 1 indicate that a particular attribute is present, a value equal to 0 indicates the attribute is not present.

1	1	1	1	1	1	1	1	0	0
0	1	1	0	0	1	1	1	0	1
0	1	1	1	1	1	1	1	1	0
1	1	1	1	1	1	1	0	1	1
0	1	1	1	1	1	1	1	1	1

a. Compute the population proportion.
b. A random sample of 15 items produced the following numbers: 1 1 1 0 0 1 0 0 1 1 0 0 0 1 0. Compute the

sample proportion and the sampling error present in your sample.

c. What is the range of extreme sampling error for a sample of 15 taken from this population?

d. How would the range of extreme sampling error change if the sample size was set to 30? Discuss the advantages of having a larger sample size.

Business Applications

6-3. The state transportation department has conducted a study of drivers to determine whether they were carrying proof of liability insurance in the car. The data are located in a file called **Liabins**. Treat the data in this file as a population rather than a sample. There is interest on the part of the state insurance department regarding the age of the participants in the study.

   a. (1) Develop a histogram (using 8 classes) for the age variable. (2) Describe the symmetry/skewness, the center, the dispersion, and any atypical groupings that you discover. (3) Compute the mean and standard deviation for the population.

   b. A simple random sample of 10 was selected from the population. It produced the following numbers: 18 18 68 58 42 22 55 61 31 36.

      Compute the sample mean. Discuss how this value compares with the population mean.

   c. Why do you suppose the sample mean differs from the population mean? What would have to be true in order for the two measures to be equal?

6-4. Refer to Problem 3. Five different samples of 10 were selected from the population. The samples were as follows:

65 20 69 31 18 35 20 36 61 65	37 58 27 31 18 67 50 48 49 26
38 42 29 66 43 44 26 50 70 72	44 48 33 79 61 39 22 65 19 38
65 22 76 26 27 32 24 32 21 24	

   a. For each sample, compute the mean and sampling error.

   b. Determine the mean of the sampling errors and the standard deviation of the sampling errors.

   c. Suppose the sampling errors were normally distributed and the values you calculated in part b were approximations of their respective parameters. Determine the maximum and minimum values of the entire set of possible sample errors—not just the 5 you computed in part a.

6-5. The Golden Calendar Company has a population of 32 customers. These customers are brokers who in turn sell the calendars to stores and catalogs. The following data reflect the number of calendars sold to each of the 32 customers last year. These data are also contained in the file called **Golden** on the CD-ROM that accompanies this text.

41,591	48,600	48,348	60,977	41,591	48,600	48,348	60,977
26,226	51,269	21,519	20,124	26,226	51,269	21,519	20,124
36,526	51,836	40,444	43,572	36,526	51,836	40,444	43,572
47,091	31,444	39,580	67,452	47,091	31,444	39,580	67,452

   a. Develop a histogram (using 6 classes) showing the shape of the distribution. Describe the symmetry/skewness, the center, and the dispersion of the data.

   b. Compute the population mean and standard deviation.

   c. Suppose that Golden managers selected 4 customers to take part in a special promotional test. The test is designed to increase the number of calendars that the customer will purchase next year. The simple random sample of 4 was obtained from this population. The data were as follows.

40,444	21,519	67,452	47,091

    (1) Calculate the sample mean number of calendars sold.

    (2) How much sampling error is present in this sample?

   d. A second simple random sample of 4 was obtained from the population of 32 customers. The data obtained were as follows.

36,526	51,836	20,124	43,572

    (1) Determine the sampling error for this sample.

    (2) Explain why sampling error occurs and why the sampling error in part d is different than the sampling error in part c.

    (3) Discuss the ramifications of sampling error. What problems might it cause in this case where the promotion is intended to increase calendar sales next year?

   e. Take a sample of size $n = 8$ from the original population.

    (1) Compute the sampling error.

    (2) Compare the sampling error for this sample with those for the two samples of $n = 4$.

    (3) Without regard to the results you obtained here, explain how a smaller sample can have a smaller sampling error than a larger sample from the same population. (Hint: In Excel, use the Sampling feature under Tools—Data Analysis. In Minitab, use the Calc—Random Data—Sample from the Columns options.)

6-6. A regional hospital collected data to analyze patients who had been admitted during a particular week. The data in the file called **Patients** reflect all patients admitted during the week in question.

   a. Calculate the population proportion of female patients. Develop a bar chart that displays the relative proportions of males and females.

   b. A simple random sample of 20 patients was obtained from this population. The sample obtained was:

| M | F | M | M | M | F | F | F | F | F |
| M | F | M | F | F | F | M | M | F | F |

Compute the sample proportion of female patients.

c. Referring to part b, what is the sampling error for this sample? Why might the sample proportion be different than the population proportion?

d. A second sample of 20 was obtained from the population. The sample obtained was:

| F | F | F | M | F | M | M | M | M | F |
| F | F | M | F | F | M | F | M | F | M |

(1) Determine the sample proportion of female patients.

(2) Compute the sampling error in this sample.

(3) Compare the sampling error here to that computed in part c. If the two are different, why are they different? Is this to be expected? Explain.

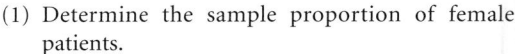

6-7 Referring to Problem 6, determine the range in potential sampling error that could result from a sample of 20 people. What would the range of potential sampling error be for samples of 10? Explain why this range is wider than when the sample size was 20.

■ 6-2: THE BASICS OF SAMPLING DISTRIBUTIONS

Section 6-1 introduced the fundamental concepts of sampling error. A sample selected from a population will not match the population perfectly. This means that the sample value (statistic) likely will not equal the population value (parameter). If this difference is due only to the fact that the sample is not a perfect representation of the population it is referred to as sampling error.

Sampling Distributions

In business applications, decision makers select a single sample from the population. They compute the sample value and use it to make decisions about the entire population. For example, the Nielsen Company takes a single sample of television viewers to determine the percentage that are watching a particular program during a particular week. It is important to realize the selected sample is only one of many possible samples that could have been selected from the same population. The sampling error will differ depending on which sample is selected. If, in theory, you were to select all possible samples of a given size and compute the sample value for each one, these values would vary above and below the true population value. If we graphed these values as a grouped data frequency distribution, the graph would be the **sampling distribution**.

SAMPLING DISTRIBUTION

A distribution of the possible values of a statistic for a given size sample selected from a population.

In this section, we introduce the basic concepts of sampling distributions. We will use an Excel tool to select repeated samples from the same population for demonstration purposes only. The same thing can be done using Minitab.

CONSTRUCTING THE SAMPLING DISTRIBUTION FOR $\bar{x}$

Aims Investment Company

Aims Investment Company handles employee retirement funds, primarily for small companies. The data file called **AIMS** contains data that represent the number of mutual funds in each client's portfolio. The file contains data for all 200 customers for the Aims Investment Company; therefore, these customers represent a population of 200. Figure 6-1 shows a graph of the population distribution of the funds owned per client and important numerical measures for the population.

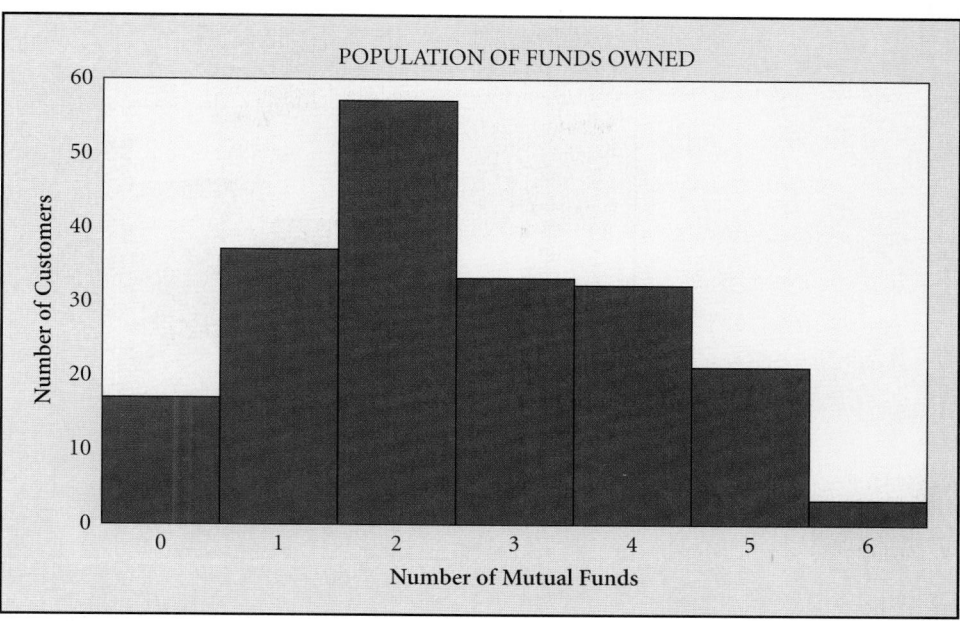

FIGURE 6-1
Distribution of Mutual Funds for the Aims Investment Company

Population Mean = μ = 2.505 funds owned
Population Standard Deviation = σ = 1.507 funds owned

The average number of mutual funds in a portfolio is 2.505 funds. The standard deviation is 1.507 funds. The graph in Figure 6-1 indicates that the population is spread between 0 and 6 funds with more customers owning 2 funds than any other number. Suppose the controller at Aims Investment Company plans to select a random sample of 10 accounts. In Excel, we can use the **Sampling** tool to assist in this process.[2] Figure 6-2 shows the resulting sample and the sample mean. To illustrate the sampling distribution concept, we repeat this process 500 times generating 500 different samples of size 10. After each sample, we compute the sample mean. Figure 6-3 shows the frequency histogram for these sample means.

Note, the horizontal axis represents the $\bar{x}$ values. The graph in Figure 6-3 is not a complete sampling distribution since it is based on only 500 samples out of the many possible

FIGURE 6-2
Excel Output for the Aims Investment Company First Sample Size n = 10

Excel Instructions:

1. Open file: AIMS.xls
2. Click on the Tools tab
3. Select the Data Analysis option
4. Select Sampling
5. Indicate the population data range and sample size

	A	B	C	D
		Number of Mutual Fund		**Sample**
1	**Cutomer Number**	**Accounts**		**n = 10**
2	19100	4		2
3	5034	4		1
4	29824	1		3
5	44955	0		1
6	44230	5		0
7	47923	5		4
8	725	2		2
9	20371	3		1
10	43162	4		1
11	6929	1		3
12	12252	4		
13	2274	2	Mean =	1.8
14	1619	0		

Microsoft Excel - AIMS.xls
File Edit View Insert Format Tools Data PHStat
D14

[2]The same thing can be achieved in Minitab by using the **Sample from Columns** option under **Calc—Random Data** options.

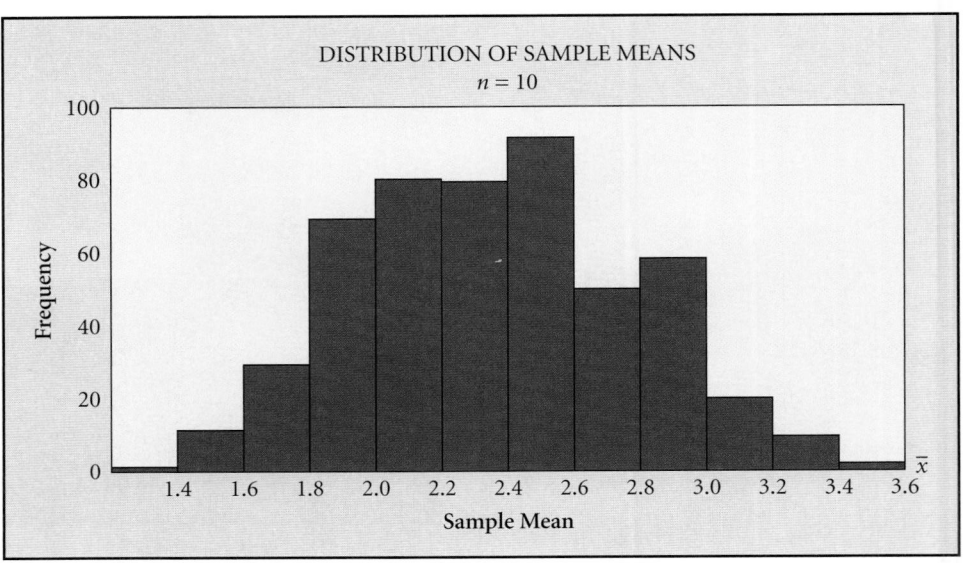

FIGURE 6-3
Histogram of Sample Means
for Aims Investment
Company

samples that could be selected. However, it gives us an idea of what the sampling distribution will look like.

Look again at the population distribution in Figure 6-1 and compare it with the shape of the frequency distribution in Figure 6-3. While the population distribution is somewhat skewed, the sampling distribution is taking the shape of a "bell curve" or normal distribution.

Note, also, the population mean for the 200 individual customers in the population is $\mu = 2.505$ mutual funds. If we average the 500 sample means in Figure 6-3, we get 2.41. This value is the *mean of the sample means*. It is reasonably close in value to the population mean. Although beyond the scope of this text, it can be shown that the average of all possible sample means will equal the population mean. When the average of all the possible values of a sample statistic equals a parameter, we call that statistic an *unbiased estimator* of that parameter.

Also, the population standard deviation is $\sigma = 1.507$ mutual funds. This measures the variation in the number of mutual funds between individual customers. When we compute the standard deviation of the 500 sample means, we get 0.421which is considerably smaller than the population standard deviation. As we will show shortly, this will always be the case.

Now suppose we increase the sample size from $n = 10$ to $n = 20$ and select 500 different samples. Figure 6-4 shows the distribution of the 500 different sample means.

The distribution in Figure 6-4 is even more bell-shaped than what we observed in Figure 6-3. As the sample size increases, the distribution of sample means will become shaped more like a normal distribution. The average sample mean for these 500 samples is 2.53, and the standard deviation of the different sample means is 0.376.

Keep in mind the distributions shown in Figures 6-3 and 6-4 are not true sampling distributions since they are developed from only 500 sample means. A true sampling distribution would be developed from the sample means of all possible samples that could be selected from the population.

SAMPLING FROM NORMAL POPULATIONS

We can again use Excel to illustrate some additional sampling distribution concepts by first generating a normally distributed population.[3] Recall from Chapter 5 that many popula-

Excel and
Minitab Tutorial

---

[3]The same task can be performed in Minitab using the **Calc—Random Data** option. However, you will have to generate each sample individually which would take time.

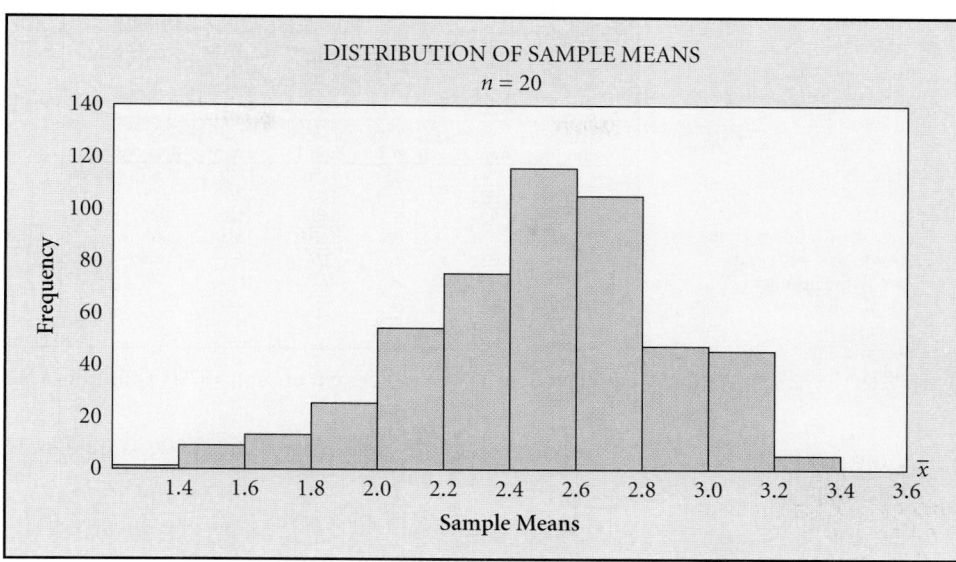

FIGURE 6-4
Histogram of Sample Means
for Aims Investment
Company

tions closely approximate a normal distribution so you may well find yourself sampling from such a distribution.

Figure 6-5 shows a simulated population that is approximately normally distributed with a mean equal to 1,000 and a standard deviation equal to 200. The data range is from 250 to 1,800. Next, we select 2,000 samples of size 10 from the population and compute the sample mean for each sample. A few of these sample means are shown in Figure 6-6. These sample means can then be graphed as a frequency histogram as shown in Figure 6-7. This histogram represents the sampling distribution. It, too, is approximately normally distributed.

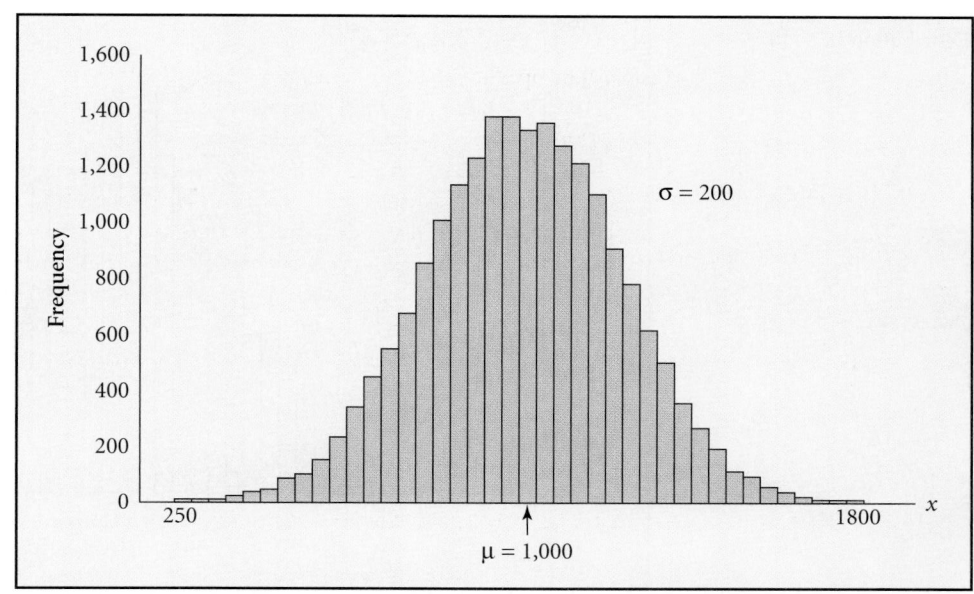

FIGURE 6-5
Simulated Normal
Population Distribution

Excel Instructions:

1. Click on the Tools tab
2. Select the Data Analysis option
3. Then select the Random Number Generation option
4. Indicate the number of variables (in this case, the sample size—10) and specify the number of samples = 2,000
5. Specify a normal distribution and enter the mean and standard deviation

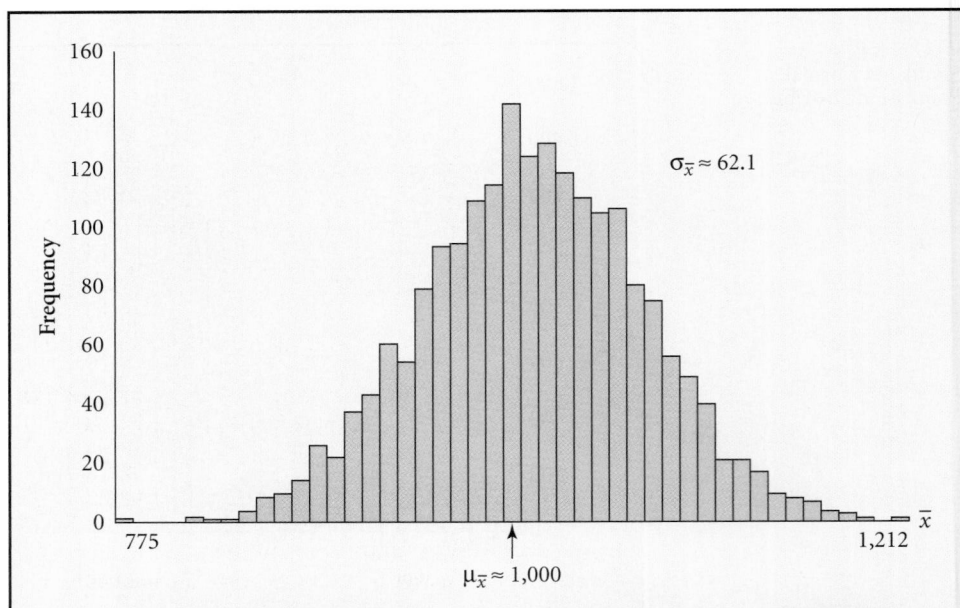

	A	B	C	D	E	F	G	H	I	J	K
	Item 1	Item 2	Item 3	Item 4	Item 5	Item 6	Item 7	Item 8	Item 9	Item 10	Mean
2	940	744	1049	1255	1240	1347	563	953	1219	783	1009
3	862	662	631	804	845	576	886	919	1027	927	814
4	935	926	1269	983	963	897	1394	1173	1475	869	1088
5	1332	678	1108	1180	1384	983	895	1135		152	1077
6	711	831	696	927	994	1006	935	1439		53	904
7	484	1290	744	869	1152	1093	1175	1119		77	943
8	1139	1065	812	952	1026	1112	1028	818	1377	1097	1042
9	1014	1166	1172	873	815	1222	760	688	1142	1128	998
10	1441	1289	1261	1023	1000	1091	995	789	645	1166	1070

Formula for mean — =AVERAGE(A2:J2)

Mean for each sample

FIGURE 6-6   Excel Output of Samples ($n = 10$) from a Normal Distribution

We next compute the average of the 2,000 sample means as follows.

The mean of sample means

$$\mu_{\bar{x}} \approx \frac{\sum \bar{x}}{2,000} = \frac{2,000,178}{2,000} \approx 1,000$$

The mean of these sample means is approximately 1,000. This is the same as the population mean.

We also compute the standard deviation of the sample means as follows.

note: not n - 1 ??

$$\sigma_{\bar{x}} \approx \sqrt{\frac{\sum (\bar{x} - \mu_{\bar{x}})^2}{2,000}} = 62.1$$

We see the standard deviation of the sample means is 62.1. This is much smaller than the population standard deviation, which is 200. The largest sample mean was just over 1,212 and the smallest sample mean was just under 775. Recall, however, that the population ranged from 250 to 1,800. The variation in the sample means will always be less than the variation for the population as a whole.

We have used this simulated example to illustrate how a sampling distribution is developed. Currently, we are assuming the population is normally distributed; the population

FIGURE 6-7
Approximated Sampling Distribution ($n = 10$)

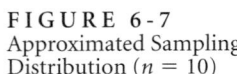

forms a continuous distribution and has an uncountable number of values. Therefore, we simply could not obtain all possible samples from this population. As a result, we would be unable to construct the true sampling distribution. Fortunately, an important statistical theorem exists that overcomes this obstacle.

THEOREM 6-1

If a population is normally distributed, with mean μ and a standard deviation σ, the sampling distribution of $\bar{x}$ is also normally distributed with a mean equal to the population mean ($\mu_{\bar{x}} = \mu$) and a standard deviation equal to the population standard deviation divided by the square root of the sample size ($\sigma_{\bar{x}} = \dfrac{\sigma}{\sqrt{n}}$).

In Theorem 6-1, the quantity $\sigma_{\bar{x}} = \dfrac{\sigma}{\sqrt{n}}$ is called the *standard deviation of the sampling distribution.* Another term that is given to this quantity is the *standard error of the sample mean* since it is the measure of the standard deviation of the potential sampling error.

Suppose we again use the simulated population shown in Figure 6-5 with $\mu = 1,000$ and $\sigma = 200$. We are interested in seeing what the sampling distribution will look like for different size samples. For example, if the sample size is 10 (as we simulated earlier), Theorem 6-1 indicates that the sampling distribution will have a mean equal to 1,000 and a standard deviation equal to:

$$\sigma_{\bar{x}} = \frac{200}{\sqrt{10}} = 63.2$$

For the 2,000 samples, the mean $\bar{x}$ is almost exactly 1,000 and the standard deviation of the $\bar{x}$ values is 62.1, close to the theoretical value of 63.2.

If we were to take a sample of 5, Theorem 6-1 indicates the sampling distribution will be normally distributed with a mean equal to 1,000 and a standard deviation equal to:

$$\sigma_{\bar{x}} = \frac{200}{\sqrt{5}} = 89.4$$

For a sample size of 20, the sampling distribution will be centered at $\mu_{\bar{x}} = 1,000$ with a standard deviation equal to:

$$\sigma_{\bar{x}} = \frac{200}{\sqrt{20}} = 44.7$$

Notice, as the sample size is increased, the standard deviation of the sampling distribution is reduced. This means the potential for extreme sampling error is reduced when larger sample sizes are used. Figure 6-8 shows sampling distributions for sample sizes of 5, 10, and 20. When the population is normally distributed, the sampling distribution of $\bar{x}$ will always be normal and centered at the population mean. Only the spread in the distribution changes as the sample size changes.

THE CENTRAL LIMIT THEOREM

Theorem 6-1 applies when the population distribution is a normal (bell-shaped) distribution. While there are many situations in business where this will be the case, there are also many situations where the population is not normally distributed. For example, incomes in a region tend to be right skewed. Some distributions, such as people's weight, are bimodal (a peak weight group for males and another peak weight group for females).

What does the sampling distribution of $\bar{x}$ look like when the population is not normally distributed? The answer is, . . . it depends. It depends on what the shape of the population is and what size sample is selected. To illustrate, suppose we have a U-shaped population like the one in Figure 6-9 with mean = 14.00 and standard deviation equal to 3.00. Now, we

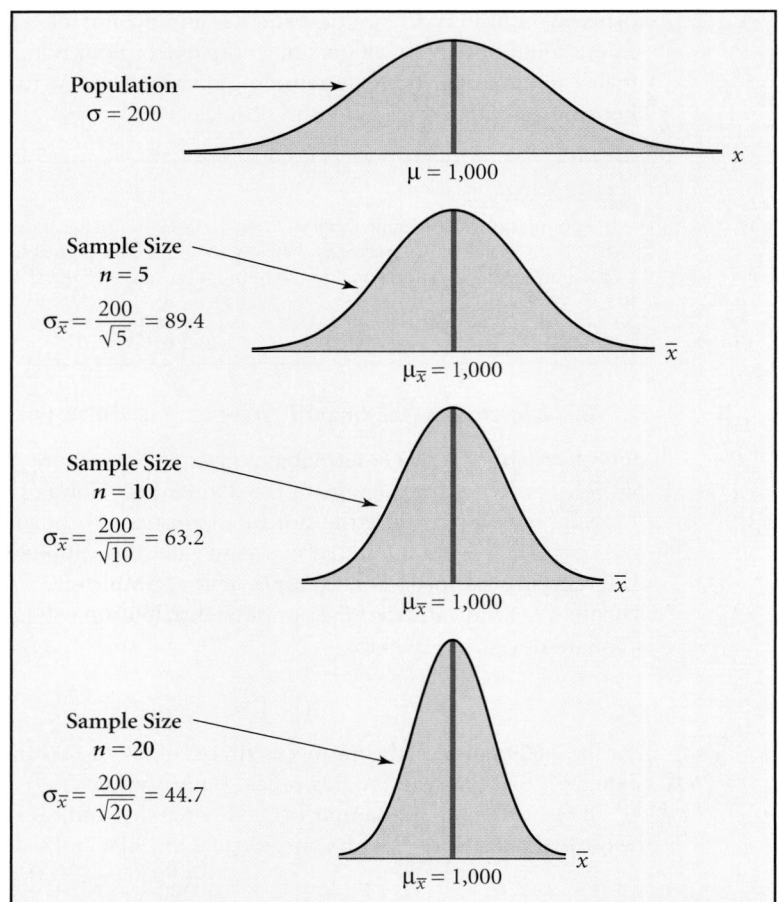

FIGURE 6-8
Theorem 6-1 Examples

FIGURE 6-9
Simulated Nonnormal
Population

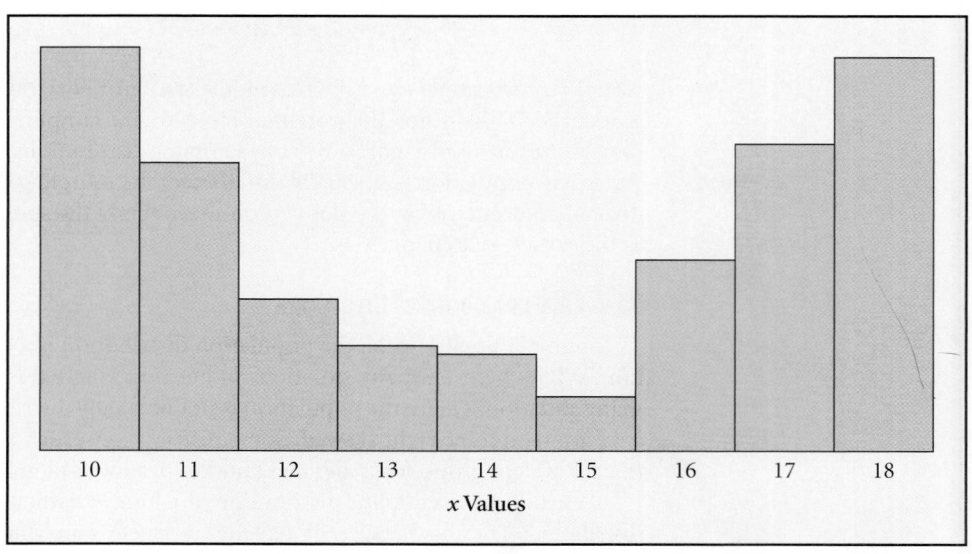

$\mu = 14.00$
$\sigma = 3.00$

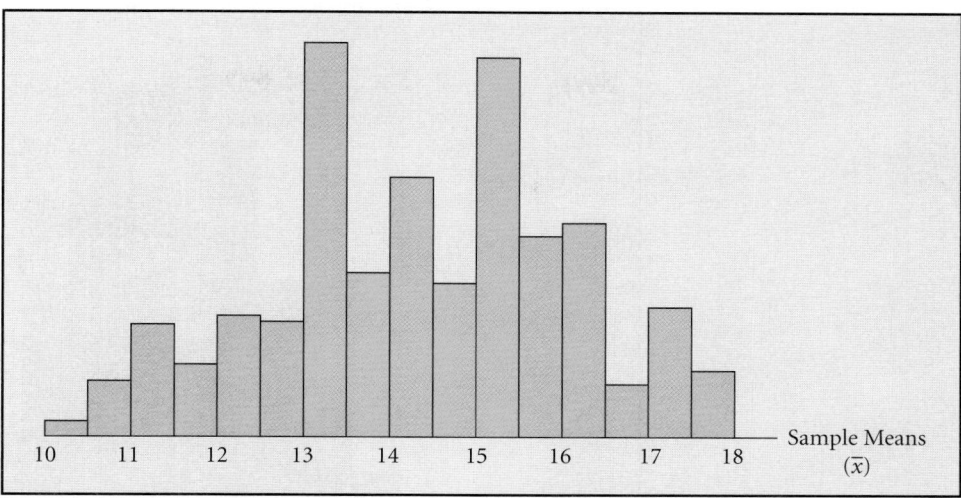

FIGURE 6-10
Frequency Distribution of $\bar{x}$
Values ($n = 3$)

14.02 = Average of sample means

1.82 = Standard deviation of sample means

select 3,000 simple random samples of size 3 and compute the mean for each sample. These $\bar{x}$ values are graphed in the histogram as shown in Figure 6-10.

The number of all possible samples of size 3 obtained from the population is, of course, considerably larger than 3,000. Therefore, we would not expect that this sample's result would produce the exact same results as if we had actually taken all the possible samples of size 3. However, the results would be reasonably close to the value that would be obtained for the average of all the possible means. The average of these 3,000 sample means is:

$$\frac{\sum \bar{x}}{3,000} = 14.02 \approx \mu_{\bar{x}}$$

Notice this value is approximately equal to the population mean of 14.00. Next we compute the standard deviation as:

$$\sigma_{\bar{x}} \approx \sqrt{\frac{\sum (\bar{x} - \mu_{\bar{x}})^2}{3,000}} = 1.82$$

The standard deviation of the sampling distribution is less than the standard deviation for the population which was 3.00. This will always be the case.

The frequency distribution of $\bar{x}$ values for the 3,000 samples of size 3 looks different than the population distribution which is U-shaped. Suppose we increase the sample size to 10 and take 3,000 samples from the same U-shaped population. The resulting frequency distribution of $\bar{x}$ values is shown in Figure 6-11. Now the frequency distribution looks very much like a normal distribution. The average of the sample means is still equal to 14.02, which is very close to the population mean. The standard deviation for this sampling distribution is now reduced to 0.97.

This example is not a special case. Instead it illustrates a very important statistical concept called the **Central Limit Theorem**.

THEOREM 6-2: *THE CENTRAL LIMIT THEOREM*

For samples of n observations taken from a population with mean μ and standard deviation σ, regardless of the population's distribution, provided the sample size is sufficiently large, the distribution of the sample means $\bar{x}$ will be approximately normal with a mean equal to the population mean ($\mu_{\bar{x}} = \mu$). Further, the standard deviation will equal the population standard deviation divided by the square root of the sample size ($\sigma_{\bar{x}} = \dfrac{\sigma}{\sqrt{n}}$). The larger the sample size, the better the approximation to the normal distribution.

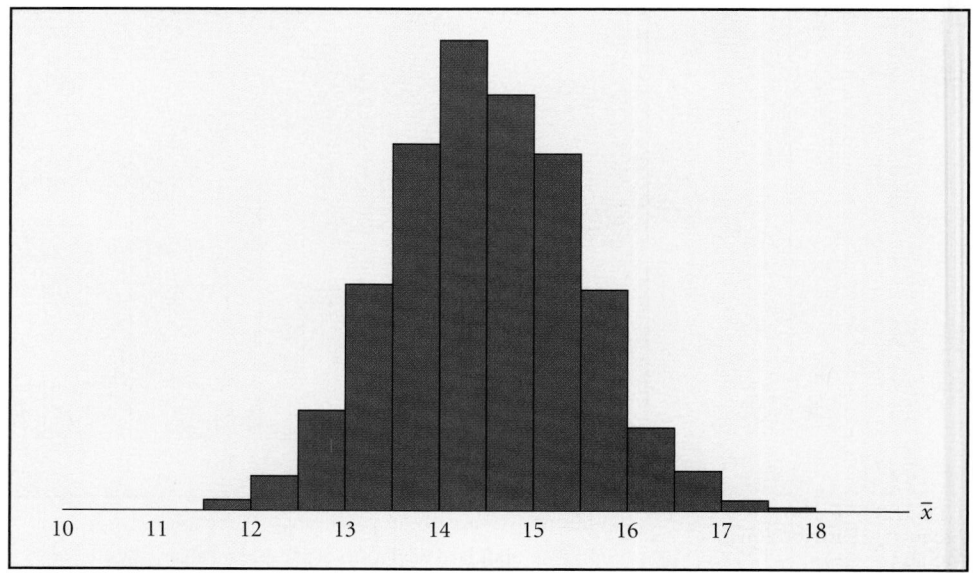

FIGURE 6-11
Frequency Distribution of $\bar{x}$ Values ($n = 10$)

14.02 = Average of sample means

.97 = Standard deviation of sample means

The Central Limit Theorem is very important since with it we know the shape of the sampling distribution even though we may not know the shape of the population distribution. The one catch is that the sample size must be "sufficiently large." What is a sufficiently large sample size?

FIGURE 6-12
Central Limit Theorem with a Rectangular Population

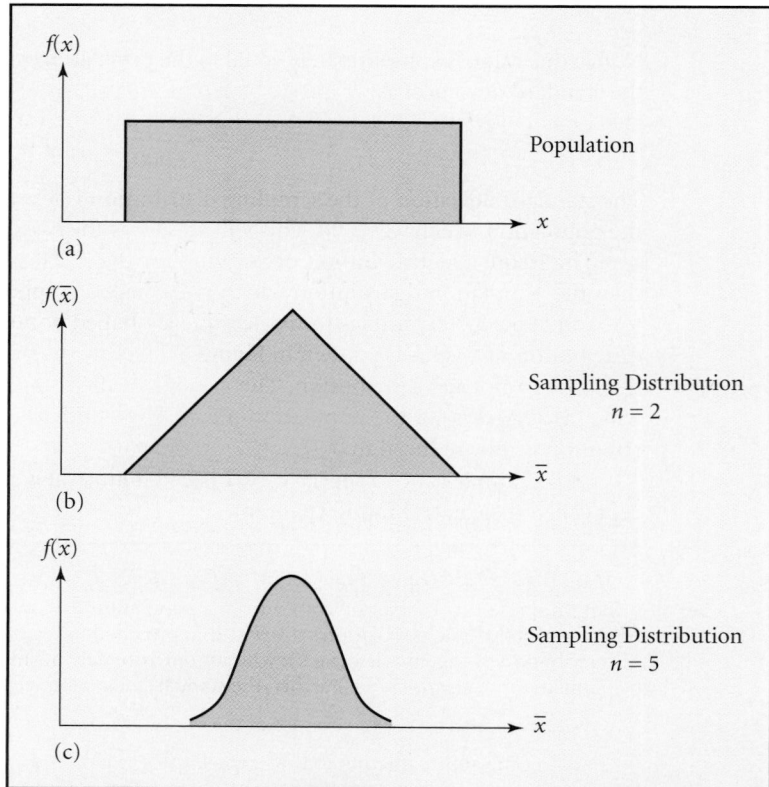

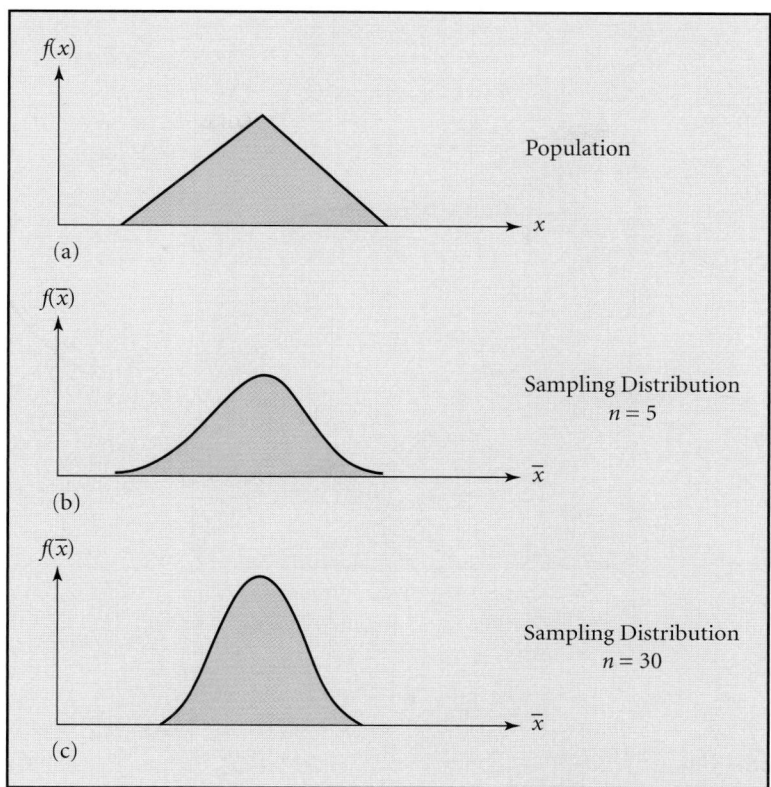

FIGURE 6-13
Central Limit Theorem with
a Triangular Population

The answer depends on the shape of the population. If the population is quite symmetric, then sample sizes as small as 2 or 3 will provide a normally distributed sampling distribution. If the population is highly skewed or otherwise irregularly shaped, the required sample size will be larger. Recall the example of the U-shaped population. The frequency distribution obtained from samples of 3 was shaped differently than the population but not like a normal distribution. However, for samples of 10, the frequency distribution was a very close approximation to a normal distribution. Figures 6-12 through 6-14 show some examples of the Central Limit Theorem concept. Simulation studies indicate that even for very strange looking populations, samples of 25 to 30 produce sampling distributions that are approximately normal. Thus, *a conservative definition of a sufficiently large sample size is $n \geq 30$.* The Central Limit Theorem is illustrated in the following examples.

EXAMPLE 6-5

CENTRAL LIMIT THEOREM

Moline Insurance

Moline Insurance, a company with headquarters in Illinois, recently conducted a study of car damages. A sample of 100 automobile claim files was selected from the thousands of claims in Moline's files. The dollar damages paid to repair each car were recorded as shown in Table 6-4.

Suppose the company knows the population of all claim files has the following parameters:

$$\mu = \$4,560 \text{ and } \sigma = \$600$$

The mean for this sample is:

$$\bar{x} = \frac{\sum x}{100} = \$4,527.77$$

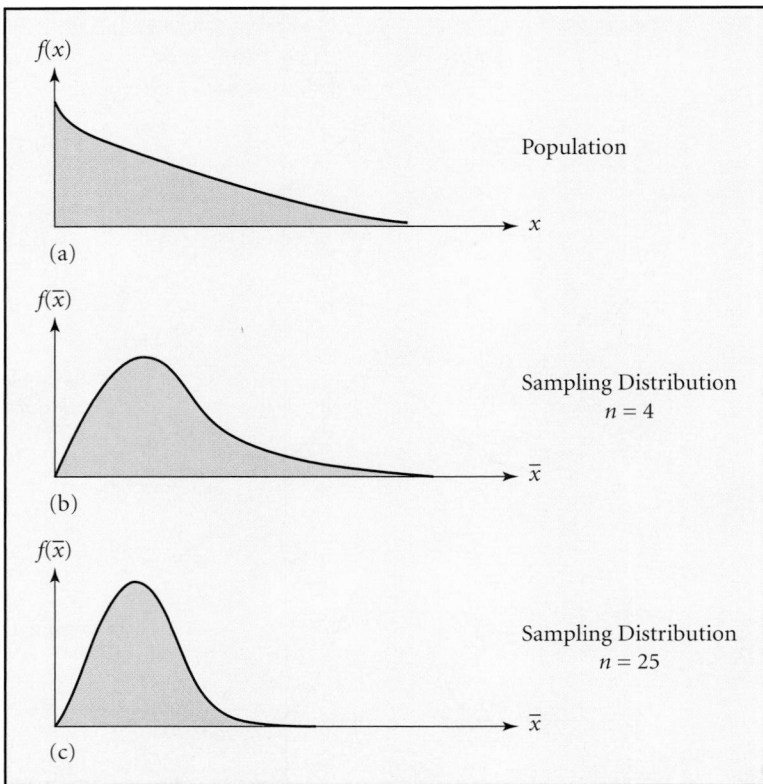

FIGURE 6-14
Central Limit Theorem with
a Skewed Population

The sampling error in this case is:

$$\text{Sampling Error} = \$4{,}527.77 - \$4{,}560.00 = -\$32.23$$

Since the company wishes to use this sample to help set its rate structure, there is concern that the sampling error may be unusually large for this population. To help determine this, the managers wish to know the probability of observing an $\bar{x} \le \$4{,}527.77$, given that the population mean is $\$4{,}560.00$. The Central Limit Theorem can be used to help find this probability even though we do not know the shape of the population distribution.

We know the sampling distribution will be approximately normal with:

$$\mu_{\bar{x}} = \mu = \$4{,}560$$

and

$$\sigma_{\bar{x}} = \frac{\sigma}{\sqrt{n}} = \frac{600}{\sqrt{100}} = 60$$

TABLE 6-4   Insurance Payments for 100 Claims

$4,483.95	$4,992.97	$3,906.07	$4,197.44	$5,718.97	$4,484.87	$3,800.40	$5,500.79	$4,402.45	$4,613.89
5,190.25	4,487.37	4,118.90	5,841.33	4,570.86	5,475.73	3,851.05	4,157.62	3,563.31	5,256.10
5,105.74	5,545.20	4,523.56	4,207.26	5,082.41	4,820.87	4,493.93	4,309.38	4,409.71	4,146.40
4,765.37	3,915.06	5,041.89	4,191.81	4,166.32	4,424.53	5,374.26	3,753.40	4,185.92	5,173.52
4,665.91	3,833.69	4,605.51	3,736.42	4,819.91	4,845.52	4,307.68	5,075.28	3,312.88	4,248.25
5,175.07	3,323.43	4,711.53	4,550.84	4,763.23	3,717.65	4,813.38	3,730.37	5,670.43	4,440.64
4,751.75	3,982.61	3,456.37	4,687.57	3,850.04	4,670.01	4,835.79	4,630.92	3,889.10	3,642.36
5,347.96	5,297.90	4,765.81	3,786.70	4,949.20	5,145.17	4,696.74	4,423.50	4,750.20	4,836.45
5,012.67	4,005.24	6,009.68	4,804.32	4,235.20	3,781.62	4,087.37	5,050.94	4,090.43	3,825.02
4,604.22	4,875.80	4,102.92	3,722.66	3,870.87	5,539.77	4,835.68	4,066.16	3,611.93	5,649.96

Now, to find $P(\bar{x} \leq \$4,527.77)$, we use the concepts introduced in Chapter 5 for finding probabilities with a normal distribution. We begin by converting to the standard normal distribution. We compute the z-value using Equation 6-7.

---

z-VALUE FOR SAMPLING DISTRIBUTION OF $\bar{x}$

$$z = \frac{\bar{x} - \mu}{\dfrac{\sigma}{\sqrt{n}}}$$

6-7

where:

$\bar{x}$ = Sample mean
μ = Population mean
σ = Population standard deviation
n = Sample size

$$z = \frac{\bar{x} - \mu}{\dfrac{\sigma}{\sqrt{n}}} = \frac{4,527.77 - 4,560}{\dfrac{600}{\sqrt{100}}} = \frac{-32.23}{60} = -0.54$$

Additional Example 6-a

Central Limit Theorem

Now go to the standard normal table in Appendix D for $z = -0.54$. We find $P(-0.54 \leq z \leq 0) = 0.2054$. Subtract this from 0.50 to get the desired probability of 0.2946 as shown in Figure 6-15. Thus, there is nearly a 30% chance of getting a sample mean as small or smaller than $4,527.77 from this population. Although the managers might want to look at other characteristics of the sample, this evidence suggests that this sampling error is not unusual for the population of all claim values.

FIGURE 6-15
Insurance Claims Pay-Out Distribution of the Sample Mean

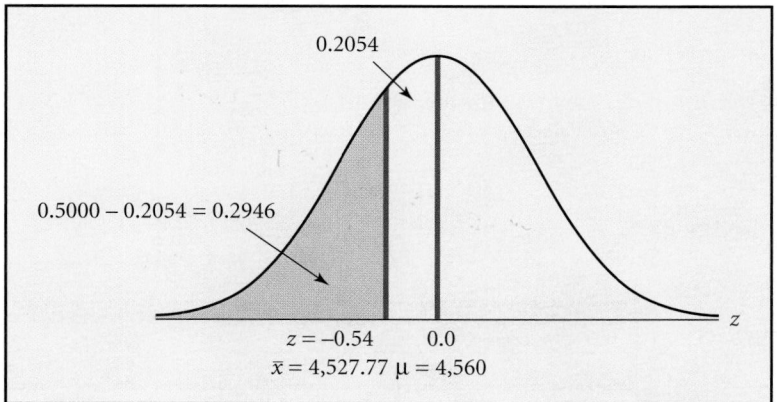

TOOLS OF QUALITY

SAMPLING DISTRIBUTIONS OF $\bar{x}$

The CD-ROM that accompanies this text contains a file named ECCO, which contains data on warranty claims and other information such as shift, manufacturing plant, and reason code. These data, representing all 110 claims that were received during the previous quarter, were collected by the ECCO quality manager for their backup alarm product.

As part of the company's Total Quality Management efforts, the quality manager selects a sample of 50 warranty complaints each quarter. She then calls each of these customers to conduct a complete interview on the customer's use of the product and level of overall satisfaction with ECCO.

In this example, the manager wants a sample of 50 from the population of 110. Figure 6-16 shows the resulting sample data generated using Minitab. The sampling was done *without replacement*.[4]

The manager is interested in knowing whether her sample has similar attributes to the population of warranty claims with respect to claim size. To determine this, she first computes μ and σ for the population.

$$\mu = \frac{\sum x}{N} = \$272.45 \text{ and } \sigma = \sqrt{\frac{\sum (x - \mu)^2}{N}} = \$53.27$$

Next, the manager computes the mean for the sample of 50 values as follows.

$$\bar{x} = \frac{\sum x}{n} = \$267.70$$

This random sample has sampling error equal to:

Sampling Error $= (\$267.70 - \$272.45) = -\$4.75$

Although the sampling error appears to be small, we can utilize the Central Limit Theorem and the knowledge that the sampling distribution will be approximately normal to determine the probability of observing a sample mean of $267.70 or less. However, we need to make one change in our methodology due to the fact the sample size ($n = 50$) is large relative to the size of the population ($N = 110$). We need to modify how we compute the standard deviation of the sampling distribution and z-value using what is known as the **finite population correction factor** as shown in Equation 6-8.

Excel and Minitab Tutorial

z-VALUE ADJUSTED FOR THE FINITE POPULATION CORRECTION FACTOR

The finite population correction factor is used to modify the standard deviation of the sampling distribution when the sampling is performed without replacement and when the sample size is greater than 5% of the population size.

$$z = \frac{\bar{x} - \mu}{\frac{\sigma}{\sqrt{n}}\sqrt{\frac{N - n}{N - 1}}} \qquad \text{6-8}$$

where:

N = Population size

n = Sample size

$\sqrt{\frac{N - n}{N - 1}}$ = Finite population correction factor

[handwritten: FCF is always less then 1.]

FIGURE 6-16
FIGURE 6-16
Minitab Sample Output for ECCO Satisfaction Study

Minitab Instructions:

1. Open file: Ecco.mtw
2. Click on Calc tab
3. Select Random Data option
4. Select Sample from Columns
5. Indicate Sample Size
6. Identify variable to be sampled from
7. Determine location for sample values

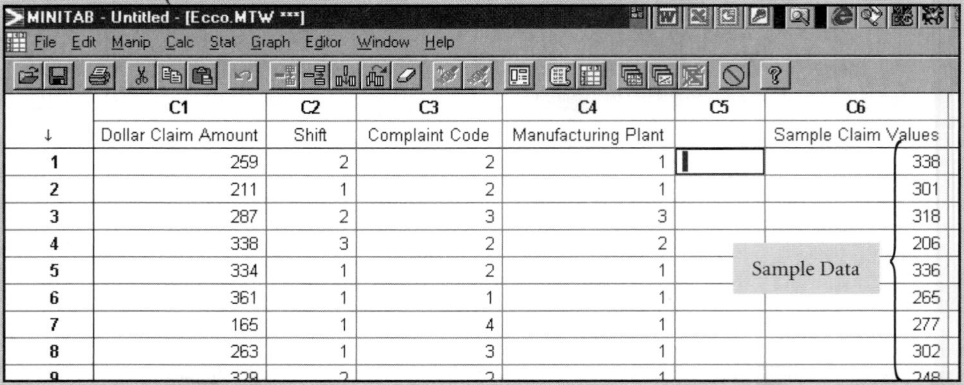

> MINITAB - Untitled - [Ecco.MTW ***]
File Edit Manip Calc Stat Graph Editor Window Help

↓	C1 Dollar Claim Amount	C2 Shift	C3 Complaint Code	C4 Manufacturing Plant	C5	C6 Sample Claim Values
1	259	2	2	1		338
2	211	1	2	1		301
3	287	2	3	3		318
4	338	3	2	2		206
5	334	1	2	1	Sample Data	336
6	361	1	1	1		265
7	165	1	4	1		277
8	263	1	3	1		302
9	329	2	2	1		248

[4]Excel also contains a Sampling option under Tools. However, Excel's sampling is done *with* replacement. This means that the same item can be selected more than one time in a sample.

In this example, the sample of 50 far exceeds the 5% limit on the population size of 110 so we use Equation 6-8 as follows.

$$z = \frac{\bar{x} - \mu}{\dfrac{\sigma}{\sqrt{n}}\sqrt{\dfrac{N - n}{N - 1}}}$$

$$z = \frac{267.70 - 272.45}{\dfrac{53.27}{\sqrt{50}}\sqrt{\dfrac{110 - 50}{109}}} = -0.85$$

The sample mean is 0.85 standard error below the true population mean. As shown in Figure 6-17, the chance of a sample selected from this population having a mean equal to or less than \$267.70 is 0.1977. Since 0.1977 is reasonably large, there is no reason for the manager to conclude that this sample has attributes that are different from the population of claims with respect to dollar value. She can now go ahead with her customer interviews.

FIGURE 6-17
ECCO Sampling Distribution
$n = 50$

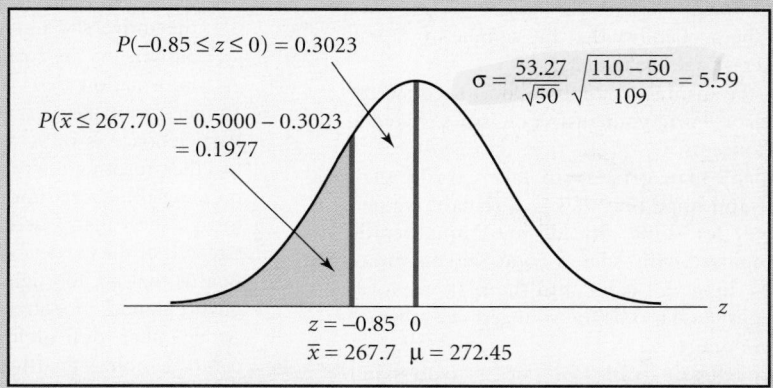

$P(-0.85 \leq z \leq 0) = 0.3023$

$P(\bar{x} \leq 267.70) = 0.5000 - 0.3023 = 0.1977$

$\sigma = \dfrac{53.27}{\sqrt{50}}\sqrt{\dfrac{110 - 50}{109}} = 5.59$

$z = -0.85 \quad 0$
$\bar{x} = 267.7 \quad \mu = 272.45$

6-2: EXERCISES

ADDITIONAL EXERCISES ON YOUR CD-ROM
Try the **ADDITIONAL EXERCISES and APPLICATION PROBLEMS** on the CD-ROM.

6-8. A population is normally distributed with mean equal to 400 and standard deviation equal to 50.
  a. Determine the probability of selecting a single value from the population that exceeds 450.
  b. Calculate the probability of selecting a random sample of size 3 that has a sample mean that exceeds 450.
  c. Explain why the probabilities are different.
  d. Determine a sample mean, say $\bar{x}_0$, so that the probability the sample mean exceeds $\bar{x}_0$ is the same as the probability that a single value from the population exceeds 450. Use a sample size of 3.

6-9. A population has a distribution of unknown shape. The mean of the population is 3,500 and the standard deviation is 600.

  a. If a sample of 100 values is selected randomly from this population, what is the probability that the sample mean will exceed 3,600?
  b. If a sample of 200 is selected from the population, what is the probability that the sample mean will exceed 3,600?
  c. Compare your answers to parts a and b and explain why the two probabilities are different.

6-10. A random sample of 100 items is selected from a population of size 350. What is the probability that the sample mean will exceed 200 if the population mean is 195 and the population standard deviation equals 20? (Hint: Use the finite population correction factor since the sample size is more than 5% of the population size.)

6-11. A population with a mean equal to 1.35 and a standard deviation equal to 0.40 is known to be very irregularly shaped. If a random sample of 49 items is selected from the population, calculate the probability that the sample mean will be less than 1.45.

Business Applications

6-12. The Adam's Food King chain employs over 3,000 people. The workers' ages are approximately normally distributed, with a mean of 31 and a standard deviation of 4.3 years. The company is thinking of introducing a healthcare package, and its insurance company wants to sample 25 workers before quoting a price.
   a. Determine the value of the standard error associated with this sample.
   b. Calculate the probability that the sample of 25 will have an average age less than 31.
   c. What can the insurance company do to reduce the standard error? Focus your answer on issues related to sampling concepts.
   d. The company managers try to take care of their employees and hope that they will remain in their employment for some time. If the employees do remain employed with Adam's Food King, approximately how long will it be until the first employee retires? (Consider 62 to be the youngest age at which an employee can retire.)

6-13. SeaFair Fashions relies on its sales force of 220 to do an initial screening of all new fashions. The company is presently bringing out a new line of swimwear and has invited 40 salespeople to its Orlando home office. An issue of constant concern to the SeaFair sales office is the volume of orders generated by each salesperson. Last year the overall company average was $417,330 with a standard deviation of $45,285.
   a. What shape do you think the distribution of all possible sample means of 40 will have? Discuss.
   b. Determine the value of the standard deviation of the distribution of the sample mean of all possible samples of size 40.
   c. Determine the probability that the sample of 40 will have a sales average less than $400,000.
   d. How would the answers to parts a, b, and c change if the home office brought 60 salespeople to Orlando? Provide the respective answers for this sample size.
   e. Each year SeaFair invites the sales personnel with sales above the 85th percentile to enjoy a complimentary vacation in Hawaii. Determine the smallest sales level for the sales personnel who were awarded a trip to Hawaii last year. (Assume the distribution of sales was normally distributed last year.)

6-14. Refer to Problem 13. SeaFair Fashions divides its sales staff into 5 regions. Each region has 44 sales personnel. As an incentive they offer a cash bonus to any region whose average is in the current year better than the third quartile for the previous year's sales. Determine the average sales a region would need to achieve for the members of the region's sales staff to receive the cash bonus. Assume $n = 44$.

6-15. A recent study by a midwestern university has concluded that the time adults spend watching television each week averages 14.6 hours with a standard deviation of 4.3 hours.
   a. Assume these values are the population parameters, and determine the probability that a sample of 100 adults from the population will average more than 15 hours of television per week. If the sample mean was 15 hours, does it seem likely that the university's conclusion concerning the population mean could be correct? Support your answer.
   b. The university obtained 3 samples of 100 adults and each sample had an average greater than 15 hours of television viewing. How likely is this assuming that the university's conclusions about the population parameters are correct? Answer part a with this new information.

6-16. Draper, Inc. makes particleboard for the building industry. Particleboard is built by mixing wood chips and resins together, forming the mix into 4 feet by 8 feet sheets, and pressing the sheets under extreme heat and pressure to form a sheet that is used as a substitute for plywood. The strength of the particleboards is tied to the board's weight. Boards that are too light are brittle and do not meet the quality standard for strength. Boards that are too heavy are strong but are difficult for the customers to work with. The company knows that there will be variation in the boards' weight. Product specifications call for the weight per sheet to average 40 pounds with a standard deviation of 1.75 pounds. During each shift, Draper, Inc. employees select and weigh a random sample of 25 boards. The boards are thought to have a normally distributed weight distribution.

   If the average of the sample slips below 39.60 pounds, an adjustment is made to the process to add more moisture and resins to increase the weight (and hopefully the strength).
   a. Assuming that the process is operating correctly according to specifications, what is the probability that a sample will indicate that an adjustment is needed?
   b. Assume the weight per sheet slips to 39 pounds. Determine the probability that the sample will indicate an adjustment is not needed.
   c. What could Draper's management do to ensure that the probability of both scenarios presented in parts a and b are not larger than 0.05? Discuss all statistical remedies of which you are aware.

6-17. Referring to Problem 16, suppose Draper, Inc. managers are concerned that the probability of overadjusting the process is too large. (That is, the probability computed in Problem 16 is too large.) If the managers want no more than a 3% chance of finding a sample that indicates an adjustment is necessary when, in fact, the process is operating according to specifications, determine the largest sample average (below 40 pounds) that would indicate that an adjustment is needed.

6-18. Referring to Problems 16 and 17, what should the cutoff be if the company wants no more than a 5% chance that a sample of 25 boards will have an average weight exceeding this cutoff?

6-19. Refer to Problems 16 through 18. A problem has arisen from the adjustment scheme used by Draper, Inc. The question is, "How much of an adjustment should be made when the scheme decides one should be made?" Currently, the adjustment is equal to the difference between the cutoff value and the mean of the sample.

    a. If the process is operating properly, determine the largest sample average weight that should occur.

    b. If the largest sample average does occur (see part a), determine the amount and direction of the adjustment to achieve the new population mean.

    c. Suppose this adjustment is made and in reality the process is operating properly. Thus, the adjustment was made and shouldn't have been. Now calculate the probability that a sample mean will be observed to be below the low-end cutoff.

    d. Can you suggest a solution to this dilemma?

6-20. Armstrong Windows makes windows for use in homes and commercial buildings. The standards for glass thickness call for glass to average 0.375 inches with a standard deviation equal to 0.050 inches. Suppose a random sample of $n = 50$ windows yields a sample mean of 0.392 inches.

    a. What is the probability of $\bar{x} \geq 0.392$ if the windows meet the standards?

    b. Based on your answer to part a, what would you conclude about the sample being representative of the population with respect to thickness?

6-21. The Jordeen Beverage Company bottles soft drinks and distributes them in the St. Louis area. Every week, a representative from the state of Missouri comes to the plant (on randomly selected days during the week) for the purpose of testing whether the average fill in the cans and bottles is acceptable. The state inspector, in looking out for consumers, selects a random sample of cans and bottles from the inventory in the plant that day. Each can (or bottle) is supposed to contain 12 ounces, but there will always be a certain amount of inherent variability from can to can. If the mean of the sample of 50 cans is less than 11.98 ounces, the company is given a $1,000 citation and the state inspector comes back again the next day and reinspects. The process continues until the company meets the standard.

    Jordeen controls the mean fill per can with a machine adjustment. They always have this set at 12 ounces. The machine does put slightly different amounts into each can. The file on the CD-ROM called **Jordeen** contains the actual fill amounts for each of the 5,000 cans in the inventory the day the state inspector arrives.

    a. Assuming that the data in the file represent the population of cans, compute the population mean fill and population standard deviation. (Note, if you are using Minitab, you will need to use the **Stack Columns** under the **Manip** menu item.)

    b. Compute the probability that a sample mean from a random sample of 50 cans will be less than 11.98 ounces.

    c. Discuss the result found in part b in terms of what it means to the Jordeen Beverage Company.

6-22. Referring to Problem 21, suppose the Jordeen managers wish to limit their chances of getting fined to no more than 5%. If the state inspector will not change the state's procedure and assuming that the standard deviation in the fill amount can't be changed, what specifically must the company do to reach the 5% level? Discuss the ramifications of making this change assuming that the company fills 500,000 cans every week for 52 weeks a year.

6-23. Referring to Problem 22, suppose the Jordeen managers are unwilling to adjust their average fill. Instead they can purchase a new filling machine that has an adjustable mean but will have a different standard deviation in fill amount than the current filling machine. What would the new machine's standard deviation have to be if the company wants no more than a 5% chance of being fined by the state inspector and assuming that the average fill is exactly 12 ounces?

6-24. Referring to Problem 22, use a statistical software package to select a random sample of 50 cans. Compute the sample mean.

    a. Assuming this is the sample the state inspector took on a particular visit to the company, what decision should the inspector reach?

    b. Repeat this process 50 times. Determine the number of times that the state inspector would have imposed the $1,000 fine even though the average fill is 12 ounces. Would you be satisfied with the state's procedure given your answer?

    c. Assume that Jordeen has an average fill exactly equal to 12 ounces and the standard deviation is the value you calculated in Problem 21. Suppose that on 4 consecutive days the state inspector found that Jordeen was not in compliance with the fill standard. Would you, as an adviser to Jordeen recommend the company institute legal proceedings against the state of Missouri? Support your answer with probability calculations and statistical reasoning.

6-25. Open the file named **Fast100** that is on the CD-ROM accompanying this text. The second column contains total sales for the past 4 quarters for these 100 companies. Assume that these 100 companies represent the population of interest.

    a. Compute the population mean and population standard deviation.

    b. Develop a frequency distribution for these data, and indicate whether the population data appear to be normally distributed.

    c. Select a random sample of 30 companies from this population. Compute the mean sales for this sample of companies. If you were asked to write a report using these 30 companies to exemplify characteristics (such as the mean) similar to those of the population, would you use this sample? Why or why not? (Hint: Compute the probability of getting a sample mean as extreme as or more extreme than the one you computed at the beginning of this part. Remember to use the finite correction factor.)

6-26. Referring to Problem 25, select a random sample of 50 companies.
   a. Find the average sales for this sample.
   b. What is the probability of getting a sample mean as extreme as or more extreme than the one found in part a assuming that the original 100 companies represent the population of interest?
   c. Compare this result with the one found in Problem 25, part c. Discuss.
   d. Determine the probability that a sample mean from a sample of size 100 would be as extreme as or more extreme than the sample mean obtained in Problem 25. Can you reconcile the probability you calculated in part c of Problem 25 with the probability you just calculated? That is to ask, "Why are the means different?"

6-27. Open the file called **Trucks** on the CD-ROM. This file contains data on trucks that have been weighed on two weigh scales—the in-ground scale at the port-of-entry (POE) and a scale that is located in the highway before the POE turn-off. This latter scale allows the trucks to be weighed as they move along the road and is referred to as a weigh-in-motion scale (WIM). Assuming the data for these 200 trucks represent the population of interest, create a new variable which is the difference between front axle WIM weight and front axle POE weight.
   a. Develop a frequency histogram for this new variable. Does this population distribution look approximately normally distributed? Describe the shape of the distribution.
   b. Compute the population mean and population standard deviation for this new variable.
   c. Select a random sample of 25 trucks. Compute the sample mean. What is the probability of getting a sample mean as extreme as or more extreme than the one you got?
   d. If the front axle WIM weight is enough different from the front axle POE weight, the WIM scale will not be useable. Determine the probability that this difference is larger than 500 pounds. (Note: This may require

that you employ procedures learned earlier in this text.) Do you think, on the basis of your calculation, that the WIM scale will be effective? Explain.

6-28. Referring to Problem 27, select a second random sample of 25 trucks.
   a. Compute the sample mean for this sample.
   b. Compare this sample mean with the one obtained in Problem 27. Write a short report describing the sampling error for these two samples. Make sure to include statements about the extent to which the two samples do or do not contain extreme sampling error.

6-29. Referring to Problems 27 and 28, suppose the data in the **Trucks** file represent a random sample of a bigger population of trucks rather than a population. Consider the new variable (difference between WIM front axle and POE front axle weights). Suppose the bigger population of all trucks has an average difference equal to 0 pounds with a standard deviation equal to 2,000 pounds.
   a. Determine the probability that the sample mean difference between WIM and POE front axle weights will be as large as or larger than the one you computed in Problem 27. Discuss.
   b. Determine the probability that the sample mean difference between WIM and POE front axle weights will be as large as or larger than the one you computed in Problem 28.
   c. Compute the probability that two random samples would have results as large as or larger than the two you just calculated. On this basis do you believe that the population mean really is zero? What would you recommend concerning the use of the WIM scale?

6-30. The file on your CD-ROM called **Cities** contains data on a sample of 100 U.S. cities. Assume the population mean unemployment rate is 5.0%.
   a. Compute the mean unemployment rate for the 100 cities.
   b. Calculate the probability of a sample of 100 cities having an unemployment rate as extreme or more extreme than the one you have computed. (Hint: In your computation, substitute the sample standard deviation for σ.)
   c. Based upon your calculation in part b, do you believe the population mean is the value it was assumed to be? Provide a rationale for your statement.

6-3: SAMPLING DISTRIBUTION OF A PROPORTION

Working with Proportions

In many instances, the objective of sampling is to estimate a population proportion. For instance, an accountant may be interested in determining the proportion of accounts payable balances that are correct. A production supervisor may wish to determine the percentage of product that is defect free. A marketing research department might want to know the proportion of potential customers who will purchase a particular product. In all these instances, the decision makers could select a sample, compute the sample proportion, and make their decision based on the sample results.

However, as shown earlier in this chapter, sample proportions are subject to sampling error just as are sample means. The concept of sampling distributions provides us a way to assess the potential magnitude of the sampling error in given situations.

In both the production supervisor and marketing research examples above, we are interested in determining the proportion (π) of all items that possess a particular attribute. We estimate this proportion with a corresponding proportion from the sample. Any statistical inference will be based on the distribution of this sample proportion, p, whose underlying distribution is the binomial. However, if the sample size is sufficiently large such that:

$$n\pi \geq 5 \text{ and } n(1 - \pi) \geq 5$$

the normal distribution can be used as a reasonable approximation to the discrete binomial distribution.[5] (Refer to the optional CD-ROM topic in Chapter 5 on the normal approximation to the binomial.) Provided we have a large enough sample size, the distribution of all possible sample proportions will be approximately normally distributed. In addition to being normally distributed, the sampling distributions will have a mean and standard error as indicated in Equations 6-9 and 6-10.

SAMPLING DISTRIBUTION OF p

$$\text{Mean} = \mu_p = \pi \qquad \text{6-9}$$

and

$$\text{Standard Error} = \sigma_p = \sqrt{\frac{\pi(1 - \pi)}{n}} \qquad \text{6-10}$$

where:

π = Population proportion
n = Sample size
p = Sample proportion

6-6

SAMPLING DISTRIBUTION

Heaton Manufacturing

Heaton Manufacturing, a company located in New England, makes Christmas ornaments. Heaton ships its ornaments to retailers throughout the United States. Because the ornaments are so fragile, they must be packed carefully. Even with special packing, Heaton executives have observed over time that 15% of the ornaments are damaged prior to reaching the retailer. There appears to be no particular pattern to the damage, and the fact that one ornament gets broken seems independent of whether any other ornament is broken.

Suppose that Heaton Manufacturing received a fax from a retail customer who indicated that 18% of the 500 ornaments she had purchased were damaged. Assume the general damage rate of 0.15 (π) still holds for the population of all ornaments. How likely is it that a sample of 500 units will contain 18% or more broken items? To answer this we first check for sample size. Since both:

$$n(\pi) = 500(0.15) = 75 \geq 5 \text{ and } n(1 - \pi) = 500(0.85) = 425 \geq 5$$

we can safely conclude that the distribution of sample proportions will be approximately normal. Using Equations 6-9 and 6-10, we can compute the mean and standard error for the sampling distribution as follows.

$$\mu_p = 0.15$$

---

[5]An application of the Central Limit Theorem provides the rationale for this statement. Recall that $p = \dfrac{x}{n}$ where x is the sum of random variables (x_i) whose values are 0 and 1. Thus, $\dfrac{x}{n} = \dfrac{\sum x_i}{n}$. Therefore, p is in reality just a sample mean. Each of these x_i can be thought of as binomial random variables from a sample of size $n = 1$. They each have a mean of $\mu = n\pi = \pi$ and a standard deviation of $\sigma = \sqrt{n\pi(1 - \pi)} = \sqrt{\pi(1 - \pi)}$. As we have seen from the Central Limit Theorem, the sample mean has an expected value of μ and a standard deviation of $\dfrac{\sigma}{\sqrt{n}}$. Thus, the sample proportion has an expected value of $\mu = \pi$ and a standard deviation of $\sigma = \sqrt{\dfrac{\pi(1 - \pi)}{n}}$.

and

$$\sigma_p = \sqrt{\frac{(0.15)(0.85)}{500}} = 0.016$$

Equation 6-11 is used to convert the sample proportion to a standardized z-value.

---

z-VALUE FOR PROPORTIONS

$$z = \frac{p - \pi}{\sigma_p}$$

6-11

where:

z = Number of standard errors p is from π
p = Sample proportion
σ_p = Standard error of the sampling distribution
$\pi = \mu_p$ = Mean of sample proportions

From Equation 6-11 we get

$$z = \frac{p - \pi}{\sigma_p} = \frac{0.18 - 0.15}{\sqrt{\dfrac{(0.15)(0.85)}{500}}} = 1.88$$

This means the 0.18 damage rate reported by the customer is 1.88 standard deviations above the average rate of 0.15. Figure 6-18 illustrates that the chances of a damage rate of 0.18 or more is only 0.0301. Since this is a very low probability, the managers at Heaton Manufacturing might want to investigate to see if there was something unusual about how this shipment was packed. While possible, it is very unlikely that a sample breakage rate of 18% or higher would occur if the company is holding to the 15% rate overall.

FIGURE 6-18
Standard Normal
Distribution for Heaton
Manufacturing

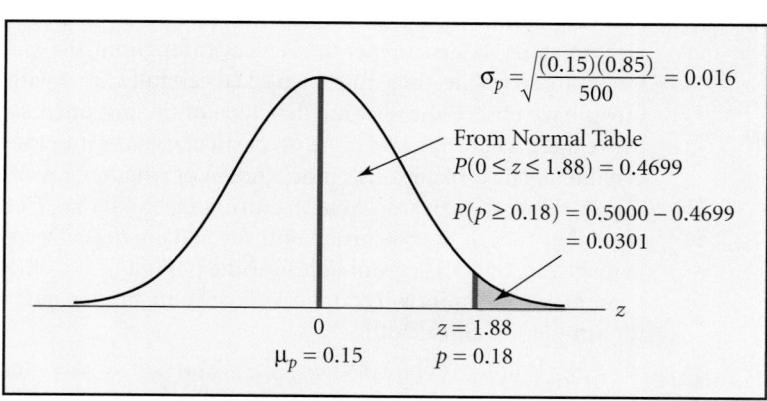

6-3: EXERCISES

ADDITIONAL EXERCISES ON YOUR CD-ROM
Try the **ADDITIONAL EXERCISES and APPLICATION PROBLEMS** on the CD-ROM.

6-31. Thirty percent of the items in a population are known to possess a particular attribute. If a random sample of 60 items is selected, what is the probability that the sample proportion of items with the attribute will exceed 0.33?

6-32. Suppose 95% of the items in a population have a particular characteristic.
   a. Find the chance that a sample of 100 items will have less than 90 items with that same characteristic.
   b. In a sample of 100 items, determine the smallest number (for all practical purposes) of items you would expect to find that possessed the particular characteristic.

6-33. Given a population where the probability of a success is $\pi = 0.40$, if a sample of 1,000 is taken:
   a. Determine the expected number of successes.
   b. What is the expected proportion of successes in the sample?
   c. Find the standard deviation of the sampling distribution of p.
   d. Calculate the probability that the proportion of successes in the sample will be less than 0.42.

6-34. Refer to Problem 33.
   a. What is the probability the proportion of successes in the sample will be greater than 0.44?
   b. Determine the probability if the sample size were reduced to 100.
   c. Suppose 5 samples of 100 items were selected. Determine the probability that 4 of the 5 samples would have sample proportions that were all greater than the population mean or that were all smaller than the population mean.

Business Applications

6-35. Tom Marley and Jennifer Griggs have recently started a marketing research firm in Jacksonville, Florida. They have contacted the Florida Democratic Party with a proposal to do all political polling for the party. Since they have just started their company, the state party chairman is reluctant to sign a contract without some test of their accuracy. He has asked them to do a trial poll in a central Florida county known to have 60% registered Democratic party voters. The poll itself had many questions. However, for the test of accuracy, only the proportion of registered Democrats was considered. Tom and Jennifer report back that from a random sample of 760 respondents, 395 were registered Democrats.

   a. Determine the probability that such a random sample would result in 395 or fewer Democrats in the sample.
   b. Based on your calculations in part a, would you recommend that the Florida Democratic Party (or anyone else for that matter) contract with the Marley/Griggs marketing research firm? Explain your answer.

6-36. A golf equipment catalog company regularly inserts coupons in the catalogs which can be redeemed for merchandise at local businesses. Historically, 8% of the coupons are redeemed. Recently the company enclosed a new style coupon in a sample of 300 catalogs. It then determined that 35 of these coupons were redeemed.
   a. What are the chances that the new style coupon has the same redemption rate as the old and the sample results were just due to sampling error? (Hint: You must calculate a specific probability here.)
   b. Would you recommend adoption of the new coupon? Justify your answer.

6-37. Micron Electronics makes personal computers that are then sold directly over the phone and over the Internet. One of the most critical factors in the success of PC makers is how fast they can turn their inventory of parts. Faster inventory turns means lower average inventory cost. Recently at a meeting, the VP of manufacturing said that there is no reason to continue offering hard disk drives that have less than a 2.0 GB storage capacity since only 10% of Micron customers ask for the smaller hard disks. After much discussion and debate about the accuracy of the VP's figure, a sample of 100 orders from the past week's sales was taken. This sample revealed 14 requests for drives with less than 2.0 GB capacity.
   a. Determine the probability of finding 14 or more requests for hard disk drives with low storage capacity if the VP's assertion is correct. Do you believe that the proportion of customers requesting hard drives with low storage capacity is smaller than 0.10? Explain.
   b. Suppose a second sample of 100 customers was selected. This sample again yielded 14 requests for less than a 2 GB drive. Combining this sample information with that in part a, what conclusion would you now reach regarding the VP's 10% claim? Base your answer on probability.

6-38. One of the major video rental chains recently made a change in its rental policies. One change is to allow the movie to be rented for 3 nights instead of 1. The marketing team that made this decision reasoned that at least 70% of the customers would return the movie by the second night anyway. A sample of 500 customers found 68% returned the movie prior to the third night.

    a. Given the marketing team's estimate, what would be the probability of a sample result with 68% or fewer returns prior to the third night?

    b. Based on your calculations, would you recommend the adoption of the new rental policy? Support your answer with statistical reasoning and calculations.

6-39. The file on your CD-ROM called **Patients** contains information for a sample of geriatric patients. During a meeting, one hospital administrator indicated that 70% of the geriatric patients are males.

    a. What is the sample proportion of male patients?

    b. Assuming that the administrator is correct, what is the probability that a sample of this size would have a sample proportion as extreme as or more extreme than the one you found in part a?

    c. Would you conclude that the administrator's assertion concerning the proportion of male geriatric patients is correct? Justify your answer.

6-40. Referring to Problem 39, the administrator believes that 80% of all geriatric patients are covered by Medicare (Code = CARE). Assume that the data in the Patients file represent a random sample of all hospital geriatric patients.

    a. What proportion of patients in the sample are covered by Medicare?

    b. Determine the probability of getting a sample proportion as extreme as or more extreme than the one you computed in part a if the administrator's 80% figure is correct.

    c. Based on the probability you computed in part b, what conclusion should the hospital administrator reach concerning the proportion of geriatric patients covered by Medicare? Discuss.

    d. Suppose you were to select one of the geriatric patients at random. Determine whether the patient's gender is independent of whether the patient is covered by Medicare. (Hint: You may have to use techniques developed in earlier chapters of this text.) Support your declaration with appropriate statistical techniques and reasoning.

6-41. The data file **Trucks** contains a sample of 200 trucks that were weighed on two scales. The WIM (weigh-in-motion) scale weighs the trucks as they drive down the highway. The POE scale weighs the trucks while they are stopped at the port-of-entry station. The makers of the WIM scale believe that their scale will weigh heavier than the POE scale 60% of the time when gross weight is considered.

    a. Create a new variable that has a value = 1 when the WIM gross weight > POE gross weight, and 0 otherwise.

    b. Determine the sample proportion of times the WIM gross weight exceeds the POE gross weight.

    c. Based on this sample, what is the probability of finding a proportion as extreme as or more extreme than that found in part b? For this calculation assume the WIM makers' assertion is correct.

    d. Based on the probability found in part c, what should the WIM makers conclude? Is their 60% figure reasonable?

6-42. Refer to Problem 41. The **Trucks** data file also contains data that indicate the speed the trucks were traveling when they crossed the WIM scale.

    a. Determine the percent of the trucks in the sample that were exceeding the 55 mph speed limit when they crossed the WIM scale.

    b. If the state highway patrol has indicated in the past that 70% of all trucks exceed the speed limit on this section of highway, do the sample data tend to support or refute the highway patrol? (Hint: Compute the probability of getting the sample proportion equal to or more extreme than the one you computed. Base your response on this probability.)

    c. Calculate the probability that the mean difference in front axle WIM weight and front axle POE weight is greater than 0 in two cases: (1) If the truck were speeding, (2) if the truck were not speeding.

    d. Based upon your calculation in part c, do you believe that at least a part of the discrepancy in weights obtained by the WIM scale is due to the speed of the vehicle being weighed? Support your answer with probability calculations and statistical reasoning.

6-43. Guidian Manufacturing supplies parts to Standard Generator which incorporates the parts in its generators. Standard wishes to negotiate a contract with Guidian concerning the proportion of defective parts it receives. It wishes the defective rate to be no larger than 0.05. Guidian has established from past performance that its defective rate is 0.076.

    a. Standard's managers propose a way of checking to determine that the defective rate (π) does not exceed 0.05. They propose sampling 150 of the parts. If more than 5 are defective, they will conclude that $\pi > 0.05$ and cancel the contract. Calculate the probability that Standard will cancel the contract even if the defective rate is 0.05. After examining this probability, Guidian refuses to sign this contract and instead proposes that the contract be canceled only if more than 10 parts are defective. Calculate the probability that the contract will not be canceled if the defective rate is what Guidian knows it to be (i.e., 0.076).

    b. Repeat the calculations in part a if the sample size is 200, instead.

    c. Using the methods outlined in parts a and b, find a sample size and a number of defectives which would cancel the contract such that the probability of cancellation is at most 0.03 when the defective rate is 0.05. Also, find the probability that the contract will be honored (i.e., not cancelled) if the defective rate is 0.076. Discuss these results.

■ SUMMARY AND CONCLUSIONS

When a manager selects a sample, it is only one of many samples that could have been selected. Consequently the sample mean, $\bar{x}$, is only one of the many possible sample means that could have been found. There is no reason to believe that the single $\bar{x}$ value will equal the population mean, μ. The difference between $\bar{x}$ and μ is called sampling error. Because sampling error exists, decision makers must be aware of how the sample means are distributed in order to discuss the potential for extreme sampling error.

This chapter has introduced two important theorems. These theorems describe the distribution of sample means taken from any population. The more important of these theorems is the Central Limit Theorem. The concepts of estimation and hypothesis testing depend heavily on the Central Limit Theorem. The important aspect of the Central Limit Theorem is that no matter how the population is distributed, if the sample size is large enough, the sampling distribution will be approximately normal.

The chapter also presented several new statistical terms, which are listed in the Key Terms section. Be sure you understand these concepts and how they apply to the material in this chapter. You will encounter these terms many times as you continue in this text.

EQUATIONS

Sampling Error—Single Mean

$$\text{Sampling Error} = \bar{x} - \mu \qquad \text{6-1}$$

Population Mean

$$\mu = \frac{\sum_{i=1}^{N} x_i}{N} \qquad \text{6-2}$$

Sample Mean

$$\bar{x} = \frac{\sum_{i=1}^{n} x_i}{n} \qquad \text{6-3}$$

Population Proportion

$$\pi = \frac{x}{N} \qquad \text{6-4}$$

Sample Proportion

$$p = \frac{x}{n} \qquad \text{6-5}$$

Single Proportion Sampling Error

$$\text{Sampling Error} = p - \pi \qquad \text{6-6}$$

z-Value for Sampling Distribution of $\bar{x}$

$$z = \frac{\bar{x} - \mu}{\frac{\sigma}{\sqrt{n}}} \qquad \text{6-7}$$

z-Value Adjusted for the Finite Population Correction Factor

$$z = \frac{\bar{x} - \mu}{\frac{\sigma}{\sqrt{n}} \sqrt{\frac{N-n}{N-1}}} \qquad \text{6-8}$$

Mean of the Sampling Distribution of p

$$\text{Mean} = \mu_p = \pi \qquad \text{6-9}$$

Sampling Distribution Standard Error of p

$$\text{Standard Error} = \sigma_p = \sqrt{\frac{\pi(1-\pi)}{n}} \qquad \text{6-10}$$

z-Value for a Proportion

$$z = \frac{p - \pi}{\sigma_p} \qquad \text{6-11}$$

■ KEY TERMS

Central Limit Theorem—For samples of n observations taken from a population with mean μ and standard deviation σ, regardless of the population's distribution, provided the sample size is sufficiently large, the distribution of the sample mean, $\bar{x}$, values will be approximately normal with a mean equal to the population mean ($\mu_{\bar{x}} = \mu$). Further, the standard deviation will equal the population standard deviation divided by the square root of the sample size ($\sigma_{\bar{x}} = \frac{\sigma}{\sqrt{n}}$). The larger the sample size, the better the approximation to the normal distribution.

Finite Population Correction Factor—A value used to modify the standard deviation of the sampling distribution when the sampling is performed without replacement and when the sample size is greater than 5% of the population size.

Parameter—A measure computed from the entire population.

Population Proportion—The fraction of values in a population which have a specific attribute.

Sample Proportion—The fraction of items in a sample that have the attribute of interest.

Sampling Distribution—A distribution of the possible values of a statistic for a given size sample selected from a population.

Sampling Error—The difference between a value (a statistic) computed from a sample and the corresponding value (a parameter) computed from the population.

Simple Random Sample—A sample selected in such a manner that each possible sample of a specified size has an equal chance of being selected.

Statistic—A measure computed from a sample that has been selected from a population.

Theorem 6-1—If a population is normally distributed, with mean μ and a standard deviation σ, the sampling distribution of $\bar{x}$ is also normally distributed with a mean equal to the population mean ($\mu_{\bar{x}} = \mu$) and a standard deviation equal to the population standard deviation divided by the square root of the sample size ($\sigma_{\bar{x}} = \frac{\sigma}{\sqrt{n}}$).

CHAPTER EXERCISES

SOLVED PROBLEMS ON YOUR CD-ROM
Try the WORKED-OUT EXERCISES and BUSINESS
APPLICATIONS on the CD-ROM.

Conceptual Questions

6-44. Explain in your own words what is meant by the term sampling distribution.

6-45. Discuss why the sampling distribution will be less variable than the population distribution. Give a short example to illustrate your answer.

6-46. Discuss why the standard error of a sampling distribution is considered a measure of average sampling error.

6-47. Discuss (using examples of your own) what effect the finite correction factor has on the computation of the standard error of the sampling distribution as the sample size gets small relative to the size of the population.

6-48. The Central Limit Theorem indicates that the sampling distribution of $\bar{x}$ will have a standard deviation of $\sigma_{\bar{x}} = \dfrac{\sigma}{\sqrt{n}}$.

Discuss why the sampling distribution of $\bar{x}$ should have less variation than the population distribution.

6-49. Under what conditions should the finite population correction factor be used in determining the standard error of a sampling distribution?

6-50. A researcher has collected all possible samples of size 150 from a population and listed the sample means for each of these samples.
  a. If the average of the sample means is 450.55, what would be the numerical value of the true population mean? Discuss.
  b. If the standard deviation of the sample means is 12.25, determine the standard deviation of the population from which the samples came. To perform this calculation, assume the population has a size of 1,250.

6-51. In Problem 50, a researcher collected all possible samples of 150 and found that the average of the sample means was 450.55. The researcher recognized that the sample means will vary around the true population mean. Consequently, she found the standard deviation of the sample means to be 30.56.
  a. Discuss this number. What term is used to describe this number?
  b. Based on the 30.56 value, determine the population standard deviation.

6-52. Suppose we are told the sampling distribution developed from a sample of size 400, has a mean of 56.78, and a standard error of 9.6. If the population is known to be normally distributed, what are the population mean and population standard deviation? Discuss how these values relate to the values for the sampling distribution.

6-53. If a population is known to be normally distributed, what size sample is required to ensure that the sampling distribution is normally distributed?

6-54. Suppose a population is normally distributed. What is the probability of finding a sample mean, $\bar{x}$, that is greater than the population mean?

Business Applications

6-55. The Doran Maintenance Company recently selected a random sample of businesses in the Dallas, Texas, area and asked the businesses to report their monthly budgets for office maintenance. The sample was randomly selected and contained 200 businesses. The mean budget for the sample was $750.00 per month.
  a. Does this indicate that the true average maintenance budget for all businesses in the Dallas area is $750.00 per month? Discuss.
  b. Give the generic term for measurements of which the $750.00 figure is an example. Also, identify the generic term for the population measurement that this sample measure is trying to estimate.
  c. Determine the probability that the sample mean budget of a sample of 200 businesses would equal the population mean it was trying to estimate. Explain why this occurs. That is, identify the characteristic of the sample mean that makes this probability so small. (Hint: You may be thinking that you need a standard deviation to calculate this probability. It is not necessary given an important characteristic of the sample mean for such large sample sizes.)

6-56. The Hardcone Baking Company recently performed a market study from the sample of 400. It asked people how much they spent on bakery products per week. The average of this sample was $3.45.
  a. Calculate the probability that a sample of 400 would produce a sample mean of $3.45. You may wish to refer to the hint in Problem 55.
  b. Calculate the probability that two samples of 400 would both produce sample means of $3.45.
  c. Review the answers to parts a and b. Is it reasonable to expect that another sample of size 400 would result in the same sample average? Discuss why or why not.

6-57. Recently, a school system in the Midwest performed a study of its students' performance on mathematics examinations. If the population of all examination scores is thought to be normally distributed, with a mean of 68 points and a standard deviation of 12 points:

a. What are the mean and standard deviation for the sampling distribution of $\bar{x}$ if the sample size is 100? Discuss why the sampling distribution has a smaller standard deviation than the population.

b. Suppose the school system takes a second sample of size 500. What is the relationship between the sampling distributions of the two sample means? Illustrate using graphs.

6-58. The time it takes a mechanic to tune an engine is known to be normally distributed with a mean of 45 minutes and a standard deviation of 14 minutes.

a. Determine the mean and standard error of a sampling distribution for a sample size of 20 tune-ups. Draw a picture of the sampling distribution.

b. Calculate the largest sampling error you would expect to make in estimating the population mean with the sample size of 20 tune-ups.

c. The mechanic charges $60 an hour for labor. Determine the largest and smallest amount of labor charges this mechanic would have for 20 tuneups.

6-59. The money spent by individuals for recreation in a particular target population is normally distributed.

a. How much will the standard error be reduced if the sample size is doubled? Discuss.

b. The z-value for a particular person's expenditure for recreation is 2.50. Determine the proportion of individuals who spend more on recreation than does this individual.

6-60. Suppose the interest earned on savings accounts by individuals at a particular bank has a distribution that may be skewed to the right. The bank asserts that the population mean is $450.00 earned per year, with a standard deviation of $67.00.

a. Describe the sampling distribution for a sample of size 100. Also show the sampling distribution in graphical form.

b. An audit has been conducted on the bank's savings accounts. One hundred accounts were sampled. The mean interest earned for the sample was $313. Do you believe the bank's assertion to be an exaggeration? Support your answer with calculation and statistical reasoning.

6-61. The population distribution for family incomes in the Canadian province of British Columbia is unknown but has a mean of $21,500 and a standard deviation of $1,700.

a. A sample of size 200 is to be selected and the sample mean calculated. Describe the sampling distribution both in terms of its general shape and descriptive measures.

b. If the sample size was actually 60 instead of 200, how would the sampling distribution be affected? Illustrate with a graph, indicating the mean and standard error.

c. What is the probability that a sample of $n = 60$ selected randomly from the population will have a mean equal to or greater than $21,300?

6-62. The Galusha C.P.A. Firm performs audits for the Alien Tool Company. As part of an audit, the accountant in charge selected a random sample of 300 accounts from the 2,000 accounts receivable on the Alien Company books. He was particularly interested in the average account balance.

a. If the computer records indicate that the true average balance for all 2,000 accounts is $786.98, with a standard deviation of $356.75, describe the sampling distribution of the sample mean.

b. Draw an illustration of the sampling distribution.

c. Describe the sampling distribution for the mean if the accountant changes the sample to 500 accounts. Also discuss why it is not necessary to know the shape of the population distribution.

d. The accountant's sample of 500 produced a mean of $795.20. If the computer records are correct with regard to the standard deviation of the account balances, do you believe the figure given for the average of the account balances? Support your answer with probability calculations and rationale.

e. Assume the population of account balances was, in fact, normally distributed. Determine the interquartile range for the account balances.

6-63. The engineering staff for the Bentrim Manufacturing Company is considering sampling 30 bolts produced by a supplier for the company to determine the average diameter. The population is 200 bolts, the population standard deviation is known to be 0.015 inches, and the output measures are normally distributed.

a. Determine the standard error of the sampling distribution.

b. The staff is troubled by bolts that do not fit the parts Bentrim is producing. Therefore, they wish to develop a method of determining when the bolts are too narrow or broad to fit the parts they are producing. If the mean diameter of bolt population is 0.75 inches, determine the largest average diameter a sample of 30 bolts should produce.

c. The staff has concluded that if the average they calculate from their sample is larger than the 95th percentile of the average bolts' width, they will return the shipment of bolts and seek another supplier of bolts. What will be the minimum average width that will cause Bentrim to return the shipment?

6-64. Dan Eyko works for the *Morning Star* newspaper. He recently selected a random sample of 40 issues of the daily newspaper during the past year. He was interested in determining the average number of column-inches devoted to hard news. Suppose the true standard deviation for the number of inches of hard news is 8 inches and the mean is 140 inches.

a. Calculate the standard error of the sampling distribution.

b. The *Morning Star* has 140 column-inches per page. Determine the probability that Dan Eyko's sample will have a sample mean larger than the equivalent of 1 page.

c. If the *Morning Star* wishes to have a 90% chance of having at least 1 page of hard news in their newspaper, what must be the value for the average number of column-inches of hard news?

d. Suppose the *Morning Star* achieves their goal (as stated in part c). Dan Eyko selects 3 samples of 40 to assure himself the goal was achieved. Determine the probability that at least 2 of these samples produce a sample mean of 140 column-inches.

6-65. Referring to Problem 64, suppose Dan Eyko selected a sample of 40 issues and found a mean equal to 130 inches. Based on the probability of this value or something more extreme, what should he conclude about the hard news trend?

6-66. The Chair Company repairs old furniture and restores it to "better than original" condition. Records indicate the time it takes to refinish and otherwise restore a standard dining room set is normally distributed, with a mean of 30 hours and a standard deviation of 5 hours. Recently a customer complained that he was charged too much for work performed by The Chair Company. To settle the argument, the manager of the company offered the customer the following option. The company will select a random sample of past work performed on tables similar to the customer's. If the sample mean based on 5 randomly selected work times turns out to be less than the time required for his table, the Chair Company will refund his money. If the mean of this sample turns out to be greater than or equal to his billed time, he will pay the company half again the amount of the bill.

a. Taking into account the mean and standard deviation of all work times on file, do you think the manager is wise to make such an offer if this customer's billed time was 32 hours? Discuss why or why not.

b. What would be your response if the customer's billed time was 34 hours? Supply probability calculations and statistical reasoning to support your answer.

6-67. Consider the Chair Company example in Problem 66. A customer was billed for 32 hours of labor.

a. Determine the probability of a single customer being billed for this many hours or more.

b. Calculate the probability that a sample of 5 customers will average 32 hours of labor or more for their projects.

6-68. The Swim and Racquet Club is in the process of establishing a policy for how long a court may be reserved at any one time. The club pro has said that she thinks the average time required to complete a tennis match at the Swim and Racquet Club is 90 minutes with a standard deviation of 10 minutes. To help make this decision, the club managers have selected a random sample of 100 tennis matches and determined that the mean time for completion is 75 minutes. The managers' spokesperson maintains that these data supports the club's pro and is preparing to put the maximum time to reserve a court to be 90 minutes. They argue that it is quite understandable that a sample of size 100

would produce a sample mean of 75 minutes. After all, 75 is only 1.5 standard deviations below the mean of 90 minutes.

a. Calculate the probability that a sample mean of 75 or something more extreme would occur if the club pro is correct in her assessment of mean and standard deviation.

b. Discuss the club spokesperson's logic.

6-69. The Environmental Protection Agency (EPA) requires all U.S. automobile makers to test their cars for mileage in the city and on the highway. One company has indicated that a certain model will get 25 mpg in the city and 32 mpg on the highway. However, not all cars of a given model will get the same mileage; these mileage ratings are simply averages. Furthermore, because there is variation among cars, the manufacturer has discovered that the standard deviation is 3 mpg for city driving and 2 mpg for highway driving.

Given this information, suppose the San Francisco Police Department has purchased a random sample of 64 cars from this company. The police officers have driven these cars exclusively in the city and have recorded an average of 24.25 mpg. Based on this sample information, what would you conclude about the EPA city driving mileage rating average for this car? Base your response on the probability of getting a sample mean of 24.25 mpg or less.

6-70. Refer to Problem 69. The police chief has asked his officers to drive the cars to Los Angeles and back when a trip is required for official business to determine how the cars perform in highway driving. The 64 cars averaged 34 mpg.

a. What can the chief conclude about the advertised highway mileage? Explain your answer.

b. Determine the maximum and minimum average mpg you would expect to obtain from the 64 cars if the manufacturer's claims are correct.

c. The distance between Los Angeles and San Francisco is approximately 400 miles. Determine the average cost of gasoline for such a round trip between the two cities. Assume the officers are able to purchase gasoline for $1.599 per gallon.

6-71. The Mason Construction Company has built a total of 50 homes in the Seattle area and claims to have built each home in an average time of 35 days, with a standard deviation of 10 days. A prospective customer has interviewed a random sample of 40 of the 50 homeowners about the quality of construction. One of the questions asked of the homeowners was how long it took the builder to construct their homes. The 40 responses averaged 36.1 days.

a. If Mason Construction's claim is correct, determine the longest average time you would (for all practical purposes) expect to see for the construction of the 40 houses.

b. Suppose the sample average obtained from the 40 homeowners can be considered a good approximation of the population average. Calculate the smallest sample average you would expect to see from the sample of 40 houses.

c. What would you conclude concerning Mason's claimed average time to construct homes? Base your answer on the probability of getting a sample mean of 36.1 or more days given the stated population mean of 35 days.

6-72. The Sullivan Advertising Agency has determined that the average cost to develop a 30-second commercial is $20,000. The standard deviation is $3,000. Suppose a random sample of 50 commercials is selected and the average cost is $20,300.

a. What are the chances of finding a sample mean this high or higher if the population parameters are as stated?

b. Sullivan's has budgeted $2,250,000 to finance the development of its next 100 commercials. Is this a realistic figure? Determine the chances that Sullivan's will overrun its budget.

6-73. Referring to Problem 72, suppose the Sullivan Advertising Agency is interested in establishing a pricing policy for prospective customers of 30-second commercials. Recall the mean cost is $20,000, with a standard deviation of $3,000.

a. What are the chances of a given commercial costing between $19,500 and $22,000?

b. What is the probability of a sample of 36 commercials having an average cost between $19,500 and $22,000? Explain why this probability is different than the probability found in part a.

c. One customer claims her records show that Sullivan's has charged her company an average of $22,500 for 30-second commercials, and they are outraged by this high billing. Sullivan's contends the customer is mistaken; that the figure she is using is simply the cost of the most recent 30-second commercial. Discuss this argument from both perspectives. Support your discussion with statistical calculations and reasoning.

6-74. The Baily Hill Bicycle Shop sells mountain bikes and offers a maintenance program to its customers. The manager has found the average repair bill during the maintenance program's first year to be $15.30, with a standard deviation of $7.00.

a. What is the probability a random sample of 40 customers will have a mean repair cost exceeding $16.00?

b. What is the probability the mean repair cost for a sample of 100 customers will be between $15.10 and $15.80?

c. The manager has decided to offer a spring special. He is aware of the mean and standard deviation for repair bills last year. Therefore, he has decided to randomly select and repair the 50 bicycles for $14 each. He notes that this is not even 1 standard deviation below the mean price to make such repairs. He asks your advice. Is this a risky thing to do? Base your answer on statistical calculations relevant to the data given. It is tempting to talk about many other issues that should be made known. However, restrict your comments to those based upon your statistical calculations.

6-75. As part of a marketing study, the Food King Supermarket chain has randomly sampled 150 customers. The average dollar volume purchased by the customers in this sample was $33.14.

a. Before sampling, the company assumed that the distribution of customer purchases had a mean of $30.00 and a standard deviation of $8.00. If these figures are correct, what is the probability of observing a sample mean of $33.14 or greater? What would this probability indicate to you concerning the assumed distribution of customer purchases?

b. A Food King market has approximately 800 customers a day on weekends. Recently, just before closing on a Saturday evening, the market was robbed of its receipts for the day. The store manager wishes to estimate how much their losses were so they can file an insurance claim. You have been called upon to provide this figure. Respond. Support your estimate with probability calculations and reasoning.

6-76. The Bendbo Corporation has a total of 300 employees in its two manufacturing locations and the headquarters office. A study conducted 5 years ago showed the average commuting distance to work for Bendbo employees was 6.2 miles, with a standard deviation of 3 miles. Recently, a follow-up study based on a random sample of 100 employees indicated an average travel distance of 5.9 miles.

a. Assuming that the mean and standard deviation of the original study hold, what is the probability of obtaining a sample mean of 5.9 miles or less?

b. Based on this probability, do you think the average travel distance may have decreased?

c. A second random sample of 40 was selected. This sample produced a mean travel distance of 5.9 miles. If the mean for all employees is 6.2 miles and the standard deviation is 3 miles, what is the probability of observing a sample mean of 5.9 miles or less?

d. Discuss why the probabilities differ in parts a and c even though the sample results were the same in each case.

e. Determine the probability that two samples, one of size 100 and the other of size 40, would have mean travel times of 5.9 miles or less if the study conducted 5 years ago was correct.

6-77. An automatic saw at a local lumber mill cuts 2 × 4s to an average length of 120 inches. However, since the saw is a mechanical device, not all 2 × 4s are exactly 120 inches. In fact, the distribution of lengths has a variance of 0.64. The saw operator took a sample of 36 boards.

a. If the saw is set correctly, what is the probability the average length of the sample boards is more than 120.2 inches?

b. What is the probability the sample mean length is less than 119.73 inches?

c. What should the saw operator conclude if she finds the sample to have an average length of 120.3 inches?

d. An order has been received for 1,000 2 × 4s. However, the purchaser has declared that he will refuse the shipment if any boards are more than 1.5 inches different than the stated average. Is this a good proposition for the lumber company? Support your opinion with statistical calculations and reasoning. You may have to make some assumptions to justify your calculations. Do so but specify what they are.

6-78. The manager for quality control at Bixby Electronics recently reviewed a contract the company has with one of the suppliers of a particular component part. According to the contract, the defective rate in the components is to be no more than 7%. A large quantity of the components has just arrived at Bixby Electronics. As part of the regular receiving process, a random sample of 100 parts was selected. In this sample 12% of the parts were found to be defective.

    a. What is the probability of 12% or more of the components being defective if the true percentage defective in the population is actually 7%?

    b. Based on the probability you have computed, what should the quality control manager conclude about the entire shipment of components with respect to the 7% defective limit?

    c. Calculate the value for control limits for the quality control procedure. The control limits are established at 3 standard deviations from the mean.

    d. Determine the probability that a sample proportion from a sample of size 100 would be beyond the control limits if the true rate of defective items is 7%.

6-79. A random sample of 344 people is selected from the adult population in Houston, Texas.

    a. What is the probability that less than 22% of the sample favor a state lottery if the true percentage for the entire population who favor one is 32%?

    b. Based on the results in part a, do you believe that the sample was selected using a statistically valid method? Justify your response.

6-80. The Republican Election Committee maintains that 34% of the members of the AFL-CIO labor union are registered Republicans, but a random sample of 300 members shows a sample proportion of 28% registered Republicans.

    a. What statistical term is given to the difference between the 28% and the 34% if the 34% figure is correct.

    b. How likely is it that a sample of this size would contain 28% if the 34% figure is correct?

6-81. The average of all accounts payable for a large national electronics firm has been estimated to be $2,755.00 with a standard deviation of $375.00.

    a. Determine the probability that a random sample of 36 accounts payable would have a sample mean (1) greater than $2,850.00; (2) less than $2,700.00; and (3) between $2,650.00 and $2,750.00.

    b. Suppose the company's internal auditor has decided to review all accounts receivable balances that are at or above the 90th percentile. What cutoff should she use in selecting which accounts to review? Assume that these accounts have a normal distribution.

6-82. Suppose that 45% of all computer users in Seattle have made at least one purchase using the Internet. You have just conducted a random sample of 49 computer users in Seattle and have found that 18 of them have made at least one purchase using the Internet.

    a. Does your sample proportion surprise you? How likely are you to see a sample proportion this small or smaller if the true population proportion is 0.45?

    b. Compute the maximum sampling error you could experience in such a sample.

6-83. The file **High Desert Banking** contains information regarding consumer, real estate, and small commercial loans made last year by the bank. Use your computer software to:

    a. Construct a frequency histogram of loans made last year. Does the population distribution appear to be normally distributed?

    b. Compute the population mean for all loans made last year.

    c. Compute the population standard deviation for all loans made last year.

    d. Select a simple random sample of 36 loans. Compute the sample mean. By how much does the sample mean differ from the population mean? Use the Central Limit Theorem to determine the probability that you would have a sample mean this small or smaller and the probability that you would have a sample mean this large or larger.

6-84. Referring to Problem 83, what proportion of all loans made last year were real estate loans?

    a. Select a random sample of 36 loans. What proportion were real estate loans? What is the standard deviation of the sample proportion p?

    b. What is the probability of getting a sample proportion greater than or equal to 0.25 for samples of 36? How would this change for samples of 49?

6-85. Marketing research indicates that 37% of all customers of a nationwide pizza chain are college students.

    a. What is the probability that a random sample of 625 customers of the pizza chain would contain 250 or more people who are college students?

    b. A local pizzeria wishes to attract college students. The pizzeria advertises in the college newspaper that it will give a coffee mug displaying the local college's insignia to every customer who presents a student I.D. from that college on a certain Saturday. Normally the pizzeria has approximately 100 customers on Saturdays. If the pizzeria stocks 50 coffee mugs, determine the probability that they will have enough coffee mugs to give to the students if the advertisement doesn't work (i.e., doesn't attract a larger percentage of students).

6-86. The file **Best-Companies** contains selected information from the 100 best companies for U.S. employees as determined by *Fortune* magazine. Use this file to perform the following:

   a. Calculate the average number of U.S. employees for all 100 companies.

   b. Calculate the population standard deviation for the variable number of U.S. employees.

   c. Select a simple random sample of 36 companies. Compute the average number of U.S. employees for the sample. Is the sample mean identical to the population mean? Would you expect it to be? Why or why not?

   d. Compute the standard error of the sampling distribution of the mean for a sample size of 36. Is this value larger than or smaller than the population standard deviation?

   e. What is the probability that for a sample of 36 you would get a sample mean that is at least 15,000 employees?

6-87. A sample of 500 business professionals found that 30% chose an airline based on price.

   a. If the population proportion of all business professionals who select an airline based on price is 0.27, then what is the probability that we would find a sample proportion of 0.30 or more?

   b. If the population proportion of all business professionals who select an airline based on price is 0.29, then what is the probability that we would find a sample proportion of 0.30 or more?

   c. If you had to decide whether the proportion of business professionals who select an airline based on price was at most 0.27 or greater than 0.27, what would you conclude? Justify your answer statistically.

6-88. When its ovens are working properly, the time required to bake fruit pies at Ellardo Bakeries is normally distributed with a mean of 45 minutes and a standard deviation of 5 minutes. Yesterday, a random sample of 16 pies had an average baking time of 50 minutes.

   a. If Ellardo's ovens are working correctly, how likely is it that a sample of 16 pies would have an average baking time of 50 minutes or more?

   b. Would you recommend that Ellardo inspect its ovens to see if they are working properly? Justify your answer.

   c. Ellardo's can bake 4 pies at once. Employees, however, need to plan the day's baking. So they must estimate the greatest amount of time it will take to complete the pie baking so that they can do their other baking tasks. Determine the greatest amount of time (for all practical purposes) that will be required to bake 16 pies.

6-89. If the true proportion of home computer users who would purchase an additional telephone line for Internet use is 0.27, then what is the probability that a random sample of 500 computer users would produce a sample proportion between 0.25 and 0.29?

6-90. The file on your CD-ROM called **Cozine** contains data on weights of garbage trucks. Assume these data represent the population of interest. Suppose the landfill manager plans to select a random sample of 30 truck weights and from that will develop a report to the county commissioners.

   a. Determine the population mean and population standard deviation.

   b. Develop a frequency histogram for these data.

   c. Write a paragraph that describes the population.

   d. Select a random sample of 30 weights. Compute the sample mean weight.

   e. Compute the probability of getting a sample mean as extreme as or more extreme than the one you got.

   f. Based on the probability computed in part e, does it appear that this sample may have attributes, such as the mean, similar to those of the population or is the sampling error too great? Discuss.

6-91. The Celltone Company offers cell phone service with two plans for customers, the Basic Plan and the Business Plan. When the owners first devised the idea of offering the two plans, they felt that 40% of all customers would select the Business Plan. The data file called **Celltone** contains data for a random sample of 200 customers.

   a. Compute the sample proportion of Business Plan customers.

   b. What is the probability that a sample will contain a proportion as extreme as or more extreme than the one computed in part a if the 40% figure is correct for the population?

   c. Based on the result in part b, what conclusion should the owners reach about their assumption regarding Business Plan customers? Discuss.

CASE 6-A

Carpita Bottling Company

Don Carpita owns and operates Carpita Bottling Company in Lakeland, Wisconsin. The company bottles soda pop and beer, and also distributes the products in the counties surrounding Lakeland.

   The company has four bottling machines, which can be adjusted to fill bottles at any mean fill level between 2 ounces

and 72 ounces. The machines exhibit some variation in actual fill from the mean setting. For instance, if the mean setting is 16 ounces, the actual fill may be slightly more or slightly less than that amount.

   Three of the four filling machines are relatively new and their fill variation is not as great as that of the older machine.

Don has observed that the standard deviation in fill for the three new machines is about 1% of the mean fill level when the mean fill is set at 16 ounces or less and 0.5% of the mean at settings exceeding 16 ounces. The older machine has a standard deviation of about 1.5% of the mean setting regardless of the mean fill setting. However, the older machine tends to underfill bottles more than overfill, so the older machine is set at a mean fill slightly in excess of the desired mean to compensate for the propensity to underfill. For example, when 16-ounce bottles are to be filled, the machine is set at a mean fill level of 16.05 ounces.

The company can simultaneously fill bottles with two brands of soda pop using two machines, and it can use the other two machines to bottle beer. Although each filling machine has its own warehouse and the products are loaded from the warehouse directly on a truck, products from two or more filling machines may be loaded on the same truck. However, an individual store almost always receives bottles on a particular day from just one machine.

On Saturday morning Don received a call at home from the J. R. Summers Grocery store manager. She was very upset because the shipment of 16-ounce bottles of beer received yesterday contained several bottles that were not adequately filled. The manager wanted Don to replace the entire shipment at once.

Don gulped down his coffee and prepared to head for the store to check out the problem. He started thinking how he could determine which machine was responsible for the problem. If he could at least determine whether it was the old machine or one of the new ones, he could save his maintenance people a lot of time and effort checking all the machines.

His plan was to select a sample of 64 bottles of beer from the store and measure the contents. Don figured that he might be able to determine, on the basis of the average contents, whether it is more likely that the beer was bottled by a new machine or by the old one.

The results of the sampling showed an average of 15.993 ounces. Now Don needs some help in determining whether a sample mean of 15.993 ounces or less is more likely to come from the new machines or the older machine.

CASE 6-B

Truck Safety Inspection

The Idaho Department of Law Enforcement, in conjunction with the federal government, recently began a truck inspection program in Idaho. The current inspection effort is limited to an inspection of only those trucks that visually appear to have some defect when they stop at one of the weigh stations in the state. The proposed inspection program will not be limited to trucks with visible defects, but it will potentially subject all trucks to a comprehensive safety inspection.

Jane Lund of the Department of Law Enforcement is in charge of the new program. She has stated that the ultimate objective of the new truck inspection program is to reduce the number of trucks with safety defects operating in Idaho. Ideally, all trucks passing through, or operating within, Idaho would be inspected once a month, and substantial penalties applied to operators if safety defects were discovered. Ms. Lund is confident that such an inspection program would, without fail, reduce the number of defective trucks operating on Idaho's highways. However, each safety inspection takes about an hour, and because of limited money to hire inspectors, Ms. Lund realizes that all trucks cannot be inspected. She also knows it is unrealistic to have trucks wait to be inspected until trucks ahead of them have been checked. Such delays would cause problems with the drivers.

In meetings with her staff, Jane has suggested that before the inspection program begins, the number of defective trucks currently operating in Idaho needs to be estimated. This estimate can be compared with later estimates to see if the inspection program has been effective. To arrive at this initial estimate, Ms. Lund thinks that some sort of sampling plan to select representative trucks from the population for all trucks in Idaho must be developed. She has suggested that this sampling be done at the eight weigh stations near Idaho's borders, but she is unsure how to establish a statistically sound sampling plan that is practical to implement.

CASE 6-C

Houston Nut and Candy Company

Bruce Houston wanted to get away from the office and start on a much-needed vacation that he and his family had been planning for some time. He really needed to get his packing done if they were going to make their 8:00 P.M. flight for Honolulu. But he also knew that he needed to get a potential problem straightened out before he left, or he wouldn't be able to enjoy the sun and beaches of Hawaii.

Earlier in the day, Helen Stahl in quality assurance had dropped by his office with several e-mail messages she had received from customers in the past few days. The three e-mail messages all contained essentially the same message: "Your gourmet mixed nuts contain too many peanuts!" Helen indicated that as far as she knew there was nothing wrong with the production process. The company's standard calls for no more than 30% peanuts in the gourmet mix. Obviously, some cans will contain more, some less, but overall the proportion should not exceed 30%. The production line controls this by starting with fixed quantities of nuts that go into the storage vats that lead to the filling machine.

Helen assured Bruce that the vats started with 30% peanuts, 30% cashews, and 40% walnuts and other varieties. These nuts are thoroughly mixed and then the cans are filled. According to Helen, the contents of each can be considered a random sample of the total production.

While Helen waited in his office, Bruce called one of the unhappy customers to see what the basis of his complaint was. This customer indicated that of the 345 nuts in a can, there were 125 peanuts while they would have expected no more than 103. A call to a second customer indicated that of 360 nuts in the can, 144 were peanuts. Bruce called the third customer and heard similar results.

After Helen left, Bruce decided to assign Helen two tasks. First he wanted her to determine the chances of other customers getting the results that were reported by the unhappy customers if the process proportion of peanuts is really 30%. Second, Bruce reasoned that if the vats started out with 30% peanuts, about half the cans would have more than 30% and half would have less than 30% by chance. He decided to have Helen open a random sample of 100 cans. For each can, she was to record whether the can contained more than 30% peanuts. Then, he wanted her to compute the probability of finding whatever result she found assuming that the proportion of cans with more than 30% peanuts was equal to 0.50. Finally, he wanted her to write him a short report summarizing the results along with suggestions for how they might improve things if improvement was needed. (The data file **Nuts** contains the results of the sample of 100 cans.)

Bruce e-mailed these instructions to Helen, shut off his lights, said good-bye to Gladys at the front desk, and headed for home.

CASE 6-D

High Country

Ed Sharperson returned to his office dumbfounded by the reception he received on the carefully crafted marketing plan he created for High Country Ale, a potential new entry in the non-alcoholic beer market. Ed contended a well-planned entry into this market had a high probability of success for two reasons:

1. Recent data showed that the North American public is increasing its beer consumption.
2. The health and safety concerns about alcohol continue.

Ed's in-house testing has indicated that the product development group has done an outstanding job designing a

process for removing the alcohol from beer and that the average person could not tell the difference between High Country Ale and any of the leading brands. His marketing campaign would be based on a take-off of the famous Schlitz Beer commercials of the early 1980s. The Schlitz commercials, which were run live, involved 100 Budweiser drinkers who were given two unidentified glasses of beer and asked to indicate which they liked better. Since the typical person cannot tell the difference between beers, about 50% said they preferred Schlitz.

Ed's plan was to run a series of live commercials, have 100 beer drinkers taste an unidentified glass of High Country Ale and each of the leading brands, find 50% preferring High

Country Ale, and follow this with a campaign featuring the slogan, "Nonalcoholic—but tastes like real beer."

Christina Horowitz, the vice president of marketing, complimented Ed on his "open-minded approach to marketing campaigns"—a phrase that always made him uneasy. She then asked a series of questions that Ed was unable to answer directly, such as, "What procedures are you going to use to select the 100 people for the ad to ensure that the viewers do not think we have stacked the deck?" "While the overall average may well be 50%, getting one group that had only 45%, or 40%, or even 35% prefer High Country Ale would be hard to explain. Could that happen?" "What would be the implica-tions of a series of taste tests, all of which resulted in less than 50% preferring High Country? How about three or four tests where less than 40% prefer High Country? Could anything like this happen?" "Also, viewers would probably not believe a group that showed 65% or 70% preferring High Country Ale. Could that happen?"

Ed assured her none of these issues would be a problem, but Christina said she needed more than his statement to approve the marketing campaign. Ed walked back to his office thinking about how some people always see problems where none exist. But he also vowed to be able to provide logical answers to her questions.

■ GENERAL REFERENCES

1. Albright, S. Christian, Wayne L. Winston, and Christopher Zappe, *Data Analysis and Decision Making with Microsoft Excel* (Pacific Grove, CA: Duxbury, 1999).
2. Berenson, Mark L., and David M. Levine, *Basic Business Statistics: Concepts and Applications*, 7th ed. (Upper Saddle River, NJ: Prentice Hall, 1999).
3. Cochran, William G., *Sampling Techniques*, 3d ed. (New York, NY: Wiley, 1977).
4. Dodge, Mark, and Craig Stinson, *Running Microsoft Excel 2000* (Redmond, WA: Microsoft Press, 1999).
5. Hogg, R. V., and Elliot A. Tanis, *Probability and Statistical Inference*, 5th ed. (Upper Saddle River, NJ: Prentice Hall, 1997).
6. Johnson, Richard A., and Dean W. Wichern, *Business Statistics: Decision Making with Data* (New York, NY: Wiley, 1997).
7. *Microsoft Excel 2000* (Redmond, WA: Microsoft Corporation, 1999).
8. *Minitab for Windows Version 13* (State College, PA: Minitab, Inc., 2000).

ESTIMATING POPULATION VALUES

CHAPTER OUTCOMES

After studying the material in Chapter 7, you should be able to:

7-1: Distinguish the difference between a point estimate and a confidence interval estimate.

7-2: Construct and interpret a confidence interval estimate for a single population mean using both the standard normal and *t* distributions.

7-3: Determine the required sample size for estimating a single population mean.

7-4: Establish and interpret a confidence interval estimate for a single population proportion.

WHY YOU NEED TO KNOW

Regardless of where in business you find yourself working, you will have a need to know population values *(parameters)* to assist you in your decision making. An accountant needs to know the percentage of accounts payable accounts with correct balances. A marketing manager needs to know the average income in her target market area. A manufacturing manager needs to know the average machine downtime at a machine center in his plant. The programming manager at a major television network needs to know the percentage of potential viewers who watch his station's programs so that he knows which programs to retain and which to cancel. A restaurant manager needs to know the percentage of customers who will order the daily special so she knows how many orders to have available. A taxi company needs to know the difference in average miles per gallon between two models of taxicabs under consideration for purchase.

In these cases, and many others like them, decision makers need to know a population parameter. But gaining access to the entire population is extremely expensive, time consuming and, in many cases, infeasible. Therefore, an alternative approach is to select a sample from the population. The sample data are used to compute the desired statistic that forms an estimate of the corresponding population parameter.

Chapter 1 discussed various sampling techniques including both statistical and nonstatistical methods. Chapter 6 introduced the concepts of sampling error and sampling distributions. Chapter 7 builds on these concepts and introduces the steps needed to develop and interpret statistical estimations of various population values. The concepts introduced here will be very useful. You will undoubtedly need to estimate population parameters as a regular part of your managerial decision making activities. In addition, you will receive estimates that other people have developed which you will need to evaluate prior to relying on them as inputs to your decision making process. Was the sample size sufficiently large to provide usable estimates of the population parameter? How confident can I be that the estimate matches the population parameter of interest? These, and other similar questions, can all be answered using the concepts and tools presented in this chapter.

■ 7-1: POINT AND CONFIDENCE INTERVAL ESTIMATES

No doubt, you have either been a respondent to, or have seen the results of a political poll taken during an election year. These polls attempt to determine the percentage of voters who will favor a particular candidate or a particular issue. For example, suppose a poll indicates that 62% of the people over 18 years of age in your state favor limiting property taxes to 1% of the market value of the property. The pollsters have not contacted every person in the state, but rather have sampled only a relatively few people to arrive at the 62% figure. In statistical terminology, the 62% is the **point estimate** for the true population percentage who favor the property tax limitation.

POINT ESTIMATE
A single number determined from a sample that is used to estimate the corresponding population parameter.

The Environmental Protection Agency (EPA) tests automobile models sold in the United States to determine their mileage ratings. Following the testing, each model is assigned an EPA mileage rating based on the test mileage. This rating is actually a point estimate for the true average mileage of all cars of the given model.

Cost accountants make detailed studies of their company's production process to determine the costs of producing each product. These costs are often found by selecting a sample of items and following each item through the complete production process. The costs at each step in the process are determined, and the total cost is found when the process is completed. The accountants calculate the average cost for the items sampled and use this figure as the point estimate for the true average cost of all items produced. The point estimate becomes the basis for assigning a selling price to the finished product.

Which point estimator the decision maker uses depends on the population characteristic the decision maker wishes to estimate. However, regardless of the population value being estimated, we always expect **sampling error**.

SAMPLING ERROR

The difference between a value (a statistic) computed from a sample and the corresponding value (a parameter) computed from the population.

Confidence Interval Estimate of the Mean, σ Known

Chapter 6 discussed sampling error. We cannot eliminate sampling error, but we can deal with it in our decision process. For example, when cost accountants use $\bar{x}$, the average cost of a sample of items, to establish the average production cost, the point estimate, $\bar{x}$, will most likely not equal the population mean, μ. But with $\bar{x}$ as their only information, they will have no way of determining how large the sampling error is.

To overcome this problem with point estimates, the most common procedure is to calculate an interval estimate known as a **confidence interval.**

CONFIDENCE INTERVAL

An interval developed from sample values such that if all possible intervals of a given width were constructed, a percentage of these intervals, known as the confidence level, would include the true population parameter.

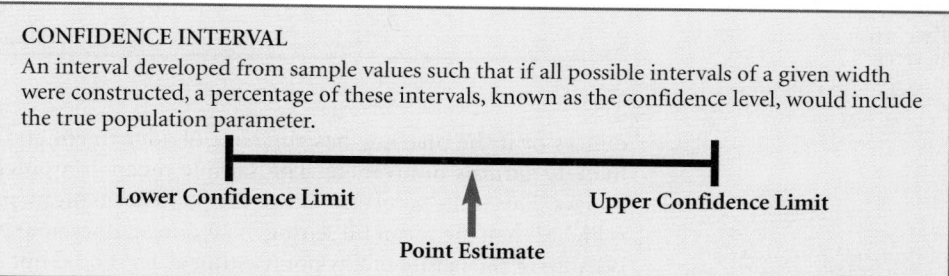

Lower Confidence Limit   Upper Confidence Limit

Point Estimate

The method for computing the upper and lower confidence limits is shown in the next example.

OPTIONAL CD-ROM TOPIC How Estimation Is Like Playing Darts and Horseshoes—An Analogy
It may be helpful to relate statistical estimation concepts to two common games. You will be surprised by the similarities. For more information, go to the CD-ROM.

EXAMPLE 7-1

INTERVAL ESTIMATION

Excel and Minitab Tutorial

Nagel Beverage Company

The production manager of the Nagel Beverage Company is responsible for monitoring the filling operations of soft drink cans. His company has recently installed a new machine. The filling machine has an adjustment that allows the operator to adjust the mean fill level. However, no matter what the mean setting, the individual cans will vary with respect to the actual volume. The machine has been carefully tested and is known to fill cans with a standard deviation of $\sigma = 0.2$ ounces.

The filling machine has been adjusted to fill cans at an average of 12 ounces. After running the machine for several hours, a sample of 100 cans is selected and the volume in each can is measured in the company's quality lab. Figure 7-1 shows the frequency histogram of the sample data. (The data are in a file on your CD-ROM called **Nagel-Beverage.**) Notice, the distribution seems to be centered at a value higher than 12 ounces.

The manager will use the sample data to estimate the mean fill amount for all cans filled by this machine. Based on this estimate, he will determine if the average is still 12

Excel Instructions:

1. Open file: Nagel–Beverage.xls
2. Create bins (upper limit of each class)
3. Select Tools
4. Select Histogram
5. Define data and bins ranges
6. Label bins as desired
7. Check Chart Output

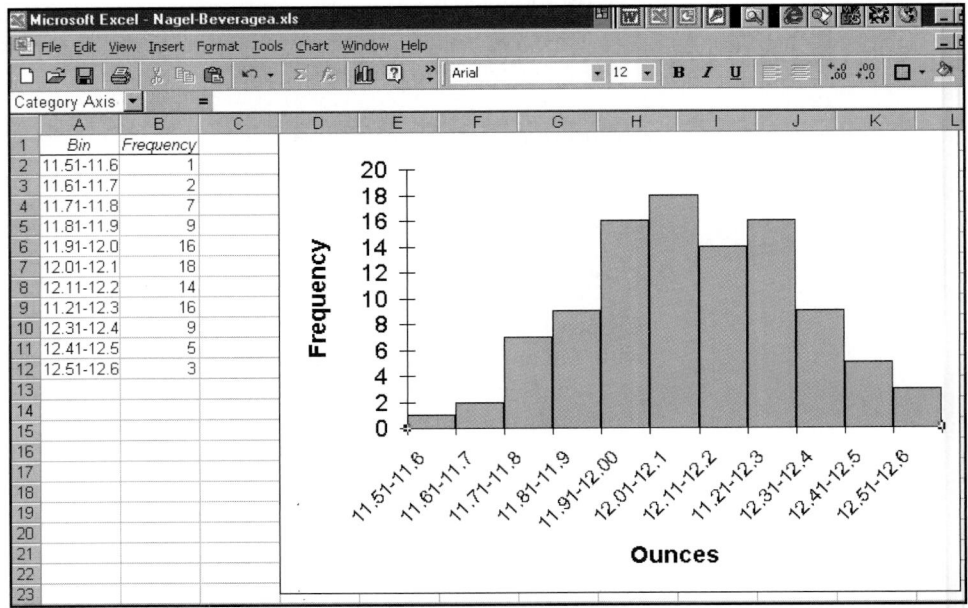

Bin	Frequency
11.51-11.6	1
11.61-11.7	2
11.71-11.8	7
11.81-11.9	9
11.91-12.0	16
12.01-12.1	18
12.11-12.2	14
11.21-12.3	16
12.31-12.4	9
12.41-12.5	5
12.51-12.6	3

FIGURE 7-1
Excel Histogram for Nagel Beverage

ounces or if the machine has gone out of adjustment and is now putting in more or less than 12 ounces on average. The sample mean computed from 100 cans is $\bar{x} = 12.09$ ounces. This is the *point estimate* of the population mean, μ. The fact that the sample mean is higher than the mean fill setting of 12 ounces does not necessarily mean that μ is not 12. Because of the nature of any point estimate, he should not expect a particular $\bar{x}$ to equal μ.

He also knows from the Central Limit Theorem that the distribution of all possible sample means will be approximately normally distributed around the population mean. This is illustrated in Figure 7-2.

Although the machine has been set to fill cans with $\mu = 12$ ounces, the mean fill level may have changed if the equipment has gone out of adjustment. Based on $\bar{x} = 12.09$ ounces, is μ still 12 ounces or has it shifted? To answer this question, the manager can develop a *confidence interval* for μ. This estimate will take the form:

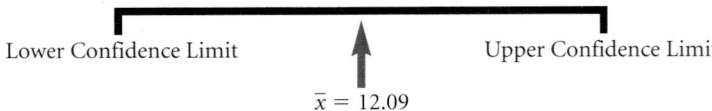

Lower Confidence Limit   Upper Confidence Limit

$\bar{x} = 12.09$

FIGURE 7-2
Sampling Distribution of $\bar{x}$

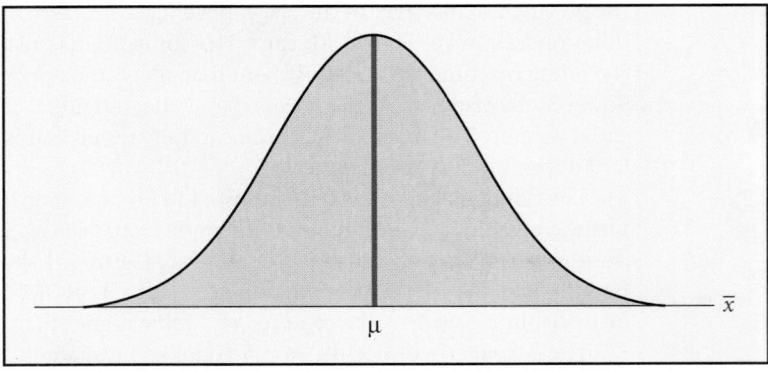

The key now is to determine the upper and lower limits of the interval. The method for computing these values depends on whether the population standard deviation, σ, is known or unknown. We first consider situations where σ is known.

There are two cases that must be considered. In the first case, in which the sample is drawn from a normal distribution with a mean of μ and a standard deviation of σ, the sampling distribution of the sample mean is a normal distribution with a mean of μ and a standard deviation of $\sigma/\sqrt{n}$. This is true for any sample size.

The second case is that in which the population does not have a normal distribution. Chapter 6 addressed these specific circumstances. Recall that in such cases, the Central Limit Theorem can be invoked if the sample size is sufficiently large ($n \geq 30$). In such cases, the sampling distribution is also a normal distribution with a mean of μ and a standard deviation of $\sigma/\sqrt{n}$.

In both cases, a confidence interval can be constructed from a basic probability statement. Consider the following equation represented by Figure 7-3 concerning the standard normal distribution.[1]

$$P(-1.96 \leq z \leq 1.96) = 0.95$$

The z-values have a normal distribution with a mean of 0 and a standard deviation of 1. Thus, 95% of the z-values are within 1.96 standard deviations of their mean, 0. Given that the sampling distribution of $\bar{x}$ is also normally distributed, then 95% of the possible sample means must be within 1.96 standard deviations of the population mean, μ. Since the standard deviation of the distribution of sample means is $\dfrac{\sigma}{\sqrt{n}}$, there is a 95% chance that the sample mean will be within $\pm 1.96\dfrac{\sigma}{\sqrt{n}}$ of the population mean, μ. Thus, 95% of all interval estimates formed as

$$\bar{x} - 1.96\frac{\sigma}{\sqrt{n}} \text{\qquad\qquad} \bar{x} + 1.96\frac{\sigma}{\sqrt{n}}$$

will contain the population mean. This concept can be generalized to any probability by replacing the value 1.96 with the appropriate z-value.

FIGURE 7-3
Critical Value for a 95% Confidence Interval

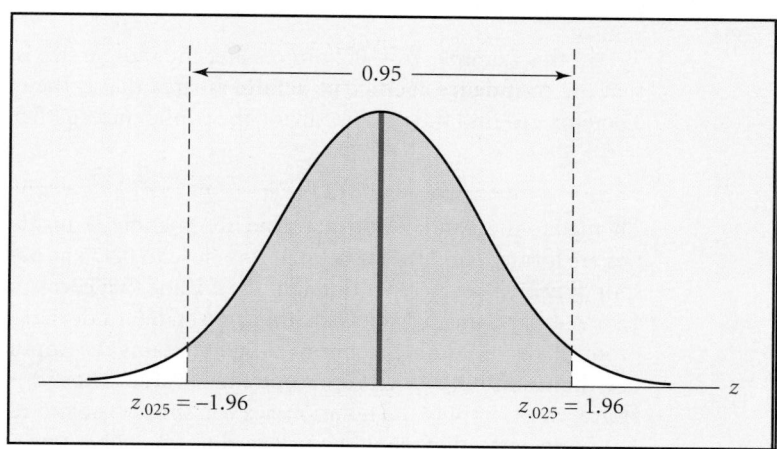

$z_{.025} = -1.96$ $z_{.025} = 1.96$

[1]Look to the standard normal distribution table for $z = 1.96$. The value there is 0.4750 which corresponds to $P(0 \leq z \leq 1.96)$. Then, likewise, $P(-1.96 \leq z \leq 0) = 0.4750$. The sum of these two probabilities $= 0.95$.

Theorem 6-1 →

CONFIDENCE INTERVAL CALCULATION

All confidence interval estimates can be constructed using the same logic just shown. The general format is shown in Equation 7-1.

CONFIDENCE INTERVAL (GENERAL FORMAT)

Point Estimate $\pm$ (Critical Value)(Standard Error)   **7-1**

The first step in developing a confidence interval estimate is to specify the **confidence level** that is needed to determine the *critical value*.

CONFIDENCE LEVEL

Percentage greater than 50 and less than 100 that corresponds to the percentage of all possible confidence intervals, based on a given size sample, that will contain the true population value.

CONFIDENCE COEFFICIENT

The confidence level divided by 100%—i.e., the decimal equivalent of a confidence level.

EXAMPLE 7-2

INTERVAL ESTIMATION

Nagel Beverage (continued)

Suppose the Nagel Beverage manager specifies a 95% confidence level. This means the width of the interval estimate will be computed such that, of all the possible confidence intervals that could be created from a given sample size, 95% will contain the true mean fill level. The higher the confidence level, the better we feel about the one interval estimate that we will compute.

Once we decide on the confidence level, the next step is to determine the *critical value*. If the population standard deviation is known and the population is normally distributed, or if the sample size is large enough to comply with the Central Limit Theorem requirements, the *critical value is a z-value* from the standard normal table. Equation 7-2 shows a modified form of the general format for a confidence interval.

CONFIDENCE INTERVAL (GENERAL FORMAT)—σ KNOWN

Point Estimate $\pm$ z (Standard Error)   **7-2**

In this example, $\sigma = 0.2$ ounces and the sample size is 100. In Figure 7-3 you can see that the **confidence coefficient** defines an area that is the middle 95% of the distribution. Therefore, to find the z-value, divide the confidence coefficient by 2 giving:

$$\frac{0.95}{2} = 0.475$$

Then go to the standard normal table in Appendix D. Inside the table, where the probabilities are located, find the value that is as close to 0.475 as possible and determine the corresponding z-value. Here we find that the z-value that corresponds to a probability of 0.475 is 1.96. A sample mean that falls within 1.96 standard deviations of the population mean will produce a 95% confidence interval that contains the population mean. Some statisticians use the notation $z_{\alpha/2}$ to represent the z-value where $1 - \alpha =$ confidence coefficient. However, to simplify the notation, we will simply use z to represent the critical value.

Note, instead of using the standard normal table, you can also find the critical z-value using Excel's NORMSINV function by inserting a probability equal to $\alpha/2$. The critical z-value is the absolute value of the function result. For example, for a 95% confidence interval $\alpha = 0.05$ and $\alpha/2 = 0.025$. Then NORMSINV(0.025) $= -1.96$. The critical z is $|-1.96| = 1.96$.

The next step is to compute the *standard error* of the sampling distribution for $\bar{x}$. In Chapter 6, you learned the standard error of the sampling distribution for $\bar{x}$ is $\frac{\sigma}{\sqrt{n}}$. Then Equation 7-3 is used to compute the confidence interval estimate of a single population mean.

CONFIDENCE INTERVAL ESTIMATE FOR μ (σ KNOWN)

$$\bar{x} \pm z \frac{\sigma}{\sqrt{n}}$$

7-3

where:

z = Critical value from the standard normal distribution table
σ = Population standard deviation
n = Sample size

Recall the sample of 100 cans produced a sample mean, $\bar{x} = 12.09$. Thus, the 95% confidence interval estimate for the population mean is:

$$\bar{x} \pm z \frac{\sigma}{\sqrt{n}}$$

$$12.09 \pm 1.96 \frac{0.20}{\sqrt{100}}$$

$$12.09 \pm 0.039$$

$$12.051 \text{ ounces} \longrightarrow 12.129 \text{ ounces}$$

Thus, based on this sample information, the Nagel manager believes that the true mean fill for all cans is within the following range:

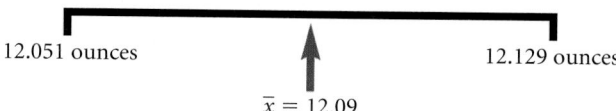

12.051 ounces   12.129 ounces

$\bar{x} = 12.09$

Since this interval does not contain the target mean of 12 ounces, the manager should conclude that the filling equipment is out of adjustment and is putting in too much soda, on average.

SPECIAL MESSAGE ABOUT INTERPRETING CONFIDENCE INTERVALS

There is a subtle distinction to be made here. Beginning students often wonder if it is permissible to say, "There is a 0.95 probability that the population mean is between 12.051 and 12.129 ounces." This may seem to be the logical consequence of constructing a confidence interval. However, we must be very careful to attribute probability only to random events or variables. Since the population mean is a fixed value, there can be no probability statement about the population mean. The confidence interval we have computed will either contain the population mean or it will not. If you were to produce all the possible confidence intervals using each possible sample mean from the population, 95% of these intervals would contain the population mean.

As shown in Equation 7-4, the quantity on the right of $\pm$ in Equations 7-2 and 7-3 is called the **margin of error**. The margin of error defines the relationship between the sample mean and the population mean.

MARGIN OF ERROR
The largest possible sampling error at the specified level of confidence.

Excel Simulation

Confidence
Interval
Estimation

MARGIN OF ERROR (ESTIMATE FOR μ WITH σ KNOWN)

$$e = z\frac{\sigma}{\sqrt{n}}$$

7-4

where:

$$e = \text{Margin of error}$$
$$z = \text{Critical value}$$
$$\frac{\sigma}{\sqrt{n}} = \text{Standard error of the sampling distribution}$$

In this example, the margin of error is:

$$e = 1.96\frac{0.2}{\sqrt{100}} = 0.039$$

Thus, with 95% confidence managers at Nagel Beverage can conclude that the true population mean fill is no more than 0.039 ounces from the sample mean of 12.09 ounces.

IMPACT OF THE CONFIDENCE LEVEL

Nagel Beverage (continued)

In the Nagel Beverage example, the manager specified a 95% confidence level. Instead, suppose he is willing to settle for 80% confidence. This will impact the critical value. To determine the new critical value, divide 0.80 by 2 giving 0.40. Go to the standard normal table and locate a probability value (area under the curve) that is as close to 0.40 as possible. The corresponding z-value is 1.28.[2] The 80% confidence interval estimate is:

$$\bar{x} \pm z\frac{\sigma}{\sqrt{n}}$$

$$12.09 \pm (1.28)\frac{0.2}{\sqrt{100}}$$

$$12.09 \pm .026$$

12.064 ounces ——————————— 12.116 ounces

Thus, based on this sample information and the 80% confidence interval, we believe that the true average fill level is between 12.064 ounces and 12.116 ounces.

By lowering the confidence level, the method used to produce the interval is less likely to contain the population mean. However, on the positive side, the margin of error has been reduced from 0.039 ounces to 0.026 ounces. For equivalent size samples from a population:

1. If the confidence level is decreased, the margin of error is reduced.
2. If the confidence level is increased, the margin of error is increased.

Lowering the confidence level is one way to reduce the margin of error. However, by examining Equation 7-4, you will note that there are two other values that affect the margin of error. One of these is the population standard deviation. The more the population's standard deviation, σ, can be reduced, the smaller the margin of error will be. In a business environment large standard deviations for measurements related to the quality of a product, for instance are not desired. In fact, corporations spend considerable effort to decrease the variation in their products. Typically, all avenues for reducing the standard deviation should be pursued before thoughts of reducing the confidence level are entertained.

EXAMPLE
7-3

**INTERVAL
ESTIMATION**

---

[2]You can also use Excel's NORMSINV function = NORMSINV(0.10) = 1.281.

However, there are many situations where reducing the population standard deviation is not possible. In these cases, another step that can be taken to reduce the margin of error is to increase the sample size. As you learned in Chapter 6, an increase in sample size reduces the standard deviation of the sampling distribution. This can be the most direct way of reducing the margin of error as long as obtaining an increased sample is not prohibitively costly or unattainable for other reasons.

IMPACT OF SAMPLE SIZE

EXAMPLE 7-4

INTERVAL ESTIMATION

Nagel Beverage (continued)

We have seen in the Nagel Beverage example that the margin of error can be reduced if we are willing to reduce our confidence level. The downside of this is that we don't feel as confident about any conclusion we draw when it is based on reduced confidence. Suppose the Nagel Beverage Company production manager decided to increase the sample to 400 cans. This is a four-fold increase over the original sample size. We learned in Chapter 6 that an increase in sample size reduces the standard deviation of the sampling distribution since the

standard deviation is computed as $\dfrac{\sigma}{\sqrt{n}}$. Thus, without adversely impacting his confidence

level, the manager can reduce the margin of error by increasing his sample size.

Assuming that by chance the sample mean for the larger sample size is found to be $\bar{x} = 12.09$ ounces, then the new 95% confidence interval estimate is:

$$12.09 \pm 1.96 \, \frac{0.2}{\sqrt{400}}$$

$$12.09 \pm 0.0196$$

$$12.0704 \text{ ounces} \underline{\hspace{3cm}} 12.1096 \text{ ounces}$$

Based on the sample information and the 95% confidence interval, the manager estimates the true population mean to be between 12.0704 ounces and 12.1096 ounces. Notice that by increasing the sample size to 400 cans, the margin of error is reduced from the original 0.039 ounces to 0.0196 ounces. The production manager now believes that 95% of the possible sample means would be within ± 0.0196 ounces of the true population mean.

He was able to achieve this reduction in margin of error without reducing the confidence level. However, the downside is that taking a sample of 400 cans instead of 100 cans will cost more money and take more time. That's the trade-off. Absent the possibility of reducing the population standard deviation, if he wants to reduce the margin of error, he must either reduce the confidence level or increase the sample size or some combination of each. If he is unwilling to do so, he will have to accept the larger margin of error.

Confidence Interval Estimates—σ Unknown

In the Nagel Beverage Company example, the manager was dealing with a filling machine that had a known standard deviation in fill volume. You may encounter applications when the standard deviation is known. However, in most cases, if you don't know the population mean, you also will not know the standard deviation. When this occurs you need to make a minor, but important, modification to the confidence interval estimation process.

EXAMPLE 7-5

INTERVAL ESTIMATION

Excel and Minitab Tutorial

Heritage Software

Heritage Software, a maker of educational and business software, operates a service center in Tulsa, Oklahoma, where employees respond to customers calling with questions and problems that relate to the various software packages the company sells. Heritage has enjoyed a competitive advantage because it has the correct staffing to meet the call demand. Recently, a team of Heritage managers and employees were charged with studying call data and making staffing recommendations to upper management.

One factor of interest to the team was the average length of time service representatives spend with customers. Since the company does not have an automated system for tracking the length of time calls take, the team decided that a sample of 100 calls would be collected and the population mean call time would be estimated based on the sample data. Not only did the team not know the average length of time, μ, they also didn't know the standard deviation of service time length, σ, either.

When the population standard deviation is known, the sampling distribution of the mean has only one unknown parameter: its mean, μ. This is estimated by $\bar{x}$. However, when the population standard deviation is unknown there are two unknown parameters, μ and σ, that must be estimated by $\bar{x}$ and s, respectively. This doesn't affect the general format for a confidence interval as shown earlier as Equation 7-1:

$$\text{Point Estimate} \pm (\text{Critical Value})(\text{Standard Error})$$

However, not knowing the population standard deviation does affect the critical value. Recall that when σ is known and the population is normally distributed or the Central Limit Theorem applies, the critical value is a z-value taken from the standard normal table. But when σ is not known, the critical value is a *t-value* taken from a distribution called the **Student's t-distribution.**

Excel Simulation

t-Distribution

STUDENT'S t-DISTRIBUTION

A family of distributions that is bell-shaped and symmetric like the standard normal distribution but with greater area in the tails. Each distribution in the t-family is defined by its degrees of freedom. As the degrees of freedom increase, the t-distribution approaches the normal distribution.

Since the specific t-distribution chosen is based upon its *degrees of freedom*, it is important to understand what the term degrees of freedom means. Recall that the sample standard deviation is an estimate of the population's standard deviation and is defined as follows.

$$s = \sqrt{\frac{\sum (x - \bar{x})^2}{n - 1}}$$

Therefore, if we wish to estimate the population standard deviation we must first calculate the sample mean. The sample mean is itself an estimator of a parameter, namely the population mean. The sample mean is obtained from a sample of n randomly chosen (and, therefore, independent) data values. Once the sample mean has been obtained there are only $n - 1$ independent pieces of data information left in the sample.

To illustrate, examine a sample of size $n = 3$ in which the sample mean is calculated to be 12. This implies that the sum of the three data values equals 36 (3×12). If you know that the first two data values are 10 and 8, respectively, then the third data value must be 18. Similarly, if you know that the first two data values were 18 and 7, respectively, the third data value must be 11. You are free to choose any two of the three data values. In general, if you must estimate k parameters before you are able to estimate the population's standard deviation from a sample of n data values, you have the freedom to choose any $n - k$ data values before the remaining k values are determined. This value, $n - k$, is called the **degrees of freedom.**

DEGREES OF FREEDOM

The number of independent data values available to estimate the population's standard deviation. If k parameters must be estimated before the population's standard deviation can be calculated from a sample of size n, the degrees of freedom are equal to $n - k$.

When the population is normally distributed, the t-value represents the number of estimated standard errors $\bar{x}$ is from μ, as shown in Equation 7-5.

$$t\text{-VALUE}$$

$$t = \frac{\bar{x} - \mu}{\frac{s}{\sqrt{n}}} \qquad \qquad 7\text{-}5$$

where:

$\bar{x}$ = Sample mean
μ = Population mean
s = Sample standard deviation
n = Sample size

Appendix F contains a table of t-values that correspond to specified tail areas and different degrees of freedom. The t-table is used to determine the critical value when we do not know the population standard deviation. Note, in Equation 7-5 we use the sample standard deviation, s, to estimate the population standard deviation, σ. The fact that we are estimating σ is the reason the t-distribution is more spread out (i.e., has a larger standard deviation) than the normal distribution (see Figure 7-4). By estimating σ, we are introducing more uncertainty into the estimation process; so to achieve the same level of confidence requires a larger number of standard deviations. As the sample size increases, our estimate of σ becomes better and the t-distribution converges to the z-distribution.

We should emphasize that the t-distribution is based on the assumption that the population is normally distributed. Although beyond the scope of this text, it can be shown that as long as the population is reasonably symmetric, the t-distribution can be used.

The managers at Heritage Software are willing to assume the population of call times is approximately normal.[3] Table 7-1 shows the sample data for 100 calls. (These data are on your CD-ROM in a file called **Heritage.**)

Heritage's sample mean and standard deviation are:

$$\bar{x} = 7.52 \text{ minutes}$$
$$s = 4.41 \text{ minutes}$$

If the managers need a single valued estimate of the population mean, they would use the point estimate, $\bar{x} = 7.52$ minutes. However, they should realize that this point estimate is subject to sampling error. To take the sampling error into account, the managers can con-

FIGURE 7-4
t-Distribution and Normal Distribution

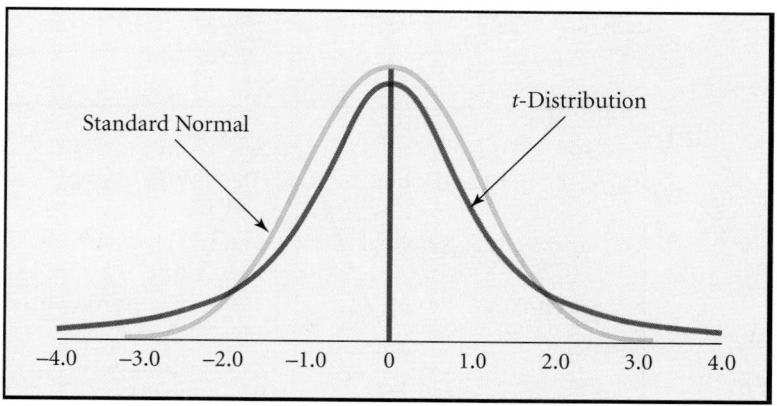

[3]Chapter 14 introduces a statistical technique called goodness-of-fit that can be used to test whether the sample data could have come from a normally distributed population.

7.1	12.4	0.4	13.9	13.5	1.4	7.6	5.5	6.6	2.5
13.6	11.0	11.0	10.8	9.9	4.7	1.3	7.6	10.2	4.3
1.4	3.7	0.8	15.3	3.2	13.8	8.4	16.9	3.6	7.7
3.6	14.6	6.4	6.8	7.4	2.5	9.4	17.1	10.0	1.9
1.9	8.8	9.1	5.0	11.0	3.4	7.8	9.8	9.8	6.5
11.6	8.5	14.3	6.1	1.7	5.5	12.8	8.3	11.2	4.5
1.7	6.1	0.4	15.6	5.0	13.9	0.1	7.8	4.7	11.6
16.9	3.3	9.1	16.6	5.3	11.1	4.4	6.7	2.7	7.9
2.6	6.1	9.7	10.2	4.4	7.3	5.5	1.3	7.0	13.7
7.7	6.9	12.5	5.8	0.9	11.8	8.1	3.3	6.7	2.4

TABLE 7-1
Sample Call Times for
Heritage Software

struct a confidence interval estimate. Equation 7-6 shows the formula for the confidence interval where the standard deviation is unknown.

CONFIDENCE INTERVAL (σ UNKNOWN)

$$\bar{x} \pm t \frac{s}{\sqrt{n}}$$

7-6

where:

$\bar{x}$ = Sample mean
t = Critical value from the t-distribution with $n - 1$ degrees of freedom
s = Sample standard deviation
n = Sample size

The first step is to specify the desired confidence level. For example, suppose the Heritage team specifies a 95% confidence level. Dividing 0.95 by 2 we get:

$$\frac{0.95}{2} = 0.475$$

Subtracting 0.475 from 0.500 we get 0.025. This is the upper tail area to use when getting the t-value from the t-table in Appendix F. Next, go to the row corresponding to $n - 1$ ($100 - 1 = 99$) degrees of freedom. Go across to the column headed 0.025 to get the t-value equal to 1.9842. Figure 7-5 illustrates the t-distribution and the critical value. Note, the t-value from the lower tail is -1.9842 as shown in Figure 7-5. You can also get the t-critical value by using Excel's TINV function. For this example, enter TINV(.05,99) to get 1.9842.

FIGURE 7-5
The Critical t-Value for
Heritage Software

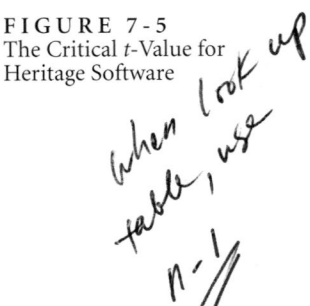

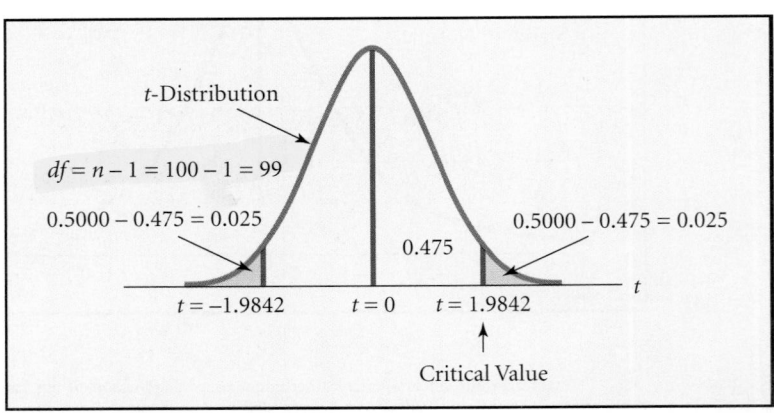

	A	B
1	Column1	
2		
3	Mean	7.522
4	Standard Error	0.441401762
5	Median	7.2
6	Mode	11
7	Standard Deviation	4.414017616
8	Sample Variance	19.48355152
9	Kurtosis	-0.713044427
10	Skewness	0.310531409
11	Range	17
12	Minimum	0.1
13	Maximum	17.1
14	Sum	752.2
15	Count	100
16	Confidence Level(95.0%)	0.875837014

$\bar{x} = 7.522$

Confidence interval estimate 7.52 ± 0.876
6.644 ———— 8.396

Margin of error

FIGURE 7-6
Excel Output for the Heritage Example

The Heritage team can now compute the 95% confidence interval estimate using Equation 7-6 as follows:

$$\bar{x} \pm t\frac{s}{\sqrt{n}}$$

$$7.52 \pm 1.9842\frac{4.41}{\sqrt{100}}$$

$$7.52 \pm 0.875$$
6.645 min. ——————— 8.395 min.

Therefore, based on the random sample of 100 calls and a 95% confidence interval, the Heritage Software team has estimated the true average time per call to be between 6.645 minutes and 8.395 minutes.

Excel and Minitab have procedures for computing the confidence interval estimate of the population mean. The Excel output is shown in Figure 7-6. Note that the margin of error is printed. You will actually have to use it and the sample mean to compute the upper and lower limits. Figure 7-7 shows the results when Minitab is used to compute the 95% confidence interval estimate for the Heritage Company. The Excel and Minitab results are slightly different from the manual computations due to rounding differences.

FIGURE 7-7
Minitab Output for the Heritage Example

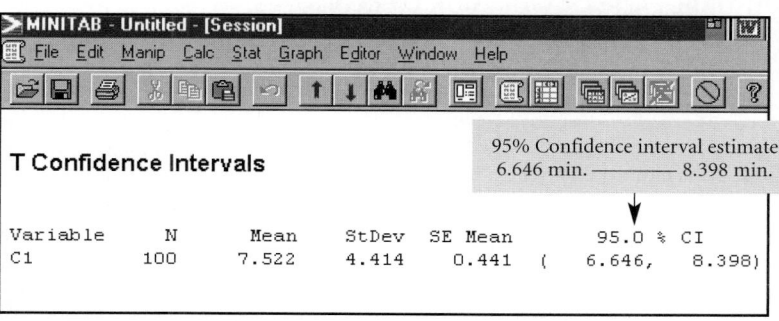

T Confidence Intervals

95% Confidence interval estimate
6.646 min. ——————— 8.398 min.

Variable	N	Mean	StDev	SE Mean	95.0 % CI
C1	100	7.522	4.414	0.441	(6.646, 8.398)

ESTIMATION WITH LARGER SAMPLE SIZES

We saw earlier that a change in sample size can affect the margin of error in a statistical estimation situation when the population standard deviation is known. This is also true in applications where the standard deviation is not known. In fact, the effect of a change is compounded because the change in sample size affects both the calculation of the standard error and the critical value from the *t*-distribution.

The *t*-distribution table in Appendix F shows degrees of freedom up to 100. Observe that for any confidence level, as the degrees of freedom increase, the *t*-value gets smaller as it approaches a limit equal to the *z*-value from the standard normal table in Appendix D for the same confidence level. Therefore, if you need to estimate the population mean with a sample size exceeding 121, one option is to find the critical value in the *z*-table and then use Equation 7-7 to develop the confidence interval.

CONFIDENCE INTERVAL—LARGE SAMPLES WITH σ UNKNOWN

$$\bar{x} \pm z\frac{s}{\sqrt{n}} \qquad\qquad 7\text{-}7$$

where:

$\bar{x}$ = Sample mean
z = Value from the standard normal distribution
s = Sample standard deviation
n = Sample size

A second option is to use the Excel TINV function to get the critical *t*-value as mentioned earlier for any specified degrees of freedom and then use equation 7-6.[4]

Hopefully, you have noticed the format for confidence interval estimates for μ is essentially the same regardless of whether the population standard deviation is known or not. The basic format is always:

Point Estimate $\pm$ (Critical Value)(Standard Error)

Later in this chapter, we introduce estimation examples where the population value of interest is π, the population proportion. Regardless of the parameter of interest, the same confidence interval format is used. In addition, the trade-offs between margin of error, confidence level, and sample size that were discussed in this section also apply to every other estimation situation.

7-1: EXERCISES

ADDITIONAL EXERCISES ON YOUR CD-ROM
Try the ADDITIONAL EXERCISES and APPLICATION PROBLEMS on the CD-ROM.

7-1. Assume a sample of size *n* has been obtained from a normal distribution. Determine the critical value in each of the following cases:

a. Confidence coefficient = 0.95, $n = 35$, $s = 2.3$
b. Confidence coefficient = 0.90, $n = 31$, $\sigma = 3.6$

c. Confidence coefficient = 0.98, $n = 15$, $s = 4.7$
d. Confidence coefficient = 0.99, $n = 36$, $s = 4.6$
e. Confidence coefficient = 0.88, $n = 56$, $\sigma = 7.9$
f. Confidence coefficient = 0.90, $n = 41$, $s = 1.6$

---

[4]Minitab also has a *t*-distribution function that can be used to obtain a *t*-value for any number of degrees of freedom and any confidence level.

7-2. Assume a sample of size n has been obtained from a normal distribution. Determine the confidence level for each of the following intervals:

a. $\bar{x} \pm 2.086 \dfrac{3}{\sqrt{21}}$ where $n = 21$ and $s = 3$

b. $\bar{x} \pm 1.645 \dfrac{3}{\sqrt{11}}$ where $n = 11$ and $\sigma = 3$

c. $\bar{x} \pm 3.1465$ where $n = 30$ and $s = 7$

d. $\bar{x} \pm 0.6502$ where $n = 40$ and $\sigma = 2.5$

e. $\bar{x} \pm 7.4714$ where $n = 6$ and $s = 12.4$

7-3. Determine the 90% confidence interval estimate for the population mean of a normal distribution given the following information:

a. $\bar{x} = 102.36$, $n = 17$, $\sigma = 1.26$

b. $\bar{x} = 56.33$, $n = 21$, $s = 22.4$

c. $\bar{x} = 1.65$, $e = 1.756$

Business Applications

7-4. The Traveler Rent-A-Car Company is interested in estimating the mean number of miles its cars are driven on a particular holiday. It has 23,000 cars nationwide and samples 200 cars on the holiday in question. The mileage for each car was recorded. The following data were computed from the sample data:

$$\bar{x} = 54.5 \text{ miles}$$
$$s = 14.0 \text{ miles}$$

a. Produce a 95% confidence interval estimate for the mean miles driven for each car.

b. Traveler's vice president of operations received a report from a city in the company's southwestern region. It indicated the location had rented 200 cars during the holiday and had received $2,500 in fees charged for mileage. Assume that Traveler charges $0.25 per mile as a mileage fee. On the basis of the confidence interval calculated in part a, would you say that the vice president should investigate the billing practices of the location? Support your opinion with statistical reasoning and logic.

7-5. Referring to Problem 4, suppose the Traveler Rent-A-Car Company wishes to decrease the margin of error in the estimate for average miles driven per car per day. Discuss the three options available to the managers, and provide an example for each case that demonstrates your options actually do decrease the margin of error.

7-6. The First National Bank is considering a survey of its customers for the purpose of estimating the mean number of checks written per month. A sample of 360 customers was selected. The following sample values were recorded:

$$\bar{x} = 33.4$$
$$s = 11.2$$

a. Provide a 90% confidence interval estimate for the mean number of checks written and interpret the estimate.

b. Suppose a mistake was made in counting the number of customers that was surveyed, and the actual sample size was 36, not 360. Recompute the 90% confidence interval estimate, and compare it to the estimate developed in part a. Why are the estimates different even though the sample mean and standard deviation did not change?

c. First National is interested in opening another branch. Its demographic studies indicate that the branch will attract about 2,000 customers who will have checking accounts. The bank is attempting to prepare a system that would process the checks these customers would write. Would it be reasonable for them to install a system that would process 65,000 checks per month? Explain your answer and the logic that led you to this answer.

7-7. Agri-Beef, Inc., is a large midwestern farming operation. The company has been a leader in employing statistical analysis techniques in its business. Recently, John Goldberg, operations manager, requested that a random sample of cattle be selected and that these cattle be fed a special diet. The cattle were weighed before the start of the new feeding program and at the end of the feeding program. John wished to estimate the average daily weight gain for cattle on the new feed program. Two hundred cattle were tested, with the following sample results:

$$\bar{x} = 1.2 \text{ lb. per day gain}$$
$$s = 0.50 \text{ lb.}$$

a. Obtain a 95% confidence interval estimate for the true average daily weight gain.

b. Provide a 90% confidence interval estimate for the true average daily weight gain.

c. Discuss the difference between the two estimates found in parts a and b and indicate the advantages and disadvantages of each.

d. John is considering adopting this new diet. However, the weight gain comes at a price. To feed 200 cows for one month, the diet would cost approximately $1,000 more than their current feed program. If the price of beef on the hoof has been close to $0.20 a pound, would such a program be cost effective for Agri-Beef? Support your answer with calculations and statistical reasoning.

7-8. The Evergreen Company operates retail pharmacies in 10 eastern states. Recently, the company's internal audit department selected a random sample of 300 prescriptions issued throughout the system. The objective of the sampling was to estimate the average dollar value of all prescriptions issued by the company. The following data were collected:

$$\bar{x} = \$56.92$$
$$s = \$8.00$$

a. Determine the 90% confidence interval estimate for the true average sales value for prescriptions issued by the company. Interpret the interval estimate.

b. One of Evergreen's retail outlets recently reported that it had a monthly revenue of $29,568 from 528 prescriptions. Are such results to be expected? Do you believe that the retail outlet should be audited? Support your answer with calculations and logic.

7-9. Marine World—Africa USA is a facility located near San Francisco, California, where people can see animals from the ocean and from Africa on display and performing in shows. Customers pay for a day ticket and can stay as long as they wish. The management is interested in determining the average length of time customers spend at the park per day. They select a simple random sample of customers and ask them, as they leave the park, what time they arrived. They then determine the length of stay for each customer. A total of 144 customers were selected at random with the following sample results:

$$\bar{x} = 311 \text{ minutes}$$
$$s = 72 \text{ minutes}$$

a. Obtain a 90% confidence interval estimate for the mean time spent at the park. Interpret the interval estimate.
b. If park administration wishes to reduce the margin of error from that which you determined in part a, what options exist to do so? Discuss.

7-10. The Apex Entertainment Company owns and operates movie theaters in Wyoming. The president of the company is concerned that home videocassette recorders are hurting business because people can simply rent a movie and watch it at home. He has directed a staff member to estimate the mean number of movies rented by people in Wyoming in December. A phone survey involving a random sample of 300 homes in Wyoming was conducted, with the following results:

$$\bar{x} = 2.4 \text{ movies}$$
$$s = 1.6 \text{ movies}$$

a. Develop and interpret the 95% confidence interval estimate for the true mean number of movies rented per month.
b. The company president recalls that people in Wyoming watched 2.5 movies per month on average before movie rentals became popular. Determine the proportion of the residents of Wyoming homes that rent more than 2.5 movies per month. Assume that the population mean and standard deviation are approximately the same as those obtained from the sample and that the number of rentals per month has an approximate normal distribution.

7-11. A major American pharmaceutical company has randomly sampled 14 customers who have had prescriptions for one of their new pain killing drugs for 2 months. There is concern that the drug may elevate the user's heart rate. Each of the customers in the sample had his or her heart rate measured after using the drug for 1 week. All people in the

sample had heart rates of 55 prior to taking the drug. The following data were recorded for the 14 customers:

| 50 | 70 | 60 | 70 | 90 | 72 | 50 |
| 80 | 85 | 55 | 66 | 70 | 80 | 40 |

a. Suppose that you have just started working in the marketing department of the pharmaceutical company. You were given the following instructions: "Based on these sample data construct a 90% confidence interval estimate for the true mean heart rate for the company's drug customers. Interpret the estimate."
b. Referring to your answer in part a, can the estimate be applied to all potential drug customers? Explain why or why not.
c. Refer to your calculations in part a. Was the concern expressed justified? Justify your answer. If you conclude the average heart rate did not increase, determine the probability that a sample mean at least as large as the one obtained in your sample could actually have been obtained.

7-12. The Simmons Furniture Company selected a random sample of 9 sofas that were made at its Memphis factory. Each sofa was subjected to a test process that simulated people sitting on the cushions. The test requires that a heavy object be repeatedly dropped on the cushion until the fabric wears out. The following data reflect the number of drops that were recorded for each of the 9 sofas:

13,356	12,742	15,345
9,459	10,634	14,309
14,098	11,245	12,652

a. Obtain a 95% confidence interval estimate for the mean number of drops until the sofa cushions wear out. Interpret the result.
b. Simmons wishes to advertise that the sofa fabric will last at least 20 years. If a sofa is sat upon an average of once a day, could Simmons justify their proposed advertisement? Justify your answer.
c. Review parts a and b. How many possible values can the variable "number of drops" realistically have? Technically, could this population actually have a normal distribution? (Hint: Refer to the discussion of the normal distribution in Chapter 5.)

7-13. The Aims Investment Company is interested in estimating the average number of mutual funds its customers have in their portfolios. A random sample of investment customers is located in a file called **Aims** on your CD-ROM.
a. Based on the sample data, construct a 90% confidence interval estimate for the mean number of mutual funds for all their customers. Interpret this interval.
b. In an effort to diversify its customers' portfolios, Aims has been encouraging its agents to advise its cus-

tomers to have at least three mutual funds in their portfolios. If the mean for all of the customers is as large as the upper confidence limit in part a, estimate the proportion of its customers that actually have at least three mutual funds in their portfolios.

7-14. Refer to Problem 13.

a. Suppose that the interval estimate you computed has a margin of error that is greater than Aims management wants. Discuss what options are open to the Aims Company. What are the advantages and disadvantages of each option?

b. How many possible values can the variable "number of mutual funds in a customer's portfolio" realistically have? Technically, could this population actually have a normal distribution? Discuss.

7-15. The Ajax Taxi Company operates taxicabs in the Manhattan area of New York City. The dispatch manager is interested in estimating the average number of miles driven per vehicle per week. Each week for 40 weeks, she sampled 4 taxis and recorded their weekly miles. At the end of 40 weeks, she had accumulated a sample of 160 values.

a. Using the sample data in the file **Ajax** on your CD-ROM, compute the 98% confidence interval estimate for the mean miles per week per vehicle. Interpret your estimate.

b. Do you see any potential problems with the way the dispatch manager has collected the sample data? Discuss.

7-16. The file on your CD-ROM named **Banks** contains data for a group of U.S. banks. These banks are defined to be the population of interest. Suppose you have been hired as an economist for one of the banks on this list. You are interested in estimating the mean revenue per employee for all banks in the population. For the purposes of this exercise, a random sample of 10 banks from the list was selected and the following data were obtained:

Revenue (millions of dollars):	$13,219	10,098	5,270	4,585	2,078
Number of employees:	56,600	33,962	21,652	21,227	10,622

Revenue (millions of dollars):	$ 1,893	1,250	1,215	2,503	6,568
Number of employees:	7,755	5,114	7,496	10,311	24,595

a. Based on this information develop a 95% confidence interval estimate for the mean revenue per employee. Interpret the estimate. (Hint: Since the sample is large relative to the size of the population, you will need to use the finite population correction factor to adjust the standard error—See Chapter 6.)

b. Now compute the population mean revenue per employee and determine whether the interval estimate was accurate.

c. Construct a histogram of the data revenue per employee. Divide the data into 7 classes. Does this population appear to have a normal distribution? Can you justify the use of the t-distribution in the construction of the previous confidence interval?

7-17. Refer to Problem 16 and take a second random sample of 10 banks' revenues.

a. Compute the 95% confidence interval estimate for the mean revenue per employee and interpret it.

b. Compare this estimate to the one you computed in Problem 16.

c. Compare this interval estimate to the true population mean. Was this an accurate estimate? Make sure that you define what you mean by "accurate" in this context.

7-18. The Ecco Company makes electronics products for distribution throughout the world. As quality manager, you are interested in the warranty claims that are made by customers who have experienced problems with Ecco products. The file on your CD-ROM called **ECCO** contains data for a random sample of warranty claims.

a. You are to develop and interpret a 90% confidence interval estimate for the mean dollar claim.

b. Suppose a customer makes a warranty claim of $305. Note that this observation is outside the confidence interval you constructed in part a. Is this possible? Has a mistake been made in the calculation of the confidence interval or is such an occurrence possible?

c. Calculate the probability that an observation as extreme as $305 or more extreme could have come from a normal distribution whose mean and standard deviation are the same as that contained in the **ECCO** file.

7-19. Referring to Problem 18, develop and interpret a 95% confidence interval estimate for the mean warranty claim amount for only those products that were made on the graveyard shift (shift 3 in the data file). There has been some concern within Ecco management that the graveyard shift's workmanship was not of the caliber of the other two shifts. Using the confidence interval you have calculated and any other statistical techniques required, address this issue.

7-20. Refer to Problem 19. Ecco's quality control manager has been concerned with the source of what he believes to be high warranty claims at the Boise site. He believes that corrosion may be the source.

a. Develop and interpret a 95% confidence interval estimate for the mean warranty claim amount for products produced at the Boise site (manufacturing site 1). Do this for each of the complaint sources (complaint codes 1–4). Now compute the 95% confidence interval estimate for mean warranty claims for each site for those cases where the complaint was based on corrosion. How do these interval estimates compare? Discuss.

b. Write a letter to the quality control manager that addresses his concern about the source of the high warranty claims. Identify, if possible, what complaint is producing the highest warranty claims. Discuss the implications of the four confidence intervals concerning the average warranty claims for each complaint type.

7-2: DETERMINING THE APPROPRIATE SAMPLE SIZE

We have discussed the trade-offs that are present in all estimation applications: the desire to have a high confidence level, a low margin of error, and a small sample size. The problem is that these three objectives conflict. For a given sample size, a high confidence level will tend to generate a large margin of error. For a given confidence level, a small sample size will result in an increased margin of error. Reducing the margin of error requires either reducing the confidence level or increasing the sample size or both.

A common question from business decision makers that are planning an estimation application using statistical sampling is, "How large a sample size do I really need?" To answer this question, we usually begin by asking a couple of questions of our own.

1. How much money do you have budgeted to do the sampling?
2. How much will it cost to select each item in the sample?

The answers to these questions provide the upper limit on the sample size that can be selected. For instance, if the decision maker indicates that she has a $2,000 budget for selecting the sample and it will cost about $10 per unit to collect the sample, the sample size upper limit is $2,000/$10 = 200 units.

Keeping in mind the estimation trade-offs discussed earlier, the issue should be fully discussed with the decision maker. For instance, is a sample of 200 sufficient to give the desired margin of error at a specified confidence level? Is 200 more than is needed to achieve the desired margin of error?

Therefore, before we can give a firm answer about what sample size is needed, the decision maker must specify her confidence level and a desired margin of error. Then the required sample size can be computed.

Determining Sample Size, σ Known

Mission Valley Power Company

EXAMPLE 7-6

SAMPLE SIZE

Consider the Mission Valley Power Company (MVP) in Northwest Michigan which has over 6,000 residential customers. In response to a request by the Michigan Public Utilities Commission, MVP needs to estimate the average kilowatts of electricity used by customers on February 1. The only way to get this number is to select a random sample of customers and take a meter reading after 5:00 PM on January 31 and again after 5:00 PM on February 1. The commission has specified that any estimate presented in the utility's report must be based on a 95% confidence level. Further, the margin of error must not exceed ±30 kilowatts. Given these requirements, what size sample is needed?

To answer this question, we start with Equation 7-4 for the margin of error.

$$e = z\frac{\sigma}{\sqrt{n}}$$

We next substitute into this equation the values we know. For example, the margin of error, e, was specified to be 30 kilowatts. The confidence level was specified to be 95%. The z-value for 95% is 1.96 (refer to the standard normal table in Appendix D.) This gives us:

$$30 = 1.96\frac{\sigma}{\sqrt{n}}$$

We need to know the population standard deviation. MVP might know this value from other studies that it has conducted in the past or from similar studies done by other utility companies. Assume for this example that σ, the population standard deviation, is 200 kilowatts. We can now substitute $\sigma = 200$ into the equation for e as follows.

$$30 = 1.96\frac{200}{\sqrt{n}}$$

We now have a single equation with one unknown, n, the sample size. Doing the algebra to solve for n, we get:

$$n = \frac{1.96^2(200)^2}{30^2} = 170.74 \approx 171 \text{ customers}$$

→ *rounded up to next whole number*

Thus, to meet the requirements of the Public Utilities Commission, a sample of $n = 171$ customers should be selected. Equation 7-8 is used to determine the required sample size for estimating a single population mean when σ is known.

SAMPLE SIZE REQUIREMENT—ESTIMATING μ WITH σ KNOWN

$$n = \frac{z^2\sigma^2}{e^2} = \left(\frac{z\sigma}{e}\right)^2 \qquad \text{7-8}$$

where:

z = Critical value for the specified confidence level
e = Desired margin of error
σ = Population standard deviation

If MVP feels that the cost of sampling 171 customers will be too high, it might appeal to the Public Utilities Commission to allow for a higher margin of error or a lower confidence level. For example, if the confidence level is lowered to 90%, the z-value is lowered to 1.645 as found in the standard normal table.[5]

We can now use Equation 7-8 to determine the revised sample size requirement.

$$n = \frac{1.645^2(200)^2}{30^2} = 120.27 \approx 121$$

→ *always round up*

MVP will need to sample only 121 (120.27 rounded up) customers if it is required to have a confidence level of 90% rather than 95%.

Determining Sample Size, σ Unknown

Equation 7-8 assumes that you know the population standard deviation. While this might be the case in some applications, most likely we won't know the standard deviation. To get around this problem, three approaches can be used. One is to use a value for σ which is considered to be at least as large as the true σ. This will provide a conservatively large sample size.

The second option is to select a **pilot sample,** a sample from the population that is used explicitly to estimate σ.

PILOT SAMPLE
A sample taken from the population of interest of a size smaller than the anticipated sample size that is used to provide an estimate for the population standard deviation.

The third option is to use the range of the population to estimate the population's standard deviation. Recall both the empirical rule in Chapter 3 and also Chapter 6's examination of the normal distribution. Both sources suggest that $\mu \pm 3\sigma$ contains virtually all of the data values of a normal distribution. If this were the case, then $\mu - 3\sigma$ would be approximately the smallest value and $\mu + 3\sigma$ would be approximately the largest value in the data set. Remember that the Range = R = Maximum Value −

---

[5]You can also use the Excel function, NORMSINV, to determine the z-value.

Minimum Value. So, $R \approx (\mu + 3\sigma) - (\mu - 3\sigma) = 6\sigma$. We can, therefore, obtain an estimate of the standard deviation as:

$$\sigma \approx \frac{R}{6}$$

We can also use a procedure that produces a larger estimate of the standard deviation, which will lead to a larger and more conservative sample size. This involves dividing the range by 4 instead of 6.

We seldom know the standard deviation of the population. However, often we have a very good idea about the largest and smallest values of the population. So this third method can be used in many instances in which you do not wish to, or cannot, obtain a pilot sample or you are unable to offer a conjecture concerning a conservatively large value of the standard deviation.

7-7

SAMPLE SIZE

Georgia Lumber Mill

Consider the Georgia Lumber Mill where the manager wishes to know the average diameter of logs that are cut by the mill. Not only does she not know μ, she also does not know the population standard deviation. She wants a 90% confidence level and is willing to have a margin of error of 0.50 inches in estimating the true mean diameter.

To use Equation 7-8 we need a value for σ. To get this value, a pilot sample of 100 logs is selected from which the mill manager calculates the sample standard deviation, s. Suppose for the pilot sample, $s = 4.8$ inches. The mill manager now uses this estimate in place of σ in Equation 7-8 as follows.

$$n = \frac{1.645^2(4.8)^2}{0.50^2} = 249.39 \approx 250$$

Thus, using the 4.8 inch value for σ, the required sample size is 250 logs. The 100 logs already selected in the pilot sample can be included in the total, so the manager really needs 150 additional logs in the sample. Note, if the standard deviation for the sample of 250 logs is larger than 4.8 inches, the actual margin of error will exceed the 0.50 desired level.

Suppose the following statistics were computed from the 250-log sample.

$$\bar{x} = 12.91 \text{ inches}$$
$$s = 4.98 \text{ inches}$$

Given the larger sample size $(n = 250)$, we now use Equation 7-7 to produce the 90% confidence interval estimate.

$$\bar{x} \pm z\frac{s}{\sqrt{n}}$$

$$12.91 \pm 1.645\frac{4.98}{\sqrt{250}}$$

$$12.91 \pm 0.518$$
$$12.392 \text{ inches} \text{———————} 13.428 \text{ inches}$$

The mill manager can conclude that the average log diameter is between 12.392 inches and 13.428 inches on the basis of this 90% confidence interval. The margin of error in the estimate is ± 0.518 inches, slightly larger than the desired 0.50 inches due to the sample standard deviation being slightly higher than that found for the pilot sample.

7-2: EXERCISES

ADDITIONAL EXERCISES ON YOUR CD-ROM
Try the ADDITIONAL EXERCISES and APPLICATION PROBLEMS on the CD-ROM.

7-21. A study is being planned to estimate the mean number of inches that trees will grow per year in a forest. The analysts wish to have 90% confidence and want to estimate the mean within ±0.20 inches. A pilot study was conducted which showed a sample standard deviation equal to 0.80 inches. What size sample is needed for this study?

7-22. The standard deviation of a population is thought to be somewhere in the interval (250, 300). The population mean is to be estimated using a confidence interval with a 90% confidence level. The desired margin of error is 20.
   a. Calculate the required sample size using the smallest value of the standard deviation perceived to be possible.
   b. Repeat the calculation in part a using the largest value of the standard deviation perceived to be possible.
   c. Note that a standard deviation of 300 is 20% larger than a standard deviation of 250. Determine the percentage increase in the sample size required by a 20% increase in the standard deviation.

7-23. Determine the sample size for estimating a population mean. The confidence level is to be 95%, and the desired margin of error is 1,000.
   a. If the population standard deviation is thought to be 13,700, calculate the required sample size.
   b. The cost of obtaining the sample has become an issue for this analysis, so a pilot sample is obtained. The standard deviation of the pilot sample is 12,500. Calculate the sample size required to estimate the population mean using the pilot sample's standard deviation to estimate the population standard deviation.

Business Applications

7-24. The Longmont Computer Leasing Company leases computers and peripherals like laser printers. The printers have a counter that keeps track of the number of pages that are printed. The company wishes to estimate the mean number of pages that will be printed in a month on its leased printers. The plan is to select a random sample of printers and record the number on each printer's counter at the beginning of May. The number on the counter will be recorded again at the end of May, and the difference will be the number of copies on that printer for the month. The company wants the estimate to be within plus or minus 100 pages of the true mean with a 95% confidence level.

   a. The standard deviation in pages printed is thought to be about 1,400 pages. How many printers should be sampled?
   b. Suppose that the conjecture concerning the size of the standard deviation is off (plus or minus) by as much as 10%. What percentage change in the required sample size would this produce?

7-25. Arco Manufacturing makes electronic pagers. As part of the company's quality efforts, the company wishes to estimate the mean number of days the pager is used before repair is needed. A pilot sample of 40 pagers indicates a sample standard deviation of 200 days. The company wishes its estimate to have a margin of error of no more than 50 days and the confidence level must be 95%.
   a. Given this information, how many additional pagers should be sampled?
   b. The pilot study was initiated because of the costs involved in sampling. Each sampled observation costs approximately $10 to obtain. Originally, it was thought that the population's standard deviation may be as large as 300. Determine the amount of money saved by obtaining the pilot sample.

7-26. The Northwest Pacific Phone Company wishes to estimate the average number of minutes its customers spend on long distance calls per month. The company wants the estimate made with 99% confidence and a margin of error of no more than 5 minutes.
   a. A previous study indicated that the standard deviation for long distance calls is 21 minutes per month. What should the sample size be?
   b. Company records indicate that the longest long distance call recorded (except for a few that were considered to be extreme outliers) was 149 minutes. The shortest long distance call for our purposes can be considered to be 0 minutes. Calculate a conservatively large sample size required to estimate the average length of long distance calls.
   c. Do you have any doubts about the standard deviation obtained from the earlier study? If the conservatively large sample size was used instead, what would be the impact on the properties of the accompanying confidence interval?

7-27. Refer to Problem 26.
   a. Determine the required sample size if the confidence level were changed from 99% to 90%.

b. What would be the required sample size if the confidence level was 95% and the margin of error was 8 minutes?

7-28. The quality manager at Ecco Company, a maker of backup alarms for use on industrial vehicles like forklifts, is interested in estimating the mean dollar volume for warranty claims for products made in Boise on the day shift. He has taken a pilot sample. The data for the pilot sample are in a file called **ECCO.**

   a. Assuming that the manager wishes to estimate the mean warranty amount to within ±$8.00 with 90% confidence, how many additional claims must be selected to develop the estimate?

   b. Suppose the sample size determined in part a is more than the manager is willing to use. What options are open to the manager? Discuss.

   c. Referring to parts a and b, suppose the manager wishes to cut the total sample size in half. For each option available to the manager show specifically what must be done to achieve the reduction in sample size.

7-29. The loan manager at High-Desert Bank wishes to estimate the mean loan amount for the commercial customers of his bank following an advertising promotion that was intended to raise the mean loan amount to $67,500. A couple of weeks ago, an intern from the nearby college collected a random sample of customers (commercial and retail). These data are in a file called **High-Desert Bank.**

   a. Use the data in this sample to develop a 95% confidence interval estimate for the population mean loan amount for commercial customers. Based on the sample data, was the promotion a success? Explain your answer.

   b. Referring to part a, suppose the loan manager would like to maintain the 95% confidence interval but with a margin of error that is 40% of the existing margin of error. How many, if any, additional loan customers must be sampled?

   c. Refer to parts a and b. Suppose the manager feels the new required sample size is too large, but he does not want to increase the margin of error. What must he do? Assuming he wants to cut the required sample size by 15%, what specifically will be required? Discuss the impact of these trade-offs.

7-30. The state Department of Transportation is experimenting with a new scale for weighing trucks. This new scale is called a Weigh-in-Motion (WIM) scale because it weighs trucks while they are driving down the highway. The traditional method is called a static scale that is at the port-of-entry (POE). The trucks pull into the scale, stop, and are weighed. The POE scale is assumed to provide accurate weights.

   a. The state has set up a test area on one stretch of highway. The WIM scale is located about 0.50 miles before the POE scale. A sample of trucks are weighed on the WIM scale and then immediately on the POE scale. Some trucks were weighed in each of several months beginning in February. These data are in the file called **Trucks.** Suppose that the objective of the department is to estimate the mean difference between WIM gross weight and POE gross weight for those trucks that were weighed in February. (Note: February trucks have a Month Code = 2.) The estimate is to be based on 95% confidence. Using the sample data, develop this estimate and interpret it. (Hint: Compute a new variable that is WIM Gross − POE Gross.)

   b. Referring to part a, suppose the department wants the margin of error reduced to no more than 50 pounds with 95% confidence. Use the sample data already collected as a pilot sample. How many more trucks would be needed to estimate the February mean difference? Comment on this result.

   c. Assuming the value in part b is considered unreasonably large, what must be done to cut the required sample size? Discuss the pros and cons of each alternative.

7-31. Refer to Problem 30.

   a. Suppose the department wishes to estimate the speed of vehicles crossing the WIM scale with 99% confidence and with a margin of error equal to ±1.5 mph. Use as the sample all trucks weighed in the study. Is the current sample size sufficient or will more trucks need to be sampled? If more are needed, how many more?

   b. Using the range (difference between the largest and smallest speeds), determine a conservatively large sample size required to produce the specified confidence interval.

   c. The department has estimated that it will cost an average of $10.00 per sample reading to obtain the information. They have a budget of $1,500 to collect the required data. Examine the calculations in part b. (1) Will the department be able to construct the sample within their budget? (2) Examine the possible alternatives to help the department collect a sample. Make any recommendations you have to the department.

▪ 7-3: ESTIMATING A POPULATION PROPORTION

The previous sections have illustrated the methods for developing confidence interval estimates when the population value of interest was the mean. However, you will encounter many situations where the value of interest is the proportion of items in the population that possess a particular attribute. The *population proportion* is represented by π (pi). The point estimate for π is the *sample proportion, p,* which is computed using Equation 7-9.

In Chapter 6 we introduced the sampling distribution for proportions. We indicated then that when the sample size is sufficiently large, the standard error for p is computed using Equation 7-10. Also, the sampling distribution will be approximately normally distributed and centered at the true population proportion, π.

SAMPLE PROPORTION
$$p = \frac{x}{n} \qquad \textbf{7-9}$$
where:
x = Number of occurrences
n = Sample size

STANDARD ERROR FOR p
$$\sigma_p = \sqrt{\frac{\pi(1-\pi)}{n}} \qquad \textbf{7-10}$$
where:
π = Population proportion
n = Sample size

Confidence Interval Estimates for Proportions

To develop the confidence interval estimate for a population proportion we use the basic equation for establishing all confidence intervals:

$$\text{Point Estimate} \pm (\text{Critical Value})(\text{Standard Error})$$

However, since the standard error relies on the unknown population proportion, π, we must use an estimate of the standard error. We substitute the sample proportion for the population proportion. The confidence interval that we produce will be an approximate confidence interval. The specific format for *confidence intervals involving the population proportion* is shown in Equation 7-11.

CONFIDENCE INTERVAL FOR π
$$p \pm z\sqrt{\frac{p(1-p)}{n}} \qquad \textbf{7-11}$$
where:
p = Sample proportion
n = Sample size
z = Critical value from the standard normal distribution

EXAMPLE 7-8

INTERVAL ESTIMATION

Quick-Lube

The Quick-Lube Company operates a chain of oil change outlets in several states. Like its competitors, Quick-Lube recommends that owners have their oil changed every 3 months or 3,000 miles, whichever comes first. When a customer comes in for service, the date of service and the mileage on the car are recorded. A computer program tracks the customers and, when the 3-month time frame nears, a reminder card is sent to the customer.

Quick-Lube recently hired a consulting company to help design a new reminder card that they hoped would prove more effective at getting customers to return for their next oil change. The company experimented with two card types that contained different formats and messages. One card focused on getting customers to bring their cars in for a basic oil change. The other card contained more information about other products and services.

The marketing manager is interested in estimating the *proportion* of customers who return for an oil change after receiving card 1. A sample of 100 customers received this card. Of these, 62 actually returned to have their oil changed within 1 month after the card was mailed. Equation 7-9 is used to compute the sample proportion.

$$p = \frac{x}{n} = \frac{62}{100} = 0.62$$

If the managers need a point estimate for the true population proportion, the best value to use would be 0.62. However, they know that this value is subject to sampling error and that the true proportion is likely to be either higher or lower than 0.62.

For the Quick-Lube example, the standard error computed using Equation 7-10 is

$$\sigma_p = \sqrt{\frac{(0.62)(1 - 0.62)}{100}} = 0.049$$

Using Equation 7-11, the Quick-Lube managers can develop an approximate 90% confidence interval estimate for the population proportion as follows.

$$p \pm z\sqrt{\frac{p(1 - p)}{n}}$$

$$0.62 \pm 1.645\sqrt{\frac{(0.62)(1 - 0.62)}{100}}$$

$$0.62 \pm 0.080$$

$$0.54 \text{———————} 0.70$$

Based on this sample of 100 customers using a 90% confidence interval, the manager estimates that the true percentage of customers who will respond to the reminder card will be between 54% and 70%.

The Epstein Corporation

EXAMPLE 7-9
INTERVAL ESTIMATION

Excel and Minitab Tutorial

The Epstein Corporation, based in Philadelphia, is considering offering its employees the option of a health maintenance organization (HMO) rather than their current health insurance plan. However, the human resources manager does not want to enter into an agreement with the HMO unless a sizable proportion of the employees plan on switching. To gather information on this, the manager has sent out a survey to 300 employees selected at random from the over 10,000 employees across the world. The employees were given information about both insurance plans and asked to indicate whether, if given the choice, they would switch to the HMO. Of the 300 employees surveyed, 205 returned their survey with 58 indicating that they would switch to the HMO.[6]

Based on this sample information the manager can develop a 95% confidence interval estimate for the proportion of all employees who will switch to the HMO. The PHStat Add-in for Excel provides a procedure for performing the calculations directly. Figure 7-8 shows the results.

FIGURE 7-8
Excel (PHStat) Output—
Epstein Example

Excel (PHStat) Instructions

1. Open file: Epstein.xls
2. Click on PHStat
3. Select Confidence Intervals
4. Input Sample Size and Number of Successes
5. Provide Title

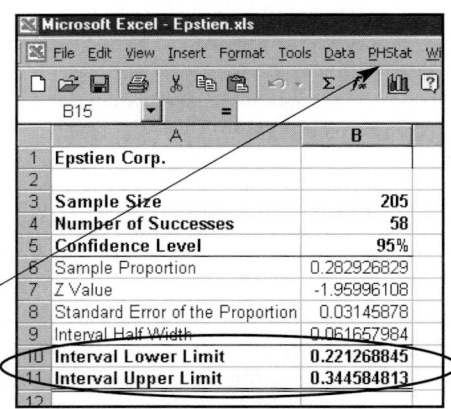

95% Confidence interval estimate

0.221 ——————— 0.345

---

[6]The people who did not return the surveys are nonrespondents. Every effort should be made to reduce the number of nonresponses. High nonresponse rates can distort the population estimates.

Thus, based on the sample data using a 95% confidence interval, the human resources manager can conclude that between 22.1% and 34.5% of all employees will switch to the HMO. Note, if the manager is concerned that the margin of error is too large, she can lower her confidence level or increase the size of the sample.

Determining the Required Sample Size

Changing the confidence level affects the width of the interval. Likewise, changing the sample size will affect the interval width. An increase in sample size will reduce the standard error and reduce the interval width. A decrease in the sample size will have the opposite effect. In many applications, decision makers would like to determine a required sample size prior to doing the sampling. As was the case for estimating the population mean, the required sample size in a proportion application is based on the desired margin of error, the desired confidence level, and the variation in the population. The *margin of error, e,* is computed using Equation 7-12.

MARGIN OF ERROR FOR ESTIMATING π

$$e = z\sqrt{\frac{\pi(1 - \pi)}{n}} \qquad \text{7-12}$$

where:

π = Population proportion
z = Critical value from standard normal distribution
n = Sample size

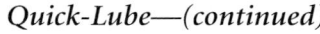

Quick-Lube—(continued)

EXAMPLE 7-10

INTERVAL ESTIMATION

Suppose the Quick-Lube managers want a margin of error, $e = \pm0.04$, and 95% confidence ($z = 1.96$). These two values can be specified. However, the population variation is outside their control and must be determined. In Equation 7-12, the population proportion, π, determines the variation in the population. The closer π is to 0.50, the greater is the variation since $\pi(1 - \pi)$ is greatest when $\pi = 0.50$.

However, if the managers already knew the value for π they wouldn't need to estimate it, and the sample size issue wouldn't come up. Two methods are frequently used to overcome this problem. First, a *pilot sample* can be taken, and p for the sample is substituted for π. An alternative approach is to use a conservative value for π. For example, if the managers have reason to believe that the population proportion, π, will be about 0.60, they could use a value for π a little closer to 0.50, say 0.55. If they don't have a good idea of what π is, the conservative thing to do is use $\pi = 0.50$. This will give a sample size that is at least large enough to meet their requirements.

Equation 7-12 can be rewritten such that the unknown sample size value, n, is alone on the left of the equal sign as shown in Equation 7-13.

SAMPLE SIZE FOR ESTIMATING π

$$n = \frac{z^2\pi(1 - \pi)}{e^2} \qquad \text{7-13}$$

where:

π = Value used to represent the population proportion
e = Desired margin of error
z = Critical value from the standard normal table

Suppose the Quick-Lube managers use the sample of 100 cards as the pilot sample with $p = 0.62$ used to represent π in Equation 7-13. For 95% confidence, the z-value is 1.96

and the margin of error, e, is equal to 0.04. Substitute these values into Equation 7-13 and solve for the required sample size.

$$n = \frac{1.96^2(0.62)(1 - 0.62)}{0.04^2} = 565.676 = 566$$

The pilot sample of 100 can be included. Therefore, Quick-Lube managers need to send out an additional 466 cards to randomly selected customers. If this is more than they can afford or wish to include in the sample, the margin of error can be increased or the confidence level can be reduced.

7-3: EXERCISES

ADDITIONAL EXERCISES ON YOUR CD-ROM
Try the ADDITIONAL EXERCISES and APPLICATION PROBLEMS on the CD-ROM.

7-32. Compute the 95% confidence interval estimate for π based on a sample size of 400 where the sample proportion, p, is equal to 0.30.

7-33. A sample of size 100 was selected from a population. Out of this sample, 47 had a particular attribute.
   a. Is the sample size large enough so that the sampling distribution of the sample proportion can be approximated with a normal distribution? Support your answer with calculations and reasons.
   b. Based on these sample data, construct and interpret the 95% confidence interval estimate for the population proportion.

7-34. A random sample of 300 items was selected from a population. Of this sample, 88 items possessed a desired attribute.
   a. Determine the approximate sampling distribution of the sample proportion. Make sure to specify its mean and standard deviation.
   b. Construct and interpret the 85% confidence interval estimate for the population proportion.

7-35. Assume that a decision maker wants to estimate a population proportion with 90% confidence and a margin of error of ±0.03. The decision maker has obtained a pilot sample of 100. This pilot sample's proportion is 0.50.
   a. What sample size will be sure to achieve the desired results? How many additional observations must the decision maker obtain?
   b. If it is impossible to alter the sample size, can you alter the confidence level of the confidence interval to achieve the same result? If you can, determine the confidence level that would achieve those same results.

7-36. Referring to Problem 35, suppose a pilot sample of 50 items was selected and 22 items had the attribute of interest.
   a. How many more items need to be sampled to meet the confidence level and margin of error requirements?
   b. Determine the confidence level that would achieve the same results without altering the sample size.

Business Applications

7-37. The corporate operations manager for the Phillips Oil Company has his staff working on a new service station layout plan that would potentially alter the ratio of regular unleaded pumps that are placed at a station in comparison to the other gasoline levels (premium, super premium, etc.). As part of the staff's analysis, they are interested in estimating the difference in the population proportions of customers who purchase unleaded regular (as opposed to premium or diesel) gasoline in eastern states versus western states. They have considerably more experience with the eastern states. The proportion of customers who purchase unleaded regular gasoline in the eastern states is known to to be 0.75. They have sampled 900 western-state customers; 643 of the western-state customers purchased regular unleaded gasoline.
   a. Using a 95% confidence level, determine the estimate for the population proportion of western-state customers who purchase unleaded regular.
   b. On the basis of this confidence interval, would you recommend that Phillips Oil use a different ratio of regular unleaded pumps in the western states than in the eastern states? Support your answer with the confidence interval and the logic that accompanies it.

7-38. Refer to Problem 37.
   a. Determine the margin of error for the confidence interval.
   b. Determine the margin of error if the sample size were cut in half, but the sample proportion remained the same.
   c. Suppose now that the sample size were not cut in half. However, you still wish to have a confidence interval with the same margin of error determined in part b. Determine the confidence level to accomplish this.

7-39. Most major airlines allow passengers to carry two pieces of luggage (of a certain maximum size) onto the plane.

However, their studies show that the more carry-on baggage passengers have, the longer it takes the plane to unload and load passengers. One regional airline is considering changing its policy to allow only one carry-on per passenger. Before doing so, the airline decided to collect some data. Specifically, a random sample of 1,000 passengers was selected. Researchers observed the passengers and noted the number of bags each person carried on the plane. Out of the 1,000 passengers, 345 had more than one bag.

a. Based on this sample, develop and interpret a 95% confidence interval estimate for the proportion of the traveling population that would have been impacted had the "one-bag" limit been in effect. Discuss your result.

b. The domestic version of Boeing's 747 has a capacity for 568 passengers. Determine an interval estimate of the number of passengers you would expect to board the plane with more than one carry-on. Assume the plane is at its passenger capacity.

7-40. Referring to Problem 39, suppose the airline also noted whether the passenger was male or female. Out of the 1,000 passengers observed, 690 were males. Of this group, 280 had more than one bag.

a. Using these data, obtain and interpret a 95% confidence interval estimate for the proportion of male passengers in the population who would have been affected by the "one-bag" limit. Discuss.

b. If the Boeing 747 had a passenger list of which one half were females, determine an interval estimate of the number of females who would be carrying more than one piece of luggage on board. Assume the aircraft is at its capacity for passengers.

7-41. Referring to Problems 39 and 40, suppose the airline decides to conduct a survey of its customers to determine their opinion of the proposed "one-bag" limit. The plan calls for a random sample of customers on different flights to be given a short written survey to complete during the flight. One key question on the survey will be: "Do you approve of limiting the number of carry-on bags to a maximum of one bag per passenger?" Airline managers expect that only about 15% will say "yes."

a. Based on this assumption, what size sample should the airline take if it wants to develop a 95% confidence interval estimate for the population proportion who will say "yes" with a margin of error of ±0.02?

b. Recall that in Section 7-3 you were given advice about choosing a parameter's value if you were uncertain. You were counseled to use a value that was near the assumed value of the parameter but that would produce a conservatively large sample size. If you were to adjust the airline managers' expectation by 5%, would you adjust it up ($\pi = 0.20$) or down ($\pi = 0.10$)? Support your answer with calculations and reasons. Determine the required sample size with the 5% adjustment to the conjectured population proportion.

c. After determining the sample size, write a short report which outlines the general method you would suggest

the airline use to determine which passengers are included in the survey.

7-42. Refer to Problem 41. Suppose the sample size you determined (in Problem 41, part a) was selected, and 270 people answered "yes" to the key question.

a. Construct the confidence interval estimate for the population proportion. What is the margin of error?

b. Discuss why the margin of error is different than the expected ± 0.02.

7-43. A major manufacturer of athletic footwear is considering a new marketing campaign directed at working women. The idea is to create the impression that athletic footwear is comfortable and appropriate to wear to work. Part of the motivation for this idea came from a survey of 499 women conducted for the American Orthopedic Foot and Ankle Society. This survey revealed that 23% wear athletic shoes to work.

a. Use this information to develop a 90% confidence interval estimate for the population proportion of women who wear athletic shoes to work. Interpret your findings.

b. The mass media usually references the information contained in a confidence interval by reciting the point estimate for the parameter of interest followed by a specification of the margin of error. Write a short description of the media release summarizing the confidence interval in part a.

7-44. The same survey of 499 women for the American Orthopedic Foot and Ankle Society revealed that 38% wear flats to work. (See Problem 43.)

a. Use this sample information to develop a 99% confidence interval for the population proportion of women who wear flats to work.

b. Suppose the society wishes to estimate the proportion of women who wear athletic shoes to work and the proportion of women who wear flats to work within a margin of error of ±0.01 with 95% confidence. Determine the sample size required if only one sample is to be obtained.

7-45. A local radio station is interested in estimating the percentage of a target market that has a favorable impression of its morning show. The marketing department wishes to estimate this proportion within ± 0.03 of the true population value and have a confidence level of 98%. A pilot sample of 40 people was selected, and the proportion in this sample with a favorable impression was 0.45.

a. Based on this information, how many more people must be surveyed?

b. Determine the margin of error in the pilot sample. Assume a confidence level of 98%.

7-46. Refer to Problem 45. Suppose the station managers can't afford to survey as many people as required and have indicated that the maximum sample size can be 700 people. Assuming that the sample size is cut to 700:

a. Without changing the confidence level, indicate specifically what must be changed and by how much.

b. Without changing the margin of error, indicate specifically what must be changed and by how much.

■ SUMMARY AND CONCLUSIONS

By the time you have reached this point you may be wondering how you are ever going to keep all these different estimation processes straight. If you try to memorize them, you probably won't be able to do it. However, if you develop an understanding of the basic logic of estimation, it is very manageable.

Remember, your first objective is to estimate a population value based on information from a sample. There are two types of estimates: point estimates and interval estimates. Point estimates are subject to potential sampling error. Point estimates are almost always different from the population value. A confidence interval estimate takes into account the potential for sampling error and provides a range within which we believe the true population value falls. There is a common format for all confidence interval estimates:

Point Estimate ± (Critical Value) (Standard Error)

The point estimate is at the center of the interval. The amount that we add and subtract to the point estimate is called the margin of error.

While this format is always used, there are slightly different formulas that we use depending on what population value we are estimating and certain other conditions. You shouldn't try to memorize these formulas. Instead, you should focus on sorting out the characteristics of the application at hand. Once you do that, you can locate the appropriate formula to determine the interval estimate. The key will be on correctly interpreting the results and applying these results to your decision situation.

Figure 7-9 contains a diagram that you should find useful as you work the problems and cases at the end of this chapter and later on when you encounter estimation applications in your work.

EQUATIONS

Confidence Interval (General Format)

Point Estimate ± (Critical Value)(Standard Error) **7-1**

Confidence Interval (General Format)—σ Known

Point Estimate ± z (Standard Error)   **7-2**

Confidence Interval for μ (σ Known)

$$\bar{x} \pm z \frac{\sigma}{\sqrt{n}} \qquad \text{7-3}$$

Margin of Error (Estimate for μ with σ Known)

$$e = z \frac{\sigma}{\sqrt{n}} \qquad \text{7-4}$$

t-Value

$$t = \frac{\bar{x} - \mu}{\frac{s}{\sqrt{n}}} \qquad \text{7-5}$$

Confidence Interval (σ Unknown)

$$\bar{x} \pm t \frac{s}{\sqrt{n}} \qquad \text{7-6}$$

Confidence Interval—Large Samples with σ Unknown

$$\bar{x} \pm z \frac{s}{\sqrt{n}} \qquad \text{7-7}$$

Sample Size Requirement—Estimating μ with σ Known

$$n = \frac{z^2 \sigma^2}{e^2} = \left(\frac{z\sigma}{e}\right)^2 \qquad \text{7-8}$$

Sample Proportion

$$p = \frac{x}{n} \qquad \text{7-9}$$

Standard Error for p

$$\sigma_p = \sqrt{\frac{\pi(1-\pi)}{n}} \qquad \text{7-10}$$

Confidence Interval for π

$$p \pm z \sqrt{\frac{p(1-p)}{n}} \qquad \text{7-11}$$

Margin of Error for Estimating π

$$e = z \sqrt{\frac{\pi(1-\pi)}{n}} \qquad \text{7-12}$$

Sample Size for Estimating π

$$n = \frac{z^2 \pi(1-\pi)}{e^2} \qquad \text{7-13}$$

FIGURE 7-9
Flow Diagram for Confidence
Interval Estimation
Alternatives

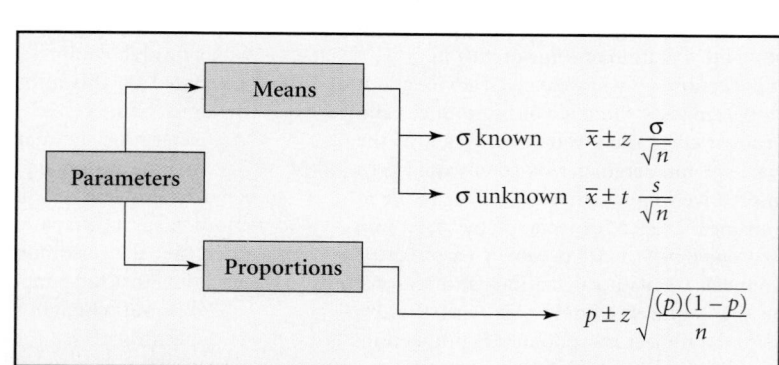

■ KEY TERMS

Confidence Coefficient—The confidence level divided by 100%—i.e., the decimal equivalent of a confidence level.

Confidence Interval—An interval developed from sample values such that if all possible intervals of a given width were constructed, a percentage of these intervals, known as the confidence level, would include the true population parameter.

Confidence Level—Percentage greater than 50 and less than 100 that corresponds to the percentage of all possible confidence intervals, based on a given size sample, that will contain the true population value.

Degrees of Freedom—The number of independent data values available to estimate the population's standard deviation. If k parameters must be estimated before the population's standard deviation can be calculated from a sample of size n, the degrees of freedom are equal to $n - k$.

Margin of Error—The largest possible sampling error at the specified level of confidence.

Pilot Sample—A sample taken from the population of interest of a size smaller than the anticipated sample size that is used to provide an estimate for the population standard deviation.

Point Estimate—A single number determined from a sample that is used to estimate the corresponding population value.

Sampling Error—The difference between the population value and the sample value.

Student's t-distribution—Family of distributions that is bell-shaped and symmetric like the standard normal distribution but with greater area in the tails. Each distribution in the t-family is defined by its degrees of freedom. As the degrees of freedom increase, the t-distribution approaches the normal distribution.

CHAPTER EXERCISES

SOLVED PROBLEMS ON YOUR CD-ROM
Try the WORKED-OUT EXERCISES and BUSINESS APPLICATIONS on the CD-ROM.

Conceptual Questions

7-47. In a situation in which our objective is to estimate the population mean, if a small sample is used and the population standard deviation is unknown, we are hit with a "double whammy" when it comes to the margin of error. Explain what the "double whammy" is and why it occurs. (Hint: Consider the sources of variation in the margin of error.)

7-48. When a decision maker is interested in estimating a single population proportion, why is the margin of error greater when the sample proportion is near 0.50 for a given confidence level? (Note: If you have had a calculus class, you may wish to use the tools acquired there to prove the result. If not, a few sample calculations of the margin of error for various sample proportions should point the way.)

7-49. An insurance company in Iowa recently conducted a survey of its automobile policy customers to estimate the mean miles these customers commute to work each day. The result based on a random sample of 300 policyholders indicated the population mean was between 3.5 and 6.7 miles. This interval estimate was constructed using 95% confidence.

    a. After receiving this result, one of the managers was overheard telling a colleague that 95% of all customers commute between 3.5 and 6.7 miles to work each day. How would you respond to this statement? Is it correct? Why or why not? Discuss.

    b. Another manager was overheard to say that she was 95% confident that the mean of the 300 policyholders was between 3.5 and 6.7. How would you respond to this statement? Is it correct? Why or why not? Discuss.

7-50. Referring to Question 49, suppose a third manager is overhead telling another colleague that there is a 95% chance that the true average commute for all policyholders is between 3.5 and 6.7 miles per day. Comment on this statement. Is it a correct statement? Discuss why or why not.

Business Applications

7-51. A survey of 619 adults who are not retired revealed that 38% of them favored allowing the federal government to invest a portion of the Social Security Trust Fund in the stock market (*USA Today*: July 27, 1998). Use this information to construct a 99% confidence interval for the proportion of working adults who favor such investments.

7-52. A random sample of 48 individuals who purchased items over the Internet revealed an average purchase amount of $178 with a standard deviation of $27. Use this sample information and a 95% confidence level to provide the following:

    a. A point estimate of the average purchase amount.

    b. The margin of error of the point estimate you provided in part a.

    c. An interval estimate for the population mean.

7-53. Chambre Corporation makes a variety of products including electrical surge protectors. It is considering developing a special model surge protector that will be mounted internally in a PC at the time of manufacture. However, before doing this, the company needs convincing data to help make the sale to the computer makers. The company contracted with a national survey research firm to conduct a survey of PC owners to determine several issues related to PC ownership and the need for a surge protector. A key question on the survey asked the respondent to indicate the total value of the PC that he or she purchased most recently. The objective is to develop a 95% confidence interval estimate for the mean value for all PCs owned in the market. The desired margin of error is not to exceed ±$100. A previous study indicated that the standard deviation for PC value would be approximately $300. Based on this, what size random sample should be taken? Justify this required sample size.

7-54. Referring to Problem 53, suppose the survey research firm did select the size sample you computed and found the following sample information:

$$\bar{x} = \$1,345.78 \text{ and } s = \$257.90$$

a. Compute the desired confidence interval estimate and interpret the estimate.
b. Indicate why the margin of error is smaller than the desired ±$100 amount.
c. Based on the preceding sample information, determine the smallest and largest prices being paid for a PC.
d. What assumption about the distribution of the PC prices allows you to produce the estimate in part c?

7-55. Referring to Problems 53 and 54, suppose a second question on the survey asked whether the PC owners already had an external surge protection device attached to their primary PC.
a. Comment on whether the sample size used to estimate the mean PC value will work if the company wants to estimate the proportion of PC owners who have a surge protector in use.
b. What size sample would be needed if they want to estimate this proportion with 95% confidence and with a margin of error not to exceed ±0.01? Note, since nothing is currently known about the rate at which surge protectors are used, use the most conservative value for π to compute the required sample size.

7-56. Refer to Problem 55.
a. Suppose the new sample size is implemented, and the survey results reveal that 18% of those sampled have a surge protector in use. Construct and interpret the 95% interval estimate.
b. Also comment on why the margin of error is different than the requested ±0.01.

7-57. A U.S. senator has asked her staff to conduct a study to determine whether people would be in favor of raising the retirement age as a way to save the Social Security system.
a. If you seek to have a 95% confidence interval for your estimate with a margin of error of 4 percentage points, how large a sample should you select? Produce a conservatively high sample size.
b. Note, there is general agreement among some legislators that the percentage of the public in agreement with this proposed change to Social Security will not exceed 20%. Assuming this to be true, how large a sample should you select?

7-58. Referring to Problem 57, suppose the survey is conducted in the senator's home state and 37.9% indicate that they would favor the proposal.
a. Use the sample size determined in Problem 57 part a to construct the confidence interval estimate. Interpret the estimate.
b. Suppose the statistic is an accurate representation of the population's parameter. Consider the next five letters received by the senator on this subject, and calculate the probability that at least three of them will favor the proposal. Discuss your results.

7-59. Referring to Problems 57 and 58, the senator's staff also broke the sample data down by age. Of the 130 responses from individuals over 50 years of age, 33 supported raising the minimum age for Social Security benefits.
a. Based on this information construct and interpret a 95% confidence interval estimate for the proportion of people over 50 years of age in the state who favor the concept of raising the minimum Social Security age.
b. Based on the 95% confidence interval you have constructed, determine the largest possible proportion of people over 50 years old who favor the concept of raising the minimum Social Security age. (Hint: You must consider the maximum proportion and margin of error.)

7-60. The Future-Vision Company is considering applying for a franchise to market satellite television dish systems in a Florida market area. As part of the company's research into this opportunity, staff in the new acquisitions department conducted a survey of 548 homes selected at random in the market area. They asked a number of questions on the survey. The data for some of the variables are in a file called **Future-Vision**. One key question asked whether the household was currently connected to cable TV.
a. Using the sample information, what is the 92% confidence interval estimate for the true proportion of households in the market area that subscribe to cable television?
b. Determine the largest value a 92% confidence interval would estimate to be the true proportion of households in the market area that subscribe to cable television.

7-61. Referring to Problem 60, the new acquisitions department manager is also interested in estimating the mean household income for those homes that currently do not have cable TV.
a. Based on the sample data, develop a 95% confidence interval estimate for the mean income and interpret this estimate.

b. The acquisitions department manager needs an estimate with a small margin of error. The largest he can tolerate for his purposes is $250. Determine the confidence level that would be associated with such a small margin of error assuming all other components of the margin of error remain fixed.

7-62. The Jordeen Bottling Company recently did an extensive sampling of its soft drink inventory where 5,000 cans were sampled. Employees weighed each can and used weight as a surrogate measure to determine the fluid ounces in the cans. The data are in a file on your CD-ROM called **Jordeen**.

    a. Based on these sample data, should the company conclude that the mean volume is 12 ounces? Base your conclusion on a 95% confidence interval estimate and discuss.

    b. Suppose the population mean is equal to the sample mean you obtained. Determine the proportion of the soft drink cans that are being filled with more than 12 ounces of liquid. What assumption(s) were necessary in order to validate the calculation you furnished in part a?

7-63. A survey was taken to determine the average amount young professionals living in Denver have invested in stock mutual funds outside of retirement accounts. The survey results showed lower and upper confidence interval limits of $25,114 and $26,068, respectively.

    a. If the confidence interval was based on a sample size of 1,024 young professionals and a known population standard deviation of $7,543, then what is the confidence level for the estimate of the population mean amount invested?

    b. Assume that the distribution of the amount of money invested in mutual funds by these young professionals is normally distributed. Determine the largest and smallest amounts that any young professional in the Denver area has invested in mutual funds.

7-64. A survey conducted by the NPD Group for Quaker Oats (*USA Today*: *http://www.usatoday.com/snapshot/life/lsnap074.htm*) revealed that 70% of those people who use oatmeal as a cereal put something on it. Suppose this estimate was based on a sample of 1,024 people who eat oatmeal for breakfast.

    a. Use the study's findings to calculate the 95% confidence interval for the true proportion of breakfast oatmeal eaters who put something on their oats.

    b. Calculate the largest the margin of error could possibly be when estimating the proportion of oatmeal eaters who don't eat it plain with the sample proportion given at the beginning of the problem. Assume a 95% confidence level.

7-65. A travel agency would like to estimate the proportion of domestic travelers who select an airline based on the price of the ticket to the desired destination.

    a. If the travel agency would like to be 94% confident of being within ±4% of the true population proportion, then what size sample should they take? (Assume that they have no knowledge about what the proportion might be and want to make sure they have a large enough sample size to meet their needs.)

    b. Suppose an experienced travel agent indicates the possible proportion of travelers who select an airline based on ticket price is between 0.40 and 0.85. Determine the required sample size under these conditions.

7-66. Referring to Problem 65, suppose the travel agency considered the sample to be too large. Its managers have now decided they can afford to take a sample that is at most 350 people. If they don't want to alter their level of confidence, specifically what options are open to them?

7-67. A sample of 441 shoppers selected from people within the city of San Luis Obispo revealed that 76% made at least one purchase at a discount store last month.

    a. Based on this sample information what is the 90% confidence interval for the population proportion of shoppers who made at least one discount store purchase last month?

    b. The city of San Luis Obispo has a population of 35,000 people. It does not have a discount store. Therefore, shoppers travel outside of the city to make purchases at discount stores. Determine a 90% confidence interval for the number of shoppers who made at least one discount store purchase last month.

7-68. A company wishes to obtain the sample size required to determine its average ordering lead time to within 1 day with 95% confidence.

    a. If the standard deviation of lead times is known to be 7 days, determine the required sample size.

    b. Determine the largest and smallest lead times you could expect from this company. What assumption(s) must you make to validate your answer?

7-69. Open the file **High-Desert Banking**. Assume that these data reflect the population of all loans in the bank's portfolio.

    a. Select a random sample of 49 loans. Use this sample to construct a 90% confidence interval for the population mean of all loans in the High-Desert Bank's portfolio. (Hint: Remember to use the finite population correction factor since the sample is large relative to the size of the population.)

    b. Repeat this process 9 more times for a total of 10 samples, each of size 49.

    c. Compute the actual population mean for all loans in the portfolio. How many of the 10 confidence intervals that you constructed contain the population mean? How many intervals would you expect to contain the true population mean in the long run?

7-70. Paper-R-Us is a national distributor of printer and copier paper for commercial use. The data file called **Sales** contains the annual, year-to-date sales values for each of the company's customers. Suppose the internal audit department has decided to audit a sample of these accounts. Specifically, they have decided to sample 36 accounts. However, before they actually conduct the in-depth audit (a process that involves tracking all transactions for each sampled account), they want to be sure that the sample they have selected is representative of the population.

    a. Compute the population mean.

    b. Use all the data in the population to develop a frequency distribution and histogram.

c. Calculate the proportion of accounts for customers in each region of the country.

d. Based on the random sample of 36 accounts, develop a frequency distribution for these sample data. Compare this distribution to that of the population. (Hint: You might want to consider using relative frequencies for comparison purposes.)

e. Using the data from part d construct a 95% confidence interval estimate for the population mean of sales per customer. Discuss how you would use this interval estimate to help determine whether the sample is a good representative of the population. (Hint: You may want to use the finite correction factor since the sample is large relative to the size of the population.)

f. Use the information developed in parts a through e to draw a conclusion about whether the sample is a representative sample of the population. What other information would be desirable? Discuss.

7-71. In 1998, the University of Michigan conducted a study of college basketball players in the United States. A total of 758 players responded to the survey. Among these, 316 were female athletes. The study found that 546 athletes admitted to gambling since entering college. A total of 465 of the respondents said they had placed bets on sports, and 266 of the male athletes said they had bet on sports. Finally, 22 of the male athletes admitted to one or more of the following: providing inside information for gambling purposes, betting on a game in which they were playing, or shaving points for money. (Sources: *Idaho Statesman* and *Associated Press*, January 12, 1999.)

a. Develop a 95% confidence interval estimate for the proportion of all athletes who have gambled while in college. Interpret.

b. Develop a 99% confidence interval estimate for the proportion of male athletes who have gambled while in college. Interpret.

c. Construct and interpret a 95% confidence interval estimate for the proportion of male students who have shaved points, provided inside information, or bet on their own game.

d. Based on your responses to parts a through c, write a short report to the NCAA on the subject of gambling by student athletes.

7-72. The president of Morgan Fabrics, a nationwide manufacturer of fabric material for the garment industry, has recommitted the company to better serving its customers. One key measure of customer satisfaction is the proportion of on-time deliveries. The company did not use this measure in the past, so the president has no idea right now of what the company's previous on-time delivery rate has been. To establish this benchmark, the customer service manager has sampled 400 customer orders from this past year. Of these, 310 showed that the delivery had reached the customer by the promised date. Use these sample data to construct a 90% confidence interval of the true proportion of on-time deliveries for this company. Interpret this interval and discuss whether you feel this will be a good benchmark against which they can compare their future on-time delivery performance.

7-73. A random sample of 25 sports utility vehicles (SUVs) for the same year and model revealed the following miles per gallon (MPG) values:

12.4	13.0	12.6	12.1	13.1
13.0	12.0	13.1	11.4	12.6
9.5	13.25	12.4	10.7	11.7
10.0	14.0	10.9	9.9	10.2
11.0	11.9	9.9	12.0	11.3

Assume that the population distribution for mpg for this model year is normally distributed.

a. Use the sample results to develop a 95% confidence interval estimate for the population mean miles per gallon.

b. Determine the average number of gallons of gasoline the SUVs previously described would use to travel between Los Angeles and San Francisco, California—a distance of approximately 400 miles.

7-74. One of the major U.S. producers of household products recently surveyed 64 adults in order to estimate the proportion of adults who prefer mint-flavored toothpaste to plain toothpaste. The motive behind the survey was to aid in its production planning efforts. The results of the survey are contained in a file called **Toothpaste**.

a. Use these sample data to construct a 99% confidence interval of the population proportion of adults who prefer mint-flavored toothpaste. Explain how this might help the company plan its toothpaste production.

b. Suppose that you are the production manager for a relatively small toothpaste manufacturing company. You produce only mint-flavored and plain toothpaste. You are trying to decide what proportion of each of these you should produce. You would like the proportion of production to match that of the consumer's preference. You do, however, have a slightly larger profit margin on plain toothpaste. Determine the proportions of each type of toothpaste that you will produce. Support your answer with statistical reasoning related to the confidence interval produced in part a.

7-75. The brokerage firm of Gallusha, Higgins & Morton is considering buying another brokerage firm in the northeast. One factor that plays a part in the price it would be willing to pay for this firm is the cash balances of the current clients. The data file called **Gallusha** contains cash balance data as of a particular point in time for a sample of customers in the firm.

a. Assuming the population of cash account balances from which this sample was taken is normally distributed, construct a 96% confidence interval of the mean cash balance for all accounts for this firm.

b. Suppose that Gallusha representatives look at the confidence interval computed in part a and feel that the margin of error is too large. If they want to reduce the margin of error by 40%, what would be the required sample size, assuming that no change in confidence level takes place?

CASE 7-A

Duro Industries, Inc.

Rochelle Phillips was more nervous than she had been for a long time. Today was the day she would have to prepare an interim report to management on the new production process she had been testing at Duro Industries, Inc., a producer of bricks and paver blocks. Rochelle had started work at the company's Memphis plant right out of college, and she had worked her way up to assistant plant manager in charge of production during her 22 years with the company.

She knew her report could result in significant changes at Duro Industries. The company had been in business for 75 years and had established a solid regional reputation for quality and reliability in the manufacturing and delivery of its products. But the brick industry was changing rapidly. In addition to competition from other regional companies, Duro was facing increased competition from large foreign firms that were looking for ways to take Duro's best customers. Furthermore, there were fundamental changes underway in how brick companies managed their production processes.

Brick companies had traditionally relied on manual labor to move bricks through the manufacturing process. Duro was no different, employing hundreds of workers to help move bricks and paver blocks through the various manufacturing steps. But some foreign competitors, most notably Australian firms, were using vector drives to provide the precision motion control necessary to automatically move different quantities and configurations through the process accurately and repeatedly with less manual labor than before. This produced both cost savings and faster production times. If domestic firms adopted the same technology, the resulting cost savings could give them a competitive advantage in price and delivery times over Duro.

The CEO of Duro had notified Rochelle that her plant would be expected to evaluate the feasibility of undertaking this new approach to moving product through the process. If successful, Rochelle would head up the implementation team at the other Duro facilities in the United States. She was concerned that the implementation would be difficult and expensive. Furthermore, she was uncertain whether the expenditure on the vector drives would have a quick enough payback. Duro was convinced that the company had to at least investigate the feasibility of such a process, and the company was initially interested in the productivity improvements that might arise from such a plan.

Rochelle contacted a company that produced electric motors and vector drives, and its consultants told her that it would be possible to set up an experiment that would allow her to estimate whether the new process could increase production. Rochelle began to make plans for the test. She decided that once the new equipment was in place and the workers were trained in the new process, the experiment would run for 50 days. Each day's output would be recorded. The file called **Duro** contains the production output each day at the Memphis plant.

Rochelle needs to prepare a report that analyzes the data for the test period at the Memphis plant. The financial analysts at Duro headquarters believe the purchase can be justified if the equipment will lead to an average increase in production of at least 10,000 bricks per day. (Note: In Chapter 9, Rochelle will be asked to compare the output at the Memphis plant to that at a comparable plant in Birmingham, Alabama.)

CASE 7-B

Management Solutions, Inc.

The round trip to the "site" was just under 360 miles which gave Fred Kitchener and Mike Kyte plenty of time to discuss the next steps in the project. The "site" is a rural stretch of highway in Idaho where two visibility sensors are located. The project is part of a contract Fred's company, Management Solutions, Inc., has with the state of Idaho and the Federal Highway Administration. Under the contract, among other things, Management Solutions, Inc. is charged with evaluating the performance of a new technology for measuring visibility. The larger study involves determining whether visibility sensors can be effectively tied to electronic message signs that would warn motorists of upcoming visibility problems in rural areas.

Mike Kyte, a transportation engineer and professor at the University of Idaho, has been involved with the project as a consultant to Fred's company since the initial proposal. Mike is very knowledgeable about visibility sensors and traffic systems. Fred's expertise is in managing projects like this one where it is important to get people from multiple organizations to work together effectively.

As the pair headed back toward Boise from the "site," Mike was more excited than Fred had seen him in a long time. Fred reasoned that the source of excitement was that they had finally been successful in getting solid data to compare the two visibility sensors in a period of "low" visibility. The previous day at the site had been very foggy. The Scorpian Sensor is a tested technology that Mike had worked with for some time in urban applications. However, it had never been installed in such a remote location as this stretch of highway on I-84 which connects Idaho and Utah. The other sensor produced by the Vanguard company measures visibility in a totally new way using laser technology.

The data that excited Mike so much were collected by the two sensors and fed back to a computer system at the port-of-entry near the test site. The measurements were collected every 5 minutes for the entire 24-hour day. As Fred took advantage of the 75 mph speed limit through southern Idaho, Mike kept glancing at the data on the printout he had made of the first few 5-minute time periods. (See Figure 7-10.) The Scorpian system not only provided visibility readings, but it also provided other weather related data such as temperature, wind speed, wind direction, and humidity.

Mike's eyes went directly to the two visibility columns. Ideally, the visibility readings for the two sensors would be the same at any 5-minute period, but they weren't. After a few exclamations of surprise from Mike, Fred suggested that they come up with an outline for the report they would have to make from these data for the project team meeting next week. Both agreed that a full descriptive analysis of all the data including graphs and numerical measures was necessary. In addition, Fred wanted to use these early data to provide an estimate for the mean visibility provided by the two sensors. They agreed that estimates were needed for the day as a whole and also for only those periods when the Scorpian system showed visibility under 1.0 mile. They also felt that the analysis should look at the other weather factors, too, but they weren't sure just what was needed.

As the lights in the Boise Valley became visible, Mike agreed to work up a draft of the report including narrative based on the data in a computer file called **Visibility**. Fred said that he would set up the project team meeting agenda, and Mike could make the presentation. Both men agreed that the data were strictly a sample and that more low visibility data would be collected when conditions occurred.

FIGURE 7-10
Visibility Sensor Data for Management Solutions, Inc.

Microsoft Excel - Visibility.xls

	A	B	C	D	E	F	G	H	I
1	Time	Wind Spd	Wind Dir	Peak Gust	Air Temp	Rel Hum	Scorpian Visibility		Vanguard Visibility
2	12:02:24 AM	1	320	5	35	84	3.25		1.0998
3	12:07:24 AM	3	302	6	35	84	3.14		1.0998
4	12:12:18 AM	3	311	5	35	85	2.75		1.0998
5	12:17:18 AM	5	293	8	36	87	2.96		0.99618
6	12:22:24 AM	5	294	7	34	88	2.83		0.774225
7	12:27:24 AM	5	294	6	35	90	2.68		0.70962
8	12:32:18 AM	4	293	5	33	91	2.03		0.51226
9	12:37:24 AM	5	297	6	34	93	1.82		0.37356

GENERAL REFERENCES

1. Berenson, Mark L., and David M. Levine, *Basic Business Statistics: Concepts and Applications,* 7th ed. (Upper Saddle River, NJ: Prentice Hall, 1999).
2. Dodge, Mark, and Craig Stinson, *Running Microsoft Excel 2000* (Redmond, WA: Microsoft Press, 1999).
3. Hogg, Robert V., and Elliot A. Tanis, *Probability and Statistical Inference,* 5th ed. (Upper Saddle River, NJ: Prentice Hall, 1997).
4. Marx, Morris L., and Richard J. Larsen, *Mathematical Statistics and Its Applications,* 3d ed. (Upper Saddle River, NJ: Prentice Hall, 2000).
5. *Microsoft Excel 2000* (Redmond, WA: Microsoft Corporation, 1999).
6. *Minitab for Windows Version 13* (State College, PA: Minitab, Inc., 2000).
7. Siegel, Andrew F., *Practical Business Statistics,* 4th ed. (Burr Ridge, IL: Irwin, 2000).

CHAPTER 8

INTRODUCTION TO HYPOTHESIS TESTING

CHAPTER OUTCOMES

After studying the material in Chapter 8, you should be able to:

8-1: Formulate null and alternative hypotheses for applications involving a single population mean, proportion, or variance.

8-2: Correctly formulate a decision rule for testing a null hypothesis.

8-3: Know how to use the test statistic, critical value, and *p*-value approach to test the null hypothesis.

8-4: Know what Type I and Type II errors are.

8-5: Be able to compute the probability of a Type II error.

WHY YOU NEED TO KNOW

Chapter 7 introduced the steps required to estimate the value of a population mean or proportion based on data from a simple random sample. Based on those estimates, decision makers are able to draw inferences about the population without having to conduct a costly and time-consuming census. Estimation is required when the decision maker may have no specific knowledge of the population value but seeks to gain that knowledge.

However, many times managers know what a population value should be because of company policy or contract specification and must be able to use sample information to determine whether the policy or contract specification is being satisfied. For instance, large metropolitan areas are required to report air pollution levels on a daily basis. They must state whether they have exceeded federal standards on different pollution measures. They cannot possibly sample all the air in the metropolitan area, yet they are required to report whether the city's air quality meets federal standards. When CPA firms perform audits they issue a final report stating whether the audited firm followed generally acceptable accounting procedures. They are unable to audit every transaction so must make the statement based on a sample of transactions. Even

construction crews pouring foundations for large buildings need to determine whether the concrete meets specifications. Taking core samples (long cylinders cut from the poured foundation) and testing these samples does this. The core samples provide information that building inspectors and construction managers use to decide whether construction work can continue, or whether foundations must be further reinforced.

Imagine for a moment that you are the buyer for a company that makes home thermostats (which are used to regulate the heating and cooling systems in homes). A new producer of a major electronic component used in your thermostats claims that no more than 3% of its components will have a sensing error of 2 degrees or more. Before you buy 100,000 units, you might want to test the manufacturer's claim. Since you could not feasibly test each component, you would select a sample and use the sample information to decide whether to make the purchase.

This chapter introduces statistical techniques used to test claims about population values. You need to have a solid understanding of these techniques in order to use sample information effectively in their decision making.

■ 8-1: HYPOTHESES TESTS FOR MEANS

By now you know that information contained in a sample is subject to sampling error. The sample mean will likely not equal the population mean. Thus, in situations where you need to test a claim about a population mean by using the sample mean, you can't simply compare the sample mean to the claim and reject the claim if $\bar{x}$ and the claim are different. Instead, you need a testing procedure that incorporates the potential for sampling error.

Statistical hypothesis testing provides managers with a structured analytical method for making decisions of this type. It lets them make decisions in such a way that the probability of errors can be controlled, or at least measured. Even though statistical hypothesis testing does not eliminate the uncertainty in the managerial environment, the techniques involved often allow managers to identify and control the level of uncertainty.

The techniques presented in this chapter assume the data were selected using an appropriate statistical sampling process.

Formulating the Hypotheses

NULL AND ALTERNATIVE HYPOTHESES

In hypothesis testing, two hypotheses are formulated. One is the **null hypothesis**.

> **NULL HYPOTHESIS** H_o
> The statement about the population value that will be tested. The null hypothesis will be rejected only if the sample data provide substantial contradictory evidence.

The null hypothesis is represented by H_0 and should contain an equality sign, such as "$=$," "$\leq$," or "$\geq$." The second hypothesis is the **alternative hypothesis** (represented by H_A).

ALTERNATIVE HYPOTHESIS H_a or H_1

The hypothesis that includes all population values not covered by the null hypothesis. The alternative hypothesis is deemed to be true if the null hypothesis is rejected.

Based on the sample data, we either reject H_0 or we do not reject H_0.

EXAMPLE 8-1

HYPOTHESIS TESTING

The State Insurance Fund

The State Insurance Fund administers the workmen's compensation system. The agency is under legislative inquiry based on complaints from companies covered by the fund. The major source of complaint is that the average processing time exceeds the legally mandated average of 25 days. The fund managers believe they are within the 25 day average response, although they admit for some complicated claims the response time may be longer.

Since the legislative committee has requested a quick reply, the fund managers cannot gather information from all claims filed this year and, therefore, must formulate a response based on a sample of claims. As indicated earlier, when a decision is based on sample results, sampling error must be expected. Without considering the effect of sampling error, the managers can't simply say that if the sample mean is 25 days or less then the population mean is also. Likewise, if the sample mean exceeds 25 days, that does not automatically indicate the population mean exceeds 25 days.

To account for the potential sampling error, the managers need to formally test whether the sample value supports the conclusion that the population mean is less than or equal to 25 days or supports the conclusion that the average time exceeds 25 days. The first step is to express these two possibilities using formal hypothesis testing terms.

In this example, concluding that the mean processing time is greater than 25 days would imply that something is wrong, and the fund managers need to change their operating procedures. Making these changes would be expensive and time consuming. Thus, the default position is that no change is needed. In this case, the null and alternative hypotheses are stated as:

Format

Null hypothesis	$H_0: \mu \leq 25$ days
Alternative hypothesis	$H_A: \mu > 25$ days

→ always population mean, for our class!

where μ is the mean claim-processing time.

This formulation for the null and alternative hypotheses puts the burden of proof on those filing the complaint. Unless the sample mean is "substantially" greater than 25 days, no action will be taken to change the system.

THE RESEARCH HYPOTHESIS

Another way to think about formulating the null and alternative hypotheses is to consider research applications. Companies such as Intel, Gillette, Dell Computers, and 3M continually bring out new and improved products. However, before introducing a new product the companies want to be sure the new product is superior. They want sufficient evidence of the new product's superiority. The default position is that the existing product or process is at least as good as the new one. The burden of proof rests with the new idea. Only if the sample test results are "substantially" better for the new product or process will it be deemed superior. In these situations, when the decision maker has control over how the null and alternative hypotheses are stated, the alternative hypothesis should be the **research hypothesis**.

RESEARCH HYPOTHESIS   *"statistical evidence"*

The hypothesis the decision maker attempts to demonstrate to be true. Since this is the hypothesis deemed to be the most important to the decision maker, it will not be declared true unless the sample data strongly indicates that it is true.

If the research hypothesis forms the alternative hypothesis, a decision to reject the null hypothesis would indicate that there is statistical evidence to believe that the research hypothesis is true.

Types of Statistical Errors

Because of the potential for sampling error, two possible errors can occur when a hypothesis is tested. These are called **Type I** and **Type II errors**. These errors show the relationships between what actually exists (a state of nature) and the decision made based on the sample information.

TYPE I ERROR
Rejecting the null hypothesis when it is, in fact, true.

also known as alpha or producer risk

TYPE II ERROR
Failing to reject the null hypothesis when it is, in fact, false. *beta error, consumer risk*

Figure 8-1 shows the possible actions and states of nature associated with any hypothesis-testing application. As you can see, there are three possible outcomes: no error (correct decision), Type I error, and Type II error. Only one of these outcomes will occur for a hypothesis test. From Figure 8-1, if the null hypothesis is true and an error is made, it must be a Type I error. On the other hand, if the null hypothesis is false and an error is made, it must be a Type II error.

Many statisticians argue that you should never use the phrase "accept the null hypothesis." Instead you should use "*do not reject* the null hypothesis." Thus, the only two hypothesis testing decisions would be *reject* H_0 or *do not reject* H_0. This is similar reasoning to that used in a jury verdict to acquit a defendant when the verdict is "not guilty" rather than innocent. Just because the evidence is insufficient to convict does not necessarily mean that the defendant is innocent.

This thinking is appropriate when hypothesis testing is employed in situations where some future action is not dependent on the results of the hypothesis test. However, in most business applications, the purpose of the hypothesis test is to direct the decision maker to take one action or another based on the results of the test. For instance, in the State Insurance Fund example, if the sample data do not lead the managers to reject that $\mu \leq 25$ days, the State Insurance Fund managers will write a report to the legislature indicating that the customer assertions are not supported. Therefore, no changes will be made in the claims evaluation process. Although they have "not rejected" the null hypothesis, their actions are consistent with what would have taken place if they had "accepted" the null hypothesis. Thus, in this text, where hypothesis testing is applied to decision-making situations, *not rejecting* the null hypothesis is essentially the same as *accepting* it.[1]

FIGURE 8-1
The Relationship Between Decisions and States of Nature

"*Fail to reject*" us = *accept*

		State of Nature	
		Null Hypothesis True	Null Hypothesis False
Decision	Conclude Null True (Don't reject H_0)	Correct Decision $1 - \alpha$	Type II Error β
	Conclude Null False (Reject H_0)	Type I Error α	Correct Decision $1 - \beta \rightarrow$ power value

[1]Whichever language you use, you should make an effort to understand both arguments and make an informed choice. If your instructor requests that you reference the action in a particular way, it would behoove you to follow his or her instructions. Having gone through this process ourselves, we prefer to state the choice as "don't reject the null hypothesis." This terminology will be used throughout this text.

EXAMPLE

8-2

HYPOTHESIS
TESTING

The State Insurance Fund (continued)

In the State Insurance Fund hypothesis test, a Type I error would occur if the sample data lead the managers to conclude that $\mu > 25$ days (H_0 is rejected) when the truth is that $\mu \leq 25$ days. The result would be that the managers would undertake an effort to change the system when no changes were actually required. This would be a costly waste of resources.

A Type II error would occur if the sample evidence leads the managers to incorrectly conclude that $\mu \leq 25$ days (H_0 is not rejected) when the truth is that the mean response time exceeds 25 days. The outcome is that nothing would be done to the system when changes were actually needed.

Establishing the Decision Rule

The objective of a hypothesis test is to use sample information to decide whether to reject or not reject the null hypothesis about a population parameter. How do decision makers determine whether the sample information supports or refutes the null hypothesis? The answer to this question is the key to understanding statistical hypothesis testing.

In hypotheses tests for a single population mean, the sample mean, $\bar{x}$, is used to test the hypotheses under consideration. Depending on how the null and alternative hypotheses are formulated, certain values of $\bar{x}$ will tend to support the null hypothesis while other values will appear to contradict it. In the State Insurance Fund example the null and alternative hypotheses were formulated as:

$$H_0: \mu \leq 25 \text{ days}$$
$$H_A: \mu > 25 \text{ days}$$

Values of $\bar{x}$ less than or equal to 25 days would tend to support the null hypothesis. By contrast, values of $\bar{x}$ above 25 days would tend to refute the null hypothesis. The larger the value of $\bar{x}$, the greater the evidence that the null hypothesis should be rejected. However, since we expect some sampling error, do we want to reject H_0 for any value of $\bar{x}$ that is greater than 25 days? Probably not. But should we reject H_0 if $\bar{x} = 26$ days, or $\bar{x} = 30$ days, or $\bar{x} = 35$ days? At what point do we stop attributing the result to sampling error?

CRITICAL VALUE AND SIGNIFICANCE LEVEL

The job of the decision maker is to establish a cutoff point, called a **critical value**, that is the demarcation between failing to reject and rejecting the null hypothesis. When the critical value is stated in terms of the sample mean it is labeled $\bar{x}_\alpha$.

Establishing the decision rule.

> **CRITICAL VALUE**
> The value of a statistic corresponding to a given significance level. This cutoff value, $\bar{x}_\alpha$, determines the boundary between those samples resulting in a test statistic that leads to rejecting the null hypothesis and those that lead to a decision not to reject the null hypothesis.

does not say "accept"

Recall from the Central Limit Theorem (see Chapter 6) that, for large samples, the distribution of the possible sample means is approximately normal with a center at the population mean, μ. The null hypothesis in our example is $\mu \leq 25$ days. Figure 8-2 shows the distribution of possible sample means for the State Insurance Fund if $\mu = 25$ days. In order to perform the hypothesis test for the State Insurance Fund, we need to determine the critical value, $\bar{x}_\alpha$. For example, the critical value, $\bar{x}_\alpha$, might be located as shown in Figure 8-3. The shaded area represents the rejection region. When $\bar{x} > \bar{x}_\alpha$, H_0 is rejected. Since $\bar{x}$ can exceed $\bar{x}_\alpha$ even if H_0 is true ($\mu \leq 25$), the area in the rejection region represents the maximum probability of a Type I statistical error. This probability is called the **significance level** and is given the symbol α (alpha).

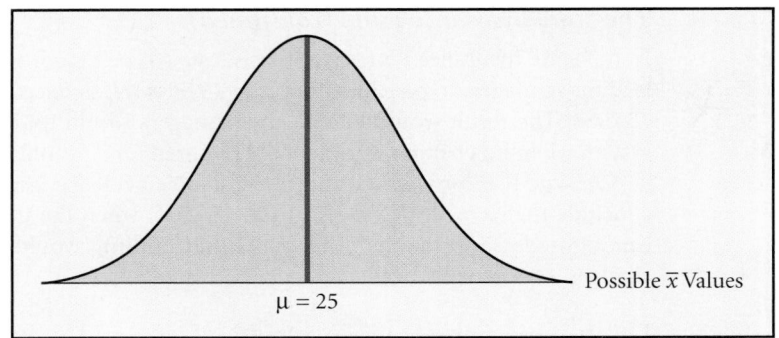

FIGURE 8-2
Sampling Distribution of $\bar{x}$
for the State Insurance Fund

[handwritten note] Effect of pre establishing the value of α + β before analysis

---

SIGNIFICANCE LEVEL
The maximum probability of committing a Type I statistical error. The probability is denoted by the symbol α.

To determine the critical value, we must specify the significance level, α. The value of α is determined based on the costs involved in committing a Type I error. If making a Type I error is costly, we will want the probability of a Type I error to be small. If a Type I error is less costly, then we can allow a higher probability of a Type I error.

However, in determining α, we must also take into account the probability of making a Type II error, which is given the symbol β (*beta*). For a fixed sample size, the two error probabilities, α and β are inversely related.[2] That is, if we reduce α, then β will increase. Thus, in setting α, you must consider both sides of the issue.

Calculating the specific dollar costs associated with making the Type I and Type II errors is often difficult and may require a subjective management decision. Therefore, any two managers might well arrive at different alpha levels. However, in the end, the choice for alpha must reflect the decision maker's best estimate of the costs of these two errors.[3]

The State Insurance Fund (*continued*)

Suppose the managers decide they are willing to incur a 0.10 probability of committing a Type I error. Assume also that the population standard deviation, σ, for processing claims is 3 days and the sample size is 64 claims. The critical value can be stated in either

EXAMPLE 8-3

HYPOTHESIS TESTING

FIGURE 8-3
Critical Value for the State
Insurance Fund Example

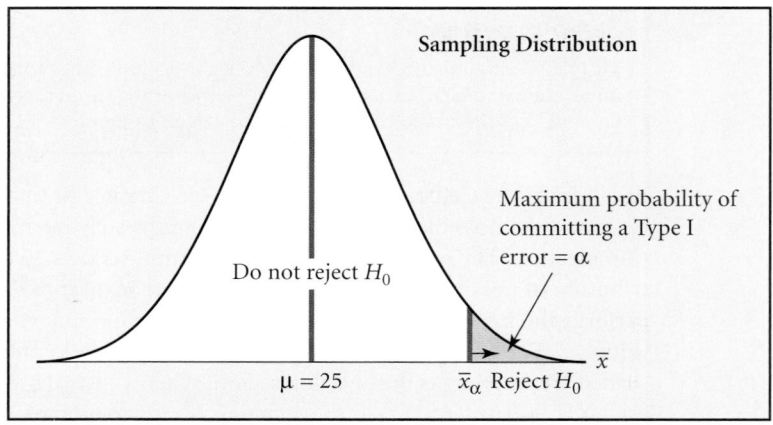

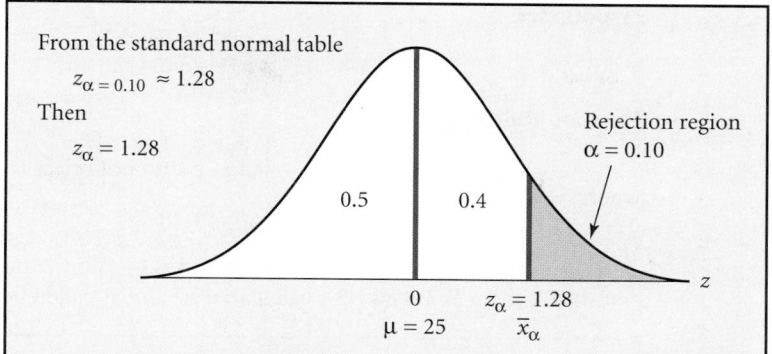

FIGURE 8-4
Establishing the Critical Value
as a *z*-Value

of two ways. First, we can establish the critical value as the number of standard deviations the critical value, $\bar{x}_\alpha$, is from μ. Figure 8-4 shows that if the rejection region on the upper end (as indicated by the alternative hypothesis) of the sampling distribution has an area of 0.10, the *z*-value determined from the standard normal table (or by using Excel's NORMSINV function) corresponding to the critical value is 1.28. If the sample mean lies more than 1.28 standard deviations above $\mu = 25$ days, H_0 should be rejected; otherwise we will not reject H_0. Having found the critical value in terms of a *z*-value, we can also express it in the same units as the sample mean. In the Insurance Fund example, the critical value, $\bar{x}_\alpha$, can be stated in terms of days such that, if $\bar{x}$ is greater than the critical value, we should reject H_0. If $\bar{x}$ is *less than or equal to the critical value*, we should not reject H_0. Figure 8-5 shows how the critical value, $\bar{x}_\alpha$, is determined using this method. If $\bar{x} > 25.48$ days, H_0 should be rejected and changes made in the process. Any sample mean less than or equal to 25.48 means that the null hypothesis should not be rejected. To conduct the hypothesis test, you can use two approaches. You can calculate a *z*-value and compare it to the critical value, z_α. Alternatively, you can calculate the sample mean, $\bar{x}$, and compare it to the critical value, $\bar{x}_\alpha$. It makes no difference which approach you use in establishing the critical value as long as you use the corresponding statistic to make your decision.

Suppose $\bar{x} = 26$ days. How we test the null hypothesis depends on the procedure we used to establish the critical value. First, using the *z*-value method, we establish the following decision rule.

FIGURE 8-5
Determining the Critical
Value for the State Insurance
Fund Example

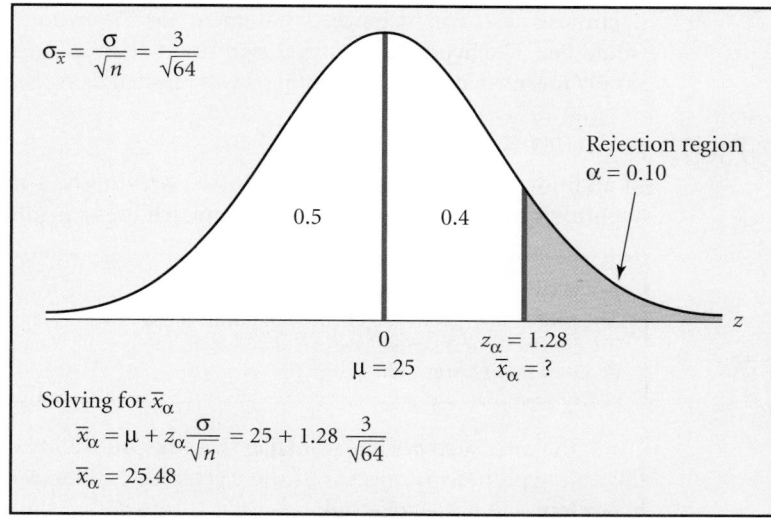

Hypotheses:

$$H_0: \mu \leq 25 \text{ days}$$
$$H_A: \mu > 25 \text{ days}$$
$$\alpha = 0.10$$

Decision Rule:

If $z > z_\alpha$, reject H_0
If $z \leq z_\alpha$, do not reject H_0

where:

$$z_\alpha = 1.28$$

Recall that the number of claims tested is 64 and the population standard deviation is assumed known at 3 days. The calculated z-value is called the *test statistic*.

TEST STATISTIC

A function of the sampled observations that provides a basis for testing a statistical hypothesis.

 *(handwritten: "3 approaches :")*

The z test statistic is computed as follows.

$$z = \frac{\bar{x} - \mu}{\dfrac{\sigma}{\sqrt{n}}} = \frac{26 - 25}{\dfrac{3}{\sqrt{64}}} = 2.67$$

The sample mean is 2.67 standard deviations above the hypothesized mean. Since $z = 2.67$ is greater than the critical value $z_\alpha = 1.28$, we clearly reject H_0.

Now we use the second approach, which established (see Figure 8-5) a decision rule as follows.

Decision Rule:

If $\bar{x} > \bar{x}_\alpha$, reject H_0.
If $\bar{x} \leq \bar{x}_\alpha$, do not reject H_0.

then:

If $\bar{x} > 25.48$ days, reject H_0.
If $\bar{x} \leq 25.48$ days, do not reject H_0.
Since $\bar{x} = 26 > 25.48$, H_0 should be rejected.

Note that the two methods yield the same conclusion, as they always will if you perform the calculations correctly. We have found that academic applications of hypothesis testing tend to use the z-value method while organizational applications of hypothesis testing use the $\bar{x}$ approach.

You will often come across a different language used to express the outcome of a hypothesis test. For instance, a statement for the hypothesis test presented previously would be, "The hypothesis test was significant at an α (or significance level) of 0.10." This simply means that the null hypothesis was rejected using a significance level of 0.10.

p-VALUES

In addition to the two methods discussed previously, a third approach for conducting hypothesis tests also exists. This third approach uses a ***p*-value** instead of a critical value.

***p*-VALUE**

The probability (assuming the null hypothesis is true) of obtaining a test statistic at least as extreme as the test statistic we calculated from the sample. The *p*-value is also known as the *observed significance level*.

If the calculated *p*-value is smaller than the probability in the rejection region (α), then the null hypothesis is rejected. If the calculated *p*-value is equal to or greater than α, the hypothesis will not be rejected.

The *p*-value approach is popular today because *p*-values are usually computed by statistical software packages, including Excel and Minitab. The advantage to reporting test results using a *p*-value is that it provides more information than simply stating that the null hypothesis is or is not rejected. The decision maker is presented with a measure of the degree of significance of the result (i.e., the *p*-value). This allows the reader the opportunity to evaluate the *extent* to which the data disagree with the null hypothesis, not just whether or not it disagrees.

State Insurance Fund (continued)

In the State Insurance Fund example, recall that $\bar{x} = 26$ days based on the sample of 64 claims. The population standard deviation, σ, is assumed known with a value of 3 days. We first determine the test statistic *z*-value.

$$z = \frac{\bar{x} - \mu}{\dfrac{\sigma}{\sqrt{n}}} = \frac{26 - 25}{\dfrac{3}{\sqrt{64}}} = 2.67$$

To compute the *p*-value manually for this hypothesis test we first go to the standard normal table in Appendix D to find the probability for a *z*-value of 2.67. In this case, the calculated *p*-value is the probability that the test statistic, *z*, is at least 2.67. From the standard normal distribution table, the $P(z \geq 2.67) = 0.5000 - 0.4962 = 0.0038$. Thus, we would report a *p*-value to 4 decimal places of 0.0038. Since $0.0038 < 0.10$, the null hypothesis should be rejected. This is the same conclusion reached earlier using the critical-value approach. Small *p*-values provide evidence to reject the null hypothesis. The smaller the *p*-value, the stronger the sample evidence is to reject.

Figure 8-6 demonstrates the relationship between the *p*-value and the rejection region. You can see that if the test statistic (*z* or $\bar{x}$) is in the rejection region then the *p*-value must be smaller than the significance level, α. In either case, the null hypothesis is rejected. Conversely, if the *p*-value is larger than the significance level, the test statistic cannot be in the rejection region. Either way the null hypothesis is not rejected. Whatever decision is reached using the test statistic approach must also be reached by the *p*-value approach.

Why do we need three methods to test the same hypothesis when they all give the same result? The answer is that we don't. However, you need to be aware of all three methods, since you will encounter each in business situations. The *p*-value approach is especially important since many statistical software packages output a *p*-value that you can use to test a hypothesis quite easily. Plus using a *p*-value means you don't need probability distribution tables. This text will use both test statistic approaches, as well as the *p*-value approach to hypothesis testing.

EXAMPLE 8-4

p-VALUES

FIGURE 8-6
Relationship Between the *p*-Value and the Rejection Region—State Insurance Fund Example

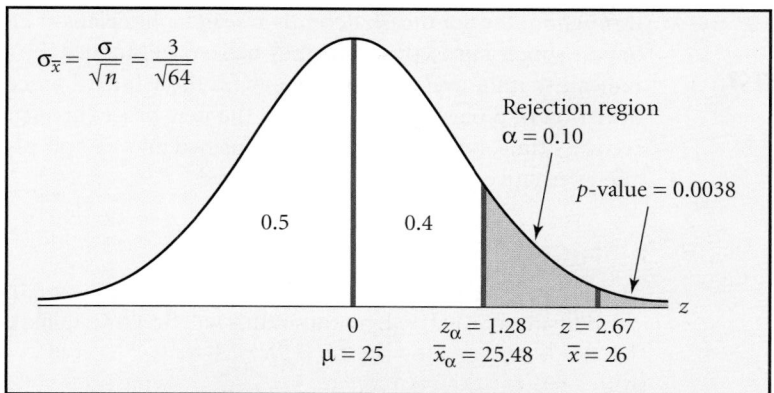

Excel Simulation

Hypothesis
Testing

SUMMARY OF THE HYPOTHESIS TESTING PROCESS
The hypothesis testing process discussed in this section can be summarized in 6 steps:

1. Determine the null hypothesis and the alternative hypothesis.
2. Determine the desired significance level (α).
3. Define the test method and sample size and determine a critical value.
4. Select the sample, calculate $\bar{x}$, and calculate the z-value or p-value. (We strongly suggest you draw a picture showing where in the distribution the rejection region(s) occurs.)
5. Establish a decision rule comparing the sample statistic, $\bar{x}$ or z, with the critical value, $\bar{x}_\alpha$ or z_α. Alternatively, compare the p-value to alpha.
6. Reach a conclusion regarding the null hypothesis.

With only minor modifications, these 6 steps can be used as a template to test null hypotheses in any of the applications introduced throughout the remainder of this text. We urge you to become well acquainted with the hypothesis testing process, as it is a fundamental part of statistical decision making.

One-Tailed Hypothesis Tests

In the State Insurance Fund example, the null hypothesis could be refuted only if the sample mean was too large (that is, too far to the right of $\mu = 25$ days). Consequently, the critical value, $\bar{x}_\alpha$, was placed in the right-hand (upper) tail of the normal curve. That example illustrates a **one-tailed hypothesis test**.

ONE-TAILED HYPOTHESIS TEST
A hypothesis test in which the entire rejection region is located in one tail of the test statistic distribution.

A one-tailed hypothesis test will assume one of two forms, depending on the way the null and alternative hypotheses are stated. Examples of these two forms are:

1	2
$H_0: \mu \leq 50$	$H_0: \mu \geq 16$
$H_A: \mu > 50$	$H_A: \mu < 16$

In either case, the entire rejection area will be in one tail of the sampling distribution.

EXAMPLE **8-5**

ONE-TAILED TEST

Elgin Heart Institute

The Elgin Heart Institute performs many open-heart surgery procedures at its 10 facilities throughout the Southeast. Recently research physicians at Elgin have developed a new heart bypass surgery procedure that they believe will reduce the average recovery time. Records indicate that the average recovery rate for the standard procedure is 42 days with a standard deviation of 5 days. To test whether the new procedure actually results in a lower average recovery time, the procedure was performed on a sample of 36 patients. The following null and alternative hypotheses are formulated:

$$H_0: \mu \geq 42$$
$$H_A: \mu < 42$$

The researchers wish to test the hypothesis using a 0.05 level of significance. As indicated by the alternative hypothesis, this will be a one-tailed test with the rejection region in the lower (left-hand) tail of the sampling distribution. The average recovery time for the 36 patients was 40.2 days. The critical value for this test is:

$$\mu - z_\alpha \frac{\sigma}{\sqrt{n}} = 42 - 1.645 \frac{5}{\sqrt{36}} = 40.629$$

Thus, if $\bar{x} < 40.629$ days, the null hypothesis should be rejected. Since $\bar{x} = 40.2$ is less than 40.629 there is sufficient evidence to conclude that the new heart bypass procedure does result in a shorter average recovery period.

Two-Tailed Tests

Cranston Peanuts

Sometimes the null hypothesis is stated as a direct equality, as shown here in an example involving the Cranston Peanut Company. Cranston grows and packages salted and unsalted unshelled peanuts in 16-ounce sacks. The company's filling process strives for an average fill amount equal to 16 ounces. However, not all sacks contain exactly 16 ounces, and the population standard deviation is known to be 0.80 ounces. Each day, company inspectors select a random sample of 40 peanut sacks and measure the weight in each sack. Based on the average fill amount in the sample, they test the following null and alternative hypotheses:

$$H_0: \mu = 16 \text{ ounces}$$
$$H_A: \mu \neq 16 \text{ ounces}$$

They plan to use a significance level equal to 0.10. Notice that the company is concerned that the true average fill may be greater than 16 ounces (lost profit) or less than 16 ounces (shortchanging customers). In this situation, the rejection region is established in both tails of the sampling distribution. We can establish critical values for both tails of the distribution as shown in Figure 8-7. The null hypothesis will be rejected if the test statistic falls in either tail of the distribution. The size of the rejection region is determined by α.

Each tail has an area equal to $\frac{\alpha}{2}$. To determine the critical values, the significance level is divided in two. Half of the significance level ($\alpha/2$) would be placed in the upper tail and half in the lower tail. The critical value in terms of z-values would, therefore, be $\pm z_{\alpha/2} = \pm z_{0.05} = \pm 1.645$.

EXAMPLE

8-6

TWO-TAILED TEST

FIGURE 8-7
Rejection Regions for Two-Tailed Hypothesis Test

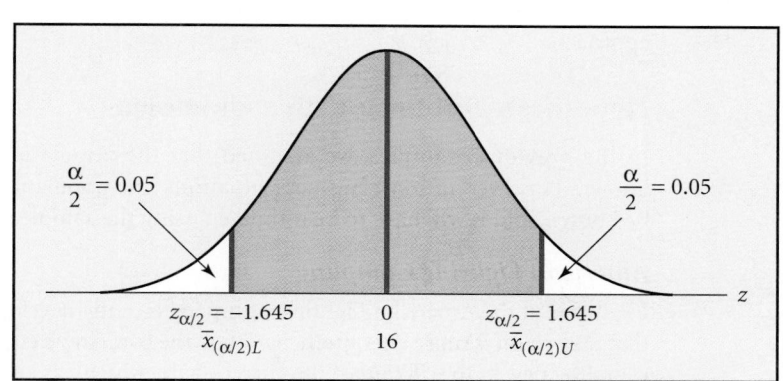

The two critical values in terms of the sample means are denoted as $\bar{x}_{(\alpha/2)L}$ and $\bar{x}_{(\alpha/2)U}$. These denote the lower and upper critical values, respectively. They are obtained as follows.

$$\bar{x}_{(\alpha/2)L} = \mu - z_{\alpha/2}\frac{\sigma}{\sqrt{n}} = 16 - 1.645\frac{0.80}{\sqrt{40}} = 15.792 \text{ and}$$

$$\bar{x}_{(\alpha/2)U} = \mu + z_{\alpha/2}\frac{\sigma}{\sqrt{n}} = 16 + 1.645\frac{0.80}{\sqrt{40}} = 16.208, \text{ respectively.}$$

If $15.792 \le \bar{x} \le 16.208$, the null hypothesis should not be rejected and the filling process should be left alone. However, if $\bar{x}$ falls outside either of these critical values, the company should conclude it has a problem with its filling process. Suppose on a particular day, the sample mean for 40 sacks is 16.42 ounces. The null hypothesis will be rejected and the process will be adjusted.

p-VALUE FOR TWO-TAILED TEST

The p-value for a **two-tailed hypothesis test** is computed in a manner similar to that for a one-tailed test.

> **TWO-TAILED HYPOTHESIS TEST**
> A hypothesis test in which the rejection region is split between the two tails of the test statistic's distribution.

First, determine the z test statistic as follows.

$$z = \frac{\bar{x} - \mu}{\dfrac{\sigma}{\sqrt{n}}} = \frac{16.42 - 16}{\dfrac{0.80}{\sqrt{40}}} = 3.32$$

Next, find $P(z > 3.32)$ using either the standard normal table in Appendix D or Excel's NORMSDIST function. In this case since $z = 3.32$ exceeds the table values, we will use the NORMSDIST(3.32) which gives 0.9995. This is $P(z \le 3.32)$. Then $P(z > 3.32) = 1 - 0.9995 = 0.0005$. However, since this is a two-tailed hypothesis test, the p-value is found by multiplying the 0.0005 value by 2 (to account for the chance that our sample result could have been on either side of the distribution). This is:

$$\text{p-value} = 2(0.0005) = 0.0010$$

Since the p-value $= 0.0010 <$ alpha $= 0.10$, the sample data lead us to reject the null hypothesis. This, of course, is the same decision we reached using the critical value approach.

Hypothesis Test for μ with σ Unknown

In the previous examples, we assumed that the population standard deviation, σ, was known. However, in most business situations, the population standard deviation will not be known, and it will have to be estimated using the sample standard deviation, s.

HYPOTHESIS TEST

American Lighting Company

Engineers at the American Lighting Company recently developed a new three-way lightbulb that they claim is more energy efficient than the company's current three-way bulb. They also claim the new bulb will outlast the current bulb, which has an average lifetime of 700 hours.

Before beginning full-scale production on the new lightbulbs, the company will test them to determine if they really do exceed the current bulb's mean life of 700 hours. This becomes the research hypothesis. The company will not begin full-scale production unless the sample data provide convincing evidence that the average life of the new bulbs does exceed 700 hours. If the new bulbs are determined to be no better than the existing bulbs, they will not be produced. A random sample of 100 new lightbulbs was selected, and the following sample results were reported.

$$\bar{x} = 702 \text{ hours}$$
$$s = 15 \text{ hours}$$

To test the claim about the bulbs, formulate the null and alternative hypotheses as follows.

Hypotheses

$$H_0: \mu \leq 700 \text{ hours}$$
$$H_A: \mu > 700 \text{ hours (claim)}$$
$$\alpha = 0.05$$

Note that we have placed the claim in the alternative hypothesis. This was done because the company would not begin production unless the data provided sufficient evidence that the new bulbs were better. This puts the burden on the new product to show that it is superior to the old product.

Figure 8-8 shows the results of the hypothesis test. When the population standard deviation, σ, is unknown, the appropriate test statistic is a t-distribution with $n - 1$ degrees of freedom. Note also that s, the sample standard deviation, is used in place of σ in computing the test statistic. As Figure 8-8 shows, the sample mean is only 1.33 estimated standard errors above the hypothesized mean. Thus the difference between $\bar{x}$ and the hypothesized mean is not sufficient to reject H_0. American Lighting may have a superior bulb in terms of energy efficiency, but it cannot conclude the same thing for the average life.

Dairy Fresh Ice Cream

Consider the Dairy Fresh Ice Cream plant in Pittsburgh, Pennsylvania. The plant produces ice cream sold under the Dairy Fresh brand name and a number of store brand names throughout the East. The production process is highly automated. The filling machine for the 64-ounce cartons is good but not perfect. There is some variation in the actual amount of ice cream that goes into the 64-ounce carton. The machine can go out of adjustment and put a mean amount either less than 64 ounces or more than 64 ounces in the cartons.

EXAMPLE

8-8

HYPOTHESIS TEST

FIGURE 8-8
Hypothesis Test for the
American Lighting Company

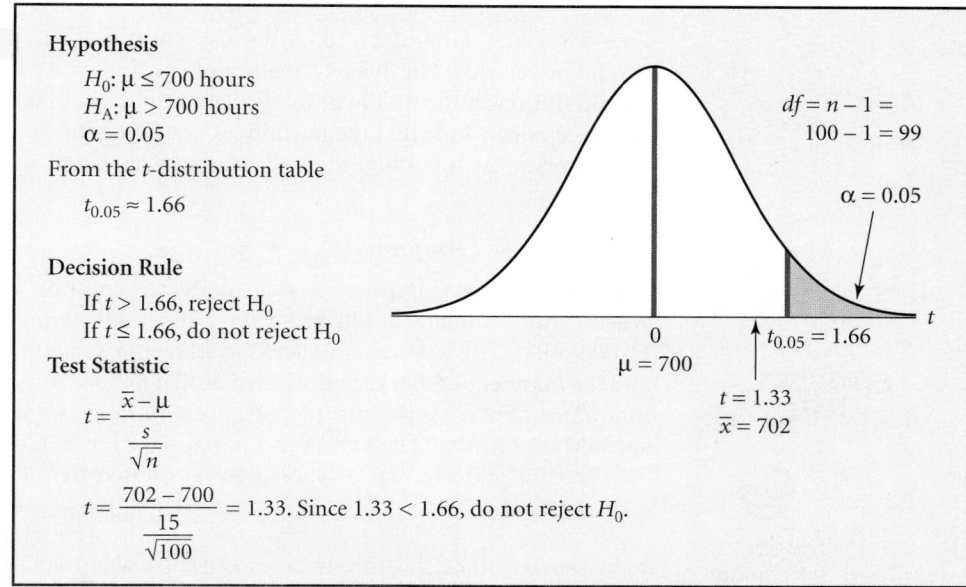

Hypothesis

$H_0: \mu \leq 700$ hours
$H_A: \mu > 700$ hours
$\alpha = 0.05$

From the t-distribution table

$t_{0.05} \approx 1.66$

$df = n - 1 =$
$100 - 1 = 99$

$\alpha = 0.05$

Decision Rule

If $t > 1.66$, reject H_0
If $t \leq 1.66$, do not reject H_0

Test Statistic

$$t = \frac{\bar{x} - \mu}{\frac{s}{\sqrt{n}}}$$

$$t = \frac{702 - 700}{\frac{15}{\sqrt{100}}} = 1.33. \text{ Since } 1.33 < 1.66, \text{ do not reject } H_0.$$

$t_{0.05} = 1.66$

0
$\mu = 700$

$t = 1.33$
$\bar{x} = 702$

To monitor the filling process, the production manager selects a sample of 30 ice-cream cartons filled during each day. The sample information is used to test the following null and alternative hypotheses.

$$H_0: \mu = 64 \text{ ounces} \quad \text{(Machine is in adjustment)}$$
$$H_A: \mu \neq 64 \text{ ounces} \quad \text{(Machine is out of adjustment)}$$

Due to potential sampling error, the sample mean may exceed 64 ounces or be less than 64 ounces. The production manager will not reject the null hypothesis as long as the difference appears to be due to sampling error. If the difference becomes too extreme, however, the null hypothesis will be rejected and the machine will be readjusted.

In establishing the decision rule, the production manager must decide which values of $\bar{x}$ will tend to refute the null hypothesis. In this example, values of $\bar{x}$ that are either too large or too small should lead to rejecting the null hypothesis, and the rejection region is divided into two tails. (Although not required, the general convention is to divide the rejection region equally between the two tails of the sampling distribution. The examples and problems in this text will follow this pattern.)

Suppose the production manager specifies an $\alpha = 0.05$, meaning that she is willing to have a maximum 5% chance of rejecting the null hypothesis when it is really true. A particular day's sample of 30 cartons resulted in a sample mean of 64.12 ounces, with a sample standard deviation of 0.50 ounces. Figure 8-9 illustrates the decision rule. Since σ is unknown, if we assume that the population distribution is approximately normally distributed, the t-distribution can be used to establish the critical values. First, from the t-distribution table (Appendix F) we find the t-values for $n - 1 = 29$ degrees of freedom and tail areas of $\alpha/2 = 0.025$ as:

$$t_{0.025, \, 29} = \pm 2.045$$

We compute the critical values, $\bar{x}_{\frac{\alpha}{2}L}$ and $\bar{x}_{\frac{\alpha}{2}U}$, as follows:

$$\bar{x}_{(\alpha/2)L} = \mu - t_{\alpha/2} \frac{s}{\sqrt{n}} = 64 - 2.045 \, (0.5/\sqrt{30}) = 63.813$$

$$\bar{x}_{(\alpha/2)U} = \mu + t_{\alpha/2} \frac{s}{\sqrt{n}} = 64 + 2.045 \, (0.5/\sqrt{30}) = 64.187$$

Finally, we state the decision rule as:

If $63.813 \leq \bar{x} \leq 64.187$, do not reject H_0. Otherwise reject H_0.

Figure 8-9 shows that if $\bar{x} < 63.813$ ounces or if $\bar{x} > 64.187$ ounces, the null hypothesis should be rejected. On this day, the sample mean $\bar{x} = 64.12$, so the production manager should not reject the null hypothesis. Based upon these sample data, there is insufficient evidence to conclude that the machine is not filling the cartons with a mean of 64 ounces of ice cream. At this time, she will take no action and will let the process continue to operate.

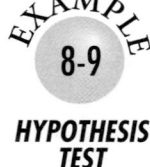

8-9

**HYPOTHESIS
TEST**

Excel and
Minitab Tutorial

Franklin Tire Company

The Franklin Tire Company recently conducted a test on a new tire design to determine whether the company could make the claim that the mean tire mileage would exceed 60,000 miles. The test was conducted in Alaska. A random sample of 100 tires was tested and the number of miles each tire lasted until it no longer met the federal government minimum tread thickness was recorded. Figure 8-10 shows some of the sample data in an Excel spreadsheet format. The data (shown in thousands of miles) are in a file called **Franklin**.

The null and alternative hypotheses to be tested are:

$$H_0: \mu \leq 60 \text{ (60,000 miles)}$$
$$H_A: \mu > 60$$
$$\alpha = 0.05$$

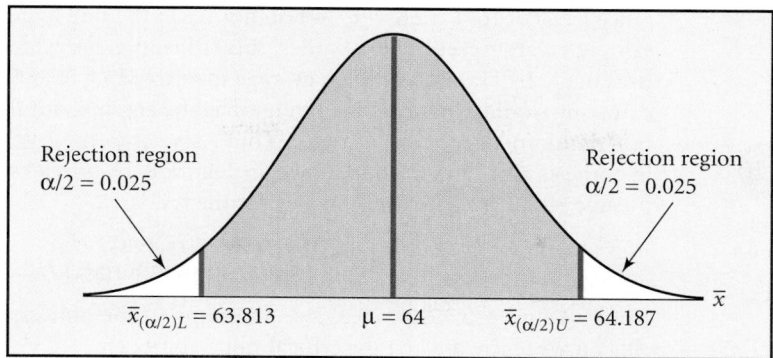

FIGURE 8-9
Decision Rule for Dairy
Fresh: A Two-Tailed Test

Excel does not have a special procedure for testing hypotheses for single population means. However, the Excel add-in software called PHStat on the CD-ROM that accompanies this text has the necessary hypothesis testing tools. Figure 8-11 shows the Excel and PHStat output.[4] The sample mean, based on a sample of 100 tires, is 60.17 (60,170 miles) and the sample standard deviation is 4.701 (4,701 miles). The test statistic, t, equals 0.3616. The critical value for $\alpha = 0.05$ and 99 degrees of freedom is 1.66. We denote the critical value of an upper-tail test with a significance level of α as t_α. For a lower-tail test, use a critical value of $-t_\alpha$.

Using the critical value approach, the decision rule is:

> If the test statistic $> 1.66 = t_\alpha$, reject H_0
> Otherwise, do not reject H_0

The t-test statistic shown in Figure 8-11 is computed as follows:

$$t = \frac{\bar{x} - \mu}{s/\sqrt{n}} = \frac{60.17 - 60}{\dfrac{4.701}{\sqrt{100}}} = 0.3616$$

FIGURE 8-10
Tires Test Data for Franklin
Tire Company

	Miles (000)	
1	Miles (000)	
2	61	
3	74	
4	63	
5	58	
6	59	
7	65	
8	58	
9	54	
10	58	

Excel Instructions:
1. Open file: Franklin.xls

FIGURE 8-11
Excel (PHStat) Output for
Frankin Tire Hypothesis Test
Results

Excel (PHStat) Instructions:

1. Open file: Franklin.xls
2. Click on PHStat tab
3. Select One Sample Tests, t-test for Mean, Sigma Unknown
4. Enter Hypothesized Mean
5. Check "Sample Statistics Unknown"
6. Check One-Tailed Test

	A	B
1	Franklin Tire Co.	
2		
3	Null Hypothesis $\mu=$	60
4	Level of Significance	0.05
5	Sample Size	100
6	Sample Mean	60.17
7	Sample Standard Deviation	4.701289314
8	Standard Error of the Mean	0.470128931
9	Degrees of Freedom	99
10	t Test Statistic	0.361602932 ◄ — Test Statistic
11		
12	**Upper-Tail Test**	
13	Upper Critical Value	1.660391717
14	p-Value	0.359209694 ◄ — p-value
15	Do not reject the null hypothesis	

Since $t = 0.3616 < 1.66$, do not reject H_0
Since p-value $= 0.3592 > \alpha = 0.05$, do not reject H_0

[4]This test can be done in Excel without the benefit of the PHStat add-ins. Please refer to the Excel tutorial on your CD-ROM for the specifics.

Since $t = 0.3616 < 1.66 = t_\alpha$, we do not reject the null hypothesis. Thus, even though the sample mean exceeds 60,000 miles, this is insufficient evidence to conclude that the new tires made by Franklin have an average life exceeding 60,000 miles. Based on this test, the company would not be justified in making the claim about the new tires.

Franklin Company managers could also use the p-value approach to test the null hypothesis since the output shown in Figure 8-11 provides the p-value. In this case, the p-value $= 0.3592$. The decision rule for the test is:

Addirional
Example 8-a

Hypothesis
Test

If p-value $< \alpha$, reject H_0
Otherwise, do not reject H_0

Since p-value $= 0.3592 > 0.05$, we do not reject the null hypothesis. This is the same conclusion we reached using the critical value approach.

This section has introduced the basic concepts of hypothesis testing. There are several ways to test a null hypothesis. Each method will yield the same result so it does not matter which method you use.

8-1: EXERCISES

ADDITIONAL EXERCISES ON YOUR CD-ROM
Try the ADDITIONAL EXERCISES and APPLICATION PROBLEMS on the CD-ROM.

8-1. Determine the p-values associated with the following test statistic for a two-tailed test.
   a. $z = 2.97$
   b. $z = 1.98$
   c. $z = 3.01$
   d. $z = 4.58$
   e. $z = -1.58$

8-2. Given the following null and alternative hypotheses:

$$H_0: \mu \leq 200$$
$$H_A: \mu > 200$$
$$\alpha = 0.05$$

and

$$\bar{x} = 204.50 \qquad \sigma = 45.00 \qquad n = 200$$

   a. Establish the appropriate decision rule for the test statistics $\bar{x}$ and z.
   b. Indicate the appropriate decision based on the sample information and each of the decision rules.
   c. Which of the hypotheses will not be declared true unless the sample data strongly indicate that it is true?

8-3. Given the following null and alternative hypotheses:

$$H_0: \mu \geq 4,000$$
$$H_A: \mu < 4,000$$
$$\alpha = 0.05$$

and

$$\bar{x} = 3,980 \qquad s = 205 \qquad n = 100$$

   a. Establish the appropriate decision rule.
   b. Indicate the appropriate decision based on the sample information and each of the decision rules using both the p-value and $\bar{x}$.

8-4. Determine the p-values associated with the following test statistics for an upper-tailed test.
   a. $z = 1.45$
   b. $z = 2.33$
   c. $z = -1.87$
   d. $z = 0$
   e. $z = -4.59$

Business Applications

8-5. A telemarketing company located in Los Angeles has established a guideline stating that the average time for each completed call should be no more than 4 minutes. Recently the operations manager was concerned that calls were taking too long. The operations manager did not wish to assert that the calls were taking too long if the sample data did not strongly indicate this. A sample of 12 calls was selected and the following times (in seconds) were recorded.

194	278	302	140	245	234	268	208	302	190	320	255

   a. Construct the appropriate null and alternative hypotheses.

b. Based on the sample data, what should the operations manager conclude? Test at the 0.10 significance level using the *p*-value approach.

c. Suppose you wished to conduct the test in part b using $\bar{x}$ as the test statistic. Calculate the critical value, $\bar{x}_\alpha$.

d. Consider your answer to part c. What values of the population mean could have been specified in the null hypothesis so that you would not reject the null hypothesis?

8-6. A mail-order business prides itself in its ability to fill customers' orders in 6 calendar days or less on the average. Periodically, the operations manager selects a random sample of customer orders and determines the number of days required to fill their orders. Based upon this sample information, he decides whether the desired standard is being met. He will assume that the average number of days to fill customers' orders is 6 or less unless the data strongly suggest otherwise.

a. Establish the appropriate null and alternative hypotheses.

b. On one occasion where a sample of 40 customers was selected, the average number of days was 6.65, with a sample standard deviation of 1.5 days. Can the operations manager conclude that his mail-order business is achieving its goal? Use a significance level of 0.025 to answer this question.

8-7. Refer to Problem 6.

a. Calculate the *p*-value for this test. Conduct the test using this *p*-value.

b. Determine the largest significance level that would lead the operations manager to conclude that the mail-order business does not fill customers' orders in 6 calendar days or less on the average.

c. The operations manager wishes to frequently monitor the efficiency of his mail-order service. Therefore, he does not wish to repeatedly calculate *t*-values to conduct the hypothesis tests. Obtain the critical value, $\bar{x}_\alpha$, so that the manager can simply compare the sample mean to this value to conduct the test. Use $\bar{x}$ as the test statistic to conduct the test.

8-8. The makers of Mini-Oats Cereal have an automated packaging machine that can be set at any targeted fill level between 12 and 32 ounces. Every box of cereal is not expected to contain exactly the targeted weight, but the average of all boxes filled should. At the end of every shift (8 hours), 16 boxes are selected at random and the mean and standard deviation of the sample are computed. Based on these sample results, the production control manager determines whether the filling machine needs to be readjusted or whether it remains all right to operate. Use $\alpha = 0.05$.

a. Establish the appropriate null and alternative hypotheses to be tested.

b. At the end of a particular shift during which the machine was filling 24-ounce boxes of Mini-Oats, the sample mean of 16 boxes was 24.32 ounces, with a standard deviation of 0.70 ounces. Assist the production control manager in determining if the machine is achieving its targeted average.

c. Why do you suppose the production control manager would prefer to make this hypothesis test a two-tailed test? Discuss.

8-9. Reconsider Problem 8.

a. Conduct the test using a *p*-value as the test statistic.

b. Considering the result of the test, which of the two types of errors in hypothesis testing could you have made?

c. Suppose the average of all boxes filled was in fact 24 ounces. Determine the probability that this test procedure will tell the production control manager that the machine is meeting its targeted goal. (Hint: Consider the complement of the event for which you wish to calculate the probability.)

8-10. The makers of a new home furnace system claim that if the furnace is installed, homeowners will observe an average fuel bill of no more than $80.00 per month during January if their house has between 2,200 and 2,400 square feet of heated living space. A consumer agency plans to test this claim by taking a random sample of homes of this size where the new furnace has just been installed.

a. Establish the appropriate null and alternative hypotheses.

b. If the desired significance level for the test is 0.05, what should be concluded about the company's claim if the following sample results are observed?

$$\bar{x} = \$81.40 \qquad s^2 = 625 \qquad n = 64$$

Use the *p*-value to conduct this hypothesis test. Verify using the $\bar{x}$ critical value approach.

c. Rather than letting the manufacturer's claim dictate the formulation of the null and alternative hypotheses, suppose the consumer agency wishes to place the burden of proof on the manufacturer. Reformulate the null and alternative hypotheses and test using the sample data from part b. Discuss the merits of both approaches.

8-11. Reconsider Problem 10 and examine it from the manufacturer's point of view. Suppose they wish to demonstrate that the claim they have been making is true. They do not want to make their claim unless the data suggest strongly that the claim is true.

a. From the manufacturer's point of view, what would the research hypothesis be?

b. State the null and alternative hypotheses that the manufacturer will use to conduct the relevant hypothesis test.

c. If the desired significance level for the test is 0.05, would you advise the company to make its claim if the following sample results are observed?

$$\bar{x} = \$71.77 \qquad s^2 = 400 \qquad n = 24$$

Support your answer with a hypothesis test using $\bar{x}$ as your test statistic. Verify this using the p-value approach.

8-12. The Cell Tone Company sells cellular phones and airtime in several northwest states. At a recent meeting, the marketing manager stated that the average age of its customers is under 40. This came up in conjunction with a proposed advertising plan that is to be directed toward a young audience. Before actually completing the advertising plan, Cell Tone decided to randomly sample customers. Among the questions asked in the survey of 50 customers in the Jacksonville, Florida, area was the customers' age. The following data are also available in a data file called **Cell Phone Survey.**

35	57	51	20	34
46	57	34	37	34
31	33	38	44	38
50	74	42	52	36
19	36	74	32	21
24	60	35	58	28
25	32	43	29	38
27	33	63	25	29
25	32	43	25	34
50	42	37	28	36

a. Based on the statement made by the marketing manager, formulate the appropriate null and alternative hypotheses.

b. The marketing manager must support his statement concerning average customer age in an upcoming board meeting. Using a significance level of 0.10, provide this support for the marketing manager.

c. Consider the result of the hypothesis test you conducted in part b. Which of the two types of hypothesis test errors could you have committed? How could you discover if you had, indeed, made this error?

8-13. Reconsider Problem 12.

a. Calculate the critical value, $\bar{x}_\alpha$.

b. Use the critical value, $\bar{x}_\alpha$, to determine the p-value and conduct the test using the p-value.

c. Note that the sample data list the customer's age to the nearest year. (1) If we denote a randomly selected customer's age (to the nearest year) as x_i, is x_i a continuous or discrete random variable? (2) Is it possible that x_i has a normal distribution? Consider your answers to (1) and (2) and the fact that $\bar{x}$ must have a normal distribution to facilitate the calculation in part b. Does this mean that the calculation you have performed in part b is inappropriate? Explain your answer.

8-14. The Haines Lumber Company makes plywood for the furniture industry. One product it makes is $\frac{3}{4}$-inch oak veneer panels. It is very important that the panels conform to the $\frac{3}{4}$-inch specification. Each hour, 5 panels are selected at random and measured. After 20 hours a total of 100 panels have been measured. The thickness measures are shown in the following table. These data are also in a file called **Haines.**

HOUR	PANEL 1	PANEL 2	PANEL 3	PANEL 4	PANEL 5
1	0.745	0.715	0.762	0.794	0.792
2	0.808	0.687	0.747	0.788	0.721
3	0.733	0.702	0.697	0.724	0.731
4	0.689	0.737	0.742	0.759	0.743
5	0.744	0.743	0.796	0.752	0.749
6	0.739	0.816	0.781	0.828	0.734
7	0.806	0.705	0.771	0.782	0.814
8	0.752	0.738	0.775	0.743	0.778
9	0.710	0.728	0.707	0.743	0.753
10	0.755	0.744	0.823	0.700	0.732
11	0.675	0.799	0.715	0.734	0.778
12	0.769	0.782	0.773	0.712	0.720
13	0.776	0.765	0.725	0.747	0.759
14	0.772	0.759	0.726	0.813	0.770
15	0.757	0.780	0.781	0.735	0.726
16	0.789	0.717	0.706	0.777	0.774
17	0.823	0.799	0.795	0.758	0.755
18	0.769	0.754	0.722	0.699	0.780
19	0.768	0.774	0.761	0.723	0.793
20	0.745	0.728	0.729	0.741	0.740

a. Formulate the appropriate null and alternative hypotheses relative to the thickness specification.

b. Based on the sample data, what should the company conclude about the status of its product meeting the thickness specification? Test at a significance level of 0.01. Discuss your results in a report to the production manager.

c. Reconsider the test statistic you used in part b. (1) Specify its distribution including the distribution's parameter(s). (2) If the test statistic is to have this distribution, the population must have a specific distribution. Specify this distribution. (3) Produce a histogram of the preceding sample data. Use five classes. (4) Does the histogram of the sample data suggest that the population has the required distribution? (5) What do the answers to (1)–(4) suggest concerning the validity of the hypothesis test you conducted in part b?

8-15. Refer to the information in Problem 14.

a. The production manager has looked at the results of your test. He wishes to know what the chances are that the panels conform to specifications but the test has determined otherwise. Furnish this information to the manager.

b. The manager wishes to know what the error alluded to in part a is called. He also wishes to know how you could know for certain whether such an error has been made. How would you respond to the manager's questions?

8-16. The Wilson Company uses a great deal of water in the process of making industrial milling equipment. To comply with the Federal Clean Water laws, it has a water purification system through which all wastewater passes before being discharged into a settling pond on the company's property. To determine whether the company is complying with the federal requirements, sample measures are taken on a random basis. One requirement is that the average pH level not exceed 7.4. A sample of 95 pH measures has been taken. The data for these measures are shown in a file called **Wilson Water.** Government inspectors do not wish to accuse The Wilson Company of violating federal requirements unless the data strongly suggest that this is the case.

  a. Considering the requirement for pH level, state the appropriate null and alternative hypotheses.

  b. Discuss why it is appropriate to form the hypothesis with the federal standard as the null hypothesis.

  c. Based on the sample data of pH levels, what should the government inspectors conclude about its current status on meeting the federal requirement? Test the hypothesis at the 0.05 level. Discuss your results in a memo to the company's environmental relations manager.

8-17. Reconsider Problem 16. Suppose you were the operations  manager for Wilson Company. You wish to demonstrate that the average pH level is less than 7.4. However, you do not wish to say that the average pH level is less than 7.4 unless the data strongly suggests that that is the case.

  a. Define the research hypothesis for the operations manager's test of hypothesis.

  b. State the appropriate null and alternative hypotheses for this test.

  c. The sample of 95 pH measures has been taken. The data for these measures are shown in the file called **Wilson Water**. Calculate the *p*-value for this test and conduct a test of hypothesis to determine if the average pH level is less than 7.4. (Be careful that you calculate the appropriate probability here. You will have to determine which probability is the correct probability to calculate on the basis of the null and alternative hypotheses.)

■ 8-2: TYPE II ERRORS

Section 8-1 provided several examples that illustrated how hypotheses and decision rules for tests of the population mean are formulated. In these examples, we determined the critical values by first specifying the significance level: the maximum probability of committing a Type I error. As we indicated, if the cost of committing a Type I error is high, the decision maker would want to specify a small significance level.

This logic provides a basis for establishing the critical value for the hypothesis test. However, it ignores the possibility of committing a Type II error. Recall that a Type II error occurs if a false null hypothesis is not rejected. The probability of a Type II error is given the symbol β, the Greek letter beta. We discussed in Section 8-1 that for a fixed sample size α and β are inversely related. That is, if we make α smaller, β will increase. However, the two are not reciprocally proportional. That is, cutting α in half will not necessarily double β.

Calculating Beta

Once α has been specified for a hypothesis test involving a particular sample size, β cannot also be specified. Rather, the β value is fixed, and all the decision maker can do is calculate it. However, β is not a single value. Since a Type II error occurs when a false null hypothesis is not rejected (refer to Figure 8-1), there is a β value for each possible population value for which the null hypothesis is false. To calculate β, we must first specify a "what if" value for the true population value. Then, β is computed conditional on that population value being true. Keep in mind that β is computed prior to actually taking the sample, so its value is not dependent on the sample outcome.

For instance, if the null hypothesis is that the mean income for a population is equal to or greater than \$30,000, then β could be calculated for any value of μ less than \$30,000. We would get a different β for each value of μ. An example will help clarify this concept.

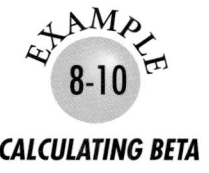

CALCULATING BETA

The American Lighting Company (continued)

Recall the example involving the American Lighting Company that had developed a new lightbulb. The thought was that this new bulb would last more than 700 hours on average. If a hypothesis test based on a random sample of $n = 100$ lightbulbs could confirm this, the company would use this claim in its advertising. The null and alternative hypotheses are:

$$H_0: \mu \leq 700 \text{ hr.}$$
$$H_A: \mu > 700 \text{ hr.}$$

Therefore, the null hypothesis is false for all possible values of $\mu > 700$ hours. Thus, for each of the infinite number of possibilities, a value of β can be determined.

Suppose we assume that μ is actually 701 hours. If we use a significance level of 0.05, we calculate beta using the following steps:

COMPUTING β

1. Draw a picture of the hypothesized sampling distribution showing the rejection region and the acceptance region found by specifying the significance level. This distribution will have a mean equal to the numerical value specified in the null hypothesis. We refer to this distribution as "the hypothesized sampling distribution."
2. Determine the critical value, $\bar{x}_\alpha$.
3. Immediately below the hypothesized sampling distribution, draw the sampling distribution whose mean is that for which you want to determine beta. Let us refer to this distribution as "the sampling distribution under H_A." Note that the hypothesized sampling distribution and the "sampling distribution under H_A" will have the same shape and spread. Only the mean value will be different.
4. Extend the critical value(s) from the hypothesized sampling distribution down to the sampling distribution under H_A and shade the rejection region.
5. The unshaded area in the sampling distribution under H_A is the graphical representation of beta, the probability of committing a Type II error. Find this area as you have always found the area under the curve of a normal distribution.

FIGURE 8-12
Beta Calculation for True
$\mu = 701$

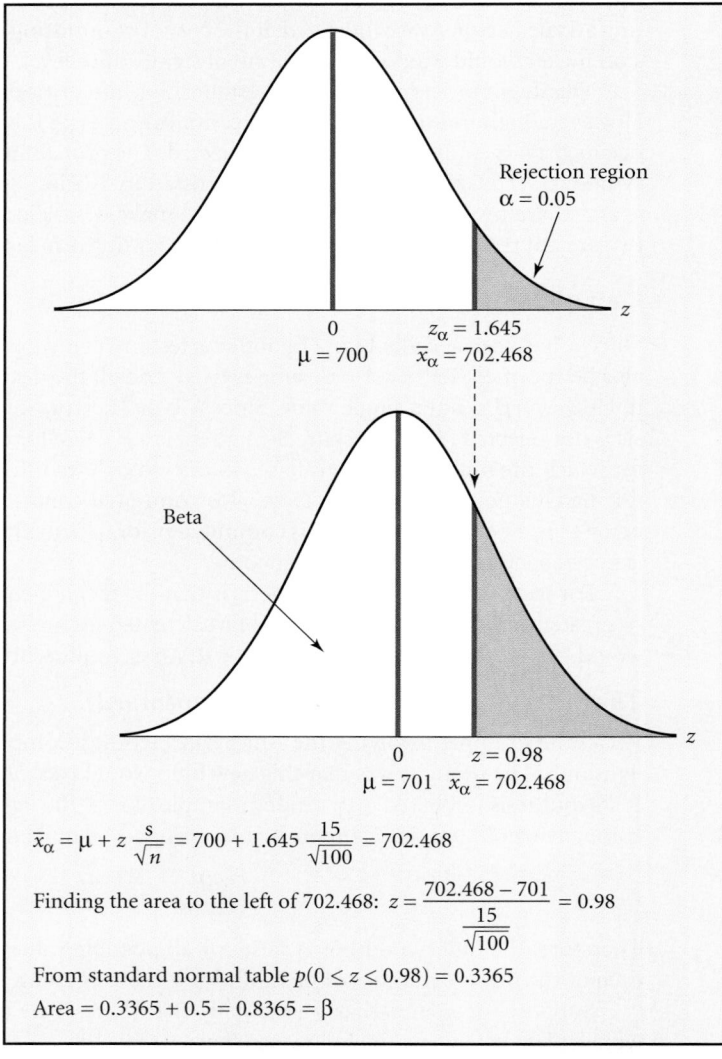

$$\bar{x}_\alpha = \mu + z\,\frac{s}{\sqrt{n}} = 700 + 1.645\,\frac{15}{\sqrt{100}} = 702.468$$

Finding the area to the left of 702.468: $z = \dfrac{702.468 - 701}{\dfrac{15}{\sqrt{100}}} = 0.98$

From standard normal table $p(0 \le z \le 0.98) = 0.3365$

Area $= 0.3365 + 0.5 = 0.8365 = \beta$

Figure 8-12 shows how β is determined if the value of μ selected from H_A is 701 hours. Note, since $n = 100$ is a large sample size, we have used the standard normal distribution to compute β. Thus, by specifying the significance level to be 0.05, the chance of committing a Type II error is approximately 0.8365. This means that if the true population mean is 701 hours there is nearly an 84% chance that the sampling plan American Lighting is using will not reject the assumption that the mean is 700 hours or less.

Figure 8-13 shows that if the "what if" mean value moves farther from the hypothesized mean ($\mu = 704$), beta becomes smaller. The greater the difference between the mean specified in H_0 and the mean selected from H_A, the easier it is to tell the two apart, and the less likely we are to not reject the null hypothesis when it is actually false. Of course the opposite is also true. As the mean selected from H_A moves increasingly closer to hypothesized mean, the harder it is for the hypothesis test to distinguish between the two.

OPTIONAL CD-ROM TOPIC Developing and Interpreting Operating Characteristic Curves
Operating Characteristic Curves show the probability of committing a Type II error for specified levels of the true population value. For more information, go to the CD-ROM.

FIGURE 8-13
Beta Calculation for True $\mu = 704$

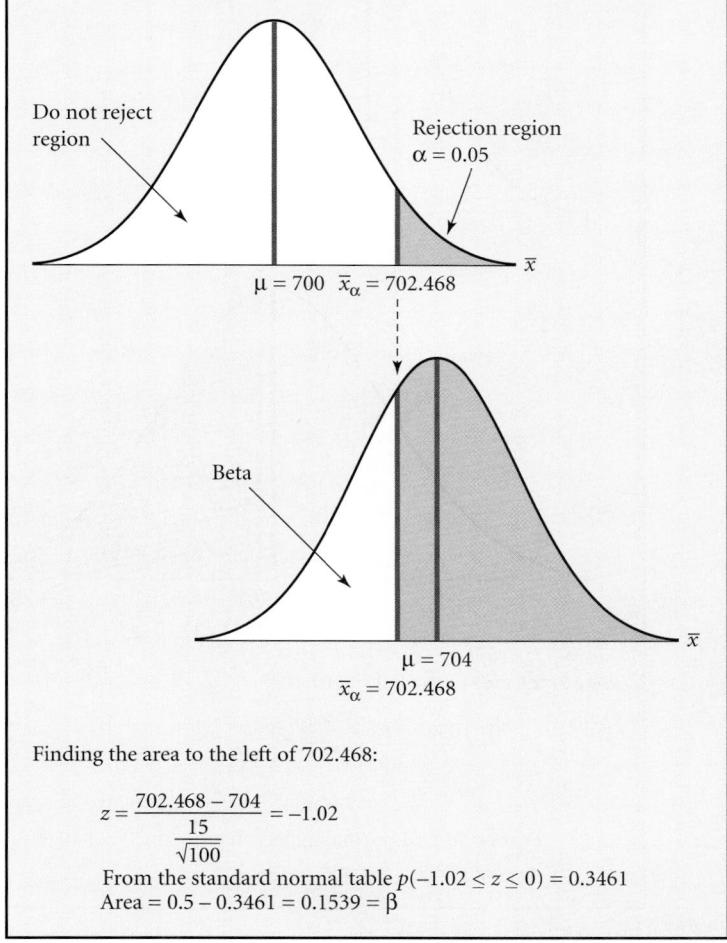

Do not reject region

Rejection region $\alpha = 0.05$

$\mu = 700 \quad \bar{x}_\alpha = 702.468$

Beta

$\mu = 704$
$\bar{x}_\alpha = 702.468$

Finding the area to the left of 702.468:

$$z = \frac{702.468 - 704}{\frac{15}{\sqrt{100}}} = -1.02$$

From the standard normal table $p(-1.02 \leq z \leq 0) = 0.3461$
Area $= 0.5 - 0.3461 = 0.1539 = \beta$

Controlling Alpha and Beta

Ideally, we want both alpha and beta to be as small as possible. While we can set alpha at any desired level, for a specified sample size and standard deviation the calculated value of beta depends on the population mean chosen from the alternative hypothesis and the significance level. For a specified sample size, reducing alpha will increase beta. However, we can control the size of both alpha and beta if we are willing to increase the sample size.

8-11

CALCULATING BETA

Additional
Example 8-b

Calculating Beta

The American Lighting Company (continued.)

In the American Lighting Company example, a sample of 100 lightbulbs was planned. In Figure 8-12, we showed that beta = 0.8365 when the "true" population mean was 701 hours. This is a very large probability and might be unacceptable to the company. However, assuming $\sigma = 15$, if the company is willing to incur the cost associated with a sample size of 500 bulbs, the probability of a Type II error could be reduced to 0.5596 as shown in Figure 8-14. This is a big improvement and is due to the fact that the standard error $\left(\dfrac{\sigma}{\sqrt{n}}\right)$ is reduced because of the increased sample size.

FIGURE 8-14
Beta Calculation for True μ and $n = 500$

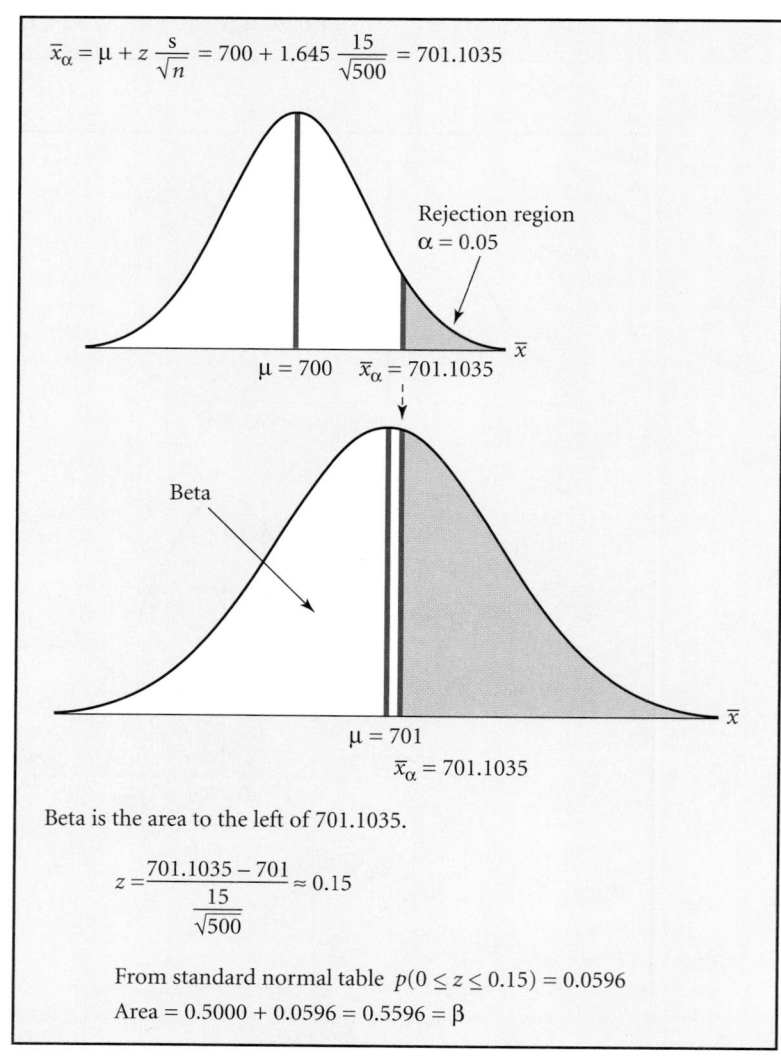

$$\bar{x}_\alpha = \mu + z\,\frac{s}{\sqrt{n}} = 700 + 1.645\,\frac{15}{\sqrt{500}} = 701.1035$$

Rejection region
$\alpha = 0.05$

$\mu = 700 \quad \bar{x}_\alpha = 701.1035$

Beta

$\mu = 701$
$\bar{x}_\alpha = 701.1035$

Beta is the area to the left of 701.1035.

$$z = \frac{701.1035 - 701}{\dfrac{15}{\sqrt{500}}} \approx 0.15$$

From standard normal table $p(0 \le z \le 0.15) = 0.0596$
Area $= 0.5000 + 0.0596 = 0.5596 = \beta$

Power of the Test

In the previous examples, we have been concerned with the chance of making a Type II error. We would like beta to be as small as possible. If the null hypothesis is false, we want to reject it. Another way to look at this is that we would like the hypothesis test to have a high probability of rejecting a false hypothesis. This concept is expressed by what is called the **power** of the test.

> **POWER**
> The probability that the hypothesis test will reject the null hypothesis when the null hypothesis is false.

When the alternative hypothesis is true, the power of the test is computed using Equation 8-1.

> **POWER**
>
> $$\text{Power} = 1 - \beta$$
>
> 8-1

EXAMPLE
8-12

CALCULATING POWER

The American Lighting Company (continued)

In the American Lighting Company example, when 100 bulbs were selected and the true population mean was assumed to be 701, the probability of a Type II error was 0.8365 (See Figure 8-12). In this case the power of the test was:

$$\text{Power} = 1 - 0.8365 = 0.1635$$

If the true mean is 701 hours, there is only a 16.35% chance the test will reject the null hypothesis that the mean is 700 or fewer hours. However, when the sample size is increased to 500 bulbs, the probability of a Type II error dropped to 0.5596 (see Figure 8-14). The power of this test is:

$$\text{Power} = 1 - 0.5596 = 0.4404$$

Therefore, the chance is increased to just over 44% of detecting that the null hypothesis is false when $\mu = 701$.

Power increases as the sample size increases. Power also increases when the population mean selected from H_A is farther from the population mean specified in H_0.

8-2: EXERCISES

Additional
Exercises

8-18. You are given the following null and alternative hypotheses:

$$H_0: \mu \leq 4{,}000$$
$$H_A: \mu > 4{,}000$$
$$\alpha = 0.05$$

a. If the population mean is 4,004, determine the value of beta. Assume that the population standard deviation is known to be 20 and the sample size is 40.

b. Referring to part a, calculate the power of the test.

c. Referring to parts a and b, what could be done to increase power and reduce beta if the true population mean is 4,004? Discuss.

d. Indicate clearly the decision rule that would be used to test the null hypothesis and determine what decision should be made if the sample mean is 4,002.

8-19. You are given the following null and alternative hypotheses:

$$H_0: \mu = 1.20$$
$$H_A: \mu \neq 1.20$$
$$\alpha = 0.10$$

a. If the true population mean is 1.25, determine the value of beta. Assume the population standard deviation is known to be 0.50 and the sample size is 60.

b. Referring to part a, calculate the power of the test.

c. Referring to parts a and b, what could be done to increase power and reduce beta when the true population mean is 1.25? Discuss.

d. Indicate clearly the decision rule that would be used to test the null hypothesis and determine what decision should be made if the sample mean is 1.23.

Business Applications

8-20. The Arrow Tire and Rubber Company plans to warranty its new mountain bike tire for 12 months. However, before it does this, the company wants to be sure that the mean lifetime of the tires is at least 18 months under normal operations. It will put the warranty in place unless the sample data strongly suggest that the mean lifetime of the tires is less than 18 months. The company plans to test this statistically using a random sample of tires. The test will be conducted using an alpha level of 0.03.

a. If the population mean is actually 16.5 months, determine the probability the hypothesis test will lead to incorrectly accepting the null hypothesis. Assume that the population standard deviation is known to be 2.4 months and the sample size is 60.

b. If the population mean is actually 16.3, calculate the chance of committing a Type II error.

8-21. Refer to Problem 20.

a. Without calculating the probability, state whether the probability of a Type II error would be larger or smaller than that calculated in part b if you were to calculate it for a mean of 15 months. Justify your answer.

b. Suppose the company decides to increase the sample size from 60 to 100 tires. What can you expect to happen to the probabilities calculated in Problem 20?

8-22. The union negotiations between labor and management at the Stone Container paper mill in Minnesota hit a snag when management asked labor to take a cut in health insurance coverage. As part of its justification, management claimed that the average monthly amount of insurance claims filed by union employees did not exceed $250 per employee. The union's chief negotiator requested that a sample of 100 employees' records be selected and that this claim be tested statistically. The claim would be accepted if the sample data did not strongly suggest otherwise. The significance level for the test was set at 0.10.

a. State the null and alternative hypotheses.

b. Before the sample was selected, the negotiator was interested in knowing the power of this test if the mean amount of insurance claims was $260. (Assume the standard deviation in claims is $70.00, as determined in a similar study at another plant location.) Calculate this probability for the negotiator.

c. Referring to part b, how would the power of the test change if an alpha = 0.05 is used?

d. Suppose alpha is left at 0.10, but the standard deviation of the population is $50.00 rather than $70.00. What will be the power of the test? State the generalization that explains the relationship between the answers to part b and d.

e. Referring to part d, based on the probability computed, if you were the negotiator, would you be satisfied with the sample size used in this situation? Explain why or why not.

8-23. The makers of Mini-Oats Cereal have an automated packaging machine that can be set at any targeted fill level between 12 and 32 ounces. At the end of every shift (8 hours), 16 boxes are selected at random and the mean and standard deviation of the sample are computed. Based on these sample results, the production control manager determines whether the filling machine needs to be readjusted or whether it remains acceptable to operate. Previous data suggest the fill level has a normal distribution with a standard deviation of 0.65 ounces. Use $\alpha = 0.05$. Recall the test was a two-sided test to determine if the mean fill level was equal to 24 ounces.

a. Calculate the probability that the test procedure will detect that the average fill level is not equal to 24 ounces when in fact it equals 24.5 ounces.

b. On the basis of your calculation in part a would you suggest a change in the test procedure? Explain what change you would make and the reasons you would make this change.

8-24. The X-John Company makes batteries specifically designed for cell phones. Recently, the R & D department at the company sent a memo to upper management indicating they had come up with a new battery design that would be less expensive to build. However, there was concern about the lasting power of the battery. The senior managers were well aware that trade publications constantly conduct tests on cell phone components like batteries. If X-John were to begin marketing the new battery and it was shown to last less than the current industry standard of 30 hours, there would be serious bad publicity and sales would decline. Therefore, it wanted to conclude that the average length of life of the battery was longer than the current industry standard only if the sample data strongly indicated this was the case.

Before the new battery is put into production, the company planned to test a sample of 100 batteries (simulating the type of test the trade publications would perform). The X-John company wanted to make this a conservative test, so they have set up the following null and alternative hypotheses:

$$H_0: \mu \le 30$$
$$H_A: \mu > 30$$

a. Explain why this hypothesis format would be considered a conservative test. Why not set up the null and alternative hypotheses as follows?

$$H_0: \mu \ge 30$$
$$H_A: \mu < 30$$

b. Suppose there is reason to believe that $\sigma = 5$ hours. Before actually testing the null hypothesis at an alpha $= 0.05$, what is the probability that the test would lead to accepting the null hypothesis when the true mean life of the new battery is 31 hours? Discuss the ramifications to the company if this error is made.

c. Determine the probability that the test would correctly indicate that the mean life of the new battery is greater than the industry standard when in fact the mean life of the new battery was 31 hours.

8-25. Referring to Problem 24, suppose the X-John Company actually tests a random sample of 100 batteries. The sample data are in the file called **X-John** and are also listed as follows.

				BATTERY LIFE					
42.2	34.0	29.9	26.0	29.6	19.7	26.5	35.7	29.7	29.4
30.9	26.1	42.8	39.8	30.3	38.3	29.5	37.2	29.1	28.1
27.4	28.4	30.0	28.7	35.3	32.1	31.6	28.9	44.1	26.1
35.0	31.3	30.0	30.5	34.3	26.3	31.3	32.2	28.2	26.4
26.8	39.1	32.8	26.6	32	30.7	38.8	30.1	30.5	30.3
33.2	32.8	34.6	31.8	29.5	30.7	31.4	32.3	30.8	30.9
38.5	24.6	37.8	31.1	27.5	29.6	28.9	32.7	29.4	21.3
31.2	30.2	26.4	34.3	21.7	26.8	26.6	28.2	33.7	37.3
29.4	19.6	32.2	22.3	21.6	25.1	33.9	26.2	29.2	24.8
25.2	37.9	32.9	29.6	35	33.3	25.1	30.4	25.6	38.2

a. Based on the sample data and an alpha level equal to 0.05, what decision should the company make about the null and alternative hypotheses?

b. What actions should the company take based on this result? Discuss.

c. The R & D department has indicated that an earlier version of this battery lasted in the range of 28.3 to 29.7 hours. If the improvements made have no effect on the length of life of the batteries, this range would be the most likely range for the current batteries. Determine the range of values for the probability of a Type II error if the improvements made no effect on the length of life of the batteries.

8-26. Refer to Problem 25. X-John's upper management faces a quandary. As mentioned, if X-John were to begin marketing the new battery and the battery was shown to last less than the current industry standard of 30 hours, there would be serious bad publicity and sales would decline.

Previous experience in the industry has led the marketing department to believe that X-John's sales could decline as much as $1.5 million with bad publicity. If, however, they can demonstrate that the new battery exceeds the company standard, X-John's experience indicates an increase in sales of $4 million. If the hypothesis test indicates the average life of the batteries is less than the industry standard, X-John will not produce the battery and will not have the indicated increase in sales. If, however, the test indicates that the average life of the batteries is at least as long as the industry standard, they will market the new battery.

a. Express a Type I error in the context of this problem. (A general definition is not desired. You are required to state what a Type I error is with respect to this hypothesis test.)

b. Express a Type II error in the context of this problem.

c. Given that you now know what a Type I error is for this problem and the consequences of such an error, provide the expected loss of sales a Type I error would produce. (Hint: Recall the definition of expected value.)

d. Upper management has instructed you to choose a test procedure so the expected loss due to a Type I error equals the expected loss due to a Type II error. Choose the probability of a Type II error (β) that will produce these results.

8-27. The Wainwright Lawn and Garden Company's marketing manager believes that the average income of the company's customers is less than $30,000. This claim was made by the manager as he defended his selection of product brands aimed at lower-income customers. To verify the claim, a random sample of 400 customers was selected and a survey was conducted to determine income levels. It is assumed that σ is equal to the sample standard deviation, $4,000, and the significance level is 0.10.

a. If the actual mean income is $30,200, determine the probability that the test will mistakenly lead the managers to believe that the mean is less than $30,000.

b. Based on your calculation in part a, what can be done to reduce the chances of making a Type II error? Explain.

8-3: HYPOTHESES TESTS FOR PROPORTIONS

So far this chapter has focused on hypothesis tests about a single population mean. While many decision problems involve a test of a population mean, there are also cases where the value of interest is the population proportion. For example, a production manager might consider the proportion of defective items produced on an assembly line in order to determine whether the line should be restructured or not. Likewise, a life insurance salesperson's performance assessment might include the proportion of existing clients who renew their policies.

Testing a Single Population Proportion

The basic concept of hypothesis testing for proportions is the same as for means.

1. The null and alternative hypotheses are stated in terms of a different population parameter, now π instead of μ, and the sample values become p instead of $\bar{x}$.
2. The null hypothesis should be a statement concerning the parameter that includes an equality.

3. The significance level of the hypothesis test again determines the size of the rejection region.
4. The test can be one- or two-tailed depending on the situation being addressed.

HYPOTHESIS TESTING

First American Bank and Title

The internal auditors at First American Bank and Title Company routinely test the bank's system of internal controls. Recently, the audit manager undertook an examination of the loan documentation on the bank's 22,500 outstanding automobile loans. The bank's procedures require that the file on each auto loan account contain certain specific documentation, such as a list of applicant assets, statement of monthly income, list of liabilities, and certificate of automobile insurance. If an account contains all the required documentation, then that account is determined to be in compliance with bank procedures.

The audit manager has established a 1% noncompliance rate as the bank's standard. This means that if *more than* 1% of the 22,500 loans do not have appropriate documentation, then the internal controls are not effective and steps would need to be taken to improve the situation. The audit staff does not have enough time to examine all 22,500 files to determine the noncompliance rate. As a result, the audit staff selects a random sample of 600 files, examines them, and determines the number of files that are not in compliance with bank documentation requirements. Based on the sample findings, the manager will reach a conclusion about whether the bank exceeds the 1% noncompliance rate for the population of all 22,500 loan files. The manager will not take steps to improve the noncompliance rate unless the sample data indicate that the noncompliance rate exceeds 1%. The default position is that the internal controls are effective. Thus, the null and alternative hypotheses are stated as follows.

$$H_0: \pi \leq 0.01 \quad \text{(Internal Controls Are Effective)}$$
$$H_A: \pi > 0.01 \quad \text{(Internal Controls Are Not Effective)}$$

Suppose the sample of 600 accounts uncovered 9 files with inadequate loan documentation. The question is whether 9 out of 600 is sufficient to conclude that the bank has a problem. To answer this question statistically, we need to recall a lesson from Chapter 6: The sampling distribution for the population proportion is approximately normal with mean π and standard deviation $\sqrt{\dfrac{\pi(1-\pi)}{n}}$ provided that n is large [i.e., $n\pi \geq 5$ and $n(1-\pi) \geq 5$].

The bank's auditors have a general policy of performing these tests with a significance level (alpha) equal to 0.02. This means they are willing to reject a true null hypothesis 2% of the time. In this case, if a Type I statistical error is committed, the internal controls will be determined to be ineffective when, in fact, they are working as intended.

Once the null and alternative hypotheses and the significance level have been specified, we can formulate the decision rule for this test. Figure 8-15 shows how the decision rule is developed. Notice the critical value, p_α, is 2.05 standard deviations above $\pi = 0.01$. Thus, if the sample proportion, p, exceeds 0.0182, the null hypothesis should be rejected.

Since there were 9 deficient files in the sample of 600 files, this means that $p = 9/600 = 0.015$. Since $0.015 < 0.0182$, the null hypothesis should not be rejected based on these sample data. Therefore, the auditors have no reason to conclude the system of internal controls is ineffective.

Alternatively, we could have based the test on a test statistic (z) with a standardized normal distribution. This test statistic is calculated using Equation 8-2

$$z = \frac{0.015 - 0.01}{0.004} = 1.25$$

As was established in Figure 8-15, the critical value, z_α, is 2.05. We reject the null hypothesis only if $z > z_\alpha$. Since $z = 1.25 < 2.05 = z_\alpha$, we don't reject the null hypothesis. This, of course, was the same conclusion we reached when we used p as the test statistic. Both test statistics must yield the same decision.

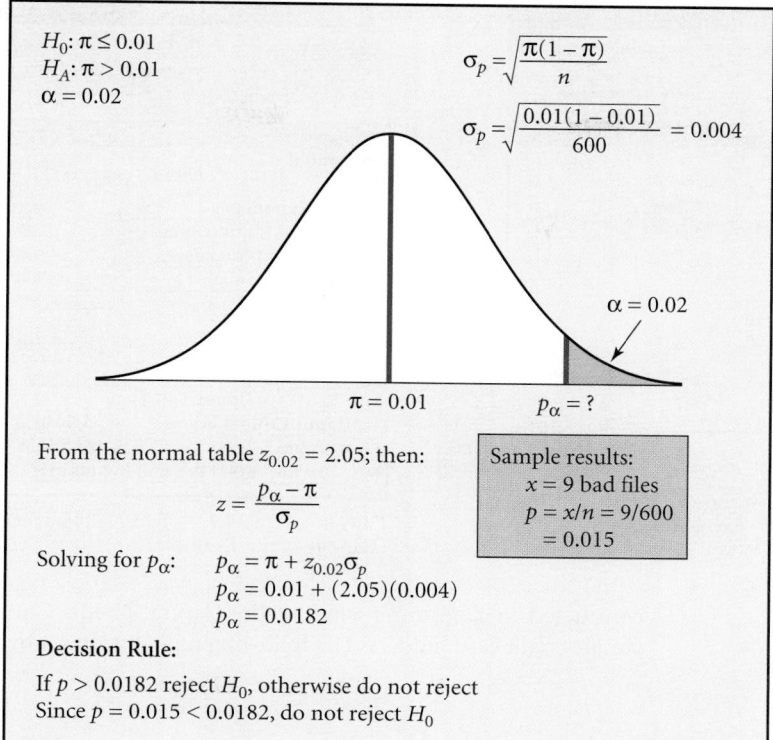

$H_0: \pi \leq 0.01$
$H_A: \pi > 0.01$
$\alpha = 0.02$

$$\sigma_p = \sqrt{\frac{\pi(1-\pi)}{n}}$$

$$\sigma_p = \sqrt{\frac{0.01(1-0.01)}{600}} = 0.004$$

$\alpha = 0.02$

$\pi = 0.01$ $p_\alpha = ?$

From the normal table $z_{0.02} = 2.05$; then:

$$z = \frac{p_\alpha - \pi}{\sigma_p}$$

Solving for p_α:
$p_\alpha = \pi + z_{0.02}\sigma_p$
$p_\alpha = 0.01 + (2.05)(0.004)$
$p_\alpha = 0.0182$

Sample results:
$x = 9$ bad files
$p = x/n = 9/600$
$\quad = 0.015$

Decision Rule:

If $p > 0.0182$ reject H_0, otherwise do not reject
Since $p = 0.015 < 0.0182$, do not reject H_0

FIGURE 8-15
Decision Rule for First
American Bank and Title
Example

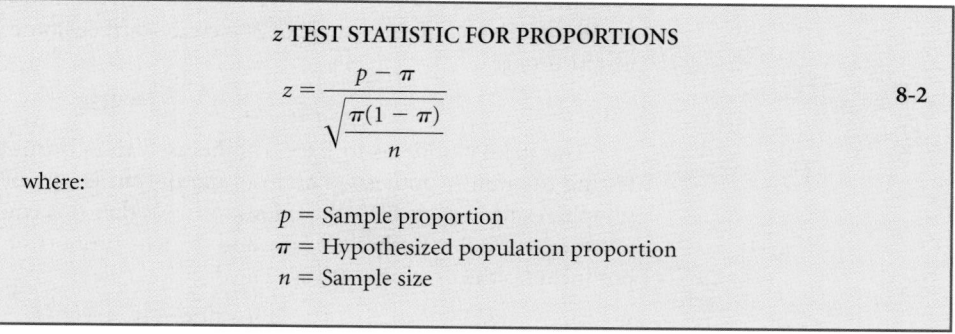

z TEST STATISTIC FOR PROPORTIONS

$$z = \frac{p - \pi}{\sqrt{\dfrac{\pi(1-\pi)}{n}}}$$

8-2

where:

p = Sample proportion
π = Hypothesized population proportion
n = Sample size

Minitab contains a tool for performing hypothesis tests for proportions. Excel does not, but through the use of Excel formulas the test can be performed. In addition, the PHStat Excel add-ins that accompany this text contain a test for proportions procedure. The next example uses PHStat. Please examine the Excel and Minitab tutorials on the CD-ROM for examples using Excel and Minitab.

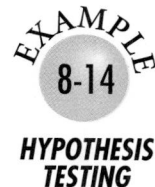

EXAMPLE
8-14

HYPOTHESIS TESTING

Excel and
Minitab Tutorial

Capital Credit Corporation

Capital Credit Corporation provides a variety of services, including credit cards, to customers in its market area. A regional TV station recently reported that banks in the area have been slow to grant credit cards to women. In fact, the station claimed that fewer than 20% of the credit cards issued by area banks and financial institutions are granted to women.

The marketing manager for Capital Credit believes that his bank has a better record than that. He has asked that a sample of 300 customers be selected and a statistical test be

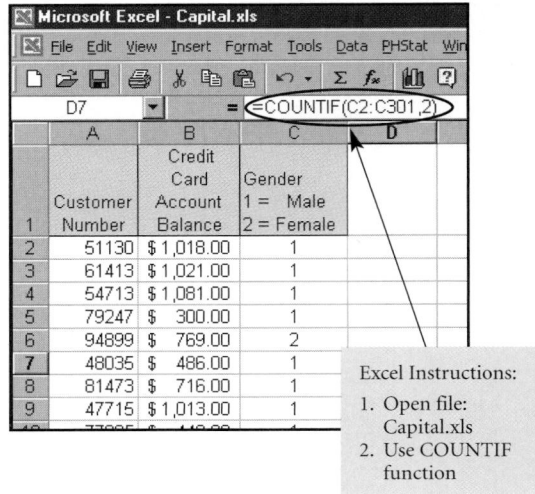

FIGURE 8-16 Excel Worksheet for Capital Credit Corporation Data

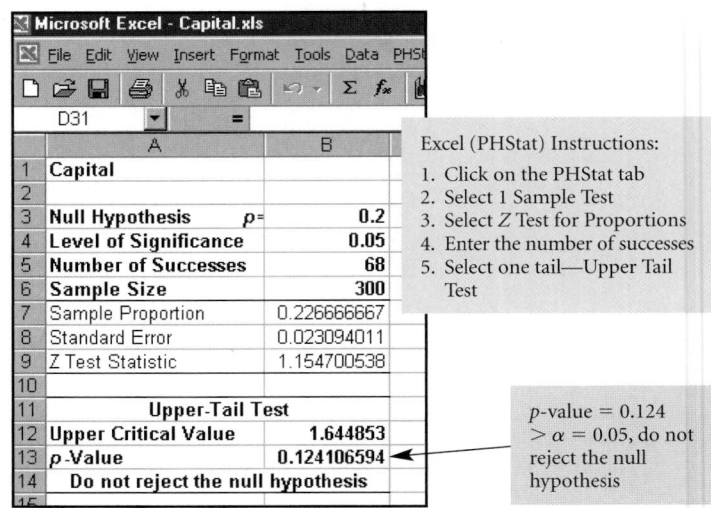

FIGURE 8-17 Excel (PHStat) Output Hypothesis Test Results (Capital Credit Example)

conducted to determine whether the Capital Credit Corporation has more than 20% female credit card holders. The following null and alternative hypotheses are established.

$$H_0: \pi \le 0.20$$
$$H_A: \pi > 0.20$$

The manager wants the test conducted at the significance level of 0.05. The sample data are contained in a file called **Capital**. A partial listing of the data is shown in Figure 8-16. Note the Excel function, COUNTIF, is used to determine how many female customers there are in the sample. In the sample of 300 credit card customers, 68 were females. The sample proportion is:

$$p = \frac{68}{300} = 0.227$$

The PHStat add-ins to Excel can be used to perform the required computations for testing the null hypothesis. The resulting output is shown in Figure 8-17. Although this sample result exceeds 0.20, the question is whether this could be due to sampling error or whether the null hypothesis is false and the true proportion exceeds 0.20. The PHStat output includes the p-value $= 0.124$. The decision rule is:

If p-value $< \alpha$, reject H_0
Otherwise, do not reject

Since p-value $= 0.124 > 0.05$ the data do not lead the Capital Credit Corporation to reject the null hypothesis. Thus, based on the data, the company should not conclude that more than 20% of its credit card customers are female.

8-3: EXERCISES

Additional Exercises

8-28. Note the following null and alternative hypotheses:

$$H_0: \pi \le 0.24$$
$$H_A: \pi > 0.24$$

Test the null hypothesis based on a random sample of $n = 100$, where $p = 0.27$. Assume an $\alpha = 0.05$ level.

a. Use p_α as the critical value to test the hypothesis. Be sure to show clearly the decision rule.

b. Use z as the test statistic to test the hypothesis.

8-29. Note the following null and alternative hypotheses:

$$H_0: \pi \ge 0.50$$
$$H_A: \pi < 0.50$$

Test the null hypothesis based on a random sample of 200 where $p = 0.47$. Use $\alpha = 0.10$.

  a. Use the *p*-value approach to test the hypothesis. State the decision rule.

  b. Use p_α as the critical value to conduct the test of hypothesis.

Business Applications

8-30. The College of Business at a state university has a computer literacy requirement for all graduates: Students must show proficiency with a computer spreadsheet software package and with a word-processing software package. To assess whether students are computer literate, a test is given at the end of each semester. The test is designed so that at least 70% of all students who have taken a special microcomputer course will pass the test. Suppose that, in a random sample of 100 students who have recently finished the microcomputer course, 63 pass the proficiency test.

  a. Using a significance level of 0.05, what conclusions should the administrators make regarding the difficulty of the test?

  b. Describe a Type II error in the context of this problem.

8-31. A shopping center developer claims in a presentation to a potential client that at least 40% of the adult female population in a community visit the center one or more times a week. To test her research hypothesis, the developer selected a random sample of 100 households with an adult female present and asked if they visit the center at least one day per week. Thirty-eight of the 100 respondents replied "yes" to the question.

  a. Based on the sample data and a significance level of 0.05, what should be concluded about the developer's claim? Show the decision rule and your analysis clearly.

  b. Suppose, instead, that the developer is unwilling to refute her claim unless the sample data strongly indicated it was not true. Calculate a *p*-value and use this to conduct the appropriate test.

8-32. A large number of complaints have been received in the past 6 months regarding airlines losing passengers' baggage. The airlines claim the problem is nowhere near as great as the newspaper articles have indicated. In fact, one airline spokesperson claimed that no more than 1% of all bags fail to arrive at the destination with the passenger. To test this claim, 800 bags were randomly selected at various airports in the United States when they were checked with this airline. Of these, 6 bags failed to reach the destination when the passenger (owner) arrived.

  a. Is this sufficient evidence to refute the airline spokesperson's claim? Test using a significance level of 0.05. Discuss.

  b. Estimate the largest and smallest proportion of bags that fail to arrive at the proper destination using a technique for which 95% confidence applies.

8-33. The AJ Fitness Center has surveyed 1,214 of its customers. Of particular interest is whether over 60% of the customers who express overall service satisfaction with the club (represented by codes 4 or 5) are female. If this is not the case, the promotions director feels she must initiate new exercise programs that are designed specifically for women. Should the promotions director initiate the new exercise programs? Support your answer with the relevant hypothesis test utilizing a *p*-value to perform the test. The data are found in a data file called **AJ Fitness**.

8-34. A computer manufacturer has a dial-up 800 number which customers can use to call for help with problems related to their computers. The service manager expects that the proportion of calls that will be answered within 5 minutes exceeds 0.90. Recently a survey was conducted of 70 calls. The data file called **Customer Service** contains the evaluation (Yes or No) on whether the call was answered within 5 minutes.

  a. State the appropriate null and alternative hypotheses.

  b. Carry out the hypothesis test using a significance level of 0.10. Show the decision rule and the result of the test.

  c. Construct a 90% confidence interval estimate for the proportion of calls that were answered in 5 minutes. Do you see any relationship between the confidence interval you constructed and the test you conducted in part b? State any generalization you may determine.

8-35. At the annual meeting of the Golf Equipment Manufacturer's Association, a speaker made the claim that over 30% of all golf clubs being used by nonprofessional United States Golf Association members are "knock-offs." These "knock-offs" are clubs that look very much like the more expensive originals such as Big Bertha drivers, but are actually nonauthorized copies that are sold at a very reduced rate. This claim prompted the association to conduct a study to see if the problem was as big as the speaker said. A random sample of 400 golfers was selected from the USGA membership ranks. The players were called and asked to indicate the brand of clubs they used and several other questions. Out of the 400 golfers, data were collected from 294 of them. Based on the response to club brand, a determination was made whether the club was "Original" or a "Copy." The data are in a file called **Golf Survey**.

  a. Based on the sample data, what conclusion should be reached if the hypothesis is tested at a significance level of 0.05? Show the decision rule.

  b. Determine whether a Type I or Type II error for this hypothesis test would be more severe. Given your determination, would you advocate raising or lowering the significance level for this test? Explain your reasoning.

8-36. Referring to Problem 35, one of the USGA officials has stated that the use of "knock-off" golf clubs is even greater among the high handicap players. He went on to state that at least 40% of all golfers with handicaps 20 and above use the unauthorized copies. This claim will be accepted unless the sample data indicate strongly that it is incorrect. Use the data in the file **Golf Survey** to test this claim.

  a. Confirm that the sample proportion's distribution can be approximated by a normal distribution.

  b. Based on the sample data, what should the USGA conclude about the use of "knock-off" clubs by the high handicap golfers? Is the official's statement justified?

8-4: HYPOTHESES TESTS FOR VARIANCES

In the previous sections of this chapter we concentrated on examples involving the population mean or proportion. However, in many cases you will be as interested in the spread of the population as in its central location. For instance, military planes designed to penetrate enemy defenses have a ground-following radar system. The radar tells the pilot exactly how far the plane is above the ground. A radar unit that is correct *on the average* is useless if the readings are distributed widely around the average value. Many airport shuttle systems have stopping sensors to deposit passengers at the correct spot in a terminal. A sensor that, *on the average*, lets passengers off at the correct point could leave many irritated people long distances up and down the track. Therefore, many product specifications involve both an average value and some limit on the variation that the individual values can have. For example, the specification for a steel push pin may be an average length of 1.78 inches plus or minus 0.01 inches. A company using these pins would be interested in both the average length and how much these pins vary in length.

Usually when we think of measuring the variation, the standard deviation is used as the measure since it is measured in the same units as the mean. Ideally, in the ground-following radar example, we would want to test to see whether the standard deviation is at or below a certain level as determined by the product specifications. Unfortunately, there is no statistical test that directly tests the standard deviation. However, there is a test called the chi-square test that can be used to test the population variance instead. We can convert any standard deviation application into one involving the variance as shown in the following example.

Hypothesis Test for σ^2

H & L Machines

EXAMPLE 8-15

HYPOTHESIS TESTING

H & L Machines provides service for all types of copy machines. Based on past records and manufacturer recommendations, the company determined the mean service time for a Kodak Image Source 85 should be 2 hours with a standard deviation not to exceed 0.5 hours if the staff is properly trained. Past data indicate that the 2 hour average is being achieved. However, there is concern that the variability may be excessive. The service schedule is built around the assumption of $\mu = 2$ hours and $\sigma = 0.5$ hours. If the service time standard deviation exceeds 0.5 hours, the service schedule gets disrupted.

The service manager has decided to select a sample of service calls and use the sample data to determine whether the service time standard deviation exceeds 0.5 hours. The methodology for conducting such a test is generally the same as for testing a population mean or proportion.

Ideally the manager would like to test the following null and alternative hypotheses.

$$H_0: \sigma \leq 0.5$$
$$H_A: \sigma > 0.5$$

Since there is no statistical technique for directly testing hypotheses about a population standard deviation, she will use a test for a population variance. We first convert the standard deviation to a variance by squaring the standard deviation, and we restate the null and alternative hypotheses as follows.

$$H_0: \sigma^2 \leq 0.25$$
$$H_A: \sigma^2 > 0.25$$

As with all hypothesis tests, the decision to reject or accept the null hypothesis will be based on the value computed from the sample. In testing hypotheses about a single population variance, the appropriate sample value is s^2, the *sample variance*.

To test a null hypothesis about a population variance, we compare s^2 with the hypothesized population variance, σ^2. To do this, we need to standardize the distribution of the sample variance in much the same way we used the z-distribution and the t-distribution when testing hypotheses about the population mean. If we are sampling from a normal distribution, the standardized distribution for sample variances is a *chi-square distribution*. The chi-square distribution is a continuous distribution of a standardized random variable computed by using Equation 8-3.

Excel Simulation

Chi-Square
Distribution

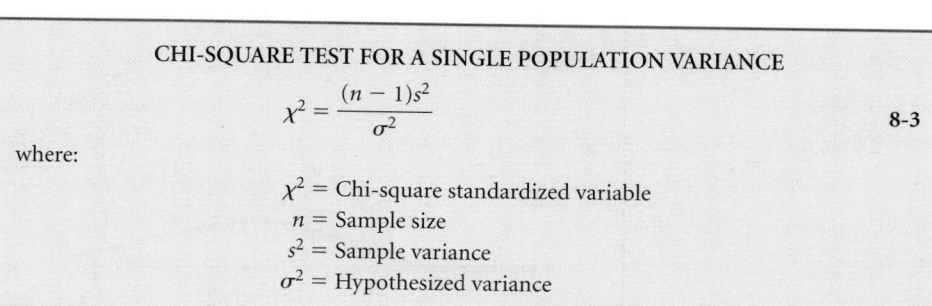

CHI-SQUARE TEST FOR A SINGLE POPULATION VARIANCE

$$\chi^2 = \frac{(n-1)s^2}{\sigma^2}$$

8-3

where:

χ^2 = Chi-square standardized variable
n = Sample size
s^2 = Sample variance
σ^2 = Hypothesized variance

Examining Equation 8-3, you will note that this test statistic can be rewritten as:

$$\chi^2 = \frac{(n-1)s^2}{\sigma^2} = \frac{(n-1)\dfrac{\sum(x-\bar{x})^2}{n-1}}{\sigma^2} = \frac{\sum(x-\bar{x})^2}{\sigma^2} = \sum\left(\frac{x-\bar{x}}{\sigma}\right)^2$$

If the sample is obtained from a normal distribution, the last expression inside the parentheses is essentially a z-value. Recall that $z = \dfrac{x-\mu}{\sigma}$. Therefore, χ^2 is the sum of squared z-values. When a z-value from a normal distribution is squared, it produces a chi-squared variable with one degree of freedom. The sum of n independent chi-squared variables is also a chi-squared random variable with n degrees of freedom. Here, however, we must estimate the population mean with the sample mean (since μ is unknown) before we estimate the population variance using s^2. You may recall from the discussion concerning degrees of freedom in Chapter 7 that this reduces the degrees of freedom by 1. Therefore, the distribution of χ^2 is a chi-squared distribution with $n-1$ degrees of freedom.

The central location and shape of the standardized chi-square distribution depend on the hypothesized variance and the degrees of freedom, $n-1$. Figure 8-18 illustrates chi-square distributions for various degrees of freedom. Note that as the degrees of freedom increase, the chi-square distribution becomes more symmetrical.

FIGURE 8-18   Chi-Square Distributions

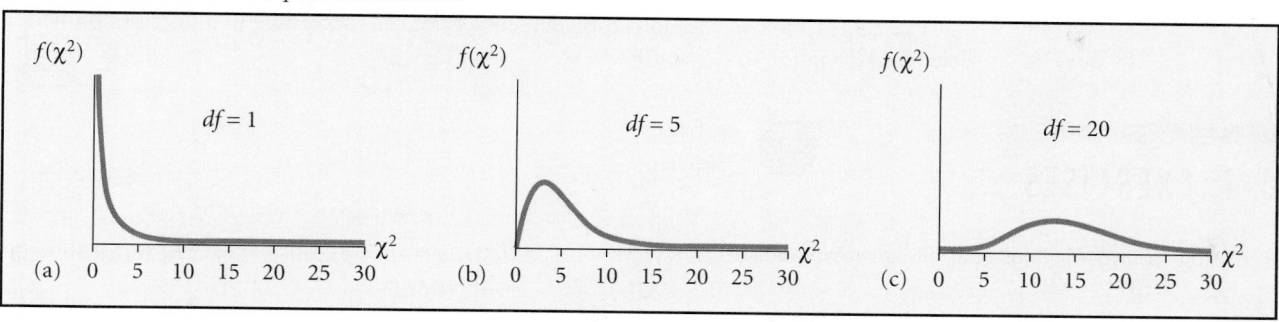

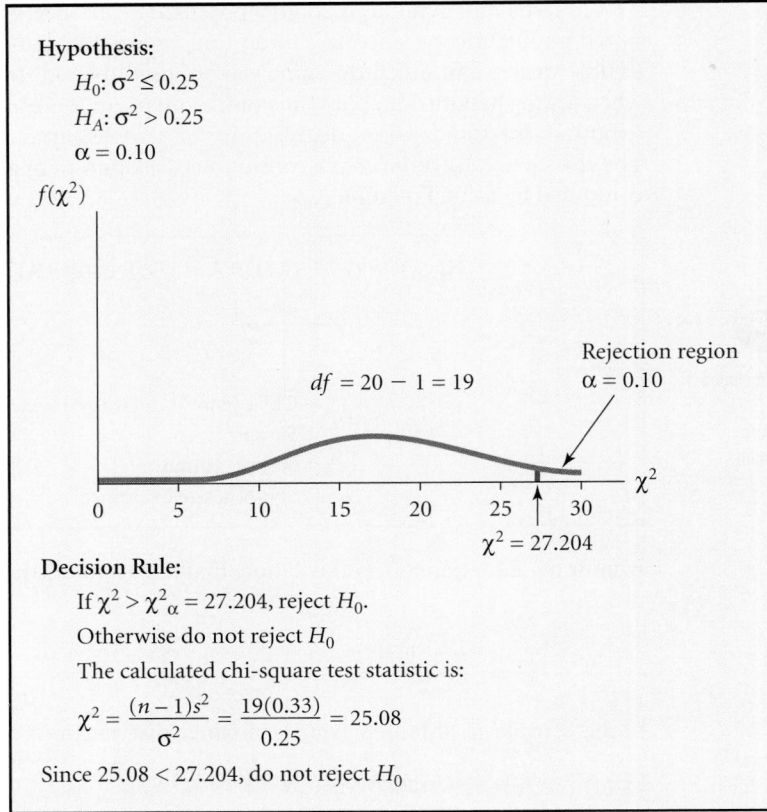

Hypothesis:

$H_0: \sigma^2 \leq 0.25$

$H_A: \sigma^2 > 0.25$

$\alpha = 0.10$

$f(\chi^2)$

$df = 20 - 1 = 19$

Rejection region
$\alpha = 0.10$

χ^2

0   5   10   15   20   25   30

$\chi^2 = 27.204$

Decision Rule:

If $\chi^2 > \chi^2_\alpha = 27.204$, reject H_0.

Otherwise do not reject H_0

The calculated chi-square test statistic is:

$$\chi^2 = \frac{(n-1)s^2}{\sigma^2} = \frac{19(0.33)}{0.25} = 25.08$$

Since $25.08 < 27.204$, do not reject H_0

FIGURE 8-19
Chi-Square Test for One
Population Variance for the
H & L Machines Example

Returning to the H & L Machines example, suppose the dispatch manager took a sample of 20 service calls and found a variance of 0.33 hours squared. Figure 8-19 illustrates the hypothesis test at a significance level of 0.10.

Appendix G contains a table of chi-square values for various levels of significance and degrees of freedom. The chi-square table is used in a manner similar to the use of the t-distribution table. For example, to find the critical value, χ^2_α, for the H & L Machines example, first determine the degrees of freedom, $n - 1 = 20 - 1 = 19$, and the desired significance level, 0.10. Now go to the chi-square table under the column headed 0.10 and find the χ^2 value in this column that intersects the row corresponding to the appropriate degrees of freedom. You should find the critical value of 27.204.

As you can see in Figure 8-19, the chi-square test statistic, calculated using Equation 8-3, is 25.08. This falls to the left of the rejection region. Thus the manager should not reject the null hypothesis based on these sample data. She will conclude, based on these results, that the service representatives should complete their service calls according to a distribution with a standard deviation of 0.5 hours or less.

Additional
Example 8-c

Chi-Square Test

Additional
Exercises

8-4: EXERCISES

8-37. Note the following null and alternative hypotheses:

$$H_0: \sigma^2 \leq 40$$
$$H_A: \sigma^2 > 40$$

a. Test if $n = 10$, $s = 7$ and $\alpha = 0.05$. Be sure to show the decision rule.

b. Test if $n = 30$, $s^2 = 54$ and $\alpha = 0.10$. Show the decision rule.

8-38. Note the following null and alternative hypotheses:

$$H_0: \sigma^2 \geq 300$$
$$H_A: \sigma^2 < 300$$

a. Test if $n = 20$, $s = 12.5$ and $\alpha = 0.05$. Be sure to show the decision rule.

b. Test if $n = 15$, $s^2 = 195$ and $\alpha = 0.10$. Show the decision rule.

Business Applications

8-39. The Hagluud Corporation manufactures paint and stain products for interior and exterior home and commercial applications. The new "Apple Wood Stain" product is thought to be a real improvement over some of the company's previous products. One criterion of a quality stain is the consistency of coverage per gallon. Hagluud hopes the standard deviation will not exceed 20 square feet per gallon. The company R&D department will assume the standard deviation does not exceed 20 square feet unless the data strongly suggest otherwise. To test this, they have selected a random sample of 12 gallons and found the following coverage in square feet:

| 245 | 302 | 240 | 280 | 255 | 300 | 290 | 240 | 300 | 270 | 230 | 300 |

a. Perform a hypothesis test to determine if the consistency of coverage for the paint is as desired by the R&D department of Hagluud. Write a one-paragraph conclusion for the manager stating your conclusions concerning the product's coverage consistency.

b. Determine the probability that a sample variance as large as or larger than the sample variance obtained from this sample would occur when sampling from a normal distribution with a variance of 20 square feet. Provide the statistical term for the quantity you just calculated. (Hint: You will need to use the chi-square table by locating the probability corresponding to the computed χ^2 value.)

8-40. Airlines face the challenging task of keeping their planes on schedule. One key measure is the number of minutes a plane deviates from the targeted arrival time. Ideally, the measure for each arrival will be 0 minutes indicating that the plane arrived exactly on time. However, experience indicates that even under the best of circumstances there will be inherent variability. Suppose one major airline has set standards that require the planes to arrive, on average, on time with a standard deviation not to exceed 2 minutes. To determine whether these standards are being met, each month the airline selects a random sample of 12 airplane arrivals and determines the number of minutes early or late the flight is. The times for last month, rounded to the nearest minute, are:

| 3 | −7 | 4 | 2 | −2 | 5 | 11 | −3 | 4 | 6 | −4 | 1 |

a. State the appropriate null and alternative hypotheses for testing the standard regarding the mean value. Test the hypothesis using a significance level equal to 0.05. What assumption will be required?

b. State the appropriate null and alternative hypotheses regarding the standard deviation. Use the sample data to conduct the hypothesis test with $\alpha = 0.05$.

c. Discuss the results of both tests. What should the airline conclude regarding its arrival standards? What factors could influence the arrival times of flights?

d. What must you assume concerning the distribution of the number of minutes a plane deviates from arrival time so that the hypothesis tests you conducted are valid?

e. Examine the sampling procedure used. Could this qualify as a random sample of all time deviations? To what population does the result apply?

8-41. A software design firm has recently developed a prototype educational computer game for children. One of the important factors in the success of a game like this is the time it takes the child to play the game. Two factors are important: the mean time it takes to play, and the variability in time required from child to child. Experience indicates that the mean time should be 10 minutes or less and the standard deviation should not exceed 4 minutes. The company has decided to test this prototype with 10 children selected at random from the local school district. The following values represent the time (rounded to the nearest minute) each child spent until completing the game.

| 9 | 14 | 11 | 8 | 13 | 15 | 11 | 10 | 7 | 12 |

a. The developers of the software will assume the mean time to completion of the game is 10 minutes or less unless the data strongly suggest otherwise. State the appropriate null and alternative hypotheses for testing the requirement regarding the mean value.

b. Referring to part a, test the hypothesis using a significance level equal to 0.10. What assumption will be required?

c. The developers of the software will assume the standard deviation of the time to completion of the game does not exceed 4 minutes unless the data strongly suggest otherwise. State the appropriate null and alternative hypotheses regarding the standard deviation. Use the sample data to conduct the hypothesis test with a significance level = 0.10.

8-42. Reconsider Problem 41. Suppose the software designers wished to take a more aggressive approach to their hypothesis test. They do not wish to market the software unless the data conclusively demonstrate that the standard deviation of the time to completion of the game does not exceed 4.

a. State the research hypothesis, the null hypothesis, and the alternative hypothesis for this hypothesis test.

b. Calculate (or place bounds) on the p-value for this hypothesis test.

c. Use the p-value you produced in part b to conduct the appropriate hypothesis test.

8-43. The Fillmore Institute has established a service designed to help charities increase the amount of money they collect from direct mail solicitations. Its consulting is aimed at increasing the mean dollar amount returned from each giver and also reducing the variation in amount contributed from giver to giver. The Badke Foundation collects money for heart disease research. Over the last 8 years, records show that the average contribution per returned envelope is $14.25 with a standard deviation of $6.44. The Badke Foundation directors decided to try the Fillmore services on a test basis. It used the recommended letters and other request materials and sent out 1,000 requests. From these, 166 were returned. The data showing the dollars returned per giver are in the file called **Badke**.

Based on the sample data, what conclusions should the Badke Foundation reach regarding the Fillmore consulting services? Use appropriate hypothesis tests with a significance level = 0.05 to reach your conclusions.

8-44. Reconsider Problem 43. Suppose that you worked for the Badke Foundation. The director of the foundation has asked you to demonstrate to the Fillmore Institute that contributions you received while you used its services had the same mean and standard deviation as when you weren't using its services.

Conduct the appropriate hypothesis tests to test the research hypotheses specified by the foundation director.

SUMMARY AND CONCLUSIONS

This chapter has introduced the fundamentals of hypothesis testing. The focus has been on hypothesis tests for decisions with large sample sizes. The concepts presented in this chapter provide decision makers with tools for using sample information to decide whether a given null hypothesis should be rejected.

In this chapter we have concentrated on examples of hypothesis tests involving a single population mean or population proportion. In following chapters you will see the hypothesis testing methodology is basically the same for all situations. The central issue is always to determine whether the sample information tends to support or refute the null hypothesis.

We have emphasized the importance of recognizing that when a hypothesis is tested, an error might occur. Type I and Type II statistical errors have been discussed. We have shown how to calculate the probability of committing each type of error for applications involving a single population mean.

You have probably noticed that the statistical estimation techniques discussed in Chapter 7 and hypothesis testing have much in common. Both estimation and hypothesis test-

ing are used extensively by business decision makers. Estimation procedures are most useful when the decision makers have little or no idea of the value of a population parameter and are primarily interested in determining these values. On the other hand, hypothesis testing is used when a claim about a population value needs to be tested. Estimation and hypothesis testing are the central components of statistical inference and will be used throughout the remaining chapters of this text.

EQUATIONS

Power

$$\text{Power} = 1 - \beta \qquad \text{8-1}$$

z-Test Statistic for Proportions

$$z = \frac{p - \pi}{\sqrt{\dfrac{\pi(1 - \pi)}{n}}} \qquad \text{8-2}$$

Chi-Square Test Statistic

$$\chi^2 = \frac{(n - 1)s^2}{\sigma^2} \qquad \text{8-3}$$

KEY TERMS

Alternative Hypothesis—The hypothesis that includes all population values not covered by the null hypothesis. The alternative hypothesis is deemed to be true if the null hypothesis is rejected.

Critical Value(s)—The value(s) of a statistic corresponding to a given significance level. This cutoff value, $\bar{x}_\alpha$, determines the boundary between those samples resulting in a test statistic that leads to rejecting the null hypothesis and those that lead to a decision not to reject the null hypothesis.

Hypothesis—A supposition used to investigate properties of the parameter(s) or shape of a distribution or process.

Null Hypothesis—The statement about the population value that will be tested. The null hypothesis will be rejected only if the sample data provide substantial contradictory evidence.

One-Tailed Hypothesis Test—A hypothesis test in which the entire rejection region is located in one tail of the test statistic distribution.

p-Value—The probability (assuming the null hypothesis is true) of obtaining a test statistic at least as extreme as the test statistic we calculated from the sample. The p-value is also known as the *observed significance level*.

Power—The probability that the hypothesis test will reject the null hypothesis when the null hypothesis is false.

Research Hypothesis—The hypothesis the decision maker attempts to demonstrate to be true. Since this is the hypothesis deemed to be the most important to the decision maker, it will not be declared true unless the sample data strongly indicate that it is true.

Significance Level—The maximum probability of committing a Type I statistical error. The probability is denoted by the symbol α.

States of Nature—The uncertain events over which decision makers have no direct control.

Statistical Inference—The process by which decision makers reach conclusions about a population based on sample information collected from the population.

Test Statistic—A function of the sampled observations that provides a basis for testing a statistical hypothesis.

Two-Tailed Hypothesis Test—A hypothesis test in which the rejection region is split between the two tails of the test statistic's distribution.

Type I Error—Rejecting the null hypothesis when it is, in fact, true.

Type II Error—Failing to reject the null hypothesis when it is, in fact, false.

CHAPTER EXERCISES

SOLVED PROBLEMS ON YOUR CD-ROM
Try the WORKED-OUT EXERCISES and BUSINESS APPLICATIONS on the CD-ROM.

Conceptual Questions

8-45. Discuss the two types of statistical errors that can occur when a hypothesis is tested. Illustrate what you mean by using a business example for each.

8-46. Discuss the issues that a decision maker should consider when determining the significance level to use in a hypothesis test.

8-47. What is meant by the term *critical value* in a hypothesis-testing situation? Illustrate what you mean with a business example.

8-48. Discuss why it is necessary to use an estimate of the standard error for a confidence interval and not for a hypothesis test concerning a population proportion.

8-49. What is the maximum probability of committing a Type I error called? How is this probability determined? Discuss.

8-50. Recall that the power of the test is the probability that the null hypothesis is rejected when H_0 is false. Explain whether or not power is definable if the given parameter was the value specified in the null hypothesis.

8-51. Go to the library and, in a journal related to your declared major, locate two articles that use hypothesis testing. Discuss the problem being addressed, how the hypothesis was formulated, and any conclusions drawn based on the statistical test.

8-52. Examine the test statistic used in testing a population proportion. Why is it impossible to test the hypothesis that the population proportion equals 0 using such a test statistic? Try to determine a way that such a test could be conducted.

8-53. Consider a time when you had to make a personal decision. Discuss to what extent your decision followed this process: (1) Formulate hypothesis, (2) Gather data, (3) Make decision.

Business Applications

8-54. The Ohio State Tax Commission attempts to set up payroll-tax withholding tables such that by the end of the year, an employee's income tax withholding is about $100 below his or her actual income tax owed to the state. The commission director claims that when all the Ohio tax returns are in, the average additional payment will be less than or equal to $100.

A random sample of 50 accounts revealed, on average, an additional payment of $114 with a sample standard deviation of $50.

  a. Testing at a significance level of 0.10, do the sample data refute the director's claim?

  b. Determine the largest sample mean (with the same sample size and standard deviation) that would fail to refute the director's claim.

8-55. The TSR Testing Service prepares real estate license examinations for several states. Wisconsin officials are considering hiring this company to devise a test for their real estate brokers' license requirements. Wisconsin requires that the average test score be exactly 70 points. In order to evaluate the test prepared by TSR Testing, Wisconsin officials have selected a random sample of 60 potential brokers and have administered the exam. They found that the mean score was 68.55 points.

  a. State the appropriate null and alternative hypotheses.

  b. Assuming that the true standard deviation is 10 points and the hypothesis is to be tested at a significance level of 0.08, on the basis of the sample data should the Wisconsin officials consider requiring TSR Testing Service to restructure their test? Describe what a Type II error would be in the context of this problem.

8-56. The Cherry Hill Growers Association operates a fruit warehouse in California. Because of the volume of cherries that arrive at the warehouse during the picking season, the growers have agreed that instead of weighing each box of cherries, they would assume that the average box weighs 20 pounds. The total weight is then simply the number of boxes times 20 pounds.

Past studies have shown that the standard deviation of weight from box to box is 0.5 pound. Suppose the manager of the warehouse has decided to select a random sample of 70 boxes of cherries from a particular grower's crop. He suspects that the grower may be underfilling the boxes and is concerned with detecting this problem, if it is the case. He is not concerned if the average box contains more than 20 pounds.

a. Would the warehouse manager be justified in concluding that underfilling of the boxes is occurring if the sample mean was 19.62? Use a significance level of 0.05.

b. Determine the probability that a sample mean less than or equal to 19.62 would be obtained from a sample of size 70 if the population mean was 20 pounds. What is the statistical term for the value you calculated?

8-57. Refer to Problem 56.

a. Discuss which type of hypothesis testing error would be more important to the warehouse manager.

b. Discuss which type of error would be more important to the grower.

8-58. The Lazer Company has a contract to produce a part for Boeing Corporation that must have an average diameter of 6 inches and a standard deviation of 0.10 inch. The Lazer Company has developed the process that will meet the specifications with respect to the standard deviation, but it is still trying to meet the mean specifications. A test run (considered a random sample) of parts was produced, and the company wishes to determine whether this latest process that produced the sample will consistently produce parts meeting the requirement of average diameter equal to 6 inches.

a. Specify the appropriate research, null, and alternative hypotheses.

b. Develop the decision rule assuming that the sample size is 200 parts and the significance level is 0.01.

c. What should the Lazer Company conclude if the sample mean diameter for the 200 parts is 6.018 inches? Discuss.

8-59. Tom Morgan operates a gas station in a suburban area of Boston. He is thinking of installing a mechanism on his self-service pumps that will not allow more than 10 gallons to be pumped without having the pump restarted. He hopes this will cut down on theft without making the honest customers angry.

The marketing representative for the new mechanism claims that if Tom's station is typical, the average fill-up is no more than 10 gallons. Tom has decided to select a random sample of 200 customers and test to determine whether the marketing rep's claim is true. He is willing to accept the claim unless the data strongly indicate that the claim is not true.

a. If the sample results show a mean of 10.32 gallons per fill-up, with a sample standard deviation of 2.9 gallons, what should Tom conclude about the population mean? Use a significance level of 0.05. Discuss your results.

b. Calculate a relevant 95% confidence interval for the average fill-up.

8-60. The owners of Fit and Trim, a fitness and diet club, would like to advertise that their clients lose at least 10 pounds, on average, during their first 3 months of membership at the club. The sample resulted in the following summary statistics:

$$\bar{x} = 9.1 \text{ lb.}$$
$$s = 0.4 \text{ lb.}$$
$$n = 20$$

a. If the desired significance level is 0.05, what should be concluded about this claim if the previously shown results are observed? Be sure to first set up the appropriate decision rule.

b. What assumption(s) must you make about the population's distribution in order that your results in part a are valid?

8-61. The Oasis Chemical Company develops and manufactures pharmaceutical drugs for distribution and sale in the United States. The pharmaceutical business can be very lucrative when useful and safe drugs are introduced into the market. Whenever the Oasis research lab considers putting a drug into production, the company must actually establish the following sets of null and alternative hypotheses:

SET 1	SET 2
H_0: The drug is safe.	H_0: The drug is effective.
H_A: The drug is not safe.	H_A: The drug is not effective.

Take each set of hypotheses separately.

a. Discuss the considerations that should be made in establishing alpha and beta.

b. For each set of hypotheses, describe what circumstances would suggest that a Type I error would be of more concern.

c. For each set of hypotheses, describe what circumstances would suggest that a Type II error would be of more concern.

8-62. The personnel manager for a large airline has claimed that, on the average, workers are asked to work no more than 3 hours overtime per week. Past studies show the standard deviation in overtime hours per worker to be 1.2 hours.

Suppose the union negotiators wish to test this claim by sampling payroll records for 250 employees. They believe that the personnel manager's claim is untrue, but they want to base their conclusion on the sample results.

a. State the research, null, and alternative hypotheses and discuss the meaning of Type I and Type II errors in the context of this case.

b. Establish the appropriate decision rule if the union wishes to have no more than a 0.01 chance of a Type I error.

c. The payroll records produced a sample mean of 3.15 hours. Do the union negotiators have a basis for a grievance against the airline? Support your answer with a relevant statistical procedure.

8-63. A major U.S. tire manufacturer has developed a new design that will allow the owner to drive on a punctured tire for some miles without having to stop and change the tire. The R&D engineers claim that at least 90 percent of the tires will function for 50 or more miles after being punctured. However, they do not wish to assert this claim to the public if the sample data indicate otherwise. To conduct the test, a sample of 100 tires is selected with the following results:

$x = 87$ tires performed as claimed

a. State the appropriate research, null, and alternative hypotheses.

b. What conclusion should the company reach assuming it wants to test the hypothesis with a significance level of 0.05?

8-64. Referring to Problem 63, suppose the company is also worried about the variability in miles that a driver can travel on a punctured tire. It would be a problem if the average was 50 miles, but some drivers could safely travel 100 miles and others would only get a few miles out of their tire. The R&D engineers claim the standard deviation does not exceed 8 miles. Again, they do not wish to assert this claim to the public if the sample data indicate otherwise.

a. State the appropriate research, null, and alternative hypotheses.

b. Based on the data collected for a sample of 100 tires shown in Problem 63, in which the actual miles was recorded with a mean of 78.5 and a standard deviation of 28.4 miles, what conclusions should the company reach about its tires? Discuss.

8-65. At a recent meeting of the budget committee at the Winter Corporation, the marketing manager made a pitch for a larger department budget by stating that more money was needed in advertising to improve the company's image. This prompted the president of the company to establish a task force to measure public opinion about the company.

This task force planned to use a well-established instrument for measuring public perception of companies like Winter. Past studies using this particular instrument indicated that a company should receive at least an average 40-point overall rating to consider that it has a positive image in the public eye. The task force will assume that the company's image is positive unless the sample data indicate otherwise.

The task force randomly sampled 300 people within the market area and found that the average rating received was 38.98, with a sample standard deviation of 5.3 points.

a. Establish the appropriate research, null, and alternative hypotheses.

b. Assuming that the test is to be conducted with a significance level equal to 0.10, what conclusion should

the Winter Corporation reach with respect to its average company rating by all the members of the population? Discuss.

c. Reflect upon Type I and Type II errors in the context of this problem. Which of these would you expect to be of more importance to the task force? Explain your reasoning.

8-66. The managing partner of Patton and Associates, a CPA firm, has a basic knowledge of hypothesis testing. One of his clients, a retail store, would like Patton to perform an audit of the daily cash register tape against the actual dollar amount in the till.

The client recognizes that occasionally an error is going to occur. As long as the error is in the store's favor, the store manager is not concerned. However, when the store comes up short, the store manager is very concerned.

The Patton managing partner has indicated that he will perform the audit via sampling and hypothesis testing with the following hypotheses:

$H_0: \mu \geq \$0$ error; the store at least comes out even on the average

$H_A: \mu < \$0$ error; the store loses some money on the average

From past experience in this kind of audit, the CPA thinks the critical value should be set at $-\$2$. Therefore, if the average discrepancy between cash register tape and actual dollars is $2 or more at the store's expense, the null hypothesis will be rejected. If the null hypothesis is rejected, the appropriate clerk will be dismissed.

The CPA partner realizes that his client wants to be very sure any such employee is fired, but only if the firing is truly justified. Consequently, he is concerned with knowing the probability of a Type II error for various values of the true, but unknown, population mean.

a. If the sample size is 47 days and the standard deviation is known to be $4, what is the probability of a Type II error if the true mean is actually $-\$1.507$?

b. Calculate β for a sample size of 64 days. The standard deviation remains $4, the critical value is held at $-\$2$, and the true mean is $-\$1.50$.

c. Why has an increase in sample size caused an increase, rather than a decrease, in probability of a Type II error? Discuss how this undesirable event happened and how you could have prevented it from happening in this case. (Consult the following article if you need some help: Herbert H. Tsang, "The Effects of Changing Sample Size on the Alpha and Beta Errors: A Pedagogic Note," *Decision Sciences* 8 (October 1977): 757–59.)

8-67. In a recent management-union negotiating process at a large national tire manufacturing company, one of the points made by management was that the average number of dollars in healthcare benefits used per worker was $417 per year. It also indicated that the standard deviation was $200 per employee. Assuming that the standard deviation figure is correct, the union decided to select a random sample of 100 employee health records and test to determine whether the management assertion was correct. It planned to test at a significance level of 0.08.

   a. From the union's perspective, what should the research hypothesis be?

   b. Based on your response to part a, set up the correct null and alternative hypotheses.

   c. If the sample mean for the 100 workers was $403, what should the union conclude about the claim made by management? Discuss.

8-68. The Bell Corporation is the parent corporation that franchises automobile lube and oil change centers around the United States. The standard set forth by the Bell Corporation is that at least 80 percent of all cars will have their lube and oil service completed in 10 minutes or less.

   Periodically, representatives from the Bell Company visit the franchises and perform a compliance test on this standard. They randomly select 150 cars (without the local operator's knowledge) and record how long it takes to service each car.

   a. Establish the appropriate null and alternative hypotheses.

   b. Determine the decision rule assuming that the company performs the compliance test using a significance level of 0.05.

   c. Determine if the franchise is operating within its standard. In the sample, 108 cars were serviced in 10.0 minutes or less.

8-69. Suppose the manager in charge of compliance auditing for the Bell Corporation (see Problem 68) has decided that a larger sample size is necessary and thus has decided to select a random sample of 200 cars rather than 150.

   a. What general impact will this have on the probability of committing a Type II error for any level of the true mean?

   b. What impact will this have on the probability of committing a Type I error? Discuss.

8-70. The maker of Quick Lite, ready-to-light charcoal briquettes, bases its claim to fame on the premise that its product, on average, will ignite within three tries. A consumer awareness group would like to test the charcoal maker's claim and reach its own opinion about the product.

   A sample of 150 buyers was asked to use the charcoal three times during the summer and record how many times it took before the briquettes caught fire. The sample revealed an average of 3.5 tries with a sample standard deviation of 0.2 tries.

   a. Testing at a significance level of 0.08, decide what the consumer group should conclude about Quick Lite's claim.

   b. Which type of error associated with hypothesis tests would the consumer awareness group be most interested in avoiding? Explain your reasoning.

8-71. A manufacturer of computer terminals claims that its product will last at least 50 weeks without needing repairs. The Quast Corporation is considering purchasing a great many of these computer terminals. However, it does not wish to purchase the computer terminals if the manufacturer's claim is untrue. A Quast data processing manager has determined that given the price of the terminal and the total dollars involved, Quast should ask for some quality control records from the manufacturer.

   Suppose the manufacturer produces records of a random sample of 30 terminals. The average time before the first breakdown was 48 weeks with a standard deviation equal to 12 weeks.

   a. Establish the appropriate research, null, and alternative hypotheses.

   b. Determine the appropriate decision rule and indicate whether the sample information justifies rejecting the manufacturer's claim. Use a significance level of 0.05.

   c. Discuss the ramifications of this decision and the potential costs of being wrong.

   d. Which type of hypothesis test error would Quast be more interested in avoiding? Explain your reasons.

8-72. Referring to Problem 71, suppose the sample mean of the 30 terminals had been 45 weeks rather than 48.

   a. What is the probability of finding a sample mean as small as or smaller than 45 if the true mean is 50 weeks?

   b. Now that you have determined the probability in part a, what does this mean to you with respect to whether the terminals can be expected to average at least 50 weeks before the first breakdown?

   c. "If the probability of a sample result, given the null hypothesis, is too small, the null hypothesis should be rejected." Comment on this statement with respect to your answers in parts a and b.

   d. What relationship does the significance level have with a probability of a "too small" sample result, as discussed in part c?

8-73. The Softsoap Company recently developed a new soap product designed for use in automatic washing machines. The marketing department would like to claim in its advertisements that the new soap will save the average homeowner at least 10 ounces of soap per month. It will make this claim unless the sample data strongly indicate otherwise. Before setting up the advertising plan, it decided to test the product in a random sample of 70 homes for a period of 1 month. The selected homeowners were asked to record how much soap they had used the month before. Then they were asked to keep track of their soap usage with the new Softsoap product. They were asked to keep their washing procedures the same as before the test.

   a. Establish the null and alternative hypotheses to be tested considering the objectives of the marketing department.

   b. Assuming that the population standard deviation is known to be 3 ounces saved per month, what is the decision rule for the hypothesis test if the test is to be conducted with a significance level of 0.10?

   c. Suppose the sample shows that the average savings is 9.5 ounces. What conclusion should the Softsoap marketing department reach with respect to its desired advertising claim? Discuss.

d. With respect to the decision reached in part c, comment on which statistical error may have been committed and what it would mean to the Softsoap Company.

8-74. The Larson & Sons Company sells dwarf fruit trees through the mail. It claims that the average pear tree will produce at least 2.5 bushels of pears the second year after it has been planted. If the desired significance level is 0.05, what should be concluded if the following data were recorded for a sample of 40 trees showing the number of bushels produced the second year after planting? The data are also in the file named **Larson**.

1.6	3.3	4.0	2.6	2.6	2.8	3.2	2.9
3.4	2.4	3.0	3.9	2.7	3.3	2.6	1.9
2.8	3.0	2.8	1.6	3.0	2.5	1.9	3.0
3.0	4.5	1.0	2.3	1.8	2.9	0.4	3.6
2.0	2.5	2.2	2.6	2.4	1.8	3.5	2.0

8-75. Referring to Problem 74, the company also claims its trees provide a consistent volume of fruit and that the standard deviation does not exceed 0.50 pounds.

a. Based on the sample data in the file called **Larson**, what should be concluded concerning the consistency contention if the test is conducted using a significance level of 0.05? Discuss.

b. Construct a histogram of the sample data using 6 classes.

c. Do the sample data appear to have come from a normal distribution? Would this impact the validity of your test in part a? Explain your reasoning.

8-76. The United States federal government has issued requests for proposals to cities around the country that might wish to serve as the site of a wind energy research facility. This facility would employ about 100 people and would be a boost to the economy of any city, but especially smaller cities.

The government required that the average wind speed year round in the selected city be at least 10 mph. In response to this, Cheyenne, Wyoming, submitted a bid for the research facility. Its proposal reached the finalist stage. The last step in the selection process was for the federal government to select a random sample of 300 days from the National Weather Service records for the city to determine whether it met the average wind-speed requirements. The government will deny Cheyenne's proposal if the data strongly suggest that the average wind speed is less than 10 mph.

a. If the average wind speed for the sampled days was 9.68 mph, with a standard deviation of 4.8 mph, what should the federal government conclude about the average wind speed in Cheyenne? Use a significance level of 0.03. Discuss your conclusions.

b. With which type of hypothesis error would Cheyenne officials be more concerned? If you were an official from Cheyenne and had to choose a significance level, would you choose 0.01, 0.025, 0.05, or 0.10? Explain your reasoning.

c. Answer the questions in part b assuming you were a federal government official. Explain your reasoning.

8-77. The Rainbow Company operates coin-operated candy machines in Lincoln, Nebraska. When the company first started using the so-called "talking" machines, it expected daily revenue per machine to be at least $63, on the average. Suppose a sample of 100 machines was selected in the Lincoln area over a period of time after the new machines had been installed and the average revenue per machine was $59.85 with a standard deviation of $12.40.

a. Formulate the appropriate null and alternative hypotheses for this situation.

b. Establish the critical value and decision rule using the z-value approach, assuming the significance level is 0.05.

c. Determine if the Rainbow Company's expectations have been met.

d. If the average daily revenue was in fact $63, determine the probability that the sample mean would be at most $59.85. Give the statistical term that refers to the probability calculated.

8-78. The Inland Empire Food Store Company has stated in its advertising that the average shopper will save $5.00 or more per week by shopping at Inland stores. A consumer group has decided to test this assertion by sampling 50 shoppers who currently shop at other stores. The group selects the customers and then notes each item purchased at their regular store. These same items are then priced at the Inland store and the total bill is compared. The following data reflect savings at Inland for the 50 shoppers. Note that those cases where the bill was higher at Inland are marked with a minus sign. The data are contained in the file **Inland Foods**.

$14.00	$2.54	$11.33	$12.02	$4.55
12.00	8.45	−0.75	12.04	1.83
−5.04	2.80	2.09	−3.10	8.02
12.10	3.31	2.20	4.65	1.03
2.93	9.75	1.73	−1.54	9.80
3.56	3.29	1.34	−4.08	9.70
10.02	1.33	4.56	−1.52	3.25
−0.85	−5.02	2.19	−3.45	0.65
1.90	2.43	0.43	2.54	0.03
2.10	−0.56	7.89	−0.65	1.34

a. Set up the appropriate null and alternative hypotheses to test Inland's claim.

b. Using a significance level of 0.05, develop the decision rule and test the hypothesis. Can Inland Empire support its advertising claim?

c. Which type of hypothesis error would the consumer group be more interested in controlling? Which type of hypothesis error would the company be more interested in controlling? Explain your reasoning.

8-79. The Falcon Speedreading Course advertises that the average increase in reading speed for graduates of the course is at least 200 words per minute.

a. What should an independent reviewer conclude if a sample of 15 graduates showed an average improvement of 190 words per minute with a standard deviation equal to 40? Test at the significance level of 0.10.

b. Consider the fact that you do not know the population's standard deviation and that the sample size is small. What assumption must you make concerning the population to validate your analysis in part a?

8-80. Referring to Problem 79, suppose the sample standard deviation is 20 words per minute rather than 40.

    a. Assuming that the sample mean was unchanged and the significance level was unchanged, what conclusion should be reached with respect to the speed-reading course offered by Falcon?

    b. Discuss why the change in standard deviation would have this effect on the conclusion reached, considering that the sample mean did not change.

8-81. The maker of Super Saver paint advertises that its product will average at least 900 square feet per gallon coverage. A consumer group that regularly tests these types of claims has budgeted enough money to sample 24 gallons of paint. It uses a significance level of 0.10 to test claims like the one made by Super Saver.

    a. State the null and alternative hypotheses to be tested.

    b. If the sample mean was 890 square feet with a sample standard deviation equal to 80 square feet, what should the consumer group conclude? Discuss.

    c. Reflect upon the propensity to file legal suits in this country. If you were the analyst for the consumer group, which type of hypothesis error would you be most interested in controlling? If you were a manager for the maker of Super Saver paint, which type of hypothesis error would you be more interested in controlling?

    d. Consider the fact that you do not know the population's standard deviation and that the sample size is small. What assumption must you make concerning the population to validate your analysis in part a?

8-82. Referring to Problem 81, the maker of Super Saver paint also has claimed that the standard deviation in coverage is 70 feet or less.

    a. Based upon the sample results in Problem 81, part b, what should the consumer group conclude concerning the maker's claim if the test is conducted using a significance level of 0.05?

    b. Regardless of the sample size used in such hypothesis tests, the population must have a specific characteristic to validate your test. Describe this characteristic.

8-83. The R&P Insurance Company provides insurance coverage for automobile owners at a fixed premium. If customers are poor risks, R&P would like to deny them coverage. However, if the customers are good risks, R&P would like to have the business. Each time an individual applies for insurance, R&P is faced with the following null and alternative hypotheses:

H_0: The applicant is a good risk.
H_A: The applicant is a poor risk.

a. Given that R&P has recently been suffering decreasing profits, how would you go about assessing levels for α and β?

b. Discuss the factors that you consider important in arriving at this decision.

c. How would your responses change if R&P were a new company anxious to grow and expand? Discuss your reasoning.

8-84. The Oat Crunch Cereal Company has a machine that automatically fills 16-ounce boxes of cereal. This machine may be set to any mean fill, but the standard deviation of fill is known to be 0.5 ounces. The machine occasionally gets out of adjustment, even though the mean has been set at the desired fill level. The production manager has the responsibility of testing samples of filled cereal boxes to see whether the average fill has deviated from the desired level.

    a. Suppose the average fill level has been set at 16.2 ounces. If a sample of 60 boxes is tested and found to average 16.36 ounces, what should the production manager conclude about the machine's adjustment? Test at a significance level of 0.05.

    b. Suppose the average fill setting is 16.2 ounces, but instead of a sample of 60 boxes, the sample size is 400 boxes. What conclusion should the production manager reach if the sample mean is the same as before, 16.36 ounces? Test at a significance level of 0.05.

    c. Why are the conclusions different even though the sample mean was the same for both parts a and b? Discuss.

    d. Consider the impact on the company of a larger mean fill level in this problem. If you were an analyst for the Oat Crunch Company and had to choose a significance level from 0.01, 0.025, 0.05, or 0.10, which would you choose? Explain your reasoning.

8-85. Referring to Problem 84, suppose the Oat Crunch Company begins to suspect that the filling machine standard deviation exceeds 0.50 ounces. A random sample of 20 cartons is selected. The average fill is 16.0 ounces with a sample standard deviation equal to 0.68 ounces.

    a. Based on the sample data, what should the Oat Crunch Company conclude concerning its suspicions about the filling machine variability if the company tests the hypothesis using a significance level of 0.05?

    b. Consider the impact on the company of a larger standard deviation for the filling machine in this problem. If you were an analyst for the Oat Crunch Company and had to choose a significance level from 0.01, 0.025, 0.05, or 0.10, which would you choose? Explain your reasoning.

8-86. The Cajun King restaurant manager is thinking about running a coupon advertisement in the local newspaper in which the restaurant offers a free soft drink with the purchase of a meal. The manager believes that at least 30% of the coupons will be redeemed. Before running the ad, he has a student group at a local high school distribute 200 coupons to a random sample of homes in the market area. Fifty-four coupons were redeemed.

a. What should the owner conclude concerning his pre-conception of the redemption rate assuming that the test is based on a significance level of 0.10? Be sure to state the appropriate null and alternative hypotheses.

b. Construct a 90% confidence interval for the proportion of coupons that will be redeemed. Suppose it costs the owner of Cajun King $0.10 for each free soft drink and that he distributes 5,000 coupons. Determine the owner's minimum and maximum cost of the free-drink offer.

8-87. A story ran recently in a major newspaper that claimed that over 70% of all employees at least one time a year call in sick when they are not actually sick. The story described this as a way for employees to get extra vacation days. Suppose a follow-up study was conducted in which 400 employees were selected at random and asked (confidentially) to indicate whether they had called in sick when they were not sick during the past year. A total of 292 employees admitted that they had done this.

a. State the appropriate null and alternative hypotheses to test the claim made in the newspaper story.

b. Based on the sample data and a significance level of 0.05, what should be concluded about the newspaper's claim? Use the p-value approach to test the hypothesis.

8-88. Assuming the data in the files labeled **Cities** are a random sample of cities in the United States, use these data to test an economist's claim that the average white-collar 1998 earnings in U.S. cities was less than $25,000. Testing at a significance level of 0.05, do these sample data support or refute this contention? Discuss your results.

8-89. Referring to Problem 88, the same economist has claimed that the average manufacturing salary in U.S. cities in 1998 exceeded $26,100. Based on the sample data, can this claim be supported or refuted at a significance level of 0.05? Discuss your conclusion.

8-90. The data in the file labeled **Fast100** represent various characteristics for companies that were determined to be the 100 fastest growing companies in the United States. The average profit for these companies during the previous year was $31.936 (in millions of dollars).

a. Select a random sample of 20 companies from this list of 100.

b. Compute the mean and standard deviation for profit for these sample data.

c. Use these sample data to test the hypothesis that population mean is equal to $31.936 million. Use a significance level of 0.05. (Hint: Remember that the finite correction factor must be used when the sample size is large relative to the size of the population.)

8-91. A market research company was recently hired to conduct a survey of cell phone owners to determine whether the Nokia brand had a market share of at least 35%. Use the sample data contained in the file called **Cell Phone Survey** to reach a conclusion using a significance level of 0.05. Be sure to state the null and alternative hypotheses.

8-92. A study was conducted by the state transportation department to determine whether a "weigh-in-motion" (WIM) scale could be used in place of the static scale currently used at port-of-entry (POE) locations across the state. The WIM scale weighs trucks as they drive over the scale rather than making them stop at the POE to be weighed. State officials think that the mean speed of trucks crossing the WIM scale would exceed the posted speed limit of 65 miles per hour. Based on these sample data in the file labeled **Trucks**, what conclusion can be reached concerning the preconception about the average speed? Test at an $\alpha = 0.10$.

8-93. Reconsider Problem 92. A published report indicates the average length of trucks (WIM total length) on the state highway exceeds 60 feet. Based on the sample data, can this claim be supported or refuted? Test at an $\alpha = 0.05$.

8-94. Reconsider Problem 92. Compute a new variable that is the difference between column F and column C. If the WIM scale is effective, the average difference should be 0. Based on these sample data, what can be concluded? Test at an $\alpha = 0.05$.

CASE 8-A

Campbell Brewery, Inc., Part 1

Don Campbell and his younger brother Edward purchased Campbell Brewery from their father in 1983. The brewery makes and bottles beer under two labels and distributes it throughout the Southwest. Since purchasing the brewery, Don has been instrumental in modernizing operations.

One of the latest acquisitions is a filling machine that can be adjusted to fill at any average fill level desired. Since the bottles and cans filled by the brewery are exclusively the 12-ounce size, when they received the machine Don set the fill level to 12 ounces and left it that way. According to the manufacturer's specifications, the machine would fill bottles or cans around the average, with a standard deviation of 0.15 ounces.

Don just returned from a brewery convention where he attended a panel discussion related to problems with filling machines. One brewery representative discussed a problem her company had. It failed to learn that its machine's average fill went out of adjustment until several months later when its cost accounting department reported some problems with beer production in bulk not matching output in bottles and cans. It turns out that the machine's average fill had increased from 12 ounces to 12.07 ounces. With large volumes of production, this deviation meant substantial loss in profits.

Another brewery reported the same type of problem, but in the opposite direction. Its machine began filling bottles with slightly less than 12 ounces on the average. Although the consumers could not detect the shortage in a given bottle, the state and federal agencies responsible for checking the accuracy of packaged products discovered the problem in their testing and substantially fined the brewery for the underfill.

These problems were a surprise to Don Campbell. He had not considered the possibility that the machine might go out of adjustment and pose these types of problems. In fact, he became very concerned because the problems of losing profits and potentially being fined by the government were ones that he wished to avoid, if possible. Following the convention, Don and Ed decided to hire a consulting firm with expertise in these matters to assist them in setting up a procedure for monitoring the performance of the filling machine.

The consultant suggested that they set up a sampling plan whereby once a month they sample some number of bottles and measure their volumes precisely. If the average of

the sample deviates too much from 12 ounces, they should shut the machine down and make the necessary adjustments. Otherwise, they should let the filling process continue. The consultant identified two types of problems that can occur from this sort of sampling plan:

1. They may incorrectly decide to adjust the machine when it is not really necessary to do so.
2. They may incorrectly decide to allow the filling process to continue when, in fact, the true average has deviated from 12 ounces.

After carefully considering what the consultant told them, Don indicated that he wanted no more than a 0.02 chance of the first problem occurring because of the costs involved. He also decided that if the true average fill had slipped to 11.99 ounces, he wanted no more than a 0.05 chance of not detecting this with his sampling plan. He wanted to avoid problems with the state and federal agencies. Finally, if the true average fill had actually risen to 12.007 ounces, he wanted to be able to detect this 98% of the time with his sampling plan. Thus, he wanted to avoid the lost profits that would result from such a problem.

In addition, Don needs to determine how large a sample size is necessary to meet his requirements.

■ GENERAL REFERENCES

1. Berenson, Mark L., and David M. Levine, *Basic Business Statistics: Concepts and Applications*, 7th ed. (Upper Saddle River, NJ: Prentice Hall, 1999).
2. Dodge, Mark, and Craig Stinson, *Running Microsoft Excel 2000* (Redmond, WA: Microsoft Press, 1999).
3. Hogg, Robert V., and Elliot A. Tanis, *Probability and Statistical Inference*, 5th ed. (Upper Saddle River, NJ: Prentice Hall, 1997).
4. Marx, Morris L., and Richard J. Larsen, *Mathematical Statistics and Its Applications*, 3d ed. (Upper Saddle River, NJ: Prentice Hall, 2000).
5. *Microsoft Excel 2000* (Redmond, WA: Microsoft Corporation, 1999).
6. Siegel, Andrew F., *Practical Business Statistics*, 4th ed. (Burr Ridge, IL: Irwin, 2000).

CHAPTER 9

Hypothesis testing and estimation for two population parameters

CHAPTER OUTCOMES

After studying the material in Chapter 9, you should be able to:

9-1: Use sample data to test hypotheses that two population variances are equal.

9-2: Discuss the logic behind, and demonstrate the techniques for, using sample data to test hypotheses and develop interval estimates about the difference between two population means for both independent and paired samples.

9-3: Carry out hypotheses tests and establish interval estimates, using sample data, for the difference between two population proportions.

WHY YOU NEED TO KNOW

Chapter 8 introduced the concepts of hypothesis testing and illustrated its application through examples involving a single population parameter. But in many business decision-making situations, managers must decide between two or more alternatives. For example, farmers must decide which of several brands and types of wheat to plant. Fleet managers in large companies must decide which model and make of car to purchase next year. Airlines must decide whether to purchase replacement planes from Boeing or Airbus. When deciding on a new advertising campaign a company may need to evaluate proposals from competing advertising agencies. Hiring decisions may require a personnel director to select one employee from a list of applicants. Production managers are often confronted with decisions concerning whether to change a production process or leave it alone. Each day consumers purchase a product from among several competing brands.

The difficulty in such situations is that the decision maker must make the decision based on limited (sample) information. Fortunately, there are statistical tools that can help decision makers use sample information to compare different populations (alternative choices). In this chapter, we introduce these tools and techniques by discussing methods that can be used to make statistical comparisons between two populations. In Chapter 10, we will discuss some methods to extend this comparison to more than two populations. Whether we are discussing cases involving two populations or cases with more than two populations, the techniques we present are all extensions of the statistical tools used in estimation and hypothesis testing involving a single population parameter as introduced in Chapters 7 and 8.

■ 9-1: HYPOTHESIS TESTS FOR TWO POPULATION VARIANCES

In Chapter 8, we introduced hypothesis testing involving single population values. Regardless of whether we are interested in a population mean, population proportion, or a population variance, the same basic steps are used to conduct the tests.

> **HYPOTHESIS TESTING STEPS**
> 1. Formulate the null and alternative hypotheses in terms of the population parameter of interest. Remember that the null hypothesis should contain the equality.
> 2. Determine the level of significance.
> 3. Determine the critical value of the test statistic.
> 4. Select the sample and compute the test statistic.
> 5. Compare the calculated test statistic to the critical value and reach a conclusion.

The logic of hypothesis testing is that if the sample result is "significantly" different from the hypothesized population value, then the hypothesis should be rejected. This same logic applies to hypothesis tests involving more than one population value.

Hypothesis Test for Two Variances

Chapter 8 introduced a method for testing hypotheses involving a single population standard deviation. Recall that in order to conduct the test, we had to first convert the standard deviation to the variance. Then we used the chi-square distribution to determine whether the sample variance led us to reject the null hypothesis. However, decision makers are often faced with decision problems involving two population standard deviations. While there is no hypothesis test that directly tests standard deviations, there is a procedure that can be used to test whether two populations have equal variances. We can formulate null and alternative hypotheses of the following forms. Note, the three different forms are equivalent and may be used interchangeably depending on your preference.

TWO-TAILED TEST	UPPER ONE-TAILED TEST	LOWER ONE-TAILED TEST
Format 1		
$H_0: \sigma_1^2 - \sigma_2^2 = 0$ $H_A: \sigma_1^2 - \sigma_2^2 \neq 0$	$H_0: \sigma_1^2 - \sigma_2^2 \leq 0$ $H_A: \sigma_1^2 - \sigma_2^2 > 0$	$H_0: \sigma_1^2 - \sigma_2^2 \geq 0$ $H_A: \sigma_1^2 - \sigma_2^2 < 0$
Format 2		
$H_0: \sigma_1^2 = \sigma_2^2$ $H_A: \sigma_1^2 \neq \sigma_2^2$	$H_0: \sigma_1^2 \leq \sigma_2^2$ $H_A: \sigma_1^2 > \sigma_2^2$	$H_0: \sigma_1^2 \geq \sigma_2^2$ $H_A: \sigma_1^2 < \sigma_2^2$
Format 3		
$H_0: \dfrac{\sigma_1^2}{\sigma_2^2} = 1$	$H_0: \dfrac{\sigma_1^2}{\sigma_2^2} \leq 1$	$H_0: \dfrac{\sigma_1^2}{\sigma_2^2} \geq 1$
$H_A: \dfrac{\sigma_1^2}{\sigma_2^2} \neq 1$	$H_A: \dfrac{\sigma_1^2}{\sigma_2^2} > 1$	$H_A: \dfrac{\sigma_1^2}{\sigma_2^2} < 1$

In order to test a hypothesis involving two population variances, we first compute the sample variances. We then compute the test statistic shown as Equation 9-1.

Excel Simulations
F-Distribution

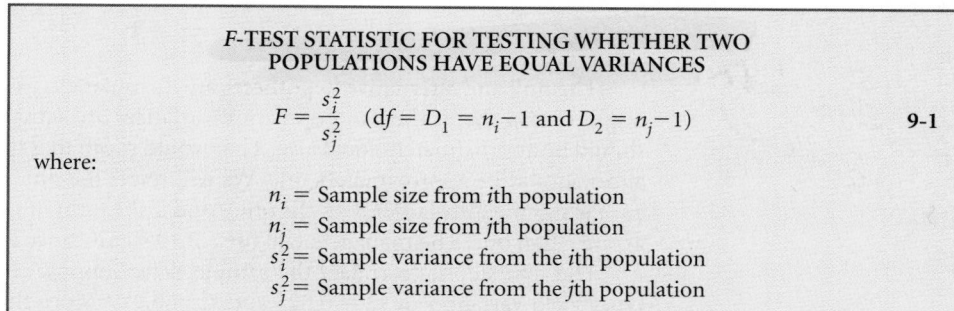

F-TEST STATISTIC FOR TESTING WHETHER TWO POPULATIONS HAVE EQUAL VARIANCES

$$F = \frac{s_i^2}{s_j^2} \quad (\text{d}f = D_1 = n_i - 1 \text{ and } D_2 = n_j - 1)$$ 9-1

where:

n_i = Sample size from ith population
n_j = Sample size from jth population
s_i^2 = Sample variance from the ith population
s_j^2 = Sample variance from the jth population

Analyzing this test statistic requires that we introduce a new distribution called the F-distribution. If the null hypothesis is true, the populations are normally distributed, and the two sample variances are independent, the value computed as the ratio of the two sample variances will come from the F-distribution. While beyond the scope of this book, statistical theory shows the F-distribution is in fact equal to the ratio of two independent chi-square distributions. Like the chi-square and the t-distributions, the appropriate F-distribution is determined by its degrees of freedom. However, the F-distribution has two sets of degrees of freedom, D_1 and D_2, that depend on the sample sizes for the variances in the numerator and denominator, respectively, in Equation 9-1.

The test statistic shown in Equation 9-1 is formed as the ratio of two sample variances. There are a couple of key points to remember when formulating this ratio.

1. For a two-tailed test, always place the larger sample variance in the numerator. This will make the calculated F-value greater than 1.0 and push the F-value toward the upper tail of the F-distribution.
2. For a one-tailed test, look to the alternative hypothesis. For the population that is *predicted* (based upon the alternative hypothesis) to have the largest variance, place that sample variance in the numerator.

The following examples will illustrate the specific methods used to test for a difference between two population variances.

EXAMPLE
9-1

TESTING TWO VARIANCES

E. Coli Bacteria Testing

Recently there have been several national scares involving meat contaminated with E. coli bacteria. The recommended preventative measure is to make sure the meat is heated to the required temperature when cooked. However, different meat patties, cooked for the same amount of time, will have different final temperatures, partially caused by variations in the patties but also partially caused by variations in burner temperatures. A regional fast-food chain is considering replacing its current burners with a new digitally controlled model. The company presently is evaluating two competing burners from which it will make its final decision. The chain's managers have decided to select the model that provides the smaller variation in final meat temperature. If they conclude that no difference exists in variation, they will use price, warranty, and service factors to make their decision.

In a preliminary test, the purchasing agents for the chain have arranged to sample 11 batches of meat cooked by burner model 1 and 13 batches of meat cooked by burner model 2 to see whether a difference in temperature variation between the two exists. Ideally, they would like a test that compares standard deviations, but no such test exists. Instead, they must convert the standard deviations to variances. The hypotheses are:

Hypotheses:

$$H_0: \sigma_1^2 = \sigma_2^2 \quad \text{or} \quad H_0: \frac{\sigma_1^2}{\sigma_2^2} = 1 \quad \text{or} \quad H_0: \sigma_1^2 - \sigma_2^2 = 0$$

$$H_A: \sigma_1^2 \neq \sigma_2^2 \qquad\quad H_A: \frac{\sigma_1^2}{\sigma_2^2} \neq 1 \qquad\quad H_A: \sigma_1^2 - \sigma_2^2 \neq 0$$

The null and alternative hypotheses are formulated as a two-tailed test. Intuitively, you might reason that if the two population variances are actually equal, the sample variances should be approximately equal also. That would mean that the ratio of the two sample variances should be approximately one. We will reject the null hypothesis if one sample variance is significantly larger than the other and if the ratio of sample variances is significantly greater than one. The managers will use a 0.10 significance level.

The first step is to collect the sample data. Suppose the samples for the two burner types yield variances of $s_1^2 = 0.025$ and $s_2^2 = 0.017$. Since this is a two-tailed test, we form the test statistic using Equation 9-1 by placing the larger sample variance in the numerator. Thus, the calculated F-value is:

$$F = \frac{s_1^2}{s_2^2} = \frac{0.025}{0.017} = 1.471$$

If this value exceeds the critical F from the F-distribution table in Appendix H, the null hypothesis is rejected. The critical F-value is determined by locating the F table for the desired alpha level and the correct degrees of freedom. This requires the following thought process:

1. If the test is two-tailed, use the F table corresponding to $\alpha/2$. For example, if $\alpha = 0.10$ for a two-tailed test, the appropriate F table is the one with the upper tail area equal to 0.05.
2. If the test is one-tailed, use the F table corresponding to the significance level. If $\alpha = 0.05$ for a one-tailed test, use the F table with the upper-tail area equal to 0.05.

In this example, the test is two-tailed and α is 0.10. Thus, we go to the F table in Appendix H for the upper-tail area equal to 0.05.

The next step is to determine the appropriate degrees of freedom. In Chapter 7 we showed that the degrees of freedom of any test statistic are equal to the number of independent data values available to estimate the population variance. We lose one degree of freedom for each parameter we are required to estimate. For both the numerator and denominator in Equation 9-1, we must estimate the population mean using $\bar{x}$ before we calculate s^2. In each case, we lose one degree of freedom. Therefore, we have two distinct degrees of freedom, D_1 and D_2, where D_1 is equal to the sample size for the variance in the numerator of the F-test statistic minus one $(n_i - 1)$ and D_2 is equal to the sample size for the variance in the denominator minus one $(n_j - 1)$. Recall that for a two-tailed test, the larger sample variance will be placed in the numerator of the F-statistic. Therefore, burner model 1 is in the numerator with a sample size of 11, $D_1 = 11 - 1 = 10$ and model 2 is in the denominator with $D_2 = 13 - 1 = 12$.

The F table is arranged in columns and rows. The columns correspond to the D_1 degrees of freedom and the rows correspond to the D_2 degrees of freedom. For this example, the critical F-value, at the intersection of $D_1 = 10$ and $D_2 = 12$ degrees of freedom, is 2.75 as shown in Figure 9-1. If you prefer you can use Excel's FINV function to determine the critical F-value.[1]

Figure 9-2 on page 339 summarizes the hypothesis test. Note the decision rule is:

If the calculated $F > 2.75$, reject H_0
Otherwise, do not reject H_0

Since the F-value $= 1.471 \leq 2.75$, the conclusion is that the null hypothesis cannot be rejected based on these sample data; that is we cannot conclude that there is a difference in the population variances. Unless further testing is performed that shows otherwise, the purchasing agents have no reason to conclude the two burners cook meat patties with different temperature variances. Thus, they can use price or other factors to make the decision between the two competing models.

Bank ATM Machines

One-tailed tests involving two population variances are performed in a similar manner to the two-tailed tests. The systems development group for a midwestern bank has developed a new software algorithm for the ATM machines at its branch banks. Although reducing average transaction time is an objective with the software, the systems programmers in charge of the project are also concerned with reducing the variability in transaction speed. They believe that their original algorithm (population 1) will have a larger standard deviation for the transaction time than the new software (population 2). To test this, they have performed 7 test runs using the original software and 11 test runs using the new system. Note that although the managers are interested in testing the standard deviation of transaction time, they must perform the test as a test of variances since no method exists for testing standard deviations directly. Thus, the null and alternative hypotheses are:

$$H_0: \sigma_1^2 \leq \sigma_2^2 \qquad \text{or} \qquad \sigma_1^2 - \sigma_2^2 \leq 0$$
$$H_A: \sigma_1^2 > \sigma_2^2 \qquad\qquad\quad \sigma_1^2 - \sigma_2^2 > 0$$

The hypothesis is to be tested using a significance level of 0.01. The sample data for the test runs are in a data file called **ATM**. Excel has a procedure for performing this test. Figure 9-3 shows the Excel results. The sample variances were:

$$s_1^2 = 612.68$$
$$s_2^2 = 51.49$$

Figure 9-3 shows Excel output for the one-tailed hypothesis test for this situation using a significance level of 0.01. Recall that in a two-tailed test, placing the largest sample variance in the numerator and the smaller variance in the denominator forms the F-ratio. In a one-tailed test, we look to the alternative hypothesis to determine which sample variance should go in the numerator. In this example, population 1 (the original software) is thought to have the larger variance. Then the sample variance from population 1 forms the

EXAMPLE
9-2

TESTING TWO VARIANCES

Excel and Minitab Tutorial

---

[1]The FINV function is $= \text{FINV}(0.05,10,12) = 2.753$

FIGURE 9-1
F-Distribution Table (Upper
Tail = 0.05)

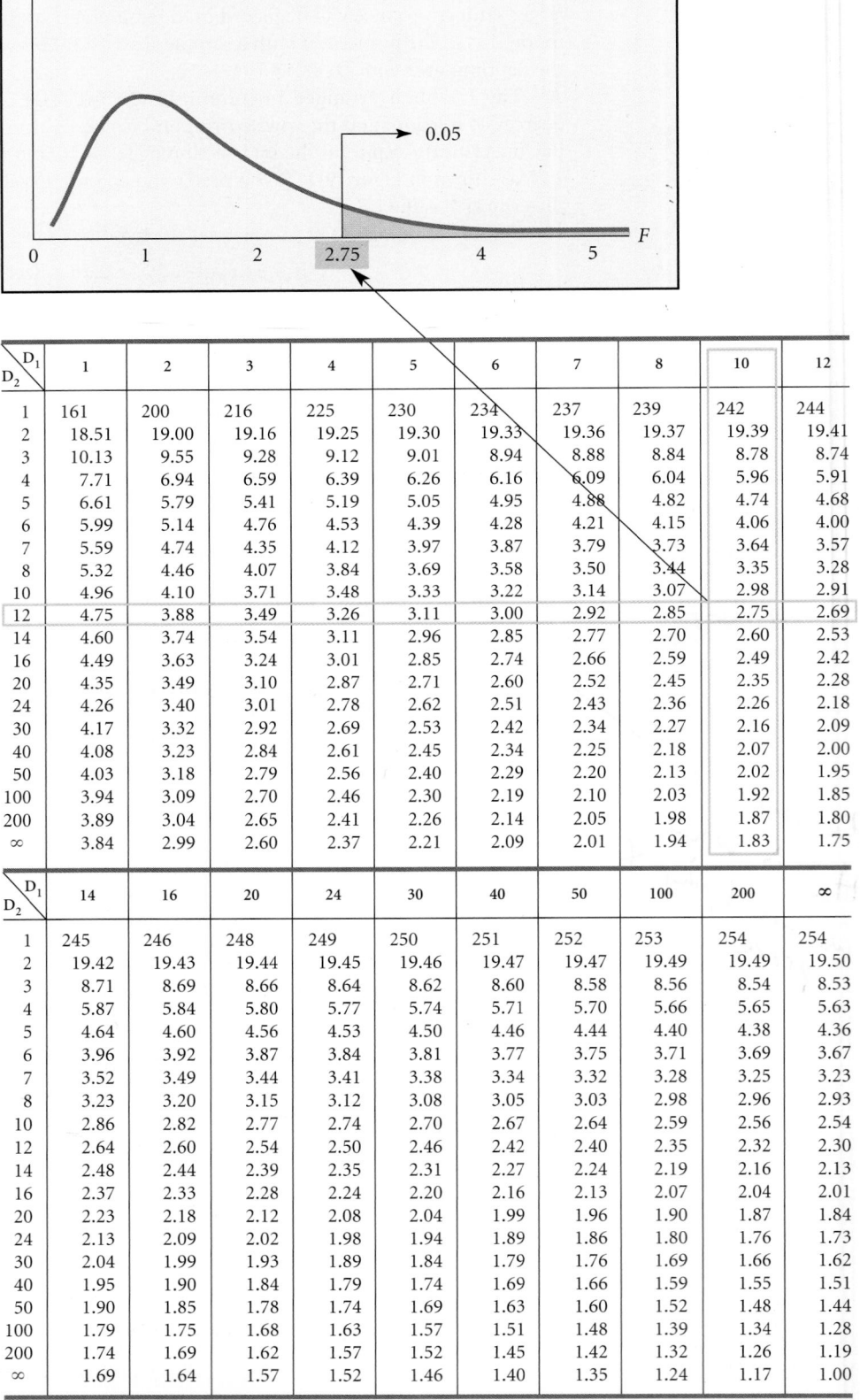

D_1 / D_2	1	2	3	4	5	6	7	8	10	12
1	161	200	216	225	230	234	237	239	242	244
2	18.51	19.00	19.16	19.25	19.30	19.33	19.36	19.37	19.39	19.41
3	10.13	9.55	9.28	9.12	9.01	8.94	8.88	8.84	8.78	8.74
4	7.71	6.94	6.59	6.39	6.26	6.16	6.09	6.04	5.96	5.91
5	6.61	5.79	5.41	5.19	5.05	4.95	4.88	4.82	4.74	4.68
6	5.99	5.14	4.76	4.53	4.39	4.28	4.21	4.15	4.06	4.00
7	5.59	4.74	4.35	4.12	3.97	3.87	3.79	3.73	3.64	3.57
8	5.32	4.46	4.07	3.84	3.69	3.58	3.50	3.44	3.35	3.28
10	4.96	4.10	3.71	3.48	3.33	3.22	3.14	3.07	2.98	2.91
12	4.75	3.88	3.49	3.26	3.11	3.00	2.92	2.85	2.75	2.69
14	4.60	3.74	3.54	3.11	2.96	2.85	2.77	2.70	2.60	2.53
16	4.49	3.63	3.24	3.01	2.85	2.74	2.66	2.59	2.49	2.42
20	4.35	3.49	3.10	2.87	2.71	2.60	2.52	2.45	2.35	2.28
24	4.26	3.40	3.01	2.78	2.62	2.51	2.43	2.36	2.26	2.18
30	4.17	3.32	2.92	2.69	2.53	2.42	2.34	2.27	2.16	2.09
40	4.08	3.23	2.84	2.61	2.45	2.34	2.25	2.18	2.07	2.00
50	4.03	3.18	2.79	2.56	2.40	2.29	2.20	2.13	2.02	1.95
100	3.94	3.09	2.70	2.46	2.30	2.19	2.10	2.03	1.92	1.85
200	3.89	3.04	2.65	2.41	2.26	2.14	2.05	1.98	1.87	1.80
∞	3.84	2.99	2.60	2.37	2.21	2.09	2.01	1.94	1.83	1.75

D_1 / D_2	14	16	20	24	30	40	50	100	200	∞
1	245	246	248	249	250	251	252	253	254	254
2	19.42	19.43	19.44	19.45	19.46	19.47	19.47	19.49	19.49	19.50
3	8.71	8.69	8.66	8.64	8.62	8.60	8.58	8.56	8.54	8.53
4	5.87	5.84	5.80	5.77	5.74	5.71	5.70	5.66	5.65	5.63
5	4.64	4.60	4.56	4.53	4.50	4.46	4.44	4.40	4.38	4.36
6	3.96	3.92	3.87	3.84	3.81	3.77	3.75	3.71	3.69	3.67
7	3.52	3.49	3.44	3.41	3.38	3.34	3.32	3.28	3.25	3.23
8	3.23	3.20	3.15	3.12	3.08	3.05	3.03	2.98	2.96	2.93
10	2.86	2.82	2.77	2.74	2.70	2.67	2.64	2.59	2.56	2.54
12	2.64	2.60	2.54	2.50	2.46	2.42	2.40	2.35	2.32	2.30
14	2.48	2.44	2.39	2.35	2.31	2.27	2.24	2.19	2.16	2.13
16	2.37	2.33	2.28	2.24	2.20	2.16	2.13	2.07	2.04	2.01
20	2.23	2.18	2.12	2.08	2.04	1.99	1.96	1.90	1.87	1.84
24	2.13	2.09	2.02	1.98	1.94	1.89	1.86	1.80	1.76	1.73
30	2.04	1.99	1.93	1.89	1.84	1.79	1.76	1.69	1.66	1.62
40	1.95	1.90	1.84	1.79	1.74	1.69	1.66	1.59	1.55	1.51
50	1.90	1.85	1.78	1.74	1.69	1.63	1.60	1.52	1.48	1.44
100	1.79	1.75	1.68	1.63	1.57	1.51	1.48	1.39	1.34	1.28
200	1.74	1.69	1.62	1.57	1.52	1.45	1.42	1.32	1.26	1.19
∞	1.69	1.64	1.57	1.52	1.46	1.40	1.35	1.24	1.17	1.00

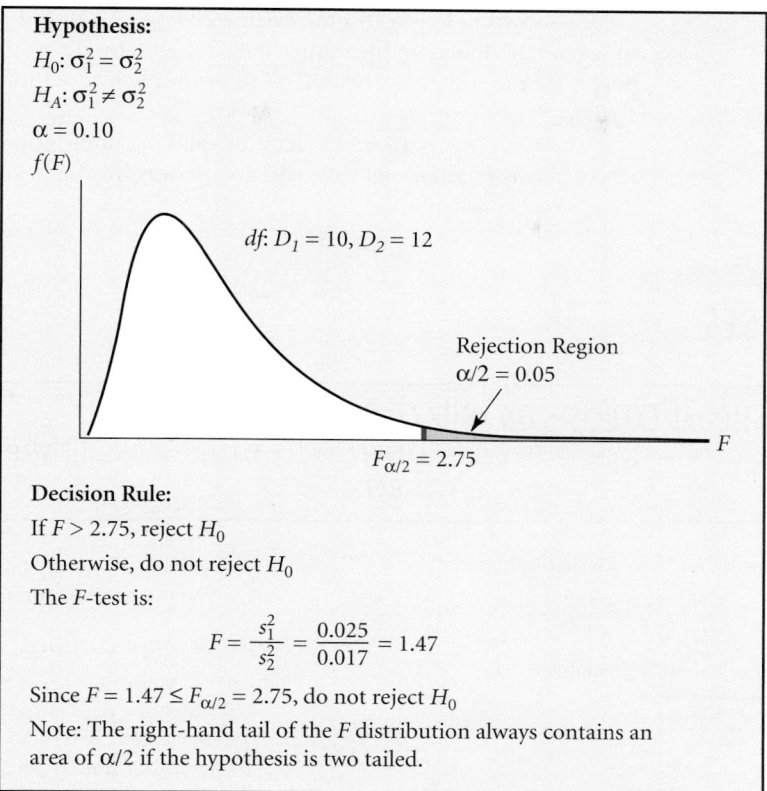

Hypothesis:

$H_0: \sigma_1^2 = \sigma_2^2$

$H_A: \sigma_1^2 \neq \sigma_2^2$

$\alpha = 0.10$

$f(F)$

df: $D_1 = 10, D_2 = 12$

Rejection Region
$\alpha/2 = 0.05$

$F_{\alpha/2} = 2.75$

Decision Rule:

If $F > 2.75$, reject H_0

Otherwise, do not reject H_0

The F-test is:

$$F = \frac{s_1^2}{s_2^2} = \frac{0.025}{0.017} = 1.47$$

Since $F = 1.47 \leq F_{\alpha/2} = 2.75$, do not reject H_0

Note: The right-hand tail of the F distribution always contains an area of $\alpha/2$ if the hypothesis is two tailed.

FIGURE 9-2
F-Test for the E. Coli Example

numerator regardless of the size of the sample variances. Excel correctly computes the calculated F-ratio.

In this one-tailed example, the numerator represents population 1 and the denominator represents population 2. This means that the degrees of freedom are $D_1 = 7 - 1 = 6$ and $D_2 = 11 - 1 = 10$. The calculated F-ratio is:

$$F = \frac{612.68}{51.49} = 11.898$$

Using the F-table in Appendix H or Excel's FINV function you can determine $F_{.01} = 5.39$ for this one-tailed test with $\alpha = 0.01$.

FIGURE 9-3
Excel Output F-Test Example
of ATM Transaction Time

Excel Instructions:

1. Open file: ATM.xls
2. Click on Tools
3. Select Data Analysis
4. Select F-Test Two-Sample for Variances
5. Define data ranges
6. Indicate significance level = 0.01

Microsoft Excel - ATM.xls

File Edit View Insert Format Tools Data PHStat Window Help

Arial   10   B U

E13   =

	A	B	C	D	E	F
1	Original Software	New System		F-Test Two-Sample for Variances		
2	38.9	22.8				
3	23.2	20			Original Software	New System
4	49.2	26.5		Mean	46.55714286	29.8
5	66.8	37.9		Variance	612.6761905	51.494
6	65.5	27.2		Observations	7	11
7	74.6	39.6		df	6	10
8	7.7	34.1		F	11.89801123	
9		39.4		P(F<=f) one-tail	0.000473972	
10		20.9		F Critical one-tail	5.38580025	
11		30.3				
12		29.1				

Since the calculated $F = 11.898 > F_{.01} = 5.39$ we reject the null hypothesis and conclude that the variance for population 1 exceeds the population 2 variance.

As shown in Figure 9-3 the calculated $F = 11.898 > F_{.01} = 5.39$, so the null hypothesis is rejected. Based on the sample data, the systems development staff has evidence to support their claim that the new ATM algorithm will result in reduced transaction time variability.

There are many business decision-making applications where you will need to test whether two populations have equal variances. In the next section, we illustrate more of these situations.

9-1: EXERCISES

ADDITIONAL EXERCISES ON YOUR CD-ROM
Try the ADDITIONAL EXERCISES and APPLICATION PROBLEMS on the CD-ROM.

9-1. Given the following null and alternative hypotheses:

$$H_0: \sigma_1^2 = \sigma_2^2$$
$$H_A: \sigma_1^2 \neq \sigma_2^2$$

and the following sample information:

SAMPLE 1	SAMPLE 2
$n_1 = 11$	$n_2 = 21$
$s_1 = 19$	$s_2 = 23$

a. If $\alpha = 0.02$, state the decision rule for the hypothesis.
b. Test the hypothesis and indicate whether the null hypothesis should be rejected.

9-2. Given the following null and alternative hypotheses:

$$H_0: \sigma_1^2 = \sigma_2^2$$
$$H_A: \sigma_1^2 > \sigma_2^2$$

and the following sample information:

SAMPLE 1	SAMPLE 2
$n_1 = 15$	$n_2 = 11$
$s_1 = 230$	$s_2 = 210$

a. If $\alpha = 0.10$, state the decision rule for the hypothesis.
b. Test the hypothesis and indicate whether the null hypothesis should be rejected.

9-3. You are given two random samples with the following information:

ITEM	SAMPLE 1	SAMPLE 2
1	19.6	21.3
2	22.1	17.4
3	19.5	19.0
4	20.0	21.2
5	21.5	20.1
6	20.2	23.5
7	17.9	18.9
8	23.0	22.4
9	12.5	14.3
10	19.0	17.8

Based on these samples, test at $\alpha = 0.10$ whether the true difference in population variances is equal to 0.

Business Applications

9-4. The McBurger Company operates fast-food stores throughout the United States and in 14 other countries. Management is very concerned about making sure that a standard of quality service is achieved. For instance, they are interested in whether there is a difference in standard deviation in service times for customers who use the drive-through window versus those who go inside to the service counter.

The McBurger store in Knoxville, Tennessee, recently was the subject of evaluation. A sample of 13 drive-through customers was selected and a sample of 9 inside-counter customers was selected. The time (in minutes) needed for each customer to be served was recorded. The following statistics were computed from the sample data.

DRIVE-THROUGH	WALK-IN
$\bar{x} = 4.5$	$\bar{x} = 4.0$
$s = 2.0$	$s = 1.2$

a. State the appropriate null and alternative hypotheses for testing the equality of the variances.
b. Based on a significance level of 0.10, determine the appropriate decision rule and determine if there is a difference in standard deviation in service times for customers who use the drive-through window versus those who go inside to the service counter.

9-5. A national TV telethon committee is interested in determining whether donations given by males have greater variability in amount than do the donations of females. To test this, random samples of 25 males and 25 females were selected from people who donated during last year's telethon. The following statistics were computed from the sample data:

MALES	FEMALES
$\bar{x} = \$12.40$	$\bar{x} = \$8.92$
$s = \$ \ 2.50$	$s = \$1.34$

a. State the null and alternative hypotheses to be tested.

b. Based on a significance level of 0.05, do donations from males have greater variability than do the donations of females?

9-6. The First Night Stage Company operates a small nonprofit theater group in Milwaukee, Wisconsin. Each year the company solicits donations to help fund its operations. This year, it obtained the help of a marketing research company in the city. This company's representatives proposed two different solicitation brochures. They are interested in determining whether there is a difference in the standard deviation of dollars returned between the two brochures. To test this, a random sample of 20 people was selected to receive brochure A and another random sample of 20 people was selected to receive brochure B. The data

are contained in the file called **First-Night**. Based on these sample data, what should the First Night Company conclude about the two brochures with respect to their variability? Test using a significance level of 0.02.

9-7. The Celltone Company is in the business of providing cellular phone coverage. Recently it conducted a study of its customers who have purchased either the "Basic Plan" or the "Business Plan" service. At issue is the number of minutes of use by customers during the midnight to 7:00 AM time period Monday through Friday over a 4-week period. Celltone managers believe the standard deviation in minutes used by Business Plan customers will be less than that for the Basic Plan customers. Data for this study are in a file called **Celltone**. Assume that the managers wish to test this using a 0.05 level of significance.

a. State the appropriate null and alternative hypotheses.

b. Determine if the standard deviation in minutes used by Business Plan customers is less than that for the Basic Plan customers using an alpha level equal to 0.05.

■ 9-2: HYPOTHESES TESTS AND ESTIMATION FOR TWO POPULATION MEANS

In this section we examine applications in which we are interested in the difference between two population means by building on the statistical inference concepts introduced in Chapters 7 and 8.

Recall that in our discussion in Chapters 7 and 8 of estimation and hypothesis testing involving a single population mean, we introduced procedures that applied when the population standard deviation was assumed to be known. The standard normal distribution z-values were used in developing the interval estimate and in establishing the critical value for the hypothesis test. We also indicated that you would rarely know the value for σ if you didn't know the value for μ. Therefore, we spent most of our discussion in Chapters 7 and 8 focusing on situations and techniques that do not require that σ be known. These techniques involved the t-distribution and are merely extensions of the methods used when σ is known.

The same issues apply when you are dealing with the difference between two population means. Techniques exist that can be used to estimate $\mu_1 - \mu_2$ or test hypotheses about the difference between two population means where we assume that σ_1 and σ_2 are known. These techniques utilize the standard normal distribution. The CD-ROM that accompanies this text contains a complete discussion of these techniques, and we encourage you to review this material. However, rarely will we have the opportunity to use these methods because σ_1 and σ_2 are almost never known, but instead must be estimated from samples from the two populations. The remaining discussion in this section introduces the hypothesis testing and estimation techniques you will use when the population standard deviations are unknown.

OPTIONAL CD-ROM TOPIC Estimation and Hypothesis Tests Involving Two Population Means When σ_1 and σ_2 Are Known

There may be rare instances in which you are interested in estimating $\mu_1 - \mu_2$ or testing a null hypothesis regarding $\mu_1 - \mu_2$ when the variances of the two populations are known. For more information, go to the CD-ROM.

Hypothesis Tests for Two Population Means, When σ_1 and σ_2 Are Unknown—Independent Samples

In most situations in which we have a need to test whether two populations have the same or different means, we will not know the values for the two population standard deviations. Instead, we will estimate σ_1 and σ_2 using s_1 and s_2, computed from samples selected from the two populations. When this is the case, the t-distribution is used to establish the critical value. We first consider situations in which the samples are considered to be **independent samples**.

> **INDEPENDENT SAMPLES**
>
> Samples selected from two or more populations in such a way that the occurrence of values in one sample has no influence on the probability of the occurrence of values in the other sample(s).

EXAMPLE 9-3

HYPOTHESIS TESTING

Retirement Investing

A major political issue for the past decade has involved questions about the long-term future of the Social Security system. Many people who have entered the workforce in the last 20 years believe the system will not be solvent when they retire and are thus actively investing in their own retirement accounts. One investment alternative is a tax-sheltered annuity (TSA) marketed by life insurance companies. Certain people, depending on occupation, qualify to deposit part of their paychecks in a TSA and pay no federal income tax on this money until it is withdrawn. While the money is on deposit, the insurance companies invest it in either stock or bond portfolios. If the portfolios perform well, the TSA accounts grow. A second alternative open to many people is a plan known as a 401(k), in which employees contribute a portion of their paycheck to purchase stocks, bonds, or mutual funds. In some cases employers match all or part of the employee contribution. In many 401(k) systems the employees can control how their funds are invested.

A recent study in North Carolina investigated the question of whether employees with equivalent annual incomes covered by the two plans [TSA or 401(k)] differ in their average annual contributions. A random sample of 15 people from the population of adults who are eligible for a TSA investment was selected. A second sample of 15 people was selected from the population of adults in North Carolina who have 401(k) plans. The variable of interest is the dollar amount of money invested in the retirement plan during the previous year. The samples are considered to be independent since the amount invested by one group should have no influence on the amount invested by the other.

Hypothesis tests involving means from two independent populations can be formulated in several ways depending on whether the test is two-tailed or one-tailed.

TWO-TAILED TEST	UPPER ONE-TAILED TEST	LOWER ONE-TAILED TEST
Format 1		
$H_0: \mu_1 - \mu_2 = 0.0$	$H_0: \mu_1 - \mu_2 \leq 0.0$	$H_0: \mu_1 - \mu_2 \geq 0.0$
$H_A: \mu_1 - \mu_2 \neq 0.0$	$H_A: \mu_1 - \mu_2 > 0.0$	$H_A: \mu_1 - \mu_2 < 0.0$
Format 2		
$H_0: \mu_1 = \mu_2$	$H_0: \mu_1 \leq \mu_2$	$H_0: \mu_1 \geq \mu_2$
$H_A: \mu_1 \neq \mu_2$	$H_A: \mu_1 > \mu_2$	$H_A: \mu_1 < \mu_2$

In this example, in which we are interested in testing whether the mean dollars invested in TSAs and 401(k) programs are the same or different, the hypothesis test will be two-tailed.

Specifically, we wish to test the following null and alternative hypotheses using a significance level of 0.05.

Hypotheses:

$$H_0: \mu_1 - \mu_2 = 0 \quad \text{or} \quad \mu_1 = \mu_2$$
$$H_A: \mu_1 - \mu_2 \neq 0 \quad \text{or} \quad \mu_1 \neq \mu_2$$

where:

μ_1 = Mean dollars invested by the TSA eligible population during the past year

μ_2 = Mean dollars invested by the 401(k) eligible population during the past year

The sample results are:

TSA ELIGIBLE	401(K) ELIGIBLE
$n_1 = 15$	$n_2 = 15$
$\bar{x}_1 = \$2,255$	$\bar{x}_2 = \$2,140$
$s_1 = \$\ 645$	$s_2 = \$\ 708$

To determine whether we should reject the null hypothesis and conclude that $\mu_1 \neq \mu_2$ (one population has a higher mean than the other), we need to first calculate the test statistic using Equation 9-2.

---

t-TEST STATISTIC (EQUAL POPULATION VARIANCES) *2 df lost in this analysis)*

$$t = \frac{(\bar{x}_1 - \bar{x}_2) - (\mu_1 - \mu_2)}{s_p\sqrt{\dfrac{1}{n_1} + \dfrac{1}{n_2}}}, df = n_1 + n_2 - 2 \qquad \text{9-2}$$

where:

$\bar{x}_1$ and $\bar{x}_2$ = Sample means from populations 1 and 2
$\mu_1 - \mu_2$ = Hypothesized difference between population means
n_1 and n_2 = Sample sizes from the two populations
s_p = Pooled standard deviation

The test statistic is based upon two important assumptions:

1. Each population has a normal distribution.[2]
2. The two population variances, σ_1^2 and σ_2^2, are equal.

If the equal variance assumption holds, then both s_1^2 and s_2^2 are estimators of the same population variance, σ^2. To only use one of these, say s_1^2, to estimate σ^2 would be disregarding the information obtained from the other sample. To use the average of s_1^2 and s_2^2, if the sample sizes were different, would ignore the fact that more information about σ^2 is obtained from the sample having the larger sample size. We, therefore, use a weighted average of s_1^2 and s_2^2, denoted as s_p^2, to estimate σ^2, where the weights are the degrees of freedom associated with each sample. The square root of s_p^2 is known as the **pooled standard deviation** as shown in Equation 9-3, and will be a value somewhere between the two sample standard deviations. Notice that the sample size we have available to estimate σ^2 is $n_1 + n_2$. However, to produce s_p, we must first calculate s_1^2 and s_2^2. This requires that we estimate μ_1 and μ_2 using $\bar{x}_1$ and $\bar{x}_2$, respectively. In Chapter 7 we showed that the degrees of freedom

---

[2]In Chapter 14 we will introduce a technique called goodness-of-fit which we can use to test whether the sample data come from a population that is normally distributed.

POOLED STANDARD DEVIATION

$$s_p = \sqrt{\frac{(n_1 - 1)s_1^2 + (n_2 - 1)s_2^2}{n_1 + n_2 - 2}}$$ 9-3

where:

s_1^2 = Sample variance from population 1
s_2^2 = Sample variance from population 2
n_1 and n_2 = Sample sizes from populations 1 and 2, respectively

---

equal the sample size minus the number of parameters needed to estimate the population variance. Therefore, the degrees of freedom must equal $n_1 + n_2 - 2$.

ARE THE POPULATION VARIANCES EQUAL?

Before proceeding to test whether the population means are equal, we need to test to determine the validity of the equal variances assumption. The F-test introduced in Section 9-1 can be used to make this determination. The null and alternative hypotheses are:

$$H_0: \sigma_1^2 = \sigma_2^2$$
$$H_A: \sigma_1^2 \neq \sigma_2^2$$

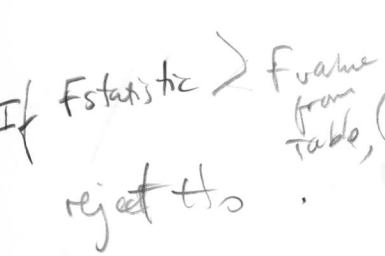

If F-statistic > F-value from Table, reject H0.

Using $\alpha = 0.10$, we form the test statistic using Equation 9-1. Recall that when we have a two-tailed test for variances, as in this case, we put the larger sample variance in the numerator giving:

$$F = \frac{708^2}{645^2} = \frac{501,264}{416,025} = 1.205$$

The critical value from the F-distribution table in Appendix H for $D_1 = (15 - 1 = 14)$ and $D_2 = (15 - 1 = 14)$ degrees of freedom, and upper tail equal to $\alpha/2 = 0.05$, is 2.484. Since $F = 1.205 < 2.484$, based on the sample data there is insufficient evidence to conclude that the population variances are different. This means we can proceed to test whether the population means are equal using the t-test statistic in Equation 9-2.

ARE THE POPULATION MEANS EQUAL?

We are now in a position to complete the hypothesis test to determine whether the mean dollar amount invested by TSA employees is equal to the mean amount invested by 401(k) employees.

First, using Equation 9-3 we find the pooled standard deviation.

$$s_p = \sqrt{\frac{(n_1 - 1)s_1^2 + (n_2 - 1)s_2^2}{n_1 + n_2 - 2}} = \sqrt{\frac{(15 - 1)645^2 + (15 - 1)708^2}{15 + 15 - 2}} = 677.23$$

Note, the pooled standard deviation is part way between the two sample standard deviations. Now, keeping in mind that the hypothesized difference between μ_1 and μ_2 is 0, we compute the t-test statistic using Equation 9-2 as follows.

$$t = \frac{(\bar{x}_1 - \bar{x}_2) - (\mu_1 - \mu_2)}{s_p\sqrt{\frac{1}{n_1} + \frac{1}{n_2}}} = \frac{(2{,}255 - 2{,}140) - (0.0)}{677.23\sqrt{\frac{1}{15} + \frac{1}{15}}} = 0.465$$

This indicates that the difference in sample means is 0.465 standard errors above the hypothesized difference of 0. To complete the hypothesis test, we next determine the critical value from the t-distribution table in Appendix F (or use Excel's TINV function) with degrees of freedom equal to $n_1 + n_2 - 2 = 15 + 15 - 2 = 28$, and alpha = 0.05 for the two-tailed test. The appropriate t-value is 2.048.

Since $t = 0.465 \leq 2.048$, the null hypothesis should not be rejected. The difference in sample means is attributed to sampling error. Figure 9-4 summarizes this hypothesis test. Based on the sample data, there is no statistical justification to believe that the mean annual investment by individuals who are eligible for the tax shelter annuity option is different than for those individuals who are eligible for the 401(k) plan.

WHAT IF THE POPULATION VARIANCES ARE NOT EQUAL?

In this example, the *F*-test led us to conclude that population variances could be equal and we carried out the hypothesis test for two population means using Equation 9-2. However, if the sample data lead to the conclusion that the variances are not equal, the *t*-test statistic is computed using a slightly different format, shown in Equation 9-4.

---

t-TEST STATISTIC (POPULATION VARIANCES ARE NOT EQUAL)

$$t = \frac{(\bar{x}_1 - \bar{x}_2) - (\mu_1 - \mu_2)}{\sqrt{\dfrac{s_1^2}{n_1} + \dfrac{s_2^2}{n_2}}}$$

9-4

FIGURE 9-4
Hypothesis Test of the Two Population Means for the North Carolina Investment Study

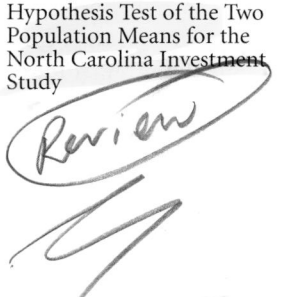
Review

Hypothesis:

$H_0: \mu_1 - \mu_2 = 0$
$H_A: \mu_1 - \mu_2 \neq 0$
$df = n_1 + n_2 - 2 = 15 + 15 - 2 = 28$

Rejection Region
$\alpha/2 = 0.025$

Rejection Region
$\alpha/2 = 0.025$

$t_{\alpha/2} = -2.048$ 0 $t_{\alpha/2} = 2.048$

t

$t = 0.465$

Decision Rule:

If $t > 2.048$, reject H_0 $\bar{x}_1 - \bar{x}_2 = (2{,}255 - 2{,}140) = 115$
If $t < -2.048$, reject H_0
Otherwise do not reject H_0

Test Statistic:

$$t = \frac{(\bar{x}_1 - \bar{x}_2) - (\mu_1 - \mu_2)}{s_P \sqrt{\dfrac{1}{n_1} + \dfrac{1}{n_2}}} = \frac{(2{,}255 - 2{,}140) - (0.0)}{677.23 \sqrt{\dfrac{1}{15} + \dfrac{1}{15}}} = 0.465$$

where:

$$s_P = \sqrt{\frac{(n_1 - 1)s_1^2 + (n_2 - 1)s_2^2}{n_1 + n_2 - 2}} = \sqrt{\frac{(15 - 1)645^2 + (15 - 1)708^2}{15 + 15 - 2}} = 677.23$$

Once you have computed the *t*-test statistic using Equation 9-4, that value is compared to the critical *t*-value from the *t*-distribution with degrees of freedom computed using Equation 9-5. (If Equation 9-5 yields a noninteger value, round down to the next lower integer.) If the *t*-test statistic falls in the rejection region, the null hypothesis is rejected, otherwise you do not reject.

DEGREES OF FREEDOM FOR *t*-TEST STATISTIC WITH UNEQUAL POPULATION VARIANCES

$$\frac{(s_1^2/n_1 + s_2^2/n_2)^2}{\left(\dfrac{(s_1^2/n_1)^2}{n_1 - 1} + \dfrac{(s_2^2/n_2)^2}{n_2 - 1}\right)} \qquad 9\text{-}5$$

9-4

HYPOTHESIS TESTING

Excel and Minitab Tutorial

Television Viewer Incomes

Both Excel and Minitab have procedures for performing the necessary calculations to test hypotheses involving two population means. Consider the situation in which managers for a local network television affiliate were preparing for a national television advertising conference. The theme of the managers' presentation was the advantage to businesses that advertise on network TV rather than on cable. The managers believe the mean household income for cable subscribers is less than for those who do not subscribe. Thus, by advertising on network stations, the business could reach a higher income audience.

However, the managers had no actual data to support their contention. In the spirit of friendly cooperation, the network managers joined forces with the local cable provider, Future-Vision, to survey a total of 548 households in the market area. The results of the survey are contained in the **Future-Vision** file on your CD-ROM. Figure 9-5 shows some of the data in the Excel worksheet.

Both Excel and the PHStat add-ins that accompany this text contain procedures for performing the calculations we are going to need to determine whether the managers' belief about incomes of cable subscribers can be justified.[3] We first formulate the null and alternative hypotheses to be tested. (Population 1 is cable subscribers.)

FIGURE 9-5
Excel Worksheet for Future-Vision Company Income Survey

	A	B	C	D	E	F
1	Household	Number of People	Household Annual Income	Current Cable Subscriber	Years at This Address	
2	1	5	35000	Yes	10	
3	2	2	29000	Yes	1	
4	3	1	25000	No	8	
5	4	1	31000	Yes	13	
6	5	3	39000	Yes	13	
7	6	7	35000	No	6	
8	7	2	32000	Yes	9	
9	8	4	44000	No	7	
10	9	1	36000	Yes	16	

---

[3]The data in the file Future-Vision will need to be unstacked before using either of the **Tool—Data Analysis—*t*-test:Two Samples** procedures. The PHStat add-ins contain an Unstack procedure under **Data Preparation**.

$$H_0: \mu_1 - \mu_2 \geq 0.0$$
$$H_A: \mu_1 - \mu_2 < 0.0$$

Population 1 defines cable subscribers in Future-Vision's market area (labeled "Yes"). Population 2 (labeled "No") defines those households that are not cable TV subscribers. The test is to be conducted using a 0.05 significance level.

The first step is to test to see whether we can assume that the populations have equal variances. You can use Excel to compute the sample variance for each sample and manually perform the F-test as discussed in Section 9-1, making sure the population with the larger sample variance is put in the numerator, or you can use the Excel tool for testing two variances. Figure 9-6 shows the Excel output to test the following null and alternative hypotheses:

$$H_0: \sigma_1^2 = \sigma_2^2$$
$$H_A: \sigma_1^2 \neq \sigma_2^2$$

The sample variances for the two samples are $s_1^2 = 35,810,898.46$ and $s_2^2 = 47,065,996.50$. As seen in Figure 9-6, the F-test leads us to reject the null hypothesis, and we now conclude that the population variances are not equal. We now proceed to test the original hypothesis for the difference in population means, but we must use the t-test for unequal population variances (Equations 9-4 and 9-5). Both Excel and Minitab have procedures for carrying out this hypothesis test. Figure 9-7 shows the Excel output for the Future-Vision example. The mean income for the sample of 404 cable subscribers is $32,589.11 while the mean for the sample of 144 noncable households is $33,395.83. At issue is whether this difference in sample means ($32,589.11 − $33,395.83 = −$806.72) is sufficient to conclude that the population means are not equal. Figure 9-7 shows that the "t-Stat" value, which is the calculated test statistic (or t-value, based on Equation 9-4), is equal to −1.2515. This means that the difference in sample means (−$806.72) is 1.2515 standard errors below the hypothesized difference of 0. The one-tail t-critical value for alpha = 0.05 is shown in Figure 9-7 to be −1.6517. (The value is negative since the rejection region is in the lower tail of the sampling distribution.) Since the t-stat value = −1.2515 > −1.6517, we do not reject the null hypothesis. Thus, the sample data do not provide sufficient evidence to conclude the mean income for cable TV households is less than the mean income for noncable households. Figure 9-8 shows the hypothesis test results in graphical form.

FIGURE 9-6
PHStat Test for Equality of Two Variances for Future-Vision

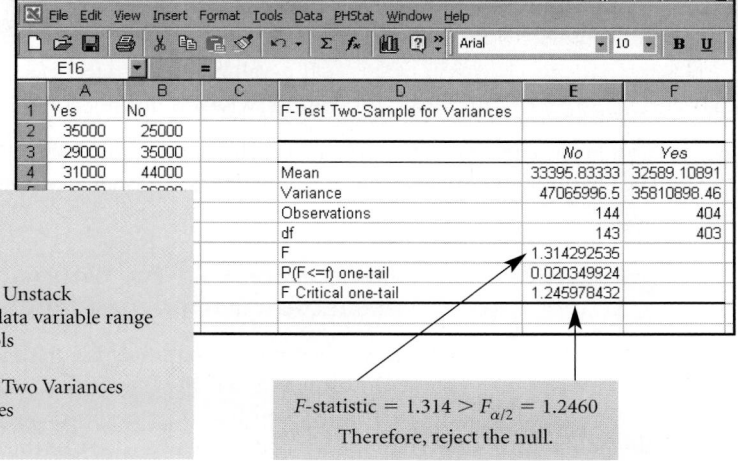

Excel Instructions:

1. Open file: Future-Vision.xls
2. Select PHStat
3. Click on Data Preparation and Unstack
4. Define grouping variable and data variable range
5. With unstacked data select Tools
6. Select Data Analysis
7. Select F-Test for Differences in Two Variances
8. Enter data range for two variables
9. Select alpha level

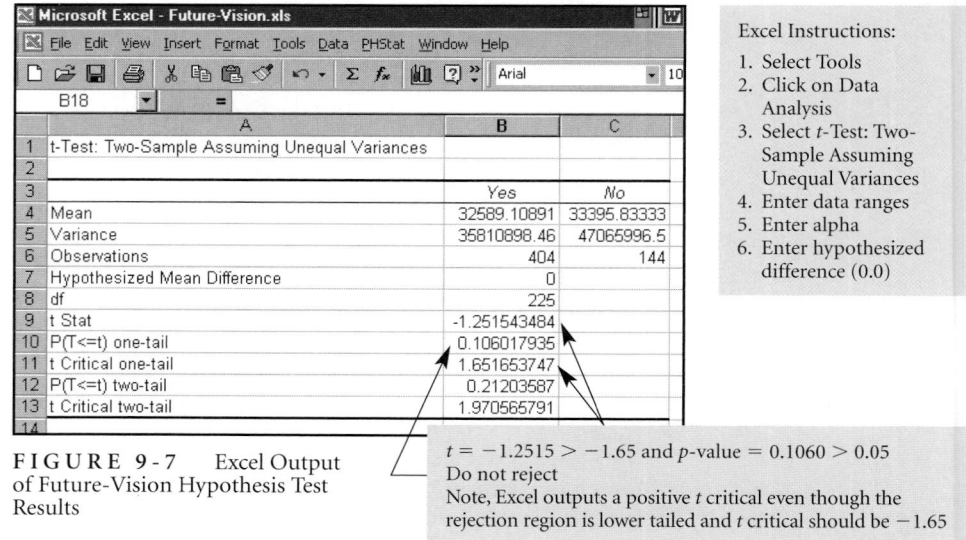

Excel Instructions:
1. Select Tools
2. Click on Data Analysis
3. Select *t*-Test: Two-Sample Assuming Unequal Variances
4. Enter data ranges
5. Enter alpha
6. Enter hypothesized difference (0.0)

FIGURE 9-7   Excel Output of Future-Vision Hypothesis Test Results

$t = -1.2515 > -1.65$ and *p*-value $= 0.1060 > 0.05$
Do not reject
Note, Excel outputs a positive *t* critical even though the rejection region is lower tailed and *t* critical should be -1.65

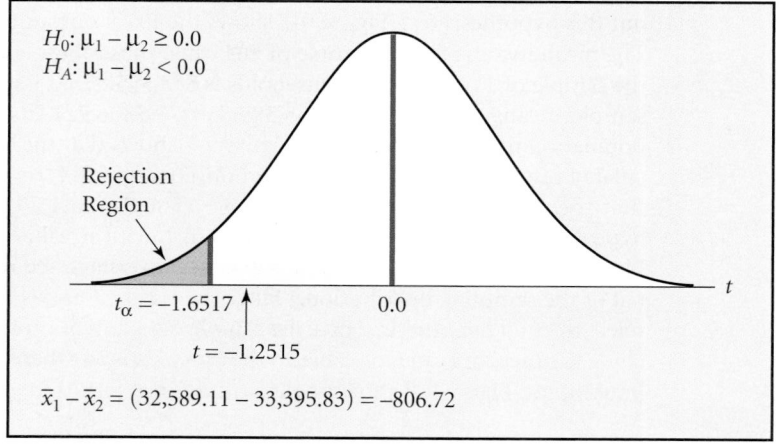

FIGURE 9-8
Future-Vision Hypothesis Test

The Excel output shown in Figure 9-7 also provides the *p*-value for the one-tailed test that could also be used to test the null hypothesis. Recall, if the calculated *p*-value is less than alpha, the null hypothesis should be rejected. The decision rule is:

$$\text{If } p\text{-value} < 0.05, \text{ reject } H_0$$
$$\text{Otherwise, do not reject } H_0$$

From Figure 9-7, the *p*-value for the one-tailed test is 0.1060. Since $0.1060 > 0.05$, the null hypothesis is not rejected. This is the same conclusion we reached using the test statistic approach.

Additional Example 9-a

Hypothesis Test for Difference in Two Population Means

Estimating the Difference Between Two Population Means When σ_1 and σ_2 Are Unknown—Independent Samples

In the previous examples, we were interested in testing to determine whether two populations have equal means. However, you will also run into situations in which your objective is to estimate the difference between two population means rather than to test whether there is a difference. As we mentioned at the beginning of this section, your CD-ROM contains a discussion of the estimation and hypothesis testing methods that are used when the two population standard deviations are known. We turn our attention here to the more common situations in which the standard deviations are not known and must be estimated from the sample data.

You should recall from Chapter 7 that there are two types of estimates, point estimates and confidence interval estimates. If we are attempting to estimate the difference between two population means, $\mu_1 - \mu_2$, the point estimate is the difference between the two sample means, $\bar{x}_1 - \bar{x}_2$. However, point estimates are subject to sampling error. To incorporate the potential for sampling error, a confidence interval estimate can be developed. The general form for the confidence interval estimate is:

$$\text{Point Estimate} \pm \text{Critical Value (Standard Error)}$$

because σ unknown.

If the populations from which the samples are selected are assumed to be normally distributed, the critical value will be a *t*-value from the *t*-distribution. As we discussed earlier in this section, the formula for the standard error depends on whether the population variances are equal. Expression 9-6 shows the confidence interval formula when $\sigma_1^2 = \sigma_2^2$.

CONFIDENCE INTERVAL ESTIMATE
FOR $\mu_1 - \mu_2$ – STANDARD DEVIATIONS UNKNOWN AND $\sigma_1^2 = \sigma_2^2$

$$(\bar{x}_1 - \bar{x}_2) \pm t_{\alpha/2} s_p \sqrt{\frac{1}{n_1} + \frac{1}{n_2}} \qquad \textbf{9-6}$$

where:

$$s_p = \sqrt{\frac{(n_1 - 1)s_1^2 + (n_2 - 1)s_2^2}{n_1 + n_2 - 2}} = \text{Pooled standard deviation}$$

$t_{\alpha/2}$ = critical value from the *t*-distribution for the desired confidence
level and degrees of freedom equal to $n_1 + n_2 - 2$

Equation 9-7 shows the confidence interval when $\sigma_1^2 \neq \sigma_2^2$.

CONFIDENCE INTERVAL ESTIMATE
FOR $\mu_1 - \mu_2$ – STANDARD DEVIATIONS UNKNOWN AND $\sigma_1^2 \neq \sigma_2^2$

$$(\bar{x}_1 - \bar{x}_2) \pm t_{\alpha/2} \sqrt{\frac{s_1^2}{n_1} + \frac{s_2^2}{n_2}} \qquad \textbf{9-7}$$

where:

$t_{\alpha/2}$ = Critical value from the *t*-distribution for the desired confidence level

and degrees of freedom equal to $\dfrac{(s_1^2/n_1 + s_2^2/n_2)^2}{\left(\dfrac{(s_1^2/n_1)^2}{n_1 - 1} + \dfrac{(s_2^2/n_2)^2}{n_2 - 1}\right)}$

If the sample sizes from each sample are large (n_1 and $n_2 > 30$) the standard normal distribution can be used to obtain the critical value as shown in Expression 9-8. However, Expressions 9-6 and 9-7 can be used for any size samples.

CONFIDENCE INTERVAL ESTIMATE FOR $\mu_1 - \mu_2$ – LARGE SAMPLE SIZES

$$(\bar{x}_1 - \bar{x}_2) \pm z_{\alpha/2} \sqrt{\frac{s_1^2}{n_1} + \frac{s_2^2}{n_2}} \qquad \textbf{9-8}$$

where:

$z_{\alpha/2}$ = Critical value from the standard normal distribution
for the desired confidence level

EXAMPLE 9-5

INTERVAL ESTIMATION

Excel and Minitab Tutorial

Insurance Crash Tests

Consider a major automotive insurance company that supervised a study to determine the difference in mean vehicle damage for a well-known import luxury car and a comparably priced U.S. model. The study involved driving the vehicles at a speed of 15 mph into a solid brick wall. The company would then have a panel of insurance adjusters compute the cost, including parts and labor, to return the car to its original condition. Because there will be variation in damage costs from car to car, the insurance company will have to crash more than one car of each make.

The sampling costs will be very high. The budget will allow for 9 import cars and 9 domestic cars. The objective is to estimate the difference in mean damage. The population standard deviations are not known, but since the sample sizes are small, Equation 9-8 should not be used. Instead, the interval estimate will be developed using either Equation 9-6 or 9-7 depending on whether we can assume that the population variances are equal.

The insurance crash tests produced the data shown in Figure 9-9.

The first step in analyzing the data is to compute the mean and standard deviations for the two samples. This is done in Excel as shown in Figure 9-10 and provides the following values:

$$\bar{x}_1 = \frac{\sum x}{n_1} = \$8{,}072.39 \qquad \bar{x}_2 = \frac{\sum x}{n_2} = \$7{,}508.45$$

$$s_1 = \sqrt{\frac{\sum(x - \bar{x}_1)^2}{n_1 - 1}} = \$1{,}304.12 \qquad s_2 = \sqrt{\frac{\sum(x - \bar{x}_2)^2}{n_2 - 1}} = \$813.11$$

If the insurance executives need only a point estimate for the difference between the true mean damage for the two car types, they would use the following.

$$\bar{x}_1 - \bar{x}_2 = (\$8{,}072.39 - \$7{,}508.45) = \$563.94$$

Additional Example 9-b

Large Sample Estimation

This indicates that the import car sustains an average of \$563.94 more damage than the U.S. car. However, point estimates are subject to sampling error. Instead of relying on the point estimate, the executives may wish to develop a 90% confidence interval estimate for the difference.

To develop the interval estimate, they would first test to see whether population variances are equal using the F-test introduced in Section 9-1. The F-test statistic is formed as

FIGURE 9-9
Crash Test Data

Microsoft Excel - Book1

File Edit View Insert Format Too

B12 =

	A	B
1	Import Cars	American Cars
2	$7,599.77	$7,994.65
3	$6,622.32	$7,215.24
4	$8,144.26	$6,827.58
5	$9,176.47	$7,869.19
6	$9,098.35	$7,397.06
7	$9,633.13	$8,176.50
8	$5,716.41	$8,850.29
9	$7,665.82	$7,144.77
10	$8,995.02	$6,100.74

Excel Instructions:

1. Open file: Crash.xls

FIGURE 9-10 Excel Descriptive Statistics for Crash Test Data

Microsoft Excel - Book1

File Edit View Insert Format Tools Data PHStat Window Help

Arial

G15 =

	A	B	C	D
1	*Import Cars*		*American Cars*	
2				
3	Mean	8072.394444	Mean	7508.446667
4	Standard Error	434.7080905	Standard Error	271.0377064
5	Median	8144.26	Median	7397.06
6	Mode	#N/A	Mode	#N/A
7	Standard Deviation	1304.124271	Standard Deviation	813.1131191
8	Sample Variance	1700740.115	Sample Variance	661152.9444
9	Kurtosis	-0.444965074	Kurtosis	0.135147313
10	Skewness	-0.672852303	Skewness	-0.090825421
11	Range	3916.72	Range	2749.55
12	Minimum	5716.41	Minimum	6100.74
13	Maximum	9633.13	Maximum	8850.29
14	Sum	72651.55	Sum	67576.02
15	Count	9	Count	9

Excel Instructions:

1. Open file: Crash.xls
2. Click on Tools
3. Select Descriptive Statistics
4. Define data range
5. Select Summary Statistics

the ratio of the two sample variances with the larger variance in the numerator when the test is two tailed. The calculated F-value is:

$$F = \frac{1{,}304.12^2}{813.11^2} = 2.572$$

The critical value from the F table in Appendix H for an upper-tail area equal to 0.05 and degrees of freedom, $D_1 = 8$ and $D_2 = 8$ is 3.44. Since $F = 2.572 < 3.44$, we should not reject the hypothesis of equal variances. Therefore, our 90% confidence interval estimate for the difference in mean damage for the two car models is developed using Equation 9-6:

$$(\bar{x}_1 - \bar{x}_2) \pm t_{\alpha/2}s_p\sqrt{\frac{1}{n_1} + \frac{1}{n_2}}$$

We first need to find the pooled standard deviation.

$$s_p = \sqrt{\frac{(n_1 - 1)s_1^2 + (n_2 - 1)s_2^2}{n_1 + n_2 - 2}} = \sqrt{\frac{(9 - 1)(1{,}304.12)^2 + (9 - 1)(813.11)^2}{9 + 9 - 2}}$$

$$s_p = 1{,}086.71$$

Note, the pooled standard deviation, s_p, has a value between the two sample standard deviations. Next, the t-value for a 90% confidence interval with $9 + 9 - 2 = 16$ degrees of freedom is 1.7459. (See the t-distribution in Appendix F or use the TINV in Excel.) Substituting these values into Equation 9-6 gives:

$$(\$8{,}072.39 - \$7{,}508.45) \pm (1.7459)(1{,}086.71)\sqrt{\frac{1}{9} + \frac{1}{9}}$$

$$\$563.94 \pm \$894.39$$

$$-\$330.45 \text{ —————— } \$1{,}458.33$$

Thus, the insurance executives estimate, based on the sample data and 90% confidence, that the difference in mean damage for import and domestic cars will be, on average, between $-\$330.45$ and $\$1,458.33$. Since this interval contains 0, the data do not provide conclusive evidence to suggest that the foreign models sustain more damage than the domestic models or vice-versa.[4]

Paired Samples Hypothesis Testing and Estimation

The previous examples in this section introduced the methods by which decision makers can test whether two populations have equal means when the samples are selected from normally distributed populations and the samples are independent. In each example, the samples were independent since the sample values from one population did not have the potential to influence the probability that values would be selected from the second population.

However, there are instances in business where you would want to use **paired samples** to control for sources of variation that might otherwise distort the conclusions of a study.

PAIRED SAMPLES

Samples that are selected such that each data value from one sample is related (or matched) with a corresponding data value from the second sample. The sample values from one population have the potential to influence the probability that values will be selected from the second population.

---

[4]While neither Excel nor PHStat has procedures for directly determining the confidence interval estimate for the difference between two population means, a formula can be written using the output from Figure 9-10. Please refer to the Excel tutorial on the CD-ROM for specifics. Minitab does contain a procedure for directly performing the estimate.

EXAMPLE 9-6

HYPOTHESIS TESTING

Testing Engine Oil

A major oil company is interested in testing to determine if there is a difference in average mileage for automobiles using regular engine oil compared with a synthetic oil product. The company believes that the mean miles per gallon will be higher when the synthetic oil is used. However, the marketing managers realize that a consumer will not be convinced the increased mileage makes any difference unless the increase is noticeable. The managers assume that they will have a hard time selling the public on the benefits of synthetic oil if it increases the mileage only by, say, 0.01 miles per gallon. After conferring with the market research section, the managers have concluded that they will have to demonstrate the mileage has increased by more than 1 mile per gallon.

The company would use a paired sample approach to control variation in mileage that might be due to the fact that cars and drivers are different. A random sample of 10 motorists (and their cars) was selected to participate in the study. Each car was filled with gasoline, the oil was drained, and new, regular oil was added. The car was driven 200 miles on a specified route. The car was then filled with gasoline and the miles per gallon were computed.

After the 10 cars completed this process, the same steps were performed with the exception being that synthetic oil was used. The fact that the same cars and drivers are used to test both types of oil means that the miles per gallon measurements for synthetic oil and for regular engine oil will mostly likely be related. The two samples are not independent, but they are instead considered to be paired samples. Thus, we will compute d, the paired difference between the values from each sample ($d = x_{syn} - x_{reg}$). The null and alternative hypotheses are stated as follows.

$$H_0: \mu_d \leq 1.0$$
$$H_A: \mu_d > 1.0$$

Equation 9-9 is used to compute d, the **paired difference.**

PAIRED DIFFERENCE

$$d = x_1 - x_2$$ **9-9**

where:

d = Paired difference

x_1 and x_2 = Values from sample 1 and 2, respectively

Figure 9-11 shows the Excel spreadsheet for this engine oil study with the paired differences ($x_{syn} - x_{reg}$) computed. The data are in the file on your CD-ROM called **Engine-Oil.**

The first step to test the hypothesis is to compute the **mean paired difference,** $\bar{d}$, using Equation 9-10.

FIGURE 9-11
Excel Worksheet for Engine Oil Study

Microsoft Excel - Engine-Oil.xls

File Edit View Insert Format Tools Data

	A	B	C
1	Synthetic	Original	d
2	19.8	20.7	-0.9
3	28.8	25.8	3
4	20.4	27.8	-7.4
5	18.7	14.9	3.8
6	23.4	21.6	1.8
7	27.1	21.1	6
8	28.4	28	0.4
9	21.4	13	8.4
10	26.4	24.4	2
11	19.9	14.3	5.6

MEAN PAIRED DIFFERENCE

$$\bar{d} = \frac{\sum_{i=1}^{n} d_i}{n}$$ **9-10**

where:

d_i = ith paired difference value

n = Number of paired differences

Using Equation 9-10 we determine $\bar{d}$ as follows.

Excel Instructions:

1. Open file: Engine-Oil.xls

$$\bar{d} = \frac{\sum d}{n} = \frac{22.7}{10} = 2.27$$

The $\bar{d}$ value measures the average paired difference. The value $\bar{d} = 2.27$ indicates that the average difference in mileage using synthetic versus regular oil is 2.27 miles per gallon.

The next step is to compute the **standard deviation for the paired differences** using Equation 9-11.

STANDARD DEVIATION FOR PAIRED DIFFERENCES

$$s_d = \sqrt{\frac{\sum_{i=1}^{n}(d_i - \bar{d})^2}{n - 1}}$$

9-11

where:

$d_i = i$th paired difference
$\bar{d}$ = Mean paired difference

The standard deviation for the paired differences is:

$$s_d = \sqrt{\frac{\sum(d - \bar{d})^2}{n - 1}} = \sqrt{\frac{172.8}{10 - 1}} = 4.382$$

We are now ready to complete the hypothesis test by computing the test **statistic for the paired difference test** using Equation 9-12.

---

t-TEST STATISTIC FOR PAIRED DIFFERENCES

$$t = \frac{\bar{d} - \mu_d}{\frac{s_d}{\sqrt{n}}} \qquad df = n - 1$$

9-12

where:

$\bar{d}$ = Sample mean paired difference
μ_d = Hypothesized paired difference
s_d = Sample standard deviation of paired differences
n = Number of paired differences (sample size)

The test statistic obtained from Equation 9-12 has a t-distribution with $n - 1$ degrees of freedom. Employing Equation 9-12 we get:

$$t = \frac{\bar{d} - \mu_d}{\frac{s_d}{\sqrt{n}}} = \frac{2.27 - 1.0}{\frac{4.382}{\sqrt{10}}} = 0.9165$$

Additional Example 9-c

Paired Sample Test Using Minitab

Figure 9-12 shows the results of the hypothesis test using alpha = 0.05 for the one-tailed test. Note that the critical value from the t-table with an upper-tail area equal to 0.05 and 9 degrees of freedom is 1.833. Since $t = 0.9165 < 1.833$, we do not reject the null hypothesis. Thus, based on the sample data, there is insufficient evidence to conclude that the synthetic oil increases the mean mpg by more than 1 mpg over the original oil.[5]

The computations required for the paired sample t-test can be done in Excel using the Descriptive Statistics option on the column of d values. Likewise, both Excel and Minitab have procedures for performing the paired sample t-test directly from the original data. Figure 9-13 illustrates the Excel output for the engine oil example. Notice that both the calculated t and critical t values are shown as well as the p-value.

---

[5]Please take notice that this paired sample test is actually the same as the one sample test introduced in Chapter 8, but in this case we are performing the analysis on the computed d values.

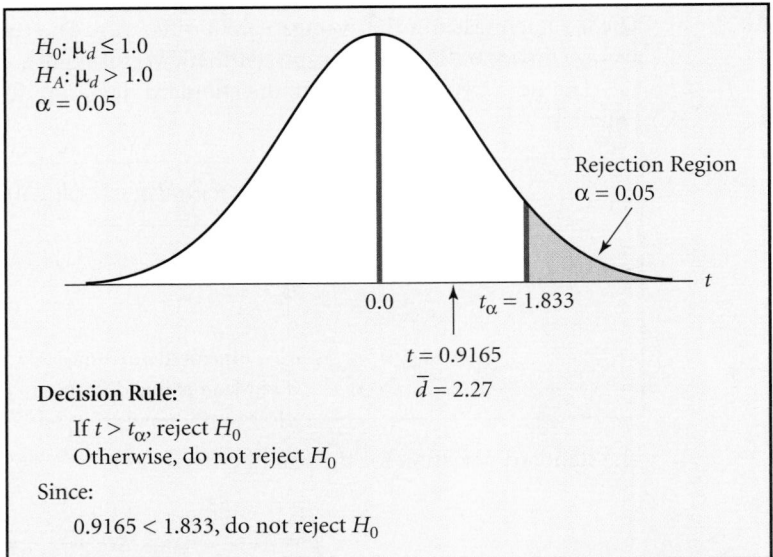

FIGURE 9-12
Paired Sample Hypothesis Test

ISSUES WITH EXCEL

In an earlier Excel caution, we pointed out that Excel does not contain a provision for automatically excluding missing values from computations. This can cause you problems if you are not careful. The *t-Test: Paired Two Sample for Means* procedure located in the *Tools, Data Analysis* option in Excel is designed to perform all the calculations required to complete the paired sample test shown in Figure 9-13. If there are no missing values in either sample, Excel works nicely.

However, under at least one special situation, the Excel results are incorrect. This happens if one or more values in the first sample are missing and the *same number* of values are missing in the second sample. (The missing values do not need to be from the same cases.) In any other situation where missing values are present, Excel gives an error message and refuses to do the calculations. But when the same number of values are missing from both samples, Excel will give an incorrect answer. Thus, before using Excel to con-

FIGURE 9-13
Excel Paired Sample Results for the Engine Oil Example

Excel Instructions:

1. Open file: Engine-Oil.xls
2. Select Tools
3. Click on Data Analysis
4. Select *t*-Test: Paired Two Sample for Means
5. Define data range for two variables
6. Specify Hypothesized value for paired difference
7. Specify alpha

Microsoft Excel - Engine-Oil.xls

File Edit View Insert Format Tools Data PHStat Window Help

E17

	A	B	C
1	t-Test: Paired Two Sample for Means		
2			
3		Synthetic	Original
4	Mean	23.43	21.16
5	Variance	15.23788889	30.68266667
6	Observations	10	10
7	Pearson Correlation	0.617880842	
8	Hypothesized Mean Difference	1	
9	df	9	
10	t Stat	0.9165409	
11	P(T<=t) one-tail	0.191642761	
12	t Critical one-tail	1.833113856	
13	P(T<=t) two-tail	0.383285521	
14	t Critical two-tail	2.262158887	

Since calculated $t = 0.9165 < t$ Critical $= 1.833$, do not reject the null hypothesis.

duct the paired sample test, make sure that cases with missing values have been excluded from your analysis.

Woodmill Corporation

EXAMPLE 9-7

INTERVAL ESTIMATION

Excel and Minitab Tutorial

Consider an example involving the Woodmill Corporation near Duluth, Minnesota. Woodmill makes wood windows and wood moldings for the building industry. It purchases dried dimension lumber (2×8, 2×10, 2×12, etc.) from lumber producers such as Boise Cascade, Potlatch, and Weyerhaeuser. The first step in the manufacturing process is to rip the lumber lengthwise into narrower pieces that can be used to make window frames and molding products.

As each board comes to the ripsaw, the operator must make a decision regarding the widths to cut the board. This decision is based on the distribution of knots and other features in the board. The objective is to create products with the greatest downstream value. To enhance the value of the cut boards, the operator must be highly trained in determining the best cuts to rip. Even then, there is a great chance that less than optimal decisions will be made.

A company in Redmond, Washington, has developed an optical scanner that the company says is capable of determining what the cut widths should be to generate "optimum" value from the wood. A computer signals an automated ripsaw which then cuts the boards to the dimensions indicated by the scanner. As you might expect, this scanner system is expensive, costing approximately $1.5 million. However, if the scanner would add sufficient value to the process, Woodmill would be interested in buying one.

As part of a larger study, Woodmill selected a random sample of 100 boards. These boards were sent to Redmond and run through the scanner. However, instead of actually running the boards through the ripsaw in Redmond, a computer file was generated that showed the projected value of each board assuming that it was ripped according to the scanner specifications. The file showed the board number and the projected dollar value. The boards were then returned to Duluth where they were run through the manual ripsaw process. The ripsaw operator made his decisions and the boards were ripped. Once ripped, the dollar value for each board was determined.

Figure 9-14 shows the data for the first few boards. The full data set is in a file called **Woodmill** on the CD-ROM that accompanies this text.

The two samples in this case are referred to as paired samples and are not independent because the sample data for both the scanner and the manual process were generated from the same set of boards. The test was set up this way in order to block out any effect that might occur due to variation in the quality of the original boards. Had the test run one set of boards through the scanner and a different set of boards through the manual process, any difference between the values from the two processes might be due to the original quality of the boards used. If by chance the scanner system was given higher quality boards, the value after ripping would tend to be higher even though the scanner might be no more effective than the manual rip process.

When paired samples are used, the difference (d) between the two sample values on a case-by-case basis must be computed. The difference variable's population must be approximately normally distributed. Figure 9-15 illustrates the d values for the first few boards.

The managers at the Woodmill Corporation are interested in estimating the mean difference between the value obtained using the scanner and the value obtained using their current manual ripsaw process. When dealing with paired samples, Equation 9-13 is used to generate the confidence interval estimate.

FIGURE 9-14
Excel Worksheet of Woodmill Data

Microsoft Excel - Woodmill.xls

File Edit View Insert Format Tools

G16

	A	B	C
1	Board	Scanner	Manual
2	ID	Value	Value
3	1	$15.23	$6.07
4	2	$31.07	$14.02
5	3	$18.44	$21.33
6	4	$18.32	$24.78
7	5	$32.11	$17.48
8	6	$47.65	$32.34
9	7	$16.11	$6.85
10	8	$30.28	$23.48
11	9	$21.18	$18.35

Excel Instructions:
1. Open file: Woodmill.xls

PAIRED CONFIDENCE INTERVAL ESTIMATE

$$\bar{d} \pm t_{\alpha/2} \frac{s_d}{\sqrt{n}}$$

9-13

Excel Instructions:

1. Open file:
   Woodmill.xls
2. Compute paired
   differences

	Board ID	Scanner Value	Manual Value		Paired Differences
1	Board	Scanner	Manual		Paired
2	ID	Value	Value		Differences
3	1	$15.23	$6.07		$9.16
4	2	$31.07	$14.02		$17.05
5	3	$18.44	$21.33		-$2.89
6	4	$18.32	$24.78		-$6.46
7	5	$32.11	$17.48		$14.63
8	6	$47.65	$32.34		$15.31
9	7	$16.11	$6.85		$9.26

E3   =B3-C3

FIGURE 9-15
Excel Output of Woodmill
Paired Differences

The managers want a 95% confidence interval estimate. The following sample statistics are computed from the sample of 100 paired differences using Excel's Descriptive Statistics tool:

$$\bar{d} = 7.10 \qquad \text{and} \qquad s_d = 10.95$$

The t-value for 95% confidence and $100 - 1 = 99$ degrees of freedom from the t-distribution table in Appendix F is 1.9842. You can also use Excel's *TINV* function to get the critical t-value. Using Equation 9-13, the confidence interval estimate is:

$$\bar{d} \pm t_{\alpha/2}\frac{s_d}{\sqrt{n}}$$

$$7.10 \pm 1.9842\frac{10.95}{\sqrt{100}}$$

$$7.10 \pm 2.172$$

$$4.928 \text{——————} 9.272$$

Figure 9-16 shows the Excel output. Based on the sample results and using the 95% confidence interval, the Woodmill managers can conclude that the mean difference per board value is between $4.93 and $9.27 higher when the scanner is used versus using the

Additional Example 9-d

Paired Sample Estimation

FIGURE 9-16
Excel Paired Differences—
Woodmill Output

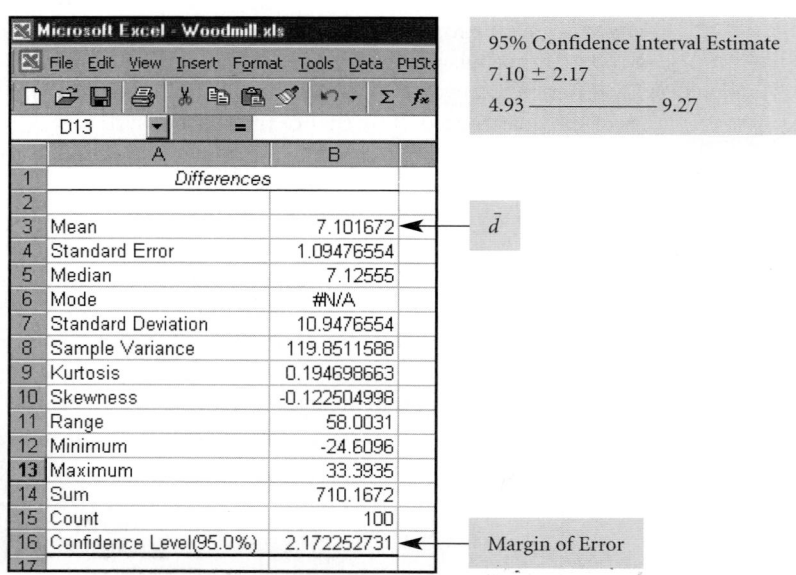

95% Confidence Interval Estimate

$$7.10 \pm 2.17$$

$$4.93 \text{——————} 9.27$$

	A	B	
1		Differences	
2			
3	Mean	7.101672	← $\bar{d}$
4	Standard Error	1.09476554	
5	Median	7.12555	
6	Mode	#N/A	
7	Standard Deviation	10.9476554	
8	Sample Variance	119.8511588	
9	Kurtosis	0.194698663	
10	Skewness	-0.122504998	
11	Range	58.0031	
12	Minimum	-24.6096	
13	Maximum	33.3935	
14	Sum	710.1672	
15	Count	100	
16	Confidence Level(95.0%)	2.172252731	← Margin of Error

Excel Instructions:

1. Open file: Woodmill.xls
2. Compute paired differences using Excel formula
3. Select Tools
4. Click on Data Analysis
5. Select Descriptive Statistics
6. Define data range
7. Click on Summary Statistics

existing manual method. Using the conservative $4.93 difference, we see that $1,500,000/$4.93 = 304,260 boards would have to be run in order to pay for the scanner system purchase price. This represents about 3 months' production. What decision would you recommend for Woodmill?

9-2: EXERCISES

ADDITIONAL EXERCISES ON YOUR CD-ROM
Try the ADDITIONAL EXERCISES and APPLICATION PROBLEMS on the CD-ROM.

9-8. Given the following null and alternative hypotheses:

$$H_0: \mu_1 - \mu_2 = 0$$
$$H_A: \mu_1 - \mu_2 \neq 0$$

and the following sample information:

SAMPLE 1	SAMPLE 2
$n_1 = 100$	$n_2 = 120$
$s_1 = 20$	$s_2 = 24$
$\bar{x}_1 = 430$	$\bar{x}_2 = 405$

a. Develop the appropriate decision rule, assuming a significance level of 0.05 is to be used.
b. Test using an alpha value = 0.05 to determine whether the population variances are equal.
c. Test the null hypothesis and indicate whether the sample information leads you to reject or fail to reject the null hypothesis that the population means are equal. Use the test-statistic approach.

9-9. Given the following null and alternative hypotheses:

$$H_0: \mu_1 - \mu_2 \geq 0$$
$$H_A: \mu_1 - \mu_2 < 0$$

and the following sample information:

SAMPLE 1	SAMPLE 2
$n_1 = 16$	$n_2 = 25$
$s_1 = 32$	$s_2 = 30$
$\bar{x}_1 = 2,456$	$\bar{x}_2 = 2,460$

a. Develop the appropriate decision rule to test that the populations have equal variances, assuming a significance level of 0.05 is to be used.
b. Conduct the hypothesis test to determine whether the two populations have equal variances using the decision rule developed in part a. (Use a 0.05 level of significance.)

9-10. The following sample data have been collected from a paired sample from two populations. The claim is that the first population mean will exceed the mean of the second population.

Ho : $\mu_d \leq 0$
Has $\mu_d > 0$

SAMPLE 1	SAMPLE 2	SAMPLE 1	SAMPLE 2
50	38	43	31
47	44	46	38
44	38	72	39
48	37	40	54
40	43	55	41
36	44	38	40

a. State the appropriate null and alternative hypotheses.
b. Based on the sample data, what should you conclude about the null hypothesis? Test at a significance level of 0.01.
c. Suppose these samples had been obtained independently. Conduct the test and determine if the results would be different.

9-11. The following sample data have been collected from a paired sample from two populations. The claim is that the first population mean will equal the mean of the second population. This claim will be assumed to be true unless the data strongly suggest otherwise.

SAMPLE 1	SAMPLE 2	SAMPLE 1	SAMPLE 2
4.4	3.7	2.6	4.2
2.7	3.5	2.4	5.2
1.0	4.0	2.0	4.4
3.5	4.9	2.8	4.3
2.8	3.1		

a. State the appropriate null and alternative hypotheses.
b. Based on the sample data, what should you conclude about the null hypothesis? Test using $\alpha = 0.10$.
c. Calculate a 90% confidence interval for the difference in the population means. Are the results from the confidence interval consistent with the outcome of your hypothesis test? Explain why.

9-12. Given the following information:

$$n_1 = 25 \qquad n_2 = 25$$
$$\bar{x}_1 = 0.145 \qquad \bar{x}_2 = 0.107$$
$$s_1 = 0.06 \qquad s_2 = 0.08$$

a. Determine the 90% confidence interval estimate for the difference between population means. Interpret the estimate.

b. Determine the 95% confidence interval estimate for the difference between population means. Interpret the estimate.

c. How would the answers to parts a and b differ if the sample sizes were doubled? Discuss what factors affect your answer.

Business Applications

9-13. The State College registrar is interested in determining whether there is a difference of more than 1 hour between male and female students in average number of credit hours taken during a term. She has selected a random sample of 60 males and 60 females and observed the following sample information:

MALE	FEMALE
$\bar{x} = 13.24$ credits	$\bar{x} = 14.65$ credits
$s = 1.2$ credits	$s = 1.56$ credits

a. Provide the registrar with the information she is seeking by performing a hypothesis test based on a 0.05 significance level.

b. Calculate the probability that if there is an average difference of 1 hour between the number of credit hours taken by male and female students, a difference as great as or greater than that observed between these two samples would occur. Specify the statistical term used to describe the probability calculated.

9-14. The marketing manager for a major retail grocery chain is wondering about the location of the stores' dairy products. She believes that the mean amount spent by customers on dairy products per visit is higher in stores where the dairy section is in the central part of the store compared with stores that have the dairy section at the rear of the store. To consider relocating the dairy products, the manager feels that the increase in the mean amount spent by customers must be at least $0.25. To determine whether relocation is justified, her staff selected a random sample of 25 customers at stores where the dairy section is central in the store. A second sample of 25 customers was selected in stores with the dairy section at the rear of the store. The following sample results were observed.

CENTRAL DAIRY	REAR DAIRY
$\bar{x} = \$3.74$	$\bar{x} = \$3.26$
$s = \$0.87$	$s = \$0.79$

a. Conduct a hypothesis test with a significance level of 0.05 to determine if the manager should relocate the dairy products in those stores displaying their dairy products in the rear of the store.

b. If a statistical error associated with hypothesis testing was made in this hypothesis test, what error could it have been? Explain.

9-15. The makers of ink cartridges for color ink-jet printers have developed a new system for storing the ink. They think the new system will result in a longer lasting product. In order to determine whether this is the case, a test was developed in which a sample of 35 new cartridges was selected. The new cartridges were installed in a printer, and test pages were run until the cartridge was empty. The same thing was done for a sample of 30 original cartridges. The following data were observed.

NEW CARTRIDGE	EXISTING CARTRIDGE
$\bar{x} = 288$ pages	$\bar{x} = 279$ pages
$s = 16.23$ pages	$s = 15.91$ pages

a. Based on the sample data and a significance level equal to 0.10, determine if the new system will result in a longer lasting product. Write a short statement that discusses the results of the test.

b. Calculate a 90% confidence interval for the difference between these two population means. Are the results of the hypothesis test consistent with the confidence interval you produced? Explain.

9-16. A random sample of 256 credit unions that offer credit cards revealed that the average annual fee charged by the credit union was $12.56 with a standard deviation of $2.33. A random sample of 225 federally chartered banks offering credit cards showed that the average annual fee was $22.48 with a standard deviation of $6.18.

a. Construct a 90% and a 95% confidence interval estimate for the true difference in means between the annual fees charged for credit cards by credit unions and federally chartered banks.

b. Could the federally chartered banks be accused of having an average annual fee that is $10 more than that of credit unions? Support your answer using your knowledge of probability and statistics.

9-17. A marketing consulting firm was recently hired by a large retail clothing chain to study the buying habits of the chain's customers. As part of the study, the consultant selected a random sample of male customers and another random sample of female customers. The sampled customers were observed to determine how long they spent in the store per visit. The following data were recorded:

MALES	FEMALES
$n = 250$	$n = 350$
$\bar{x} = 24$ minutes	$\bar{x} = 53$ minutes
$s = 11$ minutes	$s = 32$ minutes

a. Based on these sample data, what is the 90% confidence interval estimate for the difference between true average shopping times for males and females? Does the confidence interval you constructed lead you to believe that there is a difference in how long males and females spend in the store per visit?

b. Referring to the sample data, construct a 95% confidence interval estimate for the difference in mean time spent in the store for males versus females.

Given the confidence interval in part a, would you have expected this confidence interval to indicate a difference in the mean time spent in the store for males versus females? Provide the reasoning you used to reach your answer.

c. The marketing department has held the belief that women spend on average 20 minutes longer shopping than do men. Is the marketing department's belief substantiated by your calculations? Explain the logic of your answer.

d. Estimate the proportion of men who spend at least as much time as the average of the women's sample.

9-18. Two companies that manufacture batteries for electronics batteries have submitted their batteries to an independent testing agency. The agency tested 200 of each company's batteries and recorded the length of time the batteries lasted before failure. The following results were determined.

COMPANY A	COMPANY B
$\bar{x} = 41.5$ hours	$\bar{x} = 39.0$ hours
$s = 3.6$	$s = 5.0$

a. Based on these data, determine the 95% confidence interval to estimate the difference in average life of the batteries for the two companies. Do these data indicate that one company's batteries will outlast the other company's batteries on average? Explain.

b. Suppose the manufacturers of each of these batteries wished to warranty their batteries. One small company to which they both ship batteries receives shipments of 200 batteries weekly. If the average length of time to failure of the batteries is less than a specified number the manufacturer will refund the company's purchase price of that set of batteries. What value should each manufacturer set if they wish to refund money for, at most, 5% of the shipments?

9-19. The owner of Fortee Bakery is interested in determining the difference in the average purchase amount per customer at his two locations. To estimate the difference, he has selected a random sample of 50 customer receipts at each location. The following data are available:

LOCATION 1	LOCATION 2
$\bar{x} = \$5.26$	$\bar{x} = \$6.19$
$s = \$0.89$	$s = \$1.05$

a. What is the point estimate for the difference between mean purchase amount at the two locations? Comment on the advantages and disadvantages of using a point estimate only in this case.

b. Assuming that the owner wishes to develop a 95% confidence interval estimate for the difference in mean purchase amount, what will the standard error for the difference between sample means be?

c. Compute the 95% confidence interval estimate. Determine if there is a difference in the average purchase amount per customer at his two locations.

d. Referring to parts b and c, suppose the owner wishes to reduce the margin of error, what are his options? Discuss.

9-20. Wilson Construction and Concrete Company is known as a very progressive company that is willing to try new ideas to improve its products and service. One of the key factors of importance in concrete work is the time it takes for the concrete to "set up." The company is considering a new additive that can be put in the concrete mix to help reduce the set-up time. Before going ahead with the additive, the company plans to test it against the current additive. To do this, 14 batches of concrete are mixed using each of the additives. The following results were observed.

OLD ADDITIVE	NEW ADDITIVE
$\bar{x} = 17.2$ hours	$\bar{x} = 15.9$ hours
$s = 2.5$ hours	$s = 1.8$ hours

a. Use these sample data to construct a 90% confidence interval estimate for the difference in mean set-up time for the two concrete additives. On the basis of the confidence interval produced, do you agree that the new additive helps reduce the set-up time for cement? Explain your answer.

b. Assuming that the new additive is slightly more expensive than the old additive, do the data support switching to the new additive if the managers of the company are primarily interested in reducing average set-up time?

9-21. Referring to Problem 20, suppose Wilson's managers repeat the test with 14 more batches of concrete using each additive. They then combined the information from the two tests giving a sample size of 28 batches for each additive. The following results were observed.

OLD ADDITIVE	NEW ADDITIVE
$\bar{x} = 18.4$ hours	$\bar{x} = 15.2$ hours
$s = 2.9$ hours	$s = 1.6$ hours

a. Use these sample data to construct a 90% confidence interval estimate for the difference in mean set-up time for the two concrete additives. On the basis of this confidence interval, do you agree that the new additive helps reduce the set-up time for cement? Explain your answer.

b. Compare this interval with the one computed in Problem 20. Discuss why the standard error for the estimate is lower when the samples are combined.

c. Assuming that the new additive is slightly more expensive than the old additive, do the new data support switching to the new additive if the managers of the company are primarily interested in reducing average set-up time?

9-22. The First Night Stage Company operates a small nonprofit theater group in Milwaukee, Wisconsin. Each year the company markets Christmas candy to help fund its operations. This year, it has obtained the help of a marketing research company in the city. This company has proposed two different candy brochures. Brochure B costs an average of $0.35 more to produce than does brochure A. The theater group is trying to determine which brochure will produce the higher sales. To determine this, a random sample of 20 people was selected to receive brochure A, and another random sample of 20 people was selected to receive brochure B. The sales data (including sales tax) are contained in the file called **First-Night.**

   a. Based on these sample data, which brochure should the First Night Company adopt? Use $\alpha = 0.01$ for whatever statistical inference techniques you use.

   b. Referring to the statistical inference techniques you used in part a, what assumptions are required?

9-23. For years there has been a debate over whether children suffer any long-term negative effects when they are placed in child care facilities while their parents work. A recent study of 6,000 children, reported in the March 1999 issue of *Developmental Psychology,* found "no permanent negative effects caused by their mother's absence." In fact, the study indicated that there might be some positive benefits from the day care experience. To investigate this premise, a nonprofit organization called Child Care Connections conducted a small study in which children were observed playing in a neutral setting (not at home or at a day care center.) Over a period of 20 hours of observation, 15 children who do not go to day care and 21 children who have spent much time in day care were observed. The variable of interest was the total minutes of play in which the child was actively interacting with other students. Child Care Connections' leaders hoped to show that the children who had been in day care would have a higher mean time in interactive situations than the stay-at-home children. A file called **Children** contains the results of the study.

   a. Test the hypothesis that the children who have been in day care have a higher mean time in interactive situations than the stay-at-home children. Use a significance level of 0.05.

   b. Based on the outcome of the hypothesis test, which statistical error might have been committed?

9-24. A regional airport is considering the purchase of a new visibility sensor system to be used in conjunction with the air traffic control equipment. The managers have narrowed the choices down to two suppliers, Vanguard and Scorpian. To help make the final selection, the two suppliers agreed to participate in a test. The two sensors were temporarily installed side-by-side at the airport. Visibility readings from each sensor were recorded on 5-minute intervals for a 24-hour period. The resulting data are in a file called **Visibility.**

   a. State the appropriate null and alternative hypotheses to be tested by the airport managers.

   b. Discuss whether the samples can be treated as independent or if they are, in fact, paired samples. Be sure to state your reasoning.

   c. Perform the hypothesis test assuming that samples are independent using a significance level of 0.05. Discuss the results.

   d. Perform the hypothesis test assuming that the samples are paired. Use a significance level of 0.05 and discuss your results. How does the conclusion compare with the one reached in part c?

   e. Comment on whether it would be possible to reach a different conclusion using a paired sample test versus a test assuming independent samples. Explain your answer.

9-25. The managers of a regional bank in Florida believe that customers who regularly use their ATM card (regular is defined as at least one time per week) are more profitable to the bank overall than are customers who do not regularly use their ATM card. A sample of 200 of the bank's customers in each category was selected. An audit was performed to determine the 1999 profit generated from each customer. The following sample data were observed:

REGULAR ATM	NON-ATM USERS
$\bar{x} = \$142.76$	$\bar{x} = \$133.19$
$s = \$\ 30.31$	$s = \$\ 33.92$

   a. State the appropriate null and alternative hypotheses.

   b. Using an alpha level equal to 0.05, what conclusion should the bank's managers reach based on the sample data? Discuss your results in a short written statement.

   c. Calculate a 95% confidence interval for the difference of the average profit produced by these two groups. If you were one of the bank's managers, which of the two (hypothesis test or confidence interval) statistical inference procedures would you prefer in this situation? Explain.

9-26. The California State Highway Patrol recently conducted a study on a stretch of interstate highway south of San Francisco to determine whether the mean speed for California vehicles exceeded the mean speed for out-of-state vehicles. It would consider an average speed difference of at least 5 mph to be a significant increase in speed. A total of 140 California cars were included in the study while 75 out-of-state cars were included. Radar was used to measure the speed. The data file called **Speed-Test** contains the data collected by the California Highway Patrol.

   a. Determine the research hypothesis. Specify the alternative and null hypotheses that would be derived from the research hypothesis.

   b. Using a significance level equal to 0.10, would the average speed of California drivers be considered to be "significantly larger" by the California Highway Patrol? Discuss the results of this test in a short written statement.

9-27. The Sunbeam Corporation makes a wide variety of appliances for the home. One product is a digital blood pressure gauge. For obvious reasons the blood pressure readings made by the monitor need to be accurate. When a new model is being designed, one of the crucial steps is to test it. To do this, a sample of people is selected. Each person has his/her systolic blood pressure taken by a highly respected physician. They then immediately have their systolic blood pressure taken using the Sunbeam monitor. If the mean blood pressure is the same for the monitor as that determined by the physician, the monitor is determined to pass the test.

In a recent test, 15 people were randomly selected to be in the sample. The blood pressure readings for these people, using both methods, are also contained in the data file called **Sunbeam.**

PHYSICIAN	MONITOR	PHYSICIAN	MONITOR
112	126	116	116
109	108	120	118
139	116	111	114
141	123	123	108
120	138	114	130
99	123	121	123
128	119	132	127
118	122		

a. Based on the sample data and a significance level equal to 0.05, what conclusion should the Sunbeam engineers reach regarding the latest blood pressure monitor? Discuss your answer in a short written statement.

b. Consider the context of this problem. Does it make sense to you that any deviation from the equality between the mean blood pressure readings would be of interest? Examine the data to determine a, perhaps, more reasonable criterion.

c. Calculate a 95% confidence interval for the paired difference between the two mean blood pressure readings. Based on your criterion of part b, would you consider the Sunbeam blood pressure monitor to be a good substitute for a doctor's blood pressure reading? Explain.

9-28. The data file called **Cities** contains a random sample of cities in the United States. Use these sample data to estimate the difference in average SAT scores for city versus suburban dwellers. (Hint: Are the samples independent or paired?)

a. Compute the point estimate for the difference in mean SAT scores. On the basis of this point estimate alone, could you conclude that there is as much as 150 points difference in the average SAT scores for people living in the suburbs versus people living in cities? Explain your answer.

b. Based on the sample data, calculate a 95% confidence interval estimate for the difference between mean SAT scores for city versus suburban dwellers. On the basis of this confidence interval alone, could you conclude that there is as much as 150 points difference in the average SAT scores between people living in the two areas? Explain your answer.

c. Referring to part b, suppose the confidence level is changed to 80%. What is the impact on the interval estimate? Discuss why this impact occurred.

9-29. The file on the CD-ROM titled **Banks** contains data on a sample of U.S. banks. You are asked to develop a 95% confidence interval estimate for the difference in mean number of employees per bank for banks that had profits above $1 billion dollars versus those that had profits under $1 billion. (Data listed under "Profits" in the data file are in units of millions of dollars.) Interpret your results. Do these data provide evidence to suggest that there is a difference between the two groups of banks? Discuss. (Hint: You may need to reorganize the data prior to developing the interval estimate.)

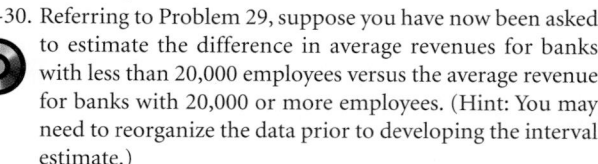

9-30. Referring to Problem 29, suppose you have now been asked to estimate the difference in average revenues for banks with less than 20,000 employees versus the average revenue for banks with 20,000 or more employees. (Hint: You may need to reorganize the data prior to developing the interval estimate.)

a. Develop a 95% confidence interval estimate and interpret.

b. Now, repeat the estimation but use 30,000 employees as the cut-off for the two populations of banks. Interpret your estimate.

c. Write a short statement that compares the estimates obtained in parts a and b.

9-31. The ECCO Company makes back-up alarms for equipment such as forklifts. As its quality manager, you are concerned about how large the difference is in average warranty claims for products made at the Boise location versus the Salt Lake City location. Sample warranty data are contained in a file called **ECCO** on the CD-ROM. Develop a 98% confidence interval estimate for the difference in mean warranty amounts for the two locations. Interpret your results. Do these results suggest that you need to focus on one location or the other? Discuss.

9-32. The marketing manager for the Capital Credit Union is considering developing an advertising campaign directed at female credit card customers. However, before continuing with the effort, she wants to know what the difference in average credit card balances is between male and female customers. She asked the database manager to select a random sample of 300 customers. These data are in the file called **Capital** on the CD-ROM.

a. Use the sample data to construct a 95% confidence interval estimate for the difference in mean credit card balances for males and females.

b. Interpret the interval estimate and write a business letter to the marketing manager discussing the conclusions that could be reached from this estimate.

c. Suppose the marketing manager decides that a higher confidence is needed. Specifically, she decides that a 99% confidence interval is needed. What is the revised confidence interval estimate? Explain what factors might have caused her to want the higher confidence level.

9-33. Freedom Hospital is in the midst of contract negotiations with its resident physicians. There has been a lot of discussion about the hospital's ability to pay and the way patients are charged. The doctors' negotiator recently mentioned that the geriatric charge system does not make sense and that there may be a difference in the way males are charged versus females. To look into this, the hospital has collected a random sample of patient data for 138 patients. The data are in a file called **Patients**. The operations manager wants to use these data to develop an estimate for the difference in average charges between males and females.

a. Construct a 95% confidence interval estimate for the difference in average charges. What does this imply about how male and female patients are charged? Is there substance to the negotiator's comments? Discuss.

b. The manager is now interested in estimating the difference between average charges for male and female patients, but only for patients who have Medicare as their principal payer. Construct the 95% confidence interval estimate. Is there a difference in how male and female patients are charged for this group?

9-34. The operations manager at Cozine Corporation was recently asked by the city council to compare the loaded weight of his company's garbage trucks as they arrive at the landfill with the weight of the competitor's trucks. The city council has received a report from Toner Garbage, Inc. that indicates a random sample of 200 trucks averaged 39,700 pounds with a standard deviation equal to 3,920 pounds. Cozine has collected a sample of 200 trucks. (The data are in a file called **Cozine**.)

a. Use these sample data and the data from Toner Garbage, Inc. to develop a 90% confidence interval estimate for the difference in average weight of the trucks from the two companies.

b. The company that operates the landfill charges the firms $20 per visit to the landfill plus a rate based on the weight of the truck at the time it arrives at the landfill. Determine the mean difference the landfill company will charge the Cozine versus the Toner Garbage Company for hauling 500,000 pounds in garbage. (Hint: The charge based on the pounds will be the same for both companies. The number of trips, however, will vary between the two companies. You must determine what this difference will be, on average.)

9-35. One of the nation's largest supermarket chains is considering changing the way it displays signs and information to make it more efficient for customers to find the items they want. The measure of success is the time it takes for customers to complete their shopping. Obviously, if a customer knows pretty much where everything is already in the store, the signs don't matter. Also, the managers know that some customers are just faster shoppers than others, regardless of the signs and information. Thus, the chain has decided to conduct a test to see how much improvement the new signs provide.

To conduct the test, the managers have selected a sample of 20 customers who regularly shop at a particular store in Denver. These 20 people are flown to Seattle where they are given a list of groceries to buy and are taken to store A, which has the store's old sign and information system. They are then asked to shop in the store until they fill the list (each customer had a different list of items). They are not told that the time it takes to complete the list is an issue. They are told that when the list is complete, they will be going to a nice restaurant for dinner. The next day, they are taken to store B, given the same list of items as the previous day, and repeat the process. Store B uses the new sign system. The layouts for stores A and B are different from each other and both are different from the Denver store where these customers usually shop.

The data file called **Food-chain** contains the results for the 20 people.

a. Based on these sample data, construct a 95% confidence interval estimate for the mean difference in time for the two sign systems. Interpret your result and discuss what this means for the food chain.

b. Comment on the method used to conduct this test. What were the strengths and what were the weaknesses?

9-3: ESTIMATION AND HYPOTHESIS TESTS FOR TWO POPULATION PROPORTIONS

The previous section illustrated the methods for testing hypotheses and developing estimates involving two population means. There are many business situations in which these methods can be applied. However, there are other instances involving two populations in which the measures of interest are not the population means. For example, Chapter 8 introduced the methodology for testing hypotheses involving a single population proportion. This section extends that methodology to tests involving hypotheses about the difference between two population proportions. In addition, we will look at confidence interval estimation involving two population proportions.

Hypothesis tests involving two population proportions can be formulated in several ways depending on whether the test is two-tailed or one-tailed.

TWO-TAILED TEST	UPPER ONE-TAILED TEST	LOWER ONE-TAILED TEST
Format 1		
$H_0: \pi_1 - \pi_2 = 0.0$ $H_A: \pi_1 - \pi_2 \neq 0.0$	$H_0: \pi_1 - \pi_2 \leq 0.0$ $H_A: \pi_1 - \pi_2 > 0.0$	$H_0: \pi_1 - \pi_2 \geq 0.0$ $H_A: \pi_1 - \pi_2 < 0.0$
Format 2		
$H_0: \pi_1 = \pi_2$ $H_A: \pi_1 \neq \pi_2$	$H_0: \pi_1 \leq \pi_2$ $H_A: \pi_1 > \pi_2$	$H_0: \pi_1 \geq \pi_2$ $H_A: \pi_1 < \pi_2$

Hypothesis Test for Two Population Proportions

EXAMPLE 9-8

HYPOTHESIS TESTING

Excel and Minitab Tutorial

Pomona Fabrication, Inc.

Pomona Fabrication, Inc., produces handheld hair dryers that several major retailers sell as in-house brands. Pomona was an early entrant into this market and has developed substantial manufacturing and technological skills. However, in recent years the firm has faced increased competition from both domestic and foreign manufacturers. Pomona has been forced to reduce its prices, and this, coupled with ever increasing production costs, has caused a substantial reduction in the company's profit margin.

A critical component of a handheld hair dryer is the motor-heater unit. This component accounts for the majority of the dryer's cost and also for a majority of the product's reliability problems. Product reliability is extremely important to Pomona since the company currently offers a standard 1-year warranty. Of course, Pomona is also interested in reducing production costs.

Pomona's research and development department has recently developed a new motor-heater unit with fewer parts than the current unit. Since the new motor-heater unit requires fewer parts than the existing unit, the company will be able to realize a 15% cost savings per hair dryer. However, the company's vice president of product development is unwilling to authorize the new component unless it is more reliable than the motor-heater currently being used.

The research and development department has decided to test samples of both units to see if the new, redesigned motor-heater is more reliable than the current unit. Two hundred fifty units of each type will be tested under conditions that simulate 1 year's use, and the proportion of each type that fails within that time will be recorded. This leads to the formulation of the following null and alternative hypotheses.

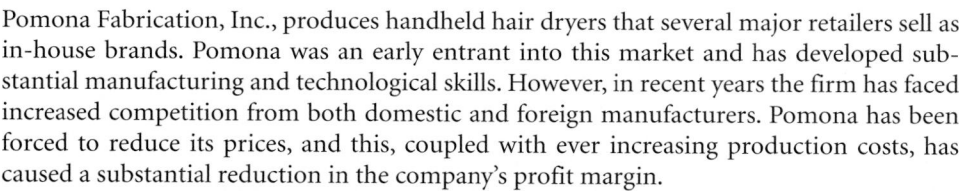

$$H_0: \pi_1 - \pi_2 \geq 0.0 \quad \text{or} \quad H_0: \pi_1 \geq \pi_2$$
$$H_A: \pi_1 - \pi_2 < 0.0 \qquad\qquad H_A: \pi_1 < \pi_2$$

where

$\pi_1 = $ Population proportion of new dryer type that fails in simulated 1-year period

$\pi_2 = $ Population proportion of existing dryer type that fails in simulated 1-year period

The null hypothesis states that the new motor-heater is no better than the current motor-heater. The alternative states that the new unit has a smaller proportion of failures within 1 year than does the current unit. In other words, the alternative states that the new unit is more reliable. This is the research hypothesis. The company wants clear evidence before changing units. If the null hypothesis is rejected, the company will conclude that the new motor-heater unit is more reliable than the old unit and should be used in producing the hair dryers. To test the null hypothesis, we can use the test statistic approach.

The test statistic is based on the sampling distribution of $p_1 - p_2$. In Chapter 6 we showed that when $n\pi \geq 5$ and $n(1 - \pi) \geq 5$, the sampling distribution of the sample proportion is approximately normally distributed with a mean equal to π and a variance equal to $\dfrac{\pi(1 - \pi)}{n}$. Likewise, in the two-sample case, the sampling distribution of $p_1 - p_2$ will also be approximately normal if $n_1\pi_1 \geq 5$, $n_1(1 - \pi_1) \geq 5$, $n_2\pi_2 \geq 5$, and $n_2(1 - \pi_2) \geq 5$. Since π_1 and π_2 are unknown, we substitute the sample proportions, p_1 and p_2 to determine whether the sample size requirements are satisfied.

The mean of the sampling distribution of $p_1 - p_2$ is the difference of the population proportions, $\pi_1 - \pi_2$. The variance is, however, the sum of the variances, $\dfrac{\pi_1(1 - \pi_1)}{n_1} + \dfrac{\pi_2(1 - \pi_2)}{n_2}$. Since the test is conducted using the assumption that the null hypothesis is true, we assume that $\pi_1 = \pi_2 = \pi$ and estimate their common value, π, using a pooled estimate shown in Equation 9-14.[6] The z-test statistic for the difference between two proportions is given as Equation 9-15.

POOLED ESTIMATOR FOR OVERALL PROPORTION (TESTS OF TWO PROPORTIONS)

$$\bar{p} = \frac{n_1 p_1 + n_2 p_2}{n_1 + n_2} = \frac{x_1 + x_2}{n_1 + n_2} \qquad \text{9-14}$$

where: x_1 and x_2 = number of successes from samples 1 and 2 with desired characteristic.

TEST STATISTIC FOR DIFFERENCE IN POPULATION PROPORTIONS

$$z = \frac{(p_1 - p_2) - (\pi_1 - \pi_2)}{\sqrt{\bar{p}(1 - \bar{p})\left(\dfrac{1}{n_1} + \dfrac{1}{n_2}\right)}} \qquad \text{9-15}$$

where:

$(\pi_1 - \pi_2)$ = Hypothesized difference in proportions from population 1 and 2, respectively
p_1 and p_2 = Sample proportions for samples selected from population 1 and 2
$\bar{p}$ = Pooled estimator for the overall proportion

The reason for taking a weighted average in Equation 9-14 is to give more weight to the larger sample if the samples are of different sizes. Note that the numerator is the total number of successes in the two samples and the denominator is the total sample size. Again, the pooled estimator, $\bar{p}$, is used when the null hypothesis indicates there is no difference between the population proportions.

Assume that Pomona is willing to use a significance level of 0.05 and that 55 of the new motor-heaters and 75 of the originals failed the 1-year test. Figure 9-17 illustrates the decision rule development and the hypothesis test. As you can see, Pomona should reject the null hypothesis based upon the sample data. Thus, the firm should conclude that the new motor-heater is more reliable than the old one. Since the new one is also less costly, the company should now use the new unit in the production of hair dryers.

The p-value approach to hypothesis testing could also have been used to test Pomona's hypothesis. In this case the calculated value of the test statistic, -2.04, results in a p-value of 0.0207 ($0.5 - 0.4793$) from the standard normal table. Since this p-value is smaller than the significance level of 0.05, we would reject the null hypothesis. Remember, whenever your p-value is smaller than the alpha value, your sample contains evidence to reject the null hypothesis.

---

[6]The procedure utilized when the hypothesized difference is not 0 is an optional topic examined on the CD-ROM.

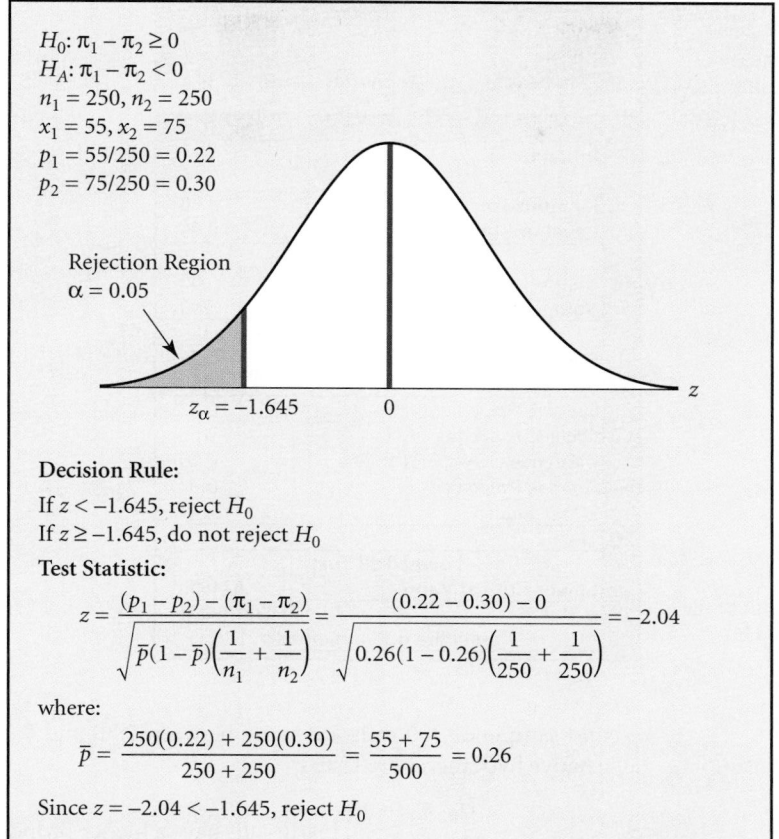

$H_0: \pi_1 - \pi_2 \geq 0$
$H_A: \pi_1 - \pi_2 < 0$
$n_1 = 250, n_2 = 250$
$x_1 = 55, x_2 = 75$
$p_1 = 55/250 = 0.22$
$p_2 = 75/250 = 0.30$

Rejection Region
$\alpha = 0.05$

$z_\alpha = -1.645$ \quad 0 \quad z

Decision Rule:
If $z < -1.645$, reject H_0
If $z \geq -1.645$, do not reject H_0

Test Statistic:

$$z = \frac{(p_1 - p_2) - (\pi_1 - \pi_2)}{\sqrt{\bar{p}(1-\bar{p})\left(\frac{1}{n_1} + \frac{1}{n_2}\right)}} = \frac{(0.22 - 0.30) - 0}{\sqrt{0.26(1-0.26)\left(\frac{1}{250} + \frac{1}{250}\right)}} = -2.04$$

where:

$$\bar{p} = \frac{250(0.22) + 250(0.30)}{250 + 250} = \frac{55 + 75}{500} = 0.26$$

Since $z = -2.04 < -1.645$, reject H_0

FIGURE 9-17
Hypothesis Test of Two
Population Proportions
for Pomona Fabrication

OPTIONAL CD-ROM TOPIC Tests for Two Proportions When Hypothesized Difference Is Not Zero
You may encounter applications in which the hypothesized difference between two population proportions is different than zero. This requires a slight adjustment in the hypothesis testing process. For more information, go to the CD-ROM.

Both Minitab and the PHStat add-ins to Excel contain procedures for performing hypothesis tests involving two population proportions. Figure 9-18 shows the PHStat output for the Pomona example. The output contains both the z-test statistic and the p-value. As we observed from our manual calculations, the difference in sample proportions is sufficient to reject the null hypothesis indicating there is no difference in population proportions.

Wilson Sales and Distribution Company

The Wilson Sales and Distribution Company is a contract provider of telephone solicitations. In this capacity, the sales staff makes "cold calls" to people in various target markets in an attempt to sell a product or service for Wilson's clients. The more sales that are made, the more revenue Wilson receives. At issue is whether calls made between 6:00 and 7:00 P.M. are more effective than calls made later in the evening.

The company conducts a test to help address this issue. Two hundred calls are made at random between 6:00 and 7:00 P.M. and the number of sales orders received recorded. A

EXAMPLE 9-9

HYPOTHESIS TESTING

Excel (PHStat) Instructions:

1. Click on the PHStat tab
2. Select the Two-Sample Tests option
3. Select Z Test for Differences in Two Proportions
4. Enter sample size and number of occurrences for each population

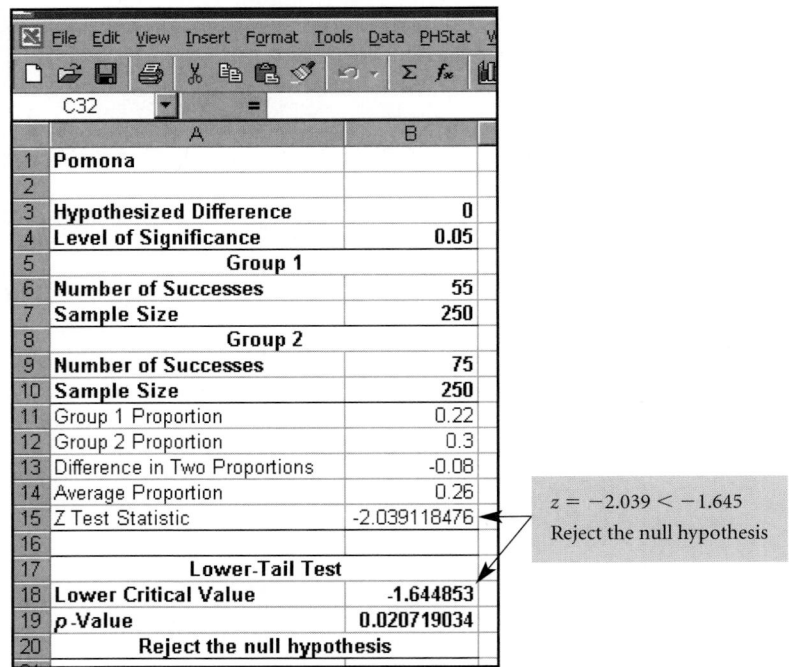

FIGURE 9-18
Excel (PHStat) Output of the Two Proportions Test for Pomona Fabrication

second sample of 200 calls are made between 7:30 and 8:30 P.M. The following null and alternative hypotheses are tested:

$$H_0: \pi_1 \leq \pi_2$$
$$H_A: \pi_1 > \pi_2 \text{ (early calls have a higher proportion of orders)}$$

The test is conducted using a 5% significance level.

The following sample data are observed:

EARLY CALLS	LATER CALLS
$n_1 = 200$	$n_2 = 200$
$x_1 = 14$	$x_2 = 9$
$p_1 = 14/200 = 0.07$	$p_2 = 9/200 = 0.045$

This is a one-tailed, upper tail test. The critical z-value from the standard normal table for alpha = 0.05 is 1.645. We can use Equation 9-15 to compute the z-test statistic. However, we first use Equation 9-14 to determine the pooled estimate for the overall proportion:

$$\bar{p} = \frac{n_1 p_1 + n_2 p_2}{n_1 + n_2} = \frac{200(0.07) + 200(0.045)}{200 + 200} = 0.0575$$

Then using Equation 9-15 we get:

$$z = \frac{(0.07 - 0.045) - (0)}{\sqrt{0.0575(1 - 0.0575)\left(\dfrac{1}{200} + \dfrac{1}{200}\right)}} = 1.074$$

This means that the difference in the two sample proportions is 1.074 standard errors above zero. Since $1.074 \leq 1.645$, the null hypothesis is not rejected. Thus, based on these sample data, the company has no basis for inferring that the early time slot for calls is superior to the later time. Consequently it will continue making calls throughout the evening rather than concentrating on the 6:00 to 7:00 P.M. slot.

Estimating the Difference Between Two Population Proportions

INTERVAL ESTIMATION

V. C. Elroy Agency

National advertising agencies spend a significant amount of time determining whether proposed advertisements will appeal to different market segments before they are introduced to the public through national media outlets. Recently, the V.C. Elroy Agency in Chicago developed an advertising campaign for a national fast-food chain. Among many issues, the ad managers were interested in determining the difference in the proportion of males versus females that would find the ads appealing.

Obviously, there was no way to gauge the attitudes of the entire populations of men and women who would eventually see or hear the ads. Instead, the Elroy agency commissioned a study in which a random sample of 425 men and 370 women were exposed to the advertising campaign. At the end, they were asked to indicate, with either a yes or no response, whether they "liked" the ads. For each group, the variable x is used to indicate the number in the sample who said "Yes." The results were:

MEN	WOMEN
$n_m = 425$	$n_w = 370$
$x_m = 240$	$x_w = 196$

Based on these sample data, the sample proportions are:

$$p_m = \frac{240}{425} = 0.565 \text{ and } p_w = \frac{196}{370} = 0.530$$

The point estimate for the difference in population proportions is:

$$p_m - p_w = 0.565 - 0.530 = 0.035$$

So, the single best estimate for the difference in the proportion of men versus women who liked the ad campaign is 0.035. However, all point estimates are subject to sampling error. A confidence interval estimate for the difference in population proportions can be developed using Equation 9-16 provided the sample sizes are sufficiently large. A rule of thumb for "sufficiently large" is that, as with hypothesis testing, np and $n(1 - p)$ exceed 5 for both samples. (Note that the standard error for the difference in proportions is computed differently in Equation 9-16 than it was in Equation 9-15. Equation 9-15 for hypothesis testing assumed that there was no difference between the population proportions so we used the pooled estimator. However, in interval estimation, we do not make any assumption about the difference between population proportions. Thus, the pooled estimator is not used and the standard error is computed as shown under the square root sign in Equation 9-16.)

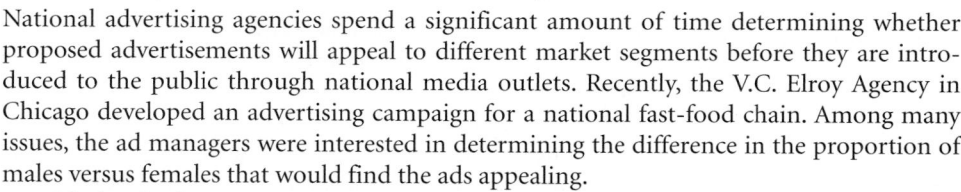

CONFIDENCE INTERVAL ESTIMATE FOR $\pi_1 - \pi_2$

$$(p_1 - p_2) \pm z_{\alpha/2} \sqrt{\frac{p_1(1 - p_1)}{n_1} + \frac{p_2(1 - p_2)}{n_2}}$$

9-16

where:

p_1 = Sample proportion from population 1
p_2 = Sample proportion from population 2
$z_{\alpha/2}$ = Critical value from the standard normal table

The Elroy managers can substitute the sample results into Equation 9-16 to establish a 95% confidence interval estimate as follows.

$$(0.565 - 0.530) \pm 1.96 \sqrt{\frac{0.565(1 - 0.565)}{425} + \frac{0.530(1 - 0.530)}{370}}$$

$$0.035 \pm 0.069$$

$$-0.034 \underline{\qquad\qquad 0.035 \pm 0.069 \qquad\qquad} 0.104$$

Thus, based on the sample data and using a 95% confidence interval, the managers estimate that the true difference in the proportion of males versus females who like the ad campaign is between −0.034 and 0.104. At one extreme 3.4% more females like the ad than males. At the other extreme, 10.4% more males like the ad than females. Since 0 is included in the interval, there may be no difference between males and females based on these data. Based on these sample data, the managers are not able to conclude that one group or the other has a stronger preference for the fast-food ad campaign.

9-3: EXERCISES

ADDITIONAL EXERCISES ON YOUR CD-ROM
Try the ADDITIONAL EXERCISES and APPLICATION PROBLEMS on the CD-ROM.

9-36. Note the following null and alternative hypotheses:

$$H_0: \pi_1 = \pi_2$$
$$H_A: \pi_1 \neq \pi_2$$

and the following sample information:

SAMPLE 1	SAMPLE 2
$n_1 = 100$	$n_2 = 100$
$x_1 = 30$	$x_2 = 34$

Using an $\alpha = 0.05$ and the sample information, what should be concluded with respect to the null and alternative hypotheses? Conduct the hypothesis test using a p-value approach. Be sure to clearly show the decision rule.

9-37. Note the following null and alternative hypotheses:

$$H_0: \pi_1 - \pi_2 = 0.05$$
$$H_0: \pi_1 - \pi_2 \neq 0.05$$

and the following sample information:

SAMPLE 1	SAMPLE 2
$n_1 = 200$	$n_2 = 150$
$x_1 = 87$	$x_2 = 80$

Using an $\alpha = 0.10$ and the sample information, what should be concluded with respect to the null and alternative hypotheses? Be sure to clearly show the decision rule.

9-38. The following information was obtained from samples of two populations:

POPULATION 1	POPULATION 2
$n_1 = 300$	$n_2 = 400$
$x_1 = 88$	$x_2 = 136$

a. Determine if the sample sizes are large enough so that the sampling distribution of the difference between the sample proportions is approximately normally distributed.
b. Calculate and interpret an 80% confidence interval estimate for the difference between the two population proportions.

Business Applications

9-39. Recently a nationwide television network commissioned a polling service to poll homeowners across the United States. Among the issues to be addressed in the survey was whether there is a difference in the proportions of homes that watch a national news broadcast depending on whether the household is headed by two parents or a single parent. The study surveyed 1,200 homes. In 745 of these, the head of household involved two parents. In the others, the household was headed by a single parent. The survey results showed that 62% of the households headed by two parents tuned in a national network news program, whereas 49% of those homes headed by a single parent did so.

  a. Can the distribution of the difference between the sample proportions of households headed by 1 and 2 parents that tune in a national network news program be approximated by a normal distribution? Provide calculations and reasons for your answer.

  b. Based on these data, what could the network conclude overall? State the null and alternative hypotheses and test at a significance level equal to 0.05.

9-40. The United Way Organization raises money for community charity activities. Recently in one community, the fund-raising committee was concerned with whether there is a difference in the proportion of employees who give to United Way, depending on whether the employer is a private business or a government agency. A random sample of people who had been contacted about contributing last year was selected. Of those contacted, 70 worked for a private business and 50 worked for a government agency. Of the 70 private-sector employees, 22 had contributed funds to United Way and 19 of the government employees in the sample had contributed.

  a. Based on these sample data and $\alpha = 0.05$, what should be concluded? Be sure to show the decision rule.

  b. Construct a 95% confidence interval for the difference between the proportion of private business and government agency employees who contribute to United Way. Do the hypothesis test and the confidence interval produce compatible results? Explain and give reasons for your answer.

9-41. Most major airlines allow passengers to carry 2 pieces of luggage (of a certain maximum size) onto the plane. However, their studies show that the more carry-on baggage passengers have, the longer it takes the plane to unload

and load passengers. One regional airline is considering changing its policy to allow only 1 carry-on per passenger. Before doing so, it decided to collect some data. Specifically, a random sample of 1,000 passengers was selected. The passengers were observed and the number of bags each carried onto the plane was counted. The passengers were divided into two groups—those with less than 2 bags and those with 2 or more bags. The sample found that 404 passengers had less than 2 bags. Of these, 181 people responded "yes" to a question about whether the airline should limit the number of bags to 1. Of those in the group with 2 or more bags, 123 indicated "yes" to the question. Using this information, construct and interpret a 95% confidence interval estimate for the difference in proportion of "yes" responses for the two groups. Do you find the results surprising?

9-42. Vintner Mortgage Company in Chicago, Illinois, markets residential and commercial loans to customers in the region. Recently, the company's board of directors asked whether the company had experienced a difference in the proportion of loan defaults between residential and commercial customers. To prepare an answer to this question, company officials selected a random sample of 200 residential loans and 105 commercial loans. The loans were analyzed to determine their status. A loan that is still being paid was labeled "Active" while a default loan was labeled "Default." The resulting data are in a file called **Vintner**.

  a. Based on the sample data and a significance level equal to 0.05, does there appear to be a difference in the proportion of loan defaults between residential and commercial customers?

  b. Prepare a short response to the Vintner board of directors. Include a graph of the data that supports your statistical analysis in your report.

  c. Provide any necessary assumptions or verifications necessary for the validity of the procedure used in part a.

■ SUMMARY AND CONCLUSIONS

The process of using sample information to reach conclusions about the population from which the sample was selected is used extensively in business decision making. This inferential analysis takes on two forms: estimation and hypothesis testing. Chapter 7 introduced the fundamentals of statistical estimation. There we discussed how to formulate and interpret confidence interval estimates for a variety of population values involving one population.

Chapter 8 introduced hypothesis testing where we were interested in a single population value. It presented the basic concepts and discussed the types of statistical errors that can be made when a hypothesis is tested using sample information. In Chapter 9 we have extended the discussion of hypothesis testing and estimation to situations involving two populations. We specifically looked at situations where the difference between two population means was the issue of

concern. In some instances the samples from the two populations are considered independent. In other cases, to control for potential sources of variation, we paired the samples and used a paired-sample test to determine whether the population means were different.

In addition to tests about the difference in population means, Chapter 9 introduced hypothesis testing and estimation for the difference in two population proportions and hypothesis testing for the difference between two population variances. The latter test involved a new distribution referred to as the F-distribution.

Chapter 10, on Analysis of Variance, will extend the hypothesis testing discussion to situations involving multiple populations. With analysis of variance (ANOVA), the F-distribution will again be used to help us determine whether the means from three[7] or more populations are equal.

---

[7]In reality, the ANOVA procedure can also be used to test two means. However, since we have already developed tests for that case, this presentation of ANOVA will examine tests of more than two means.

EQUATIONS

F-Test Statistic for Testing Whether Two Populations Have Equal Variances

$$F = \frac{s_i^2}{s_j^2} \qquad \text{9-1}$$

t-Test Statistic (equal population variances)

$$t = \frac{(\bar{x}_1 - \bar{x}_2) - (\mu_1 - \mu_2)}{s_p\sqrt{\frac{1}{n_1} + \frac{1}{n_2}}}, \, df = n_1 + n_2 - 2 \qquad \text{9-2}$$

Pooled Standard Deviation

$$s_p = \sqrt{\frac{(n_1 - 1)s_1^2 + (n_2 - 1)s_2^2}{n_1 + n_2 - 2}} \qquad \text{9-3}$$

t-Test Statistic (Population Variances Are Not Equal)

$$t = \frac{(\bar{x}_1 - \bar{x}_2) - (\mu_1 - \mu_2)}{\sqrt{\frac{s_1^2}{n_1} + \frac{s_2^2}{n_2}}} \qquad \text{9-4}$$

Degrees of Freedom for t-Test Statistic with Unequal Population Variances

$$\frac{(s_1^2/n_1 + s_2^2/n_2)^2}{\left(\frac{(s_1^2/n_1)^2}{n_1 - 1} + \frac{(s_2^2/n_2)^2}{n_2 - 1}\right)} \qquad \text{9-5}$$

Confidence Interval Estimate for $\mu_1 - \mu_2$—Standard Deviations Unknown and $\sigma_1^2 = \sigma_2^2$

est. diff bet 2 means

$$(\bar{x}_1 - \bar{x}_2) \pm t_{\alpha/2} s_p \sqrt{\frac{1}{n_1} + \frac{1}{n_2}} \qquad \text{9-6}$$

Confidence Interval Estimate for $\mu_1 - \mu_2$—Standard Deviations Unknown and $\sigma_1^2 \neq \sigma_2^2$

$$(\bar{x}_1 - \bar{x}_2) \pm t_{\alpha/2} \sqrt{\frac{s_1^2}{n_1} + \frac{s_2^2}{n_2}} \qquad \text{9-7}$$

Confidence Interval Estimate for $\mu_1 - \mu_2$—Large Sample Sizes (n_1 and $n_2 > 30$)

$$(\bar{x}_1 - \bar{x}_2) \pm z_{\alpha/2} \sqrt{\frac{s_1^2}{n_1} + \frac{s_2^2}{n_2}} \qquad \text{9-8}$$

Paired Difference

$$d = x_1 - x_2 \qquad \text{9-9}$$

Mean Paired Difference

Ho: ud ≤ 1

Ha: $u_d > 1$

$$\bar{d} = \frac{\sum_{i=1}^{n} d_i}{n} \qquad \text{9-10}$$

Standard Deviation for Paired Differences

$$s_d = \sqrt{\frac{\sum_{i=1}^{n}(d_i - \bar{d})^2}{n - 1}} \qquad \text{9-11}$$

t-Test Statistic for Paired Differences

$$t = \frac{\bar{d} - \mu_d}{\frac{s_d}{\sqrt{n}}} \qquad df = n - 1 \qquad \text{9-12}$$

Paired Confidence Interval Estimate

$$\bar{d} \pm t_{\alpha/2} \frac{s_d}{\sqrt{n}} \qquad \text{9-13}$$

Pooled Estimator for Overall Proportion

$$\bar{p} = \frac{n_1 p_1 + n_2 p_2}{n_1 + n_2} = \frac{x_1 + x_2}{n_1 + n_2} \qquad \text{9-14}$$

Test Statistic for Difference in Population Proportions

$$z = \frac{(p_1 - p_2) - (\pi_1 - \pi_2)}{\sqrt{\bar{p}(1 - \bar{p})\left(\frac{1}{n_1} + \frac{1}{n_2}\right)}} \qquad \text{9-15}$$

Confidence Interval Estimate for $\pi_1 - \pi_2$

$$(p_1 - p_2) \pm z_{\alpha/2} \sqrt{\frac{p_1(1 - p_1)}{n_1} + \frac{p_2(1 - p_2)}{n_2}} \qquad \text{9-16}$$

◼ KEY TERMS

Independent Samples—Samples selected from two or more populations in such a way that the occurrence of values in one sample has no influence on the probability of the occurrence of values in the other sample(s).

Paired Samples—Samples that are selected such that each data value from one sample is related (or matched) with a corresponding data value from the second sample. The sample values from one population have the potential to influence the probability that values will be selected from the second population.

CHAPTER EXERCISES

SOLVED PROBLEMS ON YOUR CD-ROM
Try the WORKED-OUT EXERCISES and BUSINESS
APPLICATIONS on the CD-ROM.

Business Applications

9-43. As purchasing agent for the Horner-Williams Company, you have primary responsibility for securing high-quality raw materials at the best possible price. One particular material that the Horner-Williams Company uses a great deal is aluminum. After careful study, you have been able to reduce the prospective vendors to two. You are uncertain whether these two vendors produce aluminum that is equally durable.

To compare durability, the recommended procedure is to put pressure on the aluminum until it cracks. The vendor whose aluminum requires the greater average pressure will be judged to be the one that provides the more durable product.

To carry out this test, 14 pieces of aluminum from vendor 1 and 14 pieces from vendor 2 were selected at random. The following results in pounds per square inch were noted.

VENDOR 1	VENDOR 2
$n_1 = 14$	$n_2 = 14$
$x_1 = 2,345$ psi	$x_2 = 2,411$ psi
$s_1 = 300$	$s_2 = 250$

Before testing the hypothesis about the difference in population means, you were concerned about whether the assumption of equal population variances was satisfied.
   a. Based on the sample data, what would you conclude if you tested at the significance level of 0.10?
   b. Would your conclusion differ if you tested at a significance level of 0.02? Discuss.
   c. What would be the largest significance level that would cause the null hypothesis to be rejected?

9-44. The Campbell Electronics owners have decided to place an advertisement on television to be shown three times during a live broadcast of the local university's football game. They are hoping that their average sales per day will increase so that they will recoup the cost of the advertisements during the 7 days after the football game. The advertisements cost a total of $3,500. The sales for each of the 7 days after the ad was placed are to be compared with the sales for the 7 days immediately prior to running the ad. The following data, representing the total dollar sales each day, were collected.

SALES BEFORE THE AD	SALES AFTER THE AD
$1,765	$2,045
1,543	2,456
2,867	2,590
1,490	1,510
2,800	2,850
1,379	1,255
2,097	2,255

   a. What assumptions must be made about the population distributions in order to test the hypothesis using the t-distribution?
   b. Based on the sample data, what conclusions should be reached with respect to average sales before versus after the advertisement? Use an alpha = 0.05.
   c. Suppose the Campbell Electronics Company wished to verify whether the assumption of equal population variances was satisfied when it performed the two-sample t-test. Based on the sample data, what should the company conclude if the significance level 0.02 is used?

9-45. The Fister Corporation makes ribbons for computer printers. It is currently considering changing from the current model to a new model expected to last just as long, on average, as the current model. However, the new model is thought to be more consistent in terms of how long the individual ribbons will last.

To test this claim, random samples of 21 current-model and 17 new-model ribbons were selected and tested on the company's quality testing equipment. The following results (measured in tens of thousands of characters) were recorded.

CURRENT	NEW
$n = 21$	$n = 17$
$s = 3.45$	$s = 2.87$

Be sure to state clearly the null hypothesis, alternative hypothesis, and decision rule. Test the hypotheses using $\alpha = 0.05$. Also discuss the results.

9-46. The production control manager at Ashmore Manufacturing is interested in determining whether there is a difference in the standard deviation of product diameter for part #XC-343 for units made at the Trenton, New Jersey, plant versus those made at the Atlanta, Georgia, plant. The Trenton plant is highly automated and thought to provide better quality control. Thus, the parts produced there should be less variable than those made in Atlanta.

A random sample of 15 parts was selected from those produced last week at Trenton. The standard deviation for these parts was 0.14 inches. A sample of 13 parts was selected from those made in Atlanta. The sample standard deviation for these parts was 0.202 inches.

    a. Based on these sample data, is there sufficient evidence to conclude that the Trenton plant produces parts that are less variable than those of the Atlanta plant? Test using $\alpha = 0.05$.

    b. Consider the scenario that the Trenton plant is discovered to have a smaller variability than the Atlanta plant. Management, on this basis, decides that they must expend a large amount of money to upgrade the machinery in Atlanta. Suppose also that, in reality, the difference in the observed variability between the two plants is a result of sampling error. Specify the type of error associated with hypothesis testing that was made. How would you modify the hypothesis procedure to guard against such an error?

9-47. Bach Photographs is a photography business with studios in two locations. The owner is interested in monitoring business activity closely at the two locations. Among the factors in which he is interested is whether the variation in customer orders per day for the two locations is the same. A random sample of 11 days' orders for the two locations showed the following data.

LOCATION A			LOCATION B		
$444	$478	$501	$233	$127	$230
200	400	350	299	250	300
167	250	300	800	340	400
300	600		780	370	

    a. Based on the sample data, test the appropriate hypothesis, using an $\alpha = 0.02$ level. Be sure to state the decision rule.

    b. The owner wishes to know the difference between the average amount in customer orders per day for the two locations. He has no idea what this difference might be. What procedure would you suggest under these circumstances? Explain your reasoning.

    c. Using the procedure you selected in part b, discuss the results.

9-48. Hamilton Bank & Trust operates banks throughout Wisconsin. Management is very concerned about making sure that a standard of quality service is achieved. For instance, they are interested in whether there is a difference in standard deviation in service times for customers who use the drive-up window versus those who go inside to the teller windows.

One branch in Madison recently was the subject of evaluation. A sample of 13 drive-through customers was selected and a sample of 9 inside customers was selected. The time (in minutes) it took each customer to be serviced

was recorded. The following statistics were computed from the sample data.

DRIVE-THROUGH	WALK-IN
$\bar{x} = 8.5$	$\bar{x} = 8.0$
$s = 2.0$	$s = 1.2$

    a. Based on a significance level of 0.10, determine the appropriate decision rule for testing the equality of the variances and conduct the test.

    b. Suppose the managers are also interested in testing whether there is a difference in average time it takes to service the two types of customers. State the appropriate null and alternative hypotheses and test using $\alpha = 0.05$. Based upon part a, comment on the validity of this latter test concerning the population means.

9-49. A local restaurant is interested in determining whether the dollar value of lunches ordered by males has greater variability than that for female customers. To conduct the test, random samples of 25 males and 25 females were selected from people who had lunch during the last month. The following statistics were computed from the sample data.

MALES	FEMALES
$\bar{x} = \$12.40$	$\bar{x} = \$8.92$
$s = \$2.50$	$s = \$1.34$

    a. Based on a significance level of 0.05, determine the decision rule and test whether males' lunch costs have greater variability than those for females.

    b. Suppose the manager is also interested in determining whether there is a significant difference in average amount of the lunch between men and women. The managers believe that only a difference of $1.00 or more would be considered important. State the appropriate null and alternative hypotheses and test using $\alpha = 0.05$.

9-50. A book publisher claims that undergraduates are more likely to buy used textbooks than are graduate students. The publisher's marketing department selected two random samples of 200 undergraduate students and 100 graduate students, respectively, at Arizona State University. The students were asked whether they had purchased a used textbook this term. Of the undergraduates, 138 said "yes," while 59 of the graduate students said "yes."

    a. Using a significance level of 0.05, what should the publisher conclude?

    b. Based on the results of this survey, should the publisher extend its conclusions to all undergraduates and graduate students at any university? Discuss.

9-51. A National Collegiate Athletic Association (NCAA) policy requires that athletes progress toward a degree to remain eligible to play varsity sports. One athletic conference is considering defining progress as a situation where at least 75% of the credit hours taken by the student are taken in courses leading toward the declared major at his or her institution.

One of the college officials from this conference complained that this was too strict a requirement. He stated that less than 75% of the credit hours taken by the student body as a whole would be counted toward the declared major for the student taking those credits. To test this, a random sample of 420 individual 3-credit-hour courses taken by students at the university was selected using the computerized transcript file. Each of the 3-credit-hour courses was evaluated to determine whether it would apply toward the degree program for the student involved. In 386 instances the course did apply toward degree requirements.

   a. Based on the sample results, could you conclude that less than 75% of the credit hours taken by the student body as a whole are counted toward the declared major for the student taking those credits? Test at a significance level of 0.05.

   b. Estimate the largest and smallest percentage of the 3-credit-hour courses that would apply toward the degree program for the student involved. Base this on the approximate distribution of the sample proportion.

9-52. Referring to Problem 51, suppose the same college official also claimed that there is no difference between athletes and nonathletes in terms of the proportion of credits taken that apply toward graduation. To test this, two additional samples were selected. First a random sample of 200 courses taken by athletes was selected. Of these, 144 were judged to count towards the degree of the person taking the course. The second sample consisted of 500 courses taken by nonathletes. Of these, 402 were deemed to apply towards graduation requirements of the students involved.

   a. Using a significance level equal to 0.05, what conclusion should be reached about the official's claim regarding athletes and nonathletes?

   b. Combine the findings for Problem 51 and the findings in this problem in a letter to the NCAA.

9-53. In planning for the university graduation, the chairperson based her seat assignments on the assumption that the proportion of undergraduates attending would exceed the proportion of graduate students attending graduation. A member of the graduation committee suggested that before making firm plans, they should survey students to see whether the assumption of the chairperson is correct. A sample of 80 undergraduates showed that 46 planned to attend while a sample of 60 graduate students showed 26 planned to attend.

   a. Based on the sample data, what conclusions should the committee reach concerning the proportion of graduate students and undergraduates that plan to attend the ceremony? Assume they plan to test the hypothesis using a significance level of 0.05. Discuss.

   b. Suppose there are 2,000 undergraduates and 500 graduate students who are eligible to graduate. Determine the number of seats that should be reserved for the graduate and undergraduate students. Explain your answer.

9-54. The First Night Stage Company operates a small nonprofit theater group in Milwaukee, Wisconsin. Each year the company solicits candy sales to help fund its operations. This year, it obtained the help of a marketing research company in the city. This company's representatives proposed two different sales brochures. They are interested in determining whether there is a difference in the standard deviation of funds received between the two brochures. To test this, a random sample of 20 people was selected to receive brochure A and another random sample of 20 people was selected to receive brochure B. The data are contained in file called **First-Night**.

   a. State the appropriate null and alternative hypotheses.

   b. Based on these sample data, what should the First Night Company conclude about the two brochures with respect to their variability? Test using an alpha level = 0.02.

   c. Referring to this hypothesis test, what assumptions are required? Based on these assumptions and your answer to part b, would it be possible to use a two-sample t-test procedure to test if the mean sales amount is different between those receiving brochures A and B? Explain.

9-55. The manager of a local engine repair service is considering mailing out a large number of discount coupons. Two types of coupons would be mailed. The first offers discounts on engine tune-ups. The second offers discounts on brake work. Before doing the mass mailing, a sample of 90 potential customers was selected to receive the tune-up coupon and a sample of 90 potential customers received the brake work coupon. A total of 11 engine tune-up coupons were redeemed and 15 brake work coupons were redeemed. The owner is interested in determining whether this sample information indicates that there will be a difference in the proportion of coupons of the two types that will be redeemed after the mass mailing is done.

   a. Based on the sample data and a significance level equal to 0.05, what conclusion should the owner reach? Conduct the hypothesis test using the p-value approach.

   b. Discuss in terms the shop owner can understand what Type I and Type II errors are as they relate to this situation. Also discuss the relative costs associated with each type of error. Which type of error might have been committed in this case?

9-56. The makers of Hot Mix Chili in Houston, Texas, have a product that, by seasoning standards, is one of the hottest on the market. They have marketed this product under the assumption that there is no difference between regions of the country in their preference for spicy foods. The marketing manager decided that she would test this assumption by taking samples of 280 people in Ohio and 280 people in Arizona and letting them taste Hot Mix Chili and a milder variety offered by a competitor. The people were asked to select which chili they liked better based on the criterion of seasoning. The results showed that 81 from Ohio preferred Hot Mix Chili and 74 from Arizona preferred Hot Mix Chili.

a. Determine if the sample difference of the proportion of people from Arizona and Ohio who prefer Hot Mix Chili can be properly approximated with a normal distribution.

b. Using a significance level of 0.10, what conclusions should the marketing manager reach based on these sample data?

9-57. Last year the city of Bellingham in Selina County, Georgia, undertook a campaign to consolidate the city and county governments. The premise was that proportionately more people in the city would favor the concept than in the outlying county area; this was because the county people might expect a tax increase from the consolidation even though the proponents of the plan promised a tax reduction in the long run. A polling agency was hired to conduct a study of this issue. It randomly selected 100 people in the city and 75 people in the county. It found 62 city dwellers and 36 county dwellers favoring the plan.

Based on the sample results, what should be concluded about the proportions favoring the consolidation when the city residents are compared with the county residents? Use a significance level of 0.10.

9-58. U.S. automakers have been criticized in some circles for poor quality of U.S. cars compared with their foreign competitors. In fact, one trade publication has indicated that the percentage of U.S.-made cars having serious mechanical troubles within 2 years from purchase is greater than that for foreign cars after 5 years from purchase. If this allegation were to be substantiated, it would be a severe blow to the U.S. automakers' efforts to contradict their poor quality image. To test this claim, a random sample of 60 U.S. car owners and another sample of 70 foreign car owners was selected. It found that 12 owners of U.S. cars had severe mechanical problems within the first 2 years and 13 foreign car owners had severe mechanical problems within the first 5 years of ownership.

a. What would a Type I and a Type II error be in this situation? Provide an assessment of the relative costs of each.

b. Based on a significance level of 0.02, what conclusion should be reached? Discuss.

9-59. The Wilcox Company sells breakable china through a mail-order system that has been very profitable. One of its major problems is freight damage. It insures the items at shipping, but the inconvenience to the customer when a piece gets broken can cause the customer to avoid placing another order in the future. Thus, packaging is important to the Wilcox Company.

In the past, the company has purchased two different packaging materials from two suppliers. The assumption was that there would be no difference in proportion of damaged shipments resulting from use of either packaging material. The sales manager recently decided a study of this issue should be done. Therefore, a random sample of 300 orders using shipping material 1 and a random sample of 250 orders using material 2 were pulled from the files. The

number of damaged parcels, x, was recorded for each material as follows.

MATERIAL 1	MATERIAL 2
$n_1 = 300$	$n_2 = 250$
$x_1 = 19$	$x_2 = 12$

a. Is the normal distribution a good approximation for the distribution of the difference between the sample proportions? Provide support for your answer.

b. Based on the sample information and an alpha = 0.03 level, what should the Wilcox Company conclude?

9-60. The makers of a new chemical fertilizer claim that hay yields will average 0.40 tons more per acre if this fertilizer is used than if the leading brand is used. The agricultural testing service at Oregon State University was retained to test this claim. A random sample of 52 acre-sized plots was selected and the new fertilizer was applied. A second sample of 40 acre-sized plots was selected and the leading fertilizer was used. The following sample data (in tons per acre) were observed.

CURRENT LEADING BRAND	NEW PRODUCT
$n_1 = 40$	$n_2 = 52$
$\bar{x}_1 = 4.3$ tons/acre	$\bar{x}_2 = 5.2$ tons/acre
$s_1 = 0.8$ tons	$s_2 = 0.7$ tons

a. If alpha is set at 0.05, what conclusion should be reached with respect to the claim made by the new fertilizer's company? Discuss.

b. Determine the largest significance level at which this test could indicate that the new hay yields would average greater than 0.40 tons per acre more if this fertilizer is used than if the leading brand is used.

9-61. Referring to Problem 60, the issue of yield variability is important. The makers of the new fertilizer claim that its product will result in a lower standard deviation in the tons of product per acre versus the current leading brand. The data collected to test the mean production can also be used to test whether the claim about variability is true.

a. Based upon the sample data and a significance level equal to 0.05, what should be concluded about the variability of the two fertilizers? Discuss.

b. Are any assumptions necessary to validate the hypothesis test you conducted in part a? Explain your response.

9-62. The Fitness Service Company provides financial services for people in Wisconsin and Ohio. Recently at a sales meeting, the statement was made that there is no difference in the average whole life insurance coverage for clients in the two states. The company managers decided to test this claim since the conclusion could affect the sales promotion that was being planned.

To test the claim, a random sample of 65 clients was selected from Wisconsin and another sample of 85 clients was selected from Ohio, with the following sample results:

WISCONSIN	OHIO
$\bar{x} = \$58,740$	$\bar{x} = \$54,900$
$s = \$24,800$	$s = \$27,920$

a. State the appropriate null and alternative hypotheses.

b. Assuming that a significance level equal to 0.05 is used, based on the sample data what should the Fitness Service Company conclude? Conduct the hypothesis test using a p-value approach. Discuss.

9-63. Referring to Problem 62, the Fitness Company is also interested in determining whether there is a difference in the standard deviation in whole life coverage for clients in Wisconsin versus Ohio. If a difference exists in variability, the marketing program can be tailored to reduce that variability.

a. State the appropriate null and alternative hypotheses.

b. Using a significance level of 0.10, what conclusion should the company reach with respect to the standard deviations for clients in Wisconsin and Ohio? Discuss.

9-64. The makers of Bounce Back glass backboards for basketball gymnasiums have claimed that their board is at least as durable, on the average, as the leading backboard made by Swoosh Company. Products Testing Services of Des Moines, Iowa, was hired to verify this claim. It selected a random sample of 50 backboards of each type and subjected the boards to a pressure test to determine how much weight hung from a basketball rim it would take to break the fiberglass backboard. The following results were determined from the testing process.

SWOOSH	BOUNCE BACK
$\bar{x} = 691$ lb	$\bar{x} = 653$ lb
$s = 112$ lb	$s = 105$ lb

a. Assuming that the more pounds needed to break the backboard, the better it is, state the appropriate null and alternative hypotheses.

b. At a significance level of 0.01, what conclusion should be reached with respect to the claim made by the Bounce Back Company? Discuss.

c. Suppose the hypothesis test was conducted at a significance level of 0.10 instead of 0.01. Would this change the conclusion reached based on the sample data? If so, discuss why; if not, discuss why not.

9-65. Referring to Problem 64, suppose the Bounce Back Company also claims that its boards are more consistent than the Swoosh boards in terms of strength. Specifically, the Bounce Back Company claims the standard deviation in weight required to break its boards is less than that for the Swoosh boards.

a. State the appropriate null and alternative hypotheses.

b. Based on the sample data and an alpha of 0.05, what should Products Testing Services conclude about the variability of the two boards? Discuss your results in a letter to the two companies.

9-66. The Barton Family Bakery makes and sells a variety of specialty breads at its 5th Street location. The production scheduler believes that white bread outsells the wheat bread. Specifically, he believes that the average number of white loaves sold per day exceeds the average number of wheat loaves. To test this, a sample of past days' sales was selected. The data are contained in the data file called **Bakery**.

a. State the appropriate null and alternative hypotheses.

b. Based on the sample data, what conclusions should the production manager reach about the sales of white and wheat bread? Test the hypothesis using a significance level of 0.05. Discuss your results in a report that uses appropriate graphs.

9-67. Referring to Problem 66, do the sample data provide evidence to suggest that sales of white bread are more or less variable than sales of wheat bread? State the appropriate null and alternative hypotheses and test using a significance level of 0.10.

9-68. The Capital Bank Marketing Department has recently conducted a study of a sample of the bank's customers. At issue is whether there is a difference between the mean credit card balance between female and male customers. If they find that the two groups differ, they will target the lower group with a marketing campaign designed to increase their use of the credit card. The sample data for this study are in the file called **Capital**.

a. Based on the sample data, what conclusion should the Capital Bank reach about the mean balances for males and females? Test using a significance level of 0.05.

b. Is there reason to believe that the two groups differ with respect to variability of account balance? State the appropriate null and alternative hypotheses and test using $\alpha = 0.02$.

CASE 9-A

Green Valley Assembly Company

The Green Valley Assembly Company assembles consumer electronics products for manufacturers that need temporary extra production capacity. As such, it has periodic product changes. Since the products Green Valley assembles are marketed under the label of well-known manufacturers, high quality is a must.

Tom Bradley of the Green Valley personnel department has been very impressed by recent research concerning job enrichment programs. In particular, he has been impressed with the increases in quality that seem to be associated with these programs. However, some studies have shown no significant increase in quality and imply that the money spent on such programs has not been worthwhile.

Tom has talked to Sandra Hansen, the production manager, about instituting a job enrichment program in the assembly operation at Green Valley. Sandra was somewhat pessimistic about the potential, but she agreed to introduce the program. The plan was to implement the program in one wing of the plant and continue with the current method in the other wing. The procedure was to be in effect for 6 months. Following that period, a test would be made to determine the effectiveness of the job enrichment program.

After the 6-month trial period, a random sample of employees from each wing produced the following output measures.

OLD	JOB-ENRICHED
$n_1 = 50$	$n_2 = 50$
$\bar{x}_1 = 11/\text{hr}$	$\bar{x}_2 = 9.7/\text{hr}$
$s_1 = 1.2/\text{hr}$	$s_2 = 0.9/\text{hr}$

Both Sandra and Tom wonder whether the job enrichment program has affected production output. They would like to use these sample results to determine whether the average output has changed and to determine whether the employees' consistency was affected by the new program.

A second sample from each wing was selected. The measure was the quality of the products assembled. In the "old" wing, 79 products were tested and 12% were found to be defectively assembled. In the "job-enriched" wing, 123 products were examined and 9% were judged defectively assembled.

With all these data, Sandra and Tom are beginning to get a little confused. However they realize that there must be some way to use the information in order to make a judgment about the effectiveness of the job enrichment program.

CASE 9-B

U-Need-It Rental Agency

Richard Fundt has operated the U-Need-It Rental Agency in a northern Wisconsin city for the past 5 years. One of the biggest rental items has always been chainsaws; lately the demand for these saws has increased dramatically. Richard buys chainsaws at a special industrial rate and then rents them for $10 per day. The chainsaws are used an average of 50 to 60 days per year. Although Richard makes money on any chainsaw, he obviously makes more on those saws that last the longest.

Richard worked for a time as a repairperson and can make most repairs on the equipment he rents, including chainsaws. However, he would also like to limit the time he spends making repairs. U-Need-It is presently stocking two types of saws—North Woods and Accu-Cut. Richard has an impression that one of the models, Accu-Cut, does not seem to break down as much as the other. Richard presently has 8 North Woods saws and 11 Accu-Cut saws. He decides to keep

track of the number of hours each is used between major repairs. He finds the following values.

ACCU-CUT (HOURS BEFORE BREAKDOWN)		NORTH WOODS (HOURS BEFORE BREAKDOWN)	
48 hr	46 hr	48 hr	78 hr
39	88	44	94
84	29	72	59
76	52	19	52
41	57		
24			

The North Woods sales representative has stated that the company may be raising the price of its saws in the near future. This will make them slightly more expensive than the Accu-Cut models. However, the prices have tended to move with each other in the past.

CASE 9-C

Wilson Bearing Company

The Wilson Bearing Company in Nashville, Tennessee, has a contract with one of the major appliance manufacturers to make a gear unit for clothes dryers. One of the parts that is needed to make the gear units will be purchased from another supplier. There are two prime candidates to be the supplier, and Wilson plans to purchase the parts from the one that has the less variability.

The product specifications require that the average diameter of the part be 3.5 inches with a standard deviation not to exceed 0.10 inches. Both suppliers claim they can meet these specifications. To verify this, Wilson's purchasing man-

ager, Cynthia Alley, traveled to supplier A's plant and was allowed to select a random sample of 20 parts. She measured these with a very precise caliper device. She then traveled to supplier B's location and did the same thing. The resulting data are in the file called **Wilson**.

Cynthia has a meeting scheduled for a week from Tuesday at which time she must make recommendations concerning the two suppliers. She plans to prepare a comprehensive report that addresses the capabilities of the two suppliers to meet Wilson's requirements and to determine whether differences exist between the two suppliers.

■ GENERAL REFERENCES

1. Berenson, Mark L., and David M. Levine, *Basic Business Statistics: Concepts and Applications*, 7th ed. (Upper Saddle River, NJ: Prentice Hall, 1999).
2. Cryer, Jonathan D., and Robert B. Miller, *Statistics for Business: Data Analysis and Modeling*, 2d ed. (Belmont, CA: Duxbury Press, 1994).
3. Johnson, Richard A., and Dean W. Wichern, *Business Statistics: Decision Making with Data* (New York: John Wiley & Sons, 1997).
4. Larsen, Richard J., Morris L. Marx, and Bruce Cooil, *Statistics for Applied Problem Solving and Decision Making* (Pacific Grove, CA: Duxbury Press, 1997).
5. *Microsoft Excel 2000* (Redmond, WA: Microsoft Corporation, 1999).
6. Siegel, Andrew F., *Practical Business Statistics*, 4th ed. (Burr Ridge, IL: Irwin, 2000).

ANALYSIS OF VARIANCE

CHAPTER OUTCOMES

After studying the material in Chapter 10, you should be able to:

10-1: Recognize applications that call for the use of analysis of variance.

10-2: Understand the basic logic of analysis of variance.

10-3: Be aware of several different analysis of variance designs and understand when to use each one.

10-4: Perform a single factor hypothesis test using analysis of variance manually and with the aid of Excel or Minitab software.

10-5: Conduct and interpret post-analysis of variance pairwise comparisons procedures.

10-6: Recognize when randomized block analysis of variance is useful and be able to perform the randomized block analysis.

10-7: Perform two factor analysis of variance tests with replications using Excel or Minitab and interpret the output.

WHY YOU NEED TO KNOW

Chapters 8 and 9 introduced the basics of hypothesis testing. By now you should understand that, regardless of the population parameter in question, the hypothesis testing steps are basically the same.

1. Formulate the null and alternative hypotheses.
2. Determine the level of significance.
3. Determine the critical value of the test statistic.
4. Select the sample and compute the test statistic.
5. Reject the null hypothesis, H_0, if the sample statistic falls in the rejection region; otherwise, do not reject the null hypothesis. If the test is conducted using the p-value approach, H_0 is rejected whenever the p-value is smaller than the significance level; otherwise H_0 is not rejected.

Chapter 8 focused on hypothesis tests involving a single population. Chapter 9 expanded the hypothesis testing process to include applications where differences between two populations are involved. However, you will encounter many instances where there is a need to work with more than two populations. For example, the vice president of operations at Farber Rubber, Inc., oversees production at Farber's six different U.S. manufacturing plants. Since each plant uses slightly different manufacturing processes, the vice president

needs to know if there is any difference in average strength of the products produced at the different plants.

Similarly, *Golf Digest*, a major publisher of articles devoted to golf, might wish to determine which of five major brands of golf balls have the longest mean distance off the tee. The Environmental Protection Agency (EPA) might conduct a test to determine if there is a difference in the average miles per gallon performance of cars manufactured by the big three U.S. automobile producers. In each of these cases, there is a need to test a hypothesis involving more than two population means.

This chapter introduces a tool called analysis of variance (ANOVA) which can be used to test whether there are differences among three or more population means. There are several ANOVA procedures depending on the type of test that is being conducted. Our aim in this chapter is to introduce you to the basics of ANOVA and to illustrate how to use Microsoft Excel or Minitab to help conduct hypothesis tests involving three or more population means. You will almost certainly need either to apply ANOVA in future decision-making situations or to interpret the results of an ANOVA study performed by someone else. Thus, you need to be familiar with this powerful statistical tool.

■ 10-1: ONE-WAY ANALYSIS OF VARIANCE

In Chapter 9 we introduced the t-test for testing whether two populations have the same mean when the samples from the two populations are independent. However, you will often encounter situations in which you are interested in determining whether three or more populations have equal means. To conduct this test, you will need a new tool called *analysis of variance (ANOVA)*. There are many different analysis of variance designs to fit different situations. The simplest ANOVA design is called **one-way analysis of variance**.

> **ONE-WAY ANALYSIS OF VARIANCE**
> An analysis of variance design in which independent samples are obtained from k levels of a single factor for the purpose of testing whether the k levels have equal means.

The Logic Behind One-Way ANOVA

Bayhill Marketing Company

EXAMPLE 10-1

ANOVA

The Bayhill Marketing Company is a full-service marketing and advertising firm located in San Francisco, California. While Bayhill provides many different marketing services, one of its most lucrative is coupon design. Companies that wish to increase sales often mail coupons to potential customers in their market areas. These companies hope the coupons will be redeemed and overall sales will increase. Bayhill's account managers help the company design the coupon for maximum effectiveness. The problem is that some coupon designs tend to be more effective than others.

For example, a major greeting card company that wants to develop a coupon offer for their "Special Events" card set has recently retained Bayhill. The card company negotiated a deal with the American Express credit card company to include its coupon in every American Express cardholder's monthly statement. Now a decision must be made concerning what the coupon should provide and how the coupon should be designed for maximum effectiveness. Coupon effectiveness can be determined by the percentage of coupons that are redeemed or by the dollar value of the greeting card sets purchased when a coupon is redeemed.

Bayhill's design staff originally came up with nine different designs. Through a series of meetings with the client and focus group sessions with potential customers, the list of coupon designs was reduced to four. Bayhill has arranged with American Express to do a test on these designs by sending out 200 of each coupon type to randomly selected cardholders. The purpose of this test will be to focus on the dollar value of card sets purchased when a coupon is actually redeemed. Bayhill will select a random sample from those coupons that were redeemed and determine the dollar value of greeting card sets that were purchased with each coupon. Table 10-1 shows the data that were collected for a sample of eight redemptions from each design. The values in the table are the dollar value of greeting card sets that were ordered by each customer.

In the Bayhill Marketing Company example, we are interested in determining whether the different coupon designs result in the same average order size. In other words, we are trying to determine if "coupon designs" are a possible cause of the variation we are seeing in the dollar value of the card sets ordered (the response variable). In this case, coupon design is called a **factor**.

Since we are interested only in comparing the coupon designs, the *single factor* of interest is coupon design. This factor has four categories, measurements, or strata called **levels**.

FACTOR	LEVELS
A quantity under examination in an experiment as a possible cause of variation in the response variable.	The categories, measurements, or strata of a factor of interest in the current experiment.

In our current experiment, the factor, coupon design, has four levels—designs #1, #2, #3, and #4. Since we are using only one factor here, each dollar value of card sets ordered is associated with only one level (i.e., coupon design type #1, #2, #3, or #4) as you can see in Table 10-1. Each level characterizes a population of interest.

We are interested in testing whether the four coupon designs yield the same mean dollar sales. That is, we want to determine if coupon design is a possible cause of the variation in the response variable, dollar sales.

TABLE 10-1
Bayhill Marketing Company
Coupon Order Data

Customer	COUPON DESIGN #1	#2	#3	#4	
1	$ 4.10	$ 6.90	$ 4.60	$12.50	
2	5.90	9.10	11.40	7.50	
3	10.45	13.00	6.15	6.25	
4	11.55	7.90	7.85	8.75	
5	5.25	9.10	4.30	11.15	
6	7.75	13.40	8.70	10.25	
7	4.78	7.60	10.20	6.40	
8	6.22	5.00	10.80	9.20	
					Grand Mean
Mean	$ 7.00	$ 9.00	$ 8.00	$ 9.00	$ 8.25
Variance	7.341	8.423	7.632	5.016	

Note: Data are dollar value of card sets ordered.

The null and alternative hypotheses to be tested are:

$$H_0: \mu_1 = \mu_2 = \mu_3 = \mu_4$$
$$H_A: \text{At least two population means are different}$$

The experimental design used to produce the data for this experiment is called a **completely randomized experiment.**

COMPLETELY RANDOMIZED DESIGN

An experiment is completely randomized if it consists of the independent random selection of observations representing each level of one factor.

The appropriate statistical tool for conducting the hypothesis test related to this experiment design is called analysis of variance (ANOVA). Since this ANOVA addresses an experiment with only one factor, it is termed a one-way ANOVA or one-factor ANOVA. Because the sample size for each coupon design (level) was the same, the experiment is said to have a **balanced design.**

BALANCED DESIGN

An experiment has a balanced design if the factor levels have equal sample sizes.

Analysis of variance is used to test the null hypothesis that three or more populations have the same mean. The ANOVA test is based on three assumptions:

1. All populations are normally distributed.
2. The population variances are equal.
3. The observations are independent, meaning that any one individual value is not dependent on the value of any other observation.

Then if the null hypothesis is true, the populations have identical distributions. If so, the sample means for random samples from each population should be close in value. The basic logic of ANOVA is the same as the two-sample t-test introduced in Chapter 9—the null hypothesis should be rejected only if the sample means are substantially different.

However, you may be surprised to learn that the hypothesis test for equality of the population means is in fact an F-test involving two variances. To show you what we mean, consider that in Chapter 6 we showed that the distribution of sample means for a sample of size n taken from a normally distributed population has a standard deviation, $\sigma_{\bar{x}} = \dfrac{\sigma}{\sqrt{n}}$. From this, the variance of the $\bar{x}$ values is $\sigma_{\bar{x}}^2 = \dfrac{\sigma^2}{n}$. Figure 10-1 illustrates what the sampling distribution of $\bar{x}$ values would look like. If the null hypothesis is true, the sample means from each population can be thought of as values coming from the sampling distribution in Figure 10-1. The average value of the sample means would be an estimate for μ, the mean of the sampling distribution. Likewise, the variation in the sample means would be the estimate for the variance of the sampling distribution, $\sigma_{\bar{x}}^2$.

If, as assumed, the populations have the same variance, σ^2, we can solve for σ^2 as:

$$n\sigma_{\bar{x}}^2 = \sigma^2$$

where n is the common sample size from each population. Consider the data in Table 10-1. The sample means are shown for samples of size 8. Also shown is the average of the sample means equal to 8.25. Then the estimate for $\sigma_{\bar{x}}^2$ is:

$$s_{\bar{x}}^2 = \frac{(7 - 8.25)^2 + (9 - 8.25)^2 + (8 - 8.25)^2 + (9 - 8.25)^2}{4 - 1} = 0.91667$$

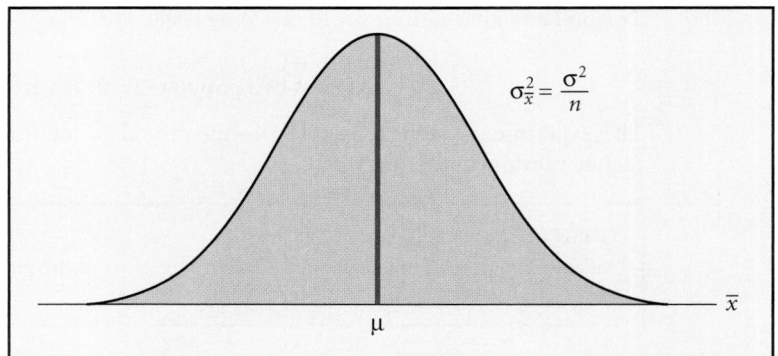

FIGURE 10-1
Sampling Distribution of $\bar{x}$

It follows that an estimate of σ^2 is $n(s_{\bar{x}}^2) = 8(0.91667) = 7.333$. This value is referred to as the *between levels (or treatments) estimate of σ^2* and is based on the premise that the null hypothesis is true and the means of the respective populations are equal.

Another approach to estimating the common variance, σ^2, is to use a pooled estimate. Since we assume that all k populations have the same variance, the average of the population variances is equal to the common population variance:

$$\sigma^2 = \frac{\sigma_1^2 + \sigma_2^2 + \cdots + \sigma_k^2}{k} = \frac{\sigma^2 + \sigma^2 + \cdots + \sigma^2}{k} = \frac{k\sigma^2}{k}$$

However, each population variance is a measure of the variation within that specific population and is not dependent on whether the means of the populations are equal. Thus, given equal sample sizes from each population the *within levels estimate of σ^2* is:

$$s^2 = \frac{s_1^2 + s_2^2 + \cdots + s_k^2}{k}$$

Based on the data in Table 10-1 for the Bayhill Marketing Company, the within levels estimate for σ^2 is:

$$s^2 = \frac{7.341 + 8.423 + 7.632 + 5.016}{4} = 7.103$$

Now, we have two estimates for the same population variance. The two estimates should have approximately the same value if the null hypothesis of equal means is true. However, if the populations have unequal means, the *between levels estimate* for σ^2 will be greater than the *within levels estimate* since the sample means will tend to differ substantially from one another. This is illustrated in Figure 10-2.

Thus, to test whether the population means are equal, we actually compare these two variance estimates. As we learned in Chapter 9, the *F*-distribution is used to test whether two variances are equal. As we will illustrate shortly, in ANOVA, the *F*-ratio is formed by taking the ratio of the between level estimate over the within level estimate. If this *F*-ratio gets too large, the null hypothesis of equal means is rejected.

PARTITIONING THE SUM OF SQUARES

Refer again to the sample data in Table 10-1. In order to understand the logic of ANOVA, you should take note of several things about the data in Table 10-1. First, the dollar values of the orders are different throughout the data table. Some values are higher; others are lower. Thus, variation exists across all customer orders. This variation is called the **total variation** in the data.

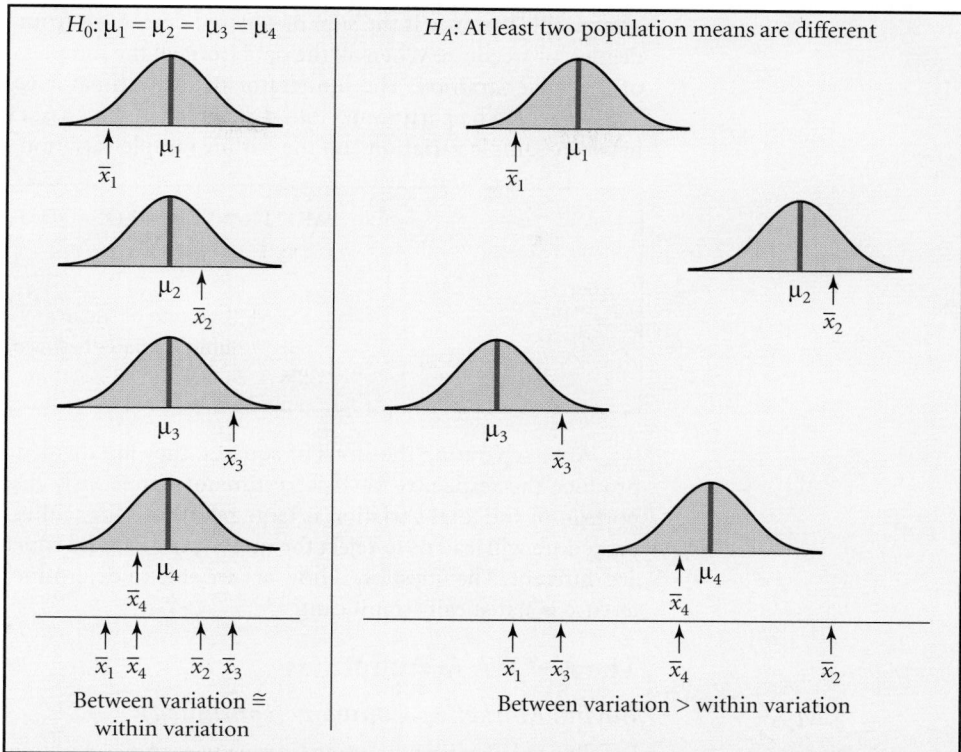

FIGURE 10-2
Variation in Sample Means

TOTAL VARIATION

The aggregate dispersion of the individual data values across the various factor levels is called the *total variation* in the data.

Next, within any particular coupon design (i.e., factor levels), not all customers ordered the same dollar value of greeting card sets. For instance, within level #1, order size ranged from $4.10 to $11.55. Similar differences occur within the other levels. The variation within each factor level is called the **within-sample variation**.

Finally, the sample means for the four coupon designs are not all equal. Thus, variation exists between the four designs' averages. This variation between the factor levels is referred to as the **between-sample variation**.

WITHIN-SAMPLE VARIATION

The dispersion that exists among the data values within a particular factor level is called the *within-sample variation*.

BETWEEN-SAMPLE VARIATION

Dispersion among the factor sample means is called the *between-sample variation*.

Recall that the sample variance is computed as:

$$s^2 = \frac{\sum_{i=1}^{n} (x_i - \bar{x})^2}{n - 1}$$

The sample variance is the sum of squared deviations from the sample mean divided by its degrees of freedom. When all the data from all the samples are included, s^2 is the estimator of the *total variation*. The numerator of this estimator is called the *total sum of squares* (TSS) and can be partitioned into the sum of squares associated with the estimators of the between-sample variation and the within-sample variation as shown in Equation 10-1.

PARTITIONED SUM OF SQUARES

$$TSS = SSB + SSW$$ **10-1**

where:

TSS = Total sum of squares
SSB = Sum of squares between
SSW = Sum of squares within

After separating the sums of squares, they are divided by their degrees of freedom to produce the respective variance estimators previously discussed. If the between-sample portion of the total variation is large relative to the within-sample variation, the ANOVA procedure will lead us to reject the null hypothesis and conclude that the population means are different. The question is how are we able to determine at what point we state any difference is statistically significant?

The ANOVA Assumptions

EXAMPLE 10-2

ANOVA

Bayhill Marketing Company (continued)

Recall in the Bayhill Marketing Company example, we are interested in testing whether the four coupon designs provide equal average dollars in orders. The following null and alternative hypotheses were given:

$$H_0: \mu_1 = \mu_2 = \mu_3 = \mu_4$$
$$H_A: \text{At least two population means are different}$$

Before we move into the ANOVA calculations, recall the three assumptions of ANOVA:

1. All populations are normally distributed.
2. The population variances are equal.
3. The sampled observations are independent.

Figure 10-3 demonstrates the first two assumptions. The populations are normally distributed and the spread (variance) is the same for each population. But in this case, the populations have different means—and the null hypothesis is false. Figure 10-4 demonstrates the same assumptions but in a case where the population means are equal—the null hypothesis is true.

You can do a rough check to determine whether the first two assumptions are satisfied by developing histograms for the sample data from each population. If the histograms appear bell shaped and if the spread is roughly the same for each, then there is evidence to suggest that the assumptions are satisfied. However, if the samples are small (as in the Bayhill Marketing Company example), the histogram approach may not be meaningful and more sophisticated approaches are needed.[1]

In Chapter 9 you learned how to test whether two populations have equal variances using the F-test. Similarly, we can hypothesize that all the population variances are equal.

$$H_0: \sigma_1^2 = \sigma_2^2 = \ldots = \sigma_k^2$$
$$H_A: \text{Not all variances are equal}$$

---

[1]Chapter 14 introduces a goodness-of-fit approach for testing whether sample data come from a normally distributed population.

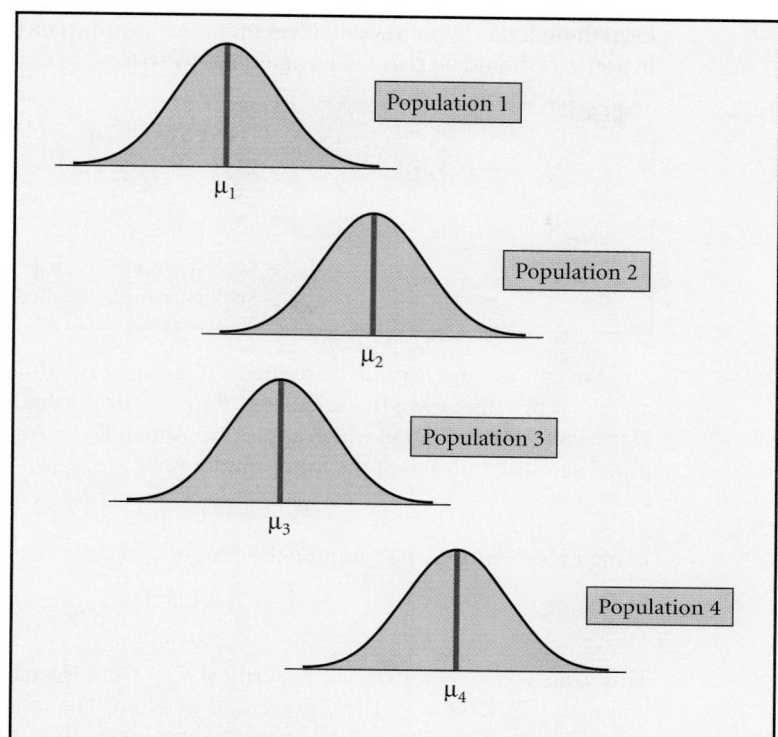

FIGURE 10-3
Normal Populations with
Equal Variances and Unequal
Means

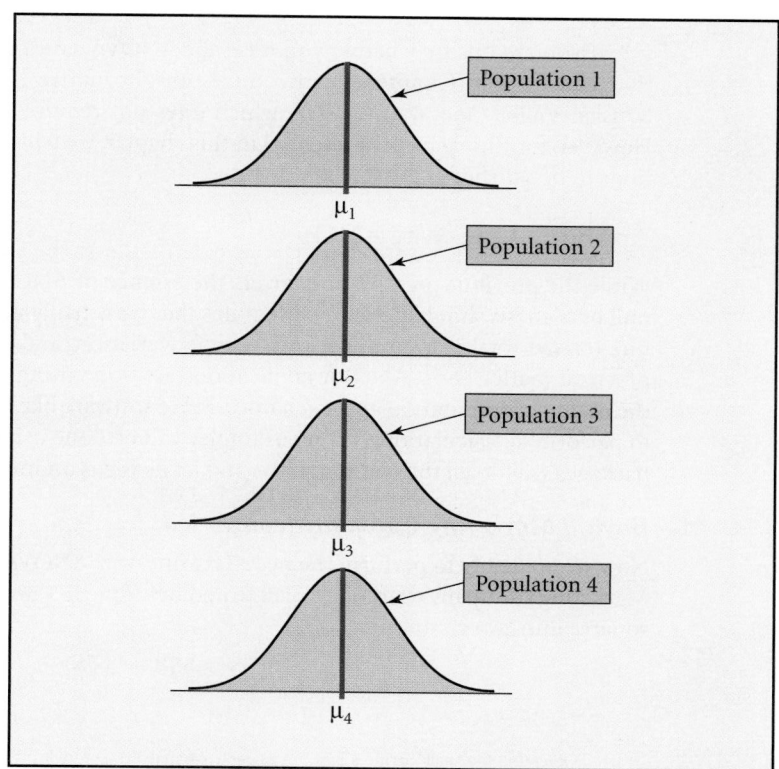

FIGURE 10-4
Normal Populations with
Equal Variances and Means

Even though this hypothesis involves more than two variances, we can test whether the null hypothesis should be rejected using Equation 10-2.

F-TEST STATISTIC

$$F = \frac{s_{max}^2}{s_{min}^2}$$

10-2

where:

$s_{max}^2 = $ Largest sample variance
$s_{min}^2 = $ Smallest sample variance

We can use the F-value computed using Equation 10-2 to test whether the variances are equal by comparing the calculated F to a critical value from a distribution known as *Hartley's F_{max} distribution* which appears in Appendix I.[2] For the Bayhill example, the computed variance for each of the four samples is:

$$s_1^2 = 7.341 \qquad s_2^2 = 8.423 \qquad s_3^3 = 7.632 \qquad s_4^2 = 5.016$$

Using Equation 10-2, we compute the F-value as:

$$F = \frac{8.423}{5.016} = 1.679$$

This value is now compared to the critical F_{max} from the table in Appendix I for $\alpha = 0.05$ and with $k = 4$ and $\bar{n} - 1 = 7$ degrees of freedom. The value, k, is the number of populations ($k = 4$). The value $\bar{n}$ is the average sample size ($\bar{n} = 8$). If $\bar{n}$ is not an integer value, then set $\bar{n}$ as the integer portion of the computed $\bar{n}$. If $F > F_{max}$, reject the null hypothesis of equal variances. If $F \leq F_{max}$, do not reject. From the Hartley's F-distribution table, the critical $F = 8.44$. Since $F = 1.679 \leq 8.44$, the null hypothesis of equal variances is not rejected.[3]

If you are unsure whether you meet the ANOVA assumptions or if your tests indicate that you do not, Chapter 15 introduces an alternative ANOVA procedure called the Kruskal-Wallis One-Way ANOVA which does not require these restrictive assumptions. However, for the examples presented in this chapter, we will consider the ANOVA assumptions to be satisfied.

Applying One-Way ANOVA

While the previous presentation covers the essence of ANOVA, to determine whether the null hypothesis should be rejected requires that we actually determine values of the estimators for the total variation, between-sample variation, and within-sample variation. As a practical matter, most ANOVA applications are done using a computer. We will illustrate the manual computation approach once. Since software like Excel and Minitab can be used to perform all calculations, future examples will be done using the computer. The software packages will do all the computations and let us focus on interpreting the results.

Bayhill Marketing Company (continued)

Now we are ready to perform the necessary one-way ANOVA computations for the Bayhill Marketing Company example. Recall from Equation 10-1, we can partition the total sum of squares into two components.

$$TSS = SSB + SSW$$

EXAMPLE

10-3

ANOVA

---

[2]Other tests for equal variances exist. For example, Minitab has a procedure that uses Bartlett and Levine's test.
[3]Hartley's F_{max} test is very dependent on the populations being normally distributed and should not be used if the populations' distributions are skewed.

The **total sum of squares** is computed as shown in Equation 10-3.

TOTAL SUM OF SQUARES

where:

$$TSS = \sum_{i=1}^{k} \sum_{j=1}^{n_i} (x_{ij} - \bar{\bar{x}})^2$$ **10-3**

TSS = Total sum of squares
k = Number of populations (levels)
n_i = Sample size from population i
x_{ij} = jth measurement from population i
$\bar{\bar{x}}$ = Grand mean (mean of all the data values)

Equation 10-3 is not as complicated as it appears. Manually applying Equation 10-3 to the Bayhill Marketing Company data shown again in Table 10-2 (Grand Mean = $\bar{\bar{x}}$ = 8.25) we compute TSS as follows.

$$TSS = (4.10 - 8.25)^2 + (5.90 - 8.25)^2 + (10.45 - 8.25)^2 + \ldots + (9.20 - 8.25)^2$$
$$TSS = 220.88$$

Thus, the sum of the squared deviations of all values from the grand mean is 220.88. Equation 10-3 can also be restated as:

$$TSS = \sum_{i=1}^{k} \sum_{j=1}^{n_i} (x_{ij} - \bar{\bar{x}})^2 = (N-1)s^2$$

where s^2 is the sample variance for all data combined and N is the sum of the combined sample sizes.

We now need to determine how much of this total sum of squares is due to between-sample sum of squares and how much is due to within-sample sum of squares. The between-sample portion is called the **sum of squares between** and is found using Equation 10-4.

SUM OF SQUARES BETWEEN

where:

$$SSB = \sum_{i=1}^{k} n_i(\bar{x}_i - \bar{\bar{x}})^2$$ **10-4**

SSB = Sum of squares between samples
k = Number of populations
n_i = Sample size from population i
$\bar{x}_i$ = Sample mean from population i
$\bar{\bar{x}}$ = Grand mean

TABLE 10-2
Bayhill Marketing Company
Coupon Order Data

Customer	COUPON DESIGN #1	#2	#3	#4	
1	$ 4.10	$ 6.90	$ 4.60	$12.50	
2	5.90	9.10	11.40	7.50	
3	10.45	13.00	6.15	6.25	
4	11.55	7.90	7.85	8.75	
5	5.25	9.10	4.30	11.15	
6	7.75	13.40	8.70	10.25	
7	4.78	7.60	10.20	6.40	
8	6.22	5.00	10.80	9.20	
					Grand Mean
Mean	$ 7.00	$ 9.00	$ 8.00	$ 9.00	$ 8.25
Variance	7.341	8.423	7.632	5.016	

Note: Data are dollar value of card sets ordered.

We can use Equation 10-4 to manually compute the sum of squares between for the Bayhill Marketing Company data in Table 10-2 as follows.

$$SSB = 8(7 - 8.25)^2 + 8(9 - 8.25)^2 + 8(8 - 8.25)^2 + 8(9 - 8.25)^2$$
$$SSB = 22$$

Once both the TSS and SSB have been computed, the **sum of squares within** (also called the sum of squares error—SSE) is easily computed using Equation 10-5. The sum of squares within can also be computed directly using Equation 10-6.

SUM OF SQUARES WITHIN

$$SSW = TSS - SSB \qquad \text{10-5}$$

or

$$SSW = \sum_{i=1}^{k} \sum_{j=1}^{n_i} (x_{ij} - \bar{x}_i)^2 \qquad \text{10-6}$$

where:

SSW = Sum of squares within samples
k = Number of populations
n_i = Sample size from population i
$\bar{x}_i$ = Sample mean from population i
x_{ij} = jth measurement from population i

For the Bayhill Marketing Company example, the SSW is:

$$SSW = 220.88 - 22$$
$$= 198.88$$

These computations are the essential first steps in performing the analysis of variance test to determine whether the population means are equal. The test is commonly performed by completing the standard format ANOVA table shown in Table 10-3. The ANOVA table contains columns for the source of variation (between and within), the sum of squares (SS), and degrees of freedom (df). The Mean Square (MS) column contains the MSB (mean square between-samples) and the MSW (mean square within-samples).[4] These values are computed by dividing the sums of squares by their respective degrees of freedom. They are actually the estimates of the respective variances that we mentioned earlier.

For the Bayhill Marketing Company example, we substitute the numerical values for SSB, SSW, and TSS, and complete the ANOVA table as shown in Table 10-4.

TABLE 10-3
One-Way ANOVA Table: The Basic Format

SOURCE OF VARIATION	SS	df	MS	F-RATIO
Between Samples	SSB	$k - 1$	MSB	$\dfrac{MSB}{MSW}$
Within Samples	SSW	$N - k$	MSW	
Total	TSS	$N - 1$		

where:

k = Number of populations
N = Sum of the sample sizes from all populations
df = Degrees of freedom
MSB = Mean square between = $\dfrac{SSB}{k - 1}$
MSW = Mean square within = $\dfrac{SSW}{N - k}$

---

[4]MSW is also known as the Mean Square for Error—MSE.

SOURCE OF VARIATION	SS	df	MS	F-RATIO
Between Samples	22	3	7.3333	$\dfrac{7.3333}{7.10286} = 1.03244$
Within Samples	198.88	28	7.10286	
Total	220.88	31		

where:

$$MSB = \text{Mean square between} = \frac{SSB}{k-1} = \frac{22}{3} = 7.3333$$

$$MSW = \text{Mean square within} = \frac{SSW}{N-k} = \frac{198.88}{28} = 7.10286$$

TABLE 10-4
One-Way ANOVA Table for
Bayhill Marketing

Restate the null and alternative hypotheses for the Bayhill Marketing Company example:

$$H_0: \mu_1 = \mu_2 = \mu_3 = \mu_4$$
$$H_A: \text{At least two population means are different}$$

Glance back at Figures 10-3 and 10-4. If the null hypothesis is true (that is, all the means are equal , Figure 10-4), MSW and MSB will be equal except for the presence of sampling error. However, the more the sample means differ (Figure 10-3), the larger the MSB becomes relative to MSW. As the MSB increases, it will tend to get larger than the MSW. When this difference gets too large, we will conclude that the population means must not be equal and the null hypothesis will be rejected. But how do we determine what "too large" is? How do we know when the difference is due to more than just sampling error?

To answer these questions, recall from Chapter 9 and Section 10-1's development "The Logic Behind One-Way ANOVA" that the F-distribution is used to test whether two populations have the same variance. In the ANOVA test, if the null hypothesis is true, the ratio of MSB over MSW forms an F-distribution with $D_1 = k - 1$ and $D_2 = N - k$ degrees of freedom. If the calculated F-ratio in Table 10-4 gets too large, the null hypothesis is rejected.

Figure 10-5 illustrates the hypothesis test for a significance level of 0.05. Since the calculated F-ratio $= 1.03244$ is less than the critical $F = 2.95$ from the F-table with 3 and 28 degrees of freedom, the null hypothesis cannot be rejected. The F-ratio indicates that the *between levels estimate* and the *within levels estimate* are not different enough to conclude that the population means are significantly different. Thus, there is insufficient statistical evidence to conclude that any one of the four coupon designs will generate higher average dollar values of the orders than any of the other three designs. Therefore, the choice of which of these four coupon designs to use can be based on other factors such as printing cost.

Hydronics Corporation

10-4

ANOVA

Excel and
Minitab Tutorial

The Hydronics Corporation makes and distributes health aid products. Currently the company's research department is experimenting with two new weight loss enhancing products that are herb based. To determine whether the products are effective, researchers at the company conducted a test using 300 human subjects over a 6-week period. All people in the study were determined to be between 30 and 40 pounds overweight.

One third of the people were randomly selected to receive a placebo that contained only vitamin C. One third of the people were randomly selected and given product #1. The remaining 100 people received product #2. None of the people knew which pill they had been assigned. Each person was asked to take the pill regularly for 6 weeks and to do everything else according to his or her normal routine. At the end of 6 weeks, the subjects were weighed and the amount of weight loss was recorded. The company is hoping to find statistical evidence that at least one of the products is an effective weight loss aid.

FIGURE 10-5
Bayhill Marketing Hypothesis Test

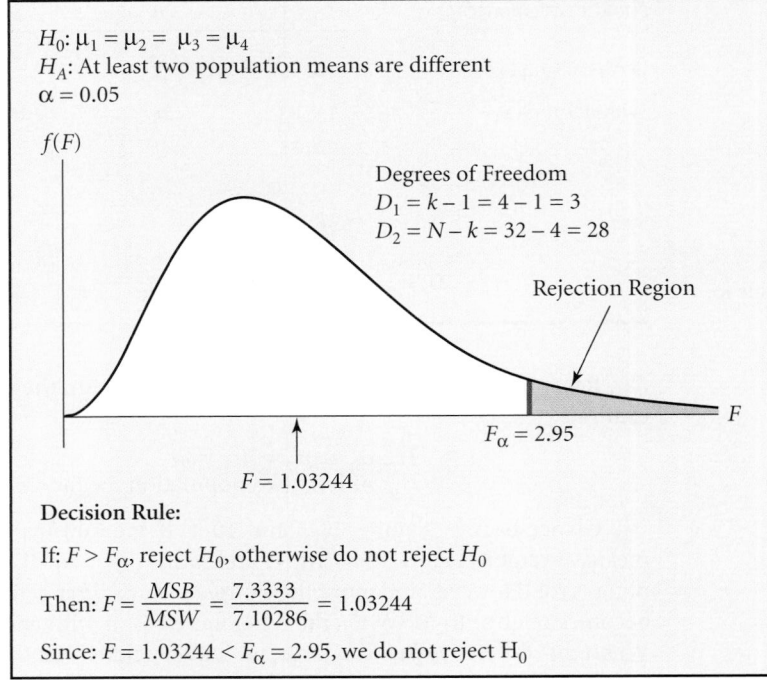

$H_0: \mu_1 = \mu_2 = \mu_3 = \mu_4$
H_A: At least two population means are different
$\alpha = 0.05$

$f(F)$

Degrees of Freedom
$D_1 = k - 1 = 4 - 1 = 3$
$D_2 = N - k = 32 - 4 = 28$

Rejection Region

$F_\alpha = 2.95$

F

$F = 1.03244$

Decision Rule:

If: $F > F_\alpha$, reject H_0, otherwise do not reject H_0

Then: $F = \dfrac{MSB}{MSW} = \dfrac{7.3333}{7.10286} = 1.03244$

Since: $F = 1.03244 < F_\alpha = 2.95$, we do not reject H_0

Figure 10-6 shows a partial listing of the data in the Excel worksheet format. Positive values indicate that the subject lost weight (in pounds), while negative values indicate the subject actually gained weight during the 6-week study period. As often happens in studies involving human subjects, people drop out for one reason or another. Thus, at the end of six weeks, 89 placebo subjects, 91 product #1 subjects, and 83 product #2 subjects were available with valid data. So, this experiment resulted in an unbalanced design (one-way ANOVA can be applied to both balanced and unbalanced designs). These data are included on the CD-ROM that accompanies this text. The file name is **Hydronics.**

The null and alternative hypotheses to be tested using a significance level of 0.05 are:

$$H_0: \mu_1 = \mu_2 = \mu_3$$
$$H_A: \text{At least two population means are different}$$

The experimental design is set up as a completely randomized design. The factor is diet supplement. This factor has three levels: placebo, product #1, and product #2. Figure 10-7

FIGURE 10-6
Excel Worksheet for the Hydronics Corp. Diet Pill Study

Excel Instructions:

1. Open file: Hydronics.xls

	A	B	C	D	E
1	Subject	Placebo	Product # 1	Product # 2	
2	1	-3.1	2.8	5.6	
3	2	-7.9	1.2	5.5	
4	3	-0.3	3.6	6.2	
5	4	4.8	-15.5	9.1	
6	5	4.4	-2.7	-2.3	
7	6	7.1	0.2	4.3	
8	7	-12.5	3.7	-1.9	
9	8	-2.7	-5.9	5.1	
10	9	3.9	-1	-6.6	
11	10	-7	13.7	-3.9	
12	11	.5	0.0	1.1	

Microsoft Excel - Hydronics
File Edit View Insert Format Tools Data Stats PHStat

Excel Instructions

1. Open file: Hydronics.xls
2. Select Tools
3. Click on Data Analysis
4. Select ANOVA: Single Factor
5. Define data range
6. Specify alpha level

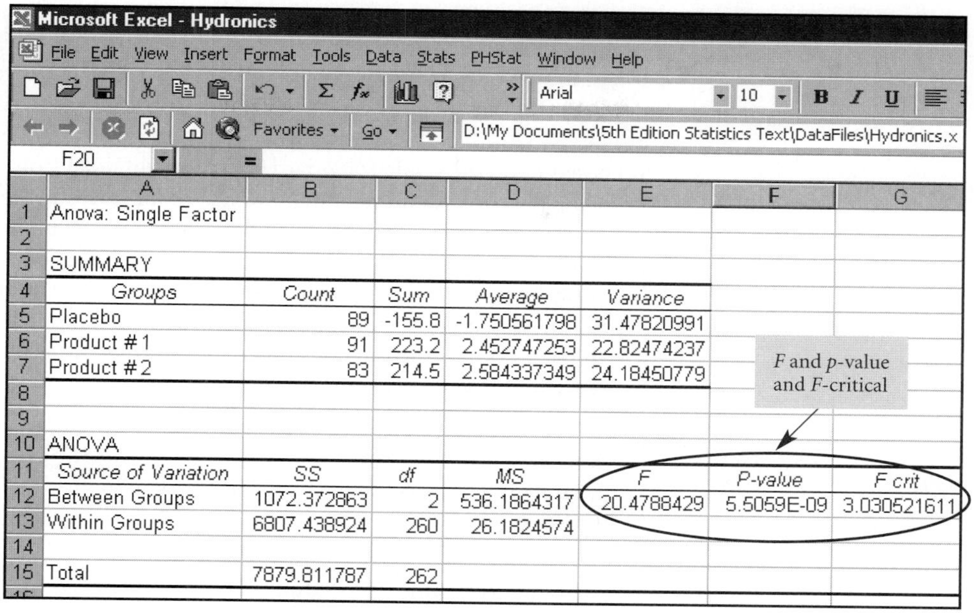

	A	B	C	D	E	F	G
1	Anova: Single Factor						
2							
3	SUMMARY						
4	Groups	Count	Sum	Average	Variance		
5	Placebo	89	-155.8	-1.750561798	31.47820991		
6	Product #1	91	223.2	2.452747253	22.82474237		
7	Product #2	83	214.5	2.584337349	24.18450779		
8							
9							
10	ANOVA						
11	Source of Variation	SS	df	MS	F	P-value	F crit
12	Between Groups	1072.372863	2	536.1864317	20.4788429	5.5059E-09	3.030521611
13	Within Groups	6807.438924	260	26.1824574			
14							
15	Total	7879.811787	262				

FIGURE 10-7
Excel Output: Hydronics Weight Loss ANOVA Results

shows the Excel analysis of variance results. The top section of the Excel ANOVA output in Figure 10-7 provides descriptive information for the three levels. The ANOVA table is listed in the second half of the output. This table looks like the one we generated manually in the Bayhill example. However, Excel also computes the *p*-value and displays the critical value, *F*-critical, from the *F*-distribution table. Thus, you can test the null hypothesis by comparing the calculated *F* to the *F*-critical or by comparing the *p*-value to the significance level.

As shown in Figure 10-7, the decision rule is:

If $F > F_{\alpha} = 3.03$, reject H_0
Otherwise, do not reject H_0

or

p-value $< \alpha$, reject H_0
Otherwise, do not reject H_0

Since $20.48 > 3.03$ (or since 5.51E-09 $< \alpha = 0.05$), we reject the null hypothesis and conclude there is a difference in the mean weight loss for people on the three treatments. At least two of the populations have different means. The top portion of Figure 10-7 shows the descriptive measures for the sample data. For example, the subjects who took the placebo actually gained an average of 1.75 pounds. Subjects on product #1 lost an average of 2.45 pounds and subjects on product #2 lost an average of 2.58 pounds.

The Tukey-Kramer Procedure for Multiple Comparisons

What does this conclusion imply about which treatment results in greater weight loss? One approach for answering this question is to use confidence interval estimates for all possible pairs of population means based on the pooling of the two relevant sample variances as introduced in Chapter 9.

$$s_p = \sqrt{\frac{(n_1 - 1)\, s_1^2 + (n_2 - 1)\, s_2^2}{n_1 + n_2 - 2}}$$

These confidence intervals are constructed using the formula also given in Chapter 9, Equation 9-6:

$$(\bar{x}_1 - \bar{x}_2) \pm t_{\alpha/2}\, s_p \sqrt{\frac{1}{n_1} + \frac{1}{n_2}}$$

which uses a weighted average of only the two sample variances corresponding to the two sample means in the confidence interval. However, in the Hydronics example, we have three samples, and thus three variances involved. If we were to use the pooled standard deviation, s_p shown previously, we would be disregarding one third of the information available to estimate the common population variance. Instead, we use a confidence interval based upon the pooled standard deviation obtained from the square root of MSW. This is the square root of the weighted average of all (three in this example) sample variances. This is preferred to the interval estimate shown previously because we are assuming that each of the three sample variances is an estimate of the common population variance.

After the one-way ANOVA has led us to reject the null hypothesis, a superior method for testing which populations have different means is called the Tukey-Kramer procedure. To understand why the Tukey-Kramer procedure is superior, we introduce the concept of an **experiment-wide error rate**.

EXPERIMENT-WIDE ERROR RATE
The proportion of experiments in which at least one of the set of confidence intervals constructed does not contain the true value of the population parameter being estimated.

The Tukey-Kramer procedure is based on the simultaneous construction of confidence intervals for all differences of pairs of treatment means. In this example, there are three different pairs of means ($\mu_1 - \mu_2, \mu_1 - \mu_3, \mu_2 - \mu_3$). The Tukey-Kramer procedure simultaneously constructs three different confidence intervals for a specified confidence level, say 95%. Intervals that do not contain zero imply that a difference exists between the associated population means.

Suppose we repeat the study a large number of times. Each time, we construct the Tukey-Kramer 95% confidence intervals. The Tukey-Kramer method assures us that in 95% of these experiments, the three confidence intervals constructed would include the true difference between the population means, $\mu_i - \mu_j$. In 5% of the experiments, at least one of the confidence intervals would not contain the true difference between the population means. Thus in, 5% of the situations, we would make at least one mistake in our conclusions about which populations have different means. This proportion of errors (0.05) is known as the experiment-wide error rate.

For a 95% confidence interval, the Tukey-Kramer procedure controls the experiment-wide error to a 0.05 level. But since we are concerned with only this one experiment (with one set of sample data), the actual error rate associated with any one of the three confidence intervals is actually less than 0.05.

The *Tukey-Kramer procedure for multiple comparisons* allows us to simultaneously examine all pairs of populations *after* the ANOVA test has been completed without increasing the true alpha level.[5] Because these comparisons are made after the ANOVA F-test, the procedure is called a post test procedure.

The first step in using the Tukey-Kramer procedure is to compute the absolute differences between each pair of sample means. Using the Excel results shown in Figure 10-7, we get the following differences.

$$|\bar{x}_1 - \bar{x}_2| = |-1.75 - 2.45| = 4.20$$
$$|\bar{x}_1 - \bar{x}_3| = |-1.75 - 2.58| = 4.33$$
$$|\bar{x}_2 - \bar{x}_3| = |2.45 - 2.58| = 0.13$$

---

[5]There are a variety of other methods for performing multiple comparison tests in ANOVA. See sources by Montgomery and Neter et al.

The Tukey-Kramer procedure requires us to compare these absolute differences to the **critical range** that is computed using Equation 10-7.

TUKEY-KRAMER CRITICAL RANGE

$$\text{Critical Range} = q_\alpha \sqrt{\frac{MSW}{2}\left(\frac{1}{n_i} + \frac{1}{n_j}\right)} \qquad \text{10-7}$$

where:

q_α = Value from Studentized range table (Appendix J) with k and $N - k$ degrees of freedom for the desired level of α [k = number of groups or factor levels, N = total number of data values from all populations (levels) combined]

MSW = Mean Square Within

n_i and n_j = Sample sizes from populations (levels) i and j, respectively

---

A critical range is computed for each pairwise comparison, but if the sample sizes are equal, only one critical range calculation is necessary since the quantity under the radical in Equation 10-7 will, therefore, be the same for all comparisons. If the calculated pairwise comparison value is greater than the critical range value, we conclude the difference is significant.

The q value from the studentized range table in Appendix J for a significance level equal to 0.05 and $k = 3$ and $N - k = 260$ degrees of freedom is approximately 3.31. Then for the placebo ($n_1 = 89$) versus product #1 ($n_2 = 91$) comparison we use Equation 10-7 to compute the critical range as follows.

$$\text{Critical Range} = q_\alpha \sqrt{\frac{MSW}{2}\left(\frac{1}{n_i} + \frac{1}{n_j}\right)}$$

$$\text{Critical Range} = 3.31 \sqrt{\frac{26.18}{2}\left(\frac{1}{89} + \frac{1}{91}\right)} = 1.785$$

Since $|\bar{x}_1 - \bar{x}_2| = 4.20 > 1.785$, we conclude that the mean weight loss for the placebo group is not equal to the mean for the product #1 group. Table 10-5 summarizes the results for the three pairwise comparisons.

From Table 10-5 we see that product #1 and product #2 both offer significantly higher average weight loss than the placebo. However, the sample data do not indicate a difference between product #1 and product #2.

The Tukey-Kramer test is further illustrated in the following example.

ANOVA

Excel and
Minitab Tutorial

Digitron, Inc.

Digitron, Inc., makes disc brakes for the automobile industry. Digitron's R&D department recently conducted a test of four different brake systems to determine if there is a difference in the average stopping distance among the different systems. In the test, 40 "identical" mid-sized cars were obtained from one of the major domestic car makers. Ten cars were fitted with brake A, 10 with brake B, and so forth. The cars were then driven on a test track. An electronic, remote switch was used to apply the brakes at exactly the same point on the

TABLE 10-5
Hydronics Pairwise
Comparisons—Tukey-
Kramer Test

	$\|\bar{x}_i - \bar{x}_j\|$	CRITICAL RANGE	SIGNIFICANT?
Placebo vs. Product #1	4.20	1.785	Yes
Placebo vs. Product #2	4.33	1.827	Yes
Product #1 vs. Product #2	0.13	1.818	No

Excel Instructions
1. Open file: Digitron.xls

FIGURE 10-8
Excel Worksheet for the
Digitron Brake Study

road. The number of feet required to bring the car to a full stop was recorded as shown in Figure 10-8. The data are in the file called **Digitron** on the CD-ROM.

The test is a one-way (single factor) test with four levels since we only care to determine whether the four brake systems have the same or different mean stopping distances.

Figure 10-9 shows the Excel output for the ANOVA. The null and alternative hypotheses are:

$$H_0: \mu_1 = \mu_2 = \mu_3 = \mu_4$$
$$H_A: \text{At least two population means are different}$$
$$\alpha = 0.05$$

Recall that the decision rule is:

If the calculated $F > F_\alpha$ reject H_0, or
If the p-value $< \alpha$ reject H_0
Otherwise, do not reject H_0

From Figure 10-9 we see that:

$$F = 3.885 > F_\alpha = 2.866, \text{ and}$$
$$p\text{-value} = 0.0167 < 0.05$$

Thus, we reject the null hypothesis and conclude that not all population means are equal.

FIGURE 10-9
Excel One-Way ANOVA
Output for the Digitron
Example

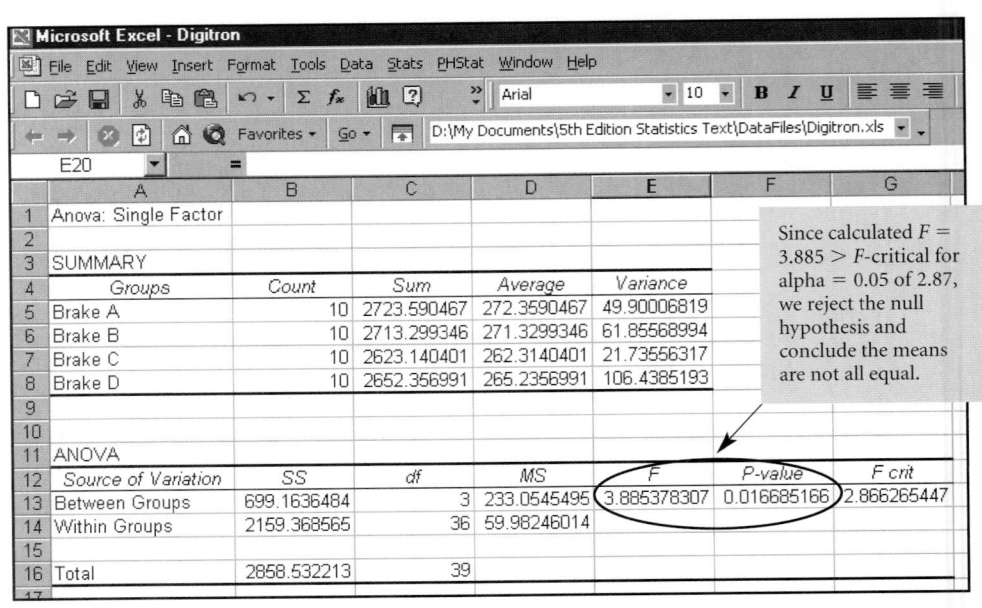

Excel Instructions

1. Open file: Digitron.xls
2. Click on Tools tab
3. Select Data Analysis option
4. Select Anova: Single Factor
5. Enter significance level and data ranges

This result indicates there is a difference in mean stopping distance between at least two of the brake systems. But which systems are different? Is one system superior to all the others? Since we have rejected the null hypothesis of equal means, we need to perform a post-ANOVA multiple comparison test. Again, Equation 10-7 for the Tukey-Kramer procedure is used to construct the critical range to which the absolute differences in all possible pairs of sample means are compared. The critical range is:[6]

$$\text{Critical Range} = q_\alpha \sqrt{\frac{MSW}{2}\left(\frac{1}{n_i} + \frac{1}{n_j}\right)} = 3.79 \sqrt{\frac{59.98}{2}\left(\frac{1}{10} + \frac{1}{10}\right)}$$

Critical Range $= 9.282$

Only one critical range is necessary since all of the sample sizes are equal. If any pair of sample means has an absolute difference, $|\bar{x}_i - \bar{x}_j|$, greater than the critical range, we can infer that a difference exists in those population means. The possible pairwise comparisons (part of a family of comparisons called *contrasts*) are:

CONTRAST			CONCLUSIONS
$\|\bar{x}_1 - \bar{x}_2\| = \|272.359 - 271.3299\|$	$= 1.029 < 9.282$		$\mu_1 = \mu_2$
$\|\bar{x}_1 - \bar{x}_3\| = \|272.359 - 262.314\|$	$= 10.045 > 9.282$		$\mu_1 \neq \mu_3$
$\|\bar{x}_1 - \bar{x}_4\| = \|272.359 - 265.2357\|$	$= 7.123 < 9.282$		$\mu_1 = \mu_4$
$\|\bar{x}_2 - \bar{x}_3\| = \|271.3299 - 262.314\|$	$= 9.016 < 9.282$		$\mu_2 = \mu_3$
$\|\bar{x}_2 - \bar{x}_4\| = \|271.3299 - 265.2357\|$	$= 6.094 < 9.282$		$\mu_2 = \mu_4$
$\|\bar{x}_3 - \bar{x}_4\| = \|262.314 - 265.2357\|$	$= 2.922 < 9.282$		$\mu_3 = \mu_4$

Therefore, based on the Tukey-Kramer procedure, we can infer that population 1 (brake system A) and population 3 (brake system C) have different mean stopping distances. Since short stopping distances are preferred, system C would be preferred over system A, but no other differences are supported by these sample data. For the other contrasts, the difference between the two sample means is insufficient to conclude that a difference in population means exists.

Fixed Effects versus Random Effects in Analysis of Variance

In the Digitron brake example, the company was testing four brake systems. These were the only brake systems under consideration. The ANOVA was intended to determine whether there was a difference in these four brake systems only. In the Hydronics weight loss example, the company was interested in determining whether there was a difference in mean weight loss for two supplements and the placebo. In the Bayhill example involving coupon designs, the company narrowed its choices to four different designs, and the ANOVA test was to determine whether there was a difference in means for these four designs only.

Thus, in each of these examples, the inferences extend only to the factor levels being analyzed, and the levels are assumed to be the only levels of interest. This type of test is called a *fixed effects analysis of variance test*.

Suppose in the Bayhill coupon example that instead of paring the list of possible coupons to a final four, the company had simply selected a random sample of four coupon designs from all possible coupon designs being considered. In that case, the factor levels included in the test would be a random sample of the possible levels. Then, if the ANOVA leads to rejecting the null hypothesis, the conclusion applies to all possible coupon designs.

---

[6]The q-value from the Studentized range table with $\alpha = 0.05$ and degrees of freedom equal to $k = 4$ and $N - k = 36$ must be approximated using degrees of freedom 4 and 40 since the table does not show degrees of freedom of 4 and 36. This value is 3.79.

The assumption is that the values within the possible levels have a normal distribution and the tested levels are a random sample of possible factor levels. When the factor levels are selected through random sampling, the analysis of variance test is called a *random effects test*.

10-1: EXERCISES

ADDITIONAL EXERCISES ON YOUR CD-ROM
Try the ADDITIONAL EXERCISES and APPLICATION PROBLEMS on the CD-ROM.

10-1. Note the following sample data:

ITEM	GROUP 1	GROUP 2	GROUP 3	GROUP 4
1	20.9	28.2	17.8	21.2
2	27.2	26.2	15.9	23.9
3	26.6	21.6	18.4	19.5
4	22.1	29.7	20.2	17.4
5	25.3	30.3	14.1	
6	30.1	25.9		
7	23.8			

a. Based on your computations for the within- and between-sample variation, develop the ANOVA table and test the appropriate null hypothesis using an $\alpha = 0.05$. Use the *p*-value approach.
b. Calculate confidence intervals for the difference between all possible pairs of levels. Use the mean square within as the estimate for the population variance.
c. Based upon the confidence intervals calculated in part b, determine which (if any) of the levels are different.
d. Why would the Tukey-Kramer procedure be preferred to the procedures calculated in parts a–c to determine the differences between the population means? State your reasons.
e. Use the Tukey-Kramer procedure to determine which populations have different means. Use alpha = 0.05.
f. What is the experiment-wide error rate for the Tukey-Kramer procedure?

10-2. Respond to each of the following questions using this partially completed one-way ANOVA table.

SOURCE OF VARIATION	SS	df	MS	F-RATIO
Between Samples		3		
Within Samples	405	___		
Total	888	31		

a. How many different populations are being considered in this analysis?
b. Fill in the ANOVA table with the missing values.
c. State the appropriate null and alternative hypotheses.
d. Based on the analysis of variance *F*-test, what conclusion should be reached regarding the null hypothesis? Test using an $\alpha = 0.05$.

Business Applications

10-3. The Green-Checker Cab Company operates 12 taxis in Seattle, Washington. The manager is interested in determining whether there is a difference in average fares collected for the day, swing, and graveyard shifts. To test whether a difference exists, she has collected a random sample of 10 observations from each shift. The following summary values have been computed from the sample data.

$$TSS = 156.764 \qquad SSB = 55.600$$

a. Develop the appropriate ANOVA table to reach the determination of interest to the manager. Test the hypothesis using an $\alpha = 0.05$.
b. How would your conclusion change if you had used a significance level of 0.01? Discuss why this change occurred.

10-4. Refer to Problem 3. The average fares for day, swing, and graveyard shifts were $28.53, $22.71, and $17.56, respectively.
a. Use the Tukey-Kramer procedure to determine which populations (shifts) have different mean fares. Use an experiment-wide significance level of 0.05.
b. Construct 95% confidence intervals for the difference between each pair of means using Equation 9-6 with MSB in place of s_p^2.
c. Compare your answer in part b to the Tukey-Kramer procedure that uses the experiment-wide error rate. Why would you prefer to use the Tukey-Kramer procedure?

10-5. As purchasing agent for the Horner-Williams Company, you have primary responsibility for securing high-quality raw materials at the best possible price. One particular material that the Horner-Williams Company uses a great deal is aluminum. After careful study, you have been able to reduce the prospective vendors to 3. It is unclear whether these 3 vendors produce aluminum that is equally durable. To compare durability, the recommended procedure is to put pressure on the aluminum until it cracks. The vendor whose aluminum requires the highest mean pressure will be judged to be the one that provides the most durable product. To carry out this test, 14 pieces from each vendor have been selected. These data are shown below and are in the file called **Horner-Williams**. (The data are pounds per square inch pressure.)

VENDOR 1	VENDOR 2	VENDOR 3
2,260	2,734	2,008
1,967	2,302	1,863
2,423	2,396	1,682
2,733	2,356	1,867
2,710	2,122	1,751
2,870	2,091	2,068
1,695	2,553	2,054
2,280	1,935	2,130
2,679	2,578	1,743
2,024	2,282	2,038
2,143	2,498	1,903
1,843	2,787	2,018
1,796	2,475	2,038
2,057	2,072	1,997

a. (1) Determine if the variance of the strength measurements for each of the 3 vendors can be considered equal. Use a significance level of 0.05. (2) Assume the distributions of the strength measurements of each of the vendors are normal. Comment on whether you would be justified if you used a one-way ANOVA procedure to determine that the mean strength of the aluminum was the same for each vendor.

b. Using a significance level of 0.05, what should the company conclude about whether there is a difference in the mean strength of the three vendors' aluminum? Use a p-value approach.

c. Based upon the results in part b and by using the Tukey-Kramer procedure for multiple comparisons, which vendor would you recommend that the Horner-Williams Company select to supply their aluminum? Discuss.

d. Horner-Williams is not satisfied with knowing that one vendor's aluminum is stronger than the others. They wish to know how much stronger the "best" vendor's aluminum is. Provide a range of values of the differences between the "best" vendor's aluminum and each of the other vendor's aluminum. (As will often be the case in a nonclass situation, you will have to choose a confidence coefficient).

10-6. Suppose as part of your job you are responsible for installing emergency lighting in a series of state office buildings. Bids have been received from 4 manufacturers of battery-operated emergency lights. The costs are about equal, so the decision will be based on the length of time the lights last before failing. A sample of 4 lights from each manufacturer has been tested with the following values (time in hours) recorded for each manufacturer.

TYPE A	TYPE B	TYPE C	TYPE D
10.2	12.7	11.2	9.2
11.2	13.3	12.6	9.8
12.5	14.3	11.9	10.9
10.2	13.2	11.2	11.2

a. Using a significance level equal to 0.01, what conclusion should you reach about the 4 manufacturers' battery-operated emergency lights? Explain.

b. If the test conducted in part a reveals that the null hypothesis should be rejected, what manufacturer should be used to supply the lights? Are there one or more manufacturers that you can eliminate based on these data? Use the appropriate test for multiple comparisons. Discuss.

10-7. A large metropolitan police force is considering changing from full-size cars to mid-size cars. The police force sampled cars from each of 3 manufacturers. The number sampled represents the number the manufacturer was able to provide for the test. Each car was driven for 5,000 miles, and the operating cost per mile computed. The operating costs, in cents per mile, for the 21 cars are provided in the data file called **Police** and are shown as follows:

CAR 1	CAR 2	CAR 3
13.3	12.4	13.9
14.3	13.4	15.5
13.6	13.1	15.2
12.8	12.8	14.5
14.0	12.7	15.7
14.6	13.2	15.3
13.9		15.0
14.5		

a. Perform an analysis of variance on these data. Assume an α level of 0.05. Do the experimental data provide evidence that the average operating costs per mile for the 3 types of police cars are different? Use a p-value approach.

b. Referring to part a, based on the sample data and the appropriate test for multiple comparisons, what conclusions should be reached concerning which type of car the police force should adopt? Discuss and prepare a report to the police chief.

c. Provide an estimate of the maximum and minimum difference in average savings per year if the police chief chooses the "best" versus the "worst" car using operating costs as a criterion. Assume that police cars are driven 30,000 miles a year. Use a 90% confidence interval.

10-8. A nationwide moving company is considering 5 different types of nylon tie-down straps. The purchasing department randomly selected straps from each company and determined their breaking strengths in pounds. The sample data are contained in the file called **Nylon**.

a. (1) Determine if the variance of the breaking strength measurements for each of the companies can be considered equal. Use a significance level of 0.05. (2) State any additional assumptions you would need to make to justify the use of a one-way ANOVA procedure to determine that the mean strength of the nylon straps was the same for each vendor. (3) Construct histograms for the data for each company. Do these samples appear to have come from normal distributions? Explain your reasons.

b. Based on your analysis, with a significance level of 0.05, can you conclude that a difference in mean breaking strengths exists among the types of nylon ropes?

c. Based on the sample data, make a recommendation regarding which company should be selected based on mean strength of the nylon straps. Discuss in a report to the purchasing manager.

10-9. A leading brewer of beer is considering 5 different types of advertising displays for a new low-calorie beer. Each display type is tested in 5 different randomly selected stores. A total of 25 stores are in the sample. The mean monthly sales (in cases) and variances for each type of display are as follows.

DISPLAY TYPE	SAMPLE MEAN	SAMPLE VARIANCE
A	98	100.75
B	77	83.00
C	84	64.75
D	103	144.25
E	91	101.00

a. Based on these sample data, can the brewery conclude that it makes a difference which type of display is used? Test using a significance level of 0.05. (Hint: Use the means and variances to determine the SSB and SSW values.)

b. Use the Tukey-Kramer procedure to determine which display type is preferred. Discuss your conclusions in a short report to the marketing manager.

10-10. Channel 9 television in Colville, Washington, recently conducted a study of television news viewers. One item of interest to Channel 9 management was whether the average age of viewers watching Channel 9 was the same as for the other two stations in Colville. The sample included 24 viewers of each station, with the following results.

$$TSS = 2,903.27 \text{ and } SSW = 713.56$$

Using a significance level of 0.05, what should Channel 9 conclude about the average ages of news viewers of the three stations? Discuss.

10-11. Ajar Mountain Ski Company operates a small snow-skiing operation with 2 chairlifts. Recently some customers have complained that the lines at chair 1 are too long. The Ajar manager has collected the following data, which represent the time spent in line for 10 randomly selected people in each of the 2 chairlifts.

CHAIR 1		CHAIR 2	
10.2	9.8	14.3	11.1
10.6	33.7	12.4	9.6
1.7	28.2	9.5	12.4
1.8	10.9	19.2	13.3
4.5	26.3	7.8	15.8

a. Use a two-sample t-test to determine whether there is a significant difference in the average times of people waiting at the 2 lifts. Test this at a significance level of 0.05.

b. Use analysis of variance to test the null hypothesis that the average waiting times at the 2 chairlifts are equal.

c. What observations can you make about the relationship between the two sample t-test and two-sample analysis of variance? Discuss.

d. Suppose you felt that the waiting time at chairlift 1 was longer than that at chairlift 2. Which of the two methods mentioned in parts b and c would you employ? Give reasons for your answer.

10-12. The Savouy Corporation recently purchased a bicycle manufacturing plant formerly owned by the American Traveling Company. American had been outfitting its bikes with tires produced by the Leach Corporation. Savouy management is considering whether to stay with Leach tires or to change to another brand. Three other brands are being considered, all of which cost about the same as the Leach tire. The criterion for tire selection will be average tread life.

Samples of 20 have been selected from the Leach tires and from brands A, B, and C. The following results were found.

$$\bar{x}_{Leach} = 111 \text{ hrs} \qquad \bar{x}_A = 126 \text{ hrs}$$
$$\bar{x}_B = 100 \text{ hrs} \qquad \bar{x}_C = 105 \text{ hrs}$$
$$TSS = 19,620$$

(Note that the sample means represent the mean hours of use until the tread was reduced to a specified level at which time the tires are discarded.)

a. Based on the sample data and using an $\alpha = 0.05$, what conclusion should the Savouy Corporation reach regarding the different brands of bicycle tires? Discuss.

b. The price of the tires is $30, $40, $20, and $25, respectively. If the bikes are to be used approximately 20 hours a week, which tires would you suggest Savouy use for their bikes? The decision should be based on yearly tire cost.

■ 10-2: RANDOMIZED COMPLETE BLOCK ANALYSIS OF VARIANCE

Section 10-1 introduced one-way analysis of variance for testing hypotheses involving two or more population means. This ANOVA method is appropriate as long as we are interested in analyzing one factor at a time and we select independent random samples from the populations. For instance, our example involving brake assembly systems at the Digitron Corporation (Figures 10-8 and 10-9) illustrated a situation in which we were interested in only one factor—type of brake assembly system. The measurement of interest was the stopping distance with each brake system. To test the hypothesis that the 4 brake systems were equal with respect to average stopping distance, 4 groups of the same make and model cars were assigned to each brake system independently. Thus, the one-way ANOVA design was appropriate.

There are, however, situations in which another factor affects the observed response in a one-way design. Often this additional factor is unknown. This is the reason for randomization within the experiment. However, there are also situations in which we know the factor that is impinging on the response variable of interest. Chapter 9 introduced the concept of paired samples and indicated that there are instances when you would want to test for differences in two population means by controlling for sources of variation that might adversely affect the analysis. For instance, in the Digitron example, we might be concerned that, even though we used the same make and model of car in the study, the cars themselves may interject a source of variability that could affect the result. To control for this, we could use the concept of *paired samples* by using the same 10 cars for each of the 4 brake systems. When an additional factor with two or more levels is involved, a design technique called *blocking* can be used to eliminate its effect on the statistical analysis of the factor of interest.

A combination of factor levels (one from each factor) is referred to as a **treatment**.

> **TREATMENT**
> A combination of one level of each factor in an experiment associated with each observed value of the response variable.

As an example, for Digitron each unique combination of one of the 10 cars and one of the 4 brake systems constitutes a treatment giving a value for the response variable.

Randomized Complete Block ANOVA

Citizen's State Bank

ANOVA

Excel and
Minitab Tutorial

Consider the following situation that recently took place in the home equity loan department of Citizen's State Bank. Homeowners can borrow money against the equity they have in their homes to use for home improvements, fund college education for their children, or for any other reason. In order to determine the maximum loan that can be made on a home, the bank has the home appraised to determine its value. The mortgage balance is subtracted from the home's value to get the equity. At Citizen's State Bank, the maximum loan is 90% of the equity.

The bank outsources the home appraisals to an appraisal company. The bank managers are aware that appraisals are not exact and are subject to the judgment and biases of the company doing the appraising. The managers also realize that some appraisal companies may overvalue homes on average while others might undervalue homes. The bank uses 3 appraisal companies: Allen & Associates, Heist Appraisal, and Appraisal International.

Bank managers wish to test the hypothesis that there is no difference in the average house appraisal by the 3 different appraising companies. One way to do this would be to select a random sample of homes for Allen & Associates to appraise. Then select a second sample of homes for Heist Appraisal to work on and a third sample of homes for Appraisal International. One-way ANOVA would be used to compare the sample means. Obviously a problem could occur if, by chance, one company received larger, higher quality homes located in better locations than the other companies. This company's appraisals would naturally be higher on average, not because they tended to appraise higher, but because the homes were simply more expensive to begin with.

Citizen's State Bank officers need to control for the variation in size, quality, and location of homes to fairly test that the three companies' appraisals are equal on the average. To do this, they select a random sample of properties and have each company appraise the same properties. In this case, the properties are called *blocks* and the test design is called a *randomized complete block design*.

The data in Table 10-6 were obtained when each appraisal company was asked to appraise the same 5 properties. The bank managers wish to test the following hypothesis.

$$H_0: \mu_1 = \mu_2 = \mu_3$$
$$H_A: \text{At least two population means are different}$$

Since the managers have chosen to have the same properties appraised by each company (block on property), the samples are not independent and a method known as *randomized complete block ANOVA* must be employed to test the hypothesis. This method is similar to the one-way ANOVA in Section 10-1. However, there is one more source of variation to be accounted for, the block variation. As was the case in Section 10-1, we must find estimators for each source of variation. Identifying the appropriate sum of squares and then dividing each by its degrees of freedom does this. As was the case in the one-way ANOVA the total sum of squares (TSS) can be partitioned. However, in this case the total sum of squares (TSS) is divided into three components instead of two, as shown in Equation 10-8.

SUM OF SQUARES PARTITIONING—RANDOMIZED COMPLETE BLOCK DESIGN

$$TSS = SSB + SSBL + SSW \qquad \textbf{10-8}$$

where:

TSS = Total sum of squares
SSB = Sum of squares between factor levels
$SSBL$ = Sum of squares between blocks
SSW = Sum of squares within levels

Both TSS and SSB are computed just as we did with one-way ANOVA using Equations 10-3 and 10-4. The **sum of squares for blocking (SSBL)** is computed using Equation 10-9.

SUM OF SQUARES FOR BLOCKING

$$SSBL = \sum_{j=1}^{n} k(\bar{x}_j - \bar{\bar{x}})^2 \qquad \textbf{10-9}$$

where:

k = Number of levels for the factor
n = Number of blocks
$\bar{x}_j$ = The mean of the jth block
$\bar{\bar{x}}$ = Grand Mean

TABLE 10-6
Citizen's State Bank Property Appraisals

| Property (Block) | APPRAISAL COMPANY | | | |
	Allen & Associates	Heist Appraisal	Appraisal International	Block Mean
1	78	82	79	79.67
2	102	102	99	101.00
3	68	74	70	70.67
4	83	88	86	85.67
5	95	99	92	95.33
Factor Level Mean	85.2	89	85.2	86.47 = Grand Mean

Note: Values are in thousands of dollars.

Finally, the **sum of squares within** (SSW) is computed using Equation 10-10. This sum of squares is what remains (or the residual) after the variation for all known factors has been removed. This residual sum of squares may be due to the inherent variability of the data, measurement error, or other unidentified sources of variation. Therefore, the sum of squares within is also known as the sum of squares of error, SSE.

SUM OF SQUARES WITHIN

$$SSW = TSS - (SSB + SSBL)$$

10-10

The effect of computing SSBL and subtracting it from TSS in Equation 10-9 is that SSW is reduced. And if the corresponding variation in the blocks is significant, the variation within the factor levels will be significantly reduced. This can make it easier to detect a difference in the population means if such a difference actually exists. If it does, the estimate for the within variability will in all likelihood be reduced. Thus, the denominator for the F-test statistic will be smaller. This will produce a larger F-test statistic, which will more likely lead to the rejection of the null hypothesis. This will depend, of course, on the relative size of SSBL and the respective changes in the degrees of freedom.

The randomized block design requires the following assumptions.

1. The populations are normally distributed.
2. The populations have equal variances.
3. The observations are independent.

Table 10-7 shows the completely randomized block ANOVA table format and equations for degrees of freedom, mean squares, and F-ratios. As you can see, we now have two F-ratios. The reason for this is that we test not only to determine whether the population means are equal, but we also can obtain an indication whether the blocking was necessary by examining the ratio of the mean square for blocks to the mean square within as shown in Table 10-7.

Although you could manually compute the necessary values for the randomized block design, both Excel and Minitab contain a procedure that will do all the computations and

TABLE 10-7
Basic Format for the Randomized Block ANOVA Table

SOURCE OF VARIATION	SS	df	MS	F-RATIO
Between Blocks	SSBL	$b - 1$	MSBL	$\dfrac{MSBL}{MSW}$
Between Samples	SSB	$k - 1$	MSB	$\dfrac{MSB}{MSW}$
Within Samples	SSW	$(k - 1)(b - 1)$	MSW	
Total	TSS	$N - 1$		

where:

k = Number of levels
b = Number of blocks
df = Degrees of freedom
N = Combined sample size
$$MSB = \text{Mean square between} = \frac{SSB}{k - 1}$$
$$MSBL = \text{Mean square blocking} = \frac{SSBL}{b - 1}$$
$$MSW = \text{Mean square within} = \frac{SSW}{(k - 1)(b - 1)}$$

Note: Some randomized block ANOVA tables put the SSB first followed by SSBL.

Excel Instructions:

1. Open file: Citizens.xls

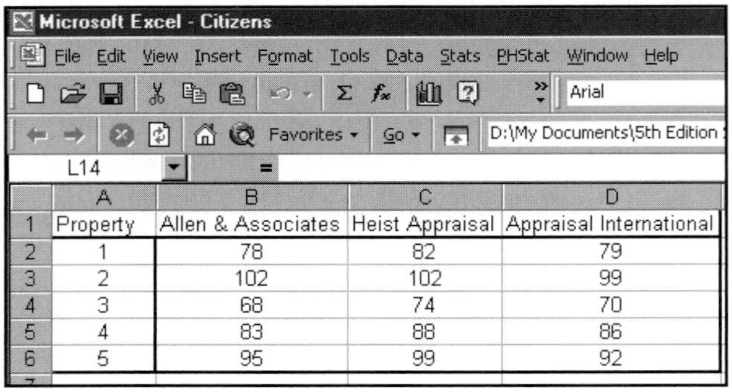

	A	B	C	D
1	Property	Allen & Associates	Heist Appraisal	Appraisal International
2	1	78	82	79
3	2	102	102	99
4	3	68	74	70
5	4	83	88	86
6	5	95	99	92

FIGURE 10-10
Excel Worksheet—Citizen's State Bank Appraisal Data

build the ANOVA table. Figure 10-10 shows the Excel worksheet with the Citizen's State Bank appraisal data. The data file is included in your CD-ROM under the name **Citizens**. (Note: The first column contains labels for each block.)

Figure 10-11 shows the resulting output. Using Excel to perform the computations frees the decision maker to focus on interpreting the results. Note, Excel refers to the randomized block ANOVA as Two-Factor ANOVA Without Replication. Minitab refers to randomized block ANOVA as Two-Way ANOVA.

The main issue is to determine whether the 3 appraisal companies differ in average appraisal values. The primary test is:

$$H_0: \mu_1 = \mu_2 = \mu_3$$
$$H_A: \text{At least two population means are different}$$
$$\alpha = 0.05$$

Using the output presented in Figure 10-11, you can test this hypothesis two ways. First, we can use the F-distribution approach. Figure 10-12 shows the results of this test.

FIGURE 10-11
Excel Citizen's State Bank Analysis of Variance Output

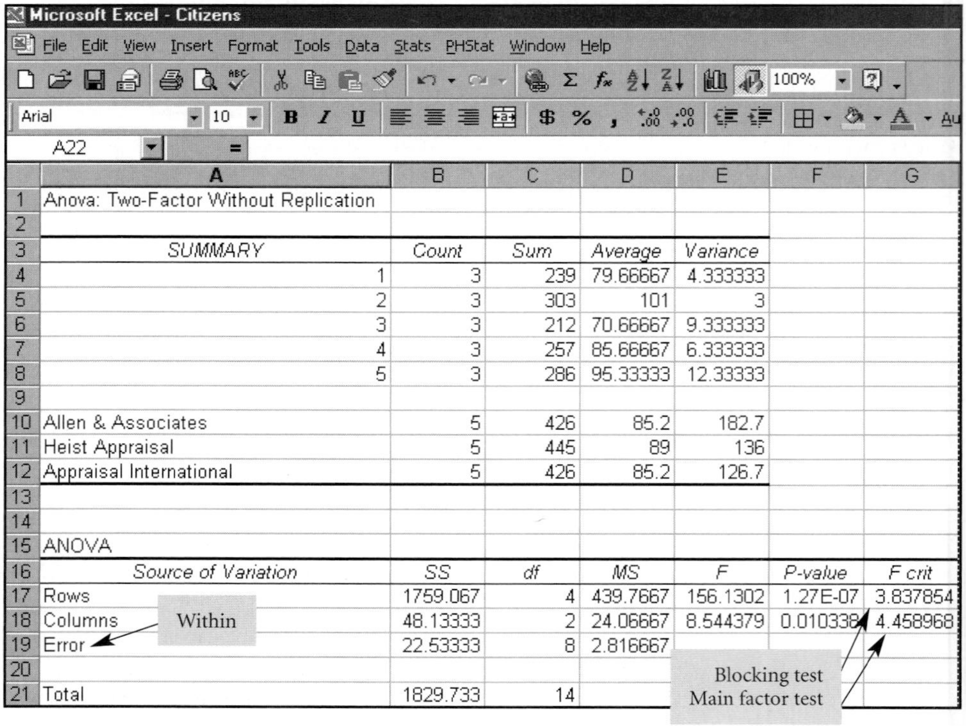

	A	B	C	D	E	F	G
1	Anova: Two-Factor Without Replication						
2							
3	SUMMARY	Count	Sum	Average	Variance		
4	1	3	239	79.66667	4.333333		
5	2	3	303	101	3		
6	3	3	212	70.66667	9.333333		
7	4	3	257	85.66667	6.333333		
8	5	3	286	95.33333	12.33333		
9							
10	Allen & Associates	5	426	85.2	182.7		
11	Heist Appraisal	5	445	89	136		
12	Appraisal International	5	426	85.2	126.7		
13							
14							
15	ANOVA						
16	Source of Variation	SS	df	MS	F	P-value	F crit
17	Rows	1759.067	4	439.7667	156.1302	1.27E-07	3.837854
18	Columns	48.13333	2	24.06667	8.544379	0.010338	4.458968
19	Error	22.53333	8	2.816667			
20							
21	Total	1829.733	14				

Excel Instructions

1. Open file: Citizens.xls
2. Click on the Tools tab
3. Select the Data Analysis option
4. Select Anova: Two-Factor Without Replication.
5. Define Data Range

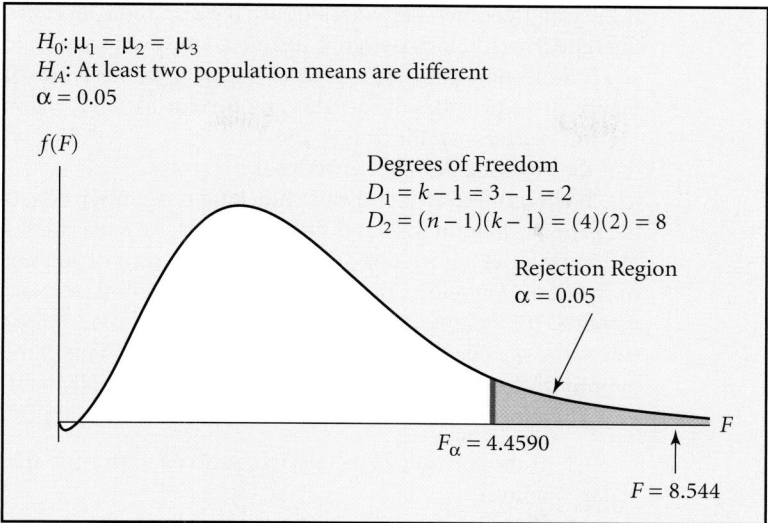

$H_0: \mu_1 = \mu_2 = \mu_3$
H_A: At least two population means are different
$\alpha = 0.05$

$f(F)$

Degrees of Freedom
$D_1 = k - 1 = 3 - 1 = 2$
$D_2 = (n - 1)(k - 1) = (4)(2) = 8$

Rejection Region
$\alpha = 0.05$

$F_\alpha = 4.4590$

$F = 8.544$

FIGURE 10-12
Appraisal Company
Hypothesis Test for Citizen's
State Bank

Based upon the sample data, we reject the null hypothesis and conclude that the 3 appraisal companies do not provide equal average values for properties.

The second approach to testing the null hypothesis is the *p*-value approach. The decision rule in an ANOVA application for *p* values is:

If *p*-value $< \alpha$, reject H_0
Otherwise, do not reject H_0

In this case, $\alpha = 0.05$ and the *p*-value in Figure 10-11 is 0.0103. Since 0.0103 $< \alpha = 0.05$, we reject the null hypothesis. Both the *F*-distribution approach and the *p*-value approach give the same result, as they must.

WAS BLOCKING NECESSARY?

Before we take up the issue of determining which company provides the highest mean property values, we need to discuss one other issue. Recall, the bank managers chose to control for variation between properties by having each appraisal company evaluate the same 5 properties. This restriction is called blocking and the properties are the blocks. The Excel analysis of variance output in Figure 10-11 contains information that allows us to test whether blocking was necessary.

If the blocking was necessary, it would mean that appraisal values are in fact influenced by the particular property being appraised. The blocks then form a second factor of interest, and we formulate a secondary hypothesis test for this factor as follows.

$H_0: \mu_{b1} = \mu_{b2} = \mu_{b3} = \mu_{b4} = \mu_{b5}$
H_A: Not all block means are equal

Note, we are using μ_{bi} to represent the mean of the ith block.

It seems only natural to use a test statistic that consists of the ratio of the mean square for blocks to the mean square within. However, certain (randomization) restrictions placed upon the complete block design make this proposed test statistic invalid from a theoretical statistics point of view. As an approximate procedure, however, the examination of the ratio MSBL/MSW is certainly reasonable. If it is large, it implies that the blocks had a large effect on the response variable and that they were probably helpful in improving the precision of the *F*-test for the primary factor's means. In performing the analysis of variance, we may also conduct a pseudo-test to see whether the average appraisals for the five properties are equal.

If the null hypothesis is "rejected," we have an indication that the blocking is necessary and the randomized block design is justified. However, we should be careful to present this only as an indication and not a precise test of hypothesis for the blocks. The Excel output in Figure 10-11 provides the F-value and p-value for this pseudo-test to determine if the blocking was a necessity. Since $F = 156.1302 > F_{0.05} = 3.838$, we definitely have an indication that the blocking design was necessary.[7]

If a hypothesis test indicates blocking is not necessary, the chance of a Type II error for the primary hypothesis has been unnecessarily increased by the use of blocking. The reason is that by blocking we not only partition the sum of squares, we also partition the degrees of freedom. Therefore, the denominator of MSW is decreased and MSW will mostly likely increase. If blocking isn't needed, the MSW will tend to be relatively larger than if we had run a one-way design with independent samples. This can lead to failing to reject the null hypothesis for the primary test when it should actually have been rejected.

Therefore, if blocking is indicated to be unnecessary follow these rules.

1. If the primary H_0 is rejected, proceed with your analysis and decision making—no concern.
2. If the primary H_0 is not rejected, redo the study without using blocking. Run a one-way ANOVA with independent samples.

Fisher's Least Significant Difference Test

EXAMPLE 10-7

ANOVA

Citizen's State Bank (continued)

The managers at Citizen's State Bank have thus far concluded the 3 appraisal companies do not all provide the same mean appraisal values. However, the ANOVA test does not indicate which companies are different from which other companies. We learned earlier that the Tukey-Kramer procedure is useful for answering these post-ANOVA questions when we have used one-way ANOVA. **Fisher's least significant difference test** is one way for testing multiple comparisons that can be used for a randomized block analysis of variance design.

If the null hypothesis has been rejected, then we can compare the absolute differences in sample means from any two populations to the *least significant difference (LSD)* as computed using Equation 10-11.

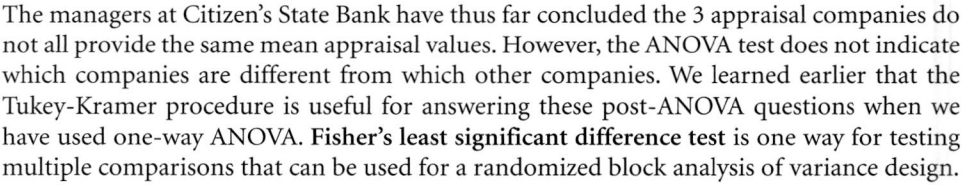

FISHER'S LEAST SIGNIFICANT DIFFERENCE FOR COMPLETE BLOCK DESIGN

$$LSD = t_{\alpha/2}\sqrt{MSW}\sqrt{\frac{2}{n}}$$

10-11

where:

$t_{\alpha/2}$ = Upper-tailed value from Student's t-distribution for $\frac{\alpha}{2}$ and $(k-1)(n-1)$ degrees of freedom

MSW = Mean square within from ANOVA table

n = Number of blocks

k = Number of levels

For each pairwise test, if the absolute difference in sample means exceeds the LSD value, the populations are inferred to have different means.

---

[7]Many authors argue that the randomization restriction imposed by using blocks means that the F-ratio really is a test for the equality of the block means plus the randomization restriction. For a summary of this argument and references see Montgomery, D.C., *Design and Analysis of Experiments,* 4th ed. (New York, NY: John Wiley & Sons, 1997) pages 175–176.

Using Equation 10-11, we compute the LSD value as follows.

$$LSD = t_{\alpha/2}\sqrt{MSW}\sqrt{\frac{2}{n}}$$

For this experiment we have $k = 3$ levels (the appraisal firms) and $n = 5$ blocks (the number of properties). We go to the t-table in Appendix F (or use Excel's TINV function) for $\frac{\alpha}{2} = \frac{0.05}{2} = 0.025$ and $(k - 1)(n - 1) = (3 - 1)(5 - 1) = 8$ degrees of freedom. Thus, $t_{\alpha/2} = 2.306$. From Figure 10-11, we see that MSW $= 2.817$ and $n = 5$ blocks. Then,

$$LSD = 2.306\sqrt{2.817}\sqrt{\frac{2}{5}}$$

$$LSD = 2.448$$

Since we have three appraisal companies, we can form the following contrasts and comparisons. (Refer to Figure 10-11 for sample means.)

ABSOLUTE DIFFERENCE	CONCLUSION
$\lvert \bar{x}_i - \bar{x}_j \rvert$	
$\lvert 85.2 - 89.0 \rvert = 3.8 > 2.448$	$\mu_1 \neq \mu_2$
$\lvert 85.2 - 85.2 \rvert = 0.0 < 2.448$	$\mu_1 = \mu_3$
$\lvert 89.0 - 85.2 \rvert = 3.8 > 2.448$	$\mu_2 \neq \mu_3$

Additional Example 10-a

Using Minitab for Randomized Block ANOVA

Therefore, from these sample data we can infer that mean appraisals from Allen & Associates (company 1) are lower than those for Heist Appraisal (company 2). Likewise, we conclude that Heist Appraisal has higher values on average than Appraisal International (company 3). However, the data do not indicate a significant difference between Allen & Associates and Appraisal International. Thus, if the bank is worried about appraisals being too high, the data suggest that Heist Appraisal may not be the firm to use.

10-2: EXERCISES

ADDITIONAL EXERCISES ON YOUR CD-ROM

Try the ADDITIONAL EXERCISES and APPLICATION PROBLEMS on the CD-ROM.

10-13. The following data were collected for a randomized block analysis of variance design with 4 populations and 8 blocks:

	GROUP 1	GROUP 2	GROUP 3	GROUP 4
Block 1	56	44	57	84
Block 2	34	30	38	50
Block 3	50	41	48	52
Block 4	19	17	21	30
Block 5	33	30	35	38
Block 6	74	72	78	79
Block 7	33	24	27	33
Block 8	56	44	56	71

a. State the appropriate null and alternative hypotheses for both groups and blocks.
b. Construct the appropriate ANOVA table.
c. Using a significance level equal to 0.05, can you conclude that blocking was necessary in this case? Use a test statistic approach.
d. Based on the data and a significance level equal to 0.05, is there a difference in population means for the 4 groups? Use a p-value approach.
e. If you found that a difference exists in part d, use the LSD approach to determine which populations have different means.

10-14 A randomized block ANOVA was performed and the following partially completed ANOVA table is available.

SOURCE OF VARIATION	SS	df	MS	F-RATIO
Between Blocks	4,560	7		
Between Samples	8,900	3		
Within Samples	___	___		
Total	23,400			

a. How many populations are being tested? How many blocks were used?
b. Using a significance equal to 0.05, what conclusion have you reached about whether blocking was necessary in this case? Be sure to state the appropriate null and alternative hypotheses.
c. What conclusion should be reached with respect to the primary null hypothesis? Test using a significance level equal to 0.05. Be sure to state the appropriate null and alternative hypotheses.
d. Given your results in part c, is it appropriate to perform a post ANOVA multiple comparisons test to determine which populations have different means? Discuss.

Business Applications

10-15. Weekly cash sales records have been collected for 4 drive-in restaurants in Topeka, Kansas, for a 6-week period. The following data were collected and are also contained in the data file called **Topeka**.

Week	DRIVE-IN 1	2	3	4
1	$1,430	$980	$1,780	$2,300
2	2,200	1,400	2,890	2,680
3	1,140	1,200	1,500	2,000
4	880	1,300	1,470	1,900
5	1,670	1,300	2,400	2,540
6	990	550	1,600	1,900

a. If the assumptions of a one-way ANOVA design are satisfied in this case, what should be concluded about the average sales at the 4 drive-in restaurants in Topeka? Use a significance level of 0.05.
b. Provide a 95% confidence interval estimate of the maximum difference in the average sales among the 4 drive-in restaurants in Topeka.
c. Discuss whether you think the assumptions of a one-way ANOVA are satisfied in this case and indicate why or why not. If they are not, what design is appropriate? Discuss.

10-16. Refer to Problem 15.

a. Perform a randomized block analysis of variance test using a significance level of 0.05 to determine whether the mean sales for the 4 drive-ins are equal.
b. Comment on any differences between these results and those in Problem 15.

10-17. Reference Problem 16.

a. Determine whether blocking on weeks was necessary in this experiment. Test at the 0.05 level and discuss why blocking may be necessary. Use a p-value approach.
b. Suppose blocking was necessary and the researcher chooses not to use blocks. Discuss what impact this could have on the results of the analysis of variance.

10-18. Refer to Problems 16 and 17.

a. Use Fisher's least significant difference procedure to determine which, if any, drive-ins have different true average weekly sales.
b. Determine if the difference between the true average weekly sales for the drive-in that sells the most and the one that sells the least could be as much as $1,400. Use a significance level of 0.01.

10-19. There are 3 commercial tax preparing offices in Bensen, Minnesota. The local Better Business Bureau has been receiving some complaints that one of the offices does not understand tax law well enough to provide expert advice. The complaints state that to safeguard itself, the preparing office overstates the tax due by the payer and thus avoids later problems with the IRS.

The Better Business Bureau has decided to invest several hundred dollars in grant money to test the claim. It has selected 8 people at random and asked that they allow each of the 3 offices to prepare their taxes using the same information. The following data show the tax bills as figured by each office. The data are also located in a data file called **Tax-test**.

RETURN	OFFICE 1	OFFICE 2	OFFICE 3
1	$ 4,376.20	$ 5,100.10	$ 4,988.03
2	5,678.45	6,234.23	5,489.23
3	2,341.78	2,242.60	2,121.90
4	9,875.33	10,300.30	9,845.60
5	7,650.20	8,002.90	7,590.88
6	1,324.80	1,450.90	1,356.89
7	2,345.90	2,356.90	2,345.90
8	15,468.75	16,080.78	15,376.70

a. Discuss why the Better Business Bureau set up this test as a randomized block design. Why did it think it was important to have all 3 offices do the returns for each of the 8 people?
b. Determine whether the blocking was necessary in this situation. Use a significance level of 0.01. State the null and alternative hypotheses.
c. Based on the sample data, can the Better Business Bureau conclude that there is a difference in the mean taxes due on tax returns? Test using a significance level of 0.01. State the appropriate null and alternative hypotheses.
d. Referring to part c, if you did conclude that a difference exists, use the Fisher's LSD approach to determine which office has the highest mean tax due.

10-20. In a local community there are 3 grocery chain stores. The 3 stores have been carrying out a spirited advertising campaign in which each claims to have the lowest prices. A local news station recently sent a reporter to the 3 stores to check prices on several items. She found that for certain items each store had the lowest price. This survey didn't really answer the question for consumers. Thus, the station set up a test in which 20 shoppers were asked to construct a shopping list for items to be used by their household during the following week. They were sent to each of the 3 chain stores to purchase the items on their list. The sales receipts from each of the 3 stores were recorded in the data file called **Groceries**.

    a. Why should this price test be conducted using the design that the television station used? What was it attempting to achieve by having the same people shop at each of the 3 grocery stores?

    b. Based on a significance level of 0.05 and these sample data, test to determine whether blocking was neces-

sary in this example. State the null and alternative hypotheses. Use a test statistic approach to provide an indication of whether blocking was effective.

    c. Based on these sample data, can you conclude the 3 grocery stores have different sample means? Test using a significance level of 0.05. State the appropriate null and alternative hypotheses. Use a p-value approach.

    d. Based on the sample data, which store has the highest average prices? Use Fisher's LSD test if appropriate.

10-21. Referring to Problem 20, suppose the same data are used 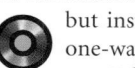 but instead of the randomized block ANOVA design, a one-way design is used.

    a. What conclusions are reached based on an $\alpha = 0.05$ level?

    b. Discuss any differences between the results using the two designs. Why might the results be different? Which design is more appropriate?

10-3: TWO FACTOR ANALYSIS OF VARIANCE WITH REPLICATION

Section 10-2 introduced an analysis of variance procedure called the randomized complete block ANOVA. This method is used when we are interested in testing whether the means for the populations (levels) for a factor of interest are equal, and we also want to control for potential variation due to a second factor. The second factor is called the blocking factor. Consider again the previous example involving the Citizen's State Bank property appraisal example in which the bank was interested in determining whether the mean property valuation was the same for 3 different appraisal companies. The company used the same 5 properties to test each appraisal company in an attempt to reduce any variability that might exist due to the properties involved in the test. The properties were the blocks in that example, but we were not really interested in knowing whether the mean appraisal was the same for all properties. The single factor of interest was the 3 appraisal companies.

However, you will encounter many situations in which there are actually two or more factors of interest in the same study. In this section, we limit our discussion to situations involving only two factors. The technique that is used when we wish to analyze two factors is called *Two Factor ANOVA with Replications*.

Two Factor ANOVA

Fly High Airlines

EXAMPLE

10-8

ANOVA

Excel and Minitab Tutorial

Like other major U.S. airlines, Fly High Airlines[8] is concerned because many of its frequent flier program members have accumulated large quantities of free miles. The airline is concerned that at some point in the future there will be a big influx of customers wanting to use their miles, and the airlines will have difficulty satisfying all the requests. Thus, Fly High recently conducted an experiment with its frequent flier program in which 3 methods for redeeming frequent flier miles were offered to a sample of 16 customers each. Each customer had accumulated over 100,000 frequent flier miles. The customers were equally divided into 4 age groups. The variable of interest was the number of miles redeemed by the customers during the 6-week period following notification of the redemption offer. Table 10-8 shows the number of miles redeemed for each person in the study. These data are also contained in the file called **Fly-High** on your CD-ROM.

[8]Name changed at request of the airline.

	CASH OPTION	VACATION	SHOPPING
Under 25 years	30,000	40,000	25,000
	0	25,000	25,000
	25,000	0	75,000
	0	0	5,000
25–40 Years	60,000	40,000	30,000
	0	25,000	25,000
	0	5,000	50,000
	25,000	25,000	0
41–60 years	40,000	25,000	25,000
	25,000	50,000	50,000
	25,000	0	0
	0	25,000	0
Over 60 years	0	45,000	30,000
	5,000	25,000	25,000
	25,000	0	25,000
	50,000	50,000	50,000

TABLE 10-8
Fly High Airlines Frequent
Flier Miles Data

Method 1 offered cash inducements to use miles. Method 2 offered discount vacation options, and method 3 offered access to a discount-shopping program through the Internet. The airline is interested in determining the effect of redemption offer approach on the number of miles that would be redeemed in a 6-week period. Further, it was interested in knowing whether the age of the customer might affect the number of miles redeemed.

A *two factor ANOVA* design is the appropriate method in this case since the airline has two factors of interest. Factor A (arbitrarily assigned) is the redemption offer type consisting of 3 levels. Factor B is the age group of the customer consisting of 4 levels. As shown in Table 10-8, there are $3 \times 4 = 12$ cells in the study. There are 4 customers in each cell. These are called the *replications* since we get 4 measurements (miles redeemed) at each combination of redemption offer (factor A) level and age level (factor B).

Two factor ANOVA is based on the same logic as all other ANOVA designs. Each factor of interest introduces variability into the experiment. As was the case in Sections 10-1 and 10-2, we must find estimators for each source of variation. Identifying the appropriate sum of squares and then dividing each by its degrees of freedom does this. As was the case in the one-way ANOVA, the total sum of squares (TSS) can be partitioned into parts. One part is due to differences in the levels of factor A (SS_A). Another part is due to the levels of factor B (SS_B). Another part is due to the *interaction* between factor A and factor B (SS_{AB}). (We will discuss the concept of interaction later.) The final component making up the total sum of squares is the sum of squares due to the inherent random variation in the data, which we now call sum of squares error (SSE). Figure 10-13 illustrates this partitioning concept. The variation due to each of these components will be estimated using the respective *mean square* obtained by dividing the sum of squares by its degrees of freedom.

If the variation accounted for by factor A and/or factor B is large relative to the error variation, we will tend to conclude that the factor levels have different means.

Table 10-9 illustrates the format of the two factor ANOVA. Three different hypotheses can be tested from the information in this ANOVA table. First, for factor A (redemption options), we have:

$$H_0: \mu_{A_1} = \mu_{A_2} = \mu_{A_3}$$
$$H_A: \text{Not all means are equal}$$

For factor B (age levels):

$$H_0: \mu_{B_1} = \mu_{B_2} = \mu_{B_3} = \mu_{B_4}$$
$$H_A: \text{Not all means are equal}$$

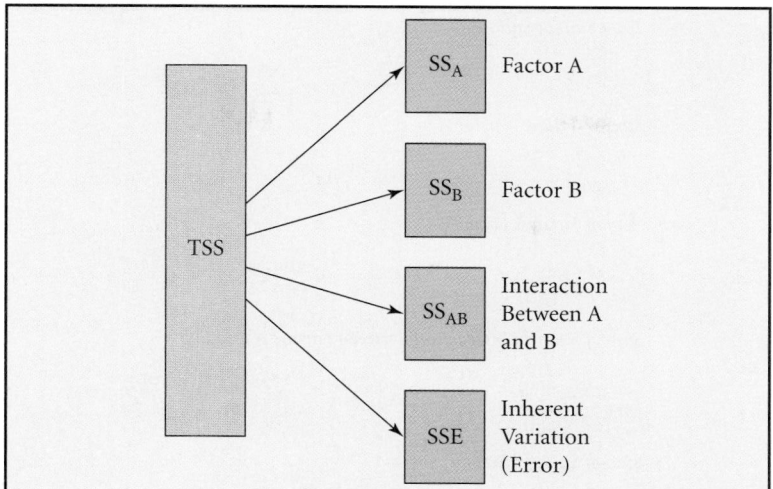

FIGURE 10-13
Two Factor ANOVA—
Partitioning of Total Sum
of Squares

Test to determine whether interaction exists between the two factors:

H_0: Factors A and B do not interact to affect the mean response
H_A: Factors A and B do interact

The necessary assumptions for the two factor ANOVA are:

1. The population values for each combination of pairwise factor levels are normally distributed.
2. The variances for each population are equal.
3. The samples are independent.
4. The observations are independent.

While all the necessary values to complete Table 10-9 could be computed manually using the equations shown in Table 10-10, it would be a time-consuming task for even a small

TABLE 10-9
Basic Format of the Two
Factor ANOVA Table

SOURCE OF VARIATION	SS	df	MS	F-RATIO
Factor A	SS_A	$a - 1$	MS_A	$\dfrac{MS_A}{MSE}$
Factor B	SS_B	$b - 1$	MS_B	$\dfrac{MS_B}{MSE}$
AB interaction	SS_{AB}	$(a - 1)(b - 1)$	MS_{AB}	$\dfrac{MS_{AB}}{MSE}$
Error	$\underline{SSE}$	$\underline{N - ab}$	MSE	
Total	TSS	$N - 1$		

where:

a = Number of levels of factor A
b = Number of levels of factor B
N = Total number of observations in all cells

$$MS_A = \text{Mean square factor A} = \frac{SS_A}{a - 1}$$

$$MS_B = \text{Mean square factor B} = \frac{SS_B}{b - 1}$$

$$MS_{AB} = \text{Mean square interaction} = \frac{SS_{AB}}{(a - 1)(b - 1)}$$

$$MSE = \text{Mean square within} = \frac{SSE}{N - ab}$$

Total Sum of Squares

$$TSS = \sum_{i=1}^{a}\sum_{j=1}^{b}\sum_{k=1}^{n'} (x_{ijk} - \bar{\bar{x}})^2$$ 10-12

Sum of Squares Factor A

$$SS_A = bn'\sum_{i=1}^{a} (\bar{x}_{i..} - \bar{\bar{x}})^2$$ 10-13

Sum of Squares Factor B

$$SS_B = an'\sum_{j=1}^{b} (\bar{x}_{.j.} - \bar{\bar{x}})^2$$ 10-14

Sum of Squares Interaction Between Factors A and B

$$SS_{AB} = n'\sum_{i=1}^{a}\sum_{j=1}^{b} (\bar{x}_{ij.} - \bar{x}_{i..} - \bar{x}_{.j.} + \bar{\bar{x}})^2$$ 10-15

Sum of Squares Error

$$SSE = \sum_{i=1}^{a}\sum_{j=1}^{b}\sum_{k=1}^{n'} (x_{ijk} - \bar{x}_{ij.})^2$$ 10-16

where:

$$\bar{\bar{x}} = \frac{\sum_{i=1}^{a}\sum_{j=1}^{b}\sum_{k=1}^{n'} x_{ijk}}{abn'} = \text{Grand mean}$$

$$\bar{x}_{i..} = \frac{\sum_{j=1}^{b}\sum_{k=1}^{n'} x_{ijk}}{bn'} = \text{Mean of each level of factor A}$$

$$\bar{x}_{.j.} = \frac{\sum_{i=1}^{a}\sum_{k=1}^{n'} x_{ijk}}{an'} = \text{Mean of each level of factor B}$$

$$\bar{x}_{ij.} = \sum_{k=1}^{n'} \frac{x_{ijk}}{n'} = \text{Mean of each cell}$$

a = Number of levels of factor A
b = Number of levels of factor B
n' = Number of replications in each cell

TABLE 10-10
Two Factor ANOVA
Equations

example because the equations for the various sum-of-squares values are quite complicated. Instead, we will use Excel to perform the two factor ANOVA.

INTERACTION EXPLAINED

Before we discuss the ANOVA results for the Fly High Airlines example, a few comments regarding the concept of factor interaction are needed. Consider our example involving the factors, miles redemption offer type and age category of customer. The response variable is the number of miles redeemed in the 6 weeks after the offer. Suppose one redemption offer type is really better and results in a higher average number of miles being redeemed. If there is no interaction between age and offer type, then customers of all ages will have uniformly higher average miles redeemed for this offer type compared to the other offer types. If another offer type yields lower average miles, and if there is no interaction, all age groups receiving this offer type will redeem uniformly lower miles on average than the other offer types. Figure 10-14 shows a graphic interpretation of a situation with no interaction between the two factors.

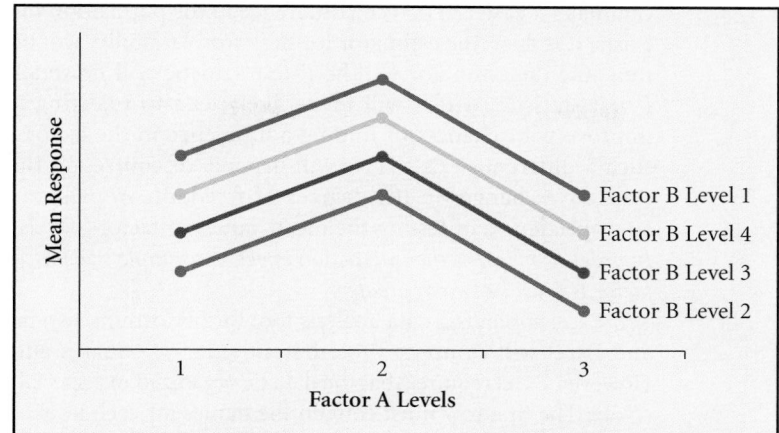

FIGURE 10-14
Differences Between Factor
Level Mean Values: No
Interaction

However, if interaction exists between the factors, we would see a graph something like the one shown in Figure 10-15. Interaction would be indicated if one age group redeemed a higher average number of miles than the other age groups with one program but a lower average number of miles than the other age groups on the other mileage redemption programs. In general, interaction occurs if the differences in the averages of the response variable for the various levels of one factor, say factor A, are not the same for each level of the other factor, say factor B. The general idea is that interaction between two factors means that the effect due to one of them is not uniform across all levels of the other factor.

Another example where potential interaction might exist occurs in plywood manufacturing where thin layers of wood called veneer are glued together to form plywood. One of the important quality attributes of plywood is its strength. However, plywood is made from different species of wood (pine, fir, hemlock, etc.) and different types of glue are available. If some species of wood work better (stronger plywood) with certain glues while other species work better with different glues, we say that the wood species and the glue type interact.

If interaction is suspected, it should be accounted for by subtracting the interaction sum-of-squares term (SS_{AB}) from the total sum-of-squares term in the ANOVA shown in Table 10-9. From a strictly arithmetic point of view, the effect of computing SS_{AB} and subtracting it from TSS is that SSE is reduced. And if the corresponding variation due to interaction is significant, the variation within the factor levels will be significantly reduced. This

FIGURE 10-15
Differences Between Factor
Level Mean Values:
Interaction Present

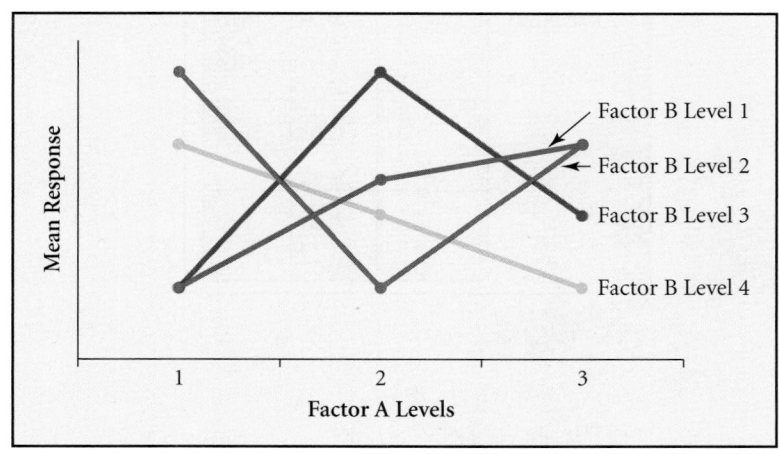

can make it easier to detect a difference in the population means if such variability actually exists. If it does, the estimator for the error variability will in all likelihood be reduced and, thus, the denominator for the F-test statistic will be smaller. This will produce a larger F-test statistic, which will more likely lead to rejecting the null hypothesis. This will improve your chances of finding a difference in the factor A and factor B mean values if such a difference exists. This will depend, of course, on the relative size of SS_{AB} and the respective changes in the degrees of freedom. We will comment later, however, on the appropriateness of testing the mean values of factors' levels if interaction is present. *Note: In order to measure the interaction effect, the sample size for each combination of factor A and factor B must be two or greater.*

Excel contains a data analysis tool for performing two factor ANOVA with replications, and Excel will compute the different sums-of-squares and complete the ANOVA table. However, Excel requires that the data be organized in a special way as shown in Figure 10-16.[9] (Note: The first row must contain the names for each level of factor A. Also, column 1 contains the factor B level names. These must be in the row corresponding to the first sample item for each factor B level.)

The Excel two factor ANOVA output for this example is actually too big to fit on one screen. The top portion of the printout shows summary information for each cell including means and variances (see Figure 10-17). At the bottom of the output (scroll down) is the ANOVA table shown in Figure 10-18. Excel changes a few labels. For example, factor A (the miles redemption options) is now referred to as *Columns*. Factor B (age groups) is referred to as *Sample*. In Figure 10-18, we see all the information necessary to test whether the 3 redemption offers (factor A) result in different mean miles redeemed.

$$H_0: \mu_{A_1} = \mu_{A_2} = \mu_{A_3}$$
$$H_A: \text{Not all means are equal}$$
$$\alpha = 0.05$$

FIGURE 10-16
Excel Data Format for Two Factor ANOVA—Fly High Airlines

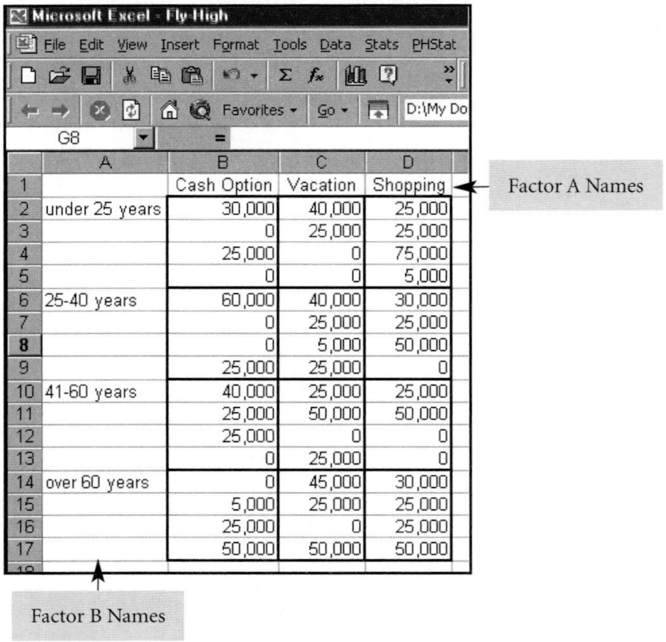

Factor A Names

Excel Instructions
1. Open file: Fly-High.xls

Factor B Names

---

[9]Minitab uses the same data input format for two factor ANOVA as for randomized block ANOVA.

Excel Instructions:

1. Open file: Fly-High.xls
2. Click on the Tools tab
3. Select Data Analysis
4. Select Anova: Two-Factor With Replication
5. Define data range (in this example, A1:D17)
6. Indicate number of rows per sample (replications)

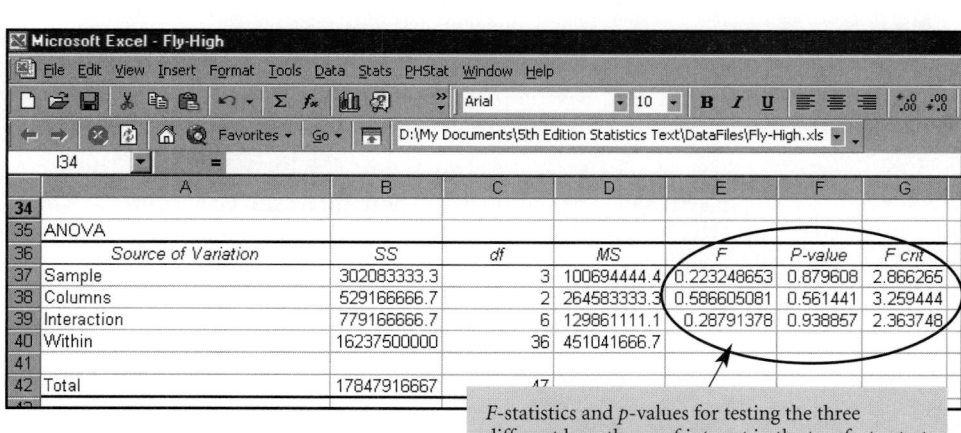

FIGURE 10-17
Excel Output (Part 1) for Two Factor ANOVA Fly High Airlines Example

Both the p-value and F-distribution approaches can be used. Since the p-value (columns) = 0.561 > α = 0.05, the null hypothesis is not rejected. (Also, F = 0.587 < F_α = 3.259, the null hypothesis is not rejected.) This means the test data do not indicate that a difference exists between the average amount of mileage redeemed for the 3 types of offers. None seems superior to the others.

We can also test to determine if age level makes a difference in frequent flier miles redeemed.

$$H_0: \mu_{B_1} = \mu_{B_2} = \mu_{B_3} = \mu_{B_4}$$
$$H_A: \text{Not all means are equal}$$
$$\alpha = 0.05$$

FIGURE 10-18
Excel Output (Part 2) for Two Factor ANOVA—Fly High Airlines Example

Excel terminology:

Sample = Factor B (age)
Columns = Factor A (program)
Within = Error

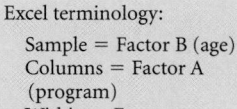

ANOVA

Source of Variation	SS	df	MS	F	P-value	F crit
Sample	302083333.3	3	100694444.4	0.223248653	0.879608	2.866265
Columns	529166666.7	2	264583333.3	0.586605081	0.561441	3.259444
Interaction	779166666.7	6	129861111.1	0.28791378	0.938857	2.363748
Within	16237500000	36	451041666.7			
Total	17847916667	47				

F-statistics and p-values for testing the three different hypotheses of interest in the two factor test

In Figure 10-18, we see that the p-value $= 0.8796 > \alpha = 0.05$. Thus, the null hypothesis is not rejected. (Also, $F = 0.2232 < F_\alpha = 2.866$.) The test data don't indicate that customer age significantly influences the average number of frequent flier miles that will be redeemed.

Finally, we can also test for interaction. The null hypothesis is that no interaction exists. The alternative is that interaction does exist between the two factors. The ANOVA table in Figure 10-18 shows a p-value of 0.939 which is greater than $\alpha = 0.05$. Based on these data, interaction between the two factors does not appear to exist. This would indicate that the differences in the average mileage redeemed between the various age categories are the same for each redemption offer type.

A Caution About Interaction

In this example the sample data indicate that no interaction between factors A and B is present. Based on the sample data, we were unable to conclude that the 3 redemption offers resulted in different average frequent flier miles redeemed. Finally, we are unable to conclude that a difference in average miles redeemed occurs over the 4 different age groups.

However, the appropriate approach is to begin first by testing for interaction. If the interaction null hypothesis is not rejected, as was the case in this example, you should proceed to test the factor A and factor B hypotheses. However, if we conclude that interaction is present between the two factors, hypothesis tests for factors A and B generally *should not* be performed. The reason is that findings of significance for either factor might be due only to interactive effects when the two factors are combined, and not to the fact that the levels of the factor differ significantly. It is also possible that interactive effects might mask differences between means of one of the factors for at least some of the levels of the other factor. If significant interaction is present, the experimenter may conduct a one-way ANOVA to test the levels of one of the factors, for example, factor A, using only one level of the other factor, factor B.

Thus when conducting hypothesis tests for a two factor ANOVA:

1. Test for interaction.
2. If interaction is present conduct a one-way ANOVA to test the levels of one of the factors using only one level of the other factor.[10]
3. If no interaction is found, test factor A and factor B.

 **OPTIONAL CD-ROM TOPIC** Experimental Design and Tukey's Method of Multiple Comparison

If the null hypothesis tests for factor A or B lead to rejecting the null hypothesis that the means are equal, you may be interested in performing a post test to determine which populations have different means. A technique called Tukey's method is among the methods that can be used for multiple comparisons. For more information, go to the CD-ROM.

---

[10]There are, however, some instances in which the effects of the factors provide important and meaningful information even though interaction is present. See Cox, D.R., *Planning of Experiments* (New York, NY: John Wiley & Sons, 1992) pages 107–108.

10-3: EXERCISES

ADDITIONAL EXERCISES ON YOUR CD-ROM
Try the ADDITIONAL EXERCISES and APPLICATION PROBLEMS on the CD-ROM.

10-22. A two factor analysis of variance design with replication has been performed. Factor A has 4 levels while factor B has 3 levels. There are 5 replications in each cell of the experiment.
   a. Determine the number of degrees of freedom for the factor A and B components of the experiment.
   b. Explain what is meant by the phrase "degrees of freedom."
   c. Determine the degrees of freedom associated with the interactive component.
   d. How many total degrees of freedom are there in this study?

10-23. Consider the following data for a two factor experiment:

		FACTOR A		
		Level 1	Level 2	Level 3
	Level 1	33	30	21
		31	42	30
		35	36	30
FACTOR B				
	Level 2	23	30	21
		32	27	33
		27	25	18

   a. Based on the sample data, do factors A and B have significant interaction? State the appropriate null and alternative hypotheses and test using a significance level of 0.05.
   b. Based on these sample data, can you conclude that the levels of factor A have equal means? Test using a significance level of 0.05.
   c. Do the data indicate that the levels of factor B have different means? Test using a significance level equal to 0.05.
   d. If you rejected the null hypothesis in either part b or part c, use Tukey's method to determine which levels have different means. (Hint: See the optional CD-ROM topic: Experimental Design and Tukey's Method of Multiple Comparison.)

10-24. Consider the following partially completed two factor analysis of variance table which is an outgrowth of a study in which factor A has 4 levels and factor B has 3 levels. The number of replications was 11 in each cell.

SOURCE OF VARIATION	SS	df	MS	F-RATIO
Factor A	345.1			
Factor B				
AB interaction	1,123.2			
Error	256.7			
Total	1,987.3			

   a. Complete the analysis of variance table.
   b. Based on the sample data, can you conclude that the two factors have significant interaction? Test using a significance level equal to 0.05.
   c. Based on the sample data, should you conclude that the means for factor A differ across the 4 levels? State the appropriate null and alternative hypotheses and test using an $\alpha = 0.05$ level.
   d. Based on the sample data, should you conclude that the means for factor B differ across the 3 levels? State the appropriate null and alternative hypotheses and test using an $\alpha = 0.05$ level.

Business Applications

10-25. A national automotive repair service is interested in studying the effect of automobile manufacturer and vehicle model on the time required to complete a brake replacement job involving all four wheels. The study was limited to the "Big Three" U.S. manufacturers (Ford, GM, and Daimler-Chrysler) and to two models (passenger cars and sport utility vehicles). Five vehicles of each model and manufacturer were tested, and the time required to complete the brake job was recorded. The data are contained in the file called **Brake-Test**. (Note, the manufacturer name has been disguised at the repair company's request.)
   a. Plot the mean brake change time for each manufacturer for each of the model types. Looking at the graphs, what conclusions do you reach about the interaction between model type and manufacturer? Discuss.
   b. Based on the sample data, is there interaction between manufacturer and model type? Test using a significance level equal to 0.05. Discuss the meaning of this result as it relates to this study.

c. Based on the sample data, can you conclude that a difference exists in mean brake repair times for passenger cars versus SUVs? Test using a significance level equal to 0.05, and state the appropriate null and alternative hypotheses.

d. Suppose a sample of 15 brake repair times were taken for passenger cars and sport utility vehicles. Test the null hypothesis that the mean difference is less than or equal to 25. Assume the decision reached in part c is a correct decision.

10-26. Refer to Problem 25.

a. What conclusions should the automobile repair company make regarding the brake repair times for the three manufacturers? Conduct this test using the p-value approach to hypothesis testing.

b. If appropriate, use the Tukey procedure for multiple comparisons with an experiment-wide significance level of 0.05. Discuss. If not appropriate, explain why not. (Hint: See the optional CD-ROM topic: Experimental Design and Tukey's Method of Multiple Comparison.)

10-27. A maker of commercial fertilizer for agricultural use has recently conducted a study of the effect of fertilizer mix and water quantity on the yield (in bushels per acre) for wheat. Three 1-acre plots were planted with the same brand of wheat seed for each of 3 fertilizer mixes and 4 levels of water quantity. The resulting sample data are in the file called **Wheat-Test**.

	MIX A	MIX B	MIX C
Water Quantity 1	87	67	89
	78	77	78
	92	58	92
Water Quantity 2	55	60	70
	67	55	67
	60	48	82
Water Quantity 3	101	90	104
	98	87	110
	89	98	98
Water Quantity 4	67	54	78
	87	67	81
	70	56	79

a. Plot the mean wheat production for each fertilizer level for each of the water quantities. Looking at the graphs, what conclusions do you reach about the interaction between fertilizer mix and water quantity? Discuss.

b. Based on the sample data, is there interaction between fertilizer mix and water quantity? Test using a significance level equal to 0.05. Use a p-value approach. Discuss the meaning of this result as it relates to this study.

c. Based on the sample data, can you conclude that a difference exists in mean wheat production across the different fertilizer levels? Test using a significance

level equal to 0.05 and state the appropriate null and alternative hypotheses.

d. Do the sample data indicate that there is a difference in mean wheat production across the 4 water quantities? Use a significance level equal to 0.05 and state the appropriate null and alternative hypotheses. Use a p-value approach.

10-28. Refer to Problem 27.

a. Can you conclude that one of the fertilizer mixes yields higher average wheat production than the others based on the sample data? If appropriate, use the Tukey procedure to make this determination. Use an experiment-wide significance level equal to 0.05. (Hint: See the optional CD-ROM topic: Experimental Design and Tukey's Method of Multiple Comparison.)

b. Fertilizer mix C costs 10% more than does mix A. Which fertilizer would you recommend? [Hint: You must determine if the mean yield of mix C is more than 10% greater than the mean yield of mix A (i.e., $A_3 > 1.10 A_1$). This will entail, in part, finding the mean and standard deviation of $1.10\bar{x}_1 - \bar{x}_3$. Refer to the optional CD-ROM topic in Chapter 4 on laws and identities for expected values and variances where we showed that $E(a_1 x_1 - a_2 x_2) = a_1 E(x_1) - a_2 E(x_2)$ and if the two variables are independent $V(a_1 x_1 - a_2 x_2) = a_1^2 V(x_1) + a_2^2 V(x_2)$.]

10-29. Mt. Jumbo Plywood Company makes plywood for use in furniture production. The first major step in the plywood process is peeling the logs into thin layers of veneer. A lathe conducts the peeling process by rotating the logs through a knife that peels the log into layers 3/8″ thick. Ideally, when a log is reduced to a 4-inch core diameter, the lathe releases the core and a new log is loaded onto the lathe. However, a problem called "spinouts" occurs if the lathe kicks out a core that has more than 4 inches left. This wastes wood and costs the company money.

Prior to going to the lathe, the logs are conditioned in a water-filled vat that is heated to warm the logs. The company is concerned that improper log conditioning may lead to excessive spin-outs. Two factors are believed to affect the core diameter: the vat temperature and the time the logs spend in the vat prior to peeling. The lathe supervisor has recently conducted a test during which logs were peeled at each combination of temperature and time. The sample data for this experiment are in the data file called **MtJumbo**. The data are the core diameters in inches.

a. Based on the sample data, is there an interaction between water temperature and vat hours? Test using a significance level of 0.01. Discuss what interaction would mean in this situation. Use a p-value approach.

b. Based on the sample data, is there a difference in mean core diameter at the 3 water temperatures? Test using a significance level of 0.01.

c. Do the sample data indicate a difference in mean core diameter across the 3 vat times analyzed in this study? Use a significance level of 0.10. Use a *p*-value approach.

d. Based on the sample data, and considering that the closer the mean core diameter is to 4 inches the better, what recommendations would you have for Mt.

Jumbo Plywood based on this study? If appropriate, use the Tukey procedure to conduct the post ANOVA tests. Use an experiment-wide significance level of 0.05. (Hint: See the optional CD-ROM topic: Experimental Design and Tukey's Method of Multiple Comparison.)

■ SUMMARY AND CONCLUSIONS

Chapter 10 has illustrated, through a wide variety of examples, that there are many instances in business where we are interested in testing to determine whether three or more populations have equal means. The technique for performing such tests is called analysis of variance. ANOVA is an extension of the two-sample *t*-test procedure introduced in Chapter 9. The basic logic is that if at least two of the sample means tend to be substantially different, then the hypothesis of equal means is rejected.

Depending upon the experimental design employed, there are different hypothesis tests that must be used. The most elementary of these experimental designs is the one-way design which is used to test whether three or more populations have equal mean values when the samples from the populations are independent. If we need to control for an outside source of variation (analogous to forming paired samples in Chapter 9), we can use the randomized complete block design. If there are two factors of interest and we wish to test to see whether the levels of each separate factor have equal means, then a two factor design with replications is used.

Regardless of which method is used, if the null hypothesis of equal means is rejected, methods exist to determine which pairs of populations have different means. Methods such as the Tukey-Kramer, Fisher's LSD, and the Tukey method allow us to examine all possible contrasts without expanding the experiment-wide significance level.

Analysis of variance is actually an array of statistical techniques used to test hypotheses related to these (and more) designs of experiment. By completing this chapter, you will have been introduced to some of the most popular ANOVA techniques.

EQUATIONS

Partitioned Sum of Squares
$$TSS = SSB + SSW \qquad \text{10-1}$$

F-Test Statistic
$$F = \frac{s_{max}^2}{s_{min}^2} \qquad \text{10-2}$$

Total Sum of Squares
$$TSS = \sum_{i=1}^{k} \sum_{j=1}^{n_i} (x_{ij} - \bar{\bar{x}})^2 \qquad \text{10-3}$$

Sum of Squares Between
$$SSB = \sum_{i=1}^{k} n_i(\bar{x}_i - \bar{\bar{x}})^2 \qquad \text{10-4}$$

Sum of Squares Within
$$SSW = TSS - SSB \qquad \text{10-5}$$
or
$$SSW = \sum_{i=1}^{k} \sum_{j=1}^{n_i} (x_{ij} - \bar{x}_i)^2 \qquad \text{10-6}$$

Tukey-Kramer Critical Range
$$\text{Critical Range} = q_\alpha \sqrt{\frac{MSW}{2}\left(\frac{1}{n_i} + \frac{1}{n_j}\right)} \qquad \text{10-7}$$

Sum of Squares Partitioning—Randomized Complete Block Design
$$TSS = SSB + SSBL + SSW \qquad \text{10-8}$$

Sum of Squares for Blocking
$$SSBL = \sum_{j}^{n} k(\bar{x}_j - \bar{\bar{x}})^2 \qquad \text{10-9}$$

Sum of Squares Within
$$SSW = TSS - (SSB + SSBL) \qquad \text{10-10}$$

Fisher's Least Significant Difference for Complete Block Design
$$LSD = t_{\alpha/2} \sqrt{MSW} \sqrt{\frac{2}{n}} \qquad \text{10-11}$$

Total Sum of Squares
$$TSS = \sum_{i=1}^{a} \sum_{j=1}^{b} \sum_{k=1}^{n'} (x_{ijk} - \bar{\bar{x}})^2 \qquad \text{10-12}$$

Sum of Squares Factor A
$$SS_A = bn' \sum_{i=1}^{a} (\bar{x}_{i..} - \bar{\bar{x}})^2 \qquad \text{10-13}$$

Sum of Squares Factor B
$$SS_B = an' \sum_{j=1}^{b} (\bar{x}_{.j.} - \bar{\bar{x}})^2 \qquad \text{10-14}$$

Sum of Squares Interaction Between Factors A and B
$$SS_{AB} = n' \sum_{i=1}^{a} \sum_{j=1}^{b} (\bar{x}_{ij.} - \bar{x}_{i..} - \bar{x}_{.j.} + \bar{\bar{x}})^2 \qquad \text{10-15}$$

Sum of Squares Error
$$SSE = \sum_{i=1}^{a} \sum_{j=1}^{b} \sum_{k=1}^{n'} (x_{ijk} - \bar{x}_{ij.})^2 \qquad \text{10-16}$$

■ KEY TERMS

Balanced Design—An experiment is said to have a balanced design if the factor levels have equal sample sizes.

Between-Sample Variation—Dispersion among the factor sample means is called the *between-sample variation.*

Completely Randomized Design—An experiment is completely randomized if it consists of the independent random selection of observations representing each level of one factor.

Experiment-Wide Error Rate—The proportion of experiments in which at least one of the set of confidence intervals constructed does not contain the true value of the population parameter being estimated.

Factor—A quantity under examination in an experiment as a possible cause of variation in the response variable

Levels—The categories, measurements, or strata of a factor of interest in the current experiment.

One-Way Analysis of Variance—An analysis of variance design in which independent samples are obtained from k levels of a single factor for the purpose of testing whether the k levels have equal means.

Total Variation—The aggregate dispersion of the individual data values across the various factor levels is called the *total variation* in the data.

Treatment—A combination of one level of each factor in an experiment associated with each observed value of the response variable.

Within-Sample Variation—The dispersion that exists among the data values within a particular factor level is called the *within-sample variation.*

CHAPTER EXERCISES

SOLVED PROBLEMS ON YOUR CD-ROM
Try the WORKED-OUT EXERCISES and BUSINESS APPLICATIONS on the CD-ROM.

Conceptual Questions

10-30. Explain the logic of analysis of variance in your own terms.

10-31. Discuss why it is appropriate to use the randomized complete block design in some circumstances. Give an example, other than those discussed in the text, where this design could be used.

10-32. In a randomized complete block ANOVA, the conclusion might be reached that blocking is not necessary.
   a. What does this imply to the decision maker?
   b. Why can this happen?
   c. What should be done if it does happen? Discuss.

10-33. Consider some decision-making situations in your major field of study, and describe two or more in which tests of one or more population variances are important.

10-34. Discuss each of the following in your own words.
   a. Within-group variation
   b. Between-group variation
   c. Total sum of squares
   d. Degrees of freedom

10-35. A one-way analysis of variance has just been performed. The conclusion reached is that the null hypothesis stating that the population means are equal has not been rejected. What would you expect the Tukey-Kramer procedure for multiple comparisons to show if it were performed for all pairwise comparisons? Discuss.

10-36. A one-way and a randomized complete blocks analysis of variance have been conducted on the same set of data.
   a. Explain the relative sizes of both analysis of variances' sum of squares and degrees of freedom.
   b. If the randomized complete blocks ANOVA concluded that blocking was unnecessary, what would you expect to be the relative size of SSB in the two ANOVAs? Explain your answer.
   c. When blocking is used unnecessarily, what impact does this have upon the components of the ANOVA? Support your answer with reasons.

10-37. In any of the multiple comparison techniques (Tukey-Kramer, LSD, etc.), the estimate of the within-sample variance uses data from the entire experiment. However, if one were to do a two-sample t-test to determine if there were a difference between any two means, the estimate of the population variances would include data from only the two specific samples under consideration. Explain this seeming discrepancy.

Business Applications

10-38. Solontactics is a large law firm with headquarters in New York City. Every day attorneys working for Solontactics must have important documents delivered to their clients and other attorneys located in and around Wall Street. Fast and reliable delivery of the documents is essential to

Solontactics, and the company currently uses several different courier services. Recently, the difficulty of working with several different couriers has led Solontactics to consider awarding an exclusive contract to a single courier service. The primary criterion in selecting a courier service will be speed of delivery. However, if no clear "winner" in terms of delivery speed can be identified, then Solontactics will examine other criteria such as price in trying to decide which courier service should be awarded an exclusive contract. To determine whether there is a difference in delivery times, Solontactics measured a random sample of 25 deliveries for each courier service. The deliveries for each courier took place over the same time period and all deliveries were made to buildings located in the same area of Wall Street. The delivery times (in minutes) were recorded for each courier and are provided in the file called **Solontactics**.

Solontactics would like to use the sample information to compare the delivery times among the 5 couriers and ultimately select a single courier service.

a. At the 0.05 level of significance, would Solontactics conclude that delivery times for the couriers are the same or different? Use the *p*-value approach.

b. If you find a difference in mean delivery times in part b, identify where the differences exist. Use a relevant multiple comparisons procedure to detect these differences.

c. Which couriers, if any, should Solontactics eliminate from further consideration?

d. Can Solontactics identify a clear "winner" in terms of delivery times, or will it be necessary to determine the winning courier service on the basis of price? Support your answer with reasons.

10-39. The materials planning group at Selser Industries is responsible for managing the inventory for all component parts and subassemblies used in the manufacture of the firm's products. Because the group monitors over 100,000 stock keeping units (SKUs), they must use a computer to assist them in their inventory control efforts. For example, the group uses the computer to calculate the requirements for all component parts of the firm's production plans. These material requirements planning (MRP) calculations are time consuming, and Selser is currently evaluating alternative MRP software packages to determine if there are significant differences in the time required by different software packages to calculate material requirements. Six software packages are being considered. Each software package was installed on Selser's computer and used to calculate the material requirements for a random sample of production plans. The results that were reported are included in the file called **Selser**.

a. Determine if the variance in the time required by different software packages to calculate material requirements can be considered equal. Use a significance level of 0.05.

b. Assume the distributions of the time required by different software packages to calculate material

requirements are normal. Comment on whether you would be justified in using a one-way ANOVA procedure to determine that the time required by different software packages to calculate material requirements was the same.

c. At the 0.01 level of significance would the materials planning group conclude that the software package makes a difference in the average times required to calculate the material plans? Use the test statistic approach.

d. At the 0.01 level of significance is there evidence to conclude that Accumat calculates material requirements plans faster than Explode? Is it possible to identify a clear winner on the basis of speed of calculation, or will Selser need to examine other criteria to decide on the "best" package?

10-40. Refer to Problem 39. Subtract 88 from all observations.

a. Conduct part c of the previous problem using these calculated differences.

b. How was the analysis affected by the transformation?

c. Determine the probability that a sample of size 18 would produce a sample mean time as large or larger than that obtained in Accumat if the true population mean time were 88.

d. Given the sample size selected for Explode, determine the smallest bound on error one would produce when trying to estimate the average time required by Explode to calculate material requirements. Assume the estimates of the appropriate parameters are sufficient for this calculation and that you wish to be 99% confident of your resulting answer.

10-41. PhoneEx provides call center services for many different companies. A large increase in its business has made it necessary to establish a new call center. One of 4 cities is being considered—Little Rock, Wichita, Tulsa, and Memphis. The new center will employ approximately 1,500 workers, and PhoneEx will transfer 75 managers from its Omaha center to the new location. One concern in the choice of where to locate the new center is the cost of housing for the managers who will be moving there. To help determine whether significant housing cost differences exist across the competing sites, PhoneEx has asked a real estate broker in each city to randomly select a list of 33 homes between 5 and 15 years old and ranging in size between 1,975 and 2,235 square feet. The prices (in dollars) that were recorded for each city are contained in the file called **PhoneEx**.

a. At the 0.05 level of significance, is there evidence to conclude that the average price of houses between 5 and 15 years old and ranging in size between 1,975 and 2,235 square feet is not the same in the 4 cities? Use the *p*-value approach.

b. At the 0.05 level of significance is there a difference in average housing price between Wichita and Little Rock? Between Little Rock and Tulsa? Between Tulsa and Memphis?

c. Determine the sample size required to estimate the average housing price in Wichita to within $500 with a 95% confidence level. Assume the sample values are sufficient for this calculation.

10-42. In an effort to improve the academic preparation of junior-high school students in the Dallas–Fort Worth metroplex, a group of concerned parents examined the number of hours per week spent doing homework by ninth grade boys and girls attending public, private (non-religious), and religious junior high schools in the area. A random sample of 15 boys and 15 girls from the 3 types of schools was selected during the semester, and the average number of weekly hours that each spent doing homework was recorded. The data are in a file called **Homework**.

The parents would like to know if the type of school makes a difference in the amount of hours students spend on homework. They would also like to determine if there is a difference in the average number of hours spent on homework by boys and girls.

    a. Is there a significant interaction effect between the type of school and the student's gender? Justify and explain your answer.

    b. At the 0.05 level of significance is there evidence of a difference in the average number of hours spent on homework by type of school? Does one type of school require significantly less hours of homework per week? If so, identify the type of school.

    c. At the 0.05 level of significance is gender a significant factor in explaining the difference in the average number of hours spent on homework?

10-43. GroBros, a regional grocery store chain located in the Intermountain West, is considering upgrading to a new series of price scanners for its checkout lanes. While scanners can save checkers a great deal of time, scanners will sometimes misread an item's price code. Before investing in one of 3 new systems, GroBros would like to determine if there is a difference in scanner accuracy. To investigate possible differences in scanner accuracy, 30 shopping baskets were randomly selected from customers at the Provo store. The 30 baskets differed from each other in both the number and types of items each contained. The items in each basket were then scanned by the 3 new scanners under consideration, as well as by the standard scanner used in all GroBros stores. Each item was also checked manually and a count was kept of the number of scanning errors made by each scanner for each basket. Each of the scannings was repeated 30 times, and the average number of scanning errors was determined. The sample data are in the data file called **GroBros**.

    a. What type of experimental design did GroBros use to test for differences among scanners? Why was this type of design selected?

    b. State the primary hypotheses of interest for this test.

    c. At the 0.01 level of significance, is there a difference in the average number of errors among the 4 different scanners?

    d. (1) Is there a difference in the average number of errors by shopping basket? (2) Was GroBros correct in blocking by shopping basket?

    e. If you determined that there is a difference in the average number of errors among the 4 different scanners, identify where those differences exist.

    f. Do you think that GroBros should upgrade from its existing scanner to scanner A, scanner B, or scanner C? What other factors may it want to consider before making a decision?

10-44. Phone Solutions provides assistance to users of a personal finance software package. Users call Phone Solutions with their questions and trained consultants provide answers and information. One concern that Phone Solutions must deal with regularly is the staffing of the call center. If the centers are understaffed, callers seeking help must wait for long periods before reaching a consultant. Many callers are unwilling to wait for more than a couple of minutes before hanging up. If the centers are overstaffed, some consultants will be idle for a large part of their shift. Phone Solutions has invested heavily in a technology to help route calls to each of the 3 centers so that a uniform number of calls are being handled at each center each day. However, the number of calls can differ depending on the day. Also, if one center takes a great deal more time to handle a caller's request, then there will be a need to redirect calls and perhaps personnel, so that a more uniform usage pattern across centers is maintained. Phone Solutions has collected data on the average length of a phone call (in minutes) for the 3 centers on 50 randomly selected days. This sample data are in a file called **Phone Solutions**.

Phone Solutions would like to determine if there is a difference in the average length of a phone call among the different call centers.

    a. State the null and alternative hypotheses of interest to Phone Solutions.

    b. Should Phone Solutions block on days? Why or why not?

    c. At the 0.05 level of significance, is there sufficient evidence to conclude that there is a difference in the average length of calls by call center?

    d. Given that Phone Solutions blocked on days, were they right in using this experimental design?

    e. If there is a difference in the average length of a call to a center, which center takes the greatest amount of time to handle calls?

    f. What might Phone Solutions do to equalize the amount of time across centers?

10-45. In order to determine whether differences exist in grocery prices charged by 3 supermarket chains located in a small city in the southwestern United States, a consumer group purchased a "typical" shopping basket of groceries from each of the 3 stores every week for 26 weeks. The "typical" basket of groceries was the same for each store in any week. The price for each basket by store for each of the 26 weeks is shown in the file called **Grocery Store**.

a. Determine if the variance in the price paid for the "typical" shopping basket among the 3 stores is equal. Use a significance level of 0.05.

b. Assume that the distributions of the price paid for the "typical" shopping basket among the 3 stores are normal. Comment on whether you would be justified if you used a one-way ANOVA procedure.

c. At the 0.05 level of significance is there evidence of a significant difference in the average price paid for the "typical" shopping basket among the 3 stores?

d. Which pairs of stores differ in the average price of the "typical" shopping basket? Does one store clearly appear to be more expensive than the others? If so, which store?

e. Are there significant differences in the average price of the shopping basket from week to week?

10-46. Jason Enterprises produces two different products. The demand for the products is high, and Jason is concerned with meeting demand in a responsive manner. To help the company meet demand faster, Jason Enterprises is considering changing the layout of its production facilities. It is currently evaluating two new layouts, a cellular configuration and a flexible flow production layout, in addition to maintaining its current production process. To determine if any benefit is achieved from the new layouts, Jason Enterprises examined the amount of time to produce its two products using each of the three production process alternatives. The times (in minutes) required to complete assembly of each finished product using the different layouts are displayed in the file called **Jason Enterprises**.

a. Is the interaction between type of product and type of production process significant? Again, establish the appropriate null and alternative hypotheses and conduct the test at the 0.01 level of significance.

b. Are there significant differences due to the type of product being assembled? Establish the appropriate null and alternative hypotheses for this question and conduct the test at the 0.01 level of significance. Use the test statistic approach.

c. Does the type of production process have a significant effect on the average time required to assemble products at Jason Enterprises? Establish the appropriate null and alternative hypotheses, and conduct the test for a significant difference at the 0.01 level of significance. Use the p-value approach.

d. How might Jason Enterprises use the information from the tests you have conducted to better manage its business? Should Jason Enterprises select a single product process for both of the products it produces, or should Jason's tailor the production process to the type of product? Comment and justify your answer.

10-47. To determine whether there is a difference in the average weekly hours of computer usage by college major, the manager of the computer laboratories at a state university in North Dakota randomly sampled observations from the computer records kept at the lab. Upon entering the lab, student computer users must enter a code that indicates their college: (1) for Engineering; (2) for Arts and Sciences; and (3) for Business. The computer then keeps track of the student's start and stop time. At the end of the semester the lab manager randomly selected the 155 records contained in the file labeled **Lab-Time**.

a. State the null and alternative hypotheses of interest to the computer laboratory manager.

b. At the 0.01 level of significance is there a difference in the average hours of weekly laboratory use by major?

c. What is the p-value for the test you conducted in part b?

d. If the average weekly amount of computer usage were actually the same for Engineering and Business, determine the probability that a difference in the sample means as large or larger than the one observed would occur. Assume the sample values obtained in this problem are sufficient for this purpose.

10-48. Hypos, a marketer of computer games, is interested in determining whether there is a difference in the average dollar amount spent on its games. It wishes to know if this difference depends on whether the customer places an order online (using the Internet), over the telephone, by mail (catalog), or in one of the company's retail stores. Hypos hopes to use this information to determine how best to advertise and market its products. The VP of marketing for Hypos randomly selected sales receipts from Internet orders, phone and catalog orders, and in-store sales. These data are contained in a file called **Hypos**.

a. Based on the sample data selected by the VP of marketing, what would be your conclusion about the average purchase amounts by customers from the different sources at the 0.01 level of significance?

b. If you concluded that differences in population means differ, identify which pairs of means differ.

c. How could Hypos use this information in its marketing and advertising programs?

10-49. Chip-O-Rama bakes and sells different types of cookies. Its managers are interested in testing whether there is an effect due to the type of cookie chip and whether margarine or butter is used in the cookie dough. The company invited 30 randomly selected groups of cookie lovers to its test center and asked them to eat as many cookies as they wanted of 4 different types (chocolate chip, white chocolate chip, butterscotch chip, and peanut butter chip) made with either butter or margarine. The company then measured the average number of cookies of each type eaten. The results are shown in the file called **Chip-O-Rama**.

a. Does there appear to be an interaction effect?

b. At the 0.05 level of significance, is there a significant difference in the average number of cookies eaten with respect to butter or margarine?

c. At the 0.05 level of significance, is there a significant difference in the average number of cookies eaten by type of cookie chip?

d. How could Chip-O-Rama use the information from this experiment in its bakery operations?

10-50. Gordon Manufacturing produces golf balls. Recently, Gordon developed a golf ball made from a space age material. This new golf ball promises greater distance off the tee. To test Gordon Manufacturing's claim, a test was set up to measure the average distance of 4 different golf balls (the new Gordon, competitor 1, competitor 2, competitor 3) hit by a driving machine using 3 different types of drivers (driver 1, driver 2, driver 3). The results (rounded to the nearest yard) are listed in the data file called **Gordon**.

a. Does there appear to be interaction between type of golf ball and type of driver?

b. Conduct a test to determine if there are significant differences due to type of golf ball.

c. Conduct a test to determine if there is a significant effect due to the type of driver used.

d. How would the results of the tests conducted be used by Gordon Manufacturing?

CASE 10-A

Consumer Information Association

Yolanda Carson is a newly hired research assistant for the Consumer Information Association. The association is a non-profit group whose major purpose is to supply information necessary to help consumers make better-informed decisions. Yolanda has been assigned to work with the group studying consumer practices in the banking industry.

Yolanda is aware of studies indicating that the interest banks charge for loans is related to demographic factors such as the size of the city in which the banks are located. She has been asked to determine whether there is a difference in consumer loan charges between major sections of the country.

Yolanda has been assured the cooperation of the American Banking Institute and has been given access to any data the institute has. However, she knows that loan charges may depend on many factors and feels compelled to study banks firsthand. In particular, she has decided to randomly select banks in all parts of the country and apply for an automobile loan at each bank selected.

Since consumer interest rates have been changing rapidly lately, Yolanda has recorded all rates in terms of the prime rate plus a certain percentage. (The prime rate is the rate large banks charge their largest corporate customers.) In the first test, Yolanda found the following values charged. These data are also contained in the data file called **Consumer Interest** and are shown as follows.

NORTHEAST	SOUTHEAST	MIDWEST	WEST
3.2	2.7	3.4	3.7
2.9	2.9	3.5	3.6
2.8	3.0	2.9	3.6
3.5	2.0	3.7	3.9
3.4	2.8	3.4	4.0
4.0	2.5	3.5	3.8
3.2	2.7	3.0	3.4
	2.9		3.8

The executive director of the Consumer Information Association is going to be holding a news conference in a few days to discuss the work the organization has been doing. He would like to be able to cite Yolanda's study as an example of its services.

CASE 10-B

West Coast Bell System

James Todd is the recently appointed director of employee benefits for West Coast Bell, a regional telephone system. The West Coast Bell medical benefits system insures over 60,000 employees and dependents. Over the last 5 years its medical costs have been increasing by over 20% annually. James knows that many companies, when facing these annual increases, have tried to pass some of the medical costs to their employees, generally by increasing the deductible allowance for each treatment visit. He has decided to look into the possibility of developing a managed-care network. Managed-care networks are a recent development in healthcare. They involve a company contracting with a group of physicians and hospitals to provide a variety of healthcare services. The company monitors the cost of the care provided to its employees and holds discussions with those whose costs are high. In some cases, the relationship between the company and either a hospital or physician will be terminated. Some companies using managed-care networks have held their healthcare cost increases to less than one-third of the previous levels.

James has recently read a study that reported on the cost of an outpatient procedure that is done to determine the extent to which a patient's arteries are closed. One hospital in Kansas City charged over $5,000 for the operation while a second, also in Kansas City, charged less than $3,000. James decided to use this operation to determine whether categories of hospitals tended to charge less for this procedure. The 4 categories of hospitals he identified were as follows: university-related, religious affiliated, municipally owned, and privately held. He contacted 10 hospitals on the West Coast in each category, asking what they charged for this operation.

Not all responded, and some who did provided data that could not readily be compared with that provided by the majority of respondents. The reported costs are shown as follows and are also contained in the file called **Hospitals**.

UNIVERSITY-RELATED	RELIGIOUS AFFILIATED	MUNICIPALLY OWNED	PRIVATELY HELD
$6,120	$4,010	$4,320	$5,100
5,960	3,770	4,650	4,920
6,300	3,960	4,575	5,200
6,500	3,620	4,440	5,345
6,250	3,280	4,900	4,875
6,695	3,680	4,560	5,330
6,475	3,350	4,610	5,415
6,250	3,250	4,850	5,150
6,880	3,400		5,380
6,550			

James plans to prepare a report on this study for presentation to the West Coast Bell committee on health and benefits.

GENERAL REFERENCES

1. Berenson, Mark L., and David M. Levine, *Basic Business Statistics: Concepts and Applications*, 7th ed. (Upper Saddle River, NJ: Prentice Hall, 1999).
2. Bowerman, Bruce L., and Richard T. O'Connell, *Linear Statistical Models: An Applied Approach*, 2d ed. (Belmont, CA: Duxbury Press, 1990).
3. Cox, D. R., *Planning of Experiments*, (New York, NY: John Wiley & Sons, 1992).
4. Cryer, Jonathan D., and Robert B. Miller, *Statistics for Business: Data Analysis and Modeling*, 2d ed. (Belmont, CA: Duxbury Press, 1994).
5. *Microsoft Excel 2000* (Redmond, WA: Microsoft Corporation, 1999).
6. Montgomery, D. C., *Design and Analysis of Experiments*, 4th ed. (New York, NY: John Wiley & Sons, 1997).
7. Neter, John, Michael H. Kutner, Christopher J. Nachtsheim, and William Wasserman, *Applied Linear Statistical Models*, 4th ed. (Homewood, IL: Richard D. Irwin, 1996).
8. Searle, S. R., and R. F. Fawcett (1970). "Expected Mean Squares in Variance Component Models Having Finite Populations." *Biometrics*, Vol. 26, pp. 243–254.

CHAPTER 11

INTRODUCTION TO LINEAR REGRESSION AND CORRELATION ANALYSIS

CHAPTER OUTCOMES

After studying the material in this chapter, you should be able to:

11-1: Calculate and interpret the simple correlation between two variables.

11-2: Determine whether the correlation is significant.

11-3: Calculate and interpret the simple linear regression coefficients for a set of data.

11-4: Understand the basic assumptions behind regression analysis.

11-5: Determine whether a regression model is significant.

11-6: Calculate and interpret confidence intervals for the regression coefficients.

11-7: Recognize regression analysis applications for purposes of prediction and description.

11-8: Recognize some potential problems if regression analysis is used incorrectly.

11-9: Recognize several nonlinear relationships between two variables and be able to introduce an appropriate transformation to apply linear regression analysis.

WHY YOU NEED TO KNOW

Although many business situations involve only one variable, in other instances decision makers need to consider the relationship between two or more variables. For example, an investment broker might be interested in the relationship between stock prices and the dividends issued by a publicly traded company. A marketing manager would be interested in examining the relationship between product sales and the amount of money spent on advertising. Consider a real estate appraiser who is interested in determining the fair market value of a home or business. He would begin by collecting data on a sample of "comparable properties" that have sold recently. In addition to the selling price, he would collect data

on other factors such as the size and age of the property. He might then analyze the relationship between the price and the other variables and use this relationship to determine an appraised price for the property in question.

Simple linear regression and correlation analysis, introduced in this chapter, are statistical techniques the broker, marketing director, and appraiser will need in their analysis. These techniques are important to decision makers who need to determine the relationship between two variables. In Chapter 12, we extend the discussion to include three or more variables. Regression analysis and correlation analysis are two of the most often applied statistical tools for business decision making.

11-1: CORRELATION

In those situations where you are interested in analyzing the relationship between two variables, the **scatter plot** or **scatter diagram** introduced in Chapter 2 is very useful.

SCATTER PLOT
A two-dimensional plot showing the values for the joint occurrence of two variables. The scatter plot may be used to graphically represent the relationship between two variables. Also known as a scatter diagram.

Figure 11-1 shows scatter plots that depict several potential relationships between values of a dependent variable, y, and an independent variable, x. A **dependent (or response) variable** is the variable whose variation we wish to explain. An **independent (or explanatory) variable** is a variable used to explain variation in the dependent variable. Figures 11-1(a) and (b) are examples of strong *linear* relationships between x and y. This means that for each unit change in the independent variable, x, the corresponding change in the dependent variable, y, will tend to be a fairly consistent amount. Note that this systematic change in y can be positive (Figure 11-1a, y increases as x increases) or negative (Figure 11-1b, y decreases as x increases). The degree of linearity exhibited depends upon the degree of consistency in the change of the y variable when the independent variable, x, changes.

DEPENDENT VARIABLE
The variable to be predicted or explained in a regression model. This variable is assumed to be functionally related to the independent variable.

INDEPENDENT VARIABLE
A variable related to a dependent variable in a regression equation. The independent variable is used in a regression model to estimate the value of the dependent variable.

Figures 11-1 (c) and (d) illustrate situations in which the relationship between the x and y variable is nonlinear. There are many possible nonlinear relationships that can occur. The scatter plot is very useful for visually identifying the nature of the relationship.

Figures 11-1 (e) and (f) show examples in which there is no identifiable relationship between the two variables. This means that as x increases, y sometimes increases and sometimes decreases, but with no discernible pattern.

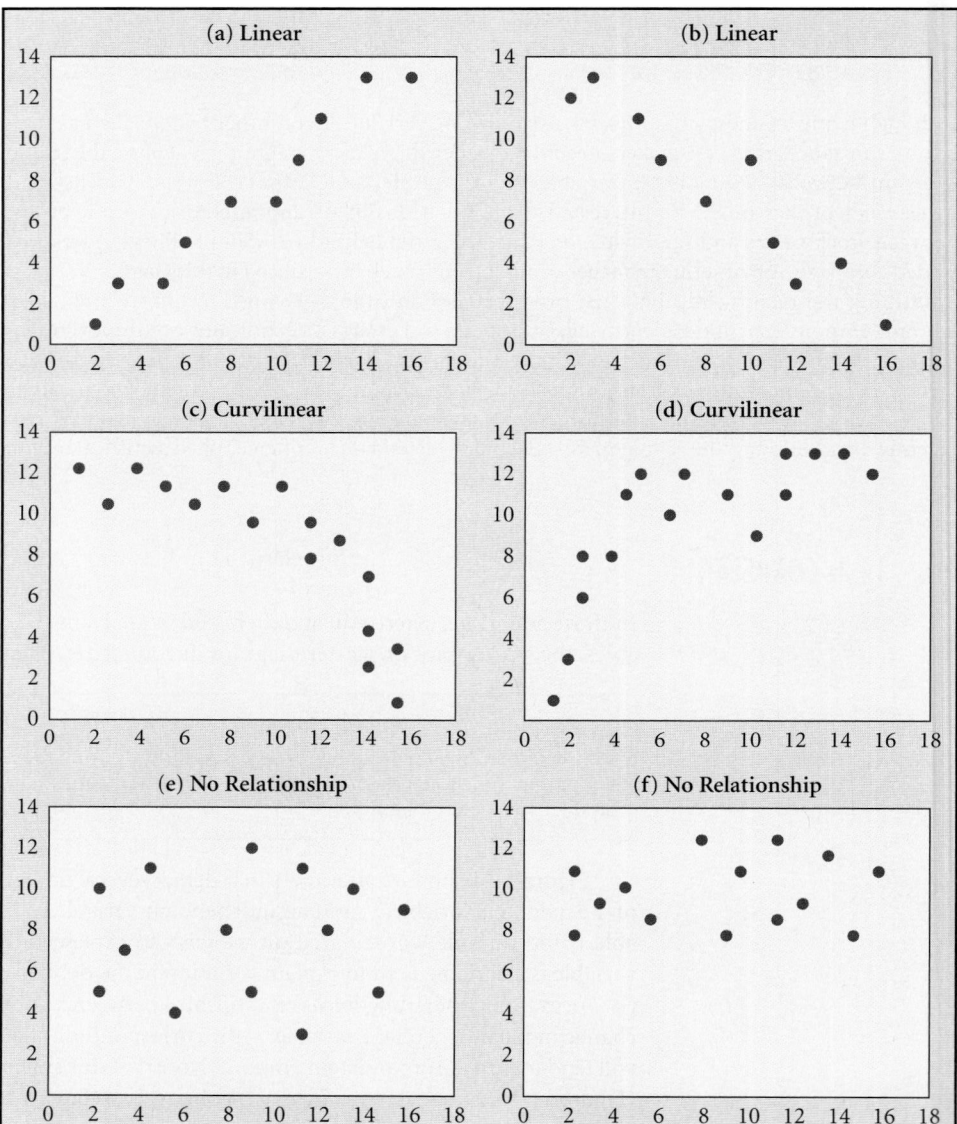

FIGURE 11-1
Two Variable Relationships

Correlation versus Regression

In analyzing the relationship between two variables, there are two basic models that we can use depending on the conditions under which the data are collected. These models are the subjects of this chapter. The first model is referred to as the *regression model*, in which the relationship between x and y assumes that the x variable takes on known values specifically selected from all the possible values for x. The y variable is a random variable observed at the different levels of x.

The second model is referred to as the *correlation model* and is used in applications where both the x and the y variable are considered to be random variables. These two models, regression and correlation, arise in practice by the way in which the data are obtained. Consider models that might apply to the relationship between the amount of sunscreen sold daily, y, as a function of the day's high temperature, x. We could select a random sample of 36 days and record the amount of sunscreen sold and the day's maximum temperature. In this case, the measurements obtained for both variables are observations from a joint distribution of x and y. An analysis of these data would be done using the correlation model approach.

Suppose instead that we decide to collect data for days with maximum temperatures of 75, 80, 85, 90, 95, and 100 degrees. We would measure the amount of daily sunscreen sold (y) for several randomly chosen days in which the maximum temperature is at each of these preselected temperatures. That is, we might pick 6 days at random from a population of days that have a maximum temperature of 75 degrees and observe the amount of sunscreen sold, and so on. Now each observation on y is from the distribution of y for a fixed x value. The analysis of these data would be done using the regression model approach.

We stress the two types of sampling because there are important differences in what can be estimated using these two methods. As we will illustrate later in this chapter, when the data have been collected at specific levels of the x variable as was suggested in the second situation, our estimates for the y variable will be conditional on the value of x we are using.[1]

The Correlation Coefficient

In addition to analyzing the relationship between two variables graphically, we can also measure the strength of the linear relationship between two variables using a measure called the **correlation coefficient.**

CORRELATION COEFFICIENT

A quantitative measure of the strength of the linear relationship between two variables. The correlation ranges from -1.0 to $+1.0$. A correlation of ± 1.0 indicates a perfect linear relationship, whereas a correlation of 0 indicates no linear relationship.

The correlation coefficient for two variables can be estimated from sample data using Equation 11-1 or the algebraic equivalent, Equation 11-2.

SAMPLE CORRELATION COEFFICIENT

$$r = \frac{\sum(x-\bar{x})(y-\bar{y})}{\sqrt{[\sum(x-\bar{x})^2][\sum(y-\bar{y})^2]}} \qquad \textbf{11-1}$$

or the algebraic equivalent:

$$r = \frac{n\sum xy - \sum x\sum y}{\sqrt{[n(\sum x^2)-(\sum x)^2][n(\sum y^2)-(\sum y)^2]}} \qquad \textbf{11-2}$$

where:

r = Sample correlation coefficient
n = Sample size
x = Value of the independent variable
y = Value of the dependent variable

The sample correlation coefficient computed using Equations 11-1 and 11-2 is called the *Pearson Product Moment Correlation.* The sample correlation coefficient, r, can range from a perfect positive correlation, $+1.0$, to a perfect negative correlation, -1.0. A perfect positive correlation is one in which a given change in the value of the x variable is accompanied by a specific amount of change in the y variable. Graphically, the x, y points will plot on a straight line. If two variables have no linear relationship, the correlation between them

---

[1]See Neter, J. et al., *Applied Linear Statistical Models,* 4th ed., p. 85; and Draper, N. R., and Smith, H., *Applied Regression Analysis,* 3d ed., p. 89, for more discussion on this subject.

is 0. Consequently, the more the correlation differs from 0.0, the stronger the linear relationship between the two variables. The sign of the correlation coefficient indicates the direction of the relationship, but it does not aid in determining the strength.

Figure 11-2 illustrates some examples of correlation between two variables. Note for the correlation coefficient to equal plus or minus 1.0, all the (x, y) points form a perfectly straight line. The more the points depart from a straight line, the weaker (closer to 0.0) the correlation is between the two variables.

Midwest Distribution Company

Midwest Distribution supplies soft drinks and snack foods to convenience stores in Michigan, Illinois, and Iowa. While Midwest Distribution has been profitable, the director of marketing has been concerned about the rapid turnover in her sales force and has implemented an exit interview procedure for departing salespeople. In the course of these interviews, she discovered a major concern with the perceived fairness of the compensation structure. The director's efforts to analyze issues associated with the company's compensation plan will require her to look for relationships in the data she has gathered.

EXAMPLE 11-1

CORRELATION COEFFICIENT

Excel and Minitab Tutorial

FIGURE 11-2
Correlation Between Two Variables

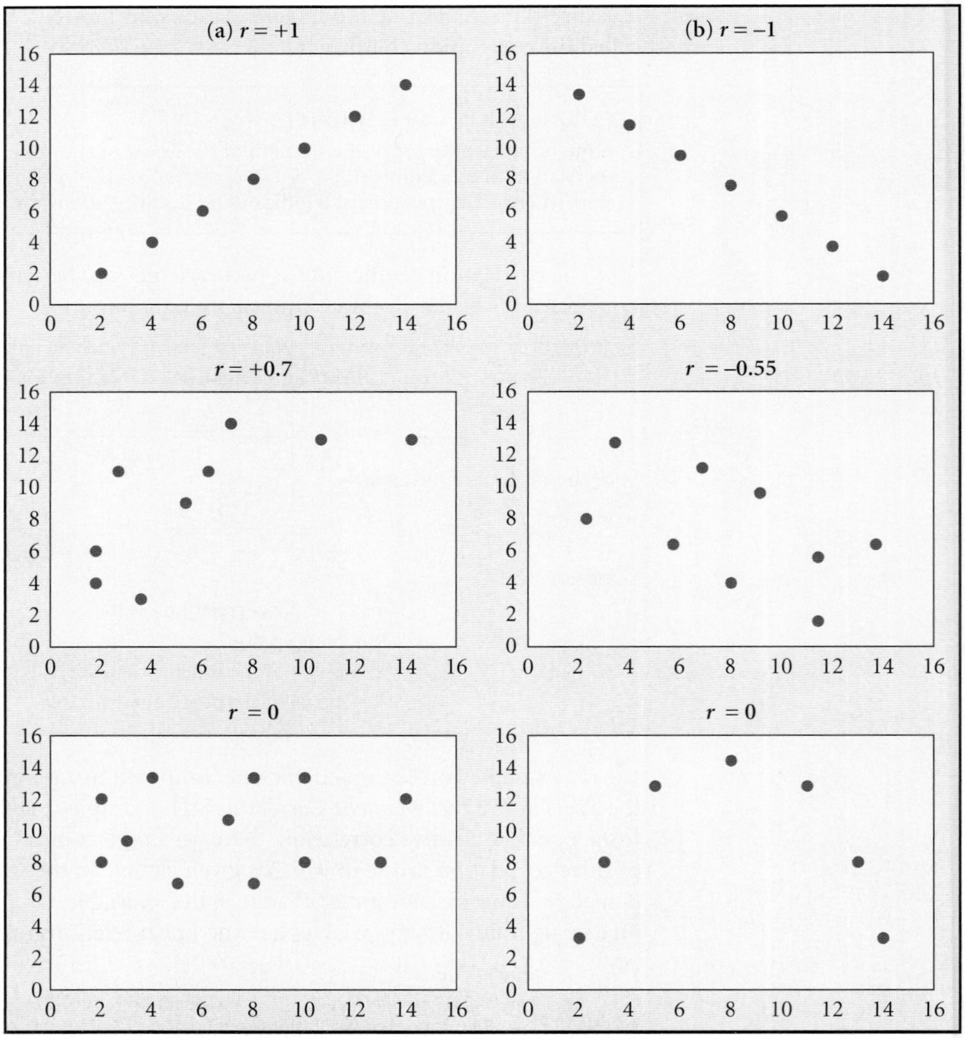

FIGURE 11-3
Data for the Midwest
Distribution Example

	A	B
1	Sales	Years with Midwest
2	487	3
3	445	5
4	272	2
5	641	8
6	187	2
7	440	6
8	346	7
9	238	1
10	312	4
11	269	2
12	655	9
13	563	6

Excel Instructions:

1. Open file: Midwest.xls

Midwest Distribution has a two-part wage structure, a base salary and a commission computed on monthly sales. Typically, about half of the total wages paid comes from the base salary that is increased based on longevity with the company. The concern expressed by departing employees is that new employees tend to be given part of the sales territory previously covered by existing employees and are assigned prime customers as a recruiting inducement. Thus, some employees are concerned that the company does not properly reward experience and commitment. The employees feel there should be a positive relationship between total compensation and years of service.

Since base salary is specifically tied to length of service, this portion of the wage structure is not an issue. At issue is the relationship between sales (on which commissions are paid) and number of years with the company. Figure 11-3 shows the data for a sample of 12 sales representatives. These data are also in the file called **Midwest** on your CD-ROM. In this form it is difficult to determine what, if any, relationship exists between sales level and years with the company. To investigate this relationship, the first step is to develop a scatter plot of the data. Both Excel and Minitab have procedures for constructing a scatter plot (refer to Chapter 2) and computing the correlation coefficient.

The scatter plot for the Midwest data is shown in Figure 11-4. Based on this plot, total sales and years with the company appear to be linearly related. However, the strength of this relationship is uncertain. That is, how close do the points come to falling on a straight line? To answer this question, we need a quantitative measure of the strength of the linear relationship between the two variables. That measure is the correlation coefficient.

Equation 11-2 is used to determine the correlation between sales and years with the company. Table 11-1 shows the manual calculations necessary to determine the correlation coefficient for sales and years that equals 0.8325. However, because the calculations are rather tedious and long, we almost always use computer software to perform the computation as shown in Figure 11-5. The $r = 0.8325$ indicates that there is a fairly strong, positive correlation between these two variables for these sample data.

FIGURE 11-4
Excel Scatter Plot of Sales
versus Years with Midwest
Distribution

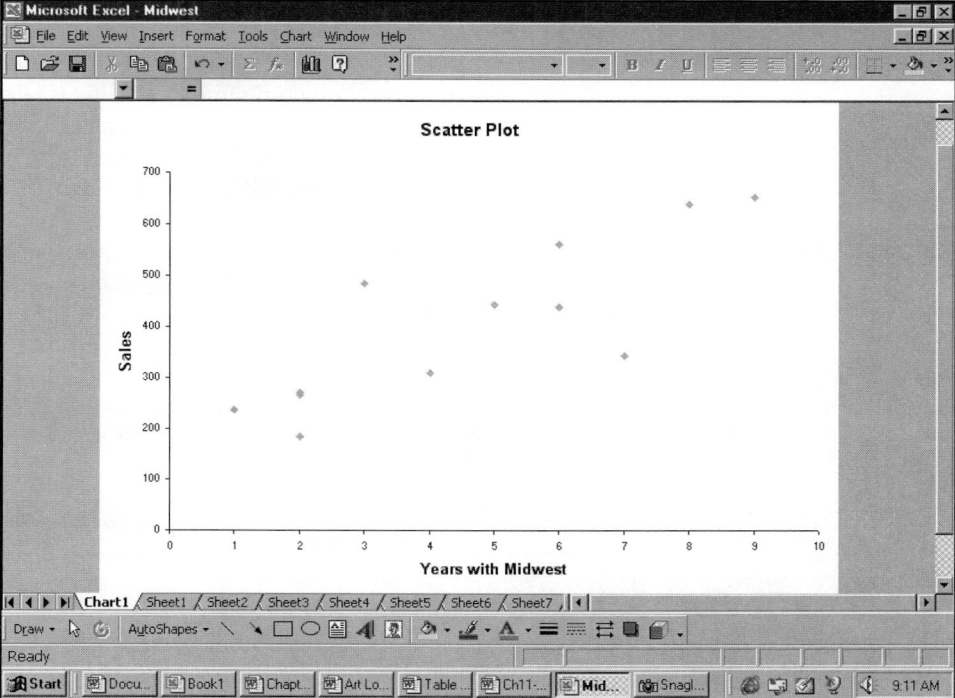

Excel Instructions:

1. Open file: Midwest.xls
2. Click on the Chart Wizard
3. Select XY Scatter
4. Select the Series tab
5. Define *x* and *y* variable
range

SALES	YEARS			
y	x	yx	y^2	x^2
487	3	1,461	237,169	9
445	5	2,225	198,025	25
272	2	544	73,984	4
641	8	5,128	410,881	64
187	2	374	34,969	4
440	6	2,640	193,600	36
346	7	2,422	119,716	49
238	1	238	56,644	1
312	4	1,248	97,344	16
269	2	538	72,361	4
655	9	5,895	429,025	81
563	6	3,378	316,969	36
$\sum = 4,855$	$\sum = 55$	$\sum = 26,091$	$\sum = 2,240,687$	$\sum = 329$

$$r = \frac{n\sum xy - \sum x \sum y}{\sqrt{[n(\sum x^2) - (\sum x)^2][n(\sum y^2) - (\sum y)^2]}}$$

TABLE 11-1
Correlation Coefficient
Calculations for the Midwest
Distribution Example

$$r = \frac{12(26,091) - 55(4,855)}{\sqrt{[12(329) - (55)^2][12(2,240,687) - (4,855)^2]}}$$

$$= 0.8325$$

SIGNIFICANCE TEST FOR THE CORRELATION

Although a correlation coefficient of 0.8325 seems quite high (relative to 0), you should remember that this value is based on a sample of 12 data points and is subject to sampling error. To illustrate what can happen, consider the scatter plot for a hypothetical situation shown in Figure 11-6. The scatter plot for the population of values indicates that there is no linear relationship between the two variables. The population correlation coefficient for these data is 0.0. We use the Greek symbol ρ (rho) to represent the population correlation coefficient. Now, suppose a random sample of values is selected from the population. (See the circled values in Figure 11-6.) These sample values appear to have a fairly strong linear relationship. In fact the correlation coefficient, r, is 0.952 based on these sample data. In this case, the sample correlation coefficient is very high, yet the two variables for the population as a whole are not correlated. This could happen if the sample data exhibit extreme sampling error. Therefore, a formal hypothesis testing procedure is needed to determine whether there is a significant positive linear relationship between sales and years with the company.

FIGURE 11-5
Excel Correlation Output
for Midwest Distribution

Excel Instructions:

1. Open file: Midwest.xls
2. Select Tools
3. Click on Data Analysis
4. Select Correlation
5. Define data range

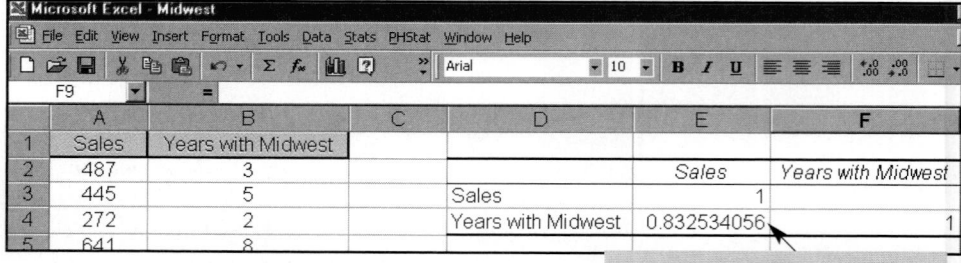

Correlation between Years and Sales

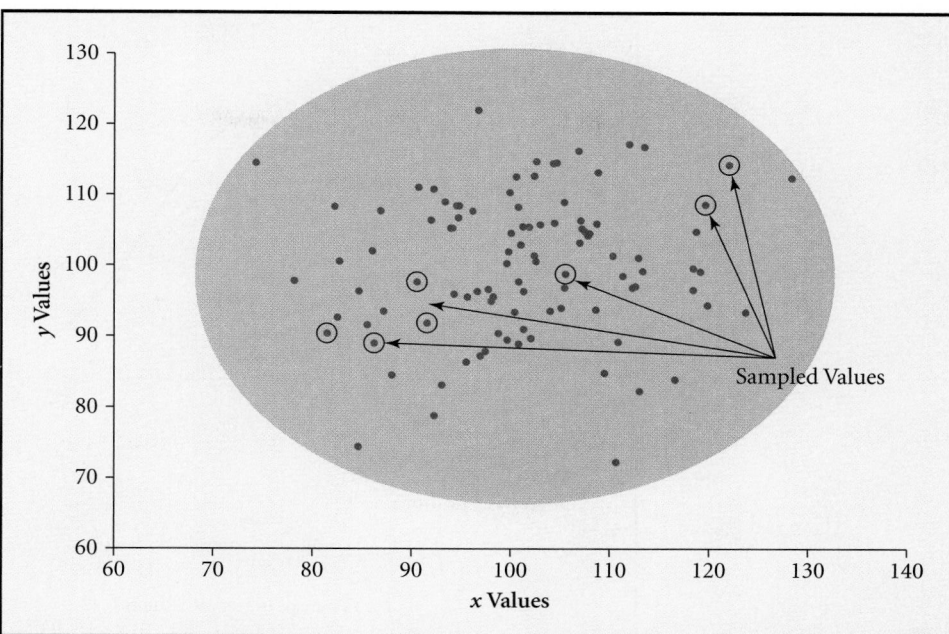

Scatter Plot—Hypothetical
Data

The null and alternative hypotheses to be tested are:

$H_0: \rho = 0.0$ (no correlation)
$H_A: \rho > 0.0$ (positive correlation exists)

We must test whether the sample data support or refute the null hypothesis. The test procedure utilizes the t-statistic in Equation 11-3

TEST STATISTIC FOR CORRELATION

$$t = \frac{r}{\sqrt{\dfrac{1 - r^2}{n - 2}}} \qquad df = n - 2 \qquad \textbf{11-3}$$

where:

t = Number of estimated standard deviations r is from 0
r = Sample correlation coefficient
n = Sample size

The degrees of freedom for this test are $n - 2$ since we lose one degree of freedom for each of the two sample means ($\bar{x}$ and $\bar{y}$ in equation 11-1) that are used to estimate the population means for the two variables. This test assumes that the two variables are selected randomly from their respective populations and that the joint distribution is normal.

Figure 11-7 shows the hypothesis test for the Midwest Distribution example using an alpha level of 0.025. Recall that the sample correlation coefficient was $r = 0.8325$. Based on these sample data, we should conclude there is a significant positive linear relationship in the population between years with the company and total sales for Midwest Distribution sales representatives. The implication is that the more years an employee has been with the company, the more sales that representative generates. This runs counter to the claims made by some of the departing employees. The manager will probably want to look further into the situation to see whether a problem might exist in certain regions.

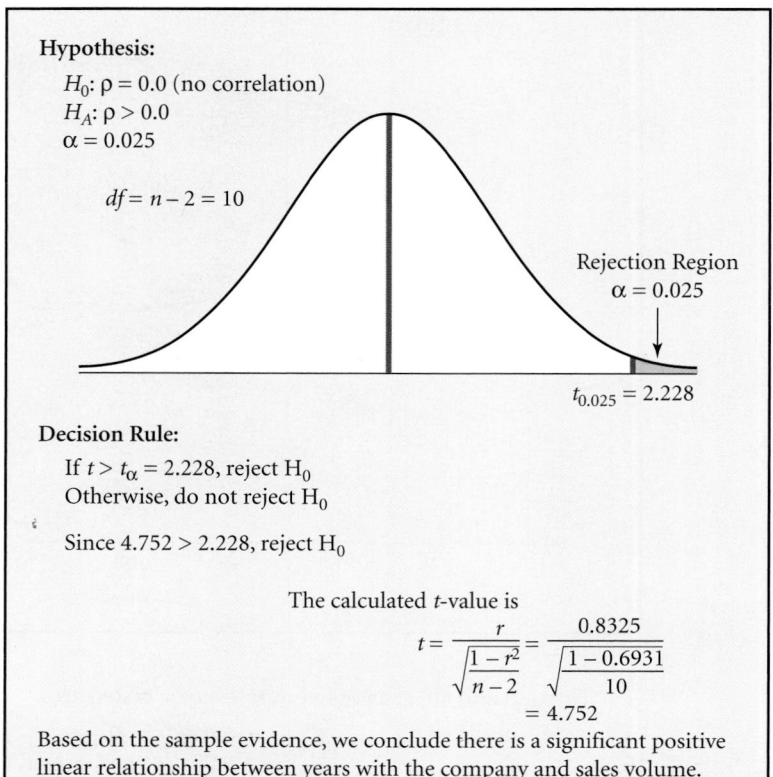

FIGURE 11-7
Correlation Significance Test for the Midwest Distribution Example

Hypothesis:
$H_0: \rho = 0.0$ (no correlation)
$H_A: \rho > 0.0$
$\alpha = 0.025$

$df = n - 2 = 10$

Rejection Region
$\alpha = 0.025$

$t_{0.025} = 2.228$

Decision Rule:
If $t > t_\alpha = 2.228$, reject H_0
Otherwise, do not reject H_0

Since $4.752 > 2.228$, reject H_0

The calculated t-value is

$$t = \frac{r}{\sqrt{\dfrac{1 - r^2}{n - 2}}} = \frac{0.8325}{\sqrt{\dfrac{1 - 0.6931}{10}}}$$

$$= 4.752$$

Based on the sample evidence, we conclude there is a significant positive linear relationship between years with the company and sales volume.

The t-test for determining whether the population correlation is significantly different from 0.0 assumes that the data are interval or ratio level and that two variables (y and x) are distributed as a *bivariate normal* distribution. Although the formal mathematical representation is beyond the scope of this text, *two variables are bivariate normal if their joint distribution is normally distributed.* Although the t-test assumes a bivariate normal distribution, it is robust—that is, correct inferences can be reached even with slight departures from the normal-distribution assumption. (See Neter et al., *Applied Linear Statistical Models* 4th ed. for further discussion of bivariate normal distributions.)

CAUSE-AND-EFFECT INTERPRETATIONS

Care must be used when interpreting the correlation results. For example, even though we found a significant linear relationship between years of experience and sales for the Midwest Distribution sales force, the correlation does not imply cause and effect. Although an increase in experience may, in fact, cause sales to change, simply because the two variables are correlated does not guarantee a cause-and-effect situation. Two seemingly unconnected variables will often be highly correlated. For example, over a period of time, teachers' salaries in North Dakota might be highly correlated with the price of grapes in Spain. Yet, we doubt that a change in grape prices will *cause* a corresponding change in salaries for teachers in North Dakota, or vice versa. When a correlation exists between two seemingly unrelated variables, the correlation is said to be **spurious**. You should take great care to avoid basing conclusions on spurious correlations.

SPURIOUS CORRELATION
A correlation between two otherwise unrelated variables.

Additional
Example 11-a

Correlation
Analysis

The Midwest Distribution marketing director has a logical reason to believe that years of experience with the company and total sales are related. That is, sales theory and customer feedback hold that product knowledge is a major component in successfully marketing a product. However, a statistically significant correlation alone does not prove that this cause-and-effect relationship exists.

11-1: EXERCISES

ADDITIONAL EXERCISES ON YOUR CD-ROM
Try the ADDITIONAL EXERCISES and APPLICATION PROBLEMS on the CD-ROM.

11-1. Develop a scatter plot for the following data.

y	x	y	x
100	88	140	100
200	120	160	90
150	200	230	125
75	100		

Based on the scatter plot, describe what, if any, relationship exists between these two variables.

11-2. You are given the following data for variables x and y:

x	y	x	y
20	16	22	21
18	12	14	10
24	18	18	10
20	17		

a. Plot these variables in scatter plot format. Based on this plot, what type of relationship appears to exist between the two variables?
b. Compute the correlation coefficient for these sample data. Indicate what the correlation coefficient measures.
c. Test to determine whether the population correlation coefficient is 0. Use the $\alpha = 0.05$ level to conduct the test. Be sure to state the null and alternative hypotheses, and show the test and decision rule clearly.
d. Refer to part c. Describe the type of hypothesis test error that could have been made in the context of this problem.   TYPE I error

Business Applications

11-3. The following information taken from the 1998 Annual Report of Baldor Electric Company shows net sales and working capital (in thousands of dollars) for the years

1988–1998. The data are also contained in the file labeled **Baldor.**

YEAR	NET SALES	WORKING CAPITAL
1988	$234,463	$ 67,168
1989	281,462	69,788
1990	294,030	75,306
1991	286,495	84,740
1992	318,930	97,343
1993	356,595	108,601
1994	418,152	118,550
1995	473,103	145,069
1996	502,875	146,975
1997	557,940	141,268
1998	589,406	176,126

a. Plot the variables net sales (y) and working capital (x) in scatter plot format. What type of relationship appears to exist between working capital and net sales?
b. Compute the correlation coefficient between working capital and net sales. What does the correlation coefficient measure?
c. Test to determine if the variable net sales declined, the variable working capital would also decline. (Hint: Think what this indicates for the value of the population correlation coefficient.) Clearly state your null and alternative hypotheses. Conduct your test at a significance level of 0.05. Be sure to state a conclusion for your test.
d. Refer to part c. Describe the type of hypothesis test error that could have been made in the context of this problem.

11-4. The following basic earnings per share (EPS) and common dividends declared data for the years 1989 to 1998 were taken from the 1998 annual report of McCormick & Company. The data are also contained in the file labeled **McCormick Dividends.**

YEAR	BASIC EPS	COMMON DIVIDENDS DECLARED
1989	$ 1.59	$ 0.19
1990	0.86	0.24
1991	1.01	0.31
1992	1.19	0.40
1993	0.90	0.45
1994	0.75	0.49
1995	1.20	0.53
1996	0.52	0.57
1997	1.30	0.61
1998	1.42	0.65

a. Plot the variables EPS and dividends in scatter plot format. What, if any, kind of relationship appears to exist between them?

b. Compute the correlation coefficient between EPS and dividends. Provide an interpretation of this coefficient.

c. Does it appear that as EPS increases, dividends decrease? Conduct a hypothesis test of the relevant parameter to answer this question. Conduct your test at a significance level of 0.025. Conduct this hypothesis test using the p-value approach.

11-5. A sample of 32 people was randomly selected, and height and weight measurements were made for each person. The correlation coefficient for the two variables was 0.80.

a. Discuss in your own words what the $r = 0.80$ means with respect to the variables height and weight. Determine whether each of the variables are fixed or randomly selected values. Explain your answer.

b. Using an $\alpha = 0.10$ level, test to determine if there exists a correlation between height and weight in the population. Conduct the test using the p-value approach. Be sure to state the null and alternative hypotheses.

11-6. A random sample of 50 bank accounts was selected from a local branch bank. The account balance and the number of deposits and withdrawals during the past month were the two variables recorded. The correlation coefficient for the two variables was -0.23.

a. Discuss what the $r = -0.23$ measures. Make sure to frame your discussion in terms of the two variables discussed here.

b. Using an $\alpha = 0.10$ level, test to determine whether there is a significant linear relationship between account balance and the number of transactions to the account during the past month. State the null and alternative hypotheses and show the decision rule.

c. Consider the decision you reached in part b. Describe the type of error you could have made in the context of this problem.

11-7. Consider the following two scenarios.

a. The number of new workers hired per week in your county has a high positive correlation with the average weekly temperature. Can you conclude that an increase in temperature causes an increase in the number of new hires? Discuss.

b. Suppose the stock price and the common dividends declared for a sample of companies have a high positive correlation. Are you safe in concluding on the basis of the correlation coefficient that an increase in the common dividends declared causes an increase in the stock price? Present other reasons than the correlation coefficient that might lead you to conclude that an increase in common dividends declared causes an increase in the stock price.

■ 11-2: SIMPLE LINEAR REGRESSION ANALYSIS

Calculus Derivation for Simple Linear Regression Model

In the Midwest Distribution example, we determined that the relationship between years of experience and total sales is linear, and statistically significant, based on the correlation analysis performed in the previous section. Since hiring and training costs have been increasing, the Midwest Distribution Company would like to use this relationship to help formulate a more acceptable wage package for the sales force.

The statistical method we will use to analyze the relationship between years of experience and total sales is *regression analysis*. When we have only two variables, a dependent variable such as sales and an independent variable such as years with the company, the technique is referred to as *simple regression analysis*. When the relationship between the dependent variable and the independent variable is linear, the technique is **simple linear regression**.

The Regression Model and Assumptions

The objective of simple linear regression (which we shall call regression analysis) is to represent the relationship between values of x and y with a model of the form shown in Equation 11-4.

SIMPLE LINEAR REGRESSION MODEL (POPULATION MODEL)

$$y = \beta_0 + \beta_1 x + \epsilon \qquad \textbf{11-4}$$

where:

y = Value of the dependent variable
x = Value of the independent variable
β_0 = Population's y-intercept
β_1 = Slope of the population regression line
ϵ = Error term, or residual (i.e., the difference between the actual y value and the value of y predicted by the population model)

The simple linear regression population model described in Equation 11-4 has four assumptions.

1. Individual values of the error terms, ϵ, are statistically independent of one another, and these values represent a random sample from the population of possible values at each level of x.
2. For a given value of x, there can exist many values of ϵ. Further, the distribution of possible ϵ values for any x value is normal.
3. The distributions of possible ϵ values have equal variances for all values of x.
4. The means of the dependent variable, y, for all specified values of the independent variable, $(\mu_{y|x})$, can be connected by a straight line called the population regression model.

Figure 11-8 illustrates assumptions 2, 3, and 4. The regression model (straight line) connects the average of the y values for each level of the independent variable, x. The actual y values for each level of x are normally distributed around the mean of y. Finally, observe that the spread of possible y values is the same regardless of the level of x. The population regression line is determined by two values, β_0 and β_1. These values are known as the population **regression coefficients**. Value β_0 identifies the y-intercept and β_1, the **regression slope coefficient** of the regression line. Under the regression assumptions, the coefficients define the true population model. For each observation, the actual value of the dependent variable, y, for any x, is the sum of two components.

$$y = \underset{\text{Linear Component}}{\beta_0 + \beta_1 x} + \underset{\text{Random Error Component}}{\epsilon}$$

The random error component, ϵ, may be positive, zero, or negative, depending on whether a single value of y for a given x falls above, on, or below the population regression line.

FIGURE 11-8
Graphical Display of Linear
Regression Assumptions

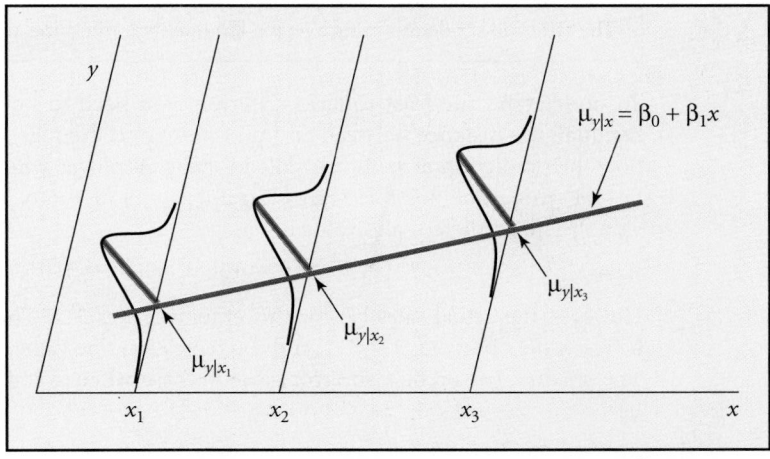

> **REGRESSION COEFFICIENTS**
> In the simple regression model, there are two coefficients: the intercept and the slope.

> **REGRESSION SLOPE COEFFICIENT**
> The average change in the dependent variable for a unit change in the independent variable. The slope coefficient may be positive or negative, depending on the relationship between the two variables.

Meaning of the Regression Coefficients

Coefficient β_1, the slope of the population regression line, measures the average change in the value of the dependent variable, y, for each unit change in x. The population slope can be either positive, zero, or negative, depending on the relationship between x and y. For example, a positive population slope of 12 ($\beta_1 = 12$) means that for a 1-unit increase in x, we can expect an average 12-unit increase in y. Correspondingly, if the population slope is negative 12 ($\beta_1 = -12$), we can expect an average decrease of 12 units in y for a 1-unit increase in x.

The population's y-intercept, β_0, indicates the mean value of y when x is 0. However, this interpretation holds only if the population could have x values equal to 0. When this cannot occur, β_0 does not have a meaningful interpretation in the regression model.

EXAMPLE 11-2

REGRESSION ANALYSIS

Midwest Distribution (continued)

In the Midwest Distribution example, the marketing manager has data for a sample of 12 sales representatives, and using correlation analysis, she has been able to establish that a significant linear relationship exists between years of experience and total sales. (Recall that the correlation between the two variables was $r = 0.8325$.) Now she would like to estimate the regression equation that defines the *true* linear relationship (i.e., the population's linear relationship) between years of experience and sales. Figure 11-4 showed the scatter plot for two variables: years with the company and sales. We need to use the sample data to estimate β_0 and β_1, the true intercept and slope of the line representing the relationship between the two variables. The *regression line* through the sample data is the best estimate of the population regression line. However, there are an infinite number of possible regression lines for a set of points. For example, Figure 11-9 shows three of the possible different lines that pass through Midwest Distribution data. Which line should be used to estimate the true regression model?

Since so many possible regression lines exist for a sample of data, we must establish a criterion for selecting the best line. The criterion used is the **least squares criterion**.

> **LEAST SQUARES CRITERION**
> The criterion for determining a regression line that minimizes the sum of squared residuals.

To understand the least squares criterion, you need to know about prediction error, or **residual**, the distance between an (x, y) point and the regression line. Figure 11-10 shows how the prediction error is calculated for the employee who was with Midwest for 4 years ($x = 4$) using one possible regression line: $\hat{y} = 150 + 60x$ (where $\hat{y}$ is the estimated sales value). The predicted sales value is:

$$\hat{y} = 150 + 60(4) = 390$$

However, the actual sales (y) for this employee was 312. Thus, when $x = 4$, the difference between the observed, $y = 312$, and the regression line value, $\hat{y} = 390$, is $312 - 390 = -78$. The residual (or prediction error) for this case when $x = 4$ is -78. Table 11-2 shows the calculated errors and sum of squared errors for each of the three regression lines shown in Figure 11-9.[2] Of these three potential regression models, the line with the equation $\hat{y} = 150 + 60x$ has the smallest sum of squared errors, or squared residuals. However, is this line the best of all possible lines? That is, would $\sum(y - \hat{y})^2$ be smaller than for any other line?

FIGURE 11-9
Possible Regression Lines

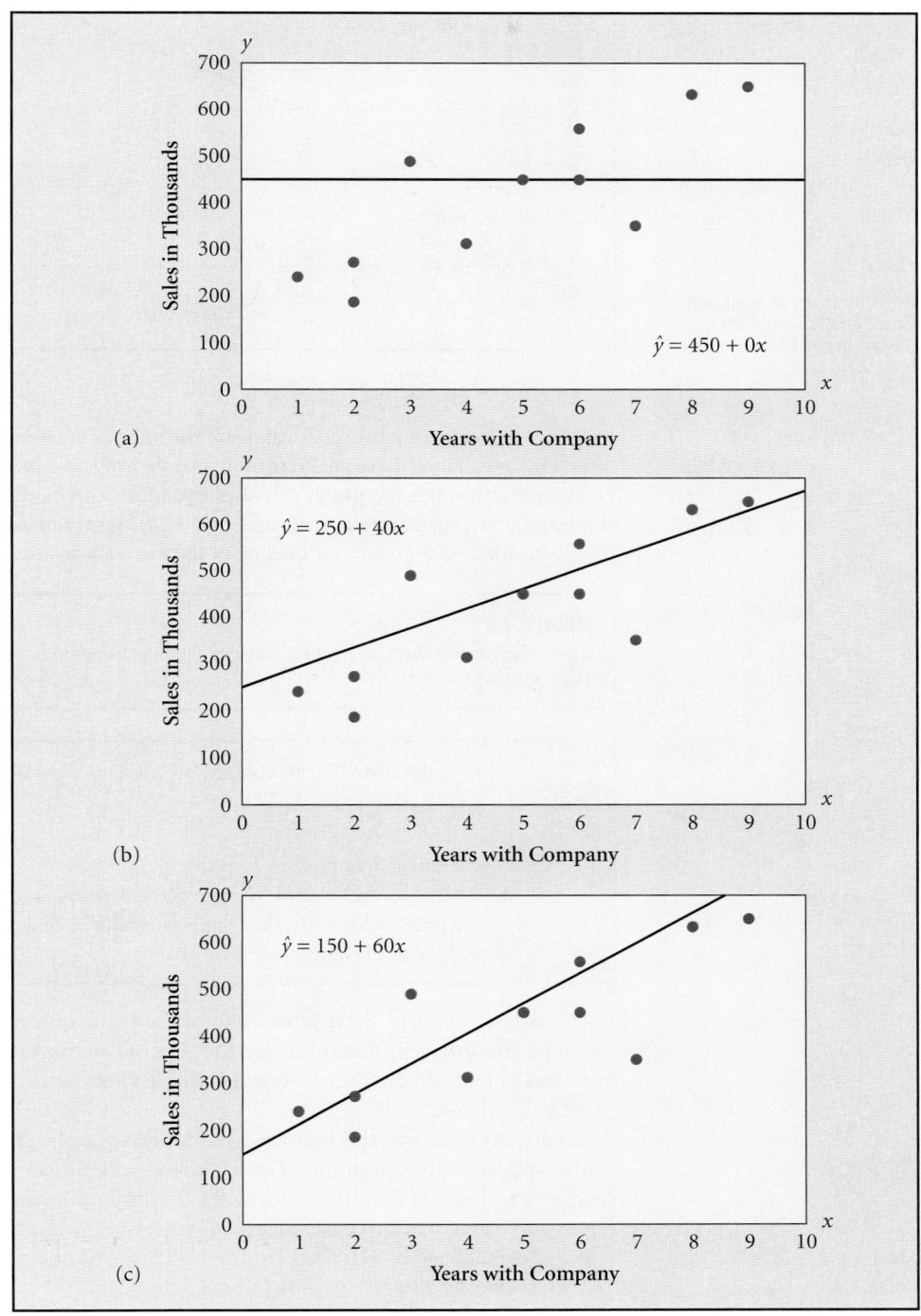

(a)

(b)

(c)

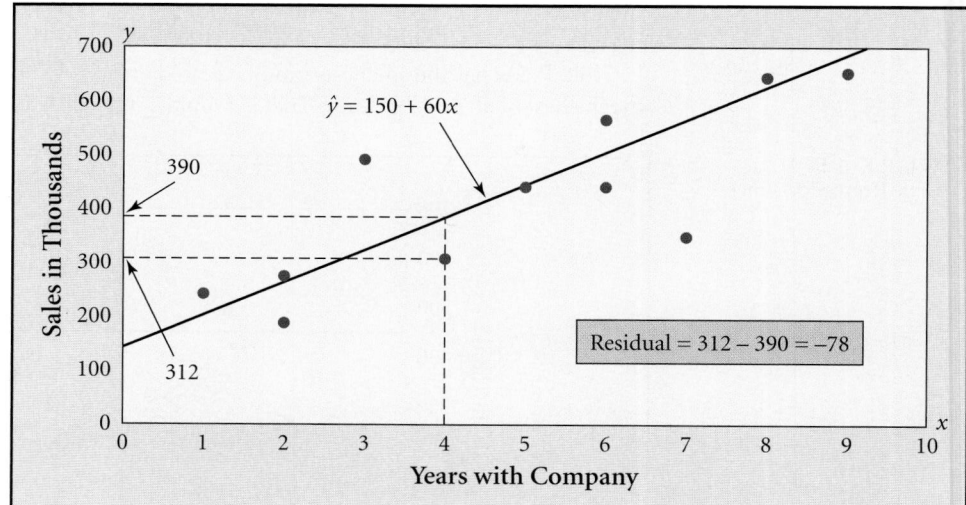

FIGURE 11-10
Computation of Regression Error for the Midwest Distribution Example

One way to determine this is to calculate the sum of squared errors for all other regression lines. However, since there are an infinite number of these lines, this approach is not feasible. Fortunately, through the use of calculus, equations can be derived to directly determine the slope and intercept estimates such that $\sum(y - \hat{y})^2$ is minimized.[3] This is accomplished by letting the estimated regression model be of the form shown in Equation 11-5.

RESIDUAL
The difference between the actual value of the dependent variable and the value predicted by the regression model.

ESTIMATED REGRESSION MODEL (SAMPLE MODEL)

$$\hat{y} = b_0 + b_1 x \qquad\qquad \textbf{11-5}$$

where:

$\hat{y}$ = Estimated, or predicted, y value
b_0 = Unbiased estimate of the regression intercept, found using Equation 11-8
b_1 = Unbiased estimate of the regression slope, found using Equation 11-6
x = Value of the independent variable

Equations 11-6 and 11-8 are referred to as the **least squares equations** since they provide the slope and intercept that minimize the sum of squared errors. Equation 11-7 is the algebraic equivalent of Equation 11-6 and is easier to use when the computation is performed using a calculator.

Table 11-3 shows the manual calculations for the least squares estimates for the Midwest Distribution example. However, you will almost always use a software package such as Excel or Minitab to perform these computations. Figure 11-11 shows the Excel regression output. In this case, the "best" regression line, given the least squares criterion, is $\hat{y} = 175.8288 + 49.9101(x)$. Figure 11-12 shows the predicted sales values and the

---

[3]The calculus derivation of the least squares equations is contained on the CD-ROM that accompanies this text under the Chapter 11 folder.

TABLE 11-2
Sum of Squared Errors for
Three Linear Equations for
Midwest Distribution

From Figure 11-9(a):
$\hat{y} = 450 + 0x$

			RESIDUAL (ERROR)	
x	$\hat{y}$	y	$y - \hat{y}$	$(y - \hat{y})^2$
3	450	487	37	1,369
5	450	445	−5	25
2	450	272	−178	31,684
8	450	641	191	36,481
2	450	187	−263	69,169
6	450	440	−10	100
7	450	346	−104	10,816
i	450	238	−212	44,944
4	450	312	−138	19,044
2	450	269	−181	32,761
9	450	655	205	42,025
6	450	563	113	12,769
				$\sum = 301{,}187$

From Figure 11-9(b):
$\hat{y} = 250 + 40x$

			RESIDUAL (ERROR)	
x	$\hat{y}$	y	$y - \hat{y}$	$(y - \hat{y})^2$
3	370	487	117	13,689
5	450	445	−5	25
2	330	272	−58	3,364
8	570	641	71	5,041
2	330	187	−143	20,449
6	490	440	−50	2,500
7	530	346	−184	33,856
1	290	238	−52	2,704
4	410	312	−98	9,604
2	330	269	−61	3,721
9	610	655	45	2,025
6	490	563	73	5,329
				$\sum = 102{,}307$

From Figure 11-9(c):
$\hat{y} = 150 + 60x$

			RESIDUAL (ERROR)	
x	$\hat{y}$	y	$y - \hat{y}$	$(y - \hat{y})^2$
3	330	487	157	24,649
5	450	445	− 5	25
2	270	272	2	4
8	630	641	11	121
2	270	187	−83	6,889
6	510	440	−70	4,900
7	570	346	−224	50,176
i	210	238	28	784
4	390	312	−78	6,084
2	270	269	−1	1
9	690	655	−35	1,225
6	510	563	53	2,809
				$\sum = 97{,}667$

LEAST SQUARES EQUATIONS (SAMPLE VALUES)

$$b_1 = \frac{\sum(x - \bar{x})(y - \bar{y})}{\sum(x - \bar{x})^2}$$

11-6

algebraic equivalent:

$$b_1 = \frac{\sum xy - \frac{\sum x \sum y}{n}}{\sum x^2 - \frac{(\sum x)^2}{n}}$$

11-7

and

$$b_0 = \bar{y} - b_1\bar{x}$$

11-8

residuals and squared residuals associated with this best simple linear regression line. Keep in mind that the residuals are also referred to as *errors* or *prediction errors*. From Figure 11-12, the sum of the squared errors is 84,834.29. This is the smallest sum of squared residuals possible for this set of sample data. No other simple linear regression line through these 12 (x, y) points will produce a smaller sum of squared residuals. Equation 11-9 presents a formula that can be used to calculate the sum of squared errors manually.

SUM OF SQUARED ERRORS

$$SSE = \sum y^2 - b_0 \sum y - b_1 \sum xy$$

11-9

Figure 11-13 shows the scatter plot of sales and years experience and the least squares regression line for Midwest Distribution. This line is the *best fit* for these sample data. Note that the regression line passes through the point corresponding to $(\bar{x}, \bar{y})$.

TABLE 11-3
Manual Calculations for Least Squares Regression Coefficients for the Midwest Distribution Example

y	x	xy	x^2	y^2
487	3	1,461	9	237,169
445	5	2,225	25	198,025
272	2	544	4	73,984
641	8	5,128	64	410,881
187	2	374	4	34,969
440	6	2,640	36	193,600
346	7	2,422	49	119,716
238	1	238	1	56,644
312	4	1,248	16	97,344
269	2	538	4	72,361
655	9	5,895	81	429,025
563	6	3,378	36	316,969
$\sum y = 4,855$	$\sum x = 55$	$\sum xy = 26,091$	$\sum x^2 = 329$	$\sum y^2 = 2,240,687$

$$b_1 = \frac{\sum xy - \frac{\sum x \sum y}{n}}{\sum x^2 - \frac{(\sum x)^2}{n}} = \frac{26,091 - \frac{55(4,855)}{12}}{329 - \frac{(55)^2}{12}}$$

$$= 49.9101$$

Then,

$$b_0 = \bar{y} - b_1\bar{x} = 4,855/12 - 49.9101(55/12) = 175.8288$$

The least squares regression line is, therefore,

$$\hat{y} = 175.8288 + 49.9101(x)$$

Estimated regression equation is
$\hat{y} = 175.8288 + 49.9101(x)$

FIGURE 11-11
Excel Midwest Distribution Regression Results

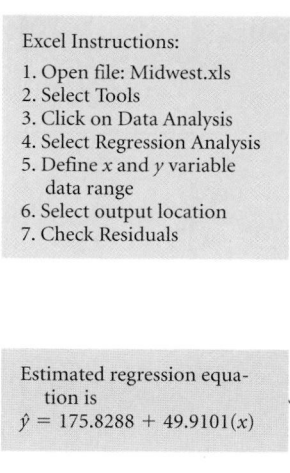

Sum of squares residual = 84,834.295

SUMMARY OUTPUT

Regression Statistics	
Multiple R	0.832534056
R Square	0.693112955
Adjusted R Square	0.662424251
Standard Error	92.10553441
Observations	12

ANOVA

	df	SS	MS	F	Significance F
Regression	1	191600.622	191600.622	22.58527906	0.000777416
Residual	10	84834.29469	8483.429469		
Total	11	276434.9167			

	Coefficients	Standard Error	t Stat	P-value	Lower 95%	Upper 95%
Intercept	175.8288191	54.98988674	3.197475563	0.00953244	53.30369475	298.3539434
Years with Midwest	49.91007584	10.50208428	4.752397191	0.000777416	26.50996978	73.3101819

Least Squares Regression Properties

Figure 11-12 illustrates two important properties of least squares regression:

1. The sum of the residuals from the least squares regression line is 0 (Equation 11-10). The total under prediction by the regression model is exactly offset by the total over prediction.

SUM OF RESIDUALS

$$\sum (y - \hat{y}) = 0$$

11-10

FIGURE 11-12
Residuals and Squared Residuals for the Midwest Distribution Example

RESIDUAL OUTPUT

Observation	Predicted Sales	Residuals	Squared Residuals
1	325.5590466	161.4409534	26063.18144
2	425.3791983	19.62080173	384.9758607
3	275.6489707	-3.648970748	13.31498752
4	575.1094258	65.89057421	4341.56777
5	275.6489707	-88.64897075	7858.640015
6	475.2892741	-35.28927411	1245.332867
7	525.1993499	-179.1993499	32112.40702
8	225.7388949	12.26110509	150.3346981
9	375.4691224	-63.46912243	4028.329502
10	275.6489707	-6.648970748	44.208812
11	625.0195016	29.98049837	898.8302828
12	475.2892741	87.71072589	7693.171437
		Sum = 0.00	84834.29

Sum of residuals equals zero
$SSE = 84,834.29$

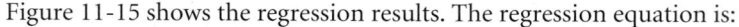

FIGURE 11-13
Least Squares Regression Line
for Midwest Distribution

2. The sum of the squared residuals (errors) is a minimum (Equation 11-11).

SUM OF SQUARED RESIDUALS

$$SSE = \sum(y - \hat{y})^2$$

11-11

This property provided the basis for developing the equations for b_0 and b_1. In addition:

3. The simple regression line always passes through the mean of the y variable, $\bar{y}$, and the mean of the x variable, $\bar{x}$. This is illustrated in Figure 11-13. So, to manually draw any simple linear regression line, all you need to do is draw a line connecting the least squares y-intercept with the $(\bar{x}, \bar{y})$ point.
4. The least squares coefficients are unbiased estimates of β_0 and β_1. Thus, the expected values of b_0 and b_1 equal β_0 and β_1, respectively.

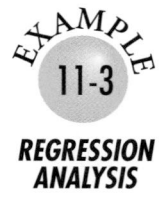

11-3

**REGRESSION
ANALYSIS**

Excel and
Minitab Tutorial

Fitzpatrick & Associates

Representatives of the investment firm Fitzpatrick & Associates are planning to make a presentation to a major retailer in Chicago in hopes of being selected to manage the retailer's pension fund monies. One part of the presentation involves an analysis of the relationship between company profits and the number of employees for 50 Fortune 500 companies in the firm's portfolio. The Fitzpatrick analysts want to model the relationship between profits and number of employees using simple linear regression analysis. The data for the analysis are contained in the file named **Fortune 50**. Figure 11-14 shows the scatter plot where the dependent variable, y, is company profits and the independent variable, x, is number of employees. There appears to be a slight positive linear relationship between the two variables.

Figure 11-15 shows the regression results. The regression equation is:

$$\hat{y} = 2{,}556.9 + 0.0048(x)$$

Excel Instructions:

1. Open file: Fortune 50.xls
2. Click on Chart Wizard
3. Select XY Scatter
4. Click on Series Tab
5. Define *x* and *y* variable range

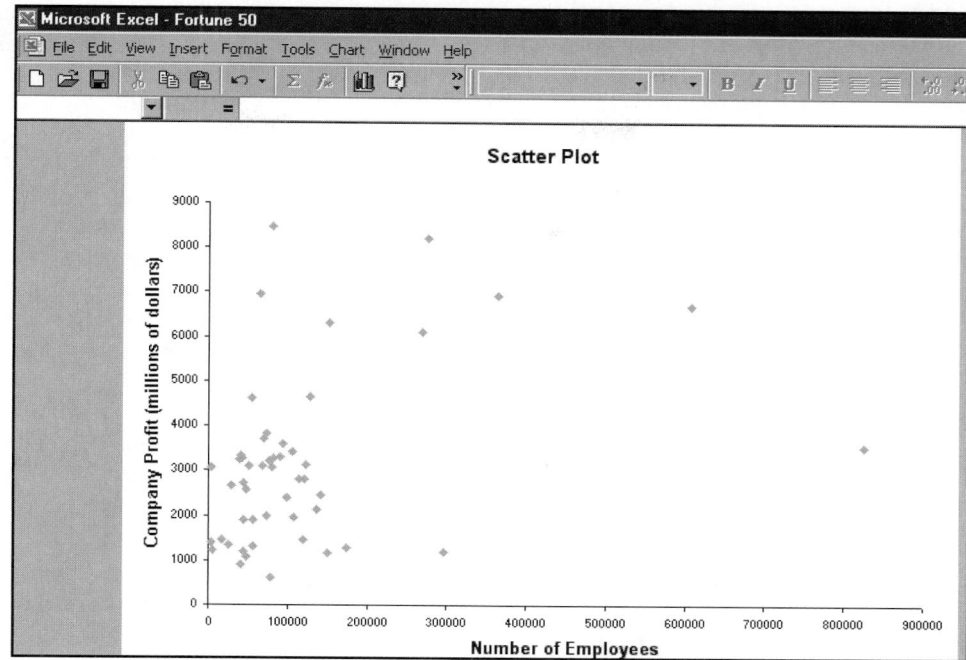

FIGURE 11-14
Excel Scatter plot for
Fitzpatrick & Associates

The regression slope is estimated to be 0.0048 which means that for each additional employee, the mean increase in company profit is 0.0048 million dollars or $4,800. Remember, this is a point estimate for the true population slope coefficient. Later in this chapter, we will discuss the concept of developing confidence interval estimators for the population slope. The intercept can be interpreted only when a value equal to zero for the *x* variable (employees) is plausible. Clearly no company has zero employees so the intercept in this case has no meaning other than it locates the height of the regression line for *x* = 0.0. You might also notice that the Excel output contains a number of statistics in addition to the regression equation. One of these is the correlation coefficient, *r*, that Excel labels

FIGURE 11-15
Excel Regression Results for
Fitzpatrick & Associates

Excel Instructions:

1. Open file: Fortune 50.xls
2. Click on Tools tab
3. Select Regression
4. Define *x* and *y* variable data range

Regression equation

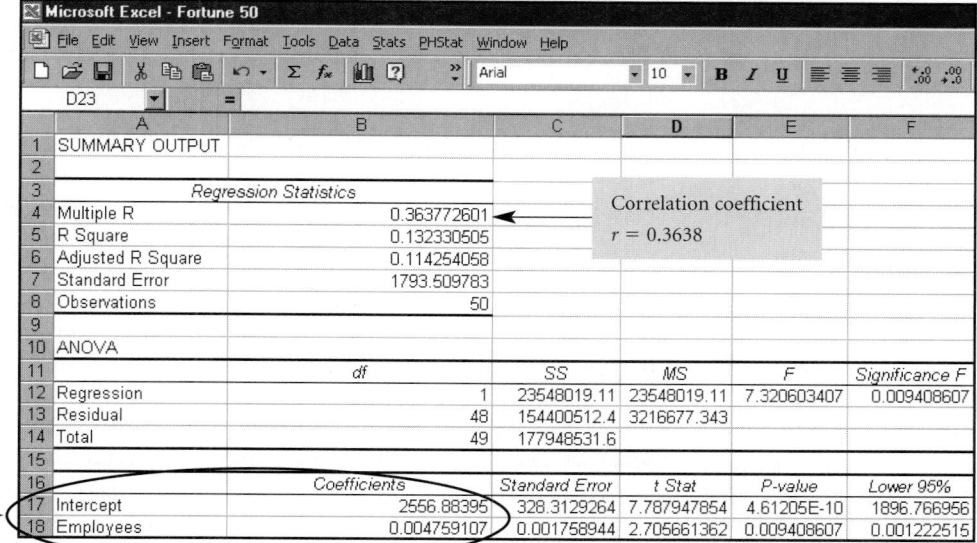

Multiple R. From Figure 11-15 we see that the correlation between profits and number of employees is 0.3638. We will discuss many of the other regression statistics later in this chapter.

Significance Tests in Regression Analysis

In Section 11-1 we pointed out that the correlation coefficient computed from sample data is a point estimate of the population correlation coefficient and is subject to sampling error. We also introduced a test of significance for the correlation coefficient. Likewise, the regression coefficients developed from a sample of data are also point estimates of the true regression coefficients for the population. The regression coefficients are also subject to sampling error. For example, due to sampling error the estimated slope coefficient may be positive or negative while the population slope is really zero. Therefore, we need a test procedure to determine whether the regression slope coefficient is statistically significant. As you will see in this section, the test for the simple linear regression slope coefficient is equivalent to the test for the correlation coefficient. That is, if the correlation between two variables is found to be significant, then the regression slope coefficient will also be significant.

THE COEFFICIENT OF DETERMINATION—R^2

SIGNIFICANCE TEST

Midwest Distribution (continued)

In the example involving the Midwest Distribution sales force, the marketing manager was interested in analyzing the relationship between the number of years an employee had been with the company (independent variable) and the sales generated by the employee (dependent variable). One of the first things we note when looking at the sample data for 12 employees (see Table 11-3, page 440) is that there is variation in sales between employees. An objective of regression analysis is to determine the extent to which an independent variable can be used to explain this variation. In this case, does number of years with the company help explain the variation in sales level from employee to employee?

The TSS (total sum of squares) introduced in Chapter 10 can be used as a component of a measure of the variation in the dependent variable. TSS is computed using Equation 11-12.

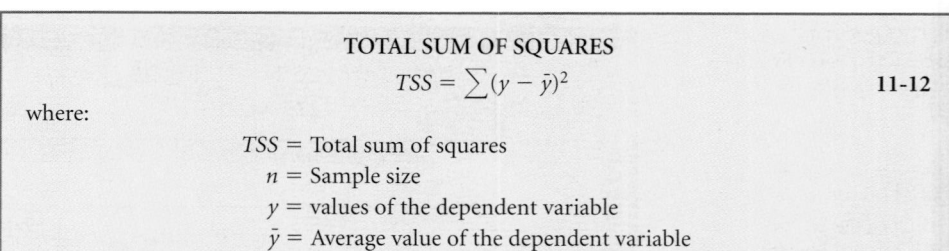

$$\text{TOTAL SUM OF SQUARES}$$
$$TSS = \sum (y - \bar{y})^2 \qquad \textbf{11-12}$$

where:

TSS = Total sum of squares
n = Sample size
y = values of the dependent variable
$\bar{y}$ = Average value of the dependent variable

For the Midwest Distribution example, the total sum of squares for sales is provided in the output generated by Excel shown in Figure 11-16. As you can see, the total sum of squares in sales that needs to be explained is 276,434.92. Note, the TSS value is in squared units and has no particular meaning.

The total sum of squares, TSS, is the sum of two other sums of squares, the sum of squares error (SSE) and the sum of squares regression (SSR). Thus:

$$TSS = SSE + SSR$$

Excel Instructions:
1. Open file: Midwest.xls
2. Click on Tools tab
3. Select Regression
4. Define *x* and *y* variable data range

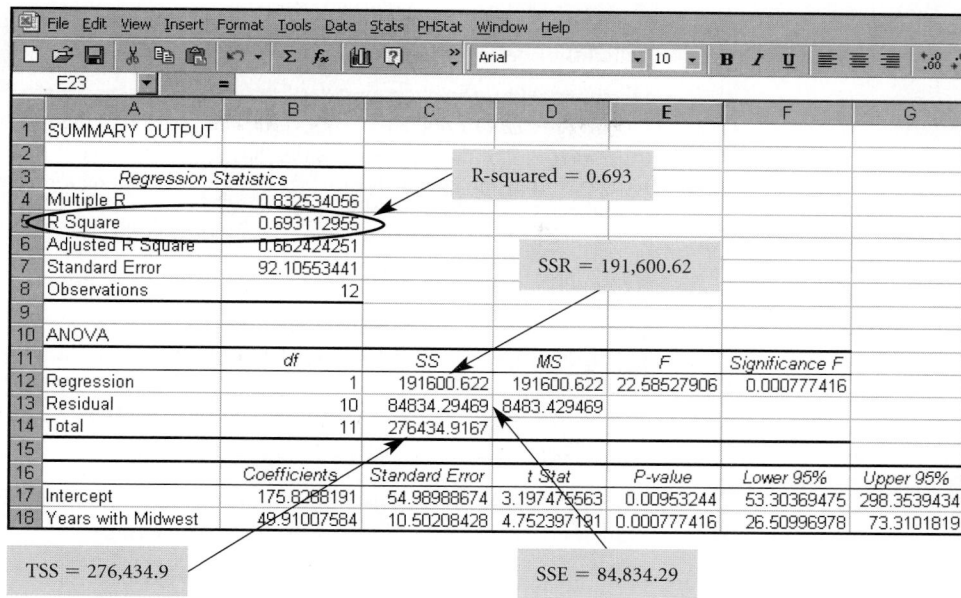

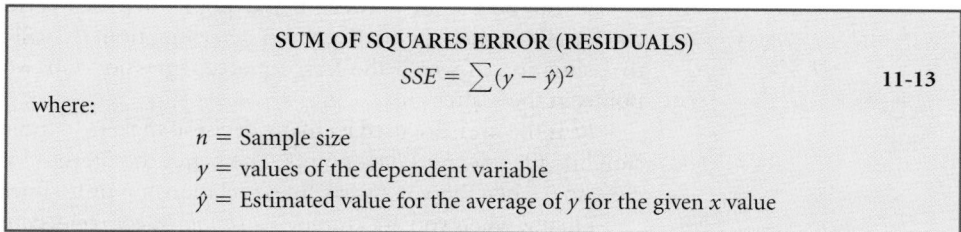

FIGURE 11-16
Excel Regression Results for Midwest Distribution

The least squares regression line is computed so that the sum of squared residuals is minimized. (Recall the discussion of the least squares equations.) The sum of squares residuals is also called the **sum of squares error** (SSE) and is defined by Equation 11-13.

SUM OF SQUARES ERROR (RESIDUALS)

$$SSE = \sum (y - \hat{y})^2$$

11-13

where:

n = Sample size
y = values of the dependent variable
$\hat{y}$ = Estimated value for the average of y for the given x value

---

SSE represents the amount of the total sum of squares in the dependent variable that *is not explained* by the least squares regression line. Excel refers to SSE as the *sum of squares residual.* This value is contained in the regression output shown in Figure 11-16.

$$SSE = \sum (y - \hat{y})^2 = 84{,}834.29$$

Thus, of the total sum of squares (TSS = 276,434.9), the regression model leaves SSE = 84,834.29 unexplained. Then, the portion of the total sum of squares that *is explained* by the regression line is called the **sum of squares regression** (SSR) and is calculated by Equation 11-14.

SUM OF SQUARES REGRESSION

$$SSR = \sum (\hat{y} - \bar{y})^2$$

11-14

where:

$\hat{y}$ = Estimated value of y for each value of x
$\bar{y}$ = Average value of the y variable

The sum of squares regression (SSR = 191,600.62) is also provided in the Excel regression output shown in Figure 11-16.

We can use these calculations to compute an important measure in regression analysis called the **coefficient of determination.**

COEFFICIENT OF DETERMINATION
The portion of the total variation in the dependent variable that is explained by its relationship with the independent variable. The coefficient of determination is also called R-squared, and denoted as R^2.

The coefficient of determination is calculated using Equation 11-15.

COEFFICIENT OF DETERMINATION (R^2)

$$R^2 = \frac{SSR}{TSS}$$

11-15

Then, for the Midwest Distribution example, the fraction of variation in sales that can be explained by the years of sales force experience is:

$$R^2 = \frac{SSR}{TSS} = \frac{191,600.62}{276,434.92} = 0.6931$$

This means that 69.31% of the variation in the sales data for this sample can be explained by the linear relationship between sales and years of experience. Notice that R-squared is part of the Excel regression output in Figure 11-16.

R^2 can be a value between 0 and 1.0. If there is a perfect linear relationship between two variables, then the coefficient of determination, R^2, will be 1.0. This would correspond to a situation in which the least squares regression line would pass through each of the points in the scatter plot.

R^2 is the measure used by many decision makers to indicate how well the linear regression line fits the (x, y) data points. The better the fit, the closer R^2 will be to 1.0. R^2 will be close to 0 when there is a weak linear relationship or no linear relationship at all.

Finally, when you are employing *simple linear regression* (a linear relationship between the one independent and one dependent variables in the model), there is an alternative way of computing R^2, as shown in Equation 11-16.

COEFFICIENT OF DETERMINATION—SINGLE INDEPENDENT VARIABLE CASE

$$R^2 = r^2$$

11-16

where:

R^2 = Coefficient of determination
r = Simple correlation coefficient

So, by squaring the correlation coefficient we can get R^2 for the simple regression model. Figure 11-16 shows the correlation, $r = 0.8325$, which is referred to as Multiple R on the Excel output. Then using Equation 11-16, we get R^2.

$$R^2 = r^2$$
$$= 0.8325^2$$
$$= 0.6931$$

SIGNIFICANCE OF THE SLOPE COEFFICIENT

Before we use the regression model to analyze the relationship between sales and years of experience, we need to determine if the overall model is statistically significant. For a simple linear regression model (one independent variable), there are two equivalent methods for making this determination.

1. Test for significance of the correlation between x and y.
2. Test for significance of the regression slope coefficient.

In Section 11-1, we discussed the first method in which a t-test is used to determine whether the population correlation coefficient is equal to 0.0. In simple regression, if the null hypothesis of zero correlation is rejected, we conclude that the two variables have a significant linear relationship. If that is the case, then the resulting regression model will also be statistically significant. However, you can directly test for the significance of the regression model.

To test the significance of the simple linear regression model, we test to determine whether the population regression slope coefficient is 0. A slope of 0 would imply that attempting to model a linear relationship between the x and y variables would be of no use in explaining the variation in y. If the linear relationship is useful, then we should reject the hypothesis that the regression slope is 0. However, because the estimated regression slope coefficient, b_1, is calculated from sample data, it is subject to sampling error. So, even though b_1 is not 0, we must determine whether its difference from 0 is greater than would generally be attributed to sampling error.

If we selected several samples from the same population, and for each sample determined the least squares regression line, we would likely get regression lines with different slopes and different y-intercepts. This is analogous to getting different sample means from different samples. Just as the distribution of possible sample means has a standard deviation, the possible regression slopes have a standard deviation, which is given in Equation 11-17.

STANDARD DEVIATION OF THE REGRESSION SLOPE COEFFICIENT (POPULATION)

$$\sigma_{b_1} = \frac{\sigma_\epsilon}{\sqrt{\sum (x - \bar{x})^2}} \qquad \text{11-17}$$

where:

σ_{b_1} = Standard deviation of the regression slope
(Called the standard error of the slope)

σ_ϵ = Population standard error of the estimate

Equation 11-17 requires that we know the *standard error of the estimate*. It measures the dispersion of the dependent variable about its mean value at each value of the dependent variable and is measured in the same units as the dependent variable. However, because we are sampling from the population, we can estimate σ_ϵ as shown in Equation 11-18.

ESTIMATOR FOR THE STANDARD ERROR OF THE ESTIMATE

$$s_\epsilon = \sqrt{\frac{SSE}{n - k - 1}} \qquad \text{11-18}$$

where:

SSE = Sum of squares error
n = sample size
k = number of independent variables in the model

Equation 11-17, the standard deviation of the regression slope, applies when we are dealing with a population. However, in most cases, such as the Midwest Distribution example, we are dealing with a sample from the population. Thus, we need to estimate the regression slope's standard deviation using Equation 11-19.

ESTIMATOR FOR THE STANDARD DEVIATION OF THE REGRESSION SLOPE

$$s_{b_1} = \frac{s_\epsilon}{\sqrt{\sum (x - \bar{x})^2}} = \frac{s_\epsilon}{\sqrt{\sum x^2 - \frac{(\sum x)^2}{n}}} \qquad \textbf{11-19}$$

where:

s_{b_1} = Estimate of the standard error of the least squares slope

$s_\epsilon = \sqrt{\dfrac{SSE}{n-2}}$ = Sample standard error of the estimate (the measure of deviation of the actual y values around the regression line)

EXAMPLE 11-5

SIGNIFICANCE TEST

Midwest Distribution (continued)

For Midwest Distribution, the Excel regression output shown in Figure 11-17 shows $b_1 = 49.91$. The question is whether this value is different enough from 0 to have not been caused by sampling error. We find the answer by looking at the value of the estimate of the standard error of the slope, calculated using Equation 11-19, also shown in Figure 11-17. The standard error of the slope coefficient is 10.50.

If the standard error of the slope is large, then the value of b_1 will be quite variable from sample to sample. On the other hand, if σ_{b_1} is small, the slope values will be less variable. However, regardless of the standard error of the slope, the average value of b_1 will equal β_1, the true regression slope, if the assumptions of the regression analysis are satisfied. Figure 11-18 illustrates what this means. Notice that when the standard error of the slope is large, the sample slope can take on values *much* different from the true population slope. As Figure 11-18(a) shows, a sample slope and the true population slope can even have different signs. However, when σ_{b_1} is small, the sample regression lines will cluster closely around the true population line [Figure 11-18(b)].

Because the sample regression slope will most likely not equal the true population slope, we must test to determine whether the true slope could possibly be 0. A slope of 0 in the linear

FIGURE 11-17
Excel Regression Results for
Midwestern Distribution

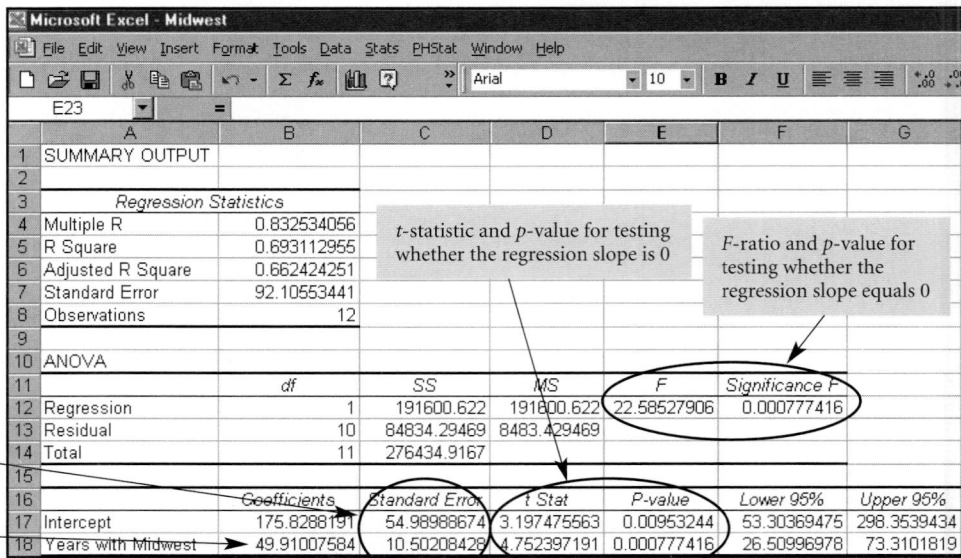

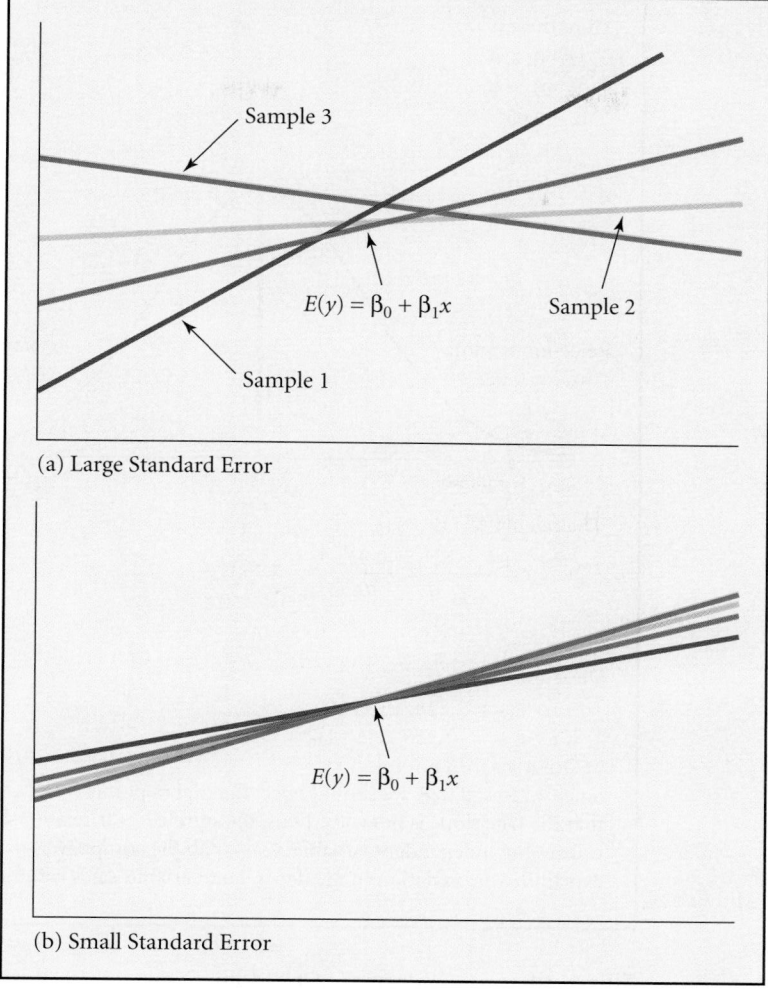

FIGURE 11-18
Standard Error of the Slope

(a) Large Standard Error

(b) Small Standard Error

model means that the independent variable will not explain any variation in the dependent variable. The null and alternative hypotheses to be tested at the 0.05 level of significance are:

$$H_0: \beta_1 = 0$$
$$H_A: \beta_1 \neq 0$$

To test the significance of a slope coefficient, we use the t-test in Equation 11-20.

TEST STATISTIC FOR TEST OF THE SIGNIFICANCE OF THE REGRESSION SLOPE

$$t = \frac{b_1 - \beta_1}{s_{b_1}} \qquad df = n - 2 \qquad \textbf{11-20}$$

where:

b_1 = Sample regression slope coefficient

β_1 = Hypothesized slope

s_{b_1} = Estimator of the standard error of the slope

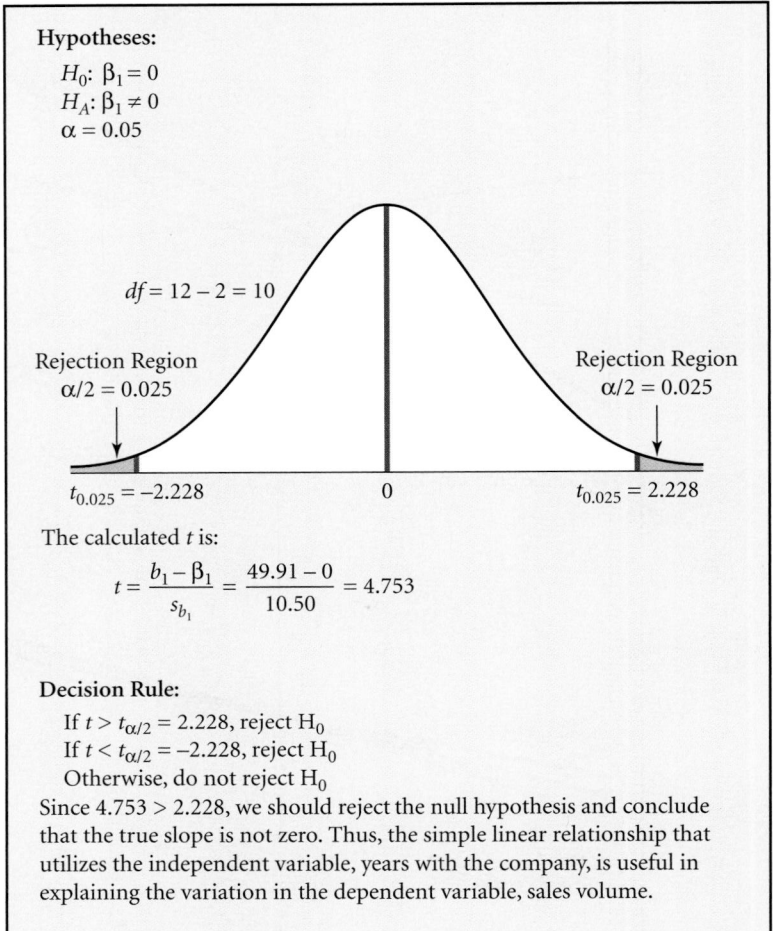

FIGURE 11-19
Significance Test of the
Regression Slope for Midwest
Distribution

Hypotheses:

H_0: $\beta_1 = 0$
H_A: $\beta_1 \neq 0$
$\alpha = 0.05$

$df = 12 - 2 = 10$

Rejection Region
$\alpha/2 = 0.025$

Rejection Region
$\alpha/2 = 0.025$

$t_{0.025} = -2.228$ 0 $t_{0.025} = 2.228$

The calculated t is:

$$t = \frac{b_1 - \beta_1}{s_{b_1}} = \frac{49.91 - 0}{10.50} = 4.753$$

Decision Rule:

If $t > t_{\alpha/2} = 2.228$, reject H_0
If $t < t_{\alpha/2} = -2.228$, reject H_0
Otherwise, do not reject H_0

Since 4.753 > 2.228, we should reject the null hypothesis and conclude that the true slope is not zero. Thus, the simple linear relationship that utilizes the independent variable, years with the company, is useful in explaining the variation in the dependent variable, sales volume.

This test has $n - 2$ degrees of freedom. Figure 11-19 illustrates this test for the Midwest Distribution example. The calculated t-value of 4.753 exceeds the critical value ($t = 2.228$) from the t-distribution in Appendix F with 10 degrees of freedom and an $\alpha/2 = 0.025$. This indicates that we should reject the hypothesis that the true regression slope is 0. Thus, years of experience can be used to help explain the variation in an individual representative's sales. (Note that the calculated t is the same value that we got in Figure 11-7 on page 432 for the test of the correlation coefficient.)

The Excel output shown in Figure 11-17 also contains the calculated t-statistic. The p-value for the calculated t-statistic is also provided. As with other situations involving two-tailed hypothesis tests, if the p-value is less than α, the null hypothesis is rejected. In this case, since p-value = 0.0008 < 0.05, we reject the null hypothesis.

ANOTHER TEST OF SIGNIFICANCE

An alternative method exists for testing whether the independent variable explains a significant portion of the variation in the dependent variable. This approach is based on the sum of squares calculations shown earlier when we introduced R^2, the coefficient of determination, and uses an analysis of variance methodology introduced in Chapter 10.

If the independent and the dependent variables are not linearly related (i.e., $\beta_1 = 0$), then the population regression model will explain none of the variation in the dependent variable. To use the analysis of variance approach, we examine two measures of variance.

The first uses the sum of squares regression value, and is called the **mean square regression** or MSR. Equation 11-21 is used to calculate MSR.

MEAN SQUARE REGRESSION

$$MSR = \frac{SSR}{k}$$

11-21

where:

SSR = Sum of squares regression

k = Number of independent variables in the model

The second variance measure uses the sum of squares error term, and is called the **mean square error** (MSE), computed using Equation 11-22.

MEAN SQUARE ERROR

$$MSE = \frac{SSE}{n - k - 1}$$

11-22

where:

SSE = Sum of squares error

n = Sample size

k = Number of independent variables in the model

Recall that Equations 11-13 and 11-14 led to the expression:

$$TSS = SSR + SSE$$

Dividing each component of this expression by its respective degrees of freedom produces the mean square. Each of the mean squares, therefore, represents the average sum of squares per degree of freedom attributable to the respective component.

The ANOVA approach is based on the idea that if the null hypothesis is false (the model does actually explain some of the variation in the dependent variable), the ratio of MSR over MSE will be "large" and will give a value in the upper tail of an F-distribution with k and $n - k - 1$ degrees of freedom.

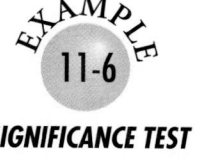

EXAMPLE 11-6

SIGNIFICANCE TEST

Midwest Distribution (*continued*)

Consider the Midwest Distribution example where a regression model was developed using years of experience as the independent variable to explain the variation in sales volume by the sales representatives. We previously used the t-test to test whether the regression slope coefficient is equal to 0.

$$H_0: \beta_1 = 0$$
$$H_A: \beta_1 \neq 0$$

The analysis of variance approach could be used to test this same hypothesis as shown in Figure 11-20. As shown there, since:

$$\frac{MSR}{MSE} = F = 22.59 > 4.96,$$

we reject the null hypothesis and conclude that the regression model is significant and $\beta_1 \neq 0$. That is, predicting sales based on the least squares regression model with number of years of experience as the independent variable would be superior to just using the overall average sales value, $\bar{y}$. The Excel regression output shown in Figure 11-17 also

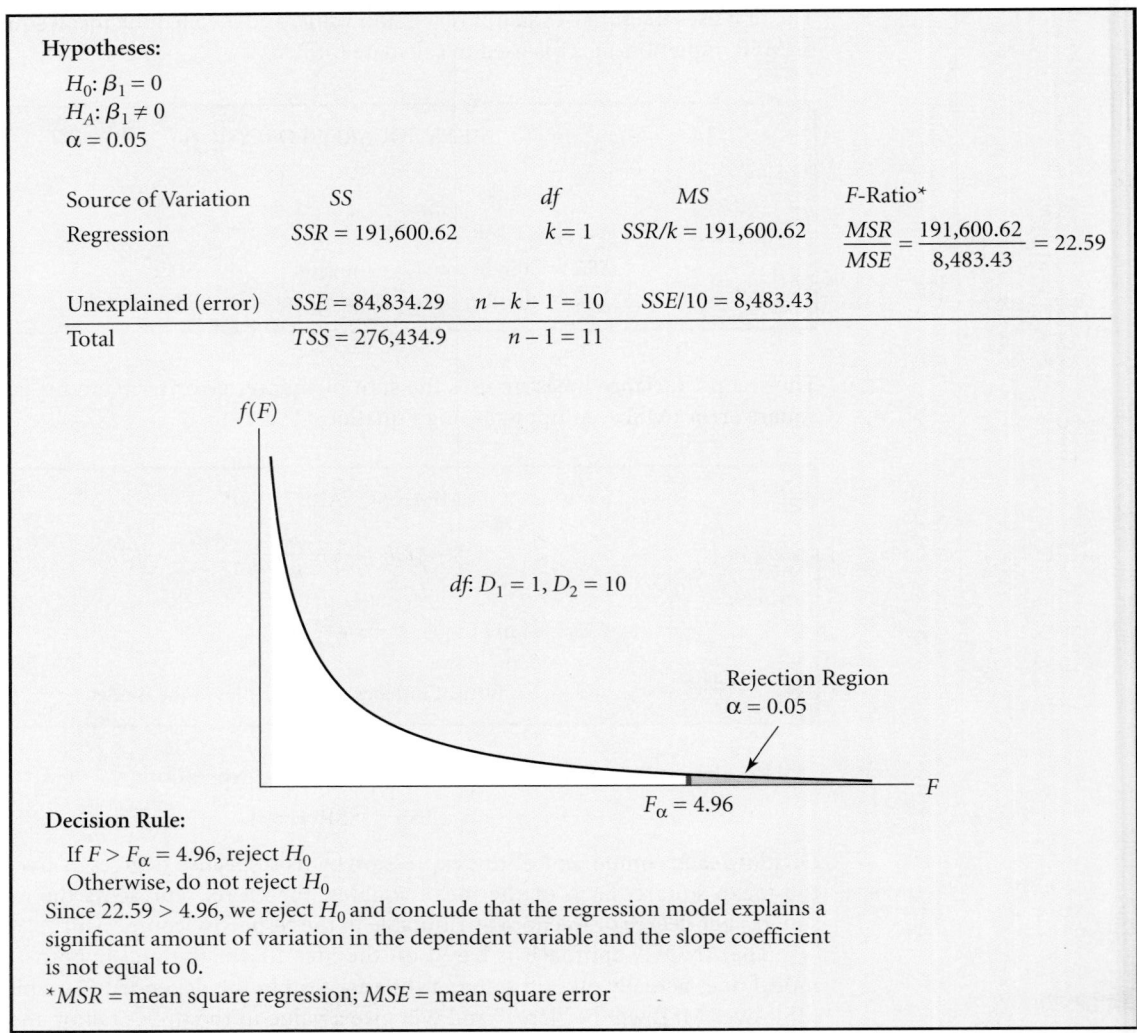

Hypotheses:

$H_0: \beta_1 = 0$
$H_A: \beta_1 \neq 0$
$\alpha = 0.05$

Source of Variation	SS	df	MS	F-Ratio*
Regression	$SSR = 191{,}600.62$	$k = 1$	$SSR/k = 191{,}600.62$	$\dfrac{MSR}{MSE} = \dfrac{191{,}600.62}{8{,}483.43} = 22.59$
Unexplained (error)	$SSE = 84{,}834.29$	$n - k - 1 = 10$	$SSE/10 = 8{,}483.43$	
Total	$TSS = 276{,}434.9$	$n - 1 = 11$		

$f(F)$

$df: D_1 = 1, D_2 = 10$

Rejection Region
$\alpha = 0.05$

$F_\alpha = 4.96$

F

Decision Rule:

If $F > F_\alpha = 4.96$, reject H_0
Otherwise, do not reject H_0
Since $22.59 > 4.96$, we reject H_0 and conclude that the regression model explains a
significant amount of variation in the dependent variable and the slope coefficient
is not equal to 0.
*MSR = mean square regression; MSE = mean square error

FIGURE 11-20   Significance Test of the Overall Regression Model for Midwest Distribution

Additional Example 11-b

Simple Regression and Correlation Analysis

shows the analysis of variance F-test as well as the significance level (p-value) for the calculated F-statistic.

Figure 11-21 outlines the steps involved in developing a simple linear regression model
and summarizes the various hypothesis tests for testing the significance of the simple linear
regression model. You should recognize that the three tests used thus far to test the significance of the linear relationship between x and y are actually equivalent. Therefore, you
need to perform only one of these tests, since they will all lead to the same conclusion.
However, you should be familiar with all three. In Chapter 12, when we introduce multiple
regression analysis with more than one independent variable, the three tests serve different
purposes.

Step 1. Develop a scatter plot of y and x. You are looking for a linear relationship between the two variables.

Step 2. Calculate the least squares regression line for the sample data.

Step 3. Calculate the correlation coefficient and the simple coefficient of determination, R^2. This value measures the proportion of variation in the dependent variable explained by the independent variable.

Step 4. Conduct one of the following three tests:

(1) Test to determine whether the true regression slope is 0. The test statistic with $df = n - k - 1$ is:

$$t = \frac{b_1 - \beta_1}{s_{b_1}} = \frac{b_1 - 0}{s_{b_1}}$$

(2) Test to see whether ρ is significantly different from 0. The test statistic is:

$$t = \frac{r}{\sqrt{\dfrac{1 - r^2}{n - 2}}}$$

(3) Test to see whether the model is significant (i.e., model's regression slope = 0). The test statistic is:

$$F = \frac{\dfrac{SSR}{k}}{\dfrac{SSE}{n - k - 1}} = \frac{MSR}{MSE}$$

Note: The three substeps (1), (2), and (3) of Step 4 are equivalent tests for the simple regression model. Only one of these tests needs to be performed.

FIGURE 11-21
Summary of Simple
Regression Steps

11-2: EXERCISES

ADDITIONAL EXERCISES ON YOUR CD-ROM

Try the ADDITIONAL EXERCISES and APPLICATION PROBLEMS on the CD-ROM.

11-8. You are given the following sample data for variables y and x.

y	140.1	120.3	80.8	100.7	130.2	90.6
x	5	3	2	4	5	4
y	110.5	120.2	130.4	130.3	100.1	
x	4	5	6	5	4	

a. Develop a scatter plot for these data and describe what, if any, relationship exists.

b. (1) Compute the correlation coefficient. (2) Test to determine whether the correlation is significant at the significance level of 0.05. Conduct this hypothesis test using the p-value approach. (3) Compute the regression equation based on these sample data and interpret the regression coefficients.

c. Use the ANOVA approach to test the significance of the overall regression model using a significance level equal to 0.05.

11-9. Refer to Problem 8.

a. Determine the proportion of the variation in the y variable explained by its linear relationship to the x variable.

b. Provide an estimate for the y variable when $x = 0$. There is a name associated with this particular y value. Provide this name.

11-10. Section 11-2 introduced three ways to test whether the relationship between a single independent variable and the dependent variable is statistically significant. Discuss each of these methods and show how they are related based on calculated values for t and F.

11-11. You are given the following results from computations pertaining to a simple linear regression application.

$$\hat{y} = 23.0 + 1.45x$$
$$SSE = 45{,}000$$
$$n = 25$$
$$\sum(x - \bar{x})^2 = 4{,}000$$

a. Based on the statistics supplied, can you conclude that there is a significant linear relationship between x and y? Test at the $\alpha = 0.05$ level. Conduct this hypothesis test using the p-value approach.

b. Interpret the slope coefficient.

Business Applications

11-12. The Apex Telephone Company recently performed a study in which 10 households were surveyed to determine the long distance charges accrued per month (y) and the number of people living at the residence (x). The sample data were determined as follows.

Charges (y)	$37.23	$23.58	$67.65	$21.74	$10.12
People (x)	4	2	3	1	2
Charges (y)	$33.43	$46.56	$67.52	$44.69	$38.14
People (x)	3	4	5	3	4

a. Develop a scatter plot for these data and describe what, if any, relationship exists.

b. Compute the correlation coefficient. Is it true that as the number of people in a household increases, the yearly long distance charges also increase? Test this hypothesis using a significance level of 0.01. Conduct this hypothesis test using the p-value approach.

c. Compute the regression equation based on these sample data, and provide an estimate of the average yearly charge for long distance service for all those households that have 5 members.

d. Compute the coefficient of determination and discuss what this value means. Conduct the appropriate test to determine whether the population coefficient of determination is equal to 0. (Hint: Recall the relationship between the coefficient of determination and another population parameter for which you know the hypothesis test procedure.)

11-13. At a recent Beach Boys concert, a survey was conducted that asked a random sample of eleven people their age and how many concerts they have attended since the first of the year. The following data were collected :

Age	24	21	34	45	23	34	47	29	20	37	42
Concerts	3	2	1	3	5	2	1	3	5	2	3

a. Develop a scatter plot for these data and describe what, if any, relationship exists between the age and the number of concerts attended by the respondents. Would you describe the model as a correlation or a regression model? Give reasons for your answer.

b. Compute the correlation coefficient. Test to determine whether the correlation is significant at the $\alpha = 0.05$ level.

c. Compute the regression equation based on these sample data if you wished to predict the number of concerts attended based upon the age of the respondents. Interpret the regression coefficients.

d. Compute the residuals and the sum of squared errors. Also compute the sum of squares for the y variable and compare the sum of squared errors to this sum. Why do you suppose the sum of squared errors is smaller? Discuss.

e. Compute the proportion of the variation in the number of the concerts attended that can be explained by the age of the Beach Boys concert attendee.

11-14. At State University, a study was done to establish whether a relationship existed between students' graduating GPA and the students' SAT score when the students originally entered the university. The sample data are reported as follows.

GPA	2.5	3.2	3.5	2.8	3.0	2.4	3.4	2.9	2.7	3.8
SAT	640	700	550	540	620	490	710	600	505	710

a. Develop a scatter plot for these data and describe what, if any, relationship exists between the two variables, GPA and SAT score.

b. Compute the correlation coefficient. Does it appear that the GPAs of students at State University is related to the SAT scores of those students? Conduct a statistical procedure to answer this question. Use a significance level of 0.01.

c. Compute the regression equation based on these sample data if you wish to predict the university GPA using the student's SAT score. Interpret the regression coefficients.

d. (1) If the administration of the university wished to admit only those students who were capable of earning a 2.0 GPA, what would be the lowest a student could score on the SAT exam and still be allowed to enter the university? (2) What assumption must be made for your answer to have validity?

e. (1) Compute the residuals and the sum of squared errors. (2) Also compute the sum of squares for the y variable and compare the sum of squared errors to this sum. (3) Why do you suppose the sum of squared errors is smaller? Discuss.

11-15. One of the editors of a major automobile publication has collected data on 30 of the best-selling cars in the United States. The data are in a file called **Automobiles**. The editor is particularly interested in the relationship between highway mileage and curb weight of the vehicles.

a. Develop a scatter plot for these data. Discuss what the plot implies about the relationship between the two variables. Assume that you wish to predict highway mileage by using vehicle curb weight.

b. Compute the correlation coefficient for the two variables and test to determine whether there is a linear relationship between the curb weight and the highway mileage of automobiles.

c. Compute the linear regression equation based on the sample data.

d. Cadillac's 1999 Sedan DeVille weighs approximately 4,012 pounds. Provide an estimate of the average highway mileage you would expect to obtain from this model.

e. The DeVille has an EPA mileage rating of 26 miles per gallon on the highway. (1) Compute the appropriate residual. (2) Calculate an estimate of the standard deviation of the model error. (3) Is the residual you calculated in part (1) unusually large or small? Support your answer with probability calculations based upon your knowledge of the statistical properties of the residuals in the simple linear regression model.

11-16. Referring to Problem 15, suppose the magazine editor wishes to examine the relationship between price of the vehicle and the horsepower of the engine.

a. Develop a scatter plot for these data. Discuss what the plot implies about the relationship between the two variables. Use price as the dependent (y) variable.

b. Compute the correlation coefficient for the two variables.

c. Compute the linear regression equation based on the sample data.

d. The 1999 Toyota Camry four-cylinder model generates 133 hp. Provide an estimate of the price of the 1999 Camry. Toyota suggested that retail price for the Camry LE 4A model was $20,278. Calculate the appropriate residual for this model of Camry.

e. Suppose that the $20,278 price listed by Toyota was actually the average price charged by its dealers throughout the nation. Obtain an estimate of the standard deviation of the prices for those automobiles having 133 hp engines.

f. (1) Compute the R-square value and discuss what this value means. (2) At a significance level of 0.01, can you conclude that engine horsepower is a good predictor of the price of an automobile?

11-17. A 1998 article in *Fortune* magazine entitled "The 100 Best Companies to Work for in America" (January 12, 1998) contained selected characteristics on the 100 companies. These data are included in the data file called **Best-Companies.** Two variables of interest are the revenues of the company and the number of hours of training per year per employee. (Note: You will need to omit companies with data marked N.A. before completing the analysis.)

a. Develop a scatter plot for these data. Discuss what the plot implies about the relationship between the two variables.

b. Provide a measurement that will give an indication of the strength of the linear relationship between revenues and the number of hours of training for employees.

c. Compute the linear regression equation based on the sample data if you wish to use the number of hours of training per employee per year to predict the revenue of the company. Interpret the slope and intercept coefficients.

d. Using a significance level of 0.01, test to determine whether the true regression slope is 0. Do your test results suggest that if companies stop training their employees their revenues will suffer? Does the result of your test indicate that there is no relationship whatsoever between revenues and the number of hours of training for employees? Discuss these two related questions.

e. Refer to part d. Describe the type of hypothesis test error that could have been made in the context of this problem.

11-18. A study has been conducted for a sample of cities in the United States. Among the data collected were the 1995 population and the 1998 unemployment rate. The data are contained in the file called **Cities.**

a. Develop a scatter plot for these data. Discuss what the plot implies about the relationship between the two variables. Assume you wish to predict the unemployment rate using the population of the city.

b. Compute the correlation coefficient for the two variables.

c. (1) Compute the linear regression equation based on the sample data. (2) Conduct a statistical procedure to determine if cities with larger populations in 1995 had higher unemployment rates in 1998.

11-19. An accountant who is performing an audit of parts inventory for a machinery company has collected the following data. The dependent variable, y, is the actual level of inventory (in hundreds of dollars) determined by the accountant. The independent variable, x, is the inventory level on the computer inventory record.

y	233.23	10.56	24.45	56.87	78.10	102.23
x	245.51	12.43	22.52	56.84	90.31	103.85
y	90.94	200.23	344.41	120.53	18.62	
x	85.56	190.86	320.74	120.25	23.88	

a. Of course the accountant wishes to know just how much agreement there is between the inventory levels determined during the audit and the levels indicated on the company records. Calculate a value for a measurement that would give the accountant the information he wishes for these sample data. Determine whether this sample indicates that such a relationship exists and is statistically significant within the population as well. Be careful to consider the type and direction of the appropriate measurement.

b. Conduct a hypothesis test to determine if the average inventory value determined by the accountant is different from that on the company's records. Again, be careful to consider the type and direction of the appropriate measurement.

c. Discuss the type and amount of information obtained in the procedures you have conducted for part a and part b above. Which procedure would be more meaningful to you?

11-20. The Skelton Manufacturing Company recently did a study of its customers. A random sample of 50 customer accounts was pulled from the computer records. Two variables were observed.

y = Total dollar volume of business this year
x = Miles customer is from corporate headquarters

The following statistics were computed.

$$\hat{y} = 2,140.23 - 10.12x$$
$$s_{b_1} = 3.12$$

a. Interpret the regression slope coefficient.

b. Using a significance level of 0.01, test to determine whether it is true that the further a business is from the corporate headquarters, the smaller is the total dollar volume of business. Conduct this hypothesis test using the p-value approach.

11-21. The data shown next and contained in the data file called **McCormick** are values (measured in millions of dollars) from the 1998 McCormick Company Annual Report.

YEAR	NET SALES	CAPITAL EXPENDI-TURES	CURRENT DEBT	LONG-TERM DEBT	SHARE-HOLDERS' EQUITY
1988	$1,099.10	$50.40	$ 49.50	$229.40	$294.30
1989	1,110.20	53.40	20.30	210.50	346.20
1990	1,166.20	58.40	30.40	311.50	364.40
1991	1,276.30	73.00	78.20	207.60	389.20
1992	1,323.90	79.30	122.60	201.00	437.90
1993	1,400.90	76.10	84.70	346.40	466.80
1994	1,529.40	87.70	214.00	374.30	490.00
1995	1,691.10	82.10	297.30	349.10	519.30
1996	1,732.50	74.70	108.90	291.20	450.00
1997	1,801.00	43.90	121.30	276.50	393.10

a. Compute the linear regression model based on the sample data if net sales are to be predicted using capital expenditures. Determine the net sales expected if McCormick has capital expenditures of $75,000,000.

b. Conduct a test to determine if McCormick's net sales increase as it increases its capital expenditure.

c. Refer to part b. Describe the type of hypothesis test error that could have been made in the context of this problem.

d. Provide a brief financial explanation of the regression slope coefficient.

11-22. Referring to Problem 21, assuming that the objective is to develop a simple linear regression model to explain the variation in net sales over the 10 years covered in the McCormick Company Annual Report, which of the other variables would make the best independent variable to use? Show the basis for your response by comparing pertinent statistics computed from the sample data.

11-23. The data in the file called **Baldor** are from that company's 1998 annual report.

a. Compute the linear regression model based on the sample data using net sales as the independent variable and working capital as the dependent variable.

b. Conduct a test to determine whether net sales can be used to predict working capital for Baldor Electric. Conduct this hypothesis test using the p-value approach.

c. Compute the R-square value and discuss how well you believe Baldor will be able to predict its net sales using its working capital.

d. Briefly discuss the conclusions of your test. What does the information, as provided by the regression slope coefficient of your estimated model, mean in a financial or business sense?

11-3: USES FOR REGRESSION ANALYSIS

Regression analysis is a statistical tool that is used for two main purposes: description and prediction. This section discusses these two applications.

Regression Analysis for Description

Car Mileage

EXAMPLE 11-7

REGRESSION ANALYSIS

In the spring of 2000, gasoline prices soared to record levels in the United States, heightening the emphasis by customers for fuel economy. As part of a larger study, analysts at one of the major automobile companies collected data on a variety of variables for a sample of 30 different cars and small trucks. Included among the data collected were the EPA highway mileage rating and the horsepower of the vehicle. Of interest is the relationship between horsepower (x) and highway mileage (y). Figure 11-22 shows a portion of the data that is contained in the file called **Automobiles**.

Excel Instructions:

1. Open file: Automobiles.xls

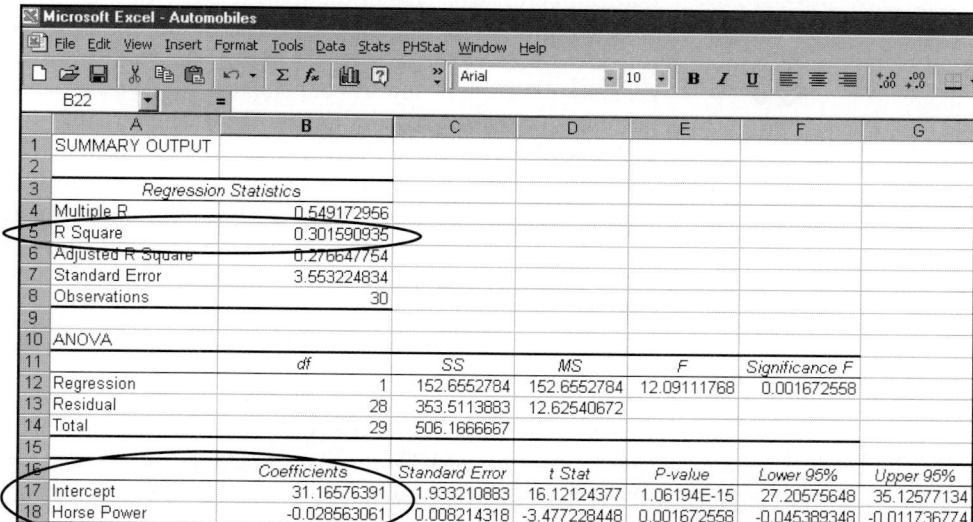

FIGURE 11-22
Automobile Mileage Study
Data

A simple linear regression model was developed using Excel as shown in Figure 11-23. For these sample data, the coefficient of determination, $R^2 = 0.3016$, indicates that knowing the horsepower of the vehicle explains 30.16% of the variation in the highway mileage. The estimated regression equation is:

$$\hat{y} = 31.1658 - 0.0286(x)$$

Before the analysts attempt to describe the relationship between horsepower and highway mileage, they first need to test whether or not there is a statistically significant linear relationship between the two variables. To do this, they can apply the *t-test* described in Section 11-2 to test the following null and alternative hypotheses at the $\alpha = 0.05$ level.

$$H_0: \beta_1 = 0$$
$$H_A: \beta_1 \neq 0$$

The calculated *t*-statistic and the corresponding *p*-value are shown in Figure 11-23. Since the *p*-value $= 0.0017 < 0.05$, the null hypothesis is rejected and the analysts can conclude that the population regression slope is not equal to 0.

The sample slope is $b_1 = -0.0286$. This means that for each one unit increase in horsepower, the highway mileage decreases by an average of 0.0286 miles per gallon. However, b_1 is subject to sampling error and is considered a *point estimate* for the true regression slope coefficient. From earlier discussions about point estimates in Chapters 7

FIGURE 11-23
Excel Regression Results for
the Automobile Mileage
Study

Excel Instructions:

1. Open file: Automobiles.xls
2. Select Tools
3. Click on Regression
4. Define y variable range
5. Define x variable range

Regression equation
$\hat{y} = 31.1658 - 0.0286(x)$

and 9, we expect that $b_1 \neq \beta_1$. Therefore, to fully describe the relationship between the independent variable, horsepower, and the dependent variable, highway miles per gallon, we need to develop a **confidence interval estimate** for β_1. Equation 11-23 is used to do this.

CONFIDENCE INTERVAL ESTIMATE FOR THE REGRESSION SLOPE

$$b_1 \pm t_{\alpha/2} s_{b_1}$$

11-23

or, equivalently:

$$b_1 \pm t_{\alpha/2} \frac{s_\epsilon}{\sqrt{\sum(x - \bar{x})^2}} \qquad df = n - 2$$

where:

s_{b_1} = Standard error of the regression slope coefficient

s_ϵ = Standard error of the estimate

The Excel regression output shown in Figure 11-23 contains the 95% confidence interval estimate for the slope coefficient which is:

$$-0.045 \text{ ———————— } -0.012$$

Additional Example 11-c

Regression Analysis for Description

Thus, at the 95% confidence level, based on the sample data, the analysts for the car company can conclude that a one unit increase in horsepower will result in a drop in mileage by an average amount between 0.012 and 0.045 miles per gallon.

There are many other situations where the prime purpose of regression analysis is description. Economists use regression analysis for descriptive purposes as they search for a way of explaining the economy. Market researchers also use regression analysis, among other techniques, in an effort to describe the factors that influence the demand for products.

Regression Analysis for Prediction

Freedom Hospital

EXAMPLE 11-8

REGRESSION ANALYSIS

Excel and Minitab Tutorial

One of the main uses of regression analysis is *prediction*. You will often encounter situations where you need to predict the value of the dependent variable based on knowing the value of the independent variable. For example, consider the administrator for Freedom Hospital who has been requested by the hospital's board of directors to develop a model that can be used to predict the total charges for a geriatric patient. The data file called **Patients** contains the data that the administrator has collected.

We've seen in the previous examples that the regression tool in Excel works fine for generating the simple linear regression equation and other useful information, but it does not provide predicted values for the dependent variable. However, both Minitab and the PHStat add-ins do provide predictions. We will illustrate the Minitab output which is formatted somewhat differently from the Excel output, but it contains the same basic information. Figure 11-24 shows the Minitab worksheet and a portion of the data.

The administrator is attempting to construct a simple linear regression model with total charges as the dependent (y) variable and length of stay as the independent (x) variable. Figure 11-25 shows the Minitab regression output. The least squares regression equation is:

$$\hat{y} = 528 + 1353(x)$$

As shown in Figure 11-25, the regression slope coefficient is significantly different from 0 ($t = 14.17$; $F = 200.89$; p-value $= 0.000$). The model explains 59.6% of the variation in the total charges (R-square $= 59.6\%$).

Minitab Instructions:
1. Open file: Patients.mtw

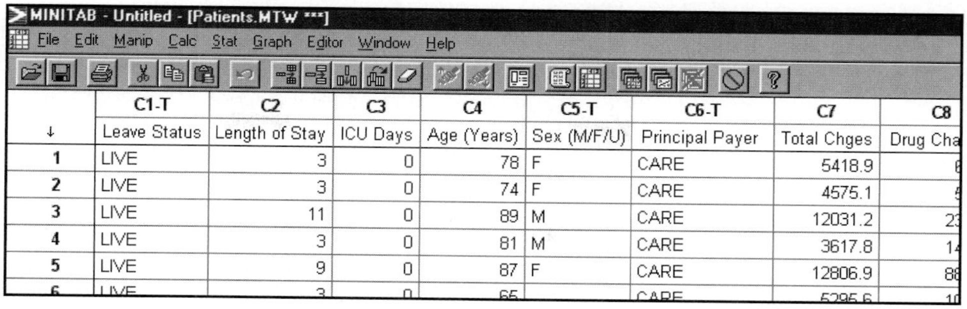

↓	C1-T Leave Status	C2 Length of Stay	C3 ICU Days	C4 Age (Years)	C5-T Sex (M/F/U)	C6-T Principal Payer	C7 Total Chges	C8 Drug Cha
1	LIVE	3	0	78	F	CARE	5418.9	
2	LIVE	3	0	74	F	CARE	4575.1	
3	LIVE	11	0	89	M	CARE	12031.2	
4	LIVE	3	0	81	M	CARE	3617.8	
5	LIVE	9	0	87	F	CARE	12806.9	

FIGURE 11-24
Minitab Worksheet for the Freedom Hospital Length of Stay Study

Notice in Figure 11-25 that Minitab has rounded the regression coefficients. The more precise values are provided in the column headed "Coef" and are:

$$\hat{y} = 527.6 + 1352.80x$$

The administrator could use this equation to predict total charges by substituting the length of stay into the regression equation for x. For example, suppose a patient has a 5 day length of stay. The predicted total charge is:

$$\hat{y} = 527.6 + 1{,}352.80(5)$$
$$\hat{y} = \$7{,}291.60$$

Note that this predicted value is a *point estimate* of the actual charges for this patient. The true charges most likely will be either higher or lower than this amount. The administrator can develop a prediction interval, similar to the confidence interval estimates developed in Chapter 7.

Confidence Interval for the Average y, Given x

The marketing manager might like a 95% confidence interval for *average* charges for all patients who stay in the hospital 5 days. The confidence interval for the expected value of a dependent variable, given a specific level of the independent variable, is determined by Expression 11-24. Observe that the specific value of x used to provide the prediction is denoted as x_p.

FIGURE 11-25
Minitab Regression Output for Freedom Hospital

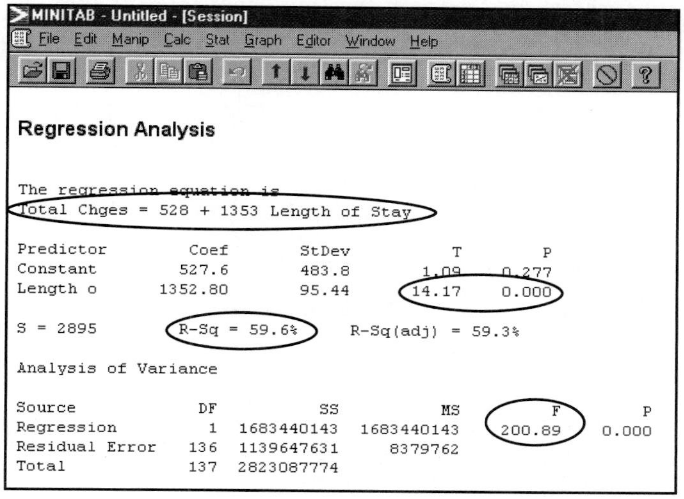

Minitab Instructions:
1. Open file: Patients.mtw
2. Click on Stat
3. Select Regression
4. Select Regression again
5. Define the Response (y) variable and the Predictor (x) variable

CONFIDENCE INTERVAL FOR $E(y)\,\big|\,x_p$

$$\hat{y} \pm t_{\alpha/2}s_\epsilon\sqrt{\frac{1}{n} + \frac{(x_p - \bar{x})^2}{\sum(x - \bar{x})^2}}$$

11-24

where:

$\hat{y}$ = Point estimate of the dependent variable

t = Critical value with $n - 2$ df

n = Sample size

x_p = Specific value of the independent variable

$\bar{x}$ = Mean of the independent variable observations in the sample

s_ϵ = Estimate of the standard error of the estimate

Although the confidence interval estimate can be manually computed using Equation 11-24, using your computer is much easier. For instance, both PHStat and Minitab have built-in options to generate the confidence interval estimate for the dependent variable for a given value of the x variable. Figure 11-26 shows the Minitab results when length of stay, x, equals 5 days. Given this length of stay, the point estimate for the mean total charges is $7,291.60, and at the 95% confidence level, the administrators believe the mean total charges will be in the interval $6,790 to $7,794.

PREDICTION INTERVAL FOR A PARTICULAR y, GIVEN x

The confidence interval shown in Figure 11-26 is for the average value of y given x_p. The administrator might also be interested in predicting the total charges for a *particular* patient with a 5 day stay rather than the average of the charges for all patients staying 5 days. Developing this 95% prediction interval requires only a slight modification to Equation 11-24. This prediction interval is given by Expression 11-25.

PREDICTION INTERVAL FOR $y\,\big|\,x_p$

$$\hat{y} \pm t_{\alpha/2}s_\epsilon\sqrt{1 + \frac{1}{n} + \frac{(x_p - \bar{x})^2}{\sum(x - \bar{x})^2}}$$

11-25

As is the case with the confidence interval application discussed previously, the manual computations required to use Equation 11-25 can be onerous. We recommend

FIGURE 11-26
Minitab Output: Freedom Hospital Confidence Interval Estimate

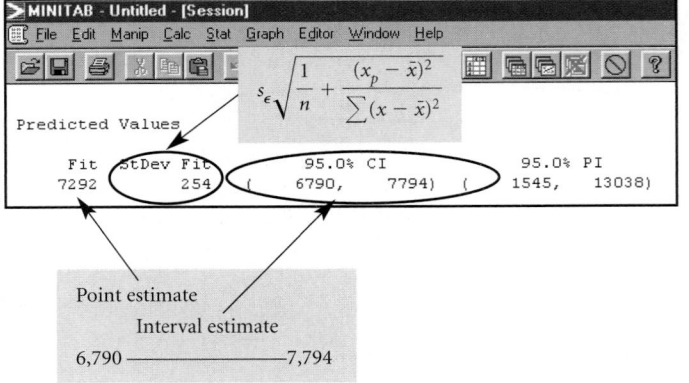

Minitab Instructions:

1. Use instruction in Figure 11-25 to get regression results
2. Before clicking OK, select Options
3. Enter value(s) of x variable in Prediction Interval for New Observations box
4. Select desired confidence level.
5. Click OK
6. Click on Confidence Limits

Excel (PHStat) Instructions:

1. Open file: Patients.xls
2. Select PHStat
3. Click on Regression
4. Select Simple Linear Regression
5. Specify y and x data ranges
6. Define x_p
7. Specify confidence level for intervals

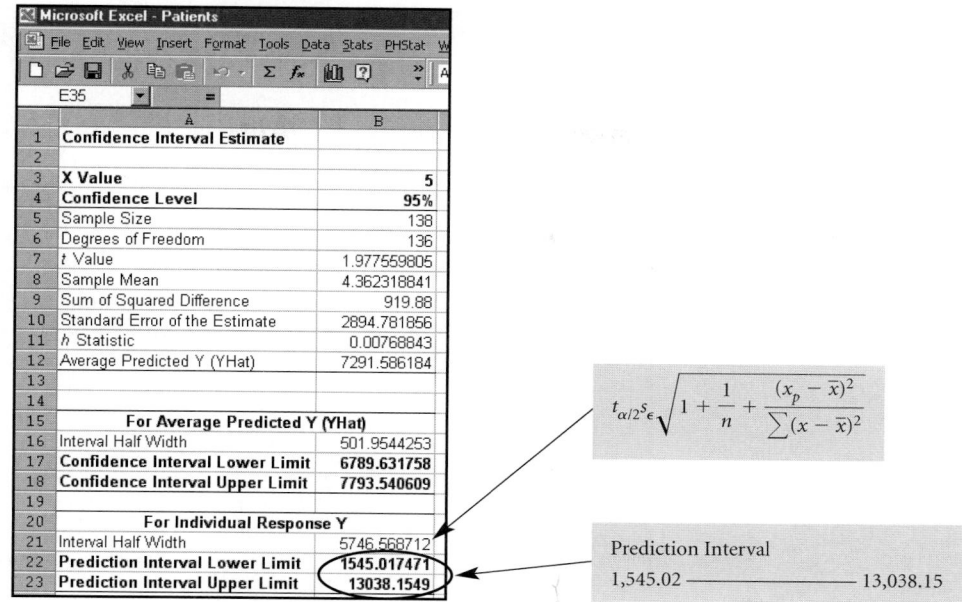

FIGURE 11-27
Excel (PHStat) Prediction Interval for Freedom Hospital

using your computer and software such as Minitab or PHStat to find the prediction interval. Figure 11-27 shows the PHStat results. Note that the same PHStat process generates both the prediction and confidence interval estimates. The same is true for Minitab.

Based upon this regression model, at the 95% confidence level, the hospital administrators can predict total charges for any patient with length of stay of 5 days to be between $1,545 and $13,038.

As you can see, this prediction has extremely poor precision. We doubt any hospital administrator will use a prediction interval that is so wide. Although the regression model explains a significant proportion of variation in the dependent variable, it is relatively imprecise for predictive purposes. To improve the precision, we might decrease the confidence requirements or increase the sample size and redevelop the model.

The prediction interval for a specific value of the dependent variable is wider (less precise) than the confidence interval for predicting the average value of the dependent variable. This will always be the case, as seen in Expressions 11-24 and 11-25. From an intuitive viewpoint, we should expect to come closer to predicting an average value than a single value.

Note, the term $(x_p - \bar{x})^2$ has a particular effect on the confidence interval determined by both Expressions 11-24 and 11-25. The farther x_p (the value of the independent variable used to predict y) is from $\bar{x}$, the greater $(x_p - \bar{x})^2$ becomes. Figure 11-28 shows two regression lines developed from two samples with the same set of x values. We have made both lines pass through the same $(\bar{x}, \bar{y})$ point; however, they have different slopes and intercepts. At $x_p = x_1$, the two regression lines give predictions of y that are close to each other. However, for $x_p = x_2$, the predictions of y are quite different. Thus, when x_p is close to $\bar{x}$, the problems caused by variations in regression slopes are not as great as when x_p is far from $\bar{x}$. Figure 11-29 shows the prediction intervals over the range of possible x_p values. The band around the estimated regression line bends away from the regression line as x_p moves in either direction from $\bar{x}$.

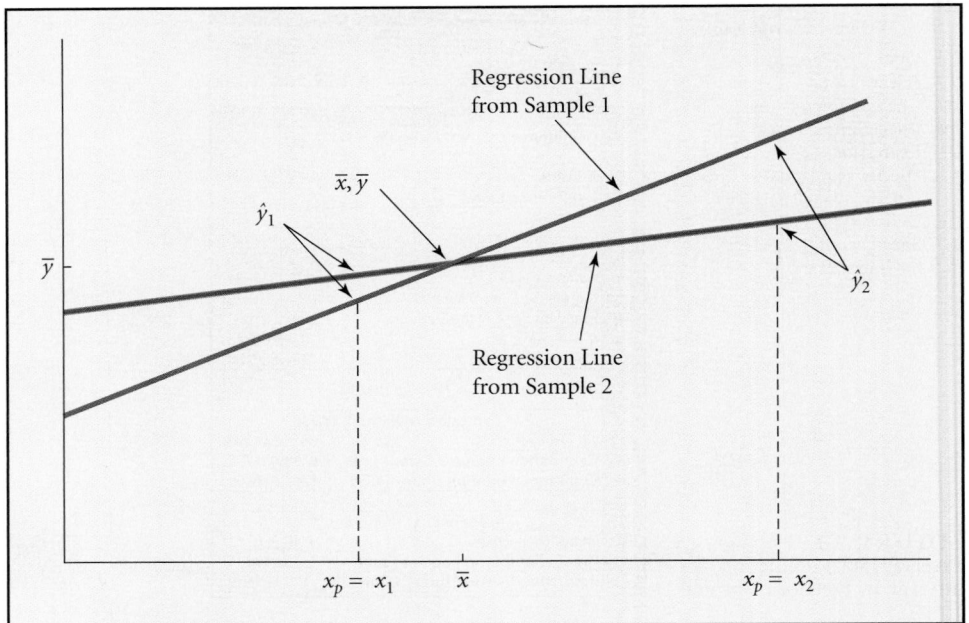

FIGURE 11-28
Regression Lines Illustrating the Increase in Potential Variation in y as x_p Moves Farther from $\bar{x}$

Residual Analysis

Recall that two assumptions associated with linear regression analysis are that the distribution of model errors is normally distributed around the mean value for all levels of x and the variance of the model errors around their mean is constant for all levels of x. Another way of stating these two assumptions is:

1. The model errors are normally distributed.
2. The model errors have a constant variance at all levels of the independent variable.

FIGURE 11-29
Confidence Intervals for $y \mid x_p$ and $E(y) \mid x_p$

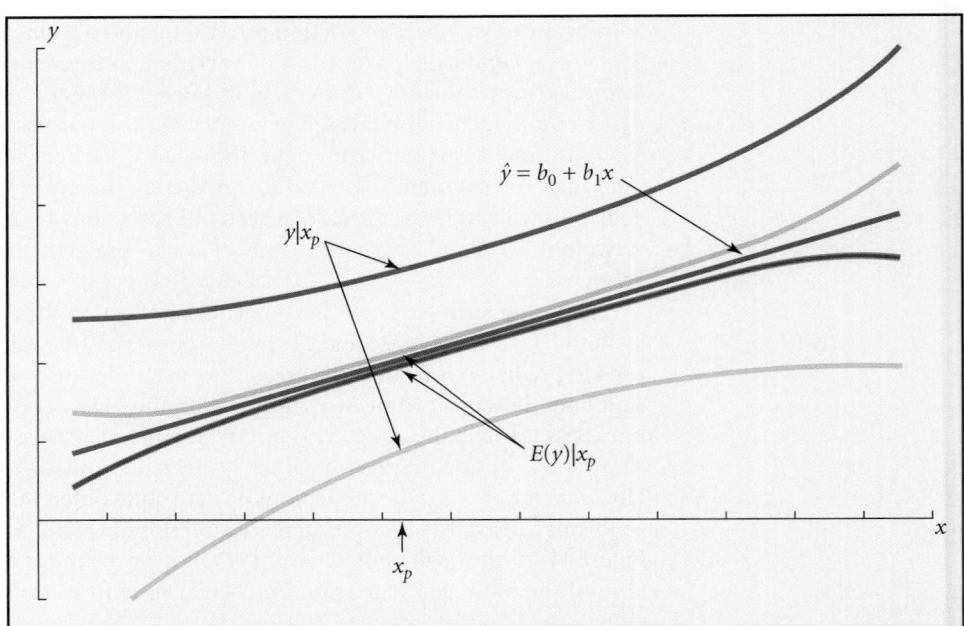

Note: The confidence interval for estimating $y \mid x_p$ is less precise than the confidence interval for estimating $E(y) \mid x_p$.

Before using a regression model for description or prediction, you should do a check to see if these assumptions are satisfied. One way to do this is by examining graphs called *residual plots.* Both Excel and Minitab can be used to generate residual plots.

EXAMPLE 11-9

RESIDUAL ANALYSIS

Excel and Minitab Tutorial

Freedom Hospital (continued)

Previously we showed the regression model constructed by the administrators at Freedom Hospital. They wanted to predict the total patient charges by knowing the patient length of stay. The resulting model was statistically significant. However, before they actually use this model, they might develop two different residual plots. The first is a *residual frequency histogram* as shown in Figure 11-30. As you can see, the histogram closely resembles a normal distribution which is one indication that the normality assumption is satisfied. Chapter 12 will introduce another type of residual plot called a *normal probability plot* that is also used to assess the normality assumption.

The second residual plot is a plot of the residuals against the y variable shown in Figure 11-31. This type of plot is discussed more fully in Chapter 12. However, for now, you would be looking for a result in which the residuals would have approximately the same spread at all levels of y. In Figure 11-31, the plot illustrates that at low values for total charges, the spread in the residuals is less than when the total charges are higher. This implies that the assumption of equal variances in the residuals is violated. We will discuss this in more detail in Chapter 12 and suggest possible steps for improving the regression model.

Common Problems Using Regression Analysis

Regression is perhaps the most widely used statistical tool other than descriptive statistical techniques. Since it is so widely used, you need to be aware of the common problems found when the technique is employed.

FIGURE 11-30
Minitab Residual Histogram for Freedom Hospital

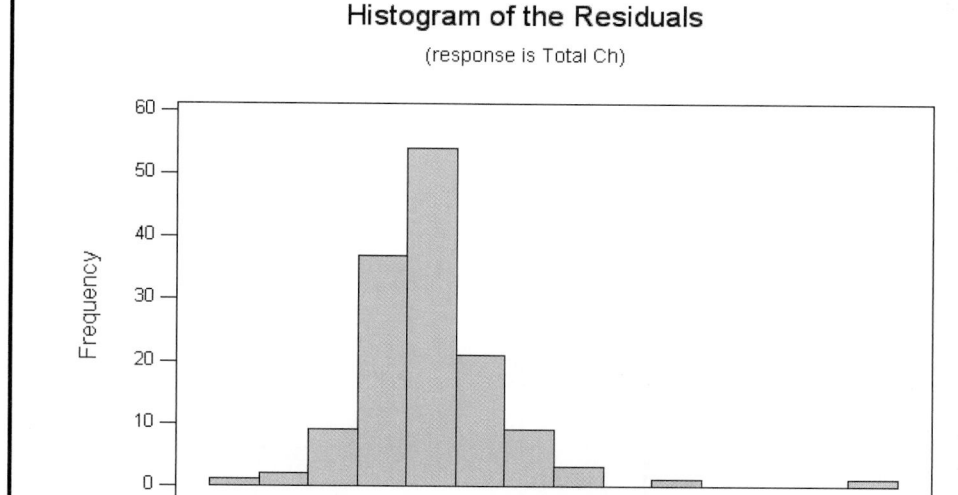

Minitab Instructions

1. Select Stat
2. Click on Regression
3. Click Regression again
4. Define the x and y variable
5. Click Graphs
6. Select graphs of interest (histogram)

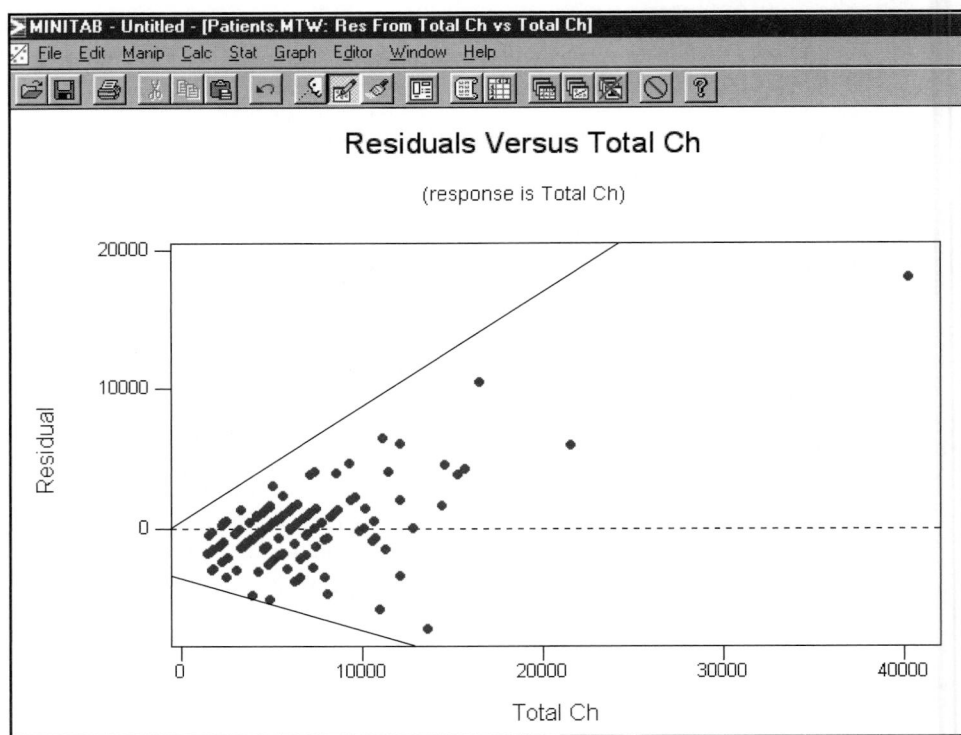

FIGURE 11-31
Minitab Residual Plot for
Freedom Hospital Example

One potential problem occurs when decision makers apply regression analysis for predictive purposes. The conclusions and inferences made from a regression line are statistically valid only over the range of the data contained in the sample used to develop the regression line. For instance, in the Midwest Distribution example, we analyzed the performance of sales representatives with 1 to 9 years of experience. Therefore, predicting sales levels for employees with 1 to 9 years of experience would be justified. However, if we were to try to predict the sales performance of someone with more than 9 years of experience, the relationship between sales and experience may be different. Since no observations were taken for experience levels beyond the 1- to 9-year range, we have no information about what might happen outside that range. Figure 11-32 shows a case where the true relation-

FIGURE 11-32
Graph for a Sales Peak at
20 Years

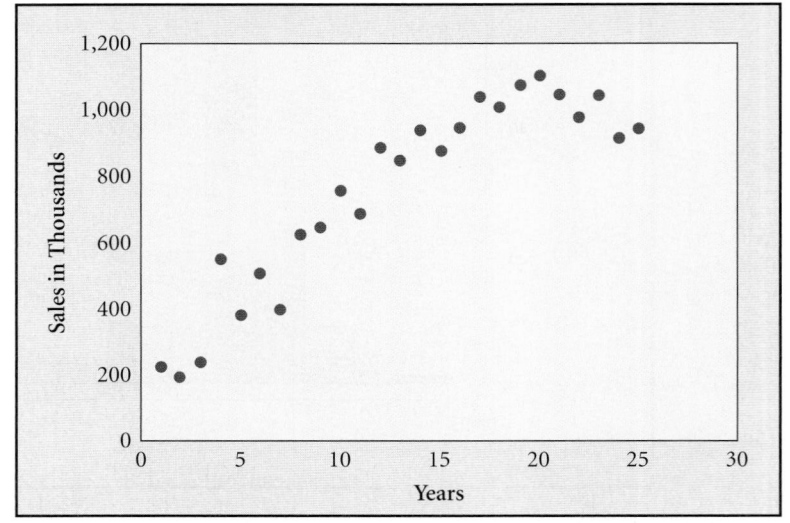

ship between sales and experience reaches a peak value at about 20 years and then starts to decline. If a linear regression equation were used to predict sales based on experience levels beyond the relevant range of data, large prediction errors could occur.

A second important consideration, one that was discussed earlier, involves correlation and causation. The fact that a significant linear relationship exists between two variables does not imply that one variable causes the other. Although there may be a cause-and-effect relationship, you should not infer that such a relationship is present based only on regression and/or correlation analysis. You should also recognize that a cause-and-effect relationship between two variables is not necessary for regression analysis to be an effective tool. What matters is that the regression model accurately reflects the relationship between the two variables and that the relationship remains stable.

Finally, many users of regression analysis mistakenly believe that a high coefficient of determination (R^2) guarantees that the regression model will be a good predictor. You should remember that R^2 is a measure of the variation in the dependent variable explained by the independent variable. While the least squares criterion assures us that R^2 will be maximized (because the sum of squares error is a minimum) for the given set of sample data, the value applies only to those data used to develop the model. Thus, R^2 measures the fit of the regression line to the sample data. There is no guarantee that there will be an equally good fit with new data. The only true test of a regression model's predictive ability is how well the model actually predicts.

Finally, we should mention that you might find a large R^2 with a large sum of squares error. This can happen if total sum of squares (TSS) is large in comparison to the SSE. Then, even though R^2 is relatively large, so too is the estimate of the model's standard error. Thus, prediction intervals may be simply too wide for the model to be used in many situations.

11-3: EXERCISES

ADDITIONAL EXERCISES ON YOUR CD-ROM
Try the ADDITIONAL EXERCISES and APPLICATION PROBLEMS on the CD-ROM.

11-24. You are given the following results from computations pertaining to a simple linear regression application.

$$\hat{y} = 5,723.0 + 145x$$
$$n = 25$$
$$s_{b_1} = 10.80$$

a. Based on the statistics supplied, can you conclude that there is a significant linear relationship between x and y? Test at a significance level of 0.05.
b. Interpret the slope coefficient.
c. Develop a 95% confidence interval estimate for the true regression slope and interpret the estimate.

11-25. The following data have been collected by an accountant who is performing an audit of paper products at a large office supply company. The dependent variable, y, is the time taken (in minutes) by the accountant to count the units. The independent variable, x, is the number of units on the computer inventory record.

y	23.1	100.5	242.9	56.4	178.7	10.5
x	24	120	228	56	190	13
y	94.2	200.4	44.2	128.7	180.5	
x	85	190	32	120	230	

a. Develop a scatter plot for these data.
b. Test to determine whether the accountant takes an average of one minute for each unit counted. Use a significance level of 0.10. Conduct this hypothesis test using the p-value approach.
c. Develop a 90% confidence interval estimate for the true regression slope and interpret this interval estimate. Does the confidence interval you generated contain the hypothesized value in the null hypothesis of part b?
d. What is the relationship between the techniques used in parts b and c?

Business Applications

11-26. The State Department of Transportation has conducted a study of 100 randomly selected vehicles in which the speed of the vehicle and age of the driver were measured. The data were collected from a stretch of highway that produces an unusually high accident rate. A regression model was developed, with vehicle speed being predicted using age as the independent variable. The results obtained were:

$$\hat{y} = 56.78 + 0.124x$$
$$s_{b_1} = 2.88$$

a. Develop a 95% interval estimate for the true regression slope and interpret.

b. Based on your response to part a, can you conclude that age and speed are linearly related? Explain your answer.

c. Construct a 98% interval estimate for the difference in speed that drivers travel whose ages are 20 years apart. (Hint: Consider carefully the parameter that would measure this difference.)

11-27. The following data have been collected by an accountant who is performing an audit of account balances for a major retail company. The population from which the data were collected represented those accounts for which the customer had indicated the balance was incorrect. The dependent variable, y, is the actual account balance as verified by the accountant. The independent variable, x, is the computer account balance.

| y | $233 | 10 | 24 | 56 | 78 | 102 | 90 | 200 | 344 | 120 | 18 |
| x | $245 | 12 | 22 | 56 | 90 | 103 | 85 | 190 | 320 | 120 | 23 |

a. Compute the least squares regression equation.

b. If the computer account balance was $100, what would you expect to be the actual account balance as verified by the accountant?

c. The computer balance for Timothy Jones is listed as $100 in the computer account record. Provide a 90% interval estimate for Mr. Jones' actual account balance.

d. Provide a 90% interval estimate for the average of all customers' actual account balances in which a computer account balance is the same as that of Mr. Jones. Interpret.

11-28. One of the editors of a major automobile publication has 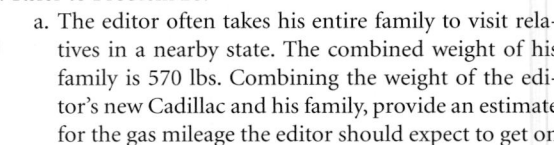 collected data on 30 of the best-selling cars in the United States. The data are in a file called **Automobiles**. The editor is particularly interested in the relationship between highway mileage and curb weight of the vehicles.

a. Develop a linear regression model where highway mileage is to be predicted using curb weight.

b. The editor just purchased a Cadillac Sedan DeVille which weighs 4,012 pounds. His previous car was a Toyota Camry which weighs 3,241 pounds. He wonders how much of a decrease in gas mileage he should expect. Provide the editor an idea of the maximum and minimum decrease in gas mileage he

should expect. You should use a procedure which will allow you to be 90% confident of your answer.

c. Provide an estimate of the gasoline mileage the editor should expect from his newly purchased car. Suppose the estimate you just provided is the true average mpg for cars that weigh the same as the Cadillac. Cadillac advertises that the Sedan DeVille has a mileage rating of 26 mpg. Determine the percentile for the DeVille's mileage rating.

d. The individual from whom the editor purchased the Cadillac said that this car got exceptional gas mileage. He claimed that this particular car got 29 mpg. Construct an appropriate 95% interval estimate that would indicate whether the seller of the Cadillac was stretching the truth or not. Comment on the seller's veracity.

11-29. Refer to Problem 28.

a. The editor often takes his entire family to visit relatives in a nearby state. The combined weight of his family is 570 lbs. Combining the weight of the editor's new Cadillac and his family, provide an estimate for the gas mileage the editor should expect to get on a trip to visit these relatives.

b. Calculate a 95% prediction interval for the average highway mileage for cars with a curb weight equal to the weight of the Cadillac after his family is inside.

c. Compute a 95% prediction interval for the actual highway mileage of this particular Cadillac with the editor's family inside.

d. Compare the prediction intervals computed in this problem to that computed in part d of Problem 28. Discuss why the intervals are different widths even though the same confidence level is used.

e. Suppose an editor for the publication wishes to predict the highway mileage of vehicles with a curb weight of 6,000 pounds. What cautions should be made before using this regression model to make that prediction? Discuss.

11-30. Referring to Problem 29, suppose the magazine editor wishes to examine the relationship between price of the vehicle and the horsepower of the engine.

a. Toyota considered increasing the horsepower in its Camry motor by 10% (recall that the horsepower for the 1999 Camry was 133). Give advice on how much the cost of the automobile should increase based solely on the increase in horsepower. Provide a minimum and maximum amount of increase you would expect with a 90% probability.

b. The Buick Riviera has an engine with 240 horsepower. Construct a 95% interval estimate of the average price of the Riviera using its horsepower as the predictor. The suggested retail price of a (1999) Riviera is $33,820. Does Buick appear to use something other than horsepower to determine its suggested retail price? Explain your reasoning.

c. The BMW Z3 roadster has an engine with 170 horsepower. Provide an estimate of the smallest and largest price you would expect to pay if you were to buy one of these vehicles.

11-31. A 1998 article in *Fortune* magazine entitled "The 100 Best Companies to Work for in America" (January 12, 1998) contained data on the 100 companies. These data are included in the data file called **Best-Companies.** Two variables of interest are the revenues of the company and the number of hours of training per year per employee. (Note: You will need to omit companies with data marked N.A. before completing the analysis.)

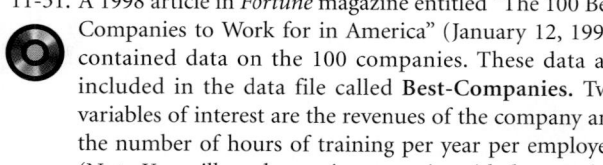

   a. Compute the linear regression equation based on the sample data if the revenue of the company is to be used to predict the number of hours of training per year per employee.
   b. Synovus Financial had 902 million dollars in revenue in a recent year. If it were to increase its revenue by 10%, what change would you expect to see in the number of hours of training per year per employee?
   c. Would you feel comfortable using the revenue of one of the 100 companies to determine the number of hours of training per year per employee with a sim-

ple linear regression model? Conduct a statistical procedure to answer this question.
   d. Synovus has 8,827 employees. Using a new regression model with number of US employees as the independent variable, predict the number of hours of training per year per employee for Synovus.
   e. Referring to part d, develop and interpret a 90% confidence interval for the average training hours per employee for companies with 8,827 employees.
   f. Referring to part e, what is the 90% confidence interval for average training hours per employee for companies with 40,000 employees? Compare this interval with the one computed in part d and discuss why the widths of the two are different.
   g. Referring to parts e and f, at what number of employees would the width of a 90% confidence interval for average training hours be minimized?
   h. Referring to parts d and e, develop and interpret a 90% prediction interval for the actual training hours per employee for Synovus Financial.

■ SUMMARY AND CONCLUSIONS

Correlation and regression analysis are two of the most frequently used statistical techniques for business decision makers. This chapter has introduced the basics of these two topics. The discussion of regression analysis has been limited to situations in which you have one dependent variable and one independent variable. In these cases, the technique for modeling the linear relationship between the two variables is referred to as simple linear regression analysis.

If two variables are correlated, then they are said to be linearly related. When that's the case, the resulting simple linear regression model will be statistically significant. That means the fraction of variation in the dependent variable that is explained by the independent variable (R-squared) is significant, and the predictions for the y variable based on values of x will be superior to using the mean of y as the predictor.

This chapter introduced the methods used to test whether the correlation is zero and whether a regression slope coefficient is zero. We also introduced you to the uses of regression for descriptive and predictive purposes and showed how to construct confidence interval estimates for the true regression slope coefficient and prediction intervals.

Chapter 12 will extend the discussion of regression analysis by showing how two or more independent variables are included in the analysis. The focus of Chapter 12 will be on building a model for explaining the variation in the dependent variable. However, the basic concepts presented in this chapter will be carried forward in the discussion in Chapter 12.

EQUATIONS

Sample Correlation Coefficient

$$r = \frac{\sum(x - \bar{x})(y - \bar{y})}{\sqrt{[\sum(x - \bar{x})^2][\sum(y - \bar{y})^2]}} \qquad \text{11-1}$$

or the algebraic equivalent:

$$r = \frac{n\sum xy - \sum x \sum y}{\sqrt{[n(\sum x^2) - (\sum x)^2][n(\sum y^2) - (\sum y)^2]}} \qquad \text{11-2}$$

Test Statistic for Correlation

$$t = \frac{r}{\sqrt{\dfrac{1 - r^2}{n - 2}}} \qquad df = n - 2 \qquad \text{11-3}$$

$H_0: \rho = 0$
$H_a: \rho \neq 0$

Simple Linear Regression Model (Population Model)

$$y = \beta_0 + \beta_1 x + \epsilon \qquad \text{11-4}$$

Estimated Regression Model (Sample Model)

$$\hat{y} = b_0 + b_1 x \qquad \text{11-5}$$

Least Squares Equations (Sample Values)

$$b_1 = \frac{\sum(x - \bar{x})(y - \bar{y})}{\sum(x - \bar{x})^2} \qquad \text{11-6}$$

algebraic equivalent: $$b_1 = \frac{\sum xy - \dfrac{\sum x \sum y}{n}}{\sum x^2 - \dfrac{(\sum x)^2}{n}} \qquad \text{11-7}$$

and $$b_0 = \bar{y} - b_1 \bar{x} \qquad \text{11-8}$$

Sum of Squared Errors

$$SSE = \sum y^2 - b_0 \sum y - b_1 \sum xy \qquad \text{11-9}$$

Sum of Residuals

$$\sum (y - \hat{y}) = 0 \qquad \text{11-10}$$

Sum of Squared Residuals (Errors)

$$\sum (y - \hat{y})^2 \qquad \text{11-11}$$

Total Sum of Squares

$$TSS = \sum (y - \bar{y})^2 \qquad \text{11-12}$$

Sum of Squares Error (Residuals)

$$SSE = \sum (y - \hat{y})^2 \qquad \text{11-13}$$

Sum of Squares Regression

$$SSR = \sum (\hat{y} - \bar{y})^2 \qquad \text{11-14}$$

Coefficient of Determination (R^2)

$$R^2 = \frac{SSR}{TSS} \qquad \text{11-15}$$

Coefficient of Determination—Single Independent Variable Case

$$R^2 = r^2 \qquad \text{11-16}$$

Standard Deviation of the Regression Slope Coefficient (Population)

$$\sigma_{b_1} = \frac{\sigma_\epsilon}{\sqrt{\sum (x - \bar{x})^2}} \qquad \text{11-17}$$

Estimator for the Standard Error of the Estimate

$$s_\epsilon = \sqrt{\frac{SSE}{n - k - 1}} \qquad \text{11-18}$$

Estimator for the Standard Deviation of the Regression Slope

$$s_{b_1} = \frac{s_\epsilon}{\sqrt{\sum (x - \bar{x})^2}} = \frac{s_\epsilon}{\sqrt{\sum x^2 - \frac{(\sum x)^2}{n}}} \qquad \text{11-19}$$

Test Statistic for Test of the Significance of the Regression Slope

$$t = \frac{b_1 - \beta_1}{s_{b_1}} \qquad df = n - 2 \qquad \text{11-20}$$

Mean Square Regression

$$MSR = \frac{SSR}{k} \qquad \text{11-21}$$

Mean Square Error

$$MSE = \frac{SSE}{n - k - 1} \qquad \text{11-22}$$

Confidence Interval Estimate for the Regression Slope

$$b_1 \pm t_{\alpha/2} s_{b_1} \qquad \text{11-23}$$

or, equivalently: $b_1 \pm t_{\alpha/2} \dfrac{s_\epsilon}{\sqrt{\sum (x - \bar{x})^2}}$

with $df = n - 2$

Confidence Interval for $E(y)\,|\,x_p$

$$\hat{y} \pm t_{\alpha/2} s_\epsilon \sqrt{\frac{1}{n} + \frac{(x_p - \bar{x})^2}{\sum (x - \bar{x})^2}} \qquad \text{11-24}$$

Prediction Interval for $y\,|\,x_p$

$$\hat{y} \pm t_{\alpha/2} s_\epsilon \sqrt{1 + \frac{1}{n} + \frac{(x_p - \bar{x})^2}{\sum (x - \bar{x})^2}} \qquad \text{11-25}$$

◼ KEY TERMS

Coefficient of Determination—The portion of the total variation in the dependent variable that is explained by its relationship with the independent variable. The coefficient of determination is also called R-squared, and denoted as R^2.

Correlation Coefficient—A quantitative measure of the strength of the linear relationship between two variables. The correlation ranges from $+1.0$ to -1.0. A correlation of ± 1.0 indicates a perfect linear relationship, whereas a correlation of 0 indicates no linear relationship.

Dependent Variable—The variable to be predicted or explained in a regression model. This variable is assumed to be functionally related to the independent variable.

Independent Variable—A variable related to a dependent variable in a regression equation. The independent variable is used in a regression model to estimate the value of the dependent variable.

Least Squares Criterion—The criterion for determining a regression line that minimizes the sum of squared residuals.

Regression Coefficients—In the simple regression model, there are two coefficients: the intercept and the slope.

Regression Slope Coefficient—The average change in the dependent variable for a unit change in the independent variable. The slope coefficient may be positive or negative, depending on the relationship between the two variables.

Residual—The difference between the actual value of the dependent variable and the value predicted by the regression model.

Scatter Plot—A two-dimensional plot showing the values for the joint occurrence of two variables. The scatter plot may be used to graphically represent the relationship between two variables. Also known as a *scatter diagram*.

Simple Linear Regression Analysis—A regression model that uses one independent variable to explain the variation in the dependent variable. The model takes the form:

$$y = \beta_0 + \beta_1 x + \epsilon$$

Spurious Correlation—A correlation between two otherwise unrelated variables.

CHAPTER EXERCISES

SOLVED PROBLEMS ON YOUR CD-ROM
Try the WORKED-OUT EXERCISES and BUSINESS APPLICATIONS on the CD-ROM.

Conceptual Questions and Assignments

11-32. Think of two variables that you believe would be negatively related in a linear manner. Describe what is meant by a negative linear relationship.

11-33. A statistics student was recently working on a class project that required him to compute a correlation coefficient for two variables. After careful work he arrived at a correlation coefficient of 0.45. Interpret this correlation coefficient for the student who did the calculations.

11-34. Referring to Problem 33, another student in the same class computed a regression equation relating the two variables. The slope of the equation was found to be −0.735. After trying several times and always coming up with the same result, she felt that she must have been doing something wrong since the value was negative and she knew that this could not be right. Comment on this student's conclusion.

11-35. If we select a random sample of data for two variables and, after computing the correlation coefficient, conclude that the two variables may have zero correlation, can we say that there is no relationship between the two variables? Discuss.

11-36. Discuss why prediction intervals that attempt to predict a particular y value are less precise than confidence intervals for predicting an average y.

11-37. If you have tested for the significance of the correlation between two variables and found that the true correlation may be 0, is it feasible to develop a simple linear regression model using the same variables and data? Will the regression model be statistically significant? Discuss.

Business Application Problems

11-38. The Farmington City Council recently commissioned a study of park users in their community. Data were collected on the age of the person surveyed and the amount of hours he or she has spent in the park in the past month. The data collected were as follows:

TIME IN PARK	AGE	TIME IN PARK	AGE
7.2	16	4.4	48
3.5	15	8.8	18
6.6	28	4.9	24
5.4	16	5.1	33
1.5	29	1.0	56
2.3	38		

Draw a scatter plot for these data and discuss what, if any, relationship appears to be present between the two variables.

11-39. Refer to Problem 38.
  a. Compute the correlation coefficient between age and the amount of time spent in the park. Provide a report to the Farmington City Council explaining what the correlation measures.
  b. Test to determine whether the amount of time spent in the park decreases with the age of the park user. Use a significance level of 0.10. Use a p-value approach to conduct this hypothesis test.

11-40. A marketing research study performed by the marketing division of the Klondike Company surveyed the income levels and expenditures on recreation for a sample of 20 people. Measurements recorded the expenditures on recreation during the previous year, y, and the total annual family income, x.

y	x	y	x
$2,425	$41,300	$1,900	$37,600
2,675	50,200	2,000	36,890
2,356	51,500	4,450	48,000
5,530	65,900	1,650	34,300
4,200	44,600	1,300	29,800
2,060	37,800	2,500	44,700
5,090	73,600	1,890	60,500
2,200	37,400	3,300	51,700
2,800	56,800	4,100	67,800
1,700	35,700	1,100	10,400

Draw a scatter plot for these data and discuss what, if any, relationship between the variables appears to exist based on the scatter plot.

11-41. Refer to Problem 40.
   a. Compute the correlation coefficient for the two variables, income and dollars spent on recreation.
   b. Test to determine whether the amount spent on recreation increases as the annual family income increases. Use a significance level of 0.025.

11-42. The Harris Corporation has recently done a study of homes that have sold in the Detroit area within the past 18 months. Data were recorded for the asking price (x) and the number of weeks (y) the home was on the market before it sold. The data collected are in the data file called **Harris**. Produce a graphical representation of these data to determine if a simple linear relationship exists between the variables. Specify the relationship indicated by the graph you produced.

11-43. Refer to Problem 42.
   a. Compute the correlation coefficient for the number of weeks the house has been on the market and the asking price of the house.
   b. Test at a significance level of 0.10 to determine whether it is true that the more expensive a house is the longer it will take to sell. Discuss your results.

11-44. Refer to Problems 42 and 43.
   a. Develop a regression model using asking price of a home as the independent variable and weeks on the market as the dependent variable.
   b. Provide an interpretation for the regression slope coefficient.
   c. Use the ANOVA approach to test whether the more expensive a house is the longer it will take to sell it. Use a significance level of 0.01. Use a test-statistic approach to conduct the hypothesis test.
   d. Use the t-test to conduct the hypothesis test indicated in part c. Use a p-value approach to conduct this test. Comment on the relationship between this hypothesis test and the one conducted in part c.

11-45. Refer to Problem 44 in which the Harris Corporation studied the relationship between the number of weeks a house stayed on the real estate market and the asking price of the house. For the regression model, develop a 95% interval estimate to determine how much longer it will take to sell a house if the price of the house is increased by $10,000. (Hint: Be very careful that you determine the parameter you are estimating and its interpretation. This parameter measures the change in the y variable for an increase in a certain number of units of the x variable. Ask yourself how many units that is.)

11-46. The Savemore Brokerage Firm of Spokane, Washington, recently studied a random sample of companies whose stock is sold on the New York Stock Exchange. Among other things, it collected data on stock price, y, and the previous year's profits, x. The following data were collected. (The x variable is measured in thousands of dollars.)

y	x	y	x
$18.70	$ 40,000	$12.60	$12,500
34.50	24,900	43.60	9,000
25.70	102,000	33.50	23,900
8.90	44,000	71.80	15,000
25.90	123,700	15.00	45,000
11.11	36,900	6.78	99,500
21.00	3,700	21.70	45,300
3.50	145,900	44.70	23,600

Draw a scatter plot for these data and discuss what, if any, relationship appears to exist between the two variables. Also comment on what other factors might be important to consider when studying stock price and earnings of the company.

11-47. The Penrose Consulting Company performs studies for universities that want to raise money through their alumni associations. As part of its work, it recently sampled 18 universities across the United States and determined the number of alumni contacts and the total dollars in gifts received from those alumni during the previous academic year. The data were recorded and are in a file called **Penrose**.
   a. Draw a scatter plot of these two variables. Based on this plot only, does it appear that a linear relationship exists between the two variables?
   b. Compute the correlation coefficient and discuss what it measures.
   c. Test to determine whether the population correlation coefficient is actually 0, using an alpha level of 0.05.
   d. Compute the least squares regression equation using money collected as the dependent variable and number of alumni contacted as the independent variable. For this model compute, and interpret, the following:
      • R-square
      • Standard error of the estimate
      • 90% confidence interval estimate for the true slope coefficient
      • 95% prediction interval for the money collected for a particular university given that 4,000 alumni are contacted
   e. Referring to part d, conduct the appropriate hypothesis test to determine whether the overall regression model explains a significant portion of the variation in the dependent variable. Use a significance level of 0.05 to conduct the test.

11-48. A company that makes a cattle feed supplement has studied 335 cattle and found the correlation between the amount of supplement feed and the daily weight gain to be 0.104 $(r = 0.104)$. Based on these results, can you conclude that increasing the amount of supplemental feed will increase the daily weight gain? Test using an alpha level of 0.01. Comment on the results.

11-49. The Smithfield Tobacco Company recently studied a random sample of 30 of its distributors and found the correlation between sales and advertising dollars to be 0.67.

a. Can the company conclude that there is a significant linear relationship between sales and advertising? If so, is it fair to conclude that advertising causes sales to increase?

b. If a regression model was developed using sales as the dependent variable and advertising as the independent variable, determine the proportion of the variation in sales that would be explained by its relationship to advertising. Discuss what this says about the usefulness of using advertising to predict sales.

11-50. The Grinfield Service Company marketing director is interested in analyzing the relationship between her company's sales and the advertising dollars spent. In the course of her analysis, she selected a random sample of 20 weeks and recorded the sales for each week and the amount spent on advertising. These data are shown as follows and are contained in the data file called **Grinfield**.

SALES	ADVERTISING	SALES	ADVERTISING
$2,050	$180	$3,250	$300
3,760	243	4,680	402
1,897	204	4,200	399
2,567	199	2,400	209
4,330	356	1,890	245
5,670	605	3,600	190
2,356	200	5,700	480
3,456	304	5,690	515
1,254	105	2,300	300
4,300	379	1,700	145

a. Identify the independent and dependent variables.

b. Draw a scatter plot with the dependent variable on the vertical axis and the independent variable on the horizontal axis.

c. The marketing director wishes to know if increasing the amount spent on advertising is related to increases in sales. As a first attempt, use a statistical test that will provide the required information. Use a significance level of 0.025.

d. Upon careful consideration, the marketing manager realizes that it takes a certain amount of time for the effect of advertising to register in terms of increased sales. She, therefore, asks you to calculate a correlation coefficient for sales of the current week against amount of advertising spent in the previous week, and conduct a hypothesis test to determine if, under this model, increasing the amount spent on advertising is related to increased sales. Again, use a significance level of 0.025.

11-51. Refer to Problem 50.

a. Develop the least squares regression equation for these variables. Plot the regression line on the scatter plot.

b. Develop a 95% confidence interval estimate for the increase in sales associated with increasing the advertising budget by $50. Interpret the interval.

c. Discuss whether it is appropriate to interpret the intercept value in this model. Under what conditions is it appropriate? Discuss.

d. Develop a 90% confidence interval for the mean sales amount achieved during all weeks in which advertising is $200 for the week.

e. Suppose you are asked to use this regression model to predict the weekly sales when advertising is to be set at $100. What would you reply to the request? Discuss.

11-52. The Rio-River Railroad, headquartered in Santa Fe, New Mexico, is trying to devise a method for allocating fuel costs to individual railroad cars on a particular route between Denver and Santa Fe. The railroad thinks that fuel consumption will increase as more cars are added to the train, but it is uncertain how much cost should be assigned to each additional car. In an effort to deal with this problem, the cost accounting department has randomly sampled 10 trips between the two cities and recorded the data in the file called **Rio-River**.

a. Draw a scatter plot for these two variables and comment on the apparent relationship between fuel consumption and the number of rail cars on the train.

b. (1) Compute the correlation coefficient between fuel consumption and the number of train cars. (2) Test Rio-River's preconception of the relation between fuel consumption and the number of train cars, using a significance level of 0.025. (3) Comment on the results of this test. Do these results necessarily indicate that adding more cars will increase the fuel usage?

c. Develop the least squares regression model to help explain the variation in fuel consumption.

d. Write a report that interprets the regression results. In the report address the issue of, on average, how much the addition of another train car will increase fuel consumption. Also, calculate the average fuel consumption, average number of cars per train, and average fuel consumption per car for the data given. Does this average equal the average increase in fuel consumption from adding an additional car using the regression model? Explain any difference.

11-53. Henry Prince has served as a consultant to the federal government for several years. Recently, he was asked to study high school students to obtain information about how television-viewing habits are related to academic performance. Possibly because Henry is always paid by the hour, he has decided to perform two studies. In the first, he collected data from 50 randomly selected students for two variables: hours of television watched per week and grade-point average during a given period. In the second study, he collected data from 100 students for two variables: number of hours per week working at a paying job and grade-point average during a given period.

Table 11-4 shows a partial computer printout for the first study. Table 11-5 shows a partial computer printout for the second study. Using the information in these printouts, and some insight of your own, your responsibility in this problem is to fill in the missing values in Tables 11-4 and 11-5.

TABLE 11-4   Study 1 Computer Printout

REGRESSION STATISTICS		MEAN TV HOURS	20
Multiple R	-0.4926		
R-Square	0.2426		
Standard Error	0.52		

	COEFFICIENTS	STANDARD ERROR	t-STAT	p-VALUE
Intercept	2.53			
TV Hours	-0.0015	0.000382		

TABLE 11-5   Study 2 Computer Printout

REGRESSION STATISTICS	
Multiple R	0.4
R-Square	0.16

ANOVA

	df	SS	MS	F	Significance F
Regression					
Residual					
Total	99	550			

COEFFICIENTS	
Intercept	2.25
Hours Worked	0.01

11-54. Referring to Problem 53, in his report, Henry Prince has indicated that the number of hours a student watches television each week is not a significant variable for explaining the variation in student grade-point average. He states that he tested this at a significance level of 0.05. Based on the information provided, do you agree with Henry's conclusion? Discuss why or why not.

11-55. Referring to Problems 53 and 54, in the random sample of 50 students in study 1, the number of hours of television ranged from a low of 8 to a high of 40 hours per week. In his report, Henry states that based on the regression model, if no hours are spent watching television, students will have an average grade-point average of 2.530. Why do you suppose he came to this conclusion? Discuss whether you agree or disagree with him and indicate why.

11-56. Referring to Problem 53, in study 2 where hours worked ranged from 0 hours to 20 hours, Henry Prince concluded that the independent variable, hours worked, and the dependent variable, grade-point average, are significantly correlated at a significance level of 0.05. Therefore, he has stated that a student can increase his or her grade-point average by working at a paying job, and students should be encouraged to do so. Further, the more hours

the student works, the higher the grade-point average will be. Support or refute Henry's statement.

11-57. Referring to Problem 53, in his report on study 2, Henry has indicated that he tested the significance of the model using the analysis of variance approach. However, he failed to include the results of the test in his report. Using the information in Table 11-5, test the null hypothesis that the regression model is not significant, using the analysis of variance approach. Use a significance level of 0.05. Discuss why a large F-ratio should lead to the rejection of the null hypothesis. Also, using the information in the analysis of variance table, determine the estimate for the standard deviation of the model error and discuss briefly what it measures.

11-58. The American Airline Company recently performed a customer survey in which it asked a random sample of 100 passengers to indicate their income and the total cost of the airfares they have purchased for pleasure trips during the past year. A regression model was developed for the purposes of determining whether income could be used as a variable to explain the variation in number of times individuals fly on airlines in a year. The following regression results were obtained.

$$\hat{y} = 0.25 + 0.0150x$$
$$s_\epsilon = 721.44$$
$$R^2 = 0.65$$
$$s_{b_1} = 0.0000122$$

a. Develop a 95% confidence interval estimate for the true regression slope and interpret this interval estimate.

b. Can the intercept of the regression equation be interpreted in this case, assuming that no one who was surveyed had an income of 0 dollars? Explain.

c. Use the information provided to perform an analysis of variance test of the significance of the regression model. Discuss your results, assuming the test is performed at the significance level of 0.05.

11-59. A manager for a major manufacturing company recently delivered a speech to other managers from around the United States. During the course of the speech, he was explaining a study his company had done with respect to sales and price of a particular product. He said his company had developed a simple regression model and found the regression slope coefficient to be − 3,456.98. He then said that this means that increasing price by 1 dollar will cause sales to drop by 3,456.98 units. Comment on this statement, indicating whether you agree or disagree with some or all of the statement.

11-60. The Briggs Bank and Trust recently performed a study of its checking account customers. One objective of the study was to determine whether it is possible to explain the variation in average checking account balance by knowing the number of checks written per month. The sample data selected are contained in the data file named **Briggs**.

a. Draw a scatter plot for these data.

b. Develop the least squares regression equation for these data.

c. Develop the 90% interval estimate for the change in the average checking account balance when a person who formerly wrote 25 checks a month doubled the number of checks they were using.

d. Test to determine if an increase in the number of checks written by an individual can be used to predict the checking account balance of that individual. Use $\alpha = 0.05$. Comment on this result and the result of part c.

11-61. The Sanders Company production manager, Bill Hendley, is in the process of performing a productivity study of the employees at the Black Hills plant. In the process of performing this study, he has selected a random sample of 20 employees who have worked for the company for 4 years or more. For each employee, he measured the number of hours of special training the employee has taken and the production rate for the employee in pieces per day produced. The following summary data are available.

$$y = \text{Pieces produced per day}$$
$$x = \text{Hours of special training}$$
$$\bar{x} = 13.50$$
$$s_\epsilon = 11.0$$
$$\bar{y} = 125.0$$
$$\hat{y} = 88.5 + 1.5x$$
$$\sum (x - \bar{x})^2 = 1,245.0$$

a. Bill has been having trouble with one of the employees at Black Hills, Jim Svede. Jim often takes naps during working hours. When questioned about this behavior, Jim asserts that these naps make him more alert and productive than the other employees. Develop a 95% confidence interval for the average daily production for people, such as Jim, who have taken 15 hours of training. Jim has an average daily production rate of 118 pieces a day. Does his assertion carry any weight?

b. Develop a 95% prediction interval for a particular individual who has taken 15 hours of special training courses. Does this interval shed any more light upon Jim Svede's assertion? Which of the two interval estimates is more appropriate to address Jim's assertion. Discuss.

11-62. A company is considering recruiting new employees from a particular college and plans to place a great deal of emphasis on the student's college grade-point average. However, the company is aware that not all schools have the same grading standards; a student at this school might have a lower (or higher) grade-point average than a student from another school, yet really be academically on par with the other student. To make this comparison between schools, the company has devised a test that it has administered utilizing a sample size of 400. With the results of the test, it has developed a regression model that it uses to predict student grade-point average. The following equation represents the model.

$$\hat{y} = 1.0 + 0.028x$$

The R^2 for this model is 0.88 and the standard error of the estimate is 0.20, based on the sample data used to develop the model. Note that the dependent variable is the grade-point average and the independent variable is test score, where this score can range from 0 to 100. For the sample data used to develop the model, the following values are known.

$$\bar{y} = 2.76$$
$$\bar{x} = 68$$
$$\sum (x - \bar{x})^2 = 148,885.73$$

a. Based on the information contained in this problem, can you conclude that as the test score increases, the GPA will also increase, using a significance level of 0.05?

b. Suppose a student interviews with this company, takes the company test, and scores 80% correct. What is the 90% prediction interval estimate for this student's grade-point average? Interpret the interval.

c. Suppose the student in part b actually has a 2.90 grade-point average at this school. Based on this evidence, what might be concluded about this person's actual grade-point average compared with other students at other schools with the same grade-point average? Discuss the limitations you might place on this conclusion.

11-63. Refer to Problem 62.

a. Suppose a second student with a 2.45 grade-point average took the test and scored 65% correct. What is the 90% prediction interval for this student's "real" grade-point average? Interpret.

b. What would be the largest difference you would expect to see between the actual grade-point average of the student in part a and that predicted by the regression equation?

11-64. Suppose the company that developed the test discussed in Problem 62 is interested in developing a 95% confidence interval estimate for the average grade-point average for students who score 88% correct on this test. Calculate this interval and interpret it.

11-65. An economist for the state government of Mississippi recently collected the data contained in the file called **Mississippi** on the percentage of people unemployed in the state at randomly selected points in time over the past 25 years and the interest rate of treasury bills offered by the federal government at each point in time.

a. (1) Develop a plot showing the relationship between the two variables. (2) Describe the relationship as being either linear or curvilinear.

b. (1) Develop a simple linear regression model with unemployment rate as the dependent variable. (2) Write a short report describing the model and indicating the important measures.

11-66. The Cooley Service Center polishes and cleans automo- biles. It has major accounts such as the Bayview Taxi Service and Bayview Police Department. It also does work for the general public by appointment. Recently, the manager decided to survey customers to determine how satisfied they were with the work performed by the Cooley Service Center. He devised a rating scale between 0 and 100, with 0 being poor and 100 being excellent service. He selected a random sample of 14 customers and asked the customers when they picked up their cars to rate the service. He also recorded the amount of time spent on each customer's car. These data are in the data file named **Cooley.**

a. (1) Draw a scatter plot showing these two variables, with the y variable on the vertical axis and the x variable on the horizontal axis. (2) Describe the relationship between these two variables.

b. (1) Develop a linear regression model to explain the variation in the service rating. (2) Write a short report describing the model and showing the results of pertinent hypothesis tests, using a significance level of 0.10.

CASE 11-A

Alamar Industries

While driving home in northern Kentucky at 8:00 P.M., Juan Alamar wondered whether his father had done him any favor by retiring early and letting him take control of the family machine tool restoration business. When his father had started the business of overhauling machine tools, both for resale and on a contract basis, American companies dominated the tool manufacturing market. Over the last 30 years the original equipment industry had been devastated, first by competition from Germany and then from Japan. While foreign competition had not yet invaded the overhaul segment of the business, Juan had heard about foreign companies establishing operations on the West Coast.

The foreign competitors were apparently emphasizing the high quality service and operations that had been responsible for their great inroads into the original equipment market. Last week Juan had attended a day-long conference on total quality management, discussing the advantages of competing for the Baldrige Award, the national quality award established in 1987. Presenters from past Baldrige winners—including Xerox, Federal Express, Cadillac, and Motorola—stressed the positive effect on their company of winning, but they said similar effects would be possible for any company. This assertion of only positive effects is what Juan questioned. He was certain that the effect on his remaining free time would not be positive.

The Baldrige Award considers seven corporate dimensions of quality. While the award is not based on a numerical score, an overall score is calculated. The maximum score is 1,000, with most recent winners scoring about 800. While Juan did not doubt the award was good for the winners, he wondered about the nonwinners. In particular, he wondered about any relationship between attempting to improve quality according to the Baldrige dimensions and company profitability. While individual company scores are not released, Juan was able to talk to one of the conference presenters to share some anonymous data, such as a company's score in the year applied, return on its investment in the year applied, and return on its investment in the year following. Juan decided to commit the company to a total quality management process if the data provided evidence that it would lead to increased profitability.

BALDRIGE SCORE	ROI APPLICATION YEAR	ROI NEXT YEAR
470	11%	13%
520	10	11
660	14	15
540	12	12
600	15	16
710	16	16
580	11	12
600	12	13
740	16	16
610	11	14
570	12	13
660	17	19

CASE 11-B

Continental Trucking

Norm Painter is the newly hired cost analyst for Continental Trucking. Continental is a nationwide trucking firm, and until recently, most of its routes were driven under regulated rates. These rates were set to allow small trucking firms to earn an adequate profit, leaving little incentive to work to reduce costs by efficient management techniques. In fact, the greatest effort was made to try to influence regulatory agencies to grant rate increases.

A recent rash of deregulation moves has made the long-distance trucking industry more competitive. Norm has been hired to analyze Continental's whole expense structure. As part of this study, Norm is looking at truck repair costs. Since the trucks are involved in long hauls, they inevitably break down. Up until now, little preventive maintenance has been done, and if a truck broke down in the middle of a haul, either a replacement tractor was sent or an independent contractor finished the haul. The truck was then repaired at the nearest local shop. Norm is sure this procedure has led to more expense than if major repairs had been made before the trucks failed.

Norm thinks that some method needs to be found for determining when preventive maintenance is needed. He believes that fuel consumption is a good indicator of possible breakdowns, and as the trucks begin running poorly they will consume more fuel. Unfortunately, the major determinants of

fuel consumption are the weight of the truck and head winds. Norm picks a sample of a single truck model and gathers data relating fuel consumption to truck weight. All trucks in the sample were in good condition. He separates the data by direction of the haul, realizing that winds tend to blow predominantly out of the west.

EAST-WEST HAUL		WEST-EAST HAUL	
Miles/Gallon	Haul Weight	Miles/Gallon	Haul Weight
4.1	41,000 lb	4.3	40,000 lb
4.7	36,000	4.5	37,000
3.9	37,000	4.8	36,000
4.3	38,000	5.2	38,000
4.8	32,000	5.0	35,000
5.1	37,000	4.7	42,000
4.3	46,000	4.9	37,000
4.6	35,000	4.5	36,000
5.0	37,000	5.2	42,000
		4.8	41,000

Although he can gather future data on fuel consumption and haul weight rapidly, now that Norm has these data, he is not quite sure what to do with them.

■ GENERAL REFERENCES

1. Berenson, Mark L., and David M. Levine, *Basic Business Statistics: Concepts and Applications*, 7th ed. (Upper Saddle River, NJ: Prentice Hall, 1999).
2. Cryer, Jonathan D., and Robert B. Miller, *Statistics for Business: Data Analysis and Modeling*, 2d ed. (Belmont, CA: Duxbury Press, 1994).
3. Draper, Norman R., and Harry Smith, *Applied Regression Analysis*, 3d ed. (New York: John Wiley & Sons, 1998).
4. Frees, Edward W., *Data Analysis Using Regression Models: The Business Perspective* (Englewood Cliffs, NJ: Prentice Hall, 1996).
5. Kleinbaum, David G., Lawrence L. Kupper, Keith E. Muller, and Azhar Nizam, *Applied Regression Analysis and Other Multivariable Methods*, 3d ed. (Belmont, CA: Duxbury Press, 1998).
6. *Microsoft Excel 2000* (Redmond, WA: Microsoft Corporation, 1999).
7. *Minitab for Windows Version 13* (State College, PA: Minitab, Inc., 2000).
8. Neter, John, Michael H. Kutner, Christopher J. Nachtsheim, and William Wasserman, *Applied Linear Statistical Models*, 4th ed. (Homewood, IL: Richard D. Irwin, 1996).

MULTIPLE REGRESSION ANALYSIS AND MODEL BUILDING

CHAPTER OUTCOMES

After studying the material in this chapter, you should be able to:

12-1: Understand the general concepts behind model building using multiple regression analysis.

12-2: Apply multiple regression analysis to business decision-making situations.

12-3: Analyze the computer output for a multiple regression model and interpret the regression results.

12-4: Test hypotheses about the significance of a multiple regression model and test the significance of the independent variables in the model.

12-5: Recognize potential problems when using multiple regression analysis and take the steps to correct the problems.

12-6: Incorporate qualitative variables into the regression model by using dummy variables.

WHY YOU NEED TO KNOW

Chapter 11 pointed out that decision makers often need to consider the relationship between two variables when analyzing a problem. Simple linear regression and correlation analyses provide a basis for analyzing the relationship between two variables. If the two variables are correlated, there is a linear relationship between them and linear regression analysis can be used to model that relationship.

As you might expect, business problems are not limited to linear relationships or to applications involving just two variables. Many practical situations involve analyzing the relationships among three or more variables, and these relationships may be nonlinear. For example, a vice president of planning for an automobile manufacturer would be interested in the relationship between her company's automobile sales and the variables that influence those sales. Included in

her analysis might be such independent or explanatory variables as automobile price, competitors' sales, and advertising, as well as such economic variables as disposable personal income, the inflation rate, and the unemployment rate. When multiple independent variables are to be included in the analysis simultaneously, the technique introduced in the chapter, referred to as multiple linear regression, is very useful. When the relationship between variables is nonlinear, we may be able to apply variable transformations that allow us to use multiple linear regression analysis to construct the model. This chapter examines the general topic of model building by extending the concepts of simple linear regression analysis. The background information provided in Chapter 11 will be very helpful in understanding and applying multiple regression analysis to business decision-making situations.

■ 12-1: INTRODUCTION TO MULTIPLE REGRESSION ANALYSIS

Chapter 11 introduced the concept of simple linear regression analysis involving a dependent variable and a single independent or explanatory variable. In those situations, we attempt to model the relationship between two variables in a population as shown in Equation 12-1.

SIMPLE LINEAR REGRESSION MODEL (POPULATION MODEL)

$$y = \beta_0 + \beta_1 x + \epsilon \qquad \text{12-1}$$

where:

y = Values of the dependent variable in the population
x = Values of the independent variable in the population
β_0 = The population regression coefficient representing the y intercept
β_1 = The population regression slope coefficient
ϵ = The random error for the observations in the population

When we have a random sample of data, the regression model represented by Equation 12-1 is estimated in the form shown as Equation 12-2.

ESTIMATED SIMPLE LINEAR REGRESSION MODEL

$$\hat{y} = b_0 + b_1 x \qquad \text{12-2}$$

where:

b_0 = Estimated y intercept
b_1 = Estimated slope coefficient

The simple regression model is characterized by two variables: y, the *dependent variable*, and x, the *independent* or *explanatory variable*. The single independent variable explains some variation in the dependent variable, but unless x and y are perfectly correlated, the proportion explained will be less than 100%. This also means that the predicted (or fitted) *y* values will often not equal the actual *y* values. Thus prediction error will be present. Another word for prediction error is **residual.**

RESIDUAL (PREDICTION ERROR)
The difference between the actual value of *y* and the predicted value of *y*, which is given by the equation:

$$e = y - \hat{y}$$

Chapter 11 indicated the model's random error (ϵ) is assumed to have a mean of 0 and a standard deviation called the **standard error of the estimate.** If this standard error of the estimate is too large, the regression model may not be very useful for prediction.

STANDARD ERROR OF THE ESTIMATE
The standard deviation of the model errors. The standard error measures the dispersion of the actual values of the dependent variable around the fitted regression plane.

In multiple regression analysis, additional independent variables are added to the regression model to explain some of the yet-unexplained variation in the dependent variable. Adding appropriate independent variables should thereby reduce the standard error of the estimate.

You will note as we proceed that multiple regression is merely an extension of simple regression analysis. However, as we expand the model for the population from one independent variable to two or more, there are some new considerations.

The general format of a **multiple regression model** is given by Equation 12-3.

MULTIPLE REGRESSION MODEL (POPULATION MODEL)

$$y = \beta_0 + \beta_1 x_1 + \beta_2 x_2 + \cdots + \beta_k x_k + \epsilon \qquad \textbf{12-3}$$

where:

β_0 = Population *y* intercept
β_j = Population regression coefficient for variable *j*; *j* = 1, 2, ..., *k*
k = Number of independent variables
ϵ = Model error

There are four general assumptions of the linear multiple regression model.

1. The regression model errors are normally distributed.
2. The mean of the model error terms is 0.
3. The model error terms have a constant variance, σ_ϵ^2, for all combinations of values of the independent variables.
4. The model error terms are independent.

Equation 12-3 represents the multiple regression model for the population. However, in most instances, you will be working with a random sample from the population. Given the assumptions just listed, the estimated multiple regression model, based on the sample data, is of the form shown in Equation 12-4.

ESTIMATED MULTIPLE REGRESSION MODEL

$$\hat{y} = b_0 + b_1 x_1 + b_2 x_2 + \cdots + b_k x_k \qquad \textbf{12-4}$$

(a) ONE INDEPENDENT VARIABLE		(b) TWO INDEPENDENT VARIABLES		
y	x_1	y	x_1	x_2
564.99	50	564.99	50	10
601.06	60	601.06	60	13
560.11	40	560.11	40	14
616.41	50	616.41	50	12
674.96	60	674.96	60	15
630.58	45	630.58	45	16
554.66	53	554.66	53	14

TABLE 12-1
Sample Data to Illustrate the
Difference Between Simple
and Multiple Regression
Models

This model is an extension of the simple regression model shown in Equation 12-2. The principal difference is that, whereas for the simple model Equation 12-2 is the equation for a straight line in a two-dimensional space, the multiple regression model forms a hyperplane (or response surface) through multidimensional space. Each regression coefficient represents a different slope. So, for a decision maker, using Equation 12-2 means a value of the dependent variable can be estimated using a value of one independent variable, but a multiple regression model requires values of two or more (k) independent variables to be known. The hyperplane represents the relationship between the dependent variable and the many independent variables.

For example, Table 12-1a shows sample data for a dependent variable, y, and one independent variable, x_1. Figure 12-1 shows a scatter plot and the regression line for the simple regression analysis for y and x_1. The points are plotted in two-dimensional space, and the regression model is represented by a line through the points such that the sum of squares of error [SSE $= \sum(y - \hat{y})^2$] is minimized.

If we add variable x_2, as shown in Table 12-1b, to the model, the resulting multiple regression equation becomes:

$$\hat{y} = 307.71 + 2.85x_1 + 10.94x_2$$

For the time being don't worry about how this equation was computed. That will be discussed shortly. Note, however, that a regression equation through the y, x_1, x_2 points forms a hyperplane through the three-dimensional space such that $\sum(y - \hat{y})^2$ is minimized. A

FIGURE 12-1
Simple Regression Line

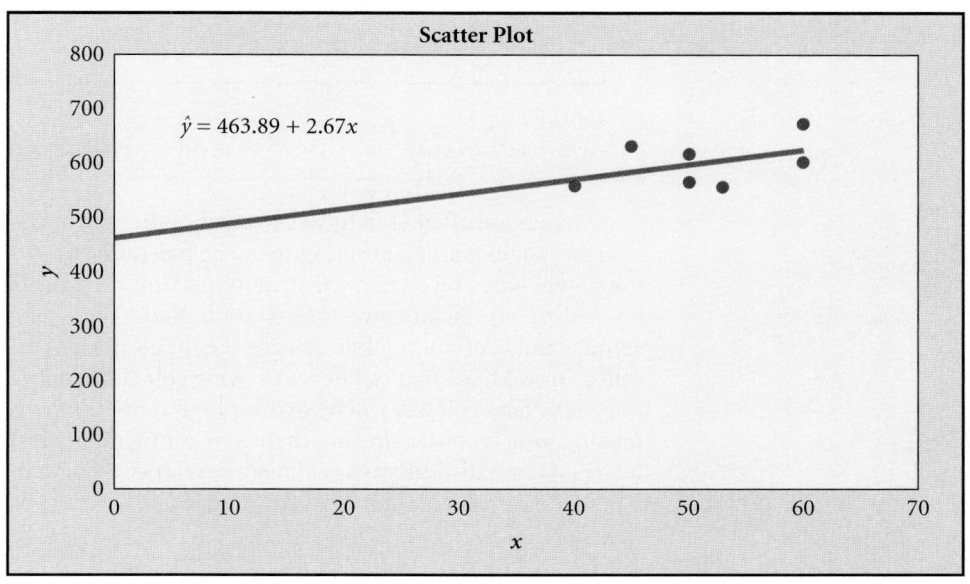

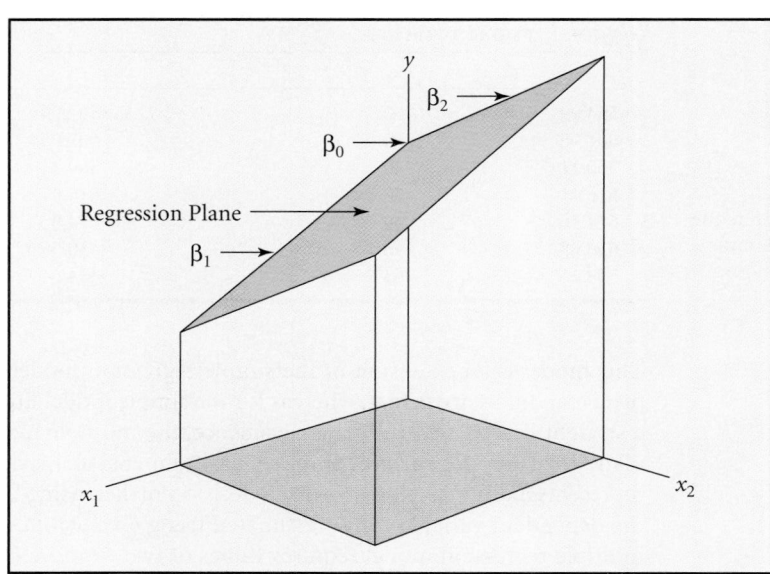

FIGURE 12-2
Multiple Regression
Hyperplane for Population

typical hyperplane is illustrated in Figure 12-2. This is the same *least squares criterion* that is used with simple linear regression. The mathematics for developing the least squares regression equation for simple linear regression involves differential calculus. (See the CD-ROM for Chapter 11.) The same is true for the multiple regression equation. Since the least squares regression coefficients are determined using matrix algebra, the mathematical derivation is beyond the scope of this text.[1]

Multiple regression analysis is virtually always performed with the aid of a computer and appropriate software. Both Minitab and Excel contain procedures for performing multiple regression. Minitab has a far more complete regression procedure. However, the PHStat Excel add-ins expand Excel's capabilities. Each software package presents the results in a slightly different format; however, the same information will appear in all regression output.

Basic Model Building Concepts

An important activity in business decision-making is referred to as **model** building.

> **MODEL**
> A representation of an actual system using either a physical or mathematical portrayal.

Models are often used to test changes in the system without actually having to change the real system. Models are also used to help describe the system or to predict the output of the system based on certain specified inputs. You are probably quite aware of physical models. Airlines use flight simulators to train pilots. Wind tunnels are used to determine the aerodynamics of automobile designs. Golf ball makers use a physical model of a golfer, called "Iron Mike," that can be set to swing golf clubs in a very controlled manner to determine how far a golf ball will fly. While physical models are very useful in business decision-making, our emphasis in this chapter is on mathematical models. In particular, we are interested in statistical models that are developed using multiple regression analysis.

---

[1]For a complete treatment of the matrix algebra approach for estimating the multiple regression coefficients, consult *Applied Linear Statistical Models* by Neter et al.

People involved in model building frequently conclude that it is both an art and a science. Determining the appropriate model is a challenging task, but it can be made manageable by employing a model-building process consisting of the following three components: model specification, model fitting, and model diagnosis.

Model Specification

Model specification, or model identification, is the process of determining the dependent variable and deciding which independent variables should be included in the model. In the context of the statistical models discussed in this chapter, this component involves the following three steps.

1. Decide what you want to do and select the dependent variable. In the previous chapter we discussed how simple linear regression analysis could be used to describe the relationship between a dependent and an independent variable.
2. List the potential independent variables for your model. Here, your knowledge of the situation you are modeling guides you in identifying potential independent variables.
3. Gather the sample data (observations) for all variables.

As with any statistical tool, the larger the sample size the better, since the potential for extreme sampling error is reduced when the sample size is large. However, at a minimum, the sample size required to develop a regression model must be at least one greater than the number of independent variables.[2] If we are thinking of developing a regression model with five independent variables, the absolute minimum number of observations required is six. Otherwise, the computer software will indicate an error has been made or will print out meaningless values. As a practical matter, the sample size should be at least four times the number of independent variables. Thus, if we have five independent variables ($k = 5$), we would want at least 20 cases to develop the regression model.

Model Building

Model building is the process of actually constructing the mathematical equation in which some or all of the independent variables are used in an attempt to explain the variation in the dependent variable.

Model Diagnosis

Model diagnosis is the process of analyzing the quality of the model you have constructed by determining how well a specified model fits the data you just gathered. You will examine such output values as R-square and the estimate of the standard deviation of the model error. At this stage, you will also assess the extent to which the model's assumptions appear to be satisfied. (Section 12-5 is devoted to examining whether a model meets the regression analysis assumptions.) If the model is unacceptable in any of these areas, you will be forced to revert to the model specification step and begin again. But you will be the final judge of whether the model provides acceptable results, and you will always be constrained by time and cost considerations.

An important consideration in practical situations is to use the simplest available model that will meet your needs. The objective of model building is to help you make better decisions. You do not need to feel that a sophisticated model is better if a simpler one will provide acceptable results.

---

[2]There are mathematical reasons for this sample size requirement that are beyond the scope of this text. In essence, Equation 12-4 won't work if the sample size is not at least one larger than the number of independent variables.

EXAMPLE 12-1

MULTIPLE REGRESSION

Excel and
Minitab Tutorial

Developing a Multiple Regression Model

First City Real Estate

First City Real Estate is an established, family owned and operated firm located in the Midwest. The owners are well aware of the trend toward national real estate chains, and many of their local competitors have been bought out or have become a franchise. First City has resisted this trend, but its owners realize they will have to adapt to the changing market. One of the recent decisions made by executives of First City is to make the firm more responsive to inquiries from people thinking about selling their house. To do so, they plan to incorporate computer technology. First City management wishes to build a model that can be used to predict sales prices for residential property.

MODEL SPECIFICATION

The dependent variable is the sales price. This is what the managers want to be able to predict. The managers met in a brainstorming session to derive a list of possible independent (explanatory) variables. Some variables, such as "condition of the house" were eliminated because of a lack of data. Others such as "curb appeal" (the appeal of the house to people as they drive by) were eliminated because the values for these variables would be too subjective and difficult to quantify. From a wide list of possibilities, the managers selected the following variables as good candidates:

$$x_1 = \text{Home size (in square feet)}$$
$$x_2 = \text{Age of house}$$
$$x_3 = \text{Number of bedrooms}$$
$$x_4 = \text{Number of bathrooms}$$
$$x_5 = \text{Garage size (\# of cars)}$$

Data were obtained for a sample of 319 residential properties that sold within the previous two months in an area served by two of First City's offices. For each house in the sample, the sales price and values for each potential independent variable were collected. Figure 12-3 shows a portion of the data as an Excel worksheet. The data are also in a file named **First City.**

MODEL FORMULATION

The regression model will be developed by including independent variables from among those for which you have complete data. There is no way to determine whether an independent variable will be a good predictor variable by analyzing the individual variables' descriptive statistics like the mean and standard deviation. Instead, we need to look at the

FIGURE 12-3
Excel Worksheet for First City
Residential Real Estate Data

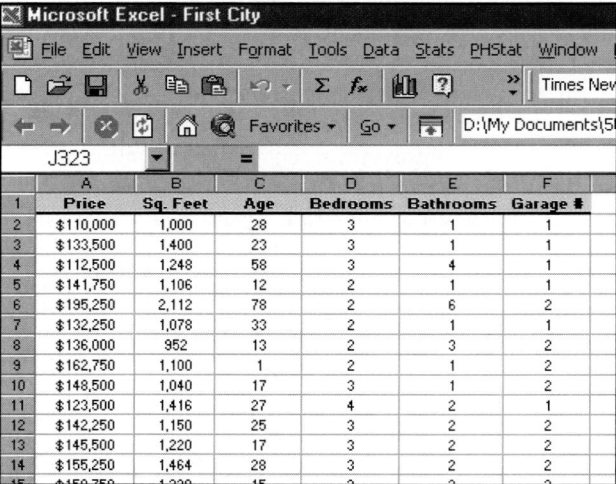

Excel Instructions:
1. Open file: First City.xls

correlation between the independent variables and the dependent variable as measured by the **correlation coefficient.**

CORRELATION COEFFICIENT

A quantitative measure of the strength of the linear relationship between two variables. The correlation coefficient, r, ranges between -1.0 and $+1.0$.

When we have multiple independent variables and one dependent variable, we can look at the correlation between all pairs of variables by developing a *correlation matrix.* Each correlation is computed using one of the equations in 12-5. The appropriate formula is determined by whether the correlation is being calculated for a predictor variable and the dependent variable or for two predictor variables, respectively.

CORRELATION COEFFICIENT

$$r = \frac{\sum (x - \bar{x})(y - \bar{y})}{\sqrt{\sum (x - \bar{x})^2 \sum (y - \bar{y})^2}} \quad \text{or} \quad r = \frac{\sum_{i=1}^{n}(x_{1i} - \bar{x}_1)(x_{2i} - \bar{x}_2)}{\sqrt{\sum_{i=1}^{n}(x_{1i} - \bar{x}_1)^2 \sum_{i=1}^{n}(x_{2i} - \bar{x}_2)^2}} \quad \text{12-5}$$

One x variable with y \qquad\qquad One x variable with another x

---

The actual calculations are done using Excel's correlation tool and the results are shown in Figure 12-4. The output provides the correlation between y and each x variable and between each pair of independent variables.[3] Recall that in Chapter 11, a t-test (see Equation 11-3) was used to test whether the correlation coefficient is statistically significant. Given degrees of freedom equal to $319 - 2 = 317$, the critical t for a two-tailed test with alpha equal to 0.02 is 2.338.[4] Any correlation coefficient generating an absolute value of $t > 2.338$ is determined to be significant.

For now, we will focus on the correlations in the first column in Figure 12-4, which measure the strength of the linear relationship between each independent variable and the dependent variable, sales price. For example, the t-statistic for price and square feet is:

$$t = \frac{r}{\sqrt{\dfrac{1 - r^2}{n - 2}}} = \frac{0.7477}{\sqrt{\dfrac{1 - 0.7477^2}{319 - 2}}} = 20.048$$

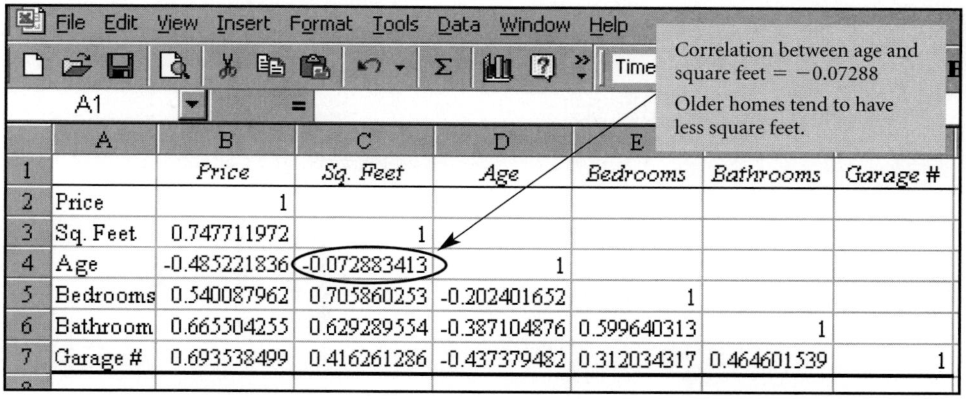

FIGURE 12-4
Excel Results Showing First City Real Estate Correlation Matrix

Excel Instructions:

1. Open file: First City.xls
2. Click on Tools
3. Select Correlation
4. Define data range and output location

Correlation between age and square feet = -0.07288
Older homes tend to have less square feet.

	Price	Sq. Feet	Age	Bedrooms	Bathrooms	Garage #
Price	1					
Sq. Feet	0.747711972	1				
Age	-0.485221836	-0.072883413	1			
Bedrooms	0.540087962	0.705860253	-0.202401652	1		
Bathroom	0.665504255	0.629289554	-0.387104876	0.599640313	1	
Garage #	0.693538499	0.416261286	-0.437379482	0.312034317	0.464601539	1

---

[3]Minitab, in addition to providing the correlation matrix, provides the p-values for each correlation. If the p-value is less than the desired alpha, the correlation is statistically significant.

[4]You can use the Excel TINV function to get the precise t-value which is 2.338 or obtain an approximation using the t-table in Appendix F.

Since 20.048 > 2.338, the correlation between sales price and square feet is statistically significant. Similar calculations for the other independent variables with price shows that all variables are statistically correlated with price. This indicates that a significant linear relationship exists between each independent variable and sales price. Variable x_1, square feet, has the highest correlation at 0.748. Variable x_2, age of the house, has the lowest correlation at -0.485. The negative correlation implies that older homes tend to have lower sales prices.

As we discussed in Chapter 11, it is always a good idea to develop scatter plots to visually see the relationship between two variables. Figure 12-5 shows the scatter plots for each independent variable and the dependent variable, sales price. In each case, the plots indicate a linear relationship between the independent variable and the dependent variable. Note that several of the independent variables (bedrooms, bathrooms, garage size) are quantitative but discrete. The scatter plots for these variables show points at each level of the independent variable rather than over a continuum of values.

FIGURE 12-5   First City Real Estate Scatter Plots

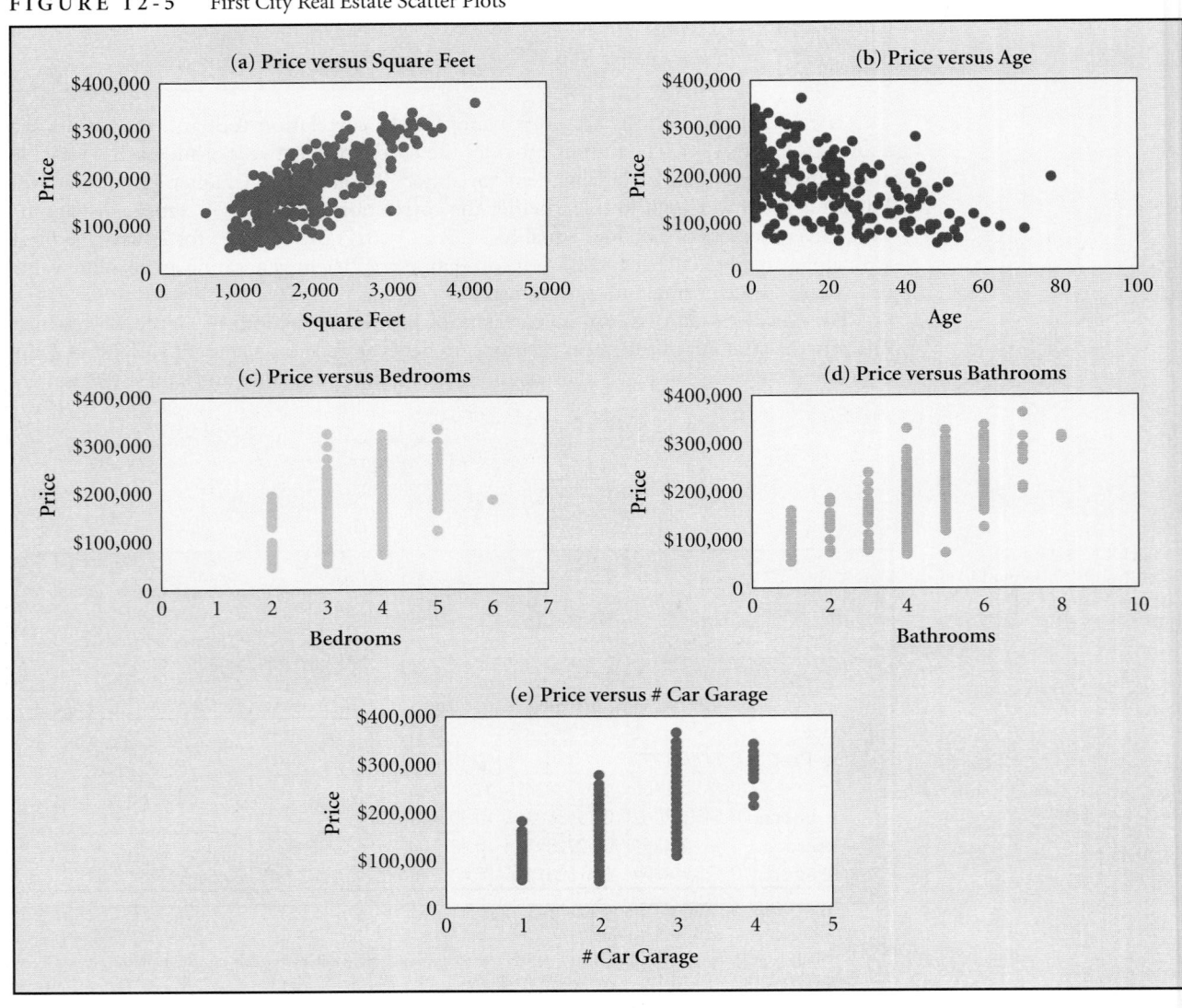

COMPUTING THE REGRESSION EQUATION

First City's goal is to develop a regression model to predict the appropriate selling price for a home, using certain measurable characteristics. The first attempt at developing the model will be to run a multiple regression computer program using all available independent variables. The regression output from Excel is shown in Figure 12-6. Minitab output is formatted slightly differently, but contains the same information.

The estimate of the multiple regression model given in Figure 12-6 is:

$$\hat{y} = 31{,}127.6 + 63.1(\text{Sq. feet}) - 1{,}144.4(\text{Age}) - 8{,}410.4(\text{Bedrooms}) + 3{,}522.0(\text{Bathrooms}) + 28{,}203.5(\text{Garage}).$$

The coefficient for each independent variable represents an estimate of the average change in the dependent variable for a one unit change in the independent variable, all other independent variables remaining constant. For example, for houses of the same age, with the same number of bedrooms, baths and garages, a one square foot increase in the size of the house is estimated to increase its price by an average of $63.10. Likewise, for houses of the same size and same number of bedrooms, bathrooms, and garages, a one year increase in the age of the house is estimated to result in an average drop in sales price of $1,144. The other coefficients are interpreted in the same way. Note, in each case, we are interpreting the regression coefficient for one independent variable while holding the other variables constant.

To estimate the value of a residential property, First Real Estate brokers would substitute values for the independent variables into the regression equation. For example, suppose a house with the following characteristics is considered.

$$x_1 = \text{Square feet} = 2{,}100$$
$$x_2 = \text{Age} = 15$$
$$x_3 = \text{Number of bedrooms} = 4$$
$$x_4 = \text{Number of baths} = 3$$
$$x_5 = \text{Size of Garage} = 2$$

FIGURE 12-6
Excel Multiple Regression Model Results for First City Real Estate

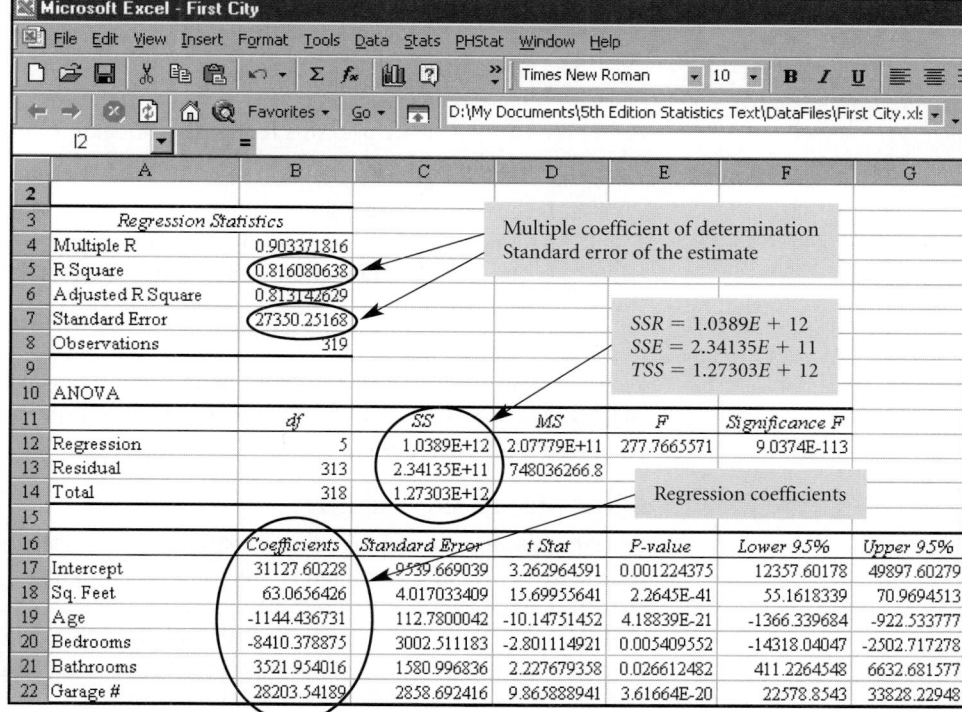

Excel Instructions

1. Open file: First City.xls
2. Click on Tools
3. Select Regression
4. Define Dependent and Independent variable range
5. Determine output location

The point estimate for the sales price is:

$$\hat{y} = 31{,}127.6 + 63.1(\text{Sq. feet}) - 1{,}144.4(\text{Age}) - 8{,}410.4(\text{Bedrooms})$$
$$+ \ 3{,}522.0(\text{Bathrooms}) + 28{,}203.5(\text{Garage})$$
$$\hat{y} = 31{,}127.6 + 63.1(2{,}100) - 1{,}144.4(15) - 8{,}410.4(4) + 3{,}522.0(3) + 28{,}203.5(2)$$
$$\hat{y} = \$179{,}802.70$$

THE COEFFICIENT OF DETERMINATION

You learned in Chapter 11 that the *coefficient of determination, R^2*, measures the fraction of variation in the dependent variable that can be explained by the dependent variable's relationship to a single independent variable. When there are multiple independent variables in the model, R^2 is also used to determine the proportion of variation in the dependent variable that is explained by the dependent variable's relationship to all the independent variables in the model. However, R^2 is now called the **multiple coefficient of determination.** Equation 12-6 is used to compute R^2 for a multiple regression model.

MULTIPLE COEFFICIENT OF DETERMINATION (R^2)

The percentage of variation in the dependent variable explained by its relationship to the independent variables in the regression model.

$$R^2 = \frac{\text{Sum of squares regression}}{\text{Total sum of squares}} = \frac{SSR}{TSS} \qquad \textbf{12-6}$$

As shown in Figure 12-6, $R^2 = 0.816$. Both SSR and TSS are included in the output in Figure 12-6. Therefore, you can use Equation 12-6 to get R^2 as follows:

$$\frac{SSR}{TSS} = \frac{1.0389E{+}12}{1.27303E{+}12} = 0.816$$

Over 81% of the variation in sales price can be explained by the multiple regression model. However, as we shall see shortly, not all independent variables are equally important to the model's ability to explain this variation.

MODEL DIAGNOSIS

Before First City actually uses this regression model to estimate the sales price of a house, there are several questions that should be answered.

1. Is the overall model significant?
2. Are the individual variables significant?
3. Is the standard deviation of the model error too large to provide meaningful results?
4. Is multicollinearity a problem?

We shall answer each of these questions in order. We will have to wait until later in the chapter before we have the tools to answer the fifth important question: Have we violated the regression model assumptions?

IS THE MODEL SIGNIFICANT?

You should keep in mind that the regression model we constructed is based upon a sample of data from the population and is subject to sampling error. Therefore, we need to test the statistical significance of the overall regression model. We have previously discussed the multiple coefficient of determination, R^2, which is a measure of how much of the variation in the dependent variable can be explained by the regression model. Since R^2 is a sample statistic, it can be used to make inferences about whether the overall model is statistically significant in explaining the variation in the dependent variable. The specific null and alternative hypotheses tested at the 0.02 significance level for First City Real Estate are:

$$H_0: \beta_1 = \beta_2 = \beta_3 = \beta_4 = \beta_5 = 0$$
$$H_A: \text{At least one } \beta_i \text{ does not equal } 0.$$

If the null hypothesis is true and all the slope coefficients are simultaneously equal to 0, the overall regression model is not useful for predictive or descriptive purposes.

In Chapter 11, we discussed the analysis of variance F-test as a method for testing whether the regression model explains a significant proportion of the variation in the dependent variable (and whether the overall model is significant). The F-test statistic for a multiple regression model is shown in Equation 12-7.

F-TEST STATISTIC

$$F = \frac{\dfrac{SSR}{k}}{\dfrac{SSE}{n - k - 1}} = \frac{MSR}{MSE} \qquad \text{12-7}$$

where:

SSR = Sum of squares regression (See Chapter 11)
SSE = Sum of squares error $\sum (y - \hat{y})^2$
n = Number of data points
k = Number of independent variables
Degrees of freedom = $D_1 = k$ and $D_2 = n - k - 1$

The analysis of variance portion of the Excel output shown in Figure 12-6 contains values for MSR and MSE and the F-value. The general format of the ANOVA table in a regression analysis is shown as follows.

ANOVA

	df	SS	MS	F	Significance F
Regression	k	SSR	$MSR = SSR/k$	MSR/MSE	computed p-value
Residual	$n - k - 1$	SSE	$MSE = SSE/(n - k - 1)$		
Total	$n - 1$	TSS			

The ANOVA portion of the Excel output from Figure 12-6 is:

ANOVA

	df	SS	MS	F	Significance F
Regression	5	$1.0389E+12$	$2.07779E+11$	277.7665571	$9.0374E-113$
Residual	313	$2.34135E+11$	748036266.8		
Total	318	$1.27303E+12$			

We can test the model's significance by either comparing the calculated F-value, 277.77, with a table value for a given alpha level and 5 and 313 degrees of freedom, or compare the p-value in the output with a specified alpha level. Since the p-value is very nearly 0, it is certainly less than $\alpha = 0.02$, and we should conclude that the regression model *does* explain a significant proportion of the variation in sales price. Thus, the overall model is statistically significant. This indicates that for estimating house sales prices, this multiple regression model is superior to using the mean house price as the estimate.

Excel and Minitab also provide a measure called the *R*-sq(adj), which is the **adjusted R-squared** value (see Figure 12-6). It is calculated by Equation 12-8.

ADJUSTED *R*-SQUARED

A measure of the percentage of explained variation in the dependent variable that takes into account the relationship between the number of cases and the number of independent variables in the regression model.

$$R\text{-sq(adj)} = R_A^2 = 1 - (1 - R^2)\left(\frac{n-1}{n-k-1}\right) \qquad \text{12-8}$$

where:

n = Sample size
k = Number of independent variables in the model

Adding independent variables to the regression model increases R^2. Thus, as the number of independent variables is increased (regardless of the quality of the variables), R^2 will increase. However, each additional variable results in the loss of one degree of freedom. This is viewed as part of the cost of adding the specified variable. The addition to R^2 may not justify the reduction in degrees of freedom. The R_A^2 value takes into account this cost and adjusts the R_A^2 value accordingly. R_A^2 will always be less than R^2. When a variable is added that does not contribute its fair share to the explanation of the dependent variable, the R_A^2 will actually decline even though R^2 will increase. The adjusted *R*-squared is a particularly important measure when the number of independent variables is large relative to the sample size. It takes into account the relationship between sample size and number of variables. R^2 may appear artificially high if the number of variables is large compared to the sample size.

In this example, in which the sample size is quite large relative to the number of independent variables, the adjusted *R*-squared is 81.3%, only slightly less than $R^2 = 81.6\%$.

ARE THE INDIVIDUAL VARIABLES SIGNIFICANT?

We have concluded that the overall model is significant. This means that *at least* one independent variable explains a significant proportion of the variation in sales price. This does not mean that *all* the variables are significant, however. To determine which variables are significant we test the following hypotheses.

$$H_0: \beta_i = 0$$
$$H_A: \beta_i \neq 0 \qquad \text{for all } i$$

We can test the significance of each independent variable using a *t*-test, as discussed in Chapter 11. The calculated *t*-value for each variable is provided on the computer printout in Figure 12-6. Recall that the *t*-statistic is determined by dividing the regression coefficient by the estimator of the standard deviation of the regression coefficient as shown in Equation 12-9.

---

t-TEST FOR SIGNIFICANCE OF EACH REGRESSION COEFFICIENT

$$t = \frac{b_i - 0}{s_{b_i}}, \qquad df = n - k - 1 \qquad \text{12-9}$$

where:

b_i = Sample slope coefficient for the *i*th independent variable
s_{b_i} = Estimate of the standard error for the *i*th sample slope coefficient

---

For example, the t-value for square feet shown in Figure 12-6 is 15.70. This was computed using Equation 12-9 as follows:

$$t = \frac{b_i - 0}{s_{b_i}} = \frac{63.06564 - 0}{4.01703} = 15.70$$

The calculated t-values should be compared to the critical t-value with $n - k - 1 = 319 - 5 - 1 = 313$ degrees of freedom which is approximately 2.364 for $\alpha = 0.02$. Since $15.70 > 2.364$, we reject the hypothesis that the regression slope for square feet is 0.

We can also look at the Excel or Minitab output and compare the p-value for each regression slope coefficient with alpha. Both the t-test and the p-value techniques will give the same results.

You should consider that these t-tests are *conditional* tests. This means the null hypothesis is that *the value of each slope coefficient is 0 given that the other independent variables are already in the model.*[5] Figure 12-7 shows the hypothesis tests for each independent variable

FIGURE 12-7
Significance Tests for Each
Independent Variable in the
First City Real Estate Example

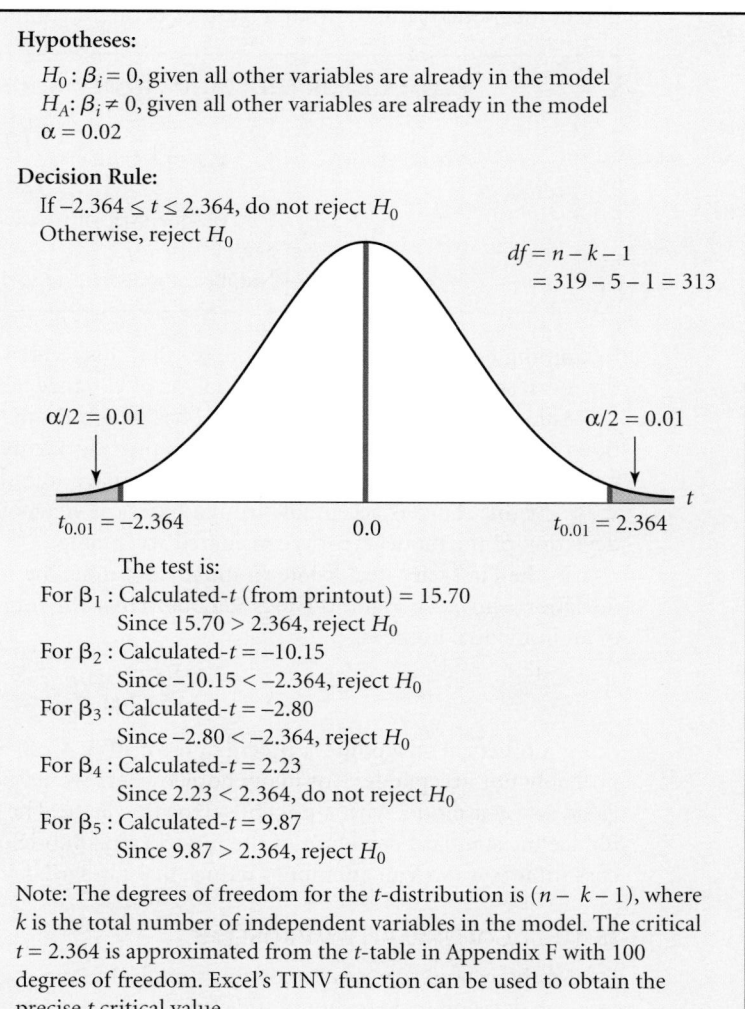

Hypotheses:

$H_0 : \beta_i = 0$, given all other variables are already in the model
$H_A : \beta_i \ne 0$, given all other variables are already in the model
$\alpha = 0.02$

Decision Rule:

If $-2.364 \le t \le 2.364$, do not reject H_0
Otherwise, reject H_0

$df = n - k - 1$
$= 319 - 5 - 1 = 313$

$\alpha/2 = 0.01$ $\alpha/2 = 0.01$

$t_{0.01} = -2.364$ 0.0 $t_{0.01} = 2.364$

The test is:
For β_1 : Calculated-t (from printout) = 15.70
Since $15.70 > 2.364$, reject H_0
For β_2 : Calculated-$t = -10.15$
Since $-10.15 < -2.364$, reject H_0
For β_3 : Calculated-$t = -2.80$
Since $-2.80 < -2.364$, reject H_0
For β_4 : Calculated-$t = 2.23$
Since $2.23 < 2.364$, do not reject H_0
For β_5 : Calculated-$t = 9.87$
Since $9.87 > 2.364$, reject H_0

Note: The degrees of freedom for the t-distribution is $(n - k - 1)$, where k is the total number of independent variables in the model. The critical $t = 2.364$ is approximated from the t-table in Appendix F with 100 degrees of freedom. Excel's TINV function can be used to obtain the precise t critical value.

[5]Note that the t-tests may be affected if the independent variables in the model are themselves correlated. A procedure known as the *sum of squares drop* F-*test,* discussed by Neter et al. in *Applied Linear Statistical Models,* should be used in this situation. Each t-test considers only the marginal contribution of the independent variables and may indicate that none of the variables in the model are significant even though the ANOVA procedure indicates otherwise.

using a 0.02 significance level. We conclude that four independent variables in the model are significant. One variable, the number of bathrooms, has a calculated t-value that just misses the rejection region. When a regression model is to be used for prediction, the model should contain no insignificant variables. If insignificant variables are present, they should be dropped and a new regression equation obtained before it is used for prediction purposes. We will have more to say about this later.

IS THE STANDARD DEVIATION OF THE REGRESSION MODEL TOO LARGE?

The purpose of developing the First City regression model is to be able to determine values of the dependent variable when corresponding values of the independent variables are known. An indication of how good the regression model is can be found by looking at the relationship between the measured values of the dependent variable and those values that would be predicted by the regression model. The standard deviation of the regression model (also called the *standard error of the estimate*), measures the dispersion of observed home sale values, y, around values predicted by the regression model. The estimate for this standard deviation of the model error, shown in Figure 12-6, can be computed using Equation 12-10.

ESTIMATE FOR THE STANDARD DEVIATION OF THE MODEL

$$s_\epsilon = \sqrt{\frac{SSE}{n - k - 1}} = \sqrt{MSE} \qquad \text{12-10}$$

where:

SSE = Sum of squares error (residual)

n = Sample size

k = Number of independent variables

Examining Equation 12-10 closely, we see that this standard deviation is the square root of the mean square error found in the analysis of variance table.

Sometimes, even though the model has a high R^2, the estimate of the standard deviation of the model error will be too large to provide adequate precision for confidence and prediction intervals. A rule of thumb that we have found useful is to examine the range $\pm 2s_\epsilon$.[6] If this range is acceptable from a practical viewpoint, the estimate of the standard deviation of the model error is considered acceptable.

In the First City Real Estate Company example, the model error's estimated standard deviation, shown in Figure 12-6, is $27,350. Thus, the rough prediction range for the price of an individual home is:

$$\pm 2(\$27,350)$$
$$\pm \$54,700$$

From a practical viewpoint, a potential error of $54,700 above or below the true value is probably not acceptable. Not many homeowners would be willing to have their appraisal value set by a model with a possible error this large. The company needs to take steps to reduce the standard deviation of the model error. Subsequent sections of this chapter discuss some ways we can attempt to reduce the standard deviation of the model error.

IS MULTICOLLINEARITY A PROBLEM?

Even if the overall regression model is significant, and if each independent variable is significant, decision makers should still examine the regression model to determine whether it appears reasonable. This is referred to as checking for *face validity*. Specifically, you should

---

[6]The actual confidence interval for prediction of a new observation requires the use of matrix algebra. However, when the sample size is large and dependent variables near the means of the dependent variables are used, the rule of thumb given in the previous paragraph is a close approximation. Refer to *Applied Linear Statistical Models* by Neter et al. for further discussion.

check to see that signs on the regression coefficients are consistent with the signs on the correlation coefficient between the independent variable and the dependent variable. Does any regression coefficient have an unexpected sign?

Before answering this question for the First City Real Estate example, we should review what the regression coefficients mean. First, the constant term, b_0, is the estimate of the model's y-intercept. If the data used to develop the regression model contain values of x_1, x_2, x_3, x_4, and x_5 that are simultaneously 0 (such as would be the case for vacant land), the constant is the mean value of y, given that x_1, x_2, x_3, x_4, and x_5 all equal 0. Under these conditions b_0 would estimate the average value of a vacant lot. However, in the First City example, no vacant land was in the sample, so the constant has no particular meaning.

The coefficient for square feet, b_1, estimates the average change in sales price corresponding to a change in house size of 1 square foot, holding the other independent variables constant. The value shown in Figure 12-6 for b_1 is 63.1. The coefficient is positive, indicating that an increase in square footage is associated with an increase in sales price. This relationship is expected. All other things being equal, bigger houses should sell for more money.

Likewise, the coefficient for x_5, the size of the garage, is positive, indicating that an increase in size is also associated with an increase in price. This is expected. The coefficient for x_2, the age of the house, is negative, indicating that an older house is worth less than a similar younger house. This also seems reasonable. However, the coefficient for variable x_3, the number of bedrooms, is $-\$8,410.4$ meaning that, if we hold the other variables constant but increase the number of bedrooms by one, the average price will *drop* by $\$8,410.4$. This would appear to run counter to conventional thinking about the housing market. Finally, variable x_4 for bathrooms has the expected positive sign, but as we discussed previously, it is not significantly different from 0 at the alpha = 0.02 level.

Referring to the correlation matrix that was shown earlier in Figure 12-4, the correlation between variable x_3, bedrooms, and y, the sales price, is $+0.540$. This indicates that, without considering the other independent variables, the linear relationship between number of bedrooms and sales price is positive. But why does the regression coefficient turn out negative in the model? The answer lies in what is called **multicollinearity**.

MULTICOLLINEARITY

A high correlation between two independent variables such that the two variables contribute redundant information to the multiple regression model. When highly correlated independent variables are included in the regression model, they can adversely affect the regression results.

Multicollinearity occurs when the independent variables overlap with respect to the information they provide in explaining the variation in the dependent variable. For example, x_3 and the other independent variables have the following correlations.

$$r_{x_3,x_1} = 0.706$$
$$r_{x_3,x_2} = -0.202$$
$$r_{x_3,x_4} = 0.600$$
$$r_{x_3,x_5} = 0.312$$

All four correlations have t-values indicating a significant linear relationship. Refer to the correlation matrix in Figure 12-4 to see that other independent variables are also correlated with each other.

The problems caused by multicollinearity, and how to deal with them, continue to be of prime concern to statisticians. From a decision maker's viewpoint, you should be aware that multicollinearity can (and usually does) exist and recognize the problems it can cause. Some of the most obvious problems and indications of severe multicollinearity are the following.

1. Incorrect signs on the coefficients
2. A sizable change in the values of the previous coefficients when a new variable is added to the model

3. A variable that was previously significant in the regression model becomes insignificant when a new independent variable is added.
4. The estimate of the standard deviation of the model error increases when a variable is added to the model.

If the independent variables in a regression model are correlated and multicollinearity is present, another potential problem is that the *t*-tests for the significance of the individual independent variables may be misleading. That is, a *t*-test may indicate that the variable is not statistically significant when, in fact, it is.

One method of measuring multicollinearity is known as the **variance inflation factor (VIF)**.

VARIANCE INFLATION FACTOR

A measure of how much the variance of an estimated regression coefficient increases if the independent variables are correlated. A VIF equal to 1.0 for a given independent variable indicates that this independent variable is not correlated with the remaining independent variables in the model. The greater the multicollinearity, the larger the VIF will be.

Equation 12-11 is used to compute the variance inflation factor for each independent variable.

VARIANCE INFLATION FACTOR

$$VIF = \frac{1}{1 - R_j^2}$$ **12-11**

where:

R_j^2 = Coefficient of determination when the *j*th independent variable is regressed against the remaining $k - 1$ independent variables

---

Both the PHStat add-in to Excel and Minitab contain options that allow you to use this factor.[7]

Figure 12-8 shows the Excel-PHStat output for the First City Real Estate data, including the variance inflation factors. While Minitab puts the VIF values for all variables on a single page, PHStat prints the VIF information for each variable on separate pages. We have consolidated these to fit on one page for simplicity of presentation.

The effect of multicollinearity is to decrease the test statistic, thus reducing the probability that the variable will be declared significant. A related impact is to increase the width of the confidence interval estimate of the slope coefficient in the regression model. Generally, if the VIF < 5 for a particular independent variable, multicollinearity is not considered a problem for that variable. VIF values ≥ 5 imply that the correlation between the independent variables is too extreme and should be dealt with by dropping variables from the model. As Figure 12-8 illustrates, the VIF values for each independent variable are less than 5, so based on variance inflation factors, no significant multicollinearity exists among the independent variables. However, the negative sign on the independent variable, bathrooms, is a concern from a descriptive standpoint. We will address this issue shortly.

CONFIDENCE INTERVAL ESTIMATION FOR REGRESSION COEFFICIENTS

Previously we showed how to determine whether the regression coefficients are statistically significant. This was necessary since the estimates of the regression coefficients are developed from sample data and are subject to sampling error. The issue of sampling error also comes into play when interpreting the regression coefficients.

---

[7]The Excel regression procedure in the data analysis tools area does not provide VIF values directly. Without PHStat, you would need to compute each regression analysis individually and record the *R*-square value to compute the VIF.

Excel Instructions:

1. Open file: First City.xls
2. Select PHStat
3. Select Regression
4. Define y variable range
5. Define x variables range
6. Check Variance Inflation Factor

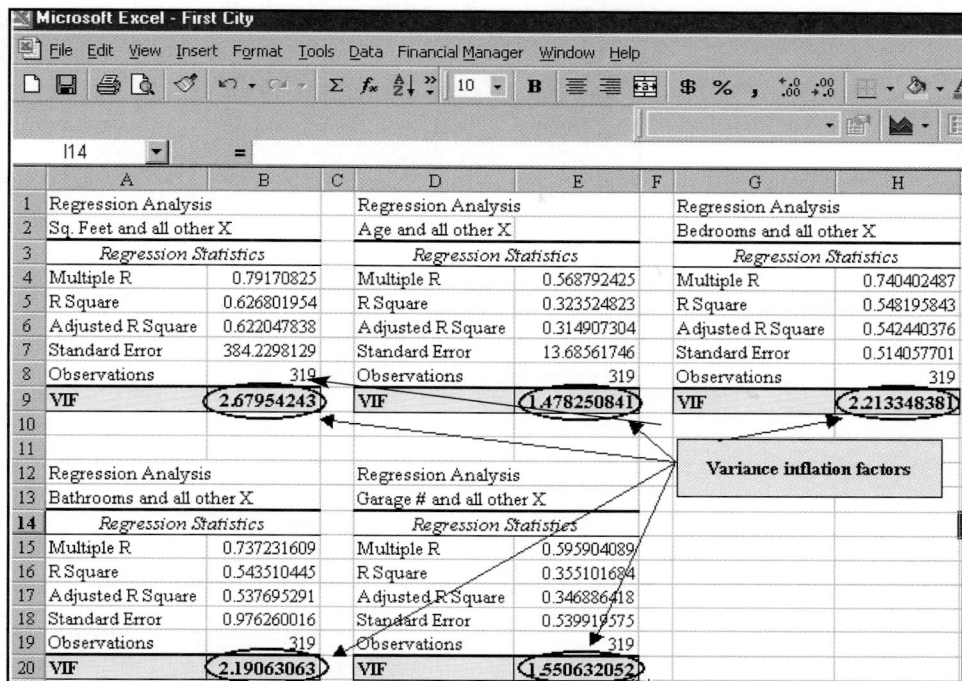

FIGURE 12-8
Excel (PHStat) Multiple Regression Model Results for First City Real Estate with Variance Inflation Factors

Consider again the regression model for First City Real Estate shown in Figure 12-9. The regression coefficients shown in Figure 12-9 are *point estimates* for the true regression coefficients. For example, the coefficient for the variable, square feet, is $b_1 = 63.07$. We interpret this to mean that, holding the other variables constant, for each increase in the size of a home by 1 square foot, the price of a house is estimated to increase by \$63.07. But like all point estimates, this is subject to sampling error. In Chapter 11 you were introduced to the concept of confidence interval estimates for the regression coefficients. That same concept applies in multiple regression models. Equation 12-12 is used to develop the confidence interval estimate for regression coefficient.

CONFIDENCE INTERVAL ESTIMATE FOR THE REGRESSION COEFFICIENT

$$b_i \pm t_{\alpha/2} s_{b_i} \qquad \text{12-12}$$

where:

b_i = Point estimate for the regression coefficient for variable x_i

$t_{\alpha/2}$ = Critical t-value for a $1 - \alpha$ confidence interval

s_{b_i} = The standard error of the ith regression coefficient

---

The Excel output in Figure 12-9 provides the confidence interval estimates for each regression coefficient. For example, the 95% interval estimate for square feet is:

$$\$55.16 \xrightarrow{\hspace{3cm}} \$70.97$$

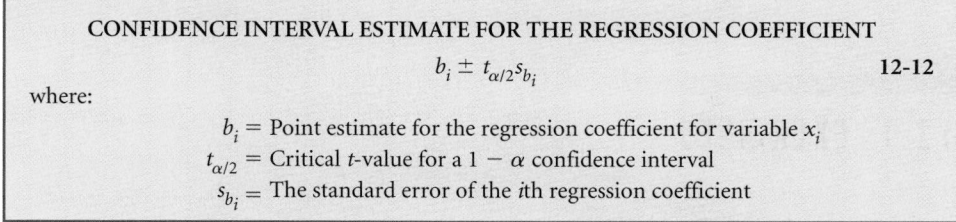

Additional Example 12-a

Developing a Multiple Regression Model

This could be computed using Equation 12-12 as:

$$b_i \pm t_{\alpha/2} s_{b_i}$$
$$63.07 \pm 1.967(4.017)$$
$$63.07 \pm 7.90$$
$$\$55.17 \xrightarrow{\hspace{3cm}} \$70.97 [8]$$

---

[8]Note: We used Excel's TINV function to get the precise t-value of 1.967. Values computed manually may differ from computer output due to rounding.

Microsoft Excel - First City

File Edit View Insert Format Tools Data Stats PHStat Window Help

Times New Roman   10   B I U

Favorites ▾   Go ▾   D:\My Documents\5th Edition Statistics Text\DataFiles\First City.xls ▾

A2   =

	A	B	C	D	E	F	G
2							
3	*Regression Statistics*						
4	Multiple R	0.903371816					
5	R Square	0.816080638					
6	Adjusted R Square	0.813142629					
7	Standard Error	27350.25168					
8	Observations	319					
9							
10	ANOVA						
11		*df*	*SS*	*MS*	*F*	*Significance F*	
12	Regression	5	1.0389E+12	2.07779E+11	277.7665571	9.0374E-113	
13	Residual	313	2.34135E+11	748036266.8			
14	Total	318	1.27303E+12				
15							
16		*Coefficients*	*Standard Error*	*t Stat*	*P-value*	*Lower 95%*	*Upper 95%*
17	Intercept	31127.60228	9539.669039	3.262964591	0.001224375	12357.60178	49897.60279
18	Sq. Feet	63.0656426	4.017033409	15.69955641	2.2645E-4	55.1618339	70.9694513
19	Age	-1144.436731	112.7800042	-10.14751452	4.18839E-2	-1366.339684	-922.533777
20	Bedrooms	-8410.378875	3002.511183	-2.801114921	0.005409552	-14318.04047	-2502.717278
21	Bathrooms	3521.954016	1580.996836	2.227679358	0.026612482	411.2264548	6632.681577
22	Garage #	28203.54189	2858.692416	9.865888941	3.61664E-20	22578.8543	33828.22948

Interval estimate for regression coefficients

FIGURE 12-9
Excel Multiple Regression
Model—First City Real Estate

We interpret this interval as follows: Holding the other variables constant, using a 95% confidence level, an increase in square feet by one foot is estimated to generate an average increase in home price of between $55.17 and $70.97. Each of the other regression coefficients can be interpreted in the same manner.

12-1: EXERCISES

Business Applications

12-1. The Western State Tourist Association gives out pamphlets, maps, and other tourist-related information to people who call a toll-free number and request the information. The association orders the packets of information from a document printing company and likes to have enough available to meet the immediate need without having too many extras sitting around taking up space. The marketing manager decided to develop a multiple regression model to be used in predicting the number of calls that will be received in the coming week. A random sample of 12 weeks is selected, with the following variables.

y = Number of calls
x_1 = Number of advertisements placed the previous week
x_2 = Number of calls received the previous week
x_3 = Number of airline tour bookings into western cities for the current week

The data that were collected are in the data file called **Western States.**

a. Identify the appropriate dependent variable for this application.

b. Produce the correlation matrix and scatter plots for each independent variable versus the dependent variable.

c. Based on the scatter plots and the correlation matrix, specify the relationship that exists between each independent variable and the dependent variable, then comment on whether you think a multiple regression model will be effectively developed from these data.

12-2. Refer to Problem 1.

a. Specify three simple linear regression equations, one for each of the respective independent variables, and then determine the estimate of each model obtained from the sample data.

b. Indicate which of the models in part a is preferred. Provide statistical analysis and reasoning to support your answer.

12-3. Refer to Problems 1 and 2.

a. Specify and then use the data to estimate a multiple regression model that contains all three independent variables.

b. What percentage of the total variation in the dependent variable is explained by the model specified in part a containing the three independent variables?

c. Test to determine whether the overall model is statistically significant. Use $\alpha = 0.05$ and use the p-value approach to conduct this test.

d. Which, if any, of the independent variables is statistically significant? Test using a significance level of 0.05.

e. Determine the adjusted R-squared and comment on what it means.

f. Determine an estimate of the standard error of the estimate and discuss whether this regression model is acceptable as a means of predicting the number of calls that will come to Western Tourist in a given week.

g. Indicate what, if any, evidence there is of multicollinearity problems with this multiple regression model. Discuss problems multicollinearity could cause in this example.

h. Determine the VIF for each variable and determine whether this measure results in different conclusions regarding the significance of the independent variables. Do the VIF calculations imply that a multicollinearity problem exists? Discuss.

12-4. The athletic director of State University is interested in developing a multiple regression model that might be used to explain the variation in attendance at football games at his school. A sample of 16 games was selected from home games played during the past 10 seasons. Data for the following factors were determined.

y = Game attendance
x_1 = Team win/loss percentage to date
x_2 = Opponent win/loss percentage to date
x_3 = Games played this season
x_4 = Temperature at game time

The data that were collected are in the file called **Football**.

a. Produce the scatter plots for each independent variable versus the dependent variable. Write a short report that discusses the relationship of each independent variable with the dependent variable.

b. Based on a correlation matrix for game attendance and the four independent variables, comment on whether you think a multiple regression model could be effectively developed from these data. Test the significance of the correlations at the 0.05 level.

12-5. Refer to Problem 4.

a. Use the sample data to develop four simple linear regression models, one for each of the independent variables.

b. Indicate which of these models is preferred. Present statistical analysis and reasoning to support your answer.

12-6. Refer to Problems 4 and 5.

a. Specify and then use the sample data to estimate the multiple regression model that contains all four independent variables.

b. What percentage of the total variation in the dependent variable is explained by the four independent variables in the model?

c. Test to determine whether the overall model is statistically significant. Use $\alpha = 0.05$.

d. Which, if any, of the independent variables is statistically significant? Use a significance level of $\alpha = 0.08$ and the p-value approach to conduct these tests.

e. Estimate the standard deviation of the model error and discuss whether this regression model is acceptable as a means of predicting the football attendance at State University at any given game.

f. Define the term multicollinearity and indicate the potential problems that multicollinearity can cause for this model. Indicate what, if any, evidence there is of multicollinearity problems with this regression model. Use the variance inflation factor to assist you in this analysis.

g. Develop a 95% confidence interval estimate for each of the regression coefficients and interpret each estimate. Comment on whether the interpretation of the intercept is relevant in this situation.

12-7. Commercial Federal Savings and Loan has been trying to gain a foothold in the southern portion of the United States. Initial plans are to open several branches throughout that region of the country in the next 5 years. The board of directors is trying to determine the effect of these plans on the company's profit margin. One of the members, Robert Williams, has recently come across an article "Entry and Probability in Rate-Free Savings and Loan Market" [*Quarterly Review of Economics and Business* (1978): 87–95]. The article relates the profit margin of savings and loan companies (y) to their net revenue in that year (x_1 in million dollars) and the number of branch offices possessed by the company (x_2). The data that were presented in the article are in the file called **Profit**.

a. Produce scatter plots of each independent variable versus the dependent variable in this data set. On the basis of these plots, determine the relationship between each independent variable and the dependent variable.

b. Determine whether Robert can use a multiple regression model containing both net revenue and number of branch offices to predict the profit margin of savings and loan companies. Use a hypothesis test with a significance level of 0.10.

c. Which, if any, of the independent variables is statistically significant? Use a significance level of $\alpha = 0.10$ and the p-value approach to conduct these tests.

d. Use a rule of thumb to determine if the standard deviation of the model error is too large for this model. Explain your reasoning in the context of this problem.

e. Produce a simple linear regression equation using net revenue to predict profit margin. Compare the sign of the slope coefficient to that of the coefficient of net revenue in the multiple regression. Discuss whether the coefficients of the two models are, and can be, different. Explain under what conditions the coefficients might have opposite signs.

12-2: USING QUALITATIVE INDEPENDENT VARIABLES

In the previous example involving the First City Real Estate Company, the independent variables were quantitative and ratio level. However, you will encounter many situations in which you may wish to use a qualitative, lower level, variable as an explanatory variable.

If the variable is nominal, and numerical codes are assigned to the categories, you already know not to perform mathematical calculations using those data. The results would be meaningless. Yet, we may wish to use marital status, gender, or geographical location as an independent variable in a regression model. If the variable of interest is coded as an ordinal variable, such as education level or job performance ranking, computing means and variances is inappropriate. Then how are these variables incorporated into a multiple regression analysis? The answer lies in using what are called **dummy** (or indicator) **variables.**

> **DUMMY VARIABLES**
> A variable that is assigned a value equal to either 1 or 0 depending on whether the observation possesses a given characteristic or not.

For instance, consider the variable gender that can take on two possible values.

male or female

Gender can be converted to a dummy variable as follows.

$$x_1 = 1 \text{ if female}$$
$$x_1 = 0 \text{ if male}$$

Thus, a data set consisting of males and females will have corresponding values for x_1 equal to 0s and 1s, respectively. Note: It makes no difference which gender is coded 1 and which is coded 0.

If a categorical variable has more than two mutually exclusive outcome possibilities, multiple dummy variables must be created. Consider the variable, marital status, with the following possible outcomes.

single   married   divorced   widowed

In this case, marital status has four values. To account for all the possibilities, you would create three dummy variables, one less than the number of possible outcomes for the original variable. They could be coded as follows.

$$x_1 = 1 \text{ if single, 0 if not}$$
$$x_2 = 1 \text{ if married, 0 if not}$$
$$x_3 = 1 \text{ if divorced, 0 if not}$$

Note that we don't need the fourth variable since we would know that a person is widowed if $x_1 = 0, x_2 = 0$, and $x_3 = 0$. If the person isn't single, married, or divorced, he or she must be widowed. *Always use one fewer dummy variables than categories.* The mathematical reason that the number of dummy variables must be one less than the number of possible responses is called the *dummy variable trap*. Perfect multicollinearity is introduced and the least squares regression estimates cannot be obtained if the number of dummy variables equals the number of possible categories.

Incorporating Dummy Variables

Business Executive Salaries

EXAMPLE 12-2

MULTIPLE REGRESSION

To illustrate the effect of incorporating dummy variables into a regression model, consider the sample data shown in Table 12-2 and displayed in the scatter plot in Figure 12-10. The population from which the sample was selected consists of executives between the ages of 24 and 60 who are working in U.S. manufacturing businesses. As shown in Table 12-2, data for annual salary and age are available. The objective is to determine whether a model can be generated to explain the variation in annual salary for business executives. Even though age and annual salary are significantly correlated ($r = 0.686$) at the alpha = 0.05 level, the coefficient of determination is only 47%. Therefore, we would likely search for other independent variables that could help us to further explain the variation in annual salary.

Suppose we can determine which of the 16 people in the sample had an MBA degree. We can create a new variable, x_2, which is a dummy variable coded as:

$$x_2 = 1 \text{ if MBA, 0 if not}$$

The data with the new variable are shown in Table 12-3. Now we would like to develop a two-variable population multiple regression model of the form:

$$y = \beta_0 + \beta_1 x_1 + \beta_2 x_2 + \epsilon$$

Using either Excel or Minitab, we get the following regression equation that is an estimate of the population model.

$$\hat{y} = 6{,}974 + 2{,}055x_1 + 35{,}236x_2$$

TABLE 12-2
Executive Salary Data

AGE	SALARY
26	$ 65,000
28	85,000
36	74,000
35	83,000
35	110,000
40	160,000
41	100,000
42	122,000
45	85,000
46	120,000
50	105,000
51	135,000
55	125,000
50	175,000
61	156,000
63	140,000

FIGURE 12-10   Executive Salary Data—Scatter Plot

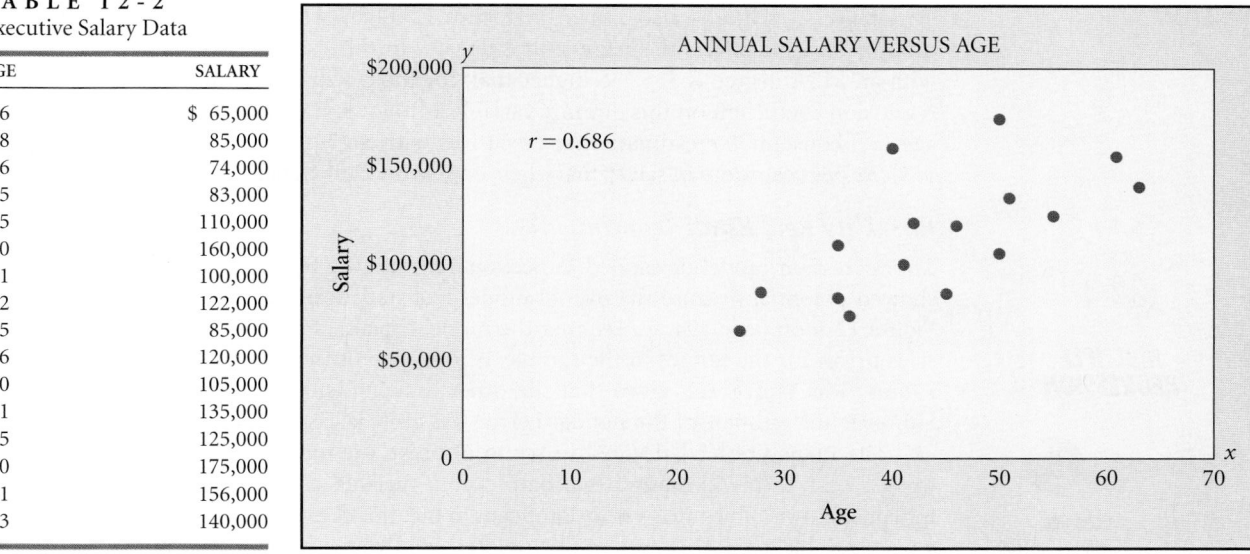

SALARY	AGE	MBA
$65,000	26	0
85,000	28	1
74,000	36	0
83,000	35	0
110,000	35	1
160,000	40	1
100,000	41	0
122,000	42	1
85,000	45	0
120,000	46	1
105,000	50	0
135,000	51	1
125,000	55	0
175,000	50	1
156,000	61	1
140,000	63	0

TABLE 12-3
Executive Salary Data
Including MBA Variable

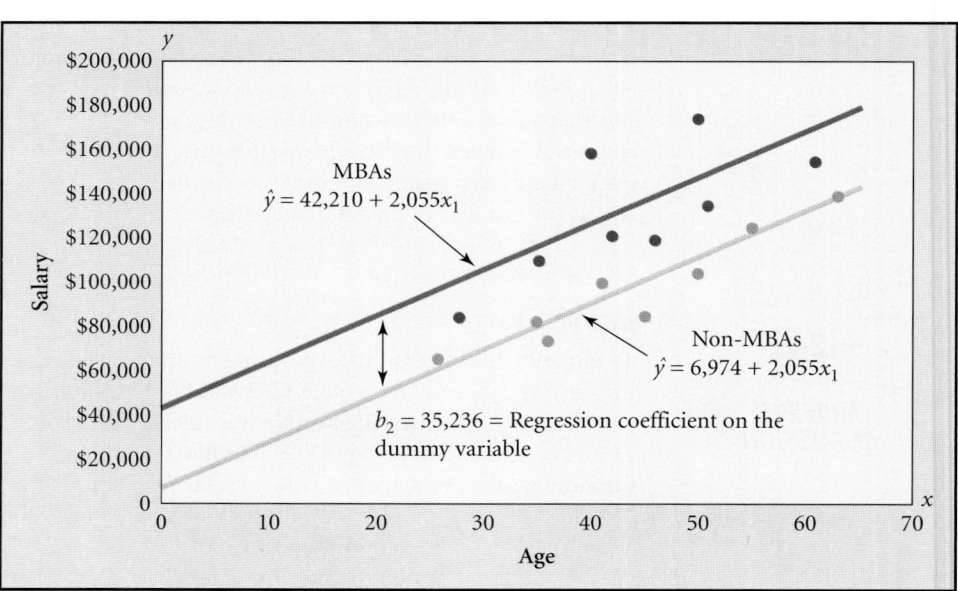

FIGURE 12-11   Impact of a Dummy Variable

Since the dummy variable, x_2, has been coded 0 or 1 depending on degree status, incorporating it into the regression model is like having two simple linear regression lines with the same slopes, but different intercepts. For instance, when $x_2 = 0$, the regression equation is:

$$\hat{y} = 6{,}974 + 2{,}055x_1 + 35{,}236(0)$$
$$= 6{,}974 + 2{,}055x_1$$

This line is shown in Figure 12-11.

However, when $x_2 = 1$ (the executive has an MBA), the regression equation is:

$$\hat{y} = 6{,}974 + 2{,}055x_1 + 35{,}236(1)$$
$$= 42{,}210 + 2{,}055x_1$$

This regression line is also shown in Figure 12-11. As you can see, incorporating the dummy variable affects the regression intercept. In this case, the intercept for executives with an MBA degree is $35,236 higher than for those without an MBA. We interpret the regression coefficient on this dummy variable as follows: Based on these data, and holding age (x_1) constant, we estimate that executives with an MBA degree make an average of $35,236 per year more in salary than their non-MBA counterparts.

First City Real Estate (continued)

12-3

MULTIPLE REGRESSION

Excel and
Minitab Tutorial

The regression model developed in Section 12-1 for the First City Real Estate Company showed potential because the overall model was statistically significant. Looking back at Figure 12-9 on page 494, we see that the model explained nearly 82% of the variation in sales prices for the homes in the sample. All but one of the independent variables (bathrooms) was significant, given that the other independent variables were in the model. However, the estimate of the standard error was quite large.

The managers have decided to try to improve the model. Initially they will do two things. First, they will remove the "bathrooms" variable as it already overlaps with other independent variables and was insignificant in the model. Second, they have decided to add a new variable, area. However, at this point, the only area variable they can get is whether the house is in the foothills or not. Since this is a categorical variable with two possible outcomes (foothills or flatland), a dummy variable can be created as follows.

$$x_5 \text{ (Area)} = 1 \text{ if foothills, } 0 \text{ if not}$$

Of the 319 homes in the sample, 249 were homes in the foothills and 70 were in the flatland. Figure 12-12 shows the revised Excel multiple regression results (using PHStat) with the variable bathrooms dropped and location added. This model does represent an improvement over the original model since the adjusted R-square increased from 0.813 to 0.902 and the estimate of the standard error of the estimate has decreased from \$27,350 to \$19,817. Based on the p-value in the analysis of variance section, the overall model is statistically significant—at least one of the regression model's coefficients is different from 0. The conditional t-tests show that all of the regression model's slope coefficients are different from 0. PHStat was used to compute the variance inflation factors. The variance inflation factors were all less than 2.0 so we don't need to be too concerned about the t-tests understating the significance of the regression coefficients. (See the Excel Tutorial on the CD-ROM for this example to see the full VIF output from PHStat. Also, the Minitab Tutorial shows how to obtain VIF results in Minitab.)

The resulting regression model is:

$$\hat{y} = 7,050.23 + 62.49(\text{Sq feet}) - 321.99(\text{Age}) - 8,830.00(\text{Bedrooms}) + 26,053.86(\text{Garages}) + 61,370.08(\text{Area})$$

Based on the sample data and this regression model, we estimate that a house with the same characteristics (square feet, age, bedrooms, and garages) is worth an average of \$61,370 more if it is located in the foothills (based on how the dummy variable was coded).

FIGURE 12-12
Excel (PHStat) Output—First City Real Estate Revised Regression Model

Excel (PHStat) Instructions:
1. Open file: First City.xls
2. Select Sheet: Homes-Sample 2
3. Click on PHStat
4. Select Regression
5. Select Multiple Regression
6. Define y and x variables ranges
7. Select Regression and Statistics Table
8. Select ANOVA and Coefficients Table
9. Select VIF option

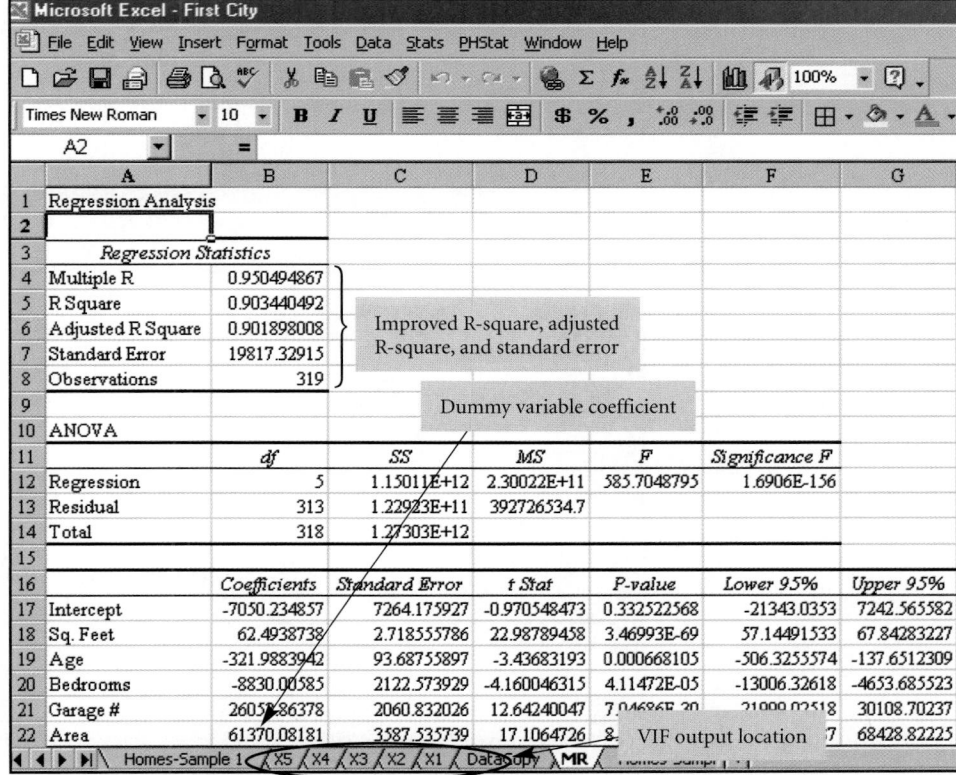

There are still signals of multicollinearity problems. The coefficient on the independent variable, bedrooms, is negative when we would expect homes with more bedrooms to sell for more. Also, the standard error of the estimate is still too large ($19,817) to provide the precision the managers would need to set prices for homes. More work needs to be done before our model is complete.

POSSIBLE IMPROVEMENTS TO THE FIRST CITY APPRAISAL MODEL

Since the standard error of the estimate is still too high, we look for ways to improve the model. At this point experience is a good teacher. We could start by identifying problems that may be contributing to the inadequacies of this model.

1. Useful independent variables may have been omitted from the model.
2. Independent variables may have been included in the model that should not have been included.

There is no sure way of determining the correct model specification. However, a recommended approach is for the decision maker to try adding new variables or removing variables from the model in an attempt to improve the results.

We begin by removing the bedrooms variable that has the incorrect sign on the regression slope coefficient in Figure 12-12. We also remove the variable, bathrooms, that was insignificant in the original model. The resulting model is shown in Figure 12-13. Now all the variables in the model have the expected signs. However, the standard error of the estimate increased slightly.

Adding other explanatory variables might help. For instance, a variable that might affect sales price of a residential property is whether the house has central air conditioning. If we can identify whether a house has air conditioning, we could add a dummy variable coded as follows.

$$\text{If air conditioning, } x_6 = 1$$
$$\text{If no air conditioning, } x_6 = 0$$

FIGURE 12-13
Excel Output for the First City Real Estate Revised Model

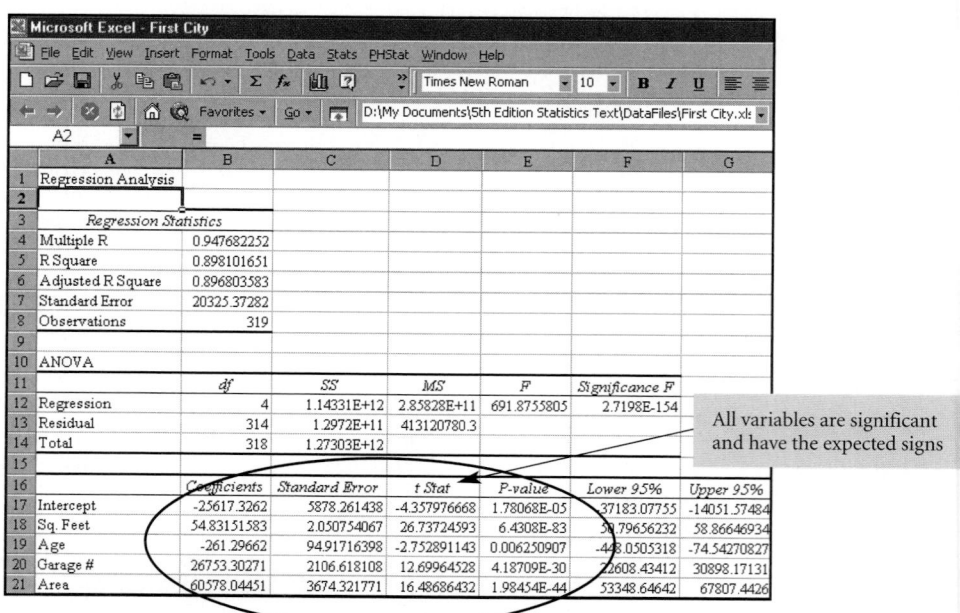

All variables are significant and have the expected signs

Other potential independent variables might include a more detailed location variable, a measure of the physical condition, or whether the house is one or two stories. Can you think of others?

The First City example illustrates that although a regression model may pass the statistical tests of significance, it may not be functional. Good appraisal models can be developed using multiple regression analysis, provided more detail is available about such characteristics as finished quality, landscaping, location, neighborhood characteristics, and so forth. The cost and effort required to obtain these data can be relatively high.

Developing a multiple regression model is more of an art than a science. The real decisions revolve around how to select the best set of independent variables for the model.

12-2: EXERCISES

ADDITIONAL EXERCISES ON YOUR CD-ROM
Try the ADDITIONAL EXERCISES and APPLICATION PROBLEMS on the CD-ROM.

Business Applications

12-8. The Polk Utility Corporation is developing a multiple regression model that it plans to use to predict customers' utility usage. The analyst currently has three quantitative variables ($x_1, x_2,$ and x_3) in the model, but she is dissatisfied with the R-square and the standard error of the estimate. Two variables that she thinks might be useful are whether the house has a gas water heater or an electric water heater and whether the house was constructed before or after the 1974 energy crisis.

Provide the model she should use to predict customers' utility usage. Specify the dummy variables to be used, the values these variables could assume, and what each value will represent.

12-9. A study was recently performed by the American Automobile Association in which it attempted to develop a regression model to explain variation in EPA highway mileage ratings of new cars. At one stage of the analysis, the estimate of the model took the following form.

$$\hat{y} = 34.20 - 0.003x_1 + 2.56x_2$$

where:

x_1 = Vehicle weight (in pounds)
x_2 = 1, if standard transmission
    = 0, if automatic transmission

a. Interpret the regression coefficient for variable x_1.
b. Interpret the regression coefficient for variable x_2.
c. Present an estimate of a model that would predict the average EPA highway mileage rating for an automobile with standard transmission as a function of the vehicle's weight.
d. Cadillac's 1999 Sedan DeVille with automatic transmission weighs approximately 4,012 pounds.

Provide an estimate of the average highway mileage you would expect to obtain from this model.
e. Discuss the effect of a dummy variable being incorporated in a regression model like this one. Use a graph if it is helpful.

12-10. A recent study by the U.S. Department of Agriculture attempted to develop a multiple regression model to explain variation in farm income. At one stage of development, the estimate of the model took the following form.

$$\hat{y} = -23,200 + 4.2x_1 + 2,345x_2 + 4,670x_3$$

where:

x_1 = Number of acres farmed
x_2 = 1, if land is row-irrigated
    = 0, if not
x_3 = 1, if land is sprinkler-irrigated
    = 0, if not

a. Interpret the regression coefficient for variable x_1.
b. Interpret the regression coefficient for variable x_2.
c. Interpret the regression coefficient for variable x_3.
d. Present an estimate of a model that would predict the average farm income for a 1,000-acre farm that irrigated using sprinklers.

12-11. The Gilmore Accounting Firm collected data in an effort  to explain variation in client profitability. The data are in the data file called **Gilmore**.

y	x_1	x_2	y	x_1	x_2
2,345	45	1	−700	34	3
4,200	56	2	3,457	45	1
278	26	3	2,478	47	1
1,211	56	2	1,975	24	2
1,406	24	2	206	32	3
500	23	3			

where:

y = Net profit earned from the client

x_1 = Number of hours spent working with the client

x_2 = Type of client:

1, if manufacturing

2, if service

3, if governmental

a. Develop a scatter plot of each independent variable against the client income variable. Comment on what, if any, relationship appears to exist in each case.

b. Run a simple linear regression analysis using only variable x_1 as the independent variable. Describe the resulting estimate fully.

c. Test to determine if the number of hours spent working with the client is useful in predicting the net profit earned by a client.

12-12. Refer to Problem 11.

a. Incorporate the client type into the regression analysis using dummy variables. Describe the resulting multiple regression estimate.

b. Test to determine if this model is useful in predicting the net profit earned by the client.

c. Test to determine if the number of hours spent working with the client is useful in this model in predicting the net profit earned by a client.

d. Considering the tests you performed in parts b and c, construct a model and its estimate for predicting the net profit earned by the client.

e. Predict the average difference in profit if the client is governmental versus one who is in manufacturing. Also state this in terms of a 95% confidence interval estimate. (Refer to Chapter 11 if needed.)

12-13. One of the editors of a major automobile publication has collected data on 30 of the best-selling cars in the United States. The data are in a file called **Automobiles**. The edi-

tor is particularly interested in the relationship between price of the vehicle and the horsepower of the engine. She thinks another variable that may have an impact on price would be the type of vehicle.

a. Specify a model that would characterize the relationship between vehicle price, horsepower, and the vehicle type. Specify the dummy variables to be used, the values these variables could assume, and what each value will represent. Note that there are 5 types of vehicles.

b. Produce an estimate of the model presented in part a.

c. Is the type of vehicle a significant predictor of the price of an automobile? Conduct an appropriate hypothesis to answer this question.

12-14. The Ajax Taxi Company operates taxicabs in the Manhattan area of New York City. The dispatch manager is interested in estimating the average number of miles driven per vehicle per week. Each week for 40 weeks, he sampled 4 taxis and recorded their weekly miles. At the end of 40 weeks, he had accumulated a sample of 160 values. Each taxi selected was from one of the 4 different types of taxis that the Ajax Taxi Company owns.

a. Using the sample data in the file **Ajax,** construct a regression model to model the average number of miles driven as a function of the 4 types of taxis that were used. Specify the dummy variables to be used, the values these variables will assume, and what each value will represent.

b. Provide a 90% confidence interval for the difference between the average mileage obtained by taxis of type II and III. Note: You must be very careful in the specification of the dummy variables if you are to construct this confidence interval.

c. Conduct a statistical procedure to determine if there is a significant difference in the average mileage of the 4 types of taxis. Be sure to do this using the regression model you have constructed for this problem.

■ 12-3: WORKING WITH NONLINEAR RELATIONSHIPS

Section 11-1 in Chapter 11 showed there are a variety of ways in which two variables can be related. Correlation and regression analysis techniques are tools for measuring and modeling linear relationships between variables. Many situations in business have a linear relationship between two variables, and regression equations that model that relationship will be appropriate to use in these situations. However, there are also many instances where the relationship between two variables will be curvilinear rather than linear. For instance, demand for electricity has grown at an almost exponential rate relative to the population growth in some areas. Advertisers believe that a diminishing-returns relationship will occur between sales and advertising if advertising is allowed to grow too large. These two situations are shown in Figures 12-14 and 12-15, respectively. They represent just two of the great many possible curvilinear relationships that could exist between two variables.

As you will soon see, models with nonlinear relationships become more complicated than models showing only linear relationships. While complicated models are sometimes necessary, decision makers should use them with caution for several reasons. First, people tend to use decision aids they understand and avoid those they don't understand. So, the

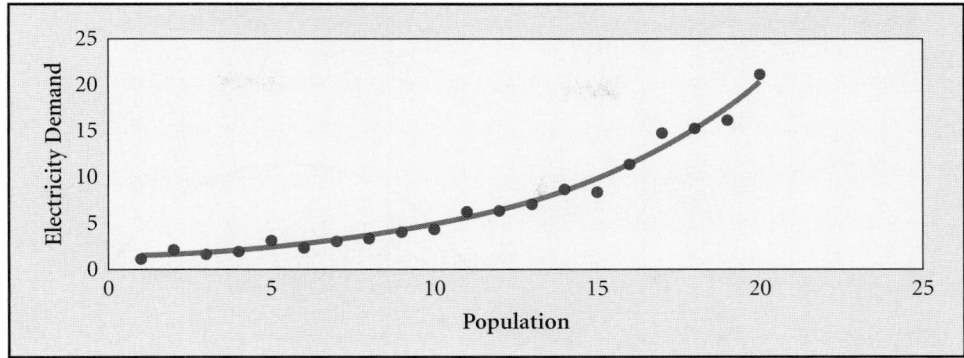

FIGURE 12-14
Exponential Relationship of Increased Demand for Electricity versus Population Growth

more complicated the model is, the less likely it is to be used. Second, the scientific principle of parsimony suggests using the simplest model possible that provides a reasonable fit of the data since complex models typically do not reflect the underlying phenomena that produced the data in the first place.

This section provides a brief introduction into how linear regression analysis can be used in dealing with curvilinear relationships. In order to model such curvilinear relationships, we must incorporate terms into the multiple regression model that will create "curves" in the model we are building. Including independent variables whose term has an exponent larger than one generates these "curves." When a model possesses such terms we refer to it as a **polynomial.** The general equation for a polynomial with one independent variable is given in Equation 12-13.

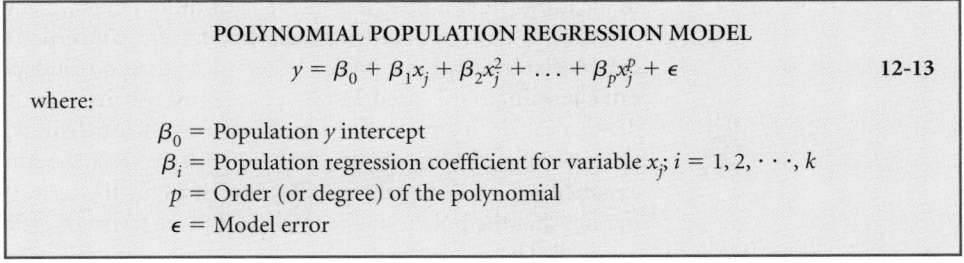

POLYNOMIAL POPULATION REGRESSION MODEL

$$y = \beta_0 + \beta_1 x_j + \beta_2 x_j^2 + \ldots + \beta_p x_j^p + \epsilon$$ **12-13**

where:

β_0 = Population y intercept
β_i = Population regression coefficient for variable x_j; $i = 1, 2, \cdots, k$
p = Order (or degree) of the polynomial
ϵ = Model error

The order, or degree, of the model is determined by the largest exponent of the independent variable in the model. For instance, the model $y = \beta_0 + \beta_1 x + \beta_2 x^2 + \epsilon$ is a second-order polynomial since the largest exponent in any term of the polynomial is two. You will note that this model contains terms of all orders less than or equal to two. A polynomial with this property is said to be a *complete* polynomial. Therefore, the previous model would be referred to as a complete **second-order regression model.**

FIGURE 12-15
Diminishing Returns Relationship of Advertising versus Sales

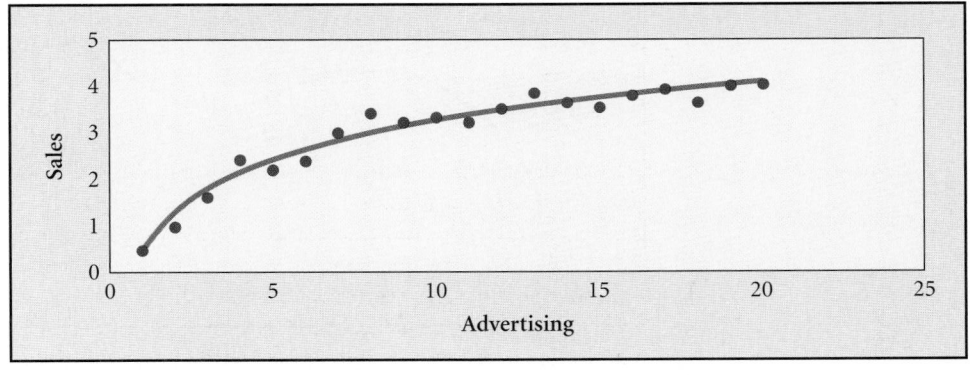

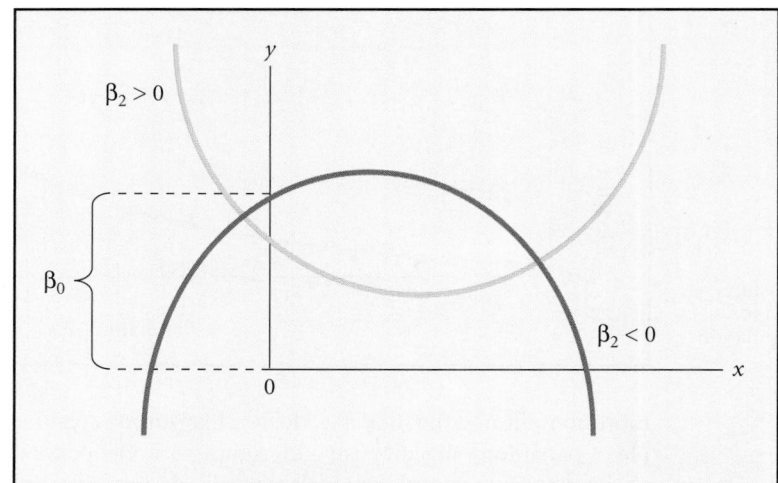

FIGURE 12-16
Second-Order Regression
Models

A second-order model produces a parabola. The parabola opens either upward ($\beta_2 > 0$) or downward ($\beta_2 < 0$) as shown in Figure 12-16. You will notice that the models in Figures 12-14 and 12-15 both possess a single "curve."

As more "curves" appear in the data, the order of the polynomial must be increased. A general (complete) third-order polynomial is given by the equation $y = \beta_0 + \beta_1 x + \beta_2 x^2 + \beta_3 x^3 + \epsilon$. This model produces a curvilinear model that reverses the direction of the initial curve to produce the second curve as shown in Figure 12-17. Note that there are two "curves" in the third-order model. In general a pth-order polynomial will exhibit $p - 1$ "curves."

Our discussion of polynomials has, thus far, concerned only models with one independent variable raised to a power. When more than one independent variable is involved, the same terminology is used. However, we must use the sum of the exponents of the independent variables in any one term to determine the order of that term. As an example, a term of the form $\beta_i x_1^2 x_2^3$ would be a fifth-order term since the sum of the independent variables' exponents ($2 + 3$) equals 5. Using similar logic, the term complete pth order polynomial implies that the polynomial contains all those terms of order p and all orders smaller than p as well. Therefore, the model:

$$y = \beta_0 + \beta_1 x_1 + \beta_2 x_2 + \beta_3 x_1^2 + \beta_4 x_2^2 + \beta_5 x_1 x_2 + \epsilon$$

FIGURE 12-17
Third-Order Regression
Models

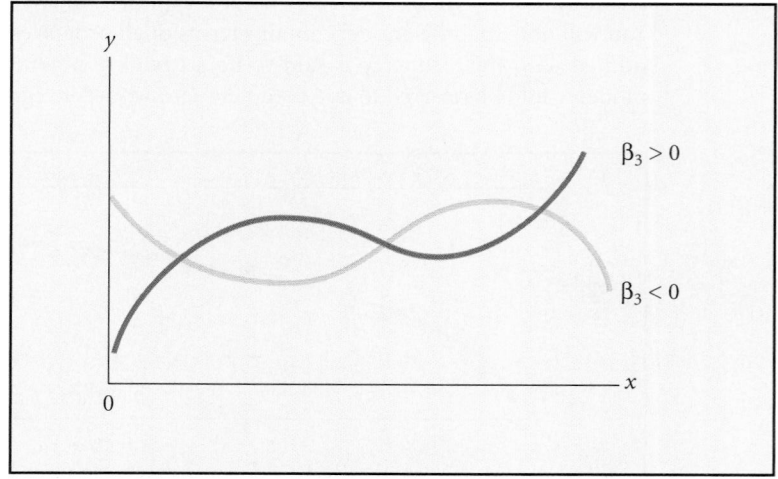

is a complete second-order model involving the independent variables x_1 and x_2. The model:

$$y = \beta_0 + \beta_1 x_1 + \beta_2 x_2 + \beta_3 x_1^2 + \beta_4 x_2^2 + \epsilon$$

is a second-order model. However, it is not a complete second-order model because it does not contain the term $\beta_5 x_1 x_2$ whose exponents of the independent variables sum to two.

Although polynomials of all orders exist in the business sector, perhaps second-order polynomials are the most common. Sharp reversals in the curvature of a relationship between variables in the business environment usually point to some unexpected or, perhaps, severe changes which were not foreseen. The vast majority of organizations try to avoid such reverses. For this reason, and the fact that this is an introductory business statistics course, we will direct most of our attention to second-order polynomials.

The following examples illustrate two of the most common instances where curvilinear relationships can be used in decision making. They should give you an idea of how to approach similar situations.

Curvilinear Relationships

Ashley Investment Services

CURVILINEAR REGRESSION

Excel and Minitab Tutorial

TABLE 12-4
Questionnaire Data for Ashley Investment Services Example

BURNOUT INDEX	SOCIALIZATION MEASURE
100	20
525	60
300	38
980	88
310	59
900	87
410	68
296	12
120	35
501	70
920	80
810	92
506	77
493	86
892	83
527	79
600	75
855	81
709	75
791	77

Ashley Investment Services has been severely shaken by a recent downturn in the stock market. To maintain profitability and save as many jobs as possible, everyone has been expected to increase the time spent analyzing new investment opportunities. The director of personnel has noticed an increased number of people suffering from what appears to be "burnout," where physical and emotional fatigue affect job performance. While he cannot do anything about pressures on the job, he has read that burnout can also be influenced by the amount of time away from the job people spend socializing with coworkers. With the help of the human resources lab at the local university, the personnel director has administered a questionnaire to employees in the company. A burnout index is computed from the responses to the survey. Likewise, the survey responses are used to determine quantitative measures of socialization. Sample data from questionnaires filled out by 20 investment advisers are shown in Table 12-4. These data are also contained in the file called **Ashley** on the CD-ROM.

Figure 12-18 presents a scatter plot of the data with the dependent variable, burnout, on the vertical axis and the independent variable, socialization, on the horizontal axis. Looking at Figure 12-18, there appears to be a linear relationship between the

FIGURE 12-18   Scatter Plot for the Ashley Investment Services Example

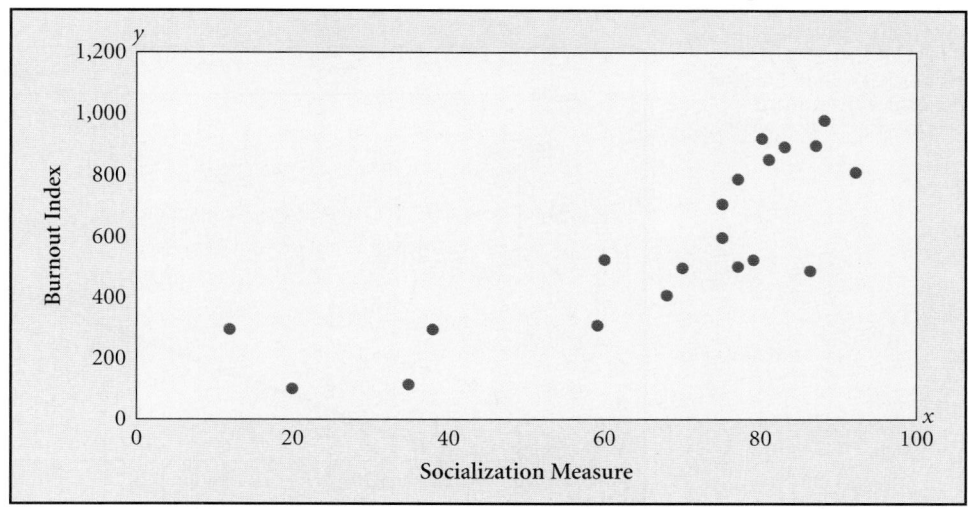

Excel Instructions:
1. Open file: Ashley.xls
2. Select Tools
3. Click on Data Analysis
4. Select Regression
5. Define y and x variable range
6. Click OK

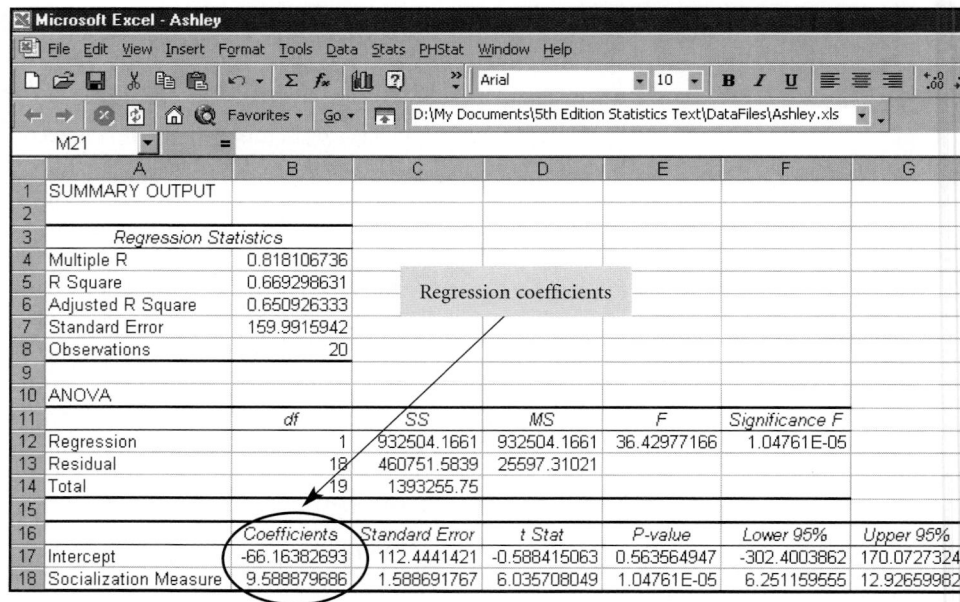

FIGURE 12-19
Excel Output of a Simple Linear Regression for Ashley Investment Services

Additional Example 12-b

Curvilinear Regression

two variables. The correlation between the two variables is $r = 0.82$, which is statistically different from 0 at any reasonable significance level. Figure 12-19 shows the regression analysis results using Excel.

The estimate of the population linear regression model shown in Figure 12-19 is:

$$\hat{y} = -66.164 + 9.5889x$$

The sample data and the regression line are plotted in Figure 12-20. The line appears to fit the data. However, a closer inspection reveals instances where several consecutive points lie above or below the line instead of having the points randomly dispersed around the regression line as we would expect given the regression analysis assumptions.

As you will recall from earlier discussions, analysis of variance can also be used to test whether the regression line explains a significant amount of variation in the dependent variable. From the Excel output in Figure 12-19, $F = 36.4298$, which is significant at the 0.00002 level with 1 and 18 degrees of freedom. We could also test the regression slope coefficient for significance, but remember that these tests are the same for the simple regression model.

FIGURE 12-20
Plot of Regression Line for the Ashley Investment Services Example

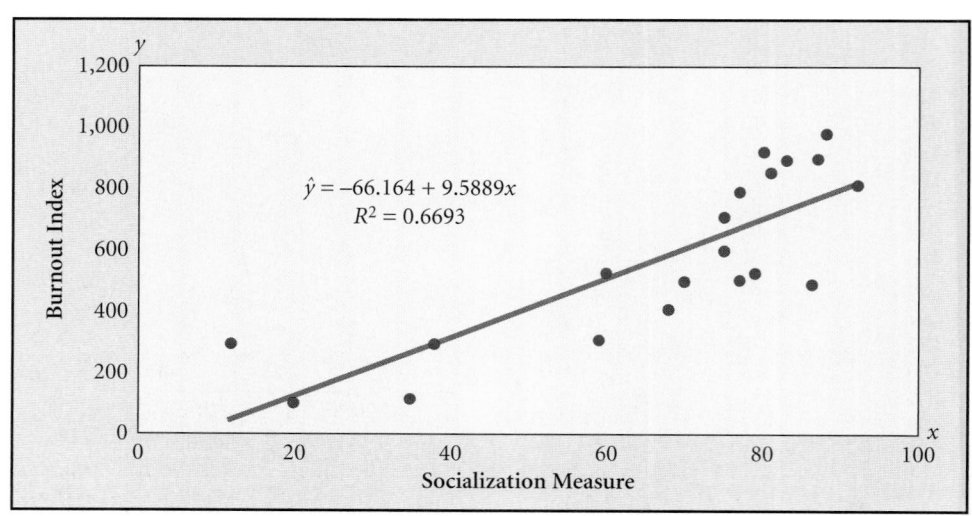

Finding instances of nonrandom patterns in the residuals for a regression model indicates the possibility of using a curvilinear relationship rather than a linear one. Looking again at the scatter plots in Figure 12-20, an exponential relationship between burnout and degree of socialization appears likely; that is, as socialization increases, the likelihood of burnout increases as well, but at an increasing rate.

While several methods exist to analyze curvilinear relationships, such as transforming the data, modern computer packages make these relationships easy to analyze. The chart wizard option of Excel has a curve fitting option that allows you to choose several possible nonlinear options, including an exponential option of the form:

$$\hat{y} = Ae^{Bx}$$

where:

A = Intercept point, or value of y when $x = 0$
e = Base of natural logarithm (approx. 2.7183)
B = Coefficient of x in the least squares model

Figure 12-21 shows the plot of this nonlinear model against the original data. Excel also gives you the option of showing the curvilinear regression equation on the output. The nonlinear regression equation is:

$$\hat{y} = 101.06e^{0.0237x}$$

Note that the exponential regression equation provides a curved line that appears to fit the data more closely than the straight line in Figure 12-20. The higher R^2 value of 0.7272 versus 0.6693 for the linear model supports this observation. Another possible approach to modeling the curvilinear nature of the data in the Ashley Investment example is with the use of polynomials. From Figure 12-21 you can see that there is one "curve" in the data. This suggests fitting the second-order polynomial:

$$y = \beta_0 + \beta_1 x_1 + \beta_2 x_1^2 + \epsilon$$

Before fitting the estimate for this population model, you will need to create the new independent variable by squaring the socialization measure variable. In either Excel or Minitab,

FIGURE 12-21
Excel Output of an
Exponential Curve Fit for
Ashley Investments

Excel Instructions:

1. Open file: Ashley.xls
2. Select Chart Wizard
3. Select XY (Scatter)
4. Use the default graph form
5. Use the Series tab and define y and x variable range
6. Click on any data value—then right click
7. Select Add Trendline
8. Select Exponential
9. Select Trend Line—Right Click
10. Select Options Tab and check equation

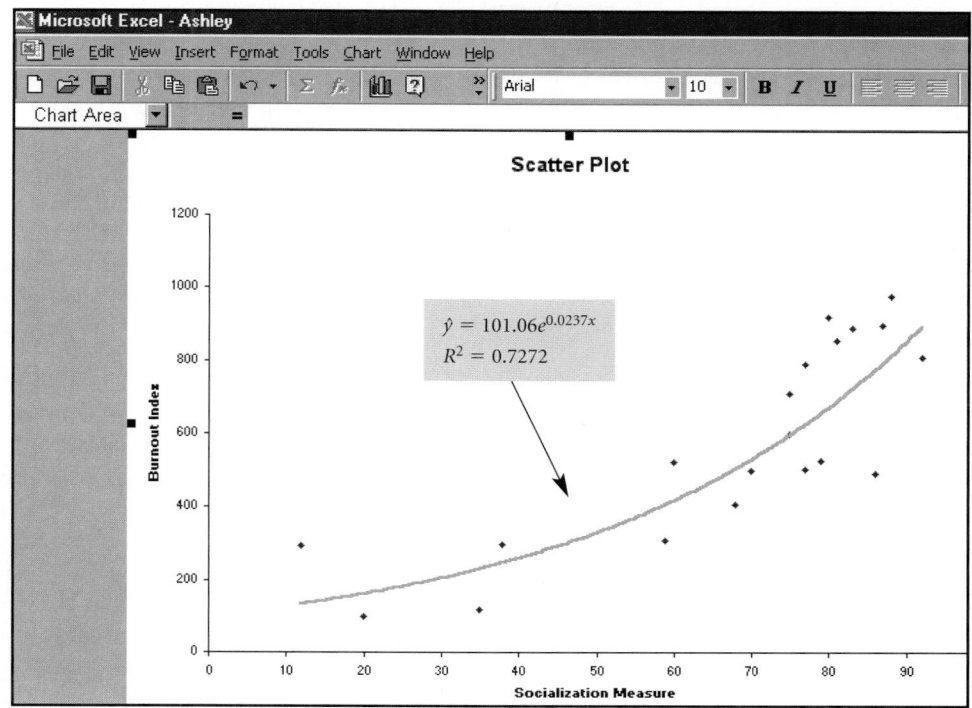

Excel Instructions:
1. Click on Tools
2. Select Data Analysis
3. Select Regression
4. Define y and x variable ranges

Microsoft Excel - Ashley

File Edit View Insert Format Tools Data Stats PHStat Window Help

Arial   10   B I U

J19   =

	A	B	C	D	E	F
1	SUMMARY OUTPUT					
2						
3	Regression Statistics					
4	Multiple R	0.860704621		R-square		
5	R Square	0.740812444				
6	Adjusted R Square	0.71031979				
7	Standard Error	145.7464665				
8	Observations	20				
9						
10	ANOVA					
11		df	SS	MS	F	Significance F
12	Regression	2	1032141.197	516070.5987	24.29478434	1.03686E-05
13	Residual	17	361114.5526	21242.0325		
14	Total	19	1393255.75			
15						
16		Coefficients	Standard Error	t Stat	P-value	Lower 95%
17	Intercept	265.6804688	184.3081377	1.441501564	0.167610901	-123.1762543
18	Socialization Measure	-6.836614826	7.720985585	-0.885458825	0.388262588	-23.12649324
19	Socialization Squared	0.153769116	0.070999741	2.165770107	0.044836957	0.003972548

FIGURE 12-22
Excel Output of a Second-Order Polynomial Fit for Ashley Investments

Additional Example 12-c

Curvilinear Regression Analysis

use the formula option to create the new variable. Figure 12-22 shows the Excel output after fitting this second-order polynomial model. Notice the second-order polynomial provides a model whose estimated regression equation has an R^2 of 0.741. This is only slightly larger than that of the exponential model's R^2 of 0.727. The two appear to be comparable models for these data. Note also that the t-value for the original independent variable, socialization measure, is only -0.89 indicating that, in the presence of the squared term, the original variable is insignificant at any reasonable level of significance.

Analyzing Interaction Effects

Ashley Investment Services (continued)

EXAMPLE
12-5

INTERACTION EFFECTS

Excel and Minitab Tutorial

The director of personnel wondered if the effects of burnout were different among male and female workers. He, therefore, identified the gender of the employees from which the data in Table 12-4 were obtained. These data are contained in the file called **Ashley-2**. A multiple scatter plot of the data is presented in Figure 12-23.

The personnel director tried to visualize the relationship between the burnout index and socialization measure for both men and women. The sketches of the result are presented in Figure 12-23. Note that both relationships appear to be curvilinear with a similar shaped curve. As we showed earlier, this type of curvilinear situation can often be modeled by the second-order polynomial:

$$y = \beta_0 + \beta_1 x_1 + \beta_2 x_1^2 + \epsilon$$

However, the regression equations that estimate this second-order polynomial for men and women are not the same. The two equations seem to have different locations and different rates of curvature. Whether an employee is a man or woman seems to change the basic relationship between burnout index (y) and socialization measure (x_1). In order to represent this difference, the equation's coefficients b_0, b_1, and b_2 must be different for men and women employees. Thus we could use two models, one for each gender. Alternatively, we

Excel Instructions:
1. Open file: Ashley-2.xls
2. Click on Chart Wizard
3. Select Scatter Plot
4. Use Series Tab
5. Identify the y variable range for males
6. Identify x variable range for males
7. Repeat steps 5 and 6 for females—use Add Series
8. Right click on each series and select Add Trend Lines, exponential option

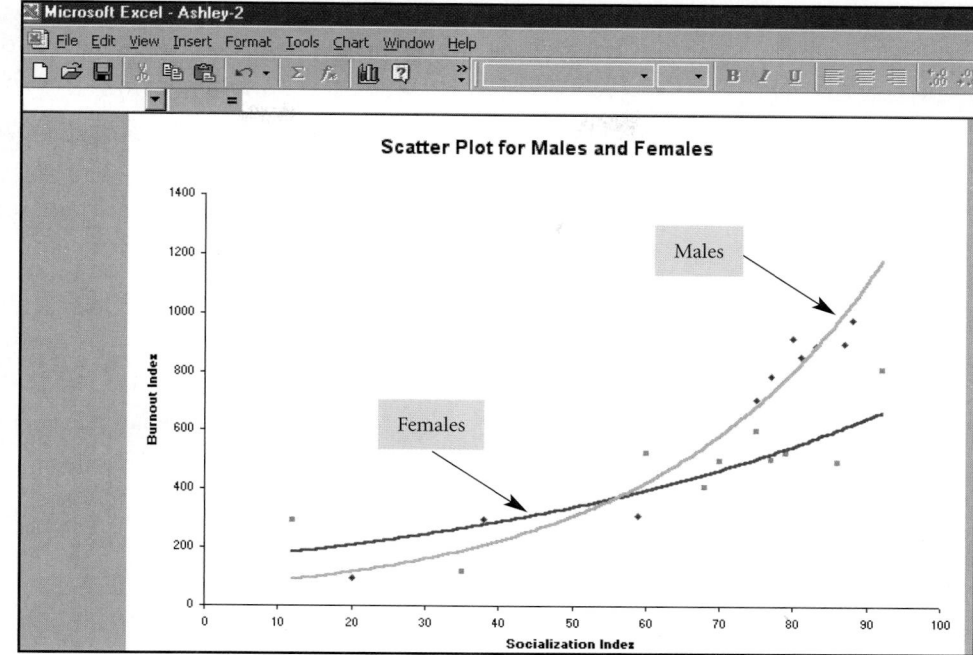

FIGURE 12-23
Excel Multiple Scatter Plot for Ashley Investments

could use one model for both males and females by incorporating a dummy independent variable with two levels shown as:

$$x_2 = 1 \text{ if a male, 0 if a female}$$

As x_2 changes values from 0 to 1 it affects the values of the coefficients b_0, b_1, and b_2. When the director fitted the second-order model for the women employees, he obtained the following regression equation.

$$\hat{y} = 291.70 - 4.61x_1 + 0.101x_1^2$$

The equation for the men employees was:

$$\hat{y} = 149.59 - 4.40x_1 + 0.159x_1^2$$

To explain how a change in gender can cause this kind of change, we must introduce the concept of **interaction.**

> **INTERACTION**
> The case in which one independent variable (such as x_2) affects the relationship between another independent variable (x_1) and a dependent variable (y).

So in our example, gender (x_2) interacts with the relationship between socialization measure (x_1) and the burnout index (y). The question is how do we obtain the interaction terms to model such a relationship? To answer this question, we first obtain the model for the basic relationship between the x_1 and y variables. The population model is:

$$y = \beta_0 + \beta_1 x_1 + \beta_2 x_1^2 + \epsilon$$

To obtain the interaction terms, multiply the terms on the right-hand side of this equation by the variable that is interacting with this relationship between y and x_1. In this case, that interacting variable is x_2. Then the interaction terms would be:

$$\beta_3 x_2 + \beta_4 x_1 x_2 + \beta_5 x_1^2 x_2$$

Notice that we have changed the coefficient subscripts so as not to duplicate those in the original model. Then the interaction terms are added to the original model to produce the **composite model**.

$$y = \beta_0 + \beta_1 x_1 + \beta_2 x_1^2 + \beta_3 x_2 + \beta_4 x_1 x_2 + \beta_5 x_1^2 x_2 + \epsilon$$

> **COMPOSITE MODEL**
> The model that contains both the basic terms and the interactive terms.

The model for women is obtained by substituting $x_2 = 0$ into the composite model. This gives:

$$\begin{aligned} y &= \beta_0 + \beta_1 x_1 + \beta_2 x_1^2 + \beta_3(0) + \beta_4 x_1(0) + \beta_5 x_1^2(0) + \epsilon \\ &= \beta_0 + \beta_1 x_1 + \beta_2 x_1^2 + \epsilon \end{aligned}$$

Similarly, for men we substitute the value of $x_2 = 1$. The model then becomes:

$$\begin{aligned} y &= \beta_0 + \beta_1 x_1 + \beta_2 x_1^2 + \beta_3(1) + \beta_4 x_1(1) + \beta_5 x_1^2(1) + \epsilon \\ &= (\beta_0 + \beta_3) + (\beta_1 + \beta_4)x_1 + (\beta_2 + \beta_5)x_1^2 + \epsilon \end{aligned}$$

This illustrates how the coefficients are changed for different values of x_2 and, therefore, how x_2 is interacting with the relationship between x_1 and y. Once we know $\beta_3, \beta_4,$ and β_5, we know the effect of the interaction of gender on the original relationship

FIGURE 12-24
Data Preparation for Estimating Interactive Effects for Second Order Model for Ashley Investments

	A	B	C	D	E	F
	Burnout Index	Socialization Measure	Socialization Squared	Gender		
1	y	x_1	x_1^2	x_2	$x_1 x_2$	$x_1^2 x_2$
2	100	20	400	1	20	400
3	980	88	7744	1	88	7744
4	310	59	3481	1	59	3481
5	900	87	7569	1	87	7569
6	920	80	6400	1	80	6400
7	892	83	6889	1	83	6889
8	855	81	6561	1	81	6561
9	709	75	5625	1	75	5625
10	791	77	5929	1	77	5929
11	300	38	1444	1	38	1444
12	810	92	8464	0	0	0
13	120	35	1225	0	0	0
14	525	60	3600	0	0	0
15	410	68	4624	0	0	0
16	296	12	144	0	0	0
17	501	70	4900	0	0	0
18	506	77	5929	0	0	0
19	493	86	7396	0	0	0
20	527	79	6241	0	0	0
21	600	75	5625	0	0	0

Excel Instructions:

1. Open file: Ashley-2.xls
2. Use Excel Formulas to create new variables

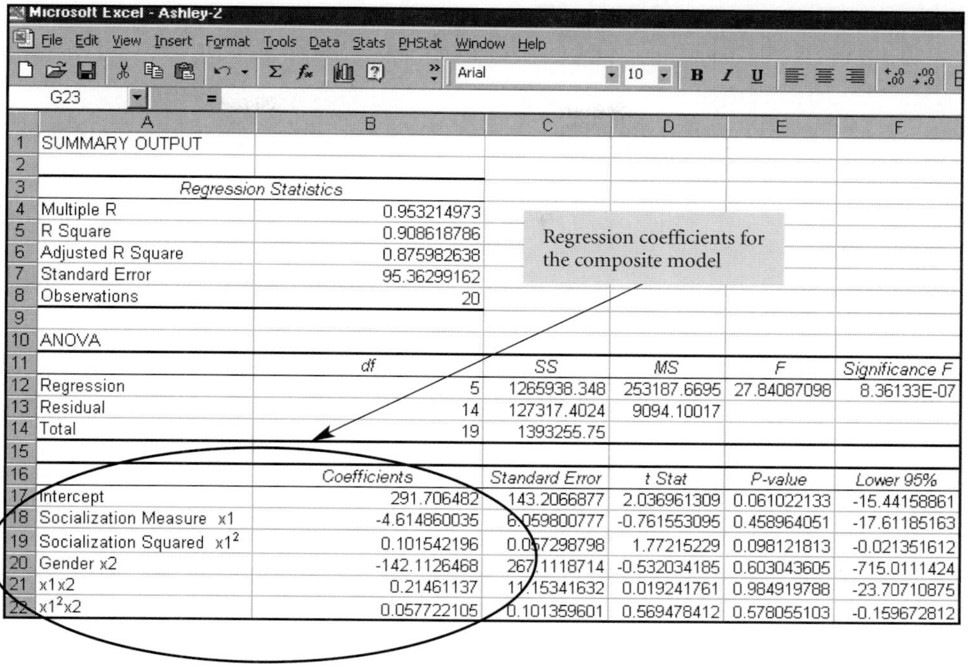

	A	B	C	D	E	F
1	SUMMARY OUTPUT					
2						
3	*Regression Statistics*					
4	Multiple R	0.953214973				
5	R Square	0.908618786				
6	Adjusted R Square	0.875982638				
7	Standard Error	95.36299162				
8	Observations	20				
9						
10	ANOVA					
11		*df*	*SS*	*MS*	*F*	*Significance F*
12	Regression	5	1265938.348	253187.6695	27.84087098	8.36133E-07
13	Residual	14	127317.4024	9094.10017		
14	Total	19	1393255.75			
15						
16		*Coefficients*	*Standard Error*	*t Stat*	*P-value*	*Lower 95%*
17	Intercept	291.706482	143.2066877	2.036961309	0.061022133	-15.44158861
18	Socialization Measure x1	-4.614860035	6.059800777	-0.761553095	0.458964051	-17.61185163
19	Socialization Squared x1²	0.101542196	0.057298798	1.77215229	0.098121813	-0.021351612
20	Gender x2	-142.1126468	267.1118714	-0.532034185	0.603043605	-715.0111424
21	x1x2	0.21461137	11.15341632	0.019241761	0.984919788	-23.70710875
22	x1²x2	0.057722105	0.101359601	0.569478412	0.578055103	-0.159672812

FIGURE 12-25
Excel Composite Model for Ashley Investments

between the burnout index (y) and the socialization measure (x_1). In order to estimate the composite model, we need to create the required variables as shown in Figure 12-24. Figure 12-25 shows the regression output for the composite model. The estimate for the composite model is:

$$\hat{y} = 291.706 - 4.615x_1 + 0.102x_1^2 - 142.113x_2 + 0.215x_1x_2 + 0.058x_1^2x_2$$

We obtain the model for females by substituting $x_2 = 0$ giving:

$$\hat{y} = 291.706 - 4.615x_1 + 0.102x_1^2 - 142.113(0) + 0.215(0) + 0.058(0)$$
$$\hat{y} = 291.706 - 4.615x_1 + 0.102x_1^2$$

For males, we substitute $x_2 = 1$ giving:

$$\hat{y} = 291.706 - 4.615x_1 + 0.102x_1^2 - 142.113(1) + 0.215x_1(1) + 0.058x_1^2(1)$$
$$\hat{y} = 149.593 - 4.40x_1 + 0.160x_1^2$$

Note, these equations for males and females are the same as we obtained earlier when we generated two separate regression models, one for each gender.

In this example we have looked at a case in which a dummy variable interacts with the relationship between another independent variable and the dependent variable. However, the interacting variable need not be a dummy variable. It can be any independent variable. Also, strictly speaking, interaction is not said to exist if the only effect of the interaction variable is to change the y-intercept of the equation relating another independent variable to the dependent variable. Therefore, when you search a scatter plot to detect interaction, you are trying to determine if the relationships produced when the interaction variable changes values are parallel or not. If the relationships are parallel, that indicates that only the y-intercept is being affected by the change of the interacting variable and that interaction does not exist. Figure 12-26 demonstrates this concept graphically.

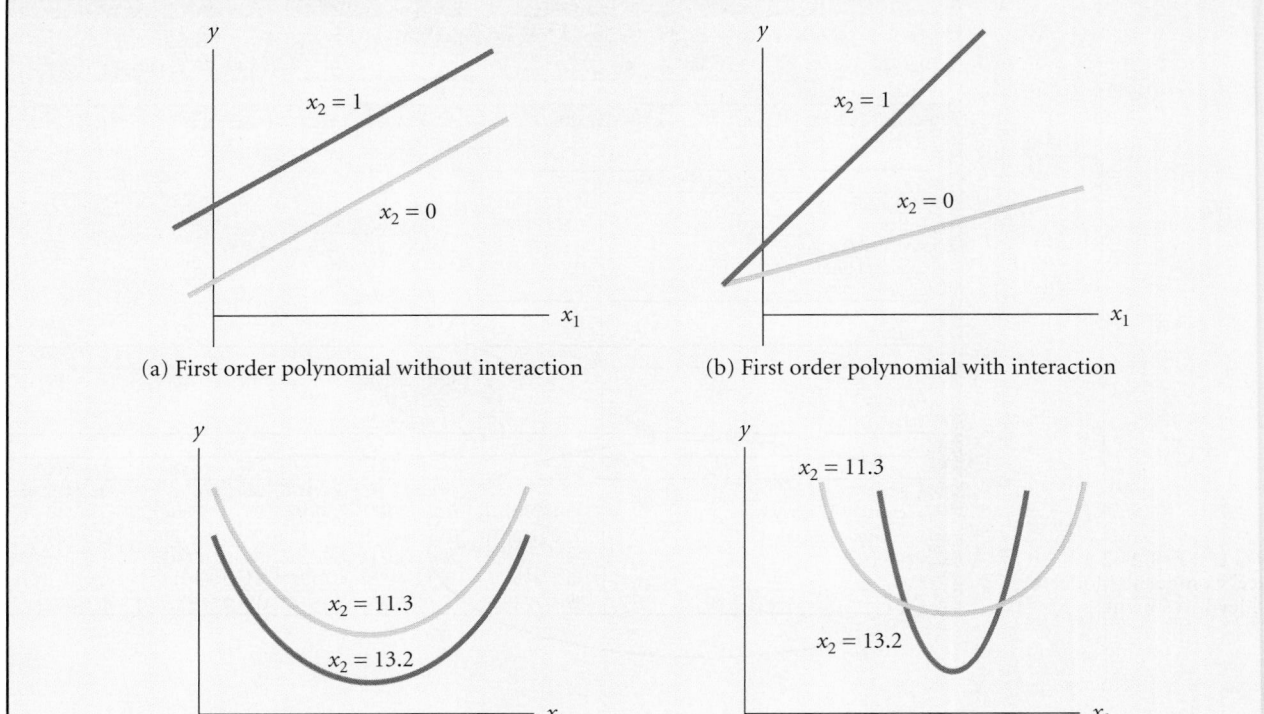

(a) First order polynomial without interaction

(b) First order polynomial with interaction

(c) Second-order polynomial without interaction

(d) Second-order polynomial with interaction

FIGURE 12-26   Graphical Evidence of Interaction

OPTIONAL CD-ROM TOPIC The Partial F-Test for Interaction

The partial F-test is useful for determining the contribution of each independent variable in the model and to assess whether interaction is present. For more information, go to the CD-ROM.

12-3: EXERCISES

ADDITIONAL EXERCISES ON YOUR CD-ROM

Try the **ADDITIONAL EXERCISES** and **APPLICATION PROBLEMS** on the CD-ROM.

Business Applications

12-15. Badeaux Brothers Louisiana Treats ships packages of Louisiana coffee, cakes, and Cajun spices to individual customers around the United States. The cost to ship these products depends primarily on the weight of the package being shipped. Badeaux charges the customers for shipping and then ships the product itself. As a part of a study of whether it is economically feasible to continue to ship products itself, Badeaux sampled 20 recent shipments to determine what, if any relationship exists between shipping costs and package weight. These data are in the file called **Badeaux**.

a. Develop a scatter plot of the data with the dependent variable, cost, on the vertical axis and the independent variable, weight, on the horizontal axis. Does there appear to be a relationship between the two variables? Is the relationship linear?

b. Compute the sample correlation coefficient between the two variables. Conduct a test, using a significance level of 0.05, to determine whether the population correlation coefficient is significantly different from 0.

c. Badeaux Brothers have been using a simple linear regression equation to predict the cost of shipping various items. Would you recommend they use a second-order polynomial model instead? Is the second-order polynomial model a significant improvement on the simple linear regression equation?

d. The Badeaux Brothers have made a decision to stop shipping products if the shipping charges exceed $100. They have asked you to determine the maximum weight for future shipments. Do this for both the first and second-order models you have developed.

12-16. Referring to Problem 15.

a. Estimate the simple linear regression model for these data.

b. Plot the simple linear regression model's estimate together with the data. Write a short report discussing this model. What improvements might you suggest?

c. Another analyst has convinced the Badeaux Brothers that they do not need to stop shipping packages. This analyst says that they need to ship bigger packages and, in so doing, reap the economy of scale. That is to say, the analyst believes that as the weight of the packages increases, the cost of shipping increases at a decreasing rate. Use a statistical technique to determine if this analyst is correct.

12-17. The State Tax Commission must download information files each morning. The time to download the files primarily depends upon the size of the file. The Tax Commission has asked your computer consulting firm to determine what, if any, relationship exists between download time and size of files. The Tax Commission randomly selected a sample of 20 days and provided the information to your firm in the file called **Tax Commission.**

a. Develop a scatter plot of the data with the dependent variable, download time, on the vertical axis and the independent variable, size, on the horizontal axis. Specify the relationship between the two variables by supplying a model that describes this relationship.

b. Compute the sample correlation coefficient between the two variables. Conduct a test, using a significance level of 0.025, to determine whether the population correlation coefficient is significantly different from 0. Use a p-value approach to conduct this test.

c. Estimate the simple linear regression model for these data. Plot the simple linear regression model together with the data. Would a nonlinear model better fit the sample data? Explain the reasons for your answer.

d. Estimate a nonlinear model and plot the model against the data. Does the nonlinear model provide a better fit than the linear model developed in part c? Describe the criterion used to reach your conclusion.

12-18. McCullom's International Grains is constantly searching out areas in which to expand its market. Such markets present different challenges since tastes in the international market are often different than domestic tastes. India is one country on which McCullom's has recently focused. Paddy is a grain used widely in India, but its characteristics are unknown to McCullom's. Charles Walters has been assigned to study this grain, and he has researched its various characteristics. During his research he came across an article, "Determination of Biological Maturity and Effect of Harvesting and Drying Conditions on Milling Quality of Paddy" (*J. of Ag. Engr. Research* (1975): 353–61). The article examines the relationship between y, the yield (kg/ha) of paddy as a function of x, the number of days after flowering at which harvesting took place. The accompanying data appeared in the article and are in a file called **Paddy.**

y	x	y	x
2,508	16	3,823	32
2,518	18	3,646	34
3,304	20	3,708	36
3,423	22	3,333	38
3,057	24	3,517	40
3,190	26	3,241	42
3,500	28	3,103	44
3,883	30	2,776	46

a. Construct a scatter plot of the yield (kg/ha) of paddy as a function of the number of days after flowering at which harvesting took place. Display at least two models that would explain the relationship you see in the scatter plot.

b. Conduct tests of hypotheses to determine if the models you selected are useful in predicting the yield of paddy.

c. Consider a model that includes the second-order term x^2. Would a simple linear regression model be preferable to the model containing the second-order term? Conduct a hypothesis test using the p-value approach to arrive at your answer.

d. Which model should Charles use to predict the yield of paddy? Explain your answer.

12-19. The Gilmore Accounting Firm collected the following data in an effort to explain variation in client profitability.

y	x_1	x_2	y	x_1	x_2
2,345	45	1	−700	34	3
4,200	56	2	3,457	45	1
278	26	3	2,478	47	1
1,211	56	2	1,975	24	2
1,406	24	2	206	32	3
500	23	3			

where:

y = Net profit earned from the client
x_1 = Number of hours spent working with the client
x_2 = Type of client:
  1, if manufacturing
  2, if service
  3, if governmental

In order to predict the net profit earned from the client, Gilmore has asked if it needs the client type in addition to the number of hours spent working with the client. You are asked to provide this information.

  a. Fit a model to the data that incorporates the number of hours spent working with the client and the type of client as independent variables. (Hint: Client type has three levels.)
  b. Fit a model to the data that uses only the number of hours spent working with the client. Based upon the results you obtained here and in part a, respond to the question posed by Gilmore.

12-20. Refer to Problem 19. The director of Gilmore Accounting has for some time now wondered if the relationship between the net profit earned from a client and the number of hours spent working with the client was different for the three client types the firm services.

  a. Construct a model that would address the issue raised by the director.
  b. Using the model derived in part a, address the issue raised by the director.

12-21. Referring to the example discussed in this chapter, First City Real Estate is an established, family-owned firm located in the Midwest. First City management wishes to build a model that can be used to predict sales price for residential property. From a wide list of possibilities, the managers selected the following as good candidates: x_1 = Home size in square feet, x_2 = Age of house, x_3 = Number of bedrooms, x_4 = Number of bathrooms, x_5 = Garage size (# of cars).

Data were obtained for a sample of 319 residential properties that sold within the previous two months in an area served by two of First City's offices. For each house in the sample, the sales price and values for each potential independent variable were collected. The data are in a file named **First City.**

  a. Construct a model that would use home size to predict the home's selling price.
  b. Use a statistical technique to determine if the number of bathrooms in the home affects the relationship between the selling price of the home and its size. (Hint: What type of terms measure such an effect?)

12-22. Refer to Problem 21. Recently the managers have begun to suspect that the age of the house has an unusual relationship to the price of the home. They conjecture that the price decreases at a decreasing rate as a function of age until the house is nearly 50 years old. Then the price begins to increase at an increasing rate.

  a. From the description just given, construct a model that would describe the relationship between the price of the home and the age of that home. Produce an estimate of such a model.
  b. Construct a scatter plot of the price of the home versus the age of the home.
  c. The manager indicates that the scatter plot seems to say that there is only a linear relationship between the price and age of the home. Produce an estimate of such a model.

■ 12-4: STEPWISE REGRESSION

One option in regression analysis is to bring all possible independent variables into the model in one step. This is what we have done in the previous sections. We use the term *full regression* to describe this approach. Another method for developing a regression model is called *stepwise regression*. Stepwise regression, as the name implies, develops the least squares regression equation in steps, either through *forward selection, backward elimination* or through *standard stepwise* regression.

Forward Selection

The forward selection procedure begins by selecting a single independent variable from all those available. The independent variable selected at step 1 is the variable that is most highly correlated with the dependent variable. An F-test is used to determine if this variable explains a significant amount of the variation in the dependent variable. The F-value that defines the beginning of the rejection region here is known as the *F-to-enter*. If the variable does explain a significant amount of the dependent variable's variation, it is selected to be part of the final model used to predict the dependent variable. If it does not, the process is terminated. If no variables were found to be significant, the researcher would have to search for different independent variables than the ones submitted initially to the stepwise procedure.

At step 2, a second independent variable is selected based on its ability to explain the remaining unexplained variation in the dependent variable. The independent variable selected in the second, and each subsequent, step is the variable with the highest **coefficient of partial determination**.

> **COEFFICIENT OF PARTIAL DETERMINATION**
> The measure of the marginal contribution of each independent variable, given that other independent variables are in the model.

Recall that the coefficient of determination (R^2) measures the proportion of variation explained by all of the independent variables in the model. Thus, after the first variable (say, x_1) is selected, R^2 will indicate the percentage of variation explained by this variable. The forward selection routine will then compute all possible two-variable regression models, with x_1 included, and determine the R^2 for each model. The coefficient of partial determination at step 2 is the proportion of unexplained variation (after x_1 is in the model) that is explained by the additional variable. The independent variable that adds the most to R^2, given the variable(s) already in the model, is the one selected. Then an F-test is conducted to determine if the proportion of unexplained variation that is explained by the additional variable is significant. This process continues until either all independent variables have been entered or the remaining independent variables do not add appreciably to R^2.

Backward elimination is just the reverse of the forward selection procedure. In the backwards elimination procedure all variables are forced into the model to begin the process. Variables are removed one at a time until no more insignificant variables are found. Once a variable has been removed from the model, it cannot be re-entered. For the forward selection procedure, the model begins with no variables. Variables are entered one at a time and once a variable is entered, it cannot be removed. (Your CD-ROM contains an optional section on backward elimination regression analysis.)

B. T. Longmont Company

EXAMPLE 12-6

FORWARD SELECTION REGRESSION

The B. T. Longmont Company operates a large retail department store in Macon, Georgia. Like other department stores, Longmont has incurred heavy losses due to shoplifting and employee pilferage. The store's security manager wants to develop a regression model to help explain the variation in monthly dollar loss. The variables the security manager is interested in are:

x_1 = Average monthly temperature (degrees Fahrenheit)
x_2 = Number of sales transactions
x_3 = Dummy variable for holiday month (1 if holiday during month, 0 if not)
x_4 = Number of employees on the store's monthly payroll
y = Monthly dollar loss attributed to shoplifting and pilferage

Table 12-5 lists the data for these variables for a random sample of 17 months from the past 10 years. The data are also in a file called **Longmont**. The correlation matrix for the data is presented in Figure 12-27. The forward selection procedure will begin by selecting the independent variable that is most highly correlated with the dependent variable. By examining the bottom row in the correlation matrix in Figure 12-27, you can see the variable x_2, number of sales transactions, is most highly correlated ($r = 0.6307$) with dollars lost. Once this variable is entered into the model, the remaining independent variables will be entered based on their ability to explain the remaining unexplained variation in the dependent variable.

MONTH	AVERAGE TEMPERATURE	NUMBER OF SALES TRANSACTIONS	HOLIDAY	EMPLOYEES	SHOPLIFTING LOSS
1	58.8	7,107	1	129	3,067
2	65.2	6,373	1	141	2,828
3	70.9	6,796	0	153	2,891
4	77.4	9,208	0	166	2,994
5	79.3	14,792	0	193	3,082
6	81	14,564	0	189	3,898
7	71.9	11,964	1	175	3,502
8	63.9	13,526	0	186	3,060
9	54.5	12,656	0	190	3,211
10	39.5	14,119	1	187	3,286
11	44.5	16,691	1	195	3,542
12	43.6	14,571	0	206	3,125
13	56	13,619	0	198	3,022
14	64.7	14,575	1	192	2,922
15	73	14,556	0	191	3,950
16	78.9	18,573	1	200	4,488
17	79.4	15,618	1	200	3,295

TABLE 12-5
Data for the B. T. Longmont Company

Figure 12-28 shows the PHStat stepwise regression output. At step 1, variable x_2, number of monthly sales transactions, enters the model. Although PHStat does not provide R^2 or an estimate of the standard error of the estimate directly, they can be computed from the output in the ANOVA section of the printout. Recall from Chapter 11 that R^2 is computed as:

$$R^2 = \frac{SSR}{TSS} = \frac{1,270,172.193}{3,192,631.529} = 0.398$$

Thus, this one independent variable explains 39.8% ($R^2 = 0.398$) of the variation in the dependent variable. The estimate of the standard error of the estimate is the square root of the mean square residual.

$$s_\epsilon = \sqrt{MSE} = \sqrt{MS \text{ Residual}} = \sqrt{128,163.96} = 358$$

Now at step 1 we test the following.

$$H_0: \beta_2 = 0 \text{ (Slope for variable } x_2 = 0)$$
$$H_A: \beta_2 \neq 0$$
$$\alpha = 0.05$$

As shown in Figure 12-28, the calculated t-value is 3.15. We compare this to the critical value from the t-distribution table (Appendix F) for $\frac{\alpha}{2} = \frac{0.05}{2} = 0.025$ and degrees of freedom equal to $n - k - 1 = 17 - 1 - 1 = 15$. This critical value is 2.131. Since

FIGURE 12-27
Excel Correlation Matrix Output for Longmont

Excel Instructions:
1. Open file: Longmont.xls
2. Click on Tools
3. Select Data Analysis
4. Select Correlation
5. Define data range

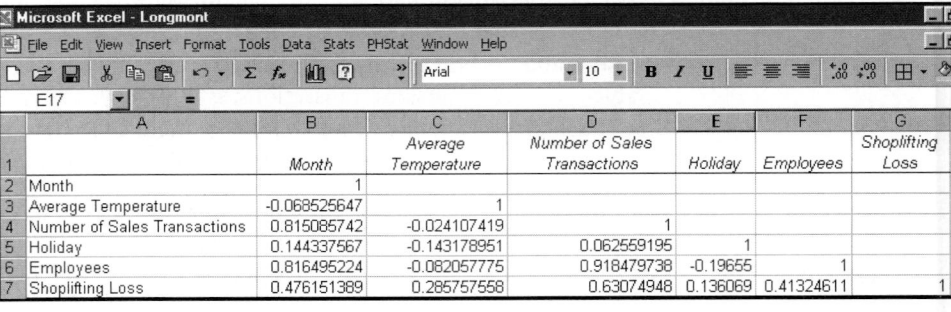

Excel (PHStat) Instructions:

1. Open file: Longmont.xls
2. Select the PHStat Tab
3. Define the *y* variable data range
4. Define the *x* variables data range
5. Select Forward Stepwise Option
6. Select *p*-value (or *t*-value) criterion
7. Set *p*-value or *t*-value to enter

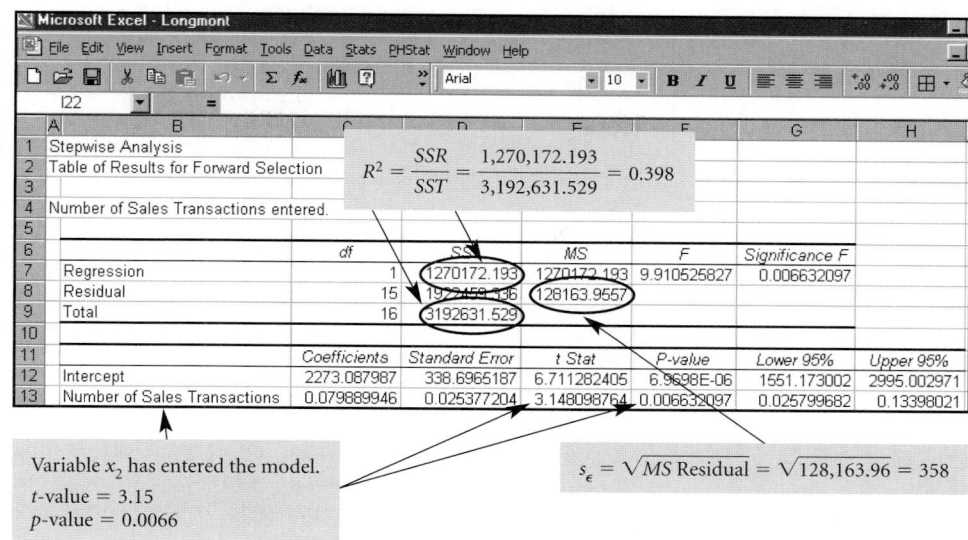

FIGURE 12-28
Excel (PHStat) Forward Selection Results for Longmont Co.—Step 1

Variable x_2 has entered the model.
t-value = 3.15
p-value = 0.0066

$s_\epsilon = \sqrt{MS \text{ Residual}} = \sqrt{128,163.96} = 358$

$t = 3.15 > 2.131$, we reject the null hypothesis and conclude that the regression slope coefficient for the variable, *number of sales transactions,* is not 0. Note also, since the *p*-value = $0.0066 < 0.05$, we would reject the null hypothesis.

The next variable to be selected will be the one that can do the most to increase R^2. If you were doing this manually, you would try each variable to see which one yields the highest R^2 given that the transactions variable is already in the model. Both the PHStat add-in software and Minitab do this automatically. As shown in Figure 12-29, the variable selected in step 2 is x_4, number of employees. Using the ANOVA section, we can determine R^2 and s_ϵ as before.

$$R^2 = \frac{SSR}{SST} = \frac{1,833,270.524}{3,192,631.529} = 0.574 \text{ and}$$

$$s_\epsilon = \sqrt{MS \text{ Residual}} = \sqrt{97,097.21} = 311.6$$

The model now explains 57.4% of the variation in the dependent variable. The *t*-values for both slope coefficients exceed $t = 2.145$ (the critical value from the *t*-distribution table with a one-tail area equal to 0.025 and $17 - 2 - 1 = 14$ degrees of freedom), so we

FIGURE 12-29
PHStat Forward Selection Results—Step 2

	A	B	C	D	E	F	G	H

Microsoft Excel - Longmont

File Edit View Insert Format Tools Data Stats PHStat Window Help

D16

	B	C	D	E	F	G	H
15							
16	Employees entered						
17							
18		df	SS	MS	F	Significance F	
19	Regression	2	1833270.524	916635.2621	9.440386786	0.002536893	
20	Residual	14	1359361.005	97097.21465			
21	Total	16	3192631.529				
22							
23		Coefficients	Standard Error	t Stat	P-value	Lower 95%	Upper 95%
24	Intercept	4600.804906	1010.544906	4.552796099	0.000451283	2433.399716	6768.210096
25	Number of Sales Transactions	0.203430952	0.055853812	3.642203536	0.002665741	0.083636333	0.323225571
26	Employees	-21.56736284	8.955880925	-2.408178829	0.030388965	-40.77583411	-2.358891569
27							
28							
29	No other variables could be entered into the model. Stepwise ends.						

conclude that both variables are significant in explaining the variation in the dependent variable, shoplifting loss.

The forward selection routine continues to enter variables as long as each additional variable explains a significant amount of the remaining variation in the dependent variable. Note, PHStat allows you to set the critical t or the significance level. Then as long as the calculated p-value for an incoming variable is less than the significance level, the variable is allowed to enter the model. Likewise, if the calculated t-statistic exceeds the critical t-value, the variable is allowed to enter.

In this example, with the p-value limit set at 0.05, neither of the two remaining independent variables would explain a significant amount of the remaining variation in the dependent variable. The procedure is, therefore, terminated. The resulting regression equation provided by forward selection is:

$$\hat{y} = 4600.8 + 0.203x_2 - 21.57x_4$$

Note, the dummy variables for holiday and temperature did not enter the model. This implies that, given the other variables, knowing whether the month in question has a holiday or knowing its average temperature does not add significantly to the model's ability to explain the variation in the dependent variable.

The Longmont Company can now use this regression model to explain variation in shoplifting losses based upon knowing the number of sales transactions and the number of employees.

OPTIONAL CD-ROM TOPIC Backward Elimination Stepwise Regression
You can also perform stepwise regression analysis by starting out with all independent variables in the model and then removing the variables one at a time. For more information, go to the CD-ROM.

Standard Stepwise Regression

The standard stepwise procedure (sometimes referred to as forward stepwise regression—not to be confused with forward selection) combines attributes of both backward elimination and forward selection. The standard stepwise method serves one more important function. If two or more variables overlap, a variable selected in an early step may become insignificant when other variables are added at later steps. The standard stepwise procedure will drop this insignificant variable from the model. Standard stepwise regression also offers a means of observing multicollinearity problems since we can see how the regression model changes as each new variable is added to the model.

The standard stepwise procedure is widely used in decision-making applications and is generally recognized as a useful regression method. However, care should be exercised when using this procedure since it is easy to rely too heavily on the automatic selection process. Remember, the order of variable selection is conditional, based on the variables already in the model. There is no guarantee that stepwise regression will lead you to the best set of independent variables from those available. Decision makers still must use common sense in applying regression analysis to make sure they have usable regression models.

First City Real Estate (continued)

Recall the First City Real Estate example in Section 12-1. First City management wished to build a model that can be used to predict sales price for residential property. The managers met in a brainstorming session to derive a list of possible independent (explana-

EXAMPLE
12-7

**STANDARD
STEPWISE**

tory) variables. From a wide list of possibilities, the managers selected the following as good candidates.

$$x_1 = \text{Home size in square feet}$$
$$x_2 = \text{Age of house}$$
$$x_3 = \text{Number of bedrooms}$$
$$x_4 = \text{Number of bathrooms}$$
$$x_5 = \text{Garage size (\# of cars)}$$

Data were obtained for a sample of 319 residential properties (file: **First City**) that sold within the previous two months in an area served by two of First City's offices. For each house in the sample, the sales price and value for each potential independent variable were collected. Figure 12-30 shows the Minitab standard stepwise regression output. At step 1, variable x_1, home size in square feet, was the first variable selected. It explains 55.91% ($R^2 = 0.5591$) of the variation in the dependent variable.

The variable selected in step 2 is x_2, age of the home, and the model now explains 74.56% of the variation in the dependent variable. The t-value, -15.22, for the coefficient is less than -1.96 (the approximate critical value for the t-distribution for $319 - 2 - 1 = 316$ degrees of freedom and $\alpha/2 = 0.05/2 = 0.025$), so we conclude the variable explains a significant amount of the remaining variation in the dependent variable, sales price. The entry of another variable into the regression model of course changes the coefficients and the associated t-values of the other variables in the regression equation. Therefore, the standard stepwise procedure now proceeds to determine if these changes have rendered any variable in the model insignificant. The procedure tests each variable in the model to determine if it should be removed from the model. If the t-value for a coefficient is less extreme than the table t-value for $n - k - 1$ degrees of freedom, the variable is removed from the model. Equivalently, the t-value could be converted into an F-value by squaring the t-value. This F-value would be compared against the critical F-value that is called the *F to remove*. In this case, the F to remove would equal $(1.96)^2$ which is very close to 4.0 which is used by Minitab as a default.

FIGURE 12-30
Minitab Standard Stepwise Output for First City Real Estate

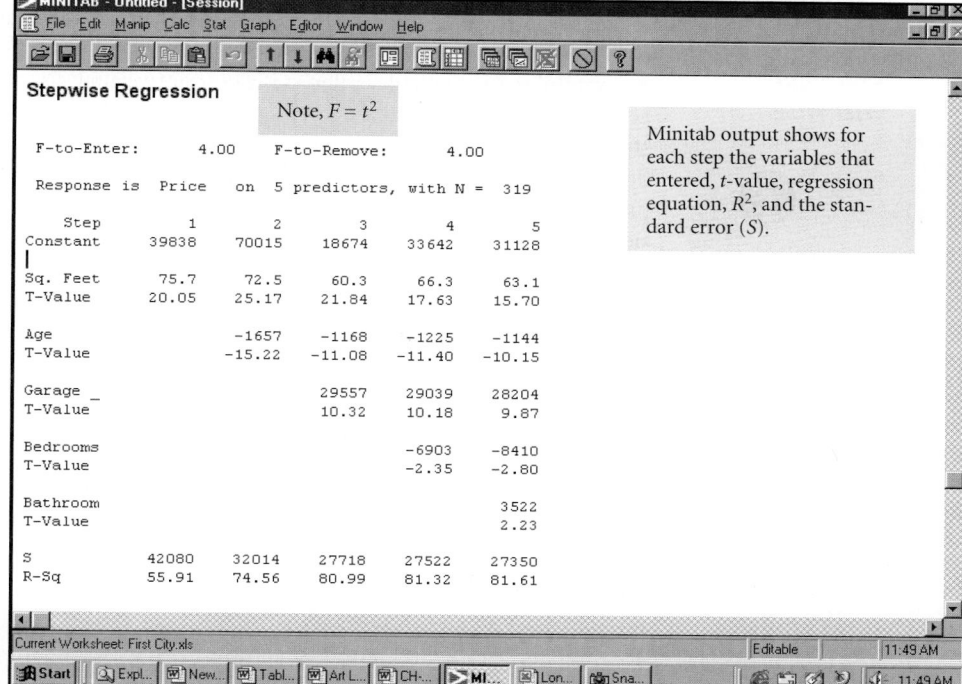

Minitab output shows for each step the variables that entered, t-value, regression equation, R^2, and the standard error (S).

Minitab Instructions:

1. Open file: First City.mtw
2. Select Stat tab
3. Select Regression
4. Click on Stepwise
5. Define y (response) variable
6. Define x variables

Note, $F = t^2$

Step	1	2	3	4	5
Constant	39838	70015	18674	33642	31128
Sq. Feet	75.7	72.5	60.3	66.3	63.1
T-Value	20.05	25.17	21.84	17.63	15.70
Age		-1657	-1168	-1225	-1144
T-Value		-15.22	-11.08	-11.40	-10.15
Garage			29557	29039	28204
T-Value			10.32	10.18	9.87
Bedrooms				-6903	-8410
T-Value				-2.35	-2.80
Bathroom					3522
T-Value					2.23
S	42080	32014	27718	27522	27350
R-Sq	55.91	74.56	80.99	81.32	81.61

Stepwise Regression

F-to-Enter: 4.00   F-to-Remove: 4.00

Response is Price on 5 predictors, with N = 319

Excel Instructions:
1. Open file: Automobiles.xls

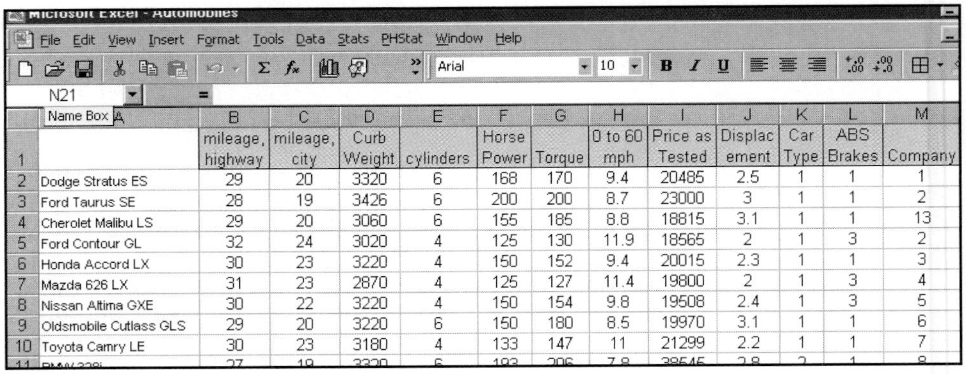

FIGURE 12-31
Motor Fan Magazine New Car Data

		mileage, highway	mileage, city	Curb Weight	cylinders	Horse Power	Torque	0 to 60 mph	Price as Tested	Displac ement	Car Type	ABS Brakes	Company
2	Dodge Stratus ES	29	20	3320	6	168	170	9.4	20485	2.5	1	1	1
3	Ford Taurus SE	28	19	3426	6	200	200	8.7	23000	3	1	1	2
4	Cherolet Malibu LS	29	20	3060	6	155	185	8.8	18815	3.1	1	1	13
5	Ford Contour GL	32	24	3020	4	125	130	11.9	18565	2	1	3	2
6	Honda Accord LX	30	23	3220	4	150	152	9.4	20015	2.3	1	1	3
7	Mazda 626 LX	31	23	2870	4	125	127	11.4	19800	2	1	3	4
8	Nissan Altima GXE	30	22	3220	4	150	154	9.8	19508	2.4	1	3	5
9	Oldsmobile Cutlass GLS	29	20	3220	6	150	180	8.5	19970	3.1	1	1	6
10	Toyota Camry LE	30	23	3180	4	133	147	11	21299	2.2	1	1	7

The stepwise regression routine continues to enter variables and remove variables until no more variables can be entered or removed from the model. In this example, the resulting regression equation provided by the standard stepwise regression procedure is:

$$\hat{y} = 31,128 + 63.1x_1 - 1,144x_2 - 8,410x_3 + 3,522x_4 + 28,204x_5$$

This model explains 81.6% of the variation in sales price and has an estimate of the standard error of the estimate equal to $27,350. This is the same result that we obtained earlier (see Figure 12-9, page 494) when all five independent variables were included at one time.

EXAMPLE
12-8

STANDARD STEPWISE

Excel and Minitab Tutorial

Motor Fan Magazine

Each year the editors of *Motor Fan Magazine* ask their staff to research various aspects of the new model cars. As one part of this research, the staff collected data on 30 new cars. A portion of these data are shown in Figure 12-31. The full data set is in the file called **Automobiles.** Of particular interest is a descriptive analysis to determine which vehicle characteristics explain the variation in highway mileage. As one part of the analysis, the magazine staff performed a standard stepwise regression analysis using highway mileage as the dependent variable and the variables, curb weight, cylinders, horsepower, torque, 0–60 mph speed, price, and displacement, as the potential independent variables. The PHStat stepwise regression results are shown in Figure 12-32.

In Figure 12-32, only two of the seven potential independent variables actually enter the model. These are curb weight and price. The other variables could not add significantly to the explanation of the variation in highway mileage. An examination of the final model at step 2 shows the heavier the car and the more expensive the car, the lower the highway mileage will be.

Best Subsets Regression

Another method for developing multiple regression models is called the *best subsets* method. As the name implies, the best subsets method works by trying possible subsets from the list of possible independent variables. The user can then select the "best" model based on such measures as *R*-square or the standard error of the estimate. Both Minitab and PHStat contain procedures for performing best subsets regression.

Final model after step 2

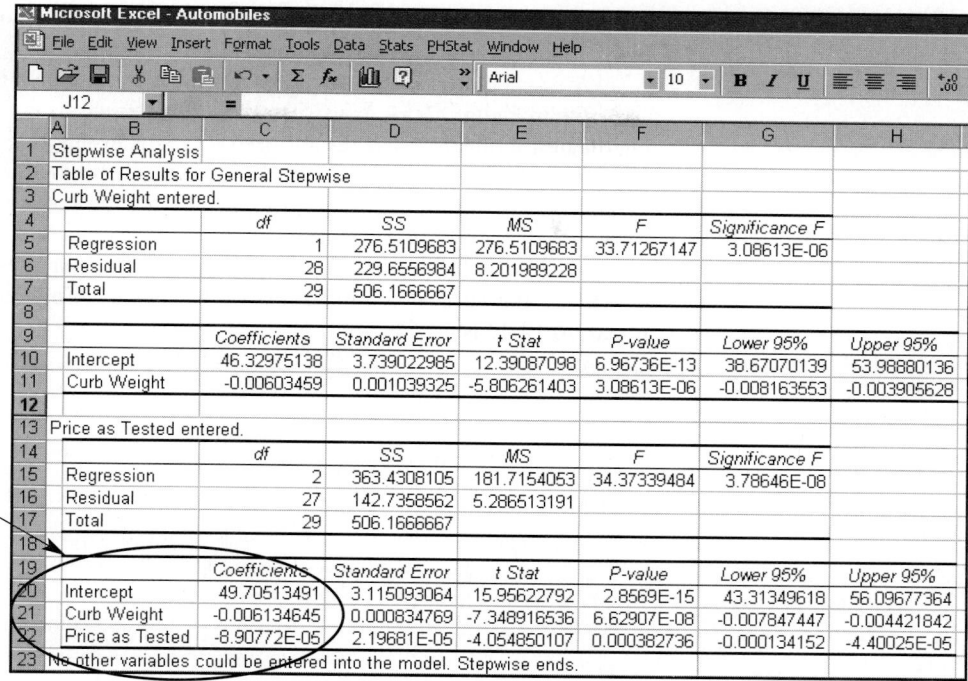

Excel (PHStat) Instructions:

1. Open file: Automobiles.xls
2. Select PHStat
3. Select Regression
4. Select Stepwise
5. Select General Stepwise
6. Define *y* variable range
7. Define *x* variables range

FIGURE 12-32
PHStat Standard Stepwise Regression Results for *Motor Fan Magazine*

EXAMPLE 12-9

BEST SUBSETS REGRESSION

Excel and Minitab Tutorial

Fortune 50 Companies

Figure 12-33 shows a portion of the data for the Fortune 50 companies that are in the file called **Fortune 50**.[9] Our objective is to develop a multiple regression model to explain the variation in total profit using the following independent variables.

x_1 = Revenue in millions of dollars
x_2 = Assets in millions of dollars
x_3 = Stockholder's equity in millions of dollars
x_4 = Number of employees in the company

FIGURE 12-33   Fortune 50 Companies Data

Excel Instructions:

1. Open file: Fortune 50.xls

[9]Note: The data are arranged so that all independent variables are in contiguous columns as required by Excel and PHStat regression procedures.

We will use the best subsets approach to determine the model. Figure 12-34 shows the PHStat best subsets regression output.

When using the best subsets approach we are given a choice of several different models as shown in Figure 12-34. As we discussed in the previous example, one criterion for selecting the best model is to use the adjusted R^2 value. Recall that this measure adjusts the coefficient of determination to account for the relationship of the sample size to the number of variables in the model. As seen in Figure 12-34, the model with the highest adjusted R^2 value ($R_A^2 = 0.636$) is the one using all four independent variables.

A second criterion that is frequently used with best subset analysis is the C_p statistic, which is a measure of the difference between the estimated model and the true model. Equation 12-14 is used to compute the C_p value.

$$C_p \text{ STATISTIC}$$

$$C_p = \frac{(1 - R_p^2)(n - T)}{1 - R_T^2} - (n - 2p) \qquad \text{12-14}$$

where:

p = Number of independent variables in the model + 1 = $k + 1$
T = 1 + The total number of independent variables to be considered for inclusion into the model
R_p^2 = Coefficient of multiple determination for the model with $p = k$ parameters
R_T^2 = Coefficient of multiple determination for the model that contains all T parameters

Additional Example 12-d

Best Subsets Regression Analysis

When a fitted model contains only random differences from the true model, the mean value of C_p will equal p. Thus, we would look for models in which the C_p value is small and close to $p = k + 1$. For instance, a model with $k = 4$ independent variables would be considered favorable if the C_p value is close to 5. As shown in Figure 12-34, the PHStat add-in to Excel generates the C_p values for each possible model. Note, the model with all four

FIGURE 12-34
PHStat Output for the Fortune 50 Companies

Microsoft Excel - Fortune 50

File Edit View Insert Format Tools Data Stats PHStat Window Help

	A	B	C	D	E	F	G
1	Fortune 50 Analysis						
2	R2T	0.666062					
3	1 - R2T	0.333938					
4	n	50					
5	T	5					
6	n - T	45					
7							Consider
8		Cp	p+1	R Square	Adj. R Square	Std. Error	This Model?
9	X1	24.32234	2	0.478149	0.467277134	1390.913	No
10	X1X2	18.09838	3	0.539178	0.519568258	1320.885	No
11	X1X2X3	19.74227	4	0.54182	0.511939081	1331.331	No
12	X1X2X3X4	5	5	0.666062	0.636378743	1149.142	Yes
13	X1X2X4	4.530245	4	0.654706	0.632187257	1155.746	No
14	X1X3	26.31995	3	0.478167	0.455961065	1405.608	No
15	X1X3X4	4.141051	4	0.657595	0.635263758	1150.903	No
16	X1X4	3.353902	3	0.648594	0.633640737	1153.461	No
17	X2	70.92332	2	0.132331	0.114254058	1793.51	No
18	X2X3	71.73089	3	0.141179	0.104633803	1803.223	No
19	X2X3X4	14.17342	4	0.583146	0.555959814	1269.873	No
20	X2X4	13.1146	3	0.576162	0.558125895	1266.772	No
21	X3	88.15173	2	0.004481	-0.016258746	1921.106	No
22	X3X4	19.50503	3	0.528739	0.508685572	1335.762	No
23	X4	19.21399	2	0.516057	0.505975135	1339.441	No

Excel (PHStat) Instructions:

1. Open file: Fortune 50.xls
2. Select PHStat
3. Click on Regression
4. Select Best Subsets
5. Define the y variable range
6. Define the x variables range

Excel (PHStat) Instructions:
1. Perform Best Subsets Regression (See Figure 12-34)
2. Select Tab for desired model (in this case ALLX tab)

Microsoft Excel - Fortune 50

File   Edit   View   Insert   Format   Tools   Data   Stats   PHStat   Window   Help

Arial   10

H21 =

	A	B	C	D	E	F	G
1	Fortune 50 Analysis						
2							
3	*Regression Statistics*						
4	Multiple R	0.816126					
5	R Square	0.666062					
6	Adjusted R Square	0.636379					
7	Standard Error	1149.142					
8	Observations	50					
9							
10	ANOVA						
11		*df*	*SS*	*MS*	*F*	*ignificance F*	
12	Regression	4	1.19E+08	29631194	22.4389	3.06E-10	
13	Residual	45	59423757	1320528			
14	Total	49	1.78E+08				
15							
16		*Coefficient*	*tandard Err*	*t Stat*	*P-value*	*Lower 95%*	*Upper 95%*
17	Intercept	549.3362	398.4223	1.378779	0.174779	-253.128	1351.8
18	Revenues ($ millions)	0.031333	0.009374	3.342666	0.001678	0.012453	0.050212
19	Employees	-0.00206	0.001932	-1.0682	0.291127	-0.00595	0.001827
20	Assets ($ million	-0.00186	0.001503	-1.23703	0.222492	-0.00489	0.001168
21	Stockholders'Equity	0.111006	0.027129	4.091732	0.000175	0.056365	0.165647

FIGURE 12-35
Excel (PHStat) Regression Output for the Fortune 50 Companies

independent variables has a C_p value equal to 5 which is our target for a model with $k = 4$ variables.[10] Note, although PH-stat suggests only models with $C_p \leq k + 1$, you should also consider the model with x_1, x_2 and x_4 since $C_p = 4.14$ is only slightly larger than $k + 1 = 4$.

Figure 12-35 shows the regression model with all four independent variables. Based on this output, 66.6% of the variation in profits can be explained by knowing the values of the four independent variables in the model. Two variables (assets and employees) are insignificant in the model.

12-4: EXERCISES

12-23. Comment on the statement, "Stepwise regression is the way to go. It will always give you the best subset of independent variables from the original list of variables. R^2 will be maximized by using stepwise regression."

12-24. Suppose you have four potential independent variables, x_1, x_2, x_3, and x_4, from which you wish to develop a multiple regression model. Using stepwise regression, x_2 and x_4 entered the model.
   a. Why did only two variables enter the model? Discuss.
   b. Suppose a full regression with only variables x_2 and x_4 had been run. Would the resulting model be dif-

ferent from the stepwise model that included only these two variables? Discuss.
   c. Comment on the statement, "The stepwise regression with the two variables will have a higher R-square than a full regression model with all four variables included."

Business Applications

12-25 The Western State Tourist Association gives out pamphlets, maps, and other tourist-related information to people who call a toll-free number and request the information. The

[10]Minitab also provides C_p values with its *Best Subsets* option.

association orders the packets of information from a document printing company and likes to have enough available to meet the immediate need without having too many extras sitting around taking up space. The marketing manager decided to develop a multiple regression model to be used in predicting the number of calls that will be received in the coming week. A random sample of 12 weeks is selected, with the following variables.

y = Number of calls
x_1 = Number of advertisements placed the previous week
x_2 = Number of calls received the previous week
x_3 = Number of airline tour bookings into western cities for the current week

These data are in the data file called **Western States.**

a. Develop the multiple regression model for predicting the number of calls received, using the full regression approach.
b. Test to determine whether the overall regression model is statistically significant at the $\alpha = 0.05$ level.
c. Write a short report discussing the overall model and indicating which of the independent variables are significant at the 0.05 level.

12-26. Refer to Problem 25.

a. Develop the correlation matrix which includes all independent variables and the dependent variable. Based on these correlations, prepare a short report that predicts the order the variables will be selected into the model if standard selection stepwise regression is used.
b. Use forward selection stepwise regression to develop a model for predicting the number of calls the company will receive. Write a report that describes what has taken place at each step of the regression process.
c. Provide the estimate of the population model derived from a standard stepwise regression procedure.
d. Compare the results of the forward selection stepwise regression results in part b, the standard stepwise regression procedure in part c, and the full regression results determined in Problem 25. Which model would you choose? Explain your answer.

12-27. The athletic director at State University was interested in developing a multiple regression model for explaining the variation in home-game football attendance. Use stan-

dard stepwise regression to develop the model. (The data are in the file called **Football.**)

a. Which variable entered the model at step 1? Discuss why this variable entered.
b. Indicate the order of variables entering the stepwise regression model. What happens to R^2 and the standard error of the estimate after each variable enters the model? Discuss.
c. Discuss the regression model at the final step. Also discuss why the model stopped at this step.
d. Test the overall significance of the regression model at the final step. Also test whether each regression coefficient is statistically significant. Use an $\alpha = 0.05$ level.

12-28. Referring to Problem 27, use the best subsets regression approach to develop a regression model for predicting home football attendance. Write a short report describing the results of this regression approach.

12-29. Lands' End is a leading direct merchant of traditionally styled casual clothing for men, women, and children, as well as soft luggage and products for the home. *Catalog Age* ranked Lands' End as the 12th largest mail-order company and the 2d largest mail-order company for apparel only. Its R&D department is constantly looking for ways to improve its products. Jeremy Walters, one of its consulting scientists, recently read an article entitled "Applying Stepwise Multiple Regression Analysis to the Reaction of Formaldehyde with Cotton Cellulose" (*Textile Research J.*, 1984, pp. 157–65). This article attempted to establish a relationship between the durable press rating of cotton with formaldehyde concentration (HCHO, x_1), a catalyst ratio (x_2), curing temperature (x_3), and curing time (x_4) to which the cotton was subjected. The data are in the data file called **Cotton.** (This problem cannot be done using Excel or PHStat.)

a. Construct scatter plots of each of the independent variables versus the durable press rating. Specify the model that would describe the relationship of each of these variables to a dependent variable.
b. Whether your scatter plots indicated such a relationship or not, develop a model using stepwise regression that could include all the dependent variables ($x_1 \ldots x_4$), their squares ($x_1^2 \ldots x_4^2$), and all possible (second-order) interaction terms ($x_1 x_2, \cdots, x_3 x_4$).
c. Perform both backward elimination and forward selection on the model submitted to the stepwise regression procedure in part b. Which of the resulting equations would you suggest in order to predict the durable press rating? Explain, giving statistical reasons for your answer.

12-5: DETERMINING THE APTNESS OF THE MODEL

In Section 12-1 we discussed the basic steps involved in building a multiple regression model. The final step is the diagnostic step in which you examine the model to determine how well it performs. We also discussed several statistics that you need to consider when performing the diagnostic step including analyzing R^2, adjusted R^2, and the standard error of the estimate. In addition, we discussed the concept of multicollinearity and the effects that can occur when multicollinearity is present. Section 12-3 introduced another diagnostic step that involves looking for potential curvilinear relationships between the independent variables and the dependent variable. We presented some basic data transformation techniques for dealing with curvilinear situations. However, a major part of the diagnostic process involves an analysis of how well the model fits the regression analysis assumptions.

The basic assumptions of multiple regression include the following.

1. The relationship between the dependent and independent variables is linear.
2. The variance of the model errors is constant over the range of the values of the independent variables.
3. The model errors are independent from observation to observation.
4. The model errors are normally distributed.

The degree to which the regression model satisfies these assumptions is called its *aptness*.

Analysis of Residuals

The residual, the difference between the actual value of the dependent variable and the value predicted by the regression model, is defined by Equation 12-15.

RESIDUAL

$$e = (y - \hat{y})$$

12-15

A residual value can be computed for each observation in the data set. A great deal can be learned about the *aptness* of the regression model by analyzing the residuals. The principal means of residual analysis is a study of residual plots. The following problems can be inferred through graphical analysis of residuals.

1. The regression function is not linear.
2. The model errors do not have a constant variance.
3. The model errors are not independent.
4. The model error terms are not normally distributed.

We will address each of these in order. The regression options in both Minitab and Excel provide extensive residual analysis. In Excel the residual options are shown on the Regression drop down box. In Minitab they are accessed in the Regression window by clicking on either the Graphs or Results button.

CHECKING FOR LINEARITY

A plot of the residuals (on the vertical axis) against the independent variable (on the horizontal axis) is useful for detecting whether a linear function is the appropriate regression function. Figure 12-36 illustrates two different residual plots. Figure 12-36(a) shows residuals that systematically depart from 0. When x is small, the residuals are negative. When x is in the midrange, the residuals are positive, and for large x values, the residuals are negative again. This type of plot suggests that the relationship between y and x is nonlinear. Figure 12-36(b) shows a plot where the residuals do not show a systematic variation from 0, implying that the relationship between x and y is linear.

If a linear model is appropriate, we expect the residuals to band around 0 with no systematic pattern displayed. If the residual plot shows a systematic pattern, it may be possible to transform the independent variable (refer to Section 12-3) such that the revised model will produce residual plots that will not systematically vary from 0.

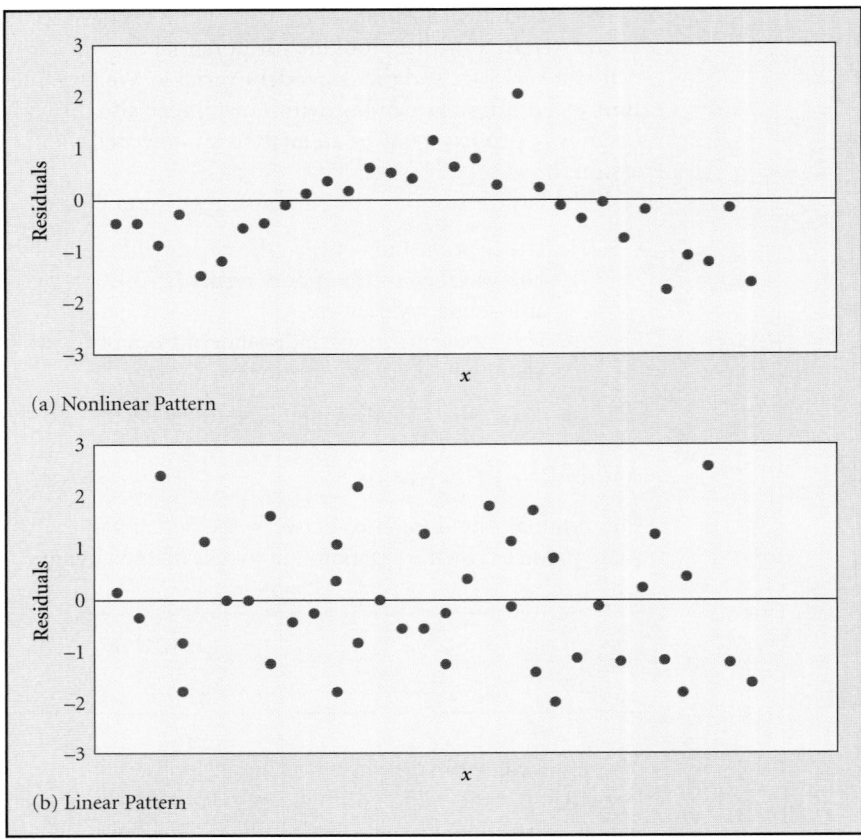

FIGURE 12-36
Residual Plots Showing
Linear and Nonlinear
Patterns

MULTIPLE REGRESSION

Excel and
Minitab Tutorial

First City Real Estate (continued)

We have been using First City Real Estate to introduce multiple regression tools throughout this chapter. Remember, the managers wish to develop a multiple regression model for predicting the sales price of homes in their market. The most recent step, done as Additional Example 12-c on your CD-ROM, involved doing a transformation on the lot size variable as log of lot size. The output for this model is shown in Figure 12-37. Notice the model now has an R^2 value of 96.9%.

There are currently four independent variables in the model: square feet, bedrooms, garages, and the log of lot size. Both Minitab and Excel provide procedures for automatically producing residual plots. Figure 12-38 shows the plots of the residuals against each of the independent variables. The transformed variable, log lot size, shows a systematic residual pattern. The residuals are positive for small values of log lot size, negative for intermediate values of log lot size, and positive again for large values of log lot size. These patterns suggest that the curvature of the relationship between sales price of homes and lot size is even more pronounced than the logarithm allows. Perhaps a second or third degree polynomial in the lot size should be pursued. (See Additional Example 12-c on the CD-ROM.)

DO THE RESIDUALS HAVE A CONSTANT VARIANCE?

Residual plots can also be used to determine whether the residuals have a constant variance. Consider Figure 12-39, on page 528, in which the residuals are plotted against an independent variable. The plot in Figure 12-39(a) shows an example in which, as x

Minitab Instructions:

1. Open file: First City-3.mtw
2. Select Stat
3. Select Regression
4. Select Regression again
5. Define *y* and *x* variables

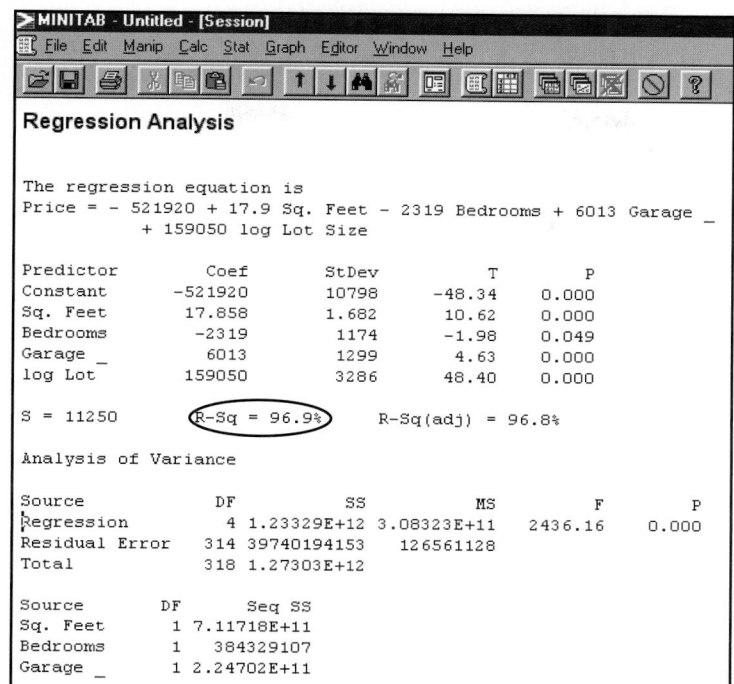

FIGURE 12-37
Minitab Output of First City
Real Estate Appraisal Model

FIGURE 12-38   First City Real Estate Residual Plots versus the Independent Variables

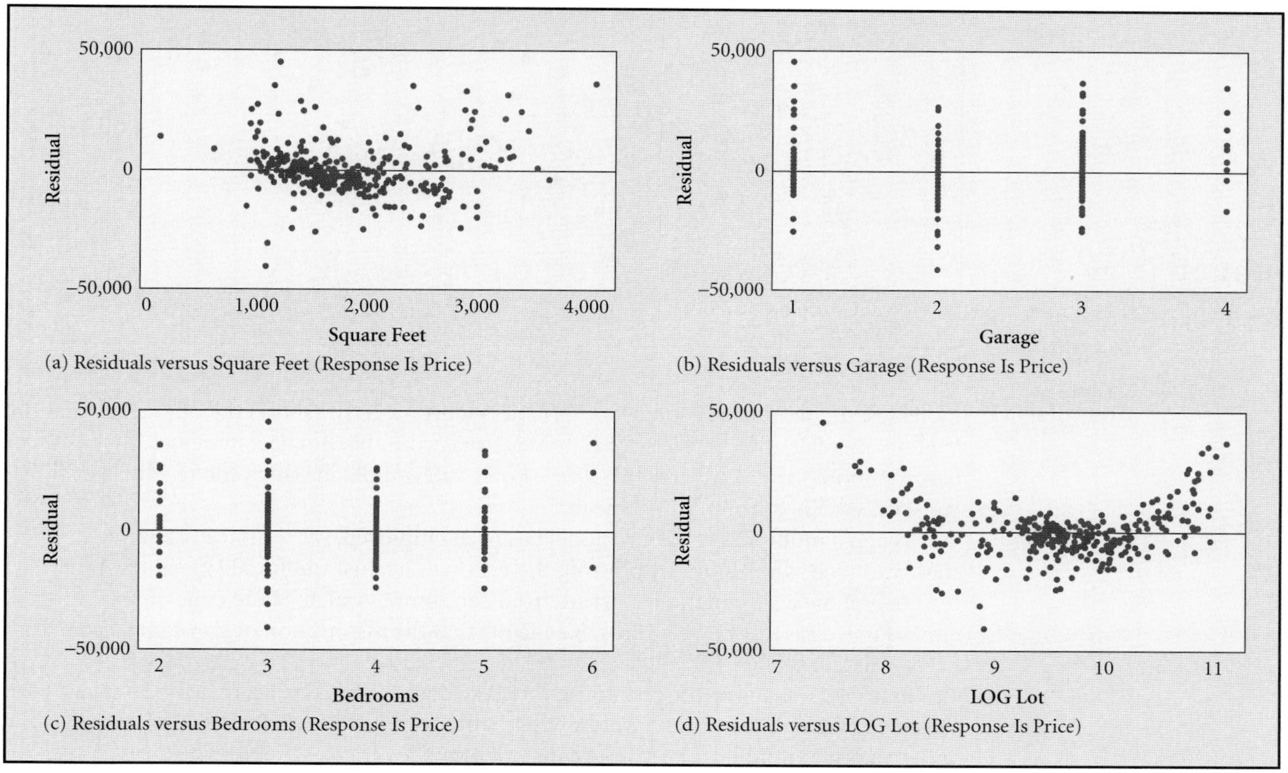

(a) Residuals versus Square Feet (Response Is Price)

(b) Residuals versus Garage (Response Is Price)

(c) Residuals versus Bedrooms (Response Is Price)

(d) Residuals versus LOG Lot (Response Is Price)

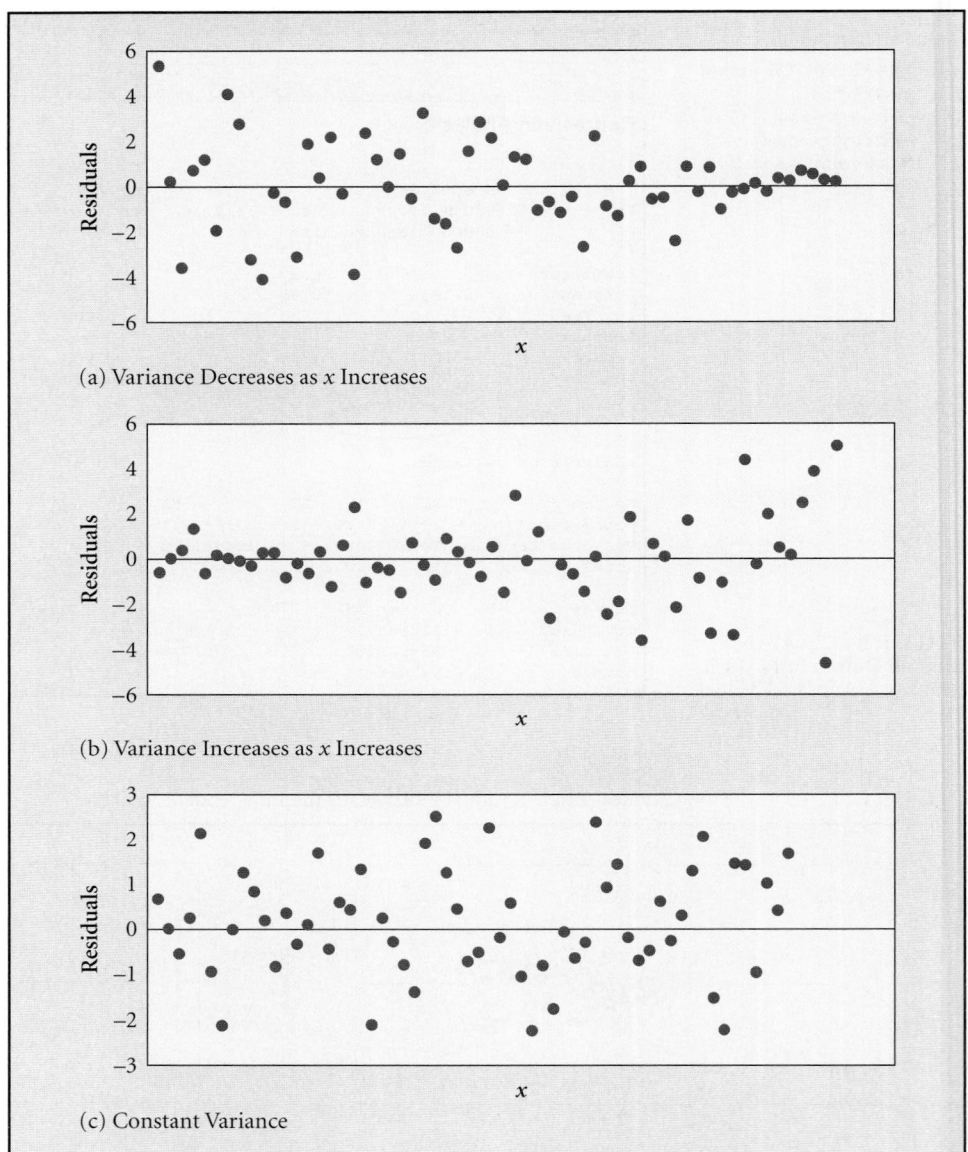

FIGURE 12-39
Residual Plots Showing
Constant and Nonconstant
Variances

increases, the residuals become less variable. Figure 12-39(b) shows the opposite situation. When x is small, the residuals are tightly packed around 0, but as x increases, the residuals become more variable. Figure 12-39(c) shows an example in which the residuals exhibit a constant variance around the 0 mean.

When a multiple regression model has been employed, we commonly analyze the constant variance assumption by plotting the residuals against the fitted ($\hat{y}$) values. When the residuals show a systematic departure from randomness such as the cone-shaped plots in either Figure 12-40(a) or 12-40(b), it suggests that the assumption of constant variance has been violated.

Figure 12-41 shows the residuals plotted against the fitted values for the First City Real Estate appraisal model. We have drawn a band around the residuals that shows that the variance of the residuals stays quite constant over the range of the fitted values.

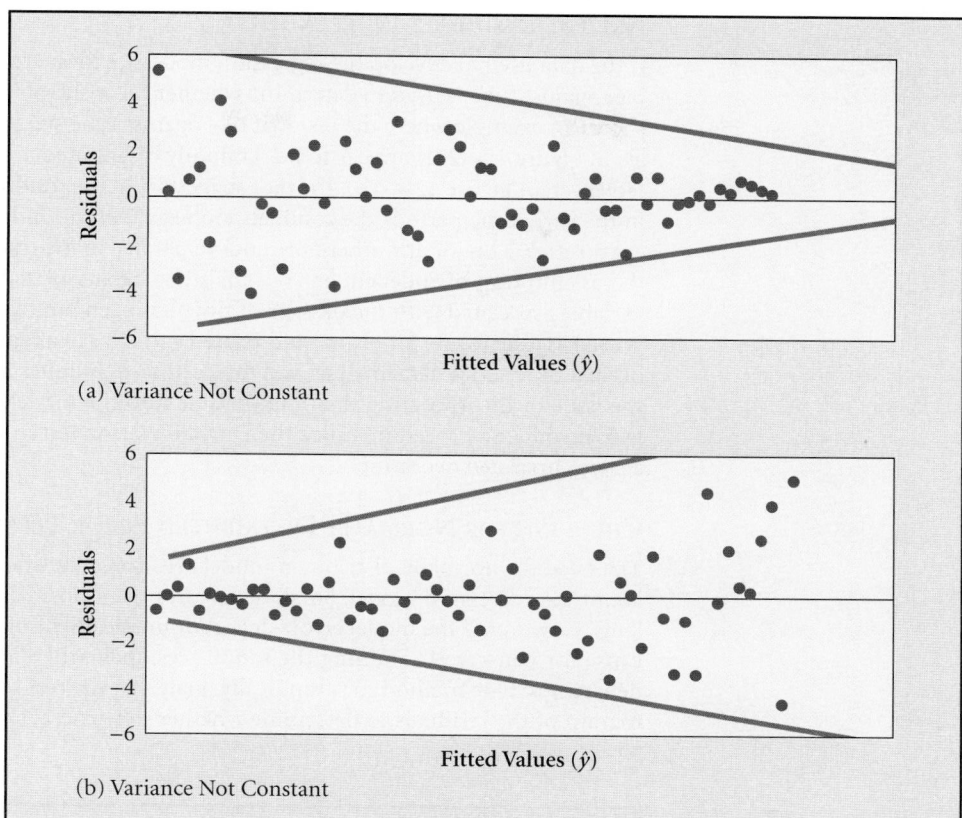

FIGURE 12-40
Residual Plots Against the
Fitted ($\hat{y}$) Values

FIGURE 12-41
Minitab Plot of Residuals
versus Fitted Values for First
City Real Estate

Minitab Instructions:

1. Open file: First City-3.mtw
2. Click on Stat
3. Select Regression
4. Identify the y variable
5. Identify the x variables
6. Select Graphs
7. Click on Residuals versus
   Fits
8. Click OK
9. Click OK

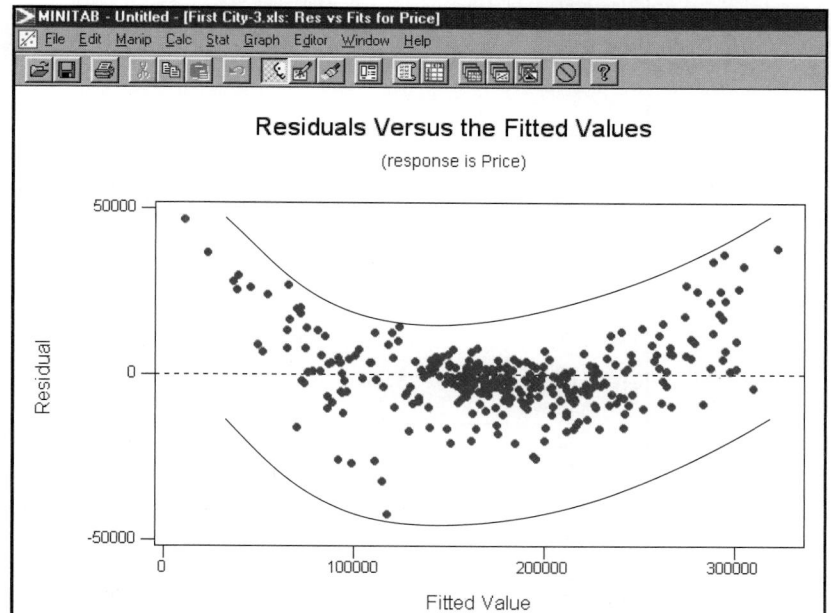

ARE THE RESIDUALS INDEPENDENT?

If the data used to develop the regression model are measured over time, a plot of the residuals against time is used to determine whether the residuals are correlated. Figure 12-42(a) shows an example where the residual plot against time suggests independence. The residuals in Figure 12-42(a) appear to be randomly distributed around the mean of 0 over time. However, in Figure 12-42(b), the plot suggests that the residuals are not independent, since in the early time periods the residuals are negative, and in later time periods the residuals are positive. This, or any other nonrandom pattern in the residuals over time, indicates that the assumption of independent residuals has been violated. Generally, this means some variable associated with the passage of time has been omitted from the model. Often, time is used as a surrogate for other time-related variables in a regression model. Chapter 16 will discuss time series data analysis and forecasting techniques in more detail and will address the issue of incorporating the time variable into the model. An Optional CD-ROM topic will introduce a procedure called the Durbin-Watson test to determine whether the residuals are correlated over time.

CHECKING FOR NORMALLY DISTRIBUTED ERROR TERMS

The need for normally distributed model errors occurs when we want to test a hypothesis about the regression model. Small departures from normality do not cause serious problems. However, if the model errors depart dramatically from a normal distribution, there is cause for concern. Examining the sample residuals will allow us to detect such dramatic departures. One method for graphically analyzing the residuals is to form a frequency histogram of the residuals to determine whether the general shape is normal. The chi-square

FIGURE 12-42
Plot of Residuals Against Time

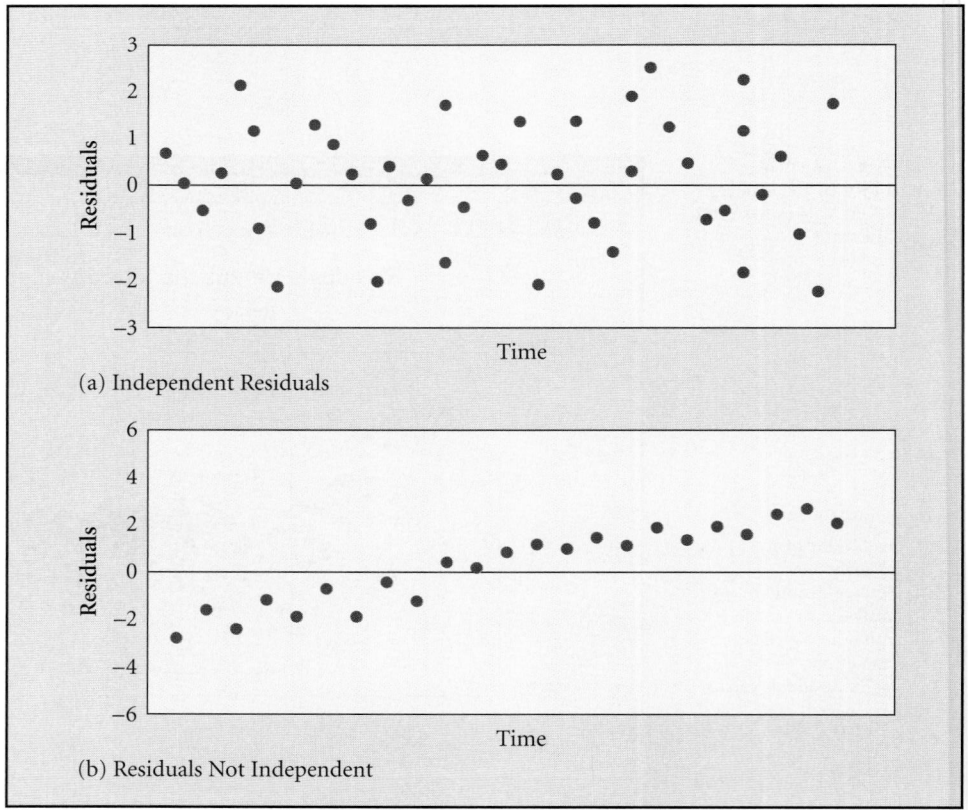

(a) Independent Residuals

(b) Residuals Not Independent

goodness-of-fit test presented in Chapter 14 can be used to test whether the residuals fit a normal distribution. An even better test for normality is the Lilliefor's test which is presented as an Optional CD-ROM topic for Chapter 14.

Another method for determining normality is to calculate and plot the **standardized residuals.** In Chapter 3 you learned that a random variable is standardized by subtracting its mean and dividing the result by its standard deviation. The mean of the residuals is zero. Therefore, dividing each residual by an estimate of its standard deviation gives the standardized residual.[11] Although the proof is beyond the scope of this text, it can be shown that the standardized residual for any particular observation for a simple linear regression model can be found using Equation 12-16.

STANDARDIZED RESIDUAL

$$sr = \frac{e}{s_\epsilon \sqrt{1 + \frac{1}{n} + \frac{(x_p - \bar{x})^2}{\sum x^2 - \frac{(\sum x)^2}{n}}}}$$

12-16

where:

e = Residual value

s_ϵ = Estimate of the standard error of the estimate

x_p = Value of x used to generate the predicted y value

Computing the standardized residual for an observation in a multiple regression model is too complicated to be done by hand. However, the standardized residuals are generated from most statistical software, including Minitab and Excel. The Excel and Minitab tutorials on your CD-ROM illustrate the methods required to generate the standardized residuals and residual plots. Because other problems such as nonconstant variance and nonindependent residuals can result in residuals that seem to be nonnormal, you should check these other factors before addressing the normality assumption.

Recall that for a normal distribution, approximately 68% of the values will fall within one standard deviation of the mean, 95% within two standard deviations of the mean, and virtually all values will fall within three standard deviations of the mean.

Figure 12-43 illustrates the histogram of the residuals for the First City Real Estate example. The distribution of residuals looks to be close to a normal distribution. Figure 12-44 shows the histogram for the standardized residuals which will have the same basic shape as the residual distribution in Figure 12-43.

Another approach for checking for normality of the residuals is to form a *probability plot.* We start by arranging the residuals in numerical order from smallest to largest. The standardized residuals are plotted on the horizontal axis and the corresponding expected value for the standardized residual is plotted on the vertical axis. While we won't delve into how the expected value is computed, you can examine the normal probability plot to see whether the plot forms a straight line at a diagonal from the lower left-hand corner. The closer the line is to linear, the closer the residuals are to being normally distributed. Figure 12-45, on page 533, shows the normal probability plot for the First City Real Estate Company example. While the graph in Figure 12-45 does not form a perfectly straight line on the diagonal from the lower left-hand corner, the fit is good enough to allow us to consider the residuals to be approximately normally distributed.

---

[11]The standardized residual is also referred to as a Studentized Residual.

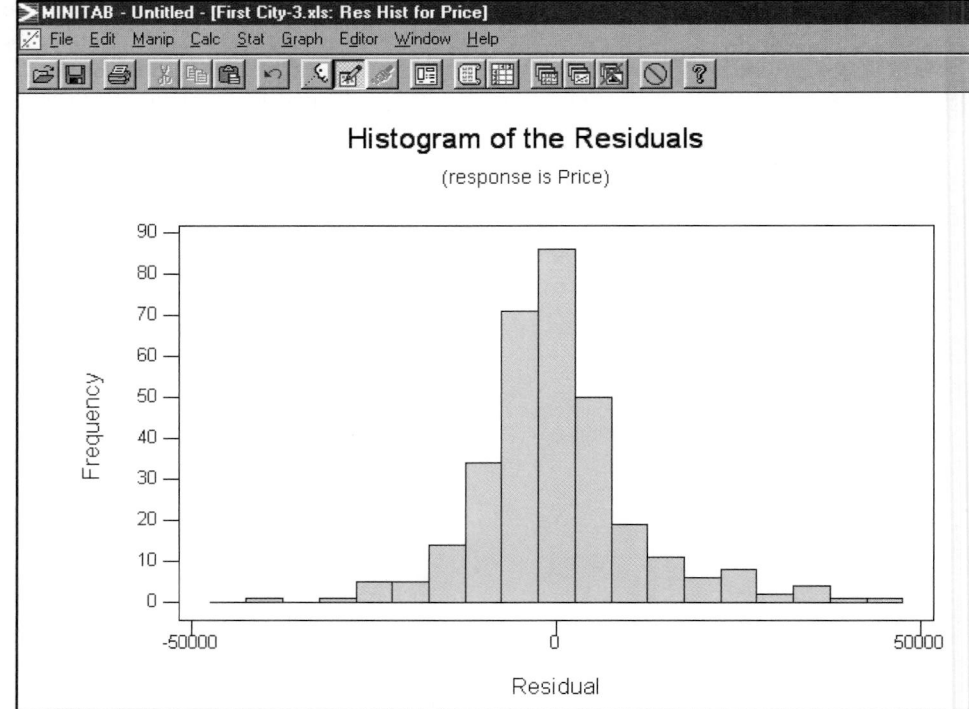

FIGURE 12-43
Minitab Histogram of
Residuals for First City Real
Estate

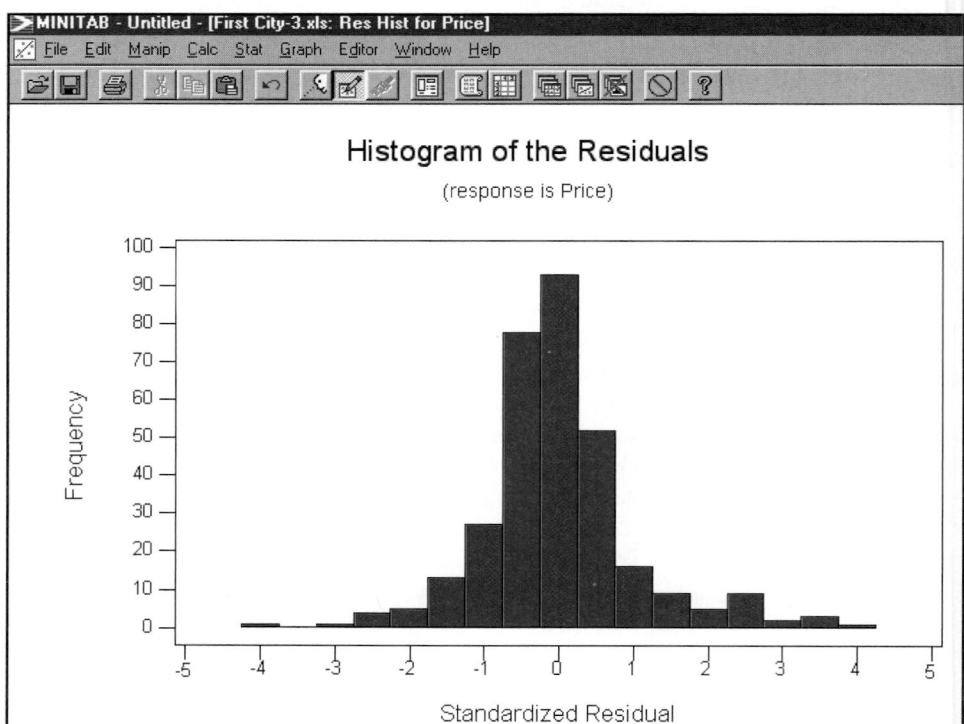

FIGURE 12-44
Minitab Histogram of
Standardized Residuals for
First City Real Estate

Minitab Instructions:

1. Open file: First City-3.mtw
2. Click on Stat
3. Click on Regression
4. Define Response (y) variable
5. Define Independent variables
6. Click on Graphs and select Normal plot of Residuals

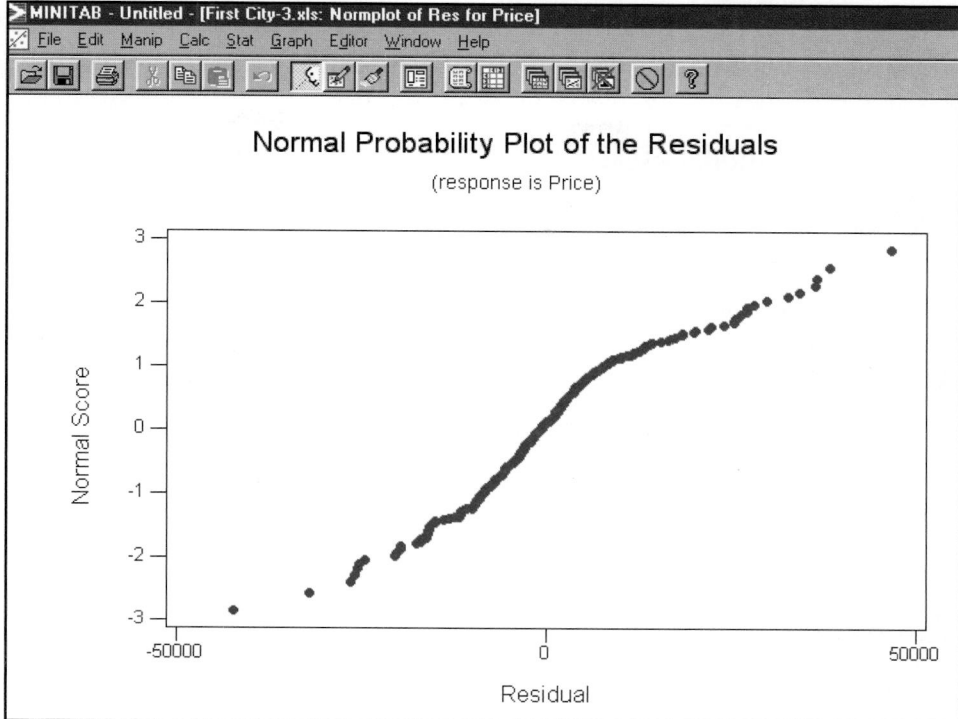

FIGURE 12-45
Minitab Normal Probability Plot of Residuals for First City Real Estate

You should be aware that Minitab and Excel format their residual plots slightly differently. However, the same general information is conveyed and you can look for the same signs of problems with the regression model.

Corrective Actions

If, based on analyzing the residuals, you decide the model constructed is not appropriate, but you still want a regression-based model, some corrective action may be warranted. There are three approaches that may work: transform some of the existing independent variables, remove some variables from the model, or start over in the development of the regression model.

Your CD-ROM contains an optional section discussing some basic approaches involved in variable transformation. The transformations of the independent variables (such as raising x to a power, taking the square root of x, or taking the log of x) are used to make the data better conform to a linear relationship. If your model suffers from both non-linearity and if the residuals have a nonconstant variance, you may want to transform both the independent and dependent variables. In cases where the normality assumption is not satisfied, transforming the dependent variable is often useful. In many instances, a log transformation works. In some instances a transformation involving the product of two independent variables will help. A more detailed discussion is beyond the scope of this text. However, you can read more about this subject in the Neter et al. reference listed at the end of the chapter.

The alternative of using a different regression model means that we respecify the model to include new independent variables or remove existing variables from the model. In most modeling situations, we are in a continual state of model respecification. We are always seeking to improve the regression model by finding new independent variables.

12-5: EXERCISES

ADDITIONAL EXERCISES ON YOUR CD-ROM

Try the ADDITIONAL EXERCISES and APPLICATION PROBLEMS on the CD-ROM.

Business Applications

12-30. The Western State Tourist Association gives out pamphlets, maps, and other tourist-related information to people who call a toll-free number and request the information. The association orders the packets of information from a document printing company and likes to have enough extras available to meet the immediate need without having too many sitting around taking up space. The marketing manager decided to develop a multiple regression model to be used in predicting the number of calls that will be received in the coming week. A random sample of 12 weeks is selected, with the following variables.

y = Number of calls
x_1 = Number of advertisements placed the previous week
x_2 = Number of calls received the previous week
x_3 = Number of airline tour bookings into western cities for the current week

The data are in the file called **Western States.**
a. Construct a multiple regression model using all three independent variables. Write a short report discussing the model.
b. Based on the appropriate residual plots, what can you conclude about the constant variance assumption? Discuss.
c. Based on the appropriate residual analysis, does it appear that the residuals are independent? Discuss.
d. Use an appropriate analysis of the residuals to determine whether the regression model meets the assumption of normally distributed error terms. Discuss.

12-31. The athletic director of State University is interested in developing a multiple regression model that might be used to explain the variation in attendance at football games at his school. A sample of 16 games was selected from home games played during the past 10 seasons. Data for the following factors were determined.

y = Game attendance
x_1 = Team win/loss percentage to date
x_2 = Opponent win/loss percentage to date
x_3 = Games played this season
x_4 = Temperature at game time

The sample data are in the file called **Football.**
a. Build a multiple regression model using all four independent variables. Write a short report that outlines the characteristics of this model.

b. Develop a table of residuals for this model. What is the average residual value? Why do you suppose it came out to this value? Discuss.
c. Based on the appropriate residual plot, what can you conclude about the constant variance assumption? Discuss.
d. Based on the appropriate residual analysis, does it appear that the model errors are independent? Discuss.
e. Can you conclude, based on the appropriate method of analysis, that the model error terms are approximately normally distributed?

12-32. Under what conditions is it desirable to plot the residuals against the predicted y values? Discuss.

12-33. In a multiple regression model, if we wish to determine whether the residuals have a constant variance, is it appropriate to plot the residuals against each x variable individually? If not, what should be done?

12-34. Charles Walters has been assigned to study paddy, an Indian grain, for a company looking to expand its grain market. He has researched the various characteristics of the grain. During his research he came across an article "Determination of Biological Maturity and Effect of Harvesting and Drying Conditions on Milling Quality of Paddy" (*J. of Ag. Engr. Research* (1975): 353–61). The article examines the relationship between y, the yield (kg/ha) of paddy as a function of x, the number of days after flowering at which harvesting took place. The data are in the file called **Paddy** and are shown as follows.

y	x	y	x
2,508	16	3,823	32
2,518	18	3,646	34
3,304	20	3,708	36
3,423	22	3,333	38
3,057	24	3,517	40
3,190	26	3,241	42
3,500	28	3,103	44
3,883	30	2,776	46

a. Fit a simple linear regression model to these data. Calculate the residuals associated with the resulting regression equation.
b. Plot the residuals against the independent variable. On the basis of this plot, determine if a linear function is the appropriate regression function to use for these data and if the residuals demonstrate a constant variance. Be sure to explain your answers using statistical concepts as support.

c. Whether you determined that a linear model is appropriate or had to select another model to fit the data, conduct a hypothesis test to determine if that model is significant.

12-35. Refer to Problem 34. Use a curvilinear model to fit the data.

a. Construct a scatter plot of the residuals versus the independent variable. Determine if the residuals possess a constant variance over the range of the values of the independent variable. Explain your answer using statistical reasoning.

b. Produce a histogram of the residuals. Based upon this histogram, do the residuals seem to possess a normal distribution? Explain your answer.

c. Determine the percent of the residuals that are: one standard deviation, two standard deviations, and three standard deviations from their mean. On this basis, do the residuals seem to possess a normal distribution? Explain your answer.

d. Produce a probability plot. Based upon this plot, do the residuals seem to possess a normal distribution? Explain your answer.

SUMMARY AND CONCLUSIONS

Multiple regression is an extension of simple regression analysis. In multiple regression, two or more independent variables are used to explain the variation in the dependent variable. Just as a manager searches for the best combination of employees to perform a job, the decision maker using multiple regression analysis searches for the best combination of independent variables to explain variation in the dependent variable.

The presentation of multiple regression analysis has largely been an analysis of computer printouts. As a decision maker, you will almost assuredly not be required to manually develop the regression model, but you will have to judge its applicability based on a computer printout. The Excel and Minitab software we have used in Chapters 11 and 12 are representative of the many software packages that are available. You no doubt will encounter printouts that look somewhat different from those shown in this text and some of the terms used may differ slightly. However, the basic information will be the same, as will be the inferences you can make from the model.

This chapter has discussed the difference between R^2 and adjusted R^2 as well as the difference between statistical significance and practical significance. As a decision maker, you must recognize that a regression model can be statistically significant yet have no practical use because the standard error of the estimate is too large or multicollinearity impacts too heavily.

As you continue your study of business you will find that multiple regression is one of the most widely used statistical tools. You will find it applied particularly to the areas of production, finance, accounting, and economics.

EQUATIONS

Simple Linear Regression Model

$$y = \beta_0 + \beta_1 x + \epsilon \qquad \text{12-1}$$

Estimated Simple Linear Regression Model

$$\hat{y} = b_0 + b_1 x \qquad \text{12-2}$$

Multiple Regression Model (Population Model)

$$y = \beta_0 + \beta_1 x_1 + \beta_2 x_2 + \cdots + \beta_k x_k + \epsilon \qquad \text{12-3}$$

Estimated Multiple Regression Model

$$\hat{y} = b_0 + b_1 x_1 + b_2 x_2 + \cdots + b_k x_k \qquad \text{12-4}$$

Correlation Coefficient

$$r = \frac{\sum (x - \bar{x})(y - \bar{y})}{\sqrt{\sum (x - \bar{x})^2 \sum (y - \bar{y})^2}}$$

or

$$r = \frac{\sum_{i=1}^{n}(x_{1i} - \bar{x}_1)(x_{2i} - \bar{x}_2)}{\sqrt{\sum_{i=1}^{n}(x_{1i} - \bar{x}_1)^2 \sum_{i=1}^{n}(x_{2i} - \bar{x}_2)^2}} \qquad \text{12-5}$$

Multiple Coefficient of Determination (R^2)

$$R^2 = \frac{\text{Sum of squares regression}}{\text{Total sum of squares}} = \frac{SSR}{TSS} \qquad \text{12-6}$$

F-Test Statistic

$$F = \frac{\dfrac{SSR}{k}}{\dfrac{SSE}{n - k - 1}} = \frac{MSR}{MSE} \qquad \text{12-7}$$

Adjusted R-Square

$$R\text{-sq(adj)} = R_A^2 = 1 - (1 - R^2)\left(\frac{n - 1}{n - k - 1}\right) \qquad \text{12-8}$$

t-Test for Significance of Each Regression Coefficient

$$t = \frac{b_i - 0}{s_{b_i}} \qquad \text{12-9}$$

Estimate for the Standard Deviation of the Model (Standard Error of the Estimate)

$$s_\epsilon = \sqrt{\frac{SSE}{n - k - 1}} = \sqrt{MSE} \qquad \text{12-10}$$

Variance Inflation Factor

$$VIF = \frac{1}{1 - R_j^2} \qquad \text{12-11}$$

Confidence Interval Estimate for the Regression Coefficient

$$b_i \pm t_{\alpha/2} s_{b_i} \qquad \text{12-12}$$

Polynomial Population Regression Model

$$y = \beta_0 + \beta_1 x_j + \beta_2 x_j^2 + \cdots + \beta_p x_j^p + \epsilon \qquad \text{12-13}$$

C_p Statistic

$$C_p = \frac{(1 - R_p^2)(n - T)}{1 - R_T^2} - (n - 2p) \qquad \text{12-14}$$

Residual

$$e = (y - \hat{y}) \qquad \text{12-15}$$

Standardized Residual

$$sr = \frac{e}{s_\epsilon \sqrt{1 + \dfrac{1}{n} + \dfrac{(x_p - \bar{x})^2}{\sum x^2 - \dfrac{(\sum x)^2}{n}}}} \qquad \text{12-16}$$

■ KEY TERMS

Adjusted *R*-Squared (R_A^2)—A measure of the percentage of explained variation in the dependent variable that takes into account the relationship between the number of cases and the number of independent variables in the regression model. Whereas R^2 will generally increase when an independent variable is added, adjusted R^2 will decrease if the added variable does not reduce the unexplained variation enough to offset the loss of degrees of freedom.

Aptness—The degree to which the regression model satisfies the following assumptions:
1. The relationship between the dependent and independent variables is linear.
2. The variance of the model errors is constant over the range of the values of the independent variables.
3. The model errors are independent from observation to observation.
4. The model errors are normally distributed.

Coefficient of Partial Determination—The measure of the marginal contribution of each independent variable, given that other independent variables are in the model.

Composite Model—The model that contains both the basic terms and the interactive terms.

Correlation Coefficient—A quantitative measure of the strength of the linear relationship between two variables. The correlation coefficient, *r*, ranges between −1.0 and +1.0.

Dummy Variables—Variables in a regression model that have two categories, valued 0 and 1. If a qualitative variable has *v* multiple categories, *v* − 1 dummy variables are formed to represent the qualitative variable in the analysis.

Interaction—The case in which one independent variable (such as x_2) affects the relationship between another independent variable (x_1) and a dependent variable (y).

Model—A representation of an actual system using either a physical or mathematical portrayal.

Multicollinearity—A high correlation between two independent variables such that the two variables contribute redundant information to the multiple regression model. When highly correlated independent variables are included in the regression model, they can adversely affect the regression results.

Multiple Coefficient of Determination (R^2)—The percentage of variation in the dependent variable explained by the independent variables in the regression model.

Multiple Regression Model for the Population—A regression model having two or more independent variables with a regression equation of the form:
$$y = \beta_0 + \beta_1 x_1 + \beta_2 x_2 + \cdots + \beta_k x_k + \epsilon$$

Polynomial Model—A model including independent variables with an exponent larger than one.

Residual (Prediction Error)—The difference between the actual value of *y* and the predicted value of *y*.

Second-Order Regression Model—A regression model in which the largest sum of the exponents of the independent variables in any one term of the model is 2.

Standard Error of the Estimate—The standard deviation of the model errors. The standard error measures the dispersion of the actual values of the dependent variable around the fitted regression plane.

Standardized Residual—The residual divided by an estimate of the residual's standard deviation.

Variance Inflation Factor—A measure of how much the variance of an estimated regression coefficient increases if the independent variables are correlated. A VIF equal to 1.0 for a given independent variable indicates that this independent variable is not correlated with the remaining independent variables in the model. The greater the multicollinearity, the larger the VIF will be.

CHAPTER EXERCISES

Conceptual Questions

12-36. Discuss in your own terms the similarities and differences between simple linear regression analysis and multiple regression analysis.

12-37. Discuss what is meant by the least squares criterion as it pertains to multiple regression analysis. Is the least squares criterion any different for simple regression analysis? Discuss.

12-38. List the basic assumptions of regression analysis, and discuss in your own terms what each means.

12-39. What does it mean if we have developed a multiple regression model and have concluded that the model is apt?

12-40. Go to the library, or use the Internet, to locate three articles using a regression model with more than one independent variable. For each article write a short summary covering the following points.
  • Purpose for using the model
  • How the variables in the model were selected
  • How the data in the model were selected
  • Any possible violations of the needed assumptions
  • The conclusions drawn from using the model

12-41. Select a company in your area that you think might use a regression model, and interview a decision maker in that company. If the company uses a regression model, outline its use. If the company does not use a regression model, discuss the alternate tools used.

12-42. A financial analyst for a Wall Street firm recently collected a random sample of 24 companies and recorded their year-end stock prices. He hopes to be able to develop a regression model that can be used to explain the variation in stock prices for these 24 firms. He plans on using financial ratios such as the debt/equity ratio as independent variables. What would you suggest to him as the maximum number of independent variables to use in the model? Discuss.

Business Applications

12-43. The managerial development director of a major corporation is trying to determine what personal abilities are necessary for a manager to move from middle- to upper-level management. Although she has been relatively successful predicting who will move rapidly from lower- to middle-management levels, she has had difficulty determining the characteristics necessary to move to the next major level. For a long time, the director has heard that the most glaring deficiency in college graduates entering the company is in communication skills, so she decides to measure whether these skills may be a determining factor.

The director decides to try to develop a multiple regression relationship between job ratings and communication ability. She picks a random sample of middle-level managers who have been in their present positions less than 5 years but more than 1 year. These managers are given a series of cases to analyze and asked to present both written and oral recommendations. They are rated by a group of top-level managers on their analyses and on their written and oral presentations. These ratings are then compared with the latest employee rating. The data are listed in the file called **Job Rating.**

Determine the multiple regression equation for these data. Write a report that summarizes the characteristics of the model.

12-44. Refer to Problem 43. One of the assumptions of multiple regression is that the independent variables are not correlated with each other. Is this assumption satisfied for these data? What do you check to see if multicollinearity is a problem? Use a significance level of 0.05.

12-45. Refer to Problem 44.
   a. Does the multiple regression model you have estimated show a significant relationship between job ratings and the three independent variables measured? How did you measure this significance? Test with a significance level of 0.05.
   b. If a middle manager were to ask you what he could do to best increase his chances of getting promoted, what would you respond?
   c. Reconsider the answer you gave in part b above. This individual wishes to know (at a 90% confidence level) what the maximum and minimum increase his job rating would realize if he increased the variable you indicated in part b by one unit. Provide this answer.

12-46. Referring to Problem 43, if you were a middle-level manager, would you be willing to have your job rating determined just on the basis of your performance on these three independent variables? Explain in statistical terms why or why not.

12-47. Referring to the regression model you developed in Problem 45, respond to each of the following.
   a. Discuss how much of the variation in job rating is explained by the three independent variables. How do you measure this factor?
   b. Are all the independent variables significant in your multiple regression relationship? How can you tell?
   c. As a test, the development director gives the same cases to a group of middle-level managers without knowing their job ratings. One of the managers received the following scores.

Case analysis	9.1
Written presentations	9.4
Verbal presentations	9.3

   Based on these data, what is the best estimate of the job rating this manager received?
   d. The personnel director comments that perhaps the regression model just developed would be a good tool to use before hiring new employees. What do you think of this idea?
   e. One manager who participated in this study is concerned with his job rating and would like to know how much his job rating should change if his written presentation score increased by a full point. You are to develop a 95% confidence interval for the regression coefficient for the independent variable, written presentation. Be sure to interpret this interval.

12-48. A publishing company in New York is attempting to develop a model that it can use to help predict sales for textbooks it is considering for future publication. The marketing department has collected data on several variables from a random sample of 15 books. These data are given in the file **Textbook.**
   a. Develop the correlation matrix showing the correlation between all possible pairs of variables.
   b. Test statistically to determine which independent variables are significantly correlated with the dependent variable, book sales. Use a significance level of 0.05.

12-49. Referring to Problem 48, develop a multiple regression model containing all four independent variables. Show clearly the regression coefficients. Write a short report discussing the model. In your report make sure you cover the following issues.
   a. How much of the total variation in book sales can be explained by these four independent variables? Would you conclude that the model is significant at the 0.05 level?
   b. Develop a 95% confidence interval for each regression coefficient and interpret these confidence intervals.
   c. Which of the independent variables can be concluded to be significant in explaining the variation in book sales? Test using an alpha level of 0.05.

d. How much, if any, does adding one more page to the book impact the sales volume of the book? Develop and interpret a 95% confidence interval estimate to answer this question.

e. Perform the appropriate analysis to determine the aptness of this regression model. Discuss your results and conclusions.

12-50. The publishing company in Problem 49 recently came up with some additional data for the 15 books in the original sample. Two new variables, production expenditures (x_5) and number of prepublication reviewers (x_6), have been added. These additional data are as follows.

BOOK	x_5	x_6	BOOK	x_5	x_6
1	$38,000	5	9	$51,000	4
2	86,000	8	10	34,000	6
3	59,000	3	11	20,000	2
4	80,000	9	12	80,000	5
5	29,500	3	13	60,000	5
6	31,000	3	14	87,000	8
7	40,000	5	15	29,000	3
8	69,000	4			

Calculate the correlation between each of these additional variables and the dependent variable, book sales. You will have to use the data from Problem 49. Then respond to each of the following statements in the form of a report to the chief editor.

a. Test the significance of the correlation coefficients using an alpha level of 0.05. Comment on your results.

b. Develop a multiple regression model that includes all six independent variables. Which, if any, variables would you recommend be retained if this model is going to be used to predict book sales for the publishing company? For any statistical test you might perform, use a significance level of 0.05. Discuss your results.

c. Use the analysis of variance approach to test the null hypothesis that all slope coefficients are 0. Test with a significance level of 0.05. What do these results mean? Discuss.

d. Do multicollinearity problems appear to be present in the model? Discuss the potential consequences of multicollinearity with respect to the regression model.

e. Discuss whether the standard error of the estimate is small enough to make this model useful for predicting the sales of textbooks.

f. Plot the residuals against the predicted value of y, and comment on what this plot means relative to the aptness of the model.

g. Compute the standardized residuals and form these into a frequency histogram. What does this indicate about the normality assumption?

h. Comment on the overall aptness of this model, and indicate what might be done to improve the model.

 The following information applies to Problems 51–60.

The J. J. McCracken Company has authorized its marketing research department to perform a study of customers who have been issued a McCracken charge card. The marketing research department hopes to be able to identify the significant variables that explain the variation in purchases. Once these variables are determined, the department intends to try to attract new customers who would be predicted to have a high volume of purchases.

Twenty-five customers were selected at random, and values for the following variables were recorded in the file called **McCracken**.

y = Average monthly purchases (in dollars) at McCracken
x_1 = Customer age
x_2 = Customer family income
x_3 = Family size

A first step in regression analysis often involves developing a scatter plot of the data. Develop the scatter plots of all the possible pairs of variables and, with a brief statement, indicate what each plot says about the relationship between the two variables.

12-51. Compute the correlation matrix for these data. Develop the decision rule for testing the significance of each coefficient. Which, if any, correlations are not significant? Use an alpha level of 0.05.

12-52. Use forward selection stepwise regression to develop the multiple regression model. The variable x_2, family income, was brought into the model. Discuss why this happened.

12-53. Test the significance of the regression model at step 1 of the computer printout. Justify the significance level you have selected.

12-54. Develop a 95% confidence level for the slope coefficient for the family income variable at step 1 of the model. Be sure to interpret this confidence interval.

12-55. Describe the regression model at step 2 of the analysis. In your discussion, be sure to discuss the effect of adding a new variable on the standard error of the estimate and on R^2.

12-56. Referring to Problem 55, suppose the manager of McCracken's marketing department questions the appropriateness of adding a second variable. How would you respond to her question?

12-57. Look at the third and final step of the regression analysis. (1) Test statistically the significance of each independent variable in the model at an alpha level of 0.05. (2) Also test the hypothesis that all slope coefficients are 0 at the alpha level of 0.05. (3) Why can the overall model be significant while some individual variables are not significant?

12-58. Looking carefully at the stepwise regression model, you can see that the value of the slope coefficient for variable x_2, family income, changes each time a new variable is added to the regression model. Discuss why this change takes place.

12-59. Analyze the regression model at step 3 and the intermediate results at steps 1 and 2. Write a report to the marketing manager pointing out the strengths and weaknesses of the model. Be sure to comment on the department's goal of being able to use the model to predict customers who will purchase high volumes from McCracken.

12-60. Plot the residuals against the predicted values of y and comment on what this plot means relative to the aptness of the model.

a. Compute the standardized residuals and graph these in a frequency histogram. What does this indicate about the normality assumption?

b. Comment on the overall aptness of this model and indicate what might be done to improve the model.

12-61. Refer to the State Department of Transportation data set called **Liabins.** The department was interested in determining the rate of compliance with the state's mandatory liability insurance law as well as other things. Assume the data were collected using a simple random sampling process. Develop the best possible linear regression model using vehicle year as the dependent variable and any or all of the other variables as potential independent variables. Assume that your objective is to develop a predictive model. Write a report that discusses the steps you took to develop the final model. Include a correlation matrix and all appropriate statistical tests. Use an $\alpha = 0.05$. If you are using a nominal or ordinal variable, remember that you must make sure it is in the form of one or more dummy variables.

12-62. Refer to Problem 61. Develop the best possible linear regression model using number of years of formal education as the dependent variable and any or all of the other variables as potential independent variables. Assume that your objective is to develop a predictive model. Write a report that discusses the steps you took to develop the final model. Include a correlation matrix and all appropriate statistical tests. Use an $\alpha = 0.05$. If you are using a nominal or ordinal variable, remember that you must make sure it is in the form of one or more dummy variables.

12-63. Refer to the data file called **Cities** in which an economist from a major east coast bank has collected data on major cities in the United States.

a. Develop a correlation matrix for all relevant variables with the Labor Market Stress Index as the dependent variable, and write a short report that discusses the correlation results. Be sure to indicate which potential independent variables appear to have the most promise in the model.

b. Develop a multiple regression model that would allow you to predict the labor market stress index based on the other variables in the database. (Note: Be careful about the SAT/ACT variables.)

c. Bring all the relevant independent variables into the model at one time. Show the model, including the intercept and regression coefficients. Look at the signs on the coefficients and indicate which, if any, seem to have inappropriate signs. Discuss.

d. Is the overall model significant? State clearly the null and alternative hypotheses and show your test procedure. Test at the $\alpha = 0.05$ level. Discuss.

e. What is the coefficient of determination? Does the model explain a significant proportion of the variation in the dependent variable? Test at an $\alpha = 0.05$ level.

f. Test each of the regression slope coefficients individually to determine which variables are significant in the model. Test at an $\alpha = 0.05$ level. Write a short report describing your results.

12-64. Referring to Problem 63, use forward stepwise regression to develop the regression model using appropriate independent variables. Write a complete report describing step-by-step what took place as the variables were entered into the model. Be sure to indicate what, if any, evidences of multicollinearity are present in the model. In your analysis, perform any appropriate tests of significance. Would you recommend that this model be used to predict a city's labor market stress index? Explain.

12-65. The objective set forth in a recent staff meeting at D. L. Green & Associates is to develop a regression model for predicting company stock price. The database called **FAST100** contains data on several potential independent variables. Construct a correlation matrix that shows the correlation between the independent variables and the dependent variable and between all possible pairs of independent variables. Write a report that discusses the correlation matrix. Which variables appear to have most promise as predictors of stock price? Discuss.

12-66. Referring to Problem 65, observe the coded variable indicating on which stock exchange the company's stock is traded. Can this variable be used directly as it is or will you need to make some modification? If so, what is that modification, and why are you making it? Given that a modification is necessary, make the modification and determine the correlation between the new variable(s) and the dependent variable. Discuss.

12-67. Referring to Problems 65 and 66, develop a multiple regression model with stock price as the dependent variable. Bring in all appropriate independent variables.

a. Identify the regression model including the intercept and slope coefficients. Comment on whether these coefficients look reasonable given the correlations in Problems 65 and 66. Discuss.

b. Is the overall model significant? State clearly the null and alternative hypotheses and show your test procedure. Test at the $\alpha = 0.10$ level. Discuss.

c. What is the coefficient of determination? Does the model explain a significant proportion of the variation in the dependent variable? Test at an $\alpha = 0.10$ level.

d. Test each of the regression slope coefficients individually to determine which variables are significant in the model. Test at an $\alpha = 0.10$ level. Write a short report describing your results.

12-68. Referring to Problem 67, use forward stepwise regression to develop the regression model using appropriate independent variables. Write a complete report describing step-by-step what took place as the variables were entered into the model. Be sure to indicate what, if any, evidence of multicollinearity is present in the model. In your analysis, perform any appropriate tests of significance. Would you recommend that this model be used as a predictive tool? Explain.

CASE 12-A

Dynamic Scales, Inc.

In 1985, Stanley Ahlon and three financial partners formed Dynamic Scales, Inc. The company was based on an idea Stanley had for developing a scale to weigh trucks in motion and thus eliminate the need for every truck to stop at weigh stations along highways. This dynamic scale would be placed in the highway approximately one-quarter mile from the regular weigh station. The scale would have a minicomputer that would automatically record truck speed, axle weights, and climate variables, including temperature, wind, and moisture. Stanley Ahlon and his partners believed that state transportation departments in the United States would be the primary market for such a scale.

Like many technological advances, developing the dynamic scale has been difficult. When the scale finally proved accurate for trucks traveling 40 miles per hour, it would not perform for trucks traveling at higher speeds. However, 8 months ago, Stanley announced that the dynamic scale was ready to be field-tested by the Nebraska State Department of Transportation under a grant from the federal government. Stanley explained to his financial partners, and to Nebraska transportation officials, that the dynamic weight would not exactly equal the static weight (truck weight on a static scale). However, he was sure a statistical relationship between dynamic weight and static weight could be determined, which would make the dynamic scale useful.

Nebraska officials, along with people from Dynamic Scales, Inc., installed a dynamic scale on a major highway in Nebraska. Each month for 6 months, data were collected for a random sample of trucks weighed on both the dynamic scale and a static scale. Table 12-6 presents these data.

Once the data were collected, the next step was to determine whether, based on this test, the dynamic scale measurements could be used to predict static weights. A complete report will be submitted to the U.S. government and to Dynamic Scales, Inc.

TABLE 12-6
Test Data for the Dynamic Scales Example

MONTH	FRONT-AXLE STATIC WEIGHT	FRONT-AXLE DYNAMIC WEIGHT	TRUCK SPEED	TEMPERA-TURE	MOISTURE
January	1,800 lb	1,625 lb	52 mph	21° F	0.00%
	1,311	1,904	71	17	0.15
	1,504	1,390	48	13	0.40
	1,388	1,402	50	19	0.10
	1,250	1,100	61	24	0.00
February	2,102	1,950	55	26	0.10
	1,410	1,475	58	32	0.20
	1,000	1,103	59	38	0.15
	1,430	1,387	43	24	0.00
	1,073	948	59	18	0.40
March	1,502	1,493	62	34	0.00
	1,721	1,902	67	36	0.00
	1,113	1,415	48	42	0.21
	978	983	59	29	0.32
	1,254	1,149	60	48	0.00
April	994	1,052	58	37	0.00
	1,127	999	52	34	0.21
	1,406	1,404	59	40	0.40
	875	900	47	48	0.00
	1,350	1,275	68	51	0.00
May	1,102	1,120	55	52	0.00
	1,240	1,253	57	57	0.00
	1,087	1,040	62	63	0.00
	993	1,102	59	62	0.10
	1,408	1,400	67	68	0.00
June	1,420	1,404	58	70	0.00
	1,808	1,790	54	71	0.00
	1,401	1,396	49	83	0.00
	933	1,004	62	88	0.40
	1,150	1,127	64	81	0.00

■ GENERAL REFERENCES

1. Berenson, Mark L., and David M. Levine, *Basic Business Statistics: Concepts and Applications,* 7th ed. (Upper Saddle River, NJ: Prentice Hall, 1999).

2. Bowerman, Bruce L., and Richard T. O'Connell, *Linear Statistical Models: An Applied Approach,* 2d ed. (Belmont, CA: Duxbury Press, 1990).

3. Cryer, Jonathan D., and Robert B. Miller, *Statistics for Business: Data Analysis and Modeling,* 2d ed. (Belmont, CA: Duxbury Press, 1994).

4. Demmert, Henry, and Marshall Medoff, "Game Specific Factors and Major League Baseball Attendance: An Econometric Study." *Santa Clara Business Review* (1977): 49–56.

5. Draper, Norman R., and Harry Smith, *Applied Regression Analysis,* 3d ed. (New York: John Wiley & Sons, 1998).

6. Frees, Edward W., *Data Analysis Using Regression Models: The Business Perspective* (Englewood Cliffs, NJ: Prentice Hall, 1996).

7. Gloudemans, Robert J., and Dennis Miller, "Multiple Regression Analysis Applied to Residential Properties." *Decision Sciences* 7 (April 1976): 294–304.

8. Kleinbaum, David G., Lawrence L. Kupper, Keith E. Muller, and Azhar Nizam, *Applied Regression Analysis and Other Multivariable Methods,* 3d ed. (Belmont, CA: Duxbury Press, 1998).

9. *Microsoft Excel 2000* (Redmond, WA: Microsoft Corporation, 1999).

10. *Minitab for Windows Version 13* (State College, PA: Minitab, Inc., 2000).

11. Neter, John, Michael H. Kutner, Christopher J. Nachtsheim, and William Wasserman, *Applied Linear Statistical Models,* 4th ed. (Homewood, IL: Richard D. Irwin, 1996).

CHAPTER 13

INTRODUCTION TO QUALITY AND STATISTICAL PROCESS CONTROL

CHAPTER OUTCOMES

After studying the material in Chapter 13, you should be able to:

13-1: Use the seven basic tools of quality.

13-2: Construct and interpret $\bar{x}$ and R charts.

13-3: Construct and interpret p-charts.

13-4: Construct and interpret c-charts.

WHY YOU NEED TO KNOW

Organizations across the United States and around the world have turned to quality management in an effort to meet the competitive challenges of the international marketplace. Although there is no set approach for implementing quality management, a commonality among most organizations is for employees at all levels to be brought into the effort as members of process improvement teams.

Successful organizations, such as Motorola and Hewlett-Packard, realize that thrusting people together in teams and then expecting process improvement to occur will generally lead to disappointment. They know that their employees need to understand how to work together as a team. In many instances, teams are formed to improve a process so that product or service quality is enhanced. However, teamwork and team building must be combined with training and education in the proper tools if employees are to be successful at making lasting process improvements. Over the past several decades a

number of techniques and methods for process improvement have been developed and used by organizations. As a group, these are referred to as the *Tools of Quality*. Many of these tools are based on statistical procedures and data analysis.

By now you have come across a number of *Tools of Quality* sections in this text. These short sections were included to illustrate how the statistical concepts in this text apply in a quality improvement setting. However, one set of quality tools known as *statistical process control charts* is so prevalent in business today, and is so closely linked to the material in Chapters 6–9, that its coverage merits a separate chapter. Today, successful managers must have an appreciation of, and a familiarity with, the role of quality in process improvement activities. This chapter is designed to introduce you to the fundamental tools and techniques of quality management and how to construct and interpret statistical process control charts.

13-1: QUALITY MANAGEMENT AND TOOLS FOR PROCESS IMPROVEMENT

From the end of World War II through about the mid-1970s, industry in the United States was kept busy meeting a pent-up demand for its products both at home and abroad. The emphasis in most companies was on getting the "product out the door." The U.S. effort to produce large quantities of goods and services led to less emphasis on quality. During this same time, Dr. W. Edwards Deming and Dr. Joseph Juran were consulting with Japanese business leaders to help them rebuild Japan's economy following World War II. Deming, a statistician, and Juran, an engineer, emphasized that quality was the key to being competitive and that quality could be best achieved by improving the processes that produced the products and delivered the services.

Employing the process improvement approach was a slow, but effective, method for improving quality, and by the early 1970s, Japanese products began to exceed those of the United States in terms of quality. The impact was felt by entire industries such as automobiles and electronics. While Juran focused on quality planning and helping businesses drive costs down by eliminating waste in processes, Deming preached a new management philosophy which has become known as **total quality management**, or TQM. There are about as many definitions of TQM as there are companies who have attempted to implement it. A representative definition and one that has been used by Hewlett-Packard beginning in the early 1980s is:

> **TOTAL QUALITY MANAGEMENT**
> A journey to excellence in which everyone in the organization is focused on continuous process improvement directed toward increased customer satisfaction.

In the early 1980s, U.S. business leaders began to realize the competitive importance of providing high quality products and services, and a *quality revolution* was underway in the United States. Deming's 14 points (see Table 13-1) reflected a new philosophy of management that emphasized the importance of leadership. The numbers attached to each point

1. Create a constancy of purpose toward the improvement of products and services in order to become competitive, stay in business, and provide jobs.
2. Adopt the new philosophy. Management must learn that it is a new economic age and awaken to the challenge, learn their responsibilities, and take on leadership for change.
3. Stop depending on inspection to achieve quality. Build in quality from the start.
4. Stop awarding contracts on the basis of low bids.
5. Improve continuously and forever the system of production and service to improve quality and productivity, and thus constantly reduce costs.
6. Institute training on the job.
7. Institute leadership. The purpose of leadership should be to help people and technology work better.
8. Drive out fear so that everyone may work effectively.
9. Break down barriers between departments so that people can work as a team.
10. Eliminate slogans, exhortations, and targets for the workforce. They create adversarial relationships.
11. Eliminate quotas and management by objectives. Substitute leadership.
12. Remove barriers that rob employees of their pride of workmanship.
13. Institute a vigorous program of education and self-improvement.
14. Make the transformation everyone's job and put everyone to work on it.

TABLE 13-1
Deming's 14 Points

do not indicate an order of importance to the points; rather the 14 points collectively are seen as necessary steps to becoming a world-class company.

Juran's role in the quality movement is virtually on a par with Deming's. Juran is noted for many contributions to TQM, including his 10 steps to quality improvement outlined in Table 13-2. Note that Juran and Deming differed with respect to the use of goals and targets. Juran is also credited with applying the **Pareto principle** to quality.

PARETO PRINCIPLE
80% of the trouble comes from 20% of the causes.

Juran urges managers to use the Pareto principle to focus on the *vital few* sources of problems and to separate the vital few from the trivial many. The Pareto chart discussed in Chapter 2 is used to display data in a way that helps managers find the most urgent problems.

There are numerous other individuals who played significant roles in the quality movement. Among these are Philip B. Crosby, who is probably best known for his book, *Quality Is Free*, in which he emphasized that in the long run, the costs of improving quality are more than offset by the reductions in waste, rework, returns, and unsatisfied customers. Kauro Ishikawa is credited with developing and popularizing the application of the *fishbone diagram* that we will discuss shortly in the section on the Basic 7 Tools of Quality. There is also the work of Masaaki Imai, who popularized the philosophy of *kaizen*, or people-based continuous improvement.

TABLE 13-2
Juran's 10 Steps to Quality
Improvement

1. Build awareness of both the need for improvement and the opportunity for improvement.
2. Set goals for improvement.
3. Organize to meet the goals that have been set.
4. Provide training.
5. Implement projects aimed at solving problems.
6. Report progress.
7. Give recognition.
8. Communicate the results.
9. Keep score.
10. Maintain momentum by building improvement into the company's regular systems.

Finally, we must not overlook the contributions of many different managers at companies such as Hewlett-Packard, General Electric, Motorola, and Federal Express. These leaders synthesized and applied many different quality ideas and concepts to their organizations in order to create world-class corporations. By sharing their successes with other firms they have inspired and motivated others to continually seek opportunities where the tools of quality can be applied to improve business processes.

The Tools of Quality for Process Improvement

Once U.S. managers realized that their businesses were engaged in a competitive battle with companies around the world, they reacted in many ways. Some managers ignored the challenge and continued to see their market presence erode. Other managers realized that they needed a system or approach for improving their firm's operations and processes. The **Deming Cycle** illustrated in Figure 13-1 has been effectively used by many organizations as a guide to their quality improvement efforts. While seemingly simple, there are at least two rather profound implications to the Deming Cycle. The first is that improvement efforts are the result of a logical process: An improvement plan must be developed, then it has to be implemented and appropriate data gathered. The data must be studied and analyzed, and finally some overall action must be taken based on the results of the study. The second implication is that this is a continual process. Once an action is taken based on the results of one improvement effort, another is planned.

Over time a collection of tools and techniques known as the *Basic 7 Tools* have been developed for quality and process improvement. Figure 13-2 illustrates a problem-solving process and shows the steps for which the tools of quality are useful. Some of these tools have already been introduced at various points throughout this text in the Tools of Quality sections. However, we will briefly discuss all Basic 7 Tools in this section. Section 13-2 will explore one of these tools, statistical process control charts (SPC), in greater depth.

PROCESS FLOWCHARTS

A flowchart is a diagram that illustrates the steps in a process. Figure 13-3 illustrates an example of a company's mail distribution process. Flowcharts provide a visualization of the process and are a good beginning point in planning a process improvement effort. A flow-

FIGURE 13-1
The Deming Cycle

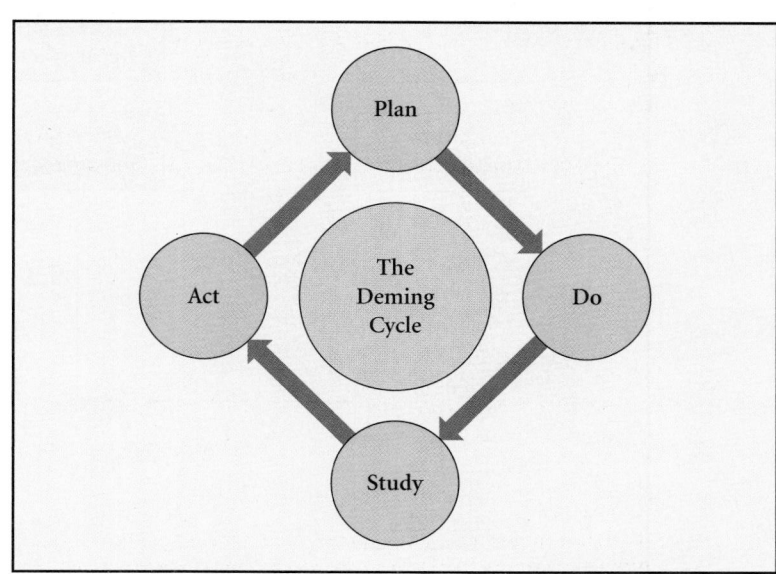

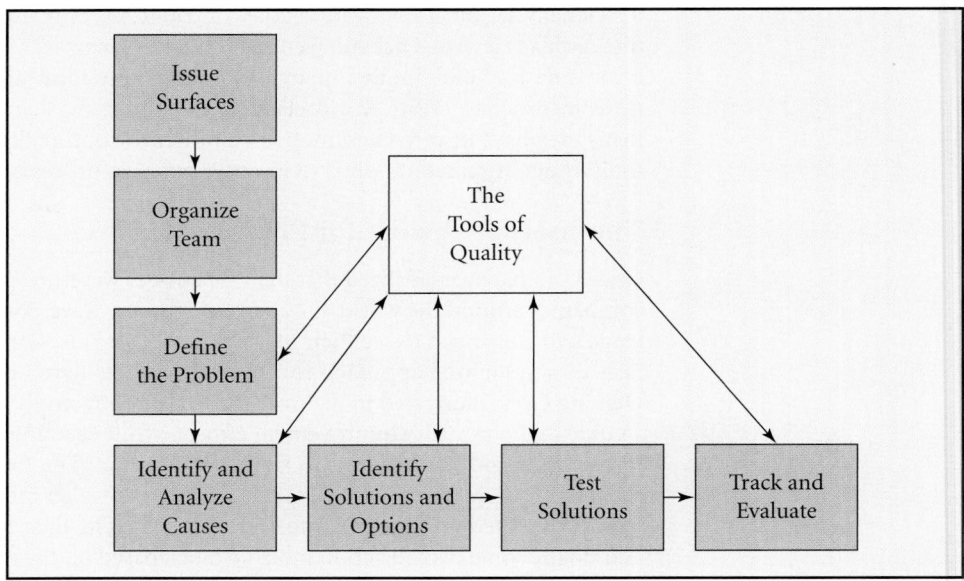

FIGURE 13-2
A Problem Solving Process

chart can be used to understand the current process and to identify opportunities for improvement.

BRAINSTORMING

One of the key components of most organizations' quality efforts is that everyone on an improvement team should contribute. Brainstorming is a tool that is used to generate ideas from the members of the process improvement team. Employees are encouraged to share any idea that comes to mind and all ideas are listed with no ideas being evaluated until all ideas are posted. Brainstorming can be either structured or unstructured. In structured brainstorming members of the team are asked for their ideas, in order, around the table.

FIGURE 13-3
A Flowchart of Mail
Distribution

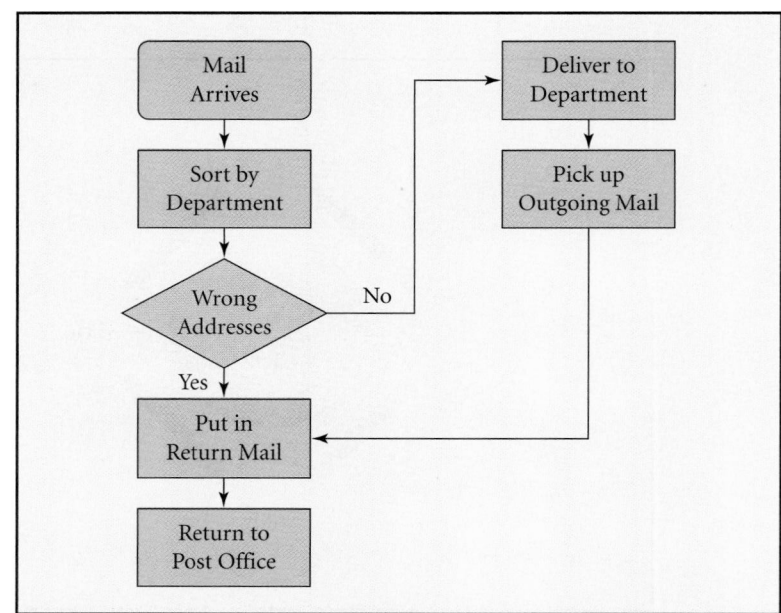

Members may pass if they have no further ideas. With unstructured brainstorming, members are free to interject ideas at any point. The *nominal group technique* is a specific type of brainstorming that follows five steps.

1. State the problem
2. Silently record ideas
3. Publicly record all ideas
4. Clarify ideas as needed
5. Silently vote on ideas

Regardless of the brainstorming method, team members can vote to determine which ideas to study further.

FISHBONE DIAGRAMS

Kauro Ishikawa from Japan is credited with developing the fishbone diagram, also called the cause-and-effect diagram or the Ishikawa diagram. The fishbone diagram can be applied as a simple graphical brainstorming tool in which the team members are given the problem and several categories of possible causes. They then brainstorm possible causes in any or all of the cause categories. Figure 13-4 illustrates an example in which a window manufacturer had a wobbly saw blade on one of its saws. For each of the four main areas of possible cause shown in Figure 13-4, the team has identified several potential issues that might affect the saw blade performance.

HISTOGRAMS

You were introduced to histograms in Chapter 2 as a method for graphically displaying quantitative data. Recall that histograms are useful for seeing the center, spread, and shape of a distribution of measurements. As a tool of quality, histograms are used to display

FIGURE 13-4
Fishbone Diagram for the Saw Blade

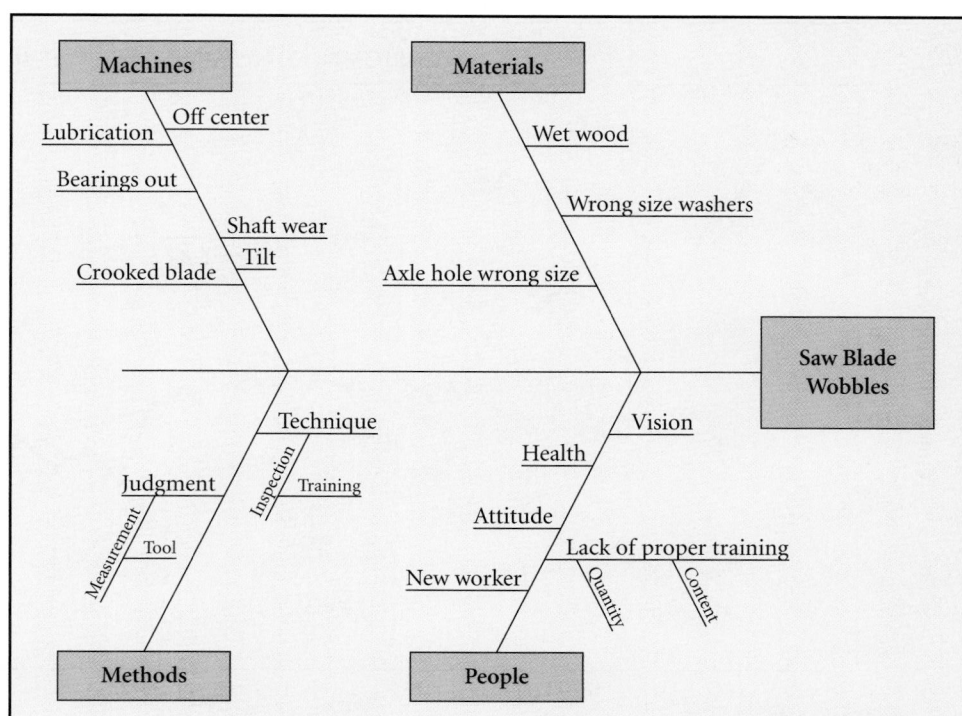

measurements to determine whether the output of a process is centered on the target value and whether the process is capable of meeting specifications.

TREND CHARTS

In Chapter 2 we illustrated the use of a line chart to display time series data. A trend chart is a line chart that is used to track output from a process over time. Figure 13-5 shows a trend chart from a major hotel chain that tracks the number of customer complaints on a daily basis. With a trend chart, the hotel managers can determine whether their training and service quality efforts are resulting in the desired downward trend in complaints.

SCATTER PLOTS

There are many instances in quality improvement efforts where you will want to examine the relationship between two quantitative variables. A scatter plot is an excellent tool for doing this. You were first introduced to scatter plots in Section 2-4 in Chapter 2. You also encountered scatter plots in Chapter 11 on regression and correlation analysis. Figure 13-6 shows an example where the hotel chain manager from the previous trend line example has graphed the number of complaints received on the vertical axis and the number of labor hours incurred by the hotels in the study. The managers are interested in determining whether complaints go down when the hotels have more service personnel working. The scatter plot shows a plot of the joint values of complaints and labor hours each day. No apparent relationship exists between the two variables.

STATISTICAL PROCESS CONTROL CHARTS

One of the most frequently used Basic 7 Tools is the statistical process control chart. SPC charts are a special type of trend chart. In addition to the data, the charts display the

FIGURE 13-5   Trend Chart of Hotel Customer Complaints

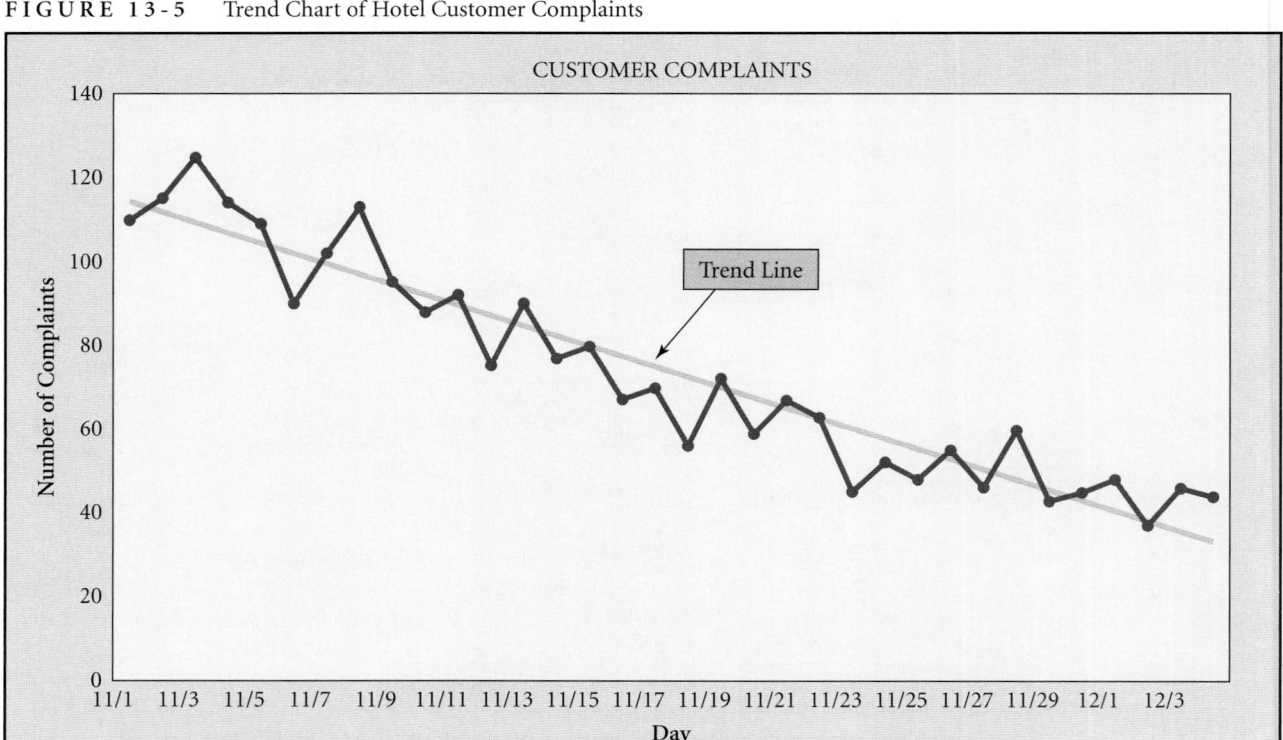

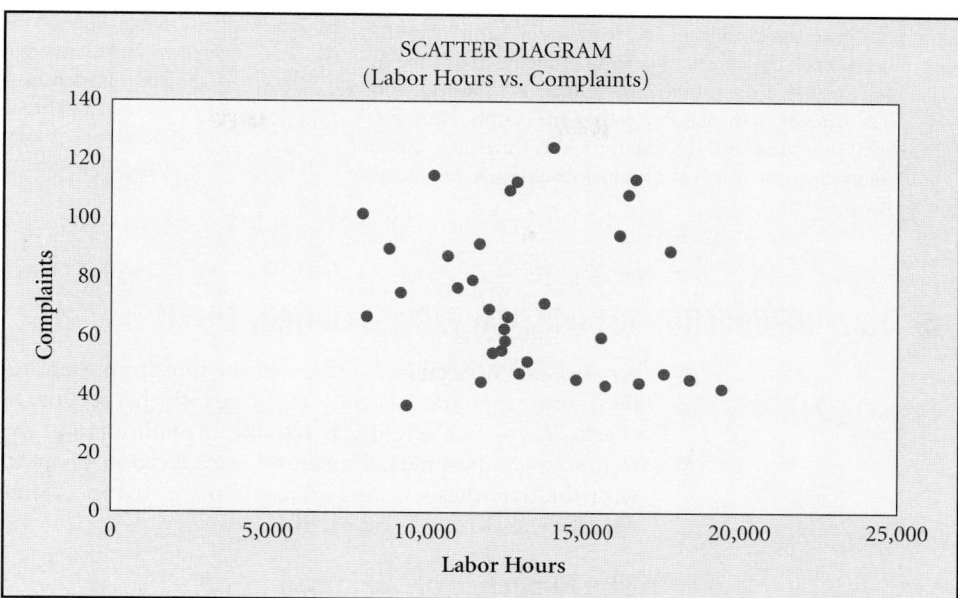

FIGURE 13-6
Scatter Plot for the Hotel
Chain

process average and the upper and lower control limits. These control limits define the range of random variation expected in the output of a process. SPC charts are used to provide early warnings when a process has gone out of control. There are several types of control charts depending on the type of data generated by the process of interest. Section 13-2 presents an introductory discussion of why control charts work and how to develop and interpret some of the most commonly used SPC charts.

Most organizations (public and private) in the United States and the developed countries of the world are involved in some form of quality improvement effort. Companies that are not will not likely survive in the competitive global marketplace that exists today. Statistics plays a key role in the efforts of organizations to improve their quality. You will have the opportunity to use the techniques presented in this chapter and throughout this text as you help your organization meet its quality challenges.

13-1: EXERCISES

13-1. Discuss the similarities and differences between Dr. Deming's 14 points and Dr. Juran's 10 steps to quality improvement.

13-2. Deming is opposed to setting quotas or specific targets for workers.
    a. Use the library or the Internet to locate information that explains his reasoning.
    b. Discuss whether you agree or disagree with him.
    c. If possible cite one or more examples based on your own experience to support your position.

13-3. Philip Crosby wrote the book, *Quality Is Free*. In it he argues that it is possible to have high quality and low price. Do you agree? Provide examples that support your position.

13-4. Develop a process flowchart that describes the registration process at your college or university.

13-5. Generate a process flowchart showing the steps you have to go through to buy a concert ticket at your school.

13-6. Assume that you are a member of a team at your university charged with the task of improving student, faculty, and staff parking. Use brainstorming to generate a list of problems with the current parking plan. After you have generated the list, prioritize the list of problems. (What criteria are you using to prioritize?)

13-7. Refer to Problem 6.
    a. Use brainstorming to generate a list of solutions for the top-rated parking problem.
    b. Order these possible solutions according to each of the following factors: cost to implement, time to implement, easiest to gain approval.
    c. Did your lists come out in a different order? Why?

13-8. Suppose the computer lab manager at your school has been receiving complaints from students about the long wait to use a computer. The "effect" is long wait times. The categories of possible causes are people, equipment, methods/rules, and the environment. Develop a fishbone diagram containing your brainstormed ideas for causes of the problem.

13-9. The city bus line is consistently running behind schedule. Develop a fishbone diagram showing the possible causes organized by such cause categories as people, methods, equipment, and the environment. Once you have finished, develop a priority order based on which cause is most likely to be the root cause of the problem.

■ 13-2: INTRODUCTION TO STATISTICAL PROCESS CONTROL CHARTS

As we stated in Section 13-1, one of the most important tools for quality improvement is the *statistical process control* (SPC) chart. In this section we provide an overview of SPC charts. As you will see, SPC is actually an application of hypothesis testing. The graphical techniques and numerical measures introduced in Chapters 2 and 3 respectively, together with the hypothesis testing concepts presented in Chapter 8, provide the background needed to understand and use SPC.

The Existence of Variation

After having studied the material in Chapters 1-12, you should be well aware of the importance of variation in business decision-making. **Inherent variation** exists naturally in the world around us. In any process or activity, the day-to-day outcomes are generally different—rarely are they exactly the same. As a practical example, think about the time it takes you to travel to your university each morning. Suppose it's about a 15-minute trip, and even though you travel the same route, your actual time will vary somewhat from day to day. You will notice variation in many daily occurrences. The next time you renew your car license plates, notice some people seem to get through faster than others. The same is true at a bank where the time to cash your payroll check varies each payday.

> **INHERENT VARIATION**
> The variation in the output of a process that exists naturally. This variation can be reduced but not eliminated.

Even in instances when variation is hard to detect, it is present. For example, when you measure a stack of $4' \times 8'$ sheets of plywood using a tape measure they are all 4 feet wide. However, when the stack is measured using an engineer's scale you may be able to detect slight variations among sheets, and using a caliper you can detect even more variation (see Figure 13-7).

So, three concepts to remember about variation are:

1. Variation is natural; it is inherent in the world around us.
2. No two products or service experiences are exactly the same.
3. With a fine enough gauge, all things can be seen to differ.

SOURCES OF VARIATION

What causes variation? Variation in the output of a process comes from variation in the inputs to the process. Let's go back to your travel time to school. Why isn't it always exactly the same? Your travel time depends on many factors, such as what route you take, how much traffic you encounter, whether or not you are in a hurry, how your car is running, etc.

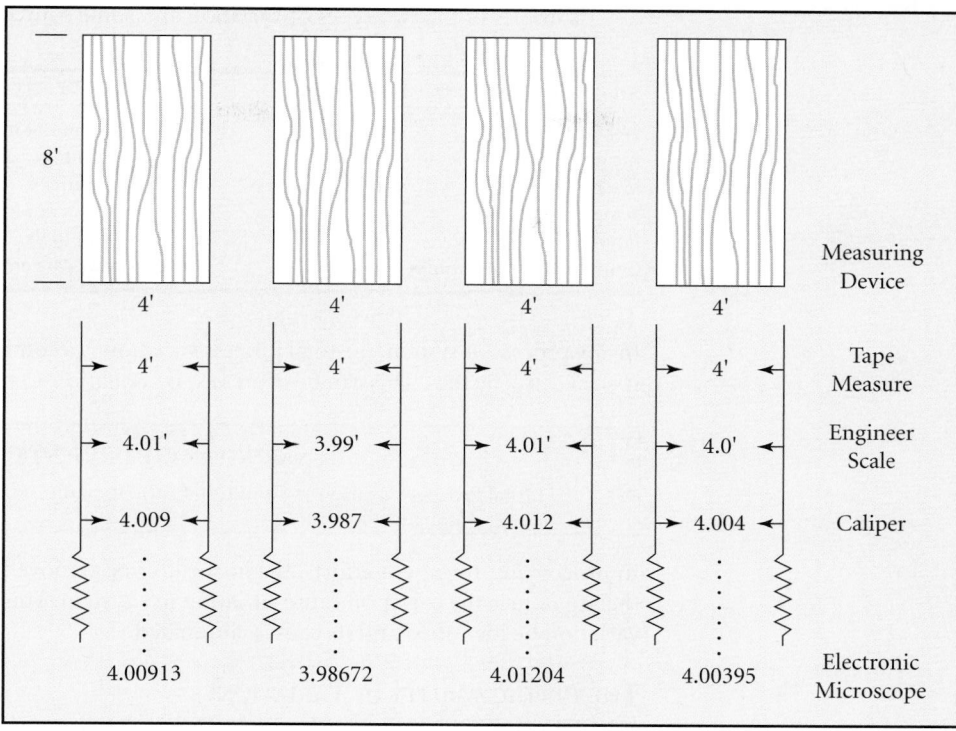

FIGURE 13-7
Plywood Variation

The six most common sources of variation are:

1. People
2. Machines
3. Materials
4. Methods
5. Measurement
6. Environment

TYPES OF VARIATION

While variation is always present, we can define two major types that occur. The first is called **common cause variation**. Other terms people use for common cause variation include normal, random, chance occurrence, inherent, and stable variation.

> **COMMON CAUSE VARIATION**
> Variation in the output of a process that is naturally occurring and expected and that may be the result of natural variation in materials, tools, machines, operators, and the environment.

The other type of variation is called **special cause variation**. This type of variation is also called nonrandom, unstable, and assignable cause variation.

In our example of travel time to school there are common causes of variation such as traffic lights, traffic patterns, weather, departure time, etc. On the days when it takes you significantly more or less time to arrive at school there are also special causes of variation occurring. These may be factors such as accidents, road construction detours, needing to stop for gas, etc.

> **SPECIAL CAUSE VARIATION**
> Variation in the output of a process that is abnormal or unexpected and which has an assignable cause. Variation in the output that is beyond that which is considered inherent to the process.

Examples of the two types of variation and some sources are given as follows.

SOURCES OF COMMON CAUSE VARIATION	SOURCES OF SPECIAL CAUSE VARIATION
Weather conditions	Equipment not maintained and cleaned
Inconsistent work methods	Poor training
Machine wear	Worker fatigue
Temperature	Procedures not followed
Employee skill levels	Misuse of tools
Computer response times	Incorrect data entry

In any process or system, the total process variation is a combination of common cause and special cause factors. This can be expressed by Equation 13-1.

VARIATION COMPONENTS

Total Process Variation = Common Cause Variation + Special Cause Variation   **13-1**

In process improvement efforts, the goal is to first remove the special cause variation and then to reduce the common cause variation in a system. This requires that the source of the variation be identified and its causes eliminated.

THE PREDICTABILITY OF VARIATION: UNDERSTANDING THE NORMAL DISTRIBUTION

Dr. W. Edwards Deming said there is no such thing as consistency. However there is such a thing as a *constant-cause system*. A system that contains only common cause variation is very predictable. Though the outputs vary, they exhibit an important feature called stability. This means that some percentage of the output will continue to lie within given limits hour after hour, day after day, so long as the constant-cause system is operating. When a process exhibits stability, it is in control.

The outputs vary in a predictable manner because measurable data, when subgrouped and pictured in a histogram, tend to cluster around the average and spread out symmetrically on both sides. This tendency is a function of the central limit theorem which you first encountered in Chapter 6. This means that the frequency distribution of most stable processes will begin to resemble the shape of the normal distribution as the values are collected and grouped into classes.

THE CONCEPT OF STABILITY

We showed in Chapter 5 that the normal distribution can be divided evenly into six sections the sum of which includes 99.7% of the data values. The width of each of these sections is called the standard deviation. The standard deviation is the primary way the spread (or dispersion) of the distribution is measured. Thus, we expect virtually all (99.7%) of the data in a stable process to fall within three standard deviations of the mean. Generally speaking, as long as the measurements fall within the three standard deviation boundary, we consider the process to be stable. This concept provides the basis for statistical process control charts.

Introducing Statistical Process Control Charts

Most cars are equipped with a temperature gauge that measures engine temperature. We come to rely on the gauge to let us know if "everything is all right." As long as the gauge points to the *normal* range, we conclude that there is no problem. However, if the gauge

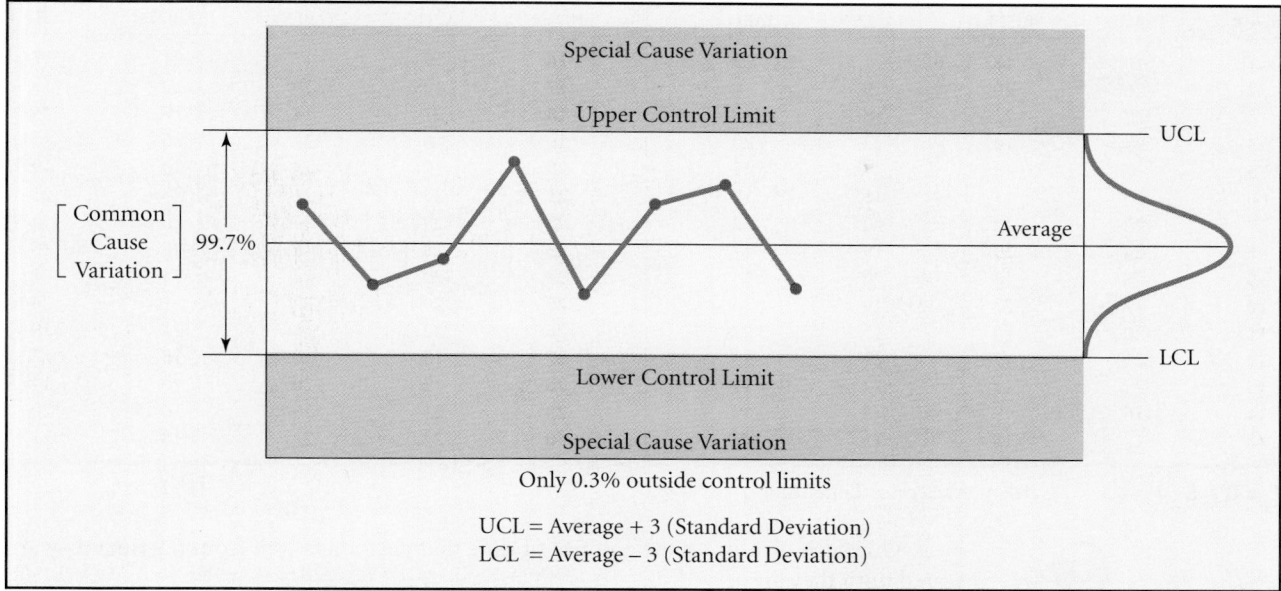

FIGURE 13-8   Process Control Chart Format

moves outside the *normal* range toward the *hot* mark, it's a signal that the engine is over-heating and something is wrong. If the gauge moves out of the normal range toward the *cold* mark, it's also a signal of potential problems.

Under typical driving conditions, engine temperature will fluctuate. The normal range on the car's gauge defines the expected temperature variation when the car is operating properly. Over time, we come to know what to expect. If something changes, the gauge is designed to give us a signal.

The engine temperature gauge is analogous to a process control chart. Like the engine gauge, process control charts are used in business to define the boundaries that represent the amount of variation that can be considered normal.

Figure 13-8 illustrates the general format of a process control chart. The upper and lower control limits define the normal operating region for the process. The horizontal axis reflects the passage of time, or order of production. The vertical axis corresponds to the variable of interest.

There are a number of different types of process control charts. In this section, we introduce four of the most commonly used process control charts.

- $\bar{x}$-chart
- R-chart (Range chart)
- p-chart
- c-chart

Each of these charts is designed for a special purpose. However, as you will see, the underlying logic is the same for each. The $\bar{x}$-chart and R-chart are almost always used in tandem. The $\bar{x}$-charts are used to monitor a process average. R-charts are used to monitor the variation of individual process values. They require that the variable of interest be quantitative. The next example shows how these two charts are developed and used.

$\bar{X}$-CHART AND R-CHART
Cattlemen's Bar and Grill

The Cattlemen's Bar and Grill in Kansas City has developed a reputation for its excellent food and service. In order to maintain this reputation, the owners have established key measures of product and service quality, and they monitor these measures on a regular

EXAMPLE 13-1

CONTROL CHARTS

HOUR	TABLE 1	TABLE 2	TABLE 3	TABLE 4	HOUR	TABLE 1	TABLE 2	TABLE 3	TABLE 4
1	16	18	21	23	**16**	19	17	21	17
2	26	20	19	19	**17**	19	19	13	16
3	20	22	18	18	**18**	21	14	17	16
4	24	16	22	20	**19**	18	17	25	18
5	17	19	24	17	**20**	20	18	20	19
6	17	17	15	18	**21**	23	21	23	21
7	22	12	20	22	**22**	20	20	20	14
8	24	19	19	17	**23**	18	18	26	15
9	18	18	20	14	**24**	20	22	23	21
10	17	23	19	15	**25**	23	22	21	24
11	20	20	17	21	**26**	22	14	21	19
12	21	17	21	23	**27**	18	20	18	22
13	22	17	22	17	**28**	19	20	16	14
14	16	19	18	19	**29**	21	19	16	20
15	17	18	15	23	**30**	22	22	18	21

TABLE 13-3 Cattlemen's Service Time Data

Excel and Minitab Tutorial

basis. One such measure is the amount of time that customers wait from the time they are seated until they are served.

Every day, each hour that the business is open, 4 tables are randomly selected. The elapsed time from when the customers are seated until their order arrives is recorded. Table 13-3 shows the data for 30 hours. The owners wish to use these data to construct an $\bar{x}$-chart and an R-chart.

The group of 4 values that are recorded each hour is referred to as a **subgroup**. In this case, each subgroup is a sample of 4 tables selected from all the tables in the establishment. The $\bar{x}$- and R-charts are typically generated from small subgroups (3 to 6 observations) and the general recommendation is that data from a minimum of 20 subgroups be gathered before a chart is constructed. Once the subgroup size is determined, all subgroups must be the same size. After the initial data have been collected, the following steps are performed to construct the two control charts.

SUBGROUP
A sample of items selected from a process. If the process is operating in control, the subgroup is free from special cause variation.

STEP 1: Calculate subgroup means and ranges. The data shown in Table 13-3 are contained in a data file called **Cattlemen** and are on the CD-ROM which accompanies this text. Figure 13-9 shows the Excel worksheet with a partial listing of the data after the means and ranges have been computed for each subgroup.

	A	B	C	D	E	F	G	H
1	Hour	Table 1	Table 2	Table 3	Table 4		Mean	Range
2	1	16	18	21	23		19.5	7
3	2	26	20	19	19		21	7
4	3	20	22	18	18		19.5	4
5	4	24	16	22	20		20.5	8
6	5	17	19	24	17		19.25	7
7	6	17	17	15	18		16.75	3
8	7	22	12	20	22		19	10
9	8	24	19	19	17		19.75	7
10	9	18	18	20	14		17.5	6

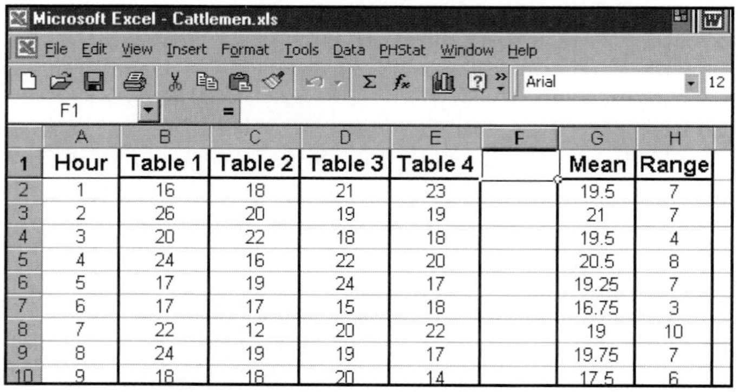

FIGURE 13-9
Excel Worksheet of Cattlemen's Service Time Data Including Subgroup Means and Ranges

Excel Instructions:

1. Open file: Cattlemen.xls
2. Use Excel formulas to compute Mean and Range values for each sample.

STEP 2: Compute the average of the subgroup means and the average range value. Next, we compute the average of the subgroup means and the average range value using Equations 13-2 and 13-3.

AVERAGE OF SUBGROUP MEANS
$$\bar{\bar{x}} = \frac{\sum_{i=1}^{k} \bar{x}_i}{k} \qquad \textbf{13-2}$$
where:
$\bar{x}_i = i$th subgroup average
$k =$ Number of subgroups

AVERAGE SUBGROUP RANGE
$$\bar{R} = \frac{\sum_{i=1}^{k} R_i}{k} \qquad \textbf{13-3}$$
where:
$R_i = i$th subgroup range
$k =$ Number of subgroups

Using Equations 13-2 and 13-3 we get:

$$\bar{\bar{x}} = \frac{\sum \bar{x}}{k} = \frac{19.5 + 21 + \cdots + 20.75}{30} = 19.24$$

$$\bar{R} = \frac{\sum R}{k} = \frac{7 + 7 + \cdots + 3}{30} = 5.73$$

STEP 3: Prepare graphs of the subgroup means and ranges as a line chart. On one graph, plot the $\bar{x}$ values in time order across the graph and draw a line across the graph at the value corresponding to $\bar{\bar{x}}$. This is shown in Figure 13-10. Likewise, graph the R values and $\bar{R}$ as a line chart as shown in Figure 13-11.

FIGURE 13-10   Line Chart for $\bar{x}$ Values for Cattlemen's Data

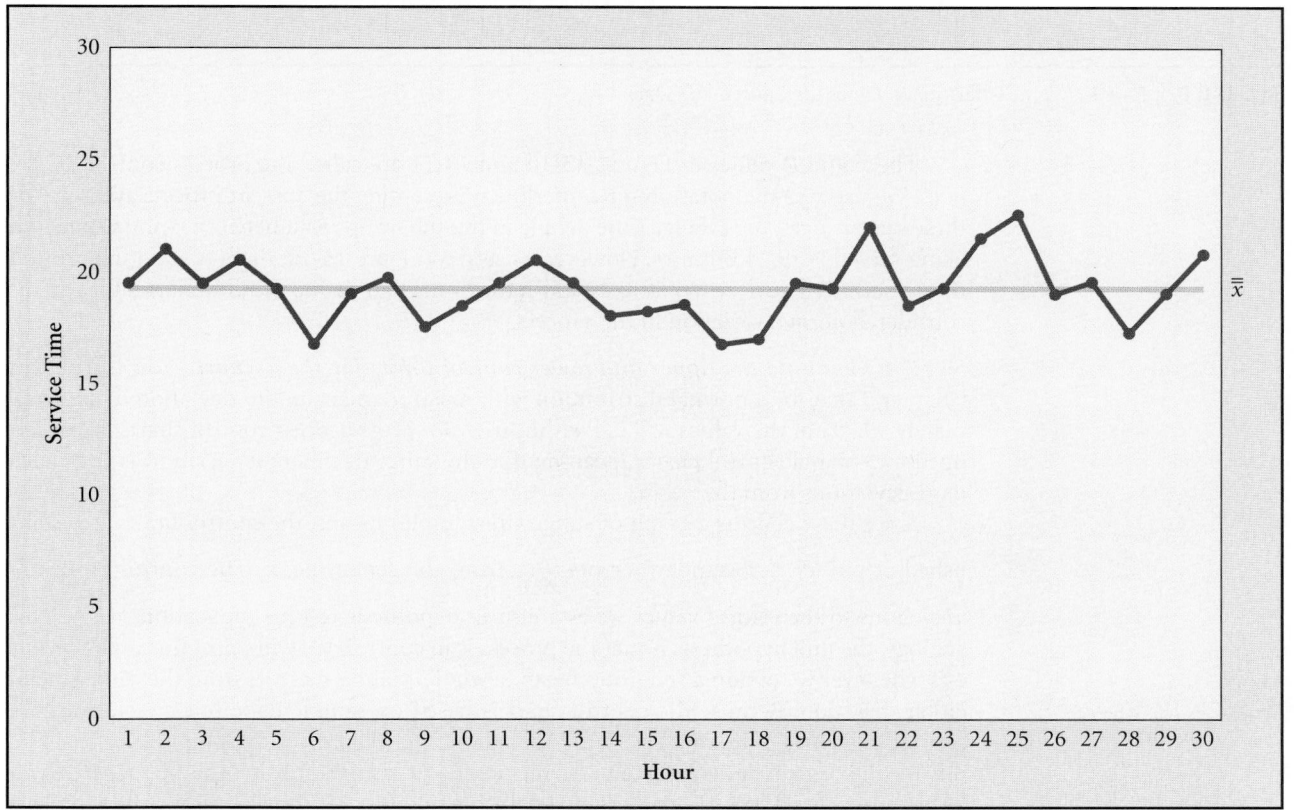

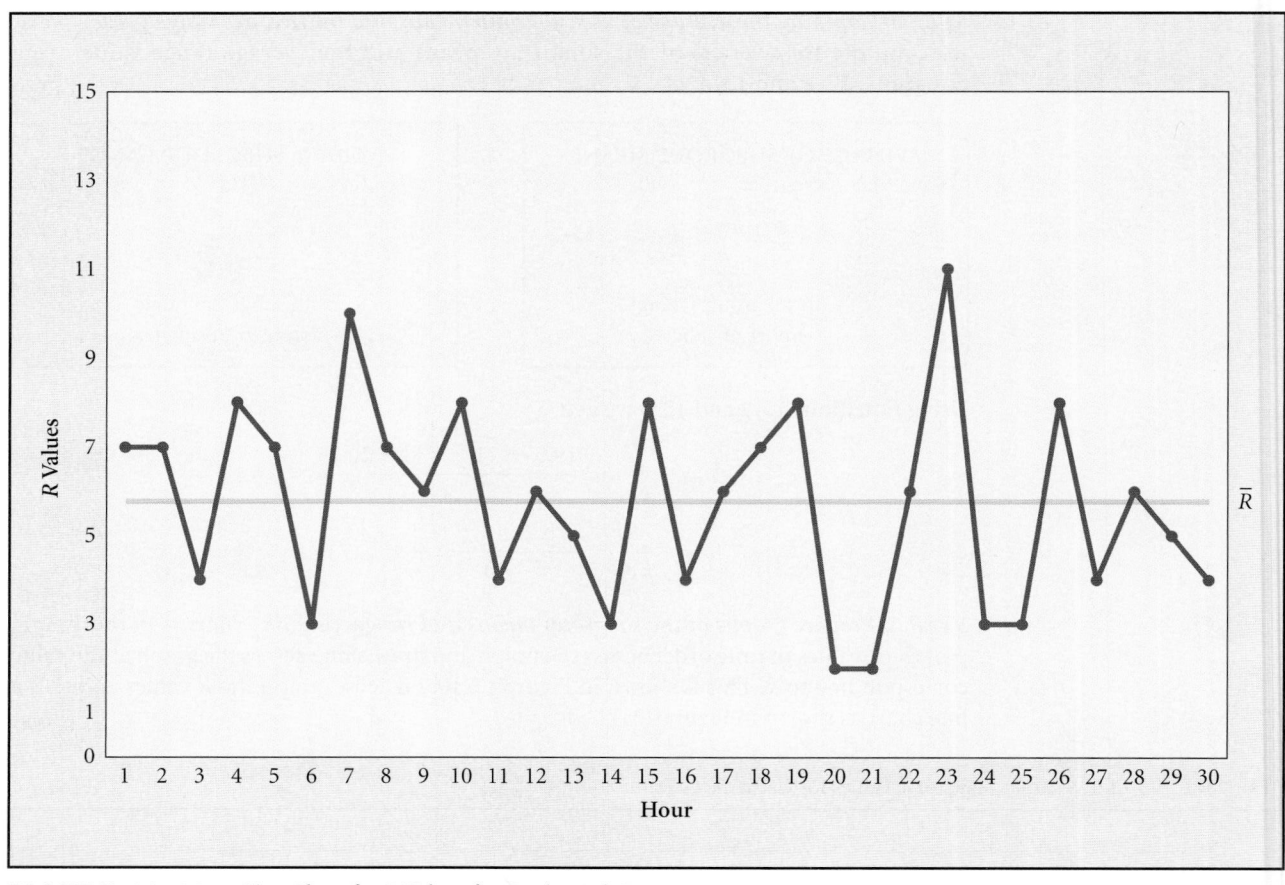

FIGURE 13-11   Line Chart for R Values for Cattlemen's Data

The $\bar{\bar{x}}$ and $\bar{R}$ values in Figures 13-10 and 13-11 are called the process control *center-lines*. We use $\bar{\bar{x}}$ as the notation for centerline representing the current process average. For these sample data, the average time people in the subgroups wait between being seated and being served is 19.24 minutes. However, as seen in Figure 13-10, there is variation around the centerline. The next step is to establish the limits that define the boundaries for what is considered *normal* variation in the process.

STEP 4: Compute the upper and lower control limits for the $\bar{x}$-chart. You learned in Chapter 5 that for a normal distribution with mean μ and standard deviation σ, approximately 99.7% of the values will fall within $\mu \pm 3\sigma$. Most process control charts are developed as 3-sigma control charts meaning that the range of inherent variation is $\pm$ 3 standard deviations from the mean.

Since the $\bar{x}$ chart is a graph of subgroup (sample) means, the control limits are established at points $\pm$ 3 standard errors $\dfrac{\sigma}{\sqrt{n}}$ from the centerline, $\bar{\bar{x}}$. The control limits are analogous to the critical values we establish in hypothesis testing applications. Using this analogy, the null hypothesis is that the process is in control. We will reject this null hypothesis whenever we obtain a subgroup mean beyond 3 standard errors from the centerline in either direction. Because the control chart is based on sample data, our conclusions are subject to error. Approximately 3 times in a thousand (0.003), a subgroup mean should be outside the control limits when, in fact, the process is still in control. If this happens, we will have committed a Type I error. The 0.003 value is the significance level for the test. This small alpha level implies that 3 sigma control charts are very conservative when it comes to

TABLE 13-4
Shewhart Factors Table

n	A_2	D_3	D_4
2	1.88	0	3.27
3	1.02	0	2.57
4	0.73	0	2.28
5	0.58	0	2.11
6	0.48	0	2.00

saying that a process is out of control. We might also conclude that the process is in control when in fact it isn't. If this happens, we have committed a Type II error.

In order to construct the control limits, we must determine an estimator for the standard error of the sample means, $\frac{\sigma}{\sqrt{n}}$. Based on what you have learned in previous chapters, you might suspect that we would use $\frac{s}{\sqrt{n}}$. However, in most applications this is not done. In the 1930s, when process control charts were first introduced, there was no such thing as pocket calculators. In order to make control charts usable by people without calculators and without statistical training, a simpler approach was needed. An unbiased estimator of the standard error of the sample means, $\frac{\sigma}{\sqrt{n}}$, that was relatively easy to calculate was developed by Walter Shewhart.[1] The unbiased estimator is $\frac{A_2}{3}\bar{R}$ where $\bar{R}$ is the mean of the subgroups' ranges and A_2 is a Shewhart factor that makes $\frac{A_2}{3}\bar{R}$ an unbiased estimator of the standard error of the sample means, $\frac{\sigma}{\sqrt{n}}$. Thus, 3 standard errors of the sample means, $3\frac{\sigma}{\sqrt{n}}$, can be estimated by $3\left(\frac{A_2}{3}\bar{R}\right) = A_2\bar{R}$. Table 13-4 displays **Shewhart** factors for various subgroup sizes. (The development of the Shewhart table is outside the scope of this text.)

Equations 13-4 and 13-5 are used to compute the upper and lower **control limits**.

UPPER CONTROL LIMIT, $\bar{x}$-CHART

$$UCL = \bar{\bar{x}} + A_2(\bar{R}) \qquad \textbf{13-4}$$

where:

A_2 = Shewhart factor for
subgroup size = n

LOWER CONTROL LIMIT, $\bar{x}$-CHART

$$LCL = \bar{\bar{x}} - A_2(\bar{R}) \qquad \textbf{13-5}$$

where:

A_2 = Shewhart factor for
subgroup size = n

For the Cattlemen's Bar and Grill example, the subgroup size is 4. Thus, the A_2 factor from the Shewhart table is 0.73. We can compute the upper and lower control limits as follows.

$$UCL = \bar{\bar{x}} + A_2(\bar{R}) \qquad\qquad LCL = \bar{\bar{x}} - A_2(\bar{R})$$
$$UCL = 19.24 + 0.73(5.73) \qquad LCL = 19.24 - 0.73(5.73)$$
$$UCL = 23.42 \qquad\qquad\qquad LCL = 15.06$$

STEP 5: Compute the upper and lower control limits for the R-chart. The D_3 and D_4 factors in the Shewhart table are used to compute the 3-sigma control limits for the R-chart. The control limits are established at points $\pm$ 3 standard errors from the centerline, $\bar{R}$. However, unlike the case for the $\bar{x}$-chart, the unbiased estimator of the standard error of the sample ranges is a constant multiplied by $\bar{R}$. The constant for the lower control limit is the D_3 value from the Shewhart table. The D_4 value from the Shewhart table is the constant for the upper control limit.

Equations 13-6 and 13-7 are used to find the UCL and LCL values. Since the subgroup size is 4 in our example, $D_3 = 0.0$ and $D_4 = 2.28$.[2]

UPPER CONTROL LIMIT, R-CHART

$$UCL = D_4(\bar{R}) \qquad \textbf{13-6}$$

where:

D_4 is taken from the Shewhart
table for subgroup size = n

LOWER CONTROL LIMIT, R-CHART

$$LCL = D_3(\bar{R}) \qquad \textbf{13-7}$$

where:

D_3 is taken from the Shewhart
table for subgroup size = n

---

[1]Shewhart was the leader of a group at the Bell Telephone Laboratories that did much of the original work in SPC. Shewhart is credited with developing the idea of control charts.

[2]Since a range cannot be negative, the constant is adjusted to indicate that the lower bound for the range must equal 0.

Excel Instructions:
1. Open file: Cattlemen.xls
2. Compute column of $\bar{x}$ and R values
3. Select PHStat
4. Click on Control Charts
5. Select R and x-bar Charts
6. Enter subgroup size
7. Define range of R values
8. Select R and x-bar chart option
9. Define range of $\bar{x}$ values

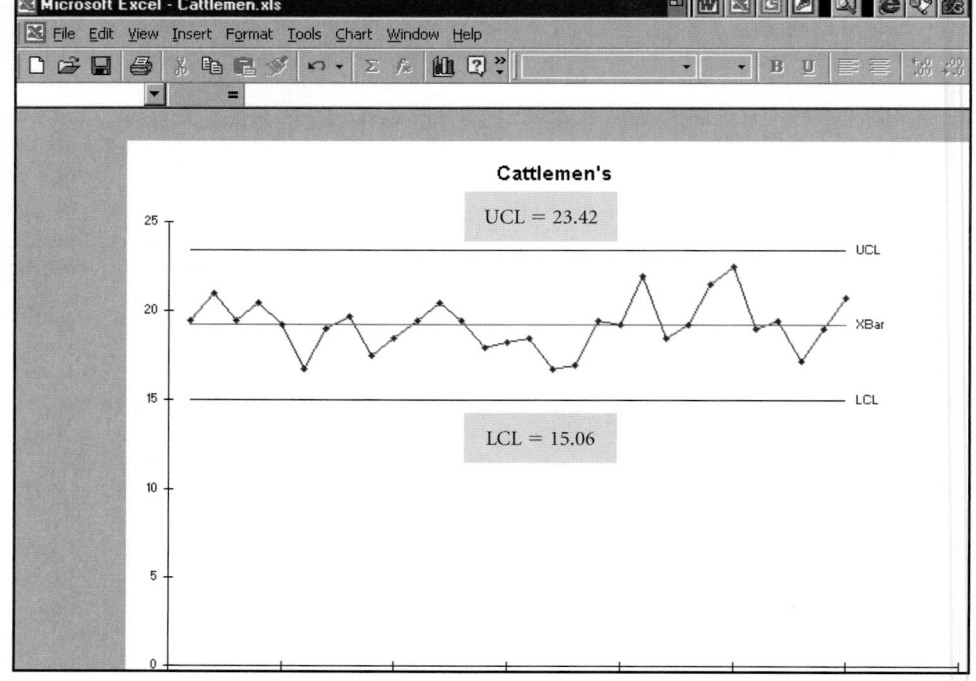

FIGURE 13-12
Excel (PHStat) Cattlemen's
$\bar{x}$-Chart Output

Using Equations 13-6 and 13-7, we get:

$$UCL = D_4(\bar{R}) \qquad LCL = D_3(\bar{R})$$
$$UCL = 2.28(5.73) \qquad LCL = 0.0(5.73)$$
$$UCL = 13.06 \qquad LCL = 0.0$$

STEP 6: Finish constructing the control chart by locating the control limits on the $\bar{x}$- and R-charts. Graph the UCL and LCL values on the $\bar{x}$- and R-charts as shown in Figure 13-12 and Figure 13-13 which were constructed using the PHStat add-in to Excel.[3]

Both students and people in industry sometimes confuse control limits and specification limits. Specification limits are arbitrary and are defined by a customer, by an industry standard, or by engineers who designed the item. The specification limits are defined as values above and below the "target" value for the item. The specification limits pertain to individual items—an item either meets specifications, or it does not. Process control limits are computed from actual data from a subgroup selected from the process. These limits define the range of inherent variation that is actually occurring in the process. The control limits are values above and below the current process average (which may be higher or lower than the "target").

Therefore, a process may be operating in a state of control, but it may be producing individual items that do not meet the specifications. Companies interested in improving quality must first bring the process under control before attempting to make changes in the process to reduce the defect level.

USING THE CONTROL CHARTS

Now that the control charts for the Cattlemen's service times have been developed, they are used to determine whether the time it takes to serve customers remains *in control*. The con-

---

[3]See the Excel and Minitab tutorial on the CD-ROM for the specific steps required to obtain the x-bar and R-charts. Minitab provides a much more extensive set of SPC options than does PHStat.

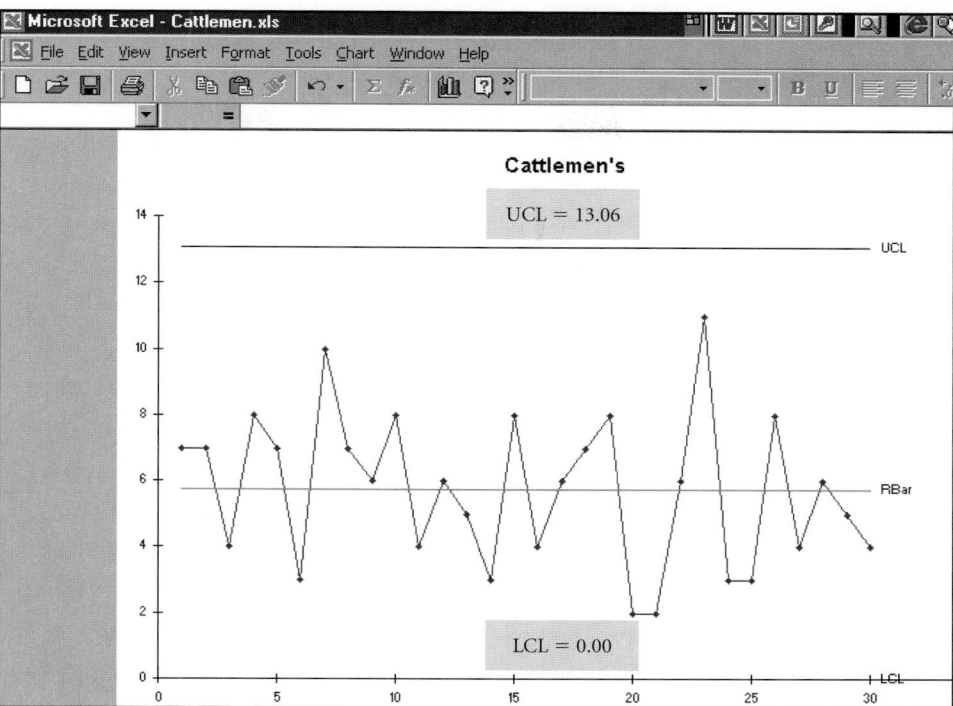

FIGURE 13-13
Excel (PHStat) Cattlemen's
R-Chart Output

cept involved is essentially a hypothesis test where the null and alternative hypotheses can be stated as:

H_0: The process is in control: The variation around the centerline is a
     result of common causes inherent in the process.
H_A: The process is out of control: The variation around the centerline is
     due to some special cause and is beyond what is normal for the process.

In the Cattlemen's Bar and Grill example, the hypothesis is tested every hour when 4 tables are selected and the service time is recorded for each table. The $\bar{x}$ and R values for the new subgroup are computed and plotted on their respective control charts.

There are three main process changes that can be detected with a process control chart.

1. The process average has shifted up (or down) from normal.
2. The process average is trending up (or down) from normal.
3. The process is behaving in such a manner that the existing variation is not random in nature.

If any of these has happened, the null hypothesis is considered false and the process is *out of control.*

The control charts are used to provide signals that something has changed. There are four primary signals that indicate a change and, if observed, cause us to reject the null hypothesis.[4] These are:

1. One or more points outside the upper or lower control limits
2. Nine or more points in a row above (or below) the center line
3. Six or more consecutive points moving in the same direction (increasing or decreasing)
4. Fourteen points in a row, alternating up and down

---

[4]There is some minor disagreement on the signals depending on which process control source you reference. Minitab actually lets the user define the signals under the option Define Tests.

HOUR	TABLE 1	TABLE 2	TABLE 3	TABLE 4	MEAN	RANGE
31	20	21	24	22	21.75	4
32	17	22	18	20	19.25	5
33	23	20	22	22	21.75	3
34	24	23	19	20	21.5	5
35	24	25	26	27	25.5	3

TABLE 13-5
Data for Hours 31–35 for
Cattlemen's Bar and Grill

These signals were derived such that the probability of a Type I error is less than 0.01. Thus, there is a very small chance that we will conclude the process has changed when in fact it has not. Note these signals are designed to detect changes 1 and 2 listed previously. Existence of nonrandom performance can be detected visually or by using a procedure called the *runs test* that is introduced in Chapter 15.

If we examine the control charts in Figures 13-12 and 13-13, we find that none of these signals occur. Thus, the process is deemed in control during the period during which the initial sample data were collected.

Suppose the Cattlemen's owners monitor the process for the next 5 hours. Table 13-5 shows these new values along with the mean and range for each hour. The means are plotted on the $\bar{x}$-chart and the range (R) values are plotted on the R-chart as shown in Figures 13-14 and 13-15.

When $\bar{x}$- and R-charts are used, we first look at the R-chart. Figure 13-15 shows the range (R) has been below the centerline ($\bar{R} = 5.7$) for 7 consecutive hours. While this doesn't quite come up to the 9 points of signal 2, the owners should begin to suspect something

FIGURE 13-14   Cattlemen's $\bar{x}$ Chart

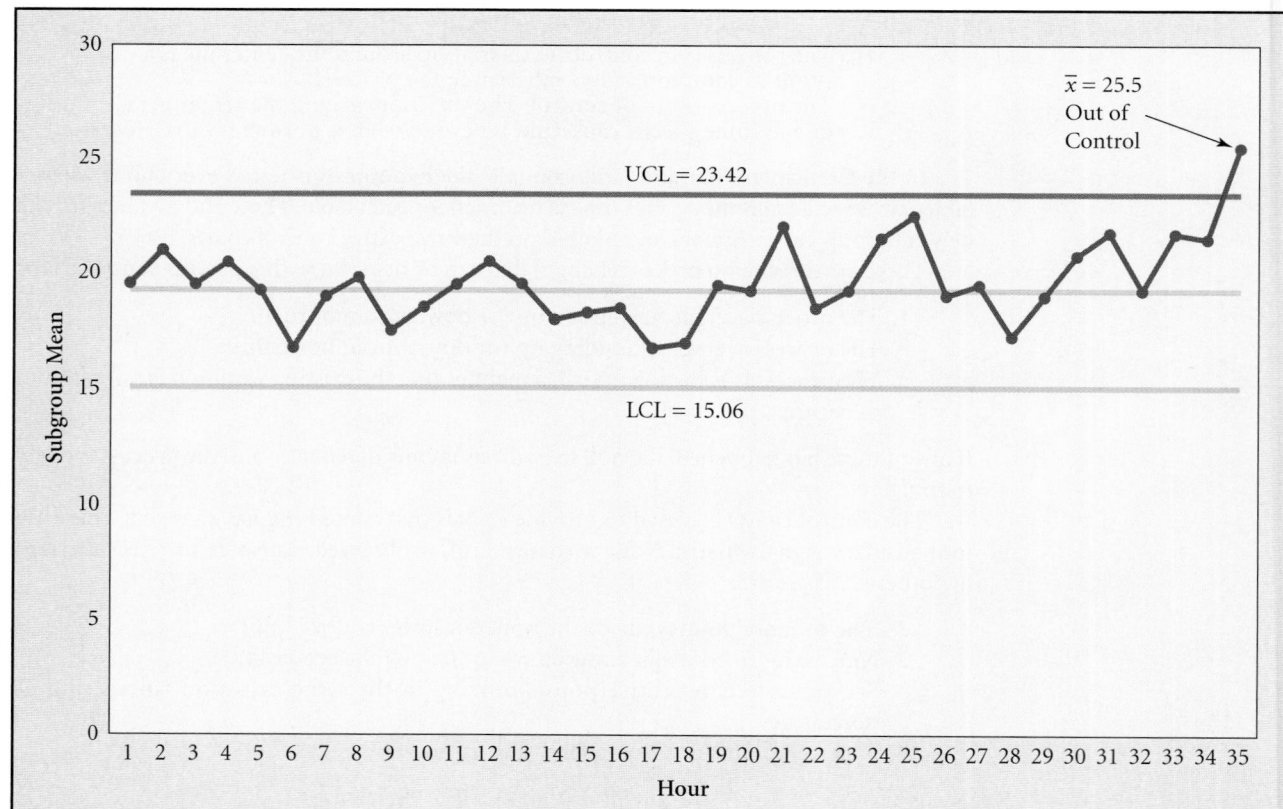

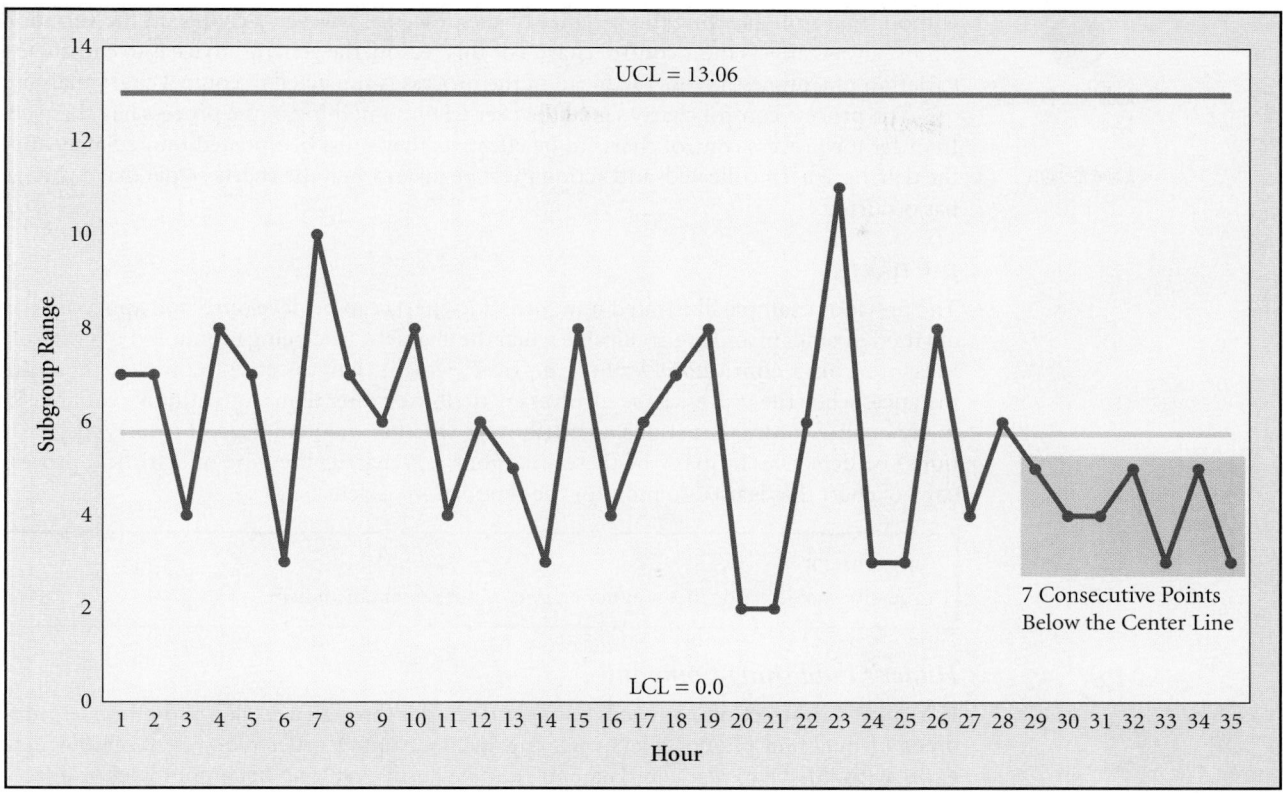

FIGURE 13-15   Cattlemen's *R*-Chart

unusual might be happening to cause a downward shift in the variation in service time between tables. Although the *R*-chart does not indicate the reason for the shift, the owners should be pleased since this would indicate greater consistency in service times. As long as the average service time is not increasing, this change in variation would actually represent a quality improvement. If this trend continues, the owners would want to study the situation that was present so that they will be able to retain these reductions in service time variability.

The $\bar{x}$-chart in Figure 13-14 indicates that the average service time is out of control because in hour 35, the mean service time exceeded the upper control limit of 23.4 minutes. The mean wait time for the 4 tables during this hour was 25.5 minutes. The chance of this happening is extremely low unless something has changed in the process. This should be a signal to the owners that a special cause exists. They should immediately investigate possible problems to determine if there has been a system change (e.g., training issue) or if this is truly a one-time event (e.g., fire in the kitchen). They could use a brainstorming technique such as the nominal group technique or a fishbone diagram to identify possible causes of the problem.

An important point is that analysis of each of the control charts should not be done in isolation. A moment's consideration will lead you to see that if the variation of the process has gotten out of control (above the upper control limit), then trying to interpret the $\bar{x}$-chart can be very misleading. Widely fluctuating variation could make it much more probable that an $\bar{x}$ value would exceed the control limits even though the process mean had not changed.

Adding (or subtracting) a given number from all of the numbers in a data set does not change the variance of that data set. So it is possible to have a shift in the mean of a process

**Additional Example
13-a**

$\bar{x}$ and R-Charts

without that shift affecting the variance of the process. However, a change in the variation almost always affects the $\bar{x}$ control chart. For this reason, the general advice is to control the variation of a process before the mean of the process is subjected to control chart analysis.

The process control charts signal the user when something in the process has changed. In order for process control charts to be effective, they must be updated immediately after the data have been collected, and action must be taken when the charts signal that a change has occurred.

p-CHARTS

The previous example illustrated how $\bar{x}$- and R-charts can be developed and applied. They are used in tandem and are applicable when the characteristic being monitored is a variable measured on a continuous scale (e.g., time, weight, length, etc.). However, there are instances when the process issue involves an **attribute** rather than a quantitative variable. In many quality control situations an attribute is whether the item is good (meets specifications) or defective. In many of these situations a *p*-chart is the type of statistical process control chart that is used to monitor the proportion of defects.

> **ATTRIBUTE**
> A quality characteristic that is either present or not present in an item.

13-2

CONTROL CHARTS

**Excel and
Minitab Tutorial**

Hilder's Publishing Company

Hilder's Publishing Company sells books and records through a catalog and processes hundreds of mail and phone orders each day. Each customer order requires numerous data entry steps. Mistakes made in data entry can be costly resulting in shipping delays, incorrect prices, or the wrong items being shipped. As part of its ongoing efforts to improve quality, Hilder's managers and employees want to reduce the number of order entry errors.

The manager of the order entry department has decided to develop a process control chart to monitor the order entry errors. She has gone back for the past 30 days and for each day selected a random sample of 100 orders. These orders were examined with the attribute being:

- Order entry is correct.
- Order entry is incorrect.

The incorrect orders, called *non-conformances*, are on the CD-ROM that accompanies this text in a file called **Hilders**. An Excel worksheet of some of the data is shown in Figure 13-16.

FIGURE 13-16
Excel Worksheet of Hilder's Data

Excel Instructions:
1. Open file: Hilders.xls

	Sample	Sample Size	Number of Orders With Errors	Fraction of Orders With Errors
2	1	100	10	0.10
3	2	100	6	0.06
4	3	100	6	0.06
5	4	100	7	0.07
6	5	100	7	0.07
7	6	100	7	0.07
8	7	100	7	0.07

Microsoft Excel - Hilders.xls

File Edit View Insert Format Tools Data PHStat Window H

G7

In developing a *p*-chart, the sample size should be large enough such that both $np > 5$ and $n(1 - p) > 5$. Unlike the $\bar{x}$- and *R*-chart cases, the sample size may differ from sample to sample. However, this complicates developing the *p*-chart.

Once the data are collected, use the following steps to construct the *p*-chart.

STEP 1: Plot the subgroup proportions as a line chart.

STEP 2: Compute the mean subgroup proportion for all samples using Equation 13-8 or 13-9 depending on whether the sample sizes are equal or not.

> **MEAN SUBGROUP PROPORTION**
>
> For equal size samples:
> $$\bar{p} = \frac{\sum_{i=1}^{k} p_i}{k} \qquad \text{13-8}$$
> where:
> p_i = Sample proportion for subgroup i
> k = Number of samples of size n
>
> For unequal sample sizes:
> $$\bar{p} = \frac{\sum_{i=1}^{k} n_i p_i}{\sum_{i=1}^{k} n_i} \qquad \text{13-9}$$
> where:
> n_i = The number of items in sample i
> $\sum_{i=1}^{k} n_i$ = Total number of items sampled in k samples

Since we have equal sample sizes, we use Equation 13-8 as follows.

$$\bar{p} = \frac{\sum p_i}{k} = \frac{0.10 + 0.06 + 0.06 + 0.07 + \cdots}{30} = \frac{2.38}{30} = 0.079$$

Thus, the average proportion of orders with errors is 0.079. This value is shown on the control chart in Figure 13-17.

STEP 3: Compute the estimate of the standard error of p using Equation 13-10.

> **ESTIMATE OF THE STANDARD ERROR FOR THE SUBGROUP PROPORTIONS**
>
> For equal sample sizes:
> $$s_p = \sqrt{\frac{(\bar{p})(1 - \bar{p})}{n}} \qquad \text{13-10}$$
> where:
> $\bar{p}$ = Mean subgroup proportion
> n = Common sample size
>
> For unequal sample sizes:
> Option 1. Compute s_p using largest sample size and s_p using the smallest sample size. Construct control limits using each value.
> Option 2. Compute a unique value of s_p for each different sample size. Construct control limits for each s_p value.

We compute s_p using Equation 13-10 as follows.

$$s_p = \sqrt{\frac{(\bar{p})(1 - \bar{p})}{n}} = \sqrt{\frac{(0.079)(1 - 0.079)}{100}} = 0.027$$

Excel (PHStat) Instructions
1. Open file: Hilders.xls
2. Click on PHStat
3. Select the Control Chart option.
4. Select P chart
5. Define the column with the number of noncon-forming values
6. Indicate the Sample Size

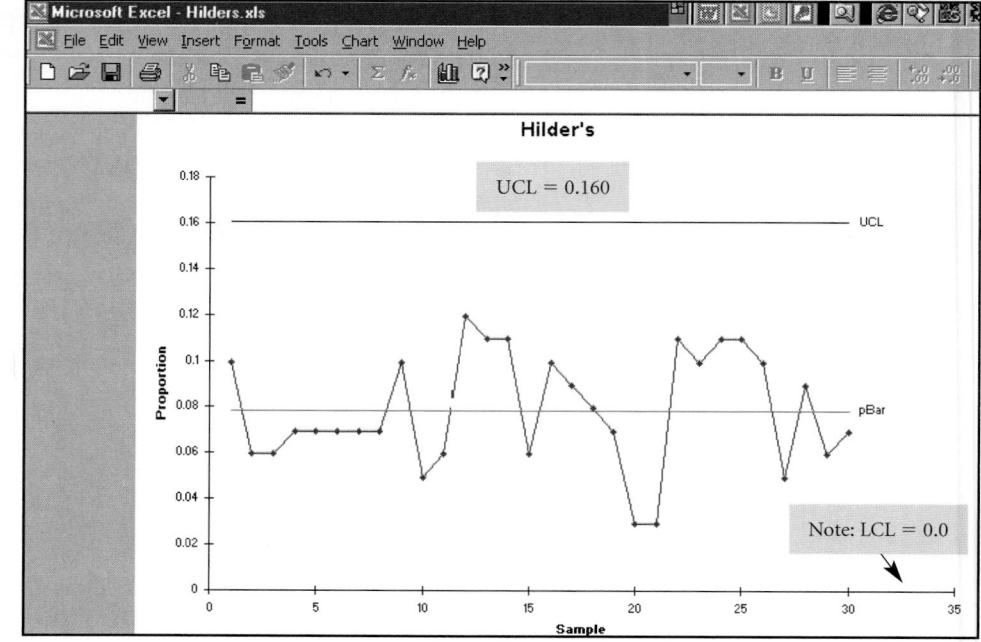

FIGURE 13-17
Excel (PHStat) p-Chart for Hilder's Publishing

STEP 4: Compute the 3-sigma control limits using Equations 13-11 and 13-12.

CONTROL LIMITS FOR p-CHART

$$UCL = \bar{p} + 3s_p \qquad \text{13-11}$$
$$LCL = \bar{p} - 3s_p \qquad \text{13-12}$$

where:

$\bar{p} =$ Mean subgroup proportion

$s_p =$ Estimated standard error of $p = \sqrt{\dfrac{(\bar{p})(1 - \bar{p})}{n}}$

Using Equations 13-11 and 13-12, we get the following control limits.

$$UCL = \bar{p} + 3s_P = 0.079 + 3(0.027) = 0.160$$
$$LCL = \bar{p} - 3s_P = 0.079 - 3(0.027) = -0.002 \to 0.0$$

Since a proportion of nonconforming items cannot be negative, the lower control limit is set to 0.0. Both upper and lower control limits are plotted on the control chart in Figure 13-17.

USING THE p-CHART

Once the control chart is developed, the same rules are used as for the $\bar{x}$- and R-charts.[5]

1. One or more points outside the upper or lower control limits
2. Nine or more points in row above (or below) the center line
3. Six or more consecutive points moving in the same direction (up or down)
4. Fourteen points in a row, alternating up and down

[5]Minitab allows the user to specify the signals. This is done in the *Define Tests* feature under Stat—Control Charts. See the Excel and Minitab Tutorial for specifics in developing a *p*-chart.

The *p*-chart shown in Figure 13-17 indicates the process is in control. None of the signals are present in these data. The variation in the nonconformance rates is assumed to be due to the common cause issues.

For future days, the managers would select a random sample of 100 orders, count the number with errors, and compute the proportion. The proportion would be plotted on the *p*-chart. For each day, the managers would use the control chart to test the hypotheses.

H_0: The process is in control: The variation around the centerline is
a result of common causes and is inherent in the process.
H_A: The process is out of control: The variation around the centerline is
due to some special cause and is beyond what is normal for the process.

The signals mentioned previously would be used to test the null hypothesis. Remember, control charts are most useful when the charts are updated as soon as the new sample data become available. When a signal of special cause variation is present, you should take action to determine the source of the problem and remove it as quickly as possible.

c-Charts

The *p*-chart just discussed is used when you select a sample of items and you determine the number of the sampled items that possess a specific attribute of interest. Each item either has that attribute or it does not. You will also encounter other situations that involve attribute data but differ from the *p*-chart applications. In these situations, you have what is called a sampling unit (or experimental unit) which could be a sheet of plywood, a door panel on a car, a textbook page, an hour of service, or any other defined unit of space, volume, time, etc. Each sampling unit could have one or more of the attributes of interest and you would be able to count the number of attributes present in each sampling unit. In cases where the sampling units are the same size, the appropriate control chart is a *c*-chart.

EXAMPLE 13-3

CONTROL CHARTS

Excel and
Minitab Tutorial

Chandler Tile Company

The Chandler Tile Company makes ceramic tile for the building industry. In recent years, there has been a big demand for tile products in private residences in kitchens and bathrooms and in commercial establishments for decorative counter and wall covering. While the demand has increased, so has the competition. The senior management at Chandler knows that three factors are key to winning business from contractors: price, quality, and service.

One quality issue is the presence of surface scratches on a tile. These scratches may be almost invisible to the naked eye under normal circumstances but if the light hits the tile just right, they can be seen. The more of these scratches on a tile, the lower the quality. The production managers wish to set up a control chart to monitor the level of scratches per tile to determine whether the production process remains in control.

One key point to remember, control charts monitor the process as it currently operates, not necessarily how you would like it to operate. Thus, a process that is in control might still yield a higher number of scratches per tile than the managers would like.

The managers may be able to assume that the number of scratches are independent of each other and that the prevailing operating conditions are consistent from tile to tile. In this case the proper control chart is a *c*-chart. Here the tiles being sampled are the same size, and the managers will tally the number of scratches per tile. However, if we asked the question "How many opportunities were there to scratch each tile?" we probably would not be able to answer this question. There are more opportunities than we could count. For this reason, the *c*-chart is based on the Poisson probability distribution which was introduced in Chapter 4. You might recall that the Poisson distribution is defined by the mean number of *successes* per interval or sampling unit of the process as shown in Equation 13-13. For this procedure, a success can be regarded as a defective, a nonconformance, or any other characteristic of interest. In the Chandler example, a success is a scratch on the tile.

MEAN FOR c-CHART

$$\bar{c} = \frac{\sum_{i=1}^{k} x_i}{k}$$

13-13

where:

x_i = Number of successes per sampling unit
k = Number of sampling units

Because the Poisson distribution is asymmetric when the mean of the sampling unit is small, we must define the sampling unit so that it is large enough to provide an average of at least 5 successes per sampling unit ($\bar{c} \geq 5$). This may require that you combine smaller sampling units into a larger unit size.

The mean and the variance of the Poisson distribution are identical. Therefore, the standard deviation of the Poisson distribution is the square root of its mean. For this reason the estimator of the standard deviation for the Poisson distribution is computed as the square root of the sample mean as shown in Equation 13-14.

STANDARD DEVIATION FOR c-CHART

$$s = \sqrt{\bar{c}}$$

13-14

Then Equations 13-15 and 13-16 are used to compute the 3-sigma (3 standard deviation) control limits for the c-chart.

---

c-CHART CONTROL LIMITS

$$UCL = \bar{c} + 3\sqrt{\bar{c}}$$

13-15

and

$$LCL = \bar{c} - 3\sqrt{\bar{c}}$$

13-16

The original plan called for the Chandler Tile Company to select one tile each hour from the production line and perform a thorough inspection to count the number of scratches. Like all control charts, at least 20 samples are needed to develop the initial control chart. After sampling 40 tiles (one each for 40 hours), the total number of scratches found was 38. Based on these results, the mean would be:

$$\bar{c} = \frac{\sum x}{k} = \frac{38}{40} = 0.95 \text{ scratches}$$

However, since the mean is less than 5, company analysts needed to form a sampling unit by combining 6 tiles. A portion of the revised data are shown in the Excel spreadsheet shown in Figure 13-18. The full data set is contained in the file called **Chandler**. The mean of these new sampling units will be 6(0.95) = 5.70 which meets the criterion of being at least 5. Note that each tile may have 0 or more scratches. Thus, each hour, 6 tiles will be inspected and the total number of scratches analyzed. Based on this result, Equations 13-13 through 13-16 are used to develop the control limits. Figure 13-19 shows the control chart that we developed using the results from the following computations.[6]

The mean is:

$$\bar{c} = \frac{\sum x}{k} = \frac{228}{40} = 5.70$$

FIGURE 13-18
Excel Worksheet for Chandler Tile Company

Excel Instructions:
1. Open file: Chandler.xls

---

[6]Neither Excel nor PHStat contains a procedure for directly developing c-charts. Refer to the Excel tutorial on the CD-ROM for specific steps needed to construct c-charts in Excel. Minitab does have a procedure for developing a c-chart. See the Minitab tutorial.

Excel Instructions:

1. Open file: Chandler.xls
2. Use Excel formula to compute centerline and UCL
3. Create a column of values corresponding to the centerline and UCL
4. Use Chart Wizard—Line Chart

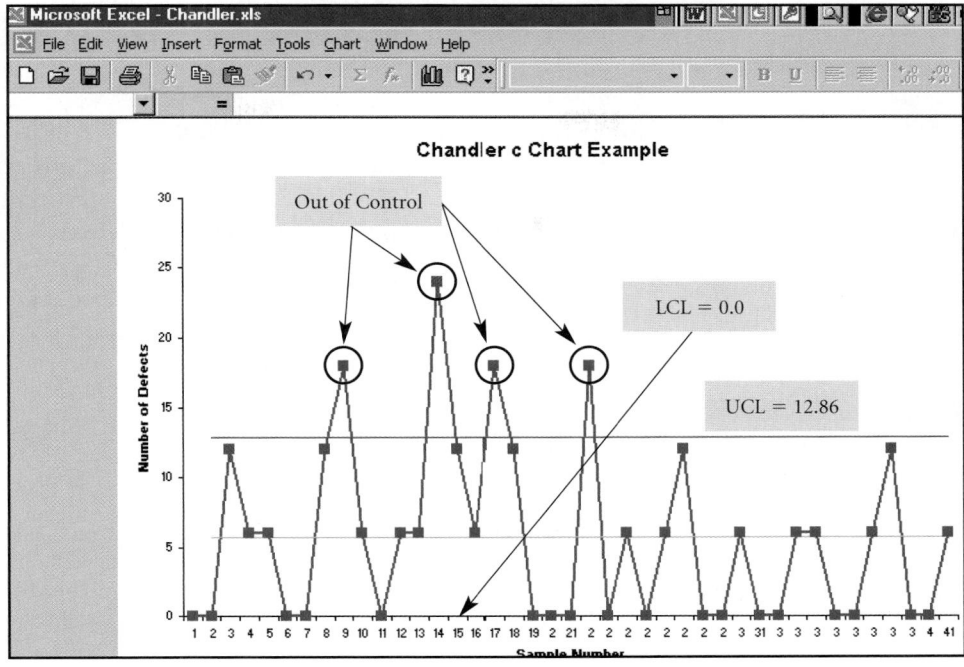

FIGURE 13-19
Excel *c*-Chart for Chandler Tile Company

The standard deviation is the square root of the mean.

$$s = \sqrt{\bar{c}} = \sqrt{5.70} = 2.387$$

Now, we compute the upper and lower 3-sigma control limits as:

$$UCL = \bar{c} + 3\sqrt{\bar{c}} = 5.7 + 3(2.387) = 12.86$$
$$LCL = \bar{c} - 3\sqrt{\bar{c}} = 5.7 - 3(2.387) = -1.46 \rightarrow 0.0$$

As with the *p*-chart, the lower control limit can't be negative. We change it to 0 which is the fewest possible scratches on a tile. The completed *c*-chart is shown in Figure 13-19.

Note in Figure 13-19 that 4 sample units of 6 tiles each had a total number of scratches that fell outside the upper control limit, 12.86. The managers need to consult production records and other information to determine what special cause might have generated these levels of scratches. If they can determine the cause, these data points should be removed and the control limits should be recomputed from the remaining 36 values. You might also note that the graph changes after sample 22. The process seems more stable from sample 23 onward. Given this, the managers might consider inspecting for another 13–15 hours and recompute the control limits using data from hours 23 and higher.

OPTIONAL CD-ROM TOPIC *u*-Charts

You will encounter situations where a *c*-chart is needed but the sampling units differ substantially in size. When this happens, the *c*-chart can't be used. Instead a control chart known as a *u*-chart is appropriate. For more information, go to the CD-ROM.

OTHER CONTROL CHARTS

Our purpose in this chapter has been to introduce you to SPC charts. We have illustrated a few of the most frequently used charts. However, there are many other types of control charts that can be used in special situations. You are encouraged to consult several of the references listed at the end of the chapter for information about these other charts.

OPTIONAL CD-ROM TOPIC Acceptance Sampling Issues and Procedures

A widely used quality control technique used to assess incoming parts and materials quality is called acceptance sampling. It is used when we are interested in determining whether an entire lot should be accepted or rejected based on a sample of items from the population. For more information, go to the CD-ROM.

13-2: EXERCISES

13-10. Data were collected on a quantitative measure with a sub-group size of 5 observations. Thirty subgroups were collected with the following results.

$$\bar{\bar{x}} = 44.52 \qquad \bar{R} = 5.6$$

    a. Determine the Shewhart factors that will be needed if x-bar and R-charts are to be developed.

    b. Compute the upper and lower control limits for the x-bar chart.

    c. Compute the upper and lower control limits for the R-chart.

13-11. Data were collected from a process where the factor of interest was whether or not the finished item contained a particular attribute. The fraction of items that did not contain the attribute was recorded. A total of 30 samples was selected. The common sample size was 100 items. The total number of nonconforming items was 270. Based on these data, compute the upper and lower control limits for the p-chart.

13-12. Fifty sampling units of equal size were inspected, and the number of nonconforming situations were recorded. The total number of instances was 449.

    a. Determine the appropriate control chart to use for this process.

    b. Compute the mean value for the control chart.

    c. Compute the upper and lower control limits.

Business Applications

13-13. The Haines Lumber Company makes plywood for residential and commercial construction. One of the key quality measures is plywood thickness. Every hour, 5 pieces of plywood are selected and the thickness is measured. The data (in inches) for the first 20 subgroups are in a file on your CD-ROM called **Haines**.

    a. Construct an $\bar{x}$-chart based on these data. Make sure you plot the centerline and both 3-sigma upper and lower control limits.

    b. Construct an R-chart based on these data.

    c. Examine both control charts and determine if there are any special causes of variation that require attention in this process.

13-14. Referring to Problem 13, suppose the process remained in control for the next 40 hours. The thickness measurements for hours 41–43 are:

Hour 41	0.764	0.737	0.724	0.716	0.752
Hour 42	0.766	0.785	0.777	0.790	0.799
Hour 43	0.812	0.774	0.767	0.799	0.821

    a. Based on these data, and the two control charts computed in problem 13, what should you conclude about the process? Has the process gone out of control? Discuss.

    b. Was it necessary to obtain your answer to Problem 13 before part a could be answered? Explain your reasoning.

13-15. The Kaiser Corporation makes aluminum at various locations around the country. One of the key factors in being profitable is keeping the machinery running. One particularly troublesome machine is the roller that flattens the sheets to the appropriate thickness. This machine tends to break down for various reasons. Consequently, the maintenance manager has decided to develop a process control chart. Over a period of 10 weeks, 20 subgroups consisting of 5 downtime measures (in minutes) were collected (one measurement at the end of each of the two shifts). The subgroup means and ranges are shown as follows and are contained in a file called **Kaiser**.

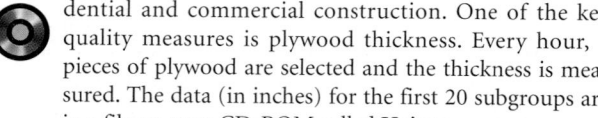

Subgroup Mean	104.8	85.9	78.6	72.8	102.6	84.8	67.0
Subgroup Range	9.6	14.3	8.6	10.6	11.2	13.5	10.8
Subgroup Mean	91.1	79.5	71.9	47.6	106.7	80.7	81.0
Subgroup Range	5.2	14.2	14.1	14.9	12.7	13.3	15.4
Subgroup Mean	57.0	98.9	87.9	64.9	101.6	83.9	
Subgroup Range	15.5	13.8	16.6	11.2	9.6	11.5	

a. Explain why an *x*-bar and *R*-chart would be appropriate in this case.

b. Determine the appropriate Shewhart factors to use for the *x*-bar and *R*-charts.

c. Find the centerline value for the *x*-bar chart.

d. Calculate the centerline value for the *R*-chart.

e. Compute the upper and lower control limits for the *x*-bar chart and construct the chart with appropriate labels.

f. Compute the upper and lower control limits for the *R*-chart and construct the chart with appropriate labels.

g. Examine the charts constructed in parts e and f and determine whether the process was in control during the period for which the control charts were developed. Explain.

13-16. Referring to Problem 15, suppose the process stays in control for the next 6 weeks (subgroups 21–32). The subgroup mean and range for subgroups 33–38 are as follows.

Subgroup	33	34	35	36	37	38
Subgroup Mean	89.0	88.4	85.2	89.3	97.2	105.3
Subgroup Range	11.4	5.4	14.2	11.7	9.5	10.2

a. Plot the ranges on the *R*-chart. Is there evidence based on the range chart that the process has gone out of control? Discuss.

b. Plot the subgroup means on the *x*-bar chart. Is there evidence to suggest that the process has gone out of control with respect to the process mean? Discuss.

13-17. The Ajax Taxi Company in Manhattan, New York, wishes to set up an $\bar{x}$-chart and an *R*-chart to monitor the number of miles driven per day by their taxi drivers. Each week, the scheduler selects 4 taxis and (without the driver's knowledge) monitors the number of miles driven. He has done this for the past 40 weeks. The data are in a file called **AJAX**.

a. Construct the $\bar{x}$-chart for these 40 subgroups. Be sure to label the chart correctly.

b. Construct the *R*-chart for these 40 subgroups.

c. Look at both control charts and determine if any of the control chart signals are present to indicate that the process is not in control. Explain the implications of what you have found for the Ajax Taxi Company.

13-18. Referring to Problem 17, the data for weeks 41–45 are in the **AJAX-Extra** file.

a. Using the control limits developed from the first 40 weeks, do these data indicate that the number of miles driven is now out of control? Explain.

b. If a change has occurred, brainstorm some of the possible reasons.

13-19. Referring to Problems 17 and 18, suppose the scheduler wishes to update the process control charts using the data for weeks 1–45.

a. What would you predict will be the impact on the control charts once the new data are included?

b. Use the data in the file called **AJAX** and **AJAX-Extra** to develop the new control charts.

c. Are any of the typical control chart signals present? Discuss.

13-20. Grandfoods, Inc., makes energy supplement bars for use by athletes and others who need an energy boost. One of the critical quality characteristics is the weight of the bars. Too much weight implies that too many liquids have been added to the mix and the bar will be too chewy. If the bars are light, the implication is that the bars are too dry. To monitor the weights, the production manager wishes to use process control charts. Data for 30 subgroups of size 4 bars are contained in a file on your CD-ROM called **Grandfoods**. Note that a subgroup is selected every 15 minutes as bars come off the manufacturing line.

a. Use these data to construct the appropriate process control chart(s).

b. Discuss what each chart is used for. Why do we need both charts?

c. Examine the control charts and indicate which if any of the process control signals are present. Discuss.

d. Develop a histogram for the energy bar weights. Discuss the shape of the distribution and the implications of this toward the validity of the control chart procedures you have used.

13-21. Referring to the process control charts developed in Problem 20, suppose data for periods 31–39 are contained in the file **Grandfoods-Extra**.

a. Based on these data, what would you conclude about the energy bar process?

b. Write a report discussing the results, and show the control charts along with the new data.

13-22. Go to any site on the Internet where values for the Dow Jones Industrial Average (DJIA) can be found. Using the weekly closing prices for Monday through Friday for weeks with no trading holidays, go back 10 weeks from last Friday. Then select the previous 30 weeks and record the values (subgroup size = 5).

a. Use the DJIA data to construct an $\bar{x}$- and an *R*-chart using the 30 weeks' data.

b. Now, use the closing prices for the 10 most recent weeks, plot the $\bar{x}$- and *R*-values on the appropriate charts computed in part a.

c. Write a short paper discussing the feasibility of using control charts to indicate when the Dow Jones Index process has incurred a special cause situation. Relate your discussion to the 10 most current weeks.

13-23. Tony Perez is the manager of one of the largest chains of service stores that specializes in oil and lubrication of automobiles, Fastlube, Inc. One of the company's stated goals is to provide a lube and oil change for anyone's automobile in 15 minutes. To monitor this aspect of Fastlube, Inc., Tony has selected a sample of 20 days and recorded the time it took 5 randomly selected employees to service an automobile. The data are located in a file called **Fastlube**.

a. Tony glanced through the data and noticed that the longest time it took to service a car was 24.14 minutes. Suppose the distribution of times to service a car was normal with a mean of 15. Use your knowledge of a normal distribution to let Tony know what the standard deviation is for the time it takes to service a car.

b. Use the **Fastlube** data to construct an $\bar{x}$ and an R-chart.

c. Based on these data, what would you conclude about the service time process?

d. Based upon your findings of the R-chart would it be advisable to draw conclusions based upon the $\bar{x}$-chart?

13-24. Regis Printing Company performs printing services for individual and business customers. Many of the jobs require that brochures be folded for mailing. The company has a machine that does the folding. The machine generally does a good job but can have problems that cause it to make improper folds. To monitor this process, the company selects a sample of 50 brochures from every order and counts the number of incorrectly folded items in each sample. Until now, nothing has been done with the 300 samples that have been collected. The data are located in a file called **Regis**.

a. What is the appropriate control chart to use to monitor this process?

b. Using the data in this file, construct the appropriate control chart and label it properly.

c. Suppose that for the next three orders, sample sizes of 50 brochures are examined with the following results.

Sample Number:	301	302	303
Number of Bad Folds	6	9	7

Plot the appropriate data to the control chart and indicate whether any of the control chart process control signals are present. Discuss your results.

13-25. Referring to Problem 24, suppose that the next sample of 50 has 14 improperly folded brochures. What conclusion should be reached based on the control chart? Discuss.

13-26. Explain why it is important to update the control charts as soon as new data become available.

13-27. The Jonestown Brick Company is concerned about the occurrences of cracks in the bricks it makes. Obviously cracks are undesirable. The more cracks, the lower the price for which the brick can be sold. Recently the production manager decided to set up a SPC chart to monitor cracks in large paver bricks the company produces. One brick is selected out of every batch of 200 bricks. The number of cracks in this brick is recorded. To construct the chart, 50 bricks were inspected and 408 cracks were observed.

a. Which control chart should be used in this application?

b. Construct the upper and lower control limits and plot these on a blank control chart.

c. Is it possible, without seeing the actual data, to determine whether the process is in control? Discuss.

13-28. Trinkle & Sons performs subcontract body paint work for one of the "Big Three" automakers. One of its recent contracts called for the company to paint 12,500 door panels. Several quality characteristics are very important to the manufacturer, one of which is blemishes in the paint. The manufacturer has required Trinkle & Sons to have control charts to monitor the number of paint blemishes per door panel. The panels are all for the same model car and are the same size. To initially develop the control chart, data for 88 door panels were collected and are provided in the data file called **CarPaint**.

a. Determine the appropriate type of process control chart to develop.

b. Develop a 3-sigma control chart.

c. Based on the control chart and the standard signals discussed in this chapter, what conclusions can you reach about whether the paint process is in control? Discuss.

13-29. Recall from Problem 23 that Tony Perez is the manager of Fastlube, Inc., one of the largest chains of service stores that specializes in oil and lubrication of automobiles. One of the company's stated goals is to provide a lube and oil change for anyone's automobile in 15 minutes. To monitor this aspect of Fastlube, Inc., Tony has selected a sample of 24 days and recorded the time it took to service 100 automobiles each day. The number of times the service was performed in 15 minutes or less (≤ 15) is given in the file called **Lubeoil**.

a. (1) Convert the sample data to proportions and plot the data as a line graph. (2) Compute $\bar{p}$ and plot this value on the line graph. (3) Compute s_p and interpret what it measures.

b. Construct a p-chart and determine if the time required for oil and lube jobs is in control.

c. Specify the signals that are used to indicate an out-of-control situation on a p-chart.

13-30. Susan Booth is the director of operations for National Skyways, a small commuter airline with headquarters in Cedar Rapids, Iowa. She has become increasingly concerned about the amount of carry-on luggage passengers have been carrying on board National Skyways' planes. She has collected data concerning the number of pieces of baggage that were taken on board over a 1-month period. The data collected are provided in the file called **Carryon**.

a. Set up a control chart for the number of carry-on bags per day.

b. Is the process in a state of statistical control? Explain your answer.

c. Suppose that National Skyways' aircraft were full for each of the 30 days. The Skyways' aircraft hold 40 passengers. Describe the control chart you would use to monitor the carry-on bags per passenger. (Hint: See CD-ROM topic on u-charts.)

13-31. Sid Luka is the service manager for Brakes Unlimited, a franchise corporation that specializes in servicing auto-mobile brakes. He wants to study the length of time required to replace the rear drum brakes of automobiles. A subgroup of 10 automobiles needing their brakes replaced was selected on each day for a period of 20 days. The time required (in hours) for this service was recorded and is presented in the file **Brakes**.

    a. Sid has been trying to get the average time required to replace the rear drum brakes of automobiles to be under 1.65 hours. Use the data Sid has collected to determine if he has reached his goal. Hint: You will have a sample size of 200.

    b. Set up the appropriate control charts to determine if this process is under control.

    c. Determine whether or not the process is under control. If the process is not under control, brainstorm suggestions that might help Sid bring it under control. What tools of quality might Sid find useful?

13-32. Wilson, Ryan, and Reed is a large CPA firm in Charleston, South Carolina. The partners have been monitoring the accuracy of their employees and wish to get the number of errors per account under statistical control. They have sampled 100 accounts for each of the last 30 days and examined them for errors. The data are presented in the file called **Accounts**.

    a. Construct the relevant control chart for the account process.

    b. What does the chart indicate about the statistical stability of the process? Give reasons for your answers.

    c. Suppose that for the next three days, sample sizes of 100 accounts are examined with the following results.

Number of Errors	6	7	9

Plot the appropriate data on the control chart and indicate whether any of the control chart signals are present. Discuss your results.

13-33. Clifford Applebee is the quality assurance engineer for Sticks and Stones. One of the items that Sticks and Stones produces is sets of pocket billiard balls. Clifford has been monitoring the finish of the pocket billiard balls. He is concerned that the sets of billiard balls are being shipped with an increasing number of blemishes. Over the last week, Clifford has selected a sample of 35 billiard balls and inspected them to determine the number of blem-ishes. The data collected by Clifford are displayed in the file called **Poolball**.

    a. What is the appropriate control chart to use to mon-itor this process?

    b. Using the data in this file, construct the appropriate control chart and label it properly.

    c. Suppose that for the next five pocket billiard balls, the following results were obtained.

Sample Number	36	37	38	39	40
Number of Blemishes	0	1	0	1	1

Plot the appropriate data to the control chart and indicate whether any of the control chart signals is present. If you discovered that the process was not under control for the last half a dozen pocket billiard balls, what would this indicate with regard to the quality of these balls?

■ SUMMARY AND CONCLUSIONS

The quality movement throughout the United States and much of the rest of the world has created great expectations among consumers. We now believe that our televisions, com-puters, stereo systems, automobiles, and even textbooks should be quality products. This quality movement experienced a slow start in the United States because many managers did not believe that there was a need to increase quality when so many units of their products were already being demanded. However, competitive pressures changed that misconception, and corporate America began to buy into the messages that had been communicated by people like W. Edwards Deming and Joseph Juran for many years. Ideas like continuous process improvement and customer focus have become a central part of the operations of many of our successful companies.

Statistics has played a key role in this transition. The enemy of quality is variation. Variation exists in every-

thing. Through the use of appropriate statistical tools and the concept of statistical reasoning, managers and employ-ees have developed a better understanding of their processes. While they haven't yet figured out how to elimi-nate variation, statistics has helped them reduce it and understand how to operate more effectively when variation exists.

Statistical process control (SPC) has played a big part in understanding variation. SPC is quite likely the most fre-quently used of the Basic 7 Tools. This chapter has intro-duced you to the basics of SPC. Hopefully, you realize that these tools are merely extensions of the hypothesis testing and estimation concepts presented in Chapters 7–9. You will very likely have the opportunity to use SPC in one form or another after you leave this course and enter the workforce.

EQUATIONS

Variation Components

$$\text{Total Process Variation} = \text{Common}$$
$$\text{Cause Variation} + \text{Special Cause Variation} \qquad \textbf{13-1}$$

Average of Subgroup Means

$$\bar{\bar{x}} = \frac{\sum\limits_{i=1}^{k} \bar{x}_i}{k} \qquad \textbf{13-2}$$

Average Subgroup Range

$$\bar{R} = \frac{\sum\limits_{i=1}^{k} R_i}{k} \qquad \textbf{13-3}$$

Upper Control Limit, $\bar{x}$-Chart

$$UCL = \bar{\bar{x}} + A_2(\bar{R}) \qquad \textbf{13-4}$$

Lower Control Limit, $\bar{x}$-Chart

$$LCL = \bar{\bar{x}} - A_2(\bar{R}) \qquad \textbf{13-5}$$

Upper Control Limit, R-Chart

$$UCL = D_4(\bar{R}) \qquad \textbf{13-6}$$

Lower Control Limit, R-Chart

$$LCL = D_3(\bar{R}) \qquad \textbf{13-7}$$

Mean Subgroup Proportion

For equal size samples:

$$\bar{p} = \frac{\sum\limits_{i=1}^{k} p_i}{k} \qquad \textbf{13-8}$$

For unequal samples:

$$\bar{p} = \frac{\sum\limits_{i=1}^{k} n_i p_i}{\sum\limits_{i=1}^{k} n_i} \qquad \textbf{13-9}$$

Estimate of the Standard Error for the Subgroup Proportions

For equal sample sizes:

$$s_P = \sqrt{\frac{(\bar{p})(1 - \bar{p})}{n}} \qquad \textbf{13-10}$$

Control Limits for p-Chart

$$UCL = \bar{p} + 3s_P \qquad \textbf{13-11}$$
$$LCL = \bar{p} - 3s_P \qquad \textbf{13-12}$$

Mean for c-Chart

$$\bar{c} = \frac{\sum\limits_{i=1}^{k} x_i}{k} \qquad \textbf{13-13}$$

Standard Deviation for c-Chart

$$s = \sqrt{\bar{c}} \qquad \textbf{13-14}$$

c-Chart Control Limits

$$UCL = \bar{c} + 3\sqrt{\bar{c}} \qquad \textbf{13-15}$$
$$LCL = \bar{c} - 3\sqrt{\bar{c}} \qquad \textbf{13-16}$$

■ KEY TERMS

Attribute—A quality characteristic that is either present or not present in an item.

c-Chart—A control chart used when the variable is an attribute and multiple attributes can occur per sampling unit.

Centerline—The average value of the plotted values on a process control chart.

Common Cause Variation—Variation in the output of a process that is naturally occurring and expected and that may be the result of natural variation in materials, tools, machines, operators, and the environment.

Control Limits—Values computed from the output measures of a process over time that define the range of inherent variation in the output. Both upper and lower control limits are computed and are typically based on the concept of being a specified number of standard deviations from the centerline.

Inherent Variation—The variation in the output of a process that exists naturally. This variation can be reduced but not eliminated.

p-Chart—A process control chart used when the variable is an attribute. The p-chart monitors the fraction of items in a sample that contain the attribute of interest.

Pareto Principle—80% of the trouble comes from 20% of the causes.

R-chart—A control chart that is used to monitor process variation when the variable of interest is a quantitative measure.

Shewhart Table—A table of factors used to compute 3-sigma control limits on certain process control charts.

Special Cause Variation—Variation in the ouput of a process that is abnormal or unexpected and which has an assignable cause. Variation in the ouput that is beyond that which is considered inherent to the process.

Statistical Process Control Chart—A chart that is used to monitor output of a process over time for the purposes of determining whether the output exhibits special cause variation.

Subgroup—A sample of items selected from a process. If the process is operating in control, the subgroup is free from special causes of variation.

Total Quality Management—A journey to excellence in which everyone in the organization is focused on continuous process improvement directed toward increased customer satisfaction.

$\bar{x}$-Chart—A chart that monitors the average value of a process over time. For each subgroup, the $\bar{x}$ value is plotted. The upper and lower control limits define the range of inherent variation in the subgroup means when the process is in control.

CHAPTER EXERCISES

Conceptual Questions

13-34. Data were collected on a quantitative measure with a sub-group size of 3 observations. Thirty subgroups were collected with the following results.

$$\bar{\bar{x}} = 2.33 \qquad \bar{R} = 0.80$$

    a. Determine the Shewhart factors that will be needed if x-bar and R-charts are to be developed.

    b. Compute the upper and lower control limits for the x-bar chart.

    c. Compute the upper and lower control limits for the R-chart.

13-35. Data were collected on a quantitative measure with sub-groups of 4 observations. Twenty-five subgroups were collected with the following results.

$$\bar{\bar{x}} = 1,345.4 \qquad \bar{R} = 209.3$$

    a. Determine the Shewhart factors that will be needed if x-bar and R-charts are to be developed.

    b. Compute the upper and lower control limits for the x-bar chart.

    c. Compute the upper and lower control limits for the R-chart.

13-36. Data were collected from a process where the factor of interest was whether or not the finished item contained a particular attribute. The fraction of items that did not contain the attribute was recorded. A total of 20 samples were selected. The common sample size was 150 items. The total number of nonconforming items was 720. Based on these data, compute the upper and lower control limits for the p-chart.

13-37. Data were collected from a process where the factor of interest was whether or not the finished item contained a particular attribute. The fraction of items that did not contain the attribute was recorded. A total of 30 samples were selected. The common sample size was 100 items. The average number of nonconforming items per sample was 14. Based on these data, construct the upper and lower control limits for the p-chart.

Business Applications

13-38. A & A Enterprises ships integrated circuits to companies that assemble computers. Because computer manufacturing operations run on little inventory, parts must be available when promised. Thus, a critical element of A & A's customer satisfaction is on-time delivery performance. To ensure that their delivery process is performing as intended, a quality improvement team decided to monitor the firm's distribution and delivery process. From the A & A corporate database, 100 monthly shipping records were randomly selected for the previous 21 months and the number of on-time shipments counted. This information is contained in the file **A & A On Time**

Shipments. Develop the appropriate 3-sigma control chart(s) for monitoring this process. Does it appear that the delivery process is in control? If not, can you suggest some possible assignable causes?

13-39. Fifi Carpets, Inc., produces carpet for homes and offices. Fifi has recently opened a new production process dedicated to the manufacture of a special type of carpet used by firms that want a floor covering for high-traffic spaces. As a part of their ongoing quality improvement activities, the management of Fifi regularly monitors their production processes using statistical process control. For their new production process Fifi managers would like to develop control charts to help them in their monitoring activities. Thirty samples of carpet sections with each section having an area of 50 square meters were randomly selected and the number of stains, cuts, snags, and tears were counted on each section. The sample data are contained in the file **Fifi Carpets**.

Use the sample data to construct the appropriate 3-sigma control chart for monitoring the production process. Does the process appear to be in statistical control?

13-40. Varians Controls manufactures a variety of different electric motors and drives. One step in the manufacturing process involves cutting copper wire from large reels into smaller lengths. For a particular motor there is a dedicated machine for cutting wire to the required length. As a part of their regular quality improvement activities, the continuous process improvement team at Varians took a sample of 5 cuttings every hour for 30 consecutive hours of operation. At the time the samples were taken, Varians had every reason to believe that its process was working as intended. The automatic machine cutting the wire records the length of each cut, and the following results are reported in the file **Varians Controls**.

    a. Develop the appropriate 3-sigma control chart(s) for this process. Does the process appear to be working as intended (in control)?

    b. A few weeks after the Varians data were sampled, a new operator was hired to calibrate the company's cutting machines. The first 5 samples taken from the machine following the calibration adjustments (samples 225–229) are shown as follows.

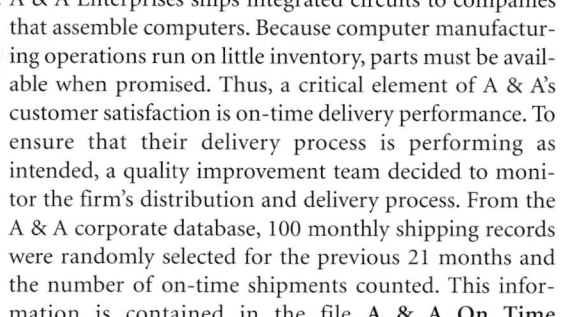

	CUTTING 1	CUTTING 2	CUTTING 3	CUTTING 4	CUTTING 5
Sample 225	0.7818	0.7760	0.7814	0.7824	0.7702
Sample 226	0.7694	0.7838	0.7675	0.7834	0.7730
Sample 227	0.7875	0.7738	0.7737	0.7594	0.7837
Sample 228	0.7762	0.7711	0.7700	0.7823	0.7673
Sample 229	0.7805	0.7724	0.7748	0.7823	0.7924

Based on these sample values, what can you say about the cutting process? Does it appear to be in control?

13-41. CC, Inc., provides billing services for the healthcare industry. To ensure that its processes are operating as intended, CC selects 100 billing records at random every day and inspects each record to determine if it is free of errors. A billing record is classified as defective whenever there is an error that requires that the bill be reprocessed and mailed again. Such errors can occur for a variety of reasons. For example, a defective bill could have an incorrect mailing address, a wrong insurance identification number, an improper doctor or hospital reference, etc. The sample data taken from the most recent 5 weeks of billing records are contained on the file **CC Inc.**

Use the sample information to construct the appropriate 3-sigma control chart. Does CC, Inc.'s billing process appear to be in control? What, if any, comments can you make regarding the performance of its billing process?

13-42. The order entry, order processing, call center for PS Industries is concerned about the amount of time that customers must wait before their calls are handled. A quality improvement consultant suggests monitoring call wait time using control charts. Using call center statistics maintained by the company's database system, the consultant randomly selects 4 calls every hour for 30 different hours and examines the wait time, in seconds, for each call. This information is contained in the file **PS Industries.**

Use the sample data to construct the appropriate control charts. Does the process appear to be in statistical control? Of what other information concerning the call center's process should the consultant be aware?

CASE 13-A

Izbar Precision Casters, Inc.

Izbar Precision Casters, Inc., manufactures a variety of structural steel products for the construction trade. Currently, there is a strong demand for their I-beam product produced at a mill outside Memphis. Beams at this facility are shipped throughout the Midwest and mid-South, and demand for the product is high due to the strong economy in the regions served by the plant. Angie Schneider, the mill's manager, wants to ensure that the plant's operations are in control and has selected several characteristics to monitor. Specifically, she collects data on the number of weekly accidents at the plant, the number of orders shipped on time, and the thickness of the steel I-beams produced.

For the number of reported accidents, Angie selected 30 days at random from the company's safety records. She, along with all the employees of the plant, is very concerned about workplace safety; and management, labor, and government officials have worked together to help create a safe work environment. As a part of their safety program, the company requires employees to report every accident regardless of how minor it may be. In fact, most accidents are very minor, but Izbar still records them and works to prevent their recurrence. Because of the company's strong reporting requirement, Angie was able to get a count of the number of reported accidents for each of the 30 sampled days. These data are shown in Table 13-6.

TABLE 13-6
Accident Data

DAY	NUMBER OF REPORTED ACCIDENTS	DAY	NUMBER OF REPORTED ACCIDENTS
1	9	16	4
2	11	17	11
3	9	18	7
4	9	19	7
5	11	20	10
6	10	21	11
7	10	22	6
8	10	23	6
9	4	24	7
10	7	25	4
11	7	26	9
12	8	27	11
13	11	28	9
14	10	29	6
15	7	30	5

To monitor the percentage of on-time shipments, Angie randomly selected 50 records from the firm's shipping and billing system every day for 20 different days over the past 6 months. These records contained the actual and promised shipping dates for each order. Angie used a spreadsheet to determine the number of shipments that were made after the promised shipment date. The number of late shipments from the 50 sampled records is then reported. These data are shown in Table 13-7.

TABLE 13-7
Late Shipments

DAY	NUMBER OF LATE SHIPMENTS	DAY	NUMBER OF LATE SHIPMENTS
1	5	11	8
2	3	12	2
3	1	13	5
4	6	14	6
5	5	15	2
6	8	16	7
7	5	17	7
8	6	18	3
9	4	19	2
10	4	20	7

Finally, to monitor the thickness of the I-beam produced at the plant, Angie randomly selected 6 I-beams every day for 30 days and had each sampled beam measured. The thickness of each beam, in inches, was recorded. All of the data collected by Angie are contained in the data file called **Izbar**. She wants to use the information she has collected to construct and analyze the appropriate control charts for the plant's production processes. She intends to present this information at the next manager's meeting on Monday morning.

a) Use the data that Angie has collected to develop and analyze the appropriate control charts for this process. Be sure to label each control chart carefully and also identify the type of control chart used.

b) Do the processes analyzed appear to be in control? Why or why not? What would you suggest that Angie do?

c) Does Angie need to continue to monitor her processes on a regular basis? How would she do this? Also, are there other variables that might be of interest to her in monitoring the plant's performance? If so, what do you think they might be?

GENERAL REFERENCES

1. Crosby, Philip B., *Quality Is Free: The Art of Making Quality Certain* (New York: McGraw-Hill, 1979).
2. Deming, W. Edwards, *Out of the Crisis* (Cambridge, MA: MIT Center for Advanced Engineering Study, 1986).
3. Evans, James R., and William M. Lindsay, *The Management and Control of Quality*, 4th ed. (Cincinnati, OH: South-Western College Publishing, 1999).
4. Gitlow, Howard, Alan Oppenheim, and Rosa Oppenheim, *Quality Management: Tools and Methods for Improvement*, 2d ed. (Burr Ridge, IL: Irwin, 1995).
5. Juran, Joseph M., *Quality Control Handbook*, 5th ed. (New York: McGraw-Hill, 1999).
6. *Microsoft Excel 2000* (Redmond, WA: Microsoft Corporation, 1999).
7. *Minitab for Windows Version 13* (State College, PA: Minitab, Inc., 2000).
8. Mitra, Amitava, *Fundamentals of Quality Control and Improvement*, 2d ed. (Upper Saddle River, NJ: Prentice Hall, 1998).

CHAPTER 14

GOODNESS-OF-FIT TESTS AND CONTINGENCY ANALYSIS

CHAPTER OUTCOMES

After studying the material in Chapter 14, you should be able to:

14-1: Utilize the chi-square goodness-of-fit test to determine whether data from a process fit a specified distribution.

14-2: Set up a contingency analysis table and perform a chi-square test of independence.

WHY YOU NEED TO KNOW

The previous 13 chapters have introduced a wide variety of statistical techniques that are frequently used in business decision making. We have discussed numerous descriptive tools and techniques, as well as large-sample estimation and hypothesis tests for one and two populations, small-sample estimation and hypothesis tests using the *t*-distribution, analysis of variance, correlation, and regression analysis. However, as we have often mentioned, these statistical tools are limited to the presence of those conditions for which they were originally developed. For example, the large-sample tests based on the standard normal distribution assume that the data can be measured at least at the interval level. The small-sample tests that employ the *t*-distribution assume that the sampled populations are normally distributed.

In those situations where the conditions just mentioned are not satisfied, we suggest using a class of statistical techniques referred to as nonparametric statistics. Several of the more widely used nonparametric techniques will be discussed in Chapter 15. These procedures will be shown to be generally the nonparametric equivalent of the classical procedures discussed in previous chapters. The obvious questions when faced with a realistic decision-making situation are "Which test do I use? Should I consider a nonparametric test?" These questions are generally followed by a third question: "Do the data come from a normal distribution?" But recall that we have

also described situations involving data from Poisson or binomial distributions. How do we know which distribution applies to our situation? Fortunately, a statistical technique called a *goodness-of-fit test* exists, which can help us answer this question. Using goodness-of-fit tests we can decide whether a set of data comes from a specific hypothesized distribution.

You will also encounter many business situations in which the level of data measurement for the variable of interest is either nominal or ordinal, not interval or ratio. For example, a bank may use a code to indicate whether a customer is a good or poor credit risk. The bank may also have data for these customers that indicate, by a code, whether each person is buying or renting a home. The loan officer may be interested in determining whether credit risk status is independent of home ownership or not. Since both credit risk and home ownership are qualitative, or categorical, variables, their measurement level is nominal and the statistical techniques introduced in Chapters 1 through 13 cannot be used to analyze this problem. We therefore need a new statistical tool to assist the manager in reaching a conclusion about the customer population. That statistical tool is contingency analysis. Contingency analysis is a widely used tool for analyzing the relationship between qualitative variables and one that decision makers in all business areas find helpful for data analysis.

■ 14-1: INTRODUCTION TO GOODNESS-OF-FIT TESTS

Many of the statistical procedures introduced in earlier chapters require that the sample data come from populations that are normally distributed. For example, when we use the *t*-distribution in confidence interval estimation or hypothesis testing about one or two population means, the population(s) of interest is (are) assumed to be normally distributed. The analysis of variance *F*-test introduced in Chapter 10 is based on the assumption that the populations are normally distributed. But how can you determine whether these assumptions are satisfied? In other instances, you may wish to employ a particular probability distribution to help solve a problem related to an actual business process. In order to solve the problem you may need to know whether the actual data from the process fit the probability distribution being considered. In such instances, a statistical technique known as a *goodness-of-fit test* can be used to help determine whether the sample data fit the specified distribution.

The term goodness-of-fit aptly describes the technique. Suppose a major retail department store is considering positioning displays at its entrances and believes customers are equally likely to use each of the four entrances to the store. This would mean that customer arrivals are *uniformly* distributed across the four entrances. Suppose a sample of 1,000 customers is observed entering the store and the entrance (A, B, C, or D) used by each customer is recorded. Table 14-1 shows the results of the sample.

If the manager's assumption about the entrances being used uniformly holds and if there was no sampling error involved, we would expect one-fourth of the customers, or

TABLE 14-1
Customer Door Entrance Data

ENTRANCE	NUMBER OF CUSTOMERS
A	260
B	290
C	230
D	220

250, to enter through each door. When we allow for the potential of sampling error, we would still expect close to 250 customers to enter through each entrance. The question is, "how good is the fit" between the sample data in Table 14-1 and the expected number of 250 people at each entrance? At what point do we no longer believe that the difference between what is actually observed at each entrance and what we expected can be attributed to sampling error? If this difference gets too big, we will reject the uniformity assumption and conclude that customers prefer some entrances to others.

Chi-Square Goodness-of-Fit Test

The *chi-square goodness-of-fit test* can be used to determine whether the sample data come from any hypothesized distribution.

GOODNESS OF FIT

Vista Health Guard

Vista Health Guard is a privately owned neighborhood health clinic providing a wide range of services to people in a Pennsylvania metropolitan community. The clinic is open 7 days a week and has offices at 25 different locations. The operations manager was recently hired from a similar position at a smaller chain of clinics in Florida. One of her responsibilities is clinic staffing. A natural concern of the operations manager is that the staffing level—consisting of physicians, nurses, and other support personnel—be balanced appropriately with the patient demand at the clinic.

Currently, the staffing level is balanced during the weekdays, Monday through Friday, with a reduced staffing level on Saturday and Sunday. The reasoning behind this, as explained by her predecessor, is that patient demand is fairly level throughout the weekday period and about 25% less on weekends, but she suspects it also has something to do with the staff wanting to have weekends free. Although she was willing to operate with this schedule for a while, she has decided to perform a study of patient demand to see whether the assumed demand pattern still applies.

To conduct the study, the operations manager requested a sample of 20 days for each day of the week, showing the number of patients in the clinic offices on each of the sample days. A portion of the data that she received is shown as follows.

DAY	PATIENT COUNT
Monday, May 6	325
Monday, October 7	379
Tuesday, July 2	456
Monday, July 15	323
Wednesday, April 3	467
.	.
.	.
.	.
etc.	etc.

TABLE 14-2
Patient Count Data for the Vista Health Guard Example

DAY	TOTAL PATIENT COUNT
Sunday	4,502
Monday	6,623
Tuesday	8,308
Wednesday	10,420
Thursday	11,032
Friday	10,754
Saturday	4,361
Total	56,000

For the 140 days observed, the total count was 56,000 patients. The total patient counts for each day of the week are shown in Table 14-2 and are graphed in Figure 14-1.

Recall that the previous operations manager at Vista Health Guard based his staffing on the premise that from Monday to Friday the patient count remained essentially the same and then for Saturdays and Sundays went down 25%. If this were actually the case, how many of the 56,000 patients would have been expected on Monday? How many on Tuesday and so forth? To figure this out, we determine weighting factors by allocating 4 units each to days Monday through Friday and 3 units each (representing the 25% reduction) to Saturday and Sunday. The total number of units is then $(5 \times 4) + (2 \times 3) = 26$

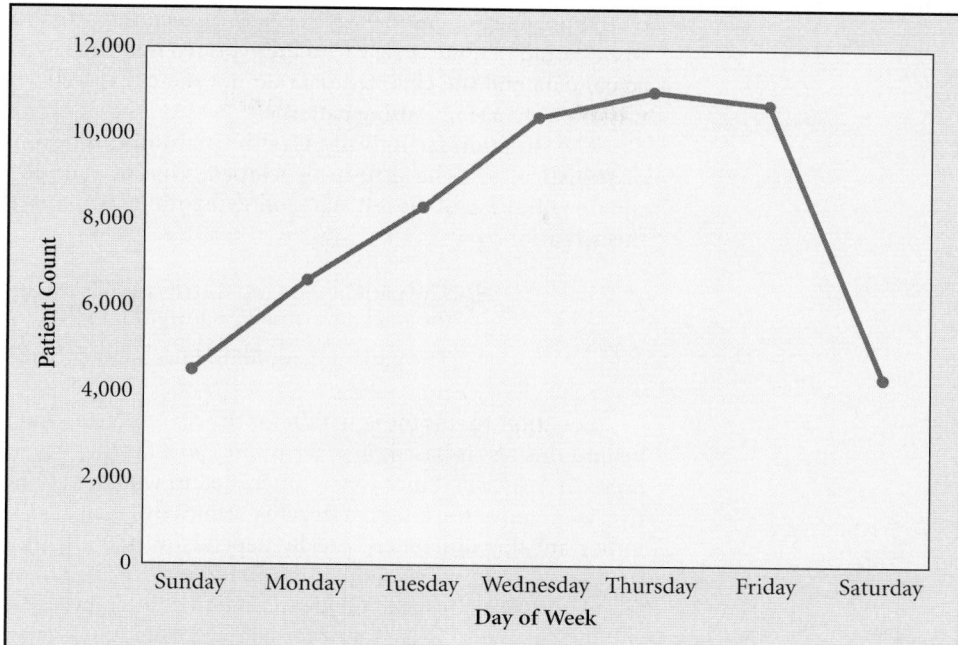

FIGURE 14-1
Graph of Actual Frequencies
for Vista Health Guard

units. The percentage of total patients expected on each weekday is 4/26 = 0.154 or 15.4% and the percentage expected on a weekend day is 3/26 = 0.115 or 11.5%. The expected number of patients on a weekday is 0.154 × 56,000 = 8,624, and the expected number on each weekend day is 0.115 × 56,000 = 6,440.

Figure 14-2 shows a graph with both the actual sample data and the expected values. With the exception of what might be attributed to sampling error, if the distribution claimed

FIGURE 14-2
Actual and Expected
Frequencies for Vista Health
Guard

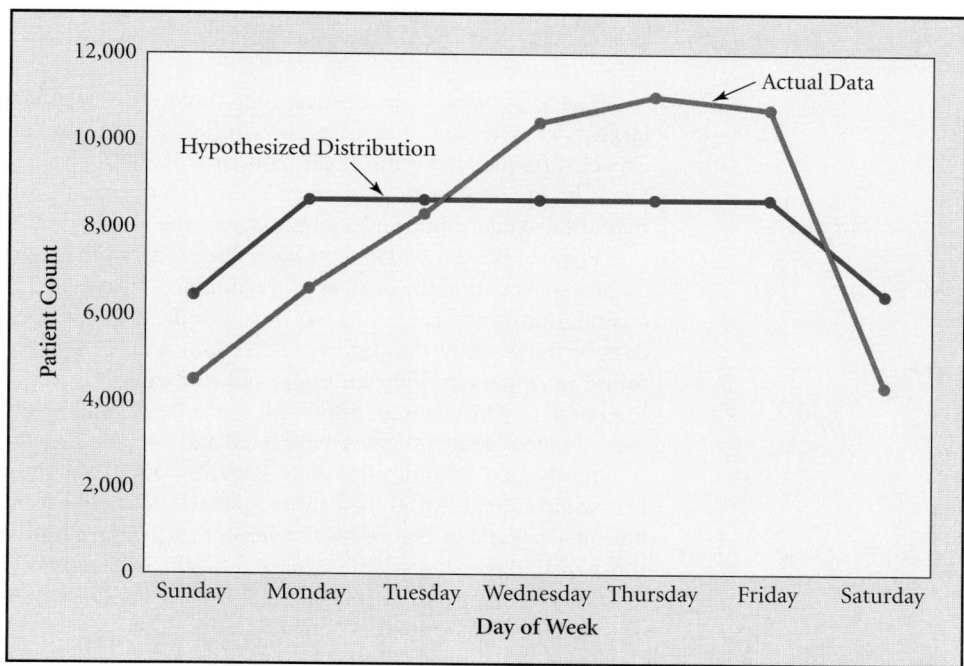

by the previous operations manager is correct, the actual frequencies for each day of the week should fit quite closely with the expected frequencies. As you can see in Figure 14-2, the actual data and the expected data do not match perfectly, but is the difference enough to warrant a change in staffing patterns?

The situation facing Vista Health Guard in this example is one for which a number of statistical tests have been developed. One of the most frequently used is the chi-square goodness-of-fit test. The following null and alternative hypotheses can represent this situation.

H_0: The patient demand distribution is evenly spread through the weekdays and 25% lower on the weekend.

H_A: The patient demand follows some other distribution.

Equation 14-1 is the equation for the chi-square goodness-of-fit test statistic. The logic behind this test is based on determining how far the actual *observed frequency* is from the *expected frequency*. Since we are interested in whether a difference exists, positive or negative, we remove the effect of negative values by squaring the differences. In addition, how important this difference is really depends on the magnitude of the expected frequency (e.g., a difference of 5 is more important if the expected frequency is 10 than if the expected frequency is 1,000) so we divide the squared difference by the expected frequency. Finally, we sum these difference ratios for all days. This sum is a statistic that has an approximate chi-square distribution.

CHI-SQUARE GOODNESS OF FIT TEST STATISTIC

$$\chi^2 = \sum_{i=1}^{k} \frac{(o_i - e_i)^2}{e_i}, \qquad df = k - 1 \qquad \text{14-1}$$

where:

k = Number of categories
o_i = Observed cell frequency for category i
e_i = Expected cell frequency for category i

The χ^2 statistic is distributed approximately as a chi-square only if the sample size is large. A sample size of at least 30 is sufficient in most cases provided that none of the expected frequencies is too small. This latter issue will be expanded upon later. If the calculated chi-square statistic gets large, this is evidence to suggest the fit of the actual data to the hypothesized distribution is not good, and the null hypothesis should be rejected.

Figure 14-3 shows the hypothesis test process and results for this chi-square goodness-of-fit test. Note that the degrees of freedom for the chi-square test are equal to $k - 1$, where k is the number of categories. In this example, we have 7 categories corresponding to the days of the week so the degrees of freedom are $7 - 1 = 6$. The critical value of 12.592 is found in Appendix G for an upper-tail test with 6 degrees of freedom and a significance level of 0.05. The test is an upper-tail test since we reject only if the calculated χ^2 statistic is large due to a poor fit between expected and actual cell frequencies.

As Figure 14-3 indicates, $\chi^2 = 3,302.7 > 12.592$, so the null hypothesis is rejected, and we should conclude that the demand pattern does not match the previously defined distribution. The data in Figure 14-3 indicate that demand is heavier than expected Wednesday through Friday and less than expected on the other days. The operations manager would now most likely wish to increase staffing on Wednesday, Thursday, and Friday to more closely approximate current demand patterns.

Hypotheses:

H_0: Patient demand is evenly spread through the weekdays and is 25% lower on weekends.
H_A: Patient demand follows some other distribution.
$\alpha = 0.05$

Total Patient Count

Day	Observed o_i	Expected e_i
Sunday	4,502	6,440
Monday	6,623	8,624
Tuesday	8,308	8,624
Wednesday	10,420	8,624
Thursday	11,032	8,624
Friday	10,754	8,624
Saturday	4,361	6,440
Total	56,000	56,000

Test Statistic:

$$\chi^2 = \sum_{i=1}^{k} \frac{(o_i - e_i)^2}{e_i} = \frac{(4{,}502 - 6{,}440)^2}{6{,}440} + \frac{(6{,}623 - 8{,}624)^2}{8{,}624} + \cdots + \frac{(4{,}361 - 6{,}440)^2}{6{,}440}$$

$$\chi^2 = 583.2 + 464.3 + \cdots + 671.2$$

$$= 3{,}302.7$$

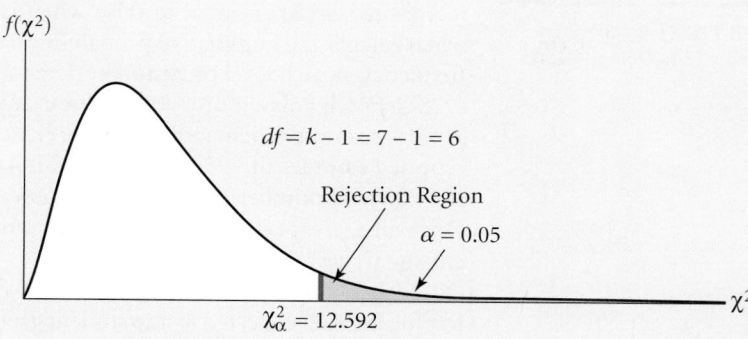

$f(\chi^2)$

$df = k - 1 = 7 - 1 = 6$

Rejection Region

$\alpha = 0.05$

$\chi^2_\alpha = 12.592$

χ^2

Decision Rule:

If $\chi^2 > 12.592$, reject H_0
Otherwise, do not reject H_0
Since $3{,}302.7 > 12.592$, reject H_0

FIGURE 14-3
Chi-Square Goodness-of-Fit
Test for Vista Health Guard

EXAMPLE 14-2

GOODNESS OF FIT

Excel and
Minitab Tutorial

Internet Service Provider

The students in a computer information systems class at State University have established their own Internet service provider (ISP) company for use by their university's students, faculty, and staff. Customers of the ISP will connect to the students' service by telephone lines.

One of the first things the students will need to do is to estimate potential demand for their service. When the student group proposed the original project, they performed a survey of likely student and faculty customers. They then estimated the demand during the late afternoon and evening hours to average 10 customers and follow a Poisson distribution.[1]

---

[1]Refer to Chapter 4 for a review of the Poisson distribution.

NUMBER OF REQUESTS	FREQUENCY
0	0
1	2
2	1
3	3
4	4
5	3
6	8
7	6
8	11
9	7
10	18
11	14
12	17
13	18
14	25
15	28
16	23
17	17
18	9
19 and over	11
Total	225

TABLE 14-3
Internet Line Demand Data

Using this information, the students configured a system that would be capable of handling a total of 20 users simultaneously. The student in charge of customer service recently indicated that there appears to be a problem since he often receives complaints from users who receive a busy signal when they attempt to connect to the system. The student thinks the demand distribution may be changing because the system designed for 20 users should be adequate to handle a Poisson-distributed demand with a mean of 10 users in almost all situations.

To determine whether the demand distribution has changed, the students have collected data from the monitoring system on the number of customers using the system and the number of calls that have been denied for 225 randomly selected periods during the past 2 months. These data are shown in Table 14-3.

The chi-square goodness-of-fit test can be used to test whether the current demand distribution is Poisson distributed with a mean equal to 10. The first step is to determine the expected number of times each level of customer demand would occur if the Poisson distribution with mean equal to 10 applies. To do this, go to the Poisson distribution table in Appendix C for the column headed $\lambda t = 10.0$, and determine the probability associated with each number of customers for 0, 1, 2, 3, 4 . . . . For example, $P(x = 0) = 0.0000$; $P(x = 1) = 0.0005$; $P(x = 2) = 0.0023$, etc. When a large number of probabilities must be determined, it is easier to use a computer, rather than a table, to determine the probability values. The use of the Excel function *POISSON (x, Mean, Cumulative)* is illustrated in Figure 14-4. The value, x, represents the number of customers demanding service. The *mean* is the expected value of the distribution. The argument *Cumulative* represents a logical value set either equal to false when calculating individual probabilities, or to true when calculating cumulative probabilities, and is illustrated in Figure 14-4. The expected frequency at each level of customer demand is determined by multiplying the sample size (225) by each Poisson probability. For example, the expected frequency when there will be $x = 10$ customers demanding ISP services is $(225)(0.1251) = 28.15$. This means that in repeated samples of 225 time periods, if $\lambda t = 10.0$ and the Poisson distribution applies, the expected number of times 10 customers would demand ISP services would be 28.15. Once all the expected frequencies are computed, Equation 14-1 is used to compute the chi-square test statistic.

Figure 14-4 presents all the expected frequencies and the chi-square goodness-of-fit test for the data collected by the student group. Although Excel does not have a tool for performing goodness-of-fit tests directly, we have used Excel to determine the Poisson probabilities and to compute the expected cell frequencies and chi-square statistic. As Figure 14-4 shows, the students should reject the hypothesis that the demand distribution is Poisson distributed with a mean equal to 10.

THE EXPECTED CELL FREQUENCIES

The chi-square goodness-of-fit test compares the actual cell frequencies with the expected cell frequencies. The test statistic from Equation 14-1:

$$\chi^2 = \sum_{i=1}^{k} \frac{(o_i - e_i)^2}{e_i}$$

is approximately chi-squared distributed if the expected cell frequencies are large. Since the expected cell frequencies are used in computing the test statistic, the general recommendation is that the goodness-of-fit test be performed only when all expected cell frequencies exceed 5. A more thorough explanation of this requirement will be given in the Chi-Square Test Limitations discussion of Section 14-2.

ADJUSTING FOR SMALL EXPECTED FREQUENCIES

Notice, in Figure 14-4 several of the expected cell frequencies (e_i) are smaller than 5. When this happens, the cells should be combined in a meaningful way such that the expected cell frequencies do exceed 5. For example, we can combine the cells corresponding to demand

Excel Instructions:

1. Use Excel Poisson Function and Equations.

Hypotheses:

H_0: The demand distribution is Poisson distributed with a mean equal to 10.
H_A: The demand distribution is not Poisson distributed with a mean equal to 10.
$\alpha = 0.05$

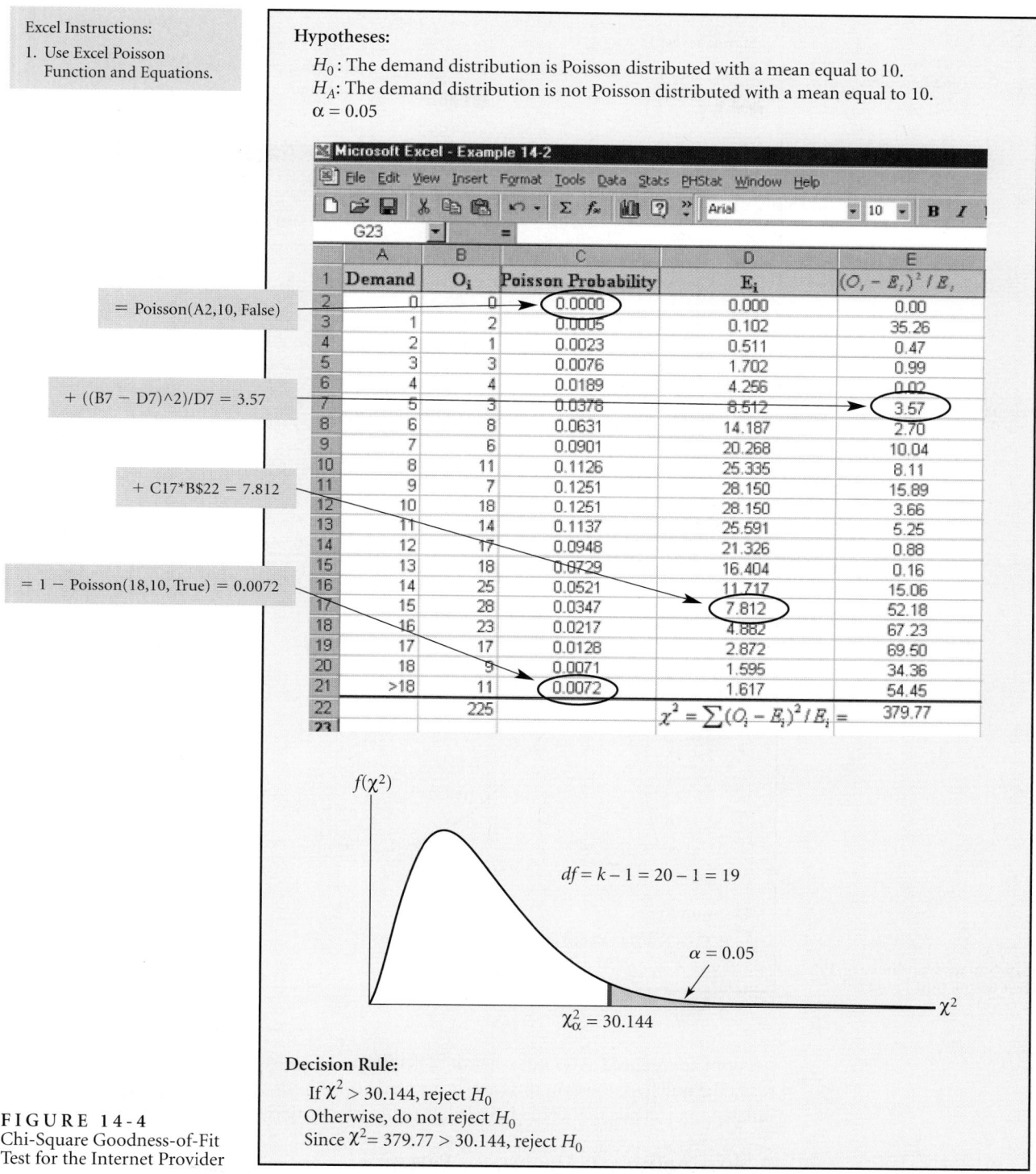

= Poisson(A2,10, False)

+ ((B7 − D7)^2)/D7 = 3.57

+ C17*B$22 = 7.812

= 1 − Poisson(18,10, True) = 0.0072

	Demand	O_i	Poisson Probability	E_i	$(O_i - E_i)^2/E_i$
2	0	0	0.0000	0.000	0.00
3	1	2	0.0005	0.102	35.26
4	2	1	0.0023	0.511	0.47
5	3	3	0.0076	1.702	0.99
6	4	4	0.0189	4.256	0.02
7	5	3	0.0378	8.512	3.57
8	6	8	0.0631	14.187	2.70
9	7	6	0.0901	20.268	10.04
10	8	11	0.1126	25.335	8.11
11	9	7	0.1251	28.150	15.89
12	10	18	0.1251	28.150	3.66
13	11	14	0.1137	25.591	5.25
14	12	17	0.0948	21.326	0.88
15	13	18	0.0729	16.404	0.16
16	14	25	0.0521	11.717	15.06
17	15	28	0.0347	7.812	52.18
18	16	23	0.0217	4.882	67.23
19	17	17	0.0128	2.872	69.50
20	18	9	0.0071	1.595	34.36
21	>18	11	0.0072	1.617	54.45
22		225		$\chi^2 = \sum(O_i - E_i)^2/E_i =$	379.77
23					

$df = k - 1 = 20 - 1 = 19$

$\alpha = 0.05$

$\chi_{\alpha}^2 = 30.144$

Decision Rule:

If $\chi^2 > 30.144$, reject H_0
Otherwise, do not reject H_0
Since $\chi^2 = 379.77 > 30.144$, reject H_0

FIGURE 14-4
Chi-Square Goodness-of-Fit Test for the Internet Provider

levels $x \leq 4$ and sum the expected frequencies for 0, 1, 2, 3, and 4 to get 6.58. Likewise, we can combine the cell for demand of 16 or more to give an expected cell frequency for $x \geq 16$ totaling 10.97.

Figure 14-5 illustrates the revised goodness-of-fit test where all expected cell frequencies exceed 5. Notice that the number of cells is reduced from $k = 20$ to $k = 13$ so the degrees of

Excel Instructions:

1. Use Excel Poisson Function and Equations

Hypotheses:

H_0: The demand distribution is Poisson distributed with a mean equal to 10.
H_A: The demand distribution is not Poisson distributed with a mean equal to 10.
$\alpha = 0.05$

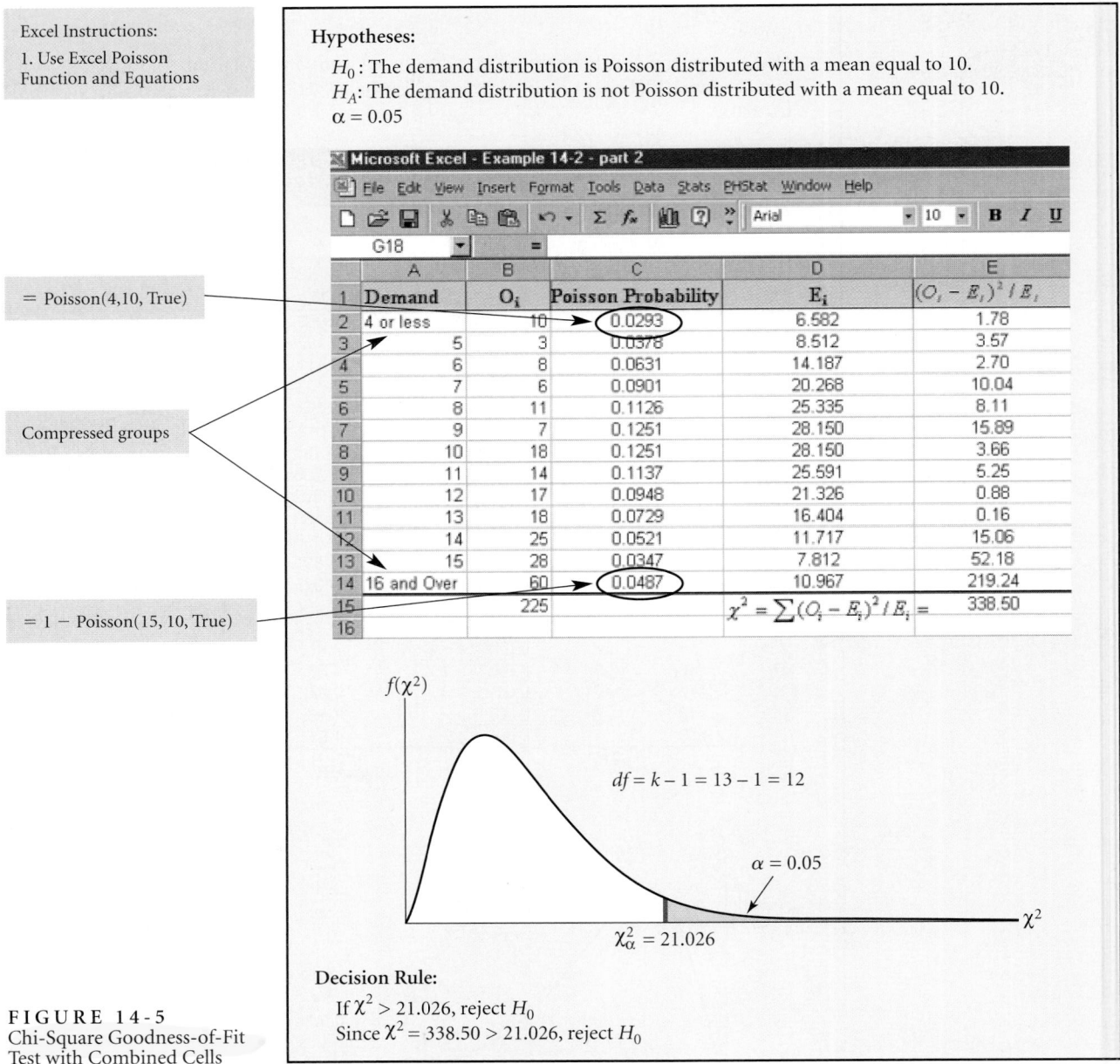

= Poisson(4,10, True)

Compressed groups

= 1 − Poisson(15, 10, True)

	A	B	C	D	E
1	**Demand**	O_i	**Poisson Probability**	E_i	$(O_i - E_i)^2 / E_i$
2	4 or less	10	0.0293	6.582	1.78
3	5	3	0.0378	8.512	3.57
4	6	8	0.0631	14.187	2.70
5	7	6	0.0901	20.268	10.04
6	8	11	0.1126	25.335	8.11
7	9	7	0.1251	28.150	15.89
8	10	18	0.1251	28.150	3.66
9	11	14	0.1137	25.591	5.25
10	12	17	0.0948	21.326	0.88
11	13	18	0.0729	16.404	0.16
12	14	25	0.0521	11.717	15.06
13	15	28	0.0347	7.812	52.18
14	16 and Over	60	0.0487	10.967	219.24
15		225		$\chi^2 = \sum (O_i - E_i)^2 / E_i =$	338.50
16					

$f(\chi^2)$

$df = k - 1 = 13 - 1 = 12$

$\alpha = 0.05$

$\chi^2_\alpha = 21.026$

Decision Rule:

If $\chi^2 > 21.026$, reject H_0
Since $\chi^2 = 338.50 > 21.026$, reject H_0

FIGURE 14-5
Chi-Square Goodness-of-Fit Test with Combined Cells

freedom are reduced. Also note that the calculated test statistic drops in value. While we still reject the null hypothesis in this case, by properly combining cells we guard against having an inflated test statistic that could have led us to incorrectly reject the null hypothesis.

A NOTE ABOUT THE DEGREES OF FREEDOM

A point should be made with respect to employing the chi-square goodness-of-fit test. If the distribution and parameters are specified in the hypothesis, the degrees of freedom are the number of cells minus 1. This was the case for the student example since the null hypothesis involved the distribution type (Poisson) and the parameter, $\lambda t = 10.0$. However, if one or more parameters are left unspecified in the null hypothesis, they must be estimated from the sample data. This will reduce the degrees of freedom by 1 for each estimated parameter.

To illustrate, suppose that the students had originally hypothesized that the demand distribution was Poisson distributed, but did not specify the mean of the distribution. The chi-square goodness-of-fit test is used as before, however we must estimate the mean of the distribution from the sample data. This sample mean is $\bar{x}$ and is used to determine the Poisson probabilities. The degrees of freedom would be computed as the number of cells minus 2 in this case, since we must estimate the mean of the distribution from the sample data. We lose an additional degree of freedom for each parameter we have to estimate.

Woodtrim Products, Inc.

Woodtrim Products, Inc., a company based in the northeast, makes wood moldings, door frames, and wood frame window products. It purchases lumber in dimensions ranging from 2 by 6 to 2 by 12 from mills throughout New England and eastern Canada.

The first step in the production process is to use a machine called a ripsaw to rip the dimension lumber into narrower strips ranging from 2 3/8 inches to 3 7/8 inches wide. Different widths are used for different products. For example, wider pieces with no imperfections are used to make door and window frames. Once the operator makes the rip decisions, they are locked into a computer and the saw is automatically adjusted to cut the board at the desired widths. The saw's manufacturer claims that the saw will generate cuts such that the average deviation from target will be 0, and the distribution of differences from target will be normally distributed with a standard deviation equal to 0.01 inches.

The company has recently become concerned that the ripsaw may not be cutting to the manufacturer's specifications since downstream in the production process, operators at other machines are finding excessive numbers of ripped pieces that are too wide or too narrow.

A "quality improvement team," QIT, has started to investigate the problem. Team members selected a random sample of 300 boards just as they came off the ripsaw. To provide a measure of control, the only pieces sampled in the initial study were pieces with stated widths of 2 7/8 (2.875) inches. Each piece was measured for width at a point halfway from each end. A portion of the data and the differences between the target 2.875 inches and the actual measured width are shown in Figure 14-6. The full data set is contained in the file called **Woodtrim**. The team can use these data and the chi-square goodness-of-fit procedure to test the following null and alternative hypotheses.[2]

H_0: The distribution of differences is normally distributed with $\mu = 0$ and $\sigma = 0.01$

H_A: The distribution of differences *is not* normally distributed with $\mu = 0$ and $\sigma = 0.01$

EXAMPLE 14-3

GOODNESS-OF-FIT EXAMPLE

Excel and Minitab Tutorial

FIGURE 14-6
Woodtrim Products, Inc. Test Data

Excel Instructions:
1. Open file: Woodtrim.xls

	A	B	C	D
1	Sample	Actual Width	Target Width	Difference
2	1	2.870	2.875	-0.005
3	2	2.863	2.875	-0.012
4	3	2.885	2.875	0.010
5	4	2.872	2.875	-0.003
6	5	2.891	2.875	0.016
7	6	2.893	2.875	0.018
8	7	2.868	2.875	-0.007
9	8	2.861	2.875	-0.014
10	9	2.889	2.875	0.014

Microsoft Excel - Woodtrim Example
File Edit View Insert Format Tools Data Stats PHStat Window
D2   = =+B2-C2

[2]More effective tests exist for testing whether sample data come from a normally distributed population. For example, refer to Lilliefors' test in an optional section on the CD-ROM.

Excel Instructions:

1. Open file: Woodtrim.xls (See Figure 14-6)
2. Define Classes (Column J)
3. Determine Observed Frequencies [i.e., cell K5 formula is = COUNTIF(D2:D301, "< 0.0") − sum(K3:K4)]
4. Determine Normal Distribution probabilities assuming the mean = 0.0 and st. dev. = 0.01 [i.e., cell L5 formula is = NORMDIST(0,0,0.01,TRUE) − SUM(L$3:L4)]
5. Determine Expected Frequencies by multiplying normal probability by the sample size ($n = 300$)
6. Compute values for chi-square in column N [cell N5 formula is = (K5 − M5)^2/M5]
7. Sum column N to get chi-square statistic
8. Find p-value using CHITEST function [cell N11 formula is = CHITEST(K3:K8,M3:M8)]

	Microsoft Excel - Woodtrim Example			
	File Edit View Insert Format Tools Data Stats PHStat Window Help			
				Arial ▾ 10 ▾ B I U ≡ ≡ ≡ $
D2	= =+B2-C2			

	J	K	L	M	N
1					
2	Class	O Observed Frequency	Normal Distribution Probability	E Expected Frequency	(O-E)²/O
3	less than -.02	0	0.022750062	6.83	6.825018611
4	-.02 and under -.01	42	0.135905198	40.77	0.037012725
5	-.01 and under 0.00	133	0.34134474	102.40	9.141790055
6	0.00 and under .01	75	0.34134474	102.40	7.333227046
7	.01 and under .02	47	0.135905198	40.77	0.951483681
8	.02 and over	3	0.021400095	6.42	1.821891392
9	Total	300			
10				Total =	26.11042351
11				p-value	0.0001

FIGURE 14-7   Woodtrim Example—Goodness-of-Fit Test—Excel Results

This example differs slightly from the previous examples since the hypothesized distribution is continuous rather than discrete. Thus, we organize the data into a grouped data frequency distribution (see Chapter 2) as shown in Figure 14-7. We have chosen to use $k = 6$ classes. The number of classes is your choice. However, remember that the expected cell frequencies must be greater than 5 or the classes will have to be combined.

Although Excel does not have a tool for performing a goodness-of-fit test directly, through the use of Excel functions and formulas, we can perform the test. (The Excel tutorial on the CD-ROM takes you through the specific steps required to complete this example.) Figure 14-7 shows the normal distribution probabilities, expected cell frequencies, and the chi-square calculation. The calculated chi-square statistic is $\chi^2 = 26.11$. The p-value associated with $\chi^2 = 26.11$ and $6 - 1 = 5$ degrees of freedom is 0.0001. Therefore, since the p-value = 0.0001 is less than any reasonable level of significance, we reject the null hypothesis and conclude that the ripsaw is not currently meeting the manufacturer's specification. The saw errors are not normally distributed with a mean equal to 0 and a standard deviation equal to 0.01.

Note, in this case, since the null hypothesis specified both the mean and the standard deviation, the normal distribution probabilities were computed using these values. However, if either or both had not been specified, the sample values would be used in the probability computation. You would lose one additional degree of freedom for each parameter that is estimated from the sample data.

Minitab has a procedure for performing a goodness-of-fit test for a normal distribution. In fact it offers three different approaches, none of which are exactly the chi-square approach just outlined. Although this text does not discuss the goodness-of-fit methods used by Minitab, their objective is the same: to determine whether observed sample data appear to have come from a normally distributed population. Figure 14-8 shows the Minitab results for the Woodtrim example. Consistent with our Excel results, this output illustrates that the null hypothesis of normality should be rejected since the p-value < 0.01.

OPTIONAL CD-ROM TOPIC   Lilliefors' Test for Normal Distributions

A very effective goodness-of-fit test for testing whether sample data come from a normal distribution is the Lilliefors' Test for Normal Distributions. For more information, see the CD-ROM.

Minitab Instructions:

1. Open file: Woodtrim.mtw
2. Select Stat
3. Select Basic Statistics
4. Select Normality Test
5. Define Variable
6. Select Test Option (We selected the Kolmogorov-Smirnov Normality test)

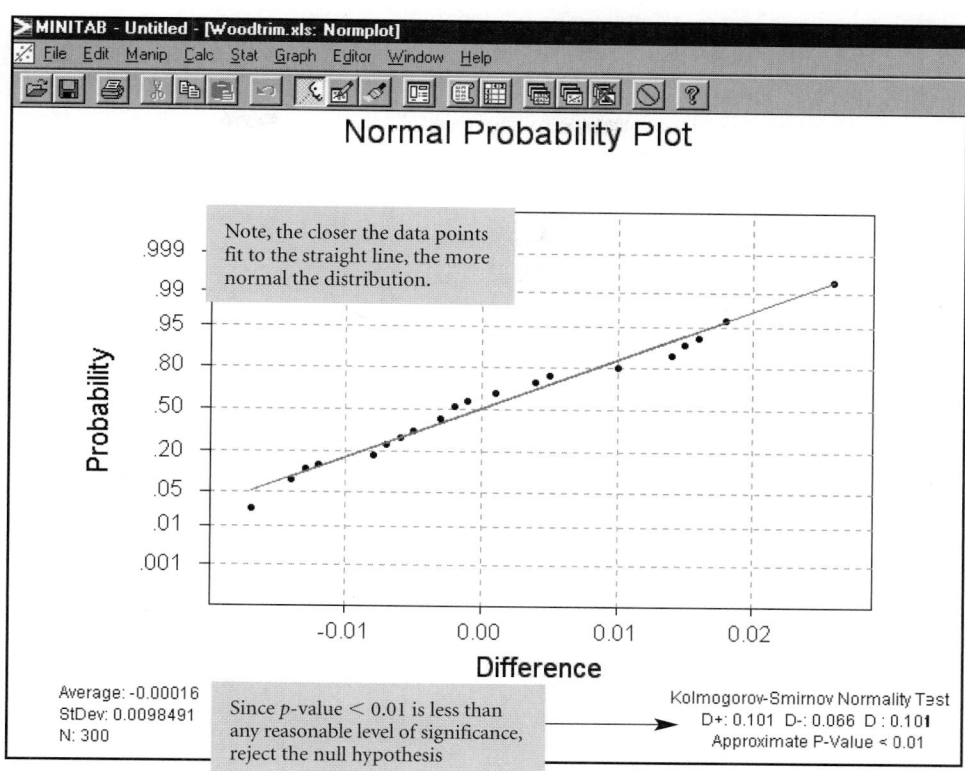

FIGURE 14-8
Woodtrim Example—Test of Normal Distributed Ripsaw Cuts—Minitab Output

14-1: EXERCISES

ADDITIONAL EXERCISES ON YOUR CD-ROM

Try the ADDITIONAL EXERCISES and APPLICATION PROBLEMS on the CD-ROM.

14-1. Daily sales volumes in dollars have been grouped as follows. Can you conclude that the sales are uniformly distributed? Test at $\alpha = 0.05$.

SALES	FREQUENCY
$500 and under $1,000	40
$1,000 and under $1,500	63
$1,500 and under $2,000	55
$2,000 and under $2,500	50
$2,500 and under $3,000	61

14-2. The following data reflect the number of customers that use an ATM machine per hour. The claim is that the hourly usage rate is Poisson distributed with a mean equal to 5 per hour.

9	7	8	7	8
4	8	5	8	9
11	7	7	8	8
8	11	8	8	12
7	11	8	8	11
9	9	8	9	8
7	6	8	6	12
8	5	7	10	7
7	5	9	8	9
7	7	9	7	8

a. State the appropriate null and alternative hypotheses.
b. Using $\alpha = 0.10$, what conclusion should be reached about the population distribution based upon the sample data?

Business Applications

14-3. The Baltimore Steel and Pipe Company recently developed a new pipe product for a customer. According to specifications, the pipe is supposed to have an average outside diameter of 2.00 inches with a standard deviation equal to 0.10 inches, and the distribution of outside diameters is to be normally distributed. Before going into full-scale production, the company selected a random sample of 30 sections of pipe from the initial test run. The following data were recorded.

PIPE SECTION	DIAMETER (INCHES)	PIPE SECTION	DIAMETER (INCHES)
1	2.04	16	1.96
2	2.13	17	1.89
3	2.07	18	1.99
4	1.99	19	2.13
5	1.90	20	1.90
6	2.06	21	1.91
7	2.19	22	1.95
8	2.01	23	2.18
9	2.05	24	1.94
10	1.98	25	1.93
11	1.95	26	2.08
12	1.90	27	1.82
13	2.10	28	1.94
14	2.02	29	1.96
15	2.11	30	1.81

   a. Using a significance level of 0.01, perform the appropriate test. (Hint: If you are using Excel, either employ the chi-square approach discussed in Example 14-3 or the Lilliefors' method discussed in the optional section on your CD-ROM. If you are using Minitab, use the Kolmogorov-Smirnov method shown in Figure 14-8.)

   b. Based on these data, should the company conclude that it is meeting the product specifications? Explain your reasoning.

14-4. A pharmaceutical company is planning to market a drug that is supposed to help reduce blood pressure. The company claims that if the drug is taken properly, the amount of blood pressure loss will be normally distributed with a mean equal to 10 points on the diastolic reading with a standard deviation equal to 4.0. One hundred patients were administered the drug, and data were collected showing the reduction in blood pressure at the end of the test period. The data are located in the file labeled **Blood Pressure**.

   a. Using a goodness-of-fit test and a significance level equal to 0.05, what conclusion should be reached with respect to the distribution of diastolic blood pressure reduction? Discuss. (Hint: If you are using Excel, employ either the chi-square approach discussed in Example 14-3 or the Lilliefors' method discussed in the optional section on your CD-ROM. If you are using Minitab, use the Kolmogorov-Smirnov method shown in Figure 14-8.)

   b. Conduct a hypothesis test to determine if the standard deviation for this population is 4.0. Use a significance level of 0.10.

   c. Given the results of the two tests in parts a and b, is it appropriate to construct a confidence interval based upon a normal distribution with a population standard deviation of 4.0? Explain your answer.

   d. If appropriate, construct a 99% confidence interval for the mean reduction in blood pressure. Based upon this confidence interval does an average diastolic loss of 10 seem reasonable for this procedure? Explain your reasoning.

14-5. The manager at the Sacramento, California, airport recently conducted a study of passengers departing from the airport to determine regional airline usage. A random sample of 100 passengers was selected. The data are in the file called **Airline Passengers**. An earlier study showed the following usage by airline.

Delta	20%
Horizon	10%
Northwest	10%
Skywest	3%
Southwest	25%
United	32%

   a. If the manager wishes to determine whether the airline usage pattern has changed from that reported in the earlier study, state the appropriate null and alternative hypotheses.

   b. Based on the sample data, what should be concluded? Test using a significance level of 0.01.

14-6. The owners of Clair's Deli are considering remodeling their facility to include a drive-through window. There would be room for 3 cars in the proposed drive-through lane. However, they are concerned that the capacity may be too low during their busy hours between 11:00 A.M. and 1:30 P.M. One of the factors they need to know is the distribution of the length of time needed to fill an order for cars coming to the drive-through. In order to collect information on this, the owners have received permission from another deli in a nearby town to collect some data at that deli's drive-through. The data in the file called **Clair's Deli** reflect the service time per car.

   a. Based on these sample data, is there sufficient evidence to conclude that the distribution of service time is not normally distributed? Test at an $\alpha = 0.05$ level. (Hint: If you are using Excel, either employ the chi-square approach discussed in Example 14-3 or the Lilliefors' method discussed in the optional section on your CD-ROM. If you are using Minitab, use the Kolmogorov-Smirnov method shown in Figure 14-8.)

   b. Examine whether the drive-through lane will be able to handle customers during its busy times. The owners' experience has indicated that approximately 3 customers arrive in each 10-minute period during their busy hours. (1) Calculate the average time between arrivals during the busy hours. (2) Assuming the mean and standard deviation of the previous data are satisfactory estimates of their corresponding population parameters, calculate the probability that the time to fill an order will be no larger than the arrival time calculated in (1).

14-7. Referring to Problem 6, the number of cars that arrive in each 10-minute period is another factor that will determine whether the deli will have the capacity to handle the drive-through business. In addition to studying the service times, the owners also counted the number of cars that arrived at the deli in the nearby town in a sample of 10-minute time periods. These data are shown as follows.

3	2	0
2	3	3
3	3	3
0	2	3
0	3	3
1	1	0
2	4	9
1	2	4
2	1	1
4	1	3

Based on these data, is there evidence to conclude that the arrivals are not Poisson distributed? State the appropriate null and alternative hypotheses, and test using a significance level of 0.025.

14-2: INTRODUCTION TO CONTINGENCY ANALYSIS

In Chapters 8 and 9 you were introduced to hypothesis tests involving one and two population proportions. While these techniques are useful in many cases, you will also encounter many situations involving multiple population proportions. For example, a major mutual fund company offers six different mutual funds. The president of the company may wish to determine if the proportion of customers selecting each mutual fund is related to the four sales regions in which the customers reside. A hospital administrator, who collects service satisfaction data from patients, might be interested in determining whether there is a significant difference in patient rating by hospital department. A personnel manager for a large corporation might be interested in determining whether there is a relationship between level of employee job satisfaction and job classification. In each of these cases the proportions relate to characteristic categories of the variable of interest. The six mutual funds, four sales regions, hospital departments, and job classifications are the specific categories.

These situations involving categorical data call for a new statistical tool known as *contingency analysis* to help in making decisions when multiple proportions are involved. Contingency analysis can be used when the level of data measurement is either nominal or ordinal and the values are determined by counting the number of occurrences in each category.

2 × 2 Contingency Tables

Dalgarno Photo, Inc.

EXAMPLE 14-4

CONTINGENCY ANALYSIS

During the 1998–1999 academic year, Dalgarno Photo, Inc., undertook the task of surveying yearbook representatives at colleges and universities in its market area. A major part of Dalgarno Photo's business comes from taking photographs for college yearbooks in the eastern United States. A first-year MBA student was hired to develop a survey that would be administered as a mail questionnaire to the yearbook representatives at the colleges and universities.

The primary objective of the survey was to solicit objective views regarding a variety of issues related to the photography and publishing activities associated with yearbook development. For instance, the survey was designed to obtain information about what photographer and publisher services the schools currently use and what factors are most important in making these selections.

The respondents were unaware that Dalgarno Photo had sent the survey that was mailed to representatives at 850 colleges and universities. A total of 221 usable responses were returned. The survey instrument contained 30 questions, which were coded into 137 separate variables. For our purposes here, we will focus on 2 of the 137 variables obtained through the survey. They are:

> Source of university funding
> Gender of the yearbook editor

Among his many interests in this study, Dalgarno's marketing manager has questioned whether funding source and gender of the yearbook editor are related in some manner. To analyze this issue, we examine the two variables more closely. Source of university funding is a categorical variable coded as follows.

$$1 = \text{Private funding}$$
$$2 = \text{Public-funded}$$

Of the 221 respondents who provided data for this variable, 155 came from privately funded colleges or universities and 66 were from public-funded institutions.

The variable, gender of the yearbook editor, is also a categorical variable with two response categories, coded as follows.

$$1 = \text{Male}$$
$$2 = \text{Female}$$

Of the 221 responses to the survey, 164 were from females and 57 were from males.

In cases like this, where the variables of interest are both categorical and the decision maker is interested in determining whether a relationship exists between the two, a statistical technique known as contingency analysis is useful. To employ contingency analysis, we set up a two-dimensional table called a **contingency table**. The contingency table for these two variables is shown in Table 14-4.

CONTINGENCY TABLE

A table used to classify sample observations according to two or more identifiable characteristics. Also called a *crosstabulation table*.

Table 14-4 shows that 14 of the respondents were males from schools that are privately funded. The numbers at the extreme right and along the bottom are called the *marginal frequencies*. For example, 57 respondents were males and 155 respondents were from privately funded institutions.

The issue of whether there is a relationship between responses to these two variables is formally addressed through a hypothesis test where the null and alternative hypotheses are stated as follows.

H_0: Gender of yearbook editor is independent of the college's funding source
H_A: Gender of yearbook editor *is not* independent of the college's funding source

If the null hypothesis is true, the population proportion of yearbook editors from private institutions that are males should be equal to the proportion of male editors from state-funded institutions and should also equal the overall population proportion of male editors. To illustrate, we can use the sample data to determine the sample proportion of male editors as follows.

TABLE 14-4
Contingency Table for Dalgarno Photo

GENDER	SOURCE OF FUNDING		
	Private	*Public*	
Male	14	43	57
Female	141	23	164
	155	66	221

$$p_M = \frac{\text{Number of male editors}}{\text{Number of respondents}} = \frac{57}{221}$$
$$= 0.2579$$

Then, if the null hypothesis is true, we would expect 25.7919% of the 155 privately funded schools, or 39.98 schools, to have a male yearbook editor. We would also expect 25.7919% of the 66 state-funded schools, or 17.02, to have male yearbook editors. (Note that the expected numbers need not be integer values. Also the expected frequencies in any column or row add to the marginal frequency.) We can use this reasoning to determine the expected number of respondents in each cell of the contingency table as shown in Table 14-5.

You can simplify the calculations needed to produce the expected values for each cell. Note that the first cell's expected value, 39.98, was obtained by the following calculation.

$$e_{11} = 0.2579(155) = 39.98$$

However, since the probability, 0.2579, is calculated by dividing the row total, 57, by the grand total, 221, the calculation can be represented as:

$$e_{11} = \frac{(\text{Row total})(\text{Column total})}{\text{Grand total}} = \frac{(57)(155)}{221} = 39.98$$

As a further example we can calculate the expected value for the next cell in the same row. The expected number of male yearbook editors in public-funded schools is:

$$e_{12} = \frac{(\text{Row total})(\text{Column total})}{\text{Grand total}} = \frac{(57)(66)}{221} = 17.02$$

Keep in mind that the row and column totals (the marginal frequencies) must be the same for the expected values as for the observed values. Therefore, when there is only one cell left in a row or a column for which you must calculate an expected value, you can obtain it by subtraction. As an example, the expected value, e_{12}, could have been calculated as:

$$e_{12} = 57 - 39.98 = 17.02$$

Allowing for sampling error, we would expect the actual frequencies in each cell to approximately match the corresponding expected cell frequencies when the null hypothesis is true. The greater the difference between the actual and the expected frequencies, the more likely the null hypothesis of independence is false and should be rejected. The statistical test to determine whether the sample data support or refute the null hypothesis is given by Equation 14-2.

CHI-SQUARE CONTINGENCY TEST STATISTIC

$$\chi^2 = \sum_{i=1}^{r}\sum_{j=1}^{c} \frac{(o_{ij} - e_{ij})^2}{e_{ij}} \qquad df = (r-1)(c-1) \qquad \textbf{14-2}$$

where:

o_{ij} = Observed frequency in cell (i, j)
e_{ij} = Expected frequency in cell (i, j)
r = Number of rows
c = Number of columns

T A B L E   1 4 - 5
Contingency Table for
Dalgarno Photo

GENDER	SOURCE OF FUNDING		
	Private	*Public*	
Male	Actual = 14	Actual = 43	57
	Expected = 39.98	Expected = 17.02	
Female	Actual = 141	Actual = 23	164
	Expected = 115.02	Expected = 48.98	
	155	66	221

Do not be confused by the double summation in Equation 14-2; it merely indicates that all rows and columns must be used in calculating χ^2. As was the case in the goodness-of-fit tests, the degrees of freedom are the number of independent data values obtained from the experiment. In any given row, once you know $c - 1$ of the data values, the remaining data value is determined. For instance, once you know that 14 of the 57 male editors were from privately funded institutions, you know that 43 were from public-funded institutions. Similarly, once $r - 1$ data values in a column are known, the remaining data value is determined. Therefore, the degrees of freedom are obtained by the expression $(r - 1)(c - 1)$.

Figure 14-9 presents the hypotheses and test results for this example. As was the case in the goodness-of-fit tests, the test statistic has a distribution that can be approximated by the chi-square distribution if the expected values are larger than 5. Note that the calculated chi-square statistic is compared to the critical value of χ^2 for an $\alpha = 0.05$ and $(2 - 1)(2 - 1) = 1$ degree of freedom. Since $\chi^2 = 76.188 > 3.841$, the null hypothesis of independence should be rejected. Dalgarno Photo representatives should conclude the gender of the yearbook editor and the school's source of funding are not independent. By examining the data in Figure 14-9, you can see that private schools are more likely to have female editors while public schools are more likely to have male yearbook editors.

 **OPTIONAL CD-ROM TOPIC The Phi Coefficient for 2 × 2 Contingency Tables**

Although the chi-square contingency test helps you determine whether the responses to one variable are independent of the responses to a second variable, it does not measure the strength of the relationship when the hypothesis of independence is rejected. A statistical tool known as the phi coefficient for 2 × 2 tables is used for that purpose. For more information, go to the CD-ROM.

$r \times c$ Contingency Tables

Benton Industries

Benton Industries manufactures carpets and draperies in the Atlanta area. Benton Industries pays market wages, provides competitive benefits, and offers other attractive options for employees in an effort to reduce turnover and create a satisfied workforce. At a recent meeting, several supervisors complained that employee absenteeism was becoming a problem. In response to these complaints, the human resource manager conducted a study involving a random sample of 500 employees. One aspect of this study was to determine whether there is a relationship between absenteeism and marital status. Absenteeism during the past year was broken down into three levels.

1. Zero Absences
2. 1–5 Absences
3. Over 5 Absences

Marital status was divided into four categories.

1. Single   2. Married   3. Divorced   4. Widowed

Hypotheses:

H_0: Gender of yearbook editor is independent of college's funding source.
H_A: Gender of yearbook editor is not independent of college's funding source.
$\alpha = 0.05$

	Private	Public
Male	Actual = 14 Expected = 39.98	Actual = 43 Expected = 17.02
Female	Actual = 141 Expected = 115.02	Actual = 23 Expected = 48.98

Test Statistic:

$$\chi^2 = \sum_{i=1}^{r} \sum_{j=1}^{c} \frac{(o_{ij} - e_{ij})^2}{e_{ij}} = \frac{(14 - 39.98)^2}{39.98} + \frac{(43 - 17.02)^2}{17.02}$$
$$+ \frac{(141 - 115.02)^2}{115.02} + \frac{(23 - 48.98)^2}{48.98} = 76.188$$

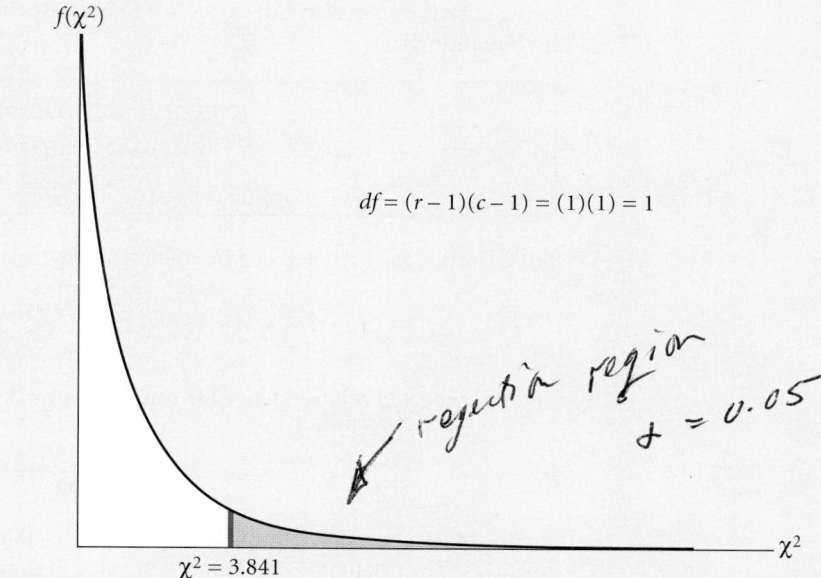

$$df = (r - 1)(c - 1) = (1)(1) = 1$$

$\chi^2 = 3.841$

rejection region
$\alpha = 0.05$

Decision Rule:

If $\chi^2 > 3.841$, reject H_0
Otherwise, do not reject H_0
Since $76.188 > 3.841$, reject H_0

FIGURE 14-9
Chi-Square Contingency
Analysis Test for Dalgarno
Photo

Table 14-6 shows the contingency table for the sample of 500 employees. The data are also shown in the file called **Benton**. The null and alternative hypotheses to be tested are:

H_0: Absentee behavior is independent of marital status
H_A: Absentee behavior *is not* independent of marital status

As with 2×2 contingency analysis, the test for independence can be made using the chi-square test, where the expected cell frequencies are compared to the actual cell frequencies using Equation 14-2. The logic of the test says that if the actual and expected frequencies

| MARITAL STATUS | ABSENTEE RATE | | | Row Totals |
	Zero	1-5	Over 5	
Single	84	82	34	200
Married	50	64	36	150
Divorced	50	34	16	100
Widowed	16	20	14	50
Column Total	200	200	100	500

Additional
Example 14-a
r x c Contingency
Tables

T A B L E   1 4 - 6
Contingency Table for
Benton Industries

closely match, then the null hypothesis of independence is not rejected. However, if the actual and expected cell frequencies are substantially different overall, the null hypothesis of independence is rejected. The calculated chi-square statistic is compared to a table critical value for the desired significance and degrees of freedom equal to $(r - 1)(c - 1)$.

The expected cell frequencies are determined assuming that the row and column variables are independent. This means, for example, that the probability of a married person being absent over 5 days during the year is the same as the probability of any employee being absent over 5 days. An easy way to compute the expected cell frequencies, e_{ij}, is given by Equation 14-3.

EXPECTED CELL FREQUENCIES

$$e_{ij} = \frac{(i\text{th Row total})\,(j\text{th Column total})}{\text{Total sample size}}$$

14-3

For example, the expected cell frequency for row 1, column 1 is:

$$e_{11} = \frac{(200)(200)}{500} = 80$$

and the expected cell frequency for row 2, column 3 is:

$$e_{23} = \frac{(150)(100)}{500} = 30$$

Figure 14-10 shows the completed contingency table with the actual and expected cell frequencies. The calculated chi-square test value is computed as follows.

$$\chi^2 = \sum_{i=1}^{r}\sum_{j=1}^{c} \frac{(o_{ij} - e_{ij})^2}{e_{ij}}$$

$$= \frac{(84 - 80)^2}{80} + \frac{(82 - 80)^2}{80} + \cdots + \frac{(20 - 20)^2}{20} + \frac{(14 - 10)^2}{10}$$

$$= 10.88$$

The degrees of freedom are $(r - 1)(c - 1) = (4 - 1)(3 - 1) = 6$. You can use the chi-square table in Appendix G to get the chi-square critical value for $\alpha = 0.05$ and 6 degrees of freedom or you can use Excel's CHIINV function [CHIINV(0.05,6) = 12.592]. Since the calculated chi-square value (10.88) shown in Figure 14-10 is less than 12.592, we cannot reject the null hypothesis. Based on these sample data, there is *insufficient evidence* to conclude that absenteeism and marital status are not independent.

Excel Instructions:
1. Open file: Benton.xls
2. Compute Expected cell frequencies using Excel formula.
3. Compute Chi-square statistic using Excel formula

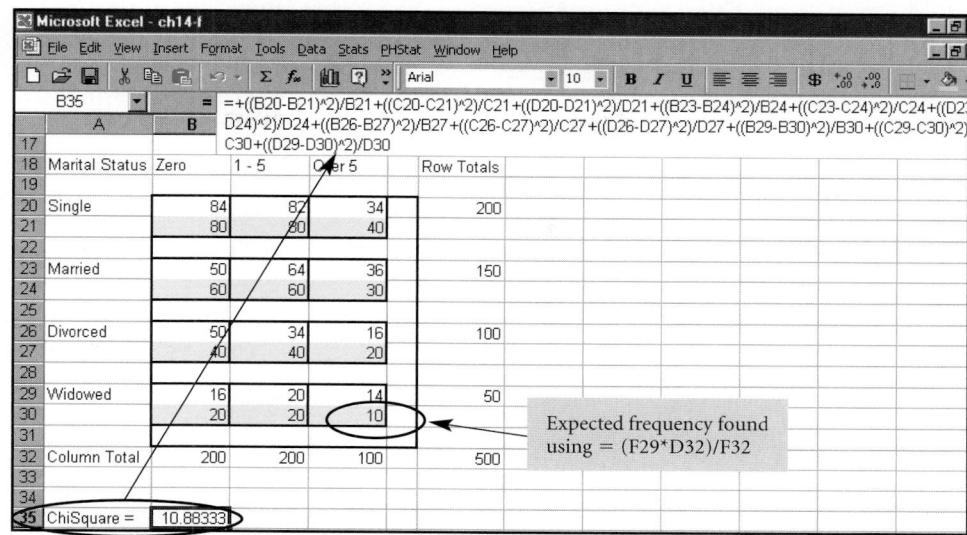

FIGURE 14-10
Excel Output—Benton Industries Contingency Analysis Test

Chi-Square Test Limitations

The chi-square distribution is only an approximation for the true distribution for contingency analysis. We use the chi-square approximation because the true distribution is impractical to compute in most instances. However, the approximation (and, therefore, the conclusion reached) is quite good when all expected cell frequencies exceed 5.0. When expected cell frequencies drop below 5.0, the calculated chi-square value tends to be inflated and may inflate the true probability of committing a Type I error beyond the stated significance level. As a rule, if the null hypothesis is not rejected, you do not need to worry when the expected cell frequencies drop below 5.0.

There are two alternatives that can be used to overcome the small expected cell frequency problem. The first is to increase the sample size. This may increase the marginal frequencies in each row and column enough to increase the expected cell frequencies. The second option is to combine the categories of the row and/or column variables. If you do decide to group categories together, there should be some logic behind the resulting categories. You don't want to lose the meaning of the results through poor groupings. You will need to examine each situation individually to determine whether the option of grouping classes to increase expected cell frequencies makes sense.

OPTIONAL CD-ROM TOPIC Cramer's Contingency Coefficient

A measure of the strength of the relationship between two variables when there are more than two levels for either of the variables is called Cramer's Contingency Coefficient. For more information, go to the CD-ROM.

14-2: EXERCISES

ADDITIONAL EXERCISES ON YOUR CD-ROM
Try the **ADDITIONAL EXERCISES** and **APPLICATION PROBLEMS**
on the CD-ROM.

14-8. A contingency analysis table has been constructed from data obtained in a phone survey of customers in a market area in which respondents were asked to indicate whether they owned a domestic or foreign car and whether or not they were a member of a union. The following contingency table is provided.

	UNION	
CAR	*Yes*	*No*
Domestic	155	470
Foreign	40	325

a. Use the chi-square approach to test whether type of car owned (domestic or foreign) is independent of union membership. Test using an $\alpha = 0.05$ level.
b. Calculate the *p*-value for this hypothesis test.

14-9. In a recent study of college graduates, it was hypothesized that income was independent of the number of different employers the person has worked for since graduation. The data collected were as follows.

	NUMBER OF EMPLOYERS				
INCOME LEVEL	*1*	*2*	*3*	*4*	*5 or more*
Under $30,000	3	4	3	2	3
30,000 < 40,000	5	3	7	3	2
40,000 < 50,000	2	5	3	6	1
50,000 < 60,000	1	7	9	3	4
≥ 60,000	1	3	11	7	4

Assuming that these data reflect observed frequencies, what can be concluded about the hypothesis? Test at an $\alpha = 0.05$ level.

Business Applications

14-10. A study of automobile drivers was conducted to determine whether the number of traffic citations issued during a 3-year period was independent of the gender of the driver. The following data were collected.

	GENDER OF DRIVER	
CITATIONS ISSUED	*Male*	*Female*
0	240	160
1	80	40
2	32	18
3	11	9
Over 3	5	4

a. Using an $\alpha = 0.05$ level, determine whether the two variables are independent.
b. A friend of yours claims to know a person who was included in the study. He has told you that his friend had more than one citation during the study period. Calculate the probability that the acquaintance of your friend is a female.

14-11. A bank in Midvale, Wisconsin, recently did a study of its customers to determine whether the number of transactions in a checking account was independent of the marital status of the customer. The following data were obtained.

	NUMBER OF TRANSACTIONS				
MARITAL STATUS	*0–10*	*11–20*	*21–30*	*31–40*	*Over 40*
Single	13	23	19	20	11
Married	6	15	33	45	27
Divorced	4	19	22	20	15
Other	2	11	8	5	2

a. Based on these data, what should the bank conclude? Test at an $\alpha = 0.05$ level.
b. (1) Are there any cells that have expected values smaller than 5? (2) Suggest an appropriate way to combine cells in a meaningful way such that the expected cell frequencies do exceed 5. (3) Repeat part a using the reconstructed contingency table.
c. Given the decision reached in part a, was it necessary to implement the procedure indicated in part b? When is it unnecessary to combine cells even though some of them have expected values smaller than 5?

14-12. In a recent labor negotiation, the union officials collected data from a sample of union members regarding how long they had been with the company and how long they would be willing to stay out on strike if a strike were called. The following data were collected.

TIME WITH COMPANY	STRIKE LENGTH TOLERATION		
	Under 1 Week	*1–4 Weeks*	*Over 4 Weeks*
Under 1 year	23	6	3
1–2 years	19	15	8
2–5 years	20	23	19
5–10 years	4	21	29
Over 10 years	2	5	18

a. Based on these data, can the union conclude that the strike length toleration is independent of time with the company? Test at the $\alpha = 0.05$ level.

b. Consider two groups: those employed with the company at most 5 years, and those employed with the company more than 10 years. Do the data suggest that the proportion of employees that would be willing to stay out on strike for at least a week if a strike were called is larger for the first group? Conduct an appropriate hypothesis test to determine this.

14-13. The table below classifies a stock's price change as up, down, or no change for both today's and yesterday's prices. Price changes were examined for 100 days. A financial theory states that stock prices follow what is called a "random walk." This means, in part, that the price change today for a stock must be independent of yesterday's price change. Test the hypothesis that daily stock price changes for this stock are independent. Let $\alpha = 0.05$.

| | | PRICE CHANGE PREVIOUS DAY | |
	Up	No Change	Down
PRICE CHANGE TODAY Up	14	16	12
No Change	6	8	6
Down	16	14	8

14-14. An AceCo Precision Products metal fabrication shop operates three shifts. The accompanying data give the distribution of accidents among the three shifts by type of accident.

| | | ACCIDENT TYPE | |
		Behavior-Based	Equipment Related
Shift	Day	270	80
	Swing	190	25
	Graveyard	96	24

Test the hypothesis that shift and accident type are independent. Let $\alpha = 0.01$.

14-15. A random sample of 980 heads of households was taken from the customer list for State Bank and Trust. Those sampled were asked to classify their own attitudes and their parents' attitudes toward borrowing money as follows.

A: Borrow only for real estate and car purchases
B: Borrow for short-term purchases such as appliances and furniture
C: Never borrow money

The following table indicates the responses from those in the study.

| | | RESPONDENT | |
		A	B	C
PARENT	A	240	80	20
	B	180	120	40
	C	180	80	40

a. Test the hypothesis that the respondents' borrowing habits are independent from what they believe their parents' attitudes to be. Let $\alpha = 0.01$.

b. Calculate a 99% confidence interval for the difference between the proportion of respondents who never borrow money and whose parents never borrowed money and the proportion of respondents who never borrow money and whose parents borrowed money for short-term purchases. Are the results of this confidence interval compatible with the conclusion you reached in part a?

14-16. A major appliance manufacturer provides four washing machine models: standard, deluxe, superior, and XLT. The marketing manager has recently conducted a study on the purchasers of the washing machines. The study recorded the model of appliance purchased and the credit account balance of the customer at the time of purchase. The sample data are in the following table. Based on these data, is there evidence of a relationship between the account balance and the model of washer purchased? Use a significance level of 0.025. Conduct the test using a p-value approach.

| | WASHER MODEL PURCHASED | | | |
CREDIT BALANCE	Standard	Deluxe	Superior	XLT
Under $200	10	16	40	5
$200–$800	8	12	24	15
Over $800	16	12	16	30

14-17. ECCO (Electronic Controls Company) makes backup alarms that are used on such equipment as forklifts and delivery trucks. The quality manager recently performed a study involving a random sample of 110 warranty claims. One of the questions the manager wanted to answer was whether there is a relationship between the type of warranty complaint and the plant at which the alarm was made. The data are in the file called ECCO.

a. Calculate the expected values for the cells in this analysis. Suggest a way in which cells can be combined to assure that the expected value of each cell is at least 5 so that as many level combinations of the two variables as possible are retained.

b. Using a significance level of 0.01, conduct a relevant hypothesis test and provide an answer to the manager's question.

14-18. Referring to Problem 17, can the quality control manager conclude that the type of warranty problem is independent of the shift the alarm was made? Test using a significance level of 0.05. Discuss your results.

■ SUMMARY AND CONCLUSIONS

This chapter has introduced two very useful statistical tools: goodness-of-fit tests and contingency analysis. Goodness-of-fit testing is used when a decision maker wishes to determine whether sample data come from a population having specific characteristics. Two goodness-of-fit procedures were introduced in this chapter—the chi-square goodness-of-fit test and the optional Lilliefors' test included on the CD-ROM. Both tests rely on the idea that if the distribution of the sample data is substantially different from the hypothesized population distribution, then the population distribution from which these sample data came must not be what was hypothesized. The Lilliefors' test (see the CD-ROM optional topic) is particularly useful for determining whether a population is normally distributed when the raw data from the sample are available. The chi-square goodness-of-fit test is most effective when the sample data have been organized into a grouped frequency distribution.

Contingency analysis is a frequently used statistical tool that allows the decision maker to test whether responses to two variables are independent. Market researchers, for example, use contingency analysis on survey research data when at least one of the variables of interest is categorical. For instance, marketers may be interested in determining whether attitude about the quality of their company's product is independent of the gender of the customer. By using contingency analysis and the chi-square contingency test, they can make this determination based on the sample of customers. If either or both of the variables are continuous in nature, they must be recoded before contingency analysis can be performed. Most software can facilitate this recoding process.

EQUATIONS

Chi-Square Goodness of Fit Test Statistic

$$\chi^2 = \sum_{i=1}^{k} \frac{(o_i - e_i)^2}{e_i}, \qquad df = k - 1 \qquad \textbf{14-1}$$

Chi-Square Contingency Test Statistic

$$\chi^2 = \sum_{i=1}^{r} \sum_{j=1}^{c} \frac{(o_{ij} - e_{ij})^2}{e_{ij}}, \qquad df = (r - 1)(c - 1) \qquad \textbf{14-2}$$

Expected Cell Frequencies

$$e_{ij} = \frac{(i\text{th Row total})(j\text{th Column total})}{\text{Total sample size}} \qquad \textbf{14-3}$$

■ KEY TERMS

Chi-Square Goodness-of-Fit Test—A test utilizing the chi-square distribution to determine whether sample data come from a specific hypothesized population distribution.

Contingency Table—A table used to classify sample observations according to two or more identifiable characteristics. Also called a crosstabulation table.

SOLVED PROBLEMS ON YOUR CD-ROM

Try the WORKED-OUT EXERCISES and BUSINESS APPLICATIONS on the CD-ROM.

CHAPTER EXERCISES

ADDITIONAL EXERCISES ON YOUR CD-ROM

Try the ADDITIONAL EXERCISES and APPLICATION PROBLEMS on the CD-ROM.

Conceptual Questions and Assignments

14-19. Go to the library and locate a journal article using either contingency analysis or a goodness-of-fit test. Discuss the article, paying particular attention to the reasoning behind using the particular statistical test.

14-20. Go to the library and find a marketing research book (or borrow one from a friend). Does it discuss either of the tests considered in this chapter? If yes, outline the discussion. If no, determine where in the text such a discussion would be appropriate.

14-21. In some of the problems in this chapter, we have asked you to provide analysis for a 2 × 2 contingency table. In addition, you were also requested to conduct a hypothesis test concerning two populations' proportions on the same data. Discuss the relative merits of these two procedures for analyzing 2 × 2 contingency tables.

Business Applications

14-22. Linda Stevens, the manager of Arlington Super Discount, always keeps four checkout stands open. However, she frequently notices lines for registers 1 and 2. She is not sure whether the layout of the store channels customers into these registers or whether the checkout clerks in these lines are simply slower than the other two.

Linda kept a record of which stands 2,000 shoppers chose for checkout. The shoppers checked out of the four stands according to the following pattern.

STAND 1	STAND 2	STAND 3	STAND 4
677	550	402	371

a. Based on these data, can Linda conclude that an equal number of shoppers are likely to use each of the stands? (Use $\alpha = 0.05$.)
b. A friend suggested that you could just as well conduct four hypothesis tests that the proportion of customers visiting each stand is equal to one-fourth. Discuss the merits of this suggestion.

14-23. A manufacturer of packaged food has decided to market a new cake mix. This venture is rather risky since the new mix will compete with three established brands. The production manager argues that quality will sell the new mix. The marketing manager states that the typical consumer cannot tell the difference between brands and that the critical factor in selling the mix will be the advertising campaign.

To test the marketing manager's contention, the four brands of cakes were baked under equal conditions. Shoppers were randomly stopped in several supermarkets and asked to sample each cake and indicate which of the four tasted the best. The cake that was first tasted was randomly determined. The following data show how many shoppers rated each brand the tastiest.

BRAND			
A	B	C	New
37	23	27	41

Which contention do these data support? Use a Type I error rate of 0.01.

14-24. Cooper Manufacturing, Inc., of Dallas, Texas, has a contract with the U.S. Air Force to produce a part for a new fighter plane being manufactured. The part is a bolt that has specifications requiring that the length be normally distributed with a mean of 3.05 inches and a standard deviation of 0.015 inch. As part of the company's quality control efforts, each day Cooper's engineers select a random sample of 100 bolts produced that day and carefully measure the bolts to determine whether the production is within specifications. The following data were collected yesterday.

LENGTH (INCHES)	FREQUENCY
Under 3.030	5
3.030 and under 3.035	16
3.035 and under 3.040	7
3.040 and under 3.050	20
3.050 and under 3.060	36
3.060 and under 3.065	8
Over 3.065	8

Based on these sample data, what should Cooper's engineers conclude about the production output if they test using an α of 0.01? Discuss. (Hint: Refer to Example 14-3 and to the special CD-ROM topic pertaining to Lilliefors' test.)

14-25. The Cooper Company discussed in Problem 24 has a second contract with a private firm for which it makes fuses for an electronic instrument. The quality control department at Cooper periodically selects a random sample of 5 fuses and tests each fuse to determine whether it is defective. Based on these findings, the production process is either shut down (if too many defectives are observed) or allowed to run. The quality control department believes that the sampling process follows a binomial distribution, and it has been using the binomial distribution to compute the probabilities associated with the sampling outcomes.

The contract allows for at most 5% defectives. The head of quality control recently compiled a list of the sampling results for the past 300 days in which 5 fuses were tested, with the following frequency distribution for the number of defectives observed. She is concerned that the binomial distribution with a sample size of 5 and a probability of defectives of 0.05 may not be appropriate.

NUMBER OF DEFECTIVES	FREQUENCY
0	209
1	33
2	43
3	10
4	5
5	0

a. Calculate the expected values for the cells in this analysis. Suggest a way in which cells can be combined to assure that the expected value of each cell is at least 5.
b. Using a significance level of 0.10, what should the quality control manager conclude based on these sample data? Discuss.
c. Conduct a hypothesis test to determine if the proportion of defectives satisfies the contract.

14-26. Ralph Rogers has developed a highly successful practice as an acupuncture specialist. Ralph's success is built on his money-back guarantee. If his treatment wears off, he will treat you again. His accountant, in trying to set up an allowance for the future visits account, hypothesizes that a patient's likelihood of demanding a retreatment is related to the price of the original treatment. The following data show the relationship between price and return treatment.

		PRICE		
		High	Medium	Low
	In less than 2 years	46	53	56
RETREATMENT	In 2–5 years	83	75	92
	None in 5 years	127	119	149

a. What should the accountant conclude regarding the hypothesis? (Use $\alpha = 0.05$.)
b. What factors that the accountant apparently has not considered might be important to the analysis?

14-27. A regional cancer treatment center has had success treating localized cancers with a linear accelerator. While admissions for further treatment nationally average 1.7 per patient per year, the center's director thinks that readmissions with the new treatment are Poisson distributed, with a mean of 1.2 per patients per year. He has collected the following data on a random sample of 300 patients.

READMISSIONS LAST YEAR	PATIENTS
0	139
1	87
2	48
3	14
4	8
5	1
6	1
7	0
8	2
	300

a. Adjust the data so that you can test the director's claim using a test statistic whose sampling distribution can be approximated by a chi-square distribution.
b. Assume the Type I error rate is to be controlled at 0.05. Do you agree with the director's claim? Why? Conduct a statistical procedure to support your opinion.

14-28. The J. Scholten CPA firm performed a study of last year's income-tax business. In one part of the study, the accountants collected data on their clients' net taxable incomes and the associated tax payments. These data are shown in the following table, where, for example, there are 50 clients whose taxable incomes were $10,000 or less and who paid $3,000 or less in taxes.

TAXABLE INCOME	TAXES			
	$0–$3,000	$3,001–$5,000	$5,001–$10,000	Over $10,000
$0–10,000	50	0	0	0
$10,001–$20,000	42	30	0	0
$20,001–$40,000	40	65	33	28
Over $40,000	28	52	47	39

a. Based on these data, can Scholten conclude that its clients' net taxable incomes are independent of the income taxes paid? Test at $\alpha = 0.05$.
b. If the taxes paid and income earned are not independent, then based upon an examination of the data what conclusions do you reach? Discuss.

14-29. Scholten also studied the time its accountants took to complete another sample client's tax returns and related this time to the taxes paid by the client. Scholten managers were interested in determining whether a relationship exists between these two variables or whether they could consider the two variables independent. The following data are available.

NO. WORK HOURS	TAXES			
	$0–$3,000	$3,001–$5,000	$5,001–$10,000	Over $10,000
0–2	52	55	30	27
3–4	47	55	30	31
Over 4	35	37	55	35

Based on these data, what should the Scholten firm conclude? Use $\alpha = 0.10$.

14-30. An instructor at a major university indicates that test scores in an introductory sociology class have been normally distributed since he started using a graduate student to grade his tests. To test this claim, a random sample of 300 test scores was selected from the previous academic year. These are shown as follows.

TEST SCORE	FREQUENCY
Under 30	20
30 and under 40	35
40 and under 50	40
50 and under 60	35
60 and under 70	105
70 and under 80	60
80 or more	5

Based on these sample data, can you conclude that the test scores are normally distributed at $\alpha = 0.05$? Note that you need to compute the sample mean and standard deviation. (Hint: Refer to Example 14-3 and to the special CD-ROM topic pertaining to Lilliefors' test.)

14-31. The State Transportation Department recently conducted a study of motorists in Idaho. Two main factors of interest were whether the vehicle was insured with liability insurance and whether the driver was wearing his/her seatbelt. A random sample of 100 cars was stopped at various locations throughout the state. The data are in the file called **Liabins**. The investigators were interested in determining whether seatbelt status is independent of insurance status.

a. Calculate the expected values for the cells in this analysis. Suggest a way in which cells can be combined to assure that the expected value of each cell is at least 5 so that as many level combinations of the two variables as possible are retained.

b. Test to determine if seatbelt status is independent of insurance status. Use a significance level of 0.05. Show the contingency table and the test statistic.

14-32. Referring to Problem 31, can the investigators conclude that knowledge of the liability insurance law is independent of the respondent's gender? Test at the $\alpha = 0.05$ level. Discuss.

14-33. Refer to Problem 32.

a. Based on the sample data, can the investigators conclude that the distribution of the time drivers have lived in Idaho is normally distributed? Test using an appropriate goodness-of-fit test at an $\alpha = 0.05$ level.

b. Construct a 95% confidence interval for the average time drivers have lived in Idaho.

14-34. Assume that you are preparing a speech for a trade conference and intend to use information from the **Cities** file. At one point in your speech, you would like to provide an estimate of the mean population growth rate between 1990 and 1995. However, based on your knowledge of estimation, you know that since the population standard deviation is unknown, you must be able to assume that the distribution of growth rates is normally distributed.

a. Using $\alpha = 0.10$, would you be justified in making the normal distribution assumption?

b. Based on your answer to part a, if appropriate, develop a 95% confidence interval estimate for the mean population growth rate between 1990 and 1995. Interpret your result.

14-35. Refer to Problem 34. Using contingency analysis, can you consider the cities' labor market stress index to be statistically independent of the 1998 unemployment rate?

a. Break each variable into appropriate categories. Produce two equally spaced intervals for the labor market stress index and three equally spaced intervals for the unemployment rate. Construct a contingency table using these intervals.

b. Conduct the hypothesis test to determine if you can consider the cities' labor market stress index to be statistically independent. Use $\alpha = 0.025$.

14-36. Refer to Problem 35.

a. Break the variables labor market stress index and 1998 unemployment rate into a different set of categories and conduct the test again.

b. Did the results change this time? Discuss why it is possible for the contingency analysis results to differ depending on how the categories are formed for a continuous random variable.

14-37. Data were recently collected on several variables for the 100 fastest-growing companies in the United States. The data are in a file called **Fast100**. A recent claim made in a major business publication has stated that the mean P/E ratio exceeds 25.0 for all growth companies. Assuming that these data represent a random sample of companies:

a. Test to determine whether the distribution of P/E ratios is normally distributed. Use $\alpha = 0.05$ level to test the hypothesis.

b. If the result in part a warrants doing so, conduct the appropriate hypothesis test for the claim made by the business publication. Use $\alpha = 0.05$ to conduct the test.

14-38. Referring to Problem 37, can you conclude that stock price is independent of the exchange on which the stock is traded? Break the stock price into three categories and test at $\alpha = 0.10$.

14-39. Referring to Problem 38, is the annual 3–5 year growth rate for companies in this study described by a uniform distribution? Test using an appropriate goodness-of-fit method using $\alpha = 0.05$.

CASE 14-A

American Oil Company

Chad Williams sat back in his airline seat to enjoy the hour flight between Los Angeles and Oakland, California. The hour would give him time to reflect upon his upcoming trip to Australia and the work he had been doing the past week in Los Angeles.

Chad is one of six men on a crew for the American Oil Company who literally walk the earth searching for oil. His college degrees in geology and petroleum engineering landed him the job with American, but he never dreamed he would be doing the exciting work he now does. Chad and his crew spend several months in special locations around the world using highly sensitive electronic equipment for oil exploration purposes.

The upcoming trip to Australia is one that Chad has been looking forward to since it was announced that his crew would be going there to search the Outback for oil. In preparation for the Australia trip, the crew has been in Los Angeles at American's engineering research facility working on some new equipment that will be used in Australia in search of oil.

Chad's thoughts centered on the problem he was having with a particular component part on the new equipment. The specifications called for 200 of the components, each having a diameter of between 0.15 and 0.18 inches. The only available supplier of the component in New Jersey manufactures the components to specifications calling for normally distributed output with a mean of 0.16 inches and a standard deviation of 0.02 inches.

Chad faces two problems. First, he is unsure that the supplier actually does produce parts with the mean of 0.16 inches and standard deviation of 0.02 inches according to a normal distribution. Second, if that is the case, he needs to determine how many components to purchase if enough acceptable components are to be received to make two oil exploration devices.

The supplier has sent Chad the following data for 330 randomly selected components. Chad believes that the supplier is honest and that he can rely on the data.

DIAMETER (INCHES)	FREQUENCY
Under 0.14	5
0.14 and under 0.15	70
0.15 and under 0.16	90
0.16 and under 0.17	105
0.17 and under 0.18	50
Over 0.18	10
Total	330

Chad needs to have a report ready for Monday indicating whether he believes the supplier delivers at its stated specifications and, if so, how many of the components American should order to have enough acceptable components to outfit two oil exploration devices.

CASE 14-B

Bentford Electronics, Part 1

On Saturday morning Jennifer Bentford received a call at her home from the production supervisor at Bentford Electronics Plant #1. The supervisor indicated that she and the supervisors from Plants #2, #3, and #4 had agreed that something must be done to improve company morale and, thereby, increase the production output of their plants. Jennifer Bentford, president of Bentford Electronics, agreed to set up a Monday morning meeting with the supervisors to see if, together, they could arrive at a plan for accomplishing these objectives.

By Monday each supervisor had compiled a list of several ideas, including a 4-day work week and interplant competition of various kinds. A second meeting was set for Wednesday to discuss the issue further.

Following the Wednesday afternoon meeting, Jennifer Bentford and her plant supervisors agreed to implement a weekly contest called the NBE Game of the Week. The plant turning out the most production each week would be considered the NBE Game of the Week winner and would receive 10 points. The second-place plant would receive 7 points, and the third- and fourth-place plants would receive 3 points and 1 point, respectively. The contest would last 26 weeks. At the end of that period, a $200,000 bonus would be divided among the employees in the four plants proportional to the total points accumulated by each plant.

The announcement of the contest created a lot of excitement and enthusiasm at the four plants. No one complained about the rules since the four plants were designed and staffed to produce equally.

At the close of the contest, Jennifer Bentford called the supervisors into a meeting, at which time she asked for data to determine whether the contest had significantly improved productivity. She indicated that she had to know this before she could authorize a second contest. The supervisors, expecting this response, had put together the following data.

UNITS PRODUCED	BEFORE-CONTEST	DURING-CONTEST
(4 Plants Combined)	Frequency	Frequency
0–2,500	11	0
2,501–8,000	23	20
8,001–15,000	56	83
15,001–20,000	15	52
	105 days	155 days

Jennifer examined the data and indicated that it looked like the contest was a success, but she wanted to base her decision to continue the contest on more than just an observation of the data. "Surely there must be some way to statistically test the worthiness of this contest," Jennifer stated. "I have to see the results before I will authorize the second contest."

■ GENERAL REFERENCES

1. Berenson, Mark L., and David M. Levine, *Basic Business Statistics Concepts and Applications*, 7th ed. (Upper Saddle River, NJ: Prentice Hall, 1999).
2. Conover, W. J., *Practical Nonparametric Statistics*, 3d ed. (New York: Wiley, 1999).
3. Marascuilo, Leonard, and M. McSweeney, *Nonparametric and Distribution Free Methods for the Social Sciences* (Monterey, CA: Brooks/Cole, 1977).
4. *Microsoft Excel 2000* (Redmond, WA: Microsoft Corporation, 1999).
5. *Minitab for Windows Version 13* (State College, PA: Minitab, Inc., 2000).

CHAPTER 15

INTRODUCTION TO NONPARAMETRIC STATISTICS

CHAPTER OUTCOMES

After studying the material in Chapter 15, you should be able to:

15-1: Recognize when and how to use the runs test when testing for randomness.

15-2: Know when and how to perform a Mann-Whitney U test.

15-3: Recognize the situations for which the Wilcoxon signed rank test applies and be able to use it in a decision-making context.

15-4: Perform nonparametric analysis of variance using the Kruskal-Wallis one-way ANOVA.

WHY YOU NEED TO KNOW

A major electronics firm is considering building a new assembly plant in the southeastern United States. Housing prices are particularly important in picking the plant's location because the company would like affordable housing to be available for employees who transfer to the new location. The company has taken a sample of real estate listings from the four cities in contention for the new plant and would like to make a statistically valid comparison of home prices based on this sample information. This comparison would then be used to help determine where the new assembly plant should be located. The same company is also considering what type of employee evaluation system to use in the new plant. It has been experimenting with a group-based, rather than an individual-based, employee evaluation system in one of its plants. As a part of this experiment the firm has gathered questionnaire data from employees who were asked to rate their experience with the evaluation system as being one with which they were *Very Satisfied, Satisfied, No Opinion, Dissatisfied,* or *Very Dissatisfied.*

In previous chapters, you were introduced to a wide variety of statistical techniques that would seem to be useful statistical analysis tools for this company. However, many of the techniques discussed earlier are not appropriate for the situation facing this company. For instance, hypothesis tests involving small samples and an unknown population standard deviation utilize the *t*-distribution. However, using the *t*-distribution in that situation assumes the population from which the sample is selected is normally distributed. If a small-sample application involves testing the difference between two population means, the *t*-distribution is used under the assumption that both populations are normally distributed. The analysis of variance *F*-test introduced in Chapter 10 is based on the assumption that all populations are normally distributed and the population variances are equal. In addition, each of these techniques requires the variables of interest to be either interval or ratio level.

While in many instances these underlying conditions are satisfied, you will encounter other situations where either the level of data measurement is too low or the distribution assumptions are clearly violated. This is the case for both of the issues facing the electronics company mentioned previously. Housing prices are generally right skewed since most locations have a few very expensive houses, and the employee questionnaire answers were measured on an ordinal, not on an interval or ratio scale. To handle cases such as the two mentioned here, a class of statistical tools called nonparametric statistics has been developed.

■ 15-1: TESTING FOR RANDOMNESS USING THE RUNS TEST

Up to this point, the text has presented a wide array of statistical tools both for describing data and for drawing inferences about a population based on sample information from that population. These tools are widely used in decision-making situations. However, you will also encounter decision situations in which major departures from the required assumptions exist. For example, many populations, such as family income levels and house prices, are highly skewed. In other instances, the level of data measurement will be too low (ordinal or nominal) to warrant use of the techniques presented in earlier chapters. In cases such as these, the alternative is to employ a **nonparametric statistical procedure** that has been developed to meet specific inferential needs. Such procedures have fewer restrictive assumptions concerning data level and underlying probability distributions. There are a great many nonparametric procedures that cover a wide range of situations. The purpose of this chapter is to introduce you to the concept of nonparametric statistics and illustrate some of the more frequently used methods.[1]

> **NONPARAMETRIC STATISTICAL PROCEDURES**
> Statistical methods that do not explicitly concern themselves with population distributions and/or parameters.

The Runs Test

The **runs test** is frequently used to determine whether a sequence of values has the property of randomness.

---

[1]See *Applied Nonparametric Statistics* by Wayne W. Daniel in the chapter references for a discussion of the technical difference between nonparametric statistics and distribution-free statistics.

> **RUNS TEST**
>
> A statistical procedure used to determine whether the pattern of occurrences of two types of observations is determined by a random process.

RUNS TEST

Idaho Hunting Permits

All states regulate hunting and fishing through some government agency. Generally, a license is required to fish on the state's streams, rivers, and lakes. Likewise, a hunting license is required to hunt birds and big game. In some states, additional permits are required to hunt certain species of animals or to hunt female deer and elk. In Idaho and some other states, these permits are usually granted based on a random drawing from the list of those hunters that apply.

Idaho is a state of approximately 1 million people. Each year nearly 300,000 big-game hunting licenses are sold. Over half of these license holders pay an additional fee to be part of a drawing for special permits to hunt antelope, cow elk, mountain sheep, and mountain goats. The number of permits granted is far less than the number of applicants.

Idaho is a relatively large state geographically. The state capital and the headquarters of all government agencies for the state are located in Boise. For that and several other reasons, most of the state's economic development occurs in and around Boise. As a result, there is an anti-Boise bias in other parts of the state. The drawing each year for special hunting permits is conducted using computer software at the Idaho Department of Fish and Game located in Boise. Possibly because of the anti-Boise feeling, a few years ago hunters from other parts of the state banded together to challenge the Idaho Fish and Game's system for allocating hunting permits. They charged that the system favored the Boise area hunters.

To answer these charges and to verify the validity of software used for drawing licenses, the Fish and Game Department hired a consultant to perform an independent audit of the system. Figure 15-1 shows a flowchart of the steps involved in making the permit selections. For each class of permit, a file exists with applications ordered by hunting license number. The file typically contains applicants from around the state depending on the type of permit and the location for which it will be valid. The computer program uses an algorithm to generate a uniform random number between 0.0 and 1.0. This random number is then multiplied by the number of applicants in the file. The product, rounded to the nearest integer value, corresponds to an applicant in the file who will receive the hunting permit. For the purposes of this example, suppose 500 hunters applied for a certain permit and are arranged from 1 to 500 in the file, according to hunting license number. If the computer program generated a "random" number between 0.0 and 1.0 of 0.34509, the product of this number and 500 is

$$0.34509 \times 500 = 172.54500$$

The product is rounded to 173. Therefore, the 173rd person in the applicant file would receive the permit. If additional permits are available, a second uniform random number is generated and the process continues.

As long as the system generates random numbers between 0.0 and 1.0, the selection of hunters to receive permits would not favor hunters from any particular part of the state. The auditors needed a technique for testing whether the computer program generated numbers that pass the test of randomness. One such technique is the *runs test*. The runs test utilizes a sample to test whether the population data are random by examining the number of **runs** in the sample.

> **RUN**
>
> A succession of occurrences of a certain type preceded and followed by occurrences of the alternate type or by no occurrences at all.

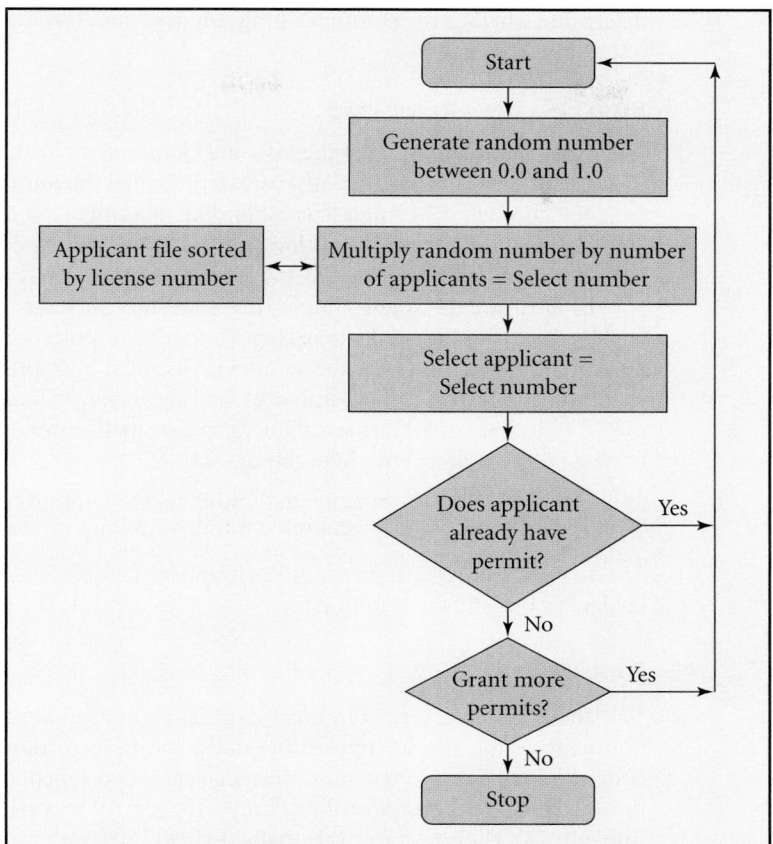

FIGURE 15-1
Hunting Permit Selection
System for the State of Idaho

Based on the logic of the runs test, if too few or too many runs are observed in the sample, the hypothesis of randomness is rejected. For example, suppose the "final bell" stock price for a certain stock is tracked for 20 trading days. The final bell price is compared to the opening price with A = above the opening price and B = below the opening price, and the following sequence is observed.

Run 1	Run 2
A A A A A A A A A A	B B B B B B B B B B

In this case, only two runs occurred in the 20 observations. Even though half the values are A and half are B, if we were expecting the stock prices to occur in a random sequence, these results suggest otherwise—there are too few runs! Suppose the following results occur for 20 observations.

A B A B A B A B A B A B A B A B A B A B

This shows 20 runs, since the stock price is alternating above and below the opening price each day. Again, even though half the values are A and half are B, this pattern indicates there are probably too many runs and suggests that the stock prices are not occurring randomly.

The runs test can be easily applied to the Idaho Fish and Game permit audit by assigning a "+" code to any random number greater than 0.50000 and a "−" code to any random number less than 0.50000. (Note the chance of a number being exactly 0.50000 is very small, so we have not included it in the coding methodology.) The runs test can be used to determine whether the computer program generates too many or too few runs to pass the test of randomness.

SMALL-SAMPLE RUNS TEST

In employing the runs test in the Fish and Game example, the consultant could select a statistical sample from the population and let n_1 equal the number of occurrences of one kind (e.g., the number of "+" signs corresponding to numbers > 0.50000). Let n_2 equal the number of occurrences of the other kind (e.g., "−" signs corresponding to numbers < 0.50000). If both n_1 and n_2 are less than 20, the small-sample runs test must be used.

To illustrate the small-sample runs test, suppose a sample of 20 numbers was generated by the Idaho Fish and Game Department's computer software. These values are shown in Table 15-1. Observe that the sample items must be kept in the sequence in which they occur. In this example, the number of "+" signs is $n_1 = 9$ and the number of "−" signs is $n_2 = 11$. Both n_1 and n_2 are less than 20, so the small-sample runs test is used to test the following null and alternative hypotheses.

H_0: Computer-generated numbers are random between 0.0 and 1.0
H_A: Computer-generated numbers are not random

To perform the test, we count the number of runs of "+" and "−" over the sequence of 20 data points shown as follows.

	− − −	+	−	+ +	− −	+ +	− − −	+ +	− −	+ +
Runs:	1	2	3	4	5	6	7	8	9	10

There are $r = 10$ runs in these data. The question is whether 10 runs are considered too many or too few to support the null hypothesis of randomness. Since we care about either too many or too few runs, the runs test is two-tailed. For the small-sample runs test, this question can be answered by comparing $r = 10$ to a critical value in the runs table in Appendix K. The runs table is actually divided into two parts: part (a) is used to locate the lower limit critical value and part (b) the upper limit critical value. Note that the runs table in Appendix K is for $\alpha = 0.05$.

To use the runs table, first go to part (a) and locate in the leftmost column a number corresponding to $n_1 = 9$, the number of "+" signs. Then locate in the top row the value $n_2 = 11$, the number of "−" signs. The value at the intersection of this row and column is 6. Therefore,

If $r \le 6$, we reject H_0

Next, go to part (b) of the runs table and locate $n_1 = 9$ in the leftmost column and $n_2 = 11$ across the top row. The intersection of the row and column is at the critical value 16. Thus,

If $r \ge 16$, we reject H_0

TABLE 15-1
Idaho Department of Fish and Game "Random" Numbers

SEQUENCE	NUMBER	CODE	SEQUENCE	NUMBER	CODE
1	0.34561	−	11	0.67201	+
2	0.42789	−	12	0.23790	−
3	0.36925	−	13	0.24509	−
4	0.89563	+	14	0.01467	−
5	0.25679	−	15	0.78345	+
6	0.92001	+	16	0.69112	+
7	0.58345	+	17	0.46023	−
8	0.23114	−	18	0.38633	−
9	0.12672	−	19	0.60914	+
10	0.88569	+	20	0.95234	+

Hypotheses:

H_0: Computer-generated numbers are random between 0.0 and 1.0
H_A: Computer-generated numbers are not random
$\alpha = 0.05$

Test Statistic:

$$r = 10 \text{ runs}$$

Critical Values from Runs Table in Appendix K.

Possible
Runs: 1 2 3 4 5 6 | 7 8 9 10 11 12 13 14 15 | 16 17 18 19 20

              Reject   Do not reject   Reject
              H_0 H_0 H_0

Decision Rule:

If: $r \leq 6$ or $r \geq 16$, reject H_0
Otherwise, do not reject H_0

Since $r = 10$, we do not reject the null hypothesis. Based on the sample data, we cannot dispute the claim that the computer-generated numbers are random.

FIGURE 15-2
Small-Sample Runs Test for the Idaho Fish and Game Example

Additional
Example 15-a

Using Minitab for the Small-Sample Runs Test

EXAMPLE
15-2

RUNS TEST

Since $r = 10$ falls between the critical values, these sample data do not refute the null hypothesis that the computer-generated numbers are random between 0.0 and 1.0 at the $\alpha = 0.05$ level. Figure 15-2 shows the runs test in summary form.

In conclusion, based in part on the runs test, the independent audit supported the Idaho Fish and Game Department's methodology for drawing hunting permits. There was no reason to believe that hunters from the Boise area received special consideration.

LARGE-SAMPLE RUNS TEST
Healthy Heart Corporation

In using the runs test for randomness, if either n_1 or n_2 exceeds 20, the runs tables in Appendix K cannot be used. Instead, an approximation method utilizing the normal distribution has been developed. To demonstrate the large-sample runs test, consider the following production control example involving the Healthy Heart Corporation which processes a wide variety of reduced calorie products at numerous plants around the country. The company produces both hard and soft yogurt at its plant in Salem, Massachusetts. A machine that inserts yogurt into each carton is used to fill the 24-ounce hard yogurt cartons. Ideally, each carton would contain exactly 24 ounces, but since all processes exhibit some variation, this is not the case. Instead, the filling machine produces yogurt cartons with weights varying around an average of 24 ounces. The production manager is interested in determining whether the fill weights are randomly distributed around the 24-ounce average or whether there is some pattern or dependency relationship between successive cartons.

As a test, the fill machine operator selected 100 successive cartons from the day shift production. These data, coded "O" for over 24 ounces and "U" for under 24 ounces, are

TABLE 15-2
Healthy Heart Hard Yogurt
Data (in sequential order)

OOO U OO U O UU OO UU OOOO UU O UU OOO
UUU OOOO UU OO UUU O UU OO UUUUU
OOO U O UU OOO U OOOO UUU O UU OOO U
OO UUU O U OO UUU O UU OOOO UUU OOO

shown in Table 15-2. A careful check of these data shows that there are $n_1 = 53$ "O's," $n_2 = 47$ "U's," and a total of $r = 45$ runs. Remember that the data are maintained in sequential order.

The large-sample runs test is based on a normal approximation for the sampling distribution of r where the mean is given by Equation 15-1 and the standard deviation by Equation 15-2.

MEAN AND STANDARD DEVIATION FOR r

$$\mu_r = \frac{2n_1 n_2}{n_1 + n_2} + 1 \qquad \text{15-1}$$

$$\sigma_r = \sqrt{\frac{(2n_1 n_2)(2n_1 n_2 - n_1 - n_2)}{(n_1 + n_2)^2(n_1 + n_2 - 1)}} \qquad \text{15-2}$$

where:

n_1 = Number of occurrences of first type
n_2 = Number of occurrences of second type

The test statistic for this test is shown in Equation 15-3.

TEST STATISTIC FOR LARGE-SAMPLE RUNS TEST

$$z = \frac{r - \mu_r}{\sigma_r} \qquad \text{15-3}$$

Additional
Example 15-b
on CD-ROM

Using Minitab for
the Large-Sample
Runs Test

The derivation of these equations is beyond the scope of the text. However, we can substitute our values for n_1 and n_2 into Equations 15-1 and 15-2 to solve for the mean and standard deviation as follows.

$$\mu_r = \frac{2 \times 53 \times 47}{53 + 47} + 1$$
$$= 50.82$$

$$\sigma_r = \sqrt{\frac{(2 \times 53 \times 47)(2 \times 53 \times 47 - 53 - 47)}{(53 + 47)^2(53 + 47 - 1)}}$$
$$= 4.957$$

We see from these computations that for a sample of size 100 with 53 occurrences of one kind and 47 of the second kind, the expected, or mean, number of runs is 50.82 with a standard deviation of just under 5.0. Recall that we found $r = 45$ runs in the data in Table 15-2. Figure 15-3 shows the large-sample runs test based on the normal approximation approach. The calculated z-value of -1.174 does not fall in the rejection region for a 0.05 level of significance. Therefore, based on these sample data, the production manager has no basis for rejecting the premise that the process is filling hard yogurt cartons with randomly distributed weights on either side of 24 ounces.

Hypotheses:

H_0: Yogurt carton fill amounts are randomly distributed above and below the 24-ounce level.

H_A: Yogurt carton fill amounts are not randomly distributed above and below the 24-ounce level.

$\alpha = 0.05$

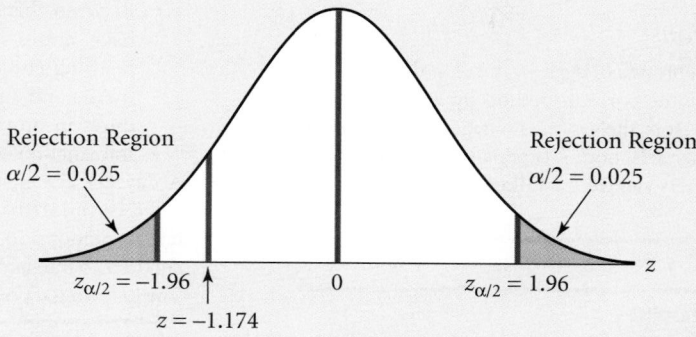

Rejection Region
$\alpha/2 = 0.025$

Rejection Region
$\alpha/2 = 0.025$

$z_{\alpha/2} = -1.96$ 0 $z_{\alpha/2} = 1.96$

$z = -1.174$

Test Statistic:

$$z = \frac{r - \mu_r}{\sigma_r} = \frac{45 - 50.82}{4.957} = -1.174$$

Decision Rule:

If $z < -1.96$ or $z > 1.96$, reject H_0
Otherwise, do not reject H_0
Since $z = -1.174$, we do not reject H_0

FIGURE 15-3
Large-Sample Runs Test for
the Healthy Heart Company

15-1: EXERCISES

ADDITIONAL EXERCISES ON YOUR CD-ROM

Try the ADDITIONAL EXERCISES and APPLICATION PROBLEMS on the CD-ROM.

15-1. A process has generated the following sequence of positive and negative values.

PPP	N	PP	NN	P	NN	PP	N	PP	NN	PPP
NN	PP	N	P	N	PP	NNN	P	NN	P	N

  a. State the appropriate null and alternative hypotheses for testing whether the sequence meets the status of randomness.
  b. Based on these sample data and a significance level equal to 0.05, what is the maximum number of runs that would be allowed before the null hypothesis is rejected?
  c. Based on these sample data and a significance level equal to 0.05, what is the minimum number of runs

that would be allowed before the null hypothesis is rejected?
  d. How many runs are present in these data?
  e. Based upon your responses to parts b, c, and d, what conclusion should be reached with respect to the null hypothesis?

15-2. A sample of items made on an assembly line are classified as either "G" for good or "D" for defective. The following sequence was observed.

GGG	D	GG	DD	G		DD	GG	D	GG	DD	GGG	
DD	GG	D	G	D		GG	DDD	G	DD	G		DDD
GG	D	GG	DD	GGG	DD		G		DD	GG	D	GG
D		GG	DD	G		DD	GGG	DD		GG	D	G

a. State the appropriate null and alternative hypotheses for testing whether the sequence meets the status of randomness.

b. Use an appropriate approximation to test the hypothesis that the sequence exhibits randomness. Use a significance level of 0.05.

c. Approximate the p-value for this hypothesis test.

Business Applications

15-3. A store sells two brands of eggs, brand X and brand Y. In order to analyze the current method by which eggs are arranged on the store shelves, the manager is interested in whether customer selection of brands is random. A sample of 20 customers yielded the following sequence of egg brand selection.

X X Y Y Y X Y X X Y Y Y Y X Y Y Y Y X Y X X

Based on these results:

a. How many runs are there in the data?

b. Using $\alpha = 0.05$, test the hypothesis that egg brand selection is random between the two brands. Be sure to state the appropriate null and alternative hypotheses.

15-4. An obstetrician has been accused by a consumer advocacy group of doing too many C-sections as the method of delivery. The case is currently under review by the regional medical examiner board. As part of the analysis, the board has selected 50 consecutive births for which this doctor was the physician of responsibility. The births were denoted as *C* for C-section and *N* for normal delivery. The intent is to use these particular data to determine whether the sequence of C-section and normal births is random. The board surmises that if the type of birth show a pattern then the doctor may be using some criterion other than the patient's best interest (such as financial gain) to determine the type of birth. The resulting data are in a file called **Babies** and are shown as follows.

NN	CCC	N	C	NN		CC	N C	N
CCCC	NNNN	C		NNN	C		N	C NN CCC
NN	C		NNN	CCC	NNNNNN	C		

a. Suppose the type of birth procedure selected was chosen randomly. Determine the largest and smallest number of runs you would expect to see for a sample size with the same number of C-section and normal births.

b. Conduct a hypothesis test to determine if the sequence of births is nonrandom. Does the doctor appear to be using something other than a random process to select the method of birth? Explain.

15-5. Referring to Problem 4, suppose that typically 25% of the babies delivered in this area are delivered using the C-section approach.

a. Based on the sample data for the doctor, does his proportion of C-section deliveries exceeds the 25% standard? State the appropriate null and alternative

hypotheses and test using $\alpha = 0.05$. (Hint: Refer to Chapter 8 for hypothesis testing involving a single population proportion.)

b. Determine a range of values for the proportion of C-section deliveries that the doctor in question performs. The range should exhibit a 95% confidence level.

c. Between this current problem and Problem 4 you have addressed different characteristics of the birthing choices made by the doctor. Discuss the merits and shortcomings of both statistical procedures in providing the regional medical examiners information concerning the issue at hand.

15-6. A daycare center operator is interested in determining whether children's preference for playing with trucks or dolls is random. To test this, she has observed 15 individual children go into a room with a truck and a doll on the floor. The following represents the sequence of first toy selection.

T T T D T D T T D D D T T D T

a. How many runs are present in these data?

b. Test the hypothesis of randomness at the $\alpha = 0.05$ level. Discuss whether children's preference for playing with trucks or dolls is random.

15-7. A department store operator is interested in determining whether the payment method for merchandise is randomly distributed between the store's credit card and a major bank card. He has observed 300 consecutive credit card sales and found 145 using the store card and 155 using a major credit card. The number of runs observed in the sample was 35.

a. Based on these data, use the runs test to determine whether the payment method for merchandise is randomly distributed between the store's credit card and a major bank card. Use a significance level of 0.10.

b. Determine the p-value for this test.

c. Test to determine if the proportion of credit card sales is different for the store card versus the major credit card.

15-8. The Farwest Bank is currently involved in a comprehensive study of its service capabilities. One component of this study involves an analysis of the customers' use of the drive-in teller facility and the inside service area. Over a 2-day period, 568 cars arrived at the bank. If a car's occupant(s) used the drive-in teller, a "D" was recorded for that car. If the occupant(s) went inside the bank, an "I" was recorded. The resulting data are in a file called **Farwest**. At issue is whether the use of bank service facilities is random. Note, occupants in 361 of the 568 cars used the inside services, and over the sequence of 568 cars arriving there were 262 runs of inside or drive-in use.

a. State the appropriate null and alternative hypotheses for testing whether the sequence meets the status of randomness.

b. Establish the appropriate rejection region(s) to conduct the test specified in part a. Use a significance level of 0.10.

c. Given the number of runs in these data, what conclusion should be reached regarding the null hypothesis? Conduct the test using a p-value approach.

15-9. A bank operations manager has claimed that the arrivals of male and female customers to the drive-in window at a particular branch are random. To test this, she has observed 400 consecutive arrivals and recorded whether the driver was male or female. Of the 400, 302 were female and 98 were male. Further, there were 77 runs of male or female in the sample. Based on these data, what should the manager conclude? Use $\alpha = 0.05$.

15-10. Cedar Rapids Electronics has been tracking its weekly sales for the last 15 weeks. Management thinks there is evidence that the company's sales are increasing. However, they think that something more complex than a simple increase in sales is happening. Perhaps some cyclical effect is exhibiting itself. A method that is used in Time Series Analysis (to be discussed in Chapter 16) to determine if the sequence of data values is exhibiting something besides a trend (upward or downward movement in the series) involves the use of *first differences*. The first differences of a sequence of data values $x_1, x_2, \ldots, x_n$ are:

$$d_i = x_i - x_{i-1} \text{ for } i = 2, 3, \ldots, n$$

The last 15 weeks sales data (in \$1,000s) are given as follows.

WEEK	SALES	WEEK	SALES
1	300	9	410
2	295	10	430
3	330	11	450
4	345	12	460
5	350	13	475
6	370	14	480
7	390	15	500
8	400		

a. Determine the 14 first differences for the sales data.
b. If the only component in this sequence of data is the increasing trend in the sales, the first differences should be random fluctuations about the mean of the first differences, $\bar{d}$. Determine the number of runs of the sequence of first differences above and below $\bar{d}$.
c. Test to determine if a random process produces the sequence of first differences above and below $\bar{d}$.
d. Does the pattern of the runs of the first differences support the conjecture voiced by the man-

agement of Cedar Rapids Electronics? Explain your reasoning.

15-11. Both Excel and Minitab have random number generator functions. In Minitab, select *Calc—Random Data—Bernoulli* and generate 50 random numbers using a probability of success = 0.40. In Excel, select *Tools—Data Analysis—Random Number Generation—Bernoulli* and generate 50 random numbers using a p-value = 0.40. The output will be a list of 0 and 1 values. Your objective is to test whether these values are randomly generated using the runs test.

a. State the appropriate null and alternative hypotheses for testing whether the sequence meets the status of randomness.
b. Based on these sample data and a significance level equal to 0.05, what is the maximum number of runs that would be allowed before the null hypothesis is rejected?
c. Based on these sample data and an alpha level equal to 0.05, what is the minimum number of runs that would be allowed before the null hypothesis is rejected?
d. Given the number of runs in these data, what conclusion should be reached regarding the null hypothesis?

15-12. The Robinson Control Company manufactures temperature control units. During the past 10 years, it has seen increasing sales almost every year. However, the company has begun to suspect that something other than this linear trend upward is occurring in its sales. The last 10 years' control unit sales data (in thousands of units) for Robinson's are given as follows.

YEAR	SALES	YEAR	SALES
1990	450	1995	520
1991	435	1996	540
1992	480	1997	550
1993	495	1998	560
1994	500	1999	580

a. Determine the 9 first differences for the control unit sales data.
b. If the only component in this sequence of data is the increasing trend in the sales of the control units, the first differences should be random fluctuations about the mean of the first differences, $\bar{d}$. Determine the number of runs of the sequence of first differences above and below $\bar{d}$.
c. Test to determine if a random process produces the sequence of first differences above and below $\bar{d}$.

15-2: NONPARAMETRIC TESTS FOR TWO POPULATION CENTERS

Chapters 8, 9, and 10 introduced a variety of hypothesis testing tools and techniques. Included were tests involving two or more population means. These tests carried with them several assumptions and requirements. For situations in which you are testing about the difference between two population means, the Student t-distribution was employed. The assumptions for the t-distribution are that the two populations are normally distributed.

The data are also restricted to being interval or ratio level. While in many situations these assumptions and data requirements will be satisfied, you will often encounter situations where that is not the case.

In this section we introduce two nonparametric techniques that do not require such stringent assumptions and data requirements, the *Mann-Whitney U test* and the *Wilcoxon matched-pairs signed rank test*. Both tests can be used with ordinal (ranked) data and neither requires that the populations be normally distributed.

The Mann-Whitney U Test

Blaine County Highway District

The Blaine County Highway District (BCHD) was recently formed to consolidate the street and highway maintenance and construction activities in Blaine County. Formerly, the urban division took care of all the streets and roads in the county's largest city, and the rural division handled all street and road work outside that city. The urban and rural divisions had separate management, and because of the perceived duplication of managerial activities, the county commissioners mandated that the two divisions consolidate into one. However, the work force of the BCHD at present remains divided between the rural and urban divisions.

A few months following the consolidation, several rural division supervisors began claiming that the urban division employees wasted gravel from the county gravel pit. They claimed the urban division used more gravel per mile of road maintenance than the rural division. In response to these claims, the BCHD materials manager decided to perform a test. He selected a random sample of weeks from the district's job cost records from work performed by the urban (U) division and a random sample of work performed by the rural (R) division. The data in Table 15-3 represent the yards of gravel used per mile of road for each week sampled.

Even though the data are of a ratio-level measurement, the manager is not willing to make the normality assumptions necessary to employ the two-sample *t*-test discussed in Chapter 9. However, a nonparametric technique called the Mann-Whitney U test will allow him to compare the gravel use of the two divisions.

The Mann-Whitney U test is one of the most popular nonparametric tests and can be used to compare samples from two populations in those cases where the following assumptions are satisfied.

1. The two samples are independent and random.
2. The value measured is a continuous variable.
3. The measurement scale used is at least ordinal.
4. If they differ, the distributions of the two populations will differ only with respect to the central location.

The fourth point is instrumental in setting your null and alternative hypotheses. We are interested in determining whether two populations have the same or different centers where the center can be defined as either the mean or the median. In situations where the level of data measurement is interval or ratio, the hypothesis can be stated in terms of the mean or the median. However, when the data level is ordinal, the hypothesis must be stated in terms of the median. In this situation, the variable of interest is cubic yards of gravel used. This is a ratio-level variable so the materials manager has decided to test the following hypotheses stated in terms of the population means.

$H_0: \mu_1 \leq \mu_2$ (Mean urban gravel use is no greater than mean rural use)
$H_A: \mu_1 > \mu_2$ (Mean urban gravel use exceeds mean rural use)
$\alpha = 0.05$

The first step in testing this hypothesis using the Mann-Whitney U test is to combine the raw data from the two samples into one set of numbers, then rank the numbers in this set from low to high. The two samples are then separated again, listing each observation with

EXAMPLE 15-3

MANN-WHITNEY U TEST

TABLE 15-3
Yards of Gravel per Mile for the Blaine County Highway District

URBAN	RURAL
460	600
830	652
720	603
930	594
500	1,402
620	1,111
703	902
407	700
1,521	827
900	490
750	904
800	1,400

the rank it had been assigned in the pooled data set. This leads to the rankings as shown in Table 15-4. The logic of the Mann-Whitney U test centers on the idea that if the sum of the rankings of one group differs greatly from the sum of the rankings of the second group, we should conclude that there is a difference in central locations of the populations. Similarly, if the sum of the rankings of the first group is significantly larger than the sum of the rankings of the second group, we should conclude that the central location of the population of the first group is larger than that of the central location of the population of the second group.

Note that we expect no ties to occur since the values are considered to have come from continuous distributions. However, in practical applications ties will sometimes occur. When they do occur we give tied observations the mean of the rank positions for which they are tied. For instance, if the lowest 4 data points had been 460, each of the four 460s would receive a rank of $(1 + 2 + 3 + 4)/4 = 10/4 = 2.5$.[2]

We calculate a U-value for each sample as shown in Equations 15-4 and 15-5.

$$\textbf{U-STATISTICS}$$

$$U_1 = n_1 n_2 + \frac{n_1(n_1 + 1)}{2} - \sum R_1 \qquad \textbf{15-4}$$

$$U_2 = n_1 n_2 + \frac{n_2(n_2 + 1)}{2} - \sum R_2 \qquad \textbf{15-5}$$

where:

n_1 and n_2 are the two sample sizes

$\sum R_1$ and $\sum R_2 =$ Sum of ranks for samples 1 and 2, respectively

For our example using the ranks in Table 15-4,

$$U_1 = 12(12) + \frac{12(13)}{2} - 142$$
$$= 80$$
$$U_2 = 12(12) + \frac{12(13)}{2} - 158$$
$$= 64$$

Note that $U_1 + U_2 = n_1 n_2$. This is always the case and provides a good check on the correctness of the rankings in Table 15-4.

TABLE 15-4
Ranking of Yards of Gravel per Mile for the Blaine County Highway District Example

URBAN ($n_1 = 12$)		RURAL ($n_2 = 12$)	
Yards of Gravel	*Rank*	*Yards of Gravel*	*Rank*
460	2	600	6
830	16	652	9
720	12	603	7
930	20	594	5
500	4	1,402	23
620	8	1,111	21
703	11	902	18
407	1	700	10
1,521	24	827	15
900	17	490	3
750	13	904	19
800	14	1,400	22
	$\sum R_1 = 142$		$\sum R_2 = 158$

[2]G. E. Noether provides an adjustment when ties occur. He, however, points out that using the ties has little effect unless a large proportion of the observations are tied or there are a large number of ties. See the General References at the end of this chapter.

The Mann-Whitney U tables in Appendix L ($n < 9$) and Appendix M ($9 \leq n \leq 20$) give the lower tail of the U-distribution. For a two-tailed test, you should select the smaller U-value as your test statistic. This will force you toward the lower tail. If the U-value is smaller than the critical value in the Mann-Whitney U table, you will reject the null hypothesis.

For one-tailed tests like our Blaine County example, you need to look at the alternative hypothesis to determine whether U_1 or U_2 should be selected as the test statistic. Recall that:

$$H_A: \mu_1 > \mu_2$$

If the alternative hypothesis indicates that population 1 has a higher mean, as in this case, then U_1 is selected as the test statistic. If population 2 is expected to have a higher mean, then U_2 would be selected as the test statistic. The reason is that the population with the larger mean should have the larger sum of ranked values, thus producing the smaller U-value. It is very important to note that this logic must be made in terms of the alternative hypothesis and not on the basis of the U's obtained from the samples.

Now, we select the U-value that the alternative hypothesis indicates should be the smaller and call this U. Since population 1 (urban) should have the smaller U-value if the alternative hypothesis is true, the sample data give a $U = 80$. This is actually higher than the U-value for the rural population, but we still use it as the test statistic because the alternative hypothesis indicates that $\mu_1 > \mu_2$.

For sample sizes less than 9, use the Mann-Whitney U table in Appendix L. For sample sizes between 9 and 20, the null hypothesis can be tested by comparing U with the appropriate critical value given in the Mann-Whitney U table in Appendix M. We begin by locating the part of the table associated with the desired significance level. In this case, we have a one-tailed test with $\alpha = 0.05$. Go across the top of the Mann-Whitney U table to locate the value corresponding to the sample size from population 2 and down the left side of the table to the sample size from population 1.

Additional
Example 15-c

Using Minitab for
the Mann-Whitney
U Test

In the Blaine County example, both sample sizes are 12, so we will use the Mann-Whitney table in Appendix M. Go across the top of the table to $n_2 = 12$ and down the left-hand side to $n_1 = 12$. The intersection of these column and row values gives a critical value $U_\alpha = 42$. We can now form the decision rule as follows.

If $U \leq U_\alpha = 42$, reject H_0

Otherwise, do not reject H_0

Additional
Example 15-d

Mann-Whitney U
Test with Ordinal
Data

Now since $U = 80 > 42$, we do not reject the null hypothesis. Therefore, based upon the sample data we can conclude the mean yards of gravel per mile used by the urban division is no more than that used by the rural division on construction jobs.

Mann-Whitney U Test—Large Samples

When you encounter a situation with sample sizes in excess of 20, the previous approaches to the Mann-Whitney U test cannot be used because of table limitations. However, the U-statistic approaches a normal distribution as the sample sizes increase, and the Mann-Whitney U test can be conducted using a normal approximation where the mean and standard deviation for the U-statistic are as given in Equations 15-6 and 15-7, respectively.

MEAN AND STANDARD DEVIATION FOR U-STATISTIC

$$\mu = \frac{n_1 n_2}{2} \qquad \text{15-6}$$

$$\sigma = \sqrt{\frac{(n_1)(n_2)(n_1 + n_2 + 1)}{12}} \qquad \text{15-7}$$

where:

n_1 and n_2 = Sample sizes from populations 1 and 2, respectively

Equations 15-6 and 15-7 are used to form the *U*-test statistic in Equation 15-8.

MANN-WHITNEY *U*-TEST STATISTIC

$$z = \frac{U - \dfrac{n_1 n_2}{2}}{\sqrt{\dfrac{(n_1)(n_2)(n_1 + n_2 + 1)}{12}}}$$

15-8

15-4

LARGE-SAMPLE MANN-WHITNEY

Excel and Minitab Tutorial

Future-Vision

Consider the example presented previously in Chapter 9 involving the managers for a local network television affiliate who were preparing for a national television advertising conference. The theme of the presentation by the managers was to center around the advantage for businesses to advertise on network TV rather than on cable. The managers believe that median household income for cable subscribers is less than the median for those who do not subscribe. So, by advertising on network stations, the business could reach a higher income audience.

The managers are concerned with the median (as opposed to the mean) income because, as you discovered in Chapter 3, data such as household income are notorious for having large outliers. In such cases, the median is a preferable measure of the center of the data. The large outliers are also an indication that the data do not have a symmetric (such as the normal) distribution—a reason to use a nonparametric procedure such as the Mann-Whitney test.

In the spirit of friendly cooperation, the network managers joined forces with the local cable provider, Future-Vision, to survey a total of 548 households (144 nonsubscribers and 404 cable subscribers) in the market area. The results of the survey are contained in the **Future-Vision** file. Figure 15-4 shows some of the data in an Excel worksheet.[3] The income data must be converted to ranks. The data and ranks are in a file called **Future-Vision-Ranks** and are shown in Figure 15-5. Note, when data are tied in value, they share the same rank. For example, if four values are tied for the fifth position, each one is assigned the average of rankings 5, 6, 7, and 8 or (5 + 6 + 7 + 8)/4 = 6.5.

FIGURE 15-4   Excel Worksheet for the Future-Vision Income Study

	B	C	D	E
1	Number of People	Househol d Annual Income	Current Cable Subscriber	Years at This Address
2	5	35000	Yes	10
3	2	29000	Yes	1
4	1	25000	No	8
5	1	31000	Yes	13
6	3	39000	Yes	
7	7	35000	No	
8	2	32000	Yes	

Excel Instructions:

1. Open file: Future-Vision.xls.

FIGURE 15-5   Ranked Values—Future-Vision Example

	A	B
1	Non Cable	Cable
2	17.5	391
3	391	160.5
4	518	265
5	416.5	472.5
6	391	306.5
7	459.5	416.5
8	440.5	213
9	416.5	497.5
10	391	40

Values represent ranks of income by cable versus noncable TV subscription

Excel Instructions:

1. Open file: Future-Vision-Ranks.xls

---

[3]Excel does not have a Mann-Whitney procedure but the calculations can be performed using Excel formulas. See the Excel tutorial on the CD-ROM.

We first formulate the null and alternative hypotheses to be tested.

$H_0: \tilde{\mu}_2 \geq \tilde{\mu}_1$
$H_A: \tilde{\mu}_2 < \tilde{\mu}_1$ (Claim: cable median income < noncable median income)
$\alpha = 0.05$

Next, we use the data in the file **Future-Vision-Ranks** to compute the U-value. The sum of the ranks for noncable subscribers is 41,204, and the sum of the ranks for cable subscribers is 109,222. Based on sample sizes of 144 noncable subscribers and 404 cable subscribers, we compute the U-value as follows.

$$U_1 = 144(404) + \frac{144(145)}{2} - 41,204 = 27,412$$

$$U_2 = 144(404) + \frac{404(405)}{2} - 109,222 = 30,764$$

Since the alternative hypothesis predicts that population 1 (non–cable subscribers) will have a higher median, U_1 is selected to be U. Thus, $U = 27,412$.

We can now substitute appropriate values into Equations 15-6 and 15-7 as follows.

$$\mu = \frac{n_1 n_2}{2} = \frac{(144)(404)}{2} = 29,088$$

and

$$\sigma = \sqrt{\frac{(n_1)(n_2)(n_1 + n_2 + 1)}{12}} = \sqrt{\frac{(144)(404)(144 + 404 + 1)}{12}} = 1,631.43$$

The test statistic is computed using Equation 15-8 as follows.

$$z = \frac{U - \frac{n_1 n_2}{2}}{\sqrt{\frac{(n_1)(n_2)(n_1 + n_2 + 1)}{12}}} = \frac{27,412 - 29,088}{\sqrt{\frac{(144)(404)(144 + 404 + 1)}{12}}} = \frac{-1,676}{1,631.43}$$

$$z = -1.027$$

Figure 15-6 shows the results of the hypothesis test. As can be seen, the null hypothesis is not rejected. This means the claim that noncable families have higher median incomes than cable families is not supported by the sample data.

Although the Mann-Whitney U test can be performed in Excel (see the tutorial on the CD-ROM) it requires you to construct the formulas—there is no tool for doing the test

FIGURE 15-6
Future-Vision Hypothesis Test

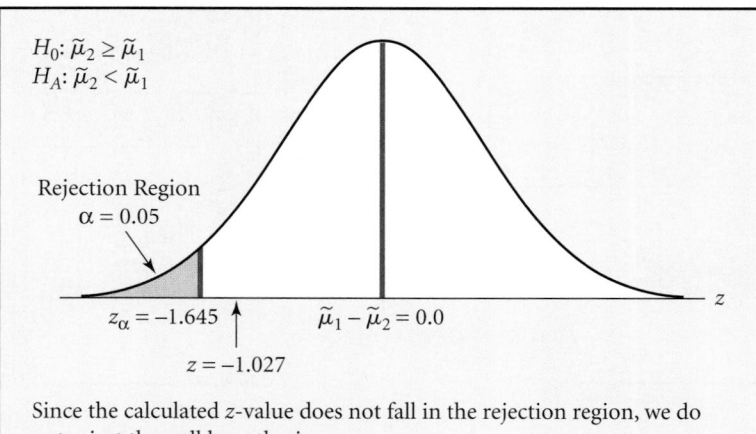

$H_0: \tilde{\mu}_2 \geq \tilde{\mu}_1$
$H_A: \tilde{\mu}_2 < \tilde{\mu}_1$

Rejection Region
$\alpha = 0.05$

$z_\alpha = -1.645$

$\tilde{\mu}_1 - \tilde{\mu}_2 = 0.0$

z

$z = -1.027$

Since the calculated z-value does not fall in the rejection region, we do not reject the null hypothesis.

Minitab Instructions:

1. Open file: Future-Vision.mtw
2. Click on Manip
3. Select Stack/Unstack
4. Select Unstack One Column
5. Define Income Variable and Subscriber Status Variable
6. Select the Stat tab
7. Select the Nonparametrics option
8. Then select the Mann-Whitney option. Minitab tests whether the two population medians are equal.
9. Define columns containing samples
10. Specify Greater Than alternative hypothesis

```
MINITAB - Untitled - [Session]
File  Edit  Manip  Calc  Stat  Graph  Editor  Window  Help

Non-Cabl   N = 144      Median =          32000
Cable      N = 404      Median =          31000
Point estimate for ETA1-ETA2 is          1000
95.0 Percent CI for ETA1-ETA2 is (0,2000)
W = 41204.0
Test of ETA1 = ETA2  vs  ETA1 > ETA2 is significant at 0.1522
The test is significant at 0.1517 (adjusted for ties)

Cannot reject at alpha = 0.05
.
```

p-value
Since 0.1517 > 0.05, do not reject H_0

FIGURE 15-7   Minitab Output for the Mann-Whitney Test for Medians

directly. However, Minitab does contain a procedure for performing the Mann-Whitney U test. We can use the original income data in the file **Future-Vision**, but the income values must first be *unstacked* using Minitab's *unstack procedure* under the *Manip* tab. This creates one column with incomes for noncable families and another column with the income for the cable families in the sample. The Minitab Mann-Whitney test checks whether the two populations have equal *medians*. In this example, the null and alternative hypotheses are:

H_0: $\tilde{\mu}_2 \geq \tilde{\mu}_1$
H_A: $\tilde{\mu}_2 < \tilde{\mu}_1$ (Claim: Median income for cable is less than median for noncable)

Figure 15-7 illustrates the Minitab output. The key output in this case is the statement:

"The test is significant at 0.1517 (adjusted for ties)"

The value, 0.1517, is the *p*-value adjusted for ties. (Although beyond the scope of this text, Minitab makes an appropriate adjustment to the *p*-value when there are data values that have tied ranks.) If the *p*-value is less than alpha, we should reject the null hypothesis. Since 0.1517 > $\alpha = 0.05$, we do not reject the null hypothesis.

The Wilcoxon Matched-Pairs Signed Rank Test

The Mann-Whitney U test is a very useful nonparametric technique. However, as discussed in the Blaine County Highway District example, its use is limited to those situations where the samples from the two populations are independent. As we discussed in Chapter 9, you will encounter decision situations in which the samples will be paired and are not independent. When the samples are paired, the Mann-Whitney U test cannot be employed.

A nonparametric test called the Wilcoxon matched-pairs signed rank test has been developed for situations in which you have related samples and are unwilling or unable (due to data level limitations) to use the paired-sample *t*-test. It is useful when the two related samples have a measurement scale that allows us to determine not only whether the pairs of observations differ, but also the magnitude of any difference. The Wilcoxon matched-pairs test can be used in those cases where the following assumptions are satisfied.

1. The differences are measured on a continuous variable.
2. The measurement scale used is at least interval.
3. The distribution of the population differences is symmetric about their median.

15-5

WILCOXON TEST

The Quick-Calc Company

To illustrate the Wilcoxon test, consider the Quick-Calc Financial Corporation that develops and markets software add-ins for common personal computer spreadsheet packages. The add-ins allow users to perform complicated financial analyses across large sets of data faster and more efficiently. To differentiate its product from the other packages on the mar-

SUBJECT	BEFORE QUICK-CALC TRAINING	AFTER QUICK-CALC TRAINING
1	24 hours	11 hours
2	20	18
3	19	23
4	20	15
5	13	16
6	28	22
7	15	8

TABLE 15-5
Quick-Calc Financial
Corporation: Time to
Complete Analysis

ket, Quick-Calc has built many macros into its software. According to Quick-Calc, once a user learns the macro keystrokes, complicated financial computations become much easier to perform.

As part of its product development testing program, software engineers at Quick-Calc Financial have selected a focus group of 7 people who frequently use spreadsheet packages. Each is given a set of complicated financial and accounting data and asked to prepare a detailed analysis. While the focus group is performing the analysis, a systems program is used to determine the amount of time needed to complete the analysis. Once the analysis is complete, these same 7 individuals are given a training course in Quick-Calc add-ins. Following the training course, they are then given a similar set of data and asked to do the same analysis. Again the systems software will determine the time needed to complete the analysis. The data are shown in Table 15-5.

You should recognize that the samples in this application are not independent since the same subjects are used in both cases. If the software engineers performing the analysis are unwilling to make the normal distribution assumption required of the paired-sample t-test, they can use the Wilcoxon matched-pairs signed rank test. The hypothesis being tested is:[4]

$$H_0: \tilde{\mu}_b \leq \tilde{\mu}_a$$
$$H_A: \tilde{\mu}_b > \tilde{\mu}_a \text{ (Median time will be smaller \textit{after} the Quick-Calc training)}$$

SMALL-SAMPLE WILCOXON TEST

When the sample sizes are less than 25, testing this hypothesis using the Wilcoxon test requires that we convert the data in Table 15-5 to differences as shown in Table 15-6. Some explanation for Table 15-6 is needed. First, the column of differences, d, gives the "before minus after" differences. The next column is the rank of the d-values from low to high. Note that the ranks are determined without considering the sign on the d-value. However, once the rank is determined, the original sign on the d-value is attached to the rank. For example, $d = 13$ is given a rank of 7, while $d = -4$ has a rank of -3.

TABLE 15-6
Quick-Calc Financial
Corporation Ranked Data

SUBJECT	BEFORE TRAINING	AFTER TRAINING	d	RANK OF d	RANKS WITH SMALLER EXPECTED SUM
1	24	11	13	7	
2	20	18	2	1	
3	19	23	-4	-3	3
4	20	15	5	4	
5	13	16	-3	-2	2
6	28	22	6	5	
7	15	8	7	6	
					$T = 5$

[4]The hypothesis could also be stated in terms of the population means since the variable (time) is ratio level.

The final column is titled "Ranks with Smaller Expected Sum." To determine the values in the final column, we take the absolute values of either the positive or the negative ranks depending upon which group has the smaller expected sum of absolute valued ranks. A logical process similar to that used in the Mann-Whitney U test must be used to identify the appropriate sum. The differences are computed by taking "*before training*" minus "*after training*" times. We look to the alternative hypothesis, which is:

$$H_A: \tilde{\mu}_b > \tilde{\mu}_a$$

Since the before median is predicted to exceed the after median, we would expect the positive differences to exceed the negative differences. Therefore, the negative ranks should have the smaller sum and should therefore be used in the final column as shown in Table 15-6.

Of course, for a two-tailed test, we would just choose the smaller sum for the test statistic. To detail the procedure for this example, we begin with the ranks with the minus signs.

$$-3$$
$$-2$$

Now take the absolute value of each of these and sum them.

$$|-3| = 3$$
$$|-2| = 2$$
$$\sum = T = 5$$

For the final column, we enter these ranks and label the sum, T. The values 3 and 2 are written in the final column. These values are summed to give $T = 5$.

Under the logic of the Wilcoxon test, if the alternative hypothesis were true we would expect most d-values to be positive. The sum of the absolute values of the negative ranks should then be quite small. So, the null hypothesis should be rejected, in this case, if the sum of the negative ranks is sufficiently small. The Wilcoxon test for this example, therefore, focuses on the T-value obtained in Table 15-6. If it gets too small, the null hypothesis is rejected.

To determine whether T is sufficiently small to reject the null hypothesis, we consult the Wilcoxon table of critical T-values in Appendix N. If the calculated T is less than or equal to the critical T from the table, the null hypothesis is rejected. For instance, with $\alpha = 0.025$ for our one-tailed test and $n = 7$, we get a critical value of 2. Since $T = 5 > 2$, we do not reject H_0. Based on these sample data, the Quick-Calc Company has no basis for stating that its product will reduce the median time required to perform complicated financial computations.

TIES IN THE DATA

If the two measurements of an observed data pair have the same values and, therefore, a d-value of 0, that case is dropped from the analysis and the sample size is reduced accordingly. You should note that this procedure favors rejecting the null hypothesis since we are eliminating cases where the two sample points have exactly the same values.

If two or more d-values have the same absolute values, we assign the same rank to each one using the same approach as with the Mann-Whitney U test. For example, if we have two d-values that tie for ranks 4 and 5, we average them as $(4 + 5)/2 = 4.5$ and assign both a rank of 4.5. Studies have shown that this method of assigning ranks to ties has little effect on the Wilcoxon test results. For a more complete discussion of the effect of ties on the Wilcoxon matched-pairs signed rank test, please see the text by Marascuilo and McSweeney referenced at the end of this chapter.

LARGE-SAMPLE WILCOXON TEST

If the sample size (number of matched pairs) exceeds 25, the Wilcoxon table of critical *T*-values cannot be used. However, for large samples, the distribution of *T*-values is approximately normal with a mean and standard deviation given by Equations 15-9 and 15-10, respectively.

WILCOXON MEAN AND STANDARD DEVIATION

$$\mu = \frac{n(n+1)}{4} \qquad \text{15-9}$$

$$\sigma = \sqrt{\frac{n(n+1)(2n+1)}{24}} \qquad \text{15-10}$$

where:

$$n = \text{Number of paired values}$$

The **Wilcoxon test statistic** is given by Equation 15-11.

WILCOXON TEST STATISTIC

$$z = \frac{T - \dfrac{n(n+1)}{4}}{\sqrt{\dfrac{n(n+1)(2n+1)}{24}}} \qquad \text{15-11}$$

Then, the *z*-value is compared to the critical value from the standard normal table in the usual manner.

Visibility Sensors

A regional airport is considering the purchase of a new visibility sensor system to be used in conjunction with the air traffic control equipment. The managers have narrowed the choices down to two suppliers, Vanguard and Scorpian. To help make the final selection, the two suppliers agreed to participate in a test. The two sensors were temporarily installed side-by-side at the airport. Visibility readings (in miles) from the sensors were recorded at 5-minute intervals for a 24-hour period and are contained in the file called **Visibility**. At issue is whether there is a difference in mean visibility readings from the two sensors. (Note: Since visibility is a ratio-level variable, the hypothesis test could be framed in terms of mean or median visibility.) The Excel worksheet displaying a portion of the sample data is shown in Figure 15-8.

EXAMPLE 15-6

WILCOXON TEST

Excel and
Minitab Tutorial

FIGURE 15-8
Excel Worksheet of Visibility
Sensor Data

	A	B	C	D	E	F	G	H	I
1	**Time**	**Wind Spd**	**Wind Dir**	**Peak Gust**	**Air Temp**	**Rel Hum**	**Scorpian Visibility**		**Vanguard Visibility**
2	12:02:24 AM	1	320	5	35	84	3.25		1.0998
3	12:07:24 AM	3	302	6	35	84	3.14		1.0998
4	12:12:18 AM	3	311	5	35	85	2.75		1.0998
5	12:17:18 AM	5	293	8	36	87	2.96		0.99618
6	12:22:24 AM	5	294	7	34	88	2.83		0.774225
7	12:27:24 AM	5	294	6	35	90	2.68		0.70962
8	12:32:18 AM	4	293	5	33	91	2.03		0.51226
9	12:37:24 AM	5	297	6	34	93	1.82		0.37356
10	12:42:24 AM	6	303	7	34	94	1.29		0.2104

Excel Instructions:

Open file: Visibility.xls

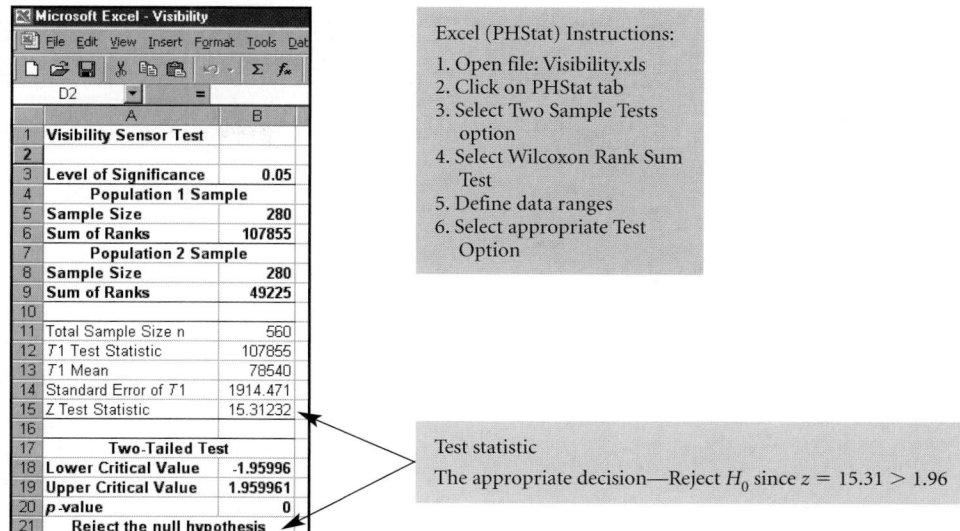

FIGURE 15-9
Excel (PHStat) Output of
Wilcoxon Test Results for
Visibility Sensor

The null and alternative hypotheses are:

$$H_0: \mu_1 = \mu_2$$
$$H_A: \mu_1 \neq \mu_2$$
$$\alpha = 0.05$$

If the airport managers were willing to assume the two visibility sensors provide paired differences that are normally distributed, the paired sample t-test discussed in Chapter 9 should be used to test this hypothesis. Suppose, however, the managers are not willing to make the normal distribution assumption. Then the Wilcoxon test should be used.

The PHStat Add-Ins for Excel that accompany this text contain a procedure for performing the Wilcoxon matched-pairs signed rank test for large samples.[5] Figure 15-9 illustrates the PHStat output for this example. Based on the sample data, the null hypothesis should be rejected. The two sensors do not provide the same mean visibility measures. Further investigation into which one is more accurate is needed.

15-2: EXERCISES

ADDITIONAL EXERCISES ON YOUR CD-ROM
Try the **ADDITIONAL EXERCISES** and **APPLICATION PROBLEMS**
on the CD-ROM.

15-13. From a recent study we have collected the following data from two independent random samples.

POPULATION 1		POPULATION 2	
405	425	300	435
450	275	340	390
290	380	400	225
370	330	250	210
345	500	270	395
460	215	410	315

a. Based on these sample data, can you conclude that the two populations have equal medians? Use $\alpha = 0.05$ and test using the t-distribution. What assumptions are needed to use this distribution? (Hint: Refer to Chapter 9.)

b. Suppose we do not wish to make the assumptions indicated in part a. Use the appropriate nonparametric test to determine whether the populations have equal medians. Test at $\alpha = 0.05$.

[5]The Mann-Whitney procedure in Minitab will provide equivalent results to the Wilcoxon test in PHStat Add-Ins to Excel.

15-14. You are given two dependent samples with the following information.

ITEM	SAMPLE 1	SAMPLE 2
1	234	245
2	221	224
3	196	194
4	245	267
5	234	230
6	204	198

Based on these paired samples, test at the $\alpha = 0.05$ level whether the true median paired difference is 0.

15-15. Consider the following data for two paired samples.

CASE #	SAMPLE 1	SAMPLE 2
1	258	304
2	197	190
3	400	500
4	350	340
5	237	250
6	400	358
7	370	390
8	130	100

a. Test the following null and alternative hypotheses at an $\alpha = 0.05$ level.

$$H_0: \tilde{\mu}_1 = \tilde{\mu}_2$$
$$H_A: \tilde{\mu}_1 \neq \tilde{\mu}_2$$

b. Answer part a if the samples were independent samples from normal distributions with equal variances.

Business Applications

15-16. The makers of the Plus 20 Hardcard, a plug-in hard disk unit on a PC board, have recently done a marketing research study in which they asked two independently selected groups to rate the Hardcard on a scale of 1 to 100, with 100 being perfect satisfaction. The first group consisted of professional computer programmers. The second group consisted of home computer users. The company hoped to be able to say that the product would receive the same median ranking from each group. The following summary data were recorded.

PROFESSIONALS	HOME USERS
$n = 10$	$n = 8$
Sum of ranks $= 92$	Sum of ranks $= 79$

Based on these data, what should the company conclude? Test at the $\alpha = 0.02$ level.

15-17. The Acme Speed Reading Company claims that graduates of its program have a higher average reading speed per minute than people who did not take the course. An independent agency conducted a study to determine whether this claim was justified. Researchers from the agency selected a random sample of people who had taken the speed reading course and another random sample of people who had not taken the course. The agency was unwilling to make the assumption that the populations were normally distributed. Therefore, a nonparametric test was needed. The following summary data were observed.

WITH COURSE	WITHOUT COURSE
$n = 7$	$n = 5$
Sum of ranks $= 42$	Sum of ranks $= 36$

Assuming that higher ranks imply more words per minute being read, what should the testing agency conclude based on the sample data? Test at an $\alpha = 0.05$ level.

15-18. The tax commission for a Midwestern state recently conducted a study to determine whether there is a difference in average deductions taken for charitable contributions depending on whether the tax return was filed as a single or joint return. A random sample from each category was selected, with the following results.

SINGLE	JOINT
$n = 6$	$n = 8$
Sum of ranks $= 43$	Sum of ranks $= 62$

Based on these data, what should the tax commission conclude? Use an $\alpha = 0.05$ level.

15-19. Property taxes are based on assessed values of property. In most states, the law requires that assessed values be "at or near" market value of the property. In one Washington State county, a tax protest group has claimed that assessed values are higher than market values. To address this claim, the county tax assessor, together with representatives from the protest group, have selected 15 properties at random which have sold within the past 6 months. Both parties agree that the sale price was the market value at the time of the sale.

The assessor then listed the assessed values and the sales values side-by-side as shown.

HOUSE	ASSESSED VALUE	MARKET VALUE
1	$102,000	$ 98,000
2	76,000	82,400
3	49,000	54,300
4	98,500	98,500
5	114,000	118,000
6	135,000	130,000
7	205,000	198,900
8	87,500	90,000
9	50,000	49,800
10	123,000	122,000
11	78,500	80,000
12	145,000	150,900
13	67,000	65,200
14	119,000	120,700
15	234,000	220,000

a. Assuming that the population of assessed values and the population of market values have the same shape distribution and that they may differ only with respect to means, state the appropriate null and alternative hypotheses.

b. Test the hypotheses using an $\alpha = 0.01$ level.

c. Do the data presented in the table appear to have been sampled from a continuous or a discrete distribution?

d. Discuss why one would not assume that the samples were obtained from normal distributions for this problem. What characteristic about the market values of houses would lead you to conclude that these data were not normally distributed?

15-20. A cattle feedlot operator has collected data for 40 matched pairs of cattle (matched on weight, age, gender, and species) showing weight gain on two different feed supplements. His purpose in collecting the data is to determine whether there is a difference in the distributions of weight gain for the two supplements. He has no preconceived idea about which supplement might produce higher weight gain. He wishes to test using $\alpha = 0.05$.

a. State the appropriate null and alternative hypotheses.

b. Assuming that the T-value for these data is 480, what, if anything, should be concluded concerning which supplement might produce higher weight gain? Conduct the test using a p-value approach.

15-21. Radio advertisements have been stressing the virtues of an audiotape program to help children learn to read. To test whether this tape program can cause quick improvement in reading ability, 10 children were given a nationally recognized reading test that measures reading ability. The same 10 children were then given the tapes to listen to for 4 hours spaced over a 2-day period. The children were then tested again. The test scores observed were as follows.

CHILD	BEFORE	AFTER
1	60	63
2	40	38
3	78	77
4	53	50
5	67	74
6	88	96
7	77	80
8	60	70
9	64	65
10	75	75

a. State the appropriate null and alternative hypotheses.

b. Test whether this tape program produces quick improvement on reading ability. Use $\alpha = 0.025$.

15-22. The First Night Stage Company operates a small non-profit theater group in Milwaukee, Wisconsin. At each performance members of the company solicit donations to help fund their operations. In the past they have simply "passed the hat." This year, they have obtained the help of a marketing research company in the city. This company has proposed a different solicitation technique. The hope is that the alternative technique will increase the median donation received from people at the performances. To test this, a random sample of 20 performances was selected at which "the hat was passed" and another random sample of 20 performances was selected on which to try the alternative technique. The data are contained in a file called **First-Night**.

a. Traditionally, the donations obtained during the performances are quite low. However, on some nights, a generous benefactor will contribute a large amount. Select an appropriate analysis technique. Based on the selected technique and these sample data, what should the First Night Company conclude about the two fund-raising techniques with respect to their capability to attract donations? Test using a significance level of 0.01.

b. Referring to this hypothesis test, what assumptions are required?

c. Suppose the populations from which these sample data were obtained have normal distributions. (1) Conduct the appropriate hypothesis test. (2) Was the result different from that in part b? (3) Which test procedure would you prefer for this test? Explain your reasoning.

15-23. For at least the past 20 years there has been a debate over whether children who are placed in child-care facilities while their parents work suffer as a result. A recent study of 6,000 children, discussed in the March 1999 issue of *Developmental Psychology*, found "no permanent negative effects caused by their mother's absence." In fact, the study indicated that there might be some positive benefits from the day-care experience. To investigate this premise, a nonprofit organization called Child Care Connections conducted a small study in which children were observed playing in neutral settings (not at home or at a day-care center). Over a period of 20 hours of observation, 15 children who do not go to day care and 21 children who have spent much time in day care were observed. The variable of interest was the total minutes of play in which the child was actively interacting with other students. Child Care Connections leaders hoped to show that the children who had been in day care would have a higher mean time in interactive situations than the stay-at-home children. A file called **Children** contains the results of the study.

a. State the appropriate null and alternative hypotheses.

b. Test the null hypothesis using a significance level of 0.05, and write a short statement that describes the results of the test. Conduct this test without making any assumptions about the shape of the populations.

c. Based on the outcome of the hypothesis test, which statistical error might have been committed?

15-24. The California State Highway Patrol recently conducted a study on a stretch of interstate highway south of San Francisco to determine whether the mean speed for California vehicles exceeded the mean speed for out-of-state vehicles. A total of 140 California cars were included in the study while 75 out-of-state cars were included. Radar was used to measure the speed. The data file called **Speed-Test** contains the data collected by the California Highway Patrol.

a. Past studies have indicated that the speeds at which both out-of-state and California drivers drive have normal distributions. However, the CHP is unwilling to make this assumption for these new data. Using a significance level equal to 0.10, obtain the results desired by the California Highway Patrol. Use a *p*-value approach to conduct the relevant hypothesis test. Discuss the results of this test in a short written statement.

b. Describe in the context of this problem what a Type I error would be.

15-25. The Sunbeam Corporation makes a wide variety of appliances for the home. One product is a digital blood pressure gauge. For obvious reasons, the blood pressure readings made by the monitor need to be accurate. When a new model is being designed, one of the steps is to test it. To do this, a sample of people is selected. Each person has his/her systolic blood pressure taken by a highly respected physician. They then immediately have their systolic blood pressure taken using the Sunbeam monitor. If the mean blood pressure is the same for the monitor as it has been determined by the physician, the monitor passes the accuracy test.

In a recent test, 15 people were randomly selected to be in the sample. The blood pressure readings for these people using both methods are contained in the data file called **Sunbeam**.

a. State the appropriate null and alternative hypotheses.

b. Based on the sample data and a significance level equal to 0.05, what conclusion should the Sunbeam engineers reach regarding the latest blood pressure monitor if they are unwilling to assume that the readings are normally distributed? Discuss your answer in a short written statement.

c. Conduct the test described in part b as a paired-*t* test.

d. Discuss which of the two procedures in parts b and c is more appropriate to analyze the data presented in this problem.

15-26. The Hersh Corporation is considering two word-processing systems for its computers. One factor which will influence its decision is the ease of use in preparing a business report. Consequently, 9 typists were selected from the clerical pool and asked to type a typical report using both word-processing systems. The typists then rated the systems on a scale of 0 to 100. The resulting ratings are in the data file called **Hersh**.

a. Which measurement level describes the data collected for this analysis?

b. Could a normal distribution describe the population distribution from which these data were sampled? Which measure would be appropriate to describe the center of the populations from which these data were sampled?

c. Choose the appropriate hypothesis procedure to determine if there is a difference in the measures you selected in part b between these two word-processing systems. Use a significance level of 0.10.

d. Which word-processing system would you recommend the Hersh Corporation adopt? Support your answer with statistical reasoning.

15-27. The Montgomery Athletic Shoe Company has developed a new shoe sole material that the company thinks will provide superior wear compared with the old material it has been using for its running shoes. The company selected 10 cross-country runners and supplied each runner with a pair of shoes. Each pair has one sole made of the old material and one sole made of the new material. The shoes were monitored until the soles were worn out. The following lifetimes (in hours) were recorded for each material.

RUNNER	OLD MATERIAL	NEW MATERIAL
1	45.5	47.0
2	50.0	51.0
3	43.0	42.0
4	45.5	46.0
5	58.5	58.0
6	49.0	50.5
7	29.5	39.0
8	52.0	53.0
9	48.0	48.0
10	57.5	61.0

a. If the populations from which these samples were taken could be considered to have normal distributions, determine if the soles made of the new material have a longer mean lifetime than those made from the old material. Use a significance level of 0.05.

b. Suppose you were not willing to consider that the populations have normal distributions. Make the determination requested in part a.

c. Given only the information in the heading of this problem, which of the two procedures indicated in parts a and b would you choose to use? Give reasons for your answer.

■ 15-3: KRUSKAL-WALLIS ONE-WAY ANALYSIS OF VARIANCE

Section 15-2 showed that the Mann-Whitney U test is a useful nonparametric procedure for determining whether two independent samples are from populations with the same median. However, as discussed in Chapter 10 many decisions involve comparing more than two populations. Chapter 10 introduced one-way analysis of variance (ANOVA) and showed how, if the assumptions of normally distributed populations with equal variances are satisfied, the *F*-distribution can be used to test the hypothesis of equal population means. However, what if decision makers are not willing to assume normally distributed populations? In that case, they can turn to a nonparametric procedure to compare the populations. *Kruskal-Wallis one-way analysis of variance* is the nonparametric counterpart to the one-way analysis of variance procedure presented in Chapter 10. It is applicable any time the variables in question satisfy the following conditions.

1. They have a continuous distribution.
2. The data are at least ordinal.
3. The samples are independent.
4. The samples come from populations whose only possible difference is that at least one may have a different central location than the others.

The East Hope Medical Center

KRUSKAL-WALLIS

The East Hope Medical Center is considering acquiring a distributed client-server computer system to handle its on-line data-processing activities, including patient scheduling, facility assignment, and general accounting and billing. Based on cost and performance standards, the medical center's information systems manager has reduced the possible suppliers to three. One critical factor in the decision is downtime (the time when the system is nonoperational). When the system goes down, the online applications are halted and normal hospital activities are interrupted. The information systems manager has received, from each supplier, a list of firms that are using the computer system East Hope Medical is considering. From these lists, the manager selected random samples of 9 users of each computer system. In a telephone interview, she found the number of hours of downtime in the previous month for each system. The downtimes are shown in Table 15-7. At issue is whether the centers of the three populations are different. Since the variable, hours of downtime, is ratio level, the hypothesis can be set up in terms of means or medians. In this case, we use means.

The null and alternative hypotheses to be tested are:

$$H_0: \mu_1 = \mu_2 = \mu_3$$
$$H_A: \text{Not all population means are equal}$$

The information systems manager is not willing to assume that the downtime populations are normally distributed, thus the one-way ANOVA procedure introduced in Chapter 10 won't be used. Instead, she will turn to the nonparametric Kruskal-Wallis one-way ANOVA procedure that does not require the normality assumption.

To use the Kruskal-Wallis analysis of variance here, we first replace each downtime measurement by its *relative ranking* within all groups combined. The smallest downtime is given a rank of 1, the next smallest a rank of 2, and so forth, until all downtimes for the three systems have been replaced by their relative rankings. Table 15-8 shows these rankings

TABLE 15-7
System Downtimes for the East Hope Medical Center Example (Hours/Month)

SYSTEM A	SYSTEM B	SYSTEM C
4.0	6.9	0.5
3.7	11.3	1.4
5.1	21.7	1.0
2.0	9.2	1.7
4.6	6.5	3.6
9.3	4.9	5.2
2.7	12.2	1.3
2.5	11.7	6.8
4.8	10.5	14.1

TABLE 15-8
Rankings of System Downtimes for the East Hope Medical Center Example

SYSTEM A	SYSTEM B	SYSTEM C
11	19	1
10	23	4
15	27	2
6	20	5
12	17	9
21	14	16
8	25	3
7	24	18
13	22	26
Sum of ranks = 103	Sum of ranks = 191	Sum of ranks = 84

for the 27 observations. Notice the rankings are summed for each computer system. The Kruskal-Wallis test will determine whether these sums are so different that it is not likely that they came from populations with equal means.

If the samples actually do come from populations with equal means (that is, the three systems have the same per-month mean downtime), then the H-statistic, calculated by Equation 15-12, will be distributed as a chi-square variable with $k - 1$ degrees of freedom, where k equals the number of samples under study.

H-STATISTIC

$$H = \frac{12}{N(N + 1)}\sum_{i=1}^{k}\frac{R_i^2}{n_i} - 3(N + 1), \text{ with } df = k - 1 \qquad \textbf{15-12}$$

where:

N = Sum of the sample sizes in all samples
k = Number of samples
R_i = Sum of ranks in the ith sample
n_i = Size of the ith sample

If H is larger than χ^2 from the chi-square distribution with $k - 1$ degrees of freedom in Appendix G, the hypothesis of equal means should be rejected. Figure 15-10 presents the hypotheses and statistical test for East Hope Medical Center. The Kruskal-Wallis one-way analysis of variance shows that the information systems manager should conclude, based on the sample data, that the three computer systems *do not* have equal mean downtimes. From this analysis, the supplier of system B would most likely be eliminated from consideration unless other factors such as price or service offset the apparent longer downtimes.

OPTIONAL CD-ROM TOPIC Performing Multiple Comparisons
If the Kruskal-Wallis procedure leads you to reject the null hypothesis, you may be interested in determining which pairs of populations have different medians. A method involving the Mann-Whitney U test can be used. For more information, go to the CD-ROM.

EXAMPLE 15-8

KRUSKAL-WALLIS

Excel and
Minitab Tutorial

Amalgamated Sugar

Amalgamated Sugar has recently begun a new effort referred to as total productive maintenance (TPM). The TPM concept is to increase the overall operating effectiveness of the company's equipment. One component of the TPM process attempts to reduce unplanned machine downtime. The first step is to gain an understanding of the current downtime situation. To do this, a sample of 20 days has been collected for each of the three shifts (day, swing, and graveyard). The variable of interest is the minutes of unplanned downtime per shift per day. The minutes are tabulated by summing the downtime minutes for all equipment in the plant. The data are in the file called **Amalgamated**. The null hypothesis is that there is no difference between median downtime on the three shifts. The Kruskal-Wallis one-way ANOVA procedure can be used to test whether the medians are equal as follows.

$$H_0: \tilde{\mu}_1 = \tilde{\mu}_2 = \tilde{\mu}_3$$
$$H_A: \text{Not all population medians are the same}$$
$$\alpha = 0.05$$

Both Minitab and Excel (using the PHStat add-ins) can be used to perform a Kruskal-Wallis nonparametric analysis of variance test. Figure 15-11, on page 630, illustrates the

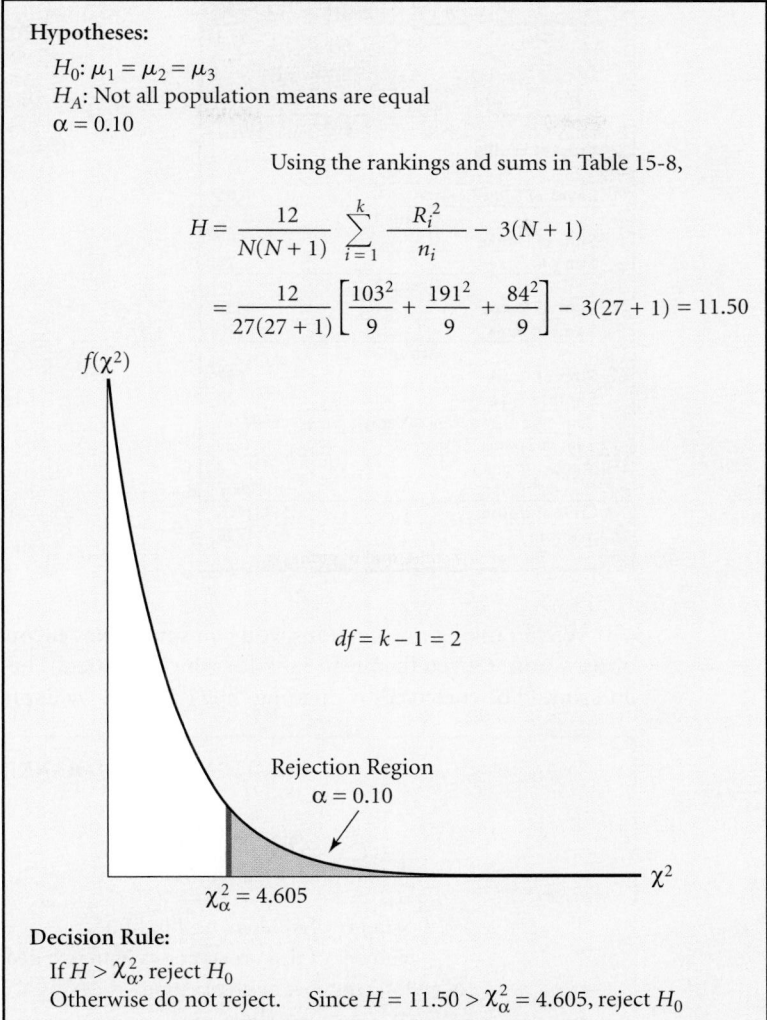

Hypotheses:

$H_0: \mu_1 = \mu_2 = \mu_3$
$H_A:$ Not all population means are equal
$\alpha = 0.10$

Using the rankings and sums in Table 15-8,

$$H = \frac{12}{N(N+1)} \sum_{i=1}^{k} \frac{R_i^2}{n_i} - 3(N+1)$$

$$= \frac{12}{27(27+1)} \left[\frac{103^2}{9} + \frac{191^2}{9} + \frac{84^2}{9} \right] - 3(27+1) = 11.50$$

$f(\chi^2)$

$df = k - 1 = 2$

Rejection Region
$\alpha = 0.10$

$\chi_\alpha^2 = 4.605$

χ^2

Decision Rule:
If $H > \chi_\alpha^2$, reject H_0
Otherwise do not reject.   Since $H = 11.50 > \chi_\alpha^2 = 4.605$, reject H_0

FIGURE 15-10
Kruskal-Wallis One-Way
Analysis of Variance Test for
East Hope Medical Center

**Additional
Example 15-e**

**Kruskal-Wallis One-
Way ANOVA**

Excel output for these sample data[6]. The calculated H-statistic is 0.185902, which is well below the chi-square critical value of 5.99, and the p-value of 0.911238 far exceeds an alpha of 0.05. Thus, based on the sample data, the three shifts do not appear to differ with respect to median equipment downtime. The company can now begin to work on steps that will reduce the downtime across the three shifts.

Limitations and Other Considerations

The Kruskal-Wallis one-way analysis of variance does *not* require the assumption of normality and is, therefore, often used instead of the analysis of variance technique discussed in Chapter 10. However, the Kruskal-Wallis test as discussed here applies only if the sample size from each population is at least 5, the samples are independently selected, and each population has the same distribution except for a possible difference in location. While the Kruskal-Wallis test can be used for samples from two distributions, its use is usually limited to comparing sample values from 3 or more populations.

[6]In Minitab, the variable of interest must be in one column. A second column contains the population identifier. In Excel, the data are placed in separate columns by population. The column headings identify the population.

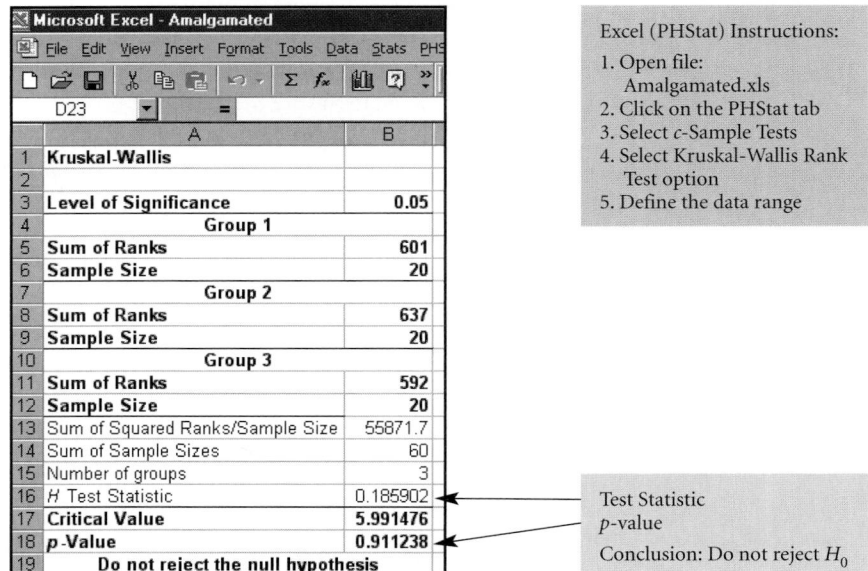

FIGURE 15-11
Excel (PHStat) Kruskal-Wallis
ANOVA Output for
Amalgamated Sugar

When ranking observations, you will sometimes encounter ties. When ties occur, each observation is given the mean rank for which it is tied. The H-statistic is influenced by ties and should be corrected by dividing the H-statistic by Expression 15-13.

CORRECTION FOR TIED RANKINGS

$$1 - \frac{\sum_{i=1}^{g}(t_i^3 - t_i)}{N^3 - N}$$

15-13

where:

g = Number of different groups of ties

t_i = Number of tied observations in the ith tied group of scores

N = Total number of observations

The correct formula for calculating the Kruskal-Wallis H-statistic when ties are present is Equation 15-14.

Correcting for ties increases H and thus makes rejecting the null hypothesis more likely than if the correction is not used. A rule of thumb is that if no more than 25% of the observations are involved in ties, the correction factor is not required. Note, if you use Minitab to perform the Kruskal-Wallis test, the adjusted H-statistic is provided. The PHStat add-in to Excel for performing the Kruskal-Wallis test does not provide the adjusted H-statistic. However, the adjustment is necessary only when the null hypothesis is not rejected and the H-statistic is "close" to the rejection region. In that case, making the proper adjustment could lead to rejecting the null hypothesis.

H-STATISTIC CORRECTED FOR TIED RANKINGS

$$H = \frac{\dfrac{12}{N(N+1)}\sum_{i=1}^{k}\dfrac{R_i^2}{n_i} - 3(N+1)}{1 - \dfrac{\sum_{i=1}^{g}(t_i^3 - t_i)}{N^3 - N}}$$

15-14

15-3: EXERCISES

ADDITIONAL EXERCISES ON YOUR CD-ROM
Try the ADDITIONAL EXERCISES and APPLICATION PROBLEMS on the CD-ROM.

15-28. You are given the following sample data.

ITEM	GROUP 1	GROUP 2	GROUP 3
1	10	8	13
2	9	6	12
3	11	8	12
4	12	9	11
5	13	10	13
6	12	10	15

   a. State the appropriate null and alternative hypotheses for determining whether a difference exists in the median value for the 3 populations.
   b. Based on the sample data, use the Kruskal-Wallis ANOVA procedure to test the null hypothesis using $\alpha = 0.05$. What conclusion should be reached?

15-29. You are given the following sample data.

GROUP 1	GROUP 2	GROUP 3
21	17	29
25	15	38
36	34	28
35	22	27
33	16	14
23	19	26
31	30	39
32	20	36

   a. State the appropriate null and alternative hypotheses to test whether there is a difference in the medians of the 3 populations.
   b. Based on the sample data and a significance level of 0.05, what conclusion should be reached about the medians of the 3 populations if you are not willing to make the assumption that the populations are normally distributed?
   c. Test the hypothesis stated in part a assuming that the populations are normally distributed with equal variances.
   d. Given the type of data presented in the heading to this problem, which of the procedures described in parts b and c would you select to analyze the data? Explain your reasoning.

Business Applications

15-30. A study was conducted by the sports department of a national network television station in which the objective was to determine whether a difference exists between median annual salaries of NBA basketball players, NFL football players, and major league baseball players. The analyst in charge of the study believes that the normal distribution assumption is violated in this study. Thus, she thinks that a nonparametric test is in order.

The following summary data have been collected.

NBA	NFL	BASEBALL
$n = 20$	$n = 30$	$n = 40$
$\sum R_i = 1,705$	$\sum R_i = 1,090$	$\sum R_i = 1,300$

   a. Why would the sports department address the median as the parameter of interest in this analysis as opposed to the mean? Explain your answer.
   b. What characteristics of the salaries of professional athletes suggest that such data are not normally distributed? Explain.
   c. Based on these data, what can be concluded about the median salaries for the 3 sports? Test at $\alpha = 0.05$. Assume no ties.

15-31. Referring to Problem 30, suppose that there were 40 ties at 8 different salary levels. The following table shows how many scores were ties at each salary level.

LEVEL	T	LEVEL	T
1	2	5	8
2	3	6	10
3	2	7	6
4	4	8	5

   a. Given the results in the previous problem, is it necessary to use the H-value adjusted for ties?
   b. If your answer to part a is yes, conduct the test of hypothesis using this adjusted value of H. If your answer is no, explain why not.

15-32. The American Beef Growers Association is trying to promote the consumption of beef products. The organization performs numerous studies, the results of which are often used in advertising campaigns. One such study involved a quality perception test. Three grades of beef were involved: choice, standard, and economy. A random sample of people was provided a piece of choice-grade beefsteak and asked to rate its quality on a scale of 1 to 100. A second sample of people was given a piece of standard-grade beefsteak, and a third sample was given a piece of economy-grade beefsteak, with instructions to rate the beef on the 100-point scale. The following data were obtained.

CHOICE	STANDARD	ECONOMY
78	67	65
87	80	62
90	78	70
87	80	66
89	67	70
90	70	73

a. What measurement level do these data possess? Would it be appropriate to assume that such data could be obtained from a normal distribution? Explain your answers.

b. Based on the sample data, what conclusions should be reached concerning the median quality perception scores for the 3 grades of beef? Test using $\alpha = 0.01$.

15-33. As purchasing agent for the Horner-Williams Company, you have primary responsibility for securing high-quality raw materials at the best possible price. One particular material the Horner-Williams Company uses a great deal is aluminum. After careful study, you have been able to reduce the prospective vendors to 3. It is unclear whether these 3 vendors produce aluminum that is equally durable.

To compare durability, the recommended procedure is to put pressure on the aluminum until it cracks. The vendor whose aluminum requires the highest mean pressure will be judged to be the one that provides the most durable product. To carry out this test, 14 pieces from each vendor have been selected. These data are in the file called **Horner-Williams**. (The data are pounds per square inch pressure.)

a. State the appropriate null and alternative hypotheses.

b. Using $\alpha = 0.05$, what should the company conclude about whether there is a difference in the mean strength of the 3 vendors' aluminum? Conduct the test without making any assumption about the shape of the population.

15-34. Suppose as part of your job you are responsible for installing emergency lighting in a series of state office buildings. Bids have been received from 4 manufacturers of emergency lights. The costs are about equal, so the decision will be based on the length of time the lights last before failing. A sample of 4 lights from each manufacturer has been tested with the following values (time in hours) recorded for each manufacturer.

TYPE A	TYPE B	TYPE C	TYPE D
1,024	1,270	1,121	923
1,121	1,325	1,201	983
1,250	1,426	1,190	1,087
1,022	1,322	1,122	1,121

a. State the appropriate null and alternative hypotheses.

b. Using $\alpha = 0.01$, what conclusion should you reach about the median length of time the lights last before failing for the 4 manufacturers? Explain.

15-35. A large metropolitan police force is considering changing from full-size to mid-size cars. The police force sampled cars from each of 3 manufacturers. The number sampled represents the number that the manufacturer was able to provide for the test. Each car was driven for 5,000 miles, and the operating cost per mile was computed. The operating costs, in cents per mile, for the 21 cars are provided in the data file called **Police** and are shown as follows.

CAR 1	CAR 2	CAR 3
13.3	12.4	13.9
14.3	13.4	15.5
13.6	13.1	15.2
12.8	12.8	14.5
14.0	12.7	15.7
14.6	13.2	15.3
13.9		15.0
14.5		

a. Perform the appropriate analysis of variance test on these data. Assume a significance level of 0.05. State the appropriate null and alternative hypotheses. Do the experimental data provide evidence that the median operating costs per mile for the 3 types of police cars are different?

b. Use the procedure outlined in the Optional CD-ROM topic on multiple comparisons to determine which car the police force should choose on the basis of median operating costs.

15-36. A nationwide moving company is considering 5 different types of nylon tie-down straps. The purchasing department randomly selected straps from each company and determined their breaking strengths in pounds. The sample data are contained in the file called **Nylon**.

a. Determine the appropriate null and alternative hypotheses.

b. Based on an appropriate analysis, with a Type I error rate of 0.05, can you conclude that a difference exists among the median breaking strength of the types of nylon straps?

c. Based on the sample data, can you make a recommendation regarding which company should be selected based on mean strength of the nylon straps? Discuss in a report to the purchasing manager.

OPTIONAL CD-ROM TOPIC Spearman Rank Correlation

The correlation coefficient introduced in Chapter 11 assumed that the data for the two variables are at least interval scaled and the joint distribution of the variables is bivariate normal. However, a nonparametric correlation coefficient called the Spearman Rank Correlation does not have these data restrictions. For more information, go to the CD-ROM.

■ SUMMARY AND CONCLUSIONS

Many people make the mistake of learning one or two statistical techniques and then using these techniques in all situations. Surprisingly, some people even get emotional about being able to analyze a particular problem using their favorite technique. As a future manager and decision maker, you cannot afford the luxury of defining a problem situation so you can apply your favorite technique. Statistics should be an aid to decision making, not an end in itself.

Many powerful statistical tools discussed in this book rest on the assumptions that the data being analyzed can be measured by at least an interval scale and that the underlying populations being analyzed are normal. If these assumptions come close to being satisfied, many of the tools discussed prior to this chapter apply and are useful. However, in many practical situations these assumptions just do not apply. In such cases the tools discussed in this chapter may be appropriate. In any case, nonparametric statistical tests should be part of every decision maker's tools. There are many other nonparametric statistical techniques that have been developed for specific applications. Many are aimed at situations involving small samples. You should consult the references at the end of the chapter for further reading and discussion.

EQUATIONS

Mean and Standard Deviation for r

$$\mu_r = \frac{2n_1 n_2}{n_1 + n_2} + 1 \qquad \text{15-1}$$

$$\sigma_r = \sqrt{\frac{(2n_1 n_2)(2n_1 n_2 - n_1 - n_2)}{(n_1 + n_2)^2 (n_1 + n_2 - 1)}} \qquad \text{15-2}$$

Test Statistic for Large-Sample Runs Test

$$z = \frac{r - \mu_r}{\sigma_r} \qquad \text{15-3}$$

U-Statistics

$$U_1 = n_1 n_2 + \frac{n_1(n_1 + 1)}{2} - \sum R_1 \qquad \text{15-4}$$

$$U_2 = n_1 n_2 + \frac{n_2(n_2 + 1)}{2} - \sum R_2 \qquad \text{15-5}$$

Mean and Standard Deviation for U-Statistic

$$\mu = \frac{n_1 n_2}{2} \qquad \text{15-6}$$

$$\sigma = \sqrt{\frac{(n_1)(n_2)(n_1 + n_2 + 1)}{12}} \qquad \text{15-7}$$

Mann-Whitney U-Test Statistic

$$z = \frac{U - \dfrac{n_1 n_2}{2}}{\sqrt{\dfrac{(n_1)(n_2)(n_1 + n_2 + 1)}{12}}} \qquad \text{15-8}$$

Wilcoxon Mean and Standard Deviation

$$\mu = \frac{n(n + 1)}{4} \qquad \text{15-9}$$

$$\sigma = \sqrt{\frac{n(n + 1)(2n + 1)}{24}} \qquad \text{15-10}$$

Wilcoxon Test Statistic

$$z = \frac{T - \dfrac{n(n + 1)}{4}}{\sqrt{\dfrac{n(n + 1)(2n + 1)}{24}}} \qquad \text{15-11}$$

H-Statistic

$$H = \frac{12}{N(N + 1)} \sum_{i=1}^{k} \frac{R_i^2}{n_i} - 3(N + 1) \qquad \text{15-12}$$

Correction for Tied Rankings

$$1 - \frac{\sum_{i=1}^{g}(t_i^3 - t_i)}{N^3 - N} \qquad \text{15-13}$$

H-Statistic Corrected for Tied Rankings

$$H = \frac{\dfrac{12}{N(N + 1)} \sum_{i=1}^{k} \dfrac{R_i^2}{n_i} - 3(N + 1)}{1 - \dfrac{\sum_{i=1}^{g}(t_i^3 - t_i)}{N^3 - N}} \qquad \text{15-14}$$

■ KEY TERMS

Kruskal-Wallis One-Way Analysis of Variance—A nonparametric test to determine whether two or more populations have equal distributions. The data must be at least ordinal level and the samples must be independent.

Mann-Whitney U Test—A nonparametric test, based on ranks, used to determine whether two populations have equal distributions.

Nonparametric Statistical Procedures—Statistical methods that do not explicitly concern themselves with population distributions and/or parameters.

Run—A succession of occurrences of a certain type preceded and followed by occurrences of the alternate type or by no occurrences at all.

Runs Test—A statistical procedure used to determine whether the pattern of occurrence of two types of observations is determined by a random process.

Wilcoxon Test—A nonparametric test based on dependent samples to determine whether two populations have equal distributions.

CHAPTER EXERCISES

SOLVED PROBLEMS ON YOUR CD-ROM
Try the WORKED-OUT EXERCISES and BUSINESS
APPLICATIONS on the CD-ROM.

Conceptual Questions and Assignments

15-37. Discuss the data conditions that would lead you to use the Kruskal-Wallis test as opposed to the analysis of variance procedure introduced in Chapter 10. Present an example illustrating these conditions.

15-38. Locate two journal articles in the library that use one of the nonparametric tests discussed in this chapter. Prepare a brief outline of the articles paying particular attention to the reasons given for using the particular test.

15-39. Find an organization that you think would be interested in data that would violate the measurement scale or known distribution assumptions necessary to use the statistical tools found in Chapters 9 and 10 (retail stores are good candidates). Determine to what extent this organization considers these problems and whether it uses any of the techniques discussed in this chapter.

15-40. As an example of how the sampling distribution for the Mann-Whitney test is derived, consider 2 samples with sample sizes $n_1 = 2$ and $n_2 = 3$. The distribution is obtained under the assumption that the 2 variables, say x and y, are identically distributed. Under this assumption each x measurement is equally likely to obtain one of the ranks between 1 and $n_1 + n_2$.

  a. List all the possible sets of 2 ranks that could be obtained from 5 ranks. Calculate the Mann-Whitney U-value for each of these sets of 2 ranks.

  b. The number of ways in which we may choose n_1 ranks from $n_1 + n_2$ is given by the combination of $n_1 + n_2$ things taken n_1 at a time. Calculate this combination for the n_1 and n_2 given in this problem. The probability that each of the Mann-Whitney U's

will occur is obtained by computing the reciprocal of this number. Find this probability.

  c. List all the possible Mann-Whitney U-values you obtained in part a. Then using parts a and b, calculate the probability that each of these U-values occurs thereby producing the sampling distribution for the Mann-Whitney U-statistic when $n_1 = 2$ and $n_2 = 3$.

15-41. Let us examine how the sampling distribution of the Wilcoxon test statistic is obtained. Consider the sampling distributions of the positive ranks as our example from a sample size of 4. The ranks to be considered are, therefore, 1, 2, 3, and 4. Under the null hypothesis the differences to be ranked are distributed symmetrically about 0. Thus, each difference is just as likely to be positively as negatively ranked.

  a. For a sample size of 4, there are $2^4 = 16$ possible sets of signs associated with the 4 ranks. List the 16 possible sets of ranks that could be positive—e.g., (none), (1), (2), . . . (1, 2, 3, 4). Each of these sets of positive ranks (under the null hypothesis) has the same probability of occurring.

  b. Calculate the sum of the ranks of each set specified in part a.

  c. Using parts a and b produce the sampling distribution for the Wilcoxon test statistic when $n = 4$.

Business Applications

15-42. The H. F. Houston Company is the parent franchiser for a nationwide fast-food chain with corporate headquarters in Austin, Minnesota. For the past few months the company has undertaken a new advertising study. Initially, company executives selected 22 of its retail outlets that were similar with respect to sales volume, profitability, location, climate, economic status of customers, and experience of store management. Each of the outlets was randomly assigned one of two advertising plans promoting a new sandwich product. The accompanying data represent the number of the new sandwiches sold during the specific test period at each retail outlet.

Houston executives want you to determine which of the two advertising plans leads to the larger average sales levels for the new product. They are not willing to make the assumptions necessary for you to use the t-test. They do not wish to have an error rate of more than 0.05.

ADVERTISING PLAN 1	ADVERTISING PLAN 2
1,711	2,100
1,915	2,210
1,905	1,950
2,153	3,004
1,504	2,725
1,195	2,619
2,103	2,483
1,601	2,520
1,580	1,904
1,475	1,875
1,588	1,943

15-43. Two small regional life insurance companies are being studied by the Triangle Life Insurance Company as candidates for a possible merger. Triangle can merge with only one of these regional companies at this time and, as part of its study, wishes to determine whether there is a difference in the average annual premiums received by the two regional companies. The following data represent sample policy premiums for each company.

COMPANY 1		COMPANY 2	
$246	$310	$300	$295
211	450	305	320
235	502	308	330
270	311	325	240
411	200	340	360

Do these data indicate a difference in mean annual premiums for the two companies? Test with a significance level of 0.10.

15-44. Refer to Problem 43.
   a. Apply the t-test to determine whether the data indicate a difference between annual premiums for the two regional companies. Use a significance level of 0.10.
   b. Indicate what assumptions must be made to apply the t-test.

15-45. The Style-Rite Company of Atlanta makes windbreaker jackets for people who play golf and who are active outdoors during the spring and fall months. The company recently developed a new material and is in the process of test marketing jackets made from the material. As part of this test-marketing effort, 10 people were each supplied with a jacket made from the original material and asked to wear it for 2 months, washing it at least twice during that time. A second group of 10 people was given a jacket made from the new material and asked to wear it for 2 months with the same washing requirements.

Following the 2-month trial period, the individuals were asked to rate the jackets on a scale of 0 to 100, with 0 being the worst performance rating and 100 being the best. The ratings for each material are shown as follows.

ORIGINAL MATERIAL		NEW MATERIAL	
76	80	55	69
34	10	90	91
70	46	72	95
23	67	17	86
45	75	56	74

The company expects that, on the average, the performance ratings will be superior for the new material.
   a. Do the sample data support this belief at a significance level of 0.05? Discuss.
   b. Examine the data given in the table. What characteristics of these data sets would lead you to reject the assumption that the data came from populations that had normal distributions and equal variances?

15-46. A study was recently conducted by the Bonneville Power Association to determine attitudes regarding the association's policies in the United States' western states. One part of the study asked respondents to rate the performance of the BPA on its responsiveness to environmental issues. The following responses were obtained for a sample of 12 urban residents and 10 rural residents. The ratings are on a 1 to 100 scale, with 100 being perfect.

URBAN		RURAL	
76	50	55	77
90	20	80	68
86	30	94	35
60	82	40	59
43	75	85	
96	84	92	

Based on the sample data, should the BPA conclude that there is no difference between the urban and rural residents with respect to median environmental rating? Test using a significance level of 0.02.

15-47. Referring to Problem 46, perform the appropriate parametric statistical test and indicate the assumptions necessary to use this test that were not required by the nonparametric tests. Use a significance level of 0.02. (Refer to Chapter 9 if needed.)

15-48. The Miltmore Corporation performs consulting services for companies that think they have image problems. Recently, the Bluedot Beer Company approached Miltmore. Bluedot executives were concerned that the company's image, relative to its two closest competitors, had diminished. Miltmore conducted an image study in which a random sample of 8 people was asked to rate

Bluedot's image. Five people were asked to rate competitor A's image, and 10 people were asked to rate competitor B's image. The image ratings were made on a 100-point scale, with 100 being the best possible rating. The results of the sampling were:

BLUEDOT	COMPETITOR A	COMPETITOR B
40	95	50
60	53	80
70	55	82
40	92	87
55	90	93
90		51
20		63
20		72
96		88

a. Based on these sample results, should Bluedot conclude there is an image difference among the three companies? Use a significance level equal to 0.05.
b. Should Bluedot infer that its image has been damaged by last year's federal government recall of its product? Discuss why or why not.

15-49. A major car manufacturer is experimenting with 3 new methods of pollution control. The testing lab must determine whether the 3 methods produce equal pollution reductions. Readings from a calibrated carbon monoxide meter are taken from groups of engines randomly equipped with 1 of the 3 control units. The following data are in the file called **Pollution**.
   a. Determine whether the 3 pollution-control methods will produce equal median pollution readings.
   b. If your finding in part a indicates a significant difference, determine which of these methods has the greatest pollution reduction. Conduct each test at a significance level of 0.01. (Hint: Refer to the optional section on your CD-ROM for performing multiple comparisons.)

15-50. During the production of a textbook, there are many steps between when the author first begins preparing the manuscript and when the book is finally printed and bound. Tremendous effort is made to minimize the number of errors of any type in the text. One type of error that is especially difficult to eliminate is the typographical error that can creep in when the book is typeset. The Prolythic Type Company does contract work for many publishers. As part of its quality control efforts, the company charts the number of corrected errors per page in its manuscripts. In one particularly difficult book to typeset, the following data were observed for a sample of 15 pages (in sequence):

Page	1	2	3	4	5	6	7	8	9	10	11	12	13	14	15
Errors	2	4	1	0	6	7	4	2	9	4	3	6	2	4	2

a. Based on these sample data, can the operations manager conclude that the occurrence of errors is random? Test at a significance level of 0.05 and use the mean as the cut-off for determining the two groups.
b. Produce a graph that displays the variable $(e_i - \mu_e)$ versus the page number where e_i = number of errors on page i and μ_e is the mean number of errors in these 15 pages. Do you detect anything systematic in the sequence of number of errors per page? Speculate on reasons for the pattern (if any) that you see.

15-51. The catering manager at a major league baseball park is interested in determining whether the requests for beer or soda follow some pattern or are random. He has observed 12 customers who arrive at a concession stand and place their beverage order. Letting B = beer and S = soda, the following data are observed.

B	B	B	S	B	B	B	B	S	S	S	S

Test for randomness at the 0.05 significance level.

15-52. A computer component manufacturer maintains a wide variety of control charts (see Chapter 13). One particular chart seems to be in control according to the operator. Her reasoning is that none of the points fall outside the control limits. However, an internal quality consultant thinks that it would be wise to examine the control chart in more detail to see whether the points do, in fact, exhibit a random pattern around the center line. In doing this study, the consultant studied the 100 most recent points and found 21 runs. Of the 100 points, 44 were above the center line and 56 were below the center line.
   a. State the appropriate null and alternative hypotheses.
   b. Based on the sample data, what conclusion should be reached at an $\alpha = 0.01$ level?

15-53. A local golf course has undertaken a service quality improvement effort. As one part of this effort, the course professional would like to be able to satisfy more customers by giving them tee times as close as possible to their preferred times to play. One question is whether players' preferences for morning versus afternoon tee times are random from call to call. To study this, a sample of 200 consecutive calls was monitored. The callers were asked to indicate morning or afternoon preference. Out of the 200 calls, 94 indicated a preference for afternoon times and 106 wanted morning times. Further, the calls showed 130 runs.
   a. State the appropriate null and alternative hypotheses to be tested.
   b. Based on $\alpha = 0.05$, what conclusion should be reached regarding whether or not time preferences are random? Discuss.
   c. Do the majority of golfers prefer morning tee times? Use a relevant test procedure to determine this.

15-54. A business statistics instructor at State University has been experimenting with her testing procedure. This term, she has taken the approach of giving two tests over each section of material. The first test is a problem-oriented exam, where students have to set up and solve an applications problem. The exam is worth 50 points. The second test, given a day later, is a multiple-choice test, testing the concepts introduced in the section of the text covered by the exam. This exam is also worth 50 points.

In one class of 15 students, the observed test scores over the first section of material in the course are contained in the file called **State University**.

   a. If the instructor is unwilling to make the assumptions for the paired-sample t-test, what should she conclude based on these data about the distribution of scores for the two tests if she tests at a significance level of 0.05?

   b. In the context of this problem, define a type II error.

15-55. A computer chip manufacturer is experimenting with a new wafer-cleaning compound. In this business, the problem with any cleaning compound is that while it may remove dust particles from the wafers, the compound can also leave some of its own particles. To test the effectiveness of the new compound, the engineer in charge of the project selected a random sample of 26 wafers. He first used an electromagnetic process to count the number of particles on each wafer. He next used the cleaner on each of the 26 wafers and recounted the particles on each wafer. He expects that there will be significantly fewer particles after the cleaner is applied.

The engineer is unwilling to make the normality assumption required for the paired-sample t-test.

   a. Indicate the appropriate null and alternative hypotheses to be tested.

   b. Differences were formed by subtracting the reading after the cleaner was applied from the reading made before the cleaner was applied. The calculated test statistic for these data is 298. Based on this result, what decision should be made using a significance level of 0.05? Discuss. (Note that there were no differences of 0.)

   c. Calculate the p-value for this hypothesis test. Interpret the meaning of this p-value in the context of this problem.

15-56. Two brands of tires are being tested for tread wear. To control for vehicle and driver variation, 1 tire of each brand is put on the front wheels of 10 cars. The cars are driven under normal driving conditions for a total of 15,000 miles. The tread wear is then measured using a very sophisticated instrument. The data that were observed are in a file called **Tread Wear**. (Note that the larger the number, the less wear in the tread.)

   a. State the appropriate null and alternative hypotheses to be tested.

   b. What would be the possible objection in this case for employing the paired-sample t-test? Discuss.

   c. Assuming that the decision makers in this situation are not willing to make the assumptions required to perform the paired-sample t-test, what decision should be reached using the appropriate nonparametric test if a significance level of 0.05 is used? Discuss.

15-57. Pinnacle Capital offers a wide range of financial services, including the ability for customers to be involved in day trading activities—moving in and out of stocks in a mat-

ter of minutes in an effort to take advantage of price volatility. Of interest to Pinnacle is whether the market listing (New York Stock Exchange or NASDAQ) of day-traded stocks is random. A sample of 30 trades produced the following market listing sequence.

Trade 1	Trade 2	Trade 3	Trade 4	Trade 5	Trade 6
NYSE	NYSE	NASDAQ	NASDAQ	NASDAQ	NASDAQ
Trade 7	Trade 8	Trade 9	Trade 10	Trade 11	Trade 12
NASDAQ	NYSE	NASDAQ	NASDAQ	NASDAQ	NYSE
Trade 13	Trade 14	Trade 15	Trade 16	Trade 17	Trade 18
NYSE	NASDAQ	NASDAQ	NYSE	NASDAQ	NASDAQ
Trade 19	Trade 20	Trade 21	Trade 22	Trade 23	Trade 24
NASDAQ	NASDAQ	NASDAQ	NASDAQ	NASDAQ	NASDAQ
Trade 25	Trade 26	Trade 27	Trade 28	Trade 29	Trade 30
NYSE	NYSE	NYSE	NASDAQ	NASDAQ	NASDAQ

   a. Based on these 30 sampled trades, how many runs are there in the data? How many runs would you expect if the market listing of day-traded stocks were random between the New York Stock Exchange and NASDAQ?

   b. Using an alpha value of 0.01, test the hypothesis that the market listing of day-traded stocks is random between the New York Stock Exchange and NASDAQ.

15-58. Lower interest rates have increased the number of people refinancing their home mortgage loans. In an effort to determine cash flow projections, the loan manager at East South Central Home & Thrift is interested in knowing whether the selection of a 15- or 30-year mortgage is random. A sample of 40 of last month's refinance applications revealed the following sequence of mortgage terms (15 or 30).

Sample 1	30	Sample 11	15	Sample 21	15	Sample 31	30
Sample 2	15	Sample 12	15	Sample 22	30	Sample 32	30
Sample 3	15	Sample 13	15	Sample 23	15	Sample 33	15
Sample 4	15	Sample 14	15	Sample 24	30	Sample 34	30
Sample 5	15	Sample 15	15	Sample 25	30	Sample 35	15
Sample 6	15	Sample 16	30	Sample 26	15	Sample 36	15
Sample 7	30	Sample 17	30	Sample 27	15	Sample 37	15
Sample 8	30	Sample 18	30	Sample 28	15	Sample 38	15
Sample 9	15	Sample 19	30	Sample 29	15	Sample 39	30
Sample 10	15	Sample 20	15	Sample 30	15	Sample 40	15

   a. How many runs are there in the data?

   b. Does it appear that the refinancing choice between a 15-year or a 30-year mortgage is random? Support your answer by conducting the appropriate statistical test. Use the p-value approach to conduct the hypothesis test.

15-59. An x-bar chart (see Chapter 13) is used to monitor a process that fills maple syrup bottles. When the process is filling correctly (in statistical control) the average fill in an 8-ounce bottle of syrup is 8.03 ounces. The last 15 samples taken revealed the following subgroup means, listed in order of occurrence from left to right.

7.95	8.02	8.07	8.06	8.05	8.04	7.97	8.01
8.04	8.05	8.08	8.11	7.99	8.00	8.02	

a. How many runs are there below the process center-line (8.03)?

b. How many runs are there above the process center-line (8.03)?

c. At the 0.01 level of significance is there evidence to suggest that the process is not random?

15-60. The manager of credit card operations for a small regional bank has determined that last year's median credit card balance was $1,989.32. A sample of 18 customer balances this year revealed the following.

Sample 1	Sample 2	Sample 3	Sample 4	Sample 5	Sample 6
1,827.85	1,992.75	2,012.35	1,955.64	2,023.19	1,998.52

Sample 7	Sample 8	Sample 9	Sample 10	Sample 11	Sample 12
2,003.75	1,752.55	1,865.32	2,013.13	2,225.35	2,100.35

Sample 13	Sample 14	Sample 15	Sample 16	Sample 17	Sample 18
2,002.02	1,850.37	1,995.35	2,001.18	2,252.54	2,035.75

a. Based on the 18 customer balances sampled, how many runs are there in the data? Based on this, can the manager conclude that the sample was randomly selected? (Use $\alpha = 0.05$.)

b. At the 0.05 level of significance, is there evidence to suggest that the median credit card balance for the bank's customers has increased over last year?

c. Based on the findings in part b, how could this information be useful to the manager of the credit card department?

d. We will presume that you had to decide which hypothesis test procedure you would implement to answer the question in part b. Discuss the alternatives you considered and the reasons for the selection you made.

15-61. High Fuel Company markets a gasoline additive for automobiles that it claims will increase a car's miles per gallon (MPG) performance. In an effort to determine whether or not High Fuel's claim is valid, a consumer-testing agency randomly selected 8 makes of automobiles. Each car's tank was filled with gasoline and driven around a track until empty. Then the car's tank was refilled with gasoline and the additive, and the car was driven until the gas tank was empty again. The miles per gallon were measured for each car with and without the additive. The results are reported in the data file called **High Fuel**.

The testing agency is unwilling to accept the assumption that the underlying probability distribution is normally distributed, but it would still like to perform a statistical test to determine the validity of High Fuel's claim.

a. State the null and alternative hypotheses of interest to the testing agency.

b. What statistical test would you recommend the testing agency use in this case? Why?

c. Conduct the test that you believe to be appropriate. Use a significance level of 0.05.

d. State your conclusions based on the test you have just conducted. Is High Fuel's claim supported by the test's findings?

15-62. A company assembles remote controls for television sets. The company's design engineers have developed a revised design that they think will make it faster to assemble the controls. To test whether the new design leads to faster assembly, 14 assembly workers were randomly selected and each worker was asked to assemble a control using the current design and then asked to assemble a control using the revised design. The times in seconds to assemble the controls are shown in a file called **Remote Control**. The company's engineers are unable to assume that the assembly times are normally distributed, but they would like to test whether assembly times are faster using the revised design.

a. What statistical test do you recommend the company use? Why?

b. State the null and alternative hypotheses of interest to the company.

c. At the 0.05 level of significance, is there any evidence to support the engineers' belief that the revised design reduces assembly time?

d. How might the results of the statistical test be used by the company's management?

CASE 15-A

Bentford Electronics, Part 2

On Saturday morning Jennifer Bentford received a call at her home from the production supervisor at Bentford Electronics Plant #1. The supervisor indicated that she and the supervisors from Plants #2, #3, and #4 had agreed that something must be done to improve company morale and, thereby, increase the production output of their plants. Jennifer Bentford, president of Bentford Electronics, agreed to set up a Monday morning meeting with the supervisors to see if, together, they could arrive at a plan for accomplishing these objectives.

By Monday each supervisor had compiled a list of several ideas, including a 4-day work week and interplant competition of various kinds.

After listening to the discussion for some time, Jennifer Bentford asked if anyone knew if there was a difference in average daily output for the 4 plants. When she heard no positive response, she told the supervisors to select a random sample of daily production reports from each plant and test whether there was a difference. They were to meet again on Wednesday afternoon with test results.

By Wednesday morning the supervisors had collected the following data on units produced.

PLANT #1	PLANT #2	PLANT #3	PLANT #4
4,306	1,853	2,700	1,704
2,852	1,948	2,705	2,320
1,900	2,702	2,721	4,150
4,711	4,110	2,900	3,300
2,933	3,950	2,650	3,200
3,627	2,300	2,480	2,975

The supervisors had little trouble collecting the data, but they were at a loss as to how to determine whether there was a difference in the output of the 4 plants. Jerry Gibson, the company's research analyst, told the supervisors that there were statistical procedures that could be used to test hypotheses regarding multiple samples if the daily output was distributed in a bell shape (normal distribution) at each plant. The supervisors expressed dismay because none thought his or her output was normal. Jerry Gibson indicated that there were techniques that did not require the normality assumption, but he did not know what they were.

The meeting with Jennifer Bentford was scheduled to begin in 3 hours, so the supervisors needed some statistical analysis help immediately.

■ GENERAL REFERENCES

1. Berenson, Mark L., and David M. Levine, *Basic Business Statistics Concepts and Applications*, 7th ed. (Upper Saddle River, NJ: Prentice Hall, 1999).
2. Conover, W. J., *Practical Nonparametric Statistics*, 3d ed. (New York: Wiley, 1999).
3. Daniel, Wayne W., *Applied Nonparametric Statistics* (Boston: Houghton Mifflin, 1978).
4. Dunn, O. J., "Multiple Comparisons Using Rank Sums," *Technometrics* 6 (1964), 241–52.
5. Marascuilo, Leonard A., and Maryellen McSweeney, *Nonparametric and Distribution-free Methods for Social Sciences* (Pacific Grove, CA: Brooks/Cole, 1977).
6. *Microsoft Excel 2000* (Redmond, WA: Microsoft Corporation, 1999).
7. *Minitab for Windows Version 13* (State College, PA: Minitab, Inc., 2000).
8. Noether, G. E., *Elements of Nonparametric Statistics*, (New York: John Wiley & Sons, 1967).

ANALYZING AND FORECASTING TIME-SERIES DATA

CHAPTER OUTCOMES

After studying the material in Chapter 16, you should be able to:

16-1: Apply the basic steps in developing and implementing forecasting models.

16-2: Identify the components present in a time series.

16-3: Use smoothing-based forecasting models including single and double exponential smoothing.

16-4: Apply trend-based forecasting models, including linear trend, nonlinear trend, and seasonally adjusted trend.

WHY YOU NEED TO KNOW

No organization, large or small, can function effectively without a demand forecast for the goods or services it provides. A retail clothing store must forecast the demand for the shirts it sells by shirt size. The concessionaire at Dodger Stadium in Los Angeles must forecast each game's attendance to determine how many soft drinks and hot dogs to have on hand. Your state's elected officials must forecast tax revenue in order to establish a budget each year. These are only a few of the instances in which forecasting is required. For many organizations, the success of the forecasting effort will play a major role in determining the general success of the organization.

When you graduate and join an organization in the public or private sector, you will almost certainly be required to prepare forecasts or to use forecasts provided by someone else in the organization. You won't have access to a crystal ball on which to rely for an accurate prediction of the future. However, once you have learned the material presented in this chapter, you will have a basic understanding of forecasting and of how and when to apply various forecasting techniques. We urge you to focus on the material in this chapter and take with you the tools that will give you a competitive advantage over those who are not familiar with forecasting and its application to business.

■ 16-1: INTRODUCTION TO FORECASTING AND TIME-SERIES ANALYSIS

Decision makers often confuse forecasting and planning. Planning is the process of determining how to deal with the future. On the other hand, *forecasting* is the process of predicting what the future will be like. Forecasts are used as inputs for the planning process.

Experts agree that good planning is essential for an organization to be effective. Since forecasts are an important part of the planning process, you need to be familiar with forecasting methods. There are two broad categories of forecasting techniques: qualitative and quantitative. *Qualitative forecasting* techniques are based upon expert opinion and judgment. *Quantitative forecasting* techniques are based on statistical methods for analyzing quantitative historical data. This chapter focuses on quantitative forecasting techniques.

In general, quantitative forecasting techniques are used whenever the following conditions are true: historical data relating to the variable to be forecast exist; the historical data can be quantified; and one can assume that the historical pattern will continue into the future. If these conditions do not exist, qualitative forecasting techniques may be employed.

OPTIONAL CD-ROM TOPIC Qualitative Forecasting Approaches
You will encounter many situations where a forecast is required but you do not have historical data that are quantitative. In these cases you will need to employ a qualitative forecasting technique. For more information, go to the CD-ROM.

General Forecasting Issues

Decision makers who are actively involved in forecasting frequently say that forecasting is both an art and a science. Operationally, the forecaster is engaged in the process of modeling a real-world system. Determining the appropriate forecasting model is a challenging task, but it can be made manageable by employing a model-building process consisting of the following three steps: **model specification**, **model fitting**, and **model diagnosis**.

> **MODEL SPECIFICATION**
> The process of selecting the forecasting technique to be used in a particular situation.

As we will point out in later sections, guidelines exist for determining which techniques may be more appropriate than others in certain situations. However, you may have to specify (and try) several model forms for a given situation before deciding on one that is acceptable.

> **MODEL FITTING**
> The process of determining how well a specified model fits past data.

The idea is that if the future tends to look like the past, a model must adequately fit the past data to have a reasonable chance of forecasting the future. As a forecaster, you will spend much time selecting the model's specification and estimating the model's parameters to reach an acceptable fit of the past data.

> **MODEL DIAGNOSIS**
> The process of determining how well the model fits the past data and how well the model's assumptions appear to be satisfied.

You will need to determine how well the model fits the past data, how well it performs in mock forecasting trials, and how well the model's assumptions appear to be satisfied. If the model is unacceptable in any of these areas, you will be forced to revert to the model specification step and begin again.

An important consideration when you are developing a forecasting model is to use the simplest available model that will meet your forecasting needs. The objective of forecasting is to provide good forecasts. You do not need to feel that a sophisticated approach is better if a simpler one will provide acceptable forecasts. As in football, where some players specialize in defense and others in offense, forecasting techniques have been developed for special situations, generally dependent on the **forecasting horizon**.

> **FORECASTING HORIZON**
> The number of future periods covered by the forecast; sometimes referred to as *forecast lead time*.

For the purpose of categorizing forecasting techniques in most business situations, the forecast horizon or lead-time is typically divided into four categories.

1. Immediate term—less than one month
2. Short term—one to three months
3. Medium term—three months to two years
4. Long term—two years or more

As we introduce various forecasting techniques, we will indicate the forecasting horizon(s) for which each is typically best suited.

In addition to determining the desired forecasting horizon, the forecaster must determine the **forecasting period**.

> **FORECASTING PERIOD**
> The unit of time for which forecasts are to be made.

For instance, the forecasting period might be a day, a week, a month, a quarter, or a year. Thus, the forecasting horizon consists of one or more forecasting periods. If quantitative forecasting techniques are to be employed, historical quantitative data must be available for a similar period. For instance, if we want weekly forecasts, weekly historical data must be available.

FORECASTING INTERVAL
The frequency with which new forecasts are prepared.

The **forecasting interval** is generally the same length as the forecast period. That is, if the forecast period is one week, then we will provide a new forecast each week.

Components of a Time Series

Most quantitative forecasting models have one factor in common: they use past measurements of the variable of interest to generate a forecast of the future. The past data, measured over time, are called **time-series data**. The decision maker who plans to develop a quantitative forecasting model must analyze the relevant time-series data.

TIME-SERIES DATA
Data measured over time. In most applications the period between measurements is uniform.

Software Consulting Revenues

For the past 4 years, a software support firm has been supplying consulting help to firms implementing enterprise-wide support systems such as SAP and PeopleSoft. The company's revenue forecast for next year should consider the historical pattern over the prior 4 years. The managers would be interested in determining whether demand for consulting services has tended to increase or decrease and whether there have been particular times during a year when demand is typically higher than at other times. The forecasters could determine this information by performing a time-series analysis of the historical billings.

Table 16-1 presents the time-series data for the revenue generated by a firm's billings for the 4-year period. An effective means for analyzing these data is to develop a **time-series plot**, as shown in Figure 16-1. By graphing the data, much can be observed about the firm's revenue over the past 4 years. In fact, the time-series plot is an important tool in identifying the time-series components. All time-series data exhibit one or more of the following.

1. Trend component
2. Seasonal component
3. Cyclical component
4. Random component

EXAMPLE 16-1

TIME-SERIES DATA

TABLE 16-1
Time-Series Data for Consultant's Billings (Thousands of Dollars)

Month	BILLING TOTAL			
	1997	1998	1999	2000
January	170	390	500	750
February	200	350	470	700
March	190	300	510	680
April	220	320	480	710
May	180	310	530	710
June	230	350	500	660
July	220	380	540	630
August	260	420	580	670
September	300	460	630	700
October	330	500	690	720
November	370	540	770	850
December	390	560	760	880

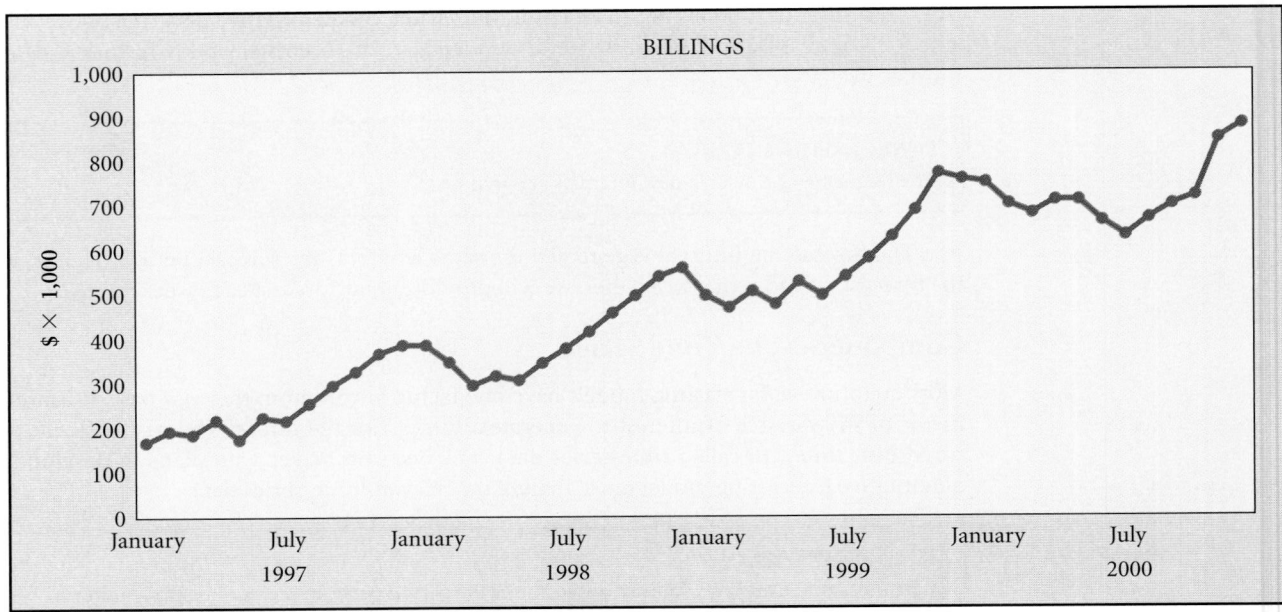

FIGURE 16-1   Time-Series Plot for Consultant Billing Data

TIME-SERIES PLOT

A two-dimensional plot of the time series. The vertical axis measures the variable of interest and the horizontal axis corresponds to the time periods.

TREND COMPONENT

A **trend** is the long-term increase or decrease in a variable being measured over time. Figure 16-1 shows the software consulting company's demand exhibited an upward trend over the 4-year period. In other situations, the time series may exhibit a downward trend.

Trends can be classified as linear or nonlinear.

LINEAR TREND

A long-term increase or decrease in a time series in which the rate of change is relatively constant.

Figure 16-1 is a good example showing a positive **linear trend**. In a *nonlinear trend*, the rate of change is not constant. Figure 16-2 shows the time-series plot of total sales for the years 1993–1999 for Albertson's, Inc., the nation's second largest grocery chain. The sales data, taken from Albertson's 1999 annual report, exhibit a positive linear trend, since sales have tended to increase at a fairly constant rate. The sales data in Figure 16-3 show that Microsoft's sales, taken from Microsoft's 1999 annual report, have exhibited a nonlinear trend between 1985 and 1999. Although sales have increased over time, the rate of increase has been much higher in recent years.

A trend can be observed when the time series is measured in any time increment such as years, quarters, months, or days. Not all of the components of a time series are evident over all time increments. For instance, you will see shortly that a seasonal component is not evident if the time series is measured in years.

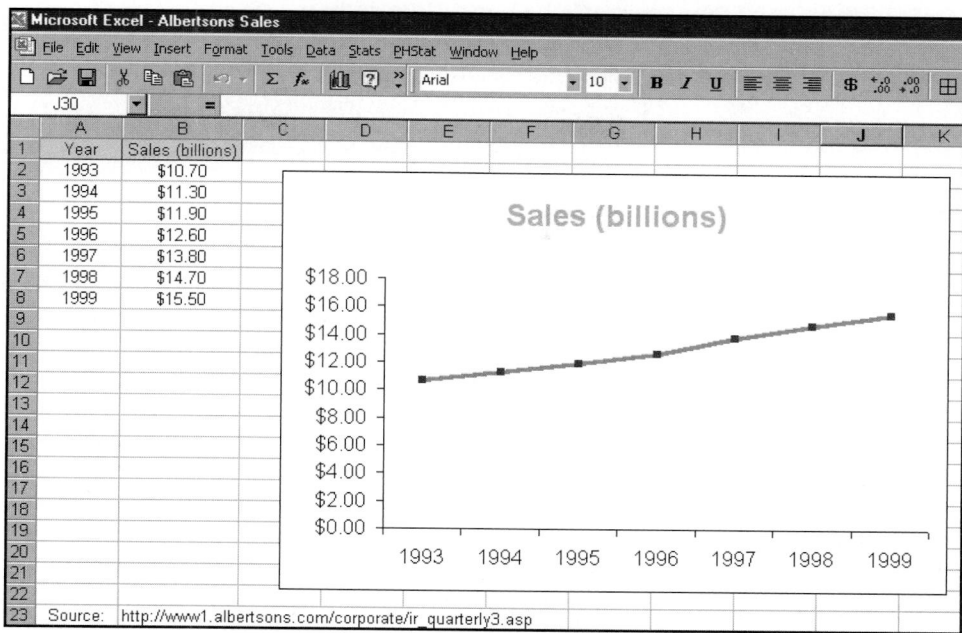

FIGURE 16-2
Albertson's, Inc.—Linear
Trend Example

SEASONAL COMPONENT

Another time series component that may be present is called the **seasonal component**. Many time series show a repeating pattern over time. For instance, Figure 16-1 showed a time series that exhibits a "wave-like" pattern. This pattern repeats itself throughout the time series. The consultant billings reach a local maximum around January and then decline to a local minimum around April. This pattern repeats itself every 12 months, and the entire pattern is not repeated more often than once every 12 months. The shortest

FIGURE 16-3
Microsoft Corporation—a
Nonlinear Trend

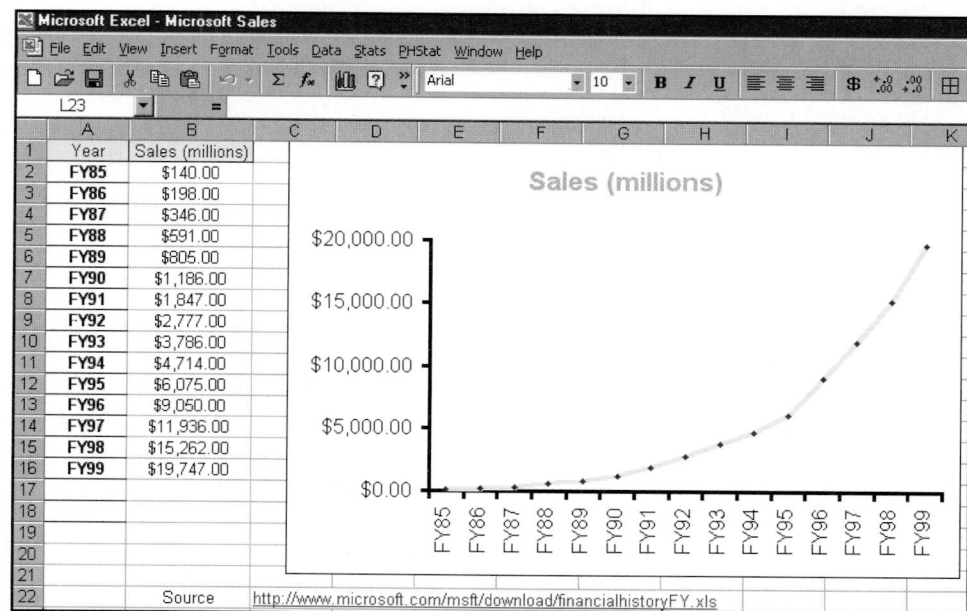

period of repetition for a pattern is known as its *recurrence period*. A seasonal component's recurrence period is at most one year.

> **SEASONAL COMPONENT**
> A pattern that is repeated throughout a time series and has a recurrence period of at most one year.

In analyzing past sales data for a retail toy store, we would expect to see that sales increase in the months leading into Christmas and then substantially decrease after Christmas. Automobile gasoline sales might show a seasonal increase during the summer months when people drive more and a decrease during the cold winter months. These predictable highs and lows at specific times during the year indicate seasonality in the data.

In order to view seasonality in a time series, the data must be measured quarterly, monthly, weekly, or daily. Annual data will not show seasonal patterns of highs and lows. Figure 16-4 shows quarterly sales data for the years 1992–1997 for the Marriott Corporation, the hotel and food service company. Notice that the data exhibit a definite seasonal pattern. The local maximums occur in March (spring). The recurrence period of the component in the time series is, therefore, one year. The December (winter) quarter tends to be low while the following quarter (spring) is the high quarter each year.

Seasonality can be observed in time-series data measured over time periods shorter than a year. For example, the number of checks processed daily by a bank may show predictable highs and lows at certain times during the month. The pattern of customers arriving at the bank during any hour may be "seasonal" within a day, with more customers arriving near opening time, around the lunch hour, and near closing time.

FIGURE 16-4   Marriott Sales by Quarter

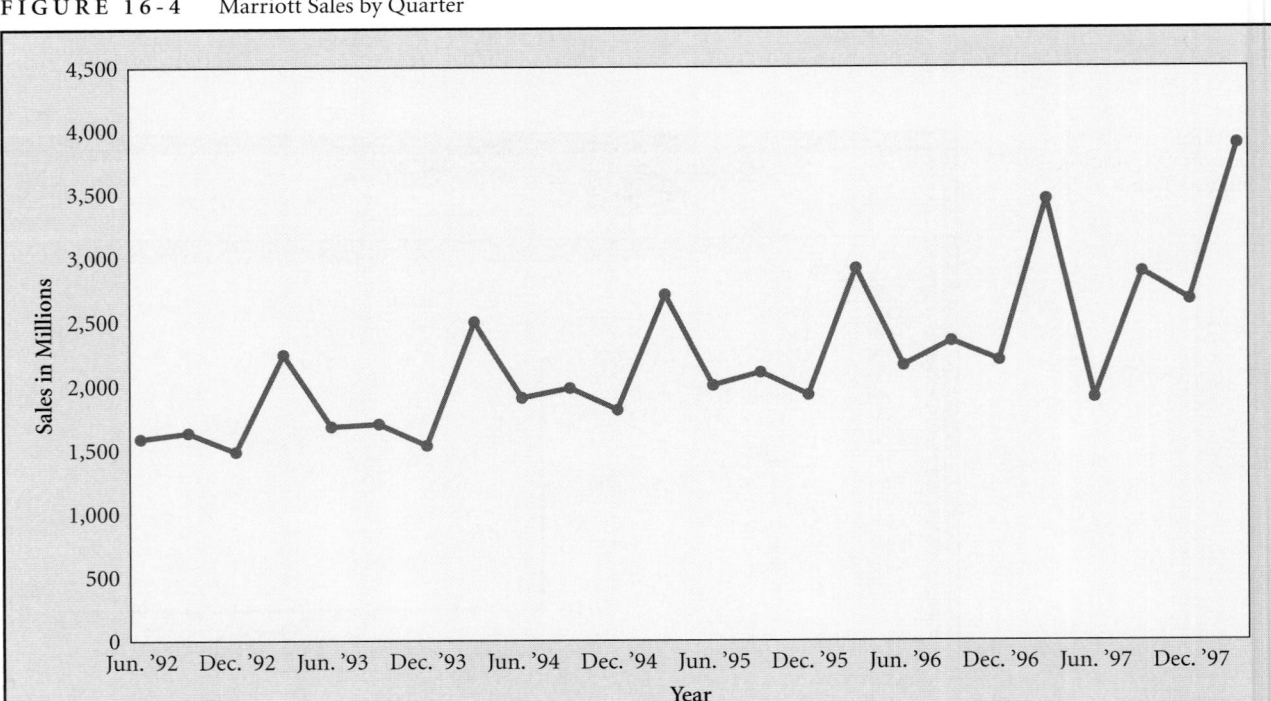

CYCLICAL COMPONENT

If you observe time-series data over a long enough period, you may see sustained periods of high values followed by periods of lower values. If the recurrence period of these fluctuations is larger than a year, the data are said to contain a **cyclical component**.

> **CYCLICAL COMPONENT**
>
> A pattern within the time series that repeats itself throughout the time series and has a recurrence period of more than one year.

National economic measures such as the unemployment rate, gross national product, stock market indexes, and personal saving rates tend to cycle. The cycles vary in length and magnitude. That is, some cyclical time series may have longer runs of high and low values than others. Also, some time series may exhibit deeper troughs and higher crests than others. Figure 16-5 shows quarterly housing starts in the United States between 1973 and 1998. Note the definite cyclical pattern with low periods around the years 1974, 1982, and 1990. Although the pattern resembles the shape of a seasonal component, the length of the recurrence period identifies this pattern as being the result of a cyclical component.

RANDOM COMPONENT

While not all time series possess a trend, seasonal, or cyclical component, virtually all time series will have a random component.

> **RANDOM COMPONENT**
>
> Changes in the time-series data that are unpredictable and cannot be associated with the trend, seasonal, or cyclical components.

FIGURE 16-5   U.S. Housing Starts, Showing a Cyclical Component

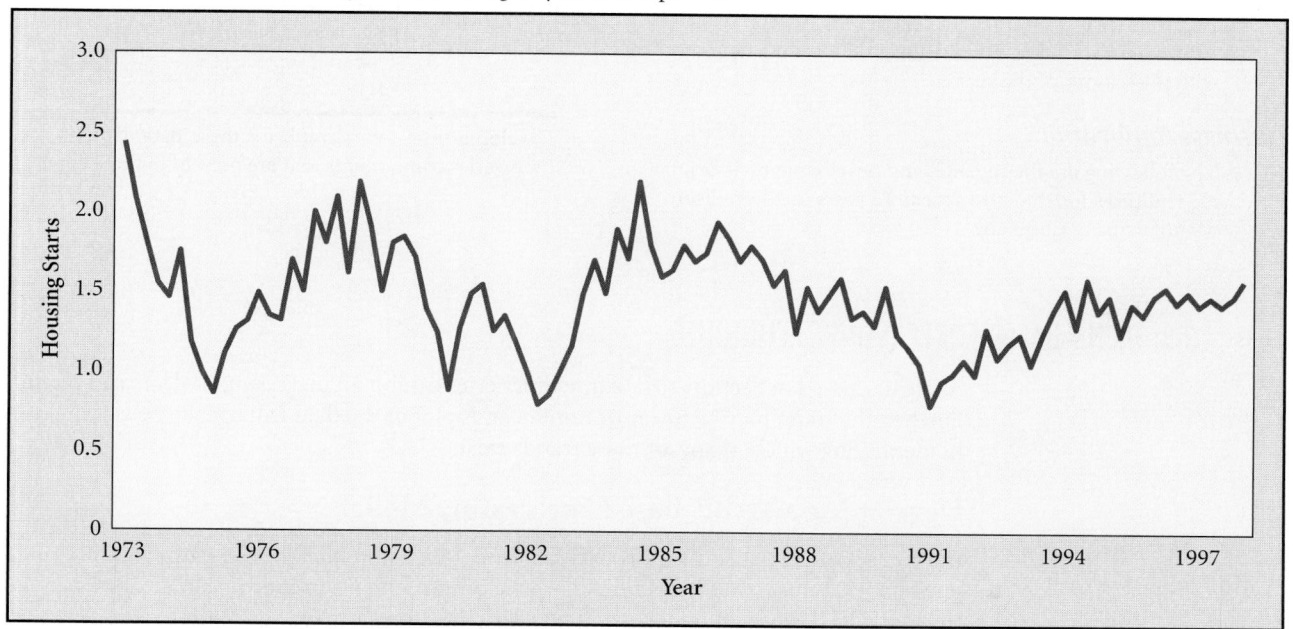

The random component is often referred to as "noise" in the data. A time series with no identifiable pattern is completely random and contains only noise. In addition to other components, each of the time series in Figures 16-1 through 16-5 contains random fluctuations.

In the following sections of this chapter, you will see how various forecasting techniques deal with the time-series components. An important first step in forecasting is to identify which components are present in the time series to be analyzed. As we have shown, constructing a time-series plot is a good first step in this process.

16-1: EXERCISES

16-1. What is the difference between planning and forecasting? Give an example of planning, and describe how forecasting would be used in the planning process.

16-2. What are the differences between quantitative and qualitative forecasting techniques? Under what conditions is it appropriate to use a quantitative technique?

16-3. Provide an example of a business decision that requires
   a. a short-term forecast
   b. a medium-term forecast, and
   c. a long-term forecast.

16-4. What is meant by time-series data? Give an example.

16-5. Explain the difference between time-series data and data that occur in regression models. Are these two types of data sets mutually exclusive? What do they have in common? How do they differ?

16-6. What is meant by the trend component of a time series? How is a linear trend different from a nonlinear trend?

16-7. Must a seasonal component be associated with the seasons (fall, spring, summer, winter) of the year? If not, provide an example of a seasonal effect that is not associated with the seasons of the year.

Business Applications

16-8. The following are the research and development (R & D) expenditures for the most recent 12 years for the Wilson Manufacturing Company.

YEAR	R&D EXPENDITURES	YEAR	R&D EXPENDITURES
1	$1,549,800	7	1,553,390
2	1,547,870	8	1,546,660
3	1,550,860	9	1,554,270
4	1,548,770	10	1,550,810
5	1,553,830	11	1,554,210
6	1,548,590	12	1,551,880

a. Graph the time series for R & D expenditures.
b. What time-series components are present? Discuss.

16-9. Ice-World is a family-oriented ice skating facility. The sales manager has the following data for the past 11 days. The data reflect the number of admissions to the Ice-World facility each day.

DAY	ADMISSIONS	DAY	ADMISSIONS
1	1,258	7	1,330
2	1,275	8	1,349
3	1,287	9	1,364
4	1,299	10	1,388
5	1,304	11	1,399
6	1,311		

Develop a time-series graph for these data. Describe the time-series components that are present in these data.

16-2: TREND-BASED FORECASTING TECHNIQUES

As we discussed in Section 16-1, some time series exhibit an increasing or decreasing trend. Further, the trend may be linear or nonlinear. A plot of the data will usually be very helpful in identifying which, if any, of these trends exist.

Developing a Trend-Based Forecasting Model

In this section, we introduce *trend-based forecasting techniques*. As the name implies, these techniques are used to identify the presence of a trend and to model that trend. Once the trend model has been defined, it is used to provide forecasts for future time periods.

16-2

TREND-BASED FORECASTING

Excel and
Minitab Tutorial

The Taft Ice Cream Company

The Taft Ice Cream Company is a family-operated company selling gourmet ice cream to resort areas, primarily on the North Carolina coast. Figure 16-6 displays the annual sales data for the past 10 years and shows the time-series plot illustrating that sales have an increasing trend in the 10-year period.

The owners of the Taft Ice Cream Company are considering expanding their ice cream manufacturing facilities. As part of the bank financing requirements, the managers are to supply a forecast of future sales. Recall from our earlier discussions that the forecasting process has three steps: (1) model specification, (2) model fitting, and (3) model diagnosis.

STEP 1: Model Specification—The time-series plot in Figure 16-6 indicates that the sales have exhibited a linear growth pattern. A possible forecasting tool is a linear trend (straight-line) model.

STEP 2: Model-fitting—Since we have specified a linear trend model, the process of fitting can be accomplished using least-squares regression analysis of a form described by Equation 16-1.

LINEAR TREND MODEL

$$y_t = \beta_0 + \beta_1 t + \epsilon_t$$ **16-1**

where:

y_t = Value of the trend at time t
β_0 = y intercept of the trend line
β_1 = Slope of the trend line
t = Time $(t = 1, 2, \dots)$

We let the first period in the time series be $t = 1$, the second period be $t = 2$, and so forth. The values for time form the independent variable with sales being the dependent variable. Referring to Chapter 11, the least squares regression coefficients for the slope and intercept are estimated by Equations 16-2 and 16-3.

FIGURE 16-6
Excel Output—Taft Ice
Cream Sales Trend Line

Excel Instructions:

1. Open file: Taft.xls
2. Select Data
3. Click on Chart Wizard
4. Select Line Graph
5. Define *x*-axis on Series Tab
6. Label Graph

Year	t	Sales
1991	1	$300,000
1992	2	$295,000
1993	3	$330,000
1994	4	$345,000
1995	5	$320,000
1996	6	$370,000
1997	7	$390,000
1998	8	$400,000
1999	9	$395,000
2000	10	$430,000

LEAST SQUARES EQUATIONS

$$b_1 = \frac{\sum_{t=1}^{n} ty_t - \frac{\sum_{t=1}^{n} t \sum_{t=1}^{n} y_t}{n}}{\sum t^2 - \frac{\left(\sum_{t=1}^{n} t\right)^2}{n}}$$ **16-2**

$$b_0 = \bar{y} - b_1 \bar{t}$$ **16-3**

where:

n = Number of periods in the time series
t = Time period (independent variable)
y_t = Dependent variable at time t

The linear regression procedures in either Excel or Minitab can be used to compute the least squares trend model. Figure 16-7 shows the Excel output for the Taft Ice Cream Company example.

The least-squares estimate of the trend model for the Taft Ice Cream Company is:

$$\hat{y}_t = b_0 + b_1 t$$
$$\hat{y}_t = 277{,}333.33 + 14{,}575.76(t)$$

For a forecasting application, we use F_t as the forecast value or predicted value at time period t. Thus:

$$F_t = 277{,}333.33 + 14{,}575.76(t)$$

STEP 3: Model Diagnosis—The linear trend regression output in Figure 16-7 allow for some conclusions about the potential capabilities of our model. The R-square = 0.912 shows that for these 10 years of data, the linear trend model explains over 91% of the variation in sales.

FIGURE 16-7
Excel Output for Taft Ice Cream Trend Model

Excel Instructions

1. Open file: Taft.xls
2. Click Tools
3. Select Data Analysis
4. Select Regression Analysis
5. Define data range for y variable
6. Define data range for the time variable ($t = 1, 2, 3, 4, \ldots 10$)
7. Indicate output location
8. Click OK

Linear trend equation
Sales = 277,333.33 + 14,575.76(t)

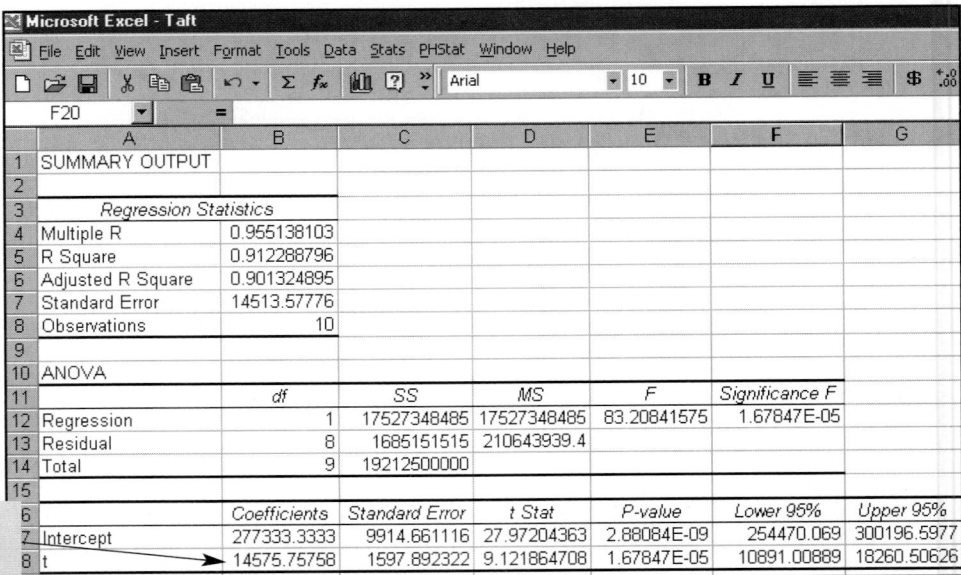

Excel Instructions:
1. Select data to be graphed
2. Click on Chart Wizard
3. Select Line option
4. Define chart format

After Constructing the Line Graph:
5. Click on the data
6. Right Click
7. Click on the Options Tab
8. Select Add Trend Line
9. Select Show Equation

FIGURE 16-8
Excel Output for Taft Ice Cream Trend Line

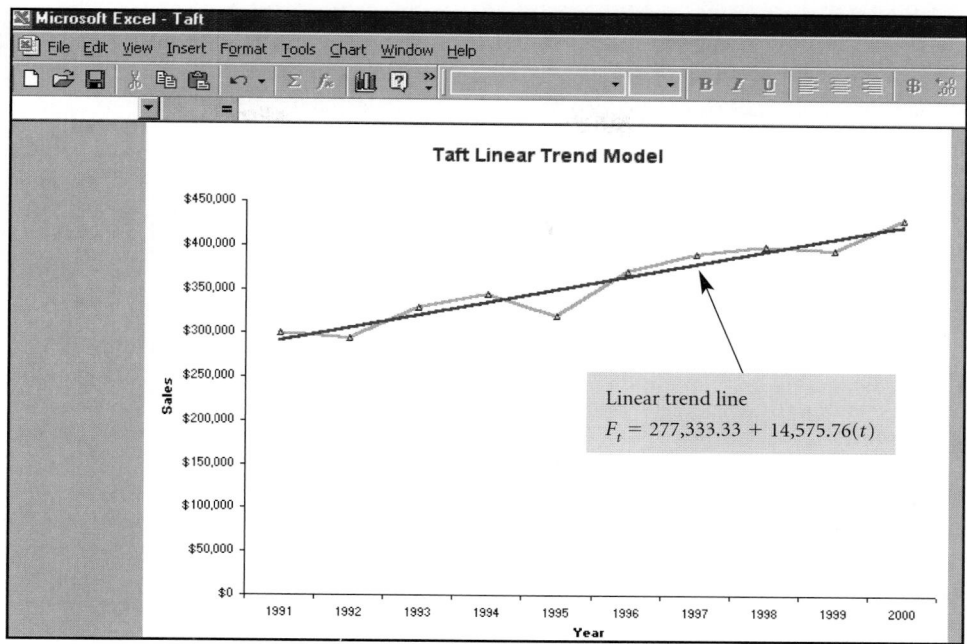

The p-value for the regression slope coefficient is 0.0000168. This means that time (t) explains a significant portion of the variation in sales. Figure 16-8 shows the Excel plot of the trend line through the data. You can see the trend model fits the historical data quite closely. Although these results are a good sign, the model diagnosis step requires further analysis.

Comparing the Forecast Values to the Actual Data

The slope of the trend line indicates the Taft Ice Cream Company has experienced an average increase in sales of $14,575.76 per year over the 10-year period. The linear trend model's fitted sales values for periods $t = 1$ through $t = 10$ can be found by substituting for t in the following forecast equation:

$$F_t = 277,333.33 + 14,575.76(t)$$

For example, for $t = 1$, we get:

$$F_t = 277,333.33 + 14,575.76(1)$$
$$= \$291,909.09$$

Note that the actual sales figure, y_1, for period 1 was $300,000. The difference between the actual sales in time t and the forecast values in time t, found using the trend model, is called the *forecast error* or the *residual*. Figure 16-9 shows the forecasts for periods 1-10 and the forecast errors at each period.

Computing the forecast error by comparing the trend-line values with actual past data is an important part of the model diagnosis step. The errors measure how closely the model fits the actual data at each point. A perfect fit would lead to residuals of 0 each time. We would like to see small residuals and an overall good fit. In addition, the residuals should exhibit no systematic patterns. Two commonly used measures of fit are the mean squared residual or **mean squared error (MSE)**, and **mean absolute deviation (MAD)**. These measures are computed using equations 16-4 and 16-5, respectively. MAD measures the average magnitude of the forecast errors. MSE is a measure of the variability in the forecast errors. The construction of MSE is the same as that for MSE in regression and analysis of variance. The forecast error is the observed value, y_t, minus the predicted value, F_t.

Excel Instructions:

1. Follow instructions on Figure 16-7
2. In the Regression Tool Template, check Residuals option

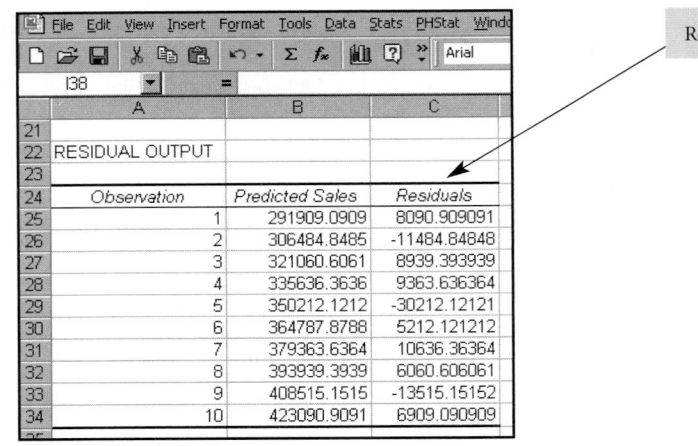

FIGURE 16-9
Excel Residual Output for Taft Ice Cream

MEAN SQUARE ERROR

$$MSE = \frac{\sum_{t=1}^{n}(y_t - F_t)^2}{n} \qquad 16\text{-}4$$

where:

y_t = Actual value at time t
F_t = Predicted value at time t
n = Number of time periods

MEAN ABSOLUTE DEVIATION

$$MAD = \frac{\sum_{t=1}^{n}|y_t - F_t|}{n} \qquad 16\text{-}5$$

where:

y_t = Actual value at time t
F_t = Predicted value at time t
n = Number of time periods

Figure 16-10 shows the MSE and MAD calculations using Excel for the Taft Ice Cream example. For example, the MAD value of 11,042 indicates that the linear trend model has an average absolute error of $11,042 per period. The MSE (in squared units) equals 168,515,152. The square root of the MSE is $12,981, and while it is not equal to the MAD

FIGURE 16-10
Excel MSE and MAD Computations for Taft Ice Cream

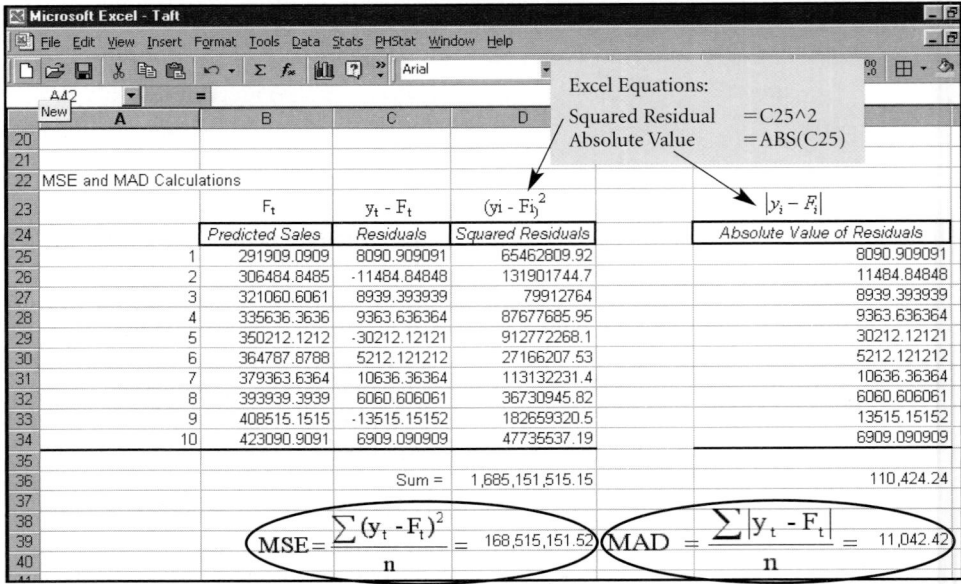

Excel Instructions:

1. Go to the Residual output section of the printout
2. Use Excel formulas to compute squared and absolute value residuals
3. Use Equations 16-4 and 16-5 to determine MSE and MAD.

value, it does provide similar information about the relationship between the forecast values and the actual values of the time series.[1]

These error measures are particularly helpful when comparing two or more forecasting techniques. We can compute the MSE and/or the MAD for each forecasting technique. The forecasting technique that gives the smallest MSE and/or MAD is generally considered to provide the best fit.

TRUE FORECASTS

While a decision maker is interested in how well a forecasting technique can fit the historical data, the real test comes with how well it forecasts future values. In the Taft example, we had 10 years of historical data. If we wish to forecast ice cream sales for year 11 using the linear trend model, we substitute $t = 11$ into the forecast equation to produce a forecast as follows.

$$F_{11} = 277{,}333.33 + 14{,}575.76(11) = \$437{,}666.69$$

This method of forecasting is called *trend projection*. To determine how well our trend model actually forecasts, we would have to wait until the actual sales amount for period 11 is known.

As we just indicated, a model's true forecasting ability is determined by how well it forecasts future values, not by how well it fits historical values. However, having to wait until after the forecast period to know how effective the forecast is doesn't help us assess a model's effectiveness ahead of time. This problem can be partially overcome by using *split samples*, which involves dividing the time series into two groups. You put the first (n_1) periods of historical data in the first group. These n_1 periods will be used to develop the forecasting model. The second group contains the remaining (n_2) periods of historical data, which will be used to test the model's forecasting ability. These data are called the *holdout data*. Usually, between 3 and 5 periods are held out, depending on the total number of available periods in the time series.

In the Taft Ice Cream example, we have only 10 years of historical data, so we will hold out the last 3 periods and use the first 7 periods to develop the linear trend model. The computations are performed as before, using Excel and Equations 16-2 and 16-3. Since we are using a different data set to develop the linear equation, we get a slightly different trend line than when all 10 periods were used.

$$F_t = 277{,}142.85 + 14{,}642.85(t)$$

This model is now used to provide forecasts for periods 8–10 by using trend projection. These forecasts are:

YEAR t	ACTUAL y_t	FORECAST F_t	ERROR $(y_t - F_t)$
8	400,000	394,285.65	5,714.35
9	395,000	408,928.50	−13,928.50
10	430,000	423,571.35	6,428.65

Then we can compute the MSE and the MAD values for periods 8–10.

$$\text{MSE} = [(5{,}714.35)^2 + (-13{,}928.50)^2 + (6{,}428.65)^2]/3 = 89{,}328{,}149.67$$

and

$$\text{MAD} = (|5{,}714.35| + |-13{,}928.50| + |6{,}428.65|)/3 = 8{,}690.50$$

These values could be compared with those produced using other forecasting techniques or evaluated against the forecaster's own standards. While smaller values are preferred, other factors should also be considered. For instance, in some cases, the forecast

---

[1]Technically, this is the square root of the average squared distance between the forecasts and the observed data values. Algebraically, of course, this is not the same as the average forecast error but it is comparable.

values might tend to be higher (or lower) than the actual values. This may imply that the linear trend model isn't the best model to use. Forecasting models that tend to over forecast or under forecast are said to contain **forecast bias**. Equation 16-6 is used as an estimator of the forecast bias.

FORECAST BIAS

$$\text{Forecast Bias} = \frac{\sum_{t=1}^{n}(y_t - F_t)}{n}$$

or:

$$\text{Forecast Bias} = \frac{\sum(\text{error})}{n}$$

16-6

The forecast bias can be either positive or negative. A positive value indicates a tendency to under forecast. A negative value indicates a tendency to over forecast. The estimated bias taken from the forecasts for periods 8–10 in our example is:

$$\text{Forecast Bias} = [(5,714.35) + (-13,928.50) + (6,428.65)]/3 = -595.17$$

This means that the model is estimated to over forecast sales by an average of $595.17.

Suppose we determine on the basis of our forecast bias estimate that the linear trend model does an acceptable job in forecasting. Then all available data (periods 1–10) would be used to develop a linear trend model (see Figure 16-7), and a trend projection would be used to forecast for future time periods by substituting appropriate values for t into the trend model.

$$F_t = 277,333.33 + 14,575.76(t)$$

However, if the linear model is judged to be unacceptable, the forecaster will need to try a different technique. For the purpose of the bank loan application, the Taft Ice Cream Company needs to forecast sales for the next 3 years (periods 11–13.) Assuming the linear trend model is acceptable, these forecasts are:

$$F_{11} = 277,333.33 + 14,575.76(11) = \$437,666.69$$
$$F_{12} = 277,333.33 + 14,575.76(12) = \$452,242.45$$
$$F_{13} = 277,333.33 + 14,575.76(13) = \$466,818.21$$

Nonlinear Trend Forecasting

As we indicated earlier, you may encounter a time series that exhibits a nonlinear trend. Figure 16-3 showed an example of a nonlinear trend. When the historical data show a nonlinear trend, you should consider using a nonlinear trend forecasting model. A common method for dealing with nonlinear trends is to use an extension of the linear trend method. This extension calls for making a data transformation before applying the least-squares regression analysis.

16-3

NONLINEAR TREND

Excel and
Minitab Tutorial

Harrison Equipment Company

Consider the situation of Harrison Equipment Company, which leases large construction equipment to contractors in the Southwest. The lease arrangements call for Harrison to perform all repairs and maintenance on leased equipment. Figure 16-11 shows the repair costs for a crawler tractor on lease to a contractor in Phoenix, for the past 20 quarters. The data are contained in the file called **Harrison**. The data are also plotted in the line chart shown in Figure 16-11.

Harrison Equipment is interested in forecasting future repair costs for the crawler tractor. Recall that the first step in forecasting is model specification. Even though the plot in Figure 16-11 indicates a sharp upward nonlinear trend, assume the forecaster starts by

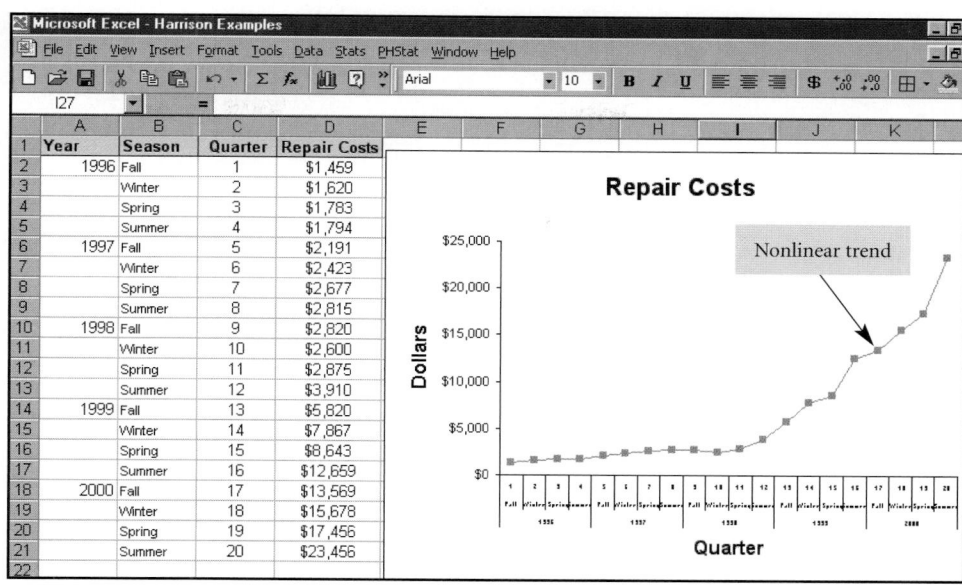

FIGURE 16-11
Excel Time-Series Plot for
Harrison Equipment Repair
Costs

Excel Instructions:

1. Open file: Harrison.xls
2. Select Repair Cost data
3. Click on Chart Wizard
4. Select Line Graph
5. Under Series Tab, define x axis labels as columns A–C
6. Complete labeling

specifying a linear trend model. As a part of the model fitting step she could use Excel's regression procedure to obtain the linear forecasting model shown in Figure 16-12:

$$F_t = -3,357.54 + 958.408\,(t)$$

The fit is pretty good with an R-square $= 0.7719$, but we need to look closer. Figure 16-13 shows the predicted values and errors for the 20 quarters of historical data and a computed MAD value equal to $2,346.44$, which is quite high given the size of the company's quarterly repair costs. Figure 16-12 shows a plot of the trend line compared with the actual data. A close inspection of the data in Figure 16-13 (high MAD value) and the graph in Figure 16-12 indicate that the linear trend model may not be best for this case. Notice in Figures 16-12 and 16-13 that the linear model under forecasts, then over fore-

FIGURE 16-12
Excel Output for the
Harrison Equipment
Company Linear Trend
Model

Forecast equation
$F_t = -3357.54 + 958.408\,(t)$

Excel Instructions:

1. Open file: Harrison.xls
2. Click on Tools tab
3. Select Regression
4. Define dependent variable
5. Define the independent variable ($t = 1, 2, 3, \ldots, 20$)
6. Check Residuals
7. Copy graph onto sheet (see Figure 16-11)

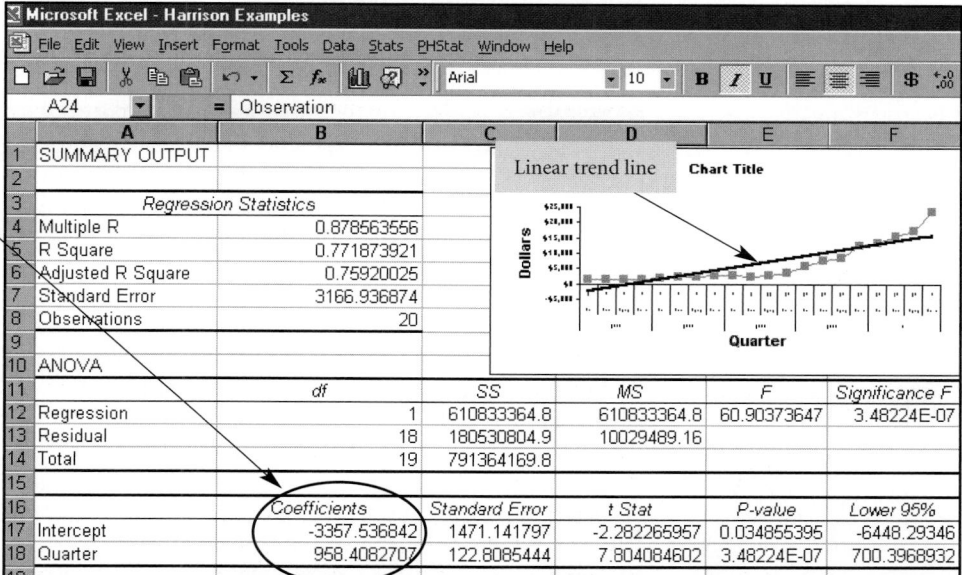

Excel Output:

1. Use Residual Output from Regression (see Figure 16-12)
2. Compute Absolute Residuals using ABS function
3. Compute MAD using formula: =SUM(D25:D44)/COUNT(D25:D44)

Microsoft Excel - Harrison Examples

D28 = =ABS(C28)

	A	B	C	D	E
24	Observation	Predicted Repair Costs	Residuals	Absolute Values	
25	1	-2,399.13	3,858.13	3,858.13	
26	2	-1,440.72	3,060.72	3,060.72	
27	3	-482.31	2,265.31	2,265.31	
28	4	476.10	1,317.90	1,317.90	
29	5	1,434.50	756.50	756.50	
30	6	2,392.91	30.09	30.09	
31	7	3,351.32	-674.32	674.32	
32	8	4,309.73	-1,494.73	1,494.73	
33	9	5,268.14	-2,448.14	2,448.14	
34	10	6,226.55	-3,626.55	3,626.55	
35	11	7,184.95	-4,309.95	4,309.95	
36	12	8,143.36	-4,233.36	4,233.36	
37	13	9,101.77	-3,281.77	3,281.77	
38	14	10,060.18	-2,193.18	2,193.18	
39	15	11,018.59	-2,375.59	2,375.59	
40	16	11,977.00	682.00	682.00	
41	17	12,935.40	633.60	633.60	
42	18	13,893.81	1,784.19	1,784.19	
43	19	14,852.22	2,603.78	2,603.78	
44	20	15,810.63	7,645.37	7,645.37	
45		Total =	0.000	2,346.44	= MAD

FIGURE 16-13
Excel Residuals and MAD Computation

casts, then under forecasts again. This pattern means that specifying a nonlinear trend may provide a better fit for these data.

To account for the nonlinear growth trend shown in Figure 16-11, which starts out slowly and then builds rapidly, the forecaster might consider transforming the time variable by squaring t to form a model of the form

$$y_t = \beta_0 + \beta_1 t^2 + \epsilon_t$$

This transformation is suggested because the growth in costs appears to be increasing at an increasing rate. Other nonlinear trends may require different types of transformations, such as taking a square root or natural log. Each situation must be analyzed separately. (See the text by Neter et al., listed in the Chapter References section, for further discussion of transformations. Also refer to the discussion on polynomial transformations in Chapter 12 of this text.) Figure 16-14 shows the Excel regression result using the transformation. Figure 16-15 shows the revised time-series plot using the t^2 transformation.

FIGURE 16-14
Excel Transformed Regression Model for Harrison Equipment

Microsoft Excel - Harrison Examples

G45 =

	A	B	C	D	E	F	G
1	SUMMARY OUTPUT						
2							
3	Regression Statistics						
4	Multiple R	0.959981211					
5	R Square	0.921563926					
6	Adjusted R Square	0.917206367					
7	Standard Error	1856.99127					
8	Observations	20					
9							
10	ANOVA						
11		df	SS	MS	F	Significance F	
12	Regression	1	729292671.4	729292671.4	211.4862445	2.16184E-11	
13	Residual	18	62071498.38	3448416.577			
14	Total	19	791364169.8				
15							
16		Coefficients	Standard Error	t Stat	P-value	Lower 95%	Upper 95%
17	Intercept	-245.255771	633.1527519	-0.387356401	0.70303438	-1575.461372	1084.94983
18	t -squared	48.43906461	3.330847009	14.54256664	2.16184E-11	41.4412093	55.43691992

Forecast equation
$F_t = -245.256 + 48.439t^2$

Excel Instructions:

1. Open file: Harrison.xls
2. Click on Tools tab
3. Select Regression
4. Define dependent variable
5. Define the independent variable (t-squared = 1, 4, 9, . . ., 400)
6. Check Residuals

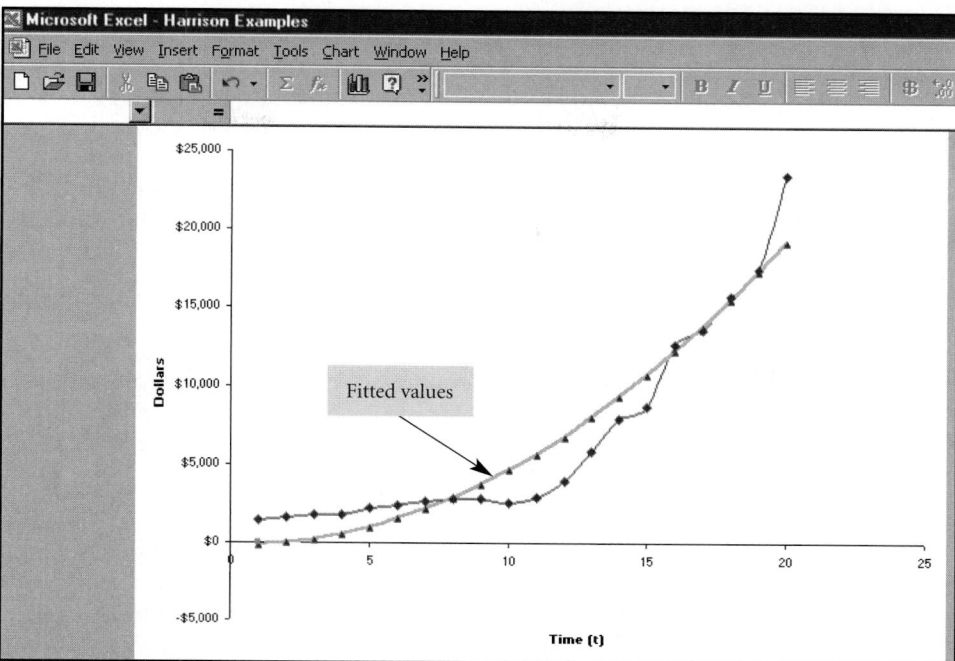

FIGURE 16-15
Transformed Model for Harrison Equipment Company

Visually, the transformed model now looks more appropriate. The fit is much better as the *R*-square value is increased to 0.922. Figure 16-16 shows the forecast values and errors for periods 1–20. The model's fit is improved, as evidenced by a reduction in the MAD from $2,346.44 (for the linear model) to $1,415.56.

Forecasts for periods 21 and 22, using this latest model, are obtained using the trend projection method.

For period $t = 21$:
$$F_{21} = -245.256 + 48.439(21^2) = \$21,116.34$$

FIGURE 16-16
Transformed Model MAD Calculation for Harrison Equipment

	A	B	C	D	E
24	*Observation*	*Predicted Repair Costs*	*Residuals*	*Absolute Values*	
25	1	-196.82	1,655.82	1,655.82	
26	2	-51.50	1,671.50	1,671.50	
27	3	190.70	1,592.30	1,592.30	
28	4	529.77	1,264.23	1,264.23	
29	5	965.72	1,225.28	1,225.28	
30	6	1,498.55	924.45	924.45	
31	7	2,128.26	548.74	548.74	
32	8	2,854.84	-39.84	39.84	
33	9	3,678.31	-858.31	858.31	
34	10	4,598.65	-1,998.65	1,998.65	
35	11	5,615.87	-2,740.87	2,740.87	
36	12	6,729.97	-2,819.97	2,819.97	
37	13	7,940.95	-2,120.95	2,120.95	
38	14	9,248.80	-1,381.80	1,381.80	
39	15	10,653.53	-2,010.53	2,010.53	
40	16	12,155.14	503.86	503.86	
41	17	13,753.63	-184.63	184.63	
42	18	15,449.00	229.00	229.00	
43	19	17,241.25	214.75	214.75	
44	20	19,130.37	4,325.63	4,325.63	
45				1,415.56 = MAD	

Excel Output:

1. Use Residual Output from Regression (see Figure 16-14)
2. Compute Absolute Residuals using ABS function
3. Compute MAD using formula:
   =SUM(D25:D44)/COUNT(D25:D44)

For period $t = 22$:
$$F_{22} = -245.256 + 48.439(22^2) = \$23,199.22$$

Using transformations often provides a very effective way of improving the fit of a time series. However, a forecaster should be careful not to get caught up in an exercise of "curve-fitting." One suggestion is that only explainable terms—terms that can be justified—be used for transforming data. For instance, in our example, we might well expect repair costs to increase at a faster rate as a tractor gets older and begins wearing out. Thus, the t^2 transformation seems to make sense.

SOME WORDS OF CAUTION

The trend projection method relies on the future behaving in a manner similar to the past. In the previous example, if equipment repair costs continue to follow the pattern displayed over the past 20 quarters, these forecasts may prove acceptable. However, if the future pattern changes, there is no reason to believe these forecasts will be close to actual costs.

Adjusting for Seasonality

In Section 16-1, we discussed seasonality in a time series. The seasonal component represents those changes (highs and lows) in the time series that occur at approximately the same interval throughout the time series. If the forecasting model that you are using does not already explicitly account for seasonality, you should adjust your forecast to take into account the seasonal component if one exists. The linear and nonlinear trend models discussed thus far do not automatically incorporate the seasonal component. Forecasts using these models should be adjusted as illustrated in the following example.

EXAMPLE
16-4

SEASONAL
ADJUSTMENT

Big Mountain Ski Resort

Most businesses associated with the tourist industry are aware that their sales are seasonal. For example, at the Big Mountain Ski Resort, business peaks at two times during the year: winter for skiing and summer for golf and tennis. These peaks can be identified in a time series if the sales data are measured on at least a quarterly basis. Figure 16-17 shows the quarterly sales data for the past 4 years in spreadsheet form. The line chart for these data is also shown. The data are in the file called **Big Mountain**.

FIGURE 16-17
Big Mountain Resort
Quarterly Sales Data

Excel Instructions:

1. Open file: Big Mountain.xls
2. Select Sales column
3. Click on Chart Wizard
4. Select Series tab
5. Define *x* axis as columns B and C

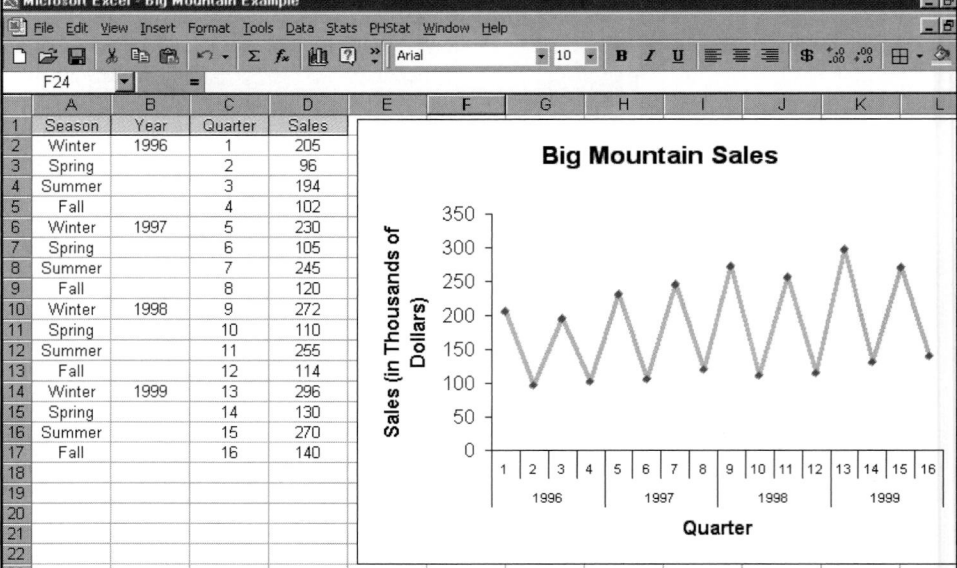

Excel and Minitab Tutorial

The time-series plot clearly shows that the summer and winter quarters are the busy times. There has also been a slightly increasing linear trend in sales over the 4 years.

Big Mountain Resort wants to forecast sales for each quarter of the coming year, and it hopes to use a linear trend model. When the historical data reflect both a trend and seasonality, the trend-based forecasting model needs to be adjusted to incorporate the seasonality. This can be done by computing **seasonal indexes**.

SEASONAL INDEX

A number used to quantify the effect of seasonality in time-series data.

For instance, when we have quarterly data, we can develop four seasonal indexes, one each for winter, spring, summer, and fall. A seasonal index below 1.00 indicates that the quarter has values that are typically below the average value for the year. On the other hand, an index greater than 1.00 indicates that the quarter's value is higher than average.

COMPUTING SEASONAL INDEXES

While there are several methods for computing seasonal indexes, the procedure introduced here is the *ratio-to-moving-average method*. This method assumes that the actual time-series data can be represented as a product of the four time-series components: trend, seasonal, cyclical, and random, which produces the **multiplicative model** shown in Equation 16-7.

MULTIPLICATIVE TIME-SERIES MODEL

$$y_t = T_t \times S_t \times C_t \times I_t \qquad \textbf{16-7}$$

where:

y_t = Value of the time series at time t
T_t = Trend value at time t
S_t = Seasonal value at time t
C_t = Cyclical value at time t
I_t = Residual or random value at time t

The ratio-to-moving-average method begins by removing the seasonal and random components S_t and I_t from the data, leaving the combined trend and cyclical components T_t and C_t. This is done by first computing successive four-period moving averages (because we have quarterly data) for the time series. Using the Big Mountain sales data in Figure 16-17, we find that the **moving average** using the first four quarters is:

$$\frac{205 + 96 + 194 + 102}{4} = 149.25$$

MOVING AVERAGES

The successive averages of n consecutive values in a time series.

This moving average is associated with the middle time period of the data values in the moving average. The middle period of the first four quarters is 2.5 (between quarter 2 and quarter 3).

The second moving average value is found by dropping the value from period 1 and adding the value from period 5 as follows.

$$\frac{96 + 194 + 102 + 230}{4} = 155.50$$

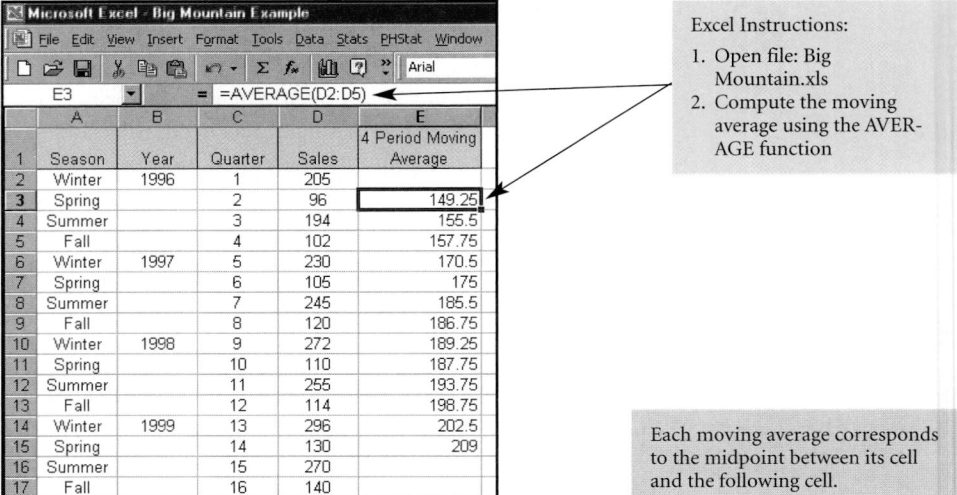

FIGURE 16-18
Seasonal Index—Step 1:
Moving Average Values for
Big Mountain Resort

Excel Instructions:
1. Open file: Big Mountain.xls
2. Compute the moving average using the AVER-AGE function

Each moving average corresponds to the midpoint between its cell and the following cell.

This moving average is associated with time period 3.5, the middle period between quarters 3 and 4.

Figure 16-18 shows the moving averages for the Big Mountain sales data in Excel spreadsheet form. We selected 4 data values for the moving average because we have quarterly data; with monthly data, 12 data values would have been used.

The next step is to compute the *centered moving averages* by averaging each successive pair of moving averages. Centering the moving averages is necessary so that the resulting moving average will be associated with one of the data set's original time periods. In this example Big Mountain is interested in quarterly sales data, (i.e., time periods 1, 2, 3, etc.). Therefore, the moving averages we have representing time periods 2.5, 3.5, etc. are not of interest to Big Mountain.[2] Centering these latter time series, however, produces moving averages for the (quarterly) time periods of interest. For example, the first two moving averages are averaged to produce the first centered moving average. We get:

$$\frac{149.25 + 155.5}{2} = 152.38$$

This centered moving average is associated with quarter 3. The centered moving averages are shown in Figure 16-19. These values estimate the $T_t \times C_t$ value.

If the number of data values used for a moving average is odd, the moving average would be associated with the time period of the middle observation. In such cases, we would not have to center the moving average as we did in Figure 16-19 since the moving averages would already be associated with one of the original time periods from the original time series.

Next, we estimate the $S_t \times I_t$ value by dividing the actual sales value for each quarter by the corresponding centered moving average, as in Equation 16-8. As an example, we examine the third time period: summer of the first year. The sales value of 194 is divided by the centered moving average of 152.38, to produce 1.273. This value is called the *ratio-to-moving-average*. Figure 16-20 shows these values for the Big Mountain data.

RATIO-TO-MOVING-AVERAGE

$$S_t \times I_t = \frac{y_t}{T_t \times C_t}$$

16-8

---

[2]Excel's tabular format does not allow the uncentered moving averages to be displayed with their "inter-quarter" time periods, e.g., 149.25 is associated with time period 2.5, 155.50 with time period 3.5, etc.

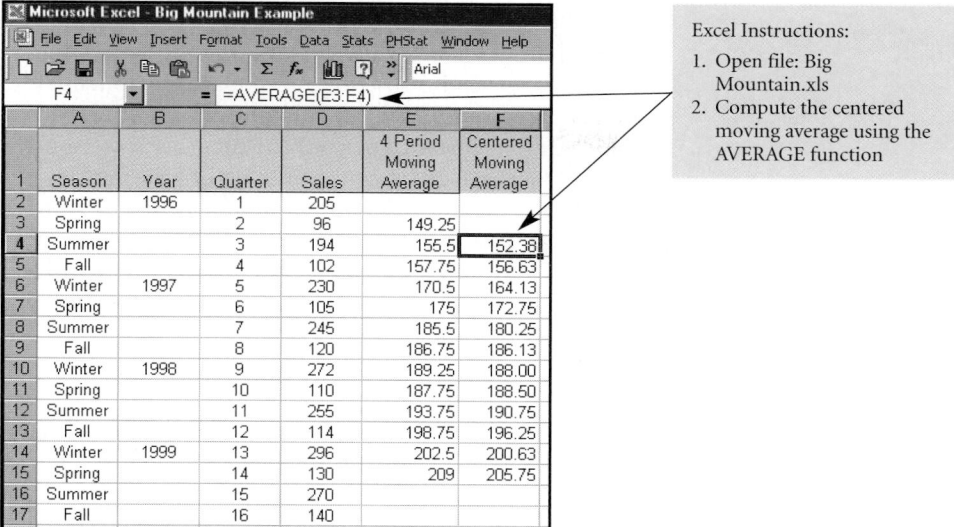

FIGURE 16-19
Seasonal Index—Step 2: Big
Mountain Resort Centered
Moving Averages

The final step in determining the seasonal indexes is to compute the mean ratio-to-moving-average value for each season. Each quarter's ratio-to-moving-averages are averaged over the years to produce the seasonal index for that quarter. Figure 16-21 shows the seasonal indexes. Thus, the seasonal index for the winter quarter is 1.441. This indicates that sales for Big Mountain during the winter are 44.1% above the average for the year. Also, sales in the spring quarter are only 60.8% of the average for the year.

One important point about the seasonal indexes is that the sum of the indexes is equal to the number of seasonal indexes. That is, the average seasonal index equals 1.0. In the Big Mountain Resort example we find:

$$\underset{1.323}{\text{Summer}} + \underset{0.626}{\text{Fall}} + \underset{1.441}{\text{Winter}} + \underset{0.608}{\text{Spring}} = 3.998 \text{ (difference from 4 due to rounding)}$$

Likewise, in an example with monthly data instead of quarterly data, we would generate 12 seasonal indexes, one for each month. The sum of these indexes would be 12.

FIGURE 16-20   Seasonal Index—Step 3: Big
Mountain Resort: Ratio-to-Moving-Averages

FIGURE 16-21   Seasonal Index—
Step 4: Big Mountain Resort: Mean Ratios

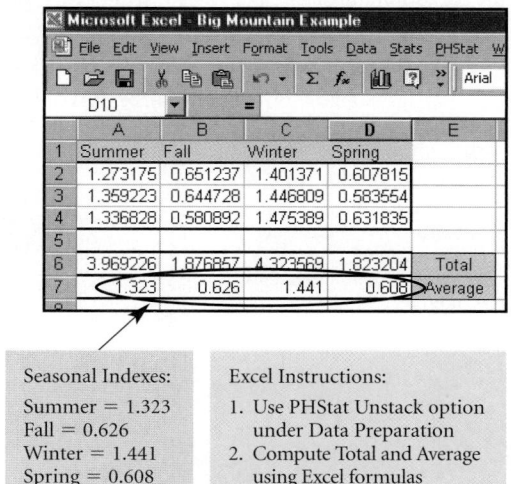

THE NEED TO NORMALIZE THE INDEXES

If the sum of the seasonal indexes does not equal the number of time periods in the recurrence period of the time series, an adjustment is necessary. In the Big Mountain Resort example, the sum of the four seasonal indexes may have been something other than 4 (the recurrence period). In such cases, we must adjust the seasonal indexes by multiplying each index by the number of time periods in the recurrence period over the sum of the unadjusted seasonal indexes. For quarterly data such as the Big Mountain Resort example, we would multiply each index by 4/(sum of the unadjusted seasonal indexes). Performing this multiplication will *normalize* the seasonal indexes. This adjustment is necessary if the seasonal adjustments are going to even out over the recurrence period.

DESEASONALIZING

A strong seasonal component may partially mask a trend in the time-series data. Consequently, to identify the trend you should first remove the effect of the seasonal component. This is called **deseasonalizing** the time series.

Again, assume that the multiplicative model shown in Equation 16-7 is appropriate.

$$y_t = T_t \times S_t \times C_t \times I_t$$

Deseasonalizing is accomplished by dividing y_t by the appropriate seasonal index, S_t, as shown in Equation 16-9.

DESEASONALIZATION

$$T_t \times C_t \times I_t = \frac{y_t}{S_t}$$

16-9

For time period 1, which is the winter quarter, the seasonal index is 1.441. The deseasonalized value for y_1 is:

$$205/1.441 = 142.26$$

FIGURE 16-22
Deseasonalized Time Series
for Big Mountain Sales Data

Excel Instructions:

1. Use Excel formula to compute Deseasonalized Sales
2. Select Chart Wizard line chart option
3. Specify x axis label as column B and C

Seasonal Indexes

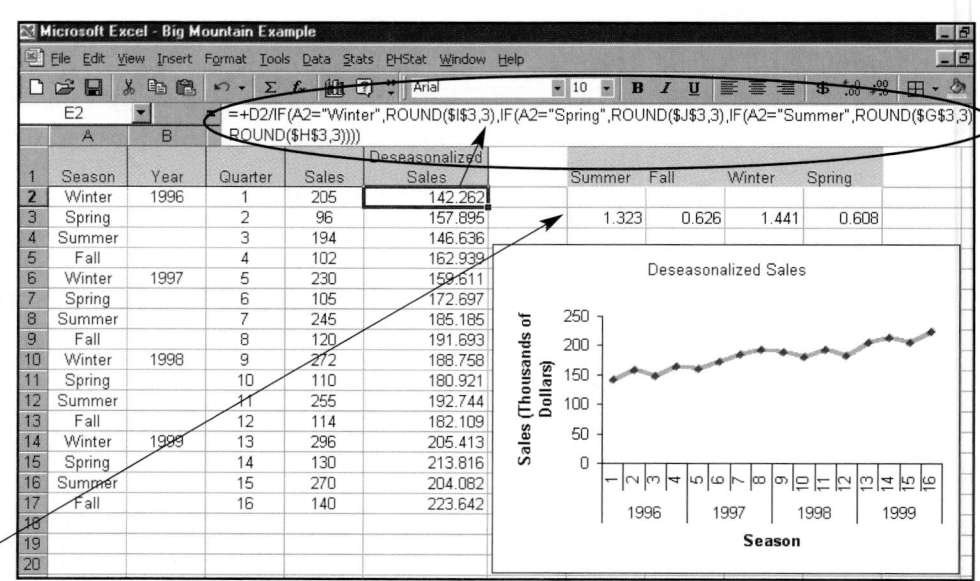

Figure 16-22 presents the deseasonalized values and the graph of these deseasonalized sales data for the Big Mountain example. This shows that there has been a gentle upward trend over the 4 years.

Once the data have been deseasonalized, the next step is to determine the trend. As in the previous examples of trend estimation, you can use either Excel or Minitab to develop the linear model for the deseasonalized data. The results are shown in Figure 16-23. The linear regression trend-line equation is

$$F_t = 142.096 + 4.683(t)$$

You can use this trend line and the trend-projection method to forecast sales for period $t = 17$.

$$F_{17} = 142.096 + 4.683(17) = 221.707 = \$221,707$$

This is a **seasonally unadjusted forecast**, because the time-series data used in developing the trend line were deseasonalized.

SEASONALLY UNADJUSTED FORECAST

A forecast made for seasonal data that does not include an adjustment for the seasonal component in the time series.

Now we need to adjust the forecast for period 17 to reflect the quarterly fluctuations. We do this by multiplying the unadjusted forecast values by the appropriate seasonal index. In this case, period 17 corresponds to the winter quarter. The winter quarter has a seasonal index of 1.441, indicating a high sales period. The adjusted forecast is:

$$F_{17} = (221.707)(1.441) = 319.48 \text{ or } \$319,480$$

The seasonally adjusted forecasts for each quarter in year 5 are:

QUARTER (YEAR 5)	t	UNADJUSTED FORECAST	INDEX	ADJUSTED FORECAST
Winter	17	221.707	1.441	319.480 = \$319,480
Spring	18	226.390	0.608	137.645 = \$137,645
Summer	19	231.073	1.323	305.710 = \$305,710
Fall	20	235.756	0.626	147.583 = \$147,583

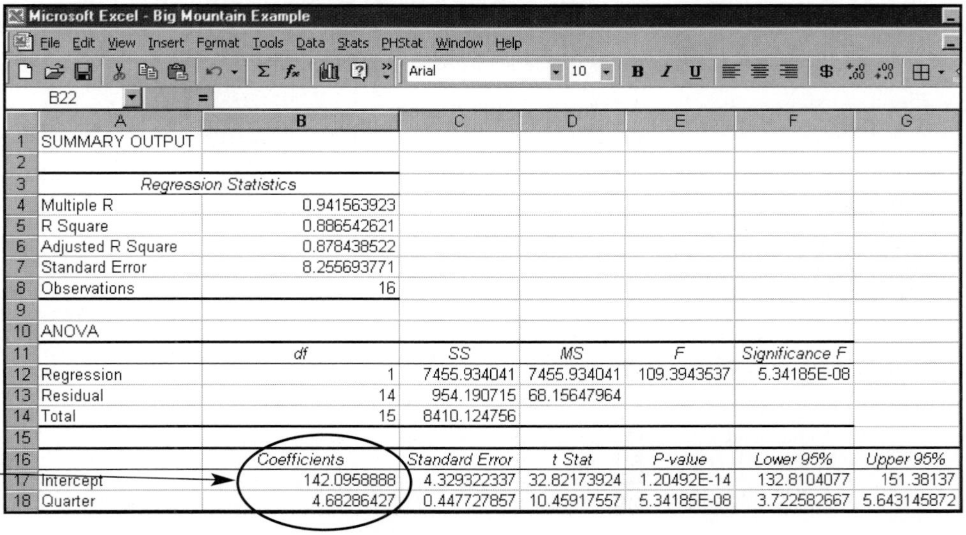

FIGURE 16-23
Regression Trend Line of Big Mountain Deseasonalized Data

Excel Instructions:

1. Select Tools
2. Click on Regression
3. Define y variable as deseasonalized data
4. Define x variable as quarter number ($t = 1$, 2, 3, . . ., 16)

Linear trend equation
$F_t = 142.096 + 4.683(t)$

	A	B	C	D	E	F	G
1	SUMMARY OUTPUT						
2							
3	Regression Statistics						
4	Multiple R	0.941563923					
5	R Square	0.886542621					
6	Adjusted R Square	0.878438522					
7	Standard Error	8.255693771					
8	Observations	16					
9							
10	ANOVA						
11		df	SS	MS	F	Significance F	
12	Regression	1	7455.934041	7455.934041	109.3943537	5.34185E-08	
13	Residual	14	954.190715	68.15647964			
14	Total	15	8410.124756				
15							
16		Coefficients	Standard Error	t Stat	P-value	Lower 95%	Upper 95%
17	Intercept	142.0958888	4.329322337	32.82173924	1.20492E-14	132.8104077	151.38137
18	Quarter	4.68286427	0.447727857	10.45917557	5.34185E-08	3.722582667	5.643145872

REVIEW OF THE SEASONAL ADJUSTMENT PROCESS

We can summarize the steps for performing a seasonal adjustment to a trend-based forecast as follows.

STEP 1. Compute each moving average from the *k* appropriate consecutive data values where *k* is the number of values in one recurrence period of the time series.

STEP 2. Compute the centered moving averages.

STEP 3. Isolate the seasonal component by computing the ratio-to-moving-average values.

STEP 4. Compute the seasonal indexes by averaging the ratio-to-moving-averages for comparable periods.

STEP 5. Normalize the seasonal indexes (if necessary).

STEP 6. Deseasonalize the time series by dividing the actual data by the appropriate seasonal index.

STEP 7. Use least-squares regression to develop the trend line using the deseasonalized data.

STEP 8. Develop the unadjusted forecasts using trend projection.

STEP 9. Seasonally adjust the forecasts by multiplying the unadjusted forecasts by the appropriate seasonal index.

You can use the seasonally adjusted trend model when the time series exhibits both a trend and seasonality. This process allows for a better identification of the trend and produces forecasts that are more sensitive to seasonality in the data.

Minitab contains a procedure for generating seasonal indexes and seasonally adjusted forecasts. Figure 16-24 shows the Minitab results for the Big Mountain Ski Resort example.

FIGURE 16-24
Minitab Output Showing Big Mountain Seasonal Indexes

Minitab Instructions:

1. Open file: Big Mountain.mtw
2. Select Stat
3. Click on Time Series
4. Select Decomposition
5. Define the variable
6. Determine seasonal length (4 quarters, 12 months, etc.)
7. Select Multiplicative Model Type
8. Use Trend plus Seasonal for Model Components
9. Generate 4 forecasts

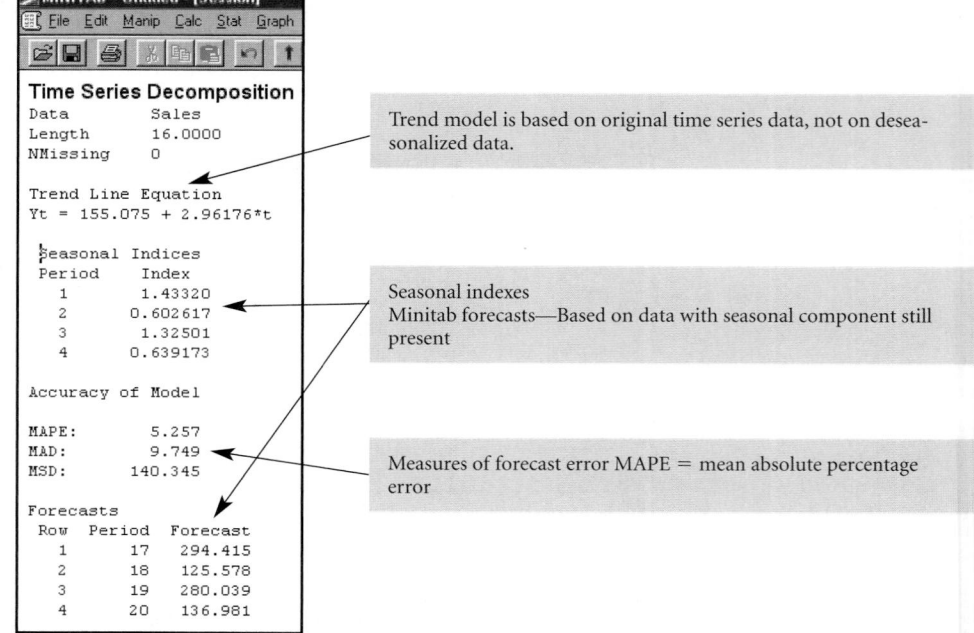

```
MINITAB - Untitled - [Session]
 File  Edit  Manip  Calc  Stat  Graph

Time Series Decomposition
Data        Sales
Length      16.0000
NMissing    0

Trend Line Equation
Yt = 155.075 + 2.96176*t

Seasonal Indices
Period    Index
  1       1.43320
  2       0.602617
  3       1.32501
  4       0.639173

Accuracy of Model

MAPE:      5.257
MAD:       9.749
MSD:     140.345

Forecasts
Row  Period  Forecast
 1     17    294.415
 2     18    125.578
 3     19    280.039
 4     20    136.981
```

Trend model is based on original time series data, not on deseasonalized data.

Seasonal indexes
Minitab forecasts—Based on data with seasonal component still present

Measures of forecast error MAPE = mean absolute percentage error

Notice that the forecast option in Minitab gives different forecasts than we showed earlier. This is because Minitab generates the linear trend model using the original sales data rather than the deseasonalized data. Our suggestion is to use Minitab to generate the seasonal indexes but then follow our outline to generate seasonally adjusted forecasts.[3]

OPTIONAL CD-ROM TOPIC Regression Based Forecasting Models

Regression models of various forms can be used to develop both short- and long-term forecasts. For more information, go to the CD-ROM.

OPTIONAL CD-ROM TOPIC Autocorrelation and the Durbin-Watson Test

When using regression analysis with time-series data, a necessary assumption is that the residuals (forecast errors) are independent from time period to time period. This means that successive residuals are uncorrelated. A test referred to as the Durbin-Watson test is used to determine if the assumption is satisfied. For more information, go to the CD-ROM.

16-2: EXERCISES

ADDITIONAL EXERCISES ON YOUR CD-ROM

Try the ADDITIONAL EXERCISES and APPLICATION PROBLEMS on the CD-ROM.

16-10. How does model specification differ from model fitting?

16-11. Consider the following set of sales data given in millions of dollars.

1997		1999	
1st quarter	152	1st quarter	217
2d quarter	162	2d quarter	209
3d quarter	157	3d quarter	202
4th quarter	167	4th quarter	221
1998		**2000**	
1st quarter	182	1st quarter	236
2d quarter	192	2d quarter	242
3d quarter	191	3d quarter	231
4th quarter	197	4th quarter	224

a. Plot these data. Based on your visual observations, what time-series components are present in the data?

b. Determine the seasonal index for each quarter.

c. Fit a linear trend model to the data for the years 1997–2000, and determine the MAD and MSE values. Comment on the adequacy of the linear trend model based on these measures of forecast error.

d. Provide a seasonally unadjusted forecast using the linear trend model for each quarter of the year 2001.

e. Use the seasonal index values computed in part b to provide seasonally adjusted forecasts for each quarter of the year 2001.

16-12. Consider the following set of inventory data given in hundreds of thousands of dollars.

---

[3]Neither Excel nor PHStat offers a procedure for automatically generating seasonal indexes. However, as shown in the Big Mountain example, you can use the spreadsheet formulas to do this. See the Excel tutorial on your CD-ROM.

1997		1999	
1st quarter	109	1st quarter	118
2d quarter	95	2d quarter	103
3d quarter	115	3d quarter	126
4th quarter	108	4th quarter	120

1998		2000	
1st quarter	115	1st quarter	130
2d quarter	110	2d quarter	127
3d quarter	120	3d quarter	138
4th quarter	116	4th quarter	135

a. Plot these data. Based on your visual observations, what time-series components are present in the data?

b. Determine the seasonal index for each quarter and convert the data to deseasonalized data.

c. Fit a linear trend model to the deseasonalized data for the years 1997–1999. Compute the MAD and MSE values for the seasonally adjusted forecasts for the year 2000. Comment on the adequacy of the linear trend model based on these measures of forecast error.

d. Provide a seasonally unadjusted forecast using the linear trend model for each quarter for the year 2001.

e. Use the seasonal index values computed in part b to provide seasonally adjusted forecasts for each quarter of the year 2001. Compare the results of the forecasts made in parts c and d.

Business Applications

16-13. Manuel Gutierrez correctly predicted the increasing need for home healthcare services due to the country's aging population. Five years ago, he started a company offering meal delivery, physical therapy, and minor housekeeping services in the New Orleans area. Since that time he has opened offices in 7 additional Gulf state cities. Manuel is presently analyzing the revenue data from his first location for the first 5 years of operation.

	REVENUE ($10,000s)				
	1996	1997	1998	1999	2000
January	23	67	72	76	81
February	34	63	64	75	72
March	45	65	64	77	71
April	48	71	77	81	83
May	46	75	79	86	85
June	49	70	72	75	77
July	60	72	71	80	79
August	65	75	77	82	84
September	67	80	79	86	91
October	60	78	78	87	86
November	71	89	87	91	94
December	76	94	92	96	99

a. Plot these data. Based on your visual observations, what time-series components are present in the data?

b. Determine the seasonal index for each month.

c. (1) Fit a linear trend model to the data for the years 1996–2000, and determine the MAD and MSE for forecasts for each of the months in 2001. (2) Conduct a test of hypothesis to determine if the linear trend model fits the existing data. (3) Comment on the adequacy of the linear trend model based on the measures of forecast error and the hypothesis test you conducted.

d. Manuel had hoped to reach $2,000,000 in revenue by the time he had been in business for 10 years. Based on results in part c, is this a feasible goal? Consider and comment on the size of the standard deviation for this prediction. What makes this standard deviation so large? How does it affect your hypothesis test?

e. Use the seasonal index values computed in part b to provide seasonal adjusted forecasts for each month of the year 2002.

16-14. The Grogan Company operates an egg farm in Wisconsin. The following data represent the number of cases of eggs (in hundreds of thousands) the company has sold in each month over the years 1999–2001. The company is considering expanding facilities and needs to provide the lending institution with a monthly sales forecast for the year 2002.

	1999	2000	2001
January	5.4	5.8	7.0
February	10.4	12.8	14.6
March	18.6	20.1	22.6
April	4.8	8.2	7.6
May	12.2	15.6	16.2
June	14.6	14.8	15.9
July	13.0	11.0	13.0
August	19.4	19.2	17.8
September	26.8	27.0	28.6
October	21.2	21.4	23.0
November	10.2	9.9	13.1
December	6.7	5.6	7.9

a. Plot these data. Based on your visual observations, what time-series components are present in the data?

b. Determine the seasonal index for each quarter.

c. Fit a linear trend model to the data for the years 1999–2001, and determine the MAD and MSE values. Comment on the adequacy of the linear trend model based on these measures of forecast error.

d. Provide a seasonally unadjusted forecast using the linear trend model for each month of the year 2002.

e. Use the seasonal index values computed in part b to provide seasonal adjusted forecasts for each month of the year 2002.

16-15. A major brokerage company has an office in Miami, Florida. The manager of the office is evaluated based on the number of new clients generated each quarter. The following data reflect the number of new customers added during each quarter between 1998 and 2001.

1998		1999	

1st quarter	218	1st quarter	250
2d quarter	190	2d quarter	220
3d quarter	236	3d quarter	265
4th quarter	218	4th quarter	241

2000		**2001**	
1st quarter	244	1st quarter	229
2d quarter	228	2d quarter	221
3d quarter	263	3d quarter	248
4th quarter	240	4th quarter	231

a. Plot the time series and discuss the components that are present in the data.

b. Referring to part a, fit the linear trend model to the data for the years 1998–2000. Then use the resulting model to forecast the number of new brokerage customers for each quarter in the year 2001. Compute the MAD and MSE for these forecasts and discuss the results.

c. Using the data for the years 1998–2000, determine the seasonal indexes for each quarter.

d. Develop a seasonally unadjusted forecast for the four quarters of the year 2001.

e. Using the seasonal indexes computed in part d, determine the seasonally adjusted forecast for each quarter for the year 2001. Compute the MAD and MSE for these forecasts.

f. Examine the values for the MAD and MSE in parts b and e. Which of the two forecasting techniques would you recommend the manager use to forecast the number of new clients generated each quarter? Support your choice by giving your rationale.

16-16. Harsin-Williams & Company is a construction company headquartered in Baton Rouge, Louisiana. A very important issue for construction companies is cash management since they tend to be paid in lump sums when projects are completed or hit milestones. However, their expenses, such as payroll, must be paid regularly. The data file called **Harsin-Williams** contains month-end cash balances (in millions of dollars) for the past 16 months. These data are also shown as follows.

MONTH	CASH BALANCE	MONTH	CASH BALANCE
1	75	9	106
2	70	10	130
3	77	11	155
4	89	12	160
5	80	13	180
6	92	14	199
7	91	15	240
8	102	16	305

a. Plot the data as a time-series graph. Discuss what the graph implies concerning the relationship between cash balance and the time variable, month.

b. Fit a linear trend model to the data. Compute the coefficient of determination for this model, and show the trend line on the time-series graph. Discuss

the appropriateness of the linear trend model. What are the strengths and weaknesses of the model?

c. Referring to part b, compute the MAD and MSE for the 16 data points.

d. Use the t^2 transformation approach and recompute the linear model using the transformed time variable. Plot the new trend line against the transformed data. Discuss whether this model appears to provide a better fit than did the model without the transformation. Compare the coefficients of determination for the two models. Which model seems to be superior using the coefficient of determination as the criterion?

e. Refer to part d. Compute the MAD and MSE for the 16 data values. Discuss how these compare to those that were computed in part c, prior to transformation. Do the measures of fit (R^2, MSE, or MAD) agree upon the best model to use for forecasting purposes?

16-17. Refer to Problem 16.

a. Use the linear trend model (without transformation) for the first 15 months and provide a cash balance forecast for month 16. Then make the t^2 transformation and develop a new linear trend forecasting model based on months 1–15. Forecast the cash balance for month 16. Now compare the accuracy of the forecasts with and without the transformation. Which of the two forecast models would you prefer? Explain your answer.

b. Provide a 95% prediction interval for the cash balance forecast for month 16 using the linear trend model both with and without the transformation. Which interval has the wider width? On this basis which procedure would you choose?

16-18. Volker Sales and Service sells and installs home security systems in the Detroit area. In order to plan for parts inventory, the company needs an accurate forecast for the number of installations it will do each month. The company's sales manager has collected data for the past 12 months. These data are in a file called **Volker** and are shown as follows.

MONTH	INSTALLATIONS	MONTH	INSTALLATIONS
1	60	7	150
2	67	8	148
3	74	9	152
4	104	10	156
5	122	11	150
6	145	12	157

a. Plot the data as a time-series graph. Discuss what the graph implies.

b. Fit a linear trend model to the data. Compute the R-square value and show the trend line on the time-series graph.

c. Transform the time variable by taking the square-root of the month number, and recompute the linear model using the transformed time variable. Discuss whether this model appears to provide a better fit than did the model without the transformation. Compare *R*-square values.

d. Compute the MAD and MSE for the 12 data values for the two models in parts b and c. Discuss which model is the better model to use for forecasting purposes. What are the strengths and weaknesses of the two models?

e. Provide forecasts for the number of installations of home security systems for the next 4 months.

f. The personnel director has been told that when 200 installations a month are reached additional service personnel will be required. Provide an estimate as to the month in which this will occur.

16-19. Referring to Problem 18, use the linear trend model (without transformation) for the first 11 months and provide a forecast of the number of installations for month 12. Then make the $\sqrt{t}$ transformation and develop a new linear trend forecasting model based on months 1–11. Forecast the cash balance for month 12. Now compare the accuracy of the forecasts with and without the transformation. Discuss.

16-3: FORECASTING USING SMOOTHING METHODS

The trend-based forecasting technique introduced in the previous section is widely used and can be very effective in some situations. However, it has a disadvantage in that it gives as much weight to the earliest data in the time series as it does to the data that are close to the period for which the forecast is required. Also, this trend approach does not provide the opportunity for the model to "learn" or "adjust" to changes in the time series.

A class of forecasting techniques called *smoothing models* is widely used to overcome these problems. These models attempt to "smooth out" the random or irregular component in the time series by an averaging process. In this section we introduce two frequently used smoothing-based forecasting techniques: single exponential smoothing and double exponential smoothing. Double exponential smoothing offers a modification to the single exponential smoothing model that specifically deals with trends.

Exponential Smoothing

The trend-based forecasting methods discussed in Section 16-2 are used in many forecasting applications. As we showed, the least-squares trend line is computed using all available historical data. Each observation is given equal input in establishing the trend line, thus allowing the trend line to reflect all the past data. If the future pattern looks like the past, the forecast should be reasonably accurate.

However, in many situations involving time-series data, the more recent the observation, the more indicative it is of possible future values. For example, this month's sales are probably a better indicator of next month's sales than would be sales from 20 months ago. However, the regression analysis approach to trend-based forecasting does not take this fact into account. The data from 20 periods ago will be given the same weight as data from the most current period in developing a forecasting model. This equal valuation can be a drawback to the trend-based forecasting approach.

With **exponential smoothing**, current observations are weighted more heavily than older observations in determining the forecast.

> **EXPONENTIAL SMOOTHING**
> A time-series smoothing and forecasting technique that produces an exponentially weighted moving average in which each smoothing calculation or forecast is dependent upon all previously observed values.

So, if in recent periods the time-series values are much higher (or lower) than those in earlier periods, the forecast will tend to reflect this difference. The extent to which the forecast reflects the current data depends on the weights assigned by the decision maker.

We will introduce two classes of exponential smoothing models: single exponential smoothing and double exponential smoothing. Double smoothing is used when the time series exhibits a linear trend; single smoothing is used when no linear trend is present in the time series. Both single and double exponential smoothing are appropriate for short-term forecasting of one or two periods into the future and for time series that are not seasonal.

SINGLE EXPONENTIAL SMOOTHING

Just as its name implies, single exponential smoothing uses one smoothing constant. Equations 16-10 and 16-11 represent two equivalent methods for forecasting using single exponential smoothing.

EXPONENTIAL SMOOTHING MODEL

$$F_{t+1} = F_t + \alpha(y_t - F_t) \qquad\qquad \textbf{16-10}$$

or:

$$F_{t+1} = \alpha y_t + (1 - \alpha)F_t \qquad\qquad \textbf{16-11}$$

where:

F_{t+1} = Forecast value for period $t + 1$
y_t = Actual value for period t
F_t = Forecast value for period t
α = Alpha (smoothing constant $0 \le \alpha \le 1$)

The logic of the exponential smoothing model is that the forecast made for the next period will equal the forecast made for this period, plus or minus some adjustment factor. The adjustment factor is determined by how far this period's forecast is from the actual value $(y_t - F_t)$, times the smoothing constant, α. The idea is that if we forecast low we will adjust next period's forecast upward, but not by the entire amount of the error.

Humbolt Electronics Company

Consider the past 10 weeks of sales figures for printed circuits at the Humbolt Electronics Company in Austin, Texas. These data and the line graph are shown in Figure 16-25. The data are in the file called **Humbolt**. Suppose the current time period is the end of week 10, and we wish to forecast sales for week 11 using a single exponential smoothing model.

**EXAMPLE
16-5**

**SINGLE EXPONENTIAL
SMOOTHING**

FIGURE 16-25
Printed-Circuit Sales Data
and Line Graph for Humbolt
Electronics

Excel Instructions:
1. Open file: Humbolt.xls
2. Select Chart Wizard Line Chart
3. Define variables and *x* axis variable

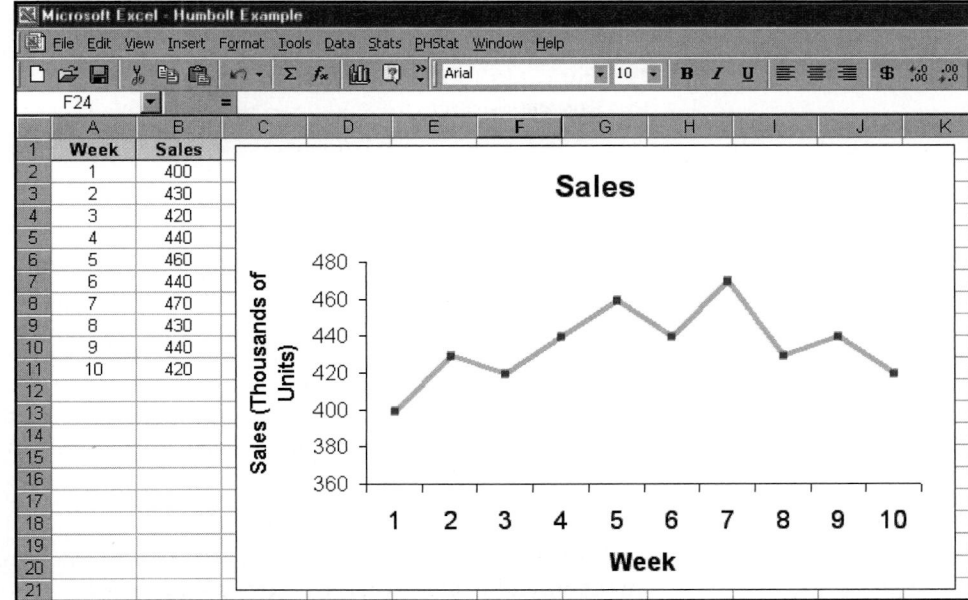

Excel and Minitab Tutorial

We start by selecting a value for α, the smoothing constant, between 0 and 1. The closer α is to 0, the less influence the current observations have in determining the forecast. Small α values will result in greater smoothing of the time series. Likewise, when α is near 1, the current observations have greater impact in determining the forecast and less smoothing will occur. There is no firm rule for selecting the value for the smoothing constant. However, in general, if the time series is quite stable, a small α should be used to lessen the impact of random or irregular fluctuations. Because the time series shown in Figure 16-25 appears to be relatively stable, we will use $\alpha = 0.20$ in this example.

The forecast value for period $t = 11$ is found using Equation 16-11 as follows.

$$F_{11} = 0.20\,y_{10} + (1 - 0.20)F_{10}$$

This demonstrates that the forecast for period 11 is a weighted average of the actual sales in period 10 and the forecast for period 10. While we know the sales for period 10, we don't know the forecast for period 10. However, we can determine it by:

$$F_{10} = 0.20\,y_9 + (1 - 0.20)F_9$$

Again, this forecast is a weighted average of the actual sales in period 9 and the forecast sales for period 9. We would continue in this manner until we get to:

$$F_2 = 0.20\,y_1 + (1 - 0.20)F_1$$

This requires a forecast for period 1. Since we have no sales data prior to period 1 from which to develop a forecast, a rule often used is to assume that $F_1 = y_1$.[4] This assumption is used to set the starting forecast value for period 1. Because setting the starting value is somewhat arbitrary, you should obtain as much historical data as possible to "warm" the model and dampen out the effect of the starting value. In our example, we have 10 periods of data to warm the model before the forecast for period 11 is made. Note that when using an exponential smoothing model, the effect of the initial forecast is reduced by $(1 - \alpha)$ in the forecast for period 2, then reduced again for period 3, and so on. After sufficient periods, any error due to the arbitrary initial forecast should be very small.

Before we actually use the exponential smoothing forecast for decision-making purposes, we want to determine how successfully the model fits the historical data. Unlike the trend-based forecast, which uses least-squares regression, there is no need to use split samples to test the forecasting ability of an exponential smoothing model, since the forecasts are "true forecasts." The forecast for a given period is made before considering the actual value for that period.

Figure 16-26 shows the results of using the single exponential smoothing equation and Excel for weeks 1 through 10. For week 1, $F_1 = y_1 = 400$. Then, for week 2 using Equation 16-11 we get:

$$F_2 = 0.20\,y_1 + (1 - 0.20)F_1$$
$$F_2 = (0.20)\,400 + (1 - 0.20)400 = 400$$

For week 3:

$$F_3 = 0.20\,y_2 + (1 - 0.20)F_2$$
$$F_3 = (0.20)430 + (1 - 0.20)400 = 406$$

Thus, at the end of week 2, after seeing what actually happened to sales in week 2, our forecast for week 3 is 406 units. This is a 6 unit increase over the forecast for week 2 of 400 units. The actual amount of sales in week 2 was 430 rather than 400. The amount of sales for week 2 was 30 units higher than the forecast for that time period. Since the actual

---

[4]Another approach for establishing the starting value, F_1, is to use the mean value for the available data. Regardless of the method used, the quantity of available data should be large enough to dampen out the impact of the starting value.

Excel Instructions

1. Open file: Humbolt.xls
2. Use Excel formulas to generate F_t and F_{t+1} using equation 16-11

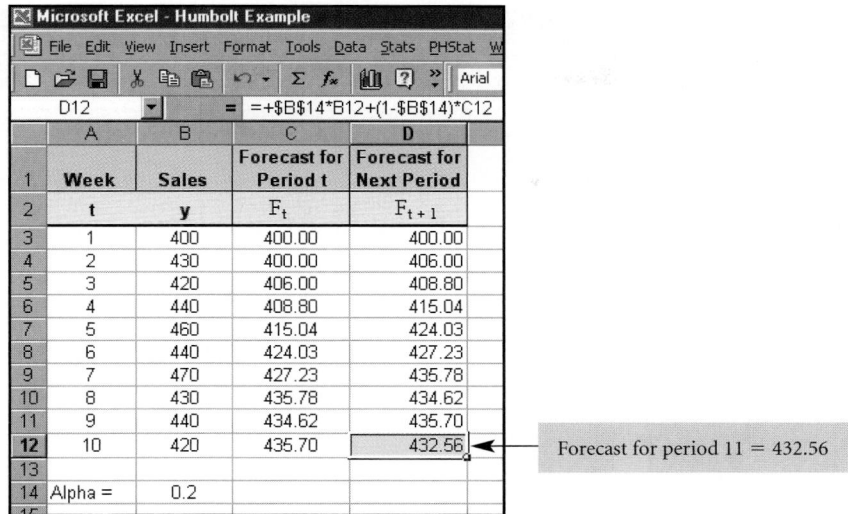

FIGURE 16-26
Humbolt Electronics Single Exponential Smoothing Excel Spreadsheet

amount of sales was larger than the forecast, an adjustment must be made. The 6 unit adjustment is calculated by multiplying the smoothing constant by this forecast error $[0.20(30) = 6]$ as specified in Equation 16-10. The adjustment compensates for the forecast error in week 2.

Continuing for week 4:

$$F_4 = 0.20\, y_3 + (1 - 0.20)F_3$$
$$F_4 = (0.20)420 + (1 - 0.20)406 = 408.80$$

Recall that our forecast for week 3 was 406. However, actual sales were again higher than forecast at 420 units, and we under forecast by 14 units. Again using Equation 16-10, the adjustment for week 4 is then $0.20(14) = 2.80$, and the forecast for week 4 is $406 + 2.80 = 408.80$. This process continues through the data until we are ready to forecast week 11 as shown in Figure 16-26.

$$F_{11} = 0.20\, y_{10} + (1 - 0.20)F_{10}$$
$$F_{11} = (0.20)420 + (1 - 0.20)435.70 = 432.56$$

Humbolt managers would forecast sales of 432,560 units for week 11. If we wished to forecast week 12 sales, we would either use the week 11 forecast or wait until the actual week 11 sales are known, and then update the smoothing equations to get a new forecast for week 12.

Figure 16-27 shows the MAD computation for the forecast model with $\alpha = 0.20$ and a plot of the forecast value versus the actual sales values. This plot shows the smoothing that has occurred.

Our next step would be to try different smoothing constants and find the MAD for each new α. The forecast for period 11 would be made using the smoothing constant that generates the smallest MAD.

In this Humbolt example, we have used Excel formulas to perform the single exponential smoothing. Both Excel and Minitab have single exponential smoothing procedures, although Minitab's procedure is much more extensive. Refer to the Excel and Minitab tutorials on the CD-ROM for instructions on each. Minitab provides optional methods for determining the initial forecast value for period 1 and a variety of useful graphs. Minitab also has an option for determining the optimal smoothing constant value.[5] Figure 16-28

---

[5]The solver in Excel can be used to determine the optimal α level to minimize the MAD.

Excel Instructions:

1. Use Excel formulas to find forecast error, absolute forecast error, and MAD
2. Use Chart Wizard, line graph option for columns B and C with Column A as *x* axis label

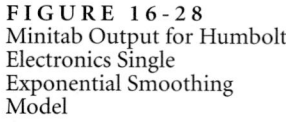

FIGURE 16-27
Humbolt Electronics MAD Computation for Single Exponential Smoothing, $\alpha = 0.20$

	Week	Sales	Forecast for Period t	Forecast for Next Period	Forecast Error	Absolute Forecast Error
1						
2	t	y	F_t	F_{t+1}	$y_t - F_t$	$|y_t - F_t|$
3	1	400	400.00	400.00	0.00	0.00
4	2	430	400.00	406.00	30.00	30.00
5	3	420	406.00	408.80	14.00	14.00
6	4	440	408.80	415.04	31.20	31.20
7	5	460	415.04	424.03	44.96	44.96
8	6	440	424.03	427.23	15.97	15.97
9	7	470	427.23	435.78	42.77	42.77
10	8	430	435.78	434.62	-5.78	5.78
11	9	440	434.62	435.70	5.38	5.38
12	10	420	435.70	432.56	-15.70	15.70
13						
14	Alpha =	0.2			Sum =	205.76
15						
16					MAD =	20.5758

Single Exponential Smoothing (alpha = .20)

Single smoothed forecasts for period *t*

shows the output generated using Minitab. This shows that the best forecast is found using an $\alpha = 0.524$. Note, MAD is decreased from 20.576 (when $\alpha = 0.20$) to 17.321 when the optimal smoothing constant is used. The forecast for period 11 is also changed from 432.56 to 430.17 when a smoothing constant of 0.524 is used rather than 0.20. In Figure 16-28, when Minitab is used to generate the optimum smoothing constant, Minitab automatically uses the average of the first two periods as the initial forecast for period 1.

A major advantage of the single exponential smoothing model is that it is easy to update. The forecast for week 12, using this model, is found by simply plugging the actual sales figure in week 11, once it is known, into the smoothing formula.

$$F_{12} = \alpha y_{11} + (1 - \alpha)F_{11}$$

FIGURE 16-28
Minitab Output for Humbolt Electronics Single Exponential Smoothing Model

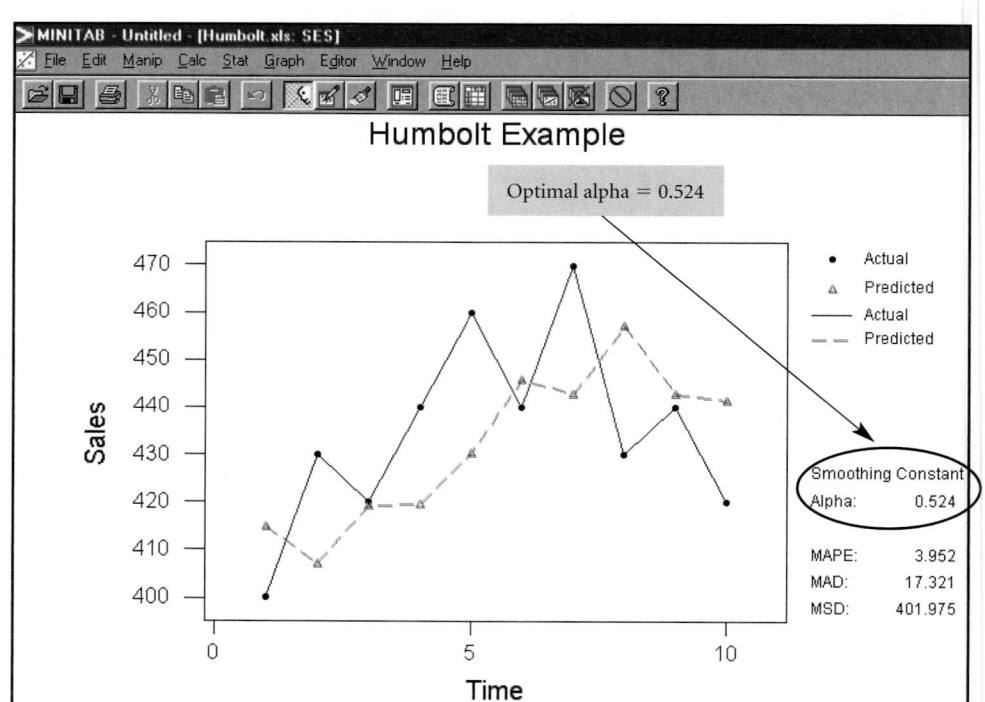

Humbolt Example

Optimal alpha = 0.524

- ● Actual
- △ Predicted
- —— Actual
- – – Predicted

Smoothing Constant Alpha: 0.524

MAPE: 3.952
MAD: 17.321
MSD: 401.975

Minitab Instructions:

1. Open file: Humbolt.mtw
2. Click on the Stat button
3. Select Time Series and Single Exp Smoothing
4. Select Optimize

We do not need to go back and recompute the entire model as would have been necessary with a trend-based regression model.

DOUBLE EXPONENTIAL SMOOTHING

When the time series has an increasing or decreasing linear trend, a modification to the single exponential smoothing model is used to explicitly account for the trend. The resulting technique is called **double exponential smoothing**. The double exponential smoothing model is often referred to as exponential smoothing with trend. In double exponential smoothing, a second smoothing constant, *beta* (β), is included to account for the trend. Equations 16-12, 16-13, and 16-14 are needed to provide the forecasts.

DOUBLE EXPONENTIAL SMOOTHING MODEL

$$C_t = \alpha y_t + (1 - \alpha)(C_{t-1} + T_{t-1}) \qquad \textbf{16-12}$$
$$T_t = \beta (C_t - C_{t-1}) + (1 - \beta)T_{t-1} \qquad \textbf{16-13}$$
$$F_{t+1} = C_t + T_t \qquad \textbf{16-14}$$

where:

y_t = Actual value in time t
α = Constant-process smoothing constant
β = Trend-smoothing constant
C_t = Smoothed constant-process value for period t
T_t = Smoothed trend value for period t
F_{t+1} = Forecast value for period $t + 1$
t = Current time period

Equation 16-12 is used to smooth the time-series data. Equation 16-13 is used to smooth the trend, and Equation 16-14 combines the two smoothed values to form the forecast for period $t + 1$.

Billingsley Insurance Company

The Billingsley Insurance Company has maintained data on the number of automobile claims filed at its Denver office over the past 12 months. These data, which are in the file called **Billingsley** on the CD-ROM, are listed and graphed in Figure 16-29. The claims manager wants to forecast claims for month 13. The time series contains a strong upward trend, so a double exponential smoothing model might be selected.

As was the case with single exponential smoothing, we must select starting values. In the case of the double exponential smoothing model, we must select initial values for C_0 and T_0 and also for the smoothing constants α and β. The choice of smoothing constant values (α and β) depends on the same issues as those discussed earlier for single exponential smoothing. That is, use larger smoothing constants when less smoothing is desired, and use values closer to 0.0 when more smoothing is desired. The larger the smoothing constant value, the more impact that current data will have on the forecast.

Suppose we use $\alpha = 0.20$ and $\beta = 0.30$ in this example. There are several approaches for selecting starting values for C_0 and T_0. The method we use here is to fit the least-squares trend to the historical data:

$$\hat{y}_t = b_0 + b_1 t$$

where the y intercept, b_0, is used as the starting value, C_0, and the slope, b_1, is used as the starting value for the trend, T_0. We can use the regression procedure in Excel or Minitab to perform these calculations giving:

$$\hat{y}_t = 34.273 + 4.1119(t)$$

So,

$$C_0 = 34.273 \quad \text{and} \quad T_0 = 4.1119$$

EXAMPLE
16-6

**DOUBLE EXPONENTIAL
SMOOTHING**

Excel and
Minitab Tutorial

Excel Instructions:

1. Open file: Billingsley.xls
2. Use Chart Wizard—Line Chart option

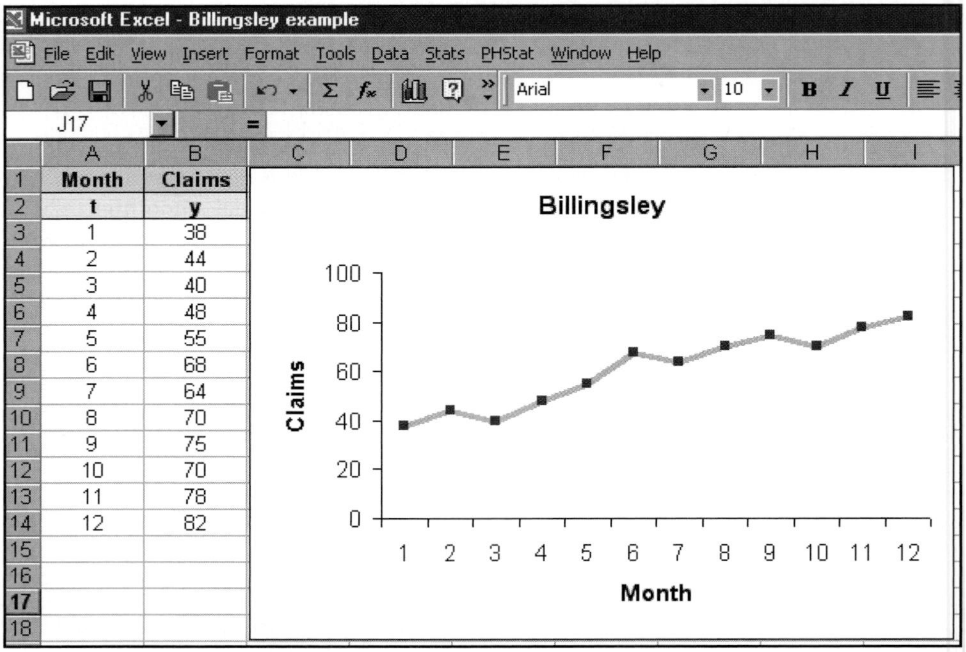

FIGURE 16-29
Excel Billingsley Insurance Company Data and Time-Series Plot

Month	Claims
t	y
1	38
2	44
3	40
4	48
5	55
6	68
7	64
8	70
9	75
10	70
11	78
12	82

Keep in mind that these are arbitrary starting values and, as with single exponential smoothing, their effect will be dampened out as you proceed through the sample data to the current period. The more historical data you have, the less impact the starting values have in the forecast.

The forecast for period 1 made at the beginning of period 1 is:

$$F_1 = C_0 + T_0$$
$$F_1 = 34.273 + 4.1119 = 38.385$$

At the close of period 1, in which actual claims were 38, the smoothing equations are updated as follows.

$$C_1 = 0.20(38) + (1 - 0.20)(34.273 + 4.1119) = 38.308$$
$$T_1 = 0.30(38.308 - 34.273) + (1 - 0.30)(4.1119) = 4.089$$

Next, the forecast for period 2 is:

$$F_2 = 38.308 + 4.089 = 42.397$$

We then repeat the process through period 12 to find the forecast for period 13. Figure 16-30 shows the results of the computations and the MAD value. The forecast for period 13 is:

$$F_{13} = C_{12} + T_{12}$$
$$F_{13} = 83.867 + 3.908 = 87.775$$

Additional Example 16-a

Double Exponential Smoothing

Based on this double exponential smoothing model, the number of claims for period 13 is forecast to be about 88. But before settling on this forecast, we would try different smoothing constants to determine whether a smaller MAD can be found.

As you can see, the computations required for double exponential smoothing are somewhat tedious and are ideally suited for your computer. Although Excel does not have a double exponential smoothing procedure, we have used Excel formulas to develop our model in conjunction with the regression tool for determining the starting values.

Excel Instructions:

1. Open file: Billingsley.xls
2. Apply equations 16-12, 16-13, and 16-14 using Excel formulas
3. Compute forecast errors and absolute forecast errors
4. Compute MAD

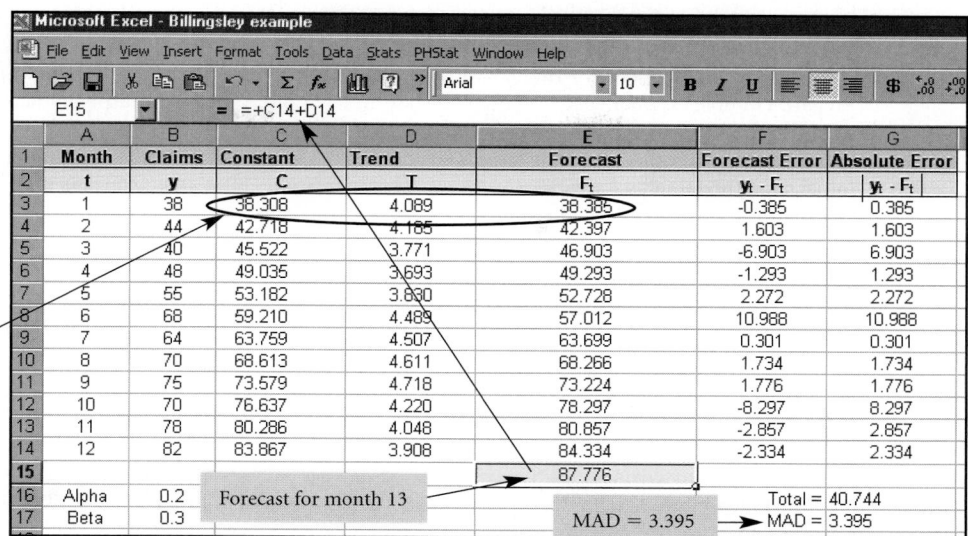

Period 1 values

FIGURE 16-30
Excel Double Exponential Smoothing Spreadsheet for Billingsley Insurance

Month	Claims	Constant	Trend	Forecast	Forecast Error	Absolute Error
t	y	C	T	F_t	$y_t - F_t$	$|y_t - F_t|$
1	38	38.308	4.089	38.385	-0.385	0.385
2	44	42.718	4.185	42.397	1.603	1.603
3	40	45.522	3.771	46.903	-6.903	6.903
4	48	49.035	3.693	49.293	-1.293	1.293
5	55	53.182	3.630	52.728	2.272	2.272
6	68	59.210	4.489	57.012	10.988	10.988
7	64	63.759	4.507	63.699	0.301	0.301
8	70	68.613	4.611	68.266	1.734	1.734
9	75	73.579	4.718	73.224	1.776	1.776
10	70	76.637	4.220	78.297	-8.297	8.297
11	78	80.286	4.048	80.857	-2.857	2.857
12	82	83.867	3.908	84.334	-2.334	2.334
				87.776		
Alpha	0.2				Total =	40.744
Beta	0.3			MAD = 3.395	MAD =	3.395

Forecast for month 13

E15 = =+C14+D14

OPTIONAL CD-ROM TOPIC **Moving Average and Weighted Moving Average Forecasting Models**

Other smoothing-based forecasting models exist. Two basic methods that are used are the moving average and weighted moving average methods. For more information, go to the CD-ROM.

16-3: EXERCISES

ADDITIONAL EXERCISES ON YOUR CD-ROM

Try the ADDITIONAL EXERCISES and APPLICATION PROBLEMS on the CD-ROM.

16-20. The following information refers to the number of guests attending the quarterly appreciation dinner sponsored by the fine arts committee at your university for the years 1999–2000.

1999		2000	
1st quarter	242	1st quarter	272
2d quarter	252	2d quarter	267
3d quarter	257	3d quarter	276
4th quarter	267	4th quarter	281

a. Prepare a single exponential smoothing forecast for the first quarter of 2001 using $\alpha = 0.10$. Let the initial forecast value for quarter 1 of 1999 be 250.

b. Prepare a single exponential smoothing forecast for the first quarter of 2001 using $\alpha = 0.25$. Let the initial forecast value for quarter 1 of 1999 be 250.

c. Calculate the MAD value for the forecasts you generated in parts a and b. Which α value provides the smaller MAD value at the end of the 4th quarter in 2000?

16-21. Enrollment in the E-Commerce course at your university has demonstrated the following enrollment figures for the past 6 semesters. (Note: Semester 1 is the oldest data; semester 6 is the most recent data.)

SEMESTER	ENROLLMENT	SEMESTER	ENROLLMENT
1	87	4	127
2	110	5	145
3	123	6	160

a. Prepare a graph of enrollment for the 6 semesters.

b. Based on the graph you prepared in part a, does it appear that a trend is present in the enrollment figures?

c. Prepare a single exponential smoothing forecast for semester 7 using $\alpha = 0.35$. Assume that the initial forecast for semester 1 is 90.

d. Prepare a double exponential smoothing forecast for semester 7 using $\alpha = 0.20$ and $\beta = 0.25$. Assume that the initial smoothed constant value is 80 and the initial smoothed trend value is 10.

e. Calculate the MAD value for the simple exponential smoothing model at the end of semester 6 and the MAD value for the double exponential smoothing model at the end of semester 6. Which model appears to be doing the better job of forecasting course enrollment?

Business Applications

16-22. The sales manager of Carl's Discount TV and Stereo Shop must decide how many 27-inch GB Super TVs to order for May. The following sales report shows the sales of the 27-inch GB Super for the months of January through April.

MONTH	SALES	MONTH	SALES
January	845	March	820
February	825	April	851

a. Use $\alpha = 0.3$ to prepare a single exponential smoothing forecast for May. Assume that your initial forecast for January is 830.

b. What is the MAD value at the end of April?

16-23. The fleet manager for a regional sales office is trying to estimate the dollar expenditure for gasoline for the next period. The past 6 months of gasoline expenditures are shown next.

MONTH	GASOLINE EXPENDITURES
April	$23,586.41
May	23,539.22
June	23,442.06
July	23,988.71
August	23,727.13
September	23,799.69

Prepare a single exponential forecast for October using $\alpha = 0.25$. Assume that your initial forecast estimate is $23,500.

16-24. The human resource manager for a medium-sized business is interested in predicting the dollar value of medical expenditures filed by employees of her company for the year 2001. From her company's database she has collected the following information showing the dollar value of medical expenditures made by employees for the previous 7 years.

YEAR	MEDICAL CLAIMS	YEAR	MEDICAL CLAIMS
1994	$405,642.43	1998	$411,085.64
1995	407,180.60	1999	412,200.39
1996	408,203.30	2000	414,043.90
1997	410,088.03		

a. Prepare a graph of medical expenditures for the years 1994–2000. Which forecasting technique do you think is more appropriate for this time series, single exponential smoothing or double exponential smoothing? Why?

b. Assume that the initial constant process value at $t = 0$ is $400,000, and the initial trend value at $t = 0$ is $5,000. Use $\alpha = 0.25$ and a $\beta = 0.15$ to produce a double exponential forecast for the medical claims data. Be sure to update your constant process value and your trend value each year.

c. Compute the MAD value for your model for the years 1994 to 2000. Also produce a graph of your forecast values.

16-25. Boondocks in Phoenix, Arizona, is one of the biggest water amusement parks in the country. The park has numerous water slides and a variety of other water related play areas for children and adults. While people are at the park, they buy food and drinks. In order for the catering manager at Boondocks to determine how much food to have on hand, she needs an accurate forecast of the number of people who will be at the park each week. Attendance data for the past 16 weeks are shown as follows and are contained in the data file called **Boondocks**.

WEEK	ATTENDANCE	WEEK	ATTENDANCE
1	14,560	9	14,745
2	18,655	10	16,778
3	15,987	11	19,456
4	13,689	12	15,789
5	15,332	13	15,602
6	16,345	14	14,556
7	17,456	15	16,344
8	16,334	16	15,617

a. Develop a times-series plot for the weekly attendance at Boondocks. Comment on the components that are visible in this time series.

b. Use the single exponential smoothing model with $\alpha = 0.25$ to develop a forecast for period 17. Assume that the initial forecast for period 1 is 15,000. Also compute the MAD value for the past 16 weeks using this forecasting model.

c. Referring to part b, change the alpha smoothing constant to 0.40 and repeat the forecasting and MAD computation processes.

d. Referring to parts b and c, write a short report to the catering manager indicating which forecasting model you would recommend and why.

16-26. Referring to Problem 25, use single exponential smoothing with a variety of alpha levels (say 0.10, 0.30, 0.50, 0.70, and 0.90) to determine the "best" value for the smoothing constant based on minimizing the MAD. (Hint: If you are using Minitab, you can use the *smoothing constant optimization* option to directly find the "best" alpha value. If you use Excel you can employ its *Data Table* feature to simultaneously calculate the MAD values for the alternative alpha values.) Discuss your results.

16-27. The sales manager at Grossmieller Importers in New York City needs to determine a monthly forecast for the number of men's golf shirts that will be sold so that he can order an appropriate amount of packing boxes. Grossmieller ships sweaters to retail stores throughout the United States and Canada. Shirts are packed 6 to a box. Data for the past 16 months are shown as follows and are also contained in the data file called **Grossmieller.**

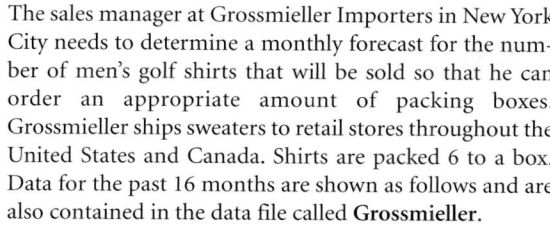

MONTH	SHIRTS SOLD	MONTH	SHIRTS SOLD
1	37,630	9	40,010
2	34,780	10	50,720
3	35,150	11	63,560
4	45,990	12	48,470
5	36,130	13	64,350
6	47,090	14	69,590
7	37,220	15	69,000
8	49,180	16	71,196

a. Plot the sales data using a time-series plot. Based on the graph, what time-series components are present? Discuss.

b. (1) Use a single exponential smoothing model with $\alpha = 0.30$ to forecast sales for month 17. Assume that the initial forecast for period 1 is 36,000. (2) Compute the MAD for this model. (3) Graph the smoothing model fitted values on the time-series plot.

c. (1) Referring to part b, try different alpha levels to determine which smoothing constant value you would recommend. (2) Indicate why you have selected this value, and then develop the forecast for month 17. (3) Compare this to the forecast you got using $\alpha = 0.30$ in part b.

16-28. Refer to Problem 27 in which the sales manager for Grossmieller Imports of New York City needs to forecast monthly sales.

a. Discuss why a double exponential smoothing model might be preferred over a single exponential smoothing model.

b. (1) Develop a double exponential smoothing model using $\alpha = 0.20$ and $\beta = 0.30$ as smoothing constants. To obtain the starting values, use the regression trend-line approach discussed in this section. (2) Determine the forecast for month 17. (3) Also compute the MAD for this model. (4) Graph the fitted values on the time-series graph.

c. Compare the results for this double exponential smoothing model with the "best" single exponential smoothing model developed in part c of Problem 27. Discuss which model is preferred.

d. Referring to part b, try different alpha and beta values in an attempt to determine an improved forecast model for monthly sales. For each model, show the forecast for period 17 and the MAD. Write a short report that compares the different models.

e. Referring to part d and to part c for Problem 27, write a report to the Grossmieller sales manager that indicates your choice for the forecasting model complete with your justification for the selection.

16-29. The sales manager has reviewed your analysis from Problem 28. You have convinced him that a double exponential forecast model is a model that will provide adequate forecasts since there is an upward trend in the number of men's golf sweaters sold. However, he has asked how confident you are in the forecast for month 17. If you cannot provide an answer to this inquiry, select a method that will provide a prediction interval with a 99% confidence level. Use this method to produce the required prediction interval.

■ SUMMARY AND CONCLUSIONS

In this chapter, we have introduced the basics of time-series analysis and forecasting. While we have included a variety of forecasting techniques, the discussion here does not cover the entire topic of forecasting. The subject of forecasting and time-series analysis could easily require one or more semester-long courses. Our objective has been to provide insight into some of the more frequently used techniques and to acquaint you with the basic terminology of forecasting and time-series analysis.

Quantitative forecasting techniques require historical data for the variable to be forecasted. The success of a quantitative model is determined by two factors.

1. How well the model fits the historical time-series data.
2. How closely the future resembles the past.

Ultimately, the best forecasting method is the one that provides the most accurate forecasts.

You will find that the techniques introduced in this chapter are used frequently as an initial basis for a forecast. However, in most cases, the decision maker will modify the forecast based on his or her own judgment and other qualitative inputs that are not considered by the quantitative model. Thus, forecasting is as much an art as it is a science. The more experience you have in a given situation, the more effective you will likely be at identifying and applying the appropriate forecasting tool.

EQUATIONS

Linear Trend Model

$$y_t = \beta_0 + \beta_1 t + \epsilon_t \qquad \textbf{16-1}$$

Least Squares Equations

$$b_1 = \frac{\sum\limits_{t=1}^{n} ty_t - \dfrac{\sum\limits_{t=1}^{n} t \sum\limits_{t=1}^{n} y_t}{n}}{\sum\limits_{t=1}^{n} t^2 - \dfrac{\left(\sum\limits_{t=1}^{n} t\right)^2}{n}}$$ 16-2

$$b_0 = \bar{y} - b_1 \bar{t}$$ 16-3

Mean Square Error

$$MSE = \frac{\sum\limits_{t=1}^{n}(y_t - F_t)^2}{n}$$ 16-4

Mean Absolute Deviation

$$MAD = \frac{\sum\limits_{t=1}^{n}|y_t - F_t|}{n}$$ 16-5

Forecast Bias

$$\text{Forecast Bias} = \frac{\sum\limits_{t=1}^{n}(y_t - F_t)}{n}$$ 16-6

or:

$$\text{Forecast Bias} = \frac{\sum(\text{error})}{n}$$

Multiplicative Time-Series Model

$$y_t = T_t \times S_t \times C_t \times I_t$$ 16-7

Ratio-to-Moving-Average

$$S_t \times I_t = \frac{y_t}{(T_t \times C_t)}$$ 16-8

Deseasonalization

$$T_t \times C_t \times I_t = \frac{y_t}{S_t}$$ 16-9

Exponential Smoothing Model

$$F_{t+1} = F_t + \alpha(y_t - F_t)$$ 16-10

or:

$$F_{t+1} = \alpha y_t + (1 - \alpha)F_t$$ 16-11

Double Exponential Smoothing Model

$$C_t = \alpha y_t + (1 - \alpha)(C_{t-1} + T_{t-1})$$ 16-12

$$T_t = \beta(C_t - C_{t-1}) + (1 - \beta)T_{t-1}$$ 16-13

$$F_{t+1} = C_t + T_t$$ 16-14

■ KEY TERMS

Alpha (α)—The smoothing constant used in exponential smoothing to indicate the relative weight placed on the most recent observations versus the historical observations.

Beta (β)—The second smoothing constant used in double exponential smoothing. It is used to weight the trend component of the model.

Cyclical Component—A pattern within the time series that repeats itself throughout the time series and has a recurrence period of more than one year.

Deseasonalizing—The process of removing the seasonal component from a time series.

Double Exponential Smoothing—An exponential smoothing forecasting model which incorporates a second smoothing constant to account for the trend in the time series.

Exponential Smoothing—A time-series smoothing and forecasting technique that produces an exponentially weighted moving average in which each smoothing calculation or forecast is dependent upon all previously observed values.

Forecast Bias—The propensity of a forecasting model on average to over forecast or under forecast the actual value of the time series.

Forecast Error—The difference between the actual value of a time series and the forecast value; also referred to as the *residual*.

Forecasting—The process of predicting the magnitude that a variable will assume at some future point in time.

Forecasting Horizon—The number of future periods covered by the forecast; sometimes referred to as the *forecast lead-time*.

Forecasting Interval—The frequency with which new forecasts are prepared.

Forecasting Period—The unit of time for which forecasts are made. The period may be a day, week, month, quarter, or year.

Linear Trend—A long-term increase or decrease in a time series in which the rate of change is relatively constant.

Mean Absolute Deviation (MAD)—The average of the absolute differences between the actual time-series values and the forecast values.

Mean Squared Error (MSE)—The average of the squared differences between actual and predicted values.

Model Diagnosis—The process of determining how well the model fits the past data and how well the model's assumptions appear to be satisfied.

Model Fitting—The process of determining how well a specified model fits past data.

Model Specification—The process of selecting the forecasting technique to be used in a particular situation.

Moving Averages—The successive averages of n consecutive values in a time series.

Nonlinear Trend—An increase or decrease in a time series where the rate of change is not constant.

Qualitative Forecasting—Forecasting techniques which are based on expert opinion and judgment.

Quantitative Forecasting—Forecasting techniques which are based on statistical methods for analyzing time-series data.

Random Component—Changes in the time-series data that are unpredictable and cannot be associated with the trend, seasonal, or cyclical components.

Ratio-to-Moving-Average Method—The actual value of the time series divided by the centered moving average; a step in the process of constructing seasonal indexes.

Residual—The difference between the actual value of the time series and the forecast value; also called the *forecast error*.

Seasonal Component—A pattern that is repeated throughout a time series and has a recurrence period of at most one year.

Seasonal Index—A number used to quantify the effect of seasonality in time-series data.

Seasonally Unadjusted Forecast—A forecast made for seasonal data that does not include an adjustment for the seasonal component in the time series.

Smoothing Constant—The value which determines the weight placed on the most current observation in an exponential smoothing model.

Splitting Samples—The process of dividing time-series data into two groups, one used to construct the model and the second used to test the ability of the model to forecast.

Time-Series Data—Data measured over time. In most applications the period between measurements is uniform.

Time-Series Plot—A two-dimensional plot of the time series. The vertical axis measures the variable of interest and the horizontal axis corresponds to the time periods. The points on the graph are frequently connected by straight-line segments.

Trend—The long-term increase or decrease in time-series data.

CHAPTER EXERCISES

SOLVED PROBLEMS ON YOUR CD-ROM
Try the WORKED-OUT EXERCISES and BUSINESS APPLICATIONS on the CD-ROM.

Conceptual Questions and Assignments

16-30. Identify three businesses in your community that might be expected to have sales that exhibit a seasonal component. Discuss.

16-31. Suppose that enrollments at a particular university have steadily declined over the past 10 years. Which time-series component would be illustrated if enrollments were graphed for this period of time? Discuss.

16-32. Discuss the difference between a cyclical component and a seasonal component. Which component is more predictable, seasonal or cyclical? Discuss and illustrate with examples.

16-33. Go to the library or use the Internet to find data showing your state's population for the past 20 years. Plot these data and indicate which of the time-series components are present.

16-34. Contact the university registrar's office for enrollment data by quarter (or semester), including summer term, for the past 6 years. Graph the data and indicate which of the time-series components are present.

Business Applications

16-35. The Malcar Autoparts Company has started producing replacement control microcomputers for automobiles. This has been a growth industry since the first control units were introduced in 1985. Sales data since the control unit was introduced are as follows.

YEAR	SALES	YEAR	SALES
1985	$ 240,000	1993	$1,570,000
1986	218,000	1994	1,947,000
1987	405,000	1995	2,711,000
1988	587,000	1996	3,104,000
1989	795,000	1997	2,918,000
1990	762,000	1998	4,606,000
1991	998,000	1999	5,216,000
1992	1,217,000	2000	5,010,000

a. Graph these data and indicate whether they appear to have a linear trend.

b. Develop a simple linear regression model with time as the independent variable. Using this regression model, describe the trend and the strength of the linear trend over the 16 years. Is the trend line statistically significant? Plot the trend line against the actual data.

c. Compute the MAD value for this model.

d. Provide the Malcar Autoparts Company an estimate of its expected sales for the next 5 years.

e. Provide the maximum and minimum sales Malcar can expect with 90% confidence for the year 2005.

16-36. Referring to Problem 35, develop a single exponential smoothing model using $\alpha = 0.20$. As a starting value use the average of the first 6 years' data. Determine the forecasted value for year 2001.

a. Compute the MAD for this model.

b. Plot the forecast values against the actual data.

c. Write a short report that discusses the potential of using the single exponential smoothing model in this application.

d. Use the same starting value but try different smoothing constants (say 0.05, 0.10, 0.25, and 0.30) in an effort to reduce the MAD value. Prepare a short report that summarizes your efforts.

e. Is it possible to answer part d of Problem 35 for this forecasting technique? Explain your answer.

16-37. Referring to Problems 35 and 36, develop a double exponential smoothing model using smoothing constants $\alpha = 0.20$ and $\beta = 0.40$. As starting values, use the least-squares trend line slope and intercept values.

a. Compute the MAD for this model.

b. Plot the forecast values against the actual data.

c. Write a short report which discusses the potential of using the double exponential smoothing model in this application.

d. Use the same starting values but try different smoothing constants [say $(\alpha, \beta) = (0.10, 0.50)$, $(0.30, 0.30)$, and $(0.40, 0.20)$] in an effort to reduce the MAD value. Prepare a short report that summarizes your efforts.

16-38. Using whatever diagnostic tools you are familiar with, determine which of the three forecasting methods utilized to forecast sales for Malcar Autoparts Company in the previous three problems provide superior forecasts. Explain the reasons for your choice.

16-39. Sunrise Sports has experienced rapidly expanding retail sales. Its sales levels for the past 12 years are:

YEAR	SALES (MILLIONS)	YEAR	SALES (MILLIONS)
1989	$1.9	1995	8.6
1990	3.1	1996	9.3
1991	2.8	1997	11.0
1992	4.5	1998	13.9
1993	5.7	1999	16.6
1994	5.8	2000	19.4

As part of the company's financial planning effort, the managers need an accurate forecast of annual sales.

a. Graph this series and describe the trend in the data.

b. Estimate a least-squares regression line to fit the data. How good a job does this line do in explaining the variation in past sales data? Comment on any patterns you see in the relationship between the actual sales values and those values predicted by the regression analysis.

c. Determine the forecast value for the year 2000.

d. Conduct a hypothesis test to determine if a long-term trend is evident in the sales data for Sunrise Sports.

e. Graph the residuals for the chosen least-squares regression line against the year. Does this graph suggest a different regression model to use for forecasting purposes? Develop the regression model that you would use to forecast sales. Provide your rationale, of course.

16-40. Referring to Problem 39, develop a single exponential smoothing model using $\alpha = 0.30$. Use as a starting value the average of the first 6 years' data. Determine the forecasted value for year 2001.

a. Compute the MAD for this model.

b. Plot the forecast values against the actual data.

c. Write a short report which discusses the potential of using the single exponential smoothing model in this application.

d. Use the same starting value but try a different smoothing constant (say 0.10, 0.20, 0.40, and 0.50) in an effort to reduce the MAD value. Prepare a short report that summarizes your efforts.

16-41. Referring to Problems 39 and 40, develop a double exponential smoothing model using smoothing constants $\alpha = 0.30$ and $\beta = 0.30$. As starting values, use the least-squares trend line slope and intercept values.

a. Compute the MAD for this model.

b. Plot the forecast values against the actual data.

c. Write a short report that discusses the potential of using the double exponential smoothing model in this application.

d. Use the same starting values but try different smoothing constants [say $(\alpha, \beta) = (0.10, 0.50)$, $(0.20, 0.40)$, and $(0.40, 0.20)$] in an effort to reduce the MAD value. Prepare a short report that summarizes your efforts.

16-42. DataNet is an Internet service where clients can find information and purchase various items such as airline tickets, stereo equipment, and listed stocks. DataNet has been in operation for 4 years. Data on monthly access calls for the time that the company has been in business are shown as follows and are also in the data file called **DataNet**.

MONTH	MONTH NUMBER	CALLS RECEIVED	MONTH NUMBER	CALLS RECEIVED
Jan.	1	23,500	25	31,000
Feb.	2	21,700	26	30,400
Mar.	3	18,750	27	29,800
Apr.	4	22,000	28	32,500
May	5	23,000	29	34,500
June	6	26,200	30	33,800
July	7	27,300	31	34,200
Aug.	8	29,300	32	36,700
Sep.	9	31,200	33	39,700
Oct.	10	34,200	34	42,400
Nov.	11	39,500	35	43,600
Dec.	12	43,400	36	47,400
Jan.	13	23,500	37	32,400
Feb.	14	23,400	38	35,600
Mar.	15	21,400	39	31,200
Apr.	16	24,200	40	34,600
May	17	26,900	41	36,800
June	18	29,700	42	35,700
July	19	31,100	43	37,500
Aug.	20	32,400	44	40,000
Sep.	21	34,500	45	43,200
Oct.	22	35,700	46	46,700
Nov.	23	42,000	47	50,100
Dec.	24	42,600	48	52,100

a. Plot these data in a times-series graph. Based on the graph, what time-series components are present in the data?

b. Develop the seasonal indexes for each month. Describe what the seasonal index for August means.

c. Fit a linear trend model to the data for months 1–48 and determine the MAD value. Comment on the adequacy of the linear trend model based on these measures of forecast error.

d. Provide a seasonally unadjusted forecast using the linear trend model for each month of the year.

e. Deseasonalize the data and develop a linear trend model. Compare this model to the model developed in part c.

f. Use the seasonal index values computed in part b to provide seasonal adjusted forecasts for months 49–52 based on the model developed in part e.

16-43. DataNet managers need to know how rapidly the monthly calls for service are increasing.

a. Provide them with an estimate (of which they can be very confident, say 99%) of the average increase in monthly calls for service.

b. The current telephone system can handle 60,000 calls a month. Provide the managers an estimate of the month in which they will have to upgrade their phone system.

16-44. Refer to Problem 43. The managers of DataNet, the Internet company where users can purchase products like airline tickets, need to forecast monthly call volumes in order to have sufficient capacity. Develop a single exponential smoothing model using $\alpha = 0.30$. As a starting value use the average of the first 6 months' data. Determine the forecasted value for month 49.

a. Compute the MAD for this model.

b. Plot the forecast values against the actual data.

c. Write a short report which discusses the potential of using the single exponential smoothing model in this application.

d. Use the same starting value but try different smoothing constants (say 0.10, 0.20, 0.40, and 0.50) in an effort to reduce the MAD value. Prepare a short report that summarizes your efforts.

e. Reflect on the type of time series for which the single exponential smoothing model is designed to provide forecasts. Does it surprise you that the MAD for this method is relatively large for this data? Explain your reasoning.

16-45. Referring to Problems 43 and 44, develop a double exponential smoothing model using smoothing constants $\alpha = 0.20$ and $\beta = 0.20$. As starting values, use the least-squares trend line slope and intercept values.

a. Compute the MAD for this model.

b. Plot the forecast values against the actual data.

c. Write a short report that discusses the potential of using the double exponential smoothing model in this application. Compare this with a linear trend model. Which forecast method would you use? Explain your rationale.

d. Use the same starting values but try different smoothing constants [say, $(\alpha, \beta) = (0.10, 0.30)$, $(0.15, 0.25)$, and $(0.30, 0.10)$] in an effort to reduce the MAD value. Prepare a short report that summarizes your efforts.

16-46. Anna Chen is the personnel manager for Datatron Corporation located in the Silicon Valley in California. She has been asked to assist the production managers in developing a staffing plan for the coming year. One factor that influences staffing is the amount of sick time taken by employees each month. The following data represent the number of sick days, by month, for the past 3 years. These data are also located in the data file called **Datatron**.

MONTH	MONTH NUMBER	SICK DAYS	MONTH NUMBER	SICK DAYS	MONTH NUMBER	SICK DAYS
Jan.	1	1,580	13	1,630	25	1,960
Feb.	2	1,608	14	1,700	26	1,880
Mar.	3	1,370	15	1,610	27	1,820
Apr.	4	1,260	16	1,590	28	1,750
May	5	1,125	17	1,498	29	1,690
June	6	1,306	18	1,540	30	1,730
July	7	1,240	19	1,580	31	1,690
Aug.	8	1,340	20	1,680	32	1,780
Sep.	9	1,090	21	1,560	33	1,670
Oct.	10	980	22	1,520	34	1,560
Nov.	11	1,260	23	1,670	35	1,760
Dec.	12	1,680	24	1,920	36	2,040

a. Plot these data in a times-series graph. Based on the graph, what time-series components are present in the data?

b. Develop the seasonal indexes for each month.

c. Fit a linear trend model to the data for months 1–36 and determine the MAD value. Comment on the adequacy of the linear trend model based on these measures of forecast error. Provide a 95% confidence interval estimate for the number of sick days for the next January.

d. Provide a seasonally unadjusted forecast using the linear trend model for each month of the year.

e. Deseasonalize the data and develop the linear trend forecasting model.

f. Use the seasonal index values computed in part b and the trend model from part c to provide seasonal adjusted forecasts for months 37–40. Compare this forecast to that made in part c.

16-47. Refer to Problem 46, in which Anna Chen was interested in forecasting the number of sick days taken by employees at Datatron each month.

a. Develop a single exponential smoothing model using $\alpha = 0.20$. As a starting value use the average of the first 6 months' data. Determine the forecasted value for month 37.

b. Compute the MAD for this model.

c. Plot the forecast values against the actual data.

d. Use the same starting value but try different smoothing constants (say, 0.10, 0.20, 0.40, and 0.50) in an effort to reduce the MAD value. Prepare a short report that summarizes your efforts.

16-48. Referring to Problems 46 and 47, develop a double exponential smoothing model using smoothing constants $\alpha = 0.30$ and $\beta = 0.20$. As starting values, use the least-squares trend line slope and intercept values.

   a. Compute the MAD for this model.

   b. Plot the forecast values against the actual data.

   c. Use a linear trend model to forecast the number of absent days for December of the third year. Compare this with the forecast obtained using the double exponential smoothing method. Discuss the two estimates' relative merits.

   d. Returning to the double exponential smoothing model you developed, use different smoothing constants [say $(\alpha, \beta) = (0.10, 0.30), (0.15, 0.25)$, and $(0.30, 0.10)$] in an effort to reduce the MAD value. Prepare a short report that summarizes your efforts.

16-49. Elliel's Quality Discount Store has applied for a line of credit with the First National Bank. This line of credit is to be used primarily for financing inventory purchases. As part of the financial application, Elliel's has been asked to provide monthly inventory levels for the past 5 years. These inventory levels (in millions of dollars) are given as follows and are also in the file called **Elliels**.

MONTH	1996	1997	1998	1999	2000
Jan.	5.2	4.7	6.6	7.1	7.0
Feb.	3.3	2.9	4.0	4.0	6.2
Mar.	2.8	3.0	3.6	2.6	4.3
Apr.	5.3	6.3	7.2	8.0	9.5
May	9.4	10.0	11.4	7.8	12.5
June	2.6	4.3	4.0	5.4	6.4
July	6.2	7.7	8.0	9.3	8.6
Aug.	7.2	7.5	6.8	8.2	8.4
Sept.	6.8	5.8	6.8	7.9	6.9
Oct.	9.7	9.6	8.9	9.3	9.8
Nov.	13.6	13.9	14.2	16.1	16.5
Dec.	11.8	11.9	12.7	13.8	14.6

   a. Determine the seasonal index number for each month.

   b. First National Bank has also asked Elliel's to provide a monthly forecast for months 61–72. Compute the least-squares trend model and determine the seasonally unadjusted forecast for months 61–72. Prepare a report discussing the forecasts for the bank loan officer.

   c. Referring to part b, prepare a seasonally adjusted forecast for months 61–72. Write a report that compares these forecasts with the unadjusted forecasts determined in part b.

   d. Discuss the advantage and reasons for incorporating the seasonal indexes into the forecasts.

16-50. The Chesterfield Company in Omaha, Nebraska, manufactures airplane parts. Sales data for the past 22 years are as follows and are also provided in the data file called **Chesterfield**.

YEAR	SALES	YEAR	SALES
1	$133,000	12	$1,335,000
2	128,000	13	1,567,000
3	202,000	14	1,234,000
4	278,000	15	1,897,000
5	388,000	16	2,300,000
6	376,000	17	2,124,000
7	504,000	18	2,579,000
8	613,000	19	3,200,000
9	745,000	20	3,106,000
10	975,000	21	3,678,000
11	1,233,900	22	3,789,000

   a. Develop a simple linear regression model with time as the independent variable.

   b. Plot the trend line against the actual data. Discuss any relationships you see between the plotted trend line and the actual data.

   c. Compute the MAD for this model.

   d. Use simple linear regression to obtain a prediction interval for the sales in year 23.

16-51. Refer to Problem 50.

   a. Develop a double exponential smoothing model to forecast year 23 sales. Use as starting values the intercept and slope coefficient from the linear trend model. Use smoothing constants with $\alpha = 0.25$ and $\beta = 0.30$.

   b. Compute the MAD for this model and compare the double smoothing model with the linear trend model developed in Problem 50. Which of these two models would you select to provide forecasts for these data? Provide the reasons for your selection.

CASE 16-A

Park Falls Chamber of Commerce

Masao Sugiyama is the recently elected president of the Chamber of Commerce in Park Falls, Wisconsin. He is the long-time owner of the only full-service hardware store in this small farming town. Being president of the Chamber has been considered largely a ceremonial post since business conditions have not changed in Park Falls for as long as anyone can remember. However, Masao has just read an article in *The Wall Street Journal* that has made him think he needs to take a more active interest in the business conditions of his town.

The article concerned Wal-Mart, the largest retailer in the United States. Wal-Mart expanded initially by locating in small towns and avoiding large suburban areas. While the Park Falls merchants have not had to deal with either Kmart or Sears since these companies have located primarily in large urban centers, Wal-Mart has recently entered the Wisconsin area. Recently, a supplier also has told Masao that both Sears and Kmart are considering locating stores in smaller towns to prevent future expansion by Wal-Mart. In addition, he knows that Wal-Mart has moved into the outskirts of metropolitan areas and now is considering smaller stores for smaller untapped markets. He has also heard that Kmart and Sears have recently had difficulty, and only Sears seems to have rebounded.

Masao has decided he needs to know more about all three retailers and so asked the son of a friend to locate the following sales data using the Compustat database.

QUARTERLY SALES VALUES IN MILLIONS OF DOLLARS (1995-1998)			
Quarter	Kmart	Sears	Wal-Mart
1	$8,015	$7,810	$17,686
2	7,845	7,926	20,417
3	9,967	10,194	24,447
4	7,501	7,463	20,440
5	8,503	8,226	22,723
6	8,041	8,440	22,914
7	10,609	10,796	27,550
8	6,975	7,995	22,772
9	7,566	9,133	25,587
10	7,212	9,067	24,644
11	9,684	12,042	25,409
12	7,263	8,732	25,409
13	7,846	9,731	28,386
14	7,315	9,752	28,777
15	9,759	13,081	35,386
16	7,515	9,163	29,819

Masao is interested in what all these data tell him. How much faster has Wal-Mart grown than the other two firms? Is there any evidence Wal-Mart's growth has leveled off? Does Sears seem to be rebounding, based on sales? Are seasonal fluctuations an issue in these sales figures? Is there any evidence that one firm is more affected by the cyclical component than the others? He needs some help in analyzing these data.

SALES VALUES		SALES VALUES		SALES VALUES	
Kmart	(million)	Sears	(million)	Wal-Mart	(million)
1988	$25,822	1988	$48,439	1988	$15,959
1989	27,496	1989	50,251	1989	20,649
1990	29,736	1990	53,793	1990	25,810
1991	32,281	1991	55,971	1991	32,601
1992	34,792	1992	57,242	1992	43,886
1993	37,942	1993	52,344	1993	55,483
1994	34,353	1994	50,837	1994	67,344
1995	34,313	1995	54,559	1995	82,494
1996	34,654	1996	34,925	1996	93,627
1997	31,437	1997	38,237	1997	98,412
1998	32,183	1998	41,296	1998	117,958

CASE 16-B

The St. Louis Companies

An irritated Roger Hatton finds himself sitting in the St. Louis airport after hearing that his flight to Chicago has been delayed—and, if the storm in Chicago continues, possibly canceled. Since he must get to Chicago if at all possible, Roger is stuck at the airport. While waiting to see if conditions improve, he decides he might as well try to get some work done, so he opens his laptop computer and calls up the CLAIMNUM file.

Roger was recently assigned as an analyst in the worker's compensation section of the St. Louis Companies, one of the biggest issuers of worker's compensation insurance in the country. Until this year, the revenues and claim costs for all parts of the company were grouped together to determine any yearly profit or loss. Therefore, no one really knew if an individual department was profitable or not. Now, however, the new president is looking at each part of the company as a profit center. The clear implication is that money-losing departments may not have a future unless they can develop a clear plan to become profitable.

When Roger asked the accounting department for a listing, by client, of all policy payments and claims filed and paid, he was told that the information is available but he may have to wait 2 or 3 months to get it. He was able to determine, however, that the department has been keeping track of the clients who file frequent (at least one a month) claims and the total number of firms that purchase worker compensation insurance. Using the data from this report, Roger divides the number of clients filing frequent claims by the corresponding number of clients. These ratios, kept in the **CLAIMNUM** file in his computer, are as follows.

YEAR	RATIO (%)	YEAR	RATIO (%)
1	3.8	12	6.1
2	3.6	13	7.8
3	3.5	14	7.1
4	4.9	15	7.6
5	5.9	16	9.7
6	5.6	17	9.6
7	4.9	18	7.5
8	5.6	19	7.9
9	8.5	20	8.3
10	7.7	21	8.4
11	7.1		

Staring at these figures, Roger feels there should be some way to use them to project what the next several years may hold if the company doesn't change its underwriting policies.

CASE 16-C

Wagner Machine Works

Mary Lindsey has recently agreed to leave her upper-level management job at a major paper manufacturing firm and return to her hometown to take over the family machine products business. The U.S. machine products industry had a strong position of world dominance until recently, when it was devastated by foreign competition, particularly from Germany and Japan. Among the many problems facing the American industry is that it is made up of many small firms which must compete with foreign industrial giants.

Wagner Machine Works, the company Mary is taking over, is one of the few survivors in its part of the state. But it, too, faces increasing competitive pressure. Mary's father let the business slide as he approached retirement, and Mary sees the need for an immediate modernization of their plant. She has arranged for a loan from the local bank, but she now must forecast sales for the next 3 years to ensure that the company has enough cash flow to repay the debt. Surprisingly, Mary finds that her father has no forecasting system in place, and she cannot afford the time, or money, to install a system like that used at her previous company.

Wagner Machine Works' quarterly sales (in millions of dollars) for the past 15 years are as follows.

	QUARTER			
Year	1	2	3	4
1986	10,490	11,130	10,005	11,058
1987	11,424	12,550	10,900	12,335
1988	12,835	13,100	11,660	13,767
1989	13,877	14,100	12,780	14,738
1990	14,798	15,210	13,785	16,218
1991	16,720	17,167	14,785	17,725
1992	18,348	18,951	16,554	19,889
1993	20,317	21,395	19,445	22,816
1994	23,335	24,179	22,548	25,029
1995	25,729	27,778	23,391	27,360
1996	28,886	30,125	26,049	30,300
1997	30,212	33,702	27,907	31,096
1998	31,715	35,720	28,554	34,326
1999	35,533	39,447	30,046	37,587
2000	39,093	44,650	30,046	37,587

While looking at these data, Mary wonders whether they can be used to forecast sales for the next 3 years. She wonders how much, if any, confidence she can have in a forecast made with these data. And she also wonders if the recent increase in sales is due to growing business or just to inflationary price increases in the national economy.

■ GENERAL REFERENCES

1. Armstrong, J. Scott, "Forecasting by Extrapolation: Conclusions from 25 Years of Research." *Interfaces*, 14, no. 6 (1984).
2. _____ "The Ombudsman: Research on Forecasting—A Quarter-Century Review, 1960–1984." *Interfaces*, 16, no. 1 (1986).
3. Bails, Dale G., and Larry C. Peppers, *Business Fluctuations: Forecasting Techniques and Applications* (Englewood Cliffs, NJ: Prentice Hall, 1982).
4. Berenson, Mark L., and David M. Levine, *Basic Business Statistics: Concepts and Applications*, 7th ed. (Upper Saddle River, NJ: Prentice Hall, 1999).
5. Bowerman, Bruce L., and Richard T. O'Connell, *Forecasting and Time Series: An Applied Approach*, 3d ed. (North Scituate, MA: Duxbury Press, 1993).
6. Brandon, Charles, R. Fritz, and J. Xander, "Econometric Forecasts: Evaluation and Revision." *Applied Economics*, 15, no. 2 (1983).
7. Cryer, Jonathan D., *Time Series Analysis* (Boston: Duxbury Press, 1986).
8. Frees, Edward W., *Data Analysis Using Regression Models: The Business Perspective* (Englewood Cliffs, NJ: Prentice Hall, 1996).
9. Granger, C. W. G., *Forecasting in Business and Economics*, 2d ed. (New York: Academic Press, 1989).
10. Makridakis, Spyros, Steven C. Wheelwright, and Rob J. Hyndman, *Forecasting: Methods and Applications* 3d ed. (New York: John Wiley & Sons, 1997).
11. McLaughlin, Robert L., "Forecasting Models: Sophisticated or Naive?" *Journal of Forecasting*, 2, no. 3 (1983).
12. *Microsoft Excel 2000* (Redmond, WA: Microsoft Corporation, 1999).
13. *Minitab for Windows Version 13* (State College, PA: Minitab, Inc., 2000).
14. Montgomery, Douglas C., and Lynwood A. Johnson, *Forecasting and Time Series Analysis*, 2d ed. (New York: McGraw-Hill, 1990).
15. Neter, John, Michael H. Kutner, Christopher J. Nachtsheim, and William Wasserman, *Applied Linear Statistical Models*, 4th ed. (Homewood, IL: Richard D. Irwin, 1996).
16. Willis, R. E., *A Guide to Forecasting for Planners* (Englewood Cliffs, NJ: Prentice Hall, 1987).

CHAPTER 17

INTRODUCTION TO DECISION ANALYSIS

CHAPTER OUTCOMES

After studying the material in Chapter 17, you should be able to:

17-1: Describe the decision-making environments of certainty and uncertainty.

17-2: Construct both a payoff table and an opportunity loss table.

17-3: Define the expected value criterion.

17-4: Apply the expected value criterion in decision situations.

17-5: Compute the value of perfect information.

17-6: Develop a decision tree and explain how it can aid decision making in an uncertain environment.

17-7: Discuss the difference between risk seeking and risk avoiding behavior.

17-8: Construct an individual risk preference function.

WHY YOU NEED TO KNOW

While this text is devoted to discussing statistical techniques managers can use to help analyze decisions, the term *decision analysis* has a specialized meaning. It applies to the set of tools, some of which are covered in this chapter, that have been developed to help managers analyze multi-stage decisions that must be made in an uncertain environment.

Putting together this set of tools has been a relatively recent development, starting in the late 1950s, initially by faculty at the Harvard Business School. The individual tools themselves are considerably older than decision analysis, however, and come from three theoretical areas of thought: (1) Bayesian statistics, (2) game theory, and (3) risk-preference analysis.

The bedrock of decision analysis was formed by the eighteenth-century work of the Reverend Thomas Bayes, one of the most enigmatic figures in scientific history. He is credited with being the first person to give a rational account of how statistical inference can be used as a process for understanding situations in the real world. But, his pioneering work was not published until after his death in 1761, and during his lifetime he was a scientific unknown. Now, however, he has become so popular that a whole group of decision analysts refer to themselves as "Bayesians."

A second contribution to modern decision analysis is the game-theory approach of John Von Neumann and Oskar Morgenstern. They demonstrated that the "correct" decision in any situation depends on the objectives of the decision maker and the actions that are likely to be taken by competitors.

The third area is the work of such economists as Milton Friedman and L. J. Savage. They showed that a person's attitude toward risk depended on the person's circumstances; and therefore different decision makers, when facing the same decision, may make different choices because of their differing risk attitudes.

Since its introduction in the late 1950s, decision analysis has become a common feature in MBA programs and has influenced thousands of decision makers in government and industry.

This chapter introduces the fundamentals of decision analysis and shows, through examples, how several basic decision analysis tools are used in the decision-making process.

◼ 17-1: DECISION-MAKING ENVIRONMENTS

In business, you will encounter a wide variety of decision situations. The analytic methods you use to deal with each situation will depend largely on the decision environment. The two primary decision environments are certainty and uncertainty.

Certainty

Sometimes you will encounter a decision situation where you can be certain of the outcome for each alternative. This type of decision environment, in which the results of each alternative are known before the decision is made, is termed a **certainty** environment.

> **CERTAINTY**
> A decision environment in which the results of selecting each alternative are known before the decision is made.

CERTAINTY

Econoprint Company

Consider a decision faced by the Econoprint Company, which makes replacement cartridges for laser printers. The national sales manager has just received a message from a regional sales representative indicating that she has negotiated a deal with a new distributor for 1 million cartridges at $5.00 each. However, the customer wants the cartridges to be packaged in groups of 6 rather than the usual 24 per package. The sales representative points out that the company can modify its packaging equipment "quite easily" to accommodate this change. She urges a quick decision, since a delay is likely to force the customer to go elsewhere, and the efforts to attract this new business will be lost.

TABLE 17-1
Econoprint Company:
Profits and Losses for
Two Alternatives

| | ALTERNATIVES | |
Revenues and Expenses	Accept Offer	Reject Offer
Revenues		
Sales (1 million × $5.00)	$5,000,000	0
Costs		
Production (1 million × $4.50)	$4,500,000	0
Selling (5% of sales)	$250,000	0
Overhead (1% of sales)	50,000	0
Profit	$200,000	0

Needing information on which to base his decision, the national sales manager contacts the industrial engineering and accounting staffs. He is told that the total production costs for the product grouped 6 to a package will be $4.50 per cartridge. Selling costs and overhead costs are 5% and 1% of sales, respectively.

Table 17-1 shows the projected profits and losses for the two decision alternatives—accept the offer or reject the offer. Since all costs and revenues are known for each alternative, the decision is straightforward: the $200,000 profit associated with accepting the offer exceeds the $0 profit associated with not accepting the offer; therefore, the offer should be accepted.

As this example shows, once a certainty model has been specified, the best decision is evident. By "best decision," we mean the alternative course of action, using all available information, that best satisfies the decision criterion. In the Econoprint Company example, the decision criterion was highest profit. Given that the decision model displayed in Table 17-1 utilized all available information, the best decision was to accept the offer. Since this is a certainty environment, the decision will result in an outcome of $200,000 profit. Thus, in a certainty environment, the best decision will always be associated with the best outcome.

Uncertainty

If business decisions were always made in a certainty environment, you would probably not need the academic training you are now receiving to be successful. How many of us would have chosen to reject the offer in the Econoprint Company example if Table 17-1 reflected the total decision picture? In reality, the typical business decision-making environment is not one of certainty but, rather, **uncertainty.**

UNCERTAINTY
A decision environment in which the decision maker does not know what outcome will occur when an alternative is selected.

The certainty environment is predicated on the fact that the outcome from each alternative course of action is known. If we choose alternative A, outcome Y will occur. If alternative B is selected, outcome Z will occur. This makes choosing between the alternatives straightforward.

However, in most business situations, while we may be able to specify the possible outcomes for each alternative, we will be uncertain about which outcome will occur. In an environment of uncertainty, the outcome that will occur from selecting an alternative course of action is not known. Consider the real estate speculator who is trying to decide whether to purchase land outside of Las Vegas, one of the fastest growing cities in the country, hoping to resell the land to a developer. If the speculator elects not to purchase the property, the net change in his financial position will be zero. He knows this for sure. However, if he chooses to buy the land, just what will the outcome be? Will he make

$10,000,000, or $20,000,000, or will he lose $5,000,000? Identifying the possible outcomes is difficult enough, but knowing for certain what outcome definitely will occur is impossible in a competitive real estate market. Thus, the speculator must decide whether to buy or not to buy in an environment of uncertainty.

Eagle Lumber Company

Consider the Eagle Lumber Company in Glenns Ferry, Wisconsin. About 3 weeks ago, the manager received 4,000 board feet of 2-inch × 6-inch tongue-and-groove knotty pine, which is used primarily for floors and ceilings. The product is hard to get, since the supplier makes only a limited quantity each month. The wholesale price for the recent shipment was $360 per thousand board feet. Two days after receiving the material, a customer came in and bought the entire shipment for $450 per thousand board feet. However, the customer wanted Eagle Lumber to store the material for 5 weeks.

Two days ago, another customer arrived and wanted to purchase as much 2-inch × 6-inch tongue-and-groove knotty pine as possible for immediate use. At that time, the only stock on hand at the lumber company was the 4,000 board feet that had already been sold. After seeing the already sold knotty pine, the new customer asked whether the manager would consider selling him the 4,000 board feet now and replacing the material before the previous customer returned to pick it up.

In a certainty environment, the decision would be relatively easy. If the lumber could be replaced at a known price before the first customer returned, the manager could resell the material and both customers would be happy. If the lumber could not be replaced before the first customer returned, the second customer would be turned away. Unfortunately, the decision environment facing Eagle's manager is not one of certainty. For one thing, he does not know whether he will be able to replace the stock within 5 weeks. Furthermore, if he is able to replace the material, he does not know exactly what the cost will be. Therefore, he is uncertain about what price to charge the second customer. He is also uncertain about whether the first customer will arrive early to take his material. As you can see, a seemingly simple situation is actually quite complex due to the uncertainties involved.

The decision-analysis techniques presented in this chapter do not eliminate the uncertainty associated with a decision, but they do provide a framework for dealing with the uncertainty. These techniques help you make good decisions under uncertain conditions, but good decisions don't necessarily result in good outcomes. For instance, suppose after considering all available information, the best decision is not to sell to the new customer. Then, a week later, the original customer calls to say he will be 6 weeks late picking up the material. If the manager had known this, he could have sold the materials to the new customer and received the additional profit. Thus, the best decision at the time did not result in a good outcome.

This concept of decision analysis is contrary to how many people view situations. The tendency is to look at the outcome and, if it is not good, we second-guess our decision. However, if we have properly used all available information in making the decision, it was a good decision. Decision makers must realize that in an uncertain environment, where they don't have total control over the outcomes of their decisions, bad outcomes will sometimes occur. Decision makers must also continually remind themselves that there is a difference between a good decision and a good outcome. *The goal of decision analysis is to focus on making good decisions, which in the long run should result in an increased number of good outcomes.*

Not all decisions require the use of decision analysis. The complexity of the decision situation usually determines the usefulness of decision analysis. The more complex the decision, the greater the potential benefit from decision analysis. Several factors affect the complexity of a decision, including the number of alternatives available to the decision maker, the number of possible outcomes associated with each alternative, and the general level of uncertainty associated with the decision. For example, marketing decisions regarding product design, product pricing, and distribution are very complex, and decision-analysis tools can be helpful to the decision maker. Of course, any decision involving product design or pricing also involves other areas in an organization, including production and finance.

Another characteristic of situations where decisions can be aided by decision analysis is that they often extend to multiple functional areas of the organization. Production decisions including process design, aggregate planning, and facilities planning all lend themselves to decision analysis because of their complexity and long-term importance to the organization. Such financial decision areas as capital budgeting, project financing, and pension investing clearly can benefit from the application of decision analysis.

The types of decisions mentioned here are only a few of those where decision analysis can be effectively applied. Throughout the remainder of this chapter we will present further examples where decision analysis can be used to aid business decision making.

17-1: EXERCISES

17-1. In decision analysis, what is the difference between a good decision and a good outcome? Do good decisions always produce the "best" outcome? Why or why not?

17-2. What is the goal of decision analysis?

17-3. Varsity Contracting has recently started negotiating to provide custodial service for a local manufacturer at several facilities in the area. The manufacturer has offered to contract for Varsity's services at the rate of $0.10 per square foot per month. To provide nightly custodial service for the 100,000-square-foot plant, Varsity would have to hire 2 more workers at $8.00 per hour. The new service would require 8 hours per night, 5 nights a week. Supplies would cost $200 per week, and overhead would be charged at 20% of the labor cost.

Given the information presented here, what decision environment exists? Why do you think so? Would you recommend that Varsity sign this contract? Explain your reasoning.

17-2: DECISION CRITERIA

When you are faced with choices between two or more options in a business situation, you are required to make a decision. Unless you are willing to flip a coin, "draw straws," or use some other random method for making the choice, you will need to establish some basis for making the decision. The criterion on which the decision is to be made needs to be established. Then, ideally, you will perform an analysis of the decision situation and make the "best" choice by weighing each decision option against the criteria you have established.

EXAMPLE
17-3

***DECISION
CRITERIA***

Fisher Fabrication

Fisher Fabrication has been in business for 10 years in eastern Tennessee. The company was started by two brothers who had worked in the electronics industry in Texas and California. They wanted to get back to where they grew up, and saw that many electronics companies were beginning to subcontract their assembly work, particularly on small volume items. They saw an opportunity to get into the subcontracting business and so decided to move back home. They found a dedicated workforce and soon employed 150 people.

The brothers concentrated on manual assembly of limited volume items such as special equipment for oil exploration, vehicle, and military contracts. Business had been extremely good until 2 years ago, when revenues began to decline slightly. By contacting past customers, the brothers determined the drop in sales was due to the increasing use by companies of surface mounted components, something the Fishers were not able to do by hand.

This finding made the brothers realize their company must invest in a surface mount machine, but they were uncertain about the extent of the investment needed. Initial research led them to identify three potential courses of action (alternatives).

A_1: A large investment, which would involve purchasing a full-scale surface mount system including robotics thus allowing them to bid on the majority of present manufacturing contracts. This equipment would give them greater capability than they now have.

A_2: A medium investment, which would give them the same general capability as alternative A_1 but which would operate at a much lower speed. This would prevent them from bidding on large contracts.

A_3: A small investment, which would limit them to bidding on less than half of the current contracts

Obviously, the alternative the Fishers select should depend on the future revenues generated by the new equipment. Consequently, the Fishers identified three potential directions that they believed the demand for surface mounted components could take. In decision-analysis terminology, these three demand levels are referred to as **states of nature**.

> **STATES OF NATURE**
> The possible outcomes in a decision situation over which the decision maker has no control.

For the Fishers, the states of nature are:

S_1: Rapidly increasing demand due to the capability of the surface mount equipment
S_2: Moderately increasing demand
S_3: Slight increase in demand as more businesses add their own surface mount capability

The Fishers would like to base their investment decision on yearly profit values, but as we can see, there will be three potential profit levels, due to the three states of nature, for each alternative. The outcome that is associated with any combination of a particular state of nature and an alternative is called a **payoff**.

> **PAYOFF**
> The outcome (profit or loss) for any combination of alternative and state of nature. The outcomes of all possible combinations of alternatives and states of nature constitute a *payoff table*.

Since the brothers' decision involves three alternatives and three states of nature, they have nine possible payoffs to consider, as shown in the payoff table (Table 17-2).

In order to decide among the three alternatives, the Fishers must have some basis for comparison and so must establish decision criteria. There are two main categories of decision criteria: *nonprobabilistic* and *probabilistic*. Nonprobabilistic criteria are used when either the probabilities associated with the possible payoffs are unknown or the decision maker lacks confidence and/or information with which to assess probabilities

TABLE 17-2
Fisher Fabrication Payoff Table

	DEMAND (STATES OF NATURE)		
Alternative	S_1 Large Increase	S_2 Moderate Increase	S_3 Small Increase
A_1 Large Investment	$6,000,000	$4,000,000	$-2,600,000
A_2 Medium Investment	2,500,000	5,000,000	-1,000,000
A_3 Small Investment	2,000,000	1,500,000	1,200,000

Note: These values are the Fishers' estimates of the profit associated with each combination of alternative and state of nature.

for the various payoffs. Probabilistic criteria incorporate the decision maker's assessment of the probability of each state of nature occurring.

Nonprobabilistic Decision Criteria

Several specific decision criteria fall into the nonprobabilistic category. One of these is the **maximax criterion**.

MAXIMAX CRITERION

An optimistic decision criterion for dealing with uncertainty without using probability. For each option, the decision maker finds the maximum possible payoff and then selects the option with the greatest maximum payoff.

For the Fisher brothers, using this criterion would mean making a major investment in surface mount equipment, since that is the alternative with the highest possible payoff, $6,000,000 per year (Table 17-2). The maximax criterion might be chosen by optimistic decision makers.

If we are not optimistic, we might select the alternative whose worst possible outcome is better than the worst possible outcome from any other alternative. This pessimistic (or conservative) criterion is called the **maximin criterion**.

MAXIMIN CRITERION

A pessimistic (conservative) decision criterion for dealing with uncertainty without using probability. For each option, the decision maker finds the minimum possible payoff and selects the option with the greatest minimum payoff.

For the Fishers, using the maximin criterion would mean selecting the small-investment alternative, since its worst outcome, $1,200,000, is better than any other alternative's worst outcome (see Table 17-2).

A disadvantage of the maximax and maximin criteria is they use only one value from the payoff table to make the decision. In analyzing the decision situation, the brothers may be interested in determining how much opportunity cost may result by making the wrong choice. For instance, suppose they decide on the medium-cost alternative and later find that the market for surface mount capability has expanded greatly. The medium-investment decision leads to a $2,500,000 yearly profit while the best decision of making a large investment (given perfect hindsight) would have earned $6,000,000. The difference between the actual payoff and the optimal payoff for a given state of nature is an **opportunity loss**; in this case, it is $3,500,000. If the Fishers decide to use the **minimax regret criterion**, they will need to know the value of the opportunity loss.

OPPORTUNITY LOSS

The difference between the actual payoff that occurs for a decision and the optimal payoff for the same state of nature.

MINIMAX REGRET CRITERION

A decision criterion that considers the costs of selecting the "wrong" alternative. For each state of nature, the decision maker finds the difference between the best payoff and each other alternative and uses these values to construct an opportunity-loss table. The decision maker then selects the alternative with the minimum opportunity loss (or regret).

Alternative	DEMAND (STATES OF NATURE)		
	S_1 Large Increase	S_2 Moderate Increase	S_3 Small Increase
A_1 Large Investment	$ 0	$1,000,000	$3,800,000
A_2 Medium Investment	3,500,000	0	2,200,000
A_3 Small Investment	4,000,000	3,500,000	0

TABLE 17-3
Fisher Fabrication:
Opportunity-Loss Table

Note: The values in this table were found by subtracting each column value in Table 17-2 from the largest value in that column: For example, if S_1 occurs, the optimal decision is A_1, yielding a payoff of $6,000,000. If A_2 is selected instead, the payoff is $2,500,000. The difference ($6,000,000 − $2,500,000) is $3,500,000, which is the opportunity loss.

TABLE 17-4
Fisher Fabrication Maximum
Regret Table

ALTERNATIVE	MAXIMUM OPPORTUNITY LOSS, OR REGRET
A_1 Large Investment	$3,800,000
A_2 Medium Investment	3,500,000 (smallest regret)
A_3 Small Investment	4,000,000

The minimax regret criterion considers the results of selecting the "wrong" alternative. The first step is to construct an opportunity-loss, or regret, table by finding, for each state of nature, the difference between the payoff for the best decision and the payoffs for all the other alternatives. Table 17-3 shows how this is done. The next step is to find the maximum regret for each alternative. These values are shown in Table 17-4. The minimax regret criterion now requires selecting the minimum of these maximum regret values. Using this criterion, we should choose the medium-investment decision, since the maximum opportunity loss of $3,500,000 is lower than the maximum opportunity loss for either of the other two alternatives.

Observe that all three criteria lead to different decisions; therefore the brothers should determine which criterion best describes their decision-making philosophy and use it to help them decide on the level of investment they should undertake.

The maximax, maximin, and minimax regret decision criteria are examples of nonprobabilistic decision criteria. Nonprobabilistic criteria do not take into account the probability associated with the outcomes for each alternative; they merely focus on the dollar value of the outcomes. The criticism of nonprobabilistic decision criteria is their failure to include important information about the chances of each outcome occurring. Decision analysts argue that if the payoff probabilities are known or can be assessed, a probabilistic decision criterion should be employed.

Probabilistic Decision Criteria

Some decision criteria take into account the probabilities associated with each outcome. One of these is the **expected-value criterion**.

> **EXPECTED-VALUE CRITERION**
> A decision criterion that employs probability to select the alternative that will produce the greatest average payoff or minimum average loss.

EXPECTED-VALUE CRITERION

The term *expected value* is often used in statistics to refer to the long-run average outcome for a given alternative. The concept of expected value was introduced in Chapter 4. In order to determine an expected value, we must have probabilities for each possible outcome. The expected value is then computed as follows.

EXPECTED VALUE

$$E(x) = \sum_{i=1}^{k} x_i P(x_i)$$ 17-1

where:

x_i = The ith outcome of the specified alternative measured in some units, such as dollars

$P(x_i)$ = The probability of outcome x_i occurring

k = number of potential outcomes

and:

$$\sum_{i=1}^{k} P(x_i) = 1.0$$ 17-2

$$0.0 \leq P(x_i) \leq 1.0$$ 17-3

Equation 17-1 shows that the expected value is the sum of the weighted outcomes for a specified alternative. This means that if the alternative is repeatedly selected, over the long run the average outcome will equal $E(x)$, the expected value.

EXAMPLE 17-4

DECISION CRITERIA

Xircom, Inc.

Consider the following simple decision situation that involves Xircom, Inc., one of the South's mobile connectivity leaders. Its products provide notebook PC users the ability to access their corporate networks. Recently, its stock has been trading in the $36 range. There has been a rumor of a merger between Xircom and one of its major competitors. Analysts think there is a 50% chance that the merger will occur. Further, if the merger occurs, analysts believe that Xircom's stock will rise by 10 points. If the merger does not occur, the analysts project that Xircom's stock will drop by 5 points. If you buy the stock and the merger occurs, you will have a profit of $10 per share. If you buy the stock and the merger does not occur, you will lose $5 per share. If you choose not to purchase the stock, you will, of course, neither gain nor lose anything. In this case, the "no-buy" option has a constant $0 payoff, and the buy alternative has uncertain outcomes. Let x_1 = $10 (merger occurs) and x_2 = −$5 (merger fails). Then, if the analysts are correct, the following probability distribution exists.

	x	$P(x)$
Merger Occurs	$10	0.50
Merger Does Not Occur	−5	0.50
		1.00

The expected value is:

$$E(x) = (\$10)(0.50) + (-\$5)(0.50) = \$2.50$$

This means that over the long run you would average $2.50 per share if you elected to purchase the stock. However, for this purchase, you would either gain $10 or lose $5. If you don't purchase the stock, the expected gain is $0, since that payoff is a constant for the "no-buy" alternative.

When applying the expected-value criterion, the best decision is to select the alternative with the highest expected payoff or the lowest expected loss. In the stock purchase example, the best decision, using the expected-value criterion, is to purchase the stock, since $2.50 > $0. The advantage of the expected-value criterion is that it takes into account the information contained in the probabilities. For instance, if the chance of a merger were only 0.10 instead of 0.50, the expected value of the buy option would be:

$$E(x) = (\$10)(0.10) + (-\$5)(0.90) = -\$3.50$$

Then, given this new information about the merger, the best decision, based on the expected-value criterion, would be the "don't-buy" option, since $0 > -\$3.50$.

The disadvantage of the expected-value criterion is that it does not take into account the decision maker's attitude toward risk. For instance, in the first case for the stock purchase example, the expected value was $2.50. Clearly, on the basis of expected value we buy the stock, since $2.50 > $0. However, if we purchase stock under these conditions, we could actually lose $5 or make $10. Thus, depending on how averse we are to losing $5, we might decide not to participate after all. Later in this chapter we will deal specifically with the issue of risk preferences.

Expected value is the decision criterion around which the techniques of decision analysis are built and is the one criterion emphasized throughout this chapter.

PROBABILITY ASSESSMENT[1]

If we are going to incorporate probability in a decision-making process, we need some method to assess the probability associated with specific outcomes. This is where a problem arises, since probability means different things to different people. Perhaps the most common situation involving probability is a simple action like flipping a coin, where, if the coin is fair, the probability of either a head or tail is 0.50. In fact, probabilities are known for most games of chance, and in casino games, serious players always know the probabilities of winning and losing. The assessment method used in these cases is called classical probability assessment. It assumes that individual outcomes are equally likely.

CLASSICAL PROBABILITY ASSESSMENT

$$P(x) = \frac{\text{Number of ways } x \text{ can occur}}{\text{Total number of ways any outcome can occur}}$$

17-4

Although classical probability assessment works well for games of chance (like dice or drawing cards), it is not appropriate for situations in which individual outcomes are not equally likely. For example, suppose your university is considering whether or not to continue to keep the computer lab open on Friday evening. The administrator agrees to do so only if 12 or more people come to use the lab. She might begin by attempting to assess the chances that 12 or more people will use the lab. The classical probability assessment method will not work, since neither denominator nor numerator values, required for using Equation 17-4, are known. However, a review of the past 50 Friday evenings shows that on 20 occasions 12 or more people were in the lab. With this information, she could use the **relative frequency of occurrence** method to assess the probabilities. This method equates the probability of an outcome occurring to the ratio of the number of times the outcome has occurred in the past to the total number of observations. In this case, the probability is $P(x \geq 12) = 20/50$. In general notation, this is stated as:

RELATIVE FREQUENCY OF OCCURRENCE PROBABILITY

$$P(x) = \frac{\text{Number of times } x \text{ occurs}}{n}$$

17-5

where:

$$n = \text{Number of observances}$$

This method of probability assessment is often used in business. For instance, a production control manager would assess the probability of a defective part being produced on a production line by examining a sample of n parts and counting how many were

---

[1]See Chapter 4 for a further discussion of probability assessment.

	MACHINE A		MACHINE B	
	Repair Cost	Probability	Repair Cost	Probability
	$ 0	0.1	$ 0	0.2
TABLE 17-5	1,000	0.5	1,000	0.3
Probability Distribution for	5,000	0.3	5,000	0.4
Monthly Repair Costs	10,000	0.1	10,000	0.1

defective. The ratio of the number of defectives to the sample size gives the probability assessment.

In order for the relative frequency of occurrence method to be appropriate, the sample size has to be sufficiently large and each observation must be taken under similar conditions. A construction firm estimating the chances of winning a bid on a project may have had only two equivalent experiences. But winning both previous bids should not lead the company to believe the chance of winning the new bid is 100% even though $P(\text{win}) = 2/2 = 1.0$. The sample size is just too small. However, the sample size might be increased by including all contract bids in the last 10 years. But even if n increases to 250, the situations for the past 250 contracts will not match this current contract; so a relative frequency of occurrence assessment would not be appropriate.

In many decision-making situations that require a probability assessment, neither the classical method nor the relative frequency of occurrence method is satisfactory. Instead, the decision maker will have to make a *subjective probability assessment*.

Subjective assessments are based upon individual experiences and available information. A subjective probability is a measure of a personal conviction that an outcome will occur. Therefore, a subjective probability assessment represents the decision maker's state of mind, or degree of belief, regarding the chance that the outcome will occur.

Decision makers constantly make subjective probability assessments and incorporate them into their decisions. When the tools of decision analysis are employed, these probability assessments must be quantified and expressed openly. For example, suppose a company manager has to decide which of two numerically controlled milling machines to purchase. One criterion to be used in the decision is monthly expected repair costs. Table 17-5 shows the possible repair costs for each machine and the subjectively assessed probability for each level. These probabilities reflect the state of mind of the manager. If someone else were to assess the probabilities, he or she would probably arrive at different assessments based on different experiences and a different state of mind.

The expected monthly repair cost for each of the two machines is computed in Table 17-6. Since lower repair costs are preferred, the best decision using the expected-value criterion is to select machine A, since $3,000 < $3,300. The expected value is computed using the decision maker's subjective probabilities. In assessing these probabilities, the decision maker should incorporate all available information and experience to accurately reflect his or her state of mind at the time the decision is being made.

TABLE 17-6
Expected-Value
Computations for Monthly
Repair Costs

MACHINE A			MACHINE B		
Repair Cost x	Probability $P(x)$	$xP(x)$	Repair Cost y	Probability $P(y)$	$yP(y)$
$ 0	0.1	$ 0	$ 0	0.2	$ 0
1,000	0.5	500	1,000	0.3	300
5,000	0.3	1,500	5,000	0.4	2,000
10,000	0.1	1,000	10,000	0.1	1,000
Expected Repair Cost		$3,000	Expected Repair Cost		$3,300

17-2: EXERCISES

Business Applications

17-4. Larry Jacava is considering producing a novelty item for golfers that will be sold through pro shops. Larry has decided on a selling price of $3.50 for the item. The item's variable cost of production is $2.00 per unit with a fixed cost of $3,750. Larry has marketed his product to local pro shops and believes the demand for the item will be either 2,000 units, 3,000 units, 4,000 units, or 5,000 units.

    a. Set up the payoff table for Larry's decision.

Determine the number of units that Larry should produce using each of the following criteria.

    b. Maximax criterion

    c. Maximin criterion

    d. Minimax regret criterion

17-5. Sal De Carlo is the manager of food sales for Coyote Stadium. For each home game Sal must decide how many hot dogs to have available for sale. The number of hot dogs sold depends on the game's attendance. Sal pays $0.75 for each hot dog and $0.15 for each hot dog bun. Hot dogs are sold to fans during the game for $1.75. Any leftover hot dogs are sold to the men's dorms for $0.25 apiece. Sal estimates that demand for hot dogs for next week's game will be either 10,000, 15,000, 20,000, or 25,000.

    a. Set up the payoff table for Sal's decision.

How many hot dogs would Sal order if he uses each of the following criteria?

    b. Maximax criterion

    c. Maximin criterion

    d. Minimax regret criterion

17-6. A real estate investor in a medium-sized Western city is considering three investments: an apartment building, a strip mall, and an office building. Returns from each investment alternative depend on future population growth. The investor has developed three growth scenarios showing the revenue from each investment alternative along with their probability of occurrence. This information is shown in the following table.

POPULATION GROWTH	PROBABILITY	APARTMENT	MALL	OFFICE
Slow	0.20	$-75,000	$15,000	-$200,000
Average	0.30	10,000	30,000	50,000
High	0.50	150,000	75,000	100,000

For the given payoff matrix, what is the best decision and its associated payoff using the following?

    a. The maximax criterion

    b. The maximin criterion

    c. The minimax regret criterion

    d. The expected-value criterion

17-7. Cooke Collectibles produces fine porcelain miniatures representing famous people and historical events. To avoid production and scheduling problems, Cooke's pol-

icy is to make all copies of a figure in one production run. In the event that the demand for any figure exceeds the number produced, the customer's money is returned along with a coupon good for $10.00 toward the purchase of another Cooke miniature. If the company makes too many figures, the extras are sold to a discount outlet, which agrees to hold them for 6 months, for $50 each. This price is half the variable production cost of a figure.

    Cooke Collectibles has recently agreed to pay $200,000 for the rights to produce a miniature representing a famous singer. The company plans to sell the figures for $250 each. The marketing department predicts that actual demand will equal one of these possible demand levels: 20,000, 40,000, 60,000, 80,000.

    a. Set up a table showing the payoffs for all combinations of production and demand.

    b. Use the maximin criterion to arrive at the appropriate decision and the associated payoff. Contrast this decision with the one made using the maximax criterion instead.

17-8. Referring to the previous problem, suppose the marketing manager at Cooke Collectibles has analyzed the possible demand levels and subjectively assessed the following probabilities for the various demand levels.

DEMAND LEVEL	PROBABILITY
20,000	0.10
40,000	0.30
60,000	0.40
80,000	0.20
	1.00

Use the expected-value criterion to arrive at the best decision for Cooke and the associated expected value.

17-9. The Special Occasions Company, a nationwide distributor of flowers and greeting cards, has just contracted with Global Floral to purchase up to 500,000 dozen red and yellow roses for sale in the week before Valentine's Day. Special Occasions supplies flower shops and other retail outlets from regional distribution centers throughout the country. The problem now facing the company is how many dozen roses to buy. If the company doesn't buy enough, it loses potential business; if it buys more than are demanded, it loses the costs of purchasing and shipping these unsold roses. Any unsold roses are given to local hospitals and retirement homes or disposed of at the area landfill.

    The contract calls for a basic payment of $150,000 plus $5 for each dozen roses bought by Special Occasions. The company's accounting department has determined that the cost of shipping the roses from Global Floral's greenhouses averages $1.50 per dozen. The marketing department has estimated the demand for roses, and its probability distribution, as follows.

DEMAND LEVEL	PROBABILITY
100,000	0.10
150,000	0.40
200,000	0.20
225,000	0.20
250,000	0.10
	1.00

Assuming the roses sell for an average of $18 per dozen, set up the payoff table and use the expected-value criterion to find how many dozen roses should actually be purchased for the next Valentine's Day sales and the associated expected profit.

17-10. Baker Enterprises, a produce wholesaler that supplies fruits and vegetables to local grocery stores and restaurants, has just received notice that a frost in Florida will have a serious impact on this winter's orange harvest. If Baker's buyer waits until the time he normally buys Florida oranges, the price could be very high. Consequently, Sara Baker, the owner, has decided to enter into a contract now. The Florida supplier will guarantee any quantity of oranges this winter, but only on the following terms.

Fixed finder's fee	$10,000
Fewer than 1,001 boxes	$3.00 per box
1,000–5,000 boxes	$2.80 per box
More than 5,000 boxes	$2.50 per box

The sales manager has identified the following possible demand levels for boxes of oranges this winter: 500, 1,000, 2,000, 4,000, 7,000. The expected selling price will be $9.00 per box, and unsold boxes will be given away.

Set up a payoff table for this decision problem and use the minimax regret decision criterion to determine how many boxes of oranges Baker Enterprises should buy.

17-11. Referring to Problem 10, suppose the managers at Baker Enterprises have discussed the situation and, on the basis of their past experience with orange sales, have assessed the following probabilities for each possible demand level.

DEMAND	PROBABILITY
500	0.15
1,000	0.20
2,000	0.20
4,000	0.30
7,000	0.15
	1.00

Incorporate these probabilities into your analysis and determine the "best decision" for Baker Enterprises as well as its expected profit for this decision, using the expected-value criterion.

17-12. Referring to Problems 10 and 11, suppose Sara Baker has found an alternative supplier of Florida oranges. The new supplier will not charge a finder's fee but will charge $4.50 per box regardless of the quantity purchased. If Sara Baker decides to buy from the new supplier, how many boxes of oranges should she buy in order to maximize expected profit? Which supplier should she choose? Explain.

17-13. Duckland Enterprises is considering bidding on one or all of the first five franchises offered by a popular Japanese fast-food operation. Each franchise requires a yearly $100,000 payment and the construction of a building at an average cost of $250,000. Duckland plans to keep the franchises for a year and, if the businesses are successful, the company should be able to sell them for $600,000 each, including the buildings. If the operations are not successful, Duckland will close them down and sell the buildings for $150,000.

  a. Use the maximax decision criterion to determine how many franchises Duckland should purchase and the associated profit.

  b. How many franchises should Duckland purchase if the maximin decision criterion is used? Determine the accompanying profit for this decision criterion as well.

  c. Suppose Duckland Enterprises has three options for constructing the buildings for its franchises. One option is to construct the buildings as originally planned, at a cost of $250,000 each. A second option is to build smaller facilities in established malls, with building expenses totaling $150,000 each. If the mall operations are not successful, Duckland can recover $100,000 of the $150,000 building cost; and if they are successful, they can be sold for $500,000 each. A third option is to construct larger buildings, at a cost of $400,000 each. If successful, these operations can be sold for $1,000,000 each; and if they are not successful, the buildings can be sold for $200,000 each. Construct a payoff table describing these new alternatives for Duckland Enterprises.

  d. Determine how many franchises Duckland should acquire under each building-cost option described in part c and determine the associated profit. Provide separate answers using the maximin and maximax decision criteria.

  e. Referring to part c, suppose Duckland Enterprises assesses the following probability distributions for the number of successful franchises at each building-cost level.

$150,000		$250,000		$400,000	
Number	P(success)	Number	P(success)	Number	P(success)
0	0.05	0	0.06	0	0.09
1	0.10	1	0.10	1	0.15
2	0.15	2	0.20	2	0.25
3	0.25	3	0.40	3	0.40
4	0.30	4	0.12	4	0.07
5	0.15	5	0.12	5	0.04

For each building alternative, use the expected-payoff criterion to determine the optimal number of franchises to purchase and the expected payoff. Then determine which building-cost level Duckland should use for its franchises.

■ 17-3: COST OF UNCERTAINTY

EXAMPLE 17-5

COST OF UNCERTAINTY

The advantage of making decisions in a certainty environment is that the best decision always yields the best outcome. In an uncertain environment, the best decision might not result in the best outcome. Thus, there is a cost of uncertainty associated with not knowing in advance which outcome will occur. An example will show what we mean.

Haroldson's

In the United States, more money is now being spent on take-out and restaurant food than is spent buying groceries. Many grocery chains, in an effort to keep up with this trend, have added extensive deli and take-out sections. Haroldson's is a regional grocery chain that has joined the movement. A popular packaged meal is made up of broiled chicken, potato salad, and a green salad. However, because of several television news specials about potentially spoiled food, Haroldson's has a company policy of giving all unsold take-out food to a local homeless shelter at the end of each day. While the company doesn't mind giving any leftover food away, it would rather sell all the meals it prepares. Therefore, the question that deli managers face is how many meals to make each day. At one particular store, the manager believes that on this Friday, the minimum demand for the broiled chicken meal will be 50 and the maximum demand will be 90. To simplify the analysis, Table 17-7 lists only 5 possible demand levels, along with the manager's subjective assessments of the probability that each of these demand levels will occur.

The fixed cost of setting up to cook the meal is $120, variable costs amount to $1.50 per meal, and the selling price is $3.70 each. With this information, we find the payoffs associated with different production levels by using the following equation.

$$\text{Payoff} = \$3.70(s) - \$120 - \$1.50(p)$$

where:

$$s = \text{Number of units sold}$$
$$p = \text{Number of units produced}$$

Thus, the payoff when production is 50 and demand is 50 is:

$$\text{Payoff} = \$3.70(50) - \$120 - \$1.50(50) = -\$10.00$$

If 70 meals are prepared and 90 are demanded, the payoff is:

$$\text{Payoff} = \$3.70(70) - \$120 - \$1.50(70) = \$34.00$$

TABLE 17-7
Haroldson's Deli Manager's Probability Assessment

DEMAND	PROBABILITY
50	0.05
60	0.10
70	0.20
80	0.40
90	0.25
	1.00

(Notice that even though demand is 90, sales are limited to 70 because only 70 were produced.) The payoffs associated with all combinations of production and demand are displayed in the *payoff table* (Table 17-8). The demand levels are labeled "states of nature," since demand is outside the control of the decision maker.

Table 17-9 shows the payoff table and the probabilities associated with each demand level. The expected values for each production alternative are shown. These are computed

TABLE 17-8
Haroldson's Payoff Table

Production	DEMAND (STATES OF NATURE)				
	50	*60*	*70*	*80*	*90*
50	$-10	$-10	$-10	$-10	$-10
60	-25	12	12	12	12
70	-40	-3	34	34	34
80	-55	-18	19	56	56
90	-70	-33	4	41	78

| | DEMAND (STATES OF NATURE) | | | | | |
Production	50 $p = 0.05$	60 $p = 0.10$	70 $p = 0.20$	80 $p = 0.40$	90 $p = 0.25$	E(Payoff)
50	$-10	$-10	$-10	$-10	$-10	$-10.00
60	-25	12	12	12	12	10.15
70	-40	-3	34	34	34	26.60
80	-55	-18	19	56	56	35.65
90	-70	-33	4	41	78	29.90

TABLE 17-9
Haroldson's Expected Values

by summing the payoffs times the probabilities. For example, the expected payoff for a production level of 80 meals is:

$$E(\text{Payoff}) = -\$55(0.05) + (-\$18)(0.10) + \$19(0.20) + \$56(0.40) + \$56(0.25)$$
$$= \$35.65$$

Therefore, in the long run, the deli manager can expect to make $35.65 if she prepares 80 broiled chicken and potato salad meals each day. The other expected values are computed in a similar manner.

From Table 17-9 we see that if the decision criterion of highest expected payoff is used, the best decision is to prepare 80 meals. This production level has a higher expected payoff than any other alternative. However, on any single day, the actual payoff from this level could be either −$55, −$18, $19, or $56. This means that for any single situation, the best decision might not give the best outcome. Thus, there is a cost of being uncertain about which demand level will occur.

If the deli manager could obtain perfect information about the demand level, her decision environment would change to one of certainty. If she knew in advance how many meals would be demanded, she could select the production level that will maximize the payoff in each case. For example, if she knew the demand was going to be 70, she would decide to prepare 70 meals, for a profit of $34.00. If she knew demand would be 90, she would decide to prepare 90, for a profit of $78.00.

However, having perfect information about what might happen does not mean that we can control what will happen. Even though the highest profit will occur when demand is 90 and production is also 90, the manager cannot *make* the demand be 90. The demand for meals is outside her control.

If the demand level is assumed to occur according to the subjectively assessed probability distribution, the *expected value under certainty (EVUC)* can be computed. We first assume we know what the demand will be for each day. Therefore, we are able to achieve the optimal decision each time. To determine our overall expected profit, we multiply the probability of each demand level times the payoff associated with the best decision *given* that demand level occurs. Therefore, if the deli manager had perfect information (certainty) about what the demand was going to be for each day, her expected payoff would be computed as follows.

$$EVUC = -\$10(0.05) + \$12(0.10) + \$34(0.20) + \$56(0.40) + \$78(0.25)$$
$$= \$49.40$$

Thus, with perfect information, the deli would make, on average, a profit of $49.40 per day.

We determined earlier that the expected payoff under uncertainty was $35.65 (the best alternative from Table 17-9). The expected cost of uncertainty is the difference between the expected payoff under perfect information and the expected payoff under uncertainty. This is:

$$\text{Expected cost of uncertainty} = \$49.40 - \$35.65 = \$13.75$$

Another term for the cost of uncertainty is the *expected value of perfect information (EVPI)*. The EVPI in this case is $13.75, which is the most the manager would be willing to pay for perfect information about the meal demand on any day. Any information that is not perfect would be worth less than $13.75 per day.

17-3: EXERCISES

Business Applications

17-14. Refer to Problem 5 concerning the number of hot dogs that Sal De Carlo should order for next week's football game (see Section 17-2). Suppose that Sal has assigned the probabilities shown next for the different demand levels.

DEMAND	PROBABILITY
10,000	0.20
15,000	0.25
20,000	0.30
25,000	0.25

   a. Set up the payoff table for Sal's decision concerning the number of hot dogs to order.
   b. What are the expected values for each decision that Sal can make?

   c. How much would Sal be willing to pay for perfect information about the number of hot dogs that will be demanded during next week's game?

17-15. Refer to Problem 7 in Section 17-2 regarding the Cooke Collectibles. How much would Cooke be willing to pay for perfect information about the number of miniatures representing a famous singer that it should produce?

17-16. Refer to the Special Occasions Company problem (Problem 9) in Section 17-2. How much should the company be willing to pay for perfect information in order to determine how many dozen roses it should order for the next Valentine's Day sales?

17-17. Refer to the Baker Enterprises problem (Problems 10 and 11) in Section 17-2. What is the maximum amount that Baker should pay for perfect information to help the company determine how many boxes of oranges to order?

◼ 17-4: DECISION-TREE ANALYSIS

When decision analysis is applied to a real business problem, the process can become quite complex. The decision maker must identify the outcomes for each decision alternative, assess probabilities associated with each outcome, assign cash flows in the form of payoffs or opportunity costs, and somehow keep the sequence of decisions and outcomes in the proper order. Decision-tree analysis is very helpful in dealing with these complex decisions in an orderly manner. A **decision tree** provides a "road map" of the decision problem. In this section, we illustrate the steps involved in using decision trees to help with the decision process.

> **DECISION TREE**
> A diagram that illustrates the correct ordering of actions and events in a decision-analysis problem. Each act or event is represented by a node on the decision tree.

EXAMPLE 17-6

DECISION TREE

Harris Publishing Company

Consider the decision facing the Harris Publishing Company, which recently received a manuscript written by a former government official about the private life of a very influential member of the U.S. government. The author will grant Harris full rights to the book for a guaranteed up-front payment of $400,000 plus a per copy royalty if the book is published. The basic question facing Harris's management is whether to sign the contract with this author or risk losing the book to another publisher. Even if they sign, Harris will publish the book only if the manuscript receives a favorable review from the editorial board. But several uncertainties make this decision difficult. The executive editor, the person ultimately responsible for making the decision, has outlined the following items for consideration.

1. There is an 80% (0.80) chance that the content of the book is accurate. If the content is accurate, the author will be paid $2.00 per copy for each hardcover book sold and $0.80 per copy for each paperback. No royalties will be paid if the manuscript is not accurate. Accuracy will be known only after the book has been published.
2. If the content is not accurate, there is a 0.90 chance that a libel suit will be filed; and if so, experience indicates the publisher will settle out of court for $1,800,000.
3. For hardcover publication, the following demand distribution has been assessed.

DEMAND	PROBABILITY
100,000 copies	0.40
1,000,000 copies	0.60

4. The fixed production costs for the hardcover book will be $700,000 before any copies are printed; the cost of printing and binding is $16.00 each. The number of copies to be printed can match any projected demand. The wholesale selling price of the hardcover book will be $24.00.
5. For paperback publication, the following demand distribution has been assessed.

DEMAND	PROBABILITY
50,000 copies	0.30
1,500,000 copies	0.70

6. The fixed costs for paperback publication are $400,000, the printing and binding cost is $2.00 per copy, and the wholesale selling price is $8.00 each.
7. The editor has assessed the probability the manuscript will get a favorable review from the editorial board as 0.80.

The decision in this case is complicated by the many uncertainties involved. In situations such as these, a decision tree can be used to provide a framework for helping make the decision. A decision tree is a diagram of the decision alternatives and outcomes arranged in the order in which they will occur. The diagram appears like a tree lying on its side, with the alternatives and outcomes forming the branches.

FIGURE 17-1
Harris Publishing Decision Tree: Step 1

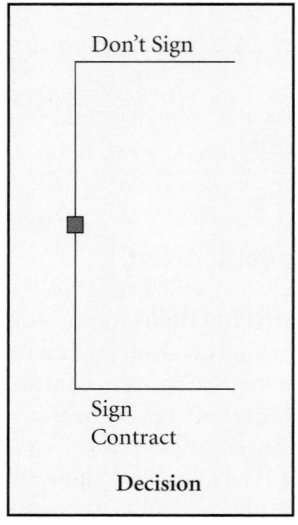

Growing the Tree

The decision tree is developed by starting with the initial decision facing the publisher: sign the contract or don't sign the contract. Figure 17-1 shows the beginnings of the decision tree. The box represents a *decision fork*, the point where a decision must be made.

If the publisher does not sign the contract, the issue is settled. There are no further branches on that side of the tree. However, if the contract is signed, other branches are needed. Keep in mind that the decision tree is a model of the decision in which alternatives (decisions) are followed by the outcomes (events) that they influence. Usually, but not always, the ordering of alternatives and outcomes follows a chronological sequence. Thus, if the contract is signed, the next step is the review by the editorial board. The outcome of this review is considered an event and is not within control of the company, since the outcome is determined by how well the book is written. A small circle is used to designate an event fork on the decision tree, as shown in Figure 17-2.

If the editorial review is unfavorable, the book will not be published. Thus, no more branches are needed if the review is unfavorable. If the manuscript review is favorable, the book will be published. Then the company must decide between hardcover or paperback books. This decision fork is shown in Figure 17-3.

Following the hardcover/paperback decision, the book will go on sale and the true demand will be known. (Recall that we assumed production can be set to match demand.)

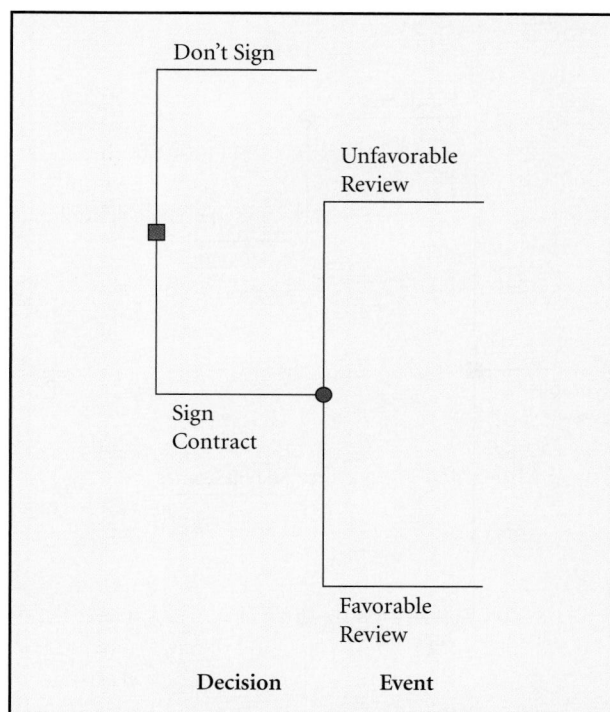

FIGURE 17-2   Harris Publishing Decision Tree: Step 2

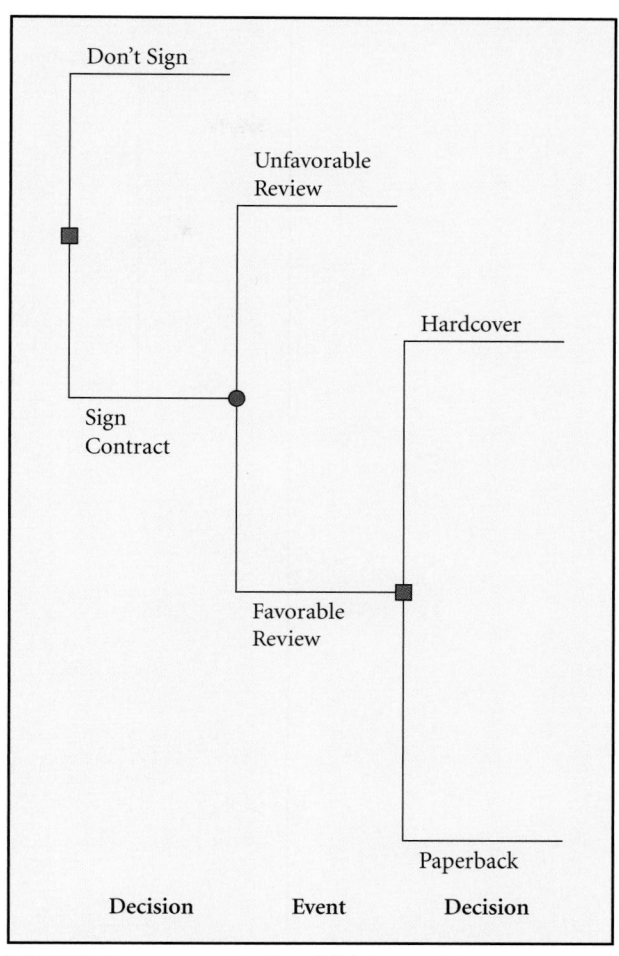

FIGURE 17-3   Harris Publishing Decision Tree: Step 3

The level of demand is an event and is not controlled by the company. Figure 17-4 shows the event forks and branches associated with demand.

After the book goes on sale, the company will find out whether the content is accurate. This is an event beyond the decision maker's control. Figure 17-5 shows these event branches. As you can see, the tree is growing.

Figure 17-6 shows the final set of branches, which relate to the possibility of a libel suit. If we have correctly described the decision problem, this tree is a model of the decision facing the Harris Publishing Company. After reaching the point when you think the tree is complete, conferring with someone who has not been involved in developing the tree can be helpful. A fresh perspective is often useful in finding oversights and inconsistencies in a decision tree. The decision tree should reflect the decision problem as accurately as possible before any further analysis is performed using the tree.

Assigning the Probabilities

The decision tree contains a number of *event forks*, represented by small circles. The branches leaving these event forks represent possible outcomes from an uncertain event. To make full use of decision-tree analysis, probabilities must be assigned to each of these event

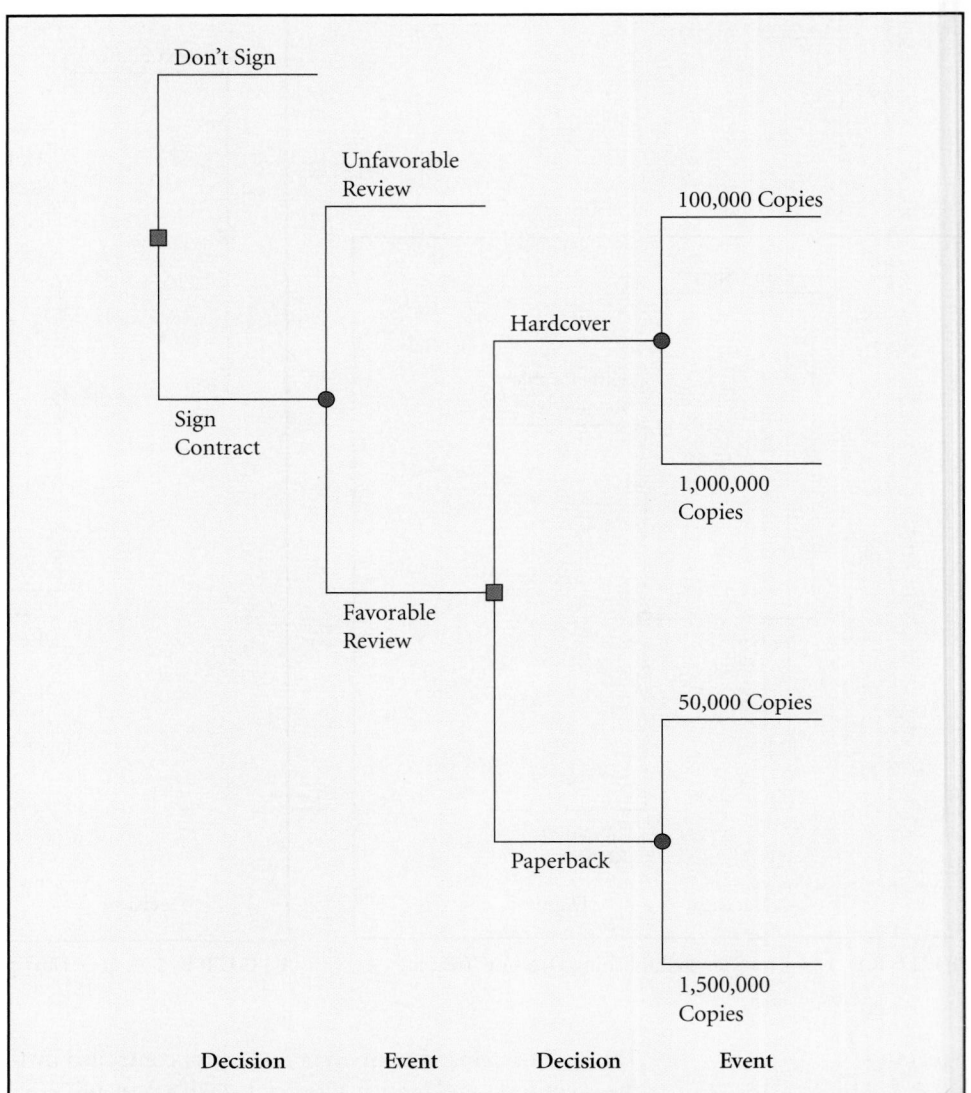

FIGURE 17-4
Harris Publishing Decision
Tree: Step 4

branches. As indicated earlier, these probabilities can come from classical assessment, relative frequency of occurrence or, most likely, subjective assessment.

In the Harris Publishing Company example, the probabilities were subjective assessments by the executive editor, based on her experience and the available information. We can summarize these as follows.

1. The probability that a manuscript review will be favorable is 0.80; unfavorable, 0.20.
2. If a hardcover edition is printed, there is a 0.40 chance that demand will be 100,000 copies and a 0.60 chance that demand will be 1 million copies.
3. If a paperback edition is printed, there is a 0.30 chance that 50,000 copies will be sold and a 0.70 chance that 1.5 million copies will be sold.
4. There is an 0.80 chance that the content of the book will prove accurate.
5. There is a 0.90 chance the publisher will be sued for libel if the book turns out not to be accurate.

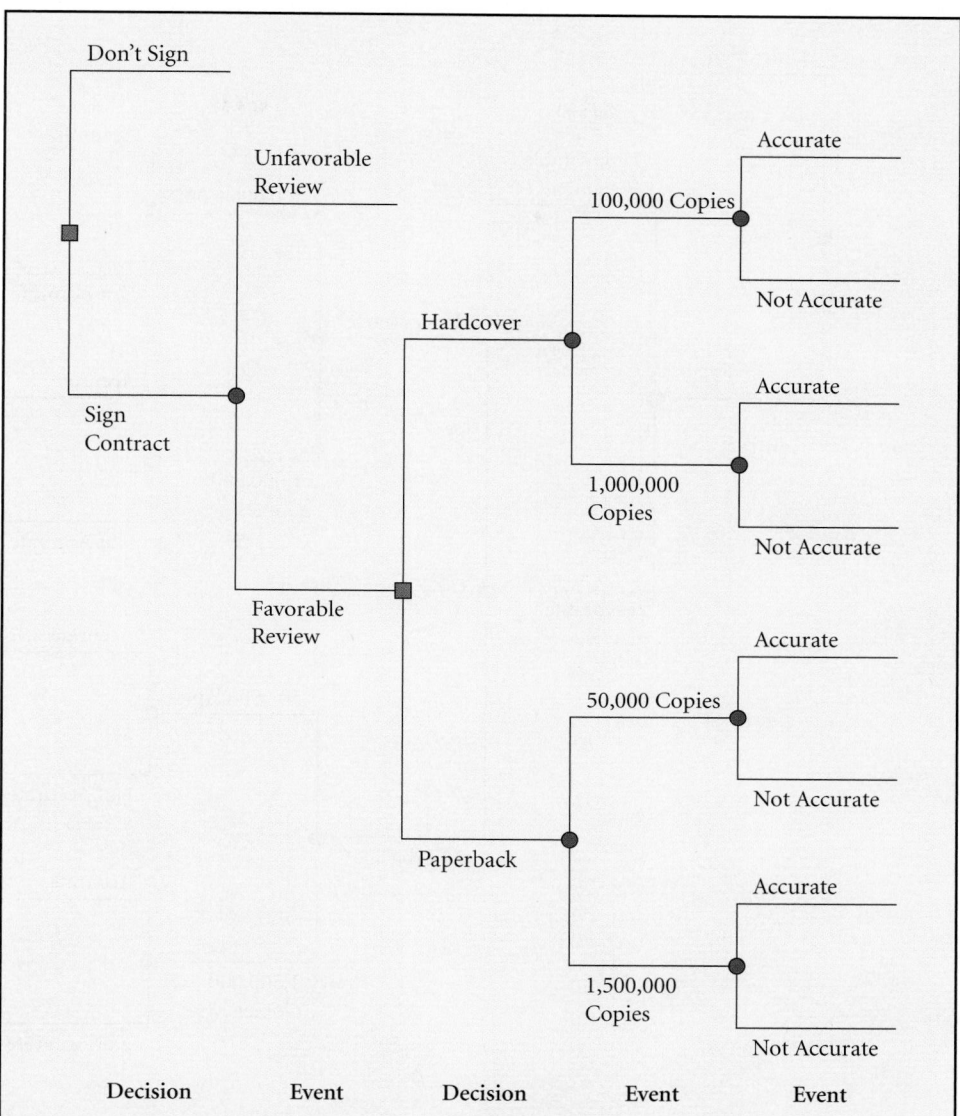

FIGURE 17-5
Harris Publishing Decision
Tree: Step 5

Figure 17-7 on page 707 shows the decision tree with the probabilities assigned. Remember, probabilities must be assigned to every event branch. The sum of the probabilities for each event fork must be 1.

Assigning the Cash Flows

Once probabilities have been assigned to each event, the next step is to assign the cash flows. A *cash flow* is defined here as any dollar change in the decision maker's asset position. For instance, any income or expense which is expressed in dollar terms is considered a cash flow. (In some applications, the "cash flows" might be expressed in something other than dollars, but in this text we will limit our definition of cash flows to dollars.) The cash flows are displayed on the tree branches indicating the time at which they will occur. Unlike probabilities, which are assigned only to events, cash flows can occur for both decisions and

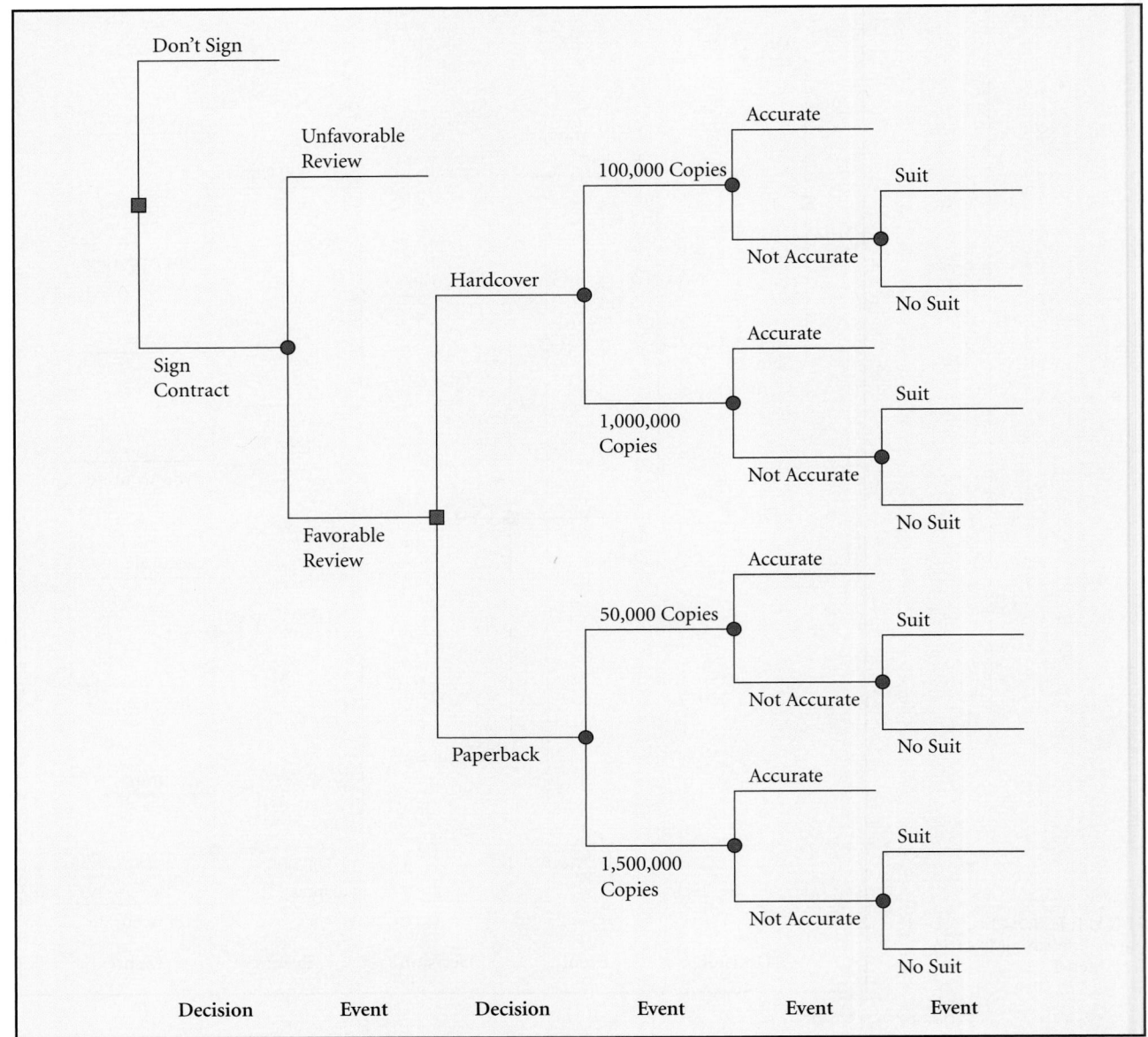

FIGURE 17-6 Harris Publishing Decision Tree: Step 6, Final Tree

events. For Harris Publishing Company, the first cash flow will occur when the author signs the contract. This will be an expense of $400,000. Figure 17-8 shows this as −$400 on the *Sign Contract* branch. The *Don't Sign Contract* branch has a cash flow of $0, indicating that if this decision is made, there will be no change in the company's asset position.

The editorial review is done by salaried staff members. Thus, we can treat this cost as part of administrative overhead and not assign any cash flows to the review branches in Figure 17-8. When the decision to publish hardcover or paperback books is made, a fixed expense occurs. The expense is $700,000 for hardcover and $400,000 for paperback. These cash flows are displayed in Figure 17-8. Next, we assign the cash flows associated with the

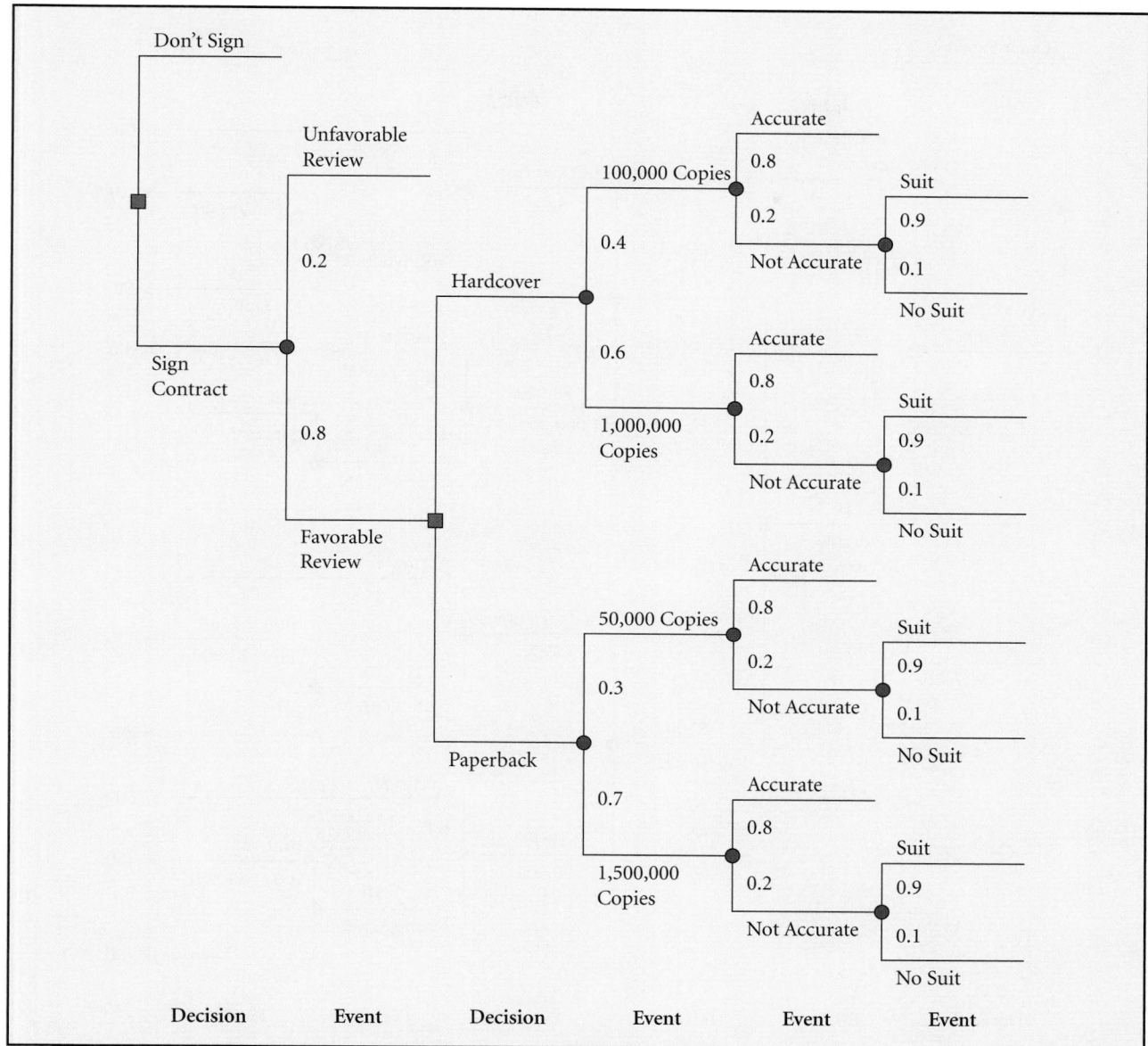

FIGURE 17-7   Harris Publishing Decision Tree: Step 7, Assigning Probabilities

demand levels for hardcover and paperback. For example, if the hardcover decision is selected and demand is 100,000 copies, the following cash flow will occur.

$$
\begin{array}{rl}
\text{Revenue: } 100,000 \text{ at } \$24.00 \text{ each} = & \$2,400,000 \\
\text{Expenses: } 100,000 \text{ at } \$16.00 \text{ each} = & \underline{-1,600,000} \\
\text{Net cash flow} = & \$ \;\;\; 800,000
\end{array}
$$

This $800,000 cash flow is shown in Figure 17-8. You may be wondering what happened to the author's royalties. These are to be paid only when the book's accuracy has been verified. For purposes of this decision, this is the same as paying the author when the books are sold and having him return the money if the book proves to be inaccurate.

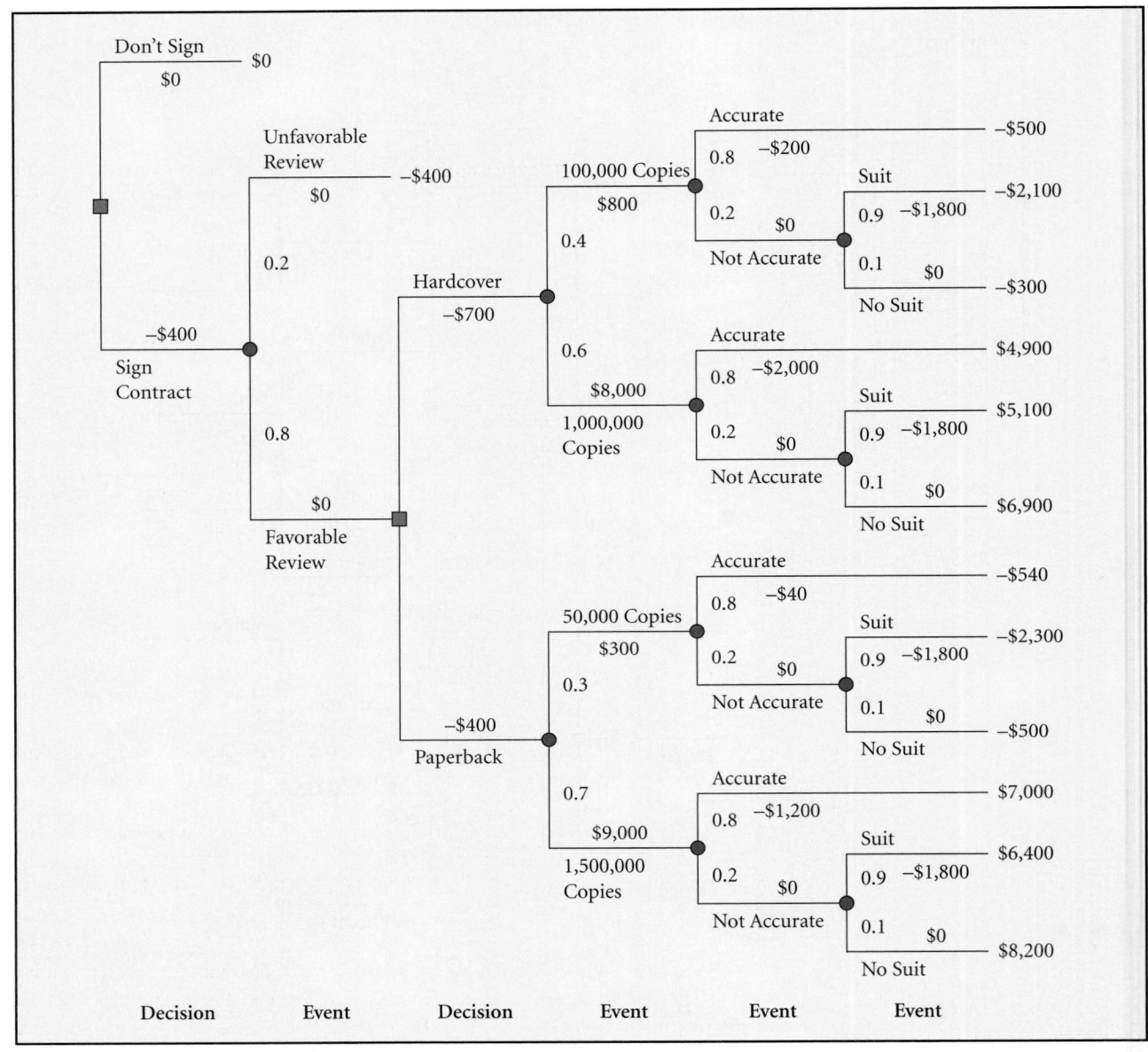

FIGURE 17-8   Harris Publishing: Assigning Cash Flows (\$ × 1,000)

If the hardcover book sells 1,000,000 copies, the cash flow will be:

$$
\begin{array}{rl}
\text{Revenues } 1,000,000 \text{ at } \$24.00 \text{ each} = & \$24,000,000 \\
\text{Expenses } 1,000,000 \text{ at } \$16.00 \text{ each} = & \underline{-16,000,000} \\
\text{Net cash flow} = & \$\ 8,000,000
\end{array}
$$

Likewise, if the paperback option is selected, the cash flow associated with 50,000 copies will be:

$$
\begin{array}{rl}
\text{Revenue } 50,000 \text{ at } \$8.00 \text{ each} = & \$400,000 \\
\text{Expenses } 50,000 \text{ at } \$2.00 \text{ each} = & \underline{-100,000} \\
\text{Net cash flow} = & \$300,000
\end{array}
$$

The total cash flow for 1,500,000 copies will be:

$$\begin{aligned} \text{Revenue } 1{,}500{,}000 \text{ at } \$8.00 \text{ each} &= \$12{,}000{,}000 \\ \text{Expenses } 1{,}500{,}000 \text{ at } \$2.00 \text{ each} &= \underline{-3{,}000{,}000} \\ \text{Net cash flow} &= \$ \ 9{,}000{,}000 \end{aligned}$$

These cash flows are shown in Figure 17-8.

Now, if the book turns out to be accurate, the publisher must pay the author royalties based on the number of books sold. For a hardcover book, the royalty rate is $2.00 per copy; for a paperback, it is $0.80 per copy. For example, if the paperback sells 1.5 million copies, the author must be paid $1,200,000. The royalty costs are shown under the branches labeled *Accurate* in Figure 17-8. If the book proves to be inaccurate, the author gets no royalties; so $0 cash flow is shown on the *Not Accurate* branch.

Finally, if the book is not accurate, the publisher might be sued for libel. In that case, the company's lawyer has told Harris that the government official who was libeled will likely settle for a payment of $1,800,000 (Figure 17-8). The editor agrees this amount is more than adequate to stop the suit. Since there are no other cash flows to be considered in this decision, the last step is to accumulate the cash flows from left to right and put the net cash flow for each branch to the right of each branch in Figure 17-8. These are called the *end values*. For example, consider the branches *Sign Contract, Favorable Review, Paperback, 50,000 Copies, Accurate, No Suit*. The end value is found as follows.

$$-400 + 0 - 400 + 300 - 40 = -540$$

Folding Back the Tree

Figure 17-9 shows the completed decision tree for Harris Publishing Company. (We have removed the intermediate values from the branches and have expressed the end values in thousands to make the numbers easier to work with.) This sets the stage for the process of *folding back the decision tree*, a process employed whenever the decision criterion being used is the expected-value criterion. Recall that Harris Publishing plans to select the alternative with the highest expected payoff.

Remember that the decision tree is a diagram of the sequence of decisions and events. To fold back the decision tree, we begin with the end values at the right of the tree and work our way back to the initial decision at the far left. To do this, we must determine the expected value of each decision branch. (Please refer to Figure 17-10 on page 711 as we discuss the foldback steps.)

Since the *Don't Sign Contract* branch has no following uncertain events, the end value of $0 is the expected value of that decision alternative. This expected value is displayed in a box near the decision fork.

The process of finding the expected value for the *Sign Contract* branch requires a little more effort. To begin, we go to each event branch where *Suit* and *No Suit* are the possible outcomes. We compute the expected values of these events by multiplying the end value times the probability of each outcome. For instance, for the event branch emanating from the *Hardcover, 100,000 Copies, Not Accurate* branch, the expected value is:

$$EV = -\$2{,}100(0.90) + (-\$300)(0.10) = -\$1{,}920$$

This expected value is displayed inside the oval between the two event branches. We use the same procedure to find expected values for all *Suit/No Suit* event branches, as shown in Figure 17-10. (Note: All dollar amounts are in thousands.)

Next, we determine the expected value of the event *Accurate/Not Accurate* in each instance in the tree where the event appears. To illustrate, we will use the event emanating from the *Hardcover, 100,000 Copies* branch. The expected value is:

$$EV = -\$500(0.80) + (-\$1{,}920)(0.20) = -\$784$$

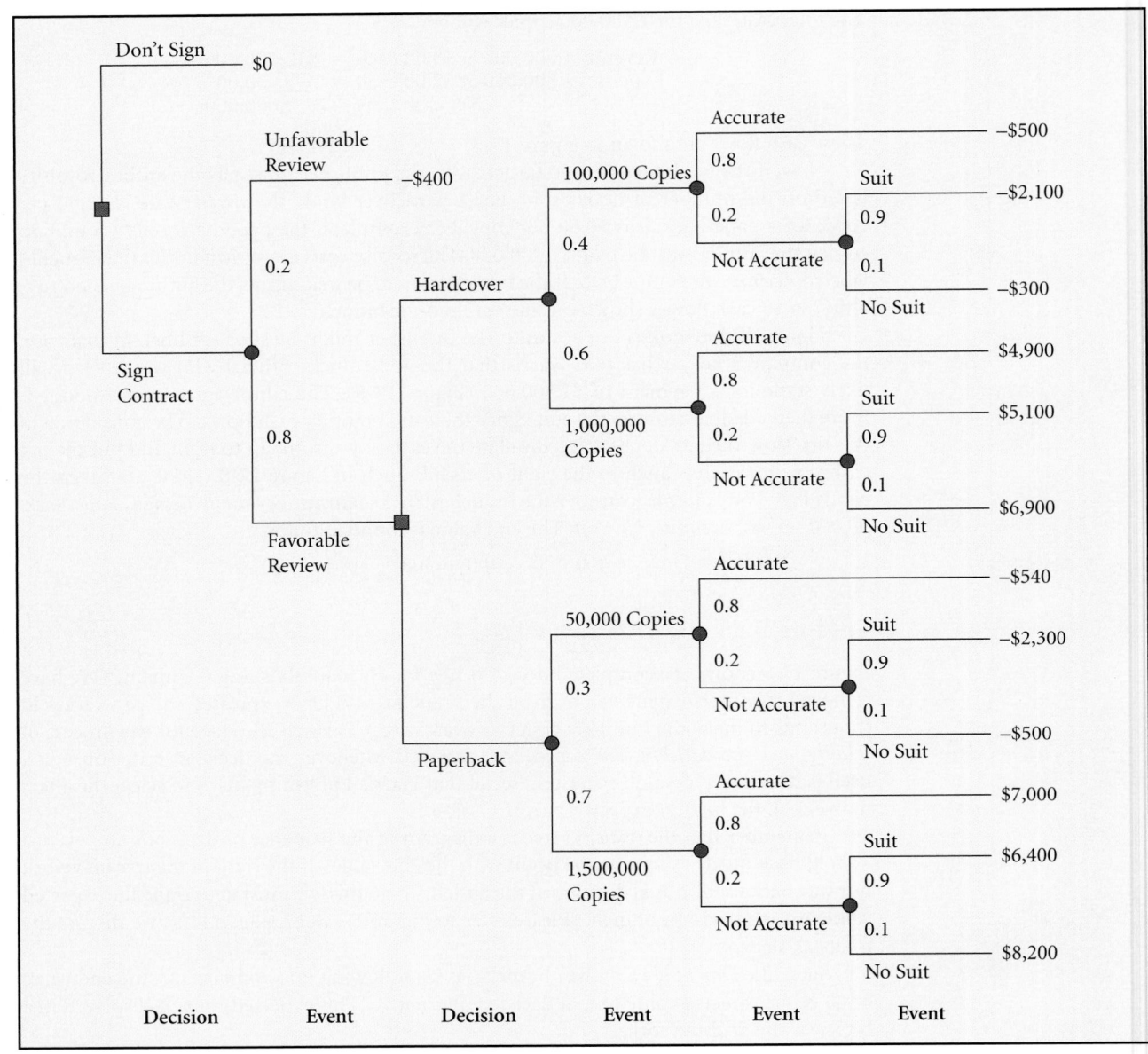

FIGURE 17-9   Harris Publishing: Final Decision Tree

This value is shown in the oval between the two event branches. Note that in computing the expected value, we used −$1,920, the expected value of the *Suit/No Suit* event. This value was multiplied by the 0.20 probability that the content of the manuscript will not be accurate. The 0.80 chance that the manuscript will be accurate is multiplied by −$500, since that is the expected value of the *Accurate* branch.

The expected value of the *Accurate/Not Accurate* event emanating from the *Hardcover, 1,000,000 copies* branch is:

$$EV = \$4,900(0.80) + \$5,280(0.20) = \$4,976$$

This value is also shown in Figure 17-10, in the oval between the two outcome branches. The same methodology is used in the lower portion of the tree. This process of moving from right to left is what we mean by "folding back the tree."

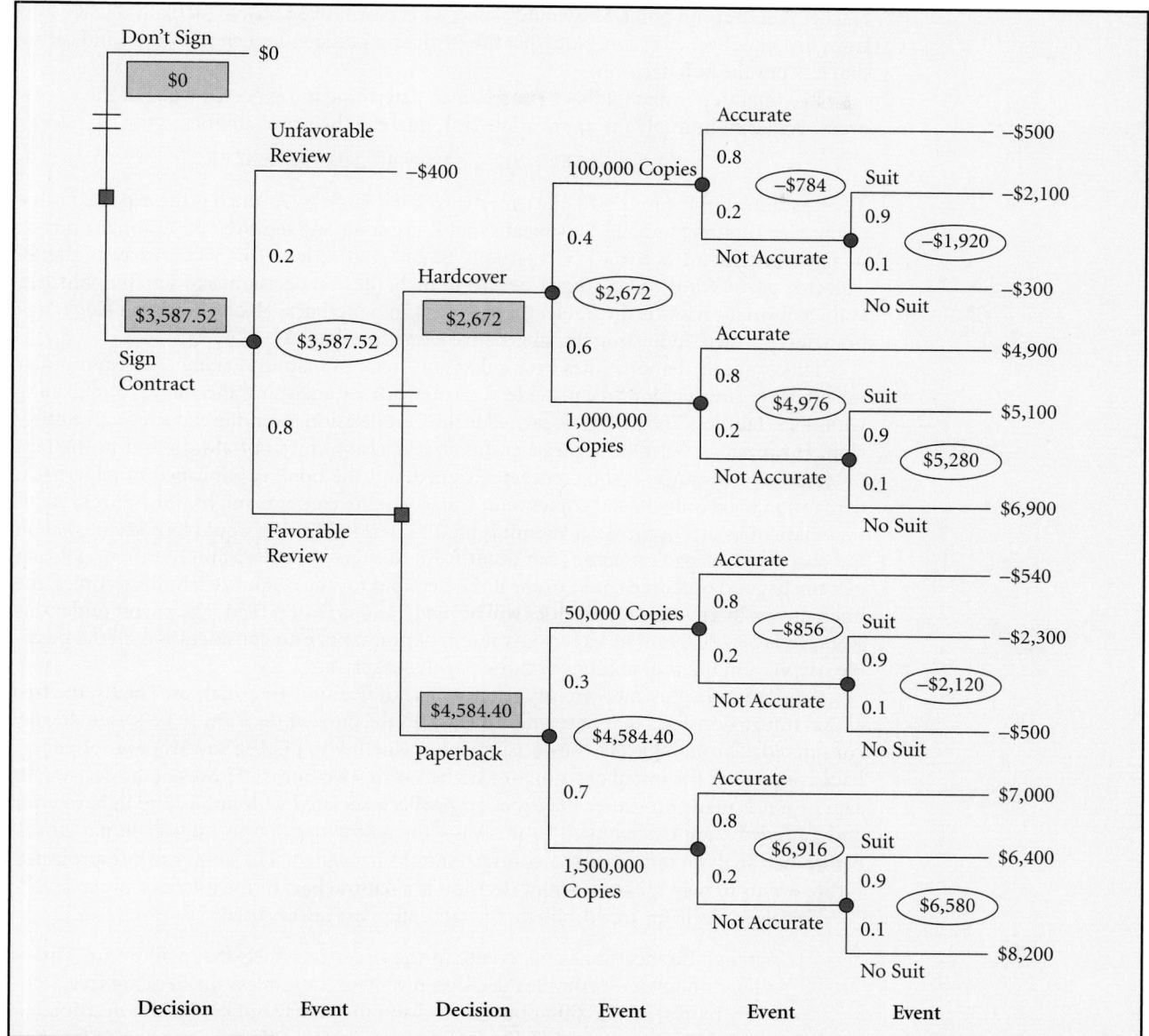

FIGURE 17-10   Harris Publishing: Folding Back the Decision Tree

We continue by determining the expected values of the demand events. For instance, the expected value for the demand event emanating from the *Hardcover* branch is:

$$EV = -\$784(0.40) + \$4,976(0.60) = \$2,672$$

This value, shown in Figure 17-10, is also the expected value of the *Hardcover* decision branch. This means that the expected value of the hardcover alternative is $2,672 (actually $2,672,000).

The expected value for the demand event emanating from the *Paperback* decision branch is:

$$EV = -\$856(0.30) + \$6,916(0.70) = \$4,584.40$$

This value, shown in Figure 17-10, is the expected value of the *Paperback* decision alternative. Since $4,584.40 > $2,672, the best decision is to select the paperback option if the editor reaches that decision point. She would expect a net payoff of $4,584.40 (actually $4,584,400) from the paperback decision. Note that the hardcover decision branch is blocked, indicating that it is not the best decision.

The final step in the foldback process is to determine the expected value of the review event. We again multiply the appropriate cash flows by their probabilities.

$$EV = -\$400(0.20) + \$4,584.4(0.80) = \$3,587.52$$

Thus, as shown in Figure 17-10, the expected value is $3,587.52, which is the expected value of the *Sign Contract* branch. This means that if the company signs the publishing contract, its expected payoff is $3,587.52 (actually $3,587,520). Since this value exceeds the $0 expected payoff for the *Don't Sign Contract* branch, the best decision is to sign the contract. If the editorial review is favorable, then publish in paperback. (Notice that the *Don't Sign* branch is blocked, indicating this alternative won't be selected.)

This example demonstrates how a decision tree can help in making a decision under uncertainty. The decision tree provides a framework for analyzing alternatives and dealing with uncertainties. The decision reached is the best decision given the expected value criterion. However, as we indicated earlier, the best decision does not always lead to the best outcome. For instance, if the contract is signed and the book is published in paperback, demand may be only 50,000 copies and, worse yet, the contents might not be accurate. If this chain of events occurred, a lawsuit is filed. Harris Publishing would lose $2,300,000 on the deal. Thus, a "bad outcome" can occur from this one-time decision. But then again, an extremely good outcome could occur if the demand for the book is 1.5 million copies, the book proves inaccurate (no royalties will be paid), and no suit is filed. The payoff under this scenario is $8,200,000. The expected-value criterion takes into consideration all the possible payoffs and the probabilities of those payoffs occurring.

This example illustrates an important virtue of decision-tree analysis. That is, the tree allows future decisions that have an influence on the current decision to be systematically considered. Chronologically, the decision about whether to publish in hardcover or paperback comes after the initial decision of whether to sign a contract. However, the decision to sign or not is made only after the expected profits associated with publishing in hardcover and paperback are determined. In this case, the editor decided to publish in paperback before her analysis indicated the contract should be signed. The ability to use projected future events to help make a current decision is a natural part of the foldback process.

To solve a decision-tree problem, the same steps are always used.

1. Arrange the decisions and events in the order in which they will occur. This is often difficult with complex decision problems, but unless the decision tree accurately represents the situation, the decision made may not be the best decision.
2. Make the necessary probability assessments and show them on the event branches. These probabilities can be determined using classical assessment, relative frequency of occurrence, or subjective techniques. (Remember, probabilities are associated with the uncertain events and not with the decision alternatives.)
3. Assign cash flows by showing costs and payoffs on the branches where they occur. Accumulate these cash flows and determine the end value for each branch of the decision tree.
4. Fold back the decision tree. At each decision fork, select the decision that maximizes expected payoff or minimizes expected cost.

Sensitivity Analysis

In a decision problem like the one facing Harris Publishing Company, uncertainty in the events is measured by the probabilities assessed for each event outcome. The expected-value criterion utilizes these probability assessments. But a question that arises when decision analysis is applied is how *sensitive* the decision is to the probabilities being assessed.

For instance, the company might want to know how much the probability of a favorable-review would have to change to make not signing the contract the best decision.

To answer this question, refer to Figure 17-10. Instead of using 0.80 for the probability of a favorable review, let the probability be p. Then the probability of an unfavorable review is $1 - p$. We next solve for p such that the expected value of the *Sign Contract* alternative ($3,587.52) is the same as the expected value of the *Don't Sign Contract* alternative, which in this case is $0.

$$0 = 4,584.40(p) + (-400)(1 - p)$$
$$0 = 4,584.40p - 400 + 400p$$
$$400 = 4,984.40p$$
$$400/4,984.40 = p$$
$$0.08025 = p$$

Thus, the probability of a favorable report would have to decrease from 0.80 to less than 0.1 in order for the best decision to be not signing the contract. This means the decision is quite insensitive to the probability assessed for a favorable editorial review, and there is probably no need to investigate this assessment any further.

Another question might be: How sensitive is the decision to publish the paperback to the probability assessment associated with the number of hardcover books that might be sold? That is, how much higher than 0.60 would the probability of selling 1 million copies have to be before the best decision would be to go with the hardcover books? The approach to answering this question is essentially the same as before. We let p = The probability of selling 1 million copies and $1 - p$ be the probability of selling 100,000 copies. We then solve for p such that the expected payoff for hardcover is equal to that for paperback: $4,584.40 (see Figure 17-10). We solve for p as follows.

$$4,584.4 = 4,976(p) + (-784)(1 - p)$$
$$4,584.4 = 4,976p - 784 + 784p$$
$$5,368.4 = 5,760p$$
$$5,368.4/5,760 = p$$
$$0.9320 = p$$

Thus, the probability of selling 1 million books would have to be higher than 0.9320 for the best decision to be to publish a hardcover book. When this is compared with the current assessment of 0.60, we see the decision is not very sensitive to this probability assessment. Depending on how much information and thought went into the original probability assessment, there does not appear to be a need to allocate substantial resources to study the hardcover demand issue further.

Sensitivity analysis can also investigate how much a cash-flow value would have to change before the decision would change. The method for determining the sensitivity of a cash-flow item is the same as for a probability. Let the cash-flow value in question equal x and then solve for x such that the decision branches have the same expected payoff.

When sensitivity analysis indicates that the resulting decision is sensitive to a probability or cash-flow value, you will want to spend extra time studying this factor before arriving at the final decision.

17-4: EXERCISES

Business Applications

17-18. Tom and Joe operate a rock quarry that provides local stone for landscaping. They currently have an offer for $50,000 to sell the quarry. They are hesitant to sell because they believe there will be an increase in demand in the next 2 years that would improve their financial situation. If they decide to keep the quarry, the present buyer would be willing to pay $30,000 in 2 years regardless of the situation. Tom and Joe think there is a 60% chance of a demand increase, at which point they could operate at a profit of

$75,000 or sell the quarry to a new buyer for $60,000. Use a decision tree to determine what they should do.

17-19. Vegetable Farms is a small, family-operated ranch that sells produce to local markets. The owners are currently trying to decide whether they should expand their operation next year. Since this is a fairly new business, the owners have assessed the following demand levels and probabilities: high (probability 0.50), medium (0.30), or low (0.20). The payoffs they expect for each demand/acreage scenario are listed. Use a decision tree to help decide whether or not to expand the farm.

	DEMAND		
Acreage	High	Medium	Low
Expanded	$100,000	$40,000	$−40,000
Same Size	50,000	40,000	30,000

17-20. Aquatech currently holds the lease to a site with good potential for geothermal development to generate electricity. Aquatech is now looking at three options for the site: (1) Sell the rights to the property for $1.5 million, (2) extend the lease for 25 years at a cost of $0.5 million, with the possibility of selling later, or (3) extend the lease and drill exploratory wells at a total cost of $2 million.

If the company decides to extend the lease in order to drill, future revenue from the site would be determined by the pressure and temperature of the water. The following chart lists the probabilities associated with the three states of nature possible, along with a projected drill revenue.

WATER TEMPERATURE	PROBABILITY	DRILL REVENUE (IN MILLIONS)
High	0.4	$5
Medium	0.4	3
Low	0.2	1

If the company extends the lease in order to sell the property later without drilling, the sale price will be determined by the demand for electricity. The following chart lists the probabilities associated with the three levels of demand and the projected sale price.

DEMAND	PROBABILITY	SALE PRICE (IN MILLIONS)
High	0.3	$2.5
Medium	0.6	2.0
Low	0.1	1.5

Use a decision tree to diagram Aquatech's alternatives and determine which option management should choose.

17-21. Paradise Springs is in the position of having to decide what size cross-country ski resort to build. The majority owners are adamant that a resort be built and that future plans for the resort should be determined by the change in net assets generated during the first 2 years of the project.

The developer has the option of building a small complex now and later expanding, if demand warrants, to a large complex. The expansion project would increase the size of a small complex to that of a large complex and could be completed in the off season to allow the resort to function as a large resort the second season. The costs of construction are as follows.

SIZE	CONSTRUCTION COST (IN MILLIONS)
Small	$2.0
Expansion (2nd year)	1.5
Large	3.0

The developer believes that demand for the resort will be either high or low and thinks there will be a fifty-fifty chance the resort will be popular in its first season. If demand is high the first year, she feels there is a 60% chance the resort will be popular its second season. If demand is low, she would not want to expand. She feels if demand is low the first year, there is a 70% chance it will remain low for the second season. The expected annual revenues for the resort are as follows.

ANNUAL OPERATIONAL PROFITS (IN MILLIONS)		
	DEMAND	
Resort Size	High	Low
Small	$2	$1
Large	3	2

Use a decision tree to determine which size the resort should develop.

■ 17-5: RISK-PREFERENCE ATTITUDES AND FUNCTIONS

Not all people select the same alternative when faced with the same decision situation. For instance, managers often disagree over which course of action should be taken by a company facing the prospect of expansion. Decision makers might reach different conclusions about whether to hire an applicant for an important position. One important reason why the choices could be different is that the decision makers have different attitudes about taking a risk. Referred to as "risk preference," the decision maker's attitude toward risk influences his or her view of the potential outcomes associated with the various alternatives. In decision analysis, the risk-preference attitudes are commonly classified as follows.

1. Risk-neutral
2. Risk-averse
3. Risk-seeking

In this section, we will discuss these three types of decision behavior and show how a decision maker's risk preference can be incorporated into the decision-analysis model.

Risk Neutral

Earlier in this chapter, the expected-value criterion was used as the primary means for deciding among alternatives. This meant that we always selected the alternative with the highest expected payoff or the lowest expected cost. Decision makers who strictly apply the expected-value criterion and select the highest payoff or lowest cost are considered **risk-neutral.**

> **RISK-NEUTRAL ATTITUDE**
> The preference for risk under which the alternative with the highest expected payoff or lowest expected cost will be selected.

For example, recalling the Xircom stock purchase example at the beginning of this chapter, suppose a risk-neutral decision maker is given the following options.

1. Buy the stock. If the merger occurs the stock will increase by $10; if the merger does not occur the stock price will decrease by $5.
2. Don't participate in the stock purchase (don't buy).

This decision is shown in Figure 17-11.

Recall that the analysts had determined that there was a 50% chance that the merger would take place. The risk-neutral decision maker would compute the expected value of both alternatives as follows.

$$E(\text{Buy}) = \$10(0.5) + (-\$5)(0.5) = \$5 - \$2.50 = \$2.50$$
$$E(\text{Don't buy}) = \$0$$

Then, choosing strictly on the basis of expected value, the decision maker would select the *Buy* alternative, since $2.50 > $0.

Consider a similar decision where the outcomes are changed to +$100 if the merger occurs and −$50 if it does not, as shown in Figure 17-12. Now the expected values of the alternatives in this case are:

$$E(\text{Buy}) = \$100(0.5) + (-\$50)(0.5) = \$25$$
$$E(\text{Don't buy}) = \$0$$

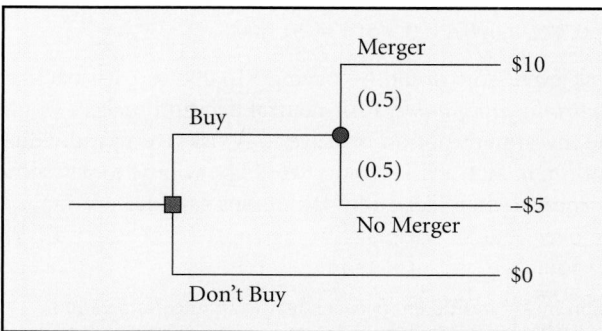

FIGURE 17-11   Xircom Stock Purchase Example

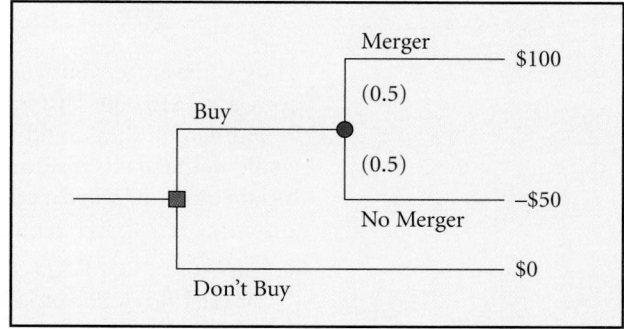

FIGURE 17-12   Xircom Stock Purchase Example

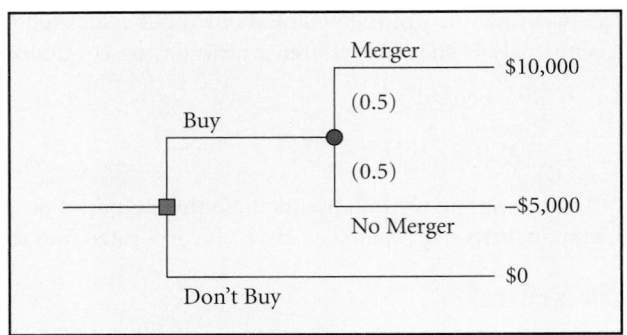

FIGURE 17-13
Xircom Stock Purchase
Example

Deciding strictly on the basis of expected value, the risk-neutral decision maker will choose to buy, since $25 > $0.

While most of us would like to see the stock price increase by $10 in the first example, our day would not be totally ruined if we lost $5. In the second example, we would very much like the $100 payoff, but the loss of $50 would hurt a bit. The risk-neutral decision maker doesn't let such thoughts affect the decision, and would make the same choice even if the game had payoffs of $10,000 and −$5,000, shown in Figure 17-13. The expected value of the *Buy* alternative is $2,500, which clearly makes the "best decision" to buy the stock. Right?

If you were faced with this latest decision situation, what would you do, given your current financial status? Just think how nice it would be to add $10,000 to your bank account—if the merger occurred. However, how would you feel if the merger didn't occur and you suddenly *had lost* $5,000? Most of us would tend to look at the values of the possible outcomes and balance our desire for the $10,000 gain versus our dislike for losing $5,000, before actually making our decision.

Considering end values and letting our attitude toward these values influence the decision means we are not risk neutral. Further, when considering the end values in a decision situation, rarely will someone be risk neutral over a wide range of decision situations. If a decision maker is not risk neutral, then he or she is said to be either a *risk avoider* or a *risk seeker*. An individual that is a risk avoider has a **risk-averse attitude**.

RISK-AVERSE ATTITUDE
The preference for risk such that the decision maker could select an alternative with a lower expected payoff in order to avoid the possibility of an undesirable outcome.

Risk Averse

Consider the following situation. An investment option exists that will require you to invest $10,000. There is a 0.50 chance that you will walk away with $20,000; but there is also a 0.50 chance that you will end up with $0. The expected value is:

$$E(\text{Payoff}) = 0.5(\$20,000) + 0.5(\$0) = \$10,000$$

Thus, on average, you would break even. You would be paying $10,000 to earn back an average of $10,000. This is an *actuarially fair gamble*. Risk-neutral decision makers would be indifferent; they could take the investment option or leave it. A risk-averse individual would not take this investment option; in fact, a risk avoider would be willing to pay some certain amount, called a **certainty equivalent**, to get out of taking this gamble.

CERTAINTY EQUIVALENT
The value that would make a decision maker indifferent between taking an uncertain gamble versus receiving that value instead of taking the gamble.

Consider your own personal situation. If you were told that you had to ante up $10,000 for an investment option where the flip of a coin would determine whether you get either $20,000 or nothing, how would you feel? Would you be willing to pay some amount right now to get out of taking the gamble? How much would you pay? The more you would be willing to pay, the more risk-averse you are for this gamble.

Most people are risk avoiders, choosing to guard against the extreme "bad" outcome. Insurance companies rely on this fact, since to be profitable they must take in more money, on average, than they pay out.

EXAMPLE 17-7

RISK AVOIDANCE

Health Insurance

Consider the decision of whether to purchase health insurance for $600 per year. The policy has a $1,000 deductible clause, meaning you pay the first $1,000 in medical bills during each year, and it covers 90% of the costs over $1,000. Figure 17-14 shows a decision tree for this situation. Suppose three possible outcomes can occur under each alternative. These outcomes and the subjectively assessed probabilities are:

MEDICAL COST	PROBABILITY
$ 100	0.90
500	0.09
25,000	0.01

The probabilities reflect the decision maker's assessment of each possible outcome. There is a high chance that the medical costs during the year will be $500 or less and only one chance in 100 that a major medical problem costing $25,000 will occur.

Figure 17-14 shows that the expected cost is $385 for the *No Insurance* alternative and $769 for the *Buy Insurance* option. On the basis of expected value, the "best decision" is not to buy insurance, since $385 < $769. However, most people will buy the insurance anyway, exhibiting a preference to avoid the risk of the potentially worst outcome.

Risk avoidance is also prevalent in business decision making. The reasons for this are at least twofold. First, since the individual is likely to be a risk avoider in many personal

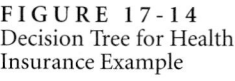

FIGURE 17-14
Decision Tree for Health Insurance Example

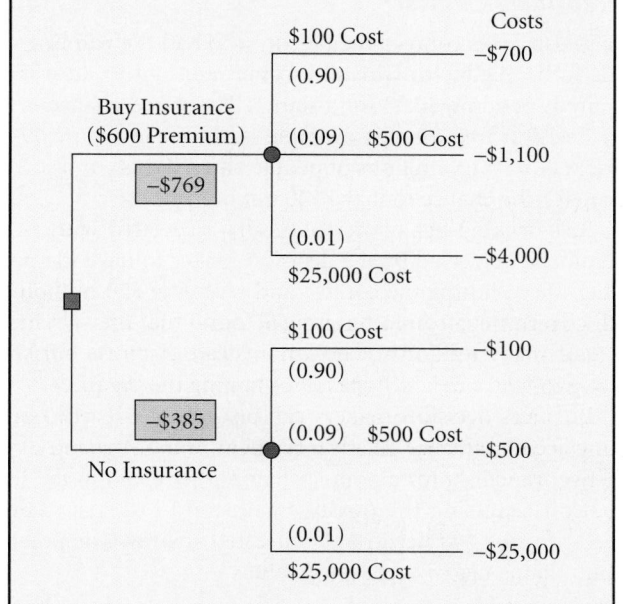

situations, this behavior will extend to business decisions, even though now it is the company's resources—not the decision maker's personal resources—that are at stake. Second, the reward structure in many organizations provides an incentive for people to avoid choosing alternatives with risky outcomes. While a good outcome may result in a bonus for the decision maker, often this bonus does not outweigh the possible consequences of an extremely negative outcome, such as being fired.

In practice, risk-avoiding behavior in an organization tends to be more prevalent at the lower and middle management levels. Often this runs counter to the desires of upper management which, publicly at least, talk about the need to take chances and being willing to fail.

Risk Seeking

Not everyone is a risk avoider. Clearly, there are many situations in which people exhibit **risk-seeking** behavior.

> **RISK-SEEKING ATTITUDE**
> The preference for risk such that the decision maker could select an alternative with a lower expected payoff in hopes of achieving an outcome with a more desirable result.

For instance, consider another investment alternative that requires a $10,000 investment. There is a 0.10 chance that you would walk away with $80,000 and a 0.90 chance that you would lose your $10,000 and end up with $0. The expected payoff is:

$$E(\text{Payoff}) = 0.10(\$80,000) + 0.90(\$0) = \$8,000$$

Thus, on average, an investor would leave with $8,000 after making a $10,000 investment, providing an expected loss of $2,000. A risk-neutral decision maker would choose not to invest; so would a risk avoider. However, some people would want to invest to have the chance at $80,000. These individuals are called risk seekers. In fact, if faced with the prospect of losing out on the investment option, a risk seeker might agree to pay some additional amount just to keep the investment opportunity open.

A good example of risk-seeking behavior is what happens when someone enters a "sweepstakes" contest sponsored by a magazine publishing company.

EXAMPLE
17-8

**RISK
SEEKING**

Sweepstakes Contest

In a sweepstakes contest, the person who had the winning number would receive $20 million. To be eligible to win, all a contestant had to do was mail in the entry form, which required spending $0.33 for a stamp. The stated chance of winning was 1 in 100,000,000. The decision tree for this example is shown in Figure 17-15. Even though the expected value was −$0.13, millions of people entered this contest. They were willing to risk a $0.33 stamp for the chance to make $20 million.

Risk-seeking behavior is typically associated with situations in which one possible outcome is perceived by the decision maker to have the potential to markedly change his or her life. Winning the contest and receiving $20 million is that type of outcome. States with government-run lotteries have found that they get more players if they offer a major prize of many millions of dollars instead of more, but smaller, prizes. People are more willing to take a risk in hopes of obtaining the big prize.

Business decision makers can also engage in risk-seeking behavior. A while ago, a young accountant saw an advertisement in the Portland *Oregonian* newspaper offering for sale five franchises for a popular hamburger chain in the Eugene area. After reviewing the situation, assessing the possible gains and losses, and determining that the decision's expected value was negative, he invested anyway. The potentially high payoff meant more to him than a negative expected value.

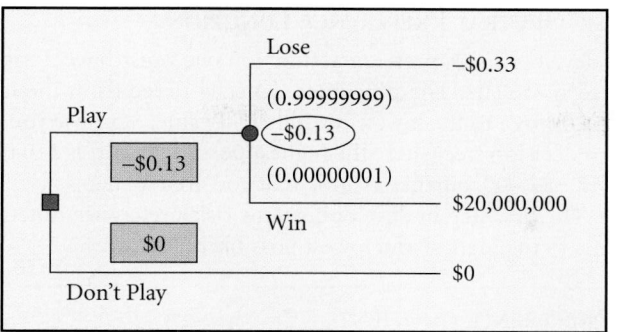

FIGURE 17-15
Decision Tree for Publisher's Sweepstakes

The same person may be risk averse in some situations and risk seeking in others, depending on the range of outcomes. For example, if you were asked to spend $1 on a lottery ticket that offered a 1 in 1,000 chance of winning $500, you might consider it, even though the expected value is −$0.50. If you play, you are a risk seeker. On the other hand, if you were offered a chance to buy a $10,000 ticket in a lottery with a 0.25 chance of netting $90,000, you might refuse the offer, even though the expected value is $15,000. If you refuse, you are exhibiting risk-averse behavior. In the first case, the range of payoffs was −$1 to $500 and the worst outcome was to lose only $1. However, when the possible loss is greater, such as the −$10,000 in the second example, you might select an alternative which would protect you against this bad outcome. Another example of an individual who is both a risk seeker and risk averse is one who purchases airline flight insurance for a gambling trip to Las Vegas.

Developing a Risk-Preference Function

The expected-value criterion suits the attitude of a risk-neutral decision maker. For this group of decision makers, the best decision is the one that maximizes the expected payoff or minimizes the expected cost. However, because not all (or even most) decision makers are risk neutral, a method for formally incorporating risk-averse and risk-seeking attitudes into the decision process is needed.

The method used in decision analysis is to develop a **risk-preference function** that describes the decision maker's relative preferences for all outcomes within a specified range. (The preference function is commonly plotted as a line or curve on a graph.)

> **RISK-PREFERENCE FUNCTION**
> A graph that describes a decision maker's preference for risk over the range of possible payoffs.

The Standard Gamble Approach

Several methods can be used to establish a decision maker's risk-preference function. The method illustrated in this text is called the **standard gamble approach**.

> **STANDARD GAMBLE APPROACH**
> The approach for assessing risk-preference functions that involves setting up a series of 50–50 gambles between two payoffs and determining the certainty equivalent for each gamble.

We begin by using a simple example to demonstrate how a standard gamble is used to develop risk-neutral, risk-averse, and risk-seeking preference functions. We will then follow with an example showing how preference functions are used in the decision-making process.

RISK-NEUTRAL PREFERENCE FUNCTION

To develop a risk-preference function, we must have a range of possible outcomes measured in dollars. The outcomes typically range from the highest possible end value on a decision tree to the lowest possible end value. Suppose you are the decision maker analyzing a decision tree where the highest possible payoff is $10,000 and the lowest possible payoff is −$2,000. Further assume that you are risk neutral.

The first step in developing your risk-preference function is to assign **preference quotients** to the highest and lowest possible outcomes.

PREFERENCE QUOTIENT
A measure of the relative utility for the outcomes of a decision on a scale between 0.0 and 1.0.

Let q represent the preference quotient. The higher the q value, the greater the relative preference for the dollar outcome. The highest possible payoff is assigned a value of $q = 1.0$, since that value is preferred over all other payoffs. The lowest possible payoff is assigned $q = 0.0$, indicating that you would prefer any other payoff over the lowest payoff. When dealing with costs instead of payoffs, we reverse this reasoning and assign a value of 1.0 to the lowest-cost alternative and 0.0 to the highest-cost alternative. For our example involving payoffs, we get:

PAYOFF	q
$10,000	1.0
−2,000	0.0

The next step in developing the risk-preference function is to pose a series of *standard gambles*. The first one is diagrammed in Figure 17-16. The alternatives are either to play a game with a 0.50 chance of winning $10,000 and a 0.50 chance of losing $2,000 or not to play the game. The payoffs associated with the *Play* alternative are the same payoffs for which we have already assigned q values. This decision is referred to as a standard gamble because the chance of each payoff occurring is set at 0.50.

You must next determine what certain outcome for the *Don't Play* branch would make you indifferent between playing and not playing. This value is termed the certainty equivalent (or CE value) of the gamble. You can think of it as the amount you would take to give up the opportunity to play the game.

The expected value of the *Play* branch is:

$$EV = \$10,000(0.50) + (-\$2,000)(0.50) = \$4,000$$

FIGURE 17-16
Assessing the Risk-Preference
Function: Standard Gamble 1

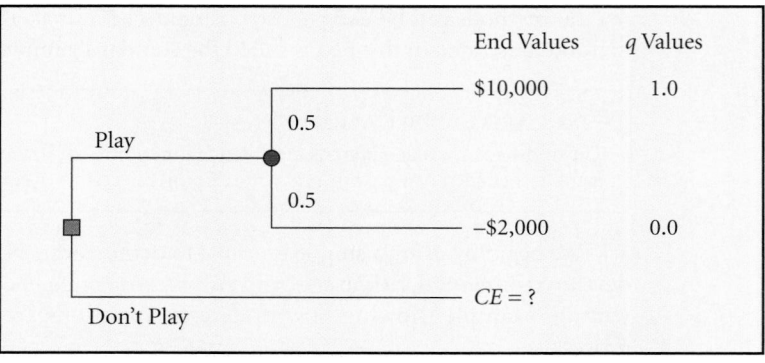

This means that, on average, you would make $4,000 by selecting the *Play* alternative. A risk-neutral decision maker always selects the option with the highest expected payoff. If the payoff for the *Don't Play* branch exceeds $4,000, then the choice would be to not play. If the payoff for the *Don't Play* alternative is less than $4,000, then the *Play* branch would be selected. Thus, for a risk-neutral decision maker, the certainty equivalent for this standard gamble is the expected value, $4,000. If the *Don't Play* branch had a certain payoff of $4,000, the risk-neutral decision maker would be indifferent between the two alternatives.

Since we are assuming you are risk neutral, the next step is to determine the q value for a payoff of $4,000. This is done by determining the expected q value for the *Play* branch based on the q values already assigned to the payoffs of $10,000 and −$2,000.

$$E(q) = 1.0(0.50) + 0.0(0.50) = 0.50$$

Thus, the preference quotient, q, for a payoff of $4,000 is 0.50. We now have the following q values.

PAYOFF	q
$10,000	1.0
4,000	0.5
−2,000	0.0

Note the decision tree may not have an end value of $4,000, but this does not present a problem, since our objective is to develop a risk-preference curve which can be used to determine the relative preference for any value between $10,000 and −$2,000. We now have three points on this preference curve.

To determine additional points, we pose a second standard gamble, as shown in Figure 17-17. The *Play* alternative now shows a 0.50 chance at $10,000 and a 0.50 chance at $4,000. We have previously assigned q values to each of these outcomes and must now determine the *CE* value for this gamble. Remember, *CE* will be the point of indifference between playing and not playing.

The expected value of the *Play* branch is:

$$EV = \$10,000(0.50) + \$4,000(0.50) = \$7,000$$

On average, the *Play* alternative will yield a $7,000 payoff. A risk-neutral decision maker would be indifferent between playing and not playing if the *Don't Play* alternative had a certain outcome of $7,000. Then, for a risk-neutral decision maker, *CE* = $7,000. We determine the q value for $7,000 by finding the expected q value for this standard gamble.

$$E(q) = 1.0(0.50) + 0.50(0.50) = 0.75$$

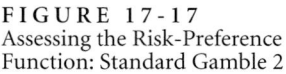

FIGURE 17-17
Assessing the Risk-Preference
Function: Standard Gamble 2

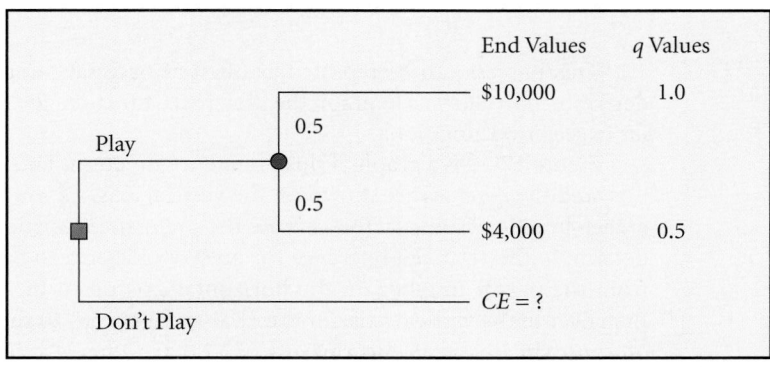

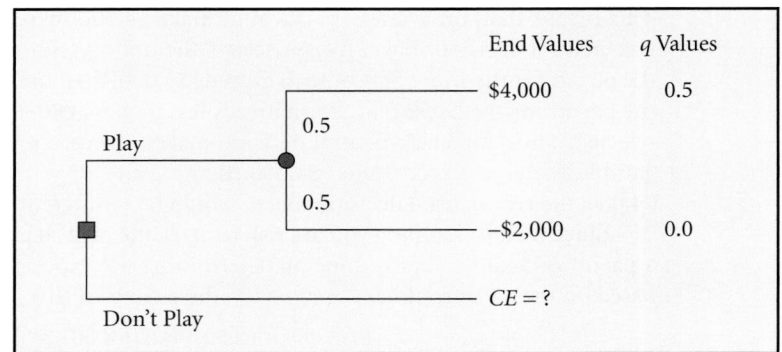

FIGURE 17-18
Assessing the Risk-Preference
Function: Standard Gamble 3

The preference quotient for a payoff of $7,000 is 0.75. We now have four values.

PAYOFF	q
$10,000	1.00
7,000	0.75
4,000	0.50
−2,000	0.00

We can pose still another standard gamble, as shown in Figure 17-18. The expected value of the *Play* branch is:

$$EV = \$4,000(0.50) + (-\$2,000)(0.50) = \$1,000$$

A risk-neutral decision maker would be indifferent between the alternatives if the certain outcome of the *Play* branch was $1,000. Thus, the *CE* for this standard gamble is $1,000. We determine the q value for a $1,000 payoff as follows.

$$E(q) = 0.50(0.50) + 0.0(0.50) = 0.25$$

The preference quotient for a $1,000 payoff is 0.25, giving the following results so far.

PAYOFF	q
$10,000	1.00
7,000	0.75
4,000	0.50
1,000	0.25
−2,000	0.00

This process can be repeated as often as necessary until enough q values have been determined to allow us to graph the preference function. Let's use the five points we have so far to see how things look.

Figure 17-19 is a graph of this preference function. The horizontal axis shows the payoffs, and the q values are shown on the vertical axis. As you can see, the risk-neutral preference function is linear. You can use the preference function graphed in Figure 17-19 to determine the relative preference for any payoff between $10,000 and −$2,000 by going from the payoff number on the horizontal axis up to the preference-function line and then over to the vertical axis, for the q value. Figure 17-20 shows how we found the q value of approximately 0.58 for a payoff of $5,000. Other q values can be determined in the same way.

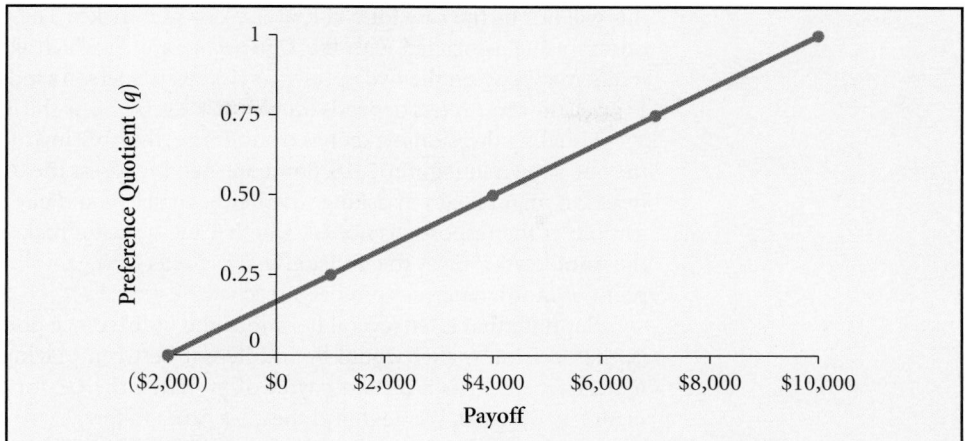

FIGURE 17-19
Risk-Neutral Preference
Function

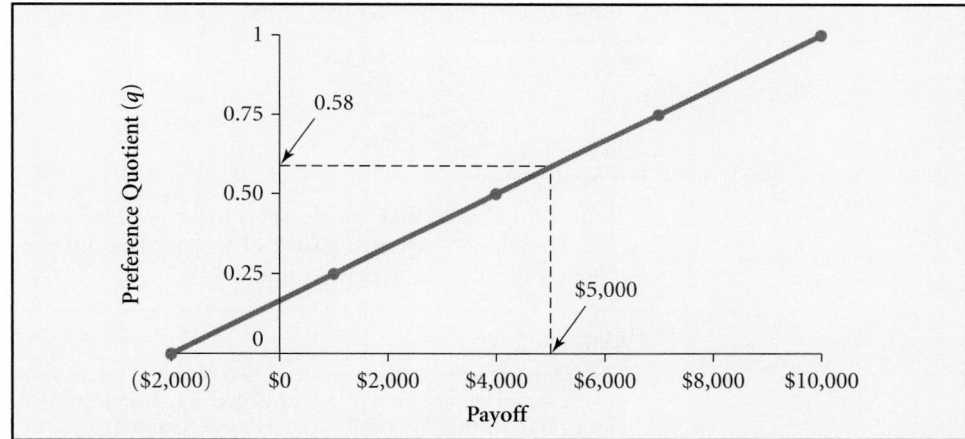

FIGURE 17-20
Risk-Neutral Preference
Function

RISK-AVERSE PREFERENCE FUNCTION

The linear preference function shown in Figure 17-19 is for a risk-neutral decision maker. The preference function is linear because the *CE* values for each standard gamble were always the expected value of the *Play* alternative. However, we indicated earlier that most decision makers are not risk neutral but instead are risk averse or risk seeking. Let's reconsider the same decision problem as before, with the highest payoff of $10,000 and the lowest payoff of −$2,000, but now suppose the decision maker is risk averse.

A risk-averse decision maker will pick a certainty equivalent that is less than the expected payoff for a standard gamble. However, there are different degrees of risk aversion. The extent to which a person is risk averse will be reflected in his or her risk-preference function.

The steps in assessing a risk-averse decision maker's preference function are essentially the same as for a risk-neutral or risk-seeking decision maker. We begin by assigning $q = 1.0$ to the highest possible payoff, in this case $10,000, and assigning $q = 0.0$ to the lowest possible payoff, −$2,000. This again gives:

PAYOFF	q
$10,000	1.0
−2,000	0.0

Next, we pose the standard gamble shown earlier in Figure 17-16. Recall that the expected value for the *Play* alternative is $4,000. A risk-neutral individual would set *CE* = $4,000. But this will not be the case for a risk-averse decision maker. The *CE* (certainty equivalent) is the certain value associated with the *Don't Play* branch which would make the decision maker indifferent between the two options. A risk-averse person's indifference point will be less than $4,000. How much less depends on how risk-averse he or she is.

Usually a decision maker has trouble directly assessing the *CE* for a standard gamble like the one shown in Figure 17-16. Someone helping assess the decision maker's risk-preference function might begin by asking whether he or she would pay $1,500 to avoid taking the play gamble. If the response is no, ask whether the decision maker would pay $500 to get out of the gamble. As long as the decision maker prefers the gamble to the certain dollar figure, the point of indifference has not been reached.

Suppose that after several iterations the indifference point is determined to be $0; that is, the decision maker would be indifferent between playing and not playing if the *Don't Play* alternative has a certain payoff of $0. Then the *CE* for the standard gamble posed in Figure 17-16 is $0. We next find the q for $0 as follows.

$$E(q) = 1.0(0.50) + 0.0(0.50) = 0.50$$

This gives us the following three values.

PAYOFF	q
$10,000	1.0
0	0.5
−2,000	0.0

You should note that this decision maker was willing to accept a $0 payoff instead of the gamble with an expected payoff of $4,000. The difference between the expected value and the *CE* is called the **risk premium**.

RISK PREMIUM

The difference between the expected value of an event and the certainty equivalent. The risk premium will be zero for a risk-neutral decision maker, positive for a risk-averse decision maker, and negative for a risk-seeking decision maker.

Risk-averse decision makers have positive risk premiums. In effect, this decision maker is willing to pay a premium, in the form of a lost expected payoff, of $4,000 to avoid the possibility of losing $2,000. The risk premium is:

$$\text{Risk premium} = \$4,000 - \$0 = \$4,000$$

Does this seem like an excessive premium to pay? Ask yourself whether today you would risk losing $2,000 for the chance to win $10,000 on the flip of a coin. If you would walk away from this gamble and take a $0 payoff, you are at least as risk averse as the decision maker in our example. If you wouldn't give up the gamble so easily, then you are less risk averse than this decision maker.

We now have three points on the preference function but need more. Our next step is to pose still another standard gamble, like the one shown in Figure 17-21. Now the decision maker must determine the certain payoff which would make him or her indifferent between playing and not playing. Using the same procedure as before, we would determine the indifference point. Assume the decision maker settles on $2,750 as the *CE* for this latest standard gamble. This means that he or she would be indifferent between taking the 50–50 gamble with payoffs of $10,000 or $0 and the sure payoff of $2,750.

The expected payoff for the gamble is:

$$EV = \$10,000(0.50) + \$0(0.50) = \$5,000$$

The difference between the expected value and the certainty equivalent is the risk premium. In this case, we get:

$$\text{Risk premium} = \$5,000 - \$2,750 = \$2,250$$

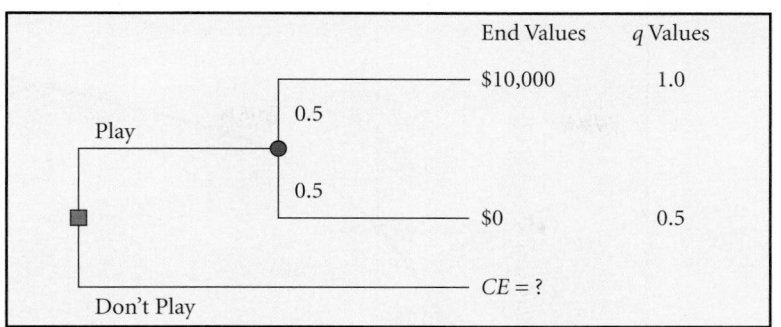

FIGURE 17-21
Assessing the Risk-Preference
Function: Standard Gamble 2

This risk premium is less than the $4,000 risk premium associated with the earlier gamble. Therefore the decision maker is not as risk averse over the range $10,000 to $0 as he or she was over the range $10,000 to −$2,000.

The q value for the $2,750 CE is:

$$E(q) = 1.0(0.50) + 0.50(0.50) = 0.75$$

We have now determined four q values.

PAYOFF	q
$10,000	1.00
2,750	0.75
0	0.50
−2,000	0.00

You should determine as many q values as necessary to feel comfortable about drawing the risk-preference function. Let's find one more value, using the standard gamble diagrammed in Figure 17-22. Suppose the CE for this gamble is determined to be −$1,250. This decision maker would be willing to pay $1,250 to avoid a 50–50 chance of losing $2,000 or breaking even.

The expected value of the gamble shown in Figure 17-22 is −$1,000, and the risk premium is:

$$\text{Risk premium} = -\$1,000 - (-\$1,250) = \$250$$

The q value for this −$1,250 CE is:

$$E(q) = 0.50(0.50) + 0.0(0.50) = 0.25$$

We now have the following q values:

PAYOFF	q
$10,000	1.00
2,750	0.75
0	0.50
−1,250	0.25
−2,000	0.00

FIGURE 17-22
Assessing the Risk-Preference
Function: Standard Gamble 3

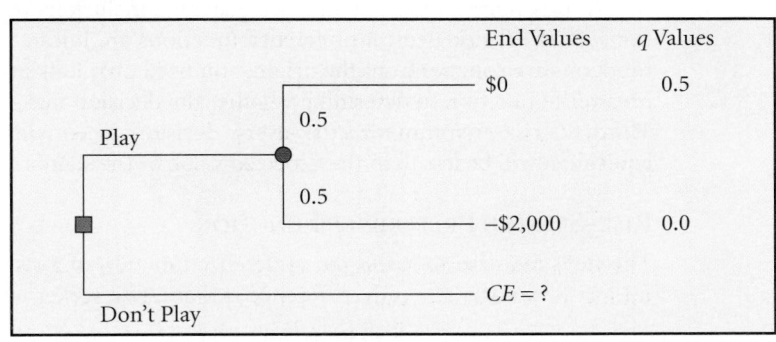

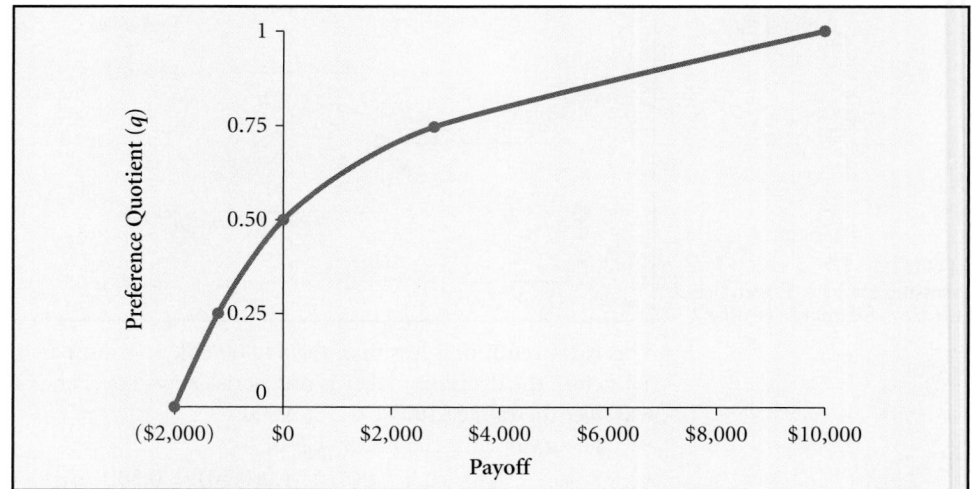

FIGURE 17-23
Risk-Averse Preference
Function

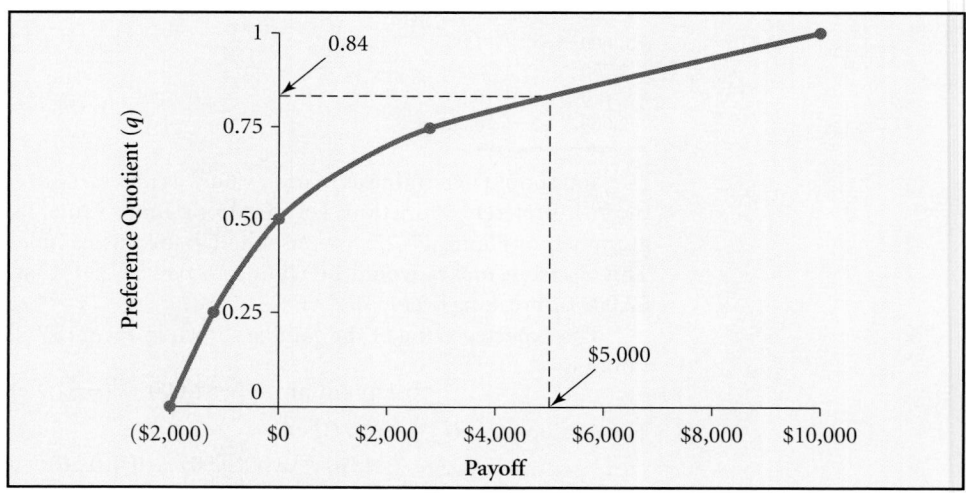

FIGURE 17-24
Determining a q Value

Figure 17-23 shows these five points connected to form the risk-preference function. Five is the minimum number of points to use for a risk-averse decision maker. We can use Figure 17-23 to determine the preference quotients for any value between $10,000 and −$2,000. For instance, Figure 17-24 shows that the q value for a payoff of $5,000 is approximately 0.84. Other q values would be determined in the same manner.

At this point, we can state three general conclusions regarding risk-preference functions. First, all risk-neutral preference functions are linear. Second, risk-averse preference functions are concave from the origin. You need only look at the general shape of the risk-preference function to determine whether the decision maker is risk neutral or risk averse. Third, the risk premium for a risk-averse decision maker will be positive, since the certainty equivalent will be less than the expected value of the standard gamble.

RISK-SEEKING PREFERENCE FUNCTION

The steps required to assess the preference function of a risk seeker are the same as those for a risk avoider. The only difference is that a risk seeker will have a certainty equivalent

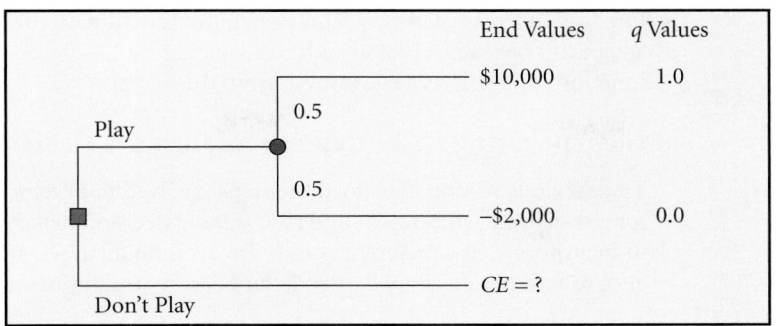

FIGURE 17-25
Assessing the Risk-Preference
Function: Standard Gamble 1

that exceeds the expected value of the standard gamble. This means that the risk premium for a risk seeker is negative. An example will show what we mean.

Let us once again consider the decision with payoffs ranging from $10,000 to −$2,000. We again set $q = 1.0$ for the $10,000 payoff and $q = 0.0$ for the −$2,000 payoff. Now we propose the standard gamble shown in Figure 17-25. The gamble has an expected value of $4,000. A risk-neutral decision maker would set the *CE* at $4,000. We saw previously that a risk-averse decision maker would have a *CE* of less than $4,000 ($0 in the earlier example).

A risk seeker will demand a certain payoff in excess of $4,000 for not playing. This demand reflects his or her desire for the $10,000 payoff. The exact *CE* chosen will depend on how much of a risk taker the decision maker is. Suppose the *Don't Play* branch would require a certain payoff of $6,500 to make the decision maker indifferent between the options of playing and not playing. Recall that the expected value of the *Play* option is $4,000; thus, $CE > EV$, indicating a negative risk premium.

$$\text{Risk premium} = \$4,000 - \$6,500 = -\$2,500$$

The preference quotient value for the *CE* of $6,500 is found as before.

$$E(q) = 1.0(0.50) + 0.0(0.50) = 0.50$$

We would continue proposing standard gambles to the risk-seeking decision maker and determine both the certainty equivalent and preference quotient for each gamble. After determining at least five preference quotients and certainty equivalents, we would be ready to determine the preference function. Figure 17-26 shows the completed risk-preference

FIGURE 17-26
Risk-Seeking Preference
Function

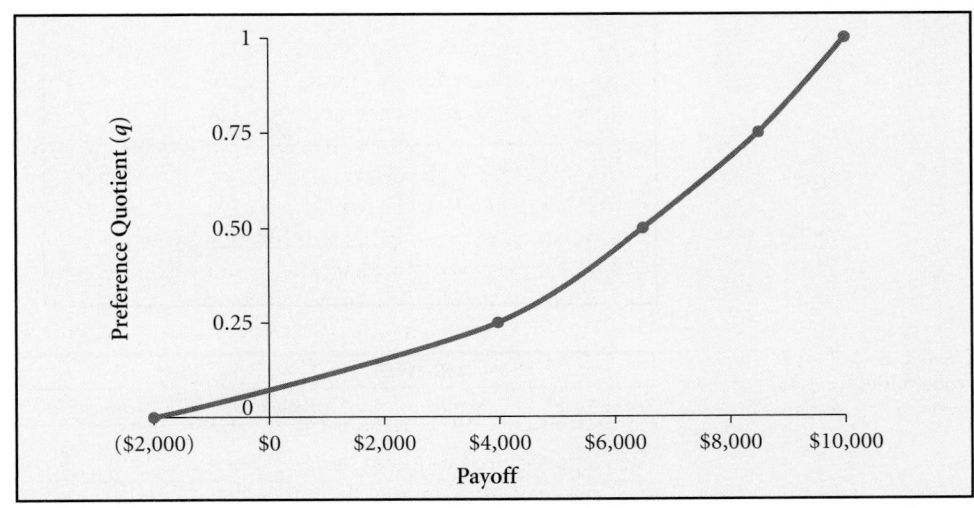

function for this risk seeker. This preference function can be used to determine q values for any payoff between $10,000 and $-$2,000. Figure 17-26 also shows that the risk-preference function for a risk seeker is convex from the origin.

Incorporating Risk Preferences Into the Decision Analysis

The previous section explained the steps involved in developing a risk-preference function for risk-neutral, risk-averse, and risk-seeking decision makers. In this section, we show how to incorporate risk preferences into the decision analysis. As you will see, once the preference function is developed, the method is very straightforward.

EXAMPLE 17-9

PERSONAL INVESTING

Personal Investing

Betty Feeney has just received a termination notice from a food processing company that is relocating its headquarters after its top management agreed to a takeover by a larger company. As a result of having been with the company for over 20 years, Betty will receive a 2-year salary termination package totaling $150,000. Betty was offered a job with another company and so is deciding what to do with the severance package. She has decided to invest the money for 5 years and then reevaluate her financial situation. She is presently trying to decide between two alternative investments: a mutual fund and resort area real estate. Figure 17-27 shows her completed decision tree. At the end of 5 years, Betty estimates her shares in the mutual fund could be sold for $300,000, $220,000, or $140,000, depending on how the stock market performs and how well the mutual fund is managed. The property could be sold at the end of the investment period for $330,000, $200,000, or $150,000, depending on the demand for real estate in the area.

FIGURE 17-27
Decision Tree for the Investment Example

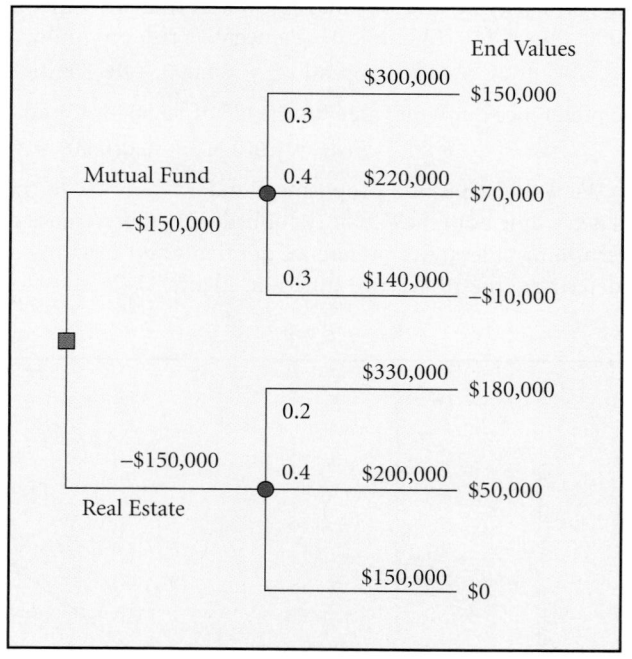

TABLE 17-10
Probabilities for Two Investment Alternatives

MUTUAL FUND			REAL ESTATE		
Selling Price	*Net Return*	*Probability*	*Selling Price*	*Net Return*	*Probability*
$300,000	$150,000	0.3	$330,000	$180,000	0.2
220,000	70,000	0.4	200,000	50,000	0.4
140,000	−10,000	0.3	150,000	0	0.4

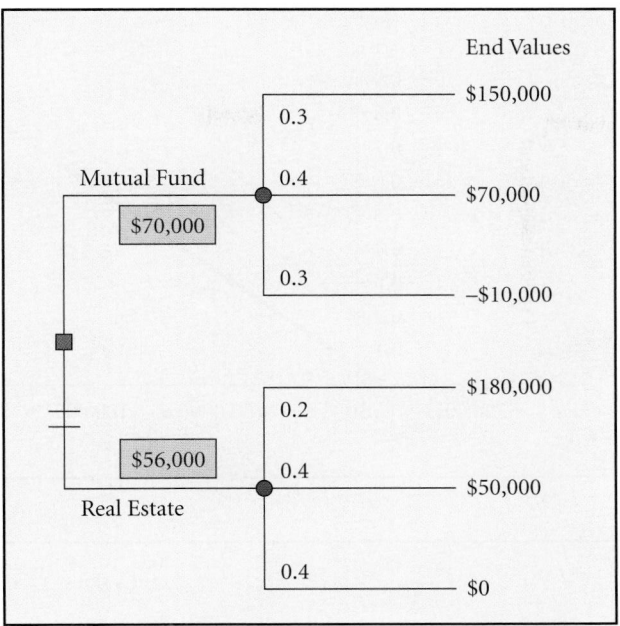

FIGURE 17-28
Folding Back the Decision
Tree for the Investment
Example

Betty has subjectively assessed the probability distributions shown in Table 17-10 on page 728. The end values to the right of the decision tree in Figure 17-27 represent Betty's projected net cash position at the end of the 5-year investment period.

A Risk-Neutral Decision Maker

Earlier in this chapter you learned how to fold back a decision tree using end values. Figure 17-28 shows the result of this foldback process for Betty's decision. We see that the expected value of the mutual fund alternative is $70,000, versus $56,000 for the real estate alternative. Thus, based upon the expected values, Betty's "best decision" is to invest in the mutual fund.

The procedure of using the end values directly in the foldback process assumes that Betty is risk neutral. Earlier, we indicated that a risk-neutral decision maker will make a decision strictly on the basis of expected value. However, for a risk-neutral decision maker, we can use an alternative method of decision-tree analysis. This method utilizes the risk-preference function.

We showed earlier that the preference function for a risk-neutral person is linear. Figure 17-29 illustrates a risk-neutral preference function that can be used for this example. Incorporating the risk-preference function into the decision-tree analysis is quite easy. You begin by substituting the q value from the preference function for each end value on the decision tree. Locating each end value on the horizontal axis on the preference-function graph does this. Then go up to the preference function and across to the vertical axis to find the preference quotient, q.

Figure 17-30 shows the decision tree with the q values to the right of the tree. The decision tree is now folded back, but we have used q values instead of dollar end values. We move from right to left, computing expected q values instead of expected payoffs. The "best decision" is the one that gives the highest expected q value. For this example, the expected q value for the mutual fund alternative is:

$$E(q) = 0.84(0.30) + 0.42(0.40) + 0(0.30) = 0.42$$

and for the real estate alternative, it is:

$$E(q) = 1.0(0.20) + 0.32(0.40) + 0.05(0.40) = 0.348$$

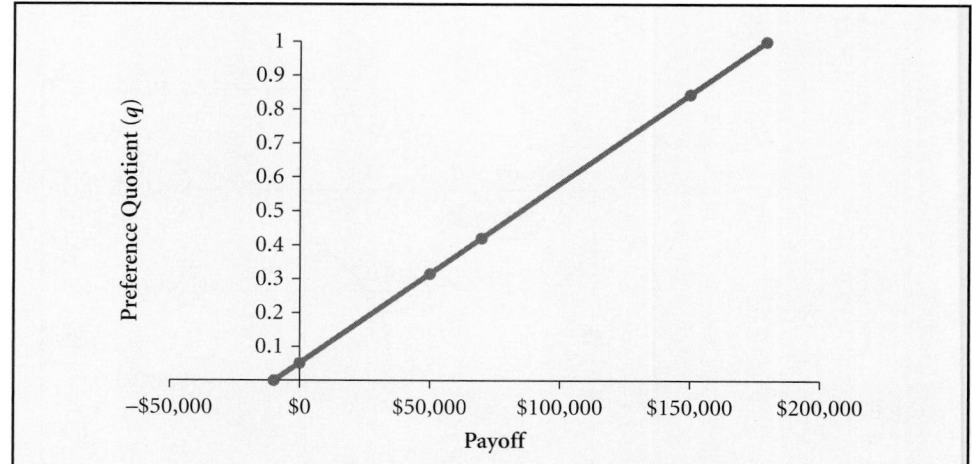

FIGURE 17-29
Risk-Neutral Preference
Function for the Investment
Example

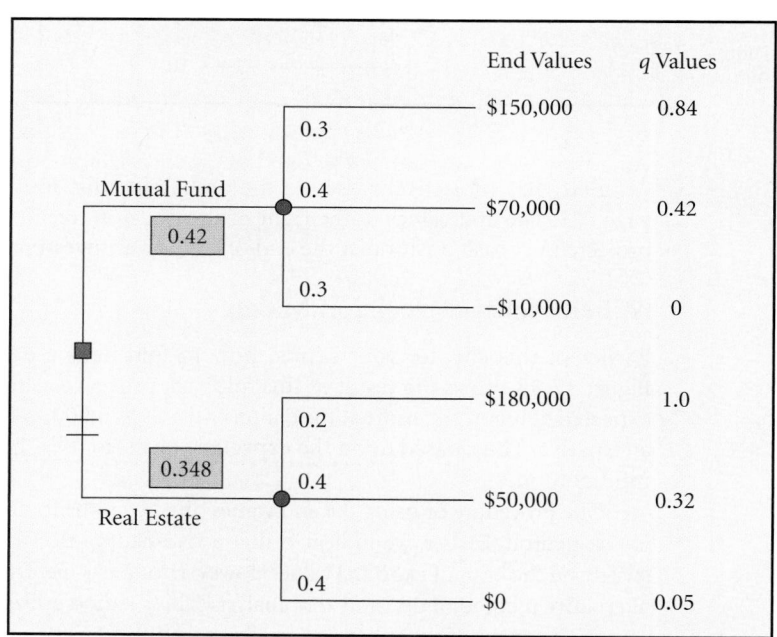

FIGURE 17-30
Folding Back the Decision
Tree, Using q Values

Then, since $0.42 > 0.348$, the "best decision" is to invest in the mutual fund.

Because a risk-neutral preference function is linear, a risk-neutral decision maker will make the same decision using dollar payoffs or q values. However, this equivalence holds only for risk-neutral decision makers.

A Risk-Averse Decision Maker

We just showed that for a risk-neutral person, using the actual dollar payoffs to fold back the decision tree leads to the same decision as using risk-preference quotients (q values). However, if the decision maker is not risk neutral, a different decision can be reached.

Risk-averse decision makers are willing to pay a risk premium to avoid alternatives with undesirable outcomes. To illustrate how we incorporate risk-averse attitudes into the decision process, suppose that Figure 17-31 shows the risk-preference function for Betty's

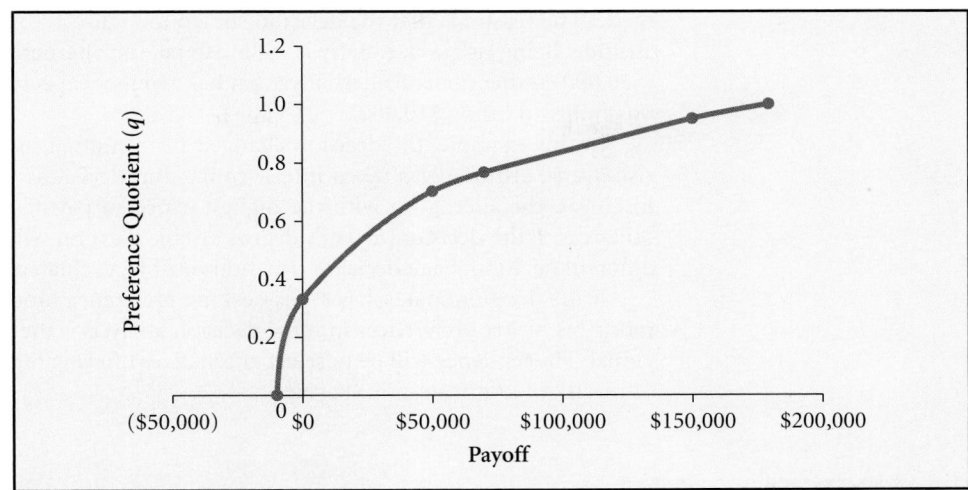

FIGURE 17-31
Risk-Averse Preference
Function for the Investment
Example

investment decision. We see that Betty is risk averse since the preference function is concave, curving up from the origin.

Figure 17-32 shows the decision tree with the q values found using Figure 17-31 on the right side. These q values are folded back instead of the dollar payoffs. The best decision at any decision fork is the one having the highest expected q value. For the mutual fund alternative:

$$E(q) = 0.95(0.30) + 0.77(0.40) + 0(0.30) = 0.593$$

For the real estate alternative:

$$E(q) = 1.0(0.20) + 0.7(0.40) + 0.33(0.40) = 0.612$$

Since $0.612 > 0.593$, the best decision for Betty, as a risk-averse decision maker, is to invest in real estate. This is a different choice than the risk-neutral decision maker would have

FIGURE 17-32
Folding Back the Decision
Tree, Using q Values

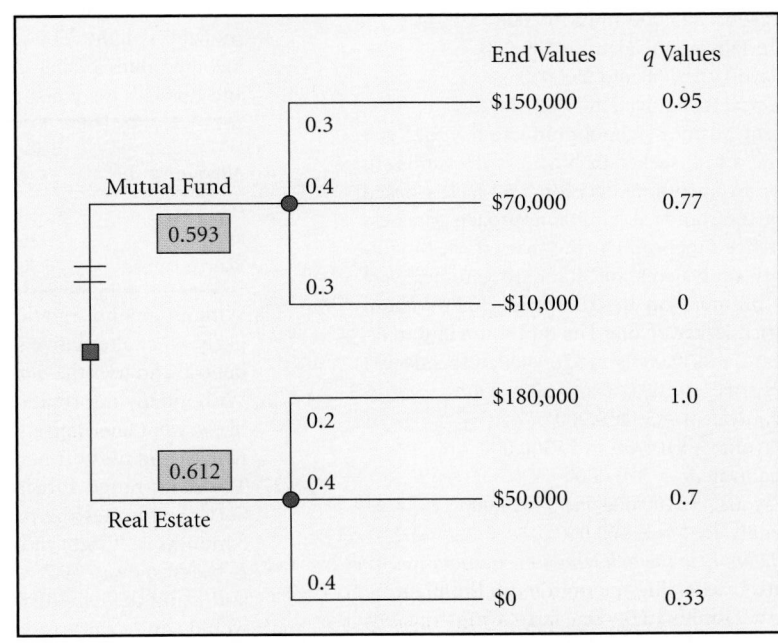

made. The reason is that the decision shown in Figure 17-32 incorporates this risk-averse attitude. Being risk averse, Betty is willing to take an alternative with a lower expected value ($56,000) rather than an alternative that has a higher expected value ($70,000) but also the possibility of losing $10,000.

In this example, the decision changed from mutual fund to real estate when Betty's risk-averse attitude was taken into account. But decisions don't always change; in some instances, the alternative with the highest expected payoff will also be the least risky. In other cases, the decision maker's degree of risk aversion will not be sufficient to lead to a different decision. Each decision situation must be evaluated independently.

If the decision maker has a risk-seeking preference function, the process for incorporating his or her preferences into the decision analysis is the same as for a risk-averse individual. The tendency will be to select alternatives offering higher potential payoffs but with more risk of low or negative payoffs.

17-5: EXERCISES

Business Applications

17-22. Use the standard gamble approach to develop your own risk-preference function for payoffs in the range of −$2,000 and $5,000. Based on the risk-preference function you have developed, indicate whether you are risk averse or risk seeking.

17-23. Based on the following standard gambles and certainty equivalents, develop the risk-preference function and indicate whether it describes a risk-averse, risk-neutral, or risk-seeking decision maker. (Note: The minimum payoff is $2,000 and the maximum is $100,000.)

    Gamble 1   Payoffs: $2,000 and $100,000
                  Certainty equivalent = $55,000
    Gamble 2   Payoffs: $55,000 and $100,000
                  Certainty equivalent = $79,000
    Gamble 3   Payoffs: $2,000 and $55,000
                  Certainty equivalent = $37,000

17-24. Suppose a recent business school graduate has told you that she will be a risk seeker in business decisions. In preparation for an upcoming decision, you have worked with her using the standard gamble approach to assess her risk-preference function. During that effort, the following certainty equivalents and standard gambles were determined. Comment on the recent graduate's claim about being a risk seeker. (Note: The minimum and maximum payoffs are −$100,000 and $300,000, respectively.)

    Gamble 1   Payoffs: −$100,000 and $300,000
             Certainty equivalent = −$10,000
    Gamble 2   Payoffs: −$10,000 and $300,000
             Certainty equivalent = $20,000
    Gamble 3   Payoffs: −$100,000 and −$10,000
             Certainty equivalent = −$60,000

Problems 25 through 32 apply to the following information.

Russell Smith is assessing his options as the planting season approaches for his 1,000-acre farm. Unfortunately,

this has been a year of low snowfall, and Russell's farm is dependent on irrigation water from the Magic Valley Reservoir. If the remaining spring snowfall in the mountains that feed the reservoir is below average, his farm will run out of irrigation water in August. If the spring snowfall is average, he will have water for the entire season, but at 75% of the normal level. If the snowfall is above average, Russell will have his normal allocation of water. Russell has three options: (1) not plant at all, and collect federal idle-land payments, (2) plant oats, and (3) plant potatoes. While not planting at all will guarantee a payment, the federal money will not cover the loan payment due at the bank. However, spending the money necessary to plant either of the two crops will be lost if the spring snowfall is light. The following table lists the potential income values arising from the three possible snow levels and Russell's three planting alternatives.

	SNOWFALL		
Alternative	Light	Average	High
Don't plant	$−10,000	$−10,000	$−10,000
Plant oats	−20,000	30,000	30,000
Plant potatoes	−50,000	10,000	60,000

17-25. Without any information about what level of snowfall is likely, what alternative should Russell choose if he is risk neutral and uses the *maximin* decision criterion?

17-26. Without any information about what level of snowfall is likely, what alternative should Russell choose if he is risk neutral and uses the *maximax* decision criterion?

17-27. The long-range forecast from the National Weather Service indicates the precipitation forecast for the next 3 months is: $P(\text{light snow}) = 0.5$, $P(\text{average snow}) = 0.3$, $P(\text{heavy snow}) = 0.2$. On the basis of this information, and using the expected-value criterion, what alternative would you recommend for Russell?

17-28. Before making his decision, Russell constructs a risk-preference function. The following are several points on his curve.

OUTCOME	PREFERENCE
−$75,000	0.00
0	0.58
10,000	0.62
40,000	0.78
100,000	1.00

Use these values to sketch the appropriate risk-preference curve for this problem and to construct a risk-preference table for the decision facing Russell.

17-29. Using the risk-preference table determined in Problem 28 and the probability assessments given in Problem 27, choose the appropriate planting strategy for Russell, using the expected-risk preference criterion.

17-30. Russell Smith's neighbor has deep wells drilled on his farm. He is willing to sell Russell extra water, which will ensure normal water levels, if the wells do not run dry. To use this potential water, Russell will have to install a temporary pipeline costing $10,000. In addition, the extra water will cost $15,000 and will be used only if snowfall is light or average. Russell assesses the probability the wells will not run dry as 75%. Draw the appropriate decision tree including this new alternative. Assess this decision tree assuming Russell is risk neutral.

17-31. Use the decision tree from Problem 30 and the risk-preference curve determined in Problem 28 to decide whether Russell should arrange to purchase water from his neighbor.

17-32. Referring to Problems 30 and 31, in addition to considering purchasing water from his neighbor, Russell is also considering the alternative of buying drought insurance for the first time. The cost of this insurance will be $5,000 and will pay off only if no water is received, starting in August. Russell estimates the payoff will be $20,000 if he receives any insurance money. Add this new factor to the decision tree. Again, assuming Russell is a risk-neutral decision maker, recommend a course of action for him.

■ SUMMARY AND CONCLUSIONS

Making decisions under uncertainty is a regular part of business. Although decision makers usually cannot eliminate uncertainty, they can use the tools of decision analysis to help deal with it.

In this chapter we explained the steps for constructing a payoff table and an opportunity-loss table. We also introduced nonprobabilistic decision criteria, such as maximin, maximax, and minimax regret. More importantly, we discussed the expected-value criterion, which utilizes probabilities assigned to the uncertain outcomes. We demonstrated how to determine the cost of uncertainty and to determine an upper limit on the value of new information using either a payoff or opportunity-cost approach.

One of the most important decision-analysis tools is the decision tree, which provides a chronological ordering of the decisions and events involved in making a decision. In this chapter, we illustrated how to use a decision tree in making a decision under uncertainty. In addition, we showed how decision-tree analysis, through the foldback process, takes into account future decisions which affect the current decision.

Not all decision makers are willing to make decisions strictly on the basis of the highest expected payoff or lowest expected cost. Many people will select an alternative which has a lower expected payoff than another alternative if doing so reduces the possibility of a bad outcome. Another decision maker will pick an alternative with a lower expected value just for the chance of a high payoff. Thus, not all decision makers are risk neutral; in fact, most are not. The majority tends to be risk avoiders, and others are risk seekers.

A decision analysis is not complete, and would not accurately model the decision maker's state of mind, if it does not take into account his or her attitude toward risk. The basics introduced in this chapter will get you started in incorporating risk preferences into decision analysis.

EQUATIONS

Expected Value

$$E(x) = \sum_{i=1}^{k} x_i P(x_i) \qquad \textbf{17-1}$$

$$\sum_{i=1}^{k} P(x_i) = 1.0 \qquad \textbf{17-2}$$

$$0.0 \le P(x_i) \le 1.0 \qquad \textbf{17-3}$$

Classical Probability Assessment

$$P(x) = \frac{\text{Number of ways } x \text{ can occur}}{\text{Total number of ways any outcome can occur}} \qquad \textbf{17-4}$$

Relative Frequency of Occurrence Probability

$$P(x) = \frac{\text{Number of times } x \text{ occurs}}{n} \qquad \textbf{17-5}$$

■ KEY TERMS

Certainty—A decision environment in which the results of selecting each alternative are known before the decision is made.

Certainty Equivalent—The value that would make a decision maker indifferent between taking an uncertain gamble versus receiving that value instead of taking the gamble.

Decision Tree—A diagram that illustrates the correct ordering of actions and events in a decision-analysis problem. Each act or event is represented by a node on the decision tree.

Expected-Value Criterion—A decision criterion that employs probability to select the alternative that will produce the greatest average payoff or minimum average loss.

Maximax Criterion—An optimistic decision criterion for dealing with uncertainty without using probability. For each option, the decision maker finds the maximum possible payoff and then selects the option with the greatest maximum payoff.

Maximin Criterion—A pessimistic (conservative) decision criterion for dealing with uncertainty without using probability. For each option, the decision maker finds the minimum possible payoff and selects the option with the greatest minimum payoff.

Minimax Regret Criterion—A decision criterion that considers the costs of selecting the "wrong" alternative. For each state of nature, the decision maker finds the difference between the best payoff and each other alternative and uses these values to construct an opportunity-loss table. The decision maker then selects the alternative with the minimum opportunity loss (or regret).

Opportunity Loss—The difference between the actual payoff that occurs for a decision and the optimal payoff for that same state of nature.

Payoff—The outcome (profit or loss) for any combination of alternative and state of nature. The outcomes of all possible combinations of alternatives and states of nature constitute a *payoff table*.

Preference Quotient—A measure of the relative utility for the outcomes of a decision on a scale between 0.0 and 1.0.

Risk-Averse Attitude—The preference for risk such that the decision maker could select an alternative with a lower expected payoff in order to avoid the possibility of an undesirable outcome.

Risk-Neutral Attitude—The preference for risk under which the alternative with the highest expected payoff or lowest expected cost will be selected.

Risk-Preference Function—A graph that describes a decision maker's preference for risk over the range of possible payoffs.

Risk Premium—The difference between the expected value of an event and the certainty equivalent. The risk premium will be zero for a risk-neutral decision maker, positive for a risk-averse decision maker, and negative for a risk-seeking decision maker.

Risk-Seeking Attitude—The preference for risk such that the decision maker could select an alternative with a lower expected payoff in hopes of achieving an outcome with a more desirable result.

Standard Gamble Approach—The approach for assessing risk-preference functions that involves setting up a series of 50–50 gambles between two payoffs and determining the certainty equivalent for each gamble.

States of Nature—The possible outcomes in a decision situation over which the decision maker has no control.

Uncertainty—A decision environment in which the decision maker does not know what outcome will occur when an alternative is selected.

CHAPTER EXERCISES

Business Applications

Problems 33 through 38 refer to the following situation.

Hatchman Electronics makes specialized fuel injection units for automobile engines. The company is presently completing its 5-year strategic plan. A major component of this plan involves analyzing the following situation.

Hatchman presently makes an injection unit that it sells to automobile manufacturers for $200. The operating profit (revenue − direct manufacturing costs) for this unit is $90. The company estimates the probability is 80% that demand for this product will continue, at the same price, for the next 5 years. But if a competitor introduces a better unit, the selling price will be dropped to $140 to maintain the company's market share. Hatchman Electronics is considering trying to develop an improved fuel injector. Whether the product is successful or not, the development costs will be amortized by adding $20 to the cost of every injector sold for the next 5 years. If the development effort is successful, the improved unit will still be sold for $200 but direct manufacturing costs will be reduced to $70. The research and development department estimates the probability of the development effort being successful is 60%.

17-33. Develop a decision tree representing the Hatchman Electronics decision situation.

17-34. Assuming the Hatchman Electronics board of directors is willing to consider this problem from a risk-neutral perspective, should they decide to develop the new product?

17-35. Since the fuel injection unit is a high-volume product for Hatchman Electronics, the company may not be willing to analyze the decision from a risk-neutral perspective. Using the preference function shown in Figure 17-33, determine the best decision about producing the new product now.

17-36. Hatchman Electronics has the option of contracting with Stewart Consultants to analyze the feasibility of developing the new fuel injection unit. The feasibility study will cost $5 million and will be added to the production cost of each of the 1 million units the company is planning to make over the next 5 years. If the study indicates the new development is feasible, the probability of the product being successfully developed will be increased to 90%. If the study indicates the new development is not feasible, the product may still be developed but the probability of its being successful drops to 20%. Hatchman's managers

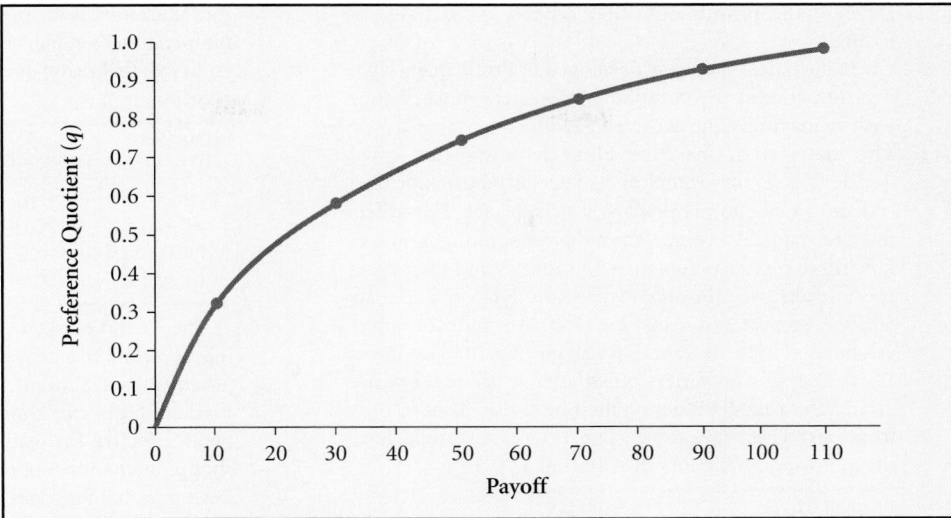

FIGURE 17-33
Risk Preference Curve for
Hatchman Electronics

don't have enough information to speculate about the probability that the feasibility study will indicate a success, so they assess each outcome—success and not a success—as being equally likely. Develop the decision tree for this new situation.

17-37. Assuming the Hatchman Electronics board of directors is still willing to consider this problem from a risk-neutral perspective, should they hire Stewart Consultants? What is the new sequence of decisions that should be taken?

17-38. Hatchman's president has read that companies that take no risks do not remain competitive in today's environment. Put yourself in the president's position and draw a risk-seeker's preference function. Using this preference function, what is the best decision about producing the new product now?

Problems 39 through 42 refer to the Far Horizons Development Corporation, which is considering building a vacation condominium project on the Maine coast. The question facing the company is how many units to build.

Because of their central-utility design, the units must be built in blocks of 10. Assume that, for each block of 10, the land will cost $200,000 and construction will cost $250,000 plus an additional $70,000 for each unit. Given that the company has decided to build, the possible production levels are as follows: 10, 20, 30, 40, 50.

Each unit will be priced at $200,000 for the regular market. However, if demand does not meet supply, Far Horizons will be forced to auction the units at an average price of $75,000.

17-39. Referring to the Far Horizons condominium project just described, set up a payoff table assuming the following possible demand levels: 0, 10, 20, 30, 40, 50.

17-40. Referring to the payoff table from Problem 39, what is the best decision if the maximin criterion is used? Show how you arrived at your answer.

17-41. What is the best decision for Far Horizons if the maximax criterion is used with the payoff table from Problem 39? Show how you arrived at your answer.

17-42. Assume that Far Horizons has assessed the following probability distribution for condominium demand.

DEMAND	PROBABILITY
0	0.05
10	0.10
20	0.25
30	0.25
40	0.20
50	0.15
	1.00

Use the expected-value criterion to determine how many units should be built. What is the expected value of this alternative?

Problems 43 through 46 refer to the following situation.

The production manager for a video-game company has been asked to help upper management decide whether or not to market a new game based on a popular cartoon character. If the new game is successful, the company will make $50 million; but if it is a failure, the company will lose an estimated $20 million in production and advertising expenses.

17-43. The video-game production manager in the situation just described believes that there is a 60% chance the new game will be successful. Construct the payoff table for the decision faced by the video-game company.

17-44. What decision should the managers of the video-game company make if they wish to maximize the expected payoff?

17-45. Suppose that marketing personnel have determined there are several levels of success and failure possible with the proposed video game. These possibilities (states of nature) and the assessed probabilities are as follows.

SUCCESS LEVEL	PROBABILITY
Excellent ($70,000,000)	0.30
Good ($50,000,000)	0.30
Fair ($10,000,000)	0.10
Poor (−$20,000,000)	0.30
	1.00

Develop the payoff table that reflects these states of nature.

17-46. Given the payoff table you developed in Problem 45, what decision should the company's managers make if they wish to maximize the expected payoff?

17-47. The manager of the Pink Flounder restaurant must decide how many orders of its specialty butter-broiled catfish to make for Thursday's lunch special. The orders must be made in advance, since the restaurant guarantees lunchtime service in less than 15 minutes and the catfish special takes 45 minutes to prepare. Each order costs $3.50 to prepare and is sold for $7.00. Any leftover orders can be used in the restaurant's fish gumbo, for a saving of $1.50. People who order catfish after it has run out are given a free catfish dinner on their next visit. Sales records from past Thursdays indicate that demand should have the following probability distribution:

DEMAND LEVEL	PROBABILITY
3	0.10
4	0.30
5	0.25
6	0.20
7	0.10
8	0.05
9 or more	0.00
	1.00

Develop a payoff table for the Pink Flounder's decision problem.

17-48. Referring to Problem 47, how many orders of catfish should be prepared on Thursday?

17-49. Referring to Problems 47 and 48, construct an opportunity-loss table for the Pink Flounder Restaurant and determine the quantity of catfish to order that will minimize the expected opportunity loss. Determine the cost of uncertainty. Discuss.

17-50. In Problems 39–42 you constructed a payoff table and used expected values to determine the appropriate number of condominiums for Far Horizons to build in Maine. Convert this table to an opportunity-loss table. Using expected opportunity loss as the decision criterion, determine how many units should be built. In this case, what is the EVPI? Suppose for $10,000 someone offered to sell the company perfect information about demand. Would the information be worth that price? Explain.

17-51. In Problems 47 and 48 you used the expected-value criterion to determine the optimal number of catfish orders to prepare. Convert the table you used in making your decision to an opportunity-loss table. Make the appropriate decision using the opportunity-loss table. What is the EVPI? What is the expected cost of uncertainty?

17-52. East Coast Imports is considering two alternative advertising and marketing plans for a new line of consumer products it buys from a manufacturer in Singapore. The first plan involves contracting with a television-shopping channel and is projected to have a monthly cost of $200,000. East Coast's marketing director has analyzed

this alternative and, after a joint meeting with the shopping-channel's manager, believes that the following probability distribution for increased revenue generated is accurate.

INCREASED REVENUE	PROBABILITY	INCREASED REVENUE	PROBABILITY
$120,000	0.10	260,000	0.20
150,000	0.10	290,000	0.10
200,000	0.20	320,000	0.10
230,000	0.20		1.00

The second marketing alternative—to rely on advertising in airline magazines and newspaper inserts—is projected to have a monthly cost of $120,000. However, the marketing director thinks that this approach would not be as effective for generating increased revenue as the shopping-channel approach. This is reflected in the following probability distribution.

INCREASED REVENUE	PROBABILITY
$ 70,000	0.10
90,000	0.10
110,000	0.25
140,000	0.25
170,000	0.20
200,000	0.10
	1.00

Because of the fear of "overkill," the company has decided not to try both approaches simultaneously. However, the managers did agree that if the print-advertising approach is chosen and results in $90,000 or less in added revenues, they can switch to the shopping channel for an additional cost of $20,000. They assume the probabilities would not be affected, but all revenue projections will be reduced by this cost.

a. Set up the appropriate decision tree for this problem.

b. Using the criterion of maximizing the expected increase in revenues, what marketing strategy should be chosen?

Problems 53 through 56 refer to the Major League Corporation, which makes sports-related items at a plant in South Carolina.

Before the baseball season, the company was approached by representatives from the Sports Connection, a company that supplies baseball items to be sold at major league parks and at sports souvenir stores. The Sports Connection has offered to contract to buy 300,000 baseball hats for $3.00 each. The company's production capacity is 500,000 hats. The problem facing Major League is whether to accept this offer or to attempt to independently sell all its baseball hats. If the demand for hats is high, the company will be able to sell hats for more than $3.00 each; but if demand is low, the hats will have to be sold for less than $3.00.

At least two uncertainties exist which will affect the demand for hats. First, if the league races are tight, the demand will be high; clear leaders early in the season will lead to low demand. Second, if the players strike this year, demand will be reduced. Using available information on injury levels and team strength analysis, Major League's executives estimate a 60% probability that the league races will be tight. In addition, the executives estimate the probability of a strike this year to be 30%. Assuming the two events, tight races and a player strike, are independent, the following table shows the possible selling prices for the company's hats and the associated probabilities.

| Player Strike | LEAGUE RACE | |
	Tight	Not Tight
No	$5.00	$2.50
	p = 0.42	p = 0.28
Yes	$4.00	$2.00
	p = 0.18	p = 0.12

17-53. Assuming Major League will sell its entire output, should it accept the Sports Connection's offer if it wishes to maximize its expected revenue?

17-54. Suppose Major League's executives believe the company will be able to negotiate the following deal with the Sports Connection: The contract price for hats will be reduced to $2.70 per hat; Major League will commit to delivering 150,000 hats at this price with the option of supplying the remaining 150,000 hats at $2.70 each after it determines whether the players will strike. This decision must be made before the status of the league races is known. This proposal, if made, will require the services of legal counsel, with a fee estimated to be $25,000. Determine the decision tree describing this situation.

17-55. Should Major League make the proposal specified in Problem 54? Base your recommendation on expected values.

17-56. Assume you are the purchasing manager for the Sports Connection. If you receive the offer proposed in Problem 54, would you recommend that it be accepted if your only other alternative is to buy 300,000 baseball hats on the open market? Assume that you have assessed the same probabilities as Major League regarding league races and player strikes. Base your conclusion on expected costs.

17-57. The Gregston Corporation has purchased a petroleum lease tract in the Pacific Ocean which may contain extensive oil deposits. Drilling a dry hole would be very expensive, so Gregston's managers are considering conducting a test to determine whether or not the geologic structure is favorable for the presence of oil. Unfortunately, the test is not perfect. Suppose Gregston's managers have determined the correct structure will be found 70% of the time when the reading is positive. Recent industry evidence with the test has shown a correct structure will be found 40% of the time when the reading is negative. Further, records show that when this test was conducted in this region in the past, 40% of the time the reading was positive. However, records also show that oil is struck for only 10% of all holes drilled worldwide.

The test will cost the company $400,000 to perform, and the cost of drilling the hole is $2 million. If Gregston does drill and hit oil, there are three possible outcomes:

OIL OUTCOME	REVENUE	PROBABILITY
Small find	$2 million	0.40
Medium find	$5 million	0.40
Large find	$10 million	0.20

Considering this information, what decision should Gregston make? Base your decision on expected profits.

17-58. In Problem 57, Gregston's managers did not take into account the fact that they had already paid $500,000 for the drilling lease. What, if any, effect does this new information have on the decision facing the company? Discuss.

17-59. Referring to Problem 58, how sensitive is the decision to the probability assessment that the tester will give a positive reading in this region of the ocean? That is, how much would this probability have to change in order to change the decision that Gregston will make?

17-60. New Age Marketing is considering two alternative advertising plans for a client. The first plan uses radio and television commercials and will cost $100,000. The account executive estimates a 40% chance that the client's revenues will increase by $80,000, a 25% chance that revenues will increase by $110,000, and a 35% chance that revenues will increase by $120,000 as a result of this advertising approach.

The second plan is to use newspaper and magazine advertisements, at a cost of $20,000. However, print media are thought to be less effective than radio and television. The account executive estimates the chances are 20% that this plan will increase revenues by $14,000, 50% that revenues will increase by $30,000, and 30% that revenues will increase by $40,000.

If the newspaper and magazine option is chosen, New Age can later take the radio and TV option, but expected revenue will decline by $10,000 from what it would have been had that been the first choice. The account executive has indicated that it would not be feasible to try the newspaper and magazine approach after first choosing radio and TV.

Use a decision-tree approach to determine what decision(s) the New Age agency should make.

Problems 61 through 66 refer to the following situation.

The Grimm Group presents in-house training seminars to organizations throughout the United States. The company currently presents seminars on three topics: quality control, material management, and just-in-time (JIT) manufacturing. The quality control seminar costs each participant $500, and the Grimm Group's gross margin (revenue − direct expenses) is 40% of this amount. The material management seminar costs $450 for each attendee and also has a 40% gross margin; the JIT seminar costs $600 and has a 35% gross margin. After 5 years of expansion, attendance at the seminars has declined more than 10% in the past year. The revenues from the three operations last year were: quality control, $1,200,000; material management, $900,000; JIT, $1,400,000.

At the yearly forecasting meeting, Graciela Grimm, the company's founder, projects that if no changes are made in marketing philosophy, revenues will be stagnant this year. She is, however, considering two options which should increase demand for the three seminars. The first option is to incorporate a computer simulation game as part of each seminar. Projections indicate that adding this type of game will increase the demand for the quality control seminar by 10% and the demand for the other two seminars by 15%. Adding a game will increase the cost associated with each seminar participant by $50; but, because the market is very competitive, the company will have to hold the line on the price change. The second option is to offer 3-day training seminars on the same topics but at 60% of the price of the 5-day seminars. Unfortunately, the cost of presenting the 3-day seminars will be reduced by only 20% from the cost of the original seminars. The president estimates the demand for the shorter seminars this year will generate revenues equal to 50% of the revenues realized from each 5-day seminar in the past year. Also, adding the shorter seminars will reduce the projected demand for the original seminars to 75% of last year's level.

17-61. Develop a decision tree describing the Grimm Group's decision situation.

17-62. Assuming President Grimm is risk neutral for this decision, what alternative would you recommend?

17-63. Assume the president's attitude about risk can be represented by the preference curve developed for a previous project (Figure 17-34). What alternative would you recommend now?

17-64. An initial market survey of the acceptance of computer simulation games indicates they are so popular that there is a 70% chance the Grimm Group will be able to raise the price of the seminars by enough to maintain its previous margins without affecting the demand. Incorporate this new information into your previous problem analysis.

17-65. Assume that Graciela Grimm is risk neutral for the decision situation as amended by Problem 64. Now what alternative would you recommend?

17-66. Referring to problem 65 and using Figure 17-34 to assess Grimm's attitude about risk, what alternative do you recommend as the decision?

FIGURE 17-34
Risk Preference Curve for the Grimm Group

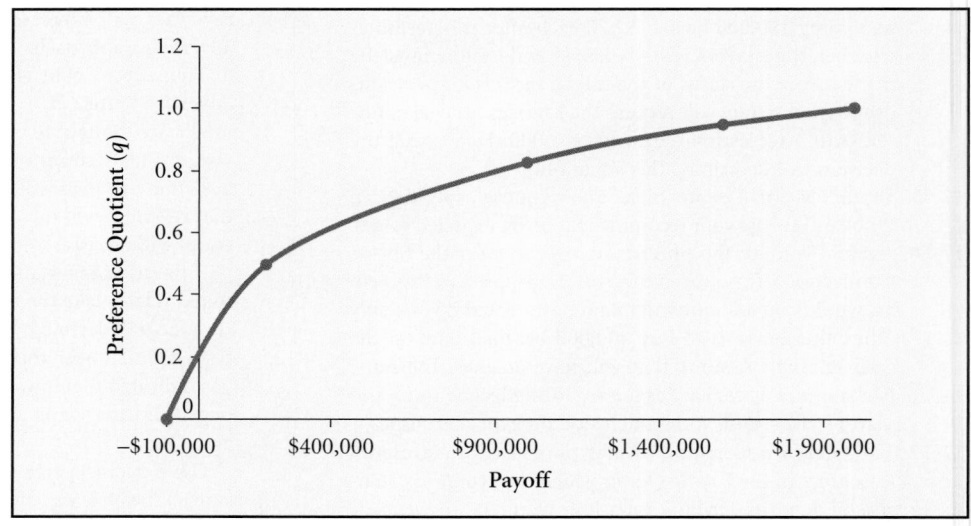

CASE 17-A

Rockstone International

Rockstone International is one of the world's largest diamond brokers. The firm purchases rough stones and has them cut and polished for sale in the United States and Europe. The diamond business has been very profitable, and from all indications it will continue to be so. However, R. B. Randall, president and chief executive officer for Rockstone, has stressed the need for effective management decisions throughout the organization if the firm is to remain profitable and competitive.

Normally, R. B. does not involve herself in personnel decisions, but today's situation is not typical. Beth Harkness, Rockstone's personnel manager, is considering whether or not to hire Hans Marquis, a world-famous diamond cutter, to replace Omar Barboa, who broke both his hands in a freak skateboard accident almost a month ago. If he is hired, Hans Marquis will be paid on a commission basis at the rate of $5,000 for each stone he cuts successfully. (Because of his professional pride, Hans will accept no fee if he is unsuccessful in cutting a stone.)

In the past, the decision of whether to hire Hans would have been simple. If he was available, he would be hired. However, 6 months ago, the Liechtenstein Corporation introduced the world's first diamond-cutting machine. This machine, which can be leased for 1 million dollars per year, is guaranteed to cut stones successfully 90% of the time.

Although Hans Marquis has an excellent reputation, Rockstone International cannot be sure about his success rate because of the extreme secrecy among people in the diamond business. Hans claims that his success rate is 95%, but he has been known to exaggerate. Rockstone executives have made the following assessments, based on all the information they could obtain.

SUCCESS RATE	PROBABILITY
0.97	0.10
0.95	0.40
0.90	0.30
0.85	0.10
0.80	0.10
	1.00

Rockstone purchases gemstones at a cost of $15,000 each. A successful cut yields four diamonds that can be sold at an average price of $35,000 each. Harry Winkler, sales and purchasing manager, reports that his projections for the next year indicate a need for 100 stones to be cut.

R. B. Randall knows there must be a way to decide whether to hire Hans Marquis or lease the new cutting machine.

CASE 17-B

Hadden Materials and Supplies, Inc., Part 1

Mark Hadden and his son, Greg, began Hadden Materials and Supplies, Inc., in the mid-1980s. Both Mark and Greg had successful careers with major U.S. corporations, but after several years of discussion they came to the conclusion that they wanted to work together in their own business. They also concluded that they wanted to be in manufacturing, where they could take advantage of their previous experience and business contacts.

From the beginning, Mark has run the production shop and Greg has concentrated on sales. About 2 years ago, they got a contract to make an electronic component for natural gas heaters. At first they made this part exclusively for one company, but about 6 months ago they started making the same component for other heater manufacturers. The component is produced in large volume and sells for $30. The variable production cost per unit is $13, making this a very profitable product for the company.

However, until recently there was no way to determine whether a component would work properly until it had actually been installed in the heater unit. Whenever the heater manufacturer found a defect, Hadden Materials and Supplies would refund the full $30 plus pay a penalty of $10. Although the company has made major improvements in its quality control program, this particular component is very difficult to build and to have work properly. As a result, the defect rate has been approximately 25%.

A week ago, the company was approached by a representative of Tech-Notics, Inc., who said her company had a device for testing components like the one Hadden makes for gas heaters. By using this tester, Hadden could determine before shipping whether or not the component would work. This was one sales call that really got Mark and Greg's attention, and the sales representative agreed to bring a unit by for a trial the next morning. Greg called their largest customer and made some arrangements to "test the tester" at the customer's plant the next afternoon.

Over the next 2 days, Mark, Greg, and the Tech-Notics sales representative tested 400 components. Of these, 320 tested positive, indicating that they would turn out to be good; however, of the 320 that tested positive, 72 ended up actually being defective. In addition, of the components that got a negative reading, 8 were found to be good. Although the testing device was not perfect, the Haddens were still encouraged.

The sales representative explained that her company preferred to lease the testers, with a financial arrangement that called for the lessor to pay $3 per test. (The tester had an automatic counter.) If the unit were sold outright, it would cost $6 million. Mark and Greg realized there was no way that they could afford to purchase the unit, so that option was immediately eliminated. However, they were interested in the lease plan and told the sales representative they would call her soon with their decision.

As Mark and Greg conferred over lunch, they estimated the heater component would remain in production for about 2 more years. During that time, they could expect orders for about 100,000 units. They also agreed that if they leased the tester, they would use it to test every component that they built. As Greg said, "Why should we lease it if we don't use it!" They also concluded that if an item tested negative, it would be scrapped and not shipped.

CASE 17-C

Hadden Materials and Supplies, Inc., Part 2

About 2 hours after Mark Hadden had phoned the Tech-Notics sales representative to tell her of his company's tentative decision, he placed a call to Diane Rogers. Diane is a former colleague of Mark's who now serves as a consultant to manufacturing companies. After Mark explained the details of the decision he and Greg had made, Diane asked whether they had considered their risk preferences in their analysis. Mark said that they thought they had, but he didn't quite know to what Diane was referring.

Before long, Mark was offering to cover the expenses if Diane and Fred, her husband, would fly out for a long weekend—and if Diane would provide some advice on this decision. They agreed to get their work out of the way Friday evening and leave the rest of the weekend for some fun and relaxation.

Friday afternoon, after making sure that Diane and Fred had arrived and were settled into their hotel, Mark arranged to drive Diane to the plant to meet with Greg. As they discussed the decision situation, Diane made some notes. She remarked that it appeared Mark and Greg had *not* formally considered their preferences for risk; instead, they had conducted their analysis as if they were risk neutral. She also noted that the decision regarding the tester should be analyzed as if only one component was being built instead of 100,000.

Diane suggested that together they try to develop a risk-preference function for this deal. First, she asked the partners to determine the highest possible addition and the biggest possible reduction in the company's net cash position that might result from the decision. Greg indicated that these ranged from a high of +$17 per unit to a low of −$26 per unit. Then Diane posed a series of questions, beginning with this one: "Suppose you are faced with an event that will give you a 50–50 chance at making $17 versus losing $26. Further suppose that you will be forced to participate. Do you want to?"

Both Mark and Greg agreed that it didn't seem like a very good deal. Diane then asked, "Suppose I will let you out of the deal for a fee. Would you pay me $20 right now to get out of the deal?"

Mark and Greg conferred and decided that they would not pay *$20* but they would pay $16 to get out of the deal. Diane wrote this down and continued asking similar questions until she finally announced, "Now we have enough information about your risk preferences to develop a risk-preference curve, which we can then use in your decision analysis."

The curve that Diane drew is shown in Figure 17-35. The group then set out to determine whether this finding would alter the decision Mark and Greg had made before conferring with Diane.

After making arrangements for an early tennis game Saturday morning, Mark asked Diane if she would take some time on Saturday to explain clearly what they had done this afternoon and why the results were the way they were, compared with the decision that Mark and Greg had reached earlier.

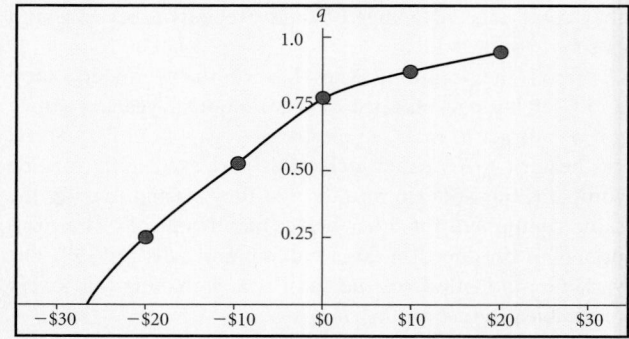

FIGURE 17-35   Risk-Preference Curve for Hadden Materials and Supplies

GENERAL REFERENCES

1. Arrow, K. J., "Utilities, Attitudes, Choices: A Review Note." *Econometrica*, 26, 1958.
2. Baird, Bruce F., *Managerial Decision Making under Uncertainty* (New York: Wiley, 1989).
3. Bell, D., "Regret in Decision Making under Uncertainty." *Operations Research*, 30, 1982.
4. Berger, P. D., and A. Gerstenfeld, "Decision Analysis for Increased Highway Safety." *Sloan Management Review* (Spring 1971).
5. Brown, R. V., "Do Managers Find Decision Theory Useful?" *Harvard Business Review* (January–February 1970).
6. Brown, R. V., A. S. Kahr, and C. Peterson, *Decision Analysis for the Manager* (New York: Holt, 1974).
7. Bunn, D. W., *Applied Decision Analysis* (New York: McGraw-Hill, 1984).
8. Davidson, F., "Dimensions of Utility in a Regional Planning Context." *Decision Sciences* (January 1974).
9. Farquhar, P., "Utility Assessment Methods." *Management Science*, 30, 1984.
10. Felson, J., *Decision Making under Uncertainty* (New York: CBS Educational and Professional Publishing, 1979).
11. Fishburn, P. C., *Utility Theory for Decision Making* (New York: Wiley, 1970).
12. Friedman, M., and L. J. Savage, "The Utility Analysis of Choices Involving Risk." *Journal of Political Economy* (August 1948).
13. Gregory, G., *Decision Analysis* (New York: Plenum, 1988).
14. Hammond, J. S., "Better Decisions with Preference Theory." *Harvard Business Review*, 45 (November–December 1967).
15. Hespos, R. F., and P. A. Strassmann, "Stochastic Decision Trees for the Analysis of Investment Decisions." *Management Science*, 11, 1965.
16. Holloway, C., *Decision Making under Uncertainty: Models and Choices* (Englewood Cliffs, NJ: Prentice Hall, 1979).
17. Howard, R. A., "An Assessment of Decision Analysis." *Operations Research*, 28, 1980.
18. Keeney, R. L., "Decision Analysis: An Overview." *Operations Research*, 30, 1982.
19. Keeney, R. L., and H. Raiffa, *Decisions with Multiple Objectives: Preferences and Value Trade-offs* (New York: Wiley, 1976).
20. Raiffa, H., *Decision Analysis* (Reading, MA: Addison-Wesley, 1968).
21. Sampson, D., *Managerial Decision Analysis* (Homewood, IL: Irwin, 1988).
22. Schlaifer, R., *Analysis of Decisions under Uncertainty* (New York: McGraw-Hill, 1969).
23. Stimson, D. H., "Utility Measurement in Public Health Decision Making." *Management Science*, 16, 1969.
24. Swalm, R. O., "Utility, Theory Insights into Risk Taking," *Harvard Business Review* (November–December 1966).
25. Ulvila, J. W., and R. V. Brown, "Decision Analysis Comes of Age." *Harvard Business Review* (September 1982).
26. Winkler, R., *Introduction to Bayesian Inference and Decision* (New York: Holt, 1972).

ANSWERS TO SELECTED ODD-NUMBERED PROBLEMS

Worked-out solutions to all the odd-numbered problems are in the **Student Solutions Manual** *that accompanies this text. Please note, many solutions were done using Excel, which outputs answers to several decimal places. The precision shown may be more than required in some instances.*

CHAPTER 1

1-1 "Estimation is a technique by which we can know about all the data in a data set whenever the data set so large that it is impractical for us to work with all the data. By looking at a subset of the larger data set estimates are formed that give us some insight into the larger data set."

1-3 Hypothesis testing is used whenever one is interested in testing claims that concern a population. Using information taken from samples, hypothesis testing evaluates the claim and makes a conclusion about the population from which the sample was taken. Estimation is used when we are interested in knowing something about all the data, but the population is too large, or the data set is too big for us to work with all the data. In estimation, no claim is being made or tested.

1-5 a Use mean or average. **b** To determine a value for the percentage of people in the market area that are senior citizens, the executives would rely on estimation. **c** The executives might want to test the hypothesis that the percentage of senior citizens in the market area is greater than the percentage of senior citizens nationwide. The executives could also test the hypothesis that the percentage of senior citizens is greater than or less than a specific value, say 27%.

1-7 Some representative examples might include estimates of the number of CEOs who will vote for a particular candidate, estimates of the percentage increase in wages for factory workers, estimates of the average dollar advertising expenditures for pharmaceutical companies in a specific year, and the expected increase in R&D expenditures for the coming quarter.

1-9 In compiling the unemployment rate, the U.S. Labor Department probably relied on telephone surveys and mail questionnaires to gather the necessary information from companies and businesses.

1-11 a Since no information was provided concerning the amount that would be donated to charities, the information was most likely obtained using a closed-end question, such as, "Do you plan on making a charitable contribution this Christmas season? Yes or No." **b** An open-end question that could be used to obtain the same information would be "How much money do you plan on giving to charity this Christmas season?"

1-13 This data could have been collected through observation or experiment. Employees of the USDA could provide periodic reports of fire ant activity in their region. Likewise, scientists studying the spread of fire ants may have conducted experiments that indicate the rate of spread in certain conditions.

1-15 Among the advantages of using a mail questionnaire are the relatively low cost and the avoidance of any interviewer-injected bias. However, mail questionnaires often suffer from low response rates (nonresponse bias), and in some cases people who feel strongly one way or the other on an issue may heavily weight responses. Written surveys may also suffer from inaccurate responses when people refuse to tell the truth about sensitive matters such as age and income.

1-25 This would not be considered a sample. You are looking at the NASDAQ for a 1-day time period, so this would be considered the entire population.

1-27 The November value is an estimate, so it is not a population. The value for October is a known value, so it is a population parameter.

1-29 a Simple random sampling **b** Cluster sampling **c** Simple random sampling **d** Stratified random sampling

1-31 In cluster sampling, the population is divided into groups, called clusters, such that the clusters each have the same characteristics as the population as a whole. In stratified random sampling, the population is divided into subgroups, called strata, so that each population item belongs to only one stratum. The objective is to form strata such that the population values of interest within each stratum are as much alike as possible.

1-33 There may be cases in which the sample size required to obtain a certain desired level of information from a simple random sample is greater than time or money will allow. In such cases, stratified random sampling has the potential to provide the desired information with a smaller sample size.

1-35 a Use cluster sampling where each area of the country (such as each national park) is used as its own sample. You could then use a random sampling technique within each cluster or use a random sampling technique to decide which clusters to look at. You could sample each *x*th number as they leave the park.

1-37 a Cluster sampling means that you could group hotels together such that you have essentially created minipopulations, and then you would use any sampling technique to determine which clusters you want to sample. You could then select every *x*th customer from the clusters you intend to sample. **b** Cluster sampling allows you to reduce the amount of sampling you need to do and also will give you a broader spectrum of the overall population. **c** It would be possible, but it would be very expensive to contact each of the customers that stayed at your hotel all over the United States.

1-39 a In this case, there is not an apparent advantage to using a systematic random sample. **b** You could use a random number generator to give you the starting point.

1-41 a Ease of use and timeliness **b** Assuming you want to use a nonstatistical method, you could actually survey the first 100 people entering the store or you could wander around the store and just ask any 100 people that you happen to observe.

1-43 a Qualitative, nominal data **b** Quantitative, ratio data **c** Quantitative, ratio data **d** Quantitative, ordinal data **e** Quantitative, ratio data **f** Quantitative, ratio data

1-45 a Ratio data **b** Nominal data **c** Nominal data **d** Ratio data **e** Interval data **f** Nominal data

1-47 a Since you are assigning a number to a group, it is qualitative data; therefore, you cannot perform mathematical calculations on these categories. **b** No **c** Ordinal **d** Cross-sectional

1-51 Primary data are collected by you or another person with whom you are closely associated, and are intended to be used for your specific purpose and use. Secondary data are collected and compiled by an outside source.

1-53 The four levels are nominal, ordinal, interval, and ratio.

1-55 a Telephone survey to people in the area would be a less costly way of determining the information rather than sending someone there to do personal interviews. **b** The population would be all the people who live in Walnut Creek and the measurement would be their response to whether they would shop at this type of store or not. **c** type of store, nominal; amount of money spent, ratio; shopper's age, ratio; shopper's income, ratio; shopper's rating of existing stores, ordinal

1-57 a Qualitative, nominal data **b** Quantitative, ratio data **c** Qualitative, nominal data **d** Quantitative, ratio data **e** Quantitative, ratio data **f** Quantitative, ordinal data

1-59 In personal interviews, people tend to give the answer they think interviewers want to hear. Interviewers can also create bias by the way they ask the question or the way they are looking at the person when they ask the question.

1-63 a This would not be a good method of sampling. Because different lifts may take you to different levels of skiing, you may be asking all expert skiers or all novice skiers. Their answers about equipment could be significantly different. **b** A better method would be to ask the questions of individuals at all ski lifts, but ask, say, every 10th person the questions. This should give you a broader audience from which to get your information.

1-65 You could set your clusters to be areas of the country; for example, Northeast, Southeast, Midwest, West, South, etc.

1-67 a You will need to select two-digit numbers. **b** 13, 22, 03, 18, 04, 27, 07, 17, 21, 08 **c** You could continue down the random number table and select the next number.

CHAPTER 2

2-1 c Mean of Data Set 1 = 5.8; mean of Data Set 2 = 5.8; the means of both data sets are the same.
d Data Set 1: 0.3667; Data Set 2: 0.33333

2-3 b Class width = 23.66, round to 25

Classes	Frequency
0 < 25	8
25 < 50	15
50 < 75	11
75 < 100	1
100 < 125	2

c

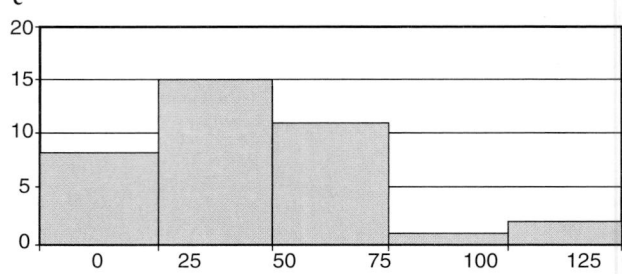

d 0.3784

2-15 a & b

Classes	Frequency	Relative Frequency
21–30	4	0.0201
31–40	4	0.0201
41–50	2	0.0101
51–60	133	0.6683
61–70	38	0.1910
71–80	3	0.0151
81–90	2	0.0101
91–100	13	0.0653

2-17 a

	KNOWLEDGE LEVEL		
	Savvy	Experienced	Novice
Online Investors	32	220	148
Traditional Investors	8	54	134

b

	KNOWLEDGE LEVEL		
	Savvy	Experienced	Novice
Online Investors	0.0533	0.3667	0.2467
Traditional Investors	0.0133	0.1967	0.2233

2-19 a

Weight	Line 1	Line 2
0 < 3	6	4
≥ 3	4	6

b

Weight	Line 1	Line 2
0 < 3	0.3	0.2
≥ 3	0.2	0.3

2-21

	Gloss	Semi-Gloss	Flat	Totals
Glidden	25	25	0	50
Everlast	50	100	50	200
Ponderosa	25	100	25	150
DuPont	0	25	75	100
Totals	100	250	150	

2-27 a

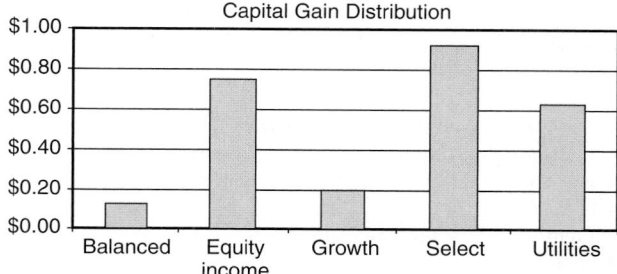

Capital Gain Distribution

2-39 b The total number of residents of cable subscribers is about three times the total number of residents not subscribing. **c** The proportion of small families is 56.25% for non–cable subscribers and 59.9% for cable subscribers.

2-47 a

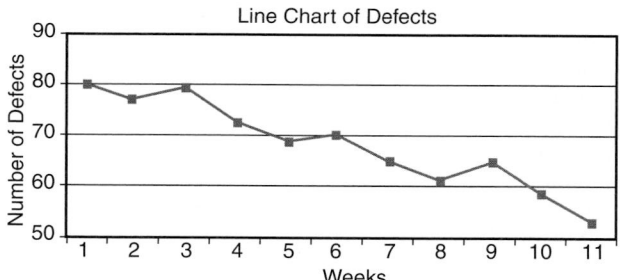

Line Chart of Defects

b About 55 or 56 **c** About week 16 or 17

2-61 b & d

Classes	Frequency	Relative Frequency	Cumulative Frequency
0–399	8	0.0234	8
400–799	12	0.0351	20
800–1,199	20	0.0585	40
1,200–1,599	50	0.1462	90
1,600–1,999	125	0.3655	215
2,000–2,399	103	0.3012	318
2,400–2,799	24	0.0702	342

e. 469 ounces of crabgrass killer
2-65 a 7 classes **b** $2,304
2-67 a 0.1029 **b** $783 per day **c** The company could hire 6 more.

2-69 a

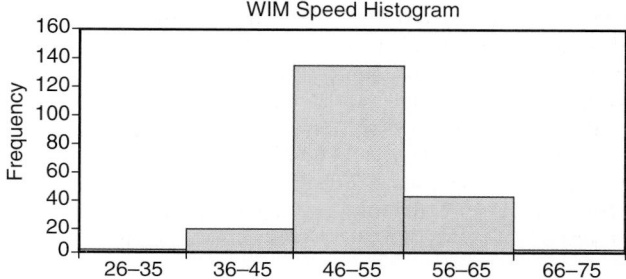

Scatter Plot of Hours and Sales

b It appears that there is a linear relationship.
d $22.76
2-75 a & b

Classes	Frequency	Relative Frequency
70,001–100,000	36	0.36
100,001–130,200	37	0.37
130,201–160,300	13	0.13
160,301–190,400	7	0.07
190,401–220,500	2	0.02
220,501–250,600	3	0.03
250,601–280,700	0	0
280,701–310,800	2	0.02

CHAPTER 3

3-1 $\mu = 5$; median = 5.5; mode = 6
3-3 a Data are right-skewed **b** 1st quartile = 18.95; 3rd quartile = 25.49
3-5 a Pre-advertising: $\bar{x} = 37.8$ years; median = 35 years; no mode. Post-advertising: $\bar{x} = 30.4$ years; median = 28.5 years; data are bi-modal at 28 and 40 **b** The pre-advertising sample is right-skewed, the post-advertising sample is right-skewed
3-7 a Mean = 42,350; median = 42,582
3-9 a 75th percentile **b** Mean = 42,261; median = 42,326
3-11 a Range = 5 **b** 5.8333, 3.1389, 1.7717 **c** 3.7667, 1.9408
3-13 a 1.26 standard deviations in the interquartile range
b −6.931
3-15 a Range = 2,440 **b** $\sigma^2 = 641,255.5$ **c** $\sigma = 800.7843$
3-17 a Range = 12; interquartile range = 5
3-19 a Mean = 11.8125; median = 12.6; mode = 12.6; interquartile range = 4.05; $s = 2.7667$ **b** 62.5% of the customer spent less than 15 minutes. With new cash registers, 93.75% of the customers spent less than 15 minutes.
3-21 a Mean = 485 DRAMs. The process used in Problem 20 outputs an average of 494.5625. **b** The current process outputs a median of 490 DRAMs. The process used in Problem 20 outputs a median of 486 DRAMs.
3-23 a

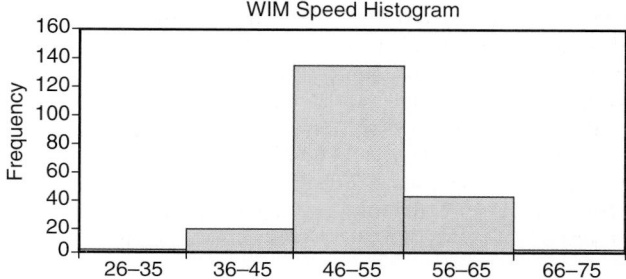

WIM Speed Histogram

b Mean = 51.875; Median = 52 **c** Standard Deviation = 5.922394; Range = 41; interquartile range = 7 **d** Proportion > 50 = 0.6150; proportion > 60 = 0.055; proportion > 70 = 0

3-25

Difference POE & WIM	
Mean	−449.92
Standard Error	81.40971
Median	−275
Mode	−690
Standard Deviation	1151.307
Sample Variance	1325508
Kurtosis	10.78195
Skewness	−2.62711
Range	8800
Minimum	−7460
Maximum	1340
Sum	−89984
Count	200

3-27 Use Excel's descriptive statistics tools to determine the answers to this problem. You can use the descriptive statistics tool to determine the interquartile range by inputting the positions, but the answer may be slightly different than doing it by hand. **a** The interquartile range = 430 **b** For males: interquartile range = 422; for females: interquartile range = 403

3-29 a 75% **b** 11% outside of three standard deviations. Half of that would be above the upper limit and half below the lower limit, which means 5.5% at most could be above the upper limit. **c** 5.5% at most could be smaller than 2,400

3-31 a Method 1: mean = 12, standard deviation = 4.848; method 2: mean = 12, standard deviation = 8.573 **b** Method 1: CV = 0.404 or 40.4%; method 2: CV = 0.714 or 71.4% **c** In this case it would be acceptable to compare standard deviations, since the means are the same.

3-33 a Growth fund: CV = 0.25 or 25%; Specialized fund: CV = 0.333 or 33.3% **b** Growth Fund **c** Growth Fund: 4–12; Specialized Fund 6–30

3-39 a Scanner **b** Scanner = 24.54%; Manual = 37.22%

3-41 The median would be preferred to the mean in data sets that have extremely high or low values that affect the mean. An example is home prices.

3-51 a Mean = 15.875 **b** Median = 14.5 **c** The mode is 12 and 16 **d** Variance = 49.5536; standard deviation = 7.0394 **f** Median, since you have an extreme outlier. **g** 17 games

3-53 a Mean = 24.7333 **b** Median = 20; data are skewed right. **c** Mode = 19 **d** Standard deviation = 11.0871 **f** Interquartile range = 15

3-55 a Mean = 530.25 **b** Median = 425 **c** The first 6 oil wells will be closed, which are those producing at 75, 100, 200, 230, 250, 250

3-57 a Mean = 364.4167 **b** Variance = 16,662.6288; standard deviation = 129.0838

3-59 a Mean = 39.0556 **b** Median = 35 **c** Variance = 219.232; standard deviation = 14.8065

3-61 a CV on Fund A = 37.88%; CV on Fund B = 43.75%

3-63 a CV of Portland plant = 13.24%; CV of San Antonio plant = 25%

3-71 b Mean = 78.51; median = 62; standard deviation = 73.82 **c** Interquartile range = 56 **d** There are no negative earnings per

share. **e** 1st quartile = 41; 2nd quartile = median = 62; 3rd quartile = 97

3-75 a

	Revenues	Profits	Employees
Mean	6,354.71	803.43	21,530.30
Median	3,428.00	401.00	11,000.00
Standard deviation	7,457.66	881.812	21,269.35

b Mellon Bank Corporation is slightly below the average for profits and revenues and slightly above the average for number of employees.

c	Revenues	Profits	Employees
Coefficient of variation	1.173564	1.097558	0.9878812

CHAPTER 4

4-1 $P(\text{Red}) = 0.25$

4-3 $P(\text{no rain}) = 0.875$

4-5 a 0.2222 **b** 0.4444

4-7 a $P(\text{Early}) = 0.1875$ **b** $P(\text{Los Angeles}) = 0.5625$ **c** $P(\text{Los Angeles with Early}) = 0.2222$; $P(\text{Early}) = 0.125$

4-9 a The subjective probability assessment method **b** No

4-11 a Yes **b** No **c** Events cannot be both mutually exclusive and independent

4-13 a 0.6613 **b** 0.4355 **c** 0.2903 **d** 0.2097

4-15 a 0.037 **b** 0.963

4-17 a 0.45 **b** 0.48

4-19 a 0.04 **b** 0.96 **c** 0.999 **d** 0.46656; 0.41990

4-21 A = 0.3913; B = 0.6087

4-23 Cost to Plant A = $4,762; cost to Plant B = $1,429; cost to Plant C = $3,809

4-25 $P(\text{Old}) = 0.2105$; $P(\text{New}) = 0.7895$

4-27 a 70 possible schedules **b** 0.25

4-29 a 0.1667 **b** 0.0278 **c** 0.6944 **d** 0.2778 **e** 0.3056

4-31 0.00072

4-33 0.0014

4-35 a 0.3333 **b** $P(\text{Boise}) = 0.9069$ $P(\text{SL}) = 0.0797$; $P(\text{Toronto}) = 0.0133$

4-37 a 138 **b** 636 **c** 25.2190

4-39 a 0.73 **b** 0.09783 **c** $29.20

4-41 a 26.70 **b** Variance = 140.1100; standard deviation = 11.8368

4-43 a 70 **b** 210 **c** 120 **d** 120

4-45 a 0.00000001 **b** 0.00000000001 **c** 0.0099 **d** 0.0199 **e** 0.4389 **f** 0.4389 **g** 0.0132 **h** 0.4142

4-47 a Binomial distribution with $n = 100$ and $p = 0.15$ **b** Binomial distribution with $n = 100$ and $p = 0.10$ **c** 0.2970 **d** 0.8365 **e** 29.7%

4-49 Expected profit = $10,500

4-51 a 0.4095 **b** 0.2262 **c** 0.5905

4-53 a 0.0028 **b** 0.0018

4-55 0.00195

4-57 a Binomial distribution with $n = 3$, $p = 0.025$ **b** 0.1426; yes, it is larger. **c** 0.84%

4-59 a 0.1755 **b** 0.6160 **c** 0.8753

4-61 a Mean = 3.1623 **b** 0.7344; 0.9627; 0.9965

4-63 a 0.0001 **b** 0.0415 **c** 0.4557

4-65 111

4-77 a e_1 = bid awarded; e_2 = bid not awarded **b** $SS = (e_1, e_2)$ **c** $SS = (e_1, e_2, e_3, e_4, e_5, e_6, e_7, e_8)$

4-79 a 0.0681 **b** 0.6375 **c** 0.5438
4-81 a 0.0020 **b** 0.0060 **c** classical probability approach
4-83 a 0.6065 **b** 0.9856 **c** 0.2231 **d** 0.0002
4-85 a 0.0009 **b** 0.0267
4-87 a 0.1841 **b** 0.0003
4-89 a 0.9997 **b** 0.2059
4-91 0.2627
4-93 a 0.49 **b** 0.40 **c** 0.11
4-95 a

x	P(x)
0	0.0778
1	0.2592
2	0.3456
3	0.2304
4	0.0768
5	0.0102

b 0.0870 **c** 2.0
4-99 a 40 **b** 80 **c** $1.80 **d** 4.0
4-101 a 0 **b** 0.0035 **c** 0.00098; $P(x > 7) = 0.1719$
4-105 a 0.2289 **b** 0.9764 **c** 0.8889
4-107 a 2 **b** 1.4142 **c** Uniform distribution
4-109 a

x	P(x)
0	0.00243
1	0.02835
2	0.13230
3	0.30870
4	0.36015
5	0.16807

b 0.00243
4-111 Expected number = 10.8; standard deviation = 1.0392
4-113 a 0.9445 **b** 0.5577 **c** 0.1768
4-115 0.964
4-117 a 0.5959 **b** 0.0708 **c** Not independent
4-119 a 0.0378 **b** 0.2503
4-121 0.3333

CHAPTER 5

5-1 a 0.5 **b** 0.1587 **c** 0.6826 **d** 0.0228
5-3 a 13.1 **b** 2.58
5-5 a $423,200 **b** 137 **c** 154 **d** 0.8340
5-7 a essentially 0 percent **b** 0.0062 **c** The number of fliers is actually a discrete variable. The normal distribution assumes that the value can take on an infinite number of possible outcomes.
5-9 a 0.0228 **b** 15.8 **c** 0.27
5-11 a 16.32 **b** 0.0228
c 0.1814; $P(x > 2 | n = 3, p = 0.1814)$ is essentially 0
5-13 a Between $2.36 and $5.86
b 90th percentile = $5.86 and 10th percentile = $2.36
5-15 a $8.93 **b** 1.55
5-17 4.32 inches
5-19 $P(x < 3.5) = 0.0495$; $P(x > 100, n = 1,000, p = .0495) = 0.0000$
5-21 b Mean = 2.452747253; standard deviation = 4.777524711
c 0.0012 **d** No, this would not be an appropriate claim. The probability of losing 12 or more pounds is only 0.12%.
5-23 a 0.0027 **b** 6.658
5-25 0.938

5-27 a 0.9817 **b** 0.1170 **c** 0.0067
5-29 a 0.5714 **b** 0.7143
5-31 0.5507
5-33 a 0.4084; yes **b** 40,840
5-35 A single point has no area, so the probability of a specific value must be zero.
5-39 b 0.2222 **c** 0.4444
5-41 a $P(x < 40) = 0.1667$; the probability that 10 would be less than 40 = 0.0000000165713. **b** No
5-43 a 4.2 **b** No
5-45 a 13 gallons **b** 0.4325
5-47 Expected weight gain would be 30,000 pounds; total price increase of $12,000
5-49 a 0.6554 **b** 0.5478 **c** 0.3967 **d** 433
5-51 a 10 feet 5.29 inches **b** 0.10; adjustment was made.
5-53 9.85% of the employees have all their sick leave paid.
5-55 a 22.08 **b** $179,600 savings
5-57 a 0.6321 **b** 0.2231 **c** 0.1733
5-63 0.1401
5-65 a 0.0721 **b** 0.0475

CHAPTER 6

6-1 a 5.8 **b** 5.8333; 0.0333 **c** −3.1333 to 2.8667
6-3 a Mean = 40.89; standard deviation = 16.97 **b** Mean = 40.9
6-5 a The data is slightly left skewed.
b Mean = 42,318.6875; standard deviation = 12,689.8732
c (1) 44,126.5; (2) 1,807.8125 **d** −4,304.1875
6-7 This range would be the same for samples of size 20 and size 10.
6-9 a 0.0475 **b** 0.0091
6-11 0.9599
6-13 a approximately normal **b** 7160.1872 **c** 0.0078
d 5846.27; $P(\bar{x} < 400,000) = 0.0015$ **e** $464,426.40
6-15 a 0.1762; population mean is probably not 14.6. **b** 0.00547
6-17 39.342
6-19 a 41.085 **b** 1.485 **c** 38.515, 1.00
6-21 a Mean = 11.9991; standard deviation = 0.2001
b 0.2514 **c** 25% chance
6-23 0.086
6-25 a Mean = 466.914; standard deviation = 805.2725
b It does not appear that the data is normally distributed.
6-29 a 0 for all practical purposes
6-31 0.305
6-33 a 400 **b** 0.4 **c** 0.0155 **d** 0.9015
6-35 a 0
6-37 a 0.0918 **b** 0.0084
6-39 a 0.4855 **b** 0
c Population proportion of male patients must be less than 70%
6-43 a 0.3336; 0.3707 **b** 0.9472; 0.0823
6-49 The finite correction factor should be used if the sample size is greater than 5% of the population size and sampling is performed without replacement.
6-51 a Standard error **b** 374.28
6-55 a No
6-57 a Mean = 68; standard deviation = 1.2
b For $n = 100$, the standard deviation is 1.2, and for $n = 500$, the standard deviation is 0.537
6-59 a 29% **b** 0.0062
6-61 a Mean = $21,500; standard deviation = $120.21
b Mean = $21,500; standard deviation = $219.47 **c** 0.8186

6-63 a 0.00253 **b** 0.7578 **c** 0.7542
6-65 $P(\bar{x} < 130) = 0$
6-67 a 0.3446 **b** 0.1867
6-69 0.0228
6-71 a 37.21 **b** 33.89
c 0.0618; Mason's claim is probably not correct.
6-73 a 0.3161; 0.8413 **b** 0; 0.2033
6-75 a 0 **b** $26,512; if you assume the company's assumption of $30 average purchases, the loss would be $24,000.
6-77 a 0.0668 **b** 0.0212 **c** 6.7%
d $P(z > 1.5/.8) = 0.0301$; $E(x) = (0.0301)(1000) = 30.1$
6-79 a 0 **b** No
6-81 a (1) 0.0643; (2) 0.1894; (3) 0.4216 **b** $3,235
6-85 a 0.0606 **b** 0.9964
6-87 a 0.0655 **b** 0.3121
6-89 0.6876
6-91 a 0.74 **b** 0

CHAPTER 7

7-1 a $t = 2.0322$ **b** $z = 1.28$ **c** $t = 2.6245$
d $t = 2.7238$ **e** $z = 1.555$ **f** $t = 1.6839$
7-3 a 101.8573 ———— 102.8627 **b** 47.8955 ———— 64.7605
c −0.106 ———— 3.406
7-7 a 1.1307 ———— 1.2693 **b** 1.1418 ———— 1.2582
d $1,370.16 ———— $1,509.84
7-9 a 301.13 ———— 320.87
7-11 a 60.1238 ———— 73.8762 **c** 0.0010
7-13 a 2.3297 ———— 2.6803 **b** 41.68%
7-15 a 406.1252 ———— 424.4748
7-19 $284.40 \pm 2.7765 (50.1228/\sqrt{5})$
7-21 44
7-23 a 722 **b** 601
7-25 a 22 **b** $620; with pilot: $770
7-27 a 48 **b** 27
7-29 a 56,441.6617 ———— 67,119.7419 **b** 898
c 909 individuals; approximately 93%
7-31 a 104; the current sample size of 200 is sufficient
b 138 **c** $1,380, which is within the budget of $1,500
7-33 a 53 **b** 0.3722 ———— 0.5678
7-35 a 751.67 or 752, which means 652 more.
b Solve the equation assuming you want a sample size of 100. Confidence level would be 45%.
7-37 a 0.6849 ———— 0.7439
7-39 a 0.3155 ———— 0.3745 **b** 179.20 ———— 212.716
7-41 a 1,225 **b** 1,537
7-43 a 0.1990 ———— 0.2610
b Point estimate = 0.23; margin of error = 0.031
7-45 a 1,493 **b** 0.1833
7-49 a This is not correct. **b** This is correct.
7-51 0.3298 ———— 0.4302
7-53 35
7-55 a Not necessarily **b** 9,604
7-57 a 601 **b** 385
7-59 a 0.1790 ———— 0.3286 **b** 33.98%
7-61 a 32,275.2905 ———— 34,516.3761 **b** approximately 34%
7-63 a 95%
b Largest amount = 28,188.1563; smallest amount = 23,023.8438
7-65 a 553 **b** 531
7-67 a 0.7265 ———— 0.7935 **b** 25,427.50 ———— 27,772.50

7-71 a 0.6883 ———— 0.7523 **b** 0.7644 ———— 0.8600
c 0.0295 ———— 0.0701
7-73 a 10.8855 ———— 14.0705 **b** 32.0564 gallons
7-75 a 2,470.9079 ———— 6,304.6921 **b** 137

CHAPTER 8

8-1 a 0.003 **b** 0.0478 **c** 0.0026 **d** 0.0000 **e** 0.1142
8-3 a If $\bar{x} < 3,966.2775$, reject H_0
b Since $3,980 > 3,966.2775$, do not reject H_0. Using Excel's TDIST function, p-value = 0.1658 > 0.05, do not reject H_0.
8-5 a $H_0: \mu \leq 240$ seconds; $H_A: \mu > 240$ seconds
b p-value = 0.3850 > 0.1, do not reject H_0
c $\bar{x}_\alpha = 259.9236$ **d** $\mu = 224.7431$
8-7 a p-value = 0.0046 < 0.025, reject H_0
b 0.0046 **c** 6.65 > 6.4797, reject H_0
8-9 a p-value = 0.0872 > 0.025 (0.05/2), do not reject H_0
b Type II error **c** 0.9128
8-11 a $80 or less **b** $H_0: \mu \geq \$80.00$; $H_A: \mu < \$80.00$
c Since $71.77 < 73.003$, reject H_0; $t = -2.0159$; p-value = 0.0278 < 0.05, so reject H_0
8-13 a $\bar{x}_\alpha = 37.6123$
b $t = -0.8052$; p-value = 0.2123 > 0.10, so do not reject H_0
8-15 a 0.01 **b** Type I error
8-17 a pH level is less than 7.4 **b** $H_0: \mu \geq 7.4$; $H_A: \mu < 7.4$ **c** $t = 10.1335$; p-value = 1 > 0.05, do not reject H_0
8-19 a 0.8 **b** 0.2 **c** Increase n
d $1.0398 < 1.23 < 1.3062$, do not reject H_0
8-21 a Type II error would be smaller.
b The probabilities from Problem 20 would get smaller.
8-23 a 0.8686 **b** 87% chance
8-25 a Since $1.3269 < 1.645$, do not reject H_0
b Based on these results, the company does not want to market the battery. **c** $P(z < 2.25) = 0.9878$; the range of a Type II error would be between 0.9878 and 1
8-27 a 0.6103 **b** Increase the sample size
8-29 a p-value = 0.1977 > 0.10, do not reject H_0
b 0.4547; since p = 0.47 > 0.4547, do not reject H_0
8-31 a Since $z = -0.4082 > -1.645$, do not reject
b p-value = 0.3409 > 0.05, do not reject
8-33 $z = 5.40$; p-value = 0, so reject H_0
8-35 a Since $z = -1.1711 > -1.645$, do not reject
8-37 a Since $11.025 < 16.919$, do not reject H_0
b Since $39.15 > 39.0875$, reject H_0
8-39 a Since $21.1551 > 19.6752$, reject H_0 **b** p-value = 0.0318
8-41 a $H_0: \mu \leq 10$; $H_A: \mu > 10$ **b** Since $1.2247 < 1.383$, do not reject H_0 **c** Since $3.75 < 14.6837$, do not reject H_0
8-43 Since $2.8553 > 1.645$ reject H_0; since $204.0936 > 195.9734$, reject H_0
8-55 a $H_0: \mu = 70$; $H_A: \mu \neq 70$ **b** Since $-1.1232 > -1.75$ and less than 1.75, do not reject H_0
8-59 a $H_0: \mu \leq 10$; $H_A: \mu > 10$; since $1.56 < 1.645$, do not reject H_0
b 9.9181 ———— 10.7219
8-63 a $H_0: \pi \geq 0.90$; $H_A: \pi < 0.90$ **b** Since $z = -1.00 > -1.645$, do not reject H_0 and conclude that the percentage is at least 90%
8-65 a $H_0: \mu \geq 40$; $H_A: \mu < 40$ **b** Since $z = -3.3334 < -1.28$, reject H_0
8-67 a Less than $417 per year **b** $H_0: \mu \geq 417$; $H_A: \mu < 417$
c Since $z = -0.70 > -1.41$, do not reject H_0

8-71 a $H_0: \mu \geq 50$; $H_A: \mu < 50$
b Since $t = -0.9129 > -1.6991$, do not reject H_0
8-73 a $H_0: \mu \geq 10$; $H_A: \mu < 10$
b Decision rule: If $z < -1.28$, reject H_0; otherwise, do not reject H_0
c Since $z = -1.3944 < -1.28$, reject H_0 **d** Type I error
8-75 a Since $99.3912 > 54.5722$, reject H_0
8-77 a $H_0: \mu \geq 63$; $H_A: \mu < 63$
b Decision rule: If $z < -1.645$, reject H_0; otherwise, do not reject H_0;
$z = -2.54$ **c** Since $-2.54 < -1.645$, reject H_0 **d** 0.0055
8-79 a Since $t = -0.9682 > -1.345$, do not reject H_0
8-81 a $H_0: \mu \geq 900$; $H_A: \mu < 900$
b Since $t = -0.6124 > -1.3195$, do not reject H_0
8-85 a Since $35.1424 > 30.1435$, reject H_0
8-87 a $H_0: \pi \leq 0.70$; $H_A: \pi > 0.70$
b Since p-value $= 0.0951 > 0.05$, do not reject H_0
8-89 Since $t = 0.5130 < 1.6939$, do not reject H_0
8-91 Since $1.0377 < 1.645$, do not reject H_0
8-93 Since $0.4020 < 1.645$, do not reject H_0

CHAPTER 9

9-1 a If the calculated $F > 4.405$, reject H_0
b Since $1.4654 < 4.405$, do not reject H_0
9-3 Since $1.1488 < 3.179$, do not reject H_0
9-5 a $H_0: \sigma_m^2 \leq \sigma_f^2$; $H_A: \sigma_m^2 > \sigma_f^2$ **b** Since $3.4807 > 1.9838$, reject H_0
9-7 a $H_0: \sigma_{Basic}^2 \leq \sigma_{Bus}^2$; $H_A: \sigma_{Basic}^2 > \sigma_{Bus}^2$
b Since $1.3246 < 1.4341$, do not reject H_0
9-9 a If the calculated $F > 2.4374$, reject H_0
b Since $1.1378 < 2.4374$, do not reject H_0
9-11 a $H_0: \mu_d = 0$; $H_A: \mu_d \neq 0$
b Since $t = -3.6387 < -1.8595$, reject H_0
c -2.1995 ——— -0.7117; yes
9-13 a $H_0: \mu_F - \mu_M \leq 1$; $H_A: \mu_F - \mu_M > 1$; $H_0: \sigma_1^2 = \sigma_2^2$;
$H_A: \sigma_1^2 \neq \sigma_2^2$; since $1.69 < 1.8459$, do not reject H_0;
since $1.6136 < 1.6579$, do not reject H_0
b $P(t > 1.6136) = 0.0546$; p-value
9-15 a $H_0: \mu_N - \mu_0 \leq 0$; $H_A: \mu_N - \mu_0 > 0$; $H_0: \sigma_1^2 = \sigma_2^2$;
$H_A: \sigma_1^2 \neq \sigma_2^2$; since $1.0406 < 2.3716$, do not reject H_0;
since $2.2491 > 1.2951$, reject H_0 **b** 2.3196 ——— 15.6804; yes
9-17 a 25.5324 ——— 32.4676; yes **b** 24.8684 ——— 33.1316;
no **c** $P(z > 41.68)$, which is essentially 0
9-19 a -0.93 **b** 0.1947 **c** -1.3116 ——— -0.5484; yes
d Increase the sample size or decrease the confidence level
9-21 a 2.1525 ——— 4.2475; yes
9-23 a $H_0: \mu_D - \mu_S \leq 0$; $H_A: \mu_D - \mu_S > 0$; $H_0: \sigma_1^2 = \sigma_2^2$; H_A:
$\sigma_1^2 \neq \sigma_2^2$; since $1.0483 < 3.1296$, do not reject H_0;
since $3.0853 > 1.6909$, reject H_0 **b** Type I error
9-25 a $H_0: \mu_R - \mu_N \leq 0$; $H_A: \mu_R - \mu_N > 0$
b Since $1.2524 < 1.3923$, do not reject H_0;
since $2.9752 > 1.6487$, reject H_0 **c** 3.2465 ——— 15.8935
9-27 a Since $-0.1526 > -2.1448$, do not reject H_0 **b** Yes
c -8.0302 ——— 6.9636; yes
9-29 27,482.7862 ——— 45,629.2098; yes
9-31 -20.8069 ——— 38.6011; no
9-33 a -713.4351 ——— 2,364.4843; no difference
b $-1,238.0438$ ——— 2,284.0386; no difference
9-35 a -10.6604 ——— 8.0604; no difference
9-37 Since $z = 0.8987 < 1.645$, do not reject H_0
9-39 a $175.52 > 5$ and $113.70 > 5$ **b** $H_0: \pi_1 - \pi_2 = 0$;
$H_A: \pi_1 - \pi_2 \neq 0$; since $z = 4.14 > 1.96$, reject H_0

9-41 0.1832 ——— 0.3000
9-43 a Since $1.44 < 2.5769$, do not reject H_0 and
conclude that the standard deviations are equal
9-45 Since $1.445 < 2.2756$, do not reject H_0
9-47 a Since $2.6134 < 4.8491$, do not reject H_0
c -120.8035 ——— 146.0761
9-49 a Since $3.4807 > 1.9838$, reject H_0
b Since $4.3716 > 2.0281$, reject H_0
9-51 a Since $7.9985 > -1.645$, do not reject H_0
b 0.8556 ——— 0.9824
9-53 a Since $1.66 > 1.645$, reject H_0
b 1,150 seats for the undergraduates
9-55 a p-value $= 0.3898 > 0.05$, so do not reject H_0
9-57 Since $1.8464 > 1.28$, reject H_0
9-59 a $n_1 p_1 = 17.78 > 5$; $n_2 p_2 = 11.42 > 5$
b Since $0.7745 < 2.17$, do not reject H_0
9-61 a Since $1.306 < 1.6333$, do not reject H_0
9-63 a $H_0: \sigma_1^2 = \sigma_2^2$; $H_A: \sigma_1^2 \neq \sigma_2^2$
b Since $1.267 < 1.4836$, do not reject H_0
9-65 a $H_0: \sigma_S^2 \leq \sigma_{BB}^2$; $H_A: \sigma_S^2 > \sigma_{BB}^2$
b Since $1.1378 < 1.6073$, do not reject H_0
9-67 Since $1.9397 < 2.8574$, do not reject H_0

CHAPTER 10

10-1 a Since p-value $= 0.000136 < 0.05$, reject H_0
b -5.4380 ——— 1.7572; 4.0299 ——— 11.6959;
0.4771 ——— 8.8087; 5.0386 ——— 14.3680;
2.1100 ——— 10.8566; -9.6541 ——— 3.2141 **c** Groups 1
and 3; Groups 1 and 4; Groups 2 and 3; and Groups 2 and 4
d The Tukey-Kramer procedure is based on the simultaneous construction of confidence intervals for all differences of pairs of treatment means.
e

	Absolute Difference	Critical Range	Significant
G1 v. G2	1.84047619	4.623216305	no
G1 v. G3	7.86285714	4.865794722	yes
G1 v. G4	4.64285714	5.208522074	no
G2 v. G3	9.70333333	5.031910377	yes
G2 v. G4	6.48333333	5.364034485	yes
G3 v. G4	3.22	5.574468157	no

f no larger than 0.05
10-3 a F-critical $= 3.3541$; since $7.4196 > 3.3541$, reject H_0
b F-critical $= 5.4881$; since $7.4196 > 5.4881$, reject H_0
10-5 a Since $7.5441 > 4.16$, reject H_0
b Since p-value $= 0.0006 < 0.05$, reject H_0
c recommend vendor 1 or vendor 2 **d** -336.8820 ——— 93.8820;
93.1894 ——— 523.9534; 214.6894 ——— 645.4534
10-7 a Since $0.00001 < 0.05$, reject H_0 **b** recommend car 3
c 1.5199 ——— 2.6421; \$455.97 ——— \$792.63
10-9 a Since $59.40217 > 2.8661$, reject H_0
b Recommendation: display type A or display type D
10-11 a Since $0.3255 < 2.1009$, do not reject H_0
b Since $0.1059 < 4.413863$, do not reject H_0
10-13 a $H_0: \mu_{\alpha_1} = \mu_{\alpha_2} = \mu_{\alpha_3} = \mu_{\alpha_4}$;
H_A: At least two population means are different;
$H_0: \mu_{b_1} = \mu_{b_2} = \mu_{b_3} = \mu_{b_4} = \mu_{b_5} = \mu_{b_6} = \mu_{b_7} = \mu_{b_8}$;
H_A: Not all block means are equal

b *ANOVA*

Source of Variation	SS	df	MS	F	p-value	F-crit
Blocks	9123.375	7	1303.339	46.87669	2.08E-11	2.487582
Groups	1158.625	3	386.2083	13.8906	3.26E-05	3.072472
Error	583.875	21	27.80357			
Total	10865.88	31				

c Since $46.87669 > 2.487582$, reject H_0
d Since p-value $0.0000326 < 0.05$, reject H_0 **e** LSD $= 5.48280844$

	Mean Difference	Absolute Mean Difference	Significant
G1 v. G2	6.625	6.625	Yes
G1 v. G3	−0.625	0.625	No
G1 v. G4	−10.25	10.25	Yes
G2 v. G3	−7.25	7.25	Yes
G2 v. G4	−16.875	16.875	Yes
G3 v. G4	−9.625	9.625	Yes

10-15 a Since $7.656659 > 3.098393$, reject H_0
b $526.2105 \text{——} 1{,}670.4555$
10-17 a Since $0.00014 < 0.05$, reject H_0
10-19 b Since $1737.192 > 4.2779$, reject H_0
c Since $7.4981 > 6.5149$, reject H_0 and conclude that at least two means are different
d LSD $= 297.4522008$; office 2 has the highest mean tax due
10-21 a Since $0.130744 < 3.1588$, do not reject H_0
10-23 a Since $0.4617 < 3.8853$, do not reject H_0
b Since $2.3766 < 3.8853$, do not reject H_0 and conclude that all means are equal **c** Since $5.7532 > 4.7472$, reject H_0

d	Absolute Differences	Critical Range	Significant
Level 1–Level 2	5.777777778	5.2462	yes

10-25 b Since $0.7085 < 3.40282$, do not reject H_0
c Since $41.1856 > 4.2597$, reject H_0 and conclude that not all means are equal **d** Since $0.9449 < 1.7011$, do not reject H_0
10-27 a no interaction **b** Since p-value $= 0.5532 > 0.05$, do not reject H_0 **c** Since $18.82389 > 3.402832$, reject H_0
d Since $39.0108 > 3.0088$, reject H_0
10-29 a Since p-value $= 0.0570 > 0.01$, do not reject H_0
b Since $2.9945 < 6.0129$, do not reject H_0
c Since p-value $= 0.4829 > 0.1$, do not reject H_0 and conclude that there is no difference in mean core diameter across the 3 vat times
10-39 a Since $1.876 < 4.3$, do not reject H_0 and conclude that all the variances are equal **b** Yes **c** Since $5.60945 > 3.202$, reject H_0
d No clear favorite
10-41 a Since the p-value $= 8.74E-30 < 0.05$, reject H_0

b	Absolute Difference	Critical Range	Significant
Wichita–Little Rock	5773.644529	1504.718895	yes
Little Rock–Tulsa	1157.565324	1504.718895	no
Tulsa–Memphis	1774.167074	1504.718895	yes

c 106
10-43 a Randomized block design **b** $H_0: \mu_1 = \mu_2 = \mu_3 = \mu_4$; H_A: At least two population means are different
c Since $3.3785 < 4.0150$, do not reject H_0

d Since $20.39312 > 1.9358$, reject H_0
e No difference between the scanners
10-45 a Since $1.4098 < 2.65$, do not reject H_0 **b** Yes
c Since $5.6880 > 3.1186$, reject H_0

d	Absolute Difference	Critical Range	Significant
Store 1–Store 2	6.52846154	5.51000017	yes
Store 1–Store 3	6.92230769	5.51000017	yes
Store 2–Store 3	0.39384615	5.51000017	no

Store 1 is more expensive than the others.

e Since $1.9921 > 1.7273$, reject H_0
10-47 a $H_0: \mu_1 = \mu_2 = \mu_3$; H_A: Not all means are equal
b Since $0.3858 < 4.7476$, do not reject H_0 **c** 0.680554 **d** 0.2730
10-49 a Since 0.53909 is < 2.74820, do not reject H_0
b Since 17.0287 is > 3.9909, reject H_0 and conclude that there is a difference in the average number of cookies eaten with respect to butter or margarine **c** Since $0.408327 < 2.7482$, do not reject H_0

CHAPTER 11

11-1 Very weak curvilinear relationship
11-3 a Strong positive correlation **b** 0.9707
c Since $12.1150 > 1.8331$, reject H_0 **d** Type I error
11-5 a Fairly strong positive linear relationship
b Since p-value essentially $= 0 < 0.1$, reject H_0
11-7 a No
11-9 a $R^2 = 0.568498$ **b** $\hat{y} = 58.7246$
11-11 a $t = 2.0744$; β_1 differs from zero **b** 1.45
11-13 a Negative linear relationship **b** $r = -0.5411$;
Since p-value $= 0.0856 > 0.05$, do not reject H_0
c $\hat{y} = 5.1569 + (-0.0751)(x)$ **d** SSE $= 12.8585$; SST $= 18.1818$
e $R^2 = 0.2928$
11-15 a Negative linear relationship **b** $r = -0.7391$; since $-5.8061 < -2.0484$, reject H_0 **c** $\hat{y} = 46.3298 + (-0.0061)(x)$
d 21.8566 **e** (1) Residual $= 4.1434$; (2) 2.8639;
(3) $P(t > 1.4468) = 0.1591$
11-17 a Weak positive linear relationship **b** $r = 0.0437$
c $\hat{y} = 5247.8610 + 15.7141(x)$ **d** Since $0.1704 < 6.9285$, do not reject H_0 **e** Type II error
11-19 a Since $34.7774 > 1.8331$, reject H_0
b Since $1218.698 > 5.117$, reject H_0
11-21 a \$1,446,133,770 **b** Since $0.6156 < 5.318$, do not reject H_0 **c** Type II
11-23 a $\hat{y} = -1858.1913 + 0.2901(x)$ **b** Since the p-value $= 7.09873E-07 < 0.1, 0.05, 0.01$, reject H_0 **c** $R^2 = 0.9422$
11-25 b Since p-value $= 0.9694 > 0.1$, do not reject H_0 and conclude that the accountant takes 1 minute to count the unit
c $0.7925 \text{——} 1.0573$; yes
11-27 a $\hat{y} = -4.7933 + 1.0488(x)$
b \$100.09; $82.19 \text{——} 117.97$ **c** $94.86 \text{——} 105.31$
11-29 a 18.8378 **b** $16.26 \text{——} 21.10$ **c** $12.33 \text{——} 25.03$
11-31 a $\hat{y} = 39.8119 + 0.0001(x)$ **b** 0.00902 **c** no; 0.0019
d 39.4296 **e** $35.17 \text{——} 43.70$ **f** $35.37 \text{——} 49.70$
g $13{,}129.73404$ **h** $-1.17 \text{——} 80.04$
11-35 No
11-39 a -0.59974 **b** Since $-2.24845 < -1.3830$, reject H_0; since p-value $= 0.025566 < \alpha = 0.10$, we reject H_0
11-41 a 0.763462 **b** Since $5.0152 > 2.1009$, reject H_0

11-43 a 0.7059 **b** Since $3.8598 > 1.3406$, reject H_0
11-45 4.9998 ——— 5.0002
11-47 a Positive linear relationship exists **b** 0.8906 **c** Since $7.8331 > 2.1199$, reject H_0 **d** $-1,676,311.93$ ——— 4,461,933.33
e Since $F = 61.3661 > 4.494$, reject H_0
11-49 a Since $t = 4.7757 > 1.7011$, reject H_0 **b** $R^2 = 0.4489$
11-51 b 480.088 ——— 484.362 **c** No
d 2,786.05 ——— 4,286.00
11-57 Since $18.6667 > 3.9381$, reject H_0; $\sqrt{MSE} = 2.1712$
11-59 Correct; $3,456.98 is an average decrease
11-61 a 105.7397 ——— 116.2603 **b** 87.2979 ——— 134.7021
11-63 a 2.491 ——— 3.149 **b** 0.6
11-65 a Linear relationship
b $\hat{y} = -19.3726 + 2.9026(x)$; $F = 285.7299$

CHAPTER 12

12-1 a The dependent variable is $y =$ number of calls. **b** Calls Received—Ads Placed Previous Week—indicates a positive linear relationship; Calls Received—Calls Received Previous Week—indicates a positive linear relationship; Calls Received—Airline Bookings—indicates a positive linear relationship
12-3 a $\hat{y} = -269.8384 + 4.9528$(Ads Placed Previous Week) $+ 0.8340$ (Calls Received the Previous Week) $+ 0.0887$(Airline Bookings) **b** $R^2 = 0.5911$ **c** Since $p\text{-value} = 0.0564 > 0.05$, do not reject H_0 and conclude that the overall model is not significant **d** p-value is $0.8169 > 0.05$, so this variable is not significant; p-value is $0.1500 > 0.05$, so this variable is not significant; p-value is $0.1445 > 0.05$, so this variable is not significant. No variables are statistically significant. **e** Adjusted $R^2 = 0.4378$ **f** 86.1868
h $VIF = 2.206$; $VIF = 1.152$

12-5 a Model 1:

		Coefficients
	Intercept	11392.04318
	Team Win/Loss Percentage	72.2162984

Model 2:

		Coefficients
	Intercept	13515.09725
	Opponent Win/Loss Percentage	36.19202811

Model 3:

		Coefficients
	Intercept	12121.05556
	Games Played	530.0185185

Model 4:

		Coefficients
	Intercept	24989.66973
	Temperature	-165.125670

b $F = 4.6001$
12-7 a There appears to be a negative linear relationship between revenues and profit margin. There appears to be a negative linear relationship between number of branch offices and profit margin. **b** Since $70.6606 > 2.5618$, conclude that the overall model is significant **c** $p\text{-value} = 0.00031 < 0.1$; $p\text{-value} = 9.508\text{E-}08 < 0.1$
d $\pm 2(0.0533)$; ± 0.1066

e

	Coefficients
Intercept	1.326160446
Revenue	-0.16913028

12-9 a As the vehicle weight increases by 1 pound, the average highway mileage rating would decrease by 0.003. **b** If the car has standard transmission, the highway mileage rating will increase by 2.56. **c** $\hat{y} = 36.76 - 0.003x_1$ **d** $\hat{y} = 22.164$ **e** The regression equation if it has an automatic transmission is $\hat{y} = 34.2 - 0.003x_1$; if the automobile has a standard transmission, the equation becomes $\hat{y} = 36.76 - 0.003x_1$.
12-11 a Positive linear relationship; negative linear relationship
b $\hat{y} = -1,012.0542 + 69.1471(x_1)$ **c** $p\text{-value} = 0.0531$; $R^2 = 0.3549$
12-13 b

	Coefficients	Standard Error	t Stat	p-value
Intercept	51053.14391	20756.30121	2.459645551	0.021495177
Horse Power (x1)	31.56438276	60.55443937	0.521256296	0.606965183
4-Door Passenger (x2)	-35646.95536	12469.101	-2.85882321	0.008656943
Luxury Cars (x3)	-20354.52784	9564.368384	-2.128162261	0.043790937
Compact Truck (x4)	-35572.07309	11959.23831	-2.974443034	0.006593708
Full-Size Truck (x5)	-31081.35603	8382.639957	-3.707824288	0.001098601

12-15 a There appears to be a curvilinear relationship between weight and cost. **b** $r = 0.9633$; since $15.2255 > 2.1009$, reject H_0 **c** Yes. The R^2 for the simple linear regression is 0.9279, and the R^2 for the second-order polynomial model is 0.9783, so students should suggest that the second-order polynomial is a significant improvement. **d** For the simple linear regression: $x = 10.998$ or 11 pounds; for the second-order polynomial model: $x = 12.121$ pounds
12-17 b Correlation coefficient $= 0.9477$; since $12.5978 > 2.445$, reject H_0 and conclude there is a relationship between file size and download time; since $p\text{-value} = 2.298\text{E-}10 < 0.05$, reject H_0

c

	Coefficients
Intercept	-4.953312705
File Size	3.812312915

d The R^2 for the simple regression model is 0.8982, while the R^2 for the second-order model is 0.9503
12-19 a

	Coefficients
Intercept	-586.2555597
Hours (x1)	22.86106295
Manufacturing (x2)	2302.267018
Service (x3)	1869.813042

b

	Coefficients	Standard Error	t Stat	p-value
Intercept	1788.9288	5304.17279	0.337268	0.74459301
Hours (x1)	-90.58866611	295.3994076	-0.30667	0.76692833
Hours^2 (x2)	2.050639421	3.769417563	0.54402	0.60125603

Yes

12-21 a

	Coefficients	Standard Error	t Stat	p-value
Intercept	39838.48333	7304.951587	5.453627291	9.94899E-08
Sq. Feet	75.69512354	3.775610524	20.04844596	2.56069E-58

b

	Coefficients	Standard Error	t Stat	p-value
Intercept	14707.19242	19848.20705	0.740983424	0.459255499
Sq. Feet	58.01379864	12.83940352	4.518418518	8.82364E-06
Bathrooms	15123.59491	4228.783207	3.576346711	0.000403138
Sq. Feet × Bathroom	-0.562809437	2.345845011	-0.239917571	0.810550207

12-23 The statement is incorrect.

12-25 b Since $F = 3.8550 < 4.0662$, conclude that the overall model is not significant.

12-27 a Team Win/Loss Percentage entered at step 1 because it had the highest correlation with the dependent variable, Game Attendance. **b** Only one step occurred in this model. $R^2 = 0.7204$; standard error of the estimate $= 1,170.9985$ **c** The final model is significant, with a p-value of 3.2237E-05 **d** The overall model is significant, with a p-value of 3.2237E-05; the Team Win/Loss Percentage with a p-value of 3.2237E-05

12-29 a There does not appear to be any type of relationship between Press Rating and HCHO. There appears to be a relationship best described by a second-order polynomial model. There does not appear to be a very significant relationship between temperature and press rate, but a third-order polynomial model seems to describe it better than any other type model. There does not appear to be a significant relationship between time and press rate. **b** $\hat{y} = 1.574 + 0.00149(x_2) + 0.0028(x_1 \times x_3)$ **c** $\hat{y} = -7.275 + 0.8(x_2) + 0.97(x_3) + 0.129(x_4) + (-0.039)(x_1^2) + (-0.0417)(x_2^2) + (-0.00039)(x_3^2) + 0.0044(x_1 \times x_3)$; $\hat{y} = 1.574 + 0.00149(x_2) + 0.0228(x_1 \times x_4)$

12-31 a

	Coefficients	Standard Error	t Stat
Intercept	14122.24086	4335.791765	3.25713079
Team Win/ Loss %	63.15325348	14.93880137	4.227464568
Opponent Win/ Loss %	10.09582009	14.31396102	0.705312811
Games Played	31.50621796	177.129782	0.177870811
Temperature	−55.4609057	62.09372861	−0.89318047

	p-value	Lower 95%
Intercept	0.0076378	4579.222699
Team Win/ Loss %	0.0014185	30.27315672
Opponent Win/ Loss %	0.4952803	−21.40901163
Games Played	0.8620577	−358.3540008
Temperature	0.3908828	−192.12835

c There appears to be a cone shape (as predicted values increase the residuals increase); therefore, the constant variance assumption has been violated. **d** The plot of the residuals against time shows a systematic variation about zero, indicating that the residuals are independent. **e** Based on the normal probability plot, which is almost a straight line, we can assume the model error terms are approximately normally distributed.

12-33 No, the residuals should not be plotted against each x individually. The residuals should be plotted against the predicted y to verify the constant variance assumption.

12-35 a The residuals do not exhibit a constant variance. When $Days^2$ is small, the variance of the residuals is large and decreases as $Days^2$ increases. **b** The residuals do not seem to possess a normal distribution. **c** Within 1 standard deviation $= 56.25\%$; within 2 standard deviation $= 100\%$; within 3 standard deviation $= 100\%$; it does not appear that the residuals are normally distributed.

d The residuals are not normally distributed.

12-43

	Coefficients	Standard Error	t Stat
Intercept	21.48048774	10.53116151	2.039707
Case Analysis Score	2.363993584	1.183937188	1.996722
Written Presentation Score	1.531347982	1.773536135	0.863443
Oral Presentation Score	3.807380091	2.493027189	1.527212

	p-value	Lower 95%
Intercept	0.066137	−1.698454194
Case Analysis Score	0.071203	−0.241835915
Written Presentation Score	0.406327	−2.372180707
Oral Presentation Score	0.154937	−1.67973853

12-45 a The calculated F is $16.6931 > 3.5874$, so conclude that the overall regression model is significant. **c** $-0.6698 \text{———} 8.2846$

12-47 a The R^2 is 0.8199 **b** None of the independent variables are significant. **c** Job rating $= 92.7959$ **e** $-2.3722 \text{———} 5.4349$

12-49

	Coefficients	Standard Error	t Stat
Intercept	−125307.8062	31082.09519	−4.031510921
Pages X1	175.8963214	39.76976966	4.422864977
Competing Books X2	−1573.777885	1995.851361	−0.788524595
Advertising Budget X3	1.591706487	0.444463005	3.581190042
Age of Author X4	1613.747496	625.0234231	2.58189923

	p-value	Lower 95%	Upper 95%
Intercept	0.002393684	−194563.0421	−56052.6
Pages X1	0.001288354	87.28373715	264.5089
Competing Books X2	0.448679286	−6020.812614	2873.257
Advertising Budget X3	0.005001797	0.601381026	2.582032
Age of Author X4	0.027327123	221.1082826	3006.387

a $R^2 = 0.8448$; since $F = 13.6076 > 3.4780$, conclude that the overall model is significant.

b

	Coefficients	Lower 95%	Upper 95%
Intercept	−125307.8062	−194563.0421	−56052.6
Pages X1	175.8963214	87.28373715	264.5089
Competing Books X2	−1573.777885	−6020.812614	2873.257
Advertising Budget X3	1.591706487	0.601381026	2.582032
Age of Author X4	1613.747496	221.1082826	3006.387

c The critical t-value would be ± 2.2281

	Coefficients	Standard Error
Intercept	−125307.8062	31082.09519
Pages X1	175.8963214	39.76976966
Competing Books X2	−1573.777885	1995.851361
Advertising Budget X3	1.591706487	0.444463005
Age of Author X4	1613.747496	625.0234231

	t Stat	p-value
Intercept	−4.031510921	0.002393684
Pages X1	4.422864977	0.001288354
Competing Books X2	−0.788524595	0.448679286
Advertising Budget X3	3.581190042	0.005001797
Age of Author X4	2.581899232	0.027327123

d 175.8963; 87.2837 ———— 264.5089

12-53	Coefficients	Standard Error	t Stat
Intercept	33.7553515	18.76904387	1.798458765
Family Income X2	0.0019913	0.000803465	2.478390013
	p-value	Lower 95%	Upper 95%
Intercept	0.08524316	−5.07132112	72.5820241
Family Income X2	0.02096854	0.000329208	0.00365339

12-55 Age X1 entered.

	df	SS	MS	F	Significance F
Regression	2	15235.41902	7617.709511	7.19814255	0.003935699
Residual	22	23282.34098	1058.288226		
Total	24	38517.76			

	Coefficients	Standard Error	t Stat
Intercept	82.8874522	25.31844215	3.273797485
Family Income X2	0.00208703	0.000719902	2.899044278
Age X1	−1.31806521	0.50826742	−2.59325141
	p-value	Lower 95%	Upper 95%
Intercept	0.00347108	30.38016058	135.394744
Family Income X2	0.00832364	0.00059404	0.00358001
Age X1	0.01659161	−2.37214845	−0.26398196

12-59 Possible points to consider in the report are: relatively low R^2 compared to 1.0; the relatively large standard error, given the size of the dependent variable; and the fact that there are many other variables that could have been included in the model.

CHAPTER 13

13-11 0.09; $UCL = 0.176$; $LCL = 0.004$
13-13 a centerline = 0.753; $UCL = 0.7961$; $LCL = 0.7104$
b R-chart centerline = 0.074; $UCL = 0.1561$; $LCL = 0.000$
13-15 a Since time is measured, the machine downtime that is being monitored is a variable characteristic and requires that both the x-bar and R-charts be used. **b** A2 = 0.58; the Shewart factors for the R-chart are D3 = 0.00 and D4 = 2.11. **c** 82.46 **d** 12.33 **e** $UCL = 89.61$; $LCL = 75.31$ **f** $UCL = 26.02$; $LCL = 0$
13-17 a $UCL = 488.574$; $LCL = 342.026$
b $UCL = 228.855$; $LCL = 0$
13-19 a Wider control limits. $LCL = 329.994$; $UCL = 501.528$; R-chart $LCL = 0.0$; $UCL = 267.875$ **b** Range chart suggests a loss of statistical control beginning in week 42.
13-23 a 3.0467 **b** $UCL = 18.8159$; $LCL = 11.3937$; R-chart $LCL = 0.0$; $UCL = 13.5264$
13-25 The new sample proportion = 0.28; out of control
13-27 a c-chart **b** The centerline = 8.16; $UCL = 16.73$; $LCL = 0$
13-29 a $\bar{p} = 0.8246$; $s = 0.038$ **b** $UCL = 0.9386$; $LCL = 0.7106$
13-31 a $P(z < −9.2448) = $ essentially 0
b $UCL = 2.9845$; LCL 1.1865; R-chart $LCL = 0.638$; $UCL = 5.162$

13-33 a c-chart; c-bar = 1.9714; $s = 1.4041$; $UCL = 6.1836$; $LCL = −2.2409$, which becomes 0
13-35 a A2 = 0.73; for the R-chart, the Shewart factors are D3 = 0 and D4 = 2.28 **b** $UCL = 1,498.189$; $LCL = 1,192.611$ **c** $UCL = 477.204$; $LCL = 0.00$
13-37 The centerline = 0.140; $UCL = 0.244$; $LCL = 0.036$
13-39 c-chart. The centerline = 23.00; standard error = 4.7958; $UCL = 37.3875$; $LCL = 8.6125$
13-41 $\bar{p} = 0.0524$; $s = 0.0223$; $UCL = 0.1193$; $LCL = −0.0145 = 0.0$

CHAPTER 14

14-1 Since $\chi^2 = 6.37174721 < 9.48772847$, do not reject H_0
14-3 a Since $\chi^2 = 3.379443 < 11.345$, we do not reject H_0; for Lilliefors' test, since the maximum absolute difference of 0.1101 < 0.187, do not reject H_0 **b** The company is meeting its product specification.
14-5 a H_0: Airline usage pattern has not changed from a previous study; H_A: Airline usage pattern has changed from a previous study **b** Since $\chi^2 = 66.4083 > 15.08632$, reject H_0
14-7 Since p-value = 0.0524 > 0.025, do not reject H_0
14-9 Since $\chi^2 = 17.54671 < 26.2962$, we do not reject H_0; p-value = 0.35110. After grouping, $\chi^2 = 8.1859 < 15.5073$, we do not reject H_0; p-value = 0.4155
14-11 a Since $\chi^2 = 28.43554 > 21.02606$, reject H_0; p-value = 0.004775 **b** Yes, there are two cells with an expected value less than 5.00. Combine the categories *Divorced* and *Other* to get a larger expected cell frequency. Since $\chi^2 = 23.94657 > 15.50731$, reject H_0
14-15 a Since 27.4510 > 13.2767, reject H_0
b −0.0175 ———— 0.0175
14-17 a One option would be to combine Salt Lake City and Toronto into one group. Also combine wiring and sound into one group. **b** Since 6.7582 < 9.2104, do not reject H_0
14-23 Since $\chi^2 = 6.625 < 11.34488$, do not reject; p-value = 0.08486
14-25 a Need to combine 2–5; since 402.3279 > 4.60518, reject

14-27 a Readmissions Last Year	Observed Frequency	Poisson Probability Distribution	Expected Frequency
0	139	0.3012	90.3583
1	87	0.3614	108.4299
2	48	0.2169	65.0579
3	14	0.0867	26.0232
4+	12	0.0338	10.1400

b Since 40.7889 > 9.4877, reject H_0
14-29 Since 19.7686 > 10.6446, reject H_0
14-31 a Combine Not Observed and Yes, and combine No and Not Required. **b** Since 0.8241 < 3.8415, do not reject H_0
14-33 Since 7.8991 > 5.9915, reject H_0 **b** 23.3715 ———— 31.1286
14-35 a

LABOR STRESS INDEX

1998 Unemployment	80–99	100–120	Total
3.2–4.5	2	9	11
4.5–5.8	6	12	18
5.8–7.1	3	1	4
Total	11	22	33

b Since $4.2614 < 9.3484$, do not reject H_0
14-37 a Since $75.6451 > 5.9915$, reject H_0
b Since $1.2758 < 1.645$, do not reject H_0
14-39 Since $179 > 16.9190$, reject H_0

CHAPTER 15

15-1 a 22 **b** 27 **c** 13 **d** 22
e Since $13 < 22 < 27$, do not reject H_0
15-3 a 11 **b** Since $6 < 11 < 16$, do not reject H_0,
and conclude that egg brand selection is random
15-5 a Since $3.103 > 1.645$, reject H_0 **b** 0.3024 ——— 0.5776
15-7 a Since $-13.4127 < -1.645$, reject H_0
b p-value is essentially 0
c Since the p-value is so large, you would not reject H_0
15-9 Since $-9.7492 < -1.96$, reject H_0
15-15 a Since $14 > 4$, do not reject H_0
b Since $-0.395 > -2.1448$, do not reject H_0
15-17 U test $= 21$
15-19 b Since $50.5 > 16$, do not reject H_0 and conclude that the medians are the same
15-21 b Since $9.5 > 6$, do not reject H_0
15-23 b Since $-2.9681 < -1.645$, reject H_0 **c** Type I error
15-25 b Since $50 > 21$, do not reject H_0
c Since $-0.1521 > t$-critical $= -2.1604$, do not reject H_0
15-27 a Since $-1.785 > t$-critical $= -1.8331$, do not reject H_0
b Since $5.5 < 6$, reject H_0 and conclude that the medians are not the same
15-31 a No
15-33 b $H = 14.854$
15-35 a $H = 13.9825$; since $13.9825 > 5.9915$, reject H_0
15-43 Since $42 > 27$, do not reject H_0 and conclude that the medians are not different
15-45 a Since $29 > 27$, do not reject H_0 and conclude that the medians are not different
15-47 Since $-0.2518 > -2.5280$, do not reject H_0
15-49 a Since $12.252 > 5.9915$, reject H_0 and conclude that not all population medians are equal
15-51 Since $r = 4$, do not reject H_0
15-53 b Since $4.1778 > 1.96$, reject H_0
c Since $0.8485 < 1.645$, do not reject H_0
15-55 b Since $3.1113 > 1.645$, reject H_0
c p-value is essentially 0; since $0 < 0.05$, you would reject H_0
15-57 a 10 runs; 13.6
b Since $-1.6036 > -2.575$, do not reject H_0
15-59 a 3 **b** 2 **c** Since $4 < 5 < 13$, do not reject H_0 and conclude that the process is random

CHAPTER 16

16-9 From the time series plot, we see that there is a positive, linear trend. We can also see that there are movements that are not attributed to the trend; in other words, random components.
16-11 b

Quarter	1	2	3	4
Seasonal Index	1.03616493	1.022034	0.96100236	0.985249

c MSE $= 36.87260447$; MAD $= 4.825696893$

d & e

Quarter	Period	Seasonally Unadjusted Forecast	Seasonal Index	Seasonally Adjusted Forecast
1	17	249.8746	1.0362	258.9113
2	18	255.8820	1.0220	261.5201
3	19	261.8895	0.9610	251.6764
4	20	267.8969	0.9852	263.9452

16-13 b

Month	January	February	March	April	May	June
Seasonal Index	0.9655	0.8891	0.8940	0.9996	1.0343	0.9307

Month	July	August	September	October	November	December
Seasonal Index	0.9842	1.0241	1.0560	1.0108	1.1191	1.1740

c MSE $= 51.6562$; MAD $= 5.1114$; since $114.12 > 4.0069$, reject H_0
d Expected revenue $= \$1,255,614$
16-15 b MSE $= 976.33861$; MAD $= 29.88694639$
c

Quarter	1	2	3	4
Seasonal Index	1.0323	0.9236	1.0823	0.9745

d

Quarter	2001 Period	Forecast
1	13	256.5620033
2	14	260.0884382
3	15	263.614873
4	16	267.1413079

e

Quarter	2001 Period	Forecast	Seasonal Index	Adjusted Forecast
1	13	256.5620	1.0323	264.8370
2	14	260.0884	0.9236	240.2300
3	15	263.6149	1.0823	285.3084
4	16	267.1413	0.9745	260.3331

Quarter	Actual	Differences	Difference Squared	Absolute Differences
1	229	-27.5620	759.6640	27.5620
2	221	-39.0884	1527.9060	39.0884
3	248	-15.6149	243.8243	15.6149
4	231	-36.1413	1306.1941	36.1413

MSE $= 959.3971$; MAD $= 29.6017$
f Recommend the deseasonalized data model
16-17 a 210.0376; 244.1914
b 161.76 ——— 258.32; 55.53 ——— 97.43
16-19 Original model: 183.7819; transformed model: 174.7804
16-21 b Yes, trend is present. **c** MAD $= 23.278$ **d** 163.69; MAD $= 7.655$ **e** The MAD for the single exponential smoothing forecast was 23.278; the MAD for the double exponential smoothing forecast was 7.655
16-23 MAD $= 153.55$; October forecast $= \$23,688.35$
16-25 b Period 17 forecast $= 15,916.90$
c Period 17 forecast $= 15,790.30$ **d** Use $\alpha = 0.25$
16-27 b Period 17 forecast $= 64,626.48$
16-29 49,781.28 ——— 92,539.22
16-35 b $\$242,385.2941$; $r = 0.9479$; since $123.9718 > 4.6001$, reject H_0 **c** MAD $= 461,216.73$

d

Year	Forecast
2001	4,929,275.00
2002	5,271,660.29
2003	5,614,045.59
2004	5,956,430.88
2005	6,298,816.18

e 5,577,229.82 ———— 7,020,402.53

16-39 b $R^2 = 0.9392$ **c** 17.031 **d** Since 12.4253 > 2.228, reject H_0

16-43 a 289.52 ———— 387.89 **b** 102.8768, or month number 103

16-45 a Forecast = 46,440.90; MAD = 5,181.12 **c** The MAD for the double exponential model is 5181.12; the MAD for the linear trend model based on deseasonalized data is 1,419.1298

d

			β		
		0.3	0.25	0.2	0.1
	0.1	5190.35	5101.89	5013.90	4823.45
α	0.15	5397.24	5258.43	5130.99	4892.37
	0.2	5538.02	5354.95	5181.12	4872.93
	0.3	5374.41	5192.38	5019.96	4709.27

16-51 a MAD = 254,886.48
b MAD = 257,898.24; no real difference

CHAPTER 17

17-3 Given that it will realize an annual profit of $69,664, Varsity should sign the contract.

17-7 a

		DEMAND		
Production	20,000	40,000	60,000	80,000
20000	$2,800,000	$2,600,000	$2,400,000	$2,200,000
40000	1,800,000	5,800,000	5,600,000	5,400,000
60000	800,000	4,800,000	8,800,000	8,600,000
80000	(200,000)	3,800,000	7,800,000	11,800,000

b Maximin: 20,000; Maximax: 80,000

17-9

			DEMAND		
Purchases	100,000	150,000	200,000	225,000	250,000
100,000	1,000,000	1,000,000	1,000,000	1,000,000	1,000,000
150,000	675,000	1,575,000	1,575,000	1,575,000	1,575,000
200,000	350,000	1,250,000	2,150,000	2,150,000	2,150,000
225,000	187,500	1,087,500	1,987,500	2,437,500	2,437,500
250,000	25,000	925,000	1,825,000	2,275,000	2,725,000

Purchases	Expected Value
100,000	1,000,000
150,000	1,485,000
200,000	1,610,000
225,000	1,582,500
250,000	1,465,000

17-11 Supply 4,000 for EV of 1,075

17-13 a Purchase 5 restaurants for a maximum profit of $1,250,000.
b Purchase no restaurants for a profit of $0. **d** Mall Option: Maximax: purchase 5 franchises for a maximum profit of 2,500,000; Maximin: purchase 0 franchises for a profit of $0.
Larger Building Option: Maximax: purchase 5 franchises for a maximum profit of 2,500,000; Maximin: purchase 0 franchises for a profit of $0.

17-15 EVPI = $1,140,000

17-17 EVPI = $7,320

17-19 The owners should expand.

17-21 The developer should build the large resort.

17-25 Max is −10,000, which is associated with don't plant.

17-27 The decision would be to plant oats.

17-29 The decision is to plant oats.

17-37 The expected value of the don't contract branch is $82. By evaluating the contract branch of the decision tree, we find an expected value of $81. So the best decision is not to sign the contract and develop the improved model.

17-41 Max = 4,250,000, which is associated with build 50.

17-43

Decision	Failure	Success
Don't Market	—	—
Market	(20,000,000)	50,000,000
Probabilities	0.4	0.6

17-45

Decision	Excellent	Good	Fair	Poor
Don't Market	—	—	—	—
Market	70,000,000	50,000,000	10,000,000	(20,000,000)
Probabilities	0.3	0.3	0.1	0.3

17-49 The number of orders that will minimize the expected opportunity loss is 6 orders at an expected loss of $3.70. ECU = $3.70

17-51 The number of orders that will minimize the expected opportunity loss is 6 orders at an expected loss of $3.70. ECU = $3.70 = EVPI

17-53 Option 1: Sign Contract: Revenue = $900,000; Option 2: Sell Independently: Revenue = $1,128,000; so, do not sign the contract.

17-55 The expected value of selling independently is $1,128,000, and the expected value of the new contract is $944,000. They should still sell independently.

17-59 $x \geq 0.66$

LIST OF TABLES

1511	4745	8716	2793	9142	4958	5245	8312	8925
6249	7073	0460	0819	0729	6806	2713	6595	5149
2587	4800	3455	7565	1196	7768	6137	4941	0488
0168	1379	7838	7487	7420	5285	8045	6679	1361
9664	9021	4990	5570	4697	7939	5842	5353	7503
1384	4981	2708	6437	2298	6230	7443	9425	5384
6390	8953	4292	7372	7197	2121	6538	2093	7629
6944	8134	0704	8500	6996	3492	4397	8802	3253
3610	3119	7442	6218	7623	0546	8394	3286	4463
9865	0028	1783	9029	2858	8737	7023	0444	8575
7044	6712	7530	0018	0945	8803	4467	0979	1342
9304	4857	5476	8386	1540	5760	9815	7191	3291
1717	8278	0072	2636	3217	1693	6081	1330	3458
2461	3598	5173	9666	6165	7438	6805	2357	6994
8240	9856	0075	7599	8468	7653	6272	0573	4344
1697	6805	1386	2340	6694	9786	0536	6423	1083
4695	2251	8962	5638	9459	5578	0676	2276	4724
3056	8558	3020	7509	5105	4283	5390	5715	8405
6887	9035	8520	6571	3233	7175	2859	1615	3349
1267	8824	5588	2821	1247	0967	4355	1385	0727
4369	9267	9377	8205	6479	7002	0649	4731	7086
2888	0333	5347	4849	5526	2975	5295	5071	6011
9893	7251	6243	4617	9256	4039	4800	9393	3263
8927	3977	6054	5979	8566	8120	2566	4449	2414
2676	7064	2198	3234	3796	5506	4462	5121	9052
0775	7316	2249	5606	9411	3818	5268	7652	6098
3828	9178	3726	0743	4075	3560	9542	3922	7688
3281	3419	6660	7968	1238	2246	2164	4567	1801
0328	7471	5352	2019	5842	1665	5939	6337	9102
8406	1826	8437	3078	9068	1425	1232	0573	7751
7076	8418	6778	1292	2019	3506	7474	0141	6544
0446	8641	3249	5431	4068	6045	1939	5626	1867
3719	9712	7472	1517	8850	6862	6990	5475	6227
5648	0563	6346	1981	9512	0659	5694	6668	2563
3694	8582	3434	4052	8392	3883	5126	0477	4034
3554	9876	4249	9473	9085	6594	2434	9453	8883
4934	8446	4646	2054	1136	1023	6295	6483	9915
7835	1506	0019	5011	0563	4450	1466	6334	2606
1098	2113	8287	3487	8250	2269	1876	3684	8856
1186	2685	7225	8311	3835	8059	9163	2539	6487
4618	1522	0627	0448	0669	4086	4083	0881	4270
5529	4173	5711	7419	2535	5876	8435	2564	3031
0754	5808	8458	2218	9180	6213	5280	4753	0696
5865	0806	2070	7986	4800	3076	2866	0515	7417
6168	8963	0235	1514	7875	2176	3095	1171	7892
7479	4144	6697	2255	5465	7233	4981	3553	8144
4608	6576	9422	4198	2578	1701	4764	7460	3509
0654	2483	6001	4486	4941	1500	3502	9693	1956
3000	9694	6616	5599	7759	1581	9896	2312	8140
2686	3675	5760	2918	0185	7364	9985	5930	9869
4713	4121	5144	5164	8104	0403	4984	3877	8772
9281	6522	7916	8941	6710	1670	1399	5961	4714
5736	9419	5022	6955	3356	5732	1042	0527	7441
2383	0408	2821	7313	5781	6951	7181	0608	2864
8740	8038	7284	6054	2246	1674	9984	0355	0775

APPENDIX B

Binomial Distribution Table

$$P(x) = \frac{n!}{x!(n-x)!} \, p^x(1-p)^{n-x}$$

n = 1

x	p = 0.01	p = 0.02	p = 0.03	p = 0.04	p = 0.05	p = 0.06	p = 0.07	p = 0.08	p = 0.09	p = 0.10	n − x
0	0.9900	0.9800	0.9700	0.9600	0.9500	0.9400	0.9300	0.9200	0.9100	0.9000	1
1	0.0100	0.0200	0.0300	0.0400	0.0500	0.0600	0.0700	0.0800	0.0900	0.1000	0
	q = 0.99	q = 0.98	q = 0.97	q = 0.96	q = 0.95	q = 0.94	q = 0.93	q = 0.92	q = 0.91	q = 0.90	
x	p = 0.11	p = 0.12	p = 0.13	p = 0.14	p = 0.15	p = 0.16	p = 0.17	p = 0.18	p = 0.19	p = 0.20	n − x
0	0.8900	0.8800	0.8700	0.8600	0.8500	0.8400	0.8300	0.8200	0.8100	0.8000	1
1	0.1100	0.1200	0.1300	0.1400	0.1500	0.1600	0.1700	0.1800	0.1900	0.2000	0
	q = 0.89	q = 0.88	q = 0.87	q = 0.86	q = 0.85	q = 0.84	q = 0.83	q = 0.82	q = 0.81	q = 0.80	
x	p = 0.21	p = 0.22	p = 0.23	p = 0.24	p = 0.25	p = 0.26	p = 0.27	p = 0.28	p = 0.29	p = 0.30	n − x
0	0.7900	0.7800	0.7700	0.7600	0.7500	0.7400	0.7300	0.7200	0.7100	0.7000	1
1	0.2100	0.2200	0.2300	0.2400	0.2500	0.2600	0.2700	0.2800	0.2900	0.3000	0
	q = 0.79	q = 0.78	q = 0.77	q = 0.76	q = 0.75	q = 0.74	q = 0.73	q = 0.72	q = 0.71	q = 0.70	
x	p = 0.31	p = 0.32	p = 0.33	p = 0.34	p = 0.35	p = 0.36	p = 0.37	p = 0.38	p = 0.39	p = 0.40	n − x
0	0.6900	0.6800	0.6700	0.6600	0.6500	0.6400	0.6300	0.6200	0.6100	0.6000	1
1	0.3100	0.3200	0.3300	0.3400	0.3500	0.3600	0.3700	0.3800	0.3900	0.4000	0
	q = 0.69	q = 0.68	q = 0.67	q = 0.66	q = 0.65	q = 0.64	q = 0.63	q = 0.62	q = 0.61	q = 0.60	
x	p = 0.41	p = 0.42	p = 0.43	p = 0.44	p = 0.45	p = 0.46	p = 0.47	p = 0.48	p = 0.49	p = 0.50	n − x
0	0.5900	0.5800	0.5700	0.5600	0.5500	0.5400	0.5300	0.5200	0.5100	0.5000	1
1	0.4100	0.4200	0.4300	0.4400	0.4500	0.4600	0.4700	0.4800	0.4900	0.5000	0
	q = 0.59	q = 0.58	q = 0.57	q = 0.56	q = 0.55	q = 0.54	q = 0.53	q = 0.52	q = 0.51	q = 0.50	

n = 2

x	p = 0.01	p = 0.02	p = 0.03	p = 0.04	p = 0.05	p = 0.06	p = 0.07	p = 0.08	p = 0.09	p = 0.10	n − x
0	0.9801	0.9604	0.9409	0.9216	0.9025	0.8836	0.8649	0.8464	0.8281	0.8100	2
1	0.0198	0.0392	0.0582	0.0768	0.0950	0.1128	0.1302	0.1472	0.1638	0.1800	1
2	0.0001	0.0004	0.0009	0.0016	0.0025	0.0036	0.0049	0.0064	0.0081	0.0100	0
	q = 0.99	q = 0.98	q = 0.97	q = 0.96	q = 0.95	q = 0.94	q = 0.93	q = 0.92	q = 0.91	q = 0.90	
x	p = 0.11	p = 0.12	p = 0.13	p = 0.14	p = 0.15	p = 0.16	p = 0.17	p = 0.18	p = 0.19	p = 0.20	n − x
0	0.7921	0.7744	0.7569	0.7396	0.7225	0.7056	0.6889	0.6724	0.6561	0.6400	2
1	0.1958	0.2112	0.2262	0.2408	0.2550	0.2688	0.2822	0.2952	0.3078	0.3200	1
2	0.0121	0.0144	0.0169	0.0196	0.0225	0.0256	0.0289	0.0324	0.0361	0.0400	0
	q = 0.89	q = 0.88	q = 0.87	q = 0.86	q = 0.85	q = 0.84	q = 0.83	q = 0.82	q = 0.81	q = 0.80	
x	p = 0.21	p = 0.22	p = 0.23	p = 0.24	p = 0.25	p = 0.26	p = 0.27	p = 0.28	p = 0.29	p = 0.30	n − x
0	0.6241	0.6084	0.5929	0.5776	0.5625	0.5476	0.5329	0.5184	0.5041	0.4900	2
1	0.3318	0.3432	0.3542	0.3648	0.3750	0.3848	0.3942	0.4032	0.4118	0.4200	1
2	0.0441	0.0484	0.0529	0.0576	0.0625	0.0676	0.0729	0.0784	0.0841	0.0900	0
	q = 0.79	q = 0.78	q = 0.77	q = 0.76	q = 0.75	q = 0.74	q = 0.73	q = 0.72	q = 0.71	q = 0.70	
x	p = 0.31	p = 0.32	p = 0.33	p = 0.34	p = 0.35	p = 0.36	p = 0.37	p = 0.38	p = 0.39	p = 0.40	n − x
0	0.4761	0.4624	0.4489	0.4356	0.4225	0.4096	0.3969	0.3844	0.3721	0.3600	2
1	0.4278	0.4352	0.4422	0.4488	0.4550	0.4608	0.4662	0.4712	0.4758	0.4800	1
2	0.0961	0.1024	0.1089	0.1156	0.1225	0.1296	0.1369	0.1444	0.1521	0.1600	0
	q = 0.69	q = 0.68	q = 0.67	q = 0.66	q = 0.65	q = 0.64	q = 0.63	q = 0.62	q = 0.61	q = 0.60	
x	p = 0.41	p = 0.42	p = 0.43	p = 0.44	p = 0.45	p = 0.46	p = 0.47	p = 0.48	p = 0.49	p = 0.50	n − x
0	0.3481	0.3364	0.3249	0.3136	0.3025	0.2916	0.2809	0.2704	0.2601	0.2500	2
1	0.4838	0.4872	0.4902	0.4928	0.4950	0.4968	0.4982	0.4992	0.4998	0.5000	1
2	0.1681	0.1764	0.1849	0.1936	0.2025	0.2116	0.2209	0.2304	0.2401	0.2500	0
	q = 0.59	q = 0.58	q = 0.57	q = 0.56	q = 0.55	q = 0.54	q = 0.53	q = 0.52	q = 0.51	q = 0.50	

continued

					$n = 3$						
x	$p = 0.01$	$p = 0.02$	$p = 0.03$	$p = 0.04$	$p = 0.05$	$p = 0.06$	$p = 0.07$	$p = 0.08$	$p = 0.09$	$p = 0.10$	$n - x$
0	0.9703	0.9412	0.9127	0.8847	0.8574	0.8306	0.8044	0.7787	0.7536	0.7290	3
1	0.0294	0.0576	0.0847	0.1106	0.1354	0.1590	0.1816	0.2031	0.2236	0.2430	2
2	0.0003	0.0012	0.0026	0.0046	0.0071	0.0102	0.0137	0.0177	0.0221	0.0270	1
3	0.0000	0.0000	0.0000	0.0001	0.0001	0.0002	0.0003	0.0005	0.0007	0.0010	0
	$q = 0.99$	$q = 0.98$	$q = 0.97$	$q = 0.96$	$q = 0.95$	$q = 0.94$	$q = 0.93$	$q = 0.92$	$q = 0.91$	$q = 0.90$	
x	$p = 0.11$	$p = 0.12$	$p = 0.13$	$p = 0.14$	$p = 0.15$	$p = 0.16$	$p = 0.17$	$p = 0.18$	$p = 0.19$	$p = 0.20$	$n - x$
0	0.7050	0.6815	0.6585	0.6361	0.6141	0.5927	0.5718	0.5514	0.5314	0.5120	3
1	0.2614	0.2788	0.2952	0.3106	0.3251	0.3387	0.3513	0.3631	0.3740	0.3840	2
2	0.0323	0.0380	0.0441	0.0506	0.0574	0.0645	0.0720	0.0797	0.0877	0.0960	1
3	0.0013	0.0017	0.0022	0.0027	0.0034	0.0041	0.0049	0.0058	0.0069	0.0080	0
	$q = 0.89$	$q = 0.88$	$q = 0.87$	$q = 0.86$	$q = 0.85$	$q = 0.84$	$q = 0.83$	$q = 0.82$	$q = 0.81$	$q = 0.80$	
x	$p = 0.21$	$p = 0.22$	$p = 0.23$	$p = 0.24$	$p = 0.25$	$p = 0.26$	$p = 0.27$	$p = 0.28$	$p = 0.29$	$p = 0.30$	$n - x$
0	0.4930	0.4746	0.4565	0.4390	0.4219	0.4052	0.3890	0.3732	0.3579	0.3430	3
1	0.3932	0.4015	0.4091	0.4159	0.4219	0.4271	0.4316	0.4355	0.4386	0.4410	2
2	0.1045	0.1133	0.1222	0.1313	0.1406	0.1501	0.1597	0.1693	0.1791	0.1890	1
3	0.0093	0.0106	0.0122	0.0138	0.0156	0.0176	0.0197	0.0220	0.0244	0.0270	0
	$q = 0.79$	$q = 0.78$	$q = 0.77$	$q = 0.76$	$q = 0.75$	$q = 0.74$	$q = 0.73$	$q = 0.72$	$q = 0.71$	$q = 0.70$	
x	$p = 0.31$	$p = 0.32$	$p = 0.33$	$p = 0.34$	$p = 0.35$	$p = 0.36$	$p = 0.37$	$p = 0.38$	$p = 0.39$	$p = 0.40$	$n - x$
0	0.3285	0.3144	0.3008	0.2875	0.2746	0.2621	0.2500	0.2383	0.2270	0.2160	3
1	0.4428	0.4439	0.4444	0.4443	0.4436	0.4424	0.4406	0.4382	0.4354	0.4320	2
2	0.1989	0.2089	0.2189	0.2289	0.2389	0.2488	0.2587	0.2686	0.2783	0.2880	1
3	0.0298	0.0328	0.0359	0.0393	0.0429	0.0467	0.0507	0.0549	0.0593	0.0640	0
	$q = 0.69$	$q = 0.68$	$q = 0.67$	$q = 0.66$	$q = 0.65$	$q = 0.64$	$q = 0.63$	$q = 0.62$	$q = 0.61$	$q = 0.60$	
x	$p = 0.41$	$p = 0.42$	$p = 0.43$	$p = 0.44$	$p = 0.45$	$p = 0.46$	$p = 0.47$	$p = 0.48$	$p = 0.49$	$p = 0.50$	$n - x$
0	0.2054	0.1951	0.1852	0.1756	0.1664	0.1575	0.1489	0.1406	0.1327	0.1250	3
1	0.4282	0.4239	0.4191	0.4140	0.4084	0.4024	0.3961	0.3894	0.3823	0.3750	2
2	0.2975	0.3069	0.3162	0.3252	0.3341	0.3428	0.3512	0.3594	0.3674	0.3750	1
3	0.0689	0.0741	0.0795	0.0852	0.0911	0.0973	0.1038	0.1106	0.1176	0.1250	0
	$q = 0.59$	$q = 0.58$	$q = 0.57$	$q = 0.56$	$q = 0.55$	$q = 0.54$	$q = 0.53$	$q = 0.52$	$q = 0.51$	$q = 0.50$	

					$n = 4$						
x	$p = 0.01$	$p = 0.02$	$p = 0.03$	$p = 0.04$	$p = 0.05$	$p = 0.06$	$p = 0.07$	$p = 0.08$	$p = 0.09$	$p = 0.10$	$n - x$
0	0.9606	0.9224	0.8853	0.8493	0.8145	0.7807	0.7481	0.7164	0.6857	0.6561	4
1	0.0388	0.0753	0.1095	0.1416	0.1715	0.1993	0.2252	0.2492	0.2713	0.2916	3
2	0.0006	0.0023	0.0051	0.0088	0.0135	0.0191	0.0254	0.0325	0.0402	0.0486	2
3	0.0000	0.0000	0.0001	0.0002	0.0005	0.0008	0.0013	0.0019	0.0027	0.0036	1
4	0.0000	0.0000	0.0000	0.0000	0.0000	0.0000	0.0000	0.0000	0.0001	0.0001	0
	$q = 0.99$	$q = 0.98$	$q = 0.97$	$q = 0.96$	$q = 0.95$	$q = 0.94$	$q = 0.93$	$q = 0.92$	$q = 0.91$	$q = 0.90$	
x	$p = 0.11$	$p = 0.12$	$p = 0.13$	$p = 0.14$	$p = 0.15$	$p = 0.16$	$p = 0.17$	$p = 0.18$	$p = 0.19$	$p = 0.20$	$n - x$
0	0.6274	0.5997	0.5729	0.5470	0.5220	0.4979	0.4746	0.4521	0.4305	0.4096	4
1	0.3102	0.3271	0.3424	0.3562	0.3685	0.3793	0.3888	0.3970	0.4039	0.4096	3
2	0.0575	0.0669	0.0767	0.0870	0.0975	0.1084	0.1195	0.1307	0.1421	0.1536	2
3	0.0047	0.0061	0.0076	0.0094	0.0115	0.0138	0.0163	0.0191	0.0222	0.0256	1
4	0.0001	0.0002	0.0003	0.0004	0.0005	0.0007	0.0008	0.0010	0.0013	0.0016	0
	$q = 0.89$	$q = 0.88$	$q = 0.87$	$q = 0.86$	$q = 0.85$	$q = 0.84$	$q = 0.83$	$q = 0.82$	$q = 0.81$	$q = 0.80$	

x	p = 0.21	p = 0.22	p = 0.23	p = 0.24	p = 0.25	p = 0.26	p = 0.27	p = 0.28	p = 0.29	p = 0.30	n − x
0	0.3895	0.3702	0.3515	0.3336	0.3164	0.2999	0.2840	0.2687	0.2541	0.2401	4
1	0.4142	0.4176	0.4200	0.4214	0.4219	0.4214	0.4201	0.4180	0.4152	0.4116	3
2	0.1651	0.1767	0.1882	0.1996	0.2109	0.2221	0.2331	0.2439	0.2544	0.2646	2
3	0.0293	0.0332	0.0375	0.0420	0.0469	0.0520	0.0575	0.0632	0.0693	0.0756	1
4	0.0019	0.0023	0.0028	0.0033	0.0039	0.0046	0.0053	0.0061	0.0071	0.0081	0
	q = 0.79	q = 0.78	q = 0.77	q = 0.76	q = 0.75	q = 0.74	q = 0.73	q = 0.72	q = 0.71	q = 0.70	

x	p = 0.31	p = 0.32	p = 0.33	p = 0.34	p = 0.35	p = 0.36	p = 0.37	p = 0.38	p = 0.39	p = 0.40	n − x
0	0.2267	0.2138	0.2015	0.1897	0.1785	0.1678	0.1575	0.1478	0.1385	0.1296	4
1	0.4074	0.4025	0.3970	0.3910	0.3845	0.3775	0.3701	0.3623	0.3541	0.3456	3
2	0.2745	0.2841	0.2933	0.3021	0.3105	0.3185	0.3260	0.3330	0.3396	0.3456	2
3	0.0822	0.0891	0.0963	0.1038	0.1115	0.1194	0.1276	0.1361	0.1447	0.1536	1
4	0.0092	0.0105	0.0119	0.0134	0.0150	0.0168	0.0187	0.0209	0.0231	0.0256	0
	q = 0.69	q = 0.68	q = 0.67	q = 0.66	q = 0.65	q = 0.64	q = 0.63	q = 0.62	q = 0.61	q = 0.60	

x	p = 0.41	p = 0.42	p = 0.43	p = 0.44	p = 0.45	p = 0.46	p = 0.47	p = 0.48	p = 0.49	p = 0.50	n − x
0	0.1212	0.1132	0.1056	0.0983	0.0915	0.0850	0.0789	0.0731	0.0677	0.0625	4
1	0.3368	0.3278	0.3185	0.3091	0.2995	0.2897	0.2799	0.2700	0.2600	0.2500	3
2	0.3511	0.3560	0.3604	0.3643	0.3675	0.3702	0.3723	0.3738	0.3747	0.3750	2
3	0.1627	0.1719	0.1813	0.1908	0.2005	0.2102	0.2201	0.2300	0.2400	0.2500	1
4	0.0283	0.0311	0.0342	0.0375	0.0410	0.0448	0.0488	0.0531	0.0576	0.0625	0
	q = 0.59	q = 0.58	q = 0.57	q = 0.56	q = 0.55	q = 0.54	q = 0.53	q = 0.52	q = 0.51	q = 0.50	

n = 5

x	p = 0.01	p = 0.02	p = 0.03	p = 0.04	p = 0.05	p = 0.06	p = 0.07	p = 0.08	p = 0.09	p = 0.10	n − x
0	0.9510	0.9039	0.8587	0.8154	0.7738	0.7339	0.6957	0.6591	0.6240	0.5905	5
1	0.0480	0.0922	0.1328	0.1699	0.2036	0.2342	0.2618	0.2866	0.3086	0.3281	4
2	0.0010	0.0038	0.0082	0.0142	0.0214	0.0299	0.0394	0.0498	0.0610	0.0729	3
3	0.0000	0.0001	0.0003	0.0006	0.0011	0.0019	0.0030	0.0043	0.0060	0.0081	2
4	0.0000	0.0000	0.0000	0.0000	0.0000	0.0001	0.0001	0.0002	0.0003	0.0005	1
5	0.0000	0.0000	0.0000	0.0000	0.0000	0.0000	0.0000	0.0000	0.0000	0.0000	0
	q = 0.99	q = 0.98	q = 0.97	q = 0.96	q = 0.95	q = 0.94	q = 0.93	q = 0.92	q = 0.91	q = 0.90	

x	p = 0.11	p = 0.12	p = 0.13	p = 0.14	p = 0.15	p = 0.16	p = 0.17	p = 0.18	p = 0.19	p = 0.20	n − x
0	0.5584	0.5277	0.4984	0.4704	0.4437	0.4182	0.3939	0.3707	0.3487	0.3277	5
1	0.3451	0.3598	0.3724	0.3829	0.3915	0.3983	0.4034	0.4069	0.4089	0.4096	4
2	0.0853	0.0981	0.1113	0.1247	0.1382	0.1517	0.1652	0.1786	0.1919	0.2048	3
3	0.0105	0.0134	0.0166	0.0203	0.0244	0.0289	0.0338	0.0392	0.0450	0.0512	2
4	0.0007	0.0009	0.0012	0.0017	0.0022	0.0028	0.0035	0.0043	0.0053	0.0064	1
5	0.0000	0.0000	0.0000	0.0001	0.0001	0.0001	0.0001	0.0002	0.0002	0.0003	0
	q = 0.89	q = 0.88	q = 0.87	q = 0.86	q = 0.85	q = 0.84	q = 0.83	q = 0.82	q = 0.81	q = 0.80	

x	p = 0.21	p = 0.22	p = 0.23	p = 0.24	p = 0.25	p = 0.26	p = 0.27	p = 0.28	p = 0.29	p = 0.30	n − x
0	0.3077	0.2887	0.2707	0.2536	0.2373	0.2219	0.2073	0.1935	0.1804	0.1681	5
1	0.4090	0.4072	0.4043	0.4003	0.3955	0.3898	0.3834	0.3762	0.3685	0.3602	4
2	0.2174	0.2297	0.2415	0.2529	0.2637	0.2739	0.2836	0.2926	0.3010	0.3087	3
3	0.0578	0.0648	0.0721	0.0798	0.0879	0.0962	0.1049	0.1138	0.1229	0.1323	2
4	0.0077	0.0091	0.0108	0.0126	0.0146	0.0169	0.0194	0.0221	0.0251	0.0284	1
5	0.0004	0.0005	0.0006	0.0008	0.0010	0.0012	0.0014	0.0017	0.0021	0.0024	0
	q = 0.79	q = 0.78	q = 0.77	q = 0.76	q = 0.75	q = 0.74	q = 0.73	q = 0.72	q = 0.71	q = 0.70	

continued

x	p = 0.31	p = 0.32	p = 0.33	p = 0.34	p = 0.35	p = 0.36	p = 0.37	p = 0.38	p = 0.39	p = 0.40	n − x
0	0.1564	0.1454	0.1350	0.1252	0.1160	0.1074	0.0992	0.0916	0.0845	0.0778	5
1	0.3513	0.3421	0.3325	0.3226	0.3124	0.3020	0.2914	0.2808	0.2700	0.2592	4
2	0.3157	0.3220	0.3275	0.3323	0.3364	0.3397	0.3423	0.3441	0.3452	0.3456	3
3	0.1418	0.1515	0.1613	0.1712	0.1811	0.1911	0.2010	0.2109	0.2207	0.2304	2
4	0.0319	0.0357	0.0397	0.0441	0.0488	0.0537	0.0590	0.0646	0.0706	0.0768	1
5	0.0029	0.0034	0.0039	0.0045	0.0053	0.0060	0.0069	0.0079	0.0090	0.0102	0
	q = 0.69	q = 0.68	q = 0.67	q = 0.66	q = 0.65	q = 0.64	q = 0.63	q = 0.62	q = 0.61	q = 0.60	

x	p = 0.41	p = 0.42	p = 0.43	p = 0.44	p = 0.45	p = 0.46	p = 0.47	p = 0.48	p = 0.49	p = 0.50	n − x
0	0.0715	0.0656	0.0602	0.0551	0.0503	0.0459	0.0418	0.0380	0.0345	0.0313	5
1	0.2484	0.2376	0.2270	0.2164	0.2059	0.1956	0.1854	0.1755	0.1657	0.1563	4
2	0.3452	0.3442	0.3424	0.3400	0.3369	0.3332	0.3289	0.3240	0.3185	0.3125	3
3	0.2399	0.2492	0.2583	0.2671	0.2757	0.2838	0.2916	0.2990	0.3060	0.3125	2
4	0.0834	0.0902	0.0974	0.1049	0.1128	0.1209	0.1293	0.1380	0.1470	0.1563	1
5	0.0116	0.0131	0.0147	0.0165	0.0185	0.0206	0.0229	0.0255	0.0282	0.0313	0
	q = 0.59	q = 0.58	q = 0.57	q = 0.56	q = 0.55	q = 0.54	q = 0.53	q = 0.52	q = 0.51	q = 0.50	

$n = 6$

x	p = 0.01	p = 0.02	p = 0.03	p = 0.04	p = 0.05	p = 0.06	p = 0.07	p = 0.08	p = 0.09	p = 0.10	n − x
0	0.9415	0.8858	0.8330	0.7828	0.7351	0.6899	0.6470	0.6064	0.5679	0.5314	6
1	0.0571	0.1085	0.1546	0.1957	0.2321	0.2642	0.2922	0.3164	0.3370	0.3543	5
2	0.0014	0.0055	0.0120	0.0204	0.0305	0.0422	0.0550	0.0688	0.0833	0.0984	4
3	0.0000	0.0002	0.0005	0.0011	0.0021	0.0036	0.0055	0.0080	0.0110	0.0146	3
4	0.0000	0.0000	0.0000	0.0000	0.0001	0.0002	0.0003	0.0005	0.0008	0.0012	2
5	0.0000	0.0000	0.0000	0.0000	0.0000	0.0000	0.0000	0.0000	0.0000	0.0001	1
6	0.0000	0.0000	0.0000	0.0000	0.0000	0.0000	0.0000	0.0000	0.0000	0.0000	0
	q = 0.99	q = 0.98	q = 0.97	q = 0.96	q = 0.95	q = 0.94	q = 0.93	q = 0.92	q = 0.91	q = 0.90	

x	p = 0.11	p = 0.12	p = 0.13	p = 0.14	p = 0.15	p = 0.16	p = 0.17	p = 0.18	p = 0.19	p = 0.20	n − x
0	0.4970	0.4644	0.4336	0.4046	0.3771	0.3513	0.3269	0.3040	0.2824	0.2621	6
1	0.3685	0.3800	0.3888	0.3952	0.3993	0.4015	0.4018	0.4004	0.3975	0.3932	5
2	0.1139	0.1295	0.1452	0.1608	0.1762	0.1912	0.2057	0.2197	0.2331	0.2458	4
3	0.0188	0.0236	0.0289	0.0349	0.0415	0.0486	0.0562	0.0643	0.0729	0.0819	3
4	0.0017	0.0024	0.0032	0.0043	0.0055	0.0069	0.0086	0.0106	0.0128	0.0154	2
5	0.0001	0.0001	0.0002	0.0003	0.0004	0.0005	0.0007	0.0009	0.0012	0.0015	1
6	0.0000	0.0000	0.0000	0.0000	0.0000	0.0000	0.0000	0.0000	0.0000	0.0001	0
	q = 0.89	q = 0.88	q = 0.87	q = 0.86	q = 0.85	q = 0.84	q = 0.83	q = 0.82	q = 0.81	q = 0.80	

x	p = 0.21	p = 0.22	p = 0.23	p = 0.24	p = 0.25	p = 0.26	p = 0.27	p = 0.28	p = 0.29	p = 0.30	n − x
0	0.2431	0.2252	0.2084	0.1927	0.1780	0.1642	0.1513	0.1393	0.1281	0.1176	6
1	0.3877	0.3811	0.3735	0.3651	0.3560	0.3462	0.3358	0.3251	0.3139	0.3025	5
2	0.2577	0.2687	0.2789	0.2882	0.2966	0.3041	0.3105	0.3160	0.3206	0.3241	4
3	0.0913	0.1011	0.1111	0.1214	0.1318	0.1424	0.1531	0.1639	0.1746	0.1852	3
4	0.0182	0.0214	0.0249	0.0287	0.0330	0.0375	0.0425	0.0478	0.0535	0.0595	2
5	0.0019	0.0024	0.0030	0.0036	0.0044	0.0053	0.0063	0.0074	0.0087	0.0102	1
6	0.0001	0.0001	0.0001	0.0002	0.0002	0.0003	0.0004	0.0005	0.0006	0.0007	0
	q = 0.79	q = 0.78	q = 0.77	q = 0.76	q = 0.75	q = 0.74	q = 0.73	q = 0.72	q = 0.71	q = 0.70	

x	p = 0.31	p = 0.32	p = 0.33	p = 0.34	p = 0.35	p = 0.36	p = 0.37	p = 0.38	p = 0.39	p = 0.40	n − x
0	0.1079	0.0989	0.0905	0.0827	0.0754	0.0687	0.0625	0.0568	0.0515	0.0467	6
1	0.2909	0.2792	0.2673	0.2555	0.2437	0.2319	0.2203	0.2089	0.1976	0.1866	5
2	0.3267	0.3284	0.3292	0.3290	0.3280	0.3261	0.3235	0.3201	0.3159	0.3110	4
3	0.1957	0.2061	0.2162	0.2260	0.2355	0.2446	0.2533	0.2616	0.2693	0.2765	3
4	0.0660	0.0727	0.0799	0.0873	0.0951	0.1032	0.1116	0.1202	0.1291	0.1382	2
5	0.0119	0.0137	0.0157	0.0180	0.0205	0.0232	0.0262	0.0295	0.0330	0.0369	1
6	0.0009	0.0011	0.0013	0.0015	0.0018	0.0022	0.0026	0.0030	0.0035	0.0041	0
	q = 0.69	q = 0.68	q = 0.67	q = 0.66	q = 0.65	q = 0.64	q = 0.63	q = 0.62	q = 0.61	q = 0.60	

x	p = 0.41	p = 0.42	p = 0.43	p = 0.44	p = 0.45	p = 0.46	p = 0.47	p = 0.48	p = 0.49	p = 0.50	n − x
0	0.0422	0.0381	0.0343	0.0308	0.0277	0.0248	0.0222	0.0198	0.0176	0.0156	6
1	0.1759	0.1654	0.1552	0.1454	0.1359	0.1267	0.1179	0.1095	0.1014	0.0938	5
2	0.3055	0.2994	0.2928	0.2856	0.2780	0.2699	0.2615	0.2527	0.2436	0.2344	4
3	0.2831	0.2891	0.2945	0.2992	0.3032	0.3065	0.3091	0.3110	0.3121	0.3125	3
4	0.1475	0.1570	0.1666	0.1763	0.1861	0.1958	0.2056	0.2153	0.2249	0.2344	2
5	0.0410	0.0455	0.0503	0.0554	0.0609	0.0667	0.0729	0.0795	0.0864	0.0938	1
6	0.0048	0.0055	0.0063	0.0073	0.0083	0.0095	0.0108	0.0122	0.0138	0.0156	0
	q = 0.59	q = 0.58	q = 0.57	q = 0.56	q = 0.55	q = 0.54	q = 0.53	q = 0.52	q = 0.51	q = 0.50	

n = 7

x	p = 0.01	p = 0.02	p = 0.03	p = 0.04	p = 0.05	p = 0.06	p = 0.07	p = 0.08	p = 0.09	p = 0.10	n − x
0	0.9321	0.8681	0.8080	0.7514	0.6983	0.6485	0.6017	0.5578	0.5168	0.4783	7
1	0.0659	0.1240	0.1749	0.2192	0.2573	0.2897	0.3170	0.3396	0.3578	0.3720	6
2	0.0020	0.0076	0.0162	0.0274	0.0406	0.0555	0.0716	0.0886	0.1061	0.1240	5
3	0.0000	0.0003	0.0008	0.0019	0.0036	0.0059	0.0090	0.0128	0.0175	0.0230	4
4	0.0000	0.0000	0.0000	0.0001	0.0002	0.0004	0.0007	0.0011	0.0017	0.0026	3
5	0.0000	0.0000	0.0000	0.0000	0.0000	0.0000	0.0000	0.0001	0.0001	0.0002	2
6	0.0000	0.0000	0.0000	0.0000	0.0000	0.0000	0.0000	0.0000	0.0000	0.0000	1
7	0.0000	0.0000	0.0000	0.0000	0.0000	0.0000	0.0000	0.0000	0.0000	0.0000	0
	q = 0.99	q = 0.98	q = 0.97	q = 0.96	q = 0.95	q = 0.94	q = 0.93	q = 0.92	q = 0.91	q = 0.90	

x	p = 0.11	p = 0.12	p = 0.13	p = 0.14	p = 0.15	p = 0.16	p = 0.17	p = 0.18	p = 0.19	p = 0.20	n − x
0	0.4423	0.4087	0.3773	0.3479	0.3206	0.2951	0.2714	0.2493	0.2288	0.2097	7
1	0.3827	0.3901	0.3946	0.3965	0.3960	0.3935	0.3891	0.3830	0.3756	0.3670	6
2	0.1419	0.1596	0.1769	0.1936	0.2097	0.2248	0.2391	0.2523	0.2643	0.2753	5
3	0.0292	0.0363	0.0441	0.0525	0.0617	0.0714	0.0816	0.0923	0.1033	0.1147	4
4	0.0036	0.0049	0.0066	0.0086	0.0109	0.0136	0.0167	0.0203	0.0242	0.0287	3
5	0.0003	0.0004	0.0006	0.0008	0.0012	0.0016	0.0021	0.0027	0.0034	0.0043	2
6	0.0000	0.0000	0.0000	0.0000	0.0001	0.0001	0.0001	0.0002	0.0003	0.0004	1
7	0.0000	0.0000	0.0000	0.0000	0.0000	0.0000	0.0000	0.0000	0.0000	0.0000	0
	q = 0.89	q = 0.88	q = 0.87	q = 0.86	q = 0.85	q = 0.84	q = 0.83	q = 0.82	q = 0.81	q = 0.80	

x	p = 0.21	p = 0.22	p = 0.23	p = 0.24	p = 0.25	p = 0.26	p = 0.27	p = 0.28	p = 0.29	p = 0.30	n − x
0	0.1920	0.1757	0.1605	0.1465	0.1335	0.1215	0.1105	0.1003	0.0910	0.0824	7
1	0.3573	0.3468	0.3356	0.3237	0.3115	0.2989	0.2860	0.2731	0.2600	0.2471	6
2	0.2850	0.2935	0.3007	0.3067	0.3115	0.3150	0.3174	0.3186	0.3186	0.3177	5
3	0.1263	0.1379	0.1497	0.1614	0.1730	0.1845	0.1956	0.2065	0.2169	0.2269	4
4	0.0336	0.0389	0.0447	0.0510	0.0577	0.0648	0.0724	0.0803	0.0886	0.0972	3
5	0.0054	0.0066	0.0080	0.0097	0.0115	0.0137	0.0161	0.0187	0.0217	0.0250	2
6	0.0005	0.0006	0.0008	0.0010	0.0013	0.0016	0.0020	0.0024	0.0030	0.0036	1
7	0.0000	0.0000	0.0000	0.0000	0.0001	0.0001	0.0001	0.0001	0.0002	0.0002	0
	q = 0.79	q = 0.78	q = 0.77	q = 0.76	q = 0.75	q = 0.74	q = 0.73	q = 0.72	q = 0.71	q = 0.70	

x	p = 0.31	p = 0.32	p = 0.33	p = 0.34	p = 0.35	p = 0.36	p = 0.37	p = 0.38	p = 0.39	p = 0.40	n − x
0	0.0745	0.0672	0.0606	0.0546	0.0490	0.0440	0.0394	0.0352	0.0314	0.0280	7
1	0.2342	0.2215	0.2090	0.1967	0.1848	0.1732	0.1619	0.1511	0.1407	0.1306	6
2	0.3156	0.3127	0.3088	0.3040	0.2985	0.2922	0.2853	0.2778	0.2698	0.2613	5
3	0.2363	0.2452	0.2535	0.2610	0.2679	0.2740	0.2793	0.2838	0.2875	0.2903	4
4	0.1062	0.1154	0.1248	0.1345	0.1442	0.1541	0.1640	0.1739	0.1838	0.1935	3
5	0.0286	0.0326	0.0369	0.0416	0.0466	0.0520	0.0578	0.0640	0.0705	0.0774	2
6	0.0043	0.0051	0.0061	0.0071	0.0084	0.0098	0.0113	0.0131	0.0150	0.0172	1
7	0.0003	0.0003	0.0004	0.0005	0.0006	0.0008	0.0009	0.0011	0.0014	0.0016	0
	q = 0.69	q = 0.68	q = 0.67	q = 0.66	q = 0.65	q = 0.64	q = 0.63	q = 0.62	q = 0.61	q = 0.60	

continued

x	p = 0.41	p = 0.42	p = 0.43	p = 0.44	p = 0.45	p = 0.46	p = 0.47	p = 0.48	p = 0.49	p = 0.50	n − x
0	0.0249	0.0221	0.0195	0.0173	0.0152	0.0134	0.0117	0.0103	0.0090	0.0078	7
1	0.1211	0.1119	0.1032	0.0950	0.0872	0.0798	0.0729	0.0664	0.0604	0.0547	6
2	0.2524	0.2431	0.2336	0.2239	0.2140	0.2040	0.1940	0.1840	0.1740	0.1641	5
3	0.2923	0.2934	0.2937	0.2932	0.2918	0.2897	0.2867	0.2830	0.2786	0.2734	4
4	0.2031	0.2125	0.2216	0.2304	0.2388	0.2468	0.2543	0.2612	0.2676	0.2734	3
5	0.0847	0.0923	0.1003	0.1086	0.1172	0.1261	0.1353	0.1447	0.1543	0.1641	2
6	0.0196	0.0223	0.0252	0.0284	0.0320	0.0358	0.0400	0.0445	0.0494	0.0547	1
7	0.0019	0.0023	0.0027	0.0032	0.0037	0.0044	0.0051	0.0059	0.0068	0.0078	0
	q = 0.59	q = 0.58	q = 0.57	q = 0.56	q = 0.55	q = 0.54	q = 0.53	q = 0.52	q = 0.51	q = 0.50	

$$n = 8$$

x	p = 0.01	p = 0.02	p = 0.03	p = 0.04	p = 0.05	p = 0.06	p = 0.07	p = 0.08	p = 0.09	p = 0.10	n − x
0	0.9227	0.8508	0.7837	0.7214	0.6634	0.6096	0.5596	0.5132	0.4703	0.4305	8
1	0.0746	0.1389	0.1939	0.2405	0.2793	0.3113	0.3370	0.3570	0.3721	0.3826	7
2	0.0026	0.0099	0.0210	0.0351	0.0515	0.0695	0.0888	0.1087	0.1288	0.1488	6
3	0.0001	0.0004	0.0013	0.0029	0.0054	0.0089	0.0134	0.0189	0.0255	0.0331	5
4	0.0000	0.0000	0.0001	0.0002	0.0004	0.0007	0.0013	0.0021	0.0031	0.0046	4
5	0.0000	0.0000	0.0000	0.0000	0.0000	0.0000	0.0001	0.0001	0.0002	0.0004	3
6	0.0000	0.0000	0.0000	0.0000	0.0000	0.0000	0.0000	0.0000	0.0000	0.0000	2
7	0.0000	0.0000	0.0000	0.0000	0.0000	0.0000	0.0000	0.0000	0.0000	0.0000	1
8	0.0000	0.0000	0.0000	0.0000	0.0000	0.0000	0.0000	0.0000	0.0000	0.0000	0
	q = 0.99	q = 0.98	q = 0.97	q = 0.96	q = 0.95	q = 0.94	q = 0.93	q = 0.92	q = 0.91	q = 0.90	

x	p = 0.11	p = 0.12	p = 0.13	p = 0.14	p = 0.15	p = 0.16	p = 0.17	p = 0.18	p = 0.19	p = 0.20	n − x
0	0.3937	0.3596	0.3282	0.2992	0.2725	0.2479	0.2252	0.2044	0.1853	0.1678	8
1	0.3892	0.3923	0.3923	0.3897	0.3847	0.3777	0.3691	0.3590	0.3477	0.3355	7
2	0.1684	0.1872	0.2052	0.2220	0.2376	0.2518	0.2646	0.2758	0.2855	0.2936	6
3	0.0416	0.0511	0.0613	0.0723	0.0839	0.0959	0.1084	0.1211	0.1339	0.1468	5
4	0.0064	0.0087	0.0115	0.0147	0.0185	0.0228	0.0277	0.0332	0.0393	0.0459	4
5	0.0006	0.0009	0.0014	0.0019	0.0026	0.0035	0.0045	0.0058	0.0074	0.0092	3
6	0.0000	0.0001	0.0001	0.0002	0.0002	0.0003	0.0005	0.0006	0.0009	0.0011	2
7	0.0000	0.0000	0.0000	0.0000	0.0000	0.0000	0.0000	0.0000	0.0001	0.0001	1
8	0.0000	0.0000	0.0000	0.0000	0.0000	0.0000	0.0000	0.0000	0.0000	0.0000	0
	q = 0.89	q = 0.88	q = 0.87	q = 0.86	q = 0.85	q = 0.84	q = 0.83	q = 0.82	q = 0.81	q = 0.80	

x	p = 0.21	p = 0.22	p = 0.23	p = 0.24	p = 0.25	p = 0.26	p = 0.27	p = 0.28	p = 0.29	p = 0.30	n − x
0	0.1517	0.1370	0.1236	0.1113	0.1001	0.0899	0.0806	0.0722	0.0646	0.0576	8
1	0.3226	0.3092	0.2953	0.2812	0.2670	0.2527	0.2386	0.2247	0.2110	0.1977	7
2	0.3002	0.3052	0.3087	0.3108	0.3115	0.3108	0.3089	0.3058	0.3017	0.2965	6
3	0.1596	0.1722	0.1844	0.1963	0.2076	0.2184	0.2285	0.2379	0.2464	0.2541	5
4	0.0530	0.0607	0.0689	0.0775	0.0865	0.0959	0.1056	0.1156	0.1258	0.1361	4
5	0.0113	0.0137	0.0165	0.0196	0.0231	0.0270	0.0313	0.0360	0.0411	0.0467	3
6	0.0015	0.0019	0.0025	0.0031	0.0038	0.0047	0.0058	0.0070	0.0084	0.0100	2
7	0.0001	0.0002	0.0002	0.0003	0.0004	0.0005	0.0006	0.0008	0.0010	0.0012	1
8	0.0000	0.0000	0.0000	0.0000	0.0000	0.0000	0.0000	0.0000	0.0001	0.0001	0
	q = 0.79	q = 0.78	q = 0.77	q = 0.76	q = 0.75	q = 0.74	q = 0.73	q = 0.72	q = 0.71	q = 0.70	

x	p = 0.31	p = 0.32	p = 0.33	p = 0.34	p = 0.35	p = 0.36	p = 0.37	p = 0.38	p = 0.39	p = 0.40	n − x
0	0.0514	0.0457	0.0406	0.0360	0.0319	0.0281	0.0248	0.0218	0.0192	0.0168	8
1	0.1847	0.1721	0.1600	0.1484	0.1373	0.1267	0.1166	0.1071	0.0981	0.0896	7
2	0.2904	0.2835	0.2758	0.2675	0.2587	0.2494	0.2397	0.2297	0.2194	0.2090	6
3	0.2609	0.2668	0.2717	0.2756	0.2786	0.2805	0.2815	0.2815	0.2806	0.2787	5
4	0.1465	0.1569	0.1673	0.1775	0.1875	0.1973	0.2067	0.2157	0.2242	0.2322	4
5	0.0527	0.0591	0.0659	0.0732	0.0808	0.0888	0.0971	0.1058	0.1147	0.1239	3
6	0.0118	0.0139	0.0162	0.0188	0.0217	0.0250	0.0285	0.0324	0.0367	0.0413	2
7	0.0015	0.0019	0.0023	0.0028	0.0033	0.0040	0.0048	0.0057	0.0067	0.0079	1
8	0.0001	0.0001	0.0001	0.0002	0.0002	0.0003	0.0004	0.0004	0.0005	0.0007	0
	q = 0.69	q = 0.68	q = 0.67	q = 0.66	q = 0.65	q = 0.64	q = 0.63	q = 0.62	q = 0.61	q = 0.60	

x	p = 0.41	p = 0.42	p = 0.43	p = 0.44	p = 0.45	p = 0.46	p = 0.47	p = 0.48	p = 0.49	p = 0.50	n − x
0	0.0147	0.0128	0.0111	0.0097	0.0084	0.0072	0.0062	0.0053	0.0046	0.0039	8
1	0.0816	0.0742	0.0672	0.0608	0.0548	0.0493	0.0442	0.0395	0.0352	0.0313	7
2	0.1985	0.1880	0.1776	0.1672	0.1569	0.1469	0.1371	0.1275	0.1183	0.1094	6
3	0.2759	0.2723	0.2679	0.2627	0.2568	0.2503	0.2431	0.2355	0.2273	0.2188	5
4	0.2397	0.2465	0.2526	0.2580	0.2627	0.2665	0.2695	0.2717	0.2730	0.2734	4
5	0.1332	0.1428	0.1525	0.1622	0.1719	0.1816	0.1912	0.2006	0.2098	0.2188	3
6	0.0463	0.0517	0.0575	0.0637	0.0703	0.0774	0.0848	0.0926	0.1008	0.1094	2
7	0.0092	0.0107	0.0124	0.0143	0.0164	0.0188	0.0215	0.0244	0.0277	0.0313	1
8	0.0008	0.0010	0.0012	0.0014	0.0017	0.0020	0.0024	0.0028	0.0033	0.0039	0
	q = 0.59	q = 0.58	q = 0.57	q = 0.56	q = 0.55	q = 0.54	q = 0.53	q = 0.52	q = 0.51	q = 0.50	

n = 9

x	p = 0.01	p = 0.02	p = 0.03	p = 0.04	p = 0.05	p = 0.06	p = 0.07	p = 0.08	p = 0.09	p = 0.10	n − x
0	0.9135	0.8337	0.7602	0.6925	0.6302	0.5730	0.5204	0.4722	0.4279	0.3874	9
1	0.0830	0.1531	0.2116	0.2597	0.2985	0.3292	0.3525	0.3695	0.3809	0.3874	8
2	0.0034	0.0125	0.0262	0.0433	0.0629	0.0840	0.1061	0.1285	0.1507	0.1722	7
3	0.0001	0.0006	0.0019	0.0042	0.0077	0.0125	0.0186	0.0261	0.0348	0.0446	6
4	0.0000	0.0000	0.0001	0.0003	0.0006	0.0012	0.0021	0.0034	0.0052	0.0074	5
5	0.0000	0.0000	0.0000	0.0000	0.0000	0.0001	0.0002	0.0003	0.0005	0.0008	4
6	0.0000	0.0000	0.0000	0.0000	0.0000	0.0000	0.0000	0.0000	0.0000	0.0001	3
7	0.0000	0.0000	0.0000	0.0000	0.0000	0.0000	0.0000	0.0000	0.0000	0.0000	2
8	0.0000	0.0000	0.0000	0.0000	0.0000	0.0000	0.0000	0.0000	0.0000	0.0000	1
9	0.0000	0.0000	0.0000	0.0000	0.0000	0.0000	0.0000	0.0000	0.0000	0.0000	0
	q = 0.99	q = 0.98	q = 0.97	q = 0.96	q = 0.95	q = 0.94	q = 0.93	q = 0.92	q = 0.91	q = 0.90	

x	p = 0.11	p = 0.12	p = 0.13	p = 0.14	p = 0.15	p = 0.16	p = 0.17	p = 0.18	p = 0.19	p = 0.20	n − x
0	0.3504	0.3165	0.2855	0.2573	0.2316	0.2082	0.1869	0.1676	0.1501	0.1342	9
1	0.3897	0.3884	0.3840	0.3770	0.3679	0.3569	0.3446	0.3312	0.3169	0.3020	8
2	0.1927	0.2119	0.2295	0.2455	0.2597	0.2720	0.2823	0.2908	0.2973	0.3020	7
3	0.0556	0.0674	0.0800	0.0933	0.1069	0.1209	0.1349	0.1489	0.1627	0.1762	6
4	0.0103	0.0138	0.0179	0.0228	0.0283	0.0345	0.0415	0.0490	0.0573	0.0661	5
5	0.0013	0.0019	0.0027	0.0037	0.0050	0.0066	0.0085	0.0108	0.0134	0.0165	4
6	0.0001	0.0002	0.0003	0.0004	0.0006	0.0008	0.0012	0.0016	0.0021	0.0028	3
7	0.0000	0.0000	0.0000	0.0000	0.0000	0.0001	0.0001	0.0001	0.0002	0.0003	2
8	0.0000	0.0000	0.0000	0.0000	0.0000	0.0000	0.0000	0.0000	0.0000	0.0000	1
9	0.0000	0.0000	0.0000	0.0000	0.0000	0.0000	0.0000	0.0000	0.0000	0.0000	0
	q = 0.89	q = 0.88	q = 0.87	q = 0.86	q = 0.85	q = 0.84	q = 0.83	q = 0.82	q = 0.81	q = 0.80	

x	p = 0.21	p = 0.22	p = 0.23	p = 0.24	p = 0.25	p = 0.26	p = 0.27	p = 0.28	p = 0.29	p = 0.30	n − x
0	0.1199	0.1069	0.0952	0.0846	0.0751	0.0665	0.0589	0.0520	0.0458	0.0404	9
1	0.2867	0.2713	0.2558	0.2404	0.2253	0.2104	0.1960	0.1820	0.1685	0.1556	8
2	0.3049	0.3061	0.3056	0.3037	0.3003	0.2957	0.2899	0.2831	0.2754	0.2668	7
3	0.1891	0.2014	0.2130	0.2238	0.2336	0.2424	0.2502	0.2569	0.2624	0.2668	6
4	0.0754	0.0852	0.0954	0.1060	0.1168	0.1278	0.1388	0.1499	0.1608	0.1715	5
5	0.0200	0.0240	0.0285	0.0335	0.0389	0.0449	0.0513	0.0583	0.0657	0.0735	4
6	0.0036	0.0045	0.0057	0.0070	0.0087	0.0105	0.0127	0.0151	0.0179	0.0210	3
7	0.0004	0.0005	0.0007	0.0010	0.0012	0.0016	0.0020	0.0025	0.0031	0.0039	2
8	0.0000	0.0000	0.0001	0.0001	0.0001	0.0001	0.0002	0.0002	0.0003	0.0004	1
9	0.0000	0.0000	0.0000	0.0000	0.0000	0.0000	0.0000	0.0000	0.0000	0.0000	0
	q = 0.79	q = 0.78	q = 0.77	q = 0.76	q = 0.75	q = 0.74	q = 0.73	q = 0.72	q = 0.71	q = 0.70	

continued

x	p = 0.31	p = 0.32	p = 0.33	p = 0.34	p = 0.35	p = 0.36	p = 0.37	p = 0.38	p = 0.39	p = 0.40	n − x
0	0.0355	0.0311	0.0272	0.0238	0.0207	0.0180	0.0156	0.0135	0.0117	0.0101	9
1	0.1433	0.1317	0.1206	0.1102	0.1004	0.0912	0.0826	0.0747	0.0673	0.0605	8
2	0.2576	0.2478	0.2376	0.2270	0.2162	0.2052	0.1941	0.1831	0.1721	0.1612	7
3	0.2701	0.2721	0.2731	0.2729	0.2716	0.2693	0.2660	0.2618	0.2567	0.2508	6
4	0.1820	0.1921	0.2017	0.2109	0.2194	0.2272	0.2344	0.2407	0.2462	0.2508	5
5	0.0818	0.0904	0.0994	0.1086	0.1181	0.1278	0.1376	0.1475	0.1574	0.1672	4
6	0.0245	0.0284	0.0326	0.0373	0.0424	0.0479	0.0539	0.0603	0.0671	0.0743	3
7	0.0047	0.0057	0.0069	0.0082	0.0098	0.0116	0.0136	0.0158	0.0184	0.0212	2
8	0.0005	0.0007	0.0008	0.0011	0.0013	0.0016	0.0020	0.0024	0.0029	0.0035	1
9	0.0000	0.0000	0.0000	0.0001	0.0001	0.0001	0.0001	0.0002	0.0002	0.0003	0
	q = 0.69	q = 0.68	q = 0.67	q = 0.66	q = 0.65	q = 0.64	q = 0.63	q = 0.62	q = 0.61	q = 0.60	

x	p = 0.41	p = 0.42	p = 0.43	p = 0.44	p = 0.45	p = 0.46	p = 0.47	p = 0.48	p = 0.49	p = 0.50	n − x
0	0.0087	0.0074	0.0064	0.0054	0.0046	0.0039	0.0033	0.0028	0.0023	0.0020	9
1	0.0542	0.0484	0.0431	0.0383	0.0339	0.0299	0.0263	0.0231	0.0202	0.0176	8
2	0.1506	0.1402	0.1301	0.1204	0.1110	0.1020	0.0934	0.0853	0.0776	0.0703	7
3	0.2442	0.2369	0.2291	0.2207	0.2119	0.2027	0.1933	0.1837	0.1739	0.1641	6
4	0.2545	0.2573	0.2592	0.2601	0.2600	0.2590	0.2571	0.2543	0.2506	0.2461	5
5	0.1769	0.1863	0.1955	0.2044	0.2128	0.2207	0.2280	0.2347	0.2408	0.2461	4
6	0.0819	0.0900	0.0983	0.1070	0.1160	0.1253	0.1348	0.1445	0.1542	0.1641	3
7	0.0244	0.0279	0.0318	0.0360	0.0407	0.0458	0.0512	0.0571	0.0635	0.0703	2
8	0.0042	0.0051	0.0060	0.0071	0.0083	0.0097	0.0114	0.0132	0.0153	0.0176	1
9	0.0003	0.0004	0.0005	0.0006	0.0008	0.0009	0.0011	0.0014	0.0016	0.0020	0
	q = 0.59	q = 0.58	q = 0.57	q = 0.56	q = 0.55	q = 0.54	q = 0.53	q = 0.52	q = 0.51	q = 0.50	

n = 10

x	p = 0.01	p = 0.02	p = 0.03	p = 0.04	p = 0.05	p = 0.06	p = 0.07	p = 0.08	p = 0.09	p = 0.10	n − x
0	0.9044	0.8171	0.7374	0.6648	0.5987	0.5386	0.4840	0.4344	0.3894	0.3487	10
1	0.0914	0.1667	0.2281	0.2770	0.3151	0.3438	0.3643	0.3777	0.3851	0.3874	9
2	0.0042	0.0153	0.0317	0.0519	0.0746	0.0988	0.1234	0.1478	0.1714	0.1937	8
3	0.0001	0.0008	0.0026	0.0058	0.0105	0.0168	0.0248	0.0343	0.0452	0.0574	7
4	0.0000	0.0000	0.0001	0.0004	0.0010	0.0019	0.0033	0.0052	0.0078	0.0112	6
5	0.0000	0.0000	0.0000	0.0000	0.0001	0.0001	0.0003	0.0005	0.0009	0.0015	5
6	0.0000	0.0000	0.0000	0.0000	0.0000	0.0000	0.0000	0.0000	0.0001	0.0001	4
7	0.0000	0.0000	0.0000	0.0000	0.0000	0.0000	0.0000	0.0000	0.0000	0.0000	3
8	0.0000	0.0000	0.0000	0.0000	0.0000	0.0000	0.0000	0.0000	0.0000	0.0000	2
9	0.0000	0.0000	0.0000	0.0000	0.0000	0.0000	0.0000	0.0000	0.0000	0.0000	1
10	0.0000	0.0000	0.0000	0.0000	0.0000	0.0000	0.0000	0.0000	0.0000	0.0000	0
	q = 0.99	q = 0.98	q = 0.97	q = 0.96	q = 0.95	q = 0.94	q = 0.93	q = 0.92	q = 0.91	q = 0.90	

x	p = 0.11	p = 0.12	p = 0.13	p = 0.14	p = 0.15	p = 0.16	p = 0.17	p = 0.18	p = 0.19	p = 0.20	n − x
0	0.3118	0.2785	0.2484	0.2213	0.1969	0.1749	0.1552	0.1374	0.1216	0.1074	10
1	0.3854	0.3798	0.3712	0.3603	0.3474	0.3331	0.3178	0.3017	0.2852	0.2684	9
2	0.2143	0.2330	0.2496	0.2639	0.2759	0.2856	0.2929	0.2980	0.3010	0.3020	8
3	0.0706	0.0847	0.0995	0.1146	0.1298	0.1450	0.1600	0.1745	0.1883	0.2013	7
4	0.0153	0.0202	0.0260	0.0326	0.0401	0.0483	0.0573	0.0670	0.0773	0.0881	6
5	0.0023	0.0033	0.0047	0.0064	0.0085	0.0111	0.0141	0.0177	0.0218	0.0264	5
6	0.0002	0.0004	0.0006	0.0009	0.0012	0.0018	0.0024	0.0032	0.0043	0.0055	4
7	0.0000	0.0000	0.0000	0.0001	0.0001	0.0002	0.0003	0.0004	0.0006	0.0008	3
8	0.0000	0.0000	0.0000	0.0000	0.0000	0.0000	0.0000	0.0000	0.0001	0.0001	2
9	0.0000	0.0000	0.0000	0.0000	0.0000	0.0000	0.0000	0.0000	0.0000	0.0000	1
10	0.0000	0.0000	0.0000	0.0000	0.0000	0.0000	0.0000	0.0000	0.0000	0.0000	0
	q = 0.89	q = 0.88	q = 0.87	q = 0.86	q = 0.85	q = 0.84	q = 0.83	q = 0.82	q = 0.81	q = 0.80	

x	p = 0.21	p = 0.22	p = 0.23	p = 0.24	p = 0.25	p = 0.26	p = 0.27	p = 0.28	p = 0.29	p = 0.30	n − x
0	0.0947	0.0834	0.0733	0.0643	0.0563	0.0492	0.0430	0.0374	0.0326	0.0282	10
1	0.2517	0.2351	0.2188	0.2030	0.1877	0.1730	0.1590	0.1456	0.1330	0.1211	9
2	0.3011	0.2984	0.2942	0.2885	0.2816	0.2735	0.2646	0.2548	0.2444	0.2335	8
3	0.2134	0.2244	0.2343	0.2429	0.2503	0.2563	0.2609	0.2642	0.2662	0.2668	7
4	0.0993	0.1108	0.1225	0.1343	0.1460	0.1576	0.1689	0.1798	0.1903	0.2001	6
5	0.0317	0.0375	0.0439	0.0509	0.0584	0.0664	0.0750	0.0839	0.0933	0.1029	5
6	0.0070	0.0088	0.0109	0.0134	0.0162	0.0195	0.0231	0.0272	0.0317	0.0368	4
7	0.0011	0.0014	0.0019	0.0024	0.0031	0.0039	0.0049	0.0060	0.0074	0.0090	3
8	0.0001	0.0002	0.0002	0.0003	0.0004	0.0005	0.0007	0.0009	0.0011	0.0014	2
9	0.0000	0.0000	0.0000	0.0000	0.0000	0.0000	0.0001	0.0001	0.0001	0.0001	1
10	0.0000	0.0000	0.0000	0.0000	0.0000	0.0000	0.0000	0.0000	0.0000	0.0000	0
	q = 0.79	q = 0.78	q = 0.77	q = 0.76	q = 0.75	q = 0.74	q = 0.73	q = 0.72	q = 0.71	q = 0.70	

x	p = 0.31	p = 0.32	p = 0.33	p = 0.34	p = 0.35	p = 0.36	p = 0.37	p = 0.38	p = 0.39	p = 0.40	n − x
0	0.0245	0.0211	0.0182	0.0157	0.0135	0.0115	0.0098	0.0084	0.0071	0.0060	10
1	0.1099	0.0995	0.0898	0.0808	0.0725	0.0649	0.0578	0.0514	0.0456	0.0403	9
2	0.2222	0.2107	0.1990	0.1873	0.1757	0.1642	0.1529	0.1419	0.1312	0.1209	8
3	0.2662	0.2644	0.2614	0.2573	0.2522	0.2462	0.2394	0.2319	0.2237	0.2150	7
4	0.2093	0.2177	0.2253	0.2320	0.2377	0.2424	0.2461	0.2487	0.2503	0.2508	6
5	0.1128	0.1229	0.1332	0.1434	0.1536	0.1636	0.1734	0.1829	0.1920	0.2007	5
6	0.0422	0.0482	0.0547	0.0616	0.0689	0.0767	0.0849	0.0934	0.1023	0.1115	4
7	0.0108	0.0130	0.0154	0.0181	0.0212	0.0247	0.0285	0.0327	0.0374	0.0425	3
8	0.0018	0.0023	0.0028	0.0035	0.0043	0.0052	0.0063	0.0075	0.0090	0.0106	2
9	0.0002	0.0002	0.0003	0.0004	0.0005	0.0006	0.0008	0.0010	0.0013	0.0016	1
10	0.0000	0.0000	0.0000	0.0000	0.0000	0.0000	0.0000	0.0001	0.0001	0.0001	0
	q = 0.69	q = 0.68	q = 0.67	q = 0.66	q = 0.65	q = 0.64	q = 0.63	q = 0.62	q = 0.61	q = 0.60	

x	p = 0.41	p = 0.42	p = 0.43	p = 0.44	p = 0.45	p = 0.46	p = 0.47	p = 0.48	p = 0.49	p = 0.50	n − x
0	0.0051	0.0043	0.0036	0.0030	0.0025	0.0021	0.0017	0.0014	0.0012	0.0010	10
1	0.0355	0.0312	0.0273	0.0238	0.0207	0.0180	0.0155	0.0133	0.0114	0.0098	9
2	0.1111	0.1017	0.0927	0.0843	0.0763	0.0688	0.0619	0.0554	0.0494	0.0439	8
3	0.2058	0.1963	0.1865	0.1765	0.1665	0.1564	0.1464	0.1364	0.1267	0.1172	7
4	0.2503	0.2488	0.2462	0.2427	0.2384	0.2331	0.2271	0.2204	0.2130	0.2051	6
5	0.2087	0.2162	0.2229	0.2289	0.2340	0.2383	0.2417	0.2441	0.2456	0.2461	5
6	0.1209	0.1304	0.1401	0.1499	0.1596	0.1692	0.1786	0.1878	0.1966	0.2051	4
7	0.0480	0.0540	0.0604	0.0673	0.0746	0.0824	0.0905	0.0991	0.1080	0.1172	3
8	0.0125	0.0147	0.0171	0.0198	0.0229	0.0263	0.0301	0.0343	0.0389	0.0439	2
9	0.0019	0.0024	0.0029	0.0035	0.0042	0.0050	0.0059	0.0070	0.0083	0.0098	1
10	0.0001	0.0002	0.0002	0.0003	0.0003	0.0004	0.0005	0.0006	0.0008	0.0010	0
	q = 0.59	q = 0.58	q = 0.57	q = 0.56	q = 0.55	q = 0.54	q = 0.53	q = 0.52	q = 0.51	q = 0.50	

$n = 11$

x	p = 0.01	p = 0.02	p = 0.03	p = 0.04	p = 0.05	p = 0.06	p = 0.07	p = 0.08	p = 0.09	p = 0.10	n − x
0	0.8953	0.8007	0.7153	0.6382	0.5688	0.5063	0.4501	0.3996	0.3544	0.3138	11
1	0.0995	0.1798	0.2433	0.2925	0.3293	0.3555	0.3727	0.3823	0.3855	0.3835	10
2	0.0050	0.0183	0.0376	0.0609	0.0867	0.1135	0.1403	0.1662	0.1906	0.2131	9
3	0.0002	0.0011	0.0035	0.0076	0.0137	0.0217	0.0317	0.0434	0.0566	0.0710	8
4	0.0000	0.0000	0.0002	0.0006	0.0014	0.0028	0.0048	0.0075	0.0112	0.0158	7
5	0.0000	0.0000	0.0000	0.0000	0.0001	0.0002	0.0005	0.0009	0.0015	0.0025	6
6	0.0000	0.0000	0.0000	0.0000	0.0000	0.0000	0.0000	0.0001	0.0002	0.0003	5
7	0.0000	0.0000	0.0000	0.0000	0.0000	0.0000	0.0000	0.0000	0.0000	0.0000	4
8	0.0000	0.0000	0.0000	0.0000	0.0000	0.0000	0.0000	0.0000	0.0000	0.0000	3
9	0.0000	0.0000	0.0000	0.0000	0.0000	0.0000	0.0000	0.0000	0.0000	0.0000	2
10	0.0000	0.0000	0.0000	0.0000	0.0000	0.0000	0.0000	0.0000	0.0000	0.0000	1
11	0.0000	0.0000	0.0000	0.0000	0.0000	0.0000	0.0000	0.0000	0.0000	0.0000	0
	q = 0.99	q = 0.98	q = 0.97	q = 0.96	q = 0.95	q = 0.94	q = 0.93	q = 0.92	q = 0.91	q = 0.90	

continued

x	p = 0.11	p = 0.12	p = 0.13	p = 0.14	p = 0.15	p = 0.16	p = 0.17	p = 0.18	p = 0.19	p = 0.20	n − x
0	0.2775	0.2451	0.2161	0.1903	0.1673	0.1469	0.1288	0.1127	0.0985	0.0859	11
1	0.3773	0.3676	0.3552	0.3408	0.3248	0.3078	0.2901	0.2721	0.2541	0.2362	10
2	0.2332	0.2507	0.2654	0.2774	0.2866	0.2932	0.2971	0.2987	0.2980	0.2953	9
3	0.0865	0.1025	0.1190	0.1355	0.1517	0.1675	0.1826	0.1967	0.2097	0.2215	8
4	0.0214	0.0280	0.0356	0.0441	0.0536	0.0638	0.0748	0.0864	0.0984	0.1107	7
5	0.0037	0.0053	0.0074	0.0101	0.0132	0.0170	0.0214	0.0265	0.0323	0.0388	6
6	0.0005	0.0007	0.0011	0.0016	0.0023	0.0032	0.0044	0.0058	0.0076	0.0097	5
7	0.0000	0.0001	0.0001	0.0002	0.0003	0.0004	0.0006	0.0009	0.0013	0.0017	4
8	0.0000	0.0000	0.0000	0.0000	0.0000	0.0000	0.0001	0.0001	0.0001	0.0002	3
9	0.0000	0.0000	0.0000	0.0000	0.0000	0.0000	0.0000	0.0000	0.0000	0.0000	2
10	0.0000	0.0000	0.0000	0.0000	0.0000	0.0000	0.0000	0.0000	0.0000	0.0000	1
11	0.0000	0.0000	0.0000	0.0000	0.0000	0.0000	0.0000	0.0000	0.0000	0.0000	0
	q = 0.89	q = 0.88	q = 0.87	q = 0.86	q = 0.85	q = 0.84	q = 0.83	q = 0.82	q = 0.81	q = 0.80	

x	p = 0.21	p = 0.22	p = 0.23	p = 0.24	p = 0.25	p = 0.26	p = 0.27	p = 0.28	p = 0.29	p = 0.30	n − x
0	0.0748	0.0650	0.0564	0.0489	0.0422	0.0364	0.0314	0.0270	0.0231	0.0198	11
1	0.2187	0.2017	0.1854	0.1697	0.1549	0.1408	0.1276	0.1153	0.1038	0.0932	10
2	0.2907	0.2845	0.2768	0.2680	0.2581	0.2474	0.2360	0.2242	0.2121	0.1998	9
3	0.2318	0.2407	0.2481	0.2539	0.2581	0.2608	0.2619	0.2616	0.2599	0.2568	8
4	0.1232	0.1358	0.1482	0.1603	0.1721	0.1832	0.1937	0.2035	0.2123	0.2201	7
5	0.0459	0.0536	0.0620	0.0709	0.0803	0.0901	0.1003	0.1108	0.1214	0.1321	6
6	0.0122	0.0151	0.0185	0.0224	0.0268	0.0317	0.0371	0.0431	0.0496	0.0566	5
7	0.0023	0.0030	0.0039	0.0050	0.0064	0.0079	0.0098	0.0120	0.0145	0.0173	4
8	0.0003	0.0004	0.0006	0.0008	0.0011	0.0014	0.0018	0.0023	0.0030	0.0037	3
9	0.0000	0.0000	0.0001	0.0001	0.0001	0.0002	0.0002	0.0003	0.0004	0.0005	2
10	0.0000	0.0000	0.0000	0.0000	0.0000	0.0000	0.0000	0.0000	0.0000	0.0000	1
11	0.0000	0.0000	0.0000	0.0000	0.0000	0.0000	0.0000	0.0000	0.0000	0.0000	0
	q = 0.79	q = 0.78	q = 0.77	q = 0.76	q = 0.75	q = 0.74	q = 0.73	q = 0.72	q = 0.71	q = 0.70	

x	p = 0.31	p = 0.32	p = 0.33	p = 0.34	p = 0.35	p = 0.36	p = 0.37	p = 0.38	p = 0.39	p = 0.40	n − x
0	0.0169	0.0144	0.0122	0.0104	0.0088	0.0074	0.0062	0.0052	0.0044	0.0036	11
1	0.0834	0.0744	0.0662	0.0587	0.0518	0.0457	0.0401	0.0351	0.0306	0.0266	10
2	0.1874	0.1751	0.1630	0.1511	0.1395	0.1284	0.1177	0.1075	0.0978	0.0887	9
3	0.2526	0.2472	0.2408	0.2335	0.2254	0.2167	0.2074	0.1977	0.1876	0.1774	8
4	0.2269	0.2326	0.2372	0.2406	0.2428	0.2438	0.2436	0.2423	0.2399	0.2365	7
5	0.1427	0.1533	0.1636	0.1735	0.1830	0.1920	0.2003	0.2079	0.2148	0.2207	6
6	0.0641	0.0721	0.0806	0.0894	0.0985	0.1080	0.1176	0.1274	0.1373	0.1471	5
7	0.0206	0.0242	0.0283	0.0329	0.0379	0.0434	0.0494	0.0558	0.0627	0.0701	4
8	0.0046	0.0057	0.0070	0.0085	0.0102	0.0122	0.0145	0.0171	0.0200	0.0234	3
9	0.0007	0.0009	0.0011	0.0015	0.0018	0.0023	0.0028	0.0035	0.0043	0.0052	2
10	0.0001	0.0001	0.0001	0.0001	0.0002	0.0003	0.0003	0.0004	0.0005	0.0007	1
11	0.0000	0.0000	0.0000	0.0000	0.0000	0.0000	0.0000	0.0000	0.0000	0.0000	0
	q = 0.69	q = 0.68	q = 0.67	q = 0.66	q = 0.65	q = 0.64	q = 0.63	q = 0.62	q = 0.61	q = 0.60	

x	p = 0.41	p = 0.42	p = 0.43	p = 0.44	p = 0.45	p = 0.46	p = 0.47	p = 0.48	p = 0.49	p = 0.50	n − x
0	0.0030	0.0025	0.0021	0.0017	0.0014	0.0011	0.0009	0.0008	0.0006	0.0005	11
1	0.0231	0.0199	0.0171	0.0147	0.0125	0.0107	0.0090	0.0076	0.0064	0.0054	10
2	0.0801	0.0721	0.0646	0.0577	0.0513	0.0454	0.0401	0.0352	0.0308	0.0269	9
3	0.1670	0.1566	0.1462	0.1359	0.1259	0.1161	0.1067	0.0976	0.0888	0.0806	8
4	0.2321	0.2267	0.2206	0.2136	0.2060	0.1978	0.1892	0.1801	0.1707	0.1611	7
5	0.2258	0.2299	0.2329	0.2350	0.2360	0.2359	0.2348	0.2327	0.2296	0.2256	6
6	0.1569	0.1664	0.1757	0.1846	0.1931	0.2010	0.2083	0.2148	0.2206	0.2256	5
7	0.0779	0.0861	0.0947	0.1036	0.1128	0.1223	0.1319	0.1416	0.1514	0.1611	4
8	0.0271	0.0312	0.0357	0.0407	0.0462	0.0521	0.0585	0.0654	0.0727	0.0806	3
9	0.0063	0.0075	0.0090	0.0107	0.0126	0.0148	0.0173	0.0201	0.0233	0.0269	2
10	0.0009	0.0011	0.0014	0.0017	0.0021	0.0025	0.0031	0.0037	0.0045	0.0054	1
11	0.0001	0.0001	0.0001	0.0001	0.0002	0.0002	0.0002	0.0003	0.0004	0.0005	0
	q = 0.59	q = 0.58	q = 0.57	q = 0.56	q = 0.55	q = 0.54	q = 0.53	q = 0.52	q = 0.51	q = 0.50	

$$n = 12$$

x	p = 0.01	p = 0.02	p = 0.03	p = 0.04	p = 0.05	p = 0.06	p = 0.07	p = 0.08	p = 0.09	p = 0.10	n − x
0	0.8864	0.7847	0.6938	0.6127	0.5404	0.4759	0.4186	0.3677	0.3225	0.2824	12
1	0.1074	0.1922	0.2575	0.3064	0.3413	0.3645	0.3781	0.3837	0.3827	0.3766	11
2	0.0060	0.0216	0.0438	0.0702	0.0988	0.1280	0.1565	0.1835	0.2082	0.2301	10
3	0.0002	0.0015	0.0045	0.0098	0.0173	0.0272	0.0393	0.0532	0.0686	0.0852	9
4	0.0000	0.0001	0.0003	0.0009	0.0021	0.0039	0.0067	0.0104	0.0153	0.0213	8
5	0.0000	0.0000	0.0000	0.0001	0.0002	0.0004	0.0008	0.0014	0.0024	0.0038	7
6	0.0000	0.0000	0.0000	0.0000	0.0000	0.0000	0.0001	0.0001	0.0003	0.0005	6
7	0.0000	0.0000	0.0000	0.0000	0.0000	0.0000	0.0000	0.0000	0.0000	0.0000	5
8	0.0000	0.0000	0.0000	0.0000	0.0000	0.0000	0.0000	0.0000	0.0000	0.0000	4
9	0.0000	0.0000	0.0000	0.0000	0.0000	0.0000	0.0000	0.0000	0.0000	0.0000	3
10	0.0000	0.0000	0.0000	0.0000	0.0000	0.0000	0.0000	0.0000	0.0000	0.0000	2
11	0.0000	0.0000	0.0000	0.0000	0.0000	0.0000	0.0000	0.0000	0.0000	0.0000	1
12	0.0000	0.0000	0.0000	0.0000	0.0000	0.0000	0.0000	0.0000	0.0000	0.0000	0
	q = 0.99	q = 0.98	q = 0.97	q = 0.96	q = 0.95	q = 0.94	q = 0.93	q = 0.92	q = 0.91	q = 0.90	

x	p = 0.11	p = 0.12	p = 0.13	p = 0.14	p = 0.15	p = 0.16	p = 0.17	p = 0.18	p = 0.19	p = 0.20	n − x
0	0.2470	0.2157	0.1880	0.1637	0.1422	0.1234	0.1069	0.0924	0.0798	0.0687	12
1	0.3663	0.3529	0.3372	0.3197	0.3012	0.2821	0.2627	0.2434	0.2245	0.2062	11
2	0.2490	0.2647	0.2771	0.2863	0.2924	0.2955	0.2960	0.2939	0.2897	0.2835	10
3	0.1026	0.1203	0.1380	0.1553	0.1720	0.1876	0.2021	0.2151	0.2265	0.2362	9
4	0.0285	0.0369	0.0464	0.0569	0.0683	0.0804	0.0931	0.1062	0.1195	0.1329	8
5	0.0056	0.0081	0.0111	0.0148	0.0193	0.0245	0.0305	0.0373	0.0449	0.0532	7
6	0.0008	0.0013	0.0019	0.0028	0.0040	0.0054	0.0073	0.0096	0.0123	0.0155	6
7	0.0001	0.0001	0.0002	0.0004	0.0006	0.0009	0.0013	0.0018	0.0025	0.0033	5
8	0.0000	0.0000	0.0000	0.0000	0.0001	0.0001	0.0002	0.0002	0.0004	0.0005	4
9	0.0000	0.0000	0.0000	0.0000	0.0000	0.0000	0.0000	0.0000	0.0000	0.0001	3
10	0.0000	0.0000	0.0000	0.0000	0.0000	0.0000	0.0000	0.0000	0.0000	0.0000	2
11	0.0000	0.0000	0.0000	0.0000	0.0000	0.0000	0.0000	0.0000	0.0000	0.0000	1
12	0.0000	0.0000	0.0000	0.0000	0.0000	0.0000	0.0000	0.0000	0.0000	0.0000	0
	q = 0.89	q = 0.88	q = 0.87	q = 0.86	q = 0.85	q = 0.84	q = 0.83	q = 0.82	q = 0.81	q = 0.80	

x	p = 0.21	p = 0.22	p = 0.23	p = 0.24	p = 0.25	p = 0.26	p = 0.27	p = 0.28	p = 0.29	p = 0.30	n − x
0	0.0591	0.0507	0.0434	0.0371	0.0317	0.0270	0.0229	0.0194	0.0164	0.0138	12
1	0.1885	0.1717	0.1557	0.1407	0.1267	0.1137	0.1016	0.0906	0.0804	0.0712	11
2	0.2756	0.2663	0.2558	0.2444	0.2323	0.2197	0.2068	0.1937	0.1807	0.1678	10
3	0.2442	0.2503	0.2547	0.2573	0.2581	0.2573	0.2549	0.2511	0.2460	0.2397	9
4	0.1460	0.1589	0.1712	0.1828	0.1936	0.2034	0.2122	0.2197	0.2261	0.2311	8
5	0.0621	0.0717	0.0818	0.0924	0.1032	0.1143	0.1255	0.1367	0.1477	0.1585	7
6	0.0193	0.0236	0.0285	0.0340	0.0401	0.0469	0.0542	0.0620	0.0704	0.0792	6
7	0.0044	0.0057	0.0073	0.0092	0.0115	0.0141	0.0172	0.0207	0.0246	0.0291	5
8	0.0007	0.0010	0.0014	0.0018	0.0024	0.0031	0.0040	0.0050	0.0063	0.0078	4
9	0.0001	0.0001	0.0002	0.0003	0.0004	0.0005	0.0007	0.0009	0.0011	0.0015	3
10	0.0000	0.0000	0.0000	0.0000	0.0000	0.0001	0.0001	0.0001	0.0001	0.0002	2
11	0.0000	0.0000	0.0000	0.0000	0.0000	0.0000	0.0000	0.0000	0.0000	0.0000	1
12	0.0000	0.0000	0.0000	0.0000	0.0000	0.0000	0.0000	0.0000	0.0000	0.0000	0
	q = 0.79	q = 0.78	q = 0.77	q = 0.76	q = 0.75	q = 0.74	q = 0.73	q = 0.72	q = 0.71	q = 0.70	

continued

x	p = 0.31	p = 0.32	p = 0.33	p = 0.34	p = 0.35	p = 0.36	p = 0.37	p = 0.38	p = 0.39	p = 0.40	n − x
0	0.0116	0.0098	0.0082	0.0068	0.0057	0.0047	0.0039	0.0032	0.0027	0.0022	12
1	0.0628	0.0552	0.0484	0.0422	0.0368	0.0319	0.0276	0.0237	0.0204	0.0174	11
2	0.1552	0.1429	0.1310	0.1197	0.1088	0.0986	0.0890	0.0800	0.0716	0.0639	10
3	0.2324	0.2241	0.2151	0.2055	0.1954	0.1849	0.1742	0.1634	0.1526	0.1419	9
4	0.2349	0.2373	0.2384	0.2382	0.2367	0.2340	0.2302	0.2254	0.2195	0.2128	8
5	0.1688	0.1787	0.1879	0.1963	0.2039	0.2106	0.2163	0.2210	0.2246	0.2270	7
6	0.0885	0.0981	0.1079	0.1180	0.1281	0.1382	0.1482	0.1580	0.1675	0.1766	6
7	0.0341	0.0396	0.0456	0.0521	0.0591	0.0666	0.0746	0.0830	0.0918	0.1009	5
8	0.0096	0.0116	0.0140	0.0168	0.0199	0.0234	0.0274	0.0318	0.0367	0.0420	4
9	0.0019	0.0024	0.0031	0.0038	0.0048	0.0059	0.0071	0.0087	0.0104	0.0125	3
10	0.0003	0.0003	0.0005	0.0006	0.0008	0.0010	0.0013	0.0016	0.0020	0.0025	2
11	0.0000	0.0000	0.0000	0.0001	0.0001	0.0001	0.0001	0.0002	0.0002	0.0003	1
12	0.0000	0.0000	0.0000	0.0000	0.0000	0.0000	0.0000	0.0000	0.0000	0.0000	0
	q = 0.69	q = 0.68	q = 0.67	q = 0.66	q = 0.65	q = 0.64	q = 0.63	q = 0.62	q = 0.61	q = 0.60	

x	p = 0.41	p = 0.42	p = 0.43	p = 0.44	p = 0.45	p = 0.46	p = 0.47	p = 0.48	p = 0.49	p = 0.50	n − x
0	0.0018	0.0014	0.0012	0.0010	0.0008	0.0006	0.0005	0.0004	0.0003	0.0002	12
1	0.0148	0.0126	0.0106	0.0090	0.0075	0.0063	0.0052	0.0043	0.0036	0.0029	11
2	0.0567	0.0502	0.0442	0.0388	0.0339	0.0294	0.0255	0.0220	0.0189	0.0161	10
3	0.1314	0.1211	0.1111	0.1015	0.0923	0.0836	0.0754	0.0676	0.0604	0.0537	9
4	0.2054	0.1973	0.1886	0.1794	0.1700	0.1602	0.1504	0.1405	0.1306	0.1208	8
5	0.2284	0.2285	0.2276	0.2256	0.2225	0.2184	0.2134	0.2075	0.2008	0.1934	7
6	0.1851	0.1931	0.2003	0.2068	0.2124	0.2171	0.2208	0.2234	0.2250	0.2256	6
7	0.1103	0.1198	0.1295	0.1393	0.1489	0.1585	0.1678	0.1768	0.1853	0.1934	5
8	0.0479	0.0542	0.0611	0.0684	0.0762	0.0844	0.0930	0.1020	0.1113	0.1208	4
9	0.0148	0.0175	0.0205	0.0239	0.0277	0.0319	0.0367	0.0418	0.0475	0.0537	3
10	0.0031	0.0038	0.0046	0.0056	0.0068	0.0082	0.0098	0.0116	0.0137	0.0161	2
11	0.0004	0.0005	0.0006	0.0008	0.0010	0.0013	0.0016	0.0019	0.0024	0.0029	1
12	0.0000	0.0000	0.0000	0.0001	0.0001	0.0001	0.0001	0.0001	0.0002	0.0002	0
	q = 0.59	q = 0.58	q = 0.57	q = 0.56	q = 0.55	q = 0.54	q = 0.53	q = 0.52	q = 0.51	q = 0.50	

n = 13

x	p = 0.01	p = 0.02	p = 0.03	p = 0.04	p = 0.05	p = 0.06	p = 0.07	p = 0.08	p = 0.09	p = 0.10	n − x
0	0.8775	0.7690	0.6730	0.5882	0.5133	0.4474	0.3893	0.3383	0.2935	0.2542	13
1	0.1152	0.2040	0.2706	0.3186	0.3512	0.3712	0.3809	0.3824	0.3773	0.3672	12
2	0.0070	0.0250	0.0502	0.0797	0.1109	0.1422	0.1720	0.1995	0.2239	0.2448	11
3	0.0003	0.0019	0.0057	0.0122	0.0214	0.0333	0.0475	0.0636	0.0812	0.0997	10
4	0.0000	0.0001	0.0004	0.0013	0.0028	0.0053	0.0089	0.0138	0.0201	0.0277	9
5	0.0000	0.0000	0.0000	0.0001	0.0003	0.0006	0.0012	0.0022	0.0036	0.0055	8
6	0.0000	0.0000	0.0000	0.0000	0.0000	0.0001	0.0001	0.0003	0.0005	0.0008	7
7	0.0000	0.0000	0.0000	0.0000	0.0000	0.0000	0.0000	0.0000	0.0000	0.0001	6
8	0.0000	0.0000	0.0000	0.0000	0.0000	0.0000	0.0000	0.0000	0.0000	0.0000	5
9	0.0000	0.0000	0.0000	0.0000	0.0000	0.0000	0.0000	0.0000	0.0000	0.0000	4
10	0.0000	0.0000	0.0000	0.0000	0.0000	0.0000	0.0000	0.0000	0.0000	0.0000	3
11	0.0000	0.0000	0.0000	0.0000	0.0000	0.0000	0.0000	0.0000	0.0000	0.0000	2
12	0.0000	0.0000	0.0000	0.0000	0.0000	0.0000	0.0000	0.0000	0.0000	0.0000	1
13	0.0000	0.0000	0.0000	0.0000	0.0000	0.0000	0.0000	0.0000	0.0000	0.0000	0
	q = 0.99	q = 0.98	q = 0.97	q = 0.96	q = 0.95	q = 0.94	q = 0.93	q = 0.92	q = 0.91	q = 0.90	

x	p = 0.11	p = 0.12	p = 0.13	p = 0.14	p = 0.15	p = 0.16	p = 0.17	p = 0.18	p = 0.19	p = 0.20	n − x
0	0.2198	0.1898	0.1636	0.1408	0.1209	0.1037	0.0887	0.0758	0.0646	0.0550	13
1	0.3532	0.3364	0.3178	0.2979	0.2774	0.2567	0.2362	0.2163	0.1970	0.1787	12
2	0.2619	0.2753	0.2849	0.2910	0.2937	0.2934	0.2903	0.2848	0.2773	0.2680	11
3	0.1187	0.1376	0.1561	0.1737	0.1900	0.2049	0.2180	0.2293	0.2385	0.2457	10
4	0.0367	0.0469	0.0583	0.0707	0.0838	0.0976	0.1116	0.1258	0.1399	0.1535	9
5	0.0082	0.0115	0.0157	0.0207	0.0266	0.0335	0.0412	0.0497	0.0591	0.0691	8
6	0.0013	0.0021	0.0031	0.0045	0.0063	0.0085	0.0112	0.0145	0.0185	0.0230	7
7	0.0002	0.0003	0.0005	0.0007	0.0011	0.0016	0.0023	0.0032	0.0043	0.0058	6
8	0.0000	0.0000	0.0001	0.0001	0.0001	0.0002	0.0004	0.0005	0.0008	0.0011	5
9	0.0000	0.0000	0.0000	0.0000	0.0000	0.0000	0.0000	0.0001	0.0001	0.0001	4
10	0.0000	0.0000	0.0000	0.0000	0.0000	0.0000	0.0000	0.0000	0.0000	0.0000	3
11	0.0000	0.0000	0.0000	0.0000	0.0000	0.0000	0.0000	0.0000	0.0000	0.0000	2
12	0.0000	0.0000	0.0000	0.0000	0.0000	0.0000	0.0000	0.0000	0.0000	0.0000	1
13	0.0000	0.0000	0.0000	0.0000	0.0000	0.0000	0.0000	0.0000	0.0000	0.0000	0
	q = 0.89	q = 0.88	q = 0.87	q = 0.86	q = 0.85	q = 0.84	q = 0.83	q = 0.82	q = 0.81	q = 0.80	

x	p = 0.21	p = 0.22	p = 0.23	p = 0.24	p = 0.25	p = 0.26	p = 0.27	p = 0.28	p = 0.29	p = 0.30	n − x
0	0.0467	0.0396	0.0334	0.0282	0.0238	0.0200	0.0167	0.0140	0.0117	0.0097	13
1	0.1613	0.1450	0.1299	0.1159	0.1029	0.0911	0.0804	0.0706	0.0619	0.0540	12
2	0.2573	0.2455	0.2328	0.2195	0.2059	0.1921	0.1784	0.1648	0.1516	0.1388	11
3	0.2508	0.2539	0.2550	0.2542	0.2517	0.2475	0.2419	0.2351	0.2271	0.2181	10
4	0.1667	0.1790	0.1904	0.2007	0.2097	0.2174	0.2237	0.2285	0.2319	0.2337	9
5	0.0797	0.0909	0.1024	0.1141	0.1258	0.1375	0.1489	0.1600	0.1705	0.1803	8
6	0.0283	0.0342	0.0408	0.0480	0.0559	0.0644	0.0734	0.0829	0.0928	0.1030	7
7	0.0075	0.0096	0.0122	0.0152	0.0186	0.0226	0.0272	0.0323	0.0379	0.0442	6
8	0.0015	0.0020	0.0027	0.0036	0.0047	0.0060	0.0075	0.0094	0.0116	0.0142	5
9	0.0002	0.0003	0.0005	0.0006	0.0009	0.0012	0.0015	0.0020	0.0026	0.0034	4
10	0.0000	0.0000	0.0001	0.0001	0.0001	0.0002	0.0002	0.0003	0.0004	0.0006	3
11	0.0000	0.0000	0.0000	0.0000	0.0000	0.0000	0.0000	0.0000	0.0000	0.0001	2
12	0.0000	0.0000	0.0000	0.0000	0.0000	0.0000	0.0000	0.0000	0.0000	0.0000	1
13	0.0000	0.0000	0.0000	0.0000	0.0000	0.0000	0.0000	0.0000	0.0000	0.0000	0
	q = 0.79	q = 0.78	q = 0.77	q = 0.76	q = 0.75	q = 0.74	q = 0.73	q = 0.72	q = 0.71	q = 0.70	

x	p = 0.31	p = 0.32	p = 0.33	p = 0.34	p = 0.35	p = 0.36	p = 0.37	p = 0.38	p = 0.39	p = 0.40	n − x
0	0.0080	0.0066	0.0055	0.0045	0.0037	0.0030	0.0025	0.0020	0.0016	0.0013	13
1	0.0469	0.0407	0.0351	0.0302	0.0259	0.0221	0.0188	0.0159	0.0135	0.0113	12
2	0.1265	0.1148	0.1037	0.0933	0.0836	0.0746	0.0663	0.0586	0.0516	0.0453	11
3	0.2084	0.1981	0.1874	0.1763	0.1651	0.1538	0.1427	0.1317	0.1210	0.1107	10
4	0.2341	0.2331	0.2307	0.2270	0.2222	0.2163	0.2095	0.2018	0.1934	0.1845	9
5	0.1893	0.1974	0.2045	0.2105	0.2154	0.2190	0.2215	0.2227	0.2226	0.2214	8
6	0.1134	0.1239	0.1343	0.1446	0.1546	0.1643	0.1734	0.1820	0.1898	0.1968	7
7	0.0509	0.0583	0.0662	0.0745	0.0833	0.0924	0.1019	0.1115	0.1213	0.1312	6
8	0.0172	0.0206	0.0244	0.0288	0.0336	0.0390	0.0449	0.0513	0.0582	0.0656	5
9	0.0043	0.0054	0.0067	0.0082	0.0101	0.0122	0.0146	0.0175	0.0207	0.0243	4
10	0.0008	0.0010	0.0013	0.0017	0.0022	0.0027	0.0034	0.0043	0.0053	0.0065	3
11	0.0001	0.0001	0.0002	0.0002	0.0003	0.0004	0.0006	0.0007	0.0009	0.0012	2
12	0.0000	0.0000	0.0000	0.0000	0.0000	0.0000	0.0001	0.0001	0.0001	0.0001	1
13	0.0000	0.0000	0.0000	0.0000	0.0000	0.0000	0.0000	0.0000	0.0000	0.0000	0
	q = 0.69	q = 0.68	q = 0.67	q = 0.66	q = 0.65	q = 0.64	q = 0.63	q = 0.62	q = 0.61	q = 0.60	

continued

x	p = 0.41	p = 0.42	p = 0.43	p = 0.44	p = 0.45	p = 0.46	p = 0.47	p = 0.48	p = 0.49	p = 0.50	n − x
0	0.0010	0.0008	0.0007	0.0005	0.0004	0.0003	0.0003	0.0002	0.0002	0.0001	13
1	0.0095	0.0079	0.0066	0.0054	0.0045	0.0037	0.0030	0.0024	0.0020	0.0016	12
2	0.0395	0.0344	0.0298	0.0256	0.0220	0.0188	0.0160	0.0135	0.0114	0.0095	11
3	0.1007	0.0913	0.0823	0.0739	0.0660	0.0587	0.0519	0.0457	0.0401	0.0349	10
4	0.1750	0.1653	0.1553	0.1451	0.1350	0.1250	0.1151	0.1055	0.0962	0.0873	9
5	0.2189	0.2154	0.2108	0.2053	0.1989	0.1917	0.1838	0.1753	0.1664	0.1571	8
6	0.2029	0.2080	0.2121	0.2151	0.2169	0.2177	0.2173	0.2158	0.2131	0.2095	7
7	0.1410	0.1506	0.1600	0.1690	0.1775	0.1854	0.1927	0.1992	0.2048	0.2095	6
8	0.0735	0.0818	0.0905	0.0996	0.1089	0.1185	0.1282	0.1379	0.1476	0.1571	5
9	0.0284	0.0329	0.0379	0.0435	0.0495	0.0561	0.0631	0.0707	0.0788	0.0873	4
10	0.0079	0.0095	0.0114	0.0137	0.0162	0.0191	0.0224	0.0261	0.0303	0.0349	3
11	0.0015	0.0019	0.0024	0.0029	0.0036	0.0044	0.0054	0.0066	0.0079	0.0095	2
12	0.0002	0.0002	0.0003	0.0004	0.0005	0.0006	0.0008	0.0010	0.0013	0.0016	1
13	0.0000	0.0000	0.0000	0.0000	0.0000	0.0000	0.0001	0.0001	0.0001	0.0001	0
	q = 0.59	q = 0.58	q = 0.57	q = 0.56	q = 0.55	q = 0.54	q = 0.53	q = 0.52	q = 0.51	q = 0.50	

n = 14

x	p = 0.01	p = 0.02	p = 0.03	p = 0.04	p = 0.05	p = 0.06	p = 0.07	p = 0.08	p = 0.09	p = 0.10	n − x
0	0.8687	0.7536	0.6528	0.5647	0.4877	0.4205	0.3620	0.3112	0.2670	0.2288	14
1	0.1229	0.2153	0.2827	0.3294	0.3593	0.3758	0.3815	0.3788	0.3698	0.3559	13
2	0.0081	0.0286	0.0568	0.0892	0.1229	0.1559	0.1867	0.2141	0.2377	0.2570	12
3	0.0003	0.0023	0.0070	0.0149	0.0259	0.0398	0.0562	0.0745	0.0940	0.1142	11
4	0.0000	0.0001	0.0006	0.0017	0.0037	0.0070	0.0116	0.0178	0.0256	0.0349	10
5	0.0000	0.0000	0.0000	0.0001	0.0004	0.0009	0.0018	0.0031	0.0051	0.0078	9
6	0.0000	0.0000	0.0000	0.0000	0.0000	0.0001	0.0002	0.0004	0.0008	0.0013	8
7	0.0000	0.0000	0.0000	0.0000	0.0000	0.0000	0.0000	0.0000	0.0001	0.0002	7
8	0.0000	0.0000	0.0000	0.0000	0.0000	0.0000	0.0000	0.0000	0.0000	0.0000	6
9	0.0000	0.0000	0.0000	0.0000	0.0000	0.0000	0.0000	0.0000	0.0000	0.0000	5
10	0.0000	0.0000	0.0000	0.0000	0.0000	0.0000	0.0000	0.0000	0.0000	0.0000	4
11	0.0000	0.0000	0.0000	0.0000	0.0000	0.0000	0.0000	0.0000	0.0000	0.0000	3
12	0.0000	0.0000	0.0000	0.0000	0.0000	0.0000	0.0000	0.0000	0.0000	0.0000	2
13	0.0000	0.0000	0.0000	0.0000	0.0000	0.0000	0.0000	0.0000	0.0000	0.0000	1
14	0.0000	0.0000	0.0000	0.0000	0.0000	0.0000	0.0000	0.0000	0.0000	0.0000	0
	q = 0.99	q = 0.98	q = 0.97	q = 0.96	q = 0.95	q = 0.94	q = 0.93	q = 0.92	q = 0.91	q = 0.90	

x	p = 0.11	p = 0.12	p = 0.13	p = 0.14	p = 0.15	p = 0.16	p = 0.17	p = 0.18	p = 0.19	p = 0.20	n − x
0	0.1956	0.1670	0.1423	0.1211	0.1028	0.0871	0.0736	0.0621	0.0523	0.0440	14
1	0.3385	0.3188	0.2977	0.2759	0.2539	0.2322	0.2112	0.1910	0.1719	0.1539	13
2	0.2720	0.2826	0.2892	0.2919	0.2912	0.2875	0.2811	0.2725	0.2620	0.2501	12
3	0.1345	0.1542	0.1728	0.1901	0.2056	0.2190	0.2303	0.2393	0.2459	0.2501	11
4	0.0457	0.0578	0.0710	0.0851	0.0998	0.1147	0.1297	0.1444	0.1586	0.1720	10
5	0.0113	0.0158	0.0212	0.0277	0.0352	0.0437	0.0531	0.0634	0.0744	0.0860	9
6	0.0021	0.0032	0.0048	0.0068	0.0093	0.0125	0.0163	0.0209	0.0262	0.0322	8
7	0.0003	0.0005	0.0008	0.0013	0.0019	0.0027	0.0038	0.0052	0.0070	0.0092	7
8	0.0000	0.0001	0.0001	0.0002	0.0003	0.0005	0.0007	0.0010	0.0014	0.0020	6
9	0.0000	0.0000	0.0000	0.0000	0.0000	0.0001	0.0001	0.0001	0.0002	0.0003	5
10	0.0000	0.0000	0.0000	0.0000	0.0000	0.0000	0.0000	0.0000	0.0000	0.0000	4
11	0.0000	0.0000	0.0000	0.0000	0.0000	0.0000	0.0000	0.0000	0.0000	0.0000	3
12	0.0000	0.0000	0.0000	0.0000	0.0000	0.0000	0.0000	0.0000	0.0000	0.0000	2
13	0.0000	0.0000	0.0000	0.0000	0.0000	0.0000	0.0000	0.0000	0.0000	0.0000	1
14	0.0000	0.0000	0.0000	0.0000	0.0000	0.0000	0.0000	0.0000	0.0000	0.0000	0
	q = 0.89	q = 0.88	q = 0.87	q = 0.86	q = 0.85	q = 0.84	q = 0.83	q = 0.82	q = 0.81	q = 0.80	

x	$p = 0.21$	$p = 0.22$	$p = 0.23$	$p = 0.24$	$p = 0.25$	$p = 0.26$	$p = 0.27$	$p = 0.28$	$p = 0.29$	$p = 0.30$	$n - x$
0	0.0369	0.0309	0.0258	0.0214	0.0178	0.0148	0.0122	0.0101	0.0083	0.0068	14
1	0.1372	0.1218	0.1077	0.0948	0.0832	0.0726	0.0632	0.0548	0.0473	0.0407	13
2	0.2371	0.2234	0.2091	0.1946	0.1802	0.1659	0.1519	0.1385	0.1256	0.1134	12
3	0.2521	0.2520	0.2499	0.2459	0.2402	0.2331	0.2248	0.2154	0.2052	0.1943	11
4	0.1843	0.1955	0.2052	0.2135	0.2202	0.2252	0.2286	0.2304	0.2305	0.2290	10
5	0.0980	0.1103	0.1226	0.1348	0.1468	0.1583	0.1691	0.1792	0.1883	0.1963	9
6	0.0391	0.0466	0.0549	0.0639	0.0734	0.0834	0.0938	0.1045	0.1153	0.1262	8
7	0.0119	0.0150	0.0188	0.0231	0.0280	0.0335	0.0397	0.0464	0.0538	0.0618	7
8	0.0028	0.0037	0.0049	0.0064	0.0082	0.0103	0.0128	0.0158	0.0192	0.0232	6
9	0.0005	0.0007	0.0010	0.0013	0.0018	0.0024	0.0032	0.0041	0.0052	0.0066	5
10	0.0001	0.0001	0.0001	0.0002	0.0003	0.0004	0.0006	0.0008	0.0011	0.0014	4
11	0.0000	0.0000	0.0000	0.0000	0.0000	0.0001	0.0001	0.0001	0.0002	0.0002	3
12	0.0000	0.0000	0.0000	0.0000	0.0000	0.0000	0.0000	0.0000	0.0000	0.0000	2
13	0.0000	0.0000	0.0000	0.0000	0.0000	0.0000	0.0000	0.0000	0.0000	0.0000	1
14	0.0000	0.0000	0.0000	0.0000	0.0000	0.0000	0.0000	0.0000	0.0000	0.0000	0
	$q = 0.79$	$q = 0.78$	$q = 0.77$	$q = 0.76$	$q = 0.75$	$q = 0.74$	$q = 0.73$	$q = 0.72$	$q = 0.71$	$q = 0.70$	

x	$p = 0.31$	$p = 0.32$	$p = 0.33$	$p = 0.34$	$p = 0.35$	$p = 0.36$	$p = 0.37$	$p = 0.38$	$p = 0.39$	$p = 0.40$	$n - x$
0	0.0055	0.0045	0.0037	0.0030	0.0024	0.0019	0.0016	0.0012	0.0010	0.0008	14
1	0.0349	0.0298	0.0253	0.0215	0.0181	0.0152	0.0128	0.0106	0.0088	0.0073	13
2	0.1018	0.0911	0.0811	0.0719	0.0634	0.0557	0.0487	0.0424	0.0367	0.0317	12
3	0.1830	0.1715	0.1598	0.1481	0.1366	0.1253	0.1144	0.1039	0.0940	0.0845	11
4	0.2261	0.2219	0.2164	0.2098	0.2022	0.1938	0.1848	0.1752	0.1652	0.1549	10
5	0.2032	0.2088	0.2132	0.2161	0.2178	0.2181	0.2170	0.2147	0.2112	0.2066	9
6	0.1369	0.1474	0.1575	0.1670	0.1759	0.1840	0.1912	0.1974	0.2026	0.2066	8
7	0.0703	0.0793	0.0886	0.0983	0.1082	0.1183	0.1283	0.1383	0.1480	0.1574	7
8	0.0276	0.0326	0.0382	0.0443	0.0510	0.0582	0.0659	0.0742	0.0828	0.0918	6
9	0.0083	0.0102	0.0125	0.0152	0.0183	0.0218	0.0258	0.0303	0.0353	0.0408	5
10	0.0019	0.0024	0.0031	0.0039	0.0049	0.0061	0.0076	0.0093	0.0113	0.0136	4
11	0.0003	0.0004	0.0006	0.0007	0.0010	0.0013	0.0016	0.0021	0.0026	0.0033	3
12	0.0000	0.0000	0.0001	0.0001	0.0001	0.0002	0.0002	0.0003	0.0004	0.0005	2
13	0.0000	0.0000	0.0000	0.0000	0.0000	0.0000	0.0000	0.0000	0.0000	0.0001	1
14	0.0000	0.0000	0.0000	0.0000	0.0000	0.0000	0.0000	0.0000	0.0000	0.0000	0
	$q = 0.69$	$q = 0.68$	$q = 0.67$	$q = 0.66$	$q = 0.65$	$q = 0.64$	$q = 0.63$	$q = 0.62$	$q = 0.61$	$q = 0.60$	

x	$p = 0.41$	$p = 0.42$	$p = 0.43$	$p = 0.44$	$p = 0.45$	$p = 0.46$	$p = 0.47$	$p = 0.48$	$p = 0.49$	$p = 0.50$	$n - x$
0	0.0006	0.0005	0.0004	0.0003	0.0002	0.0002	0.0001	0.0001	0.0001	0.0001	14
1	0.0060	0.0049	0.0040	0.0033	0.0027	0.0021	0.0017	0.0014	0.0011	0.0009	13
2	0.0272	0.0233	0.0198	0.0168	0.0141	0.0118	0.0099	0.0082	0.0068	0.0056	12
3	0.0757	0.0674	0.0597	0.0527	0.0462	0.0403	0.0350	0.0303	0.0260	0.0222	11
4	0.1446	0.1342	0.1239	0.1138	0.1040	0.0945	0.0854	0.0768	0.0687	0.0611	10
5	0.2009	0.1943	0.1869	0.1788	0.1701	0.1610	0.1515	0.1418	0.1320	0.1222	9
6	0.2094	0.2111	0.2115	0.2108	0.2088	0.2057	0.2015	0.1963	0.1902	0.1833	8
7	0.1663	0.1747	0.1824	0.1892	0.1952	0.2003	0.2043	0.2071	0.2089	0.2095	7
8	0.1011	0.1107	0.1204	0.1301	0.1398	0.1493	0.1585	0.1673	0.1756	0.1833	6
9	0.0469	0.0534	0.0605	0.0682	0.0762	0.0848	0.0937	0.1030	0.1125	0.1222	5
10	0.0163	0.0193	0.0228	0.0268	0.0312	0.0361	0.0415	0.0475	0.0540	0.0611	4
11	0.0041	0.0051	0.0063	0.0076	0.0093	0.0112	0.0134	0.0160	0.0189	0.0222	3
12	0.0007	0.0009	0.0012	0.0015	0.0019	0.0024	0.0030	0.0037	0.0045	0.0056	2
13	0.0001	0.0001	0.0001	0.0002	0.0002	0.0003	0.0004	0.0005	0.0007	0.0009	1
14	0.0000	0.0000	0.0000	0.0000	0.0000	0.0000	0.0000	0.0000	0.0000	0.0001	0
	$q = 0.59$	$q = 0.58$	$q = 0.57$	$q = 0.56$	$q = 0.55$	$q = 0.54$	$q = 0.53$	$q = 0.52$	$q = 0.51$	$q = 0.50$	

continued

$n = 15$

x	p = 0.01	p = 0.02	p = 0.03	p = 0.04	p = 0.05	p = 0.06	p = 0.07	p = 0.08	p = 0.09	p = 0.10	n − x
0	0.8601	0.7386	0.6333	0.5421	0.4633	0.3953	0.3367	0.2863	0.2430	0.2059	15
1	0.1303	0.2261	0.2938	0.3388	0.3658	0.3785	0.3801	0.3734	0.3605	0.3432	14
2	0.0092	0.0323	0.0636	0.0988	0.1348	0.1691	0.2003	0.2273	0.2496	0.2669	13
3	0.0004	0.0029	0.0085	0.0178	0.0307	0.0468	0.0653	0.0857	0.1070	0.1285	12
4	0.0000	0.0002	0.0008	0.0022	0.0049	0.0090	0.0148	0.0223	0.0317	0.0428	11
5	0.0000	0.0000	0.0001	0.0002	0.0006	0.0013	0.0024	0.0043	0.0069	0.0105	10
6	0.0000	0.0000	0.0000	0.0000	0.0000	0.0001	0.0003	0.0006	0.0011	0.0019	9
7	0.0000	0.0000	0.0000	0.0000	0.0000	0.0000	0.0000	0.0001	0.0001	0.0003	8
	q = 0.99	q = 0.98	q = 0.97	q = 0.96	q = 0.95	q = 0.94	q = 0.93	q = 0.92	q = 0.91	q = 0.90	

x	p = 0.11	p = 0.12	p = 0.13	p = 0.14	p = 0.15	p = 0.16	p = 0.17	p = 0.18	p = 0.19	p = 0.20	n − x
0	0.1741	0.1470	0.1238	0.1041	0.0874	0.0731	0.0611	0.0510	0.0424	0.0352	15
1	0.3228	0.3006	0.2775	0.2542	0.2312	0.2090	0.1878	0.1678	0.1492	0.1319	14
2	0.2793	0.2870	0.2903	0.2897	0.2856	0.2787	0.2692	0.2578	0.2449	0.2309	13
3	0.1496	0.1696	0.1880	0.2044	0.2184	0.2300	0.2389	0.2452	0.2489	0.2501	12
4	0.0555	0.0694	0.0843	0.0998	0.1156	0.1314	0.1468	0.1615	0.1752	0.1876	11
5	0.0151	0.0208	0.0277	0.0357	0.0449	0.0551	0.0662	0.0780	0.0904	0.1032	10
6	0.0031	0.0047	0.0069	0.0097	0.0132	0.0175	0.0226	0.0285	0.0353	0.0430	9
7	0.0005	0.0008	0.0013	0.0020	0.0030	0.0043	0.0059	0.0081	0.0107	0.0138	8
8	0.0001	0.0001	0.0002	0.0003	0.0005	0.0008	0.0012	0.0018	0.0025	0.0035	7
9	0.0000	0.0000	0.0000	0.0000	0.0001	0.0001	0.0002	0.0003	0.0005	0.0007	6
10	0.0000	0.0000	0.0000	0.0000	0.0000	0.0000	0.0000	0.0000	0.0001	0.0001	5
	q = 0.89	q = 0.88	q = 0.87	q = 0.86	q = 0.85	q = 0.84	q = 0.83	q = 0.82	q = 0.81	q = 0.80	

x	p = 0.21	p = 0.22	p = 0.23	p = 0.24	p = 0.25	p = 0.26	p = 0.27	p = 0.28	p = 0.29	p = 0.30	n − x
0	0.0291	0.0241	0.0198	0.0163	0.0134	0.0109	0.0089	0.0072	0.0059	0.0047	15
1	0.1162	0.1018	0.0889	0.0772	0.0668	0.0576	0.0494	0.0423	0.0360	0.0305	14
2	0.2162	0.2010	0.1858	0.1707	0.1559	0.1416	0.1280	0.1150	0.1029	0.0916	13
3	0.2490	0.2457	0.2405	0.2336	0.2252	0.2156	0.2051	0.1939	0.1821	0.1700	12
4	0.1986	0.2079	0.2155	0.2213	0.2252	0.2273	0.2276	0.2262	0.2231	0.2186	11
5	0.1161	0.1290	0.1416	0.1537	0.1651	0.1757	0.1852	0.1935	0.2005	0.2061	10
6	0.0514	0.0606	0.0705	0.0809	0.0917	0.1029	0.1142	0.1254	0.1365	0.1472	9
7	0.0176	0.0220	0.0271	0.0329	0.0393	0.0465	0.0543	0.0627	0.0717	0.0811	8
8	0.0047	0.0062	0.0081	0.0104	0.0131	0.0163	0.0201	0.0244	0.0293	0.0348	7
9	0.0010	0.0014	0.0019	0.0025	0.0034	0.0045	0.0058	0.0074	0.0093	0.0116	6
10	0.0002	0.0002	0.0003	0.0005	0.0007	0.0009	0.0013	0.0017	0.0023	0.0030	5
11	0.0000	0.0000	0.0000	0.0001	0.0001	0.0002	0.0002	0.0003	0.0004	0.0006	4
12	0.0000	0.0000	0.0000	0.0000	0.0000	0.0000	0.0000	0.0000	0.0001	0.0001	3
	q = 0.79	q = 0.78	q = 0.77	q = 0.76	q = 0.75	q = 0.74	q = 0.73	q = 0.72	q = 0.71	q = 0.70	

x	p = 0.31	p = 0.32	p = 0.33	p = 0.34	p = 0.35	p = 0.36	p = 0.37	p = 0.38	p = 0.39	p = 0.40	n − x
0	0.0038	0.0031	0.0025	0.0020	0.0016	0.0012	0.0010	0.0008	0.0006	0.0005	15
1	0.0258	0.0217	0.0182	0.0152	0.0126	0.0104	0.0086	0.0071	0.0058	0.0047	14
2	0.0811	0.0715	0.0627	0.0547	0.0476	0.0411	0.0354	0.0303	0.0259	0.0219	13
3	0.1579	0.1457	0.1338	0.1222	0.1110	0.1002	0.0901	0.0805	0.0716	0.0634	12
4	0.2128	0.2057	0.1977	0.1888	0.1792	0.1692	0.1587	0.1481	0.1374	0.1268	11
5	0.2103	0.2130	0.2142	0.2140	0.2123	0.2093	0.2051	0.1997	0.1933	0.1859	10
6	0.1575	0.1671	0.1759	0.1837	0.1906	0.1963	0.2008	0.2040	0.2059	0.2066	9
7	0.0910	0.1011	0.1114	0.1217	0.1319	0.1419	0.1516	0.1608	0.1693	0.1771	8
8	0.0409	0.0476	0.0549	0.0627	0.0710	0.0798	0.0890	0.0985	0.1082	0.1181	7
9	0.0143	0.0174	0.0210	0.0251	0.0298	0.0349	0.0407	0.0470	0.0538	0.0612	6
10	0.0038	0.0049	0.0062	0.0078	0.0096	0.0118	0.0143	0.0173	0.0206	0.0245	5
11	0.0008	0.0011	0.0014	0.0018	0.0024	0.0030	0.0038	0.0048	0.0060	0.0074	4
12	0.0001	0.0002	0.0002	0.0003	0.0004	0.0006	0.0007	0.0010	0.0013	0.0016	3
13	0.0000	0.0000	0.0000	0.0000	0.0001	0.0001	0.0001	0.0001	0.0002	0.0003	2
	q = 0.69	q = 0.68	q = 0.67	q = 0.66	q = 0.65	q = 0.64	q = 0.63	q = 0.62	q = 0.61	q = 0.60	

x	p = 0.41	p = 0.42	p = 0.43	p = 0.44	p = 0.45	p = 0.46	p = 0.47	p = 0.48	p = 0.49	p = 0.50	n − x
0	0.0004	0.0003	0.0002	0.0002	0.0001	0.0001	0.0001	0.0001	0.0000	0.0000	15
1	0.0038	0.0031	0.0025	0.0020	0.0016	0.0012	0.0010	0.0008	0.0006	0.0005	14
2	0.0185	0.0156	0.0130	0.0108	0.0090	0.0074	0.0060	0.0049	0.0040	0.0032	13
3	0.0558	0.0489	0.0426	0.0369	0.0318	0.0272	0.0232	0.0197	0.0166	0.0139	12
4	0.1163	0.1061	0.0963	0.0869	0.0780	0.0696	0.0617	0.0545	0.0478	0.0417	11
5	0.1778	0.1691	0.1598	0.1502	0.1404	0.1304	0.1204	0.1106	0.1010	0.0916	10
6	0.2060	0.2041	0.2010	0.1967	0.1914	0.1851	0.1780	0.1702	0.1617	0.1527	9
7	0.1840	0.1900	0.1949	0.1987	0.2013	0.2028	0.2030	0.2020	0.1997	0.1964	8
8	0.1279	0.1376	0.1470	0.1561	0.1647	0.1727	0.1800	0.1864	0.1919	0.1964	7
9	0.0691	0.0775	0.0863	0.0954	0.1048	0.1144	0.1241	0.1338	0.1434	0.1527	6
10	0.0288	0.0337	0.0390	0.0450	0.0515	0.0585	0.0661	0.0741	0.0827	0.0916	5
11	0.0091	0.0111	0.0134	0.0161	0.0191	0.0226	0.0266	0.0311	0.0361	0.0417	4
12	0.0021	0.0027	0.0034	0.0042	0.0052	0.0064	0.0079	0.0096	0.0116	0.0139	3
13	0.0003	0.0004	0.0006	0.0008	0.0010	0.0013	0.0016	0.0020	0.0026	0.0032	2
14	0.0000	0.0000	0.0001	0.0001	0.0001	0.0002	0.0002	0.0003	0.0004	0.0005	1
15	0.0000	0.0000	0.0000	0.0000	0.0000	0.0000	0.0000	0.0000	0.0000	0.0000	0
	q = 0.59	q = 0.58	q = 0.57	q = 0.56	q = 0.55	q = 0.54	q = 0.53	q = 0.52	q = 0.51	q = 0.50	

n = 20

x	p = 0.01	p = 0.02	p = 0.03	p = 0.04	p = 0.05	p = 0.06	p = 0.07	p = 0.08	p = 0.09	p = 0.10	n − x
0	0.8179	0.6676	0.5438	0.4420	0.3585	0.2901	0.2342	0.1887	0.1516	0.1216	20
1	0.1652	0.2725	0.3364	0.3683	0.3774	0.3703	0.3526	0.3282	0.3000	0.2702	19
2	0.0159	0.0528	0.0988	0.1458	0.1887	0.2246	0.2521	0.2711	0.2818	0.2852	18
3	0.0010	0.0065	0.0183	0.0364	0.0596	0.0860	0.1139	0.1414	0.1672	0.1901	17
4	0.0000	0.0006	0.0024	0.0065	0.0133	0.0233	0.0364	0.0523	0.0703	0.0898	16
5	0.0000	0.0000	0.0002	0.0009	0.0022	0.0048	0.0088	0.0145	0.0222	0.0319	15
6	0.0000	0.0000	0.0000	0.0001	0.0003	0.0008	0.0017	0.0032	0.0055	0.0089	14
7	0.0000	0.0000	0.0000	0.0000	0.0000	0.0001	0.0002	0.0005	0.0011	0.0020	13
8	0.0000	0.0000	0.0000	0.0000	0.0000	0.0000	0.0000	0.0001	0.0002	0.0004	12
9	0.0000	0.0000	0.0000	0.0000	0.0000	0.0000	0.0000	0.0000	0.0000	0.0001	11
	q = 0.99	q = 0.98	q = 0.97	q = 0.96	q = 0.95	q = 0.94	q = 0.93	q = 0.92	q = 0.91	q = 0.90	

x	p = 0.11	p = 0.12	p = 0.13	p = 0.14	p = 0.15	p = 0.16	p = 0.17	p = 0.18	p = 0.19	p = 0.20	n − x
0	0.0972	0.0776	0.0617	0.0490	0.0388	0.0306	0.0241	0.0189	0.0148	0.0115	20
1	0.2403	0.2115	0.1844	0.1595	0.1368	0.1165	0.0986	0.0829	0.0693	0.0576	19
2	0.2822	0.2740	0.2618	0.2466	0.2293	0.2109	0.1919	0.1730	0.1545	0.1369	18
3	0.2093	0.2242	0.2347	0.2409	0.2428	0.2410	0.2358	0.2278	0.2175	0.2054	17
4	0.1099	0.1299	0.1491	0.1666	0.1821	0.1951	0.2053	0.2125	0.2168	0.2182	16
5	0.0435	0.0567	0.0713	0.0868	0.1028	0.1189	0.1345	0.1493	0.1627	0.1746	15
6	0.0134	0.0193	0.0266	0.0353	0.0454	0.0566	0.0689	0.0819	0.0954	0.1091	14
7	0.0033	0.0053	0.0080	0.0115	0.0160	0.0216	0.0282	0.0360	0.0448	0.0545	13
8	0.0007	0.0012	0.0019	0.0030	0.0046	0.0067	0.0094	0.0128	0.0171	0.0222	12
9	0.0001	0.0002	0.0004	0.0007	0.0011	0.0017	0.0026	0.0038	0.0053	0.0074	11
10	0.0000	0.0000	0.0001	0.0001	0.0002	0.0004	0.0006	0.0009	0.0014	0.0020	10
11	0.0000	0.0000	0.0000	0.0000	0.0000	0.0001	0.0001	0.0002	0.0003	0.0005	9
12	0.0000	0.0000	0.0000	0.0000	0.0000	0.0000	0.0000	0.0000	0.0001	0.0001	8
	q = 0.89	q = 0.88	q = 0.87	q = 0.86	q = 0.85	q = 0.84	q = 0.83	q = 0.82	q = 0.81	q = 0.80	

continued

x	p = 0.21	p = 0.22	p = 0.23	p = 0.24	p = 0.25	p = 0.26	p = 0.27	p = 0.28	p = 0.29	p = 0.30	n − x
0	0.0090	0.0069	0.0054	0.0041	0.0032	0.0024	0.0018	0.0014	0.0011	0.0008	20
1	0.0477	0.0392	0.0321	0.0261	0.0211	0.0170	0.0137	0.0109	0.0087	0.0068	19
2	0.1204	0.1050	0.0910	0.0783	0.0669	0.0569	0.0480	0.0403	0.0336	0.0278	18
3	0.1920	0.1777	0.1631	0.1484	0.1339	0.1199	0.1065	0.0940	0.0823	0.0716	17
4	0.2169	0.2131	0.2070	0.1991	0.1897	0.1790	0.1675	0.1553	0.1429	0.1304	16
5	0.1845	0.1923	0.1979	0.2012	0.2023	0.2013	0.1982	0.1933	0.1868	0.1789	15
6	0.1226	0.1356	0.1478	0.1589	0.1686	0.1768	0.1833	0.1879	0.1907	0.1916	14
7	0.0652	0.0765	0.0883	0.1003	0.1124	0.1242	0.1356	0.1462	0.1558	0.1643	13
8	0.0282	0.0351	0.0429	0.0515	0.0609	0.0709	0.0815	0.0924	0.1034	0.1144	12
9	0.0100	0.0132	0.0171	0.0217	0.0271	0.0332	0.0402	0.0479	0.0563	0.0654	11
10	0.0029	0.0041	0.0056	0.0075	0.0099	0.0128	0.0163	0.0205	0.0253	0.0308	10
11	0.0007	0.0010	0.0015	0.0022	0.0030	0.0041	0.0055	0.0072	0.0094	0.0120	9
12	0.0001	0.0002	0.0003	0.0005	0.0008	0.0011	0.0015	0.0021	0.0029	0.0039	8
13	0.0000	0.0000	0.0001	0.0001	0.0002	0.0002	0.0003	0.0005	0.0007	0.0010	7
14	0.0000	0.0000	0.0000	0.0000	0.0000	0.0000	0.0001	0.0001	0.0001	0.0002	6
	q = 0.79	q = 0.78	q = 0.77	q = 0.76	q = 0.75	q = 0.74	q = 0.73	q = 0.72	q = 0.71	q = 0.70	

x	p = 0.31	p = 0.32	p = 0.33	p = 0.34	p = 0.35	p = 0.36	p = 0.37	p = 0.38	p = 0.39	p = 0.40	n − x
0	0.0006	0.0004	0.0003	0.0002	0.0002	0.0001	0.0001	0.0001	0.0001	0.0000	20
1	0.0054	0.0042	0.0033	0.0025	0.0020	0.0015	0.0011	0.0009	0.0007	0.0005	19
2	0.0229	0.0188	0.0153	0.0124	0.0100	0.0080	0.0064	0.0050	0.0040	0.0031	18
3	0.0619	0.0531	0.0453	0.0383	0.0323	0.0270	0.0224	0.0185	0.0152	0.0123	17
4	0.1181	0.1062	0.0947	0.0839	0.0738	0.0645	0.0559	0.0482	0.0412	0.0350	16
5	0.1698	0.1599	0.1493	0.1384	0.1272	0.1161	0.1051	0.0945	0.0843	0.0746	15
6	0.1907	0.1881	0.1839	0.1782	0.1712	0.1632	0.1543	0.1447	0.1347	0.1244	14
7	0.1714	0.1770	0.1811	0.1836	0.1844	0.1836	0.1812	0.1774	0.1722	0.1659	13
8	0.1251	0.1354	0.1450	0.1537	0.1614	0.1678	0.1730	0.1767	0.1790	0.1797	12
9	0.0750	0.0849	0.0952	0.1056	0.1158	0.1259	0.1354	0.1444	0.1526	0.1597	11
10	0.0370	0.0440	0.0516	0.0598	0.0686	0.0779	0.0875	0.0974	0.1073	0.1171	10
11	0.0151	0.0188	0.0231	0.0280	0.0336	0.0398	0.0467	0.0542	0.0624	0.0710	9
12	0.0051	0.0066	0.0085	0.0108	0.0136	0.0168	0.0206	0.0249	0.0299	0.0355	8
13	0.0014	0.0019	0.0026	0.0034	0.0045	0.0058	0.0074	0.0094	0.0118	0.0146	7
14	0.0003	0.0005	0.0006	0.0009	0.0012	0.0016	0.0022	0.0029	0.0038	0.0049	6
15	0.0001	0.0001	0.0001	0.0002	0.0003	0.0004	0.0005	0.0007	0.0010	0.0013	5
16	0.0000	0.0000	0.0000	0.0000	0.0000	0.0001	0.0001	0.0001	0.0002	0.0003	4
	q = 0.69	q = 0.68	q = 0.67	q = 0.66	q = 0.65	q = 0.64	q = 0.63	q = 0.62	q = 0.61	q = 0.60	

x	p = 0.41	p = 0.42	p = 0.43	p = 0.44	p = 0.45	p = 0.46	p = 0.47	p = 0.48	p = 0.49	p = 0.50	n − x
0	0.0000	0.0000	0.0000	0.0000	0.0000	0.0000	0.0000	0.0000	0.0000	0.0000	20
1	0.0004	0.0003	0.0002	0.0001	0.0001	0.0001	0.0001	0.0000	0.0000	0.0000	19
2	0.0024	0.0018	0.0014	0.0011	0.0008	0.0006	0.0005	0.0003	0.0002	0.0002	18
3	0.0100	0.0080	0.0064	0.0051	0.0040	0.0031	0.0024	0.0019	0.0014	0.0011	17
4	0.0295	0.0247	0.0206	0.0170	0.0139	0.0113	0.0092	0.0074	0.0059	0.0046	16
5	0.0656	0.0573	0.0496	0.0427	0.0365	0.0309	0.0260	0.0217	0.0180	0.0148	15
6	0.1140	0.1037	0.0936	0.0839	0.0746	0.0658	0.0577	0.0501	0.0432	0.0370	14
7	0.1585	0.1502	0.1413	0.1318	0.1221	0.1122	0.1023	0.0925	0.0830	0.0739	13
8	0.1790	0.1768	0.1732	0.1683	0.1623	0.1553	0.1474	0.1388	0.1296	0.1201	12
9	0.1658	0.1707	0.1742	0.1763	0.1771	0.1763	0.1742	0.1708	0.1661	0.1602	11
10	0.1268	0.1359	0.1446	0.1524	0.1593	0.1652	0.1700	0.1734	0.1755	0.1762	10
11	0.0801	0.0895	0.0991	0.1089	0.1185	0.1280	0.1370	0.1455	0.1533	0.1602	9
12	0.0417	0.0486	0.0561	0.0642	0.0727	0.0818	0.0911	0.1007	0.1105	0.1201	8
13	0.0178	0.0217	0.0260	0.0310	0.0366	0.0429	0.0497	0.0572	0.0653	0.0739	7
14	0.0062	0.0078	0.0098	0.0122	0.0150	0.0183	0.0221	0.0264	0.0314	0.0370	6
15	0.0017	0.0023	0.0030	0.0038	0.0049	0.0062	0.0078	0.0098	0.0121	0.0148	5
16	0.0004	0.0005	0.0007	0.0009	0.0013	0.0017	0.0022	0.0028	0.0036	0.0046	4
17	0.0001	0.0001	0.0001	0.0002	0.0002	0.0003	0.0005	0.0006	0.0008	0.0011	3
18	0.0000	0.0000	0.0000	0.0000	0.0000	0.0000	0.0001	0.0001	0.0001	0.0002	2
	q = 0.59	q = 0.58	q = 0.57	q = 0.56	q = 0.55	q = 0.54	q = 0.53	q = 0.52	q = 0.51	q = 0.50	

$n = 25$

x	p = 0.01	p = 0.02	p = 0.03	p = 0.04	p = 0.05	p = 0.06	p = 0.07	p = 0.08	p = 0.09	p = 0.10	n − x
0	0.7778	0.6035	0.4670	0.3604	0.2774	0.2129	0.1630	0.1244	0.0946	0.0718	25
1	0.1964	0.3079	0.3611	0.3754	0.3650	0.3398	0.3066	0.2704	0.2340	0.1994	24
2	0.0238	0.0754	0.1340	0.1877	0.2305	0.2602	0.2770	0.2821	0.2777	0.2659	23
3	0.0018	0.0118	0.0318	0.0600	0.0930	0.1273	0.1598	0.1881	0.2106	0.2265	22
4	0.0001	0.0013	0.0054	0.0137	0.0269	0.0447	0.0662	0.0899	0.1145	0.1384	21
5	0.0000	0.0001	0.0007	0.0024	0.0060	0.0120	0.0209	0.0329	0.0476	0.0646	20
6	0.0000	0.0000	0.0001	0.0003	0.0010	0.0026	0.0052	0.0095	0.0157	0.0239	19
7	0.0000	0.0000	0.0000	0.0000	0.0001	0.0004	0.0011	0.0022	0.0042	0.0072	18
8	0.0000	0.0000	0.0000	0.0000	0.0000	0.0001	0.0002	0.0004	0.0009	0.0018	17
9	0.0000	0.0000	0.0000	0.0000	0.0000	0.0000	0.0000	0.0001	0.0002	0.0004	16
10	0.0000	0.0000	0.0000	0.0000	0.0000	0.0000	0.0000	0.0000	0.0000	0.0001	15
	q = 0.99	q = 0.98	q = 0.97	q = 0.96	q = 0.95	q = 0.94	q = 0.93	q = 0.92	q = 0.91	q = 0.90	

x	p = 0.11	p = 0.12	p = 0.13	p = 0.14	p = 0.15	p = 0.16	p = 0.17	p = 0.18	p = 0.19	p = 0.20	n − x
0	0.0543	0.0409	0.0308	0.0230	0.0172	0.0128	0.0095	0.0070	0.0052	0.0038	25
1	0.1678	0.1395	0.1149	0.0938	0.0759	0.0609	0.0486	0.0384	0.0302	0.0236	24
2	0.2488	0.2283	0.2060	0.1832	0.1607	0.1392	0.1193	0.1012	0.0851	0.0708	23
3	0.2358	0.2387	0.2360	0.2286	0.2174	0.2033	0.1874	0.1704	0.1530	0.1358	22
4	0.1603	0.1790	0.1940	0.2047	0.2110	0.2130	0.2111	0.2057	0.1974	0.1867	21
5	0.0832	0.1025	0.1217	0.1399	0.1564	0.1704	0.1816	0.1897	0.1945	0.1960	20
6	0.0343	0.0466	0.0606	0.0759	0.0920	0.1082	0.1240	0.1388	0.1520	0.1633	19
7	0.0115	0.0173	0.0246	0.0336	0.0441	0.0559	0.0689	0.0827	0.0968	0.1108	18
8	0.0032	0.0053	0.0083	0.0123	0.0175	0.0240	0.0318	0.0408	0.0511	0.0623	17
9	0.0007	0.0014	0.0023	0.0038	0.0058	0.0086	0.0123	0.0169	0.0226	0.0294	16
10	0.0001	0.0003	0.0006	0.0010	0.0016	0.0026	0.0040	0.0059	0.0085	0.0118	15
11	0.0000	0.0001	0.0001	0.0002	0.0004	0.0007	0.0011	0.0018	0.0027	0.0040	14
12	0.0000	0.0000	0.0000	0.0000	0.0001	0.0002	0.0003	0.0005	0.0007	0.0012	13
13	0.0000	0.0000	0.0000	0.0000	0.0000	0.0000	0.0001	0.0001	0.0002	0.0003	12
14	0.0000	0.0000	0.0000	0.0000	0.0000	0.0000	0.0000	0.0000	0.0000	0.0001	11
	q = 0.89	q = 0.88	q = 0.87	q = 0.86	q = 0.85	q = 0.84	q = 0.83	q = 0.82	q = 0.81	q = 0.80	

x	p = 0.21	p = 0.22	p = 0.23	p = 0.24	p = 0.25	p = 0.26	p = 0.27	p = 0.28	p = 0.29	p = 0.30	n − x
0	0.0028	0.0020	0.0015	0.0010	0.0008	0.0005	0.0004	0.0003	0.0002	0.0001	25
1	0.0183	0.0141	0.0109	0.0083	0.0063	0.0047	0.0035	0.0026	0.0020	0.0014	24
2	0.0585	0.0479	0.0389	0.0314	0.0251	0.0199	0.0157	0.0123	0.0096	0.0074	23
3	0.1192	0.1035	0.0891	0.0759	0.0641	0.0537	0.0446	0.0367	0.0300	0.0243	22
4	0.1742	0.1606	0.1463	0.1318	0.1175	0.1037	0.0906	0.0785	0.0673	0.0572	21
5	0.1945	0.1903	0.1836	0.1749	0.1645	0.1531	0.1408	0.1282	0.1155	0.1030	20
6	0.1724	0.1789	0.1828	0.1841	0.1828	0.1793	0.1736	0.1661	0.1572	0.1472	19
7	0.1244	0.1369	0.1482	0.1578	0.1654	0.1709	0.1743	0.1754	0.1743	0.1712	18
8	0.0744	0.0869	0.0996	0.1121	0.1241	0.1351	0.1450	0.1535	0.1602	0.1651	17
9	0.0373	0.0463	0.0562	0.0669	0.0781	0.0897	0.1013	0.1127	0.1236	0.1336	16
10	0.0159	0.0209	0.0269	0.0338	0.0417	0.0504	0.0600	0.0701	0.0808	0.0916	15
11	0.0058	0.0080	0.0109	0.0145	0.0189	0.0242	0.0302	0.0372	0.0450	0.0536	14
12	0.0018	0.0026	0.0038	0.0054	0.0074	0.0099	0.0130	0.0169	0.0214	0.0268	13
13	0.0005	0.0007	0.0011	0.0017	0.0025	0.0035	0.0048	0.0066	0.0088	0.0115	12
14	0.0001	0.0002	0.0003	0.0005	0.0007	0.0010	0.0015	0.0022	0.0031	0.0042	11
15	0.0000	0.0000	0.0001	0.0001	0.0002	0.0003	0.0004	0.0006	0.0009	0.0013	10
16	0.0000	0.0000	0.0000	0.0000	0.0000	0.0001	0.0001	0.0002	0.0002	0.0004	9
17	0.0000	0.0000	0.0000	0.0000	0.0000	0.0000	0.0000	0.0000	0.0001	0.0001	8
	q = 0.79	q = 0.78	q = 0.77	q = 0.76	q = 0.75	q = 0.74	q = 0.73	q = 0.72	q = 0.71	q = 0.70	

continued

x	p = 0.31	p = 0.32	p = 0.33	p = 0.34	p = 0.35	p = 0.36	p = 0.37	p = 0.38	p = 0.39	p = 0.40	n − x
0	0.0001	0.0001	0.0000	0.0000	0.0000	0.0000	0.0000	0.0000	0.0000	0.0000	25
1	0.0011	0.0008	0.0006	0.0004	0.0003	0.0002	0.0001	0.0001	0.0001	0.0000	24
2	0.0057	0.0043	0.0033	0.0025	0.0018	0.0014	0.0010	0.0007	0.0005	0.0004	23
3	0.0195	0.0156	0.0123	0.0097	0.0076	0.0058	0.0045	0.0034	0.0026	0.0019	22
4	0.0482	0.0403	0.0334	0.0274	0.0224	0.0181	0.0145	0.0115	0.0091	0.0071	21
5	0.0910	0.0797	0.0691	0.0594	0.0506	0.0427	0.0357	0.0297	0.0244	0.0199	20
6	0.1363	0.1250	0.1134	0.1020	0.0908	0.0801	0.0700	0.0606	0.0520	0.0442	19
7	0.1662	0.1596	0.1516	0.1426	0.1327	0.1222	0.1115	0.1008	0.0902	0.0800	18
8	0.1680	0.1690	0.1681	0.1652	0.1607	0.1547	0.1474	0.1390	0.1298	0.1200	17
9	0.1426	0.1502	0.1563	0.1608	0.1635	0.1644	0.1635	0.1609	0.1567	0.1511	16
10	0.1025	0.1131	0.1232	0.1325	0.1409	0.1479	0.1536	0.1578	0.1603	0.1612	15
11	0.0628	0.0726	0.0828	0.0931	0.1034	0.1135	0.1230	0.1319	0.1398	0.1465	14
12	0.0329	0.0399	0.0476	0.0560	0.0650	0.0745	0.0843	0.0943	0.1043	0.1140	13
13	0.0148	0.0188	0.0234	0.0288	0.0350	0.0419	0.0495	0.0578	0.0667	0.0760	12
14	0.0057	0.0076	0.0099	0.0127	0.0161	0.0202	0.0249	0.0304	0.0365	0.0434	11
15	0.0019	0.0026	0.0036	0.0048	0.0064	0.0083	0.0107	0.0136	0.0171	0.0212	10
16	0.0005	0.0008	0.0011	0.0015	0.0021	0.0029	0.0039	0.0052	0.0068	0.0088	9
17	0.0001	0.0002	0.0003	0.0004	0.0006	0.0009	0.0012	0.0017	0.0023	0.0031	8
18	0.0000	0.0000	0.0001	0.0001	0.0001	0.0002	0.0003	0.0005	0.0007	0.0009	7
19	0.0000	0.0000	0.0000	0.0000	0.0000	0.0000	0.0001	0.0001	0.0002	0.0002	6
	q = 0.69	q = 0.68	q = 0.67	q = 0.66	q = 0.65	q = 0.64	q = 0.63	q = 0.62	q = 0.61	q = 0.60	

x	p = 0.41	p = 0.42	p = 0.43	p = 0.44	p = 0.45	p = 0.46	p = 0.47	p = 0.48	p = 0.49	p = 0.50	n − x
0	0.0000	0.0000	0.0000	0.0000	0.0000	0.0000	0.0000	0.0000	0.0000	0.0000	25
1	0.0000	0.0000	0.0000	0.0000	0.0000	0.0000	0.0000	0.0000	0.0000	0.0000	24
2	0.0003	0.0002	0.0001	0.0001	0.0001	0.0000	0.0000	0.0000	0.0000	0.0000	23
3	0.0014	0.0011	0.0008	0.0006	0.0004	0.0003	0.0002	0.0001	0.0001	0.0001	22
4	0.0055	0.0042	0.0032	0.0024	0.0018	0.0014	0.0010	0.0007	0.0005	0.0004	21
5	0.0161	0.0129	0.0102	0.0081	0.0063	0.0049	0.0037	0.0028	0.0021	0.0016	20
6	0.0372	0.0311	0.0257	0.0211	0.0172	0.0138	0.0110	0.0087	0.0068	0.0053	19
7	0.0703	0.0611	0.0527	0.0450	0.0381	0.0319	0.0265	0.0218	0.0178	0.0143	18
8	0.1099	0.0996	0.0895	0.0796	0.0701	0.0612	0.0529	0.0453	0.0384	0.0322	17
9	0.1442	0.1363	0.1275	0.1181	0.1084	0.0985	0.0886	0.0790	0.0697	0.0609	16
10	0.1603	0.1579	0.1539	0.1485	0.1419	0.1342	0.1257	0.1166	0.1071	0.0974	15
11	0.1519	0.1559	0.1583	0.1591	0.1583	0.1559	0.1521	0.1468	0.1404	0.1328	14
12	0.1232	0.1317	0.1393	0.1458	0.1511	0.1550	0.1573	0.1581	0.1573	0.1550	13
13	0.0856	0.0954	0.1051	0.1146	0.1236	0.1320	0.1395	0.1460	0.1512	0.1550	12
14	0.0510	0.0592	0.0680	0.0772	0.0867	0.0964	0.1060	0.1155	0.1245	0.1328	11
15	0.0260	0.0314	0.0376	0.0445	0.0520	0.0602	0.0690	0.0782	0.0877	0.0974	10
16	0.0113	0.0142	0.0177	0.0218	0.0266	0.0321	0.0382	0.0451	0.0527	0.0609	9
17	0.0042	0.0055	0.0071	0.0091	0.0115	0.0145	0.0179	0.0220	0.0268	0.0322	8
18	0.0013	0.0018	0.0024	0.0032	0.0042	0.0055	0.0071	0.0090	0.0114	0.0143	7
19	0.0003	0.0005	0.0007	0.0009	0.0013	0.0017	0.0023	0.0031	0.0040	0.0053	6
20	0.0001	0.0001	0.0001	0.0002	0.0003	0.0004	0.0006	0.0009	0.0012	0.0016	5
21	0.0000	0.0000	0.0000	0.0000	0.0001	0.0001	0.0001	0.0002	0.0003	0.0004	4
22	0.0000	0.0000	0.0000	0.0000	0.0000	0.0000	0.0000	0.0000	0.0000	0.0001	3
	q = 0.59	q = 0.58	q = 0.57	q = 0.56	q = 0.55	q = 0.54	q = 0.53	q = 0.52	q = 0.51	q = 0.50	

APPENDIX C

Poisson Probability Distribution

Values of $P(x) = (\lambda t)^x e^{-\lambda t} / x!$

					λt					
x	0.005	0.01	0.02	0.03	0.04	0.05	0.06	0.07	0.08	0.09
0	0.9950	0.9900	0.9802	0.9704	0.9608	0.9512	0.9418	0.9324	0.9231	0.9139
1	0.0050	0.0099	0.0196	0.0291	0.0384	0.0476	0.0565	0.0653	0.0738	0.0823
2	0.0000	0.0000	0.0002	0.0004	0.0008	0.0012	0.0017	0.0023	0.0030	0.0037
3	0.0000	0.0000	0.0000	0.0000	0.0000	0.0000	0.0000	0.0001	0.0001	0.0001

					λt					
x	0.10	0.20	0.30	0.40	0.50	0.60	0.70	0.80	0.90	1.00
0	0.9048	0.8187	0.7408	0.6703	0.6065	0.5488	0.4966	0.4493	0.4066	0.3679
1	0.0905	0.1637	0.2222	0.2681	0.3033	0.3293	0.3476	0.3595	0.3659	0.3679
2	0.0045	0.0164	0.0333	0.0536	0.0758	0.0988	0.1217	0.1438	0.1647	0.1839
3	0.0002	0.0011	0.0033	0.0072	0.0126	0.0198	0.0284	0.0383	0.0494	0.0613
4	0.0000	0.0001	0.0003	0.0007	0.0016	0.0030	0.0050	0.0077	0.0111	0.0153
5	0.0000	0.0000	0.0000	0.0001	0.0002	0.0004	0.0007	0.0012	0.0020	0.0031
6	0.0000	0.0000	0.0000	0.0000	0.0000	0.0000	0.0001	0.0002	0.0003	0.0005
7	0.0000	0.0000	0.0000	0.0000	0.0000	0.0000	0.0000	0.0000	0.0000	0.0001

					λt					
x	1.10	1.20	1.30	1.40	1.50	1.60	1.70	1.80	1.90	2.00
0	0.3329	0.3012	0.2725	0.2466	0.2231	0.2019	0.1827	0.1653	0.1496	0.1353
1	0.3662	0.3614	0.3543	0.3452	0.3347	0.3230	0.3106	0.2975	0.2842	0.2707
2	0.2014	0.2169	0.2303	0.2417	0.2510	0.2584	0.2640	0.2678	0.2700	0.2707
3	0.0738	0.0867	0.0998	0.1128	0.1255	0.1378	0.1496	0.1607	0.1710	0.1804
4	0.0203	0.0260	0.0324	0.0395	0.0471	0.0551	0.0636	0.0723	0.0812	0.0902
5	0.0045	0.0062	0.0084	0.0111	0.0141	0.0176	0.0216	0.0260	0.0309	0.0361
6	0.0008	0.0012	0.0018	0.0026	0.0035	0.0047	0.0061	0.0078	0.0098	0.0120
7	0.0001	0.0002	0.0003	0.0005	0.0008	0.0011	0.0015	0.0020	0.0027	0.0034
8	0.0000	0.0000	0.0001	0.0001	0.0001	0.0002	0.0003	0.0005	0.0006	0.0009
9	0.0000	0.0000	0.0000	0.0000	0.0000	0.0000	0.0001	0.0001	0.0001	0.0002

					λt					
x	2.10	2.20	2.30	2.40	2.50	2.60	2.70	2.80	2.90	3.00
0	0.1225	0.1108	0.1003	0.0907	0.0821	0.0743	0.0672	0.0608	0.0550	0.0498
1	0.2572	0.2438	0.2306	0.2177	0.2052	0.1931	0.1815	0.1703	0.1596	0.1494
2	0.2700	0.2681	0.2652	0.2613	0.2565	0.2510	0.2450	0.2384	0.2314	0.2240
3	0.1890	0.1966	0.2033	0.2090	0.2138	0.2176	0.2205	0.2225	0.2237	0.2240
4	0.0992	0.1082	0.1169	0.1254	0.1336	0.1414	0.1488	0.1557	0.1622	0.1680
5	0.0417	0.0476	0.0538	0.0602	0.0668	0.0735	0.0804	0.0872	0.0940	0.1008
6	0.0146	0.0174	0.0206	0.0241	0.0278	0.0319	0.0362	0.0407	0.0455	0.0504
7	0.0044	0.0055	0.0068	0.0083	0.0099	0.0118	0.0139	0.0163	0.0188	0.0216
8	0.0011	0.0015	0.0019	0.0025	0.0031	0.0038	0.0047	0.0057	0.0068	0.0081
9	0.0003	0.0004	0.0005	0.0007	0.0009	0.0011	0.0014	0.0018	0.0022	0.0027
10	0.0001	0.0001	0.0001	0.0002	0.0002	0.0003	0.0004	0.0005	0.0006	0.0008
11	0.0000	0.0000	0.0000	0.0000	0.0000	0.0001	0.0001	0.0001	0.0002	0.0002
12	0.0000	0.0000	0.0000	0.0000	0.0000	0.0000	0.0000	0.0000	0.0000	0.0001

continued

λt

x	3.10	3.20	3.30	3.40	3.50	3.60	3.70	3.80	3.90	4.00
0	0.0450	0.0408	0.0369	0.0334	0.0302	0.0273	0.0247	0.0224	0.0202	0.0183
1	0.1397	0.1304	0.1217	0.1135	0.1057	0.0984	0.0915	0.0850	0.0789	0.0733
2	0.2165	0.2087	0.2008	0.1929	0.1850	0.1771	0.1692	0.1615	0.1539	0.1465
3	0.2237	0.2226	0.2209	0.2186	0.2158	0.2125	0.2087	0.2046	0.2001	0.1954
4	0.1733	0.1781	0.1823	0.1858	0.1888	0.1912	0.1931	0.1944	0.1951	0.1954
5	0.1075	0.1140	0.1203	0.1264	0.1322	0.1377	0.1429	0.1477	0.1522	0.1563
6	0.0555	0.0608	0.0662	0.0716	0.0771	0.0826	0.0881	0.0936	0.0989	0.1042
7	0.0246	0.0278	0.0312	0.0348	0.0385	0.0425	0.0466	0.0508	0.0551	0.0595
8	0.0095	0.0111	0.0129	0.0148	0.0169	0.0191	0.0215	0.0241	0.0269	0.0298
9	0.0033	0.0040	0.0047	0.0056	0.0066	0.0076	0.0089	0.0102	0.0116	0.0132
10	0.0010	0.0013	0.0016	0.0019	0.0023	0.0028	0.0033	0.0039	0.0045	0.0053
11	0.0003	0.0004	0.0005	0.0006	0.0007	0.0009	0.0011	0.0013	0.0016	0.0019
12	0.0001	0.0001	0.0001	0.0002	0.0002	0.0003	0.0003	0.0004	0.0005	0.0006
13	0.0000	0.0000	0.0000	0.0000	0.0001	0.0001	0.0001	0.0001	0.0002	0.0002
14	0.0000	0.0000	0.0000	0.0000	0.0000	0.0000	0.0000	0.0000	0.0000	0.0001

λt

x	4.10	4.20	4.30	4.40	4.50	4.60	4.70	4.80	4.90	5.00
0	0.0166	0.0150	0.0136	0.0123	0.0111	0.0101	0.0091	0.0082	0.0074	0.0067
1	0.0679	0.0630	0.0583	0.0540	0.0500	0.0462	0.0427	0.0395	0.0365	0.0337
2	0.1393	0.1323	0.1254	0.1188	0.1125	0.1063	0.1005	0.0948	0.0894	0.0842
3	0.1904	0.1852	0.1798	0.1743	0.1687	0.1631	0.1574	0.1517	0.1460	0.1404
4	0.1951	0.1944	0.1933	0.1917	0.1898	0.1875	0.1849	0.1820	0.1789	0.1755
5	0.1600	0.1633	0.1662	0.1687	0.1708	0.1725	0.1738	0.1747	0.1753	0.1755
6	0.1093	0.1143	0.1191	0.1237	0.1281	0.1323	0.1362	0.1398	0.1432	0.1462
7	0.0640	0.0686	0.0732	0.0778	0.0824	0.0869	0.0914	0.0959	0.1002	0.1044
8	0.0328	0.0360	0.0393	0.0428	0.0463	0.0500	0.0537	0.0575	0.0614	0.0653
9	0.0150	0.0168	0.0188	0.0209	0.0232	0.0255	0.0281	0.0307	0.0334	0.0363
10	0.0061	0.0071	0.0081	0.0092	0.0104	0.0118	0.0132	0.0147	0.0164	0.0181
11	0.0023	0.0027	0.0032	0.0037	0.0043	0.0049	0.0056	0.0064	0.0073	0.0082
12	0.0008	0.0009	0.0011	0.0013	0.0016	0.0019	0.0022	0.0026	0.0030	0.0034
13	0.0002	0.0003	0.0004	0.0005	0.0006	0.0007	0.0008	0.0009	0.0011	0.0013
14	0.0001	0.0001	0.0001	0.0001	0.0002	0.0002	0.0003	0.0003	0.0004	0.0005
15	0.0000	0.0000	0.0000	0.0000	0.0001	0.0001	0.0001	0.0001	0.0001	0.0002

λt

x	5.10	5.20	5.30	5.40	5.50	5.60	5.70	5.80	5.90	6.00
0	0.0061	0.0055	0.0050	0.0045	0.0041	0.0037	0.0033	0.0030	0.0027	0.0025
1	0.0311	0.0287	0.0265	0.0244	0.0225	0.0207	0.0191	0.0176	0.0162	0.0149
2	0.0793	0.0746	0.0701	0.0659	0.0618	0.0580	0.0544	0.0509	0.0477	0.0446
3	0.1348	0.1293	0.1239	0.1185	0.1133	0.1082	0.1033	0.0985	0.0938	0.0892
4	0.1719	0.1681	0.1641	0.1600	0.1558	0.1515	0.1472	0.1428	0.1383	0.1339
5	0.1753	0.1748	0.1740	0.1728	0.1714	0.1697	0.1678	0.1656	0.1632	0.1606
6	0.1490	0.1515	0.1537	0.1555	0.1571	0.1584	0.1594	0.1601	0.1605	0.1606
7	0.1086	0.1125	0.1163	0.1200	0.1234	0.1267	0.1298	0.1326	0.1353	0.1377
8	0.0692	0.0731	0.0771	0.0810	0.0849	0.0887	0.0925	0.0962	0.0998	0.1033
9	0.0392	0.0423	0.0454	0.0486	0.0519	0.0552	0.0586	0.0620	0.0654	0.0688
10	0.0200	0.0220	0.0241	0.0262	0.0285	0.0309	0.0334	0.0359	0.0386	0.0413
11	0.0093	0.0104	0.0116	0.0129	0.0143	0.0157	0.0173	0.0190	0.0207	0.0225
12	0.0039	0.0045	0.0051	0.0058	0.0065	0.0073	0.0082	0.0092	0.0102	0.0113
13	0.0015	0.0018	0.0021	0.0024	0.0028	0.0032	0.0036	0.0041	0.0046	0.0052
14	0.0006	0.0007	0.0008	0.0009	0.0011	0.0013	0.0015	0.0017	0.0019	0.0022
15	0.0002	0.0002	0.0003	0.0003	0.0004	0.0005	0.0006	0.0007	0.0008	0.0009
16	0.0001	0.0001	0.0001	0.0001	0.0001	0.0002	0.0002	0.0002	0.0003	0.0003
17	0.0000	0.0000	0.0000	0.0000	0.0000	0.0001	0.0001	0.0001	0.0001	0.0001

					λt					
x	6.10	6.20	6.30	6.40	6.50	6.60	6.70	6.80	6.90	7.00
0	0.0022	0.0020	0.0018	0.0017	0.0015	0.0014	0.0012	0.0011	0.0010	0.0009
1	0.0137	0.0126	0.0116	0.0106	0.0098	0.0090	0.0082	0.0076	0.0070	0.0064
2	0.0417	0.0390	0.0364	0.0340	0.0318	0.0296	0.0276	0.0258	0.0240	0.0223
3	0.0848	0.0806	0.0765	0.0726	0.0688	0.0652	0.0617	0.0584	0.0552	0.0521
4	0.1294	0.1249	0.1205	0.1162	0.1118	0.1076	0.1034	0.0992	0.0952	0.0912
5	0.1579	0.1549	0.1519	0.1487	0.1454	0.1420	0.1385	0.1349	0.1314	0.1277
6	0.1605	0.1601	0.1595	0.1586	0.1575	0.1562	0.1546	0.1529	0.1511	0.1490
7	0.1399	0.1418	0.1435	0.1450	0.1462	0.1472	0.1480	0.1486	0.1489	0.1490
8	0.1066	0.1099	0.1130	0.1160	0.1188	0.1215	0.1240	0.1263	0.1284	0.1304
9	0.0723	0.0757	0.0791	0.0825	0.0858	0.0891	0.0923	0.0954	0.0985	0.1014
10	0.0441	0.0469	0.0498	0.0528	0.0558	0.0588	0.0618	0.0649	0.0679	0.0710
11	0.0244	0.0265	0.0285	0.0307	0.0330	0.0353	0.0377	0.0401	0.0426	0.0452
12	0.0124	0.0137	0.0150	0.0164	0.0179	0.0194	0.0210	0.0227	0.0245	0.0263
13	0.0058	0.0065	0.0073	0.0081	0.0089	0.0099	0.0108	0.0119	0.0130	0.0142
14	0.0025	0.0029	0.0033	0.0037	0.0041	0.0046	0.0052	0.0058	0.0064	0.0071
15	0.0010	0.0012	0.0014	0.0016	0.0018	0.0020	0.0023	0.0026	0.0029	0.0033
16	0.0004	0.0005	0.0005	0.0006	0.0007	0.0008	0.0010	0.0011	0.0013	0.0014
17	0.0001	0.0002	0.0002	0.0002	0.0003	0.0003	0.0004	0.0004	0.0005	0.0006
18	0.0000	0.0001	0.0001	0.0001	0.0001	0.0001	0.0001	0.0002	0.0002	0.0002
19	0.0000	0.0000	0.0000	0.0000	0.0000	0.0000	0.0001	0.0001	0.0001	0.0001

					λt					
x	7.10	7.20	7.30	7.40	7.50	7.60	7.70	7.80	7.90	8.00
0	0.0008	0.0007	0.0007	0.0006	0.0006	0.0005	0.0005	0.0004	0.0004	0.0003
1	0.0059	0.0054	0.0049	0.0045	0.0041	0.0038	0.0035	0.0032	0.0029	0.0027
2	0.0208	0.0194	0.0180	0.0167	0.0156	0.0145	0.0134	0.0125	0.0116	0.0107
3	0.0492	0.0464	0.0438	0.0413	0.0389	0.0366	0.0345	0.0324	0.0305	0.0286
4	0.0874	0.0836	0.0799	0.0764	0.0729	0.0696	0.0663	0.0632	0.0602	0.0573
5	0.1241	0.1204	0.1167	0.1130	0.1094	0.1057	0.1021	0.0986	0.0951	0.0916
6	0.1468	0.1445	0.1420	0.1394	0.1367	0.1339	0.1311	0.1282	0.1252	0.1221
7	0.1489	0.1486	0.1481	0.1474	0.1465	0.1454	0.1442	0.1428	0.1413	0.1396
8	0.1321	0.1337	0.1351	0.1363	0.1373	0.1381	0.1388	0.1392	0.1395	0.1396
9	0.1042	0.1070	0.1096	0.1121	0.1144	0.1167	0.1187	0.1207	0.1224	0.1241
10	0.0740	0.0770	0.0800	0.0829	0.0858	0.0887	0.0914	0.0941	0.0967	0.0993
11	0.0478	0.0504	0.0531	0.0558	0.0585	0.0613	0.0640	0.0667	0.0695	0.0722
12	0.0283	0.0303	0.0323	0.0344	0.0366	0.0388	0.0411	0.0434	0.0457	0.0481
13	0.0154	0.0168	0.0181	0.0196	0.0211	0.0227	0.0243	0.0260	0.0278	0.0296
14	0.0078	0.0086	0.0095	0.0104	0.0113	0.0123	0.0134	0.0145	0.0157	0.0169
15	0.0037	0.0041	0.0046	0.0051	0.0057	0.0062	0.0069	0.0075	0.0083	0.0090
16	0.0016	0.0019	0.0021	0.0024	0.0026	0.0030	0.0033	0.0037	0.0041	0.0045
17	0.0007	0.0008	0.0009	0.0010	0.0012	0.0013	0.0015	0.0017	0.0019	0.0021
18	0.0003	0.0003	0.0004	0.0004	0.0005	0.0006	0.0006	0.0007	0.0008	0.0009
19	0.0001	0.0001	0.0001	0.0002	0.0002	0.0002	0.0003	0.0003	0.0003	0.0004
20	0.0000	0.0000	0.0001	0.0001	0.0001	0.0001	0.0001	0.0001	0.0001	0.0002
21	0.0000	0.0000	0.0000	0.0000	0.0000	0.0000	0.0000	0.0000	0.0001	0.0001

continued

λt

x	8.10	8.20	8.30	8.40	8.50	8.60	8.70	8.80	8.90	9.00
0	0.0003	0.0003	0.0002	0.0002	0.0002	0.0002	0.0002	0.0002	0.0001	0.0001
1	0.0025	0.0023	0.0021	0.0019	0.0017	0.0016	0.0014	0.0013	0.0012	0.0011
2	0.0100	0.0092	0.0086	0.0079	0.0074	0.0068	0.0063	0.0058	0.0054	0.0050
3	0.0269	0.0252	0.0237	0.0222	0.0208	0.0195	0.0183	0.0171	0.0160	0.0150
4	0.0544	0.0517	0.0491	0.0466	0.0443	0.0420	0.0398	0.0377	0.0357	0.0337
5	0.0882	0.0849	0.0816	0.0784	0.0752	0.0722	0.0692	0.0663	0.0635	0.0607
6	0.1191	0.1160	0.1128	0.1097	0.1066	0.1034	0.1003	0.0972	0.0941	0.0911
7	0.1378	0.1358	0.1338	0.1317	0.1294	0.1271	0.1247	0.1222	0.1197	0.1171
8	0.1395	0.1392	0.1388	0.1382	0.1375	0.1366	0.1356	0.1344	0.1332	0.1318
9	0.1256	0.1269	0.1280	0.1290	0.1299	0.1306	0.1311	0.1315	0.1317	0.1318
10	0.1017	0.1040	0.1063	0.1084	0.1104	0.1123	0.1140	0.1157	0.1172	0.1186
11	0.0749	0.0776	0.0802	0.0828	0.0853	0.0878	0.0902	0.0925	0.0948	0.0970
12	0.0505	0.0530	0.0555	0.0579	0.0604	0.0629	0.0654	0.0679	0.0703	0.0728
13	0.0315	0.0334	0.0354	0.0374	0.0395	0.0416	0.0438	0.0459	0.0481	0.0504
14	0.0182	0.0196	0.0210	0.0225	0.0240	0.0256	0.0272	0.0289	0.0306	0.0324
15	0.0098	0.0107	0.0116	0.0126	0.0136	0.0147	0.0158	0.0169	0.0182	0.0194
16	0.0050	0.0055	0.0060	0.0066	0.0072	0.0079	0.0086	0.0093	0.0101	0.0109
17	0.0024	0.0026	0.0029	0.0033	0.0036	0.0040	0.0044	0.0048	0.0053	0.0058
18	0.0011	0.0012	0.0014	0.0015	0.0017	0.0019	0.0021	0.0024	0.0026	0.0029
19	0.0005	0.0005	0.0006	0.0007	0.0008	0.0009	0.0010	0.0011	0.0012	0.0014
20	0.0002	0.0002	0.0002	0.0003	0.0003	0.0004	0.0004	0.0005	0.0005	0.0006
21	0.0001	0.0001	0.0001	0.0001	0.0001	0.0002	0.0002	0.0002	0.0002	0.0003
22	0.0000	0.0000	0.0000	0.0000	0.0001	0.0001	0.0001	0.0001	0.0001	0.0001

λt

x	9.10	9.20	9.30	9.40	9.50	9.60	9.70	9.80	9.90	10.00
0	0.0001	0.0001	0.0001	0.0001	0.0001	0.0001	0.0001	0.0001	0.0001	0.0000
1	0.0010	0.0009	0.0009	0.0008	0.0007	0.0007	0.0006	0.0005	0.0005	0.0005
2	0.0046	0.0043	0.0040	0.0037	0.0034	0.0031	0.0029	0.0027	0.0025	0.0023
3	0.0140	0.0131	0.0123	0.0115	0.0107	0.0100	0.0093	0.0087	0.0081	0.0076
4	0.0319	0.0302	0.0285	0.0269	0.0254	0.0240	0.0226	0.0213	0.0201	0.0189
5	0.0581	0.0555	0.0530	0.0506	0.0483	0.0460	0.0439	0.0418	0.0398	0.0378
6	0.0881	0.0851	0.0822	0.0793	0.0764	0.0736	0.0709	0.0682	0.0656	0.0631
7	0.1145	0.1118	0.1091	0.1064	0.1037	0.1010	0.0982	0.0955	0.0928	0.0901
8	0.1302	0.1286	0.1269	0.1251	0.1232	0.1212	0.1191	0.1170	0.1148	0.1126
9	0.1317	0.1315	0.1311	0.1306	0.1300	0.1293	0.1284	0.1274	0.1263	0.1251
10	0.1198	0.1210	0.1219	0.1228	0.1235	0.1241	0.1245	0.1249	0.1250	0.1251
11	0.0991	0.1012	0.1031	0.1049	0.1067	0.1083	0.1098	0.1112	0.1125	0.1137
12	0.0752	0.0776	0.0799	0.0822	0.0844	0.0866	0.0888	0.0908	0.0928	0.0948
13	0.0526	0.0549	0.0572	0.0594	0.0617	0.0640	0.0662	0.0685	0.0707	0.0729
14	0.0342	0.0361	0.0380	0.0399	0.0419	0.0439	0.0459	0.0479	0.0500	0.0521
15	0.0208	0.0221	0.0235	0.0250	0.0265	0.0281	0.0297	0.0313	0.0330	0.0347
16	0.0118	0.0127	0.0137	0.0147	0.0157	0.0168	0.0180	0.0192	0.0204	0.0217
17	0.0063	0.0069	0.0075	0.0081	0.0088	0.0095	0.0103	0.0111	0.0119	0.0128
18	0.0032	0.0035	0.0039	0.0042	0.0046	0.0051	0.0055	0.0060	0.0065	0.0071
19	0.0015	0.0017	0.0019	0.0021	0.0023	0.0026	0.0028	0.0031	0.0034	0.0037
20	0.0007	0.0008	0.0009	0.0010	0.0011	0.0012	0.0014	0.0015	0.0017	0.0019
21	0.0003	0.0003	0.0004	0.0004	0.0005	0.0006	0.0006	0.0007	0.0008	0.0009
22	0.0001	0.0001	0.0002	0.0002	0.0002	0.0002	0.0003	0.0003	0.0004	0.0004
23	0.0000	0.0001	0.0001	0.0001	0.0001	0.0001	0.0001	0.0001	0.0002	0.0002
24	0.0000	0.0000	0.0000	0.0000	0.0000	0.0000	0.0000	0.0001	0.0001	0.0001

λt

x	11.00	12.00	13.00	14.00	15.00	16.00	17.00	18.00	19.00	20.00
0	0.0000	0.0000	0.0000	0.0000	0.0000	0.0000	0.0000	0.0000	0.0000	0.0000
1	0.0002	0.0001	0.0000	0.0000	0.0000	0.0000	0.0000	0.0000	0.0000	0.0000
2	0.0010	0.0004	0.0002	0.0001	0.0000	0.0000	0.0000	0.0000	0.0000	0.0000
3	0.0037	0.0018	0.0008	0.0004	0.0002	0.0001	0.0000	0.0000	0.0000	0.0000
4	0.0102	0.0053	0.0027	0.0013	0.0006	0.0003	0.0001	0.0001	0.0000	0.0000
5	0.0224	0.0127	0.0070	0.0037	0.0019	0.0010	0.0005	0.0002	0.0001	0.0001
6	0.0411	0.0255	0.0152	0.0087	0.0048	0.0026	0.0014	0.0007	0.0004	0.0002
7	0.0646	0.0437	0.0281	0.0174	0.0104	0.0060	0.0034	0.0019	0.0010	0.0005
8	0.0888	0.0655	0.0457	0.0304	0.0194	0.0120	0.0072	0.0042	0.0024	0.0013
9	0.1085	0.0874	0.0661	0.0473	0.0324	0.0213	0.0135	0.0083	0.0050	0.0029
10	0.1194	0.1048	0.0859	0.0663	0.0486	0.0341	0.0230	0.0150	0.0095	0.0058
11	0.1194	0.1144	0.1015	0.0844	0.0663	0.0496	0.0355	0.0245	0.0164	0.0106
12	0.1094	0.1144	0.1099	0.0984	0.0829	0.0661	0.0504	0.0368	0.0259	0.0176
13	0.0926	0.1056	0.1099	0.1060	0.0956	0.0814	0.0658	0.0509	0.0378	0.0271
14	0.0728	0.0905	0.1021	0.1060	0.1024	0.0930	0.0800	0.0655	0.0514	0.0387
15	0.0534	0.0724	0.0885	0.0989	0.1024	0.0992	0.0906	0.0786	0.0650	0.0516
16	0.0367	0.0543	0.0719	0.0866	0.0960	0.0992	0.0963	0.0884	0.0772	0.0646
17	0.0237	0.0383	0.0550	0.0713	0.0847	0.0934	0.0963	0.0936	0.0863	0.0760
18	0.0145	0.0255	0.0397	0.0554	0.0706	0.0830	0.0909	0.0936	0.0911	0.0844
19	0.0084	0.0161	0.0272	0.0409	0.0557	0.0699	0.0814	0.0887	0.0911	0.0888
20	0.0046	0.0097	0.0177	0.0286	0.0418	0.0559	0.0692	0.0798	0.0866	0.0888
21	0.0024	0.0055	0.0109	0.0191	0.0299	0.0426	0.0560	0.0684	0.0783	0.0846
22	0.0012	0.0030	0.0065	0.0121	0.0204	0.0310	0.0433	0.0560	0.0676	0.0769
23	0.0006	0.0016	0.0037	0.0074	0.0133	0.0216	0.0320	0.0438	0.0559	0.0669
24	0.0003	0.0008	0.0020	0.0043	0.0083	0.0144	0.0226	0.0328	0.0442	0.0557
25	0.0001	0.0004	0.0010	0.0024	0.0050	0.0092	0.0154	0.0237	0.0336	0.0446
26	0.0000	0.0002	0.0005	0.0013	0.0029	0.0057	0.0101	0.0164	0.0246	0.0343
27	0.0000	0.0001	0.0002	0.0007	0.0016	0.0034	0.0063	0.0109	0.0173	0.0254
28	0.0000	0.0000	0.0001	0.0003	0.0009	0.0019	0.0038	0.0070	0.0117	0.0181
29	0.0000	0.0000	0.0001	0.0002	0.0004	0.0011	0.0023	0.0044	0.0077	0.0125
30	0.0000	0.0000	0.0000	0.0001	0.0002	0.0006	0.0013	0.0026	0.0049	0.0083
31	0.0000	0.0000	0.0000	0.0000	0.0001	0.0003	0.0007	0.0015	0.0030	0.0054
32	0.0000	0.0000	0.0000	0.0000	0.0001	0.0001	0.0004	0.0009	0.0018	0.0034
33	0.0000	0.0000	0.0000	0.0000	0.0000	0.0001	0.0002	0.0005	0.0010	0.0020
34	0.0000	0.0000	0.0000	0.0000	0.0000	0.0000	0.0001	0.0002	0.0006	0.0012
35	0.0000	0.0000	0.0000	0.0000	0.0000	0.0000	0.0000	0.0001	0.0003	0.0007
36	0.0000	0.0000	0.0000	0.0000	0.0000	0.0000	0.0000	0.0001	0.0002	0.0004
37	0.0000	0.0000	0.0000	0.0000	0.0000	0.0000	0.0000	0.0000	0.0001	0.0002
38	0.0000	0.0000	0.0000	0.0000	0.0000	0.0000	0.0000	0.0000	0.0000	0.0001
39	0.0000	0.0000	0.0000	0.0000	0.0000	0.0000	0.0000	0.0000	0.0000	0.0001

Standard Normal Distribution Table

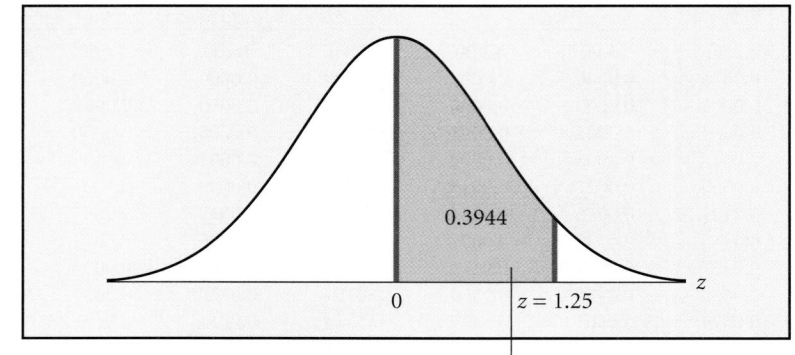

z	0	0.01	0.02	0.03	0.04	0.05	0.06	0.07	0.08	0.09
0.0	0.0000	0.0040	0.0080	0.0120	0.0160	0.0199	0.0239	0.0279	0.0319	0.0359
0.1	0.0398	0.0438	0.0478	0.0517	0.0557	0.0596	0.0636	0.0675	0.0714	0.0753
0.2	0.0793	0.0832	0.0871	0.0910	0.0948	0.0987	0.1026	0.1064	0.1103	0.1141
0.3	0.1179	0.1217	0.1255	0.1293	0.1331	0.1368	0.1406	0.1443	0.1480	0.1517
0.4	0.1554	0.1591	0.1628	0.1664	0.1700	0.1736	0.1772	0.1808	0.1844	0.1879
0.5	0.1915	0.1950	0.1985	0.2019	0.2054	0.2088	0.2123	0.2157	0.2190	0.2224
0.6	0.2257	0.2291	0.2324	0.2357	0.2389	0.2422	0.2454	0.2486	0.2517	0.2549
0.7	0.2580	0.2611	0.2642	0.2673	0.2704	0.2734	0.2764	0.2794	0.2823	0.2852
0.8	0.2881	0.2910	0.2939	0.2967	0.2995	0.3023	0.3051	0.3078	0.3106	0.3133
0.9	0.3159	0.3186	0.3212	0.3238	0.3264	0.3289	0.3315	0.3340	0.3365	0.3389
1.0	0.3413	0.3438	0.3461	0.3485	0.3508	0.3531	0.3554	0.3577	0.3599	0.3621
1.1	0.3643	0.3665	0.3686	0.3708	0.3729	0.3749	0.3770	0.3790	0.3810	0.3830
1.2	0.3849	0.3869	0.3888	0.3907	0.3925	0.3944	0.3962	0.3980	0.3997	0.4015
1.3	0.4032	0.4049	0.4066	0.4082	0.4099	0.4115	0.4131	0.4147	0.4162	0.4177
1.4	0.4192	0.4207	0.4222	0.4236	0.4251	0.4265	0.4279	0.4292	0.4306	0.4319
1.5	0.4332	0.4345	0.4357	0.4370	0.4382	0.4394	0.4406	0.4418	0.4429	0.4441
1.6	0.4452	0.4463	0.4474	0.4484	0.4495	0.4505	0.4515	0.4525	0.4535	0.4545
1.7	0.4554	0.4564	0.4573	0.4582	0.4591	0.4599	0.4608	0.4616	0.4625	0.4633
1.8	0.4641	0.4649	0.4656	0.4664	0.4671	0.4678	0.4686	0.4693	0.4699	0.4706
1.9	0.4713	0.4719	0.4726	0.4732	0.4738	0.4744	0.4750	0.4756	0.4761	0.4767
2.0	0.4772	0.4778	0.4783	0.4788	0.4793	0.4798	0.4803	0.4808	0.4812	0.4817
2.1	0.4821	0.4826	0.4830	0.4834	0.4838	0.4842	0.4846	0.4850	0.4854	0.4857
2.2	0.4861	0.4864	0.4868	0.4871	0.4875	0.4878	0.4881	0.4884	0.4887	0.4890
2.3	0.4893	0.4896	0.4898	0.4901	0.4904	0.4906	0.4909	0.4911	0.4913	0.4916
2.4	0.4918	0.4920	0.4922	0.4925	0.4927	0.4929	0.4931	0.4932	0.4934	0.4936
2.5	0.4938	0.4940	0.4941	0.4943	0.4945	0.4946	0.4948	0.4949	0.4951	0.4952
2.6	0.4953	0.4955	0.4956	0.4957	0.4959	0.4960	0.4961	0.4962	0.4963	0.4964
2.7	0.4965	0.4966	0.4967	0.4968	0.4969	0.4970	0.4971	0.4972	0.4973	0.4974
2.8	0.4974	0.4975	0.4976	0.4977	0.4977	0.4978	0.4979	0.4979	0.4980	0.4981
2.9	0.4981	0.4982	0.4982	0.4983	0.4984	0.4984	0.4985	0.4985	0.4986	0.4986
3.0	0.4987	0.4987	0.4987	0.4988	0.4988	0.4989	0.4989	0.4989	0.4990	0.4990

APPENDIX E

Exponential Distribution Table

Values of $e^{-\lambda a}$

λa	$e^{-\lambda a}$	λa	$e^{-\lambda a}$	λa	$e^{-\lambda a}$	λa	$e^{-\lambda a}$	λa	$e^{-\lambda a}$
0.00	1.0000	2.05	0.1287	4.05	0.0174	6.05	0.0024	8.05	0.0003
0.05	0.9512	2.10	0.1225	4.10	0.0166	6.10	0.0022	8.10	0.0003
0.10	0.9048	2.15	0.1165	4.15	0.0158	6.15	0.0021	8.15	0.0003
0.15	0.8607	2.20	0.1108	4.20	0.0150	6.20	0.0020	8.20	0.0003
0.20	0.8187	2.25	0.1054	4.25	0.0143	6.25	0.0019	8.25	0.0003
0.25	0.7788	2.30	0.1003	4.30	0.0136	6.30	0.0018	8.30	0.0002
0.30	0.7408	2.35	0.0954	4.35	0.0129	6.35	0.0017	8.35	0.0002
0.35	0.7047	2.40	0.0907	4.40	0.0123	6.40	0.0017	8.40	0.0002
0.40	0.6703	2.45	0.0863	4.45	0.0117	6.45	0.0016	8.45	0.0002
0.45	0.6376	2.50	0.0821	4.50	0.0111	6.50	0.0015	8.50	0.0002
0.50	0.6065	2.55	0.0781	4.55	0.0106	6.55	0.0014	8.55	0.0002
0.55	0.5769	2.60	0.0743	4.60	0.0101	6.60	0.0014	8.60	0.0002
0.60	0.5488	2.65	0.0707	4.65	0.0096	6.65	0.0013	8.65	0.0002
0.65	0.5220	2.70	0.0672	4.70	0.0091	6.70	0.0012	8.70	0.0002
0.70	0.4966	2.75	0.0639	4.75	0.0087	6.75	0.0012	8.75	0.0002
0.75	0.4724	2.80	0.0608	4.80	0.0082	6.80	0.0011	8.80	0.0002
0.80	0.4493	2.85	0.0578	4.85	0.0078	6.85	0.0011	8.85	0.0001
0.85	0.4274	2.90	0.0550	4.90	0.0074	6.90	0.0010	8.90	0.0001
0.90	0.4066	2.95	0.0523	4.95	0.0071	6.95	0.0010	8.95	0.0001
0.95	0.3867	3.00	0.0498	5.00	0.0067	7.00	0.0009	9.00	0.0001
1.00	0.3679	3.05	0.0474	5.05	0.0064	7.05	0.0009	9.05	0.0001
1.05	0.3499	3.10	0.0450	5.10	0.0061	7.10	0.0008	9.10	0.0001
1.10	0.3329	3.15	0.0429	5.15	0.0058	7.15	0.0008	9.15	0.0001
1.15	0.3166	3.20	0.0408	5.20	0.0055	7.20	0.0007	9.20	0.0001
1.20	0.3012	3.25	0.0388	5.25	0.0052	7.25	0.0007	9.25	0.0001
1.25	0.2865	3.30	0.0369	5.30	0.0050	7.30	0.0007	9.30	0.0001
1.30	0.2725	3.35	0.0351	5.35	0.0047	7.35	0.0006	9.35	0.0001
1.35	0.2592	3.40	0.0334	5.40	0.0045	7.40	0.0006	9.40	0.0001
1.40	0.2466	3.45	0.0317	5.45	0.0043	7.45	0.0006	9.45	0.0001
1.45	0.2346	3.50	0.0302	5.50	0.0041	7.50	0.0006	9.50	0.0001
1.50	0.2231	3.55	0.0287	5.55	0.0039	7.55	0.0005	9.55	0.0001
1.55	0.2122	3.60	0.0273	5.60	0.0037	7.60	0.0005	9.60	0.0001
1.60	0.2019	3.65	0.0260	5.65	0.0035	7.65	0.0005	9.65	0.0001
1.65	0.1920	3.70	0.0247	5.70	0.0033	7.70	0.0005	9.70	0.0001
1.70	0.1827	3.75	0.0235	5.75	0.0032	7.75	0.0004	9.75	0.0001
1.75	0.1738	3.80	0.0224	5.80	0.0030	7.80	0.0004	9.80	0.0001
1.80	0.1653	3.85	0.0213	5.85	0.0029	7.85	0.0004	9.85	0.0001
1.85	0.1572	3.90	0.0202	5.90	0.0027	7.90	0.0004	9.90	0.0001
1.90	0.1496	3.95	0.0193	5.95	0.0026	7.95	0.0004	9.95	0.0000
1.95	0.1423	4.00	0.0183	6.00	0.0025	8.00	0.0003	10.00	0.0000
2.00	0.1353								

APPENDIX F

Values of *t* for Selected Probabilities

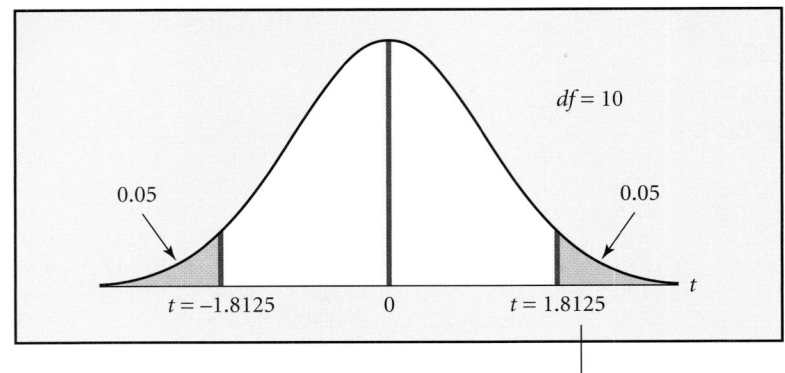

PROBABILITIES (OR AREAS UNDER *t*-DISTRIBUTION CURVE)

Conf. Level One Tail Two Tails	0.1 0.45 0.9	0.3 0.35 0.7	0.5 0.25 0.5	0.7 0.15 0.3	0.8 0.1 0.2	0.9 0.05 0.1	0.95 0.025 0.05	0.98 0.01 0.02	0.99 0.005 0.01
df					*Values of t*				
1	0.1584	0.5095	1.0000	1.9626	3.0777	6.3137	12.7062	31.8210	63.6559
2	0.1421	0.4447	0.8165	1.3862	1.8856	2.9200	4.3027	6.9645	9.9250
3	0.1366	0.4242	0.7649	1.2498	1.6377	2.3534	3.1824	4.5407	5.8408
4	0.1338	0.4142	0.7407	1.1896	1.5332	2.1318	2.7765	3.7469	4.6041
5	0.1322	0.4082	0.7267	1.1558	1.4759	2.0150	2.5706	3.3649	4.0321
6	0.1311	0.4043	0.7176	1.1342	1.4398	1.9432	2.4469	3.1427	3.7074
7	0.1303	0.4015	0.7111	1.1192	1.4149	1.8946	2.3646	2.9979	3.4995
8	0.1297	0.3995	0.7064	1.1081	1.3968	1.8595	2.3060	2.8965	3.3554
9	0.1293	0.3979	0.7027	1.0997	1.3830	1.8331	2.2622	2.8214	3.2498
10	0.1289	0.3966	0.6998	1.0931	1.3722	1.8125	2.2281	2.7638	3.1693
11	0.1286	0.3956	0.6974	1.0877	1.3634	1.7959	2.2010	2.7181	3.1058
12	0.1283	0.3947	0.6955	1.0832	1.3562	1.7823	2.1788	2.6810	3.0545
13	0.1281	0.3940	0.6938	1.0795	1.3502	1.7709	2.1604	2.6503	3.0123
14	0.1280	0.3933	0.6924	1.0763	1.3450	1.7613	2.1448	2.6245	2.9768
15	0.1278	0.3928	0.6912	1.0735	1.3406	1.7531	2.1315	2.6025	2.9467
16	0.1277	0.3923	0.6901	1.0711	1.3368	1.7459	2.1199	2.5835	2.9208
17	0.1276	0.3919	0.6892	1.0690	1.3334	1.7396	2.1098	2.5669	2.8982
18	0.1274	0.3915	0.6884	1.0672	1.3304	1.7341	2.1009	2.5524	2.8784
19	0.1274	0.3912	0.6876	1.0655	1.3277	1.7291	2.0930	2.5395	2.8609
20	0.1273	0.3909	0.6870	1.0640	1.3253	1.7247	2.0860	2.5280	2.8453
21	0.1272	0.3906	0.6864	1.0627	1.3232	1.7207	2.0796	2.5176	2.8314
22	0.1271	0.3904	0.6858	1.0614	1.3212	1.7171	2.0739	2.5083	2.8188
23	0.1271	0.3902	0.6853	1.0603	1.3195	1.7139	2.0687	2.4999	2.8073
24	0.1270	0.3900	0.6848	1.0593	1.3178	1.7109	2.0639	2.4922	2.7970
25	0.1269	0.3898	0.6844	1.0584	1.3163	1.7081	2.0595	2.4851	2.7874
26	0.1269	0.3896	0.6840	1.0575	1.3150	1.7056	2.0555	2.4786	2.7787
27	0.1268	0.3894	0.6837	1.0567	1.3137	1.7033	2.0518	2.4727	2.7707
28	0.1268	0.3893	0.6834	1.0560	1.3125	1.7011	2.0484	2.4671	2.7633
29	0.1268	0.3892	0.6830	1.0553	1.3114	1.6991	2.0452	2.4620	2.7564
30	0.1267	0.3890	0.6828	1.0547	1.3104	1.6973	2.0423	2.4573	2.7500
31	0.1267	0.3889	0.6825	1.0541	1.3095	1.6955	2.0395	2.4528	2.7440
32	0.1267	0.3888	0.6822	1.0535	1.3086	1.6939	2.0369	2.4487	2.7385
33	0.1266	0.3887	0.6820	1.0530	1.3077	1.6924	2.0345	2.4448	2.7333
34	0.1266	0.3886	0.6818	1.0525	1.3070	1.6909	2.0322	2.4411	2.7284
35	0.1266	0.3885	0.6816	1.0520	1.3062	1.6896	2.0301	2.4377	2.7238
36	0.1266	0.3884	0.6814	1.0516	1.3055	1.6883	2.0281	2.4345	2.7195
37	0.1265	0.3883	0.6812	1.0512	1.3049	1.6871	2.0262	2.4314	2.7154

PROBABILITIES (OR AREAS UNDER t-DISTRIBUTION CURVE)

Conf. Level One Tail Two Tails	0.1 0.45 0.9	0.3 0.35 0.7	0.5 0.25 0.5	0.7 0.15 0.3	0.8 0.1 0.2	0.9 0.05 0.1	0.95 0.025 0.05	0.98 0.01 0.02	0.99 0.005 0.01
df					Values of t				
38	0.1265	0.3882	0.6810	1.0508	1.3042	1.6860	2.0244	2.4286	2.7116
39	0.1265	0.3882	0.6808	1.0504	1.3036	1.6849	2.0227	2.4258	2.7079
40	0.1265	0.3881	0.6807	1.0500	1.3031	1.6839	2.0211	2.4233	2.7045
41	0.1264	0.3880	0.6805	1.0497	1.3025	1.6829	2.0195	2.4208	2.7012
42	0.1264	0.3880	0.6804	1.0494	1.3020	1.6820	2.0181	2.4185	2.6981
43	0.1264	0.3879	0.6802	1.0491	1.3016	1.6811	2.0167	2.4163	2.6951
44	0.1264	0.3878	0.6801	1.0488	1.3011	1.6802	2.0154	2.4141	2.6923
45	0.1264	0.3878	0.6800	1.0485	1.3007	1.6794	2.0141	2.4121	2.6896
46	0.1264	0.3877	0.6799	1.0482	1.3002	1.6787	2.0129	2.4102	2.6870
47	0.1263	0.3877	0.6797	1.0480	1.2998	1.6779	2.0117	2.4083	2.6846
48	0.1263	0.3876	0.6796	1.0478	1.2994	1.6772	2.0106	2.4066	2.6822
49	0.1263	0.3876	0.6795	1.0475	1.2991	1.6766	2.0096	2.4049	2.6800
50	0.1263	0.3875	0.6794	1.0473	1.2987	1.6759	2.0086	2.4033	2.6778
51	0.1263	0.3875	0.6793	1.0471	1.2984	1.6753	2.0076	2.4017	2.6757
52	0.1263	0.3875	0.6792	1.0469	1.2980	1.6747	2.0066	2.4002	2.6737
53	0.1263	0.3874	0.6791	1.0467	1.2977	1.6741	2.0057	2.3988	2.6718
54	0.1263	0.3874	0.6791	1.0465	1.2974	1.6736	2.0049	2.3974	2.6700
55	0.1262	0.3873	0.6790	1.0463	1.2971	1.6730	2.0040	2.3961	2.6682
56	0.1262	0.3873	0.6789	1.0461	1.2969	1.6725	2.0032	2.3948	2.6665
57	0.1262	0.3873	0.6788	1.0459	1.2966	1.6720	2.0025	2.3936	2.6649
58	0.1262	0.3872	0.6787	1.0458	1.2963	1.6716	2.0017	2.3924	2.6633
59	0.1262	0.3872	0.6787	1.0456	1.2961	1.6711	2.0010	2.3912	2.6618
60	0.1262	0.3872	0.6786	1.0455	1.2958	1.6706	2.0003	2.3901	2.6603
61	0.1262	0.3871	0.6785	1.0453	1.2956	1.6702	1.9996	2.3890	2.6589
62	0.1262	0.3871	0.6785	1.0452	1.2954	1.6698	1.9990	2.3880	2.6575
63	0.1262	0.3871	0.6784	1.0450	1.2951	1.6694	1.9983	2.3870	2.6561
64	0.1262	0.3871	0.6783	1.0449	1.2949	1.6690	1.9977	2.3860	2.6549
65	0.1262	0.3870	0.6783	1.0448	1.2947	1.6686	1.9971	2.3851	2.6536
66	0.1261	0.3870	0.6782	1.0446	1.2945	1.6683	1.9966	2.3842	2.6524
67	0.1261	0.3870	0.6782	1.0445	1.2943	1.6679	1.9960	2.3833	2.6512
68	0.1261	0.3870	0.6781	1.0444	1.2941	1.6676	1.9955	2.3824	2.6501
69	0.1261	0.3869	0.6781	1.0443	1.2939	1.6672	1.9949	2.3816	2.6490
70	0.1261	0.3869	0.6780	1.0442	1.2938	1.6669	1.9944	2.3808	2.6479
71	0.1261	0.3869	0.6780	1.0441	1.2936	1.6666	1.9939	2.3800	2.6469
72	0.1261	0.3869	0.6779	1.0440	1.2934	1.6663	1.9935	2.3793	2.6458
73	0.1261	0.3868	0.6779	1.0438	1.2933	1.6660	1.9930	2.3785	2.6449
74	0.1261	0.3868	0.6778	1.0437	1.2931	1.6657	1.9925	2.3778	2.6439
75	0.1261	0.3868	0.6778	1.0436	1.2929	1.6654	1.9921	2.3771	2.6430
76	0.1261	0.3868	0.6777	1.0436	1.2928	1.6652	1.9917	2.3764	2.6421
77	0.1261	0.3868	0.6777	1.0435	1.2926	1.6649	1.9913	2.3758	2.6412
78	0.1261	0.3867	0.6776	1.0434	1.2925	1.6646	1.9908	2.3751	2.6403
79	0.1261	0.3867	0.6776	1.0433	1.2924	1.6644	1.9905	2.3745	2.6395
80	0.1261	0.3867	0.6776	1.0432	1.2922	1.6641	1.9901	2.3739	2.6387
81	0.1261	0.3867	0.6775	1.0431	1.2921	1.6639	1.9897	2.3733	2.6379
82	0.1261	0.3867	0.6775	1.0430	1.2920	1.6636	1.9893	2.3727	2.6371
83	0.1260	0.3867	0.6775	1.0429	1.2918	1.6634	1.9890	2.3721	2.6364
84	0.1260	0.3866	0.6774	1.0429	1.2917	1.6632	1.9886	2.3716	2.6356
85	0.1260	0.3866	0.6774	1.0428	1.2916	1.6630	1.9883	2.3710	2.6349
86	0.1260	0.3866	0.6774	1.0427	1.2915	1.6628	1.9879	2.3705	2.6342
87	0.1260	0.3866	0.6773	1.0426	1.2914	1.6626	1.9876	2.3700	2.6335
88	0.1260	0.3866	0.6773	1.0426	1.2912	1.6624	1.9873	2.3695	2.6329
89	0.1260	0.3866	0.6773	1.0425	1.2911	1.6622	1.9870	2.3690	2.6322

continued

PROBABILITIES (OR AREAS UNDER t-DISTRIBUTION CURVE)

Conf. Level	0.1	0.3	0.5	0.7	0.8	0.9	0.95	0.98	0.99
One Tail	0.45	0.35	0.25	0.15	0.1	0.05	0.025	0.01	0.005
Two Tails	0.9	0.7	0.5	0.3	0.2	0.1	0.05	0.02	0.01
df					Values of t				
90	0.1260	0.3866	0.6772	1.0424	1.2910	1.6620	1.9867	2.3685	2.6316
91	0.1260	0.3865	0.6772	1.0424	1.2909	1.6618	1.9864	2.3680	2.6309
92	0.1260	0.3865	0.6772	1.0423	1.2908	1.6616	1.9861	2.3676	2.6303
93	0.1260	0.3865	0.6771	1.0422	1.2907	1.6614	1.9858	2.3671	2.6297
94	0.1260	0.3865	0.6771	1.0422	1.2906	1.6612	1.9855	2.3667	2.6291
95	0.1260	0.3865	0.6771	1.0421	1.2905	1.6611	1.9852	2.3662	2.6286
96	0.1260	0.3865	0.6771	1.0421	1.2904	1.6609	1.9850	2.3658	2.6280
97	0.1260	0.3865	0.6770	1.0420	1.2903	1.6607	1.9847	2.3654	2.6275
98	0.1260	0.3865	0.6770	1.0419	1.2903	1.6606	1.9845	2.3650	2.6269
99	0.1260	0.3864	0.6770	1.0419	1.2902	1.6604	1.9842	2.3646	2.6264
100	0.1260	0.3864	0.6770	1.0418	1.2901	1.6602	1.9840	2.3642	2.6259
∞	0.1260	0.3853	0.6745	1.0365	1.2816	1.6449	1.9600	2.3263	2.5758

APPENDIX G

Values of χ^2 for Selected Probabilities

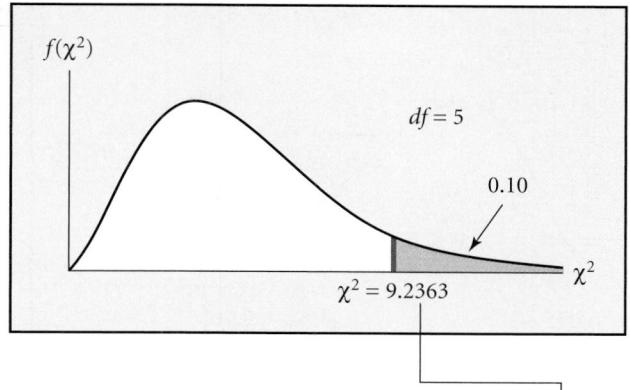

PROBABILITIES (OR AREAS UNDER CHI-SQUARE DISTRIBUTION CURVE ABOVE GIVEN CHI-SQUARE VALUES)

df	0.9	0.7	0.5	0.3	0.2	0.1	0.05	0.02	0.01
				Values of Chi-Squared					
1	0.0158	0.1485	0.4549	1.0742	1.6424	2.7055	3.8415	5.4119	6.6349
2	0.2107	0.7133	1.3863	2.4079	3.2189	4.6052	5.9915	7.8241	9.2104
3	0.5844	1.4237	2.3660	3.6649	4.6416	6.2514	7.8147	9.8374	11.3449
4	1.0636	2.1947	3.3567	4.8784	5.9886	7.7794	9.4877	11.6678	13.2767
5	1.6103	2.9999	4.3515	6.0644	7.2893	9.2363	11.0705	13.3882	15.0863
6	2.2041	3.8276	5.3481	7.2311	8.5581	10.6446	12.5916	15.0332	16.8119
7	2.8331	4.6713	6.3458	8.3834	9.8032	12.0170	14.0671	16.6224	18.4753
8	3.4895	5.5274	7.3441	9.5245	11.0301	13.3616	15.5073	18.1682	20.0902
9	4.1682	6.3933	8.3428	10.6564	12.2421	14.6837	16.9190	19.6790	21.6660
10	4.8652	7.2672	9.3418	11.7807	13.4420	15.9872	18.3070	21.1608	23.2093
11	5.5778	8.1479	10.3410	12.8987	14.6314	17.2750	19.6752	22.6179	24.7250
12	6.3038	9.0343	11.3403	14.0111	15.8120	18.5493	21.0261	24.0539	26.2170
13	7.0415	9.9257	12.3398	15.1187	16.9848	19.8119	22.3620	25.4715	27.6882
14	7.7895	10.8215	13.3393	16.2221	18.1508	21.0641	23.6848	26.8727	29.1412
15	8.5468	11.7212	14.3389	17.3217	19.3107	22.3071	24.9958	28.2595	30.5780
16	9.3122	12.6243	15.3385	18.4179	20.4651	23.5418	26.2962	29.6332	31.9999
17	10.0852	13.5307	16.3382	19.5110	21.6146	24.7690	27.5871	30.9950	33.4087
18	10.8649	14.4399	17.3379	20.6014	22.7595	25.9894	28.8693	32.3462	34.8052
19	11.6509	15.3517	18.3376	21.6891	23.9004	27.2036	30.1435	33.6874	36.1908
20	12.4426	16.2659	19.3374	22.7745	25.0375	28.4120	31.4104	35.0196	37.5663
21	13.2396	17.1823	20.3372	23.8578	26.1711	29.6151	32.6706	36.3434	38.9322
22	14.0415	18.1007	21.3370	24.9390	27.3015	30.8133	33.9245	37.6595	40.2894
23	14.8480	19.0211	22.3369	26.0184	28.4288	32.0069	35.1725	38.9683	41.6383
24	15.6587	19.9432	23.3367	27.0960	29.5533	33.1962	36.4150	40.2703	42.9798
25	16.4734	20.8670	24.3366	28.1719	30.6752	34.3816	37.6525	41.5660	44.3140
26	17.2919	21.7924	25.3365	29.2463	31.7946	35.5632	38.8851	42.8558	45.6416
27	18.1139	22.7192	26.3363	30.3193	32.9117	36.7412	40.1133	44.1399	46.9628
28	18.9392	23.6475	27.3362	31.3909	34.0266	37.9159	41.3372	45.4188	48.2782
29	19.7677	24.5770	28.3361	32.4612	35.1394	39.0875	42.5569	46.6926	49.5878
30	20.5992	25.5078	29.3360	33.5302	36.2502	40.2560	43.7730	47.9618	50.8922

APPENDIX H

F-Distribution Table:
Upper 5%
Probability
(or 5% Area) Under
F-Distribution Curve

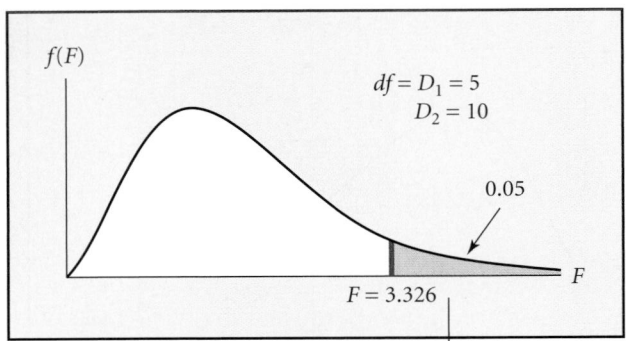

DENOMINATOR				NUMERATOR $df = D_1$						
$df = D_2$	1	2	3	4	5	6	7	8	9	10
1	161.446	199.499	215.707	224.583	230.160	233.988	236.767	238.884	240.543	241.882
2	18.513	19.000	19.164	19.247	19.296	19.329	19.353	19.371	19.385	19.396
3	10.128	9.552	9.277	9.117	9.013	8.941	8.887	8.845	8.812	8.785
4	7.709	6.944	6.591	6.388	6.256	6.163	6.094	6.041	5.999	5.964
5	6.608	5.786	5.409	5.192	5.050	4.950	4.876	4.818	4.772	4.735
6	5.987	5.143	4.757	4.534	4.387	4.284	4.207	4.147	4.099	4.060
7	5.591	4.737	4.347	4.120	3.972	3.866	3.787	3.726	3.677	3.637
8	5.318	4.459	4.066	3.838	3.688	3.581	3.500	3.438	3.388	3.347
9	5.117	4.256	3.863	3.633	3.482	3.374	3.293	3.230	3.179	3.137
10	4.965	4.103	3.708	3.478	3.326	3.217	3.135	3.072	3.020	2.978
11	4.844	3.982	3.587	3.357	3.204	3.095	3.012	2.948	2.896	2.854
12	4.747	3.885	3.490	3.259	3.106	2.996	2.913	2.849	2.796	2.753
13	4.667	3.806	3.411	3.179	3.025	2.915	2.832	2.767	2.714	2.671
14	4.600	3.739	3.344	3.112	2.958	2.848	2.764	2.699	2.646	2.602
15	4.543	3.682	3.287	3.056	2.901	2.790	2.707	2.641	2.588	2.544
16	4.494	3.634	3.239	3.007	2.852	2.741	2.657	2.591	2.538	2.494
17	4.451	3.592	3.197	2.965	2.810	2.699	2.614	2.548	2.494	2.450
18	4.414	3.555	3.160	2.928	2.773	2.661	2.577	2.510	2.456	2.412
19	4.381	3.522	3.127	2.895	2.740	2.628	2.544	2.477	2.423	2.378
20	4.351	3.493	3.098	2.866	2.711	2.599	2.514	2.447	2.393	2.348
24	4.260	3.403	3.009	2.776	2.621	2.508	2.423	2.355	2.300	2.255
30	4.171	3.316	2.922	2.690	2.534	2.421	2.334	2.266	2.211	2.165
40	4.085	3.232	2.839	2.606	2.449	2.336	2.249	2.180	2.124	2.077
50	4.034	3.183	2.790	2.557	2.400	2.286	2.199	2.130	2.073	2.026
100	3.936	3.087	2.696	2.463	2.305	2.191	2.103	2.032	1.975	1.927
200	3.888	3.041	2.650	2.417	2.259	2.144	2.056	1.985	1.927	1.878
300	3.873	3.026	2.635	2.402	2.244	2.129	2.040	1.969	1.911	1.862

DENOMINATOR $df = D_2$	NUMERATOR $df = D_1$									
	11	12	13	14	15	16	17	18	19	20
1	242.981	243.905	244.690	245.363	245.949	246.466	246.917	247.324	247.688	248.016
2	19.405	19.412	19.419	19.424	19.429	19.433	19.437	19.440	19.443	19.446
3	8.763	8.745	8.729	8.715	8.703	8.692	8.683	8.675	8.667	8.660
4	5.936	5.912	5.891	5.873	5.858	5.844	5.832	5.821	5.811	5.803
5	4.704	4.678	4.655	4.636	4.619	4.604	4.590	4.579	4.568	4.558
6	4.027	4.000	3.976	3.956	3.938	3.922	3.908	3.896	3.884	3.874
7	3.603	3.575	3.550	3.529	3.511	3.494	3.480	3.467	3.455	3.445
8	3.313	3.284.	3.259	3.237	3.218	3.202	3.187	3.173	3.161	3.150
9	3.102	3.073	3.048	3.025	3.006	2.989	2.974	2.960	2.948	2.936
10	2.943	2.913	2.887	2.865	2.845	2.828	2.812	2.798	2.785	2.774
11	2.818	2.788	2.761	2.739	2.719	2.701	2.685	2.671	2.658	2.646
12	2.717	2.687	2.660	2.637	2.617	2.599	2.583	2.568	2.555	2.544
13	2.635	2.604	2.577	2.554	2.533	2.515	2.499	2.484	2.471	2.459
14	2.565	2.534	2.507	2.484	2.463	2.445	2.428	2.413	2.400	2.388
15	2.507	2.475	2.448	2.424	2.403	2.385	2.368	2.353	2.340	2.328
16	2.456	2.425	2.397	2.373	2.352	2.333	2.317	2.302	2.288	2.276
17	2.413	2.381	2.353	2.329	2.308	2.289	2.272	2.257	2.243	2.230
18	2.374	2.342	2.314	2.290	2.269	2.250	2.233	2.217	2.203	2.191
19	2.340	2.308	2.280	2.256	2.234	2.215	2.198	2.182	2.168	2.155
20	2.310	2.278	2.250	2.225	2.203	2.184	2.167	2.151	2.137	2.124
24	2.216	2.183	2.155	2.130	2.108	2.088	2.070	2.054	2.040	2.027
30	2.126	2.092	2.063	2.037	2.015	1.995	1.976	1.960	1.945	1.932
40	2.038	2.003	1.974	1.948	1.924	1.904	1.885	1.868	1.853	1.839
50	1.986	1.952	1.921	1.895	1.871	1.850	1.831	1.814	1.798	1.784
100	1.886	1.850	1.819	1.792	1.768	1.746	1.726	1.708	1.691	1.676
200	1.837	1.801	1.769	1.742	1.717	1.694	1.674	1.656	1.639	1.623
300	1.821	1.785	1.753	1.725	1.700	1.677	1.657	1.638	1.621	1.606

DENOMINATOR $df = D_2$	NUMERATOR $df = D_1$						
	24	30	40	50	100	200	300
1	249.052	250.096	251.144	251.774	253.043	253.676	253.887
2	19.454	19.463	19.471	19.476	19.486	19.491	19.492
3	8.638	8.617	8.594	8.581	8.554	8.540	8.536
4	5.774	5.746	5.717	5.699	5.664	5.646	5.640
5	4.527	4.496	4.464	4.444	4.405	4.385	4.378
6	3.841	3.808	3.774	3.754	3.712	3.690	3.683
7	3.410	3.376	3.340	3.319	3.275	3.252	3.245
8	3.115	3.079	3.043	3.020	2.975	2.951	2.943
9	2.900	2.864	2.826	2.803	2.756	2.731	2.723
10	2.737	2.700	2.661	2.637	2.588	2.563	2.555
11	2.609	2.570	2.531	2.507	2.457	2.431	2.422
12	2.505	2.466	2.426	2.401	2.350	2.323	2.314
13	2.420	2.380	2.339	2.314	2.261	2.234	2.225
14	2.349	2.308	2.266	2.241	2.187	2.159	2.150
15	2.288	2.247	2.204	2.178	2.123	2.095	2.085
16	2.235	2.194	2.151	2.124	2.068	2.039	2.030
17	2.190	2.148	2.104	2.077	2.020	1.991	1.981
18	2.150	2.107	2.063	2.035	1.978	1.948	1.938
19	2.114	2.071	2.026	1.999	1.940	1.910	1.899
20	2.082	2.039	1.994	1.966	1.907	1.875	1.865
24	1.984	1.939	1.892	1.863	1.800	1.768	1.756
30	1.887	1.841	1.792	1.761	1.695	1.660	1.647
40	1.793	1.744	1.693	1.660	1.589	1.551	1.537
50	1.737	1.687	1.634	1.599	1.525	1.484	1.469
100	1.627	1.573	1.515	1.477	1.392	1.342	1.323
200	1.572	1.516	1.455	1.415	1.321	1.263	1.240
300	1.554	1.497	1.435	1.393	1.296	1.234	1.210

continued

(continued)

**F-Distribution Table:
Upper 1%
Probability
(or 1% Area) Under
F-Distribution Curve**

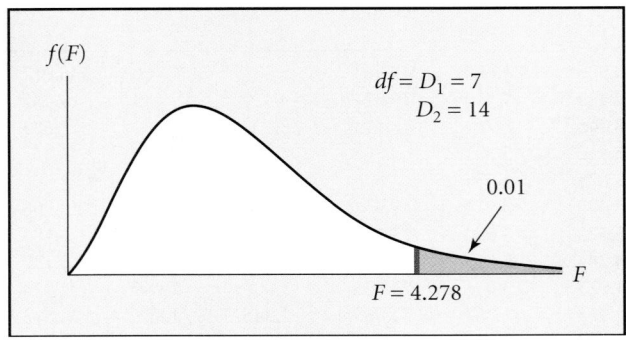

DENOMINATOR				NUMERATOR $df = D_1$							
$df = D_2$	1	2	3	4	5	6	7	8	9	10	11
1	4052.185	4999.340	5403.534	5624.257	5763.955	5858.950	5928.334	5980.954	6022.397	6055.925	6083.399
2	98.502	99.000	99.164	99.251	99.302	99.331	99.357	99.375	99.390	99.397	99.408
3	34.116	30.816	29.457	28.710	28.237	27.911	27.671	27.489	27.345	27.228	27.132
4	21.198	18.000	16.694	15.977	15.522	15.207	14.976	14.799	14.659	14.546	14.452
5	16.258	13.274	12.060	11.392	10.967	10.672	10.456	10.289	10.158	10.051	9.963
6	13.745	10.925	9.780	9.148	8.746	8.466	8.260	8.102	7.976	7.874	7.790
7	12.246	9.547	8.451	7.847	7.460	7.191	6.993	6.840	6.719	6.620	6.538
8	11.259	8.649	7.591	7.006	6.632	6.371	6.178	6.029	5.911	5.814	5.734
9	10.562	8.022	6.992	6.422	6.057	5.802	5.613	5.467	5.351	5.257	5.178
10	10.044	7.559	6.552	5.994	5.636	5.386	5.200	5.057	4.942	4.849	4.772
11	9.646	7.206	6.217	5.668	5.316	5.069	4.886	4.744	4.632	4.539	4.462
12	9.330	6.927	5.953	5.412	5.064	4.821	4.640	4.499	4.388	4.296	4.220
13	9.074	6.701	5.739	5.205	4.862	4.620	4.441	4.302	4.191	4.100	4.025
14	8.862	6.515	5.564	5.035	4.695	4.456	4.278	4.140	4.030	3.939	3.864
15	8.683	6.359	5.417	4.893	4.556	4.318	4.142	4.004	3.895	3.805	3.730
16	8.531	6.226	5.292	4.773	4.437	4.202	4.026	3.890	3.780	3.691	3.616
17	8.400	6.112	5.185	4.669	4.336	4.101	3.927	3.791	3.682	3.593	3.518
18	8.285	6.013	5.092	4.579	4.248	4.015	3.841	3.705	3.597	3.508	3.434
19	8.185	5.926	5.010	4.500	4.171	3.939	3.765	3.631	3.523	3.434	3.360
20	8.096	5.849	4.938	4.431	4.103	3.871	3.699	3.564	3.457	3.368	3.294
24	7.823	5.614	4.718	4.218	3.895	3.667	3.496	3.363	3.256	3.168	3.094
30	7.562	5.390	4.510	4.018	3.699	3.473	3.305	3.173	3.067	2.979	2.906
40	7.314	5.178	4.313	3.828	3.514	3.291	3.124	2.993	2.888	2.801	2.727
50	7.171	5.057	4.199	3.720	3.408	3.186	3.020	2.890	2.785	2.698	2.625
100	6.895	4.824	3.984	3.513	3.206	2.988	2.823	2.694	2.590	2.503	2.430
200	6.763	4.713	3.881	3.414	3.110	2.893	2.730	2.601	2.497	2.411	2.338
300	6.720	4.677	3.848	3.382	3.079	2.862	2.699	2.571	2.467	2.380	2.307

DENOMINATOR $df = D_2$	NUMERATOR $df = D_1$										
	12	13	14	15	16	17	18	19	20	24	30
1	6106.682	6125.774	6143.004	6156.974	6170.012	6181.188	6191.432	6200.746	6208.662	6234.273	6260.350
2	99.419	99.422	99.426	99.433	99.437	99.441	99.444	99.448	99.448	99.455	99.466
3	27.052	26.983	26.924	26.872	26.826	26.786	26.751	26.719	26.690	26.597	26.504
4	14.374	14.306	14.249	14.198	14.154	14.114	14.079	14.048	14.019	13.929	13.838
5	9.888	9.825	9.770	9.722	9.680	9.643	9.609	9.580	9.553	9.466	9.379
6	7.718	7.657	7.605	7.559	7.519	7.483	7.451	7.422	7.396	7.313	7.229
7	6.469	6.410	6.359	6.314	6.275	6.240	6.209	6.181	6.155	6.074	5.992
8	5.667	5.609	5.559	5.515	5.477	5.442	5.412	5.384	5.359	5.279	5.198
9	5.111	5.055	5.005	4.962	4.924	4.890	4.860	4.833	4.808	4.729	4.649
10	4.706	4.650	4.601	4.558	4.520	4.487	4.457	4.430	4.405	4.327	4.247
11	4.397	4.342	4.293	4.251	4.213	4.180	4.150	4.123	4.099	4.021	3.941
12	4.155	4.100	4.052	4.010	3.972	3.939	3.910	3.883	3.858	3.780	3.701
13	3.960	3.905	3.857	3.815	3.778	3.745	3.716	3.689	3.665	3.587	3.507
14	3.800	3.745	3.698	3.656	3.619	3.586	3.556	3.529	3.505	3.427	3.348
15	3.666	3.612	3.564	3.522	3.485	3.452	3.423	3.396	3.372	3.294	3.214
16	3.553	3.498	3.451	3.409	3.372	3.339	3.310	3.283	3.259	3.181	3.101
17	3.455	3.401	3.353	3.312	3.275	3.242	3.212	3.186	3.162	3.083	3.003
18	3.371	3.316	3.269	3.227	3.190	3.158	3.128	3.101	3.077	2.999	2.919
19	3.297	3.242	3.195	3.153	3.116	3.084	3.054	3.027	3.003	2.925	2.844
20	3.231	3.177	3.130	3.088	3.051	3.018	2.989	2.962	2.938	2.859	2.778
24	3.032	2.977	2.930	2.889	2.852	2.819	2.789	2.762	2.738	2.659	2.577
30	2.843	2.789	2.742	2.700	2.663	2.630	2.600	2.573	2.549	2.469	2.386
40	2.665	2.611	2.563	2.522	2.484	2.451	2.421	2.394	2.369	2.288	2.203
50	2.563	2.508	2.461	2.419	2.382	2.348	2.318	2.290	2.265	2.183	2.098
100	2.368	2.313	2.265	2.223	2.185	2.151	2.120	2.092	2.067	1.983	1.893
200	2.275	2.220	2.172	2.129	2.091	2.057	2.026	1.997	1.971	1.886	1.794
300	2.244	2.190	2.142	2.099	2.061	2.026	1.995	1.966	1.940	1.854	1.761

DENOMINATOR $df = D_2$	NUMERATOR $df = D_1$				
	40	50	100	200	300
1	6286.427	6302.260	6333.925	6349.757	6355.345
2	99.477	99.477	99.491	99.491	99.499
3	26.411	26.354	26.241	26.183	26.163
4	13.745	13.690	13.577	13.520	13.501
5	9.291	9.238	9.130	9.075	9.057
6	7.143	7.091	6.987	6.934	6.916
7	5.908	5.858	5.755	5.702	5.685
8	5.116	5.065	4.963	4.911	4.894
9	4.567	4.517	4.415	4.363	4.346
10	4.165	4.115	4.014	3.962	3.944
11	3.860	3.810	3.708	3.656	3.638
12	3.619	3.569	3.467	3.414	3.397
13	3.425	3.375	3.272	3.219	3.202
14	3.266	3.215	3.112	3.059	3.040
15	3.132	3.081	2.977	2.923	2.905
16	3.018	2.967	2.863	2.808	2.790
17	2.920	2.869	2.764	2.709	2.691
18	2.835	2.784	2.678	2.623	2.604
19	2.761	2.709	2.602	2.547	2.528
20	2.695	2.643	2.535	2.479	2.460
24	2.492	2.440	2.329	2.271	2.251
30	2.299	2.245	2.131	2.070	2.049
40	2.114	2.058	1.938	1.874	1.851
50	2.007	1.949	1.825	1.757	1.733
100	1.797	1.735	1.598	1.518	1.490
200	1.694	1.629	1.481	1.391	1.357
300	1.660	1.594	1.441	1.346	1.309

APPENDIX I

Critical Values of Hartley's F_{max} Test

$$\left(F_{max} = \frac{S^2_{largest}}{S^2_{smallest}} \sim F_{max_{1-a(c,v)}} \right)$$

UPPER 5% POINTS ($\alpha = 0.05$)

c / v	2	3	4	5	6	7	8	9	10	11	12
2	39.0	87.5	142	202	266	333	403	475	550	626	704
3	15.4	27.8	39.2	50.7	62.0	72.9	83.5	93.9	104	114	124
4	9.60	15.5	20.6	25.2	29.5	33.6	37.5	41.1	44.6	48.0	51.4
5	7.15	10.8	13.7	16.3	18.7	20.8	22.9	24.7	26.5	28.2	29.9
6	5.82	8.38	10.4	12.1	13.7	15.0	16.3	17.5	18.6	19.7	20.7
7	4.99	6.94	8.44	9.70	10.8	11.8	12.7	13.5	14.3	15.1	15.8
8	4.43	6.00	7.18	8.12	9.03	9.78	10.5	11.1	11.7	12.2	12.7
9	4.03	5.34	6.31	7.11	7.80	8.41	8.95	9.45	9.91	10.3	10.7
10	3.72	4.85	5.67	6.34	6.92	7.42	7.87	8.28	8.66	9.01	9.34
12	3.28	4.16	4.79	5.30	5.72	6.09	6.42	6.72	7.00	7.25	7.48
15	2.86	3.54	4.01	4.37	4.68	4.95	5.19	5.40	5.59	5.77	5.93
20	2.46	2.95	3.29	3.54	3.76	3.94	4.10	4.24	4.37	4.49	4.59
30	2.07	2.40	2.61	2.78	2.91	3.02	3.12	3.21	3.29	3.36	3.39
60	1.67	1.85	1.96	2.04	2.11	2.17	2.22	2.26	2.30	2.33	2.36
∞	1.00	1.00	1.00	1.00	1.00	1.00	1.00	1.00	1.00	1.00	1.00

UPPER 1% POINTS ($\alpha = 0.01$)

c / v	2	3	4	5	6	7	8	9	10	11	12
2	199	448	729	1036	1362	1705	2063	2432	2813	3204	3605
3	47.5	85	120	151	184	21(6)	24(9)	28(1)	31(0)	33(7)	36(1)
4	23.2	37	49	59	69	79	89	97	106	113	120
5	14.9	22	28	33	38	42	46	50	54	57	60
6	11.1	15.5	19.1	22	25	27	30	32	34	36	37
7	8.89	12.1	14.5	16.5	18.4	20	22	23	24	26	27
8	7.50	9.9	11.7	13.2	14.5	15.8	16.9	17.9	18.9	19.8	21
9	6.54	8.5	9.9	11.1	12.1	13.1	13.9	14.7	15.3	16.0	16.6
10	5.85	7.4	8.6	9.6	10.4	11.1	11.8	12.4	12.9	13.4	13.9
12	4.91	6.1	6.9	7.6	8.2	8.7	9.1	9.5	9.9	10.2	10.6
15	4.07	4.9	5.5	6.0	6.4	6.7	7.1	7.3	7.5	7.8	8.0
20	3.32	3.8	4.3	4.6	4.9	5.1	5.3	5.5	5.6	5.8	5.9
30	2.63	3.0	3.3	3.4	3.6	3.7	3.8	3.9	4.0	4.1	4.2
60	1.96	2.2	2.3	2.4	2.4	2.5	2.5	2.6	2.6	2.7	2.7
∞	1.00	1.0	1.0	1.0	1.0	1.0	1.0	1.0	1.0	1.0	1.0

Note: $S^2_{largest}$ is the largest and $s^2_{smallest}$ the smallest in a set of c independent mean squares, each based on v degrees of freedom.
Source: Reprinted from E. S. Pearson and H. O Hartley, eds., *Biometrika Tables for Statisticians,* 3d ed., 1966, by permission of the Biometrika Trustees.

APPENDIX J

Distribution of the Studentized Range

Percentage points of the studentized range, $q = (x_{D_1} - x_1)/s_{D_2}$.

$p = 0.95$

D_2 \ D_1	2	3	4	5	6	7	8	9	10
1	17.97	26.98	32.82	37.08	40.41	43.12	45.40	47.36	49.07
2	6.08	8.33	9.80	10.88	11.74	12.44	13.03	13.54	13.99
3	4.50	5.91	6.82	7.50	8.04	8.48	8.85	9.18	9.46
4	3.93	5.04	5.76	6.29	6.71	7.05	7.35	7.60	7.83
5	3.64	4.60	5.22	5.67	6.03	6.33	6.58	6.80	6.99
6	3.46	4.34	4.90	5.30	5.63	5.90	6.12	6.32	6.49
7	3.34	4.16	4.68	5.06	5.36	5.61	5.82	6.00	6.16
8	3.26	4.04	4.53	4.89	5.17	5.40	5.60	5.77	5.92
9	3.20	3.95	4.41	4.76	5.02	5.24	5.43	5.59	5.74
10	3.15	3.88	4.33	4.65	4.91	5.12	5.30	5.46	5.60
11	3.11	3.82	4.26	4.57	4.82	5.03	5.20	5.35	5.49
12	3.08	3.77	4.20	4.51	4.75	4.95	5.12	5.27	5.39
13	3.06	3.73	4.15	4.45	4.69	4.88	5.05	5.19	5.32
14	3.03	3.70	4.11	4.41	4.64	4.83	4.99	5.13	5.25
15	3.01	3.67	4.08	4.37	4.59	4.78	4.94	5.08	5.20
16	3.00	3.65	4.05	4.33	4.56	4.74	4.90	5.03	5.15
17	2.98	3.63	4.02	4.30	4.52	4.70	4.86	4.99	5.11
18	2.97	3.61	4.00	4.28	4.49	4.67	4.82	4.96	5.07
19	2.96	3.59	3.98	4.25	4.47	4.65	4.79	4.92	5.04
20	2.95	3.58	3.96	4.23	4.45	4.62	4.77	4.90	5.01
24	2.92	3.53	3.90	4.17	4.37	4.54	4.68	4.81	4.92
30	2.89	3.49	3.85	4.10	4.30	4.46	4.60	4.72	4.82
40	2.86	3.44	3.79	4.04	4.23	4.39	4.52	4.63	4.73
60	2.83	3.40	3.74	3.98	4.16	4.31	4.44	4.55	4.65
120	2.80	3.36	3.68	3.92	4.10	4.24	4.36	4.47	4.56
∞	2.77	3.31	3.63	3.86	4.03	4.17	4.29	4.39	4.47

D_2 \ D_1	11	12	13	14	15	16	17	18	19	20
1	50.59	51.96	53.20	54.33	55.36	56.32	57.22	58.04	58.83	59.56
2	14.39	14.75	15.08	15.38	15.65	15.91	16.14	16.37	16.57	16.77
3	9.72	9.95	10.15	10.35	10.52	10.69	10.84	10.98	11.11	11.24
4	8.03	8.21	8.37	8.52	8.66	8.79	8.91	9.03	9.13	9.23
5	7.17	7.32	7.47	7.60	7.72	7.83	7.93	8.03	8.12	8.21
6	6.65	6.79	6.92	7.03	7.14	7.24	7.34	7.43	7.51	7.59
7	6.30	6.43	6.55	6.66	6.76	6.85	6.94	7.02	7.10	7.17
8	6.05	6.18	6.29	6.39	6.48	6.57	6.65	6.73	6.80	6.87
9	5.87	5.98	6.09	6.19	6.28	6.36	6.44	6.51	6.58	6.64
10	5.72	5.83	5.93	6.03	6.11	6.19	6.27	6.34	6.40	6.47
11	5.61	5.71	5.81	5.90	5.98	6.06	6.13	6.20	6.27	6.33
12	5.51	5.61	5.71	5.80	5.88	5.95	6.02	6.09	6.15	6.21
13	5.43	5.53	5.63	5.71	5.79	5.86	5.93	5.99	6.05	6.11
14	5.36	5.46	5.55	5.64	5.71	5.79	5.85	5.91	5.97	6.03
15	5.31	5.40	5.49	5.57	5.65	5.72	5.78	5.85	5.90	5.96
16	5.26	5.35	5.44	5.52	5.59	5.66	5.73	5.79	5.84	5.90
17	5.21	5.31	5.39	5.47	5.54	5.61	5.67	5.73	5.79	5.84
18	5.17	5.27	5.35	5.43	5.50	5.57	5.63	5.69	5.74	5.79
19	5.14	5.23	5.31	5.39	5.46	5.53	5.59	5.65	5.70	5.75
20	5.11	5.20	5.28	5.36	5.43	5.49	5.55	5.61	5.66	5.71
24	5.01	5.10	5.18	5.25	5.32	5.38	5.44	5.49	5.55	5.59
30	4.92	5.00	5.08	5.15	5.21	5.27	5.33	5.38	5.43	5.47
40	4.82	4.90	4.98	5.04	5.11	5.16	5.22	5.27	5.31	5.36
60	4.73	4.81	4.88	4.94	5.00	5.06	5.11	5.15	5.20	5.24
120	4.64	4.71	4.78	4.84	4.90	4.95	5.00	5.04	5.09	5.13
∞	4.55	4.62	4.68	4.74	4.80	4.85	4.89	4.93	4.97	5.01

Note: D_1: Size of sample from which range obtained D_2: Degrees of freedom of independent s_{D_1}

continued

$p = 0.99$

D_1 / D_2	2	3	4	5	6	7	8	9	10
1	90.03	135.0	164.3	185.6	202.2	215.8	227.2	237.0	245.6
2	14.04	19.02	22.29	24.72	26.63	28.20	29.53	30.68	31.69
3	8.26	10.62	12.17	13.33	14.24	15.00	15.64	16.20	16.69
4	6.51	8.12	9.17	9.96	10.58	11.10	11.55	11.93	12.27
5	5.70	6.98	7.80	8.42	8.91	9.32	9.67	9.97	10.24
6	5.24	6.33	7.03	7.56	7.97	8.32	8.61	8.87	9.10
7	4.95	5.92	6.54	7.01	7.37	7.68	7.94	8.17	8.37
8	4.75	5.64	6.20	6.62	6.96	7.24	7.47	7.68	7.86
9	4.60	5.43	5.96	6.35	6.66	6.91	7.13	7.33	7.49
10	4.48	5.27	5.77	6.14	6.43	6.67	6.87	7.05	7.21
11	4.39	5.15	5.62	5.97	6.25	6.48	6.67	6.84	6.99
12	4.32	5.05	5.50	5.84	6.10	6.32	6.51	6.67	6.81
13	4.26	4.96	5.40	5.73	5.98	6.19	6.37	6.53	6.67
14	4.21	4.89	5.32	5.63	5.88	6.08	6.26	6.41	6.54
15	4.17	4.84	5.25	5.56	5.80	5.99	6.16	6.31	6.44
16	4.13	4.79	5.19	5.49	5.72	5.92	6.08	6.22	6.35
17	4.10	4.74	5.14	5.43	5.66	5.85	6.01	6.15	6.27
18	4.07	4.70	5.09	5.38	5.60	5.79	5.94	6.08	6.20
19	4.05	4.67	5.05	5.33	5.55	5.73	5.89	6.02	6.14
20	4.02	4.64	5.02	5.29	5.51	5.69	5.84	5.97	6.09
24	3.96	4.55	4.91	5.17	5.37	5.54	5.69	5.81	5.92
30	3.89	4.45	4.80	5.05	5.24	5.40	5.54	5.65	5.76
40	3.82	4.37	4.70	4.93	5.11	5.26	5.39	5.50	5.60
60	3.76	4.28	4.59	4.82	4.99	5.13	5.25	5.36	5.45
120	3.70	4.20	4.50	4.71	4.87	5.01	5.12	5.21	5.30
∞	3.64	4.12	4.40	4.60	4.76	4.88	4.99	5.08	5.16

D_1 / D_2	11	12	13	14	15	16	17	18	19	20
1	253.2	260.0	266.2	271.8	277.0	281.8	286.3	290.4	294.3	298.0
2	32.59	33.40	34.13	34.81	35.43	36.00	36.53	37.03	37.50	37.95
3	17.13	17.53	17.89	18.22	18.52	18.81	19.07	19.32	19.55	19.77
4	12.57	12.84	13.09	13.32	13.53	13.73	13.91	14.08	14.24	14.40
5	10.48	10.70	10.89	11.08	11.24	11.40	11.55	11.68	11.81	11.93
6	9.30	9.48	9.65	9.81	9.95	10.08	10.21	10.32	10.43	10.54
7	8.55	8.71	8.86	9.00	9.12	9.24	9.35	9.46	9.55	9.65
8	8.03	8.18	8.31	8.44	8.55	8.66	8.76	8.85	8.94	9.03
9	7.65	7.78	7.91	8.03	8.13	8.23	8.33	8.41	8.49	8.57
10	7.36	7.49	7.60	7.71	7.81	7.91	7.99	8.08	8.15	8.23
11	7.13	7.25	7.36	7.46	7.56	7.65	7.73	7.81	7.88	7.95
12	6.94	7.06	7.17	7.26	7.36	7.44	7.52	7.59	7.66	7.73
13	6.79	6.90	7.01	7.10	7.19	7.27	7.35	7.42	7.48	7.55
14	6.66	6.77	6.87	6.96	7.05	7.13	7.20	7.27	7.33	7.39
15	6.55	6.66	6.76	6.84	6.93	7.00	7.07	7.14	7.20	7.26
16	6.46	6.56	6.66	6.74	6.82	6.90	6.97	7.03	7.09	7.15
17	6.38	6.48	6.57	6.66	6.73	6.81	6.87	6.94	7.00	7.05
18	6.31	6.41	6.50	6.58	6.65	6.73	6.79	6.85	6.91	6.97
19	6.25	6.34	6.43	6.51	6.58	6.65	6.72	6.78	6.84	6.89
20	6.19	6.28	6.37	6.45	6.52	6.59	6.65	6.71	6.77	6.82
24	6.02	6.11	6.19	6.26	6.33	6.39	6.45	6.51	6.56	6.61
30	5.85	5.93	6.01	6.08	6.14	6.20	6.26	6.31	6.36	6.41
40	5.69	5.76	5.83	5.90	5.96	6.02	6.07	6.12	6.16	6.21
60	5.53	5.60	5.67	5.73	5.78	5.84	5.89	5.93	5.97	6.01
120	5.37	5.44	5.50	5.56	5.61	5.66	5.71	5.75	5.79	5.83
∞	5.23	5.29	5.35	5.40	5.45	5.49	5.54	5.57	5.61	5.65

Source: Reprinted with permission from E. S. Pearson and H. O Hartley, *Biometrika Tables for Statisticians* (New York: Cambridge University Press, 1954).

APPENDIX K

Critical Values of r in the Runs Test

a. Lower Tail: Too Few Runs

n_1 \ n_2	2	3	4	5	6	7	8	9	10	11	12	13	14	15	16	17	18	19	20
2											2	2	2	2	2	2	2	2	2
3				2	2	2	2	2	2	2	2	2	2	3	3	3	3	3	3
4			2	2	2	3	3	3	3	3	3	3	3	3	4	4	4	4	4
5		2	2	3	3	3	3	3	4	4	4	4	4	4	4	4	5	5	5
6		2	2	3	3	3	3	4	4	4	4	5	5	5	5	5	5	6	6
7		2	2	3	3	3	4	4	5	5	5	5	5	6	6	6	6	6	6
8		2	3	3	3	4	4	5	5	5	6	6	6	6	6	7	7	7	7
9		2	3	3	4	4	5	5	5	6	6	6	7	7	7	7	8	8	8
10		2	3	3	4	5	5	5	6	6	7	7	7	7	8	8	8	8	9
11		2	3	4	4	5	5	6	6	7	7	7	8	8	8	9	9	9	9
12	2	2	3	4	4	5	6	6	7	7	7	8	8	8	9	9	9	10	10
13	2	2	3	4	5	5	6	6	7	7	8	8	9	9	9	10	10	10	10
14	2	2	3	4	5	5	6	7	7	8	8	9	9	9	10	10	10	11	11
15	2	3	3	4	5	6	6	7	7	8	8	9	9	10	10	11	11	11	12
16	2	3	4	4	5	6	6	7	8	8	9	9	10	10	11	11	11	12	12
17	2	3	4	4	5	6	7	7	8	9	9	10	10	11	11	11	12	12	13
18	2	3	4	5	5	6	7	8	8	9	9	10	10	11	11	12	12	13	13
19	2	3	4	5	6	6	7	8	8	9	10	10	11	11	12	12	13	13	13
20	2	3	4	5	6	6	7	8	9	9	10	10	11	12	12	13	13	13	14

b. Upper Tail: Too Many Runs

n_1 \ n_2	2	3	4	5	6	7	8	9	10	11	12	13	14	15	16	17	18	19	20
2																			
3																			
4				9	9														
5			9	10	10	11	11												
6			9	10	11	12	12	13	13	13	13								
7				11	12	13	13	14	14	14	14	15	15	15					
8				11	12	13	14	14	15	15	16	16	16	16	17	17	17	17	17
9					13	14	14	15	16	16	16	17	17	18	18	18	18	18	18
10					13	14	15	16	16	17	17	18	18	18	19	19	19	20	20
11					13	14	15	16	17	17	18	19	19	19	20	20	20	21	21
12					13	14	16	16	17	18	19	19	20	20	21	21	21	22	22
13						15	16	17	18	19	19	20	20	21	21	22	22	23	23
14						15	16	17	18	19	20	20	21	22	22	23	23	23	24
15						15	16	18	18	19	20	21	22	22	23	23	24	24	25
16							17	18	19	20	21	21	22	23	23	24	25	25	25
17							17	18	19	20	21	22	23	23	24	25	25	26	26
18							17	18	19	20	21	22	23	24	25	25	26	26	27
19							17	18	20	21	22	23	23	24	25	26	26	27	27
20							17	18	20	21	22	23	24	25	25	26	27	27	28

Source: Adapted from Frieda S. Swed and C. Eisenhart, "Tables for testing randomness of grouping in a sequence of alternatives," *Ann. Math. Statist.* 14 (1943): 83–86, with the permission of the publisher.

Mann-Whitney
U Test Probabilities
($n < 9$)

	$n_2 = 3$		
U \ n_1	1	2	3
0	.250	.100	.050
1	.500	.200	.100
2	.750	.400	.200
3		.600	.350
4			.500
5			.650

	$n_2 = 4$			
U \ n_1	1	2	3	4
0	.200	.067	.028	.014
1	.400	.133	.057	.029
2	.600	.267	.114	.057
3		.400	.200	.100
4		.600	.314	.171
5			.429	.243
6			.571	.343
7				.443
8				.557

	$n_2 = 5$				
U \ n_1	1	2	3	4	5
0	.167	.047	.018	.008	.004
1	.333	.095	.036	.016	.008
2	.500	.190	.071	.032	.016
3	.667	.286	.125	.056	.028
4		.429	.196	.095	.048
5		.571	.286	.143	.075
6			.393	.206	.111
7			.500	.278	.155
8			.607	.365	.210
9				.452	.274
10				.548	.345
11					.421
12					.500
13					.579

	$n_2 = 6$					
U \ n_1	1	2	3	4	5	6
0	.143	.036	.012	.005	.002	.001
1	.286	.071	.024	.010	.004	.002
2	.428	.143	.048	.019	.009	.004
3	.571	.214	.083	.033	.015	.008
4		.321	.131	.057	.026	.013
5		.429	.190	.086	.041	.021
6		.571	.274	.129	.063	.032
7			.357	.176	.089	.047
8			.452	.238	.123	.066
9			.548	.305	.165	.090
10				.381	.214	.120
11				.457	.268	.155
12				.545	.331	.197
13					.396	.242
14					.465	.294
15					.535	.350
16						.409
17						.469
18						.531

n

$$n_2 = 7$$

U \ n_1	1	2	3	4	5	6	7
0	.125	.028	.008	.003	.001	.001	.000
1	.250	.056	.017	.006	.003	.001	.001
2	.375	.111	.033	.012	.005	.002	.001
3	.500	.167	.058	.021	.009	.004	.002
4	.625	.250	.092	.036	.015	.007	.003
5		.333	.133	.055	.024	.011	.006
6		.444	.192	.082	.037	.017	.009
7		.556	.258	.115	.053	.026	.013
8			.333	.158	.074	.037	.019
9			.417	.206	.101	.051	.027
10			.500	.264	.134	.069	.036
11			.583	.324	.172	.090	.049
12				.394	.216	.117	.064
13				.464	.265	.147	.082
14				.538	.319	.183	.104
15					.378	.223	.130
16					.438	.267	.159
17					.500	.314	.191
18					.562	.365	.228
19						.418	.267
20						.473	.310
21						.527	.355
22							.402
23							.451
24							.500
25							.549

continued

$$n_2 = 8$$

U \ n_1	1	2	3	4	5	6	7	8	t	Normal
0	.111	.022	.006	.002	.001	.000	.000	.000	3.308	.001
1	.222	.044	.012	.004	.002	.001	.000	.000	3.203	.001
2	.333	.089	.024	.008	.003	.001	.001	.000	3.098	.001
3	.444	.133	.042	.014	.005	.002	.001	.001	2.993	.001
4	.556	.200	.067	.024	.009	.004	.002	.001	2.888	.002
5		.267	.097	.036	.015	.006	.003	.001	2.783	.003
6		.356	.139	.055	.023	.010	.005	.002	2.678	.004
7		.444	.188	.077	.033	.015	.007	.003	2.573	.005
8		.556	.248	.107	.047	.021	.010	.005	2.468	.007
9			.315	.141	.064	.030	.014	.007	2.363	.009
10			.387	.184	.085	.041	.020	.010	2.258	.012
11			.461	.230	.111	.054	.027	.014	2.153	.016
12			.539	.285	.142	.071	.036	.019	2.048	.020
13				.341	.177	.091	.047	.025	1.943	.026
14				.404	.217	.114	.060	.032	1.838	.033
15				.467	.262	.141	.076	.041	1.733	.041
16				.533	.311	.172	.095	.052	1.628	.052
17					.362	.207	.116	.065	1.523	.064
18					.416	.245	.140	.080	1.418	.078
19					.472	.286	.168	.097	1.313	.094
20					.528	.331	.198	.117	1.208	.113
21						.377	.232	.139	1.102	.135
22						.426	.268	.164	.998	.159
23						.475	.306	.191	.893	.185
24						.525	.347	.221	.788	.215
25							.389	.253	.683	.247
26							.433	.287	.578	.282
27							.478	.323	.473	.318
28							.522	.360	.368	.356
29								.399	.263	.396
30								.439	.158	.437
31								.480	.052	.481
32								.520		

Source: Reproduced from H. B. Mann and D. R. Whitney, "On a test of whether one of two random variables is stochastically larger than the other," *Ann. Math Statist*, 18 (1947): 52–54, with the permission of the publisher.

APPENDIX M

Mann-Whitney U Test Critical Values ($9 \leq n \leq 20$)

Critical Values of U for a One-Tailed Test at $\alpha = 0.001$ or for a Two-Tailed Test at $\alpha = 0.002$

n_1 \ n_2	9	10	11	12	13	14	15	16	17	18	19	20
1												
2												
3									0	0	0	0
4		0	0	0	1	1	1	2	2	3	3	3
5	1	1	2	2	3	3	4	5	5	6	7	7
6	2	3	4	4	5	6	7	8	9	10	11	12
7	3	5	6	7	8	9	10	11	13	14	15	16
8	5	6	8	9	11	12	14	15	17	18	20	21
9	7	8	10	12	14	15	17	19	21	23	25	26
10	8	10	12	14	17	19	21	23	25	27	29	32
11	10	12	15	17	20	22	24	27	29	32	34	37
12	12	14	17	20	23	25	28	31	34	37	40	42
13	14	17	20	23	26	29	32	35	38	42	45	48
14	15	19	22	25	29	32	36	39	43	46	50	54
15	17	21	24	28	32	36	40	43	47	51	55	59
16	19	23	27	31	35	39	43	48	52	56	60	65
17	21	25	29	34	38	43	47	52	57	61	66	70
18	23	27	32	37	42	46	51	56	61	66	71	76
19	25	29	34	40	45	50	55	60	66	71	77	82
20	26	32	37	42	48	54	59	65	70	76	82	88

Critical Values of U for a One-Tailed Test at $\alpha = 0.01$ or for a Two-Tailed Test at $\alpha = 0.02$

n_1 \ n_2	9	10	11	12	13	14	15	16	17	18	19	20
1												
2					0	0	0	0	0	0	1	1
3	1	1	1	2	2	2	3	3	4	4	4	5
4	3	3	4	5	5	6	7	7	8	9	9	10
5	5	6	7	8	9	10	11	12	13	14	15	16
6	7	8	9	11	12	13	15	16	18	19	20	22
7	9	11	12	14	16	17	19	21	23	24	26	28
8	11	13	15	17	20	22	24	26	28	30	32	34
9	14	16	18	21	23	26	28	31	33	36	38	40
10	16	19	22	24	27	30	33	36	38	41	44	47
11	18	22	25	28	31	34	37	41	44	47	50	53
12	21	24	28	31	35	38	42	46	49	53	56	60
13	23	27	31	35	39	43	47	51	55	59	63	67
14	26	30	34	38	43	47	51	56	60	65	69	73
15	28	33	37	42	47	51	56	61	66	70	75	80
16	31	36	41	46	51	56	61	66	71	76	82	87
17	33	38	44	49	55	60	66	71	77	82	88	93
18	36	41	47	53	59	65	70	76	82	88	94	100
19	38	44	50	56	63	69	75	82	88	94	101	107
20	40	47	53	60	67	73	80	87	93	100	107	114

continued

Critical Values of U for a One-Tailed Test at $\alpha = 0.025$ or for a Two-Tailed Test at $\alpha = 0.05$

n_1 \ n_2	9	10	11	12	13	14	15	16	17	18	19	20
1												
2	0	0	0	1	1	1	1	1	2	2	2	2
3	2	3	3	4	4	5	5	6	6	7	7	8
4	4	5	6	7	8	9	10	11	11	12	13	13
5	7	8	9	11	12	13	14	15	17	18	19	20
6	10	11	13	14	16	17	19	21	22	24	25	27
7	12	14	16	18	20	22	24	26	28	30	32	34
8	15	17	19	22	24	26	29	31	34	36	38	41
9	17	20	23	26	28	31	34	37	39	42	45	48
10	20	23	26	29	33	36	39	42	45	48	52	55
11	23	26	30	33	37	40	44	47	51	55	58	62
12	26	29	33	37	41	45	49	53	57	61	65	69
13	28	33	37	41	45	50	54	59	63	67	72	76
14	31	36	40	45	50	55	59	64	67	74	78	83
15	34	39	44	49	54	59	64	70	75	80	85	90
16	37	42	47	53	59	64	70	75	81	86	92	98
17	39	45	51	57	63	67	75	81	87	93	99	105
18	42	48	55	61	67	74	80	86	93	99	106	112
19	45	52	58	65	72	78	85	92	99	106	113	119
20	48	55	62	69	76	83	90	98	105	112	119	127

Critical Values of U for a One-Tailed Test at $\alpha = 0.05$ or for a Two-Tailed Test at $\alpha = 0.10$

n_1 \ n_2	9	10	11	12	13	14	15	16	17	18	19	20
1											0	0
2	1	1	1	2	2	2	3	3	3	4	4	4
3	3	4	5	5	6	7	7	8	9	9	10	11
4	6	7	8	9	10	11	12	14	15	16	17	18
5	9	11	12	13	15	16	18	19	20	22	23	25
6	12	14	16	17	19	21	23	25	26	28	30	32
7	15	17	19	21	24	26	28	30	33	35	37	39
8	18	20	23	26	28	31	33	36	39	41	44	47
9	21	24	27	30	33	36	39	42	45	48	51	54
10	24	27	31	34	37	41	44	48	51	55	58	62
11	27	31	34	38	42	46	50	54	57	61	65	69
12	30	34	38	42	47	51	55	60	64	68	72	77
13	33	37	42	47	51	56	61	65	70	75	80	84
14	36	41	46	51	56	61	66	71	77	82	87	92
15	39	44	50	55	61	66	72	77	83	88	94	100
16	42	48	54	60	65	71	77	83	89	95	101	107
17	45	51	57	64	70	77	83	89	96	102	109	115
18	48	55	61	68	75	82	88	95	102	109	116	123
19	51	58	65	72	80	87	94	101	109	116	123	130
20	54	62	69	77	84	92	100	107	115	123	130	138

Source: Adapted and abridged from Tables 1, 3, 5, and 7 of D. Auble, "Extended tables for the Mann-Whitney statistic," *Bulletin of the Institute of Educational Research at Indiana University* 1, No. 2 (1953) with the permission of the publisher.

Critical Values of T in the Wilcoxon Matched-Pairs Signed-Ranks Test ($n \leq 25$)

	LEVEL OF SIGNIFICANCE FOR ONE-TAILED TEST		
	0.025	0.01	0.005
n	LEVEL OF SIGNIFICANCE FOR TWO-TAILED TEST		
	0.05	0.02	0.01
6	0	—	—
7	2	0	—
8	4	2	0
9	6	3	2
10	8	5	3
11	11	7	5
12	14	10	7
13	17	13	10
14	21	16	13
15	25	20	16
16	30	24	20
17	35	28	23
18	40	33	28
19	46	38	32
20	52	43	38
21	59	49	43
22	66	56	49
23	73	62	55
24	81	69	61
25	89	77	68

Source: Adapted from Table 1 of F. Wilcoxon, *Some Rapid Approximate Statistical Procedures* (New York: American Cyanamid Company, 1949), 13, with the permission of the publisher.

GLOSSARY

Adjusted R-squared (R_A^2)—A measure of the percentage of explained variation in the dependent variable that takes into account the relationship between the number of cases and the number of independent variables in the regression model. Whereas R^2 will generally increase when an independent variable is added, adjusted R^2 will decrease if the added variable does not reduce the unexplained variation enough to offset the loss of degrees of freedom.

All-inclusive classes—A set of classes that contains all the possible data values.

Alpha (α)—The smoothing constant used in exponential smoothing to indicate the relative weight placed on the most recent observations versus the historical observations. Also used to represent the probability of a Type I statistical error.

Alternative hypothesis—The hypothesis that includes all population values not covered by the null hypothesis. The alternative hypothesis is deemed to be true if the null hypothesis is rejected.

Aptness—The degree to which the regression model satisfies the following assumptions:

1. The relationship between the dependent and independent variables is linear.
2. The variance of the model errors is constant over the range of the values of the independent variables.
3. The model errors are independent from observation to observation.
4. The model errors are normally distributed.

Attribute—A quality characteristic that is either present or not present in an item.

Average or arithmetic mean—A measure of the center of the data, computed by summing all the data values and dividing by the number of values added.

Balanced design—An experiment is said to have a balanced design if the factor levels have equal sample sizes.

Bar chart—A graphical representation of a categorical data set in which a rectangle or bar is drawn over each category or class. The length of each bar represents the frequency or percentage of observations contained in a category.

Beta (β)—The second smoothing constant used to weight the trend component of the double exponential smoothing model. Also used to represent the probability of a Type II statistical error.

Between-sample variation—Dispersion among the factor sample means.

Binomial probability distribution—A distribution that gives the probability of x successes in a fixed number of independent trials. Each trial must only have two possible outcomes. The probability of a success must be constant from trial to trial.

Business statistics—A collection of tools and techniques that are used to convert data into meaningful information in a business environment.

c-Chart—A control chart used when the variable is an attribute and multiple attributes can occur per sampling unit.

Census—An enumeration of the entire set of measurements taken from the whole population.

Centerline—The average value of the plotted values on a process control chart.

Central limit theorem—For samples of n observations taken from a population with mean μ and standard deviation σ, regardless of the population's distribution, provided the sample size is sufficiently large, the distribution of the sample mean, $\bar{x}$, values will be approximately normal with a mean equal to the population mean ($\mu_{\bar{x}} = \mu$). Further, the standard deviation will equal the population standard deviation divided by the square root of the sample size. The larger the sample size, the better the approximation to the normal distribution.

Certainty—A decision environment in which the results of selecting each alternative are known before the decision is made.

Certainty equivalent—The value that would make a decision maker indifferent between taking an uncertain gamble versus receiving that value instead of taking the gamble.

Chi-square goodness-of-fit test—A test utilizing the chi-square distribution to determine whether sample data come from a specific hypothesized population distribution.

Class boundaries—The upper and lower value of each class.

Class width—The distance between the lowest possible value and the highest possible value for a frequency class.

Classical probability assessment—The method of determining probability based on the ratio of the number of ways the event of interest can occur to the total number of ways *any* event can occur when the individual elementary events are equally likely.

Closed-end questions—Questions that require the respondent to select from a short list of defined choices.

Cluster sample—A method by which the population is divided into groups, or clusters, that are each intended to be minipopulations. A simple random sample of *m* clusters is selected. The items selected from a cluster can be chosen using any probability sampling technique.

Coefficient of determination—The portion of the total variation in the dependent variable that is explained by its relationship with the independent variable. The coefficient of determination is also called R-squared, and denoted as R^2.

Coefficient of partial determination—The measure of the marginal contribution of each independent variable, given that other independent variables are in the model.

Coefficient of variation—The ratio of the standard deviation to the mean expressed as a percentage. The coefficient of variation is used to measure the relative variation in the data.

Common cause variation—Variation in the output of a process that is naturally occurring and expected and that may be the result of natural variation in materials, tools, machines, operators, and the environment.

Completely randomized design—An experiment is completely randomized if it consists of the independent random selection of observations representing each level.

Composite model—The model that contains both the basic terms and the interactive terms.

Conditional probability—The probability that an event will occur *given* that some other event has already happened.

Confidence coefficient—The confidence level divided by 100%—i.e., the decimal equivalent of a confidence level.

Confidence interval—An interval developed from sample values such that if all possible intervals of a given width were constructed, a percentage equal to the confidence level would include the true population value.

Confidence level—Percentage greater than 50 and less than 100 that corresponds to the percentage of all possible confidence intervals, based on a given size sample, that will contain the true population parameter.

Contingency table—A table used to classify sample observations according to two or more identifiable characteristics. This table is used as an intermediate step in performing contingency analysis.

Continuous data—Data whose possible values are uncountable and which may assume any value in an interval.

Continuous random variable—Random variables that can assume any of the possible values between two points.

Control limits—Values computed from the output measures of a process over time that define the range of inherent variation in the output. Both upper and lower control limits are computed and are typically based on the concept of being a specified number of standard deviations from the centerline.

Convenience sampling—A sampling technique that selects the items from the population based on accessibility and ease of selection.

Correlation coefficient—A quantitative measure of the strength of the linear relationship between two variables. The correlation ranges from -1.0 to $+1.0$. A correlation of ± 1.0 indicates a perfect linear relationship, whereas a correlation of 0 indicates no linear relationship.

Correlation matrix—A table showing the pairwise correlations between all variables (dependent and independent).

Critical value(s)—The value(s) in a hypothesis test that separate the rejection region from the acceptance region. The critical value can be in the same units as the population parameter or it can be in standardized units.

Cross-sectional data—A set of data values observed at a fixed point in time.

Cumulative frequency—The number of observations with values less than or equal to the upper limit of the class.

Cumulative relative frequency—The proportion of observations with values less-than-or-equal-to the upper limit of the class.

Cyclical component—A pattern within the time series that repeats itself throughout the time series and has a recurrence period of more than one year.

Data array—Data that have been sorted in ascending or descending order.

Data check sheets—Forms designed for easy data collection. As the data are collected, they are also displayed in a format that allows for immediate analysis.

Decision tree—A diagram that illustrates the correct ordering of actions and events in a decision-analysis problem. Each act or event is represented by a node on the decision tree.

Degrees of freedom—The number of independent data values available to estimate the population's standard deviation. If k parameters must be estimated before the population's standard deviation can be calculated from a sample of size n, the degrees of freedom are equal to $n - k$.

Demographic questions—Questions relating to the respondents' own characteristics, backgrounds, and attributes.

Dependent events—Two events are dependent if the occurrence of one event impacts the probability of the other event occurring.

Dependent variable—A variable whose values are thought to be a function of the values of another variable called the *independent variable*. On a scatter plot, the dependent variable is placed on the y-axis and is often called the response variable.

Deseasonalizing—The process of removing the seasonal component from a time series.

Discrete data—Data whose possible values are countable.

Discrete random variable—A variable that can take on a countable number of possible values along a specified interval. The values can be listed.

Double exponential smoothing—An exponential smoothing forecasting model which incorporates a second smoothing constant to account for the trend in the time series.

Dummy variables—Variables in a regression model that have two categories, valued 0 and 1. If a qualitative variable has v multiple categories, $v - 1$ dummy variables are formed to represent the qualitative variable in the analysis.

Elementary events—The most rudimentary outcomes resulting from a simple experiment.

Empirical rule—If the data distribution is bell-shaped, then the interval:

$\mu \pm 1\sigma$ contains approximately 68% of the values in the population or the sample

$\mu \pm 2\sigma$ contains approximately 95% of the values in the population or the sample

$\mu \pm 3\sigma$ contains virtually all of the data values in the population or the sample

Equal-width classes—The distance between the lowest possible value and the highest possible value in each class is equal for all classes.

Event—A collection of elementary events.

Expected-value criterion—A decision criterion that employs probability to select the alternative that will produce the greatest average payoff or minimum average loss.

Experiment—A process that produces a single outcome whose result cannot be predicted with certainty.

Experiment-wide error rate—The proportion of experiments in which at least one of the set of confidence intervals constructed does not contain the true value of the population parameter being estimated.

Experimental design—A plan for performing an experiment in which the variable of interest is defined. One or more factors are identified to be manipulated or changed so that the impact (or influence) on the variable of interest can be measured or observed.

Exponential distribution—A continuous probability distribution has the probability density function given by $f(x) = \lambda e^{-\lambda x}$, $x \geq 0$. It describes the distribution of times between occurrences for a Poisson distributed variable with mean = λ. The mean of the exponential is $1/\lambda$.

Exponential smoothing—A time-series smoothing and forecasting technique that produces an exponentially weighted moving average in which each smoothing calculation or forecast is dependent upon all previously observed values.

Factor—A quantity under examination in an experiment as a possible cause of variation in the response variable.

Finite population correction factor—A value used to modify the standard deviation of the sampling distribution when the sampling is performed without replacement and when the sample size is greater than 5% of the population size.

Forecast bias—The propensity of a forecasting model on average to over forecast or under forecast the actual value of the time series.

Forecast error—The difference between the actual value of a time series and the forecast value; also referred to as the *residual*.

Forecasting—The process of predicting the magnitude that a variable will assume at some future point in time.

Forecasting horizon—The number of periods in the future covered by the forecast; sometimes referred to as the *forecast lead-time*.

Forecasting interval—The frequency with which new forecasts are prepared.

Forecasting period—The unit of time for which forecasts are made. The period may be a day, week, month, quarter, or year.

Frequency distribution—A summary of a set of data that displays the number of observations in each of the distribution's distinct categories or classes.

Frequency histogram—A graph of a frequency distribution with the horizontal axis showing the classes, the vertical axis showing the frequency count, and (for equal class widths) the rectangles having a height equal to the frequency in each class.

Hypothesis—A supposition used to investigate properties of the parameter(s) or form of a distribution or process.

Independent events—Two events are independent if the occurrence of one event in no way influences the probability of the occurrence of the other event.

Independent samples—Samples selected from two or more populations in such a way that the occurrence of values in one sample have no influence on the probability of the occurrence of values in the other sample(s).

Independent variable—A variable that is thought to have an influence on a *dependent variable*. It is often a variable that can be controlled by the decision maker. On a scatter plot, the independent variable or *explanatory variable* is graphed on the *x*-axis.

Inherent variation—The variation in the output of a process that exists naturally. This variation can be reduced but not eliminated.

Interaction—The case in which one independent variable (such as x_2) affects the relationship between another independent variable (x_1) and a dependent variable (y).

Interquartile range—The interquartile range is a measure of variation that is determined by computing the difference between the first and third quartiles.

Interval data—The distance between two data items can be measured, on some scale, and the data have ordinal properties.

Joint frequency distribution—A summary of a bivariate set of data that displays the number of observations that exhibit the respective joint characteristics of one value taken from each of the variables that define the data set.

Kruskal-Wallis one-way analysis of variance—A nonparametric test to determine whether two or more populations have equal distributions. The data must be at least ordinal level and the samples must be independent.

Least squares criterion—The criterion for determining a regression line that minimizes the sum of squared residuals.

Left-skewed data—A data distribution is left skewed if the mean for the data is smaller than the median.

Levels—The categories, measurements, or strata of a factor of interest in the current experiment.

Line chart—A two-dimensional chart showing time on the horizontal axis and the variable of interest on the vertical axis.

Linear trend—A long-term increase or decrease in a time series in which the rate of change is relatively constant.

Mann-Whitney U test—A nonparametric test, based on ranks, used to determine whether two populations have equal distributions.

Margin of error—The largest possible sampling error at the specified level of confidence.

Maximax criterion—An optimistic decision criterion for dealing with uncertainty without using probability. For each option, the decision maker finds the maximum possible payoff and then selects the option with the greatest maximum payoff.

Maximin criterion—A pessimistic (conservative) decision criterion for dealing with uncertainty without using probability. For each option, the decision maker finds the minimum possible payoff and selects the option with the greatest minimum payoff.

Mean—A numerical measure of the center of a set of quantitative measures computed by dividing the sum of the values by the number of variables in the data.

Mean absolute deviation (MAD)—The average of the absolute differences between the actual time-series values and the forecast values.

Mean squared error (MSE)—The average of the squared differences between actual and predicted values.

Median—A center value that divides a data array into two halves.

Minimax regret criterion—A decision criterion that considers the costs of selecting the "wrong" alternative. For each state of nature, the decision maker finds the difference between the best payoff and each other alternative and uses these values to construct an opportunity-loss table. The decision maker then selects the alternative with the minimum opportunity loss (or regret).

Mode—The value in a data set that occurs most frequently.

Model—A representation of an actual system using either a physical or mathematical portrayal.

Model diagnosis—The process of determining how well the model fits the past data and how well the model's assumptions appear to be satisfied.

Model fitting—The process of determining how well a specified model fits past data.

Model specification—The process of selecting the forecasting technique to be used in a particular situation.

Moving average—The average of n consecutive values of a time series.

Multicollinearity—High correlation between two independent variables that means the two variables contribute redundant information to the multiple regression model. When highly correlated independent variables are included in the regression model, they can adversely affect the regression results.

Multiple coefficient of determination (R^2)—The percentage of variation in the dependent variable explained by the independent variables in the regression model.

Multiple regression model for the population—A regression model having two or more independent variables with a regression equation of the form:
$$y_i = \beta_0 + \beta_1 x_{1i} + \beta_2 x_{2i} + \cdots + \beta_k x_{ki} + \epsilon_i$$

Mutually exclusive classes—Classes that do not overlap so that a data value can be placed in only one class.

Mutually exclusive events—The occurrence of one event precludes the occurrence of a second event.

Nominal data—The lowest form of data; data assigned to categories which have no order associated with them.

Nonlinear trend—An increase or decrease in a time series where the rate of change is not constant.

Nonparametric statistical procedure—Statistical methods that do not explicitly concern themselves with population parameters.

Nonstatistical sampling—Those methods of selecting samples using convenience, judgment, or other nonchance processes.

Normal distribution—A bell-shaped, continuous distribution with the following properties:

1. It is *unimodal;* that is, the normal distribution peaks at a single value.
2. It is *symmetrical;* this means that 50% of the area under the curve lies left of the center and 50% lies right of the center. One side of the distribution is the mirror image of the other side.
3. The mean, median, and mode are equal.
4. The normal distribution approaches the horizontal axis on either side of the mean toward plus and minus infinity ($\pm\infty$). In more formal terms, the normal distribution is *asymptotic* to the *x*-axis.
5. The amount of variation in the random variable determines the width of the normal distribution.

Null hypothesis—The statement about the population value that will be tested. The null hypothesis will be rejected only if the sample data provide substantial contradictory evidence.

One-tailed hypothesis test—A hypothesis test in which the entire rejection region is located in one tail of the test statistic distribution.

One-way analysis of variance—An analysis of variance design in which independent samples are obtained from k levels of a single factor for the purpose of testing whether the k levels have equal means.

Open-end questions—Questions that allow respondents the freedom to respond with any value, words, or statements of their own choosing.

Opportunity loss—The difference between the actual payoff that occurs for a decision and the optimal payoff for that same decision.

Ordinal data—One notch above nominal data; the data elements can be rank-ordered on the basis of some relationship among them.

p-Chart—A process control chart used when the variable is an attribute. The p-chart monitors the fraction of items in a sample that contain the attribute of interest.

p-Value—The probability (assuming the null hypothesis is true) of obtaining a test statistic at least as extreme as the test statistic we calculated from the sample. The p-value is also known as the *observed significance level*.

Paired samples—Samples that are selected such that each data value from one sample is related (or matched) with a corresponding data value from the second sample. The sample values from one population have the potential to influence the probability that values will be selected from the second population.

Parameter—A measure computed from the entire population. As long as the population does not change, the value of the parameter will not change.

Pareto chart—A bar chart that is sorted so that the categories or classes are arranged from highest to lowest with respect to the magnitude of the displayed variable associated with each category or class.

Pareto principle—80% of the trouble comes from 20% of the causes.

Payoff—The outcome (profit or loss) for any combination of alternative and state of nature. The outcomes of all possible combinations of alternatives and states of nature constitute a *payoff table*.

Percentiles—The pth percentile in a data array is a value that divides the data set into two parts. The lower segment contains at least p% and the upper segment contains at least $(100 - p)$% of the data. The 50th percentile is the median.

Pie chart—A graph in the shape of a circle. The circle is divided into "slices" corresponding to the categories or classes to be displayed. The size of the slices is proportional to the magnitude of the displayed variable associated with each category or class.

Pilot sample—A sample taken from the population of interest of a size smaller than the anticipated sample size that is used to provide an estimate for the population standard deviation.

Point estimate—A single number determined from a sample that is used to estimate the corresponding population value.

Poisson probability distribution—A probability distribution for the possible outcomes of interest of a process where the average number of outcomes of interest per segment is λ, and the outcomes of interest are rare and random.

Polynomial model—A model including independent variables with an exponent larger than one.

Population—The set of all objects or individuals of interest or the measurements obtained from all objects or individuals of interest.

Population proportion—The fraction of values in a population which have a specific attribute.

Power—The probability that the hypothesis test will reject the null hypothesis when the null hypothesis is false.

Preference quotient—A measure of the relative utility for the outcomes of a decision on a scale between 0.0 and 1.0

Primary data—Data that are collected by you or another person with whom you are closely associated. Primary data are collected for your specific purpose and use.

Probability—The chance that a particular event will occur. The probability of an event will be a value in the range 0.00 to 1.00. A value of 0.00 means the event will not occur. A probability of 1.00 means the event will occur. Anything between 0.00 and 1.00 reflects the uncertainty of the event occurring.

Qualitative data—Data whose measurement scale is inherently categorical.

Qualitative forecasting—Forecasting techniques which are based on expert opinion and judgment.

Quantitative data—Data that are numeric and which define value or quantity.

Quantitative forecasting—Forecasting techniques which are based on statistical methods for analyzing time-series data.

Quartiles—Quartiles in a data array are those values that divide the data set into four equal-sized groups. The median corresponds to the second quartile.

R-chart—A control chart that is used to monitor process variation when the variable of interest is a quantitative measure.

Random component—Changes in the time-series data that are unpredictable and cannot be associated with the trend, seasonal, or cyclical components.

Random variable—A variable that assigns a numerical value to each outcome of a random experiment or trial.

Range—The range is a measure of variation which is computed by finding the difference between the maximum and minimum values in a data set.

Ratio data—Data that have all the characteristics of interval data but also have a true zero point (where zero means "none").

Ratio-to-moving-average method—The actual value of the time series divided by the centered moving average; a step in the process of constructing seasonal indexes.

Regression coefficients—In the simple regression model, there are two coefficients: the intercept and the slope.

Regression slope coefficient—The average change in the dependent variable for a unit change in the independent variable. The slope coefficient may be positive or negative, depending on the relationship between the two variables.

Relative frequency—The proportion of total observations contained in a given category. Relative frequency is computed by dividing the frequency in a category by the total number of observations. The relative frequencies can be converted to percents by multiplying by 100.

Relative frequency of occurrence—The method that defines probability as the number of times an event occurs, divided by the total number of times an experiment is performed in a large number of trials.

Research hypothesis—The hypothesis the decision maker attempts to demonstrate to be true. Since this is the hypothesis deemed to be the most important to the decision maker, it will not be declared true unless the sample data strongly indicates that it is true.

Residual—The difference between the actual value of the dependent variable and the value predicted by the regression model.

Right-skewed data—A data distribution is right skewed if the mean for the data is larger than the median.

Risk-averse attitude—The preference for risk such that the decision maker could select an alternative with a lower expected payoff in order to avoid the possibility of an undesirable outcome.

Risk-neutral attitude—The preference for risk under which the alternative with the highest expected payoff or lowest expected cost will be selected.

Risk-preference function—A graph that describes a decision maker's preference for risk over the range of possible payoffs.

Risk premium—The difference between the expected value of an event and the certainty equivalent. The risk premium will be zero for a risk-neutral decision maker, positive for a risk-averse decision maker, and negative for a risk-seeking decision maker.

Risk-seeking attitude—The preference for risk such that the decision maker could select an alternative with a lower expected payoff in hopes of achieving an outcome with a more desirable result.

Run—A succession of occurrences of a certain type preceded and followed by occurrences of the alternate type or by no occurrences at all.

Runs test—A statistical procedure used to determine whether the pattern of occurrence of two types of observation is determined by a random process or whether the pattern of occurrence is not random.

Sample—A subset of the population.

Sample proportion—The fraction of items in a sample that have the attribute of interest.

Sample space—The collection of all elementary outcomes that can result from a selection or decision.

Sampling distribution—A distribution of the possible values of a statistic for a given size sample selected from a population.

Sampling error—The difference between the population value and the sample value.

Scatter diagram—A two-dimensional graph of plotted points in which the vertical axis represents values of one variable and the horizontal axis represents values of the other. Each plotted point has coordinates whose values are obtained from the respective variables. Also known as a *scatter plot*.

Scatter plot—A two-dimensional plot showing the values for the joint occurrence of two variables. The scatter plot may be used to graphically represent the relationship between two variables. Also known as a *scatter diagram*.

Seasonal component—A pattern that is repeated throughout a time series and has a recurrence period of at most one year.

Seasonal index—A number used to quantify the effect of seasonality in time-series data.

Seasonally unadjusted forecast—A forecast made for seasonal data that does not include an adjustment for the seasonal component in the time series.

Secondary data—Collected and compiled by an outside source.

Second-order regression model—A regression model in which the largest sum of the exponents of the independent variables in any one term of the model is 2.

Shewhart table—A table of factors used to compute 3-sigma control limits on certain process control charts.

Significance level—The maximum probability of committing a Type I error. The probability is denoted by the symbol α.

Simple linear regression analysis—A regression model that uses one independent variable to explain the variation in the dependent variable. The model takes the form:
$$y = \beta_0 + \beta_1 x + \epsilon$$

Simple random sample—A sample selected in such a manner that each possible sample of a specified size has an equal chance of being selected.

Simple random sampling—A method of selecting items from a population such that every possible sample of a specified size has an equal chance of being selected.

Skewed data—Data sets that are not symmetric. For skewed data, the mean will be larger or smaller than the median.

Smoothing constant—The value which determines the weight placed on the most current observation in an exponential smoothing model.

Special cause variation—Something taking place in the process that causes variation in the output which is beyond that which is considered inherent to the process. The process is brought under control by removing all special causes.

Splitting samples—The process of dividing time-series data into two groups, one used to construct the model and the second used to test the ability of the model to forecast.

Spurious correlation—A correlation between two otherwise unrelated variables.

Standard deviation—The standard deviation is the positive square root of the variance.

Standard error of the estimate—The standard deviation of the model errors. The standard error measures the dispersion of the actual values of the dependent variable around the fitted regression plane.

Standard gamble approach—The approach for assessing risk-preference functions that involves setting up a series of 50–50 gambles between two payoffs and determining the certainty equivalent for each gamble.

Standard normal distribution—A normal distribution which has a mean = 0.0 and a standard deviation = 1.0.

Standard normal table—A table of standard normal distribution probabilities.

Standardized data values—The number of standard deviations a value is from the mean. The standardized data values are sometimes referred to as z-scores.

Standardized residual—The residual divided by an estimate of the residual's standard deviation.

State of nature—The possible outcome in a decision situation over which the decision maker has no direct control.

Statistic—A measure computed from a sample that has been selected from a population.

Statistical inference—The process by which decision makers reach conclusions about a population based on sample information collected from the population.

Statistical inference tools—Tools that allow a decision maker to reach a conclusion about a population of data based on a sample of data from the population.

Statistical process control chart—A chart that is used to monitor output of a process over time for the purposes of determining whether the output exhibits special cause variation.

Statistical sampling techniques—Those sampling methods that use selection techniques based on chance selections.

Stratified random sample—A statistical sampling method in which the population is divided into subgroups called *strata* so that each population item belongs to only one stratum. The objective is to form strata such that the population values of interest within each stratum are as much alike as possible. Sample items are selected from each stratum using the simple random sampling method.

Structured interview—Interview in which the questions are scripted.

Student's *t*-distribution—Family of distributions that are bell-shaped and symmetric like the standard normal distribution but with greater area in the tails. Each distribution in the *t* family is defined by its degrees of freedom. As the degrees of

freedom increase, the *t* distribution approaches the normal distribution.

Subgroup—A sample of items selected from a process. If the process is operating in control, the subgroup is free from special causes of variation.

Subjective probability assessment—The method that defines probability of an event as reflecting a decision maker's state of mind regarding the chances that a particular event will occur.

Symmetric data—Data sets whose values are evenly spread around the center. For symmetric data, the mean and the median are equal.

Systematic random sampling—A statistical sampling technique that involves selecting every *k*th item in the population after randomly selecting a starting point between 1 and *k*. The value of *k* is determined as the ratio of the population size over the desired sample size.

Tchebysheff's theorem—Regardless of how the data are distributed, *at least* $(1 - 1/k^2)$ of the values will fall within k standard deviations of the mean.

Test statistic—A function of the sampled observations that provides a basis for testing a statistical hypothesis.

Theorem 6-1—If a population is normally distributed, with mean μ and a standard deviation σ, the sampling distribution of $\bar{x}$ values is also normally distributed with a mean equal to the population mean and a standard deviation equal to the population standard deviation divided by the square root of the sample size.

Time-series data—A set of ordered data values observed at successive points in time.

Time-series plot—A two-dimensional plot of the time series. The vertical axis measures the variable of interest and the horizontal axis corresponds to the time periods. The points on the graph are frequently connected by straight-line segments.

Total quality management—A journey to excellence in which everyone in the organization is focused on continuous process improvement directed toward increased customer satisfaction.

Total variation—The aggregate dispersion of the individual data values across the various factor levels.

Treatment—A combination of one level of each factor in an experiment associated with each observed value of the response variable.

Trend—The long-term increase or decrease in time-series data.

Two-tailed hypothesis test—A hypothesis test in which the rejection region is split between the two tails of the test statistic's distribution.

Type I error—Rejecting the null hypothesis when it is, in fact, true.

Type II error—Failing to reject the null hypothesis when it is, in fact, false.

Uncertainty—A decision environment in which the decision maker does not know what outcome will occur when an alternative is selected.

Uniform distribution—A probability distribution in which the probability of a value occurring between two points, *a* and *b,* is the same as the probability between any other two points, *c* and *d,* given that the distance between *a* and *b* is equal to the distance between *c* and *d.*

Unstructured interview—Interviews that begin with one or more broadly stated questions with further questions being based on the responses.

Variance—The population variance is the average of the squared distances of the data values from the mean.

Variance inflation factor—A measure of how much the variance of an estimated regression coefficient increases if the independent variables are correlated. A VIF equal to 1.0 for a given independent variable indicates that this independent variable is not correlated with the remaining independent variables in the model. The greater the multicollinearity, the larger the VIF will be.

Variation—A set of data exhibits variation if all the data are not the same value.

Wilcoxon test—A nonparametric test based on dependent samples to determine whether two populations have equal distributions.

Within-sample variation—The dispersion that exists among the data values within a particular factor level.

$\bar{x}$-Chart—A chart that monitors the average value of a process over time. For each subgroup, the $\bar{x}$ value is plotted. The upper and lower control limits define the range of inherent variation in the subgroup means when the process is in control.

z-Value—The standardized value representing the number of standard deviations a value is from the mean. A positive z-value indicates the value is larger than the mean and negative z-value means that the value is smaller than the mean.

INDEX

LICENSE AGREEMENT

SITE LICENSE AGREEMENT AND LIMITED WARRANTY. READ THIS LICENSE CAREFULLY BEFORE OPENING THIS PACKAGE. BY OPENING THIS PACKAGE, YOU ARE AGREEING TO THE TERMS AND CONDITIONS OF THIS LICENSE. IF YOU DO NOT AGREE, DO NOT OPEN THE PACKAGE. PROMPTLY RETURN THE UNOPENED PACKAGE AND ALL ACCOMPANYING ITEMS TO THE PLACE YOU OBTAINED THEM. THESE TERMS APPLY TO ALL LICENSED SOFTWARE ON THE DISK EXCEPT THAT THE TERMS FOR USE OF ANY SHAREWARE OR FREEWARE ON THE DISKETTES ARE AS SET FORTH IN THE ELECTRONIC LICENSE LOCATED ON THE DISK.

1. GRANT OF LICENSE and OWNERSHIP: The enclosed computer programs and data files ("Software") are licensed, not sold, to you by Prentice Hall, Inc. ("We" or the "Company") in consideration of your purchase or adoption of the accompanying Company textbook, and your agreement to these terms. We reserve any rights not granted to you. You own only the disk(s) but we and/or licensors own the Software itself. This license allows you to use and display the enclosed copy of the Software on an unlimited number of computers at a single campus or branch or geographic location of an educational institution, for academic use only, so long as you comply with the terms of this Agreement and only for as long as you require the accompanying textbook as your required text. You may make one copy for back up only.

2. RESTRICTIONS ON USE AND TRANSFER: You may not transfer, distribute or make available the Software or the Documentation, except to instructors and students in your school in connection with the Course. You may not reverse engineer, disassemble, decompile, modify, adapt, translate or create derivative works based on the Software or the Documentation. You may be held legally responsible for any copying or copyright infringement which is caused by your failure to abide by the terms of these restrictions.

3. TERMINATION: This license is effective until terminated. This license will terminate automatically without notice from the Company if you fail to comply with any provisions or limitations of this license. Upon termination, you shall destroy the Documentation and all copies of the Software. All provisions of this Agreement as to limitation and disclaimer of warranties, limitation of liability, remedies or damages, and our ownership rights shall survive termination.

4. LIMITED WARRANTY AND DISCLAIMER OF WARRANTY: Company warrants that for a period of 60 days from the date you purchase this Software (or purchase or adopt the accompanying textbook), the Software, when properly installed and used in accordance with the Documentation, will operate in substantial conformity with the description of the Software set forth in the Documentation, and that for a period of 30 days the disk(s) on which the Software is delivered shall be free from defects in materials and workmanship under normal use. The Company does not warrant that the Software will meet your requirements or that the operation of the Software will be uninterrupted or error-free. Your only remedy and the Company's only obligation under these limited warranties is, at the Company's option, return of the disk for a replacement of the disk. THIS LIMITED WARRANTY IS THE ONLY WARRANTY PROVIDED BY THE COMPANY AND ITS LICENSORS, AND THE COMPANY AND ITS LICENSORS DISCLAIM ALL OTHER WARRANTIES, EXPRESS OR IMPLIED, INCLUDING WITHOUT LIMITATION, THE IMPLIED WARRANTIES OF MERCHANTABILITY AND FITNESS FOR A PARTICULAR PURPOSE. THE COMPANY DOES NOT WARRANT, GUARANTEE OR MAKE ANY REPRESENTATION REGARDING THE ACCURACY, RELIABILITY, CURRENTNESS, USE, OR RESULTS OF USE, OF THE SOFTWARE.

5. LIMITATION OF REMEDIES AND DAMAGES: IN NO EVENT, SHALL THE COMPANY OR ITS EMPLOYEES, AGENTS, LICENSORS, OR CONTRACTORS BE LIABLE FOR ANY INCIDENTAL, INDIRECT, SPECIAL, OR CONSEQUENTIAL DAMAGES ARISING OUT OF OR IN CONNECTION WITH THIS LICENSE OR THE SOFTWARE, INCLUDING FOR LOSS OF USE, LOSS OF DATA, LOSS OF INCOME OR PROFIT, OR OTHER LOSSES, SUSTAINED AS A RESULT OF INJURY TO ANY PERSON, OR LOSS OF OR DAMAGE TO PROPERTY, OR CLAIMS OF THIRD PARTIES, EVEN IF THE COMPANY OR AN AUTHORIZED REPRESENTATIVE OF THE COMPANY HAS BEEN ADVISED OF THE POSSIBILITY OF SUCH DAMAGES. IN NO EVENT SHALL THE LIABILITY OF THE COMPANY FOR DAMAGES WITH RESPECT TO THE SOFTWARE EXCEED THE AMOUNTS ACTUALLY PAID BY YOU, IF ANY, FOR THE SOFTWARE OR THE ACCOMPANYING TEXTBOOK. SOME JURISDICTIONS DO NOT ALLOW THE LIMITATION OF LIABILITY IN CERTAIN CIRCUMSTANCES, THE ABOVE LIMITATIONS MAY NOT ALWAYS APPLY.

6. GENERAL: THIS AGREEMENT SHALL BE CONSTRUED IN ACCORDANCE WITH THE LAWS OF THE UNITED STATES OF AMERICA AND THE STATE OF NEW YORK, APPLICABLE TO CONTRACTS MADE IN NEW YORK, AND SHALL BENEFIT THE COMPANY, ITS AFFILIATES AND ASSIGNEES. This Agreement is the complete and exclusive statement of the agreement between you and the Company and supersedes all proposals, prior agreements, oral or written, and any other communications between you and the company or any of its representatives relating to the subject matter. If you are a U.S. Government user, this Software is licensed with "restricted rights" as set forth in subparagraphs (a)-(d) of the Commercial Computer-Restricted Rights clause at FAR 52.227-19 or in subparagraphs (c)(1)(ii) of the Rights in Technical Data and Computer Software clause at DFARS 252.227-7013, and similar clauses, as applicable. Should you have any questions concerning this agreement or if you wish to contact the Company for any reason, please contact in writing: Prentice Hall Inc., Higher Education Division, Business Publishing Media Technology Group, One Lake Street, Upper Saddle River, NJ 07458.